301.08 L

64547

Lipset, S. M.
AUTHOR

Sociology: the progress of a
TITLE
                                        decade.

DATE LOANED	BORROWER'S NAME	DATE RETURNED
MAR 2 1 '65	Sr. Clare Marie Mitte	APR 1 0 '65
MAY 1 8 '65		MAY 1 9 '65
JUL · 5		JUL 1 9 '65
SEP 3 0 '65	Sister Mary Nivelly	OCT
	Bill Phil	

64547
Lipset

SOCIOLOGY, THE PROGRESS OF A DECADE

A COLLECTION OF ARTICLES

SOCIOLOGY

THE PROGRESS OF A DECADE

A COLLECTION OF ARTICLES

edited by

SEYMOUR MARTIN LIPSET
*Professor of Sociology, University of
California at Berkeley*

and

NEIL J. SMELSER
*Associate Professor of Sociology, Uni-
versity of California at Berkeley*

PRENTICE-HALL, INC.   *Englewood Cliffs, N. J.*

PRENTICE-HALL SOCIOLOGY SERIES
Herbert Blumer, Editor

Third printing......April, 1964

Preface

The development of an academic discipline is frequently charted in terms of its major landmarks—big, important books which consolidate existing knowledge, bring to light new discoveries, and initiate new lines of research. The publication of such books typically creates a flurry of excitement, criticism, and controversy. For sociology in recent times it is possible to identify many such landmarks: the publication of *The Polish Peasant in Europe and America* by Thomas and Znaniecki; *The Theory of the Leisure Class* by Veblen; the *Middletown* Series by the Lynds; *Management and the Worker* by Roethlisberger and Dickson; *The American Soldier* by Stouffer *et al.*; *The People's Choice* by Lazarsfeld *et al.*; *The Authoritarian Personality* by Adorno *et al.*; and *Toward a General Theory of Action* by Parsons and Shils—to name a few.

These major innovations do not, however, tell the whole story. Behind the scenes, as it were, in the learned journals, there is a continuous hum of intellectual activity. Some of this activity supplements the work of the big books. Some scholars chip away at the theories and methods underlying the major works; others point out implications not seen by the authors themselves; others conduct research based on the approaches developed in the major works. In addition, the journals show much independent activity. New techniques appear; old ones are destroyed; still others are refined; new lines of research are suggested; controversies over a significant article rise, prosper, and fall, only to be revived by some new statement. The journals also contain a significant amount of self-examination, in which scholars inquire where the field is going, why, and with what promise.

In this book we attempt to sample the major trends of the 1950's in the field of sociology as they have unfolded in the pages of the learned journals. Our sample is not without bias, naturally, because we ourselves have been exposed selectively to the field and have developed our own ideas as to its character. We also have had to apply many different, sometimes competing, criteria in selecting the articles—excellence, comprehensiveness, representativeness, and brevity. We hope we have been able, however, to tap most of the major developments as they have unfolded in the past decade.

We are solely responsible for the selections. We would like to thank Professors William Petersen and Hanan Selvin of the University of California, Berkeley, for some helpful hints. In addition, we are grateful for the diligence of Mrs. Carroll H. Harrington and Miss Pauline Jones, who attended to the

v

interminable and often tedious details of reproducing articles, writing for permissions, and reminding us of dozens of chores we surely would have neglected otherwise.

S.M.L.
N.J.S.

Table of Contents

vii

Part 2. The Major Boundaries of Social Systems

Culture and Society: The Creation and Maintenance of Cultural Patterns

Personality and Society: The Formation of Personality Through Socialization and Education

Physical and Biological Boundaries: Ecology and Demography

Part 3. The Production and Allocation of Wealth, Power, and Prestige

Economic Structures and Processes

Political Structures and Processes

The Distribution of Prestige

Part 4. The Balance Between Stability and Change in Society

Social Disorganization, Deviance, and Social Problems

Social Control and Social Change

SOCIOLOGY, THE PROGRESS OF A DECADE

A COLLECTION OF ARTICLES

Introduction

The Setting of Sociology in the 1950's

Seymour Martin Lipset and Neil J. Smelser

The growth of an intellectual tradition is not without the ironies and paradoxes that accompany all growth. The radicals and innovators in one period frequently become conservatives in the next. Indeed, the initiators of trends often come to resist the extension and consolidation of the very trends which they themselves set in motion. As a result, intellectual developments are commonly plagued by those controversies, revolutions, secessions, and accusations of heresy and subversion associated with the dynamics of religion and politics.

The recent history of the discipline of sociology has displayed some of these general characteristics. From its beginnings to the present day, sociology has evolved steadily from its policy-oriented roots toward a more strictly scientific emphasis. In large measure, the articles reprinted in this book, if matched with a comparable set of selections from the journals of fifty years ago, would reflect the complete triumph since World War I of the new "scientific sociology." This evolution, however, has left and is leaving in its trail a number of controversies and disputes which reflect the tensions inherent in such growth. In this introduc-

tory section, we shall sketch the course of this development and comment on the related intellectual turbulence which accompanied it.

Sociology's earliest concern with ways to handle social problems no doubt infused it with an energy that brought it rapidly to the fore as a major subject of research and study in the United States. Perhaps this policy-oriented side of the field accounts in part for its relatively faster development here than in Europe. At any rate, in its early days sociology was clearly devoted to dealing with the causes and cures of uniquely American problems—the pathologies associated with immigrant slums, such as family disorganization, juvenile delinquency, crime, suicide, bad housing, and so on. The immigrant and the city, both of which were disturbing to the traditional values of small-town Protestant Anglo-Saxon America, became the preoccupation of sociology. Like the applied field of social work to which it was linked, American sociology expressed deep concern with the reintegration of the society. The backgrounds of many early sociologists revealed these concerns. Many were ministers of the gospel; others were scien-

1

tists and engineers who wanted to apply "scientific methods" to the solution of social evils.

Chicago and Columbia, universities with two of the most important sociology departments,[1] reflected this emphasis. The University of Chicago, which undoubtedly had more influence than any other school until the 1930's, was best known for its extensive studies on the problems of the metropolis. This focus by Chicago is reflected in the titles of many of the books which appeared in the series of monographs sponsored by the sociology department: The Gang, The Gold Coast and the Slum, The Ghetto, The Hobo, The Jack-Roller, The Unadjusted Girl. Perhaps the most influential single piece of research was Thomas and Znaniecki's The Polish Peasant in Europe and America. Columbia, until the mid-thirties, also laid heavy emphasis on social reform. Its first professor of sociology, Franklin Giddings, who dominated Columbia sociology from the early 1890's to the late twenties, had had a religious home environment (his father was a minister) and academic training in the physical sciences. His belief, derived from Spencer, that social engineering must be based on a general social science, was an important factor in his decision to enter the new discipline of sociology. For him the relationship between sociology and social engineering was unambiguous:

Facing the facts that the physical and biological sciences have made known to us has enabled us to live more comfortably and longer than man once did. Facing the facts that the social sciences are making known to us, and will make better known, should enable us to diminish human misery and to live more wisely than the human race has lived hitherto.[2]

Correspondingly, the early course offerings at Columbia were weighted heavily in the practical direction. In addition to courses in social theory, historical sociology, and observational and statistical methods, students were required to complete work in criminology, penology, pauperism, poor laws, and the family. The graduate course in Family Organization required students to work with underprivileged families.

Gradually in the 1920's an academic field of study apart from the concerns of social workers and social reformers began to emerge more definitely. Though research still focused on the deviant and depressed, more refined methods of analysis began to replace the journalistic and problem-focused approach of the earlier work. Important developments began to stir on the theoretical level as well. Earlier sociologists had written as if the problems of society were inherent in specific institutions. More and more, American sociologists now began to develop—both on their own and under a new European influence—what came to be known as the functional approach, which views specific institutions and problems as part of an interdependent whole.

The specific character of these changes may be seen in the area of social stratification. Many early American sociologists—for example, Giddings, Sumner, and Cooley—had dealt with larger aspects of social structure such as power and class, but these subjects were not treated as foci for research. Rather they were subjects for lectures and general discussion articles.[3] Not until the Lynds'

---

[1] In choosing Chicago and Columbia for illustration, we do not intend to slight the important work done by Sumner at Yale, Cooley at the University of Michigan, Ross at the University of Wisconsin, and others. Until the 1920's, however, Chicago and Columbia had more sociology graduate students than the rest of the sociology departments combined.

[2] Franklin H. Giddings, The Scientific Study of Human Society (Chapel Hill, N. C.: The University of North Carolina Press, 1924), pp. 37-38.

[3] For a detailed exposition of the writings of the "fathers" of American sociology on social stratification, see Charles H. Page, Class and American Sociology (New York: The Dial Press, 1940).

Middletown studies were these topics treated in the light of hypotheses to be tested by actual investigation. The Middletown studies were the first empirical researches on a large scale which employed the new functional approach.[4] The work of the Lynds helped to demonstrate that specific social evils could not be analyzed apart from their structural context in society. Their rejection of the "specific-problem" approach in favor of the "functional" approach occurred during the actual course of the research. The Middletown project had begun as a study of the church in the small city, under the sponsorship of The Institute of Social and Religious Research. The Lynds, however, came to the decision that they could study the church only through an analysis of the larger system of which it is a part. As they put it, "The stubborn resistance which 'social problems' offer may be related in part to the common habit of piecemeal attack on them ... The present investigation, accordingly, set out to approach the life of the people in the city selected as a unit complex of interwoven trends of behavior."[5]

During the years that the Lynds were engaged in their pioneer research, Pitirim Sorokin, originally trained in Europe, introduced American sociologists to the myriad of detailed quantitative investigations of social mobility in Europe, and underlined, in his classic volume, Social Mobility, the close link between theory and research.[6] In addition, he brought

alive to many Americans the importance of systematic theory, an intellectual pursuit which had a long history in Europe but which had been ignored in the policy-oriented American approach.[7]

The work of the Lynds and Sorokin thus played a major role in changing the outlook of American sociology. This work set the stage for the investigation of relationships in the larger social structure. One index of this change may be seen in the concepts employed to describe the different classes of society. The early Columbia catalogues used the terms "delinquent," "depressed," and "deviant" to describe groups living in slum areas. However, in the thirties and thereafter, the sociologist came to define his problem as the analysis of differences in the behavior and values of the various classes. The question of who is the deviant in the total social structure waned correspondingly.

In the thirties, Talcott Parsons and Paul Lazarsfeld, two young men who were to play major roles in furthering such trends, entered American sociology.[8] Parsons, in his teaching at Harvard and in his famous volume, The Structure of Social Action, enlarged American scholars' awareness of the importance of systematic theory and of the work of several major European sociologists, particularly Emile Durkheim, Max Weber, and Vilfredo Pareto. While Parsons has been concerned from the beginning primarily with the elaboration of that systematic theory which goes under the name of structural-functional analysis and the theory of action, he also insisted

---

[4] In the introduction to Middletown, the Lynds specifically asserted that "the following pages aim to present a dynamic, functional study of the contemporary life of this specific American community in the light of the trends of changing behavior observable in it during the last thirty-five years." In a footnote they defined "function" as denoting "a major life-activity or something contributing to the performance of a major life-activity." This definition, while vague, is not inconsistent with later definitions of the functional approach. Robert S. Lynd and Helen Merrell Lynd, Middletown: A Study in American Culture (New York: Harcourt, Brace and Company, 1929), p. 6.

[5] Ibid., p. 3.
[6] Pitirim Sorokin, Social Mobility (New York: Harper & Brothers, 1927).

[7] Pitirim Sorokin, Contemporary Sociological Theories (New York: Harper & Brothers, 1928).

[8] Again our choice of these figures is meant to be illustrative of major intellectual trends. An exhaustive analysis of the intellectual developments of the 1930's and the decades since would have to include the important contributions of men like Warner in the field of stratification; Mayo, Roethlisberger and Dickson in industrial sociology; Lewin in the field of small groups; Ogburn in the field of technological and social change. Men trained by these scholars figure heavily in the development of the field of sociology since World War II.

on the necessary relationship between theory and empirical research. Thus, he elaborated the way in which Durkheim used suicide statistics to test many of his hypotheses concerning the social structure, and both translated and analyzed Max Weber's classic historical study, The Protestant Ethic and the Spirit of Capitalism. In the 1930's and thereafter, then, Parsons contributed not only to the development of systematic theory but also to furthering Sorokin's concern with bridging the gap between European and American theory and research.[9]

In the late twenties and early thirties Paul Lazarsfeld and a number of other young Austrian scholars had been engaged in extensive research in Vienna on the determinants of occupational choice, on buying decisions, on the effects of unemployment and insecurity on family interaction and political attitudes, and on problems of research methodology. To support this research Lazersfeld initiated patterns of securing funds for sociological research from governments and business concerns to supplement the limited sums available from foundations.

Upon his arrival in America in 1932 as a Rockefeller Fellow, Lazarsfeld attempted to interest American social scientists in the self-conscious application of research methodology and in the use of quantitative techniques, particularly the survey, in their research designs. Among those impressed with the potentialities of these methods was Robert Lynd, who introduced some of these approaches into his second major work, Middletown in Transition. Perhaps more important, he sponsored Lazarsfeld's appointment to the Columbia graduate department. This appointment was significant not only be-

cause it brought a major exponent of sophisticated research methods into one of the key centers of graduate training, but also because it was accompanied by the introduction of a sociological research institute (the Office of Radio Research, now known as the Bureau of Applied Social Research) as an adjunct to a university department. This model of a research institute linked to sociology has been adopted at most other major universities.

In a real sense, the early trends set in motion by Sorokin and Lynd have culminated in a sociology which is more consciously oriented toward the objective of building a science of society. The pace-setters in this new scientific sociology are identified both by admirers and opponents in the names of Parsons (as well as his students, such as Davis, Levy, Merton[10] and Moore, and his oft-time collaborator, Edward Shils) and Lazarsfeld (as well as names like Stouffer and Guttman). Most important sociological works today attempt to locate their concerns in

---

[9]One should not overemphasize the continuity between Sorokin and Parsons. A reading of the critical footnotes in The Structure of Social Action reveals a long list of substantive and methodological differences. Sorokin, however, in a mimeographed document privately circulated by him to various sociologists after the appearance of Parsons' The Social System (Glencoe, Ill.: The Free Press, 1951), pointed out that Parsons had studied under him and that there are many parallel concepts and analyses in their work.

[10]Robert K. Merton's position is a unique one. Having been influenced heavily both by Parsons and Lazarsfeld at different points in his career, he tends to occupy a place somewhere between the two. His own research interests, as well as his call some years ago for emphasis upon "theories of the middle range" perhaps reflect this middle position. It should be noted that Merton's appointment at Columbia was sponsored by Robert MacIver. MacIver and Lynd were appointed in 1929-30, one as a theorist, the other as a more research-oriented man. A decade later Merton and Lazarsfeld were called to Columbia to supplement the work of the two older men.

Edward A. Shils' place in American sociology is likewise difficult to classify in any simple way. For many years he has operated as an influence in the Parsonian tradition—from his early critical assistance on The Structure of Social Action to his more recent collaboration in Toward a General Theory of Action with Parsons (Cambridge, Mass.: Harvard University Press, 1951), and Working Papers in the Theory of Action, with Parsons and R. F. Bales (Glencoe, Ill.: The Free Press, 1953). His translations and commentaries on men like Weber, Mannheim, and Sorel have augmented the link between European and American sociology. In still another role, Shils has acted as a kind of mediator between the traditions of sociological analysis and the major moral, intellectual, and political problems of the day—as illustrated in his The Torment of Secrecy (Glencoe, Ill.: The Free Press, 1956).

a body of developing theory. Similarly, sociology has become methodologically more self-conscious. Technical courses in theory and methods are now required areas of study in the leading centers of graduate training. Many of the recognized younger sociologists, who will set the tone in decades to come, have received their training in the traditions which crystallized in the thirties and forties at Columbia and Harvard.

Such lines of evolution in sociology have given rise to a multi-sided polemic in the field, a polemic which rose to something of an apex in the 1950's. On the one side stand those who believe that sociology, in its theoretical and methodological aspects, should move in the direction of greater scientific adequacy, and thus take its place among the more formal social sciences (such as economics and parts of psychology) or even the physical sciences. On the other side stand a variety of critics, including, interestingly enough, Sorokin[11] and Lynd,[12] who were themselves instrumental in furthering the very trends which they now deplore. Joining these now retired scholars are younger men like Barrington Moore, Jr., of Harvard[13] and C. Wright Mills of Columbia.[14] Many sociology departments, in fact, are now divided intellectually between those who are committed to system theory and methodological formalization and their critics.

These critics share a dissatisfaction with what they view as excessive abstraction and overpreoccupation with esoteric methodology. From this general theme emerge several more specific issues:

(1) Basically the critics of preoccupation with scientific theory and method argue that all complex social systems must be analyzed primarily from a historical point of view. The analysis of the consequences of specific historical situations is a more important "explanation" of the "system" than is the effort to specify the interrelated functions which the system and its parts serve at any given time.

(2) On another level, the conflict has become a controversy between the exponents of a functionalist and equilibrium concept of society and those who prefer to view society in dialectical terms as ever-changing and in a state of permanent conflict.[15] Sociology, it is maintained, because of its preoccupation with formal theory and precise methods, has moved away from the significant social and political problems, from the analysis of social change, the nature of power, and the extent of conflict and exploitation which exists in class systems. Many important problems are ignored because they do not fit a "static" functionalist approach or because they cannot be measured precisely.

(3) A related wing of this controversy is the assertion that theoretical and methodological preoccupation leads to political sterility or political conservatism. Critics maintain that functionalism becomes an endorsement of the status quo[16] an empty body of study whose primary task is to deflect possible sources of intellectual criticism of society.

(While these three criticisms often

---

[11]Pitirim Sorokin, Fads and Foibles in Modern Sociology and Related Sciences (Chicago: H. Regnery Co., 1956).

[12]Lynd's published attack has been perhaps least explicit among the critics of "scientific sociology." For a statement of his disaffection from the organization of contemporary empirical research, however, cf. "Can Labor and Intellectuals Work Together?" in J.B.S. Hardman and Maurice F. Neufeld (eds.), The House of Labor: Internal Operations of American Unions (New York: Prentice-Hall, 1951), pp. 511-15.

[13]Barrington Moore, Jr., "The New Scholasticism," World Politics, Vol. 6 (1953-54), pp. 122-38; also "Sociological Theory and Contemporary Politics," American Journal of Sociology, Vol. 61 (1954-55), pp. 107-15. See also his Political Power and Social Theory: Six Studies (Cambridge, Mass.: Harvard University Press, 1958).

[14]C. Wright Mills, The Sociological Imagination (New York: Oxford University Press, 1959).

[15]Ralf Dahrendorf, "Out of Utopia: Toward a Reorientation of Sociological Analysis," American Journal of Sociology, Vol. 64 (1958), pp. 115-27. Lewis Coser, The Functions of Social Conflict (Glencoe, Ill.: The Free Press, 1956). Coser occupies a mixed position. While he is impatient with "functionalist" analysis, he himself uses many of the functionalist assumptions and methods in demonstrating the importance of conflict in society.

[16]Coser, op. cit.

come from the same source, they are not necessarily interrelated. We would classify ourselves, for instance, as functionalists concerned primarily with historical and comparative work and concerned with the political and moral implications of sociological research.)

This attempt to dichotomize the study of society into the study of the "imperatives" inherent in social systems on the one hand, and the study of historic sources of specific—often politically significant—patterns of behavior on the other, strikes us as erroneous. It is not necessary to consider the issue in either-or terms. As many methodologists of science have observed, the fact that something is socially significant at any given moment does not mean that studying it directly is the best means for social improvement. The cure for a given disease may come sooner by studying the fundamental body processes rather than the specific disease itself. The study of the laws of blood chemistry may, in fact, be more useful in the cure of mental illness than the development of ad hoc generalizations from the psychotherapeutic situation. In short, without a guiding body of theory and methods to enable men to relate their findings to society or its various problems, no real accumulation of valid action-relevant findings is possible.

The criticism that the efforts to formulate generalizations about systems necessarily conflicts with the analysis of historical processes also strikes us as unwarranted. Mills' and others' criticism of sociological theory for ignoring the Marxian "principle of historical specification" has recently been discussed by Louis Feuer, a student of both scientific methodology and Marxian thought. After pointing out that Marx never used the expression, "the principle of historical specificity," Feuer goes on to state:

There is, to my mind, a bit of obscurantism in "the principle of historical specification" which, at the present time, obstructs the advance of social science. The principle rightly warns us to specify clearly the variables in our sociological laws; do not, for instance, enunciate as a law for all economic systems what may be true only of a competitive capitalist one. The principle has its obvious counterpart in physics. Kepler's laws, for instance, are laws for the motions of planets, not for masses in general. But Kepler's laws turned out to be special cases of the Newtonian laws which did apply to all masses. And, in a similar sense, the laws of different societies might likewise be special cases of the operation of universal psychological and sociological laws. To specify the historical structure would simply then be to state the social initial conditions which would bound the operation of the universal laws in the specific historical situation. We cannot indeed understand how one social system evolves into another without using some guiding laws of a common human nature; the revolt of men against their society's mores and values would be otherwise unintelligible. For all Marx's presumable adherence to the "principle of historical specification," he had no hesitance about making trans-historical generalizations. He set forth general laws concerning "all ruling classes," "all ideologies," "all modes of exploitation," and "all history." As for the hypothesis that the past itself is less important for American-type societies than others, that too could be formulated in some cross-societal law. We might say, for example; for all societies composed of immigrants, the influence of the past will vary inversely with the novelty of the social circumstances.[17]

Obviously an important task of sociology is to locate generalizations which take account of the fact that all complex social systems are also historical systems. As Max Weber argued, historical explanations are crucial if we are to understand the rigidities and flexibilities built into any institution. In fact, the functionalist emphasis on key values in a social system is an effort to relate the operation of the system to elements rooted in its history. Within these historical "givens," furthermore, a certain body of theoretical propositions states what kind of system is operating, its relation with external systems, its internal

---

[17]Louis S. Feuer, "A Symposium on C. Wright Mills' 'The Sociological Imagination,'" Berkeley Journal of Sociology (Berkeley: University of California, Department of Sociology, Fall 1959), Vol. 5, No. I, pp. 122-23.

relations, its tensions, its contradictions, and so on. Sometimes, if one utilizes a stable equilibrium model, one emphasizes the self-regulating and restorative mechanisms. For other purposes, one may use dynamic (for example, moving or unstable) equilibrium models to posit conditions under which the system will move to a new state or disintegrate. And finally, no matter what sort of equilibrium model is posited, the propositions concerning the relationships among the parts of the system are verified, modified, or rejected in the light of research into specific historical sequences. As we see it, then, there is no necessary clash between systematic theory and a concern with social change and historical specificity. As Radcliffe-Brown summarized the issue over twenty-five years ago, when sociology was just entering its "modern era":

One "explanation" of a social system will be its history, where we know it—the detailed account of how it came to be—what it is and where it is. Another "explanation" of the same system is obtained by showing... that it is a special exemplification of laws of social psychology or social functioning. The two kinds of explanation do not conflict but supplement one another.[18]

Why, we might ask in conclusion, have controversies like those just sketched appeared and flourished at this particular time? A partial answer lies, we feel, in the stage of development of the discipline itself. As we have noted, and as Talcott Parsons observes in the first selection in this volume, sociology, in its brief history, has evolved gradually toward a concern with scientific canons and away from social philosophy and social problems. The two advance guards in this movement have been the development of systematic research methods and the exploration for adequate systematic theory.

While this process of differentiation of the scientific aspects of sociology from its ethical and practical background has been gradual and irregular, it has been powerful and unrelenting as well.

In broader perspective, this process of differentiation is an instance of the tendencies toward the secularization of knowledge which have characterized Western civilization for many centuries. During periods of secularization specific spheres of knowledge come to be established more nearly in accordance with an autonomous set of technical standards and a distinctive rationality. The criteria for truth become less mingled with religious, political, and practical concerns. The separation of several of the physical sciences from the religious cosmology of the sixteenth and seventeenth centuries is a classic instance of the secularization of knowledge. The recent emergence of the social sciences from their broader moral and philosophical traditions seems to be a recapitulation of this process of secularization, though the specific historical setting differs radically.

Secularization never occurs, of course, without a great deal of pain and controversy. In particular, the representatives of the older moral and intellectual traditions (from which the new form emerges) experience a sense of loss of importance and authority. Their assertions of right and truth are displaced by competing, secularized assertions, and their sphere of control is pared back. In this sense the rise of the scientific cosmology in post-Renaissance Europe marked a "defeat" for the religious cosmology, for religion no longer defined and controlled the physical universe unequivocally. As a result, the complaints are usually loudest from the parent tradition from which the secularized branch of knowledge arises:

---

[18] A. R. Radcliffe Brown, "On the Concept of Function in Social Science," *American Anthropologist*, New Series, Vol. 37 (1935), p. 401. For a similar point of view, cf. B. Malinowski, The Dynamics of Culture Change (New Haven: Yale University Press, 1945), p. 34.

...for over two centuries religion has been on the defensive, and on a weak defensive. The period has been one of unprecedented intellectual progress. In this way a series of novel situations have been produced for thought. Each occasion has found the religious thinkers unprepared. Something, which has been proclaimed to be vital, has finally, after struggle, distress, and anathema, been modified and otherwise interpreted. The next generation of religious apologists then congratulates the religious world on the deeper insight which has been gained. The result of the continued repetition of this undignified retreat, during many generations, has at last almost entirely destroyed the intellectual authority of religious thinkers. Consider this contrast: when Darwin or Einstein proclaim theories which modify our ideas, it is a triumph for science. We do not go about saying that there is another defeat for science, because its old ideas have been abandoned. We know that another step of scientific insight has been gained...[In the sixteenth and seventeenth centuries, theologians] were always attacking and defending. They pictured themselves as the garrison of a fort surrounded by hostile forces.[19]

In the recent public controversies regarding sociology a similar pattern seems to emerge. Most of the vitriol comes from the side of people who incline toward political sensitivity and broad moral concerns, who see sociology becoming less problem-oriented, less vital, less concerned, less committed, less historical, less humanistic, more sterile, and more conservative politically ---and the worse for all these things. Those with moral and ideological identifications experience a sense of loss as sociological thought strives---with varying degrees of success---for a closer approximation to standards of scientific adequacy. Furthermore, they tend to see, with the partial truth of all such insights, "empty" theory and "barren" research methods as the twin devils leading sociology away from its traditional moral, political, and practical concerns. With few exceptions, however, those identified with the more scientific side of sociology have tended more to "go about their business"; they have been (at least in public) much less defensive, aggressive, and vigorous on their side of the controversy.

---

[19] A. N. Whitehead, Science and the Modern World (New York: The New American Library, 1948), pp. 187-89.

PLAN OF THE BOOK

Since so much recent interest and controversy has focused on areas of sociological theory and sociological methods, we have decided to begin the book (after a brief introductory section on the profession itself) by presenting a number of writings on these two subjects in the past decade. We cannot pretend to mention, much less exhaust all the developments in these areas. Many contributions and discussions appeared in book form and thus lie outside the scope of this book. Our aim is to present a representative discussion from the journals of the issues which set the tone in theory and methods during the 1950's---the recurrent problem of "functionalism"; the problem of general theory; the role of values in theoretical formulation; the comparative study of societies in theory and practice; the place of quantitative and qualitative methods in empirical research; the use of surveys and interviews as instruments for research, and so on.

For organizing the remainder of the volume, our starting point has been that the proper province of sociology is the analysis of that vaguely designated land known as "social structure" or "social systems." Without attempting to define these concepts formally, we shall divide the rest of the book into three subdivisions revolving around them: (1) Research at the major "boundaries" of social systems. At these boundaries society articulates with culture, with individual personalities, and with the physical and biological environment. (2) Research on typical processes and structures in the social system itself. We have chosen to emphasize the production, allocation and consumption of three major societal resources---wealth, power, and prestige. (3) Research concerning the balance between stability and change in social systems. This involves the study of social disorganization, deviance, and social control, as well as the resolution of these several forces into processes of social change.

The Major Boundaries of Social Systems. 1. Culture. In late 1958 two eminent representatives of anthropology and sociology, the late Alfred L. Kroeber and Talcott Parsons, issued a brief "manifesto" in the American Sociological Review.[20] Its object was to carve out appropriate definitions for the familiar concepts "culture" and "social system." According to their formulation, culture should refer to the "transmitted and created content and patterns of values, ideas, and other symbolic-meaningful systems as factors in the shaping of human behavior and the artifacts produced through behavior," whereas social system should refer to "the specifically relational system of interaction among individuals and collectivities." Some have questioned the logical and empirical validity of this particular distinction.[21] Most would agree, however, that some distinction between the two must be preserved, and the relationship between culture and social systems constitutes a field worthy of research.

Many problems recur in connection with the relationship between culture and society: What kinds of controls does culture implant on social action? How is culture created, maintained, and transmitted through institutionalized structures in society? How does culture "reflect" organized social life? How do modifications of the social structure affect the cultural system, and vice-versa? In what ways do culture and social systems interpenetrate?

Many substantive subfields of sociology have congealed around analytical questions regarding the relationship between culture and society. We might mention only the sociology of knowledge, the sociology of science, the sociology of art, the sociology of literature, part of the sociology of religion, and—as a newcomer—the sociology of mass culture. Sometimes this list of sub-fields (which could be expanded by addition and further subdivision of fields) has been grouped in a larger field, the sociology of culture. In this volume we include several representative pieces of research on the creation and maintenance of cultural patterns.

2. Personality. In his contribution to Sociology Today, the stocktaking volume published in 1959, Alex Inkeles called for a greater emphasis on the interplay between personality and social structure. Defining the task of the sociologist as the explanation of action flowing from various institutional settings, Inkeles argued that this kind of explanation must rely on the fact that such action is mediated through individual personalities. "The human personality system thus becomes one of the main intervening variables in any estimate of the effects of one aspect of social structure on another."[22] A second major "boundary" of the social structure concerns, therefore, its relationship with individual personalities.

How is this relationship to be formulated? Obviously personality and social structure are mutually dependent. The bearing of social structure on personality is revealed in the processes of socialization and adjustment to social roles and organizations, social control, and the demand for value-commitments on the part of individuals in society. The reciprocal influence concerns the degree of acceptance, redefinition, and modification of these structures which stems from the exigencies of personality systems.

Almost any "substantive" sub-field of sociology can and occasionally does deal with the interplay between social structure and personality. The areas most closely concerned, however, include the sociology of child socialization, sociology of the family, sociology of the primary group, sociology of education, and sociology of sports and leisure.

[20]"The Concepts of Culture and of Social System," American Sociological Review, Vol. 23 (Oct., 1958), pp. 582-83.
[21]Richard H. Ogles, Marion J. Levy, Jr., and Talcott Parsons, "Culture and Social System: An Exchange," American Sociological Review, Vol. 24 (April, 1959), pp. 246-50.

[22]Alex Inkeles, "Personality and Social Structure," in Sociology Today, edited by Robert K. Merton, Leonard Broom, and Leonard S. Cottrell, Jr. (New York: Basic Books, 1959), p. 251.

With one exception (the article by Levinson, a psychologist) our selections in this volume display what is possibly a real bias in the field of sociology---the overemphasis of the effects of social structure on personality, and the corresponding underemphasis of the reverse effects. Perhaps this apparent bias echoes Inkeles' insistence on the greater need for research in the realm of personality and its influence on social action.

3. Physical and biological boundaries. As boundaries of the social system, culture and personality "set limits" on the extent to which social action can be pursued according to the dictates of social criteria alone. A third group of limiting conditions is found in the physical and biological exigencies of life.

The physical size of any social organization, for instance, is a serious limiting factor in the functioning of that organization. Let us suppose that for any given collectivity we wish to maximize both democracy and efficiency. As the organization expands in size, the increasing difficulties of rapid and effective interaction make for greater centralization of communication and authority. This in turn impinges on the degree of democratic control which is possible in large organizations. Similarly, in large metropolitan centers, the sheer difficulties of moving people and things from place to place impose many restrictions and imperatives on policy, planning, and public expenditure. Finally, and more indirectly, a person's physical place in a network of human relations may influence greatly the amount and kind of communication he gives and receives, and this may react in turn on his satisfaction with and his contribution to the group in question.

Biological exigencies also contribute to the structure and functioning of social systems. Most obviously, the need for procreation of the species enforces a general set of requirements for the organization of a family structure. At the other end of the life cycle, aging and infirmity impose exigencies which must be met by some kind of institutional arrangements. More broadly, such a biological phenomenon as population pressure constitutes the focus of a myriad of social problems, as the literature on underdeveloped areas reveals. In return, the social structure reacts back on the biological realm; it conditions the birth, death, and migration rates both directly and indirectly.

Substantively the concern with these kinds of problems has fallen most exclusively to the sub-fields of demography, ecology, urban sociology, and parts of organizational and small-group sociology.

The Production and Allocation of Wealth, Power, and Prestige. Any given social organization---a family, a business firm, a church---is intimately involved both at the boundaries of the social system just reviewed, and in the production and allocation of distinctively social resources and rewards. Analytically, however, these two classes of social action can be separated from one another. Without any pretense at theoretical exhaustiveness, we have taken wealth, power, and prestige as the important foci of classification of these resources and rewards. Sociology has "invaded" the provinces of economics and political science, respectively, with regard to wealth and power; the study of prestige systems (or social stratification) was originally and always has been in the sociological domain.

1. Economic structures and processes. Traditionally the science of economics has dealt with the production, distribution, exchange, and consumption of scarce goods and services. From a theoretical point of view, moreover, economists have been interested in processes within structures; that is to say, they have tended to assume that "institutions" and "tastes" are given as a starting point for analysis.[23] Some economists, especially those interested in market structure, labor relations, and economic development, have found it necessary to inquire

---

[23]Paul A. Samuelson, Economics: An Introductory Analysis (Second Edition) (New York: McGraw-Hill, 1951), p. 15.

into the occasions when institutions and tastes undergo change.

Sociologists have carried the concern with economic institutions even further in their pursuit of the following kinds of problems: the nature of economic values and ideologies, the ways in which informal organization supports or subverts the formal purposes of the firm; the expectations and conflicts which arise in specific occupational roles; the relations between labor and management; the structure of unions, and so on. As for the study of tastes, sociologists have also brought their empirical "givenness" into question, especially through the study of status symbolization. Various selections in Part III reflect the kinds of research which sociologists offer in supplement to traditional economic analysis.

2. Political structures and processes. Until very recent times the study of political science has dealt with the moral and philosophical bases of the political life on the one hand and formal political arrangements, such as constitutions, on the other. In the past few decades, however, both political scientists and political sociologists—while maintaining the preoccupation with the nature and distribution of power—have turned to many new interests. These interests include the study of voting statistics and political participation, party and machine organization, informal political processes, the working and management of public opinion, and the impingement of other institutional spheres on the political process. We include a sample of contributions in such areas by political scientists and political sociologists in the 1950's.

3. The distribution of prestige. The study of prestige has, as mentioned, a more distinctively sociological tone. In fact, the systematic approach to stratification constitutes one of those few areas which sociology does not share, in one way or another, with some other field of intellectual endeavor. Areas of concern in the study of stratification include the functional significance of systems of ranking; the relation of systems of prestige-ranking to the stratification of wealth

and power; the effects of status position on almost every conceivable kind of human behavior; the symbolization of social status, and social mobility.

The Balance Between Stability and Change in Society. In the subjects covered in the foregoing sections there has been much study of social change—voting sequences, social mobility, patterns of socialization and adjustment, population movements, and so on. Frequently, however, these are processes which occur within existing social structures. The development, crystallization, and expression of public opinion in an election campaign, for instance, involves many observable changes in attitudes and behavior. However, such change is much less far-reaching than the modification of the constitutional or electoral structure within which these processes unfold. It is this higher-level kind of change—modification in social organization, institutions and values—which forms the subject-matter of our last section.

1. Social disorganization, deviance, and social problems. First we include discussions of the problems of the malfunctioning and breakdown of social system. Historically this has been studied under the headings of social pathology or social disorganization. In the same section we include some of the phenomena which emerge from such conditions of disorganization and which constitute various kinds of deviance or social problems—alcoholism, racial conflict, illness, crime, delinquency, suicide, and some types of collective behavior.

2. Social control and social change. We shall round out our concern with the stability-change problem with the inclusion of a number of studies of social control. As a social force, control is designed first to prevent, and second to correct or neutralize the consequences of social disorganization and deviance. The resultant tug-of-war between tendencies to disorganization on the one hand and the forces of social control on the other leads to the phenomenon of social change, or the modification of social structure and values. Our final list of selections

focuses on some of the issues involved in the systematic study of social change.

The reader will notice that we have used <u>analytic</u> rather than <u>substantive</u> principles to subdivide the field of sociology. We have taken the social system as our starting point, and from there, indicated its boundaries, its major structures and processes, and its kinds of disorganization and reorganization. We have indicated roughly where the usual substantive fields of sociology (for example, family, small groups, urban sociology) fall within the analytic subdivisions, but the correspondence between the two principles of division is far from exact. The family falls first at the cultural boundary (in its capacity as transmitter of values) and second at the personality boundary (in its capacity as agency of socialization). For many societies the sociology of the family would include economic structure and process as well, especially if the family were a viable productive unit. Racial problems occupy no special analytic status, but articles concerning race relations are included under the analytic headings of prestige and social control. Small groups likewise do not form a special heading; rather we have assigned small-group research to areas such as the problem of power and the problem of deviance, depending on the analytic focus of the piece of research itself.

Why have we chosen to divide the field of sociology according to these analytic subdivisions? We feel that this procedure has several advantages over the usual listing of substantive sub-fields of sociology:

(1) By using this analytical framework we are able to avoid at least part of the embarrassing theoretical overlaps of many of the substantive areas, e.g., between social stratification and racial relations.

(2) Many of the substantive areas—sociology of delinquency, urban sociology, criminology, sociology of mental health, sociology of economic development, and others—have arisen in response to specific policy demands and social problems. We feel it wiser to attempt to organize the field in terms of the desiderata of analytic problems rather than in terms of a somewhat unsystematic accumulation of areas upon which public attention has fixed from time to time.

(3) The definition of the field in analytic rather than substantive terms also aids comparative analysis. The analytic approach suggests a comparative search for cognate processes within differing structures rather than the limitation of the subject matter of the field to particular structures. Many of the substantive subdivisions of sociology—occupational sociology, sociology of law, sociology of leisure—are in many ways bound to specific structures; they do not suggest comparative dimensions because such structures for which they are named are not found in other societies.

CRITERIA FOR SELECTION

Several different principles entered into our decision to include or exclude any given article in this volume:

(1) <u>Excellence</u> of several kinds: methodological or theoretical sophistication, relevance to major sociological problems, or comprehension of many discrete research findings.

(2) <u>Representativeness</u> in the general areas which have commanded the attention of sociologists in the decade of the 1950's.[24]

(3) <u>Accessibility</u>: If certain materials —for example, the work of Selznick on the vulnerability of elites in mass society, of Hollingshead and his collaborators on stratification and mental health, of Hughes on work, of Mills on power, of

[24] The one exception to our limitation of selections to the 1950's is "Some Principles of Stratification," by Kingsley Davis and Wilbert E. Moore, which appeared in 1945. We include it because so much controversy accumulated over this theory in the 1950's. Walter Buckley's article, "Social Stratification and The Functional Theory of Social Differentiation," is an illustrative selection from the literature of this controversy.

Riesman on social character, or of Homans on interaction—were largely readily available in book form, this argued in part for their exclusion from this volume. If, on the other hand, a piece of research was located in journals far from the usual travels of the student, we allowed it a special claim for inclusion.

(4) Length: Many excellent contributions to the field during the decade are obviously too long for inclusion in a book of selections. When a question of two appropriate selections of substantially different length arose, we more frequently decided in favor of the shorter.

These criteria obviously overlap; sometimes, in fact, they compete with each other. Hence we ask the reader to assess the net result in the volume not in terms of any one of the criteria, but as a compromise among all of them. We have attempted, using each criterion with flexibility, to assemble as comprehensive and representative a view of sociological research in the 1950's as can be given in a single volume of readings.

PART 1 The Discipline of Sociology

SOCIOLOGY THE PROFESSION: ITS SCOPE AND STYLE

Some Problems Confronting Sociology as a Profession*

Talcott Parsons

SOURCE: *American Sociological Review*, Vol. 24 (1959), pp. 547–59.

I conceive a profession to be a category of occupational role which is organized about the mastery of and fiduciary responsibility for any important segment of a society's cultural tradition, including responsibility for its perpetuation and for its further development. In addition, a profession may have responsibility for the application of its knowledge in practical situations. Roles are organized into collectivities. Professional roles are organized into two main kinds of collectivity: those in which the professional functions themselves are predominantly performed, for example, universities, colleges, and other employing organizations; and those collectivities formed by fellow-professionals for the purpose of promoting the interests of their field, that is, professional associations.

In contrast to a predominantly applied profession like medicine, sociology is universally conceived as a scientific discipline which is clearly primarily dedicated to the advancement and transmission of empirical knowledge in its field and secondarily to the communication of such knowledge to non-members and its utilization in practical affairs. The cen-

tral agency for performance of these functions is clearly a body of professionally competent personnel who have been trained in the mastery of the subject-matter and the techniques of its advancement and use, and who have been socialized into the professional role, accepting certain responsibilities and enjoying certain privileges, in the society.

Given the clear centrality of the profession's organization about a scientific discipline, the first set of problems to be raised involves the state of the discipline as a cultural complex itself and as part of a larger one. This set of problems can in turn be broken down into four questions. The most central of these concerns the extent to which the canons of scientific adequacy and objectivity have come to be established as the working code of the profession in dealing with a defined intellectual subject matter. The second concerns the present clarity of the differentiation from and relation to neighboring scientific disciplines, so that we can speak with a certain definiteness about what, as distinct from other scientists, a sociologist does. The third question concerns the differentiation of sociology as a science from sociological "practice" or application to such problems as the welfare of various categories of handicapped or disturbed people, the

*I am particularly indebted to Mrs. Carolyn Cooper, who both compiled data for this paper and competently revised and condensed the first draft.

efficiency of workers in industry, and so on, and its proper relation to this applied field. Finally, there is the problem of sociology's differentiation as a scientific discipline from and relation to the non-scientific aspects of the general culture, such as philosophy, religion, literature, and the arts, as well as the general Weltenschauung.

While these four problem areas are directly related to sociology as a discipline within the culture, it is equally important to consider the corresponding set of problems which faces sociologists individually and collectively functioning in American society. In doing so, I would give unequivocal primacy to the sociologist's role as scientist. This is to say that I conceive the first obligation of sociology as a profession to be the promotion of the discipline: on the one hand, through the investigations carried out by its members, and, on the other, through the "investment" of their capacities and energies in the training of others who will subsequently carry on this function. But this central function cannot be carried on in a social vacuum; in our type of society it is inherently linked with certain other functions which the profession cannot and should not evade.

The first of these is what may be called "citizenship" in the world of scientists and other culturally-oriented groups. This concerns the place of sociologists in universities and the responsibilities they carry outside their own departments, but also their relations with other intellectual groups---notably in neighboring disciplines---in the society at large. A second important social function carries the responsibility for facilitating the use of sociological knowledge for the practical interests of the society---the whole field of "applied" sociology. Finally, sociologists contribute to their society's general "definition of the situation." As experts in some sense in the interpretation of social events, they necessarily exercise a certain indirect influence, most conspicuously through teaching their subject to students who are not likely to become profes-

sionals in the field---a "general education" function. To their influence through formal teaching is added the influence exerted by sociologists through writing, lecturing, and other channels on the general "intellectual" concerns of the day. In the nature of the case, the more firmly sociology becomes established in the universities, the more important these three secondary social functions will become.

In this paper my main interest is to discuss the ways in which the profession of sociologist fits into the social structure, not how sociology as a discipline fits into the cultural setting. But these two topics are so closely intertwined empirically that in discussing either the other must continually be kept in mind. Precisely because of this intimate inter-relationship, it is necessary to sketch the situation of the discipline as a background for discussing the profession itself.

THE SITUATION OF SOCIOLOGY AS A DISCIPLINE

In the perspective of history, any high-level scientific knowledge of human social behavior is a very recent phenomenon, having been achieved, with such antecedent developments as those in economic theory and in statistics, largely in the present century. In this brief period, sociology has advanced with seemingly great rapidity. But cultural growth is so complex and the time so short that it almost goes without saying that the development of sociology stands at present in an early stage.

Given this situation, it is not surprising that the differentiation between social science, on the one hand, and the most closely related non- or partially-scientific components of the general culture, on the other hand, is recent, incomplete, and unstable. I refer to the differentiation of social science from both "social philosophy" and "social problems." A field of science cannot be institutionalized until a relatively clear orientation to its own investigative problems has been worked out which is not dominated by either of these two socially important but pre-dominantly non-scientific bases of concern. The third problem of differentiation, then, refers to the place of sociology within the corpus of scientific disciplines, above all those dealing with human behavior. A brief discussion of each of these three problems of differentiation seems to be in order.

First, with respect to the most general differentiation of social science from the philosophical matrix in which it had earlier been embedded, we may speak of a religious, a philosophical, and a more generally scientific aspect of this matrix. The relative predominance of these aspects partly corresponds with principal phases of Western intellectual history.

In the earliest of these phases, the differentiation of secular social thought from religious apologetics was brought about, becoming a considerable movement only in the 17th century. The primary emphasis in this first major secular phase was political in a broad and diffuse sense, dealing with secular society as a politically organized "state" contrasting with the church. Once this step had been taken, a differentiation of substantive specialties within the field could gradually develop.

Not until the late 18th century did the field of economics begin clearly to emerge from this diffuse political matrix, with Adam Smith as the first highly eminent writer leading up to the classical economics. The focus of political theory tended to become considerably narrower, centering on the phenomena of government in the increasingly differentiated type of society of the time. Thus, along with history, which refused to identify itself with any particular focus of substantive interest, in the 19th century the broad frames of reference were laid out for political science and for economics.

This intellectual situation provided the main setting for the emergence of sociology along one of its main paths namely the treatment of those more macroscopic aspects of society that were not adequately accounted for in the utilitarian tradition which had gained such promi-nence in political theory and in economics. With Comte as the most important precursor and Marx pointing up the problem of the status of "economic factors," Durkheim and Weber in Europe were the great theoretical tone-setters of the new sociological approach, being greatly preoccupied with the assessment of the institutional framework within which modern economic processes took place, and which were independent in certain ways of the operations of political organization. They were also oriented to the "collectivist" mode of thought stemming from Rousseau and from German idealism, which provided the major point of reference for their critiques of utilitarianism.[1] In general, they looked to the "ideal" as contrasted with "material" factors for the key concepts---such as values and institutionalized norms---of their analyses.

Within the "scientific" aspect of the philosophical matrix of social thought, referred to above, the phase given impetus by Darwinian biology in the second half of the 19th century had particular relevance to sociology. Spencer and the American evolutionists Sumner and Ward in particular derive from this background and its complex interrelations with utilitarianism and positivistic rationalism. But in addition to their influence on the emergence of sociology, the concept of evolution and the broad framework of the relation between competition and cooperation, laissez faire and planning, also provided the intellectual matrix from which grew anthropology in Great Britain, and which underlies much of the development of modern psychology. Of course, psychology, by way of Freud, also traces back in a complex manner to medical biology; and anthropology, especially as influenced in this country by Frans Boas, was infused by German idealist-historicist thinking. In the United States the "social psychology" of C. H.

---

[1] For a fuller discussion, see "The General Interpretation of Action," Introduction to Part 1, Section A of Theories of Society, co-edited with E. A. Shils, K. D. Naegele, and J. R. Pitts, to be published in 1961 by the Free Press.

Cooley and G. H. Mead was an important bridge between these intellectual currents.

In very schematic terms, these are the main Western intellectual trends in the developmental background of the present social sciences. It can be readily seen that the lines which distinguish them from each other are far from being very sharply drawn. From the viewpoint of the more macroscopic disciplines like political science and economics, sociology has often been treated as a residual category or as a more or less "imperialistic" summation of all knowledge about society. In Germany in particular it has tended to be identified with the philosophy of history, the main difference being sociology's greater claim to empirical standing. There has been an increasingly clear focus, however, on phenomena of values and norms and their relation to personality, independently of technical concerns, particularly of economics.

Within the complex more closely associated with Darwinian biology, there are also difficult borderline problems vis-à-vis both anthropology and psychology. The earlier anthropological concentration on the study of nonliterate peoples helped to postpone consideration of such questions, but more recently the distinction between sociology and anthropology has become less conspicuous. It is not an easy question whether the relative emphases on "culture," as made by many American anthropologists, and on social systems, as stressed by at least some sociologists, is an adequate working basis for a differentiation of the two disciplines. Psychology, however, seems clearly to focus on the study of analytically distinct components of behavior imputable to the "individual." But since virtually all human behavior is concretely both individual and social (and also cultural), here there are also formidable difficulties in drawing clear analytical lines; hence the ambiguous position of social psychology.

It seems to be in the nature of such a complex of scientific disciplines that, first, in studying empirical phenomena, any analytical classification crosscuts common sense classifications. Thus economics cannot be the theory of "business" in a simple sense, political theory the theory of "government," nor psychology the theory of individual behavior, any more than psysiology studies living organisms only and chemistry only lifeless matter. Secondly, the line cannot be drawn altogether clearly between the scientific components of this complex of disciplines and their non-scientific philosophical matrix. Such issues as positivism and the possible ontological status of the individual in the utilitarian frame of reference, for example, cannot be fully excluded from theoretical discussion in the social sciences.

These intellectual problems, which are unlikely to be easily and quickly settled, have an important bearing on the position and behavior of the professional groups involved in them. They are sources of strain both within and between disciplines. The social sciences have come to form a "family" which is well enough structured for certain working purposes, but which still leaves many areas of indeterminacy and of potential and sometimes open conflict. It may well be that only a minority of members of the relevant professional groups actively concern themselves with these problems at any given time—undoubtedly a desirable situation—but this does not justify treating the problems themselves as trivial in their implications for the professional situation.

I have suggested that the historical process by which the social science disciplines have come to be differentiated is so closely intertwined with the process by which they have gradually emerged from a more philosophical matrix that a single treatment of both trends has been necessary. Turning to the third problem of differentiation, between scientific disciplines and prescriptions for practical action, perhaps the most striking fact is the very near recency of any clear differentiation. Both political and economic theory throughout their formative periods were directly concerned with prescribing public policy and did not seriously attempt to separate even conceptually the bases of empirical generalization from the evaluative basis of policy recommendation. Marxism is a particularly important example of an economic theory that attempts no such distinction, and indeed denies its legitimacy. Max Weber was probably the first major theorist to assert the fundamental importance of carefully distinguishing between problems of scientific generalization and those of evaluation and policy, and to work out a clear methodological basis for the distinction. It is virtually only within the last generation that acceptance of this distinction has come to be generally diffused within the social science professions, and it is still quite incomplete. The strong positivistic component in the philosophical matrix underlying the social sciences has been one of the major impediments to such acceptance.

One feature of the history of American sociology, which differs from the European (especially Continental), is important in the present-day situation. European social sciences generally and sociology in particular had been primarily concerned with a highly macroscopic interpretation of society's development.[2] Hence the prominence of such general rubrics as capitalism and socialism. In the United States, however, there was considerably less concern with macroscopic interpretation.[3] The broad outline of the society and its major values were more apt to be taken for granted, with the emphasis given to particular "social problems." There was a deep concern with how actual situations deviated from values, which were above all the values of liberal Protestantism in the era when the "social gospel" was particularly prominent. Here problems associated with slums, rural life, immigration, and Negro-White relations were at the center of attention.

This kind of interest helps to explain why American sociology has been far less concerned with the borderline of philosophy than has European. It could become separated from political theory and economics more readily since these two disciplines tended to take a macroscopic view of society. Under these circumstances, the most serious problem of differentiation for American sociology has stemmed from its applied interests. In its earlier period sociology was closely identified with religiously defined ethical obligations and with philanthropy, which became institutionalized in certain aspects of community service and social work. Thus many early American sociologists were trained in the ministry, and several university departments combined sociology and social work. However, a rather early and sometimes sharp reaction developed against the latter association,[4] often resulting in the separation of the two fields, notably at the University of Chicago and later at Harvard.

Although the problem of differentiation from applied interests was particularly acute in the American case, concentration on less macroscopic problems had a special advantage. This emphasis encouraged the development of a variety of techniques for empirical research, for example, participant observation, the use of personal documents, interviewing, and questionnaire methods. That this rapid technical development coincided with a similar growth in statistics was highly important. In the general American climate of interest in empirical matters, this technical emphasis, much more pronounced than in Europe, helped significantly to speed the development of sociology as an empirical science.

It is also important that the more microscopic emphasis of American sociology brought it into relatively close touch

[2]See, e.g., Karl Mannheim, "German Sociology (1918-1933)," Politica, Vol. 1 (February, 1934), pp. 12-33.

[3]For perhaps the fullest historical account available, see Howard W. Odum, American Sociology: The Story of Sociology in the United States Through 1950, (New York: Longmans, Green, 1951).

[4]Cf. Robert C. Angell, "A Research Basis for Welfare Practice," Social Work Journal, Vol. 35 (October, 1954), pp. 145 ff.

with psychology, particularly in the over-lapping field of social psychology, and with anthropology, particularly in the study of small communities, which were the first major objects in modern society of anthropological study. Both psychology and anthropology were fields which, in different ways, were very active in developing detailed empirical research. The Continental European type of sociology would have had much more difficulty in becoming an integral part of the more general trend of empirical research than this has actually been the case in the United States. It would be hard to exaggerate the importance of a strong tradition of empirical research in bringing about the differentiation between sociology as a scientific discipline and its application to social policy.

In sum, within the last generation or so sociology has reached what is, perhaps, a first level of maturity as a scientific discipline. Although the process of differentiation is far from complete and there remain many indistinct borderline areas, sociology, along with the other social sciences, has become relatively differentiated from the philosophical matrix. It has, again with a good deal of indistinctness, achieved a fairly clearly defined place in the general cluster of scientific disciplines which deal with human behavior. It has also been disentangled from the earlier simple identification with specific practical goals in the society, to become an independent, relatively "pure" discipline with a research and theoretical tradition of its own. As we have seen, however, each of these borderlines is still highly problematical, and the unclarity of the cultural lines is a focus of strain at each point. I would say that the problem of ideological contamination is the most urgent one vis-à-vis the philosophical background; that of interdisciplinary imperialisms and conflict in relations with sister disciplines; and the problem of full commitment to pure research and training, not the formulation of social policy, vis-à-vis the applied front.

THE INSTITUTIONALIZATION OF SOCIOLOGY IN THE UNIVERSITIES

Keeping in mind these intellectual highlights, I turn to a sketch of the institutionalization of the profession in the structure of our society. According to the conception of sociology as a scientific discipline, it is evident that the central point of its institutionalization should be university faculties of arts and sciences. Here sociology established a fairly secure foothold at an early stage, and has greatly extended it since. Clearly strategic for its development was sociology's introduction around the turn of the century in the new Faculty of Political Science at Columbia University and at the University of Chicago. These two departments, each led by a man of such stature as to play a leadership role in faculty affairs—Franklin H. Giddings and Albion W. Small, respectively—have served as the most important training grounds for the second generation of American sociologists, especially those with a strong orientation to establishment of the field as a scientific discipline, and have populated many of the important posts throughout the country. A notable early offshoot of Columbia, for example, was the introduction of sociology at the University of North Carolina under the leadership of Howard W. Odum. The story, of course, has not been without its vicissitudes. Certainly Columbia and Chicago have been the most consistently successful centers of sociology from the formative years, though each has had its ups and downs. But until very recently the early initiative of Ward (late in his career) at Brown University did not lead to a comparable development there, and the Yale tradition established much earlier by Sumner long remained under his successor largely insulated from the rest of the profession.

More generally, it is of the first importance that in this country training in sociology was established concomitantly with professional training in the other social sciences. Even though the emergence of sociology as a discipline has lagged somewhat behind the other social sciences, for reasons suggested above, sociology as a profession has not had to surmount alone the difficult barrier of gaining full university status.

Another notable feature of the development of sociology in American universities was its strength, in a decisive period, in the Middle West. Here the University of Chicago did not stand alone, but bore a very close relation to the Wisconsin of Ross and Gillin, the Michigan of Cooley, the Illinois of Hayes, and the Minnesota of Vincent and somewhat later, of Chapin. This expansion may have been related to the religio-ethical complex in that part of the country, noted above. In any event, the main pattern established in the Middle West, as well as in the East, was that of departments heavily committed to the pursuit of sociological research and of training competent and committed professionals.

The last generation has seen a diffusion of this professional pattern throughout the country's major universities. Among the several important steps in this further development have been sociology's establishment at Harvard in 1931, under the chairmanship of Sorokin, and its expansion in 1946; its development at Cornell, under the leadership of Leonard S. Cottrell, Jr., building on a foundation of rural sociology under the direction of Dwight Sanderson; and the great expansion within very recent years at Berkeley, California, building partly on Teggart's historical study of social institutions.

Now for the first time, sociology has come to be recognized as one of the regular disciplines in every major university in the United States—with Johns Hopkins finally completing the roster. Only in a few elite colleges of liberal arts—for example, Amherst, Williams, and Swarthmore—has this development still failed to occur. This situation stands in sharp contrast to that in Europe, where the total number of chairs constitutes a rather small fraction of the American, with as yet only minimal recognition of sociology at Oxford and Cambridge and, on the Continent, with only about one half of the universities north of the Alps showing some interest.

If the conception of sociology as a profession organized about a scientific discipline be accepted, the importance of the broad development in the United States can scarcely be exaggerated. A secure position in university faculties of course is the structural base from which a scientifically oriented profession can most effectively operate. Sociology is thus completely involved in the situation confronting the scientific professions generally, and the social sciences particularly, in American society. Yet no other base of operations could be so advantageous for sociology's further development as a discipline and its eventual influence in the society.

If this position is to be firmly consolidated, it is crucial to have an adequate supply of able and properly trained personnel. People who entered the field in its earliest phase had highly diverse backgrounds, including the ministry, social work, journalism, and business. And their training was only minimally technical. The early expansion of the profession probably took place rather too rapidly; in the first decades of this century there were more positions available than there were trained people to occupy them, and hence a considerable influx of people without adequate professional qualification. It took time to get training programs established within the university framework.

In the last generation, however, this situation has greatly improved. The output of professionally qualified personnel has steadily increased, both through growing numbers being turned out by the same graduate schools and by new graduate training programs. For example, in the three years 1936-1938, the average number of new Ph.D. degrees reported to the American Journal of Sociology was 45 a year, compared to an annual average of 133 for the period 1955-1957. These degrees were granted by about 18 departments in the earlier period, and by about 35 departments in the recent period.

However, graduate training programs have come increasingly to include apprenticeship in empirical investigations within the framework of on-going research programs. Some of these programs have been financed by grants to individual faculty members from foundations, or more recently, from the government; some are more formally organized through such devices as Columbia's Bureau of Applied Social Research; and some are carried on by such university-based survey research organizations as the National Opinion Research Center. Whatever the varying patterns of organization, these research facilities have added enormously to the promotion of the profession's two fundamental functions—the advancement of its own discipline and the training of its core personnel. Certainly this development could not have occurred without substantial advance both in research techniques and in theoretical sophistication. It is one of the clearest indications of the discipline's gradual coming of age.

As a result of this steady increase in the quantity and quality of graduate training programs, sociology in recent years has reached, I believe, the stage of professionalization where it no longer depends so heavily on the contributions of a few outstanding individuals, a seemingly inevitable feature of the earliest stage of a profession's development. We have instead a growing body of solidly trained and competent people who provide in the aggregate a cumulative development of knowledge on which their successors can build and which is the most important hallmark of a relatively mature science.

Sociology's central operating base in university faculties raises the important problem of the place of sociology relative to its sister disciplines in these faculties. As noted above, there are many points at which, in terms of intellectual content, the borderlines are unclear. Although many of these borderline problems lack clear substantive and organi-

zational definition, the situation seems to be fairly satisfactory. From the point of view of the profession's institutionalization in the academic community, there are two conspicuous encouraging facts about the current situation. First, sociology as a "subject" has gained generally acknowledged academic "citizenship," as we have seen. Second, although there are cases in which sociology is organizationally combined with other disciplines —sometimes with the economics-political science complex, sometimes with psychology or anthropology or both—there is no threatening uniformity of the pattern in which this occurs.

Sociology's middle position in relation to the other "behavioral sciences" is clearly a highly strategic one. The professional group is in no danger of being absorbed into any of its neighbors; moreover it offers something essential to each of them. To economists and political scientists, for instance, it provides a better understanding of "institutional" factors than their own disciplines make readily available. To psychologists it contributes a focus on "social" factors not readily reducible to individual terms. Vis-à-vis anthropology, the line is not so clear, but perhaps without seeming invidious one may say that anthropologists, having derived so much of their experience from the study of relatively undifferentiated societies, can use some help in the analysis of structurally complex modern societies, a field in which sociologists have a certain "head start."

With respect to the familiar question of sociology's place in the "pecking order" of academic disciplines, we may note that (given the crudity of such a rating system) within the last generation sociology has risen substantially in relative prestige. I interpret this rise to be a consequence of its relative strengthening in all four of the variables which were distinguished at the beginning of this paper.

A final point concerning the relation of sociology to its sister disciplines concerns the increasing participation of sociologists in interdisciplinary research projects. One major type of interdisciplinary venture is the "area" study, but there is a variety of other types such as studies of organizations and local community situations. These projects provide an important setting in which the nature of the participating disciplines can become better defined.

I have briefly outlined the general strengthening of sociology's position as a scientific discipline, its establishment in university faculties, and the development of its research and training functions; and touched upon the contributions it can make to its sister disciplines. Two other main developments remain to be reviewed. Anticipating the subsequent discussion somewhat, it may first be said that sociology's contribution to our society's ideological "definition of the situation" has greatly increased in importance in recent years. The frequency with which the term "sociology" appears in popular discussions, albeit often with dubious technical justification, is an index of this situation. Secondly, although sociologists are still well behind their economist, political scientist, and psychologist colleagues, the change over the past twenty years in the extent to which they have won a place in the world of practical affairs is unmistakable. The upshot of this whole shift, to which no one factor has predominantly contributed, is that sociology may perhaps be said to have graduated from being the least respectable of the social science disciplines to being the most controversial.

SOCIOLOGY'S CONTRIBUTION TO CONTEMPORARY IDEOLOGY

An important index of the relationship which has been developing between changes in the society itself and the place of the social science professions within it is that the term sociology is coming increasingly to be a central symbol in the popular ideological preoccupations of our time. In this respect, perhaps we may say that, ideologically, a "sociological era" has begun to emerge, following an "economic" and, more recently, a "psychological" era.

Not only was the industrial economy the great new phenomenon from the latter 19th well into this century; intellectually economic theory of varying kinds provided the terms for defining the character of that period. Schools of thought ranged from the most orthodox laissez-faire capitalism through varying shades of liberalism and reformism to radical socialism, eventually crystallizing in Marxism; but underlying all these views was a common set of assumptions about the critical character of "economic factors." This ideological era, the last major phase of which was the New Deal period, was undoubtedly intimately connected with the process by which economics as a science came to be established in the academic world. The salience of economics as an ideological focus has not greatly subsided, although of course it continues to play an important role in various issues of public policy. The economic era was succeeded, in a considerably less "massive" form, by the psychological era. This shift, which came to a head in the 1930s, was signalled by the growing concern with the role of rational versus "irrational" factors in the motivation of the individual. Similarly, it was closely associated with the rapid development of psychology as a scientific discipline.

While the economic era of ideology was related to the fact of industrialization, the psychological era has been related to industrialization's consequences for the individual. If, the psychological movement challenged the adequacy of simpler-minded economic interpretations of human behavior, however, it became apparent that the understanding of the complexities and changes of our large-scale society and its "mass" phenomena require more than analysis of individual conduct. The new ideological era, which has overlapped with the psychological one, can be described as a kind of dialectic between a psychological focus of interest in the individual and a sociological focus of interest in the society. Inevitably the problem of constraints on individual freedom is a central theme in this complex. This seems to be the background of contemporary concern with the problem of "conformity." Note the striking difference between the emphasis in this case and what it was in the era of economic ideological primacy, when the essential problem—often posed as productivity _versus_ equality—was to find a basis for adequate "satisfaction of wants." Certainly, in a sense, the conformity problem is peculiar to an "affluent society."

The emergence of this broad ideological preoccupation has affected the status of the sociological profession because now the sociologist is beginning to be defined by a much broader public as an expert on intellectual problems of public concern. The fact that his expertise is viewed with a large measure of ambivalence does not detract from the significance of this point. Although the extrapolation of trends is dangerous business, it seems justified to suggest a probable connection between the emergence of this sociological focus of ideological preoccupation and the consolidation of the sociological profession within the society. If this be the case, it is clearly a major harbinger of opportunity. At the same time it is a basis for stressing the urgency of certain problems of our own position and the way in which it is likely to develop.

There is an intimate connection between the growing ideological significance of sociology and what in many respects is its oldest function, namely the teaching of college undergraduates, the large majority of whom do not expect to become professional social scientists. Clearly this teaching function has always been one of the principal responsibilities of the profession and still is. It is primarily a general education function, helping to orient the student to aspects of the world in which he lives. Naturally the character of this function has changed, with change both in the society itself and in sociology as a discipline. The more technical the discipline becomes, the greater the problem of its adaptation to general education purposes.

The problem of the relation between the profession's research and training functions at the graduate level and the undergraduate educational function presents formidable complications. It is difficult to know the proportion of sociologists in academic positions mainly engaged in each of these functions. Those serving on the faculties of liberal arts colleges with only minimal or no graduate programs are primarily involved in general education. Yet in the universities there is generally a shading off, and many faculty members devote a substantial portion of their energy to undergraduate teaching. Such shading off is undoubtedly desirable, because undergraduate work in sociology is continuous with graduate work, and also because it feeds into professional training in the neighboring disciplines. The so-called "university college" exposes its undergraduates to the influence of those who are pursuing research directly on the frontiers of their fields, thus providing opportunity for observing the actual process of culture building, rather than merely receiving the end "product."

Nevertheless there are important problems in integrating the two teaching functions. Since graduate training has come to be so highly oriented to the training of research and graduate school personnel, there has been a strong tendency for the undergraduate teaching function (where it is not merged with the graduate) to be carried out by personnel who have not been selected for careers of high professional prestige. Moreover, with increasing professionalization, the new Ph.D. who accepts a college teaching job finds it increasingly difficult to transfer to a university department. This growing rigidity of career lines has probably been accentuated by the enormous expansion of organized research facilities, so that a man who works in a university research setting early in his career has opportunities to accumulate a research record which, in competition for the higher level university appointments, cannot be matched by the man who has carried a heavy load of undergraduate teaching in an atmosphere where little research is going on—although their capabilities may be equal. There is, therefore, a tendency to make the college teacher a kind of second class citizen of the profession's academic branch.

To be sure, this is a problem shared by other academic disciplines and is in no way peculiar to sociology. But the situation may be aggravated by the recent expansion of opportunities for sociologists in other professional faculties and in non-academic fields. Thus the time seems to be approaching when we should give serious consideration to the establishment of special training programs for prospective college teachers. The profession's undergraduate teaching function is too important to be allowed to deteriorate by default.

Undergraduate teaching itself is undergoing an important shift in emphasis which increases its importance in relation to the problems of the profession. During the earlier period, the primary appeal of sociology to undergraduates lay in "social problems," including not only crime and poverty, but also such problem areas as marriage and the family. Now, even in these areas, the emphasis seems to have shifted from the problem of how to cope with clear-cut "evils" in the society, to the type of concern I have called ideological. Instead of taking for granted a clear definition of what needs to be done in our society, concern centers about what kind of a society it is, where it is going, and the like. The most important consequence of this shift is to bring the undergraduate teaching of sociology much more closely into relation with the major general intellectual preoccupations of our society.

This shift imposes a heavy responsibility on sociologists. An ideology is precisely a meeting ground between a society's value-commitments and its empirical scientific culture. In the nature of the case powerful pressures come into conflict with standards of scientific objectivity. The emergence of sociology into a central position in the focus of

ideological preoccupation means that it must serve as a primary guardian of the scientific tradition, counteracting the many tendencies to introduce biases and distortions. It must do this in a situation where its own technical resources are only partially adequate to the task, where the only honest professional answer to many questions is "we don't know," even though would-be sociologists loudly proclaim their pseudo-solutions of many problems.

Some scientific purists would advocate dealing with this situation by total withdrawal, by avoiding all connection with this wider public forum of discussion. This is feasible and often justifiable for certain purely technical specialists. For the profession as a whole, however, it is an impossible position to take. A publicly salient participation of the profession in these discussions is bound to occur somehow or other, and it is of crucial interest to the profession that enough highly competent and professionally responsible persons should be heard. This consideration applies not least to the function of teaching and writing for undergraduates.

THE APPLIED FUNCTION

The fourth principal area of the profession's involvement in the structure of the society I have called the applied function. As noted, this interest was particularly prominent in sociology's early phase, especially in the social problems field, but was followed by a rather sharp withdrawal in favor of building up the central academic core of the discipline. More recently, however, there has been a notable return to applied interests over a far broader front than before. The turning point probably lay in the attempt to mobilize social science talent for military purposes in World War II, a movement in which sociology played an appreciable though far from leading part. Developments in such fields as industrial sociology and market research have also given impetus to the steady expansion of the applied function.

During the early development of a new discipline having practical possibilities, it is common for its own professional personnel directly to undertake these practical functions, and in some professions this pattern continues and expands. Chemistry perhaps is the profession in which this pattern is most prominent; a large proportion of those with Ph.D.s in chemistry do applied technological work for industry and government, probably outnumbering the chemical engineers. A similar pattern marks the recent growth of sociology and will probably continue to do so, most importantly perhaps in industrial organization, governmental organization, especially the armed services; opinion and attitude research; and various types of social agencies concerned with criminology, health, and the like. As yet, however, by far the largest proportion of sociologists with the Ph.D. ---about 86 per cent---are employed by colleges and universities, exceeded in this respect only by history, literature, and other humanities, while a significantly smaller proportion of holders of the Ph.D. in political science and economics are so employed (76 and 69 per cent, respectively).[5]

An important and rapidly expanding bridge between non-academic and academic employment is the consultant role in various non-academic organizations. This ranges from a relatively individualized service to particular clients to a considerable amount of "conferencing" where groups of professionals, often interdisciplinary in composition, are called on to help clarify a practical problem area.

A critical difference between the development of applied functions in sociology and psychology is the lesser importance in the former of anything like "practice," in the sense of individual service for a fee. The employers of sociologists, on both full time and consulting bases, are more likely to be organizations such as business firms, governmental units, social agencies, and research offices, which as such are unlikely to need the same kind of protection against charlatanism or other exploitation needed by an individual employing professional services. Hence the sociological profession is more likely to be able to minimize the complicated problems of legal certification, licensing, or both, in which the psychologists have recently become heavily involved.[6]

A new pattern of application has recently emerged, however, in which sociologists participate along with specialists in other "basic sciences" in research and training for a range of applied professions. Historically the closest affiliation of sociology with an applied profession was that with social work. When sociology withdrew from this activity social work formed a primary al-

---

[5] According to a 1952 survey reported in "Personnel Resources in the Social Sciences and Humanities," U.S. Bureau of Labor Statistics Bulletin #1169, Table A-17, pp. 94-96. The differences are even more striking among those holding a Master's degree: of sociology Masters, 69.1 per cent were employed in colleges or universities, but only 36.8 per cent of those in political science and 46.3 per cent of those in economics were so employed. It is suggestive in this connection that a more up-to-date survey of graduate students, not yet published by N.O.R.C., shows a smaller proportion (68 per cent) of sociologist-anthropologist Ph.D. candidates intending to enter academic life. By comparison, the proportions of candidates with this intention in some other fields are: English, 82 per cent; political science, 49 per cent; economics, 48 per cent; psychology, 42 per cent; chemistry, 39 per cent. (Personal communication from James A. Davis, National Opinion Research Center.)

[6] In this case the problem stems mainly from the rapid expansion of practice in clinical psychology and the ambiguities of its relation to the practice of psychiatry. As a defense against the medical claim to a monopoly on legitimate psychotherapy, the psychologists have adopted a policy in favor of legal certification, to be implemented by certifying not functions as such but the use of the title "psychologist." This has impinged on the interests of sociologists because the certification of the title in the terms spelled out in some statutes would exclude social psychologists with sociological training and affiliation from certification and hence from performing various applied functions. This issue is currently the object of complex negotiation between the two professional associations. But it is clear that certification of the title of an academic discipline in order to define legitimate applied practice seems to involve serious complications both for the discipline itself and for those closely related to it in the scientific community.

liance with psychiatry. Only recently has the relationship been reestablished, primarily through the participation of sociologists both in the training of graduate social work students and in research bearing on social work.[7]

The primary break-through of the new pattern has occurred in the field of health, especially mental health. After the overwhelming predominance, during the first quarter of the century, of the definition of "scientific" medicine as "organic" medicine, the emergence of concern with psychological and social factors in illness and health has been a dramatic development. Within this framework, sociologists perhaps have come to take the lead more than any other "behavioral" scientists, in collaboration and friendly rivalry with the anthropologists, and apparently drawing ahead of the psychologists, although the latter constitute numerically and organizationally a more powerful group. This seems to be largely because sociology is uninvolved in claims to control the therapy of individual patients. The sociologist helps with problems that impinge on medicine and public health, but his functions cannot be seen as practice in the traditional medical sense. Hence sociology is not viewed as a threat to the psychiatric treatment of patients in the same way as is clinical psychology.

It is now well known that appointments in medical and public health organizations of various sorts constitute one of the major fields of employment for sociologists, probably the largest single field except for the central teaching-research occupation. The character of these openings varies greatly, perhaps qualitatively the most important type being appointment to faculty posts in medical schools and schools of public health. The trend is certainly toward the inclusion of sociology among the basic sciences underlying the practice of medicine, and thus toward the incorporation of sociologists, along with other behavioral scientists, in an organizational status parallel to that of

psychologists, biochemists, biophysicists, bacteriologists, and so on.

The health field, however, is only one of several applied areas in which this new pattern is emerging. Although not as yet on so large a scale, the same trend is observable in the relation of the social sciences generally, and sociology in particular, to schools of business and public administration, of education, of law, and even of divinity. Perhaps the furthest advancement along these lines so far is in business schools—the most important precursor of this development having been the linkage between rural sociology and colleges of agriculture. The two most important branches of sociology to business schools are of course industrial sociology and survey research. Probably the field in which sociology's role is most likely to grow rapidly in the near future is education, not least because of our society's present urgent need for expansion and improvement of educational facilities. The penetration of the social sciences into the field of law has been rather slow—notwithstanding such assertions as Dean Griswold's that law itself is a social science;[8] but it may be expected to accelerate and to be substantial in the long run.

Public funds have been very important in this general development. Funds available through the land-grant colleges and the agricultural experimental stations gave rural sociology considerable prominence a generation ago, and the Department of Agriculture, along with the Bureau of the Census, was the first agency of the Federal government in which social scientists gained a firm foothold. The role of the National Institutes of Health in the development of social sciences in that area is well known. One reason for predicting a major development of the social sciences in relation to education is the expectation that federal activities will greatly expand in this field and that financial aid to training and

---

[7] Angell, op. cit.

[8] Erwin N. Griswold, "Law Schools and Human Relations," Tyrrell Williams Lecture delivered at the Law School of Washington University, St. Louis, April 19, 1955, (mimeo.) p. 6.

research in the relevant professions will play a major part in this expansion.

This movement has been brought about not only by the various professional schools themselves and by the availability of public funds, but has been greatly aided in particular by the Russell Sage Foundation, which has acted as a catalyst in encouraging awareness among sociologists and the applied professions of the relevance of each others' skills. As Donald Young pointed out in 1955: "Reference has been made to the needs of the practicing professions for social science data and techniques.... It would be a pity not to respond to their need and not to take advantage of the opportunity to test our 'wares'---to identify their deficiencies and to consider where to attempt to improve them." He also posed the question of "whether the aim should be the development of practicing sociologists to take direct responsibility for determination of policy, operation of action programs, and work with clients presenting personal problems; or whether the purpose should be the development of consultants or middlemen to work closely with the applied professions already established." [9]

I believe myself that it is of the highest importance to the development of sociology that its relation to a whole series of applied functions be mediated through the professional schools which train practitioners in these functions and which form centers for "action research" aimed at yielding directly practical results. In a highly differentiated society where applied science is rapidly increasing in importance in the social as well as the natural science fields, such schools are the most appropriate point of articulation between a scientific profession and the many urgent practical social needs. In general it is sounder that the primary responsibilities for implementation should be borne by members of the applied professions rather than by scientists as such. The existence of such a

mediating structure provides a highly important protection of the scientific profession's central function against many types of diversionary pressures.

This expanding pattern of relationship with the applied professions presents an urgent problem to the sociological profession: we must try to ensure that the sociologists who are employed in these contexts meet very high standards of ability, training, and professional responsibility. In view of the rapidly expanding demand for sociologists' services, this is clearly going to be a very difficult requirement to meet.

CHANNELS OF PUBLICATION

One important facility on which a profession must depend consists of channels for publishing its research results and teaching materials, both in journals and in book form. In launching and developing the field of sociology, it was of the first importance that the American Journal of Sociology was established so early by the University of Chicago department under Small, and that in due course still other organs were established. By the time (1936) the American Sociological Review was started, there was urgent need for an additional journal, and now the range of such outlets is still widening.

It is not so easy for the profession itself to control book publishing opportunities. University presses of course have played an important part, but for a long period sociology was caught in a kind of vicious circle in which, due to the urgency of teaching needs and the limited library facilities at the undergraduate level, elementary textbooks were overemphasized, at the expense of more substantial studies. With the maturing of the field, this situation has greatly improved in recent years. The market for substantial books has widened and the output of publishable research has increased; in addition, classics in the field are being translated and reprinted, reaching a much wider public than before. The Free Press in particular has greatly increased the availability of sociological literature and has demonstrated to other publishing

[9]Donald Young, "Sociology and the Practicing Professions," American Sociological Review, Vol. 20 (December, 1955), p. 646.

houses that serious non-textbook publications in sociology have a wide market.

THE ORGANIZED PROFESSION

This review of the problems facing the sociological profession concludes with a brief consideration of its own organization in professional associations. The founders of sociology in the United States took steps very early to organize the American Sociological Society, and there has been a clear continuity of responsible leadership ever since. A generation later several regional societies were established. Today there are various other specialized groups, affiliated with the national Society, such as the Rural Sociological Society and the Society for the Study of Social Problems, each having a journal of its own.

As is usual with such enterprises, in its early years the national organization was managed informally by a member of the profession who, as Secretary, carried on most of the routine business as a voluntary contribution. But by about 1948-1950, the Society had so expanded in membership and in range of activities that a major reorganization was undertaken, resulting in the establishment of a central Office under the direction of a paid Executive Officer. Since that time the membership has more than doubled and the activities of the office have expanded enormously. [10]

As emphasized above, the main anchorage of a scientific profession in a modern society must be the universities, which alone can provide the setting for the profession's primary teaching and research functions. At the same time, the importance of strong, well-managed professional associations should not be underestimated. Through their meetings, publications, and various other channels they form the most important single type of medium through which sociologists over the country communicate with one another. Furthermore they provide a means of concerted action in promoting interests and discharging responsibilities of the profession.

A professional association differs in ideal type from a trade union in that it is not so much an "interest group" as an agency for facilitating the development of its professional field and a guardian of the technical and ethical standards of its personnel. Its criteria of membership constitute an important symbol in this respect. At the same time, sociologists, of all professional groups, should be aware of their social and cultural involvement in all of the major respects noted above. The professional association can be especially helpful in mediating our "citizenship" relations to neighboring disciplines as well as to the public at large. And perhaps most urgent now is the function of the professional association in relation to the applied fields. Here, where conflicts of interest are likely to develop between disciplines and between academic and non-academic groups, perhaps a working code of relationships particularly needs to be worked out. For example, a current practical problem is posed by the ways in which civil service job descriptions specify disciplinary titles, so that any particular group of "-ologists" may need to protect its interests by keeping the Civil Service Commission informed about the scope of the profession. This and other problems have been made the special concern of the Society's recently-formed Committee on the Profession, which will address itself to a broad range of matters concerning not only the technical development of sociology but also the place of sociologists in our society.

SUMMARY AND CONCLUSION

This review yields a fairly clear picture. Sociology is a profession centered

---

[10] The pattern of membership of the Society is of interest. For the first decade it did not exceed about 500. Then, following World War I, it reached a plateau between 1,000 and 1,500 which was not exceeded until after World War II. By the time of the reorganization in 1948-1950, it had risen to about 2,500. In 1951 more stringent qualifications for active membership were introduced, but even so, by 1958 it reached 5,783, of whom approximately 2,600 were active members. Source: Official Reports and Proceedings, as published annually in the official journal of the Society.

about a growing scientific discipline which, within the last decade or so, has reached a new level of maturity and has come to occupy an increasingly strategic place in the cluster of social sciences. The latter have acquired in this century a position in the society never before accorded to them. The technical basis of sociology has developed enormously in the last generation, with a far deeper and broader battery of research technology than before and a substantial improvement of its theory. The output of superior research results has greatly expanded at the same time that its average quality has substantially improved.

As a profession, its central working base in the universities has been greatly extended and consolidated; now every major American university has made a place for sociology. The number of professionally trained new personnel is about three times the figure of twenty years ago, and will certainly increase. Sociology has moved into a central place in current broad intellectual preoccupations. The involvement of sociologists in practical functions has greatly expanded. At least prominent beginnings have been made in establishing it as a basic science underlying a whole range of applied professions. The various professional associations have been greatly expanded and strengthened. On every essential front there has been growth and, I think, improvement.

If this be an accurate picture, it is highly gratifying, perhaps especially for those who entered the profession when its situation was much less promising. But at the same time the current state of affairs presents a number of serious difficulties and dangers which call not for complacent relaxation but for intensified effort. In conclusion, I suggest several areas in which particularly urgent problems seem to lie ahead.

(1) It should never be forgotten that the central task of a scientific profession is the development of its discipline and the training of its successors in carrying on that function. Increasing involvement in popular ideological discussions and in applied functions could readily divert attention from these functions, although of course here there need be no intense conflict. Highly qualified manpower in sociology is bound to remain scarce for a long time, since demand is apparently running well ahead of even the steadily increasing supply. In my opinion, our first priority should be the staffing of university departments with the ablest persons and the facilitation of their research on as "pure" a level as possible.

(2) Some adjustment of the relations between sociology and its neighboring disciplines has occurred, but there remain many unsettled problems. The detailed solution of these must develop mostly in terms of research, of professional writings, and of the highly variegated relationships that sociologists, individually and in small groups, form with other social scientists. Here and there a problem may become a focus of action by the organized profession, but it is highly important that there should be no retreat into a disciplinary parochialism. Perhaps most important of all is the establishment and maintenance of good interdisciplinary contacts in the universities, although such enterprises as the Center for Advanced Study in the Behavioral Sciences also contribute greatly to good interdisciplinary relations.

(3) Sociologists as a profession should prepare themselves for increased pressure stemming from the involvement of sociology in ideological controversy. Precisely because their subject is more in the public eye, it will be exposed to more distortion and misunderstanding than before. It is their responsibility to maintain high standards of scientific competence and objectivity. Some will have to serve as mediators between the profession and the public, on occasion entering the forum of discussion on their own initiative. Retreat of the whole profession into technical preoccupations could be dangerous in the long run, especially since this situation is very closely linked with undergraduate teaching, in which lies so much of the discipline's strength.

(4) We must look to further expansion of the applied functions and cope with the problems which arise here. I think that a great deal of effort should be devoted to promoting what has been called the basic science pattern of relation to many of these functions, even though this clearly means diverting an appreciable fraction of our valuable personnel. At the same time, there will be many sociologists who enter more directly into applied activities. The creation of codes for professionally proper ways of organizing such participation will, I believe, constitute one major task of our professional associations, a task closely related to the protection of sociologists' interests as these are threatened more frequently with the increase in this participation.

In sum, it seems likely that the problems facing our profession in the coming years will center on the temptations and complications which set in with relative, though incomplete success. Sociology is becoming "important." Let us hope that this accomplishment will not divert us from the main task and at the same time that we take due account of the responsibilities and opportunities presented by our growing involvement in the larger social setting. Primary concentration on the science itself is not incompatible with good citizenship in the scientific community and in the general society. The great challenge is to maintain the proper balances.

The Image of Man in the Social Sciences: The Basic Assumptions of Present-Day Research

Reinhard Bendix

SOURCE: *Commentary*, Vol. 11 (1951), pp. 187–92.

A paradox rends the social sciences today. Two contradictory views of the nature of man are asserted simultaneously. On the one hand, we are told that it is possible to know and understand more and more about the nature of man and society, for man to use this increasing body of knowledge and theory to improve his condition, to reduce unhappiness and poverty, and to increase the joy and fullness of life. On the other hand, modern social science teaches us to regard man as a creature of his drives, habits, and social roles, in whose behavior reason and choice play no decisive part. Accordingly, man's efforts to acquire knowledge about himself and society, and to use such knowledge, are beset with insuperable obstacles; men are regarded as unable to achieve objective knowledge or to be guided by it.

Of course, social scientists do not often hold either of these positions in so bold a form. Most of them gravitate to some compromise when they have occasion to reflect on the larger implications of their disciplines. Sometimes the belief in mass education---in which the social sciences are assigned a major role---is stressed; this implies that all men are capable in some measure of guiding their actions by the use of their rational faculties. At present, a more popular resolution of the dilemma is the attitude that some men are rational, but most men are not; and that the few can use their knowledge for the benefit of the many.

Despite such practical compromises the paradox remains, and the questions raised still need examination. Can reason direct human behavior? Is only a small elite capable of being guided by reason?

Must the great masses of men be manipulated by elites for their own good? How can we expand the role of reason in human affairs? In the absence of answers to these questions we are left uncertain as to the future of the social sciences. Do the social scientists propose to increase the role of reason in Everyman's guidance of his own destiny and human affairs generally? Or do they propose to expand the knowledge possessed by an elite as to the manipulation and control of the mass of the unreasonable? One view of man's nature would logically lead us to take the first course; the other would require us to take the second. No more important task faces the social sciences today than to determine by which "image of man" they are to be led.

Oddly enough, these two opposing views stem from one and the same source: the three-hundred-year-old effort to determine both the limits and the power of reason in the control of nature and human affairs.

During the 17th and 18th centuries men were inspired by a belief in human reason and human perfectibility. Steeped in theological traditions, they assumed that God, in establishing an orderly universe, had endowed man's intellect with the ability to comprehend it. To understand the laws of nature meant the possibility of controlling the forces of nature. And it seemed logical to infer that the same might be true for society.

This view was given classic expression by Francis Bacon. It seemed obvious to him that the knowledge accumulated by the proper use of reason would always be of value to mankind. "Human knowledge and human power meet in one; for where the cause is not known, the effect cannot be produced." Men must guard against "deliberate and factitious despair, which cuts the sinews and spur of industry ... all for the miserable vainglory of making it believed that whatever has not yet been discovered and comprehended can never be discovered and comprehended hereafter."

Bacon applied his view of knowledge to the study of nature; the philosophers of the Enlightenment, men like Diderot, Holbach, and Helvetius, applied it to the study of society. In applying to social affairs Bacon's faith in man's ability to acquire and use knowledge, these philosophers took for granted something that has since become less certain. Not only scientists or scholars but all men were believed capable of using scientific knowledge for a control of nature. Hence, in developing a science of society, the philosophers of the Enlightenment turned their attention to devising ways by which all men could be educated to control the forces of society. They believed that education would dispel prejudice, replace ignorance, and permit men to act rationally in human affairs. Acting within this tradition, for example, Jefferson gave education a central role in his hopes for an American democracy.

Karl Marx challenged the Enlightenment's view on both these points: he denied that knowledge was sufficient to redirect society, and that human minds could be opened to reason simply by education. With this challenge, he became the fount of one of the mainstreams of modern social science.

Marx was, of course, not the first to question the role of knowledge in society, nor was he the first to show the distorting influence that self-interest can have on our attitude towards human affairs. Previous writers had doubted the feasibility of a rational social order, and many had shown how self-interest leads to bias and prejudice in social thought. But in Marx's view the role of ideas in society and the influence of self-interest on ideas become of over-riding importance. To him the content of human history consisted in a series of class struggles, and ideas about society provided the contending classes with arsenals of symbols (ideologies) with which to fight each other. In this view, every idea was involved in this struggle and either intentionally obscured or—if analyzed as an ideology—unintentionally revealed certain aspects of society.

Marx's attitude towards human ideas and human rationality was basically skeptical. Yet Marx was not without hope. He made a heroic effort to regard man's reason as a constructive force in human history, and he believed ideas were exempt in two important ways from the distortions created by the class struggle.

First, he believed there was a way by which men could surmount their class-conditioned ideologies and be induced to submit to reason. They would do so when the social conditions (i.e. the class struggle) which had led to these ideologies were radically altered. In a classless society, in the absence of human misery and human exploitation, men would be able to see and understand society as it really was; they would have a perfect insight into the laws of social life, and in obeying these laws they would experience the ultimate freedom of controlling the forces of society deliberately.

Second, Marx believed that even before the advent of this future society, while humanity was still in the period of capitalism, there would be some men (like Marx, for example) who, having attained a "premature" scientific knowledge of their society, would not have their understanding limited by class interest: "...In times when the class struggle nears the decisive hour, the process of dissolution ...within the old society assumes such a violent glaring character, that a small section of the ruling class cuts itself adrift, and joins the revolutionary class, that class that holds the future in its hands....A portion of the bourgeois ideologists (in particular) have raised themselves to the level of comprehending theoretically the historical movement as a whole." (The Communist Manifesto.)

Marx's critique of human reason thus aimed ultimately at an enhancement of reason. While exploring the many ways in which class interest turns social thought into an apology for things as they are, he was yet confident in his own ability to see through this deception, and he believed that some "bourgeois ideologists," at first, and the masses of the working people, later, would see through it as well. With all his deep insight into the abuse of "knowledge" in society, he still believed that man could use knowledge to improve his condition.

This belief was shared by another thinker who has had an enormous influence on modern social science, Sigmund Freud. If Marx questioned the meaning of ideas apart from the material interests and actions of men, Freud questioned their meaning apart from individual strivings and emotions. The ideas and actions of an individual make sense in Freudian terms only when we see them in the context of a man's personal history. Every man seeks to increase pleasure and avoid pain; pleasure and pain are conceived as strictly organic, bodily experiences, and the most fundamental instinct around which they revolve is sex. Ideas, scientific research, artistic creations---in a word, all man's intellectual endeavors---can be analyzed as products of the psychosexual life history of the thinker involved. And since, by definition, these activities yield less pleasure than the direct gratification of our instinctual drives, men create culture at the price of sexual renunciation and sexual frustration.

This appears an even more skeptical view of the value of man's intellectual efforts, yet Freud by no means called for the abandonment of substitute gratifications (or sublimation). Rather, he hoped that man would be made happier in his renunciation of instinctual pleasure by a further expansion of reason; where the renunciation had been unconscious and led to torment, it was now to be made in the full light of intelligence and rendered harmless or at least manageable. In hoping for the psychological improvement of the individual, Freud assigned to human reason an important role. When a patient is accepted for treatment in psychoanalytic therapy, he is warned that analysis is arduous in terms of time and expense and that the emotional demands to be made upon him will be severe. But once the patient is accepted, then the success of his treatment depends upon his ability to utilize his rational insight into the origin of his present emotional difficulties. Thus psychoanalysis does take its stand on the side of human improvement through reason, however heavy may be its emphasis on the power of organic drives and on the relative weakness of human intelligence. Under favorable circumstances man is judged to be capable of assessing his personal history, and of reshaping his personal life on the basis of that assessment. To be sure, psychoanalytic therapy is by no means a purely rational process on the part of the patient; but the end product is a rational being.

Marx and Freud contributed to the destruction of the 18th-century belief in human reason and perfectibility. Yet, as we have said, they did not argue that reasoning was altogether futile or that improvement was unattainable. Knowledge or reason, they agreed, are greatly hampered by human interests and personal emotions; to the extent that they demonstrated this, "knowledge" is often less "objective" than men believed. Marx and Freud did not fully share the Baconian and Enlightenment belief that "human knowledge and power meet in one." Yet, despite this insight, they were confident that some men could attain an objective knowledge of man and history and that the scientific knowledge of the few would in the long run benefit the many. Their qualified optimism effected a compromise that combined a faith in the intelligence of the many with the conviction that, under present circumstances, there are only a few who are able to free human understanding of the distortion which results from its involvement with group interests and individual emotion.

Social scientists by and large have since, so it seems, departed from this compromise view. They are indebted to Marx and Freud for deep insights into the conditioned nature of man's quest for knowledge. But they have also gone beyond them by discarding the belief that all men have a common capacity for reason and rational action, either now or in the future.

Marx's view that ideas are embedded in self-interest and social action, taken out of the context of his philosophy of history, has come to mean that any idea must be misleading, any statement must be false, when its speaker or writer represents an interest group. And in assuming that the ideas of a man have no meaning apart from his actions and interests, these contemporary interpretations of Marx show little concern with the "abstract" meaning of the ideas a person expresses. They are concerned instead with learning who his friends are and how his ideas undermine the position of his enemies. This might be called the "pigeonhole theory of truth." The content of a statement is examined in terms of whether its source commends or condemns it.[1]

And for every idea discredited by identification with an interest group, there is another that is not taken seriously because it is "emotionally biased." This might be called the "poker-face theory of truth." To find the "true" meaning of an idea, we need to ask, not "What did he say?" but "Why did he say it?" Thus only a man who can keep a straight face while telling an outrageous lie has a chance of escaping this inquisition into his motives. For the motives of a man become immediately suspect when he reveals that his emotions are deeply involved with the ideas he expresses.[2]

But once we judge what a man says according to who his friends are, we need think of him no longer as a person but

---

[1] The most sophisticated expression of this view is contained in Karl Mannheim's Ideology and Utopia. In recent years it has influenced a species of writing that treats the history of ideas as a form of propaganda analysis. Both the telling insights and the glaring crudities of this approach are well illustrated by Karl Popper's The Open Society and Its Enemies (Princeton, 1950), and, on the other side, by Georg Lukacs's Studies in European Realism (London, 1950). A similar view has inspired much political science writing that conceives of politics in terms of "who gets what, when, and how."

[2] The psychiatric analysis of ideas is emphasized in Elton Mayo's work on human relations in industry. The same emphasis is contained in much of the work that seeks to understand the ideas that have been prominent in a nation's history in terms of a "national character structure." This literature has been summarized and examined critically by Otto Klineberg, Tensions Affecting International Understanding (Bulletin 62; New York, Social Science Research Council, 1950).

only as a member of his group. And if a person is judged in terms of his suspected motives, what he says is no longer important, and "verbalization" becomes "only" the surface manifestation of his subconscious. Reason, and efforts at reason, are thereby depreciated.

These vulgarizations have had a profound impact on the contemporary image of man, and particularly on the image of man in the social sciences. To go from Marx and Freud to the positions held in the social sciences today takes only a short step; it involves simply the abandonment of the residual hope for the governance of men by their rational faculties which Marx and Freud permitted themselves.

Yet is it not also true that the belief in science is stronger today than ever before? Would so many research projects be undertaken if those who initiated them did not believe that the findings produced would result in greater human happiness? And, indeed, most social scientists today believe that they are the true heirs of the 18th century, and are still loyal to its belief in reason and human perfectibility.

But I think that they have deceived themselves. I believe that a faith in science has superseded the earlier faith in reason.

What is the content of this faith in science, and how does it differ from the earlier faith in reason? Modern social scientists believe that economic interests and traditional beliefs, emotions and cultural conditions, distort our understanding. They no longer believe that men can rid their minds of these impediments to lucid thought: only scientists can. Social scientists have become persuaded of the ingrained irrationality of the many, and their own work repeatedly demonstrates to them how difficult it is—even for the expert—to attain objectivity. Their more intensive knowledge of the fallibility of human reason, which is itself an outgrowth of modern social science, leads many social scientists to accept as inevitable an unbridgeable gulf between themselves and the public at large. They assert that there is only one escape from

the consequences of irrationality: that is by the application of scientific method. And this method can be used effectively only by the expert few. Research has revealed the many obstacles to understanding among the mass of men. Hence social scientists are less concerned today with improving the understanding of the mass of men, and they are more intent on insuring the objectivity of their own practices. This they do by the use of specific techniques: pre-testing of questionnaires, random sampling, calculation of standard errors, and so on.

The danger of this position is that the social scientists, in their concern to be objective or scientific, run the risk of losing perspective with regard to the ends of their knowledge. That danger is present, in one form, wherever social scientists shy away from a discussion of questions (such as those concerning the purpose of social science) to which the answers must remain tentative and unverified. If the only way to achieve understanding is marked out by the scientific method, and if that method is only accessible to the expert few, then the belief in the intelligence of all men is in effect abandoned. Instead of attempting to make people more rational, contemporary social scientists often content themselves with asking of them that they place their trust in social science and accept its findings. If people do this they will presumably put themselves on safe and sure ground and become free from bias, even though they cannot share in the inquiry that leads to knowledge, and will therefore remain ignorant of the premises and facts upon which it is based.

Inevitably, the methods of research in the social sciences are difficult to handle and equally difficult to explain in short order, and this was bound to alienate the social scientist from the public to some extent: so in speaking of the effects of the social scientist's faith in science, we do not refer to his need to use technical tools. However, the social scientists also draw, from their faith in science, the conclusion that the social scientists must serve as instruments of the civil (or other) authorities, whoever they may be. This startling conclusion---expressed clearly in Alexander Leighton's Human Relations in a Changing World (Dutton, 1949)---is, as we may see in Leighton's book and elsewhere, the clear result of the belief that the social sciences as sciences must play the leading role in solving our social problems. For if we believe they must play this role as science, that is, as tools, rather than as means whereby men in general may be made more rational, as earlier social scientists believed, then we can only conclude that the contemporary social scientist should confine himself to a study of the facts pertinent to an implementation of policies, and not make suggestions of policies themselves; this is his duty as a value-free scientist, and it harms his science to do more. But further, to gain the material support necessary to expand social science as science and this expansion, to the mind of the social scientist, also means an inevitable improvement in the condition of mankind---the social scientist must gain the support of the men of affairs. And how can he do this but by convincing the man of affairs that his work holds out promise of greater success in the conscious manipulation of social forces and of the "mass mind?"

Thus, beginning with the age-old belief in the liberating power of knowledge and reason, social scientists end up by becoming protagonists of a neutral social science which will facilitate the manipulation of social forces and of the general population, regardless of who does the manipulating and for what purpose. In their eagerness to make the social sciences more scientific, social scientists persuade others and themselves that human advancement is identical with the advancement of scientific knowledge--- with their scientific knowledge.

As a result, social scientists have often become less concerned with the use to which their knowledge is put than with the question whether that use is compatible with the further development of social science. They emphasize that everything must be done to persuade policy makers that they should use the social sciences, and the problems to be investigated are often selected so as to demonstrate the usefulness or the scientific rigor of the social sciences to the political leader or administrator.

The most striking development in this respect is the increased role of the foundations and the diminished importance of university scholars. The external reason for this shift is, of course, financial, but the question is pertinent whether the allocation of large sums by foundation executives will not undermine the independent judgment of the individual social scientist with regard to what he regards as significant. Instances are known in which large funds have been allocated to a university department, not because the department but because the foundation wanted to emphasize a certain field of research. Individual social scientists have been more or less permanently diverted from their original research interests, simply because they did not resist the temptation of funds which were available for other projects.

Some thirty years ago Max Weber addressed this question of the meaning of science in his lecture, "Science as a Vocation." Weber stated that social science could serve three ends. It may enable us to control the forces of society, it provides training for future social scientists, and it makes for intellectual clarity.

It is a measure of how rapidly the 18th-century creed has disappeared in recent years that only the first and second of these ends still appear valid. A generation ago Weber had regarded "intellectual clarity" as one of the most important goals of social science. By receiving training in them the individual citizen would learn to judge alternative courses of action in the light of knowledge of their conditions and consequences. Weber believed that this was a worthy goal of the social sciences, even if they were often found to have no other apparent social utility. Yet, the majority of introductory courses in the different social sciences shows little evidence that intellectual clarity is still the goal today.

Instead, these courses give the impression that they are designed for future specialists, not for the individual who seeks clarity on social and political issues. As an impartial examination of introductory textbooks will confirm, students are treated as budding experts, which in many instances will make them poorer citizens. Robert K. Merton, in his introduction to an introductory text (Sociological Analysis, by Logan Wilson and William Kolb, Harcourt, Brace; 1949), points out that in recent years there has been a shift from an emphasis on a general, semi-philosophical "humanities" approach in sociology textbooks, to an emphasis on techniques and empirical studies. He does not, however, point up the educational implications of these changes.[3]

The serious question which we all confront is thereby posed: must we pay for the greater technical resources and the refined research methods of modern social science with the unconscious and uncritical subordination of intellectual endeavor to the dominant social and political forces of our time? Must we renounce reason for all to gain science for the few and the elites? Must we give up our faith that all men can become reasonable and instead hope that some men---the powerful---will learn to make use of the technical tools of science?

Each person who is concerned with this question will answer it in his own way. As I see it, a major desideratum is that each social scientist should be personally conscious of the link between his research and the social and political and moral forces of his society. Such consciousness can only enhance the intellectual integrity

of his work. It should enter into his selection of research problems, wherever possible. This is usually interpreted as the need to make one's values explicit as they are involved in the specific problems under discussion. We should, however, recognize that it is less our opinions on day-to-day problems and more our major underlying assumptions that call for explicit acknowledgment: our beliefs concerning the relation of knowledge and human power, the role of science in society, the position of the intellectual in the community---these are among the problems which we must clarify for ourselves.

There is nothing necessarily degrading in such work as opinion analyses for an advertising company, or anthropological field work for a colonial office, or analyses of price trends for a government agency, and when this work is useful we may properly be pleased---if nothing else is involved. But social scientists are placed in a dubious light when they claim that their work for hire is the ultimate goal of all social science research, and when they plead in extenuation for some of their "pure" work that what is not useful now may or will be useful tomorrow or the day after. It would be far more useful in the long run---from the point of view both of science and of humanity---to take one's stand on the ground that our human life is enriched by worthwhile research in the social sciences, that such research is a token of high civilization, worth preserving as an integral part of our quest for knowledge, and that this quest manifests our abiding faith in the constructive and enriching possibilities of human reason. I do not claim that this is an "objective" statement. It is rather a declaration of personal belief that in a world torn by wars of nerves, arms, and words, the universities are institutions of detachment whose academic personnel have an important service to render in the community, one for which they may properly claim recognition from the powers that be. Social scientists, to reiterate, should place their abiding faith in reason rather

---

[3] There are some notable educational tendencies which point in the opposite direction, however. An interesting discussion of this problem and some striking suggestions are contained in Philipp Frank's Modern Science and Its Philosophy (Harvard University Press, 1949). A similar humanistic emphasis in the teaching of the social sciences is found in the introductory courses taught at the University of Chicago, and at other institutions where the so-called "general" education approach has spread.

than an exclusive concern with improving the techniques of social manipulations. This is the only position worthy of the great intellectual traditions of which they are the heirs. It is also the only position consistent with the intellectual defense against the threat of totalitarianism, from without and within.

Sociology and the Intellectuals: An Analysis of a Stereotype

Bennett M. Berger

SOURCE: *Antioch Review*, Vol. 17 (1957), pp. 275-90.

(While you and i have lips and voices which
are for kissing and to sing with
who cares if some oneeyed son of a bitch
invents an instrument to measure Spring with? *

e. e. cummings

I

For some years, humanist intellectuals have been cultivating a hostile stereotype of sociology and sociologists. Like other stereotypes, this one has its foundation in fact; like other stereotypes too, its exaggerations, whether expressed in the language of annihilating wit or of earnest bludgeoning, call for some serious comment. It is surprising therefore, that the responses of sociologists have been anything but dispassionate. These responses range all the way from (1) Daniel Lerner's polemical defense of sociology in his article analyzing the book reviews of The American Soldier,[1] to (2) the posture of tolerant disdain toward the "misguided" stereotype, to (3) a sort of nervous embrace of the stereotype by sociologists themselves (which attempts—usually unsuccessfully—to demonstrate that they do too have a sense of humor), often

involving a self-parody whose furtive masochism is almost startling.

There is no real need to document the stereotype with exhaustive quotations since it is rife enough in intellectual circles for everyone to have had his own personal experience of it. The overt expression of the stereotype in print is the exception, and whole articles devoted to it are rare. The most common vehicle for its expression is the derisive "remark" and the parenthetical aside. Occasionally, one finds a curiously ambiguous statement like the following:

Popular images are rarely entirely wrong; and if the mass media and the popular mind today see the social scientist as a man with pencil and pad in hand, buttonholing hapless citizens on the street, the error is not in the observation—it is only in seeing the social scientist as the interviewer.... Today, no matter what the question put to the social scientist, he begins his answer by composing a questionnaire, which he then gets filled out by having an appropriate number of respondents interviewed. (In an introductory note by Nathan Glazer to I. L. Peretz' "The Interviewer at Work," Commentary, February, 1953, p. 195.)

One of the interesting things in this statement is the apparent convergence of images held by the "popular mind" with those held by intellectuals like Glazer. I say "apparent" because intellectuals do

[1]Daniel Lerner, "The American Soldier and the Public," in R. K. Merton and P. F. Lazarsfeld, Continuities in Social Research (The Free Press, 1950), pp. 212-251.

not often share the stereotypes of the popular mind, and the quoted instance is not one of the exceptions. Glazer does not describe a popular image in his remarks, but a stereotype held by intellectuals. Anyone who has done extensive interviewing of the "popular mind" knows that ordinary people are generally naïvely interested as well as pleased and flattered to be interviewed by a social scientist; it takes considerable sophistication to feel disdainful of and superior to the poised pencil of the interviewer. But in a curiously inverted "proof by authority" Glazer attributes an image to the popular mind in order to validate his own.

Using evidence like this demands some reading between the lines. For example, nowhere in the above quotation does Glazer explicitly state that the image supposedly held by the popular mind is an invidious one; it is largely a matter of tone, created by key connotative words like "buttonholing," and "hapless," and "appropriate." Many expressions of the stereotype are of this hit-and-run kind, and depend for their meaning and effect upon one's being "in" on the current scapegoatology. For example, the poet and critic Randall Jarrell explicates a few lines from a Robert Frost poem, then says, "if you can't feel any of this, you are a Convention of Sociologists." A remark like this would be meaningless to someone not "in" on the current stereotype; to those who are "in," and presumably a good number of readers are, it is very funny indeed. Similarly, W. H. Auden speaks to Jarrell's audience when he says:

> Thou shalt not answer questionnaires
> Or quizzes upon World-Affairs,
>   Nor with compliance
> Take any test. Thou shalt not sit
> With statisticians nor commit
>   A social science. *

There are, of course, more elaborate and heavy handed assaults, J. P. Marquand's portrait of W. Lloyd Warner in Point of No Return not being the only one. Still, it is the light touch of people like Auden and Jarrell which is most effective in spreading the stereotype.

Stereotypes, and hostile stereotypes especially, do injury to the group stereotyped, and it is or ought to be our responsibility to correct them. But stereotypes are not generally exorcised by pretending they do not exist; nor are they dispelled by polemic or a demonstration of innocence. Although founded in fact, stereotypes are nonrational, and flourish in spite of the preponderance of evidence against them. Thus arguing from facts to correct an emotional excrescence is vain. What we want to know are the conditions that have generated the stereotype and permitted it to grow. Knowing these, we can transcend polemic and use our understanding in more effective ways.

II

The stereotype of the sociologist has two dimensions, founded in contradictory beliefs which, in turn, have their source in the structure of the intellectual professions. The image of the sociologist as a pathetically ignorant and pompous bumbler (jargon-ridden, pretentious, and without insight) is based on the conviction that sociology has no special subject matter, and is therefore no science; its technical apparatus and methodological strictures are hence not only presumptuous but futile, and result only in pretentiousness and banality. The image of the sociologist as a Machiavellian manipulator, however, clearly rests on a recognition of the efficacy of scientific, especially statistical, techniques in dealing with a human subject matter. But both of these—the perceived failure as well as the perceived success of sociology—have elicited from the intellectuals a hostile response.

A. The Problem of Subject Matter: The Sociologist as Bumbler. The tendency to specialization in the intellectual professions submits them to pressure to define specifically a subject matter uniquely their own, in order to justify their existence in a profession- and specialty-conscious culture, to establish and preserve their identities with foundations

---

* Copyright 1946 by W. H. Auden. Reprinted from Nones by permission of Random House, Inc.

and university administrations, and to demonstrate their utility and their consequent right to public support. As new specializations develop, and claim professional status, entirely reasonable questions of justification can be raised. What can you do that others not trained in your profession cannot do? What competence has your training conferred on you that is denied to others because of their lack of such training? I take it that the flourishing health of the image of the sociologist as bumbler can in part be attributed to the failure of sociologists to answer these questions satisfactorily. Any discipline which claims as its special subject matter the domain of "social relations" or "social systems" or "society" or any of the other textbook-preface definitions claims not a special subject matter but the whole gamut of human experience, a claim which thousands of scholars and intellectuals are with good reason likely to dispute.[2] Louis Wirth's definition of sociology as the study of that which is true of men by virtue of the fact that they have everywhere and at all times lived a group life, strikes the eye as somewhat better, but runs into the difficulty[3] of generally assuming that pretty nearly everything that is true of men is true by virtue of this fact.

It is in part due to this failure to meet the responsibility of defining one's professional competence simply and clearly to interested laymen that sociological "jargon," for example, is met with such resistance and resentment. Laymen react with no such rancor to the technical vocabularies of mathematics, the physical

and natural sciences, and engineering because by an act of faith (based, to be sure, on a common-sense understanding of what these disciplines do) they decide that behind the jargon, which they do not understand (because it is a descriptive shorthand, familiarity with which requires special training), lies a <u>special subject matter amenable to technical treatment</u> which they <u>could</u> understand <u>if</u> they took the trouble. Thus the intelligent layman feels no shame or outrage at not being able to understand a technical article in a chemistry journal—or, for that matter, in not understanding the job specifications in a newspaper want ad for engineers. No such toleration is likely toward the technical vocabulary of sociology until it is accepted as a legitimate scientific profession.

That this acceptance is not forthcoming is due partly to the belief of many intellectuals that the technical vocabulary is not a natural concomitant of scientific enterprise, but rather an attempt to disguise the banality of the results of sociology studies: sociologists "belabor the obvious"; they lack insight, and substitute in its place a barrage of carefully "proven" platitudes. Doubtless, some sociologists do, but every intellectual discipline has its share of brilliant people, as well as hacks, and there is no reason to suppose that sociology has more than a normal complement of either.[4] That the hacks are identified <u>as representative</u> of sociology is probably due more to judgments regarding the quality of sociological prose rather than to any analysis of the significance of its contents. Certainly, the prose of sociologists may seem clumsy when compared to the efforts of those whose business it is to write well. But whereas the results of scientific endeavor can legitimately be expected to be true and important, one cannot legitimately expect either that science be

---

[2] At a recent meeting of the Western Branch of the American Oriental Society, a distinguished member introduced a resolution affirming the Branch's loyalty to the traditions of humanistic study, and barring from the pages of the society's journal what he called articles of the "social science type."

[3] I say "difficulty" not because I think this assumption may not be useful, but because (1) such an assumption places the sociologist in the role of "academic imperialist," and because (2) the implied primacy of society, or group life, over the individual runs counter to deeply rooted Western values about "the individual."

[4] This feature of the stereotype asserts only that sociologists are cliché experts. What is interesting is that there is no "objective correlative" sufficient to make comprehensible the passion with which sociologists are denounced for being—innocuous.

beautiful or that scientists be literary stylists.

In short, then, the hue and cry about the jargon and turgidity of sociological prose, about the pretentiousness of its methodology and the banality of its preoccupations, is meaningful as criticism only if one assumes that sociology has no special subject matter amenable to technical treatment; if it has not, then it must be judged by the same criteria as general essays on social and cultural topics. But as long as sociologists commit themselves to the traditions of science, and address their work not to a general literate audience, but to a community of their colleagues, these criticisms cannot seem other than beside the point. For the continuing application of aesthetic criteria of judgment to a nonaesthetic pursuit reveals only a refusal to grant to sociology the status of a science.

B. The Threat of Technique: The Sociologist as Diabolist. Stereotypes generally contain contradictory elements, and the stereotype of the sociologist is no exception. For along with his alleged gifts for the labored cliché and the clumsy, inept sentence, the sociologist is also credited with the diabolical potential of making puppets out of men, of destroying their individuality with IBM machines, of robbing them of their "individual human dignity," and presiding, finally, over their total mechanization.[5] This image of the sociologist as diabolist[6] rests not on a conviction regarding the failure to define a specific subject matter, but on a fear regarding the success of sociological techniques, particularly statistics, which is seen by some intellectuals as threatening in two ways. First, the possibility of a science of society apparently implies the possibility of human behavior being controlled or manipulated by those who know its "causes" or by those with access to this knowledge. This vision, fostered by stimulus-response psychology, nourished by the "sociological perspective," which finds the source of individual behavior in group influences (and thus runs head on into the myth of the autonomous individual), and made

fearful by reports of brain washing and by novels like 1984 and Brave New World, is perhaps responsible for the peculiar ambivalence felt by some intellectuals toward the very desirability of a science of society. Sociology is thus seen as a potential threat to democratic society. Second, and more relevant in the present context, is the fact that the application of the techniques of science to human behavior is perceived as a threat to the viability of the most basic function of intellectuals in the Western tradition: to comment on and to interpret the meaning of contemporary experience.

III

The noun "intellectual" is one of those words which, in spite of lack of concensus regarding their meaning, continue to flourish in common usage. Attempts to define the term, to ask who the intellectuals are or what the intellectuals do, while useful, have seemed to me inconclusive. Certainly some intellectuals are "detached" or "free-floating"; surely a great number are "alienated"; doubtless "neurosis" is widespread among them; "irresponsibility," although currently out of fashion, is nevertheless affirmed by some of them. There is great magic in some of their bows; but, like Philoctetes, they often carry a corresponding wound

---

[5]If it be pointed out that punch cards, IBM machines, and statistical techniques generally are merely tools, and that men who call themselves sociologists have been in the forefront of the battle against the "mechanization of man" and the "loss of individuality," then as likely as not the alternative elements of the stereotype will be invoked to damn them. The contradictions are legion. Those who believe that there cannot be a science of sociology often believe also that there ought not to be one, although if one says that there cannot be a science of sociology, then the dictum that there ought not to be one is meaningless; while if one says that there ought not to be a science of sociology, then it must be possible that there can be one.

[6]It is possible that the contradictory images of the sociologist as "bumbler" and the sociologist as "diabolist" can be related to the two traditions of sociology, the first stemming from the American tradition of social reform, the latter stemming from the conservative European tradition of aristocratic privilege and the consequent right and responsibility of the aristocracy to "control" the fate of the masses.

whose stench forces them to live some-what marginally. Finally, it is true that they create and transmit cultural values ---sometimes. There are, however, two difficulties with these and similar attempts at definition. First, the relation between the key criteria of the definitions and the perspectives of the definers is generally only too transparent. Second, and for my purposes more interesting, is that although the word is part of common usage, the attempts to define it have generally ignored this fact. I propose here first to ask not who the intellectuals are or what they do, but rather who they are thought to be---whom do people have in mind when they use the term?---and only then to go on to the other questions.

In this connection, I was present a few years ago at a forum on "The Role of the Intellectual in Modern Society" held at the Museum of Modern Art in New York. The panel members were Granville Hicks, Clement Greenberg, W. H. Auden, and Robert Gorham Davis. Auden spoke last, and at one point in his remarks he looked around at his colleagues on the platform as if to take note of the experts chosen to talk on this topic. Hicks, he said, was a novelist and literary critic; Davis was a literary critic and English professor; Greenberg was an art critic and an editor of Commentary; and Auden identified himself as a poet and critic. Had this forum been held in the Middle Ages, he pointed out, we panel members would have been mostly members of the clergy; in the sixteenth and seventeenth centuries, we would have been mostly natural scientists; in the twentieth century, we are mostly literary men.[7] Auden did not attempt to answer the question

that he had left implicit, but the question is a very leading one because the contemporary image of the intellectual is, I believe, essentially a literary one---and in two senses: he is conceived as a literary man, and this conception has been reinforced by the fact that it is literary men who have been most interested in, and who have written most on, the problem of the intellectual.

But it would be a mistake to assume that, because the intellectual is conceived in the image of the literary man, his essential property is that he is an artist or a student of literature. His identification as an intellectual rests not on the aesthetic value of his novels, plays, poems, essays, or literary criticism, but on his assumption, through them, of the role of commentator on contemporary culture and interpreter of contemporary experience.[8] But if the intellectuals are those who assume this role, Auden's implicit question still remains: Why, in our time, has it been typically literary men who have assumed the role of the intellectual? It is in attempting to answer this question that the relation between "the intellectuals" and the stereotyping of sociologists will become clear.

In our time literary men have pre-empted the intellectual's role because of (A) their maximal freedom from the parochial demands of technical specialization, (B) their freedom (within their status as literary men) to make large and uncompromising judgments about values, and (C) their maximal freedom from institutional restraints.

A. Specialization. Intellectuals, I have said, are commentators on contemporary culture and interpreters of contemporary experience; they are critics, liberal or conservative, radical or reactionary, of contemporary life. The range of their competence is not circumscribed; it includes nothing less than the entire cultural life of a people. If they are aca-

---

[7] Although one's conception of who "the intellectuals" are is largely a function of one's own intellectual level and preoccupations, the existence of subcultural phenomena does not prevent us from making statements about cultural worlds as wholes. Thus in spite of sub-cultural variations, the answer to "who are the intellectuals" is likely consistently to include: Camus, Sartre, Malraux, and de Beauvoir in France; Eliot, Auden, and the group around Encounter in England; Silone, Praz, Moravia, and Vittorini in Italy; and in the United States the writers associated with Partisan Review, Commentary, the literary quarterlies, and the "little magazines."

[8] With the publication and reception of The Lonely Crowd, David Riesman emancipated himself, in the eyes of the community of intellectuals, from bearing the burden of identification as a "sociologist"; that is to say, he became an intellectual.

demic men, they may be specialists in various subjects; but their professional specialties do not generally interfere with their being intellectuals. In the humanities, and particularly in literature, a specialty usually consists of expertise regarding a given historical period and the figures important to one's discipline who are associated with it: Dr. Johnson and the English literature of the eighteenth century; the significance of Gide in the French literature of the twentieth century; Prince Metternich and the history of Europe after 1815; Kant, Hegel, and German Idealism 1750-1820. Specialties like these do not militate against one's assuming the role of the intellectual, because the traditions of humanistic study encourage the apprehension of cultural wholes; they encourage commentary and interpretation regarding the "backgrounds"---social, cultural, intellectual, spiritual---of the subject matter one is expert about. The humanities--- and particularly literature---offer to intellectuals a professional status which impeded little if at all the fulfillment of their function as intellectuals. On the other hand, the commitment of empirical sociology to "scientific method" frequently renders it incompetent to deal with the "big problems," and often instills in sociologists a trained incapacity to say anything they cannot prove.

B. Values. In commenting on contemporary culture and in interpreting contemporary experience, intellectuals are under no seriously sanctioned injunction to be "detached" or "objective." Unlike the sociologist, who functions under the rule of strict separation between facts and values, the intellectual is expected to judge and evaluate, to praise and blame, to win adherents to his point of view and to defend his position against his intellectual enemies. In the context of free debate among intellectuals, the exercise of this function takes the form of polemics; in an academic context, it develops into the phenomenon of "schools of thought." The point is that, whereas in sociology the existence of schools of thought is an embarrassment to everyone

(since it is a constant reminder that not enough is known---in science, opinion is tolerated only where facts are not available), in the humanities the existence of schools of thought is accepted as normal and proper, because the humanities actively encourage evaluation, the development of point of view, and heterogeneity of interpretation.

C. Freedom from Institutional Restraints. Literary men have been able, more than members of other intellectual professions, to resist the tendencies toward the bureaucratization of intellectual life. This has been possible because of the large market for fiction in the United States, and because of the opportunities of selling critical and interpretive articles to the high- and the middle-brow magazines, which, in spite of repeated protestations to the contrary, continue to flourish in this country. The ability of free lance writers to support themselves without depending upon a salary from a university or other large organization maximizes their freedom to be critics of contemporary life.[9] Such opportunities are not typically available to sociologists. In addition, major sociological research is increasingly "team" research, while literary and humanistic research in universities is still largely a matter of individual scholarship. Obviously, collective responsibility for a work restrains the commentaries and interpretations of its authors; the individual humanistic scholar, usually responsible only to himself, is free from the restraints imposed by the conditions of collective research.[10]

[9] I am aware that this assertion seems to imply a view of institutions as conservative, and a view of intellectuals as liberal or radical critics of them; this implication is not intended.

[10] The question of why the intellectuals have flocked to positions in the universities in the past ten years is an interesting one. I have asserted that free-lanceness facilitates the fulfillment of the intellectual's role, and the movement to the universities apparently contradicts this assertion. One hypothesis that seems tenable to me is that, as a well-insulated intellectual institution, the university can, to a considerable extent, successfully resist the dominant social pressures. In an age dominated by radical and rebellious sentiments among the intellectuals, as were the first forty years of this

The purpose of this discussion of the intellectuals has been to highlight the fact that although sociology has arrogated to itself the right to expertise regarding society and culture, its commitment to the traditions of science (narrow specialization, objectivity, and team research) militates against sociologists assuming the role of the intellectual. The business of intellectuals has always been the critical discussion and evaluation of the affairs of contemporary men, or, if I may repeat it once more, to comment on contemporary culture and interpret contemporary experience. When the sociologist arrogates expertise regarding the affairs of contemporary men, he is perceived as saying, in effect, that he knows more about the affairs of contemporary men than the intellectual does; and once this implication is received into the community of intellectuals, the issue is joined. The fact of this implication becomes one more fact of contemporary experience to which the intellectuals can devote their critical faculties—and with considerable relish, because the implication seems to threaten the basis of their right to the position which, as intellectuals, they hold.

Even those intellectuals with sympathies for the goals of sociology often exhibit a fundamental underestimation of the consequences of its commitment to science. The characteristic plea of these people is an exhortation to "grapple with the big problems."[11] Although this advice is without doubt well intentioned, it characteristically underestimates the degree to which the mores of science and the responsibility of foundations and university research institutes can command the type of work sociologists do. I mean by this simply that the sociologist is responsible to the community of social scientists for the scientific value of his work, and that university research institutes are sensitive to charges of financing "biased" or "controversial" research (a possibility that is maximized when one deals with the "big problems"). And when the "big problems" are grappled with, for example, in books like The American Soldier and The Authoritarian Personality, or in other types of work like The Lonely Crowd, White Collar, and The Power Elite, controversy and polemic follow. For the sympathetic intellectual's exhortation to the sociologist to "grapple with the big problems" says, in effect, "don't be a scientist, be a humanist; be an intellectual." This implication is supported by the respectful (if not totally favorable) reception given by intellectuals to the works of Riesman and Mills (least encumbered with the trappings of science), and their utter hostility to works like The American Soldier, which fairly bristles with the method of science.[12]

There is one more source of the intellectual's hostility to sociology that I would like to examine, a source that was anticipated by Weber in his lecture on science as a vocation. For if it is true that intellectualization and rationalization, to which science commits itself and of which it is a part, means "that principally there are no mysterious incalculable forces that come into play,[13] but rather that one can, in principle, master

---

century, the universities may seem to be the source of reaction and apologetics for the status quo; but in the intellectual atmosphere of the last ten years, the universities seem to be a fortress (not quite impregnable) of free critical thought.

[11] Among these intellectuals, one often finds people who, by profession, are sociologists themselves; and this fact creates an added complexity. For one sector of the sociological profession is humanistic in its intellectual traditions, its characteristic substantive interests, and its methods of investigation. These sociologists often harbor the intellectual's stereotype of "the sociologist"—but in a diluted and ambivalent form, because it involves their professional loyalties, and because they are living refutations of the accuracy of the image.

[12] As "big" books, all five of these contain something of value; the point is that the works by Riesman and Mills are clearly "intellectual" works in that they use data to illustrate a "thesis." They are clearly commentaries and interpretations of contemporary experience, and as such are grist for the intellectual's mill. It is this that makes them "interesting" and reviewable in the prominent periodicals of the intellectuals. The American Soldier and The Authoritarian Personality are less "interesting" to intellectuals because their primary intent is to report facts, not to diagnose, warn, or exhort. Nothing can kill an argument as quickly as a fact.

[13] Max Weber, From Max Weber: Essays in Sociology (Oxford University Press, 1946), p. 139 (ed. by Gerth and Mills).

all things by calculation," then it is not only true, as Weber said, that "the world is disenchanted," but also true that the social scientist is perceived as challenging that tradition of humanism and art which has subsisted on the view that the world is enchanted, and that man is the mystery of mysteries. To the carriers of this tradition, every work of art and every poetic insight constitutes further proof that the world is enchanted, and that the source of man's gift to make art and to have poetic insight is a mystery made more mysterious by each illumination. The power of this tradition should not be underestimated; it is well rooted in the thinking of modern literature, with its antiscientific temper and its faith in the recalcitrance of men to yield up their deepest secrets to the generalizations of science. From Wordsworth's "to dissect is to kill," to Mallarmé's "whatever is sacred, whatever is to remain sacred, must be clothed in mystery," to Cummings' "mysteries alone are significant," the tradition has remained strong. And surely, it must have reached its apotheosis when, before a Harvard audience, Cummings made the following pronouncement:

I am someone who proudly and humbly affirms that love is the mystery of mysteries, and that nothing measurable matters "a very good God damn": that "an artist, a man, a failure," is no mere whenfully accreting mechanism, but a givingly eternal complexity —neither some soulless and heartless ultrapredatory infra-animal nor any un-understandingly knowing and believing and thinking automation, but a naturally and miraculously whole human being—a feelingly illimitable individual; whose only happiness is to transcend himself, whose every agony is to grow. (E. E. Cummings, six nonlectures, Cambridge: Harvard University Press, 1955, pp. 110-111.)

Intellectuals in this tradition seem to believe that the fulfillment of the goals of social science necessarily means that the creative powers of man will be "explained away," that his freedom will be denied, his "naturalness" mechanized, and his "miraculousness" made formula; that

Cummings' "feelingly illimitable individual" will be shown up as a quite limited and determined "social product," whose every mystery and transcendence can be formulated, if not on a pin, then within the framework of some sociological theory.[14] It is no wonder, then, that a vision as fearsome as this can provoke the simultaneous convictions that a science of society is both impossible and evil.

IV

It is no great step from the stereotypes consequent to ethnic and racial diversity to the stereotypes consequent to the diversity of occupational specialization. In those occupations which claim technical, professional status, occupations in which advanced, specialized training is necessary, it is likely that occupational stereotypes should find fertile ground because those on the "outside" have only secondary, derivative "knowledge" of the occupation. It is likely to be even more true of those professions which, like sociology, are so new that the nature of their subject matter is still being discussed by their members, and still more true if the new profession, by arrogating to itself a field of study formerly "belonging" to someone else (or to everyone else), raises, either intentionally or unintentionally by implication, invidious questions of relative competence.

Noteworthy in this regard is the fact that the social sciences which have been most active in the "interdisciplinary" tendencies of recent years are sociology, cultural anthropology, and psychology—precisely those disciplines with the most broadly defined subject matter. Each of these claims nothing less, in effect, than

---

[14]Nowhere is this made more clear than in the hostility of artists to the sociology of knowledge, art, or intellectual life. Artists resist having their work "explained" in terms of ideology, class, milieu, spirit of the age, and so forth, even when they are assured that this explanation of its sources in no way impugns the "truth" or the "integrity" of the work; somehow, the feeling persists among artists that a sociological explanation of the sources of their work makes it, in some way, "not theirs." This, I suppose, is one of the more or less rueful consequences of the belief that man is sui generis.

the totality of man's nonphysiological behavior as the field of its special competence; and it is no wonder that economics and political science, whose claims are considerably more modest (i.e., whose subject matter is relatively clearly and narrowly defined), have not found it strikingly to their interests to participate much in this convergence. For it is no doubt partly a matter of common professional interest as well as a matter of theoretical clarification that is behind this pooling of their intellectual resources by sociologists, anthropologists, and psychologists. The satire[15] (which invokes the extant stereotype) to which social scientists are submitted is of common concern to them, for the public image of the social sciences, largely created by the commentaries of intellectuals on them, is related to the amount of public support that the social sciences receive.

The stereotype of sociology and sociologists is part of a larger configuration which stereotypes social science in general; sociology, however, is the most successfully maligned of the social sciences. This special vulnerability is due largely to its relative lack of the sources of prestige available to the other social sciences. Economics commands a respect consequent to its age, to the generally accepted legitimacy of its subject matter, to its demonstrated usefulness, and to the wide variety of jobs available to people trained in it. Cultural anthropology borrows scientific prestige from physical anthropology and archeology, and gets some of its own as a result of its concern with the esoteric subject matter of primitive peoples. Political science has the prestigious correlates of law, diplomacy, and international relations. Clinical psychology has the towering figure of Freud, an affinity to medicine, and the presence of the almost mythic dimen-

sions of The Psychiatrist. Unlike economics, sociology has no hoary past, and no long line of employers clamoring for access to its skills. Unlike clinical psychology, it has no founding figure generally recognized as seminal in the history of western science; and the tenuousness of the concept of a "sick society" denies to sociology the status of a clinical discipline, and hence the prestige that accrues to The Healer. Unlike political science, it has neither an empirical nor an historical relation to the high concerns of nations, governments, or law; and unlike cultural anthropology, it has neither empirical roots nor an esoteric subject matter. Not only is sociology's subject matter not esoteric, but its traditional concern with such peripheral problems of social life as crime, delinquency, and divorce, and others conventionally classified under the rubric "social disorganization," quite likely tends, as Merton has suggested, to diminish its prestige.

Sociology, then, is <u>vulnerable</u> to stereotyping; its position in the contemporary structure of the intellectual professions exposes it to criticism from all sides. It numbers among the weaker of the social sciences, it is the bastard son of the humanities, from which it gets its subject matter, and the sciences, from which it gets its methods. Fully acknowledged by neither parent, it finds itself in the role of <u>upstart</u>, now utilizing the existing methods of science, now improvising new scientific methods, in an attempt to make the enchanted data of the humanities yield up their mysteries.

Like ethnic stereotypes, which are fostered by segregation and reinforced by the consequent cultural isolation, intellectual stereotypes are fostered by professional specialization and reinforced by the diverse (and sometimes conflicting) perspectives developed in each.[16] The lack of an intellectual perspective that

---

[15] Apparently large numbers of people find it rather amusing to indulge fantasies of anthropologists being eaten by cannibals, to hear of a sociologist who spends $10,000 to find a brothel, and to trivialize psychology by reference now to rats, now to the couch.

[16] How, for example, is a social scientist to respond to literary critic Stanley Edgar Hyman, when, in a recent article on Freud and the psychoanalytical movement, he praises Freud because, by locating the source of the neuroses in the instincts, he <u>permits the possibility of dramatic tragedy in liter-</u>

transcends the provincialism generated by the limitations of a specialized perspective makes one susceptible to clichés and stereotypic thinking about related fields of study. In race and interethnic relations, the marginal man has, with his proverbial "one foot in each culture," provided this transcendent perspective. Humanist intellectuals can fulfill this function in intellectual life by addressing their criticisms of sociology to sociologists, rather than to their own colleagues;

for it is the ironic fact that in writing to his own colleagues about sociology, the humanist intellectual himself tends to use obvious clichés to which his immersion in his own perspective binds him.[17] The kind of cross-fertilization that might be achieved by having humanist intellectual perspectives critically directed at an audience of sociologists, perhaps in a sociological journal, might go a long way toward providing this transcendent perspective.

---

ature, and condemns the neo-Freudians because, by locating the source of the neuroses in culture and society, they deny the possibility of inherent tragic flaws? Is the worth of a psychological theory to be measured in terms of how well it supports an aesthetic theory? (Stanley Edgar Hyman, "Freud and

the Climate of Tragedy," Partisan Review, Spring, 1956; see p. 211.)

[17]Arthur Schlesinger Jr.'s review of The American Soldier contains a catalogue of these clichés. See his "The Statistical Soldier," Partisan Review, 1949, p. 853.

SOCIOLOGICAL THEORY

The Myth of Functional Analysis as a Special Method in Sociology and Anthropology

Kingsley Davis

SOURCE: *American Sociological Review*, Vol. 24 (1959), pp. 757–73.

For more than thirty years now "functional analysis" has been debated among sociologists and anthropologists. Perhaps the time has come for the debate to be either settled or abandoned. My view is that it should be abandoned, because it rests on the false assumption that there is a special method or body of theory called functional analysis which can be distinguished from other methods or theories within sociology and social anthropology. It is not that the work done under the functional label is poor or unscientific (quite the contrary), but rather that the label itself signalizes and fosters the myth of a homogeneous mode of analysis distinct from other sociological modes of analysis. Not only is this assumption false, in my view, but it is increasingly a source of confusion. However strategic it may have been in the past, it has now

become an impediment rather than a prop to scientific progress.

In seeing the rationale of this thesis, one should first realize that consensus on the definition of structural-functional analysis does not exist, but that examination of the features most commonly mentioned and of the work actually done under the label shows it to be, in effect, synonymous with sociological analysis. Next, one should recognize that the issues involved in the debate over functionalism—issues with respect to problems, assumptions, methods, evidence— are the issues of sociological analysis itself. To debate them under the guise of evaluating functionalism, therefore, is to inject into the discussion a spurious obstacle to clarity and objectivity. Finally, one should undertake to see how this interpretation fits into an analysis of the history of anthropology and sociology, first with respect to the conditions under which functionalism emerged as a scholarly movement, then with respect to the subsequent circumstances that altered its role.

THE MEANING OF FUNCTIONAL ANALYSIS

Diversity and ambiguity are easily found in conceptions of functional analysis. Characteristics that the functionalists themselves regard as either accidental faults or as totally alien to their point of view—teleology, conservatism, preoccupation with social statics, assumption of complete social integration —critics often regard as the essence of the approach. Even within each camp there are differences of definition, some as wide as those between the two sides. Among the critics we find that functionalists are described on the one hand as "primarily concerned with maintaining a stable, integrated and harmonious social equilibrium,"[1] and, on the other, as deriving "'cultural necessities and imperatives' from physiological sources."[2] While one critic characterizes functionalism as using psychological explanations,[3] another praises it for at least not committing this error,[4] and a third berates it for neglecting motivation.[5]

The functionalists themselves exhibit scarcely more agreement. Although Firth points out that "all British social anthropology today is functionalist," and quotes Fortes to the effect that functionalism is "the generally accepted basis of

theory and research in British social anthropology," he admits that the off-hand definitions and the actual practice in contemporary anthropology reveal anything but agreement or clarity as to the nature of functional analysis. There is "Redfield's description of 'the functional model' as one in which a culture or society is seen as an organization of means designed to achieve ends, ...;" or the view that functionalism is properly the study of the "conjunction of cultural behaviors."[6] Radcliffe-Brown's distaste for Malinowski's functionalism is well known, and is hardly stronger than that of nonfunctionalist Kroeber.[7]

One's first impulse, when faced with this diversity, is to try to redefine structural-functional analysis clearly and consistently. But so many have tried this— notably Merton, Levy, Radcliffe-Brown —without visably improving general usage, that one is forced to view the diversity itself as an essential rather than an accidental feature of the situation, and thus as requiring explanation. If we avoid the assumption that functionalism refers to a consistent and recognizable approach within sociology, and instead entertain the hypothesis that, as most commonly defined, it is as broad as sociological analysis itself, we can understand both the extent and the limits of disagreement. We can see that the lack of agreement on functionalism reflects the lack of agreement on the issues of sociological analysis, and that the features of functionalism most commonly cited are the essentials of sociological interpretation itself.

Turning from the sheer variety of con-

---

[1]Wayne Hield, "The Study of Change in Social Science," British Journal of Sociology, 5 (March, 1954), p. 1.

[2]Dorothy Gregg and Elgin Williams, "The Dismal Science of Functionalism," American Anthropologist, 50 (October-December, 1958), p. 597.

[3]Alexander Lesser, "Functionalism in Social Anthropology," American Anthropologist, 37 (July-September, 1935).

[4]Sidney Morgenbesser, "Role and Status of Anthropological Theories," Science, 128 (August 8, 1958), p. 285.

[5]Harry C. Bredemeier, "The Methodology of Functionalism," American Sociological Review, 20 (April, 1935), pp. 173-179.

[6]Raymond Firth, "Function" in Current Anthropology, Chicago: University of Chicago Press, 1955, pp. 247-251. He gives further quotations and references showing diversity of definitions, including Fortes' claim' "that the chief innovation for which the functionalist movement stands was a contribution of the Cambridge School of anthropology—the principle of the intensive study of limited areas."

[7]A. R. Radcliffe-Brown: "As for myself, I reject it entirely, regarding it as useless and worse." "Functionalism: A Protest," American Anthropologists, 51 (April-June, 1949), p. 321. A. L. Kroeber: "I have long considered Malinowski's whole scheme of need-derivation a verbal wish-fulfilment...." "An Authoritarian Panacea," ibid., p. 318.

ceptions to the traits most frequently cited as characterizing functional analysis, we find that functionalism is most commonly said to <u>do</u> two things: to relate the parts of society to the whole, and to relate one part to another. Almost as common is the specification of <u>how</u> it does this relating—namely, by seeing one part as "performing a function for" or "meeting a need or requirement of" the whole society or some part of it. It strikes me that the first two traits simply describe what <u>any</u> science does. Every science describes and explains phenomena from the standpoint of a <u>system</u> of reasoning which presumably bears a relation to a corresponding <u>system</u> in nature. In the case of sociology, what is distinctive is the subject, not the method; for it deals with human societies whereas other disciplines deal with other kinds of systems. Given its subject, the least it could do is to relate the parts to the whole of society and to one another.

A better case of the distinctiveness of functionalism can be made on the basis of the "requirement-meeting" mode of reasoning. The distinctiveness seems to dissolve, however, when semantic problems are recognized. For this purpose Merton's characterization offers a point of departure. He describes "the central orientation of functionalism" as "the practice of interpreting data by establishing their consequences for larger structures in which they are implicated."[8] If "interpreting" here means "explanation," the sense of the statement can hardly be that in functionalism data are explained <u>solely</u> in terms of their consequences; for nothing is explained that way. Evidently the statement means that <u>among</u> the considerations used in interpretation are the consequences for larger structures. In this case, however, we have added nothing to the two characterizations discussed in the preceding paragraph. How else can data be interpreted except in relation to the larger structures in <u>which they are implicated</u>? How can data on the earth's orbit, for ex-

ample, be understood except in relation to a system in which they are involved— in this case, the solar system or the earth's climatic system? Since in science some kind of system is usually being dealt with, an analysis of the effect of one factor must always be made with the possibility in mind of a possible return effect ("feedback") on the factor itself. If, for example, the increase in fish (y) in a pond has the effect of increasing the toxicity (x) of the water, the growth of the fish population (y again) will eventually cease unless other factors intervene. This is not explaining things solely by their consequences, but rather by the way their consequences react upon them.[9]

Misunderstanding in this matter seems to arise from two sources: first from the language used in describing the relationships, second from the special problems of applying systematic analysis to human societies. As to language, if the investigator uses phrases like "has the function of," "meets the need of," or simply "is for," the words have so many connotations and ambiguities that the effect is often to obstruct rather than to facilitate the conveyance of meaning. Part of the reason is that these are words borrowed from common discourse and hence mainly used to indicate moral imperatives and volitional intent rather than sheer causal relationships. Actually, when such terms are used in natural science there is not much debate as to what is meant. An agronomist, for instance, theorizing that certain types of fruit trees die when particular trace elements are missing from the soil, may say that the trace elements "contribute to" or "have the function of" keeping fruit trees alive. He may say this without being accused of teleology, conservatism, or worse;[10] but the same phrases used in sociological or anthropological discourse are often either actually intended this way or are so interpreted. The reason relates to the second source of difficulty

---

[8] Robert K. Merton, <u>Social Theory and Social Structure</u>, Glencoe, Ill.: Free Press, 1957, p. 19.

[9] Cf. Bredemeier, <u>op. cit.</u>

[10] For an excellent account of questionable language in textbooks of natural and physical science, see A. J. Bernatowicz, "Teleology in Science Teach-

—the fact that human society is being dealt with. Terms connoting moral obligation or censure, or indicating explanation by intent, are particularly unsuited for the description of causal relationships because the meanings they stand for are properly part of the object rather than the basis of explanation. It is of course extraordinarily difficult to escape from such words, not only because nearly all language is infused with them, but because they contain conceptions and values that the observer himself has as a member of society.

It thus appears that the most nearly agreed-upon traits of functionalism are those broadly characterizing scientific analysis in general. Any distinction is due, not to method per se, but to linguistic usage and the particular subject (society). Granted the linguistic matter is superficial,[11] we find nothing to upset the view that it is another name for sociological analysis—the interpretation of phenomena in terms of their interconnections with societies as going concerns.

WHAT IS NON-FUNCTIONALISM?

The same conclusion emerges from examining that neglected concept, "non-functional analysis." Although seldom defined explicitly, this residual category seems, by implication, to include traits falling into one or the other of two classes: either they constitute some sort of reductionism and are therefore non-sociological in character, or they constitute some form of raw empiricism or sheer data manipulation and are therefore non-theoretical. In other words, whatever falls outside the domain of sociological theory falls outside the realm of functionalism.

Reductionist Theories as Non-Functional. If the word "psychological" is construed as referring to analysis in terms of the individual as a system, especially with the implication that this system is determinative of social phenomena, there is general agreement that, although it may be functional psychology, it is not functional anthropology or sociology.[12] Durkheim phrased the point characteristically: "The determining cause of a social fact should be sought among the social facts preceding it and not among the states of the individual consciousness."[13] Functionalists have typically rejected explanations of social phenomena which depended on some alleged trait of the human mind rather than on the operation of a social system. Following Durkheim, for instance, they rejected the evolutionists' individualistic theory of religion as failing to account for the cultural standardization and normative obligatoriness of religious belief and behavior.[14]

---

ing," Science, 128 (December 5, 1958), pp. 1402-1405. The author finds the infinitive verb is a common linguistic gateway to teleological and anthropomorphic phraseology. The to in these cases "is merely an abbreviation of in order to." Thus atoms "strive to attain the stable arrangement of electrons...," "the ultimate goal of stream erosion is to reduce the land surface to a nearly flat plain ...." Other key words of similar effect are "for," "has to," "must." Such language is justified as being useful in avoiding awkward circumlocutions and making for livelier reading, though Bernatowicz disagrees.

[11]Sometimes commentators come perilously near to saying that functional analysis is analysis that employs the word function. "'The function of religion is to relieve anxiety in a group.' This asserts nothing not asserted by 'Anxiety in a group is relieved if (or perhaps, only if) it practices religion,' or by 'A (sufficient, necessary, or sufficient and necessary) condition for relief of anxiety in a group is the practice of religion.' These latter statements are clearly nonfunctional." Walter Buckley (para-

phrasing Nagel), "Structural-Functional Analysis in Modern Sociology," in Howard Becker and Alvin Boskoff, editors, Modern Sociological Theory, New York: Dryden, 1957, p. 247.

[12]The occasional charge that functionalism is psychological evidently arises from an ambiguity. Insofar as the word "psychological" refers simply to mental phenomena, such as thoughts, sentiments, and attitudes, sociology and social anthropology can hardly escape dealing with psychological phenomena. "Psychological" in the sense of treating the person as a system is a different thing. It is interesting that the science of treating the personality, or the psyche, as a system is often called "functional psychology." For this reason a disorder of the individual for which no organic cause can be found, and which is thus presumably explicable in terms of the personality system, is commonly designated a "functional disorder."

[13]Emile Durkheim, Rules of Sociological Method, Glencoe, Ill.: Free Press, 1950, pp. 110-111.

[14]See W. J. Goode, Religion Among the Primitives, Glencoe, Ill.: Free Press, 1951, pp. 243-244;

If psychologistic solutions are barred from structural-functional analysis, then biologistic solutions are a fortiori barred. One form of biologism—explanation of social phenomena in terms of genetic inheritance—is generally considered to be at the opposite pole from functionalism.[15] Another form—the analysis of society by treating it literally as if it were a biological organism—has sometimes been regarded as one of the precursors of functionalism, but if the only legacy is seeing society as "composed of differentiated, interrelated structures reacting on one another and constituting an integral whole on a psycho-social, rather than a biological, level,"[16] nothing biological is left. A third kind of biologism, social Darwinism, more an epithet for a bad ideology than a name for a scientific outlook, has seldom been charged to functionalists.[17] It is identified with Spencer and the evolutionism against which functionalists were in rebellion, and with a rugged individualism hardly compatible with an emphasis on "the

functional integration of society." In fact, the critics of functionalism have accused it of paying too little attention to conflict and the struggle for power[18] —elements that the evolutionists and social Darwinists stressed.

The type of reductionism represented by technological or economic determinism is equally differentiated from functionalism. Although Marx, for instance, was occasionally called a functionalist,[19] his followers in sociology and anthropology quarrel with colleagues who wear this label. The reason usually given is their aversion to the functionalist concern with integration rather than conflict, but a more basic reason is the reductionism implicit in "materialism." Any view that sees all change in society as the consequence of technological or economic change offends functionalists because it reduces other aspects of society to epiphenomena and treats non-rational behavior as simply ignorance and error.

Similarly, the functionalist rebellion against trait-distributionism, signalized by Lowie's charge that Malinowski "flouts distribution studies,"[20] is understandable as a reaction of those interested in societies against those interested in culture traits. From the former standpoint the only significant aspect of a trait is its relation to the social system, and for many traits this aspect is trivial. In cultural anthropology, on the other hand, the existence, form, and provenience of

---

Kingsley Davis, Human Society, New York: Macmillan, 1949, p. 518; J. Milton Yinger, Religion, Society and the Individual, New York: Macmillan, 1957, Chapter 3. Psychoanalytic theories of religion and the family were criticized for similar reasons. Goode, op. cit., pp. 247-249, and E. E. Evans Pritchard, Social Anthropology, Glencoe, Ill. Free Press, 1954, pp. 44-45. As early as 1927 B. Malinowski complained that Ernest Jones "regards the [Oedipus] complex as the cause, and the whole sociological structure as the effect." Sex and Repression in Savage Society, London: Paul, Trench, Trubner, 1927, pp. 139, 130.

[15]Obviously, the biological character of the human species is relevant to the question of the limits of variation in human society—see Marion J. Levy, Jr., The Structure of Society, Princeton: Princeton University Press, 1952, pp. 16-17—but recognition of this fact by functionalists has not committed them to genetic interpretation of social variation itself. Admittedly the theoretical status of Malinowski's "needs" is open to dispute; although often accused of biologism (see cited articles by Gregg and Williams and by Radcliffe-Brown), his writings contain firm statements indicating that in his mind biological needs are necessary but not sufficient causes.

[16]Buckley, op. cit., pp. 239-240.

[17]Richard Hofstadter's Social Darwinism in American Thought, revised edition, Boston: Beacon Press, 1955, contains no reference to "functionalism" or to Robertson Smith, Durkheim, Malinowski, Radcliffe-Brown. In fact, Hofstadter thinks that so-

cial Darwinism was dead by the end of World War I, which is just about the time functionalism began to emerge as a name for a self-conscious school of thought in anthropology.

[18]See Ralf Dahrendorf, "Out of Utopia: Toward A Reorientation of Sociological Analysis," American Journal of Sociology, 64 (September, 1958); Held, op. cit.; David Lockwood, "Some Remarks on 'The Social System,'" British Journal of Sociology, 7 (June, 1956), pp. 134-146. Bredemeier, op. cit., p. 175, is one of the few critics to note that the functionalists' concern with factors governing the survival of societal elements gives them a basis of linkage with biological theory.

[19]Horace Kallen, "Functionalism," Encyclopedia of the Social Sciences, New York: Macmillan, 1931, Vol. 6, pp. 523-526.

[20]Robert H. Lowie, History of Ethnological Theory, New York: Rinehart, 1937, pp. 234-235.

traits are important per se, whether significant for the operation of society or not.

Empiricism and Data as Non-Functional. So far we have found that, among theories, those that explain social phenomena in terms derived from some other level tend to be classed as nonfunctional. Now let us recall that if a part of social science consists of theories, there must be another part that consists of observations. It appears that this part of sociology and anthropology, the sheer description and reporting of statistical relationships, is regarded as wholly outside of structural-functional analysis.

The clearest exclusion from functionalism, for instance, is the "historical approach." Insofar as this approach implies an antagonism to theoretical generalization and a preference for straight description of the past, it is opposed to the functionalists' predilection for explaining phenomena by appeal to abstract principles.[21] Of course, the attempt merely to state facts is not confined to historicism but appears in contemporary fieldwork of both the ethnographic and survey type. Such an attempt, either as methodological doctrine or as research performance, is regarded as outside of functionalism. The same is true of the empiricist doctrine that science is "nothing but" the establishment of statistical probabilities. Functional analysis is felt to involve interpretation, not simply data or data-manipulation.

CRITICAL ISSUES IN "FUNCTIONAL ANALYSIS"

If the most frequent conceptions of functionalism make it, in effect, inclusive of sociological analysis but exclusive of reductionism and sheer description, then the scientific problems of functional analysis are the same as those of sociology in general. That this is true is suggested by the kind of questions most commonly

identified with functionalism—for example: What features of social organization or behavior appear in all or nearly all societies? Why are these features so nearly universal while others are more variable? What particular features characterize each type of society, and how do they mesh together in the operation of that type? How in a concrete community are the parts of the social structure mutually congruent or incongruent, as exhibited in attitudes, roles, and conduct? Such "functional questions," when taken together, evoke a comparative science of society, because they are the most general that can be asked. The attempt to find systematic answers to them forms a framework of reasoning that can enlighten any specific inquiry, no matter how limited. Such questions, then, are not peripheral to sociological analysis, but central.

It is therefore puzzling that a distinction should be assumed between sociological and functional analysis, and that once distinguished, the latter should be considered more controversial—as witness the numerous articles and chapters dealing with "functional analysis," the most famous of which opens with this statement: "Functional analysis is at once the most promising and possibly the least codified of contemporary orientations to problems of sociological interpretation."[22] Naturally, I am not interested solely in questioning the accuracy of this notion but also in trying to explain its prevalence. I think that an explanation, though hard, is possible if one bears in mind the difficulties inherent in studying

---

[21]Evans-Pritchard characterizes functionalism as holding that "even with the best sources at his disposal, the historian can only tell us what has been the succession of accidental events by which society has become what it is." Op. cit., p. 47.

[22]Merton, "Manifest and Latent Functions," loc. cit., p. 19. Lowie, in his History of Ethnological Theory, op. cit., has a chapter on the French "sociological school" including Radcliffe-Brown, followed by a chapter on "functionalism" including Malinowski. Actually, the term "sociological" and "functional" are often used interchangeably. Most of Chapter 3 in Yinger, op. cit., entitled "A Sociological Theory of Religion," is devoted to the "functional approach," which is taken for granted as the distinctively sociological approach. Radcliffe-Brown usually avoids the term "functional analysis" in favor of "comparative sociology" or simply "sociological" inquiry or theory. Malinowski was in the habit of calling his approach indefinitely either sociological of functional.

society—difficulties arising mainly, if not exclusively, from the circumstance that the observer must analyze objectively the norms of conduct that he and others, as actors, react to emotionally. In pursuing this line of explanation, one can begin by examining some of the major criticisms of functionalism. These, as already indicated, are critical issues in sociological theory (a point well worth demonstrating further), but the fact that they are debated with reference to functional analysis, assumed to be a special method, is of prime significance for our argument. Let us start with the question of evidence.

Evidence and Functional Analysis. Critics note that functionalism "abounds in principles and categories" but offers little by way of verification. Relationships are established "intuitively by the structure of the observer's language, or are assumed to be in nature."[23] Since this is true of functionalist ethnography as well as comparative functionalist theory, there is no value in denial. There is value, however, in asking why the charge is true. In large part it is because functionalism is preëminently social theory. The broader and more general a theory, the less is the chance of proving or disproving it in its entirety.[24] Social theory, in particular, tends to be broad and complex, because the observer, reared in a society himself, comes equipped with knowledge and opinion about social matters, including abstractions of great generality. He also intui-

tively understands behavior by imagining himself in the circumstances of the actor, and he constantly deals with ideological controversies woven into learned discourse. Thus the conceptual and linguistic apparatus constituting social theory becomes extremely subtle and highly ramified. By comparison, social research seems puny indeed. One reason is that much of the theory is too ambiguous to be researchable; also public attitudes severely restrict the possible kinds of social research; and, above all research on the non-instrumental aspects of society—on norms, values, religion, and so on—has little utility precisely because, unlike research in medicine or business, it concerns goals rather than means. Functional analysis is thus vulnerable to the charge of unverified theorizing because it has the character par excellence that social theory in general has.

But beyond this there is the fact that functionalism adopts a kind of language that is peculiarly close to the purposive and moralistic reasoning of ordinary discourse, yet tries to use it in the opposite way, that is, for the disinterested analysis of exactly this type of reasoning and its related behavior. Such words as "function," "disfunction," "latent," "needs" are treacherous for the same reason that they are handy. Connected with ideas much older than sociology or anthropology, they are susceptible of easy expansion by knitting together ready-made intuitions, connations, and ambiguities. But for this reason they are strikingly inappropriate for doing the opposite of moralistic reasoning—that is, for explaining in a detached manner the moral and religious ideas and behavior of mankind. It is this paradox that lies behind many charges against functionalism. Lack of evidence, being a good scientific objection, sometimes masks the other considerations.

Evidence is especially scarce insofar as functionalism attempts to state the requisites for the existence of any society or to explain the universals of social organization. In such matters there can be no proof by co-variation, because, by

---

[23]Buckley, op. cit., p. 258, speaking particularly of Parsonian functionalism. Merton's essay, loc. cit., voices similar criticism of functionalism generally.

[24]A body of theory includes a conceptual framework which, not being in the form of evidential propositions, is not subject to verification. Furthermore, disproof of specific propositions logically related to parts of the theory need not kill the system, because the latter can be modified without necessarily changing its essentials. The broader and looser a theoretical system, the more prolific it is of propositions and the less embarrassed by their disproof. Fantastic schemes of reasoning have lasted for decades and finally died of disinterest rather than disproof. On verification and theoretical systems, see Ernest Nagel, Logic Without Metaphysics, Glencoe, Ill.: Free Press, 1956, Chapter 7.

definition, all actual societies exhibit the traits in question. Nor can functionalists create experimental societies to test the effect of omitting this or that ingredient. The analysis must therefore be heavily deductive,[25] the language of which is easily borrowed from ordinary discourse. Anybody can see, for example, that the virtually universal occurrence of incest taboos is due to their being "essential for" the nuclear family; people habitually justify basic norms in terms of their social value. The disinterestedness of functional analysis is hardly clearer when disapproved institutions like prostitution, social inequality, or political corruption are being explained, for this seems like either cynicism or satire. The best chance for real evidence is provided by "experimental" communities set up by political or religious sects or brought about by accidental conditions, by exceptional cases occurring in particular segments or classes of some societies, and by the inevitable normal variation in the concrete manifestation of any general rule. But unless the language of functionalism is remedied (which means eliminating the notion of "functionalism"), there seems no way for the analyst to escape having his deductions deliberately or unwittingly confused with moralizing.

The Three Postulates of Functionalism. In criticizing the postulation of functional unity, universal functionalism, and functional indispensability, Merton seems to charge both that these abstractions are reified in functional analysis and that they lack heuristic value in any case. Whether they are actually reified depends on how one reads the evidence.[26] Our interest lies, however, in the other question, the heuristic value of the abstractions.

This question turns on what the postulates mean. As for the first two, Merton speaks of "complete functional unity" and of "universal functionalism." Certainly it would be silly to regard such propositions as literally true, and perhaps pointless to use them as abstractions. But if the intended meaning is simply that some order in societies is assumed and that every social form should be examined from the standpoint of its possible role in societal continuity (thus assuming heuristically that each item plays such a role), the analytic value seems plain. What else could a sociologist do? If one sets out to study societies, one presumably sets out to study something that exists. If societies exist, there must be some sense in which each one more or less hangs together, and the question of how this is accomplished and not accomplished is a central one.

The third postulate is, in Merton's view, a dual one: first, that certain functions are indispensable for the persistence of a society or group; second, "that certain cultural or social forms are indispensable in fulfilling each of these functions."[27] He seemingly has no objection to the first version—evidently on the ground that functions are fewer than social forms and that therefore the assumption that some of them are indispensable is a high-level abstraction serving to evoke a theory of the basis of human societies. The second version seems more specific, thus more open to empirical test, and hence more dangerous if assumed to be true concretely. Yet if a social form is actually found in all

---

[25] "If we start with a social-system theory, defining and relating all the necessary concepts involved, ...then the functional requisites, or conditions necessary for the persistence of such a system are, ideally, implied by the system as delineated." Buckley, op. cit., p. 256.

[26] Since no functionalist has given his theory a rigorous axiomatic treatment, conclusive evidence as to whether the three abstractions are reified or even postulated cannot be produced. Merton naturally relies on quotations. Most of these are from Malinowski, whose statements are varied and careless enough to afford evidence of numerous errors.

In the case of Radcliffe-Brown, a quoted statement assuming only a "degree of harmony or consistency" seems to be the evidence for Merton's implication in the next two pages that he assumes "complete functional unity." Similarly, Clyde Kluckhohn is cited (Merton, op. cit., pp. 30-31) as "postulating functional value for all surviving forms of culture," but no reference is made to passages in the same book (Navajo Witchcraft, Cambridge, Mass.: The Museum, 1944, p. 68) where Kluckhohn discusses the "costs" and the "disruptive effects" of witchcraft.

[27] Op. cit., p. 33 (italics in original).

known societies, it would seem harmless to entertain the hypothesis that it is indispensable.[28] Such a hypothesis is not a postulate on which a system is built; it is rather a prediction resulting from theory and fact---a prediction that no society will be found which lacks the trait. The important thing is not the prediction but the sociological reasoning on which it is based. Equally of value is the opposite assumption, that there may be as yet undiscovered alternative structures that can perform the same function as the trait in question—provided, of course that this abstraction is not reified either.[29]

If Merton is correct in calling attention to the absurdity of reifying the three assumptions but not in impugning their heuristic value, the readiness of the critics of functionalism to accept and repeat the entire charge seems an over-reaction. A clue to the reason appears in the selectivity of the charge. If somebody states that a society must have economic support or biological reproduction, the proposition is taken as a harmless truism made for the purpose of facilitating a process of reasoning. If, on the other hand, it is said that normative control, attitudinal consensus, or social inequality is required, one is likely to be accused, among other things, of making an unwarranted assumption. Not only are things like consensus and inequality less tangible than economic support or reproduction, they are more closely related to ideological controversies.

The postulates are identified with functionalism, and yet Merton says they are " unnecessary to the functional orientation."[30] The same has been said of sociology, for the latter has been perennially accused of hypostatizing something called society, of treating social solidarity as

if it were the only reality or the only explanatory principle. In the case of functionalism, the idea seems to be that if the postulates can be eliminated, this orientation will be purged of some of its impurities. As I see it, the opposite course is advisable—to eliminate the notion of functionalism as a distinct method along with the confusing terminology that goes with the name, and to keep the basic heuristic assumptions that form part of a system of sociological reasoning.

A system of reasoning cannot be developed without assumptions. As long as these are not reified, it makes little difference where one starts. If one begins by asking why conflict and strife are so rife among human beings, one eventually gets around to asking why there is not even more strife than there is and hence to the problem of social control and integration. If one starts by asking how a modicum of harmony is achieved, one is soon forced to discuss conflict. Viewed in this light, there is no reason to eliminate the basic thinking represented by the three postulates discussed, but there is reason to phrase them differently and in terms less open to logical confusion and ideological attack. Also there is a need to add other assumptions.

Latent, Manifest, and Functional. The distinction between latent and manifest functions might be described as the fourth postulate of functionalism. However, although identified with functionalism by virtue of Merton's brilliant exposition, the idea of the distinction, phrased in various ways, has long been central in sociology. It was stated in 1895 by Durkheim, who spoke of "function" versus "purpose."[31] It was developed with extreme thoroughness in Pareto's discussion, in 1916, of individual utility and

---

[28]If societies were found which lacked the trait, there would be no point in assuming the trait to be indispensable.

[29]In recommending the idea of functional equivalents, Merton does not call it a postulate, but simply a concept. Op. cit., pp. 34, 36. Could the ideas of functional unity and functional indispensability also be called concepts? For interesting brief statements of the principles of functional equivalents, multi-functionality of structures, and limited

possibilities, see B. Malinowski's article, "Culture," Encyclopedia of the Social Science, Vol. 4, pp. 621-646.

[30]Op. cit., p. 25.

[31]" We use the word 'function,' in preference to 'end' or 'purpose,'... Whether there is a correspondence between the fact under consideration and the general needs of the social organism [is independent of] whether it has been intentional or not." Rules of Sociological Method, p. 95.

utility to, of, and for the community.[32] Accordingly, the distinction in no way depends upon a special functional method or requires the use of the term "function;" yet the fact that it plays a crucial role in both sociological theory and what is called functionalism deserves careful attention.

It seems to me that the scientific issue involved is the explanatory role of subjective elements (goals, norms, knowledge) and of rational and non-rational behavior. Talcott Parsons' classic typology of theoretical positions in social science rests on different ways of handling this issue.[33] For the economist, the problems are not great: he can get along analytically by taking goals as given and assuming rational behavior modified simply by ignorance and error. For the sociologist, however, the goals and sentiments and non-rational behavior are among the phenomena to be explained. He is therefore required to distinguish carefully between what the actor has in mind and what the social causes and consequences of his action may be, to keep separate always the point of view of the actor and the point of view of the observer. To the extent that he fails to do so, to the extent that he cherishes certain goals or puts his analysis in terms of them and thus adopts the role of an actor, he loses the sociological level of analysis.

Undeniably, the observer role with respect to social institutions is hard to maintain. The investigator, in trying to comprehend the subjective views of his subjects, tends to make the honest mistake of taking these views as an ultimate basis of explanation. Sometimes, in addition, social science is made to validate democracy, tolerance, peace, and other values. The functionalist movement, as I see it, represents an effort to explain social organization and behavior from a disinterested observer's point of view.

This is why the manifest-latent distinction is important. Ironically, however, the movement has fallen victim to what it sought to overcome. The inability to see purposes and sentiments as objects of explanation, the unwillingness to remain detached—these have joined the inherent discomfort of analysis from a societal rather than a psychological standpoint and have riddled the weak terminology of functionalism with criticism and confusion.

Teleology and Ideology. Teleology is one fallacy that functionalists try hard to avoid, but when they are charged with it, their language and their own and others' ambiguities make defense difficult. If we accept the dictionary definition of teleology as "the doctrine that the existence of everything in nature can be explained in terms of purpose," the distinction between manifest and latent functions is clearly contrary to it. The functional theory of incest taboos or of magical practices does not hold that these exist because their social consequences (functions) are perceived. On the contrary, the purposes the actors have in mind are treated as not necessarily including the consequences but as being part of the mechanisms by which the societal functions are accomplished. This refusal to take purposes at their face value as the basis of explanation often appears incomprehensible or reprehensible. One critic, for example, feels that the only way the consequences of an action can serve to explain its persistence is by the actor's perceiving the possible consequences and guiding his behavior accordingly.[34] To visualize the unrecognized social consequences of an action as leading, by their unrecognized effect on the conditions, to the continuous reinforcement or minimization of that action in the society, is too much against the grain of ordinary discourse.

Those interested in social protest or reform necessarily depend upon purposes as the basis of explanation, for they must

---

[32]V. Pareto, Mind and Society, New York: Harcourt, Brace, 1935, Vol. 1, Chapter 2; Vol. 4, Chapter 12.

[33]Structure of Social Action, New York: McGraw-Hill, 1937, Chapter 2-3.

[34]Bredemeier, op. cit., pp. 173, 175. This is the utilitarian position.

assign praise and blame. The feature of functionalism they find most objectionable is its refusal to rest with the imputation of motives. To explain anti-semitism for example, as due to the bad motives of either gentiles or Jews is to explain it in terms palatable to either the pro- or the anti-semite, whereas to explain it in "structural-functional" terms satisfies neither. Indeed, the actionist feels threatened by a system that subjects <u>his</u> motives to impersonal scrutiny. He defends himself by charging functionalism with various sins, one of which, ironically, is teleology. He sustains the charge by pointing out that <u>function</u> often means purpose or "final cause;" that words like <u>needs</u> and <u>requirements</u> are subjective; that <u>functional</u> or <u>disfunction</u> can often be translated "approved" or "disapproved."

Similarly, the view of functionalism as disguised ideology is most often advanced by those who are themselves ideologically oriented—as shown by the selectivity of the evidence adduced and by the purport of the theories proposed as substitutes.[35] Strictly speaking, a theory's support of a moral or political bias is independent of its scientific validity. We thus have no concern with the issue except as illustrating further that functional analysis is attacked for being sociological analysis, under the guise that it is something else. Merton, noting that functional analysis has been accused of radicalism as well as conservatism, shrewdly takes this as <u>prima facie</u> evidence that it is intrinsically neither one.[36] What interests us, however, is that in making this point he

unconsciously denies the premise that functionalism is a special kind of sociology. "Like other forms of sociological analysis," he says, functionalism "can be infused with any one of a wide range of ideological values." The only other form of sociology he mentions is Marxism, but, curiously, he finds that the Marxist theory of religion is no different from the functional theory in method or structure of analysis.

....the functionalists, with their emphasis on religion as a <u>social mechanism</u>..., may not differ materially in their <u>analytical frame-work</u> from the Marxists who, if their metaphor of "opium of the masses" is converted into a neutral statement of social fact, also assert that religion operates as a social mechanism....The point of difference appears only when <u>evaluations</u> of this commonly accepted fact come into question.[37]

If Marxist sociology does not differ methodologically from functional analysis, it seems doubtful that <u>any</u> kind of sociology does.

<u>Can Functionalism Handle Social Change?</u> The claim that functionalism cannot handle social change because it posits an integrated static society, is true by definition if "posits" means "to take literally." Here again, as with the other issues, the question for us is not who is right, but why the controversy? It seems strange indeed that the criticism should be voiced so often when in fact some of the best analyses of social change have come from people labeled as functionalists.[38] It seems even stranger when, in looking over these works, we find they do not differ in any basic way

---

[35]Gregg and Williams, <u>op. cit.</u>, condemn functionalism for not making a clear-cut distinction between good and bad. They say: "the cultural dichotomy which functionalism needs would at the outset distinguish <u>good</u> from <u>bad</u> goals, stultifying from liberating institutions, efficient from inefficient customs." (p. 608) See A. L. Kroeber's interesting comment on the article, "An Authoritarian Panacea," <u>op. cit.</u>, pp. 318-320.

[36]<u>Op. cit.</u>, pp. 38-46. A thoughtful analysis of why the functional theory of religion is radical is W. L. Kolb's "Values, Positivism, and the Functional Theory of Religion," <u>Social Forces</u>, 31 (May, 1953), pp. 305-311. "To spread the idea that a belief in ultimate validity of values is necessary but illusory,"

says Kolb, "would be to destroy society through destroying or confusing this belief." In another vein is the attack on the present writer's "functional" theory of religion by Gordon George, S. J., in "Some Sociologists Out of Bounds," <u>America</u>, 93 (January 15, 1955), pp. 397-398. "In the name of science," says George, "he [Davis] has unscientifically reduced religion to a mere device for bolstering social order." Similarly, Thomas F. O'Dea, "The Sociology of Religion," <u>American Catholic Sociological Review</u>, 15 (June, 1954), pp. 73-103.

[37]<u>Op. cit.</u>, p. 44 (italics in original).

[38]A few examples: Marion J. Levy's analyses of institutional factors in Chinese and Japanese economic development; Merton's studies of the rise of

from many studies of social change by persons opposing functionalism or at least not wearing the functionalist label.[39] Perhaps the idea of incompetence in this regard is a deduction from the fact that functionalism began as a revolt against historicism. As we shall see, however, the revolt was not against the study of change itself but against the omission of sociological analysis from such study. If it is true that functionalists have devoted less attention to social change than to statics, the same can be said of sociology and of social anthropology in general in recent decades. It happens that theories of social change, for understandable reasons, are ideologically significant. Possibly the charge of incompetence in this field represents, in part at least, still another use of functionalism as a means of criticizing sociological analysis.

THE ILLUSION OF A FUNCTIONAL METHOD

The substantive issues so far discussed all point to the conclusion that, if there is a functional method, it is simply the method of sociological analysis. Now let us examine more directly the persistent idea that it constitutes a more special method.

Functionalism and Exact Laws. Evans-Pritchard, following Radcliffe-Brown, says that functionalism rests on two propositions, one of which is "that social life can be reduced to scientific laws which allow prediction."[40] It is therefore

startling to find another functionalist, Talcott Parsons, stating the opposite. We cannot yet "develop a complete dynamic theory" of action, he says, and "therefore, the systematization of theory in the present state of knowledge must be in 'structural-functional' terms." The latter is primitive, the highest state of theory being one "permitting deductive transitions to be made from one aspect or state of a system to another." Since this is possible only in the most fragmentary way in the sciences of action at present, "there is danger of losing all the advantages of systematic theory. But it is possible to retain some of them...[by] a second best type of theory," the structural-functional.[41]

These contrasting views can be reconciled if we forget functionalism and ask how we know when theory is exact. We know it when the theory is logically tight and empirically proven. Evans-Pritchard and Radcliffe-Brown are saying that a natural science of human society <u>can be</u> developed. Parsons is saying that a rather primitive state of theorizing is about <u>all we have now</u>, but he too believes that a more exact science is possible. There is actually no contradiction, but there <u>seems</u> to be one because the same term, <u>functional analysis</u>, is used with opposite meanings.

Functional versus Causal. The occasional view that functional analysis is <u>not</u> causal analysis apparently arises from two sources: first, the image of functionalism as theory and hence as excluding raw data or pure data-manipulation; second, the Parsonian image of it as excluding exact laws too. The conclusion would not follow from the first source, except on the premise that causation is identical with evidence or statistical correlation. If, however, <u>causal analysis</u> is construed in the usual sense of discovering relationships between phenomena, there is excellent ground for stating this to be impossible in a systematic way without theory. It is the theory which provides the idea of what would be significant to

---

science; Wilbert E. Moore's work on labor and industrialization; Bellah's study of religion and change in Japan; Bryce Ryan's historical chapters on caste in Ceylon; Geoffrey and Monica Wilson's theory of change in central Africa; Schapera's studies of native transition in South Africa.

[39] I see no basic difference of method or theory between the analysis of ideology and industrialization by Reinhard Bendix, who opposes functionalism, and the analysis of Puritanism and science by Merton or the study of the family and industrialization by Levy. Nor would I know whether to classify the work on social change by Ralph Linton, E. H. Spicer, Robert Redfield, Margaret Mead, Ralph Beals, Howard Becker, Fred Cottrell, Charles Loomis, and Philip Selznick as "functionalist" or not.

[40] Evans-Pritchard, <u>op. cit.</u>, p. 49.

[41] <u>The Social System</u>, Glencoe, Ill.: Free Press, 1951, pp. 19-20.

test and the notion of the conditions under which a test would be conclusive.

While every experiment requires the use of principles of interpretation, the evidence for the truth of these principles comes ultimately through observation and experiment. But such further experiments once more require principles of interpretation, and this process is endless.[42]

Doubtless the feeling behind the separation of functional and causal analysis has some basis. Parsons' characterization of actual functional analysis as primitive theory is correct. Functional studies provide an intuitive grasp of how social structures fit together, of the principles somehow operative in going societies, much more than they provide logically precise or empirically proven propositions. The contribution of such work is that of bringing forth a framework, a point of view, in terms of which interpretation is possible. At the same time, as we have seen, verification is difficult. Some functionalists have seemed unwilling to discipline their language or test their propositions, taking instead the easy path of verbal tapestry. As a result, sociologists who have learned the techniques of empirical research come to feel that functionalism is a crank method, and they are encouraged in this by functionalists themselves who say they are engaged in non-causal analysis, whatever that is. But there will always be speculative sociological theory. From the standpoint of scientific discovery, the interesting part of theory is not the verified but the unverified propositions. A theory proved is no longer theory; it is fact. What is still unproved is speculation; it is, as commonly said, "theoretical." If the broadest theory in sociology is thrown out on the ground that it is "functionalism," and if what is recommended in its stead are neat single propositions whose validity is proved but whose significance is not, the result will be scientific ritualism.

WHY THE MYTH?

Logicians habitually explain schools of thought as due to logical blunders. Thus,

according to Ernest Nagel, "Functionalism in the social sciences has admittedly been inspired, and continues to be influenced, by the supposed character of functional analyses in physiology."[43] Nagel presents no evidence for this assertion, nor does he explain why the blunder happened to be committed and become popular at the particular time. The record shows that the functional lineage goes in direct line from William Robertson Smith, a philologist and Biblical and Semitic scholar, through Durkheim, a student of law and sociology, to Radcliffe-Brown and Malinowski, none of whom had any experience or interest in physiology. Radcliffe-Brown drew an analogy between his mode of thinking and that of physiology, but this was merely post hoc rationalization of a method he had long been using and had admittedly borrowed from Durkheim.[44] Malinowski, who became identified with "functionalism" but was a late borrower of the word "function," was even less concerned with physiology.

Actually, the rise of "functionalism" can be explained sociologically, as due to the peculiar conditions found in the sociological and anthropological professions around the turn of the century. Briefly, the key fact was the absence of a sociological point of view, and the key problem (for students dimly perceiving the idea) was how to develop and establish this point of view. We have tried to state earlier the reasons why this point of view is difficult to adopt and maintain. Suffice it

---

[42]Nagel, op. cit., p. 152.

[43]Op. cit., p. 247.

[44]In The Andaman Islanders, Cambridge· Cambridge University Press, 1922, Radcliffe-Brown first attempted "to develop a new method in the interpretation of the institutions of a primitive people." Although the book was not published until 1922, he had written it in 1910, and he says that the new method "will not perhaps seem so novel now as it would have done then" (p. ix). In this book he shows no concern with methods in physiology, but in fact states his methodological assumptions in such a way as to make them incompatible with physiological procedures—e.g., in insisting on the importance of the "meaning" of a social custom (pp. 229-235). His article, "On the Concept of Function in Social Science," in which he spoke of "an analogy between social life and organic life," did not appear until 1935. American Anthropologist, 37 (July-September, 1935), pp. 395-402.

to realize that in the discipline called "sociology" there were, concretely, two chief obstacles---the fact that various brands of encyclopedism[45] and reductionism[46] were masquerading under the name, and the fact that ethics and social reform were woven into the analysis.[47] The situation was worse in anthropology, because that field supposedly embraced man as an organism as well as human history and all of culture.[48] If sociological analysis was to receive recognition as an anthropological specialty in competition with archeology, physical anthropology, historical reconstruction, and cultural anthropology, it had to assert itself. As usual, a movement gains strength if it can rally under a special name. In this case the most appropriate name, sociology, was precluded, not only because it already designated a rival discipline, but also because, as just noted, it was tainted by contrary meanings. There was another term, however, which seemed to pick up the essence of what was meant. This was the term "function" which had

been deliberately used by Durkheim, the founder of what has often been called the "sociological school" in anthropology. Although Radcliffe-Brown explicitly adopted the term as a key concept, it was the irrepressible Malinowski who championed it so insistently that the name "functionalism"---long used in philosophical circles to designate a focus on activity rather than structure---came to be applied to the movement.[49] Malinowski made it crystal clear that he was fighting against evolutionary theory and trait-diffusion analysis---two contrary points of view that he says had dominated anthropology. Under their dominance there was little room for the study of societies as going concerns. It was his mission to make room for it under the banner of functionalism. As soon as this term came to be applied to sociological analysis in anthropology, it was also used in sociology for the same purpose.

This interpretation of the rise of functionalism explains a paradox in its history---the fact that the hardest battle for functional analysis was fought in anthropology, whereas the most effective critical and methodological discussion of it emerged in sociology. The reason for the hard initial battle in anthropology lay in the entrenched character of the competing interests in that field; the battle was

---

[45]Comte's concept of society included almost everything; Spencer's notion of sociology was that it included the other social sciences, and Ward's that it embraced all truth.

[46]Social phenomena were being "explained" in all conceivable terms except the sociological. There were organic, psychological, climatic, racial, ecological, demographic theories in abundance. After finishing two-thirds of his article on "Sociology" for the Encyclopedia of the Social Sciences, MacIver says: "The schools thus far discussed are distinguished by the fact that they applied to social phenomena the specific concepts or the specific methods of some other science or group of sciences." Vol. 14, pp. 232-247.

[47]Accounts of the "theories" of nineteenth-century sociologists are mostly accounts of what they "advocated." "Spencer was so busy throughout his life attempting to formulate a doctrine of what the state should not do that he failed to develop any coherent positive theory of the state." Harry E. Barnes, Introduction to the History of Sociology, Chicago: University of Chicago Press, 1948, p. 128. Comte's religion of positivism got in the way of his science of sociology. Le Play was mainly a social reformer who "set forth the principles of Christian morality, duty and obedience to authority as the bases of a sound economic and social organization." Gottfried Salomon, "Le Play," Encyclopedia of the Social Sciences, Vol. 9, p. 412.

[48]Franz Boas' article, "Anthropology," Encyclopedia of the Social Sciences, Vol. 2, pp. 73-110, in effect claimed for this field the whole of human knowledge.

[49]In 1931 Horace Kallen, a philosopher, noting in his article on "Functionalism," loc. cit., that a trend toward functionalism was manifesting itself in architecture, law, psychology, etc., added that "Malinowski appears to be aiming at an equally thoroughgoing functionalism in anthropology." Some of the means by which Malinowski became identified as the leader of functionalism are questionable. His writings, which owe many of their ideas to Durkheim and his followers, characteristically ignored or misrepresented these predecessors. His long article on "Culture" in the Encyclopedia of the Social Sciences, where he argued his complete case for functionalism, caricatured Durkheim and ignored Radcliffe-Brown altogether. He was so extreme and careless in his statements that the critics of functionalism found him a convenient standard-bearer for that point of view. Whenever they needed a quotation to illustrate one of the fallacies of functionalism, they could usually find one in Malinowski's writings. His readable and imaginative style of writing, his capacity for eliciting the enthusiasm of students, his prolific output---these were further factors in his acquiring the leadership of the functionalist movement.

for the <u>admission</u> of sociological analysis against the indifference or opposition of older preoccupations.[50] Subsequently the debate died down because, once this kind of work had forced its way into anthropology as functionalism, there was no longer any question of its admission, for it was then recognized as one among a plurality of distinct anthropological interests.[51] Furthermore, having been accepted as a separate type of interest, functionalist anthropology was distracted from theoretical self-criticism by its overwhelming emphasis on ethnography ---that is, on informal description and interpretation of single simple societies. "Field work" in this sense became a <u>mystique</u> among social anthropologists,[52] with the result that singularly little systematic comparison was attempted and hence not much empirically disciplined general theory. Functionalism was easily applied at the case-study level, to the analysis of particular primitive societies. Historicism in anthropology thus won a partial counter-victory over its upstart opponent, functionalism. The latter remained methodologically weak and self-

satisfied as it gained success in anthropology.[53]

In sociology, on the other hand, structural-functional analysis has been subjected to searching criticism and some codification. Since sociologists deal with complex societies, they cannot rely on informal observation and informants but have to employ a variety of research techniques. This gives them a methodological self-consciousness that makes it inevitable that any development such as functionalism will be subjected to technical scrutiny. Furthermore, the traditional interest of sociologists in systematic theory (in part a reflection of their closer ties with economics and philosophy) prompts them to examine the premises and the logic of functionalism.

[50]The first edition of A. L. Kroeber's widely used text, <u>Anthropology,</u> New York: Harcourt, Brace, 1923, contained nothing on social anthropology. At the end of the chapter on religion (p. 325) he felt uneasy enough to admit "there must be laws underlying culture phenomena"; but he said their source must lie "obviously in the human mind. The laws of anthropological data, like those of history, are the laws of psychology." Boas, in his 40,000-word article on "Anthropology" for the <u>Encyclopedia of the Social Sciences</u> (1930), makes no mention of Malinowski or Radcliffe-Brown and refers to Durkheim and Levy-Bruhl only in the bibliography. His account of the field is preoccupied with evolution, invention, and diffusion in connection with an encyclopedic array of topics running from "food" to "art" and from "economics" to "psychological aspects."

[51]The case was somewhat like establishing a new department in a university. The new department is usually strenuously opposed when the question of its admission is raised, but, once created, it is grudgingly accepted.

[52]The chief innovation for which it [the functionalist movement] stands," says Meyer Fortes, "was ...the principle of 'the intensive study of limited areas' as Haddon described it ...the study and analysis of a living community in its native habitat with reference to its total social life." <u>Social Anthropology at Cambridge Since 1900: An Inaugural Lecture,</u> Cambridge: University Press, 1953, pp. 16-17.

[53]This interpretation of the anthropologists' lack of critical interest in functional analysis differs from that of Firth. The latter attributes the lack of methodological criticism in anthropology to the fact "that so much of 'functional thinking' has passed into general currency unnoticed or at least unnamed." <u>Op. cit.,</u> pp. 245-247. However, his evidence showing <u>how</u> inconsistently and loosely the concept of function is used in contemporary anthropology makes it clear that some additional factors must have been involved. Why would anthropologists allow such slipshod thinking to pass into general currency? The additional factor, in my view, is the concentration on informal case studies of simple communities or local societies. At this superficial level it is easy to "apply" functionalism, but if this is all that is done, there is little to offer a theoretical or methodological challenge.
The popularity of functionalism in anthropology has been due in large part to the ease of applying sociological analysis to simple local societies. The latter, small and often isolated, can be "seen" as totalities. Having relatively little specialization, they facilitate the task of studying the interrelation of the parts of society. Since primitive societies also live in close dependence on nature, they can be readily regarded from the standpoint of societal survival. Being small, isolated, and relatively undifferentiated, they are more traditionalized than advanced societies, thus manifesting in startling fashion the dependence of individual behavior upon the group, the reality of society. Finally, since aboriginal societies are quite different from our own, the values and purposes of the members can be viewed by the observer as part of the phenomena to be explained, not the basis of explanation, thus the distinction between manifest and latent functions can be more easily applied. By the same token, it is easier for the ethnographer to "get away" with his interpretations. Other social scientists, being unacquainted with the society in question, cannot easily check up on him.

In both anthropology and sociology, however, and particularly in the latter field, the intensity of the attack on functionalism suggests something more than a purely technical concern. It suggests a persistence, though in more sophisticated form, of the very factors that had originally obstructed strictly sociological analysis and had given rise to reductionism and empiricism. To understand the role of these factors, we must come back to our central historical theme. Having raised the question of how the idea of functionalism as a separate method got started, we must now ask why it is that this illusion has persisted.

In a way it is appropriate to speak of functional analysis as something within anthropology, because there are branches of that field that have totally different subject-matters. A similar statement with respect to social anthropology or sociology, however, is tautological, for the reason that structural-functional analysis is sociological analysis. Realization of this tautology is coming in social anthropology, particularly in Britain,[54] but is still impeded by the confusion between cultural and social anthropology. In sociology the failure to recognize the tautology is largely due, I think, to the fact that sociologists, working mainly on their own society, often take for granted the broad knowledge and interpretation (the "theory") of this society in order to concentrate on empirical fact-finding and reporting, on practical but limited applications, on social reform, or even on research techniques per se. To the technicians in the field, functional analysis is remote and speculative theory; their antagonism to theory in general makes them critical of what seems to be the most speculative kind of all. To applied sociologists functional analysis is uncomfortable, to social reformers it is anathema, because it subjects to scrutiny the very goals for which application is made or reform intended. Such extra-scientific considerations, however, are more effective when not re-

vealed. The belief that functionalism is some special kind of theory or method permits an attack on sociological analysis which seems to be only an attack on functionalism.

REASONS FOR ABANDONMENT

The early rise of functionalism helped to make a place in sociology and anthropology for those wishing to explain social phenomena in terms of social systems, as against those who wished to make no explanation at all, to explain things in terms of some other system, or to plead a cause. Now, however, the movement that was once an asset has turned into a liability. The idea that functionalism is a special method has become a source of confusion and needless controversy. Above all, by a curious turn, it has become a convenient cloak under which the old enemies of sociological analysis can make their attack.

We have seen how difficult it is to say what functionalism is. Not only do definitions differ within each camp, but we find that so-called functionalists and professed enemies of functionalism are often doing the same kind of analysis. The name "functionalism" implies a difference of method or interpretation that does not exist. Not only is energy wasted in protracted discussion of this nebulous method, but the genuine issues are obscured. If a table is made of the theoretical issues in which there is a difference of opinion on scientific grounds alone, we shall find that the people called functionalists do not share positions, nor do the people who are non-functionalists. Yet issues are often debated as if they were an incidental battle in the warfare between the functionalists and some other camp, and some issues are meaningless apart from that supposition. For instance, we have seen that the question of "assuming" social integration or social conflict is a false issue conceived as a fight between functionalism and Marxism.[55]

---

[54] As witness Firth's view that all of social anthropology in Britain is functionalist now.

[55] To say that functionalism is wrong because it assumes integration, whereas Marxism is right because it assumes conflict, is to overlook that both are wrong as scientific theories insofar as they commit the fallacy of misplaced concreteness.

Once issues are understood to be those of sociological analysis itself, the false ones can be eliminated more effectively and the others debated more clearly.

Sociology and social anthropology are too mature to continue the archaic notion that their work is a battle between "isms." As Radcliffe - Brown says, "names ending in -ism do not apply to scientific theories, but do apply to philosophical doctrines."[56] More importantly, we have seen that the special language that gave functionalism its name is itself, if not archaic, at least so close to ordinary moralistic discourse that it tends to lead people (even some functionalists) to do what functionalism has tried to avoid —the substitution of the actor's point of view for that of the observer. To speak of the function of an institution for a society or for another institution in that society is a way of asking what the institution does within the system to which it is relevant. But, having connotations that are impossible to control, the word is more of a hindrance than a help to communication.[57] Natural scientists occasionally use the term, and others like it, to convey a quick notion of how something fits into a system; but such language is

acknowledged to be a way of conveying the general layout at the start of a discussion, not a medium for presenting systematic analysis. That the function of the heart is to pump blood through the body was doubtless a discovery when made, but if every time one establishes a relationship one has to say "the function of such and such is to do such and such" the circumlocution becomes tiresome. Why not say simply that the heart pumps blood through the system? Insofar as functionalism is defined as analysis that uses the term "function" and derivatives like "eufunction" and "disfunction," it is a semantic artificiality—a fact which doubtless explains one's embarrassment when someone in a field of physical science asks what "functionalism" is. It is worth noting that economics, the most systematic of the social sciences, has not found it necessary to evolve a special method using the concept "function" or a school of thought called "functionalism."

Let me make it clear that I do not consider the myth of functionalism as a special method in sociology or anthropology to be a catastrophe. As stated earlier, in my opinion some of the sociological work wearing the functional label is the best ever done, and some of it is poor. The quality has nothing to do with the label or with use of the term function. The designation of a school called functionalism will doubtless die out in time anyway. My effort here has simply been based on the assumption that minor gains will be made if the process of dying is not unduly prolonged.

[56] He continues: "By calling his doctrine 'functionalism' Malinowski seems to have wished to emphasize that it was the product of one mind, like any philosophical doctrine, not, like a scientific theory, the product of the cooperative thinking of a succession of scientists. Might it not prevent confusion if it were renamed Malinowskianism?" "Functionalism: A Protest," American Anthropologist, 51 (April-June, 1949), pp. 320-323.

[57] To some persons the term has the added meaning of "good," "necessary," "sole."

Some Convergences in Sociological Theory

George A. Lundberg

SOURCE: *American Journal of Sociology*, Vol. LXII (1956–57), pp. 21–27.

I

This paper purposes to show that certain theoretical formulations and research approaches that have until recently been regarded as mutually hostile, if not wholly incompatible, are, according to the most recent statements of them, highly compatible and strongly convergent. Further, this convergence has been achieved mainly through an evolution of the principal schools of thought in the direction of the theory and methods of natural science.[1] This thesis is documented by references chiefly to the sociological theory and methods of Talcott Parsons and then of S. C. Dodd. Their convergence has brought into focus and perhaps to resolution some of the principal sociological arguments of the last two decades.

I have already called attention in another paper[2] to the coalescence during the past decade in personnel and in ideology in two leading graduate schools, namely, Columbia and Harvard. I also called attention to the shift in certain quarters from skepticism regarding quantitative methods and especially sociological scales and related matters to an enthusiastic appreciation of the brilliant work of Lazarsfeld, Guttman, and Stouffer in precisely this field. In the present paper I will further illustrate this trend by an examination of the most recent statements of Parsons and his associates as found in Working Papers in the Theory of Action.[3]

The most general complaint against Parsons' theoretical formulations has been, as one writer has recently said, that it "frequently has been regarded as too difficult or overtly abstract for utilization in research."[4] In view of this widely felt difficulty, the following statement must be regarded as of revolutionary import:

The essential relations which we wish to discuss are, with the exception of the involvement of symbolism, schematically represented in Figure 3 [of Working Papers]. This shows that it is possible to regard the categories of interaction process developed by Bales and the motivational paradigm developed by Parsons, as, in all essentials, different ways of conceptualizing the same thing. The mode of organization of the scheme revolves about the "functional problems of social systems" put forward by Bales, and the pattern variables of Parsons and Shils, put together in a specific combination; the two in this context turning out to mean essentially the same thing.[5]

---

[1] The term "natural science" is here used instead of "positivism" and "neopositivism" because of the ambiguity of the latter terms. On the other hand, the "theory and methods of natural science" can be relatively sharply defined, and are here defined, as the general position expounded in the International Encyclopedia of Unified Science. For further discussion of this subject see my recent paper, "The Natural Science Trend in Sociology," American Journal of Sociology, LXI (November, 1955), 191-202.

[2] Ibid. In this paper I have dealt at some length also with the trend evident in the work of P. H. Furfey.

[3] T. Parsons, R. F. Bales, and E. A. Shils, Working Papers in the Theory of Action (Glencoe, Ill.: Free Press, 1953), chap. iii.

[4] N. S. Timasheff, Sociological Theory: Its Nature and Growth (New York: Doubleday & Co., 1955), p. 239.

[5] Parsons, Bales, and Shils, op. cit., p. 71.

My reason for regarding the above statement of such major significance is that the identification of Parsons' terminology with Bales's categories gives us, I believe for the first time, operational specifications of the meaning of these terms. Bales's categories were developed in concrete, objective research and are subject to the usual empirical checks of reliability and validity. Accordingly, we have here for the first time the basic categories of a widely studied system defined operationally so that they can be used by different investigators with some assurance of their designating the same referents. That is, Bales and other properly trained observers can agree with considerable reliability that a given instance of interactional behavior is to be designated by one rather than another of his categories. Accordingly, they are wholly compatible with the neopositivists' requirements so far as definitions of categories are concerned. The possible larger usefulness of these particular categories in the development of sociological theory is another matter. That is a subject for future determination on the basis of results secured in actual research.

Before proceeding with a more detailed analysis of the parallels between the Parsons-Bales categories and those of Dodd, let us observe first how certain subsidiary problems that have been the subject of much controversy fall out or recede to the background as the more rigorous meaning of the categories is specified. Speaking of his twelve categories, Bales says:

> The set of categories is held to form a logically exhaustive classification system. Every act that occurs is classified into one of the twelve categories. All of the categories are positively defined—that is, none of them is treated as a residual or wastebasket category for "leftovers." With competent observers and hard training, correlations between observers ranging from .75 to .95 can be obtained.[6]

Obviously, the old argument over operational definitions is here immediately relegated to the background. Description and repeated observation of the interaction process by Bales's laboratory observers has required the factoring of the interaction and the rigorous specification of what segment of behavior is to be designated by a particular category. The specifications and delimitations prescribed for observers in the laboratory instructions <u>constitute</u> operational definitions of the categories.

And what about quantification? In the first place, if certain behavior occurs in varying degrees, quantitative symbols are convenient to designate degree. Also, after having observed and described a large number of group-interaction situations, the question of the frequency of recurrence and non-recurrence arises. Some well-established statistical methods are routinely invoked by Bales to answer these questions. New techniques to suit new types of observation will doubtless be developed from time to time. In short, the traditional argument about operational definitions and quantification, which at least one writer designates as major ingredients of a school of theory called neopositivism,[7] is quietly taken care of as incidental in actual scientific work. They have nothing to do with substantive theory in any field of science but are generally accepted methods of scientific procedure. Accordingly, it is absurd to set them down as the special property or characteristic of neopositivism or any other sociological theory.

Operational definitions and quantitative techniques are not inherent in some schools of scientific thought and lacking in others. They are semantic techniques of more perfect or more precise communication, not subjects to be adopted or rejected at the outset according to what theory one decides to pursue. Thus, one by one, the major subjects of debate during the last two decades in sociological theory are quietly laid to rest or reduced

[6]R. F. Bales, "Some Uniformities of Behavior in Small Social Systems," in Paul F. Lazarsfeld and Morris Rosenberg (eds.), <u>The Language of Social Research</u> (Glencoe, Ill.: Free Press, 1955), p. 349.

[7]N. F. Timasheff, "Sociological Theory Today," <u>American Catholic Sociological Review</u>, XI (March, 1950), 26.

to their proper incidental significance. That is, when predictability is accepted as the criterion of scientific work, certain other questions become purely a matter of deciding what means and methods contribute most efficiently and reliably to the stipulated end. Operational definitions and quantitative techniques are, by this criterion, demonstrably most efficient. This does not mean either in sociology or in physics that all other concepts, including "primitive" and "literary" ones, are prohibited. They will continue to be used and will be defined with whatever degree of operationality is demanded by the results sought.

The same may be said of much of the other argument about the merits of different alleged "schools" of sociological theory. We hear about behaviorism, positivism, neopositivism, "functionalism," and, as a gratuitous insult to all the others, an "analytical" school.[8] Parsons, for example, devotes a hundred pages in his Structure of Social Action to a discussion of positivism and assures us that "it will be maintained and the attempt made in considerable detail to prove that in this sense (as a general framework for understanding human behavior) all of the variations of positivistic social thought constitute untenable positions for both empirical and methodological reasons."[9] To be sure, it never becomes very clear what the monstrous doctrine is or who

represents the various categories and subcategories of it. But traditional notions of now largely mythical sociological "schools" still persist. Thus, Timasheff, writing in 1955, still finds at least three recognizable "elements" that characterize the neopositivist theoretical framework: "quantitativism," "behaviorism," and "pragmatic philosophy."[10] By a sort of common consent, other characteristics which are usually also designated as characterizing this "school" are neglect of the "psychic component" and a preoccupation with or "aping" the natural sciences.

Consider now in the light of the above characterization the most recent exposition of their theory by Parsons and his associates. Even a cursory examination of chapter iii of Working Papers is illuminating from the point of view of what I have somewhat conservatively called "convergence" in sociological theory in the direction of positivism. The title alone of the Parsons-Bales' chapter should be alarming to those who apparently believe that, if certain words used in chemistry or physics are also employed in sociology, it constitutes strong presumptive evidence that the author is a "natural science" sociologist who proposes "to force sociology into the framework of physics." Well, the title of the Parsons-Bales chapter in question reads "The Dimensions of Action-Space." Dodd's title, "Dimensions of Society" (1942), created agitation because it was felt in some circles that the word "dimensions," since it figures prominently in physics, cannot properly be used in sociology. Today it is permissible to speak of social dimensions, especially when we measure certain aspects or characteristics of social behavior. Sociologists today are interested in what one can do with a terminology or a framework, regardless of where it has come from. But, if the above be regarded as possibly merely an accident of terminology, consider the following statements toward the end of the chapter:

---

[8]N. F. Timasheff, Sociological Theory: Its Nature and Growth (New York: Doubleday & Co., 1955), chap. viii. Timasheff classifies Parsons as among the "analytical" sociologists, the other representatives of which are Sorokin, MacIver, and Znaniecki. T. F. O'Dea ("The Sociology of Religion," American Catholic Sociological Review, June, 1954), however, attacks Parsons as a positivist.

[9]T. Parsons, The Structure of Social Action (2d ed.; Glencoe, Ill.: Free Press, 1949), p. 42. (Italics in the original.) Parsons outlines (p. 79) two principal types of positivism, "radical" and "statistical," the latter of two subclasses, "individualistic" and "sociologistic," with four subcategories of the latter. How many varieties and subvarieties of "positivism" there may be and who may be their proponents I do not know. On the other hand, the philosophical foundations of natural science as expounded in the various monographs of the International Encyclopedia of Unified Science provide a relatively well-defined universe of discourse.

[10]Op. cit., pp. 137-38.

If all this, which frankly involves a speculative element at present, is correct, then it would seem likely that there is a very important analogy between the scheme we have developed in this paper and the classical mechanics. If this supposition stands up to critical testing of a variety of sorts, it is evident that it should turn out to have far-reaching implications in that it should open up possibilities of quantitative as well as qualitative systematization which are far beyond those which the sciences of action have yet attained.

For convenience we present succinct statements of the four generalized conditions of equilibrium or laws just reviewed as follows:

1. The Principle of Inertia: A given process of action will continue unchanged in rate and direction unless impeded or deflected by opposing motivational forces.
2. The Principle of Action and Reaction: If, in a system of action, there is a change in the direction of a process, it will tend to be balanced by a complementary change which is equal in motivational force and opposite in direction.
3. The Principle of Effort: Any change in the rate of an action process is directly proportional to the magnitude of the motivational force applied or withdrawn.
4. The Principle of System-Integration: Any pattern element (mode of organization of components) within a system of action will tend to be confirmed in its place within the system or to be eliminated from the system (extinguished) as a function of its contribution to the integrative balance of the system.[11]

It will be seen that the first three of these proposed laws are identical with those of classical mechanics, and the fourth is definitely of the same type. I am not here concerned with validity or scientific value; I am merely interested in calling attention to the fact that, regardless of their merit, this is the type of formulation which fifteen years ago would have been greeted with howls of protest as representing attempts "to force sociology into the framework of physics." Yet it would be difficult to find more striking examples than these of a convergence of sociological theory and terminology in the direction of what has

hitherto been called neopositivism, behaviorism, and "natural science."

Now the proponents of sociology as a natural science have never held that the terminology and methods or theories of other sciences were to be adopted in sociology because they had been found useful in other sciences. On the other hand, we have said, and we do say, that in our search for hypotheses and for suggestions regarding methods we will and should look first to the analogous problems which we have already successfully solved. A fairly substantial victory has been won for the point of view during the last fifteen years and social scientists stand greatly to profit from it. Incidentally, in the above formulation Parsons and his associates have in effect returned to the cradle of positivism. Auguste Comte in his Positive Philosophy (1859) asserted that Newton's three laws of motion applied to social phenomena. It is true that his discussion of the point was more philosophical than mathematical. But Stuart C. Dodd as early as 1934 proposed definite operational methods of remedying the shortcoming by submitting the following formulation:

To paraphrase Newton's laws of motion in sociological terms gives:
1. Every group continues in its present status or social process until compelled by a force to change that status or process.

A version preferred by the writer as implying less of a metaphysical assumption and more of a simple agreement to standardize a definition is:
1. (a) Whatever changes in the status of a group or its process in rate or direction is called a social force.
2. Change of rate of a social process is proportional to the social force and takes place along the line of the scale in which the force is measured.
3. Forces and their total resistances are equal and opposite.

These principles in social terms are not seen as postulates of the ultimate metaphysical nature of society and its functioning. They are modestly viewed as simple proposals to standardize the meaning of social force and the units for measuring it.... Force thus is not a thing nor an active agent as it is in the popular view. Scientifically, it is that which produces a measured effect. It is a pure in-

---

[11]Parsons, Bales, and Shils, op. cit., pp. 102-3.

vented concept justified by its usefulness in dealing with phenomena. If this is understood, forces may be spoken of as political forces, or economic forces, or psychological forces, etc. as convenient designations of the agencies producing forces, i.e., stimulating people to respond.[12]

It is unnecessary to elaborate upon the striking similarity between Dodd's formulation and that by Parsons and his associates as given above. It is of great in-

vergences in the theoretical positions of Parsons and Dodd. Fortunately, in this case we need not become involved in any controversy as to who was influenced by whom, because each author readily grants his inability to read the other's works, at least until recently.

Since Bales has provided the key to a more objective understanding of Parsons' categories, a more detailed comparison now may be made between them and the

Chart I. A Comparison of the General Categories of Parsons and Dodd

	Parsons' Action*		Dodd's Transact†
1.	Actors	1.	People (Who?)
	(a) Individuals or collectivities		(a) Persons or groups
	(b) Subject-object		(b) Actors-reactors
2.	Situation	2.	Time, space, and residual factors
			(When?) (Where?) (How?)
	(a) Social objects (persons and groups)		(a) Symbolic factors (including symbols of persons and groups)
	(b) Non-social objects (physical and cultural)		(b) Material factors (physical and cultural)
3.	Orientation of (1) to (2)	3.	Actions and values‡ (orientation relating [1] to [2] (Doing what? Why?)
	(a) Motivational orientation: cognitions, cathexis, evaluative modes		(a) Motivational orientation—actions (in knowing, feeling, doing modes)
	(b) Value orientations: cognitive, appreciative, moral		(b) Value orientation—standards or desiderata in knowing, feeling, doing modes

*See T. Parsons, E. A. Shils, et al. Toward a General Theory of Action (Cambridge, Mass: Harvard University Press, 1951), pp. 56-60. Also T. Parsons, R. F. Bales, and E. Shils, Working Papers in the Theory of Action (Glencoe, Ill.: Free Press, 1953), chap. III, esp. pp. 162-72.

†See S. C. Dodd, Systematic Social Science ("Social Sciences Series," No. 16 [Beirut: American University of Beirut, 1947]). Also S. C. Dodd "A Predictive Theory of Opinion," read at the American Sociological Society meetings, September, 1953.

‡The six categories underscored represent Dodd's basic factors of a transact, or the chief classes of dimensions of any social situation. We have attempted to fit Dodd's categories into Parson's rather than vice versa, in which case the presentation of Dodd's system would be somewhat different, as indicated in the works cited.

terest to note, however, that much of the tremendously elaborate and voluminous work of Parsons can in the end be distilled into this historic formulation. This is not to minimize the importance of the steps, however circuitous they may seem, by which Parsons arrived at this conclusion. It is the possibility of the translation, as admitted by Parsons, that is important.

II

I have been concerned above with certain large and general trends and con-

categories of Dodd.

Chart I shows the principal parallels between the general systems of Parsons and Dodd. The texts referred to corroborate the validity of the parallelism exhibited in Chart I—a parallelism which seems genuine and striking.

When we turn to a more detailed comparison of the Bales-Parsons-Dodd categories as applied to the highly restricted and simple laboratory situation for which Bales's categories were adopted, the parallels may be less clear because each author uses brief, general terms from folk language to designate aspects or dimensions of quite complex social situations. The parallelism between the Bales-Parsons categories, as attested by them, is exhibited in Figure 3 of their Working

[12]S. C. Dodd, A Controlled Experiment on Rural Hygiene in Syria (Beirut, Lebanon: American Press, 1934), pp. 216-17. See also his Dimensions of Society (New York: Macmillan Co., 1942), p. 744, where essentially the same formulation is repeated.

Papers'(p. 74). In our Chart II we compare the categories of Bales and Dodd. As Chart II shows, Dodd's categories are generated by cross-classifying two generalized dimensions, viz.: (a) action in three modes (doing, feeling, knowing) against (b) interaction in four degrees (positive in two degrees and negative in two degrees). The parallels in the meaning of the categories will be more striking in some cases than in others, but it must be remembered that the full equivalence (or lack thereof) can be exhibited only after a full exposition of each system and the specific meaning adopted by each author for the terms employed in the chart. Also it must be noted that the generality of Dodd's categories, as compared with those of Bales, which are adapted to a specific laboratory situation, necessarily results in considerable dis-

parity of terminology especially when terms are taken apart from their context as in Chart II. The same is true also of the Parsons-Bales categories. The degree of actual correspondence in the three systems deserves more intensive inquiry.

Since the experimental situation for which Bales developed his categories is highly circumscribed and controlled, their adequacy for more complex and general situations is as yet undetermined. The more comprehensive systems of Parsons and Dodd profess, of course, to provide a framework for the analysis of any human social situation whatever. Most of Parsons' work deals with these more general situations, and Dodd has experimented with the applicability of his categories to very much broader social contexts as described in his published

Chart II. Convergence of Interaction Categories Between Bales and Dodd (and Parsons)

			Modes of Speech Behavior					
			"I Do..."		"I Feel..."		"I Know..."	
			DODD	BALES	DODD	BALES	DODD	BALES
Integrative Interaction	Positive	STRONG	Strongly integrative doing	1	Strongly integrative feeling	2	Strongly integrative knowing	3
				Shows solidarity		Shows tension release		Agrees
		WEAK	Weakly integrative doing	4	Weakly integrative feeling	5	Weakly integrative knowing	6
				Gives suggestion		Gives opinion		Gives orientation
	Negative	WEAK	Weakly disintegrative doing	9	Weakly disintegrative feeling	8	Weakly disintegrative knowing	7
				Asks for suggestion		Asks for opinion		Asks for orientation
		STRONG	Strongly disintegrative doing	12	Strongly disintegrative feeling	11	Strongly disintegrative knowing	10
				Shows antagonism		Shows tension		Disagrees

research.[13] More to the point in the present comparison is Dodd's application of his categories to original behavior situations.[14]

Incidentally, both systems achieve a high degree of parsimony in that Parsons and Bales have only twelve categories which are held to be logically exhaustive, whereas Dodd proposes eight concepts, one of which, however, is residual. The system claims to provide a parsimonious

way of describing in terms of eight basic concepts, and in other derivative concepts defined in terms of the original eight, the sociological essence of any situation represented by such a question as "Who does what, why, when, where, and how?" Bales's categories have so far been applied only to the communicative aspects of a group discussion under laboratory conditions. Their validity in larger and more varied situations remains to be demonstrated.

It is not the primary purpose of the present paper to attempt prematurely to evaluate one set of categories as against another: that will come about incidentally as research and experiment continue. We are interested here primarily in calling attention to a considerable fundamental parallelism in two systems hitherto assumed by many to represent incompatible systems.

---

[13]See the material analyzed in Dodd, <u>Dimensions of Society</u>.

[14]For examples see the following: "Dimensions of a Poll," <u>International Journal of Opinion and Attitude Research,</u> Vol. III, No. 3 (Fall, 1949); "On All-or-None Elements and Mathematical Models for Sociologists," <u>American Sociological Review,</u> Vol. XVII, No. 2 (April, 1952); "Can the Social Scientist Serve Two Masters?" <u>Research Studies of the State College of Washington,</u> Vol. XXI, No. 3 (September, 1953); and "A Predictive Theory of Opinion" (forthcoming).

The Approach to a General Theory of Action by Parsons and Shils

G. E. Swanson

SOURCE: *American Sociological Review*, Vol. 18, (1953), pp. 125–34.

For more than ten years, Talcott Parsons has spoken about the uses of, and the need for, general theory in sociology. Having been promised that general theory would provide sociology with all the benefits that it has supplied other disciplines ---such benefits as universality, necessity, and accuracy of proof---it was natural that sociologists awaited the publication of Parsons' and Shils' book <u>Toward a General Theory of Action</u>[1] with keen anticipation.

The published discussions and reviews of this effort of Parsons,[2] and of Parsons and Shils, to develop an approach to a general theory of action and of social systems have included much talk about style of writing, vagueness of concepts,

---

[1]Talcott Parsons and Edward A. Shils (eds.), <u>Toward a General Theory of Action</u>, Cambridge: Harvard University Press, 1951.

[2]Talcott Parsons, The Social System, Glencoe, Illinois: The Free Press, 1951. This paper deals primarily with problems raised by Parsons and Shils in their monograph "Values, Motives, and Systems of Action," in Parsons and Shils, <u>op. cit.</u>, pp. 47-275. <u>The Social System</u> extends that monograph to a more detailed account of the implications of the theory of action for sociology. Since it is based on the monograph, the comments we make here have implications for <u>The Social System</u> as well.

and unjustified psychologizing, with little attention to the assumptions that underlie their work and to the insights it may contain. Since these assumptions are the residue that is likely to have the greatest effect on the development of general sociological theory, it seems appropriate to make them explicit and to explore their implications.

At the beginning of their work the authors tell us something of what we may expect. Their theory is of "the categorial type," which means that it

...involves a system of classes which is formed to fit the subject matter, so that there are intrinsic relations among the classes, and these are in accord with the relations among the items of the subject matter. Thus, in these systems, the principles of classification, themselves, include statements of certain relationships among classes. The elements are so defined as to constitute an interdependent system ... A categorial system in this sense is always logically prior to the laws which state further relations between its elements. The laws state generalized relationships of interdependence between variables in the system. The laws presuppose the definitions of the variables, and they presuppose those relations which are logically implied by the definitions and by the kind of system in question. Insofar as specific laws can be formulated and verified, a categorial system evolves into a theoretical system.[3]

Or, again,

The present monograph is a straightforward exposition of a conceptual scheme.[4]

At no point do they claim to present a theoretical system. What they do say is that they want to try out the usefulness of certain assumptions about the bases from which a general theory of "action"[5] could be built. Their initial effort seems to be a matter of formulating some assumptions about theory building in general, and about theory-building in disciplines

concerned with "action" in particular, of presenting some primitive categories for analyzing "action," and, finally, of showing how these primitive categories, in various combinations and permutations, can be used to encompass all of the phenomena now designated in existing concepts describing action. In this way, for example, Parsons[6] tries to show how Nazi ideology may be thought of as a product of the combination of the second-order concepts of ascription and universalism or how[7] the professional relation to a client is one special case of the second-order concepts of universalism, affective neutrality, specificity, collective focus, and achievement.

By so "deriving"[8] higher level concepts from more primitive elements Parsons and Shils hope to give one kind of evidence for the fruitfulness of the primitive concepts they propose for later use in deductive systems (i.e., adequate primitive concepts should be capable of representing the differentiations in the phenomena under study), and, in a preliminary way, to show the conceptual interconnections among these variables.

The kinds of evaluation we may make of their work are limited by these intentions. It is not germane to say that they predict nothing, because no predictions are attempted or intended. But we may ask such a question as the following: How adequate are the primitive concepts proposed by Parsons and Shils for redefining and ordering the major concepts now used by sociologists? It is this problem that the present paper examines.

In one sense, the primitive concepts of Parsons and Shils are stated in the following quotation, "The frame of reference of action involves actors, a situa-

---

[3]Parsons and Shils, op. cit., p. 50.

[4]Ibid., p. 51.

[5]According to Parsons and Shils, social systems are a special case of the general theory of action. Sociology is not the study of social systems, but of that aspect "of the theory of social systems which is concerned with the phenomena of the institutionalization of patterns of value-orientation in the social system...." See Parsons, op. cit., p. 552.

[6]Ibid., pp. 191-194.

[7]Parsons and Shils, op. cit., p. 259.

[8]Parsons and Shils use "deriving" in a special sense. It does not mean an operation in which a set of conditions are stated, and from these, certain consequents are predicted. What they do seem to mean is an operation by which one seeks to show that new combinations of primitive concepts give an adequate definition of additional concepts. In this way, Nazi-type ideologies are not predicted from combinations of universalistic and ascriptive orientations, but are defined by this combination.

tion of action, and the orientation of the actor to that situation."[9] Action is behavior "oriented to the attainment of ends in situations, by means of the normatively regulated expenditure of energy."[10]

... There are four points to be noted in this conceptualization of behavior: (1) Behavior is oriented to the attainment of ends or goals or other anticipated states of affairs. (2) It takes place in situations. (3) It is normatively regulated. (4) It involves the expenditure of energy or effort or "motivation" (which may be more or less organized independently of its involvement in action). Thus, for example, a man driving his automobile to a lake to go fishing might be the behavior analyzed. In this case, (1) to be fishing is the "end" toward which our man's behavior is oriented (2) his situation is the road and the car and the place where he is (3) his energy expenditures are normatively regulated---for example, this driving behavior is an intelligent means of getting to the lake (4) but he does spend energy to get there; he holds the wheel, presses the accelerator, pays attention and adapts his action to changing road and traffic conditions. When behavior can be and is so analyzed, it is called action.[11]

Presumably, then, any behavior that involves some awareness of a goal, and that is organized to choose means for reaching such a goal which have previously been learned to be more effective rather than less effective, will be action. This is to be contrasted with behaviors without goals (if such exist) or those cases in which a goal is known, but the means to the goal are completely unknown.[12] Since few behaviors of interest to sociologists fall into these last two classifications, except as matters of degree, the distinction is probably of little moment for their work.

At any rate, it is the properties of actors' situations, and the orientations of actors to situations that will be manipu-

lated by these authors to define the conceptual battery of sociology and, we may suppose, at some later date, to predict the phenomena of social systems. These properties, then, represent the primitive concepts that will actually be used in future theory building and they are the center of our concern here.

(1) Properties of Actors. We are told very little about the properties of actors, as such, other than that they must be individuals or collectivities.[13] The actions produced are processes of "change of state in such empirical systems of action."[14] At other points, we are told that the actor behaves toward his world in terms of its "significance for direct gratification or deprivation of impulse-needs."[15] Finally, the actor must be capable of having, and of acting on, the kinds of orientation to situations that appear below.

(2) Properties of Situations. There is a little more information about the situation encountered by the actor. He[16] may find that situation consisting of "a class of social objects (individuals and collectivities) and a class of nonsocial (physical and cultural) objects."[17] Social objects may be sub-classified in two ways. The actor-subject may see these objects "solely in terms of what [an actor-object] is and irrespective of what that actor [-object] does." In the former case he is concerned with the actor-object as a complex of qualities; in the latter, as a complex of performances. The actor-subject may, secondly, see social objects as having "such a broad and undefined significance for [him] that he feels obliged to grant them any demand they make of him,"[18] or he may see social objects as having "such a narrow and clearly defined significance for [him] that [he] does

---

[9] Parsons and Shils, op. cit., p. 56.

[10] Ibid., p. 53.

[11] Ibid., p. 53.

[12] For possible examples of behavior without goals, see Norman R. F. Maier, Frustration, New York: McGraw-Hill Book Co., Inc., 1949, and the discussion of expressive behavior in Herbert Blumer "Collective Behavior," in Alfred M. Lee (ed.), New Outline of the Principles of Sociology, New York Barnes and Noble, 1946, pp. 167-222.

[13] See Blumer, op. cit., especially the discussion of the acting crowd.

[14] Parsons and Shils, op. cit., p. 56.

[15] Ibid., p. 10.

[16] To simplify the presentation, actors will be referred to as if they were individuals. The reader is asked to remember that they may be collectivities.

[17] Parsons and Shils, op. cit., p. 57.

[18] Ibid., p. 57.

not feel obliged to grant them anything that is not clearly called for in the definition of the relationship which obtains between them."[19] The first of these situations is called diffuse; the second, specific.

Nonsocial objects ("any objects which are not actors") are called "physical" if they do not interact with "the actor-subject as other actors do; and...constitute only objects, not subjects, of cognitive, cathetic and evaluative orientation."[20] When nonsocial objects have the additional property of being produced through interaction they are called "cultural." Laws, ideas, and recipes would be examples of cultural objects.

(3) Varieties of Orientations of Actors to Situations. Like the properties of situations, the orientations of actors to situations are of two major varieties. One of these is called "motivational orientation," the other, "value-orientation." Motivational orientation

refers to those aspects of the actor's orientation to his situation which are related to actual or potential gratification or deprivation of the actor's need-dispositions. We will speak of three modes of motivational orientation.

i. The cognitive mode involves the various processes by which an actor sees an object in relation to his system of need-dispositions. Thus it would include the "location" of an object in the actor's total object-world, the determination of its properties and actual and potential functions, its differentiations from other objects, and its relations to certain general classes.

ii. The cathetic mode involves the various processes by which an actor invests an object with affective significance. Thus it would include the positive or negative cathexes implanted upon objects by their gratificational or deprivational significance with respect to the actor's need-dispositions or drives.

iii. The evaluative mode involves the various processes by which an actor allocates his energy among the various actions with respect to various cathected objects in an attempt to optimize gratification. Thus it would include the processes by which an actor organizes his cognitive and cathectic orientations into intelligent plans...Evaluation is functionally necessary for the resolution of conflicts among interests and among cognitive interpretations which are not resolved automatically and which thus necessitate choice, or at least specific selective mechanisms. Value orientation refers to those aspects of the actor's orientation which commit him to the observance of certain norms, standards, criteria of selection, whenever he is in a contingent situation which allows (and requires) him to make a choice....On a cultural level we view the organized set of rules or standards as such, abstracted, so to speak, from the actor who is committed to them by his own value-orientations and in whom they exist as need-dispositions to observe these rules. Thus a culture includes a set of standards. An individual's value orientation in his commitment to these standards....
We shall speak of three modes of value-orientation, which parallel the modes of motivational orientation.

i. The cognitive mode of value-orientation involves the various commitments to standards by which the validity of cognitive judgments is established...[Among these would be the standards setting the validity of observations, the relevance of data, and the importance of problems.]

ii. The appreciative mode of value-orientation involves the various commitments to standards by which the appropriateness or consistency of the cathexis of an object or class of objects is assessed...these standards purport to give us rules for judging whether or not a given object, sequence, or pattern will have immediate gratificatory significance.

iii. The moral mode of value-orientation involves the various commitments to standards by which certain consequences of particular actions and types of action may be assessed with respect to their effects upon systems of action....Specifically, they guide the actor's choices with a view to how the consequences of these choices will affect (a) the integration of his own personality system and (b) the integration of the social systems in which he is a participant.[21]

The examination of the properties of actors, situations, and actors' orientations to situations seems to reveal that there are not three categories of properties here, but one---the orientations of

─────────

[19]Ibid., p. 58.

[20]Ibid., p. 58.

[21]Ibid., pp. 58-60.

actors to situations. Inspection of the properties of situations shows that each of them is defined by the way actors may experience it. The actor's properties are his potential for having such experiences as gratification, deprivation, or the modes of orientation. The modes of orientation, themselves, are simply additional potentialities for relating to objects. They are varieties of the more fundamental capacity of experiencing gratification and deprivation.

Some interesting implications follow from this conclusion. The present paper will discuss three of them: (1) The nature of the variables that will be used in prediction if this kind of primitive category is employed, (2) the method of prediction implied, and (3) the suitability of these particular categories for such prediction.

(1) <u>The Nature of the Variables for Use in Prediction.</u> It will be helpful to phrase this problem as one of stating the dependent variable <u>to</u> which one might predict from these categories of actors' orientations and the independent variable from which the predictions will be derived. The dependent variable is action and its varieties. The independent variable will be a predisposition of the actor to take one kind of action as against another.

(2) <u>The Method of Prediction Implied.</u> If we accept the common approach of saying that predispositions to behave are a part of any total act, then what we do in predicting action is to forecast the later phases of acts from their predispositional stages. Parsons and Shils provide no formal method to enable prediction to the predispositions themselves. The major problems of prediction that might be handled by their concepts will be those that tell us (a) the conditions under which predispositions will result in one form of action rather than another[22] and, with the

formal nature of the resulting action held constant, what will be (b) the substantive nature of the manifestations of combinations of predispositions of a particular nature (e.g., Nazi ideology being a product of ascription and universalism). It is instructive that the formal "derivations" appearing in this book are precisely of the latter type.

All current behavior theories seem to be of this kind. All of them predict in the style: Given an organism of type X with predispositions A and B, the following behavior will result; or: If one adds predisposition C to A and B, the organism's behavior will be different in <u>c</u> ways from what it would otherwise have been.

An example may be taken from a recent experiment by Festinger and Thibaut.[23] These investigators brought small populations into the laboratory and put them to work on a task that could only be solved through the reaching of some consensus among the people involved. The situation was arranged to insure that there would be considerable diversity of opinion among the participants and that these differences of opinion would be such that the participants would perceive them as falling on a single continuum. The prediction was that these conditions would force participants to communicate more frequently to those of their number holding the opinions most extremely different from those held by most group members.

If the prediction in this experiment were restated in terms of one variety of reinforcement theory, it might read like this: <u>General theory</u>: When humans are faced with a series of barriers to a desired goal, they will try to remove those barriers. <u>Operational definitions:</u> For college students at the University of Michigan, reaching a solution to the experimental problem is a goal. Persons holding divergent ideas from those of the rest of the group will prevent the achievement of consensus. Therefore they will be manipulated to remove their dif-

---

[22]For important work of this kind, see Sigmund Freud, "Psychopathology of Everyday Life," "The Interpretation of Dreams," "Wit and its Relation to the Unconscious," in A. A. Brill (ed.), <u>The Basic Writings of Sigmund Freud</u>, New York: The Modern Library, 1938, pp. 35-178, 181-549, 633-803; and John Dollard, "Under What Conditions Do Opinions Predict Behavior?" <u>Public Opinion Quarterly</u>, 12 (Winter, 1948-49), pp. 623-632.

[23]Leon Festinger and John Thibaut, "Interpersonal Communication in Small Groups," <u>Journal of Abnormal and Social Psychology</u>, 46 (January, 1951), pp. 92-99.

ferences. Epistemic correlations:[24] From the general knowledge of the experimenters through experience in our culture, these operations are valid replications of the nature and relations among the concepts of the general theory. Therefore they will provide a valid test of that theory.

What we have done here is to state that, to the extent that the theoretical and conceptual materials are validly replicated, the prediction will hold. We have placed the theoretically necessary and sufficient conditions for our prediction within the already existing behavior predispositions of the organism, and said that organisms having such predispositions will behave overtly in predictable ways.

Sociologists will remember that such writers as Herbert Spencer and Ellsworth Huntington took certain objective conditions external to the organism, assumed they would all be experienced in the same ways by all organisms, and that, as we have assumed, overt behaviors would follow from these induced predispositions. It was in large part to take account of the fact that there often was no one-to-one correspondence between the "objective" nature of the environment and the way the organism dealt with it that led psychologists as well as sociologists[25] to build theories that predicted behavior from the environment conceptualized in the terms in which it was experienced.

(3) The Suitability of These Categories for the Prediction of Action. The predispositions to behave that are specifically listed in the statement of Parsons' and Shils' "Frame of Reference" included three sub-types of the predisposition to be gratified and deprived: the cognitive, cathetic, and evaluative modes.

---

[24]For the function of epistemic correlations, see Filmer S. C. Northrop, The Logic of the Sciences and The Humanities, New York: The Macmillan Co., 1947).

[25]For a sample sociological effort of this kind, see William I. Thomas, The Unadjusted Girl, Boston: Little, Brown and Co., 1923, pp. 42-43, on "the definition of the situation."

Another kind of predisposition, the value orientations, are really derivations from the motivational modes of orientation. All that is added to the natural propensities of the organism to experience his situation through cognizing, cathecting, and evaluating is the learning of specific standards that give focus to these aspects of behavior. The two sub-classes of social objects seem to be of a different order and cannot be discussed in detail[26] in this paper. It is the three motivational modes, then, that give us most of the basic sub-types of the experiencing of gratification and deprivation, and they may be a center for our attention, since, presumably, their combinations will someday be used among the principal independent variables in predictions.

Parsons' and Shils' present use of these three aspects of behavior takes the form of arranging them into some rela-

---

[26]We have seen that the two major sub-classifications of social objects (quality-performance and specificity-diffuseness) are, in reality, additional orientations of the actors toward their worlds. Many of the objections to be raised against the other orientations used by Parsons and Shils do not apply to these. It does seem relevant, however, to ask why these are the only sub-classifications of orientation to social objects. There seems to be no criterion given by these authors that would rule out such classifications as the following from a list at this level of generality: Shall I move toward, away from, or against this object (See Karen Horney, Our Inner Conflicts, New York: W. W. Norton and Co., Inc., 1945)? Do I manipulate this object or permit myself to be manipulated by it? What are my chances of dealing successfully with this object? Is this object real or an illusion?

It also seems relevant to suggest that the two sub-classifications of social objects mentioned by Parsons and Shils and all of the additional classifications suggested above, seem to be derivations from a still more general frame of reference that sees the meanings of situations as being set by decisions as to whether objects are such things as barriers, paths, or goals, whether they occur frequently or infrequently and regularly or irregularly, or whether they are irrelevant to the action of the organism. (For an expansion of one version of such a set of constructs, see Kurt Lewin, The Conceptual Representation and the Measurement of Psychological Forces, Durham, N. C.: Duke University Press, 1938). If the classifications of social objects are, indeed, all second-order derivations from such more primitive concepts, then it should follow that the frame of reference of Parsons and Shils needs restructuring to include such concepts to make possible these and other derivations of the same order.

tively informal combinations as a basis for defining further orientations to the situation. They are "informal" in the sense that the properties of these orientations are not specified with rigor nor are the rules for their combination stated in clean, precise ways.

It is striking that these three major analytic categories are the very ones that were central to the faculty psychologies of the eighteenth and nineteenth centuries, typically expressed as in Kant's "ultimate modes of psychical functioning"---modes of knowing, feeling and willing.[27] It is certain that Parsons and Shils are far too sophisticated to resurrect the situation of the older faculty psychology, but it is impressive that the difficulties one finds in using their categories for prediction include those usually mentioned in post mortems on faculty psychology.

The experience of psychologists with these three aspects of behavior may help us to test the probable usefulness of Parsons' and Shils' scheme. As long as cognizing, cathecting, and evaluating were considered to be "ultimate and distinct functions" present in all behavior, no differential predictions could be made from them and the result was sterility. When, as Murphy[28] suggests, they were treated as "labels for complex activities which [required] further study," the possibility of hypothesis construction opened again. When psychologists abandoned using them as explanatory variables and turned to still more primitive variables, and to variables permitting a more detailed description of events---to concepts such as reward-deprivation, or to other properties of the perceptual field---the possibility of building systematic learning and personality theories appeared.

A second difficulty that psychologists found in working with this trichotomy was its arbitrary division of behavior into three parts. Since they wanted to predict the whole acts of organisms, they sought for more concepts that could be assigned dynamic properties for that task. Such notions as those connected with reinforcement were among those finally chosen. Using these ideas, it was possible to predict, for example, that all of behavior, including knowing, thinking, and deciding, would take certain forms.

The doubts of still other psychologists about the fruitfulness of thinking in terms of such distinctions as these come from empirical observation that each unit of observed behavior (a) involves perception - need-feeling - belief-emotion-etc.,[29] and that (b) these do not vary at random with reference to each other. Consequently, there is a growing emphasis on the evolving of laws of behavior that will involve "all the parameters of [behavior] simultaneously."[30] As Krech has phrased it:

... Experimentally this means that we cannot talk about "varying the stimulus condition and holding motivation constant," or "varying motivation and holding knowledge constant." Varying the stimulus conditions will vary the [organization of behavior] and therefore all of its attributes.[31]

A fourth difficulty involves the operational problems of the system. As many experimenters have made explicit, it is possible to control the things that are available for people to cognize, but it is impossible to vary such materials and hold reward constant. Hence, the recent wave of studies of the effects of social experience on perception hold the objective visual field constant while varying the reward-deprivation properties of the phenomena. Or, in learning experiments, there is a growing tendency to say that it is impossible, at least at present, to rule out the possibility of reinforcement and, hence, to judge whether learning can oc-

---

[27]See Immanuel Kant, Critique of Pure Reason, 1781; Critique of Judgment, 1790 and Critique of Practical Reason, 1788.

[28]Gardner Murphy, Historical Introduction to Modern Psychology, New York: Harcourt, Brace and Co., 1950, p. 217.

[29]David Krech, "Notes Toward a Psychological Theory," Journal of Personality, 18 (September, 1949), p. 80.

[30]Ibid., p. 80.

[31]Ibid., p. 80.

cur in its absence.[32]

We may expect extensions of Parsons' and Shils' scheme to be confronted by these four issues, but the problem that seems most critical in working with this trichotomy lies in its inability to lend itself to use as part of dynamic theories as contrasted with static descriptions. The key to this property lies, I think, in what we have already seen to be the nature of current behavior theories---that is, their prediction from predispositions present in the organism to subsequent behavior. These theories are essentially equilibrium theories, although, generally, theories of a moving or "quasi-stationary" equilibrium. This means that they conceive that the organism, if allowed to function over time in an unchanging environment, will develop a habitual, repetitive behavior pattern. The organism's behavior changes because the environment changes. And there lies the problem. As we have seen, to get around the fact that many environmental changes had no one-to-one relationship with particular organismic responses, psychologists invented a terminology that said in effect: let us bring environmental changes into our system by classifying them in terms of the properties through which these organisms experience them, and in terms of which the response of the organism is determined. Thus a hungry cat runs faster as he approaches food, not because there is anything in the food that draws him to it, but because food corresponds to an available gratification in a behavioral field in which a force or motive or need for this gratification exists. The food, and the hunger sensations induced by artificial starvation, are simply operational equivalents of the concepts of the system. The theory postulates that the environment that determines responses is the environment as experienced, and the concepts of the theory are geared to

permit the description of the environment as experienced. Terms of various systems illustrative of this include: drive, goal, valence, barrier, motive, attitude, path, sign-gestalt, reinforcement, and reward.

The point to be made is that these terms, and the theories of which they are a part, lend themselves to dynamic formulations because they unite the nature of the organism with the nature of the environment as a source of change in the organism. By contrast, cognition, cathection, and evaluation are almost exclusively intra-organismic terms. As such, they are capable of describing some events occurring within the organism, but not of relating those occurrences to the events that set them in motion and determine their direction. This means, contrary to Parsons · and Shils, that the road from these categories to a theoretical system is not simply a matter of hooking their categories to a motivational scheme, but that it will require a comprehensive redefinition of all second, third, and n-order categories in terms of some set of primitive concepts more suitable for the expression of laws of behavior. In the course of such a redefinition, it may be possible to derive by definition categories additional to those they have already defined.

One test of the fruitfulness of using the three motivational modes as part of a battery of primitive concepts of the organism's predispositions, from which we can derive other concepts that we need, is to see what Parsons and Shils have done with them. (Let us keep in mind, again, that "derive" is here used to mean "combine to produce by definition" not "to predict from the logical interrelationships among postulates.") Their answer is to be found in the definition of the "pattern variables" that play so crucial a part of their analyses of empirical data.

First, let us establish that these pattern variables are derived in the manner stated above. In their introduction of the material, Parsons and Shils say:

...There are further important conceptual entities and classificatory systems to be de-

---

[32]And Krech would probably caution that even in experiments that seem to hold certain properties of the perceptual field constant, what is held constant objectively by the experimenter may not be held constant in the experience of the subject, thus invalidating the effort to control non-reward conditions.

fined, but these, in a sense, derive from the basic terms that have already been defined. The point is that the further entities can be defined largely in terms of the entities and relationships already defined, with the introduction of a minimum of additional material.

... If one were to look back over the sections of this chapter devoted to the objects of the situation and to the orientation of the actor to the situation ..., he would see that an actor in a situation is confronted by a series of major dilemmas of orientation, a series of choices that the actor must make before the situation has a determinate meaning for him. The objects of the situation do not interact with the cognizing and cathecting organism in such a fashion as to determine automatically the meaning of the situation. Rather, the actor must make a series of choices before the situation will have a determinate meaning. Specifically, we maintain, the actor must make five specific dichotomous choices before any situation will have a determinate meaning. The five dichotomies which formulate these choice alternatives are called the pattern variables because any specific orientation (and consequently any action) is characterized by a pattern of the five choices. Three of the pattern variables derive from the absence of any biologically given hierarchy of primacies among the various modes of orientation. In the first place, the actor must choose whether to accept gratification from the immediately cognized and cathected object or to evaluate such gratification in terms of its consequences for other aspects of the action system. (That is, one must decide whether or not the evaluative mode is to be operative at all in a situation.) In the second place, if the actor decided to evaluate, he must choose whether or not to give primacy to the moral standards of the social system or subsystem. In the third place, whether or not he decides to grant primacy to such moral standards, he must choose whether cognitive or appreciative standards are to be dominant, the one set with relation to the other ....

The other pattern variables emerge from indeterminacies intrinsic to the object situation: social objects as relevant to a given choice situation are either quality complexes or performance complexes, depending on how the actor chooses to see them; social objects are either functionally diffuse (so that the actor grants them every feasible demand) or functionally specific (so that the actor grants them only specifically defined demands), depending on how the actor chooses to see them

or how he is culturally expected to see them.[33]

The present objective is to reflect on certain properties of those pattern variables derived from the orientations of the actor-subject. In this case, the following remarks will often apply to those derived from alternatives within the class of social objects[34] as well.

Parsons and Shils argue that these five derived choices are exhaustive. This claim is especially crucial, since it is said that these five choices are the most general statements of the behaviors that define all possible situations for actors. If this is true, and if our earlier statement is correct that newer behavior theories predict from the predispositions of the actor to subsequent behavior, then these choices represent the second-order categories for stating the independent variable for truly predictive theorizing.

Parsons and Shils say that there are three assumptions underlying their "contention that the five pattern-variable dilemmas are an exhaustive set."

... These assumptions are: (1) acceptance of the basic frame of reference as we have defined it; (2) acceptance of the level of generality on which we are proceeding, which is the first level of derivation from the basic frame of reference; (3) acceptance of our method of derivation through the establishment of primacies among types of interest and the resolution of ambiguities intrinsic to the world of social objects.[35]

In the absence of any clear criteria for knowing whether we are working on the "first level of derivation from the basic frame of reference" it is uncertain whether any seeming exceptions to their rule of exhaustiveness are valid, but some things come to mind that seem to be possible bases for doubting the rule. We notice, for example, that a whole set of concepts referring to organizational forms are never derived by Parsons or by Parsons and Shils from these pattern variable dilemmas or from the pattern variables. Among them are such ideas

---

[33]Parsons and Shils, op. cit., pp. 76-77.
[34]See ibid., p. 248, for a chart that illuminates these relationships.
[35]Ibid., p. 91.

as: crowd, social class, bureaucracy, social movement, mass action, community, or nation. Nor is there a derivation by definition of the inter-personal relationships subsumed under the "social processes" of three or four decades ago: cooperation, competition, conflict, assimilation, and accommodation, to say nothing of such sub-types of each as those elaborated by Simmel.[36] Nor do we find derivations by definition of the more genotypic concepts used to describe interpersonal influence, for example, authority, legitimacy, power, coordination, communication, leader, follower, prestige, or of the highly general categories for describing social systems such as integration, division of labor, mobility, or stratification. Finally, there is no derivation of a whole range of concepts such as the rate, frequency, duration, and intensity of the contacts among individuals. (In fact it is hard from this scheme to tell what it is that is in process in social life. Is it the physical movements of actors, their ideas, the modifications they make in each other's behavior, or what?)

Parsons and Parsons and Shils do use concepts such as the underived examples mentioned above. They are critical to their extension of the scheme. But, and this is the important point, these ideas appear neither in the initial concepts of the frame of reference nor are they given even an informal derivation from the orientational modes of the actor that form the prospective independent variables of a future theoretical scheme. They are brought in because they are necessary, but they are not formally related to the rest of the system.

It may be, of course, that they could be formally related, that Parsons and Shils were not interested in doing that job, or that they just did not get around to it. What seems likely is that such formal relating is difficult, if not impossible, using their present concepts.

In view of the intra-organismic nature of the basic categories of Parsons and of Parsons and Shils, it is not surprising that such use as their categories have is largely in the area of describing intra-organic events---in this case, primarily the treatment of the ideologies of populations as they presently exist in the functioning of those populations, and, further, that this treatment is a kind of Benedictean "patterns of culture" approach[37] in which the connections between the details of those ideologies and their master themes are shown largely by shrewd intuition and a kind of Verstehen rather than by formal derviation.

It seems to me that the ranges of conventional sociological concepts that they fail to derive are the very ones that tend to require some uniting of organisms with the environing conditions set by other organisms. They are the concepts that correspond to the properties of social systems as systems. There is not space here to state personal preferences for the primitive concepts from which system properties might be derived, but it can be pointed out that concepts stating the environment as experienced have been used for the description, and for the prediction, of such phenomena.[38]

The absence of derivations of terms describing the system-properties of social systems may be a function of Par-

[36]See, for example, Georg Simmel, "Superordination and Subordination," in Kurt H. Wolff (ed.). The Sociology of Georg Simmel, Glencoe, Ill.: The Free Press, 1950, pp. 181-303.

[37]Ruth Benedict, Patterns of Culture, Boston: Houghton Mifflin Co., 1934.

[38]The reader may be reminded of a very few such illustrative cases as these: The derivation by definition of integration, and a variety of stratification phenomena, in Robert F. Bales, Interaction Process Analysis, Cambridge: Addison-Wesley Press, 1950. The prediction by Mark A. May and Leonard W. Doob of competition and cooperation from behavioral states in their monograph Cooperation and Competition, New York: Social Science Research Council, 1937. John Hemphill's study of leadership and followership in his Situational Factors in Leadership, Columbus, Ohio: Ohio State University, 1949.

Sumner's statement of the behavioral nature of culture in William G. Sumner, Folkways, Boston: Ginn and Company, 1906. The classic definitions of a number of the "social processes" and of interaction, society, and group, in Robert E. Park and Ernest W. Burgess, Introduction to the Science of Sociology, Chicago: The University of Chicago Press, 1924.

sons' choice of the dependent variable for sociological theory. He states:

Sociological theory...is for us that aspect of the theory of social systems which is concerned with the phenomena of the institutionalization of patterns of value-orientation in the social system, with the conditions of that institutionalization, and of changes in the patterns, with conditions of conformity with and deviance from a set of such patterns and with motivational processes in so far as they are involved in all of these...[39]

And "institutionalization" of a social practice or standard occurs to the extent that:

See also the conceptualization by Louis Wirth of "Urbanism as a Way of Life," The American Journal of Sociology, 44 (July, 1938) pp. 1-24. For a preliminary statement of the traditional phenomena of "collective behavior" in predispositional terms, see Guy E. Swanson, "Social Change in the Urban Community," in Ronald Freedman and others, Principles of Sociology, New York: Henry Holt and Co., 1952.

None of these references are as comprehensive in attempted coverage as are Parsons and Shils, but they point the way to analyses of behavior in terms of other sets of predispositional variables. They also cast doubt on the assumption of Parsons and Shils that substantial theoretical prediction must wait until there exists a comprehensive set of categories for all major predictions. More probably, the scientist is led to a knowledge of the categories he needs, and of how they should be formulated, as a result of his attempts to predict empirical events. Such events are commonly amenable to several descriptive approaches. The choice of one of these is usually made in terms of its suitability for use in prediction.

[39]Parsons, op. cit., p. 552.

...from the point of view of any given actor in the system, it is both a mode of the fulfillment of his own need-dispositions and a condition of "optimizing" the reactions of other significant actors....[40]

While it is doubtful that the Parsons-Shils frame of reference has the categories needed to predict to this order of dependent variable, such a variable is consistent with the lack of derivation of system properties from that frame of reference, for this dependent variable describes the conditions under which an actor will come to view a given behavior as gratifying to himself and others. Thus one might be interested in the degree of integration or stratification or mobility in a population insofar as these conditions would affect its members' acquiring such a conception of the reward-deprivation qualities of a given behavior, but, presumably, one would not be interested in the prediction of these conditions for their own sake.

Parsons, and Parsons and Shils, have performed a major service in clearing away many old controversies, in showing the reasonableness of a behavioral foundation for general theory in social science as a whole and in sociology in particular, in clarifying the interrelations among many concepts, and in the insightful interpretation of particular pieces of data. However, the behavioral scheme they propose is inadequate for deriving the events they hope some time to order.

[40]Ibid., p. 38.

Metaphysical Pathos and the Theory of Bureaucracy

Alvin W. Gouldner

SOURCE: *American Political Science Review*, Vol. 49, (1955), pp. 496–507.

The conduct of a polemic focusses attention on the differences between two points of view to the neglect of their continuity and convergences. No modern polemic better exemplifies this than the controversy between the proponents of capitalism and of socialism. Each tends to define itself as the antithesis of the other; even the uncommitted bystander, rare though he be, is likely to think of the two as if they were utterly alien systems.

There have always been some, however, who have taken exception to this sharp contrast between socialism and capitalism and who have insisted that there are significant similarities between the two. One of these, the French sociologist Emile Durkheim, maintained that socialism like capitalism involved an overbearing preoccupation with economic interests. In both socialist and capitalist societies, Durkheim argued, economic concerns were at the center of attention. In Durkheim's view, neither capitalism nor socialism deemed it necessary to bridle materialistic ends; neither society subordinated pecuniary interests to some higher, governing, moral norms. Therefore, "from Durkheim's point of view," writes Talcott Parsons, "socialism and laissez-faire individualism are of the same piece."[1]

Bertrand Russell came to similar conclusions on the basis of a trip to the then newly-established Soviet Republic: "... the practical difference between socialism and capitalism is not so great as politicians on both sides suppose. Certain features will appear in the early stages of individualism under either system; and under either system certain other features will appear in its later stages."[2]

Without doubt, though, the most sophisticated formulation of this view was that conceived by the German sociologist, Max Weber. To Weber, the distinguishing characteristic of modern capitalism was the "rational organization of free labor." The pursuit of private gain, noted Weber, was well known in many earlier societies; what distinguishes present-day capitalism, he held, is the peculiar organization of the production unit, an organization that is essentially bureaucratic. This conception of capitalism, writes Parsons, "has one important concrete result; in contradistinction to Marx and most 'liberal' theories, it strongly minimizes the differences between capitalism and socialism, emphasizing rather their continuity. Not only would socialistic or-

[1] Talcott Parsons, The Structure of Social Action (New York, 1937), p. 341. For Durkheim's own statement, see his Le Socialisme (Paris, 1908), especially Ch. 2. The present writer is preparing an English translation of this volume.

[2] Bertrand and Dora Russell, Prospects of Industrial Civilization (New York, 1923), p. 14. Compare this with the discussion of Stalinist Communism by a postwar Russian refugee, G. F. Achminow, Die Macht im Hintergrund: Totengraber des Kommunismus (Ulm, 1950), which is discussed in Hans Gerth and C. Wright Mills, Character and Social Structure (New York, 1953), p. 477.

ganization leave the central fact of bureaucracy untouched, it would greatly accentuate its importance."[3]

While Marx had dwelt largely on the interrelations among production units, that is, their market ties, Weber focussed on the social relations within the industrial unit. If social relations inside of socialist and capitalist factories are fundamentally alike, in that they are both bureaucratic, then, asked Weber, does a socialist revolution yield very much of an improvement for the capitalist proletarian?

If Marx argued that the workers of the world had nothing to lose by revolting, Weber contended that they really had nothing to gain. "For the time being," he declared, "the dictatorship of the official and not that of the worker is on the march." Capitalism and socialism are thus placed under the same conceptual umbrella—bureaucracy—with the important practical result that the problem of choosing between them loses much of its point.

It is for this reason that the discussions of bureaucratic organization which are heir to the Weberian analysis must be understood as being, in part, a displacement of the controversy over socialism. Weber made it clear that questions of economic choice could no longer be treated in isolation from questions of administration. From Weber's time forward, administrative and economic choices were seen to be but two facets of the same hard problem. This has been recognized even by socialists, at least when they have been unencumbered by Communist party orthodoxy. For example, Oskar Lange once remarked, with a frankness that we hope he will never be compelled to regret, "...the real danger of socialism is that of bureaucratic organization of economic life...."[4]

It is sometimes assumed today that the Weberian outlook is at bottom anti-socialist. In effect, the argument runs, Weber's viewpoint devitalizes the myth-like appeal of socialism, draining off its ability to muster immense enthusiasms. Weber's theses are therefore held to be an "ideology" serviceable for the survival of capitalism, while Weber himself is characterized as the "Marx of the bourgeoisie."

Now all this may be true, but it is only a partial truth; for, in actuality, Weber's theories cut two ways, not one. If it is correct that his theory of bureaucracy saps the fervor of the socialist offensive, it also undermines the stamina of the capitalist bastions. If socialism and capitalism are similar in being bureaucratic, then not only is there little profit in substituting one for the other, but there is also little loss.

Considered only from the standpoint of its political consequences then, the Weberian outlook is not anti-socialist alone, nor anti-capitalist alone, it is both. In the final analysis its political slogan becomes "a plague on both your houses." If Weber is to be regarded as an "ideologist," he is an ideologist not of counter-revolution but of quiescence and neutralism. For many intellectuals who have erected a theory of group organization on Weberian foundations, the world has been emptied of choice, leaving them disoriented and despairing.

That gifted historian of ideas, Arthur O. Lovejoy, astutely observed that every theory is associated with, or generates, a set of sentiments which those subscribing to the theory could only dimly sense. Lovejoy called this the "metaphysical pathos" of ideas, a pathos which is "exemplified in any description of the nature of things, any characterization of the world to which one belongs, in terms which, like the words of a poem, evoke through their associations and through a sort of empathy which they engender, a congenial mood or tone of feeling."[5]

[3] Parsons, p. 509. See also the provocative fuller development of this argument as it applies to industrial organization: George C. Homans, "Industrial Harmony as a Goal," in Industrial Conflict, eds. Kornhauser, Dubin, and Ross (New York, 1954).

[4] Oskar Lange and Fred M. Taylor, On the Economic Theory of Socialism, ed. Lippincott (Minneapolis, 1948), p. 109.

[5] Arthur O. Lovejoy, The Great Chain of Being (Cambridge, Mass., 1948), p. 11.

As a result, a commitment to a theory often occurs by a process other than the one which its proponents believe and it is usually more consequential than they realize. A commitment to a theory may be made because the theory is congruent with the mood or deep-lying sentiments of its adherents, rather than merely because it has been cerebrally inspected and found valid. This is as true for the rigorous prose of social science as it is for the more lucid metaphor of creative literature, for each has its own silent appeal and its own metaphysical pathos.

Furthermore, those who have committed themselves to a theory always get more than they have bargained for. We do not make a commercial contract with a theory in which we agree to accept only the consignment of intellectual goods which has been expressly ordered; usually we take also the metaphysical pathos in which the theory comes packaged. In the end, the theory reinforces or induces in the adherent a subtle alteration in the structure of sentiments through which he views the world.

So too is it with the theory of organization. Paradoxically enough, some of the very theories which promise to make man's own work more intelligible to himself and more amenable to his intelligence are infused with an intangible metaphysical pathos which insinuates, in the very midst of new discoveries, that all is lost. For the metaphysical pathos of much of the modern theory of group organization is that of pessimism and fatalism.

I. EXPLANATION OF BUREAUCRACY

Nowhere does the fatalism of the theory of organization become more articulate than in its efforts to account for the development of bureaucratic behavior. One of the less challenging explanations, for example, premises a supposedly invariant human nature. Thus in an otherwise illuminating analysis, one political scientist remarks: "Civil servants are ordinary mortals; they have the defects and weaknesses typical of human nature.

Each loves, as Shakespeare said, 'his brief moment of authority'."

This, however, is difficult to reconcile with recurrent complaints, from civic leaders or business managers, that it is often hard to persuade people either to run for political office or to accept positions as foremen. Apparently there are some people who do not hanker after their brief moment of authority. [6]

In any event, it does not seem possible to account for bureaucracy in any of its forms as an outgrowth of "human nature.' This explanation cannot cope with the rudimentary fact that in some times and in some places there is much bureaucracy, but in other times and places there is little. Leaving aside the question of the validity of the argument, its practical results are again all too evident. For if bureaucracy is rooted in human nature then all hope for a remedy must be abandoned.

Much more serious as goads to pessimism are theories explaining bureaucracy as the end-product of increased size and complexity in organizations. This is by far the most popular of the interpretations. Marshall Dimock and Howard Hyde, for example, in their report to the Temporary National Economic Committee (TNEC), state: "The broadest structural cause of bureaucracy, whether in business or in government, is the tremendous size of the organization. Thus with capital or appropriations measured in hundreds of millions and in billions of dollars and personnel in tens and hundreds of thousands, it is difficult to avoid the obtrusion of the objectionable features of bureaucracy." [7]

While suggesting varied causes for the development of bureaucracy, Max Weber also interpreted it as a consequence of large size. For example, in discussing the ubiquity of bureaucratic forms Weber

---

[6] John A. Vieg, "Bureaucracy—Fact and Fiction," in Elements of Public Administration, ed. Fritz Morstein Marx (New York, 1946), p. 52.

[7] Monograph # 11, Temporary National Economic Committee, Bureaucracy and Trusteeship in Large Corporations (Washington, D. C., 1940), p. 36.

adds: "The same [bureaucratic] phenomena are found in the large-scale capitalistic enterprise; and the larger it is, the greater their role."[8] He underscores the role of size by emphasizing that "only by reversion in every field—political, religious, economic, etc.—to small-scale organization would it be possible to escape its influence."[9] Despite his consideration of other possible sources of bureaucracy, these comments suggest that Weber regarded organizational size as the controlling factor in the development of bureaucracy.

Weber's emphasis on size as the crucial determinant of bureaucratic development is unsatisfactory for several reasons. First, there are historic examples of human efforts carried out on an enormous scale which were not bureaucratic in any serious sense of the term.[10] The building of the Egyptian pyramids is an obvious example. Second, Weber never considers the possibility that it is not "large size" as such that disposes to bureaucracy; large size may be important only because it generates other social forces which, in their turn, generate bureaucratic patterns.

Of cource, in every analysis there are always intervening variables—the unknown "x"—which stand between any cause and effect. Scientific progress depends, in part, on moving away from the gross causes and coming closer to those which are more invariably connected with the object of interest. The point is that when a social scientist accepts "size" as an explanatory factor, instead of going on to ask what there is about size that

makes for bureaucracy, he is making an analytic decision. It is not a formulation unavoidably dictated by the nature of the data itself.

Significantly, though, it is a decision that leads once again to bleak pessimism. For to inform members of our society that the only way out of the bureaucratic impasse is to return to the historical past and to trade in large for small-scale organizations is, in effect, to announce the practical impossibility of coping with bureaucracy. Moreover, many people in our society believe that "bigness" symbolizes progress; to tell them that it also creates bureaucracy is to place them on the horns of a dilemma which gores no matter which way they turn. In such a position the most painless response is inaction.

Underlying this conception of the matter there is a Hegelian dialectic in which "good" and "bad" are viewed as inseparably connected opposites; bureaucracy, "the bad thing," is represented as the inescapable price that has to be paid for the good things, the efficiency and abundance of modern life. One social scientist clearly puts it this way: "Assembly line techniques offer marked advantages over those of custom craftsmanship. They also have their price. They entail the imposition of an order of progression, the fixing of a rate or rhythm of operation, and the discipline of a regular routine. Set order, fixed pace, and adherence to routine— these are the very stuff of which red tape is made. Yet they are of the essence of system, too."[11] However true or false, there can be little doubt that this is an outlook which is convenient and comfortable for bureaucrats—if not for many others.

II. THE STRUCTURAL-FUNCTIONALISTS

The fuller ramifications of this approach to bureaucracy can best be explained by turning to the analyses of industrial organization made by some of

---

[8] Max Weber: The Theory of Social and Economic Organization, translated and edited by A. M. Henderson and Talcott Parsons (New York, 1947), p. 334.

[9] Ibid., p. 338.

[10] See Reinhard Bendix, "Bureaucracy: The Problem and Its Setting," American Sociological Review, Vol. 12, pp. 502-7 (Oct., 1947). On the other hand, there are theoretically significant cases of small organizations which are highly bureaucratized, for example, the Boulton and Watt factory in 1775-1805. This "case illustrates the fact that the bureaucratization of industry is not synonymous with the recent growth in the size of business enterprises." Reinhard Bendix, "Bureaucratization in Industry," in Industrial Conflict, p. 166.

[11] Vieg, pp. 5-6.

the "structural-functionalists." This is a comparatively new and vigorous school of American sociologists, which has grown directly out of the theories of Durkheim, Weber, and others, and whose most elaborate expression is to be found in the work of Talcott Parsons.

Parsons' recent analyses of industrial bureaucracy are of sufficient importance to be quoted in full. "Though with many individual exceptions [which he does not examine], technological advance almost always leads to increasingly elaborate division of labor and the concomitant requirement of increasingly elaborate organization." He continues:

The fundamental reason for this is, of course, that with elaborate differentiation of functions the need for minute coordination of the different functions develops at the same time.... There must be a complex organization of supervision to make quite sure that exactly the right thing is done.... Feeding the various parts into the process, in such a way that a modern assembly line can operate smoothly, requires very complex organization to see that they are available in just the right quantities at the right times and places.... One of the most important phases of this process of change is concerned with the necessity for formalization when certain points of complexity are reached....

Smaller and simpler organizations are typically managed with a high degree of particularism (i.e., personal consideration) in the relations of persons in authority to their own subordinates. But when the "distance" between points of decision and of operation increases, and the number of operating units affected by decisions with it, uniformity and coordination can be attained only by a high degree of formalization....[12]

Surprisingly enough, this is an atavistic recurrence of technological determinism in which characteristic bureaucratic traits—such as an elaborate division of labor, complex organization, and formalization—are held to stem directly from technological advance. This is a form of technological determinism because bureaucracy is seen as the result of technological change, without inquiring into the motives and meanings which these

changes have for the people involved, and without wondering whether technological change would have a different impact on the formal organization of a group that had a high motivation to produce and therefore did not require close supervision. This is a form of technological determinism, because no alternative solutions are appraised or deemed possible and coordination is seen as attainable "only by a high degree of formalization...."

Here once again we are invited to draw the conclusion that those who want modern technology must be prepared to pay for it with a minute and even stultifying division of labor.

All this, though, is a theoretical tapestry devoid of even the plainest empirical trimmings. Even on logical grounds, however, it is tenuous indeed. For it is evident that organizational patterns, such as a high division of labor, are found in spheres where modern technology has made comparatively little headway. This, in fact, is a point that Weber was at pains to insist upon. And if, as he maintained, bureaucratic forms are also found in charitable, political, or religious organizations—and not solely in industry— then they certainly cannot be explained as a consequence of modern machine technology.

Beyond these logical considerations, there are also some empirical grounds for questioning the adequacy of Parsons' analysis. Peter Drucker, for example, became extremely doubtful about the necessity of a minute division of labor while observing large-scale American industry during World War II. (This is crucial for Parsons' argument, because he holds that it is through increased specialization that technology evokes the other elements of bureaucratic organization.) Drucker comments that "we have learned that it is neither necessary nor always efficient to organize all mass production in such a manner as to have the majority of workers confine themselves to doing one and only one of the elementary manipulations .... It was impossible [because of wartime shortages of skilled labor] to 'lay

[12] Talcott Parsons, The Social System (Glencoe, Illinois, 1951), pp. 507-8. Emphasis added.

out' the job in the usual assembly-line fashion in which one unskilled operation done by one unskilled man is followed by the next unskilled man. The operation was broken down into its unskilled components like any assembly-line job. <u>But then the unskilled components were put together again with the result that an unskilled worker actually performed the job of a highly skilled mechanic</u>—and did it as reliably and efficiently as had been done by skilled men."[13]

In short, lower degrees of specialization than those normally found in large-scale industry are not necessarily forbidden by modern technology. Drucker's observations must, at the very least, raise the question as to how much of the minute division of labor is attributable to technological causes. Parsons, though, gives no consideration to other factors contributing to an extreme division of labor. However, Carl Dreyfuss, a German industrial sociologist, has advanced an array of keen observations and hypotheses which meet this question directly. He writes: "the artificial complication of the rank order...permits numerous employees to feel that they hold high positions and are to a certain extent independent." Moreover, he notes that a complicated division of labor is "with its unwarranted differentiations, telescoped positions, and ramifications, diametrically opposed to efforts of rationalization."[14] In other words, Dreyfus suggests that much of the complex division of labor today is not to be explained by technological requirements, but rather in terms of the prestige satisfactions, the "psychic income," that it presumably provides workers.

In Dreyfuss' view, the "minute division of labor" also stems from management's need to <u>control</u> workers and to make themselves independent of any specific individual or group of workers. A high division of labor, said Dreyfuss, means that "individual workers and employees

can be exchanged and replaced at any time."[15] Through its use, "dependence of the employee upon the employer is greatly increased. It is much more difficult for today's employee, trained in only one particular function, to find reemployment than it was for his predecessor, a many-sided, well-instructed business man, able and fitted to fill a variety of positions."[16]

A similar view is advanced in the more recent studies of industrial organization in Yankee City, which were made by W. L. Warner and J. O. Low. "While machine processes were adopted by shoe factories primarily to reduce costs and to speed the processing, the machine has other great advantages over the human worker from the managerial point of view," comment Warner and Low.

Control problems are simplified...on two counts through mechanization: (1) machines are easier to control than human beings, and (2) mechanization tends to disrupt the social solidarity of the workers, who thereby become easier to control than they would if they were able to maintain close social relations during working hours...these factors tend to increase the subordination of the individual worker to management; from the management's viewpoint they are valuable means of social control over workers....The routinization of jobs also simplifies control of workers in another way. The individual operative today does not have the feeling of security that the oldtime craftsman derived from his special technical abilities. In most cases, today's operative is aware that only a comparatively brief training period protects him in his job from a large number of untrained individuals. The members of the supervisory hierarchy are also well aware of this fact. The psychological effect of this result of the division of labor is to intensify the subordinate position of the individual operative and to make him submit the more readily to the limitations on his behavior required by the supervisory group.[17]

It is unnecessary for our purpose here to resolve this disparity between Warner

[13] Peter Drucker, <u>Concept of the Corporation</u> (New York, 1946), pp. 183-84.

[14] Carl Dreyfuss, <u>Occupation and Ideology of the Salaried Employee</u>, trans. Eva Abramovitch (New York, 1938), p. 17.

[15] <u>Ibid</u>., p. 75.
[16] <u>Ibid</u>., p. 77.

[17] W. Lloyd Warner and J. O. Low, <u>The Social System of the Modern Factory</u> (New Haven, 1947), pp. 78, 80, 174.

and Dreyfuss, on the one hand, and Parsons, on the other. What may be suggested, however, is that there is considerable reason for holding Parsons' position to be both logically and empirically inadequate and to recognize that it has, without compelling scientific warrant, accommodated itself to the metaphysical pathos of organizational theory, which sees no escape from bureaucracy.

III. THE TRADITION OF MICHELS

There is another offshoot among the structural-functionalists which is distinguished by its concern for the problems bequeathed by Robert Michels and, as such, it is even more morosely pessimistic than others in the school. Michels, it will be remembered, focussed his empirical studies on the Social Democratic parties of pre-World War I Europe. He chose these, quite deliberately, because he wanted to see whether groups which stood for greater freedom and democracy, and were hostile to authoritarianism, were not themselves afflicted by the very organizational deformity to which they were opposed.

Michel's conclusions were, of course, formulated in his "iron law of oligarchy," in which he maintained that always and everywhere a "system of leadership is incompatible with the most essential postulates of democracy."[18] Oligarchy, said Michels, "derives from the tactical and technical necessities which result from the consolidation of every disciplined political aggregate..."[19] It is the outcome of organic necessity, and consequently affects every organization, be it socialist or even anarchist."[20]

In concluding his study, Michels remarks with a flourish of defensive pathos, "...it seemed necessary to lay considerable stress upon the pessimist aspect of democracy which is forced upon us by historical study...."[21] "The demo-cratic currents of history resemble successive waves. They break ever on the same shoals....It is probable that this cruel game will continue without end."[22]

Focussing, as Michels did, on an apparently democratic group, Philip Selznick examined the TVA, which many Americans had long believed to be an advanced expression of democratic values. Like Michels, Selznick assumes that "wherever there is organization, whether formally democratic or not, there is a split between the leader and the led, between the agent and the initiator. The phenomenon of abdication to bureaucratic directives in corporations, in trade unions, in parties, and in cooperatives is so widespread that it indicates a fundamental weakness of democracy."[23]

Selznick's study concludes that the TVA's emphasis on "decentralization" is to be best understood as a result of that agency's needs to adapt to suspicious local communities and to survive in competition with older governmental agencies based in Washington. "Decentralization" is viewed as a "halo that becomes especially useful in countries which prize the symbols of democracy."[24] In its turn, the TVA's emphasis on "participation" is explained as a catchword, satisfying the agency's needs to transform "an unorganized citizenry into a reliable instrument for the achievement of administrative goals...."[25]

Selznick, like Michels, is impressed with the similarity in the organizational devices employed by different groups, whether they are democratic or authoritarian in ideology. He asserts "...there seems to be a continuum between the voluntary associations set up by the democratic (mass) state—such as committees of farmers to boost or control agricultural production—and the citizens' associations of the totalitarian (mass) state. Indeed the devices of corporatism emerge as relatively effective responses

---

[18]Robert Michels, Political Parties (Glencoe, Ill., 1949), p. 400. Michel's work was first published in 1915.
[19]Ibid., p. 401.
[20]Ibid., p. 402.
[21]Ibid., p. 405.

[22]Ibid., p. 408.
[23]Philip Selznick, TVA and the Grass Roots (Berkeley and Los Angeles, 1949), p. 9.
[24]Ibid., p. 220.
[25]Loc. cit.

to the need to deal with the mass, and in time of war the administrative techniques of avowedly democratic countries and avowedly totalitarian countries tend to converge."[26]

In Selznick's analysis human action involves a commitment to two sets of interests: first to the goals intended, and second to the organizational instruments through which these goals are pursued. These tools are, however, recalcitrant; they generate "needs" which cannot be neglected. Hence if men persist in their ends, they are forced to satisfy the needs of their organizational instruments. They are, therefore, as much committed to their tools as to their ends, and "these commitments may lead to unanticipated consequences resulting in a deflection of original ends."[27]

For these reasons, organizational behavior must be interpreted not so much in terms of the ends that administrators deliberately seek, as in terms of the organizational "needs" which their pursuit engenders. "The needs in question are organizational, not individual, and include: the security of the organization as a whole in relation to social forces in its environment; the stability of the lines of authority and communication; the stability of informal relations within the organization; the continuity of policy and of the sources of its determination; a homogeneity of outlook with respect to the means and role of the organization."[28]

"In general," writes Selznick, "we have been concerned to formulate some of the underlying tendencies which are likely to inhibit the democratic process. Like all conservative or pessimistic criticism, such a statement of inherent problems seems to cast doubt upon the possibility of complete democratic achievement. It does cast such a doubt. The alternative, however, is the transformation of democracy into a utopian notion which, unaware of its internal dangers, is unarmed to meet them."[29] This, however, is an argu-

ment that rests upon assumptions which are not transparently self-evident and are acceptable without dispute only by those who are susceptible to its metaphysical pathos. Despite demagogic appeals to democratic symbols, there seem to be few places in either the Eastern or Western worlds in which there is a real and present danger of the "transformation of democracy into a utopian notion." Surely this is not to be expected among the class conscious working classes of Europe, the laborite masses of England, the untutored peasants of China, or among the confused and often apathetic American electorate to whom politics is something of a dirty game, to be periodically enlivened with scandals and investigations. And if this appraisal is correct, then just who is there to be "armed" with this knowledge of the internal dangers of democracy?

For some reason Selznick has chosen —and this was not forced upon him by the data—to focus on the things which harry and impede democratic aspirations, rather than on those which strengthen and energize it. It is for this reason perhaps that he is led to reiterate Michel's apologia: "Attention being focussed on the structural conditions which influence behavior, we are directed to emphasize constraints, the limitations of alternatives imposed by the system upon its participants. This will tend to give pessimistic overtones to the analysis, since such factors as good will and intelligence will be de-emphasized."[30]

Selznick chose to focus on those social constraints that thwart democratic aspirations, but neglected to consider the constraints that enable them to be realized, and that foster and encourage "good will" and "intelligence." Are these, however, random occurrences, mere historic butterflies which flit through events with only ephemeral beauty? Or are they, as much as anything else, often the unanticipated products of our "commitments"? Why is it that "unanticipated consequences" are always tacitly assumed to

[26]Loc. cit.
[27]Ibid., p. 259.
[28]Ibid., p. 252.
[29]Ibid., p. 265.

[30]Ibid., p. 252.

be destructive of democratic values and "bad"; why can't they sometimes be "good"? Are there no constraints which <u>force</u> men to adhere valorously to their democratic beliefs, which <u>compel</u> them to be intelligent rather than blind, which leave them <u>no choice</u> but to be men of good will rather than predators? The neglect of these possibilities suggests the presence of a distorting pathos.

It is the pathos of pessimism, rather than the compulsions of rigorous analysis, that lead to the assumption that organizational constraints have stacked the deck against democracy. For on the face of it there is every reason to assume that "the underlying tendencies which are likely to inhibit the democratic process" are just as likely to impair authoritarian rule. It is only in the light of such a pessimistic pathos that the defeat of democratic values can be assumed to be probable, while their victory is seen as a slender thing, delicately constituted and precariously balanced.

When, for example, Michels spoke of the "iron law of oligarchy," he attended solely to the ways in which organizational needs inhibit democratic possibilities. But the very same evidence to which he called attention could enable us to formulate the very opposite theorem—the "iron law of democracy." Even as Michels himself saw, if oligarchical waves repeatedly wash away the bridges of democracy, this eternal recurrence can happen only because men doggedly rebuild them after each inundation. Michels chose to dwell on only one aspect of this process, neglecting to consider this other side. There cannot be an iron law of oligarchy, however, unless there is an iron law of democracy.

Much the same may be said for Selznick. He posits certain organizational needs: a need for the <u>security</u> of the organization, for <u>stable</u> lines of authority and communication, for <u>stable</u> informal relationships. But for each of the organizational needs which Selznick postulates, a set of contrary needs can also be posited, and the satisfaction of these would seem to be just as necessary for the sur-

vival of an organization. If, as Selznick says, an organization must have security in its environment, then certainly Toynbee's observations that too much security can be stultifying and corrosive is at least as well taken. To Selznick's security need, a Toynbee might counterpose a need for a moderate challenge or threat.

A similar analysis might also be made of Selznick's postulated need for <u>homogeneity</u> of outlook concerning the means and role of the organization. For unless there is some heterogeneity of outlook, then where is an organization to find the tools and flexibility to cope with changes in its environment? Underlying Selznick's need for homogeneity in outlook, is there not another "need," <u>a need that consent of the governed be given</u>—at least in <u>some measure</u>—to their governors? Indeed, this would seem to be at the very core of Selznick's empirical analysis, though it is obscured in his high-level theoretical statement of the needs of organizations. And if all organizations must adjust to such a need for consent, is there not built into the very marrow or organization a large element of what we mean by democracy? This would appear to be an organizational constraint that makes oligarchies, and all separation of leaders from those led, no less inherently unstable than democratic organization.[31]

These contrary needs are just as real and just as consequential for organizational behavior as those proposed by Selznick. But they point in a different direction. They are oriented to problems of change, of growth, of challenging contingencies, of provoking and unsettling encounters. Selznick's analysis seems

---

[31] See Arthur Schweitzer, "Ideological Groups," *American Sociological Review*, Vol. 9, pp. 415-27 (Aug., 1944), particularly his discussion of factors inhibiting oligarchy. For example, "A leadership concentrating all power in its hands creates indifference among the functionaries and sympathizers as well as decline in membership of the organization. This process of shrinkage, endangering the position of the leaders, is the best protection against the supposedly inevitable iron law of oligarchy" (p. 419). Much of the research deriving from the Lewinian tradition would seem to lend credence to this inference.

almost to imply that survival is possible only in an icy stasis, in which "security," "continuity," and "stability" are the key terms. If anything, the opposite seems more likely to be true, and organizational survival is impossible in such a state.

Wrapping themselves in the shrouds of nineteenth-century political economy, some social scientists appear to be bent on resurrecting a dismal science. For the iron law of wages, which maintained that workers could never improve their material standards of life, some sociologists have substituted the iron law of oligarchy, which declares that men cannot improve their political standards of life. Woven to a great extent out of theoretical whole cloth, much of the discussion of bureaucracy and of organizational needs seems to have provided a screen onto which some intellectuals have projected their own despair and pessimism, reinforcing the despair of others.

Perhaps the situation can be illuminated with an analogy. For many years now infantile paralysis has killed and maimed scores of people. For many years also doctors, biologists, and chemists have been searching for the causes and cure of this disease. Consider the public reaction if, instead of reporting on their newest vaccines, these scientists had issued the following announcement: "We have not reached any conclusions concerning the causes of the disease, nor

has our research investigated defenses against it. The public seems to have perfectionist aspirations of flawless health, they have 'utopian' illusions concerning the possibilities of immortality and it is this—not the disease—that is the danger against which the public needs to be armed. We must remember that the human animal is not immortal and that for definite reasons his lifespan is finite." It is likely, of course, that such scientists would be castigated for having usurped the prerogatives and functions of clergymen.

This, however, seems to parallel the way in which some social scientists have approached the study of organizational pathology. Instead of telling men how bureaucracy might be mitigated, they insist that it is inevitable. Instead of explaining how democratic patterns may, to some extent, be fortified and extended, they warn us that democracy cannot be perfect. Instead of controlling the disease, they suggest that we are deluded, or more politely, incurably romantic, for hoping to control it. Instead of assuming responsibilities as realistic clinicians, striving to further democratic potentialities wherever they can, many social scientists have become morticians, all too eager to bury men's hopes.[32]

---

[32] We have sought to develop the positive implications of this approach to bureaucratic organization in Patterns of Industrial Bureaucracy (Glencoe, Ill., 1954).

SOCIOLOGICAL METHODS

The Relevance of Mathematics to Controlled Experimentation in Sociology

Leon Festinger

SOURCE: *International Social Science Bulletin*, Vol. 6, (1954), pp. 622–27.

In recent years there has been, at least in the United States, a growing enthusiasm for the possible uses of mathematics in sociology and in social psychology.

"Possible uses of mathematics" does not mean here the use of mathematics in statistics or in measurement and scale construction. What is referred to is rather the hope of being able to state empirically relevant hypotheses about social behavior in mathematical terms and to make derivations from this theory by means of rigorous mathematical manipulations. There are a number of such efforts underway which we will later describe. At present, however, the use of mathematics in the above sense is more a hope and faith than a reality. It is consequently appropriate for us first to discuss what is hoped for from such use of mathematics and why, if it becomes a reality, it will be extremely relevant to controlled experimentation.

Mathematics is, essentially, a set of techniques for deductive reasoning, and such techniques for deductive reasoning can be extremely valuable. When a theory becomes so complex that one cannot easily see all its implications, mathematics, if applicable, could enable the rigorous derivation of deductions and implications, some of which might only have been guessed at and others of which might not even have been foreseen. Sometimes, of course, "so complex" is a low degree of complexity indeed.

One might then ask why mathematics, representing, as it does, a powerful aid to theoretical reasoning, is not used all the time. The difficulty lies in the fact that one must know exactly and specifically what one is talking about and what one is saying before it can be stated in terms amenable to mathematical techniques. In other words, before mathematics can be used as an aid to theoretical thinking, the theory in question must be very specific and unambiguous. This advanced state of affairs, unfortunately, hardly exists in the fields of sociology and social psychology, and this is why the application of mathematics remains a hope rather than a reality. In fact, to convince oneself that most theoretical statements are vague and ambiguous one need only attempt to state a sociological theory in mathematical terms.

When an interrelated set of hypotheses are stated in specific and unambiguous terms, precise data are usually required to test the implications. Because controlled experimentation frequently yields information of a more precise and unequivocal nature than do other types of studies, the application of mathematics has special importance for such studies. Mathematics may help to formulate a theory to explain the results of an experiment or it may suggest controlled experiments to test some mathematically stated hypotheses. We will give a number of examples of ongoing uses of mathematics in such contexts to illustrate how it is used and what its current value seems to be.

Interest in the use of mathematics in sociology was greatly increased with the publication of the Theory of Games and Economic Behavior by von Neumann and Morgenstern.[1] Let us examine the impact which this mathematical theory of games has had on controlled experimentation. The theory of games is a mathematical system which enables one to deduce how one party in a certain restricted kind of competitive situation should act so as to produce optimal results for himself. (A great oversimplification, but this is all that is possible in a brief statement.) The theory of games leads to definitive mathematical solutions when the following conditions are met: each possible action of each competitor, and the payoff to each competitor of each combination of actions, are known to all in advance; when the number of competitors being considered is two, or one considers one of them against all the others; and when the situation is such that the gains and losses of the competitors always total to zero or some constant amount. Needless to say, this set of restrictions, when adhered to precisely, makes the theory of games quite inapplicable to sociological problems. Furthermore, the theory of games is not a theory of how people behave but is rather a theory of what, according to certain definitions, would be optimal strategy in such competition.

Peculiarly enough, however, despite these limitations, the theory of games

[1] J. von Neumann and O. Morgenstern. The Theory of Games and Economic Behavior, Princeton University Press, Princeton, 1947.

has begun to have a very interesting impact on controlled experimentation. It has, for example, enabled Dr. Morton Deutsch[2] to devise an experimental situation in which he can, with a high degree of control, study tendencies toward competitive and co-operative behaviour. The experimental situation is one suggested by the theory of games and is precisely one of those situations which cannot adequately be handled mathematically. It is a situation where the total of the winnings and losses of the two competitors or players do not add up to a constant amount. Under these circumstances one can devise a situation where, if they engage in what superficially looks like optimal strategy to each, both of them lose heavily. They can both gain only if they behave as though the other person is friendly and co-operative. The theory of games has thus enabled the development of a technique for controlled experiments on competition versus mutual trust.

Another example of the impact of the theory of games on controlled experimentation is an experiment done by Hoffman, Festinger and Lawrence.[3] Curiously enough, again a part of the theory of games which is rather inept mathematically has made impact, specifically, a part which deals with three-person games and which attempts to analyse, mathematically, the formation of coalitions. The impact on controlled experimentation again took the form of suggesting an experimental situation which could be used effectively in studying how certain factors affect competitive tendencies and how they affect coalition formation among any two of the three persons in the situation.

It is perhaps no accident that the theory of games has had this kind of impact. After all, it is not a sociological or psychological theory and can hardly be expected to deal adequately with sociologi-

cal or social psychological phenomena. It does, however, enable one to construct situations where, from an understanding of the mathematics of "optimum action," one can better compare the effects of different sociological and psychological variables.

Another instance of mathematical work which has had an impact on controlled experimentation is the development of mathematics for dealing with "group structure." The sociological problem which has been formulated in this connexion is, in its essence, a simple one although the mathematical problems involved become very complex. Considering that in any collection of persons there are different degrees and kinds of relationships among the persons, one may set out to systematize and to develop a mathematics for dealing with this variety of relations. The simplest case which can be specified is one where certain connexions or relationships among persons either do or do not exist. For example, for any pair of persons one might specify whether or not they communicate with one another or whether or not they work together. The variety of configurations and networks which can exist in a group in even this simple instance is bewildering. A mathematical system which would enable one to solve problems concerning such configurations and networks would be of obvious value. The major mathematical area which is relevant to solving these problems is what is known as the "theory of graphs" mainly developed by König,[4] but as yet of limited usefulness. Harary and Norman[5] have worked out possible uses of the mathematical theory of graphs in social psychology.

Once more its major application has been in suggesting techniques of controlled experimentation which have been

---

[2] Work now in progress at the Human Relations Research Center, New York University.

[3] P. J. Hoffman, L. Festinger and D. H. Lawrence. "Tendencies toward Group Comparability in Competitive Bargaining." Human Relations, vol. 7, 1954, p. 141-59.

[4] D. König, Theorie der Endlichen und Unendlichen Graphen. Chelsea Publishing Company, New York, 1949.

[5] F. Harary and R. Z. Norman. Graph Theory as a Mathematical Model in Social Science. Institute for Social Research, Univ. of Mich. Press, Ann Arbor, Michigan.

useful. Bavelas[6] and Leavitt[7] and others have done a number of experiments where the connexion or lack of connexion among individuals in a group is specified in terms of the possibility or lack of possibility of their communicating to one another. Experimentally this can be done with relative ease. These experiments have mainly concerned themselves with the effect of different "patterns of connexions" among the members of a group on (a) the effectiveness with which the group can solve problems; (b) the morale and satisfaction of members of the group; and (c) the emergence of leadership in the group. The actual application of mathematics to the social psychological problems involved and to the data, however, has been minimal. Thus far, the major contribution of the mathematical formulations has been to suggest the experiments in the first place.

A different, and highly interesting, attempt at applying mathematics to social processes is presently being carried out by Hays and Bush.[8] They have concerned themselves with trying to analyse a very simple, restricted, controlled situation. The problem which they put is essentially this: Given a group of three persons who, functioning as a group, are required to solve a problem which involves learning, what minimal mathematical formulation is necessary to account for the speed of learning which the group shows? Considering only one aspect of the group interaction, namely, the extent to which the individuals in the group are affected by or influenced by the other individuals in the group concerning each decision they make, it is possible to state two extreme hypotheses which must include within them all possibilities. One extreme formulation would be that each individual acts as an individual, completely unaf-

fected by what the others say or do. The other extreme is to imagine that the effect of the person who answers first is complete and exerts a definitive influence on the others in the group. The authors are able, mathematically, to derive the course of group performance under these two extreme hypotheses and are currently engaged in conducting experiments with three-person groups in appropriately restricted situations to test which of these, if either, comes appreciably close to describing what actually happens.

This, of course, represents an effective application of mathematics. A set of hypotheses has been stated specifically, certain derivations have been made mathematically, and experiments can be, and are being, conducted to test the derivations. Yet, I expect there are many who would wonder about the fruitfulness to sociology or social psychology of this kind of approach. It makes sense, then, for us to examine the limitations of this kind of endeavor without detracting from its present or potential value. First of all, the situations, and the set of hypotheses, with which this mathematical formulation deals are so narrow and circumscribed that its usefulness for broader theory in sociology and social psychology will be very limited. A proponent of this kind of endeavor might, however, feel that this is exactly the way to start; that once the mathematics is developed, and the hypotheses substantiated for such a narrow realm, the theory can then be broadened and extended.

A sceptic might also point out that even within the narrow realm dealt with by the mathematical formulation, it is almost certainly wrong. That is, neither of the extremes will turn out to be the actual state of affairs. A proponent might feel, however, that this way of proceding will eventually lead to the discovery of a correct formulation and then the hypotheses and the mathematical model will be altered appropriately.

Clearly, one cannot tell at this very early stage whether such an application is or is not fruitful. One can only hope that it will be fruitful.

---

[6] A. Bavelas. "Communication Patterns in Task-Oriented Groups." J. Accoust. Soc. Am., 22, 1950, p. 725–30.

[7] H. J. Leavitt. "Some Effects of Certain Communication Patterns on Group Performance." J. Abnorm. Psychol., 46, 1951, p. 38–50.

[8] D. G. Hays and R. R. Bush. "A Study of Group Action." Laboratory of Social Relations, Harvard University. Unpublished manuscript.

I would like to give one last example of what is probably the most ambitious, and perhaps the most promising, of the attempts at using mathematics in sociology or social psychology. This is the work of Simon,[9] and of Simon and Guetzkow.[10] These men have attempted to take existing theory in sociology or social psychology which is, to some extent at least, substantiated by empirical data, and to state such theory in mathematical terms. This has been done now in two different instances, first for a number of interrelated hypotheses stated by Homans[11] concerning determinants of friendship and group interaction, and, secondly, for a number of interrelated hypotheses stated by Festinger[12] concerning the informal processes of communication and influence in groups.

In both cases, the system of interrelated hypotheses, which were stated verbally, seemed to Professor Simon to describe what was essentially an equilibrium system, that is, one in which the interrelations among the variables was such that a change in one produced changes in others until the system reached a new point of equilibrium. He felt that such theories could be adequately handled by a system of non-linear differential equations. Translating the verbal statements of hypotheses to such equations is by no means easy. It becomes clear that the verbal statements of the hypotheses, while they may seem fairly specific, are not specific enough to allow them to be stated in terms of differential equations without a number of additional more specific assumptions. This they were able to do surprisingly well. The result is that they have produced a mathematical statement of a fairly broad theory which has accomplished several things. First, it has made clear where some of the points of vagueness and ambiguity are in the verbal statement of the theory. Second, it has shown that the deductions which were made semi-intuitively from the verbal theory can be deduced rigorously and mathematically.

This, however, is only part of what such a mathematical statement should do. The authors of the mathematical system hoped to be able to claim that:

"(a) It helps us know more precisely what mechanisms or structural relations are being postulated, sometimes calling attention to the need for further clarification of the operational meaning of definitions and statements.

"(b) It enables us to discover whether certain postulates can be derived from others, and hence can be eliminated as independent assumptions; whether additional postulates need to be added to make the system complete and the deductions rigorous; and whether there are inconsistencies among the postulates.

"(c) It assists in the discovery of inconsistencies between the empirical data and the theories used to explain them.

"(d) It lays the basis for the further elaboration of theory, and leads to deductions from the postulates that suggest further empirical studies for verification.

"(e) It aids in handling complicated, simultaneous interrelations among a relatively large number of variables, with some reduction of the obscuring circumlocutions demanded by nonmathematical language."

And indeed, if the fourth claim had been substantiated, it would have been a clear and unequivocal contribution which could not have been achieved without the aid of mathematics. If the authors had been able to show that at some point where the verbal theory was vague or ambiguous, consequently leaving a choice of formulation, different seemingly plausible as-

[9]H. A. Simon. "A Formal Theory of Interaction in Social Groups." <u>American Sociological Review</u>, 17, 1952, p. 202-10.

[10]H. A. Simon and H. Guetzkow. "Communication resulting from Pressures toward Uniformity in groups." Carnegie Institute of Technology. Unpublished manuscript.

[11]G. C. Homans. <u>The Human Group</u>. New York, Harcourt Brace, 1950.

[12]L. Festinger. "Informal Social Communication." <u>Psychological Review</u>, 57, 1950, p. 271-82.

sumptions led to different derivations which could be tested, then the mathematical formulation would have led to growth of the theory. Another valuable contribution would have been to derive from the mathematical formulation some consequence or implication which had not been foreseen because of the complexities of the system and the inability to think it through without mathematical aids. Such a contribution would have increased the value and utility of the theory. Unfortunately, neither of these two types of contribution were forthcoming, and consequently, although the work of Simon and Guetzkow is an impressive contribution and, to date, the most promising use of mathematics in social psychology, we must still look to the future to bring its promise to fruition.

One could supply still other examples of attempts to apply mathematics to sociology and social psychology, but most of them would simply duplicate the points already made. To sum up, a few things should be said about what seem to be the major difficulties in the way of using mathematics in sociology and social psychology today.

Thus far mathematics has not proven immensely useful in social psychology. The faith that it will in the future prove useful must undoubtedly stem from the fact it has been so invaluable in other sciences, mainly in the physical ones. But even in the social sciences we can find examples, such as economic theory, where mathematical formulations have been extraordinarily helpful in systematizing theory and in allowing the derivation of new and different implications, sometimes even of a quantitative nature.

Why then is there the difficulty we see in connexion with sociology and social psychology?

The opinion has been expressed that one of the difficulties lies in the fact that the mathematics which exists today has been developed largely under the spur of problems faced by the physical sciences and, consequently, may not be the mathematics needed in sociology. Thus, it might be argued that new mathematics must be developed. This may or may not turn out to be true, but it is in any event no stimulus to new mathematical developments. Before the situation is ripe for the application of mathematics, it is not possible to foresee what kind of mathematics needs to be developed to handle the problems of the new field.

This last, I think, is the crucial difficulty in applying mathematics. The theories which exist, few enough though they may be, are not specifically enough stated and the problems are not cogently enough delineated to enable us to ask sensible questions with respect to mathematics. A forced attempt to use mathematics under such circumstances easily leads to a mathematical statement which has little to do with real problems or else leads to formulations which are trivial in the sense that they perform little that could not have been performed with the verbal statement itself.

In my opinion, when we have theory which is stated with relatively few points of ambiguity and vagueness, and when this theory approaches a state of complexity which cannot be thought through unaided, then the formidable problem of finding mathematical formulations can be approached on a sensible basis with much hope for progress.

Some Functions of Qualitative Analysis in Social Research

Allen H. Barton and
Paul F. Lazarsfeld

SOURCE: *Frankfurter Beiträge zur Sociologie*, Vol. I, (1955), pp. 321–61.

THE METHODOLOGICAL PROBLEM

The advancement of research procedure in social science as elsewhere depends on making explicit what researchers actually do, and systematically analyzing it in the light of logic and of substantive knowledge. Such a "codification" of procedures points out dangers, indicates neglected possibilities, and suggests improvements. It makes possible the generalization of methodological knowledge —its transfer from one specific project or subject matter to others, from one researcher to the scientific community. Finally it makes possible a more systematic training of students, in place of simply exposing them to concrete cases of research in the hope that they will somehow absorb the right lessons.

Such a recording and analysis of procedures has gone quite far in certain parts of the social research process—in the design of experiments, in the analysis of survey data, in the scaling and measurement of social and psychological variables, and in sampling. But codification has been very unevenly applied; important parts of the research process have been neglected.

This is particularly true of the analysis of non-quantified data, "qualitative analysis," as it is often called. A great deal of social research operates with qualitative descriptions of particular institutions, situations or individuals, rather than with "largely quantified data accumulated by structured observation in empirical situations approximating (with specified deviations) the model of controlled experiment."[1] Not only is this type of research large in volume, but it plays important roles in the research process, by itself and in connection with quantitative research. This paper aims to make a start at the systematic analysis of "qualitative procedure."

The question which we would like to answer is: "What can a researcher do when confronted by a body of qualitative data—detailed, concrete, non-metric descriptions of people and events, drawn from direct observation, interviews, case-studies, historical writings, the writings of participants?" The methodologist's first step toward a systematic answer is to examine what researchers in fact have been doing with qualitative material. About 100 studies were culled for characteristic examples. An effort was then made to organize these cases in order that the most characteristic types of qualitative work could be distinguished and documented. This paper presents the resulting organization.

The reader will have no difficulty in noting that this "guide through qualitative research" is itself guided by proceeding from simple to ever more complex pro-

---

[1] Definition of quantitative research given by Daniel Lerner, "The American Soldier and the Public," in: Robert K. Merton and Paul F. Lazarsfeld, eds., Continuities in Social Research, Glencoe, Illinois, 1950, p. 220.

cedures. We begin with a discussion of the value of simple observations. We then proceed to those studies which center on ordering and classification. Our next group of examples demonstrates the various ways in which several variables are interrelated through qualitative analysis. Next we discuss cases where the analyst wants to encompass such a great number of dimensions that he cannot make them all explicit, but tries to sum them up in a general "pattern." This is probably the point at which qualitative research is most creative, most controversial, and most difficult to describe. It will be seen that we had to use a special term ("matrix formula"), to bring into relief this means of seeing the social world in a new way. Finally, we touch on the role of qualitative data in the support of theory, a topic so large that we did not dare to pursue it to any extent.

It should also be kept in mind what this paper does not attempt to do. First of all, it does not describe how qualitative research should be done; it is restricted to an organized description of what is actually being done, without expressing any judgment. Secondly, this paper, but for one point, does not make any attempt at formalization. The exception is in Section II where the use of typologies is discussed. The logic of typologies is by now so well developed that it was simple to include it in this paper. Such formalizations have considerable advantages. They indicate the underlying assumptions in a given piece of qualitative work, what points the author might have overlooked, at what points he might have contradicted himself, and so forth. There is no doubt that additional formalizations will be needed. We have, for example, distinguished various ways in which a single observation can be fruitful; however, we have not tried to bring the different possibilities into a more general context from which they can be derived. As a matter of fact, one of the hopes for the present survey is that it will facilitate further work in this direction.[2] We have

also not dealt with the problem of evidence. Under what conditions in the social sciences an assertion is proved is a very difficult question, not restricted to qualitative research. It seemed best not to touch on this issue, in a context in which all emphasis was placed on providing a picture of a kind of work which is usually considered so "private" that it defies all systematic presentation.

I. ANALYSIS OF SINGLE OBSERVATIONS

When one examines qualitative reports, one of the first types of material which catches our attention is the "surprising observation." Like the nets of deep sea explorers, qualitative studies may pull up unexpected and striking things for us to gaze on. We find that there are people who believe that they are being educated by the unrelated and trivial information presented by quiz shows.[3] Interviews with people deprived of their newspaper by a strike disclose that some do not turn to alternative sources of news, but to reading anything which is lying around the house; a major function of newspaper reading seems to be simply to fill in "gaps" in the daily routine.[4] Observers of the underworld tell us that professional thieves constitute a rather exclusive social group, with exacting standards of membership strongly reminiscent of those of lawful professions.[5] Anthro-

---

[2]The general idea of codifying existing methods of social research is now being carried out by a special project on Advanced Training in Social Research at Columbia University. Formalizations of specific pieces of qualitative writing are an essential part of this project. Available in monograph form so far are a formalization by Ernest Nagel of procedures of functional analysis in social research, and a formalization by Paul F. Lazarsfeld of certain problems of process analysis, the interaction of social variables through time. The present survey can be considered as the typical first step which has to precede a more full-fledged formalization. It is one of the documents developed by the Columbia project.

[3]Paul F. Lazarsfeld, Radio and the Printed Page, New York, 1940, pp. 74 seq.

[4]Bernard Berelson, "What 'Missing the Newspaper' Means," in: Paul F. Lazarsfeld and Frank Stanton, eds., Communications Research 1948-1949, New York, 1949, pp. 122 seq.

[5]E. H. Sutherland, The Professional Thief, Chicago 1937.

pological data of course are full of surprising observations: that Eskimos lend their wives to guests without any jealousy, that Fiji Islanders kill their chiefs when they grow old, and so on.[6]

These phenomena are of various levels: some are individual beliefs and behaviors, some are a matter of group standards and structures within a society, some involve the norms of a whole culture. In each case the qualitative researcher has simply disclosed that such-and-such a phenomenon exists. And in one way or another, to be told that such things exist has a strong impact on the reader. They all have an element of surprise.

In the next few pages we will try to clarify what this impact is, and what research functions are served by these qualitative observations which simply state the existence of something surprising. We can distinguish at least two different uses for such observations. First, the existence of a phenomenon may raise problems—that is, compel us to look for explanations, to explore its consequences, to try to fit it into our scheme of knowledge. Second, we may find in the qualitative observations an indicator of some general variable which we want to study, but cannot measure directly.

Observations Which Raise Problems. Some observations are surprising because they conflict with our expectations, either common-sense or theoretically derived. Other observations surprise us by bringing to light phenomena which are simply new and unexplained, which challenge our curiosity. Yet another important type of problem-raising observations is that which brings together under a clear label a body of "familiar" experiences which had not previously been seen as a definite, generally occurring social phenomenon—which forms for the first time, so to speak, a "social object" to be studied.

In any of these cases the result is that a problem is raised. Our attention is focussed on a phenomenon, and we are stimulated to seek explanations and inquire into consequences. To make such a problematic observation is to initiate a research process which may lead to significant advancement of our understanding of social phenomena. (Some kind of observations no doubt raise more significant questions and lead to more valuable findings than others. It would be of great value to develop "screening principles" which can direct our attention to the more significant of the surprising observations; this cannot however be gone into here.[7])

To give concrete meaning to the notion of a problematic qualitative observation, and to provide material for its further development, a number of examples can be given.

As is well known, the original experiments of the Western Electric researchers led to highly surprising quantitative results: the experimental changes in physical conditions of work in no way accounted for the changes in production in the experimental group or workers. At this point the researchers decided to go back to the very first stage of the research process, and simply gather observations about what goes on in a normal working group in a factory. This exploratory research turned up a number of surprising qualitative observations:[8]

Some work groups were characterized by "a lack of ambition and initiative and a complacent desire to let well enough alone";
The supervisory control which is set up by management to regulate and govern the workers exercises little authority...
They [the employees] firmly believe that they will not be satisfactorily remunerated for any additional work they produce over the bogey...

[6] A variety of anthropological examples is given in Margaret Mead, "Adolescence in Primitive and in Modern Society," in: Theodore M. Newcomb and Eugene L. Hartley, eds., Readings in Social Psychology, New York, 1947, pp. 6 seq.

[7] A discussion of this point is found in Robert K. Merton, Social Theory and Social Structure, Glencoe, Illinois, 1949; Chapter III, "The Bearing of Empirical Research on Sociological Theory."

[8] F. J. Roethlisberger and William J. Dickson, Management and the Worker, Cambridge, Mass., 1946, Chapter XVII.

All of these facts were in conflict with what the management and the researchers had expected. By following them up the researchers were led to their now well-known discovery of the importance of informal groups in formal organizations, and of the barriers to communication which exist between levels within organizations.

Communications research offers many examples of surprising qualitative observations. We have already mentioned the discovery of unexpected motives— for listening to quiz programs and for reading newspapers. Unexpected responses to communications are another important example. A broadcast warning the public to patronize X-ray operators and avoid "quacks" left some listeners afraid of any X-ray treatments, and others doubting whether there could be any X-ray machines in the hands of incompetent operators.[9] A film designed to impress Americans with the British war-effort left some more convinced than ever that America was bearing all the burden.[10] The discovery of such anomalous responses led to more detailed investigations of the communications process, which turned up some important general principles—for example, about the need to relate the message to the experience-world for the audience, which may be quite different from that of the communicator.

A study of how prejudiced people respond to cartoons ridiculing prejudice found an unexpected type of response.[11] Some people were neither shamed out of their prejudices nor insulted; they simply did not understand what the cartoons were driving at. When this response was investigated in detail, the "derailment

mechanism" of motivated misunderstanding was revealed (see below).

Listeners to Kate Smith's war-bond "marathon broadcast" placed remarkable emphasis on her "sincerity."[12] Considering that other professional entertainers drew no such response, and that the respondents were generally suspicious of advertising and propaganda manipulation, this seemed worth investigating. Further study suggested the importance of "the propaganda of the deed" in a propaganda-wary society—in this case, Kate Smith's presumed strain and sacrifice in making the 18-hour broadcast.

The examples so far have involved unexpected phenomena which stimulated a search for causal explanations. In other instances the problem which is raised is in the other direction—an investigation of the consequences of a certain phenomenon is stimulated. Thus one researcher interested in problems of the profession noted an "obvious" fact as raising a problem: while all professionals meet a certain proportion of failures, the trial lawyers as a group necessarily lose half their cases.[13] What must be the consequences of such a high rate of failure for these professionals, and how do they deal with it? The answers to these problems might throw light on some important problems of the professional role. The ability to take a commonplace fact and see it as raising problems is important because it can lead ultimately to such enlightenment.

Another such observation was made by Merton in his study of the Kate Smith war-bond marathon. In the content of the broadcast there was no reference to the real economic purpose of war bond buying as an anti-inflation measure. Merton saw this fact as raising problems of consequences: an opportunity to educate a large and attentive audience in economic realities had been neglected, and reliance had been placed instead upon "large delusive statements" playing upon the anxi-

[9]Paul F. Lazarsfeld and Patricia L. Kendall, "The Listener Talks Back," in Radio and Health Education, New York, 1945.

[10]Robert K. Merton and Patricia L. Kendall, "The Boomerang Response," in: Channels, Vol. XXI, No. 7 (June 1944).

[11]Patricia L. Kendall and Katherine M. Wolfe, "The Analysis of Deviant Cases in Communications Research," in: Lazarsfeld and Stanton, op. cit., pp. 158 seq. Also E. Cooper and M. Jahoda, "The Evasion of Propaganda," Journal of Psychology, Vol. XXIII, 1947, pp. 15 seq.

[12]Robert K. Merton, Mass Persuasion, New York, 1946, pp. 82 seq.

[13]Wagner Thielens, research in progress, Columbia University, Department of Sociology.

eties of those with loved ones overseas. What were "the further, more remote but not necessarily less significant effects of these techniques upon the individual personality and the society?" "Does the unelaborated appeal to sentiment which displaces the information pertinent to assessing this sentiment blunt the critical capacities of the listeners?"[14]

An example of the forming of commonplace experiences into a clearly labelled social phenomenon, and thereby creating a new object for investigation, is Adler's formulation of the concept of the inferiority complex.[15] Everyone at one time or another has experienced feelings of being inadequate, unworthy, etc., but until these private sensations had been pointed out and labelled, they could not be investigated by social science. Other examples which might be called to mind are Veblen's formulation of the concept of conspicuous consumption[16], or Sutherland's labelling of certain categories of business behavior as "white collar crime."[17] Without having actually discovered any new facts, simply by directing attention to familiar facts placed for the first time within a distinctive category, these investigators were able to raise important problems and initiate fruitful study.

The reader may have noticed that some of the examples of "surprising observations" cited are no surprise at all to him. This is as it should be. The point is that one time they were surprising, and initiated further investigation which has been sufficiently successful to render them familiar and understandable today. Another problem is that an observation may be surprising to the particular researchers, while other social scientists have known about it all along. Thus the Western Electric researchers made the "surprising discovery" that informal social

organization existed among workers. Other sociologists had long been aware of the problem of informal groups; however, the special preconceptions of American industrial sociology up to that time had kept it unaware of this whole realm of phenomena. In a still more extreme case, a finding may be new only to one particular researcher; in which case it might better be termed "self-education" than a scientific discovery.

Is there anything which a researcher can do toward making "surprising observations" other than to maintain an alert state of mind? It may seem contradictory to speak of giving instructions for making surprising observations. However, there are ways in which one can at least increase the probability of making such observations. Some of these are discussed by Jahoda, Deutsch, and Cook under the heading, "The Analysis of 'Insight-Stimulating Cases'."[18] Strangers or newcomers to a community or a country, it is suggested, may be able to pick out problematic facts which are simply taken for granted by those accustomed to the locale. Marginal individuals, or cases in transition from one stage or status to another, may present much more clearly certain problematic features of a personality-type of social system. Deviants, extreme cases, or "pure, ideal-typical" cases may have a relatively high efficiency in indicating problematic facts.

Observations Which Serve As Indicators. The first type of surprising observations discussed was those which were anomalous and unexplained, which served the function of stimulating a search for explanations. Another type of qualitative observations is challenging because we see in them indications of some large-scale phenomenon which we cannot perceive directly. Thus the occurrence of riots and protest meetings in the North during the Civil War serves as an indication that opposition to Lincoln's war policy existed; bits of shell or pottery

---

[14] Merton, Mass Persuasion, pp. 188 seq.

[15] Alfred Adler, The Neurotic Constitution, New York 1926.

[16] Thorstein Veblen, The Theory of the Leisure Class, Modern Library, New York 1934.

[17] Edwin H. Sutherland, "White-Collar Criminality," in: American Sociological Review, Vol. V, February 1940, No. 1, pp. 1 seq.; White-Collar Crime, New York 1949.

[18] Marie Jahoda, Morton Deutsch and Stuart W. Cook, Research Methods in Social Relations, New York, 1951, pp. 42 seq.

found in graves mark the routes of trade and cultural contact in the prehistoric world; a peculiar military custom indicates the caste-like nature of army organization; modes of speech may indicate complex mental patterns or cultural emphases.

Three situations can be pointed out in which one pays particular attention to qualitative indicators. They are distinguished in terms of the kind of obstacle which prevents direct observation and measurement of the underlying variable:

(1) Situations in which qualitative evidence substitutes for otherwise simple statistical information relating to past ages or inaccessible countries.
(2) Situations in which qualitative evidence is used to get at psychological data which are repressed or not easily articulated— attitudes, motives, assumptions, frames of reference, etc.
(3) Situations in which simple qualitative observations are used as indicators of the functioning of complex social structures and organizations, which are difficult to subject to direct observation.

The underlying assumption in all these cases is that a phenomenon which cannot be directly observed will nevertheless leave traces which, properly interpreted, permit the phenomenon to be identified and studied. A great historical movement, a basic personality characteristic, an essential characteristic of organizational structure, should all leave their imprint on almost any documentary material, accounts by observers, or even physical refuse, which they leave behind.

Examples of the first class (qualitative substitutes for unavailable statistical or descriptive material) would include the use of newspaper stories or other contemporary records of public demonstrations as indications of public opinion in past times of crisis.[19] Frasier's use of advertisements for slaves in ante-bellum Southern newspapers to find out about the

structure of the slave family,[20] the use of reports of refugees, Soviet press materials, and the contents of Soviet literature to provide information about life in the Soviet Union[21]; the use of archeological remains to indicate culture contacts or religious beliefs in prehistoric times.

Examples of the second class (qualitative indicators of psychological variables) include formal projective testing, the psychological analysis of personal documents or artistic works, the analysis of items of literature or entertainment as presumed projections of the traits of their audience,[22] and of course, the analysis of qualitative interviews or records of participant observation. A good example of the use of indicators for a psychological concept is found in the study of anti-prejudice cartoons mentioned earlier:

In tracing the process through which these 68 respondents arrive at their misunderstanding, we find our starting point in the fact that most of them identified with Mr. Bigott. (Footnote:) By "identification" we mean the mental process through which a subject assumes the role of another person to such an extent that actions, either verbal or behavioral, directed toward the object of identification are experienced as directed toward the identifying person. Evidence of identification with Mr. Bigott was manifested by the subject's acting in one or more of the following ways: (a) explicitly affirming identification, saying, for example, "I guess I'm a Mr. Bigott"; (b) consistently and openly sympathizing with Mr. Bigott, expressing sorrow, for example, that Mr. Bigott looked so weak and sick in the "transfusion" cartoon (c) interpreting a threat to or criticism of Mr.

[19]For a number of examples, see Paul F. Lazarsfeld, "The Obligations of the 1950 Pollster to the 1984 Historian," in: Public Opinion Quarterly, Vol. 14, No. 4 (Winter 1950–51).

[20]E. F. Frasier, The Negro Family in the United States, Chicago 1939, pp. 55 seq. This and other examples are discussed in: Robert Bower, Training Guide on the Qualitative Use of Documentary Material, New York, Bureau of Applied Social Research, 1950; mimeographed.

[21]For example: Barrington Moore, Jr., Soviet Politics: The Dilemma of Power, Cambridge, Mass., 1950; Alexander Gerschenkron, "A Neglected Source of Economic Information on Soviet Russia," in: American Slavic and East European Review, Vol. IX (February 1950).

[22]For one example: Donald V. McGranahan and Ivor Wayne, "German and American Traits Reflected in Popular Drama," in: Human Relations, Vol. I, No. 4 (August 1948), pp. 429 seq.

Bigott as referring to himself, as, for example, becoming emotionally upset by the cobweb on Mr. Bigott's head.[23]

A single conversation reported by the authors of Deep South bears witness to the depth of feeling involved in white attitudes toward Negroes in this deeply prejudiced area: A social worker described a poor-white family in which two girls

"are having babies and are not married... That isn't the end by any means. Somebody told me that this older girl was sleeping with the father..." After the recitation of the case, when the social worker was out of the room, a woman whispered to the interviewer: "Mrs. Wilson says those girls have Negro men too, but Miss Trent [the supervisor] won't let me say anything about that ... Isn't that awful?" It is significant to note from this interview that the incest situation was viewed with less horror than the infraction of the caste sex taboos.[24]

On the basis of his long participant observation, William Whyte was able to report the following striking indicator of the complete acceptance of gambling in Cornerville:

When a mother sends her small child down to the corner for a bottle of milk, she tells her to put the change on a number.[25]

Investigators studying the effects of unemployment on the psychology of the people of an Austrian village had the school children write essays on the theme, "My Future Occupation." The pervasiveness of the insecurity of the children of the unemployed, its corrosive effect on planning for the future, was indicated among other ways by the very language used. Children of employed workers would write, "I will be..." or "I want to become..." Children of the unemployed tended to use phrases like "I might become" or "I would like to be..." In the same study a small boy remarked to one of the investigators that he would like to be an Indian chief. "But

I am afraid it will be hard to get the job."[26]

The third situation—the use of simple qualitative indicators to show the attributes of complex social structures—is very clearly exemplified in Blumenthal's study of a small mining community. The speed and inclusiveness of interpersonal communication in the community was indicated

by the fact that should a death occur at nine o'clock in the morning and the information not reach a resident until late in the afternoon, his usual expression is, "I can't understand why I didn't hear that sooner," and others say to him, "Where have you been? Everybody knew that by noon."[27]

At another point Blumenthal notes the existence of conflicting qualitative indicators of the social contact between Mineville and its nearest neighbor, and concludes that one has the greater weight:

During the heyday of Crystal her people and those of Mineville were not so well acquainted as might be supposed... Hotly contested baseball games and the communities having celebrated together on the main day of festivities for each—Miner's Union Day—were not indications of far-reaching personal relations. This is shown by the measure of social distance evidenced by the fact that a young man whose reputation was such in one town that its "respectable" girls refused to associate with him could go to the other and fraternize with its "best" young woman.[28]

The existence of primary group relations within smaller units of the American army can be inferred from the following qualitative indications drawn from an interview:

We bunked together, slept together, fought together, told each other where our money was pinned in our shirts... If one man gets a letter from home the whole company reads it.[29]

---

[23]Kendall and Wolfe, op. cit., p. 163.

[24] Allison Davis, Buleigh B. Gardner and Mary R. Gardner, Deep South, Chicago, 1943, p. 116.

[25] William F. Whyte, Street Corner Society, Chicago, 1943, p. 116.

[26]M. Jahoda and H. Zeisel, Die Arbeitslosen von Marienthal, Leipzig 1932, quoted in: Jahoda, Deutsch and Cook, op. cit., pp. 298 seq.

[27]Albert Blumenthal, Small Town Stuff, Chicago, 1932, pp. 136 seq.

[28]Ibid., p. 30.

[29]Samuel Stouffer et al., The American Soldier, Princeton, 1949, Vol. II, p. 99.

The authors of The American Soldier, wanting an indicator for the complex notion of the "Army caste system," pointed to an institutionalized symbolic act:

Enlisted men selected for officer candidate school were first discharged from the Army and then readmitted in their new and very different status.

Just as it is impossible to move from one caste to another in an ethnic caste situation, so an enlisted man about to become an officer must leave the Army system before reentering in his new status. The continuation of this custom is a certain indication of the continuation of the attitudes of a "caste system" in the Army.[30]

In discussing the family structure found in Middletown's various classes, the Lynds suggest a possible indicator of the position of the husband in the family:

It may not be wholly fantastic to surmise that there may be some significance for the understanding of local marital association in the hierarchy of terms by which local women speak of their husbands. There is a definite ascent of man in his conjugal relations as one goes up in the social scale, from "my old man" through "the man," "he" (most frequent), "the mister," "John," "my husband," to "Mr. Jones." The first four are the common terms among the working class families, and the last two among business class families.[31]

The indicators which have been referred to are of many different forms. Some are linguistic, some are symbolic acts, some are documentary, some are physical objects. As substantive knowledge of linguistics, social organization and technology are applied to the problem, one may expect ever more sensitive and reliable interpretations of such qualitative indicators. To what extent interpretation of indicators will have to remain an art, and to what extent it can be made a science, is one of the important problems of qualitative research which we cannot attempt to discuss here.

[30]Ibid., Vol. I, p. 56, fn. 2. This example and others are discussed by Patricia L. Kendall and Paul F. Lazarsfeld, "Problems of Survey Analysis," in: Merton and Lazarsfeld, op. cit., pp. 183 seq.

[31]Robert S. and Helen Merrell Lynd, Middletown, New York 1929, p. 118, fn. 2.

II. CONSTRUCTION OF DESCRIPTIVE SYSTEMS

The previous section discussed what can be done with a single "point" of qualitative data; the present section considers what one does when confronted by a whole array of qualitative observations. As a first step toward understanding a field of human activity, one must organize the raw observations into a descriptive system. In some cases one has only to apply categories already set up by previous investigators or by the society itself, and proceed with the further stages of analysis. In other cases previously existing categories are clarified and revised by the attempt to apply them to a concrete body of data. And in some cases the researcher must create his own classification system for the material under study. It is this latter case which will be particularly considered here.

In terms of their formal structure, the descriptive systems created by investigators can range from crude lists of "types," each defined individually without clear logical relationship to the others, to fully systematic typologies in which each type is a logical compound of a small number of basic attributes. Between these end points are all intermediate degrees of "partial" systematization, including some sets of types which include in their definition virtually all the logical elements necessary to set up a multi-dimensional "attribute space," but in which the logical analysis has not been explicitly made. Descriptive systems may also vary in terms of their degree of concreteness or generality. A fully systematic typology may be based on dimensions of a highly limited, concrete nature, while a preliminary classification can be broad and general.

Preliminary Classifications. A classification which falls toward the unsystematized end of the continuum can be called a preliminary one, since it represents an essential first step toward the ideal of a fully systematic one. The importance of this first step from completely unordered data to a preliminary classification must never be underestimated. Until the data are ordered in some way, the analysis of relationships cannot begin; more refined categories normally develop out of the attempt to analyze relationships between preliminary categories; there is an interacting process between refinement of classification and the analysis of relationships.

A good preliminary classification must provide a workable summary of the wealth of elements in the original data, and include—even if in unsystematic form—the basic elements necessary for understanding the situation. A bad preliminary classification is one which is poor in elements and suggestiveness, which omits so many important aspects of the situation that analysis reaches a dead end, and one must go back to the original data for a new start. So long as the essential elements are suggested somewhere in the initial classification; they can be picked and recombined more logically as the analysis proceeds. The question of what it takes to make fruitful preliminary categories—whether the process can be systematized and taught, or whether it is wholly an individual art —is one of those which most needs exploring. The present discussion can only raise this question, and present a number of examples of the process.

Good examples of the use of this form of qualitative analysis—the formation of relatively unsystematized but fruitful classifications of people and situations —can be found in the work of the Chicago urban sociologists. Such an instance is Louis Wirth's suggestive notes on "Some Jewish Types of Personality." Wirth defines his purpose in using this technique as follows:

> The sociologist, in transforming the unique or individual experience into a representative or typical one, arrives at the social type, which consists of a set of attitudes on the part of the person toward himself and the group and a corresponding set of attitudes of the group toward him ... The range of personality types in a given social group is indicative of the culture of that group.[32]

Wirth's gallery of "characteristic and picturesque personalities that are met with in the average community" includes:

> the Mensch, a person of superior economic status who has "achieved his success without sacrificing his identity as a Jew";
> the allrightnick, who "in his opportunism, has thrown overboard most of the cultural baggage of his group";
> the Schlemihl, who belies the stereotype of the Jew as "the personification of the commercial spirit" by being "quite shiftless and helpless, failing miserably in everything he undertakes";
> the Luftmensch, who moves easily from one unsuccessful project to another, and whose "only apparent means of subsistence is the air he breathes";
> the Yeshiva Bochar, literally the talmudical student, the young man whose learning gives prestige irrespective of wealth or origin;
> the Zaddik, the "pious, patriarchal person ... whose exemplary conduct is pointed to as an example" and so on.[33]

The purpose of presenting these types, drawn largely from the folklore and literature of the subject group, lies in the fact that

> they are as complete an index as any at present obtainable of the culture traits ... and the culture pattern of the group ... Together they constitute the personal nuclei around which the fabric of the culture of the group is woven. A detailed analysis of the crucial personality types in any given area or cultural group shows that they depend upon a set of habits and attitudes in the group for their existence and are the direct expressions of the values of the group.[34]

Starting from these types, therefore, one can derive a classification of the values, habits and attitudes which are important to the explanation of the behavior of the group.

In much the same way, from folklore and literature as well as personal observation, C. Wright Mills draws a gallery of "white-collar types." There are types of managers:

> the "glum men" on the top of the white-collar pyramid, harrassed, cautious, careful to stay in line with the aims of the employers or other higher ups;

---

[32]Louis Wirth, "Some Jewish Types of Personality," in: Ernest W. Burgess, The Urban Community, Chicago, 1926, p. 106.

[33]Ibid., paraphrased, pp. 108 seq.
[34]Ibid.

the "old veterans" just below the top, who seek security in closely following explicit instructions, and strive for deference from those below;

the "live wire," the younger man on his way up;

the "new entrepreneur," who prospers as a fixer and go-between in a world of huge and complicated organizations, mass manipulation, and general insecurity.[35]

There are types of intellectuals,[36] of academic men,[37] and—all the way down at the bottom of the white-collar pyramid—of salesgirls: "the wolf," "the charmer," "the ingenue," "the social pretender," and so on.[38]

There is a serious purpose in pinpointing these picturesque types:

By examining white-collar life, it is possible to learn something about what is becoming more typically "American" than the frontier character probably ever was. What must be grasped is the picture of society as a great salesroom, an enormous file, an incorporated brain, a new universe of management and manipulation. By understanding these diverse white-collar worlds, one can also understand better the shape and meaning of modern society as a whole, as well as the simple hopes and complex anxieties that grip all the people who are sweating it out in the middle of the twentieth century.[39]

The general run of preliminary categories will not be as colorful and rich in suggestions as these just quoted, but they will be of the same formal nature: a simple list of discrete "types." Thus we will have lists of "types" of comic-book readers,[40] types of client-professional relations, types of appeals in a certain propaganda broadcast,[41] types of communities, etc., representing a preliminary ordering of material into a simple list of headings. As the analysis progresses, either within the original study or in the

work of replication or secondary analysis, these simple lists may be developed into more systematic and more general descriptive systems.

Somewhat further along the road to generality and systemization are the kinds of "types" found in the great deal of the speculative and theoretical literature. Typical examples here are Spranger's six "value types"—the theoretical, economic, aesthetic, social, political, and religious[42]—or von Wiese's four types of religious organizations—the ecclesia, the denomination, the sect and the cult.[43] Merton, in discussing the forms of interpersonal influence, lists the following types: coercion, domination, manipulation, clarification, provision of prototypes for imitation, advice, and exchange.[44] Kingsley Davis classifies social norms in traditional categories: folkways, mores, law, custom, morality, religion, convention, and fashion.[45] Lasswell sets up eight basic categories of values which he uses to classify institutions and leaders;[46] Malinowski sets up seven "basic needs" in terms of which cultural phenomena can be classified and so on.[47]

All of the above mentioned sets of categories are of far greater generality than those which arise in the analysis of a single empirical study of limited scope. They are the result of attempts at general analysis of a wide range of situations. On the other hand, in their formal aspect, they are similar to the other forms of preliminary categories discussed earlier. Some of them are quite

---

[35]C. Wright Mills, White Collar, New York, 1951, pp. 92 seq.

[36]Ibid., pp. 144 seq.

[37]Ibid., pp. 131 seq.

[38]Ibid., pp. 174 seq.

[39]Ibid., Introduction, p. xv.

[40]Katherine M. Wolfe and Marjorie Fiske, "The Children Talk About Comics," in: Lazarsfeld and Stanton, op. cit.

[41]For examples: Merton, Mass Persuasion, pp. 50 seq.

[42]Eduard Spranger, Types of Men, Halle 1928; for an attempt to develop measuring instruments for Spranger's concepts, see P. E. Vernon and G. W. Allport, "A Test for Personal Values," in: Journal of Abnormal and Social Psychology, Vol. 26 (1931),

[43]Leopold von Wiese and Howard Becker, Systematic Sociology, New York, 1932, pp. 214 seq.

[44]Robert K. Merton, "Patterns of Influence," in: Lazarsfeld and Stanton, op. cit., p. 218.

[45]Kingsley Davis, Human Society, New York, 1950, Ch. III.

[46]Harold D. Lasswell and Abraham Kaplan, Power and Society, New Haven, 1950, pp. 55 seq.

[47]Bronislaw Malinowski, "The Group and the Individual in Functional Analysis," in: American Journal of Sociology, Vol. XLIV, No. 6 (May 1939), pp. 938 seq.

unsystematized; others include in their definition most of the elements required to set up a logical structure of basic attributes from which they could be derived, but this has not been explicitly done.

A special kind of descriptive system which might be mentioned under this heading consists of ordered categories, which are set up as developmental stages or degrees along a continuum. Thus Piaget distinguished the stages of development of children's attitudes toward the rules of conduct, from "moral realism" in which the letter of the rule is absolute to "autonomous rationality" in which blind acceptance "withdraws in favor of the idea of justice and of mutual service." [48] Scheler sets up seven categories of knowledge which he orders along the dimension of increasing "artificiality"; (1) myth and legend; (2) knowledge implicit in the natural folk-language; (3) religious knowledge; (4) the basic types of mystical knowledge; (5) philosophical-metaphysical sciences; (7) technological knowledge. [49] In such sets of categories an ordering along one dimension is explicitly stated, while the other attributes characterizing the categories are simply listed or suggested without any systemization.

Systematic Typologies. The most highly developed form of descriptive system which can arise in a qualitative analysis is one in which each type is explicitly derived from the logical combination of basic attributes or dimensions. A simple example is the logical scheme set up by

Riesman in his study of political participation. [50] By examining a set of concrete "type cases" Riesman was led to break the concept of participation into two basic elements; emotional involvement and competence, or more simply, "caring" and "knowing." Taking each of these elements as a simple dichotomy, Riesman obtained four types of relations to politics:

		Competence	
		+	−
Affect	+	"involved"	"indignants"
	−	"inside-dopesters"	"indifferent"

Merton employs this technique in his typology of prejudice and discrimination. He starts from the usual formulation of two types of people: people who live up to the American creed of non-discrimination, and people who violate it. Merton suggests a further elaboration: that people be distinguished on one hand by whether they personally believe in the creed or not, and, on the other hand, by whether they practice discrimination or not.

...This is the salient consideration: conduct may or may not conform with individuals' own beliefs concerning the moral claims of all men to equal opportunity. Stated in formal sociological terms, this asserts that attitudes and overt behavior vary independently. Prejudicial attitudes need not coincide with discriminatory behavior. The implications of this statement can be drawn out in terms of, a logical syntax whereby the variables are diversely combined, as can be seen in the following typology. [51]

A Typology of Ethnic Prejudice and Discrimination

	ATTITUDE DIMENSION	
BEHAVIOR DIMENSION	Non-prejudiced	Prejudiced
Non-discrimination	Type I: "The All-Weather Liberal"	Type III: "The Fair-Weather Illiberal"
Discrimination	Type II: "The Fair-Weather Liberal"	Type IV: "The All-Weather Illiberal"

[48] Jean Piaget, The Moral Judgment of the Child, New York, 1932.

[49] Max Scheler, Die Wissenformen und die Gesellschaft, Leipzig, 1926, p. 62. The list given here is adapted from Merton's discussion of Scheler, in: Social Theory and Social Structure, pp. 230 seq.

[50] David Riesman and Nathan Glazer, "Criteria for Political Apathy," in: Alvin W. Gouldner, ed., Studies in Leadership, New York, 1950, pp. 535 seq.

[51] Robert K. Merton, "Discrimination and the American Creed," in: R. M. MacIver, ed., Discrim-

A mere list of the "folk-labels" of each type would appear superficially like one of the preliminary lists of categories; they are fundamentally different, however, since they are systematically derived from the cross-tabulation of two basic dimensions.

The most elaborate use of systematic typologies is found in Talcott Parsons' recent works.[52] Parsons sets forward five dichotomous attributes:

1. Affectivity—Affective neutrality;
2. Self-orientation—Collectivity orientation;
3. Universalism—Particularism;
4. Ascription—Achievement;
5. Specificity—Diffuseness.

By combining these five "pattern variables" Parsons has been able to construct general categories for describing social relations, cultural systems, and personality systems.

The process of constructing systematic typologies need only be briefly summarized here. The starting point is often a good preliminary set of categories. By examining them one derives a small number of attributes which seem to provide the basis for the distinctions made, and sets these attributes up as a multidimensional system (an "attribute-space"). This operation has been termed the "substruction" of an attribute space to a typology. One can then examine all of the logically possible combinations of the basic attributes. This serves to locate the original set of categories within the system; it often shows that some combinations have been ignored (appear as blank cells), while in other bases distinctions have been missed (the original category will overlap several cells). Of course not all of the logically possible combinations may be important or even empirically possible; it will often be necessary to restrict the combinations to be studied, or to recombine several cate-

gories to simplify the analysis. Such a recombination has been termed a "reduction," and is closely related to the operation of index formation.[53]

Partial Substructions. There remains to be mentioned a type of operation which is very frequent in qualitative analyses: the partial systematization of a concept or a set of categories. A good introduction to this operation is the well-known discussion by Simmel of envy and jealousy.[54] The situations in which these feelings arise are quite complex, and Simmel does not give an exhaustive account of them. What he does, however, is to indicate one important aspect in which the two attitudes differ: in the case of jealousy the person feels that he has a claim on the object of his desire, while in the case of envy he has no claim, only desire for the object. Simmel has thus partially substructed the attribute-space by which envy and jealously could be systematically defined; he has not done so completely, but rather only enough to make one major distinction.

A more elaborate but still partial substruction is presented in Werner Landecker's discussion of "Types of Integration and Their Measurement." Landecker begins by indicating his discontent with the undifferentiated concept of "social integration." To study the relation of integration to other variables, to find its necessary conditions and its consequences, the broad abstraction must be broken down:

Early in the exploration of a type of phenomena it seems advisable to break it up into as many subtypes as one can distinguish and to use each subdivision as a variable for research. This appears to be a more fruitful procedure than to attempt immediately to generalize about the generic type as a whole. The main advantage of subclassification in an initial phase of research is that it leads to problems of relationship among subtypes

---

ination and National Welfare, New York, 1949.— Table is adapted from Merton's, p. 103. See also Merton's Appendix to that paper: "A Note on the Use of Paradigms in Qualitative Analysis."

[52] Talcott Parsons and Edward A. Shils, Toward a General Theory of Action, Cambridge, Mass., 1951, Part 2.

[53] A more detailed discussion will be found in Paul F. Lazarsfeld and Allen H. Barton, "Qualitative Measurement in the Social Sciences," in: Daniel Lerner and Harold D. Lasswell, eds., The Policy Sciences, Stanford, California, 1951, pp. 169 seq.

[54] Georg Simmel, "The Sociology of Conflict," in: American Journal of Sociology, Vol. IX, No. 4 (January 1904), pp. 521 seq.

which would evade the attention of the investigator if he were to deal with the broader type from the very beginning. Generalizations on the higher level of abstraction will suggest themselves as a matter of course once regularities common to several subtypes are discovered.[55]

In analyzing the concept of social integration, Landecker first breaks down society into two types of elements: cultural standards, on the one hand, and persons and their behavior, on the other. The logical interrelations among these two elements give him three types of integration:

"Cultural integration": integration within the realm of cultural standards;
"Normative integration": integration between cultural standards and the behavior of persons;
"Integration among persons": integration within the realm of behavior.

This last type in turn is broken down in terms of two types of human behavior: the interchange of ideas and the interchange of services. Integration within the realm of communication is termed "communicative integration"; integration within the realm of services is termed "functional integration."

Since "integration" is a relational concept, Landecker's types can be easily represented by a relational matrix—a table, along each side of which we list the elements involved in interrelationships. The interior cells of the table then indicate the logically possible connections, including, in the main diagonal, the internal relationship within each element:

This relational scheme allows us to locate all of the types of integration proposed by Landecker. It also raises the question of further relationships not discussed and distinctions not made: e. g. the possible subdivision of "normative integration" in terms of the two spheres of behavior, the relationship between the two forms of behavior themselves, and indeed the possibility of distinguishing still other major spheres within the realm of behavior, for example the sphere of government, religion, or family life. For this reason we refer to Landecker's scheme as a "partial" substruction, one which is not fully worked through in all its logical possibilities.

An even more elaborate relational scheme is implicit in a discussion of "craftsmanship" by C. Wright Mills:

Craftsmanship as a fully idealized model or work gratification involves six major features: [1] There is no ulterior motive in work other than the product being made and the processes of its creation. [2] The details of daily work are meaningful because they are not detached in the worker's mind from the product of the work. [3] The worker is free to control his own working action. [4] The craftsman is thus able to learn from his work; and to use and develop his capacity and skills in its prosecution. [5] There is no split of work and play, or work and culture. [6] The craftsman's way of livelihood determines and infuses his entire mode of living.[56]

In effect, Mills proposes six attributes by which a job situation can be described. If all six of these attributes have the values indicated above, we have the ideal-

| | Cultural Standards | Persons and Their Behavior: | |
		Communication	Work
Cultural Standards	1. Cultural integration	2. Normative integration	
Communication		3. Communicative integration	5. ?
Work			4. Functional integration

[55]Werner S. Landecker, "Types of Integration and Their Measurement," in: American Journal of Sociology, Vol. LVI, No. 4 (January 1951), p. 332.

[56]Mills, op. cit., p. 220.

type situation of "craftsmanship." The situation of the modern industrial or office worker, Mills implies, is the opposite of the idealized craftsman in all these respects. Actually the six attributes give 64 logically possible combinations of values; the intermediate, mixed combinations however do not enter into Mills' present discussion, which deals only with the ideal-type cases and not with the whole attribute-space.

In this case each of the six attributes actually refers to a relationship—between a worker's capacities and his work, between work and leisure, etc. They can be derived from a relational matrix consisting of four elements: the worker (his capacities, his character); the work activity; the final product; and the worker's leisure activities (his "play," "culture," "general mode of living"). Each of these can act on any of the others, as summarized in the relational scheme below:

not originally considered. They are not, however, a substitute for careful study and sensitive thinking about a problem. There are any number of possible relationships or attributes which might be picked out and put into a formal scheme; the strategic act is to "feel out" those which are important, which will ultimately help to solve the problems in which we are interested. Formal analysis can then be used to clarify, develop, and communicate the results of qualitative insights.

III. QUALITATIVE DATA SUGGESTING RELATIONSHIPS

The only fully adequate way to test the existence of a relationship between two variables is through statistical analysis; to test cause-and-effect relations requires either a controlled experiment, or a rather large number of cases of "natural change" observed over time. But research which has neither statistical

	Worker	Work Activity	Final Product	Leisure
Acting on: Worker	—	(1) Gratifies (4) Develops	(1) Gratifies	
Work Activity	(3) Freely controls	—		(5, 6) Contributes to
Final Product		(2) Visibly related to	—	
Leisure		(5, 6) Contributes to		—

This scheme might suggest additional dimensions of the man-job relationship to be taken into account, to make for a more systematic classification of work situations. Still more elements might also be added—for instance, the "external rewards" which are not supposed to dominate the craftsman's approach to his work but which are obviously primary for many kinds of jobs.

Formal devices such as attribute-space and relational matrices can often help to clarify concepts which are not systematically presented; sometimes they can even suggest significant possibilities

weight nor experimental design, research based only on qualitative descriptions of a small number of cases, can nonetheless play the important role of suggesting possible relationship, causes, effects, and even dynamic processes. Indeed, it can be argued that only research which provides a wealth of miscellaneous, unplanned impressions and observations can play this role. Those who try to get suggestions for possible explanatory factors for statistical results solely from looking at tabulations of the few variables which were deliberately included in the study in advance often can make no progress; sometimes even a single written-in comment by a respondent will provide a clue to additional factors.

Finding "Factors" Influencing Action. A classic case of the use of qualitative observation to disclose possible factors influencing behavior is the Western Electric study.[57] When the experimental group of workers maintained their high production even when physical conditions were made worse than before the experiment began, it was clear that something else was affecting their production. What the real factors were was first suggested by informal conversations with and observations of the experimental group, and from then on the main research effort was focussed on qualitative interviewing and observation to discover social factors and processes.

A more recent study, the main focus of which was to uncover possible factors rather than strictly to test them, is Merton's Mass Persuasion.[58] Here some 75 people were selected who were known to have bought bonds through a Kate Smith warbond "marathon" broadcast, and interviewed in such a way as to reconstruct their experience during the broadcast as spontaneously as possible. Among the factors which stood out as possibly influential were the fact that "the all-day series of appeals emerged as a dramatic event . . . a single unified pattern"; "There was reciprocal interplay, for the audience was not only responding to Smith, but she was also responding to her audience and modifying her subsequent comments as a result"; "there was considerable qualificative evidence that belief in Smith's disinterestedness and altruism played an integral role in the process of persuasion"; "the audience's images of Smith, the class structure of our society, the cultural standards of distinct strata of the population, and socially induced expectations, feelings, tensions were all intricately involved in the patterns of response to the bond drive"; "but the cumulation of affect and emotion was not the major function of the marathon broadcasts. Above all, the presumed stress and strain of the eighteen-hour series of broadcasts served to validate Smith's sincerity . . . for an understanding of the process of persuasion, the most significant feature of these responses to the marathon is the effectiveness of this propaganda of the deed among the very people who were distrustful and skeptical of mere exhortation."

A study applying the same technique to a broader historical situation was that of Elizabeth Zerner on the factors in recent history which influenced attitudes toward Jews in France.[59] By a very small number of detailed interviews with people who were presumed to be good observers (about half concierges of apartment houses, the other half intellectuals), it was suggested that there were four main events influencing attitudes toward Jews in one manner or another: the persecutions outside France, which made people more aware of the Jews as a special group; the appearance of Jewish refugees from other countries, who were a clearly visible, different group in French society; the persecution of the French Jews during the occupation, which aroused certain feelings of guilt and a certain real danger for those who helped the Jews; the restoration of Jewish jobs and property after the Liberation, which obviously caused loss and disturbance to some non-Jews.

One special technique for discovering additional factors relevant to a given type of behavior is the examination of cases which deviate from the behavior expected in terms of known factors. Thus a purely economic-interest explanation of voting leaves poor Republicans and rich Democrats as "deviants"; by qualitative interviewing one may be able to get some idea of the factors other than economic interest which motivate voting. In the "Mr. Bigott" study of the response of prejudiced people to anti-prejudice cartoons,

---

[57]Roethlisberger and Dickson, op. cit.
[58]Merton, op. cit.

[59]Elizabeth Zerner (with Robert T. Bower), "German Occupation and Anti-Semitism in France," Public Opinion Quarterly, Vol. 11, No. 2 (Summer 1948), pp. 258 seq.

it was expected that the prejudiced would misunderstand the message of the cartoons—as indeed almost 2/3 did. But there remained deviant cases who understood the "hostile" meaning. To explain these cases, qualitative interviews were used. It appeared that such factors were involved as the degree of security in one's attitudes, the feeling that one's beliefs were socially caused and not a personal responsibility, the fact that the subject totally disidentified himself from the caricatured figure of "Mr. Bigott" and therefore was under no threat.[60]

Qualitative Suggestions of Process. The simplest form of a "process" analysis is that which looks for an intervening variable which "explains" the correlation between two other variables. In his study of an East-coast slum neighborhood, William Whyte arrived (on a qualitative basis) at the following relationship: the socially aspiring "college boys" clubs seemed to be more unstable and subject to internal conflict than those of the non-mobile "corner-boys." To explain this relationship (which could be considered quite "upside-down" from a middle-class viewpoint) Whyte introduced a third variable, "informal organization." The corner boy clubs could draw for cohesion on already existing informal organization:

The daily activities of the corner boys determined the relative positions of members and allocated responsibilities and obligations within the group.

Among the college boys on the other hand,

Outside club meetings the members seldom associated together except in pairs. Since there was no informal organization to bind the men together, there was also no common understanding upon matters of authority, responsibility, and obligation.[61]

To be able to assert this explanation with any certainty, it would be necessary for Whyte to have observed corner-boy clubs which were weak in informal organization and college-boy groups which

were strong in it; if the former were also unstable, while the latter were stable, it would constitute a certain test of the hypothesis. Whyte does not record whether he sought out such "test situations" or was familiar with a range of such cases.

In the same way the relation between membership in a corner gang and failure to rise economically was explained in terms of the impact of group relations on saving and spending habits. Whyte denies that preexisting differences in intelligence and ability explain the whole relation (again on the basis of qualitative observations which presumably held ability constant for a number of cases in each group). Whyte goes on to suggest:

The pattern of social mobility in Cornerville can best be understood when it is contrasted with the pattern of corner-boy activity. One of the most important divergences arises in matters involving the expenditure of money. The college boys fit in with an economy of savings and investment. The corner boys fit in with a spending economy. The college boy must save his money in order to finance his education and launch his business or professional career. He therefore cultivates the middle-class virtue of thrift. In order to participate in group activities, the corner boy must share his money with others. If he has money and his friend does not, he is expected to do the spending for both of them...Prestige and influence depend in part upon free spending.[62]

This observation indicates some of the factors in the process of social mobility. Of course behind each such factor uncovered are other factors—the variables which for instance determine who sticks with the boys and spends, and who breaks away, saves money, and rises.

The uncovering of possible processes can go much further than inserting a third variable in a chain. The study of anti-prejudice cartoons mentioned previously suggested a whole chain which led up to misunderstanding among the non-deviant two thirds of the prejudiced people who misunderstood:

---

[60]Kendall and Wolfe, op. cit., pp. 166 seq.
[61]Whyte, op. cit., pp. 96 seq.

[62]Ibid., p. 106.

1. Identification with Mr. Bigott and momentary understanding;
2. Desire for escape from identification;
3. Disidentification mechanism (caricaturing Mr. Bigott, making him intellectually or socially inferior);
4. Derailment of understanding: absorbtion in the derogatory characteristics of Mr. Bigott to the exclusion of understanding the point of the cartoons.[63]

In the Whyte study one finds the process of the rise of a local corner boy to political leadership traced out through a series of steps, with interacting forces noted.[64] To get a start, the corner boy must demonstrate his loyalty and ability to get results for his immediate circle of friends. Yet "if he concentrates on serving his own group, he will never win widespread support." "In order to win support he must deal with important people who influence other groups." Since he has only limited resources in terms of energy and access to official favors, he must "betray" his original friends by neglecting their interests and using his resources to help outsiders and bigshots. The result is a widespread cynicism toward "politicians" among the rank and file, which might be expected to cause constant turnover. However, according to Whyte, the politician is normally able to "trickle down" enough benefits to his followers in the district as a whole to prevent a revolt, even though his closest original friends who had the highest expectations may be badly disillusioned. The process reaches a kind of equilibrium, presumably at a level determined by the political abilities, initial "connections," and good luck of the individual politician.

In exploring for possible factors affecting some given variable, or for chains of causes and effects constituting a "process," there appear to be two basic techniques. The first attempts to obtain objective information about the sequence of events, particularly what events preceded the response under investigation.[65] The typical questions, whether addressed to a subject or used by an observer to guide his observations, are: "What happened before X? What happened just before the subject made his decision to move, vote, buy, steal, etc.? What was the frame of mind? What had been going on in the family, neighborhood, nation, world? Had he been talking with anyone, reading anything, listening to anything? Some responses will look like causal factors immediately, on the basis of our past experience or general hypotheses about human behavior. Others will only become prominent when we notice an apparent correlation between them and the criterion behavior in several cases.

The second technique is to ask people themselves to explain what happened and to give their reasons for acting as they did.[66] The basic question here is always "Why?" This technique has obvious limitations: people are often unaware of their real motives, of indirect influences, of the precise chain of causes and effects, of underlying necessary conditions. On the other hand it stands to reason that the participant knows a good deal about his own behavior, particularly about attitudes, motives, influences, "trigger events," and so on, and often can tell the outside investigator about things which he would never have guessed by himself. "Reasons" may not be the whole story, but they are an important source of information on possible factors, and in some cases a quite indispensible source, especially in the early stages of investigation. By adding to the general "why" query a set of more specific questions, focussing the respondent's attention on each of several basic aspects of the situation, "reason" questions can obtain more adequate coverage, although still limited to what the respondent himself is in a position to know.

---

[63]Kendall and Wolfe, op. cit., pp. 163 seq.
[64]Whyte, op. cit., pp. 209 seq.

[65]Robert K. Merton and Patricia L. Kendall, "The Focussed Interview," in: American Journal of Sociology, Vol. LI (1946), pp. 541 seq.; Herta Herzog, Training Guide on the Techniques of Qualitative Interviewing, New York, Bureau of Applied Social Research 1958; mimeographed.
[66]Paul F. Lazarsfeld, "The Art of Asking Why," in: National Marketing Review, Vol. I, pp. 26 seq.

Both of these techniques are combined in a technique of qualitative exploration of causal relations known as "discerning." This has been carefully described in Mirra Komarovsky's study of the effect of unemployment on the family status of the husband.[67] With only 59 case-studies to analyze, it was not possible to undertake a full-scale statistical analysis of the interrelations between all the possible variables. What was done was to take each case of apparent change due to the husband's unemployment and subject it to systematic checks: Had the change already begun before the unemployment? Did other factors arise concurrently with unemployment which might have been the real cause? Are the participants able to trace the step-by-step development of the change, the detailed links between unemployment and the altered role of the husband? If the respondents believe that unemployment was the reason for a certain change, on what evidence do they base their opinion? By these techniques it was possible to isolate with considerable promise of validity the causal relations between unemployment and family structure. The search for "possible factors" and "possible consequences" was made systematic; within the limitations of the data real precautions were taken against spurious relations.

Quasi-Statistics. Previous sections have dealt with operations of qualitative analysis which are essentially prior to quantitative research: observations which raise problems, the formulation of descriptive categories, the uncovering of possible causal factors or chains of causation for a particular piece of behavior. These operations stimulate and focus later quantitative research, and they set up the dimensions and categories along the "stub" of the tables, into which quantitative research may fill the actual frequencies and measurements.

However, one encounters very frequently in social science literature, studies which do not use the mechanism of quantitative data-collection and statistical analysis, and still make the kind of statements which quantitative research makes. These statements may be simply frequency distributions (i.e. "most Trobrianders" or even "the Trobriander" knows or believes or does so-and-so); they may be correlations (corner boys have a spending economy, while college boys have a saving economy); they may be statements of causal relationships ("If [the politician] concentrates upon serving his own group, he will never win widespread support...In order to win support, he must deal with important people who influence other groups"). Such statements, based on a body of observations which are not formally tabulated and analyzed statistically, may be termed "quasi-statistics." They include "quasi-distributions," "quasi-correlations," and even "quasi-experimental data."

Non-quantitative research of this sort is no longer logically prior to statistical research. It rather directly substitutes for statistical research, making the same kind of statements but on the basis of a recording and analysis of cases which takes place largely within the mind of the observer. This kind of research has obvious shortcomings, but it also has a place in the research process, viewed as a continuing and increasingly refined pursuit by the whole community of social scientists.

An example of the dangers of impressionistic "quasi-statistics" is given by Bernard Barber is an article on participation in voluntary associations:

American observers themselves were overwhelmed by what they did not fully understand: instance the following from Charles and Mary Beard's The Rise of American Civilization: "The tendency of Americans to unite with their fellows for varied purposes...now became a general mania...It was a rare American who was not a member of four or five societies...Any citizen who refused to affiliate with one or more associations became an object of curiosity, if not suspicion." Although in comparative perspective the United States may well be a "nation of joiners," a survey of the available data on the number of people with memberships in voluntary associations reveals the little-known

[67]Mirra Komarovsky, The Unemployed Man and His Family, New York, 1940; especially pp. 135 seq.

fact that many have not even a single such affiliation. This uniformity too holds for all types of areas in the United States, whether urban, suburban, small city, small town or rural.[68]

Barber then quotes statistics showing that in these various areas and strata of the population from one third to over two thirds of the people do not belong to any voluntary associations. As one proceeds from simple frequency distributions to correlations and then to systems of dynamic relationships between several variables, impressionistic "quasi-statistics" becomes steadily less adequate.

On the other hand it is argued that a careful observer who is aware of the need to sample all groups in the population with which he is concerned, who is aware of the "visibility bias" of the spectacular as opposed to the unspectacular case, who becomes intimately familiar with his material over a long period of time through direct observation, will be able to approximate the results of statistical investigation, while avoiding the considerable expense and practical difficulty of quantitative investigation. It has been claimed, for instance, that to provide a fully statistical basis for the conclusions which Whyte was able to draw from his observation of corner gangs and college boys groups, would require hundreds of observers studying hundreds of gangs and neighborhoods over many years.

There are some situations in which formal quantitative methods are apparently less necessary than others. When one is dealing with primitive groups with a nearly homogeneous culture, in which one set of prescribed roles is just about universally carried out by the population, it may require only the observation and interviewing of relatively few cases to establish the whole pattern. The same argument can be applied to studies of a quite homogeneous subculture within a civilized society. These methods seem to have succeeded in presenting a good first approximation at least in the description of the culture and behavior of such groups. When anthropologists now call for formal sampling, data-recording, and statistical analysis it is either to catch up finer details—the small number of deviant individuals, for instance—or to deal with situations of culture groups with less homogeneity—with groups in process of acculturation, breakdown of old norms, or the development of strong internal differentiation.

In situations of less homogeneity and simplicity, it is doubtful that quasi-statistics are anything like a full substitute for actual statistics. However they can still play an important "exploratory" function. Statistical research is too expensive and time-consuming to be applied on all fronts at once; like the 200-inch telescope it must focus on a few areas of particular interest for intensive study. Quasi-statistical studies can run ahead of the more cumbersome quantitative procedures to cover wide areas of social phenomena, and to probe into tangled complexes of relationship in search of possible "processes." They serve as a broad scanner and "finder" like the wide-angled but less powerful Schmidt telescope of Mount Wilson and Palomar. Moreover the gathering and analysis of "quasi-statistical data" can probably be made more systematic than it has been in the past, if the logical structure of quantitative research at least is kept in mind to give general warnings and directions to the qualitative observer.

Systematic Comparison. There is one special form of research into a relationship which stands on the border between statistical and quasi-statistical methods. This involves the systematic comparison of a relatively small number of cases. It differs from quasi-statistics in that the analysis of the cases proceeds along lines closely approximating those of a statistical survey or controlled experiment. However it involves too few cases to actually apply statistical tests, and it involves natural situations in which one

---

[68]Bernard Barber, "Participation and Mass Apathy in Associations," in: Gouldner, op. cit., pp. 481 seq.

cannot be certain that "other factors are equal" for the various cases beyond those factors specifically analyzed. It is as though one set up the tables for a statistical or experimental research, but had only one or two cases to fill in each cell, and perhaps had to leave some entirely empty.

This form of "comparative research" is only possible when the "cases" to be studied are social phenomena of a high order of complexity, such as wars, revolutions, large-scale social systems, forms of government. There do not exist very many cases in recorded history of such phenomena. Toynbee faced this problem in his classic "comparative analysis" of "Great Civilisations"—there were only about twenty-one such civilisations, along with a number of abortive or arrested civilisations. Weber faced the same situation in dealing with the role of religious systems in the development of society. [69]Besides the total number of available cases being small, each is a very large and complex unit which requires great time and effort to analyze. Even where there are a large number of cases, this factor may compel the researcher to restrict himself to the systematic comparison of a few. This situation arises in studying communities or large institutions. To describe any one community's social structure is such a large job that most studies have been of single cases. Only after different researchers over a generation have produced a dozen or so such studies can a "secondary analyst" undertake a comparative analysis. In the long run, it is to be hoped that data-gathering procedures on such complex "cases" can be so simplified that statistical studies will become possible. Then the intensive study of one community, factory, union, government agency, or voluntary association can give way to a quantitative study of a sample of such cases, testing the hypotheses derived from single-case studies. Of course, where the difficulty lies in the fact that there is only a handful of cases at all, the comparative method is the best we can do.

An example of systematic comparison of a small number of cases is offered by Lipset's study of the Canadian province of Saskatchewan. [70] The population of the province, mainly wheat farmers, had a remarkably high level of participation in political affairs and in seeking an explanation for this unusual behavior, comparisons were first made with areas where participation was known to be low.

The amount of participation in public affairs in the large cities of Canada and the U. S. is notoriously low. This is true even of cities like Toronto and Vancouver, which resemble Saskatchewan in giving a large vote to the new, radical C. C. F. (socialist) party. Comparing Saskatchewan with these large cities, Lipset was struck by the smallness of political units in Saskatchewan and the large number of offices to be filled in each. The average rural municipality had fewer than 400 families, with over 50 elective posts on municipal councils and school boards to be filled, while most large cities elect no more officials than that to represent their hundreds of thousands of families.

Besides the small size of Saskatchewan communities, they were relatively lacking in social stratification—almost everyone was a working farmer. In this respect too, Saskatchewan is at the opposite pole from the cities, with their wide differences in incomes and their staffs of specialists for performing normal public services. In the cities the positions of responsibility which are available tend to be monopolized by upper-class people and professionals; in Saskatchewan school boards, telephone companies, marketing agencies, etc. had to be staffed by ordinary farmers, who thereby acquired organizational and political skills unknown to the average city dweller.

Certain rural areas also are highly

[69]Arnold Toynbee, A Study of History, abridgement by D. C. Somerville, New York, 1947. Max Weber, Gesammelte Aufsatze zur Religionssoziologie, Tübingen, 1920-21. A brief outline is presented in: Talcott Parsons, The Structure of Social Action, Glencoe, Illinois, 1949, Ch. XV.

[70]Seymour Martin Lipset, Agrarian Socialism, Berkeley, 1950.

stratified, and in such areas the rate of mass participation is also low:

> Within the rural areas of the Southern States or in parts of California, where significant social and economic cleavage exists within the rural community, the wealthier and upperclass farmers are the formal community leaders, and the bulk of the poorer farmers are politically apathetic. (p. 202).

A third structural factor distinguishing Saskatchewan is its exposure to extreme economic fluctuations, due to the unstable price of its one main crop and to the recurrence of drought. In this it can be contrasted with its eastern neighbor, Manitoba, which has more diversified crops, stable markets, and more reliable weather. And it is notable that Manitoba today has much less community and political activity. Low participation is also found in the Maritime Provinces, where the farmers generally have a low standard of living, but do not experience the chronic alterations between wealth and poverty of the farmers of Saskatchewan.

Having isolated these possible sources of high participation by comparing the social structure of Saskatchewan with those of areas of low participation, we can now look for other areas which have equally favorable patterns of social characteristics. The neighboring wheat-belt areas of North Dakota and Alberta have virtually the same characteristics: small political units, little social stratification, and highly unstable economies. And both these areas have widespread community participation through local government and cooperatives, and a readiness to de-velop new political movements when confronted by economic crisis. The same structural characteristics were found in Manitoba in the 1890's, at which time the Manitoba agrarian political movement evoked widespread participation. When Manitoba's society changed through the development of a large urban center with an upper-class and specialized services, and through the diversification of agriculture which ended the complete dependence on the wheat crop, mass participation in politics fell off. Manitoba thus provides a natural "before-and-after" experiment.

Lipset notes that the same pattern of structural characteristics which exists in Saskatchewan can also be found in communities far removed from the specific conditions of the wheat belt. Merton studied an American industrial community, "Craftown," which was small in size, relatively unstratified, being mainly inhabited by workers, and faced with a series of pressing social and economic problems. This community was found to be much more politically active than neighboring urban areas; its wide spread political participation resembled that of the Saskatchewan farmers (pp. 303-304). The generalization of explanatory factors from "the wheat economy" to attributes applicable to any community obviously opens up a much wider range of cases for use in comparative analysis.

This comparative analysis of areas of high and low participation can be summarized in the following scheme:

Scheme of Factors Accounting for Political Participation

(Attributes in parentheses were not explicitly discussed in the comparisons)

Economic Fluctuations	Small Social Units	Little Stratification	Cases	Participation
+	+	+	Saskatchewan North Dakota Alberta Manitoba, 1890-1910 "Craftown"	High High High High High
(+)	(+)	–	Rural South Rural California	Low Low
(+)	–	–	Large cities in U.S. and Canada	Low
–	(+)	(+)	Maritime Provinces	Low
–	–	–	Manitoba today	Low

In the study just discussed it appears that comparisons were used not only to suggest explanatory factors but also to offer supporting evidence, as a kind of quasi-experimental test. One of the most celebrated instances of such quasi-experimental tests is found in Malinowski's study of the use of magic in the Trobriand Islands.[71] Malinowski wanted to test the old theory that primitive man uses magic because of a childlike confusion of the real and the imaginary or because of some instinctive belief in the supernatural. He found the Trobrianders engaging in some activities—for instance, fishing within the lagoons—for which their technology was adequate to permit certain economic returns and personal safety. Other activities—for instance fishing in the open sea—involved uncertainty of return and risks to life which could not be eliminated by available technological means. In the safe and certain activities, no magic was used; in the unsafe and uncertain ones, magic was used a great deal. This supported Malinowski's contention that magic was not a substitute for rational techniques, but a supplement to them when dealing with situations beyond the power of available rational technology, which created severe emotional strain.

Of course the use of comparisons of small numbers of cases as tests requires great caution; care must be taken to see that other significant factors are in fact equal, and that cases are selected in an unbiased manner.

IV. MATRIX FORMULATIONS

Sometimes the analysis of qualitative observations confronts a mass of particular facts of such great number and variety that it seems quite unworkable to treat them individually as descriptive attributes or in terms of their specific interrelationships. In such a situation the analyst will often come up with a descriptive concept on a higher level which manages to embrace and sum up a great

wealth of particular observations in a single formula. Take for instance, Ruth Benedict's description of the Zuni Indians, which mentions their avoidance of drugs and alcohol, their lack of personal visions, their placid response to divorce, their "mild and ceremonious" relation to their gods, and so on. After presenting a great many such particular facts, Benedict is able to sum them up in a single formula: The Zuni culture has an Apollonian pattern—that is, a central theme of avoidance of emotional excess. This pattern or theme permeates every aspect of Zuni life.[72] Such a formula capable of summing up in a single descriptive concept a great wealth of particular observations may be called a matrix formulation. This definition covers the notion of a "Basic pattern" of a culture, a "theme," an "ethos," a "zeitgeist" or "mentality of the time," a "national character," and on the level of the individual person a "personality type."

Matrix formulations may be applied to complex units at any level. In a study of a village of unemployed in Austria, the researchers made a collection of separate "surprising observations." Although they now had more time, the people read fewer library books. Although subject to economic suffering, their political activity decreased. Those totally unemployed showed less effort to look for work in other towns than those who still had some kind of work. The children of unemployed workers had more limited aspirations for jobs and for Christmas presents than children of employed people. The researchers faced all kinds of practical difficulties because people often came late or failed to appear altogether for interviews. People walked slowly, arrangements for definite appointments were hard to make, "nothing seemed to work any more in the village."

Out of all these observations there finally arose the over-all characterization of the village as "The Tired Community." This formula seemed clearly to express the characteristics which permeated

[71]Bronislaw Malinowski, *Magic, Science and Religion.* A brief outline is presented in Talcott Parsons, *op. cit.,* Ch. XV.

[72]Ruth Benedict, *Patterns of Culture,* New York, 1946, Ch. IV.

every sphere of behavior: although the people had nothing to do, they acted tired —they seemed to suffer from a kind of general paralysis of mental energies.[73]

In a study of a particular group—people who had been designated as "influentials" in an American community— Merton confronted the problem of explaining their diverse behaviors. Various classifications proved of no avail in accounting for the wide range of observations available. The particular behavior on which the research was focussed—the reading of news magazines—remained unexplained. In trying to order the "welter of discrete impressions not closely related one to the others," the researchers finally came up with one general theme" which distinguished the influentials: some were "cosmopolitan," primarily interested in the world outside the local community, while others were "local," primarily interested in the local community itself. Merton clearly indicates the typical function of such a matrix formulation when he declares:

All other differences between the local and cosmopolitan influences seem to stem from their difference in basic orientation...The difference in basic orientation is bound up with a variety of other differences: (1) in the structures of social relations in which each type is implicated; (2) in the roads they have travelled to their present positions in the influence-structure; (3) in the utilization of their present status for the exercise of interpersonal influence; and (4) in their communications behavior.[74]

The bulk of the article is then taken up with an elaboration of this dual matrix formulation in terms of all the specific behaviors which fit into one or the other type of orientation, the local or the cosmopolitan.

Matrix formulations can thus vary in the level of the unit which they describe, from a whole culture to a community and to a status group within a community. They are used right down to the level of individual personalities, where, for instance, a great variety of particular behaviors will be summed up in the matrix formula of an "anal personality" or a "cerebrosonic temperament." At the personality level they are often referred to as "syndromes," a term arising out of the physiological level where it refers to just the same kind of complex of individual facts all of which can be summed up in one single formula.

Another way in which the matrix formulations can vary is in terms of the relations between the elements. The elements which went into Benedict's formulation of an Apollonian culture were all alike in terms of the variable "emotional tone"—their emotional tone was low in intensity. They all went together in the same sense that one can classify in a single group all regions with a very even temperature, or all people with a high blood pressure. In a matrix formulation such as Tönnies' "Gemeinschaft," the elements seem to be involved in causal relations and processes with one another.[75] The elements of "reciprocal trust" for example can be considered as growing out of the element of "prolonged face-to-face association with the same people," as can a great many of the other characteristics of a "Gemeinschaft"-situation. In the matrix formulation of an "anal personality," the behavior characteristics are thought of as all arising out of a single basic factor, the fixation of the erotic development at a certain childish stage. In many of the culture-pattern formulations since Benedict's purely descriptive ones, we find the idea that all of the elements in the pattern are products of the pattern of child training—or even of a single element in the child training pattern. Some matrix formulations involve a mixture of descriptively related and causally related elements.

Yet another way in which matrix formulae can be differentiated could be called their "projective distance." The following examples should indicate what is meant by this dimension. In Merton's study of Mass Persuasion, it was found

---

[73]Jahoda and Zeisel, op. cit.
[74]Merton, "Patterns of Influence," op. cit., p. 191.

[75]Ferdinand Tonnies, Gemeinschaft und Gesellschaft, Leipzig, 1887. A brief summary is found in Parsons, op. cit., pp. 686 seq.

that a wide variety of remarks made by the Kate Smith devotees could be summed up in the notion of "submissiveness to the status quo."[76] They believed that it was right for some to be poor and others rich, they accepted their position in the system of stratification, they rationalized that the rich had so many troubles that it was just as well to be poor. The more general descriptive concept follows very directly from the manifest content of the respondent's statements; they could almost have made the generalization themselves.

In Cantril's study of the Psychology of Social Movements, he confronted a collection of interviews and observations of people who join all sorts of marginal political cults like the Townsend groups, Moral Rearmament, the Coughlinites, and so on.[77] Out of the welter of characteristics there emerged the general notion that all of these people were suffering from a lack of orientation to the complexities of the modern world, a need for a frame of reference within the events of their lives and for world affairs could be understandable. The matrix formulation of "need for orientation" seemed to tie together a great many diverse forms of behavior, attitudes and beliefs on the part of the members of these groups. Now this matrix formulation is further removed from the manifest content of the material than was the formulation in the previous example. There is a greater gap between the formula and what the people actually said, in talking about troubles they had and how good it made them feel that their movement told them what was wrong with the world and how it could be corrected. Here the statements and observations collected by the field work are interpreted as projections of a somewhat complex psychological state, which very few of the respondents themselves could directly articulate.

A still greater distance between the manifest content of the material and the matrix formulation which is constructed

to express its basic pattern is often found in the characterization of personality types or of the ethos of a culture. In these cases, guided by general theoretical orientations, one may use subtle indicators as a basis for a formulation which appears in some ways contradictory to the manifest content of the material. Verbal expressions and actual behavior patterns apparently indicative of feelings of superiority are interpreted, when seen in the context of more subtle indicators, as evidence of quite the opposite basic outlook. In Benedict's characterization of the Zuni as basically Apollonian, she has to explain away—on the basis of looking beneath the surface—various apparently "Dionysian" elements.[78]

There is a good deal of similarity between the rationale of the matrix formulation and Parson's discussion of the place of "secondary descriptive systems" in his scheme of social systems based on the unit act:

When a certain degree of complexity is reached, however, to describe the system in full in terms of the action scheme would involve a degree of elaboration of details which would be very laborious and pedantic to work out. This is true even if description is limited to "typical" unit acts and all the complex detailed variations of the completely concrete acts are passed over. Fortunately, as certain degrees of complexity are reached, there emerge other ways of describing the facts, the employment of which constitutes a convenient "shorthand" that is adequate for a large number of scientific purposes.

...It has been seen that the acts and action systems of different individuals, in so far as they are mutually oriented in one another, constitute social relationships. In so far as this interaction of the action systems of individuals is continuous and regular these relationships acquire certain identifiable, relatively constant properties or descriptive aspects ... It is not necessary to observe all the acts of the parties to a relationship, or all their attitudes, etc., but only enough to establish what is for the purpose in hand the relevant "character" of the relationship ...

Thus the primary function of such a secondary descriptive scheme as that of social relationship is one of scientific economy, of

---

[76]Merton, Mass Persuasion, pp. 152 seq.
[77]Hadley Cantril, The Psychology of Social Movements, New York, 1941.

[78]Benedict, op. cit., see p. 80, 83, 85, 94, 107, 112 for instances.

reducing the amount of labor of observation and verification required before adequate judgements may be arrived at. A second function... [is] to state the facts in a way that will prevent carrying unit analysis to a point where it would destroy relevant emergent properties.[79]

Parsons gives as examples of secondary descriptive schemes typologies of social relationships, personality types, and descriptive categories applied to groups. While Parsons' concept is not entirely identical with that of the matrix formulation, it illustrates much of the reasoning behind such complex descriptive concepts, which sum up and render manageable a large and varied body of individual points of data.

V. QUALITATIVE SUPPORT OF THEORY

So far we have mainly discussed ways in which qualitative data can contribute to the formulation of problems, classifications, and hypotheses. Qualitative materials are particularly suitable for this exploratory phase of research: their wealth of detailed descriptive elements gives the analyst the maximum opportunity to find clues and suggestions. For testing hypotheses, on the other hand, the ideal model would be the controlled experiment, with precise measurements on a limited number of preselected variables.

The use of controlled experiments in social science is increasing, but it remains severely limited. Recent years have also seen a great development of quantitative research, employing such rough approximations of the experimental design as the controlled observation of natural processes, or the correlational analysis of cross-sectional surveys. These techniques provide tests for certain theories. There remain, however, major areas in which theories are supported mainly by qualitative data.

The General Problem of Qualitative Support. The word "theory" has actually a number of different meanings, ranging from broad general orientations to precise propositions.[80] The theories for which qualitative support is most often used are relatively large-scale, wide-ranging systems or relationships. For example, large-scale theories of social change must rely upon the qualitative data of historical records; theories of the functioning of organizations and institutions are based largely on qualitative descriptions; theories of personality development grow out of clinical case materials. One calls to mind at once the historical theories of Marx, Weber's insitutional analysis, Freud's personality theory, and the subsequent work in their traditions.

In discussing the use of qualitative data to support theory, it should be made clear that more is involved than mere illustration. For illustration, intended to help the writer communicate the meaning of his concepts, purely imaginary examples can be used. Durkheim, for instance, in describing types of suicide, drew on examples from literature as well as real case-histories.[81] But for the use we have in mind it is important that the examples are real. Since they are not systematically sampled or precisely measured, they do not offer rigorous proof in any statistical or experimental sense. Yet according to their number, range, and relation to the reader's own experience they offer varying degrees of support or corroboration. It is this function which we wish to examine.

Psychoanalysis, Marxism, and other theories of history in general or of overall personality development are large and complicated structures. The use of qualitative data in supporting such complex theoretical systems is one of the major undeveloped areas for methodological analysis. In order to find manageable illustrations of the use of qualitative data to support theory, we will restrict ourselves to a much simpler type, which may be called "trend theories." These

[79]Parsons, op. cit., pp. 743 seq.

[80]Merton, Social Theory and Social Structure, Chapter II.

[81]Emile Durkheim, Suicide, Glencoe, Illinois, 1951; Book Two, Ch. 6.

are theories which call attention to one particular trend in society, usually derived from some underlying change in the economic or demographic structure.

We will consider three such theories. Erich Fromm has suggested that a major tendency of our time is "self-alienation," resulting from the insecurities and disruption of social bonds brought about by the rise of the market economy and industrialization. C. Wright Mills suggests that the rise of the big city and the standardization of tastes subject increasing numbers of people to status-insecurity. Lasswell proposes the "developmental construct" of the garrison state, which attempts to work out the logical implications of the tendency toward an increasing reliance on military force in international relations.

"Signs of the Times"; Qualitative Observations Supporting Trend Theories. Fromm's theory as a whole is relatively complicated, dealing with the interaction of economic structure, personality, and systems of belief.[82] We will consider one particular aspect of that theory: that the individual, rendered isolated and powerless in the face of impersonal market forces, monopolies, mass organization and recurring wars, develops "automaton conformity" as a mechanism of escape:

> This particular mechanism is the solution that the majority of normal individuals find in modern society. To put it briefly, the individual ceases to be himself; he adopts entirely the kind of personality offered to him by cultural patterns; and he therefore becomes exactly as all others are and as they expect him to be.[83]

Let us see how Fromm goes about supporting this contention derived from his trend theory. First of all, he wants to demonstrate that it is at all possible for a person to think thoughts and feel feelings which are not his own, but induced from outside. This he does by describing

a common hypnotic experiment where it is suggested to a subject that he will do certain things and have certain feelings upon awakening from the hypnotic sleep. This establishes that the phenomenon can exist; however it involves very special conditions.

Fromm then attempts to show that the same kind of behavior occurs in the daily life of many individuals. To specify what this would involve, he gives a hypothetical example of "pseudo-thinking" in daily life: the man who makes a weather prediction which he believes to be his own thinking, when he is simply repeating what he heard on the radio. He then proceeds to actual observations:

> Many persons looking at a famous bit of scenery actually reproduce the pictures they have seen of it numerous times, say on postal cards...Or, in experiencing an accident which occurs in their presence, they see or hear the situation in terms of the newspaper report they anticipate.
>
> The average person who goes to a museum and looks at a picture by a famous painter, say Rembrandt, judges it to be a beautiful and impressive picture. If we analyze his judgment, we find that he does not have any particular inner response to the picture but thinks it is beautiful because he knows that he is supposed to think it beautiful.[84]

Fromm gives a number of other observations of pseudo-thinking and feeling: the man whose face goes solemn after he leaves a party where he was "gay," children who say they "like" to go to school every day, people who believe they are marrying because they want to, while they are only conforming to other people's expectations, the case of a man who "voluntarily" follows the career set by his father, but suffers strange difficulties.

Of course Fromm's examples do not provide rigorous proof of the assertion that "the majority of normal individuals" are self-alienated. What Fromm has done is, first, to establish thoughts and feelings. Then he presented a hypothetical example to show how this might happen

---

[82]Erich Fromm, Escape From Freedom, New York, 1941; Appendix: "Character and the Social Process."

[83]Ibid., pp. 185 seq.

[84]Ibid., pp. 192 seq.

in daily life. Finally be mobilized a wide range of common observations to show that it actually does occur frequently.

Let us take another example. C. Wright Mills holds that the white-collar worker in urban, mass-production society suffers from an increasing ambiguity and insecurity of social status; he or she is unable to develop a stable self-esteem or a secure prestige-status in the eyes of others.[85] Mills presents qualitative observations from various sources. Strategically-placed specialists—e. g. personnel directors—report such surprising behavior as the following: a girl typing in a large office was deeply hurt when her chair was replaced with a new one, because the old one had her nameplate on the bottom; office workers attach great importance to objectively meaningless changes in the location of desks, etc. This suggested to Mills the intensity of the effort to retain some identity and status in a standardized environment.

Detailed interviews found other phenomena which fitted in with the notion of a "status panic": Routine clerical workers tried to conceal the nature of their own work, and borrow prestige from the firm or industry, by identifying themselves with such phrases as "I am with Saks," or "I work at Time." They saved up their salaries and spent them for an evening at expensive places of entertainment, or for a vacation at a costly resort, in order to "buy a feeling, even if only for a short time, of higher status." A salesgirl dealing with "Park Avenue" customers will try to behave with greater dignity and distinction in her off-the-job contacts than the girl who works on 34th Street.

Such qualitative observations provide support for a theory in several ways. Aside from their own weight, they may call the reader's attention to certain areas of his own experience, which may provide much additional support. Furthermore, when the observations cover many different areas of behavior they gain additional weight, because they indicate that the theory has the ability to account for a wide range of phenomena.

The notion of the "garrison state" as formulated by Lasswell also suggested a trend growing out of basic social changes; however it was unusual in being formulated not ex post facto but at a very early stage in the process. This is what Lasswell meant in describing it as a "developmental construct"—a trend theory referring not only to the immediate situation but to the future. The substance of Lasswell's theory was a set of consequences which could be expected if the world situation stimulated modern great powers, with modern economies and technology, to all-out development of military strength. Some of these consequences were relatively logical and obvious: the entire labor force would be put to work, political conflicts will be minimized in the interests of national unity, the government will become involved in more and more previously private activities. Others were more of a symbolic nature:

The distinctive frame of reference in a fighting society is fighting effectiveness. All social change is translated into battle potential.

The military are therefore compelled to become competent in the skills of technology, administration, and public relations; there is a "merging of skill" between the professional soldier and the manager of large-scale civilian enterprise.

There is intense concern with public morale and its manipulation; the military "are compelled to consider the entire gamut of problems that arise in living together under modern conditions."[86]

If one wanted in 1953 to see to what extent the predicted trend had become a reality, the developmental construct provides a guiding framework for observation. "All social change is translated into battle potential"—a study of illiteracy in America is discussed mainly in terms of "how many divisions" it costs the army.

---

[85]Mills, op. cit., Ch. 11, "The Status Panic."

[86]Harold Lasswell, "The Garrison State and Specialists on Violence," in: American Journal of Sociology (January 1941). Reprinted in: Lasswell, The Analysis of Political Behavior, London, 1947, pp. 146 seq.

"The merging of skills"—generals appear on boards of directors of large corporations, and large corporation executives appear in the defense departments. "Intense concern with public morale"— the traditional concern with the morality of school-teachers in terms of smoking, drinking, and sex shifts to a concern with treasonable ideas. In politics the traditional charges of corruption and inefficiency against opponents are replaced by charges of treason, or of failure to build enough air groups.

One or two of these might be isolated events; taken together they begin to build up a "pattern," giving some plausibility to the theory. At this point it becomes important to undertake more systematic studies of the actual extent and degree of militarization, to distinguish its progress in different spheres, etc.

From the few examples presented here, it is hoped that the reader has been able to get an idea of the intermediate role played by qualitative observations in relation to theory—as more than simply illustration, but less than definitive proof. It is likely that there are several degrees or stages of qualitative support, ranging from an initial encouragement to go on with a certain line of speculation, to a systematic examination of case material which offers some approximation to the classical canons of proof. There also may be differences in function according or the type of "theory" involved. The present analysis is only a tentative beginning; there is a great need for intensive work on additional examples of qualitative support of theory.[87]

Now that we are at the end of our survey, it is necessary to add that some of the areas we have distinguished inevitably overlap at their borders. It would be easy to find examples in which it would be difficult to decide whether they have the complexity of a matrix formula. Another set of uncertainties will sometimes arise when we have to decide whether the writer is arguing for a relationship between a few variables or whether he is supporting a rather general theory. Even the very notion of qualitative research has its haziness on the fringes; it would not be easy, e. g., to say when the comparative analysis of a few cases shades over into statistical treatment.

The present discussion is a beginning only. It has started from a simple position: that there exists this area of research which is generally considered important but which has not been analyzed methodologically. It has set forward a collection of examples both as an extensional definition of "qualitative analysis" and as material for further study. Besides collecting this material, it has made a preliminary organization of it. There are many problems left unsolved in the discussion.[88] The tentative classifications set forward here need to be tried out on additional materials; more good cases need to be collected and examined. Only after many successive phases of logical formulation and attempted application will the methodology of qualitative techniques come to possess the same usefulness to the research worker which is today possessed by quantitative methodology.

[87]Paul F. Lazarsfeld, "Remarks on Administrative and Critical Communications Research," in: Studies in Philosophy and Social Science, Vol. IX (May 1941), gives a number of further examples in the field of mass communications, especially from the work of Max Horkheimer and T. W. Adorno. In another field, Thorstein Veblen, Theory of the Leisure Class, offers a classic example of the use of qualitative observations.

[88]The authors are indebted to Professor Merton and the members of his seminar in the Sociology of Occupation for raising many of these problems in discussing an earlier draft of this paper.

The Respondent Reports on the Interview [1]

Charles F. Cannell and Morris Axelrod

SOURCE: *American Journal of Sociology*, Vol. 62, (1956), pp. 177–81.

As more and more survey interviews are being conducted with the general public and more and more people are being interviewed, their reactions take on increasing importance. If the public is annoyed or feels imposed upon by interviewers, it may eventually refuse to co-operate with agencies and social scientists who seek to collect information through personal interviews. On the other hand, if respondents enjoy participating in interviews, the door is open to wider use of sample surveys.

However, there is a further important reason for knowing how respondents react to being interviewed. This has to do with the respondent's motivation to communicate with the interviewer; that is, whether he agrees to be interviewed in the first place and, second, whether he is disposed to give accurate responses to the questions he is asked. The relationship which the interviewer succeeds in establishing with the respondent to a large extent determines the accuracy of the information the latter will supply. Moreover, the motivation established in one interview may help in gaining a second interview with the same individual, a matter of importance, since, more and more in sample surveys, the respondents are interviewed twice or more to shed light on trends.

Of course, we already know something about the public acceptance of the survey interview; for example, that the proportion who refuse to talk with the interviewer is rarely higher than 5 per cent, even in the most complicated surveys. We know further that respondents do communicate readily with interviewers and that much of their information is highly accurate.

But does the respondent after the interview is over consider that it was a profitable and enjoyable experience and that some good was served by his participation? Is he mildly tolerant of the interviewer, or does he wish he had never been involved in the first place? Is he concerned lest the interview in some way be used against him? Further, does the reaction of respondents to interviewers and to interviews vary from topic to topic or from survey to survey, depending upon the subject matter, the sponsorship of the study, and the purpose of the study? To learn the respondents' perceptions of interviews and attitudes to having been interviewed, we used three different methods of investigation. The first consisted of a letter thanking the respondent for the interview and inclosing a post card asking if he wished to have a copy of the survey report. The bottom of the post card was left blank and headed with the word "comments." This procedure was used on three national surveys of the Survey Research Center.

A second method was used in four other surveys. A letter was sent to the respondent after the interview, and a questionnaire of ten questions was in-

[1] The research reported here is part of a larger study of factors related to interviewer effectiveness. This study was made possible by a grant from the University of Michigan's Faculty Research Fund.

closed with a "thank-you" letter, questions asking the respondent about his reactions to the interview and his notions of it and the interviewer.

The third method was a personal interview with a subsample of respondents taken from a few days to two weeks after the original interview. It covered the same kind of questions that were asked in the mail questionnaire, namely, the reaction of the respondents to the interview, their perception of what the interview was about, and so forth. This method was used in a single survey, conducted in the Detroit area, Survey C.

The three methods were used to collect data in several surveys widely differing in subject matter. One, Survey A, was the Survey of Consumer Finances conducted by the Survey Research Center. In these surveys approximately three thousand interviews are taken in a national sample of cities and counties. The study consists largely of detailed financial questions on such matters as family income, liquid assets, past purchases, debts, and so forth. The interviews average about an hour in length, the range being from one-half hour in simple cases to two hours where the financial situation is complicated. The respondents are the heads of spending units (roughly equivalent to families); about 85 per cent of them were male respondents. About three-quarters of the interviewers were women.

The second, Survey B, had to do with plans for size of family. The respondents were women between eighteen and thirty-nine years old. All the interviewers were women. The subject matter covered plans and expectations of size of family, included detailed information on each of the respondent's pregnancies, family decisions on the number of children wanted and on contraceptive practices, and so forth. This study was conducted jointly by the Scripps Foundation for Research in Population Problems and the Survey Research Center.

Survey C was conducted in the Metropolitan Detroit area. Approximately eight hundred interviews were taken. About two-thirds of the interviews were conducted by first-year graduate students who had been trained in interviewing, the remainder by professional interviewers.[2] The subject was decision-making within the family and the relationship between the family and other social units. The interviews lasted approximately an hour.

Survey D, also part of the program of the Detroit Area Study, concerned aspects of community integration.

To the questionnaire mailed after the interview the highest response rate—approximately 80 per cent—was in Survey C. In Survey D it was 75 per cent. These were sent about a week after the interview. On the family study the questionnaire was sent three or four weeks after the interview was received, which means a month after the interview. The response rate for this study was about 40 per cent. On the Survey of Consumer Finances the questionnaires were sent even longer after the interview, and the rate of response dropped to about one-third. In previous years when post cards had been sent on the Survey of Consumer Finances, it has been about 50 per cent.

The number of mail questionnaires returned and included in the following analysis are: Survey A, 621; Survey B, 656; Survey C, 578; and Survey D, 521.

In order to have the mail questionnaire sufficiently short to fit conveniently on one page, two forms were used. Some questions appeared on both forms and some only on one. This means that some of the tables are based on about one-half the number of responses as reported in the tabulation above. Tables 2, 4, and 7 are based on the entire number and the remainder on one-half the number.

One of the questions was: "How interesting did you find the interview?" Table 1, summarizing the reaction of the respondents to all four studies, shows that a high proportion found the interview either very interesting or fairly interesting. The lowest response for these two categories was 91 per cent for the Survey of Consumer Finances (Survey A).

[2] This study was conducted as part of the Detroit Area Study, a graduate program of training and research of the department of sociology and the Survey Research Center of the University of Michigan.

The only difference of importance in this table is in the "Very interesting" category for the four studies: from one-half on the Survey of Consumer Finances to nearly two-thirds on the 1956 Detroit Area Study.

Of more importance, however, is the fact that the proportion of people finding the interview interesting varies but slightly from study to study, in spite of the wide variation in subject matter and the personal nature of some of the surveys. This lack of difference is surprising, the more so because, whereas the Survey of Consumer Finances consists almost entirely of questions asking for factual information, the other three surveys had a considerable number of open questions on personal attitudes.

One might expect that the response to the first question was motivated by politeness and that a more crucial question for measuring interest might be to ascertain how the respondent would feel about being reinterviewed. This query on the mail questionnaire read: "How would you feel about being interviewed again?" (Table 2).

Here, again, combining the first two categories in the table and looking only at those people who either would like or would not mind being interviewed again reveals little difference between the four studies. In each survey about three-quarters of the respondents report that they would be willing to be interviewed again. Some validation of these figures can be found in the proportion of people who do, in fact, grant reinterviews. A few years ago in the Survey of Consumer Finances 83 per cent of those interviewed permitted a second interview. This figure is generally corroborated in the experience of the Survey Research Center. The figures are roughly comparable to the proportion of respondents who <u>say</u> they would not mind being reinterviewed.

These two tables report a generally favorable response to the interviews which, however, varied greatly in the type of subject matter and in the amount of personal information asked for.

Next information on how the respond-

ents conceive of the interview was sought as a means of understanding favorable reactions. In the follow-up of the Survey of Consumer Finances a "thank-you" letter was sent, together with a post card asking the respondent whether he wished a copy of the report. About 50 per cent of the respondents responded by post card, and a high proportion asked for a copy of the report. Of course, the people who requested the report may well be different from those who did not. Sixty-five per cent of the post cards contained comments in the space provided for the purpose. A high proportion mentioned either

Table 1. How Interesting Did You Find the Interview?

| | (Per Cent) | | | |
	Survey A	Survey B	Survey C	Survey D
Very interesting . . .	49	61	59	63
Fairly interesting . .	42	32	34	29
Not too interesting. .	6	6	4	5
Not interesting at all	3	1	3	1
Did not answer	*	0	0	2
	100	100	100	100

*Less than 0.5 of 1 per cent.

Table 2. How Would You Feel About Being Interviewed Again?

| | (Per Cent) | | | |
	Survey A	Survey B	Survey C	Survey D
Would like to be interviewed again . .	14	14	19	20
Wouldn't mind being interviewed again .	64	62	50	52
Would rather not be interviewed again .	14	17	22	20
Wouldn't want to be interviewed again .	8	7	6	7
Did not answer	0	0	3	1
	100	100	100	100

the interviewer or the conducting of the interview rather than the content of the survey itself:

I found your interviewer most agreeable and courteous.

The interviewer who called on us was charming, just the right kind of a person for the work.

It was a fine interview. I thought it was interesting and worthwhile.

The very few critical comments were largely focused on the interviewer:

The interviewer could have been more adept at getting the information.

The purpose of the interview was never made clear to me, and I've wondered ever since what it was all about.

To the personal follow-up interviews conducted with a sample of respondents on the survey in Detroit came, in general, the same response, namely, that the respondents think of the interviewer rather than the content of the survey. The findings point to the importance of the relationship between interviewer and respondent. Adequate training and selection of the interviewers so that they will make the right impression on the respondents thus is a matter of first importance.

Table 3. How Friendly Was the Interviewer?

(Per Cent)

	Survey A	Survey B	Survey C	Survey D
Very friendly	84	85	85	85
Fairly friendly	13	15	15	13
Not too friendly. . . .	1	0	*	2
Not friendly at all . .	0	0	0	0
Did not answer	2	0	0	*
	100	100	100	100

*Less than 0.5 of 1 per cent.

Table 4. How Interested Did the Interviewer Seem in What You Had to Say?

(Per Cent)

	Survey A	Survey B	Survey C	Survey D
Very interested. . . .	82	75	74	76
Fairly interested. . .	15	22	23	20
Not too interested . .	2	2	2	3
Not interested at all.	1	1	1	*
Did not answer	*	0	*	1
	100	100	100	100

*Less than 0.5 of 1 per cent.

Several questions in the mail questionnaire of the four studies focused on the interviewer and the reaction of the respondents to him. Table 3 gives the answers to the query: "How friendly was the interviewer?" while Table 4 shows the tabulation of the question, "How interested did the interviewer seem in what you had to say?"

Two apparently essential characteristics of rapport are covered by these tables. The first is the impression that the interviewer was interested in what the respondent had to say. In each of the surveys nearly all the respondents felt their interviewer was at least fairly friendly, and most felt that he was very friendly.

Tables 5 and 6 are designed to show if the interviewer made the surveys clear to the respondent and whether the latter felt he was pressed into giving an interview.

In all surveys letters were sent to respondents prior to the interview stating the purpose of the study. In Survey A interviewers also were provided with reports of previous studies and with letters from the Federal Reserve Board, and a special attempt was made to gain newspaper publicity. It is not surprising, then, that the purpose of this survey was clearer to respondents than were the others. In Surveys B and C the sponsorship was less clear; there was no single sponsoring organization, and the purpose was also less specific. For example, why is information needed on family size? It is difficult to explain it briefly and explic-

Table 5. How Well Did the Interviewer Succeed in Making Clear to You What the Study Was About?

(Per Cent)

	Survey A	Survey B	Survey C	Survey D
Very clear	83	70	67	71
Fairly clear	14	26	28	25
Not so clear	1	3	3	2
Not clear at all	2	1	2	1
Did not answer	0	0	0	1
	100	100	100	100

Table 6. Did You Feel That You Were Being "Pressured" into Giving an Interview?

(Per Cent)

	Survey A	Survey B	Survey C	Survey D
No, not at all	85	87	81	84
Yes, to some extent .	12	13	15	13
Yes, very much so. .	3	0	3	3
Did not answer	*	0	1	*
	100	100	100	100

*Less than 0.5 of 1 per cent.

itly to a respondent. In spite of this, however, most respondents thought they had
either a fairly clear or a very clear understanding of the purpose.

Table 6 attempts to show whether or
not the respondents felt pressure. Prior
to the interview a letter stating the general purpose of the survey and saying
that an interviewer would call was mailed
to each respondent. In spite of this, the
interviewer had to "sell" himself and the
survey at the door. Since the interviewer
is highly motivated to obtain an interview
with each potential respondent, one might
expect the respondent to be aware at
times of some pressure to grant it. It is,
therefore, surprising that a high proportion of respondents reported feeling no
pressure at all.

Table 7 shows answers to the question:
"Were there any questions which you
thought too personal or too prying?"

Survey A, it will be remembered,
sought detailed financial information;
Survey B, detailed accounts of pregnancies and family limitation; Survey C, details about family relations; and Survey
D, facts about community integration. A
sizable proportion in each of the surveys
thought some questions were too personal. In the questionnaire, though, no
space was left for a response; a number
of people wrote in questions which they
considered too personal; in most cases
questions on income were specified. In
Survey B it was the questions having to
do with techniques of family limitation.

It seems clear, therefore, that the respondent will give information which the
interviewer desires, even though acutely

Table 7. Were There Any Questions Which You
Thought Were Too Personal or Too Prying?

| | (Per Cent) | | | |
	Survey A	Survey B	Survey C	Survey D
No	75	63	76	82
Yes.	24	36	22	15
Did not answer	1	1	2	3
	100	100	100	100

personal, as a means of maintaining the
enjoyable personal connection with the
interviewer. One is struck in reading the
comments in the follow-up interviews by
the obvious pleasure in the relationship.
There appears to be something of the
cathartic element so common in psychotherapeutic interviews. The interviewer,
establishing a permissive atmosphere,
provides the respondent an opportunity to
express himself to a receptive listener.
Even though the topic is neither personal
nor emotional, the respondent reacts positively.

It is interesting to speculate as to
whether the respondent values the relationship with the interviewer sufficiently
to take care to give an accurate report,
knowing that in so doing he can best help
him: if the relationship is viewed as
positive, the respondent will probably
not want to damage it or hurt the interviewer. There may be, of course, a point
beyond which the information requested
is a greater threat than the relationship
permits, at which time the interview must
either be broken off, the specific information refused, or the situation disguised
by inadequate or inaccurate answers.

Pitfalls in the Analysis of Panel Data: A Research Note on Some Technical Aspects of Voting[1]

Eleanor E. Maccoby

SOURCE: *American Journal of Sociology*, Vol. 61, (1956), pp. 359–62.

Voting is an extremely valuable book. However, it does appear to contain some technical analysis problems which should be discussed in the hope that future workers with panel studies will avoid the pitfalls which raise serious question about the validity of some, but not most, of the conclusions.

The central problem is one of the unreliability of measurement. In polling, there is always a group of cases in which an error has been made. The interviewer accidentally checks the wrong box, the respondent misunderstands the question, the punch-clerk punches the wrong number, etc. Let us assume for purposes of illustration that this kind of error occurs in 10 per cent of the cases and that it is random and so equally likely to happen for any case included in the study. If we are dealing with an attitude whose distribution in the population is uneven, the situation may be seen in Table 1.

In this table we see that among the 400 cases in the sample who are really "for" the issue, 40 will be erroneously classified as "against" and will be added to the "against" total. At the same time, 10 of the 100 people who are really "against" will be classified as "for." Thus the loss of the larger group is numerically greater, being only partially compensated for by errors in the opposite direction, and the distribution of opinion as measured is somewhat more evenly

divided than it would be if the measurement were free of error. The limiting case of this process would occur if the measurement had no reliability at all (so that every case was classified as though by tossing a coin), when the measured distribution would show a 50-50 split, no matter what the "true" division of opinion might be.

Now let us assume that we remeasure these cases, as is done in a panel study. To begin with, for the sake of simplicity, let us assume, further, that errors will not be made in the same case twice. Among our larger group, the "for's," there are 10 people who are there by accident. Upon remeasurement, they should revert to their proper place, the "against" column. But 10 new errors will occur to take their place. That is, there will be 10 new people who are actually "against" who will now be measured as "for." Similarly, the 40 cases who were erroneously classed as "against" in the first measure will revert to type and will be replaced by the same number of new errors. To continue the illustration, the shift of cases upon remeasurement would be as shown in Table 2. The distribution on the first measurement and the distribution on the second measurement are the same. Cases have simply changed places across the dividing line which separated "for" from "against," the same number moving from "for" to "against" as move in the opposite direction.

Occasionally, of course, an error will occur twice in succession in the same

[1] By Bernard R. Berelson, Paul F. Lazarsfeld, and William M. McPhee. Chicago: University of Chicago Press, 1954. Pp. xix +395.

case. Since the error rate is 10 per cent, among the 40 cases who were originally mismeasured "against" and are shown in Table 2 as moving to the "for" column, 4 will be mismeasured again and will remain where they were, erroneously classified in the "against" column; in addition, 1 out of the 10 originally misclassified as "for" will be mismeasured a second time and remain where it is. These 5 cases will take the place of 5 of the new errors in the second measurement. Thus, in fact, only 45 cases, rather than 50, will move each way upon remeasurement. But the distribution remains the same upon the second measurement as it was upon the first.

Suppose, now, that we select groups on the basis of their score on the first measurement and ask ourselves how many of them will get a different score upon remeasurement. Out of our 370 cases who were classified as "for" on the first measurement, 45, or about 12 per cent of those originally "for," will change over to the opposite position; out of the 130 originally classified as "against," 45, or about 35 per cent of those originally classified as "against," will change. We see from this that, while equal members of cases in each group change upon remeasurement, it will inevitably be true that a higher <u>proportion</u> of the minority group will shift.

Table 1

	Per Cent For	(N)	Per Cent Against	(N)
"True" distribution	80	(400)	20	(100)
Minus cases lost due to 10 per cent error of measurement . . .	- 8	(40)	- 2	(10)
Plus cases gained due to 10 per cent error of measurement . .	+ 2	(10)	+ 8	(40)
Distribution as measured.	74	(370)	26	(130)

Table 2

	Per Cent For	(N)	Per Cent Against	(N)
Distribution on first measurement	74	(370)	26	(130)
Minus cases which were originally mis-measured, and return to opposite column	- 2	(10)	- 8	(40)
Plus cases which were originally mismeasured, and return to this column	+ 8	(40)	+ 2	(10)
Minus error cases on second measurement, moving to opposite column	- 8	(40)	- 2	(10)
Plus error cases on second measurement, moving into this column.	+ 2	(10)	+ 8	(40)
Distribution on second measurement	74	(370)	26	(130)

Table 3

	RESPONDENT'S VOTE INTENTIONS IN JUNE			
	Same as Members of Family		Opposite from Members of Family	
	Per Cent	No.	Per Cent	No.
Actual vote in November:				
Same as intention in June.	93	(273)	66	(25)
Changed to opposite party	7	(22)	34	(13)
	100	(295)	100	(38)

In their excellent discussion of measurement errors in a test-retest situation, Hovland, Lumsdaine, and Sheffield[2] point out that, since the numerically smaller category will always contain a higher proportion of shifters upon remeasurement, there is danger of concluding that "the majority opinion has much more effect on the minority than vice versa," whereas, actually, the shifts may be attributed entirely to errors of measurement. This brings us back to Berelson et al., who have not taken measurement errors into account in their analysis and who appear to have come to some conclusions about the effects of social pressures on vote changes when the findings could be explained on the basis of the kind of error-produced shifts discussed here. Here are some examples from Voting. Table 3 is a condensation of Chart LVIII in the book, with undecided and non-voting cases omitted. The authors' comment about this table (and a similar table based upon the political preferences of the respondent's friends) is: "Changes in vote are related to the political color of such intimate groups as the family household. While there are occasional deviations, individual members of a family adjust their views toward each others'....Those with compatible associates are stable, the others unstable. As a consequence, the already high homogeneity of small groups maintains itself and even builds up still further."

Actually, there is no evidence here that the homogeneity of the family as a small group is built up further during the campaign. Thirteen people who differed with their families at the beginning of the campaign returned to the fold. But 22 people who were in the family fold at the beginning of the campaign deserted it, so that homogeneity appears to have been lessened, if any change, indeed, occurred. However, since the numbers 22 and 13 are probably not significantly different from each other, the best interpretation of Table 3 appears to be that errors of

[2]Experiments on Mass Communication (Princeton, N. J.: Princeton University Press, 1949), Appendix D.

measurement have produced a counterbalancing shift. There are certainly no grounds for believing that the family is exercising strong political pressure. The difference in <u>proportions</u> in the table would be a function of the disproportionate sizes of the groups, if only errors of measurement were involved.

Similarly, the documentation of the existence of "cross-pressures" from one's occupational group is questionable. The figures in Table 4 are taken from Chart LXII. For the non-union white-collar group, the percentage differences look impressive. But since there are far more June Republicans than June Democrats among this group, the numbers of cases shifting in the two groups are identical (Table 5).

Table 4

	Percentage of Defectors to Opposite Party in August, Among:	
	June Republicans	June Democrats
Occupation:		
Non-union white collar	4	20
Union labor............	11	14

Table 5

	Number of Defectors to Opposite Party in August, Among:	
	June Republicans	June Democrats
Occupation:		
Non-union white collar	7	7
Union labor............	13	11

These charts appear in a chapter entitled "Social Effects of the Campaign"; some of the conclusions appearing at the end of the chapter are: "Within social strata with unambiguous political preferences, the political majority is more stable than the political minority." "People under cross-pressure (e.g., between class and religion) change their vote during the campaign more than people in homogeneous circumstances." Actually, none of the shifts which appear in the tables just described can be attributed to effects of the campaign, to group pressures, or to any other force impinging upon the respondents between the first and second interviews, until we know something about how much shift would occur upon remeasurement the next day because of errors of measurement alone.

One other point may be relevant here. In our discussion so far, it has been assumed that measurement errors are random—that an error is equally likely to occur for any case in the sample. There are some kinds of error for which this is not a good assumption. Let us assume that we are dealing with the attitude of a man who vacillates a little from day to day, always remaining generally pro, for example, but sometimes feeling more so than at other times. His vacillating may depend on the interview's tone of voice when he asks the question, the topic that was uppermost in the respondent's mind just before the interviewer arrived, etc. Let us assume further that we are dealing with an attitude which is really continuous in the population, ranging from very much pro (scale point 7) to very much anti (scale point 1) but that we have chosen to treat the answers as a dichot-

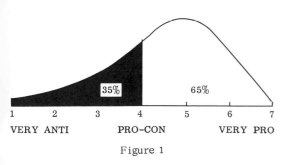

1   2   3   4   5   6   7
VERY ANTI   PRO-CON   VERY PRO

Figure 1

omy for convenience in measurement. The distribution of the population (upon first measurement) might be something like that shown in Figure 1.

The item in this illustration splits the population into two groups: 65 per cent pro and 35 per cent anti. Now let us assume that the instability of opinion is such that nearly everyone in the sample feel a little different at the time of remeasurement from the way he did the first time. The man who originally felt very pro (point 7) now feels a little less

so (point 6). Or the man at point 2 has shifted from point 2 to point 3 or 1. None of these shifts will show up in the tabulations, for none of them will take the individual across the border line which divides pros from antis. The chances that a shift in opinion will show up as a changed score from one interview to the next are obviously greater for the people who lie near the border line—in this example, for those whose opinions fall at points 3, 4, and 5. It follows that if we select a group of people who, for some reason, tend to fall near the border line, we will detect more of their changes and will therefore tend to define them as "unstable," even though other groups are changing just as much along the whole scale. It will be recognized that our earlier discussion of random errors is related to this point, for in almost all cases a higher proportion of the minority will be close to the border line than of the majority. But there are other instances in which the principle applies. For example, Table 6 presents some figures from Voting, Chart LVII.

Table 6

AUGUST TO NOVEMBER VOTE
CHANGE AMONG THOSE WHO:

	Discussed Election with Person of Same Party	Discussed Election with Person of Opposite Party
Per cent who changed to opposite party. .	1	13

We know that most people do not discuss the election during the campaign with anyone of the opposite party. It is probable that the people who do so are not such strongly convinced partisans in the first place as those who avoid cross-party discussion. In August they already lie closer to the border line of change. The chances are, then, that if they had been remeasured before they discussed the election with a person of the opposite party, more of them would have changed. The evidence is not conclusive that their change is related to their discussion with a person of different political views. A check is needed of the amount of change that would occur with simple remeasurement and no intervening events.

Clearly, it is much easier to point out problems of the sort that have been discussed than it is to offer solutions for them. Some check on test-retest reliability appears essential, however, before the errors of measurement can be isolated and the independent contribution of other factors assessed.

Obtaining such a check is not a simple matter. The "split-half" method of measuring reliability is obviously not applicable for a variable such as party preference, which is generally measured by a single question. And the "alternative-form" method also implies a group of questions devoted to the measurement of the variable being studied. Retest within a short period appears to be the only feasible method, and this has the drawback that the second measurement may be influenced by the respondent's recol-

lection of what he said on the first one. To determine the magnitude of this effect, a control group is sometimes recommended, to be measured at the same time as the second measurement, without having been exposed to the first measurement. However, even if the distribution of party preferences in such a control group were identical with the distribution in the main group upon second measurement, this would not rule out the possibility of a spurious consistency between the first and second measurements of the main group—such a consistency could occur, owing to the memory of the first response, without affecting the marginal distributions.

Further discussion should produce a solution to the problem of getting a valid measure of the error of measurement involved in panel studies. The solution would much enhance the power of the panel method.

Durkheim's Suicide *and Problems of Empirical Research*[1]

Hanan C. Selvin

SOURCE: *American Journal of Sociology*, Vol. 63, (1958), pp. 607–19.

Sixty-one years after it first appeared in print, Emile Durkheim's Suicide[2] is still a model of sociological research. Few, if any, later works can match the clarity and power with which Durkheim marshaled his facts to test and refine his theory. The stature of this work is even more impressive when one remembers that Durkheim lacked even so rudimentary a tool as the correlation coefficient.

Yet the methodology of Suicide is important to those now engaged in empirical research, not merely to historians of sociology. Durkheim recognized and solved many of the problems that beset present-day research. Others he formulated so lucidly—perhaps because he did not exile his methodology to appendixes —that their solution is relatively simple with the tools now available. To use a fashionable term, this paper will explore some of the methodological "continuities" that stem from Suicide, much as the essays based on The American Soldier[3] and

[1] I am deeply indebted to Paul F. Lazarsfeld for acquainting me with the kind of analysis on which this paper is based.

[2] Emile Durkheim, Suicide, trans. John A. Spaulding and George Simpson (Glencoe, Ill.: Free Press, 1951).

[3] Robert K. Merton and Paul F. Lazarsfeld (eds.),

The Authoritarian Personality[4] have done with these more recent classics.

"Methodology" has several meanings to sociologists. To some it means questionnaires, interviews, punched cards—the hand tools of research. To others, such as Durkheim himself and Parsons,[5] it is the assumptions and concepts used in constructing a theory. Here it will be used to mean the systematic examination of the procedures, assumptions, and modes of explanation in the analysis of empirical data.[6] This focus on Durkheim's methodology is not meant to minimize the importance of his theoretical insights; the value of methodological investigations, after all, is that they lead to more effective theorizing about social behavior. But Durkheim's theoretical development has been discussed by many authors,[7] while his analytical procedures have not received the attention they deserve.

MULTIVARIATE ANALYSIS

Central to Durkheim's methodology is his use of what has been called multivariate analysis: "the study and interpretation of complex interrelationships among a multiplicity of characteristics."[8] Much of the empirical analysis in Suicide can be viewed as the progressive introduction of additional variables. It will be useful to examine one of these analyses in detail, for it includes several of the procedures to be considered in this paper.

The first chapter on egoistic suicide (Book II, chap. ii) begins with the relation between religion and suicide rates for three groups of countries—the predominantly Protestant, the mixed Protestant and Catholic, and the predominantly Catholic.[9] But, as Durkheim points out, this comparison includes countries with radically different social conditions and requires consideration of the relation between religion and suicide within each country. Bavaria, the German state with the lowest proportion of Protestants, has the lowest proportion of suicides. And, in what may seem a mere piling-up of instances, the provinces within Bavaria also exhibit this same relationship: "Suicides are found in direct proportion to the number of Protestants and in inverse proportion to that of Catholics." Prussia and the Prussian provinces are the site of a similar analysis. Then the analysis is repeated for a third country: Switzerland. Here Durkheim takes advantage of the fact that both French- and German-speaking areas contain some cantons that are largely Catholic and others that are largely Protestant. This allows him to hold constant the effect of language as well as nationality ("race") while examining the effect of religion on suicide.

All the preceding analyses are based on data for nations or other large aggregations; thus the discussion of Bavaria cites the relatively high rate of suicides in provinces with high proportion of Protestants and the low rate in provinces with many Catholics. The implications of this procedure will be considered later; here it is important to note only that Durkheim recognized the difference between relationships based on aggregate data and those based on individual data, for he goes on to say that "in a fairly large number of cases the number of sui-

---

Continuities in Social Research: Studies in the Scope and Method of "The American Soldier" (Glencoe, Ill.: Free Press, 1950).

[4] Richard Christie and Marie Jahoda (eds.), Continuities in Social Research: Studies in the Scope and Method of "The Authoritarian Personality" (Glencoe, Ill.: Free Press, 1951).

[5] Emile Durkheim, The Rules of Sociological Method, trans. Sarah A. Solvay and John M. Mueller (Glencoe, Ill.: Free Press, 1948); Talcott Parsons, The Structure of Social Action (Glencoe, Ill.: Free Press, 1949), pp. 20-27 and chap. ix.

[6] Paul F. Lazarsfeld and Morris Rosenberg (eds.), The Language of Social Research (Glencoe, Ill.: Free Press, 1955), p. 4.

[7] Parsons, op. cit.; Harry Alpert, Emile Durkheim and His Sociology (New York: Columbia University Press, 1939), Parts II and III; Emile Benoit-Smullyan, "The Sociologism of Emile Durkheim and His School," in Henry Elmer Barnes (ed.), An Introduction to the History of Sociology (Chicago: University of Chicago Press, 1948), chap. xxvii. His chapter contains a considerable bibliography.

[8] Lazarsfeld and Rosenberg, op. cit., p. 11.

[9] This and the following two paragraphs are taken from Suicide, pp. 152-56.

cides per million inhabitants of the population of each confession has been directly determined." And he presents data on the suicide rates by religion for twelve periods of time in five countries, as well as some fragmentary data for France.

After disposing of the "deviant case" of Norway and Sweden, Durkheim considers the low suicide rate among Jews. As compared with Protestants and Catholics, Jews are more likely to live in cities and to pursue intellectual occupations—both conditions that are associated with higher suicide rates. Therefore, Durkheim reasons, if the reported rate of suicide among Jews is lower, despite these conditions, the "true" Jewish rate must be even lower than the figures reveal it to be.

As this passage makes plain, multivariate analysis meant more to Durkheim than simply considering the separate relationships between suicide and the several independent variables—religion, nationality, and language. Each new variable is progressively incorporated into the preceding analyses, so that several variables are considered jointly. The methodology of multivariate analysis is most clearly seen in the case where a relationship between one independent variable (say, religion) and the dependent variable (suicide) is "elaborated" by the introduction of a third variable or "test factor" (say, nationality). Lazarsfeld, Kendall, and Hyman have defined three major types of elaboration: explanation, interpretation, and specification.[10] Explanation is the attempt to "explain away" the apparent meaning of an observed relationship. For example, the association between religion and suicide might have been a manifestation of nationality, since countries like Germany have both a high suicide rate and many Protestants. Look-

ing into this possibility, Durkheim finds that the original association between religion and suicide persists when national differences are taken into account; nationality is therefore not an explanation of this relationship.

Once convinced that nationality and language do not explain away the association between religion and suicide, Durkheim turns to the interpretation of this relationship: what is the chain of variables connecting two such disparate phenomena as Protestantism and a high suicide rate? A spirit of free inquiry, according to Durkheim, is the most important link in this chain. Protestantism fosters free inquiry and free inquiry in turn leads to a higher rate of suicide.

Although Durkheim lacked the statistical techniques to develop these ideas rigorously, he saw their central place in theoretically oriented research. The relationship between two variables "... may not be due to the fact that one phenomenon is the cause of the other but to the fact that they are both the effects of the same cause, or, again, that there exists between them a third phenomenon, interposed but unperceived, which is the effect of the first and the cause of the second."[11]

Specification, the third mode of elaboration, identifies the conditions under which a relationship holds true in greater or less degree. For example, the effect of religion on suicide is less in the German cantons of Switzerland than in the French. Since specification appears in many forms in Suicide and since its role in the development of sociological theory differs from the other modes of elaboration, it will be considered at some length.

Specification leads to the development of multivariate theories of behavior in a way that is not true of explanation and interpretation. The aim of specification is to construct three-variable relationships—to say that, as in the example just cited, the effect of religion on suicide is greater in one place than in another. Note that this statement cannot be decomposed

[10] Paul F. Lazarsfeld, "Interpretation of Statistical Relations as a Research Operation," in Lazarsfeld and Rosenberg, op. cit., pp. 115-25; Patricia L. Kendall and Paul F. Lazarsfeld, "Problems of Survey Analysis," in Merton and Lazarsfeld, op. cit., pp. 133-96, esp. pp. 135-67; Herbert H. Hyman, Survey Design and Analysis (Glencoe, Ill.: Free Press, 1955), chaps. vi and vii.

[11] Rules, p. 131.

into a set of two-variable relationships. Explanation, on the other hand, involves a three-variable association only as an intermediate step, either toward rejecting the apparent finding or toward affirming its provisional meaning; in either case, the result is not a three-variable relationship. Interpretation, likewise, uses the three-variable association only to produce a series of two-variable relationships, to show that these relationships are linked by the variables they have in common.

This greater complexity of specification, its essential three-variable nature, leads to more complex problems in analysis. Durkheim's successes and failures in coping with some of these problems are instructive. Three problems will be considered: (1) the joint effects of group and individual characteristics on individual behavior; (2) the theoretical problems stemming from the statistical concept of "interaction"; and (3) the question of when to stop an empirical analysis.

The variety of analyses that come under the heading of specification is suggested by Hyman's classification; among other ways, one can specify a relationship according to the interest and concern of respondents, the time and place at which it occurs, or the conditions and contingencies on which it depends.[12] Durkheim's analysis provides still another type based on the "units of analysis." This type of specification of which there are several varieties, has been called "contextual analysis":[13] it involves the joint effects of an individual characteristic and a group characteristic on rates of individual behavior. In discussing the lower suicide rate among married people, Durkheim points out that in France the difference between the married and the single (his "coefficient of preservation") is greater among the men, while

in the Grand-Duchy of Oldenburg it is greater among the women.[14] That is, the social and cultural differences between France and Oldenburg are manifested in two essentially different ways: (1) They exert a <u>direct</u> effect; the over-all suicide rate is noticeably higher in France than in Oldenburg. (2) They exert an <u>indirect</u> effect; the <u>relationship</u> between sex and suicide is different in France and in Oldenburg. In other words, national characteristics have a differential impact on the sex-suicide association in the two countries, the difference between the sexes being greater in France than in Oldenburg.

Methodological devices like contextual analysis are more than ingenious ways to manipulate data. As Merton has emphasized, they are important in opening new directions for theory.[15] Durkheim's contextual analysis raises questions about the ways in which group and individual characteristics interact to affect behavior. For example, under what conditions do national characteristics produce such a marked reversal in the association between individual attributes and behavior?

The negative side of this case can also be found in <u>Suicide</u>: where Durkheim lacked adequate statistical techniques, he was occasionally led into theoretical contradictions. At one point he asserts that "the relation between the aptitude for suicide of married persons and that of widowers and widows is identically the same in widely different social groups, from the simple fact that the moral condition of widowhood everywhere bears the same relation to the moral constitution characteristic of marriage."[16] But Durkheim's data on Oldenberg and France lead to the opposite conclusion—that the relation between the suicide rates of married persons and widows and widowers was <u>not</u> the same in the two countries. What Durkheim lacked and what has since become available is a precise conception of statistical interaction, the

---

[12]Hyman, op. cit., pp. 295-311.
[13]Hanan C. Selvin and Warren O. Hagstrom, "Contextual Analysis: The Joint Effects of Group and Individual Characteristics on Behavior" (in preparation). I am indebted to Robert K. Merton for first calling my attention to the necessity of specifying the social context of a relationship between individual characteristics.

[14]Suicide, pp. 177-80.
[15]Robert K. Merton, Social Theory and Social Structure (Glencoe, Ill.: Free Press, 1949), chap. iii.
[16]Suicide, p. 307.

ways in which the association between two variables depends on the values of a third variable.[17]

Durkheim's treatment of statistical interaction and of the theoretical relationships that it measures is notably inconsistent. Sometimes, as here, he ignores the presence of interaction in his data. Elsewhere, he correctly notes its presence, remarking, for example, that seasonal differences in suicide are less pronounced in cities than in rural areas.[18] And in another place he assumes, without any evidence for or against his assumption, that the interaction of temperature and location is zero: "...if the temperature had the supposed influence, it should be felt equally in the geographical distribution of suicides."[19]

One possible reason for Durkheim's inconsistency is that he had not formalized his analytical procedures. In effect, each time he came to a case of specification, it had to be reasoned through from the beginning. Formalizations such as the Lazarsfeld-Kendall-Hyman types of elaboration enable the analyst to recognize the same principle at work in different instances and therefore to treat them similarly. Such formalizations also reveal a link between apparently disparate phenomena; thus the formal model of elaboration also illuminates the seemingly unrelated problem of when to stop an analysis.

Durkheim's treatment of "race" and suicide provides a case in point.[20] Arguing that the high rate of suicide in Germany "might be due to the special nature of German civilization," he decides to "see whether the German retains this sad primacy outside of Germany."[21] To this

end he examines the suicide rates in the provinces of Austria-Hungary, in which German-speaking people range from 1.9 to 100 per cent, and finds "not the least trace of German influence" on the suicide rate. However, a close examination of Durkheim's data, particularly of the five provinces that have high proportions of Germans and disproportionately few suicides, leads to quite different conclusions. These provinces—Upper Austria, Salzburg, Transalpine Tyrol, Carinthia, and Styria—comprise the western part of present-day Austria. If these five contiguous provinces are removed, the Spearman rank correlation for the remaining ten provinces is 0.95, indicating an almost perfect relationship between the suicide rate and the proportion of German-speaking people.

The important point here is not substantive but methodological. Durkheim stopped his analysis as soon as he found a "zero" relationship. This procedure is perhaps more common in research today. Small associations are considered a signal to turn to other matters, especially when the associations are not statistically significant. The reasoning behind this assumption is never made explicit, but it would seem to be that, if two variables are not associated when other items are left free to vary, they will not be associated when these other items are "held constant." That is, if the total association between two variables is zero, the partial association will be zero. Sometimes this is true; often it is not. Hyman's passage on the "elaboration of a zero relationship"[22] indicates that this may happen when the two partial relations are approximately equal in size and opposite in sign. For example, a surpris-

---

[17]The phenomenon of statistical interaction has been given many different names (e.g., specification, conditional relationship, differential impact, differential sensitivity, and non-additivity of effects).

[18]*Suicide*, p. 120.
[19]*Ibid.*, p. 113.
[20]*Ibid.*, pp. 86-87.

[21]By today's standards Durkheim's table shows a moderately high degree of association. The Spearman rank correlation is 0.57. In general, Durkheim regarded anything much less than perfect rank cor-

relation as "independent." The reason why he could demand and find such high levels of association, while survey researchers are content with much less impressive relationships, has to do with the differences in the numbers of cases on which the associations are based. See the discussion of "grouping" in G. Undy Yule and M. G. Kendall, *An Introduction to the Theory of Statistics* (14th ed.; New York: Hafner, 1950), pp. 313-14.

[22]*Op. cit.*, pp. 307-10.

ingly small association between job satisfaction and participation in community organizations resulted from a positive association between participation and satisfaction among members of the working class and a negative association of approximately the same size in the white-collar class.

To my knowledge, Hyman's is the only published discussion of this problem. It may be useful, therefore, to make two further points suggested by Hyman's brief treatment. First, he implies that this kind of relationship is uncommon and even accidental. Actually, it may occur frequently under certain conditions—for example, in the kind of contextual analysis discussed above, where people are assigned to groups instead of being born into them or choosing them themselves. A study of leisure-time behavior in army training companies found that many small or zero associations between behavior and an individual characteristic, such as marital status, resulted from opposite and approximately equal associations in companies with different "leadership climates."[23]

Second, still another type of elaboration of a zero relationship may be ranged alongside the two identified by·Hyman. A

tion tend to choose the Democratic party, yet the "collapsed" table of information and party affiliation without regard to education will show that, among both the more-informed, 50 per cent are Democrats. The two partial associations are positive (and about the same size); the total association is zero. Unrealistic as this example may be (although it could describe a university town with a Democratic newspaper), it does demonstrate the importance of looking into those zero associations that theory or previous research suggests should not have been zero. A zero association between two variables may therefore result from any one of three different conditions in the partial relationships: zero associations in both partials, equal and opposite associations, or associations in the same direction. Only the first of these is a signal to stop the analysis.

THE FUNCTIONS OF REPLICATION IN EMPIRICAL RESEARCH

Another multivariate procedure that is conspicuous in Suicide and that deserves intensive inquiry is replication, the systematic restudy of a given relationship in different contexts.

Again using the first chapter on egois-

Table 1. Information and Party Affiliation Education Held Constant
(Hypothetical Data)

	Less Educated		More Educated	
	Much Information	Little Information	Much Information	Little Information
Per Cent Democratic....	38	24	74	63
N...............	(200)	(100)	(100)	(200)

zero association between two variables may occur even when both partial associations are in the same direction. The hypothetical example in Table 1 shows that this case would interest the student of political behavior. At both levels of education, the people with more informa-

tic suicide as an illustration, we find that the original table relating religion and suicide is followed by no less than the seventeen replications in three pages. Why so many replications? Durkheim's answer is not altogether clear. He does demand that the facts cited to support a thesis be "numerous enough not to be attributable to accidental circumstances—not to permit another explanation—to be contradicted by no other fact."[24] But

[23]Hanan C. Selvin, The Effects of Leadership Climate on the Nonduty Behavior of Army Trainees ("University Microfilms Publications," No. 19.256 [microfilmed Ph.D. dissertation, Columbia University, 1956]), Appendix F.

[24]Suicide, p. 95.

these principles are not systematically explained. This section will therefore examine some of the uses of replications in Suicide and will consider what functions replications may serve in current research.

Durkheim's lavish use of replications is all the more noteworthy in contrast with modern survey research, where a relationship is often demonstrated only in a single table. One reason why Durkheim used so many replications is undoubtedly that his data came from official records; it cost him little more to study suicide in six countries than in one. On the other hand, in contemporary surveys the researcher must gather his own data, often at great expense, so that one community is a practical limit. However, as will be seen, this explanation rests on too narrow a conception of replications; a careful study of Durkheim's procedures will show that there are abundant opportunities for replication in every survey. A second reason for demonstrating a hypothesis in only one table is the belief that a close adherence to modern techniques of statistical inference—tests of significance, confidence intervals, and the like—guarantees the statistical soundness of the conclusions. This point of view has recently been vigorously attacked and staunchly defended.[25] Instead of repeating these arguments here, it will be shown that properly conducted replications may achieve the same ends more effectively. First, however, it is necessary to clarify the different kinds of replications.

"Unit replications" are the most frequent in Suicide; in these the original finding is re-examined for different groups of subjects—for example, the excess of military over civilian suicides is confirmed for eight different countries

of Europe.[26] Durkheim further replicates this finding within the Austro-Hungarian Empire; the military-civilian difference persists in the various military areas.[27] These two examples suggest that unit replications may be divided into two subtypes: "external replications" and "internal replications."

In external replications the conclusions of one study are tested independently in another study, usually conducted by a different investigator.[28] Cross-cultural comparisons are a familiar example. Demographers and others who work with official records also conduct external replications as a matter of course. But this procedure is difficult and expensive for anyone who must gather his own data.

Just the opposite is true of internal replications, in which a finding is restudied for smaller groups within the original set of subjects. In the passage on military and civilian suicides there are several external replications, based on the different countries, and several internal replications for areas within one country.[29] Although these replications have a geographical basis, a finding may be replicated in groups formed on any set of variables. In the chapter on anomic suicide (Book II, chapter v), Durkheim presents a table of suicide rates by occupation for eight countries. Here the various countries act as external replications for his original finding on occupations and suicide. But the same table could also serve as an internal replication of the national differences considered in the earlier chapter on egoistic suicide, the comparisons between overall national suicide rates being replicated for the comparable occupational groups within the countries.[30] Of course, all replications are not equally desirable;

[25] Hanan C. Selvin, "A Critique of Tests of Significance in Survey Research," American Sociological Review, XXII (1957), 519-27; David Gold, "Comment" and Hanan C. Sevin, "Reply," American Sociological Review, XXIII (1958), 85-86; James Beshers, "Comment" and Hanan C. Selvin, "Reply," American Sociological Review, Vol. XXIII (April, 1958).

[26] Suicide, p. 228.
[27] Ibid., p. 235.
[28] For a collection of external replications and an interesting treatment of the factors making for successful replications see Robert C. Hanson, "Evidence and Procedures Characteristics of 'Reliable' Propositions in Social Science," American Journal of Sociology, LXIII (1958), 357-70.
[29] Suicide, pp. 228-39.
[30] Ibid., p. 258.

some criteria for choosing replications will be taken up after considering the uses of replications.

Replications, properly conducted, may serve at least two functions. They may provide a more valid "test of significance" where the usual tests cannot be legitimately applied, and they may lessen the seriousness of the "ecological fallacy," in which relationships between characteristics of individuals are wrongly inferred from data about groups.

REPLICATIONS AND STATISTICAL SIGNIFICANCE

Some reasons why tests of statistical significance are inapplicable in survey research have been noted in another paper.[31] Perhaps the most important reason—and the one that bears on the use of replications—is that the tests assume an experimental situation, in which differences between subjects can be randomized. Agronomists, for example, can convert constant differences in the fertility of their experimental plots into chance differences by randomizing the assignment of their plants; in effect, they toss a coin to determine whether a plant goes into the experimental plot or the control plot. But sociologists can seldom randomize. If Catholics are more numerous in Italy and Protestants in Germany, the sociologist must cope with these stubborn facts. He cannot randomly assign Protestants and Catholics to the two countries.

Randomization turns such systematic differences, or "correlated biases," into random differences. Tests of significance can then be used to measure the probability that the observed difference between experimental and control groups could have been produced by the accidents of randomization. Without randomization, these correlated biases remain as possible sources of the observed difference between the groups, along with the experimental variable whose influence is being measured. Thus the interpretation of the difference in suicide rates between Italy and Germany as the

result of religious differences must take into account the many other differences between the two countries—education, cultural norms, and so on, which may account, in part at least, for the relationship between religion and suicide. Some of these differences could have been removed by cross-tabulation, had Durkheim had the necessary data. Others, not necessarily the least important, could not. Consequently, it appears misleading to ask for the probability that the observed relationship may be "due to change" without first being reasonably certain that correlated biases did not produce it.

Replications, properly conducted, can take care of correlated biases and random errors at the same time. When Durkheim replicates within Germany the relationship previously studied among the various countries of Europe, he is removing the host of biases correlated with nationality. And when he further replicates within Bavaria and within Prussia, constant differences between these states no longer are mixed in with the religion-suicide relationship. Finally, his replications based on individual data remove some of the provincial differences. At each level of replication, additional correlated biases are controlled: the original relationship between religion and suicide gains more and more support.

Replications can thus lessen the likelihood that correlated biases may have produced the observed result. It is necessary only that the variable on which the replications are based be theoretically relevant (i.e., that there is reason to believe it is causally related to both the independent and the dependent variable). Now what of the random factors that may have produced the observed result? Here, too, replications are useful: they lead toward a valid test of significance which is simple to understand and easy to compute.

Consider once again the seventeen replications of the relationship between religion and suicide. How likely is it that this relationship resulted from some combination of random errors? That is,

[31]Selvin, "A Critique of Significance Tests."

how often would one expect to find seventeen consecutive replications all showing Protestants more likely to commit suicide if, in fact, Protestants and Catholics are equally prone to suicide? Assuming that the replications are independent, that the outcome of one replication does not affect the outcome of another, the probability of such a series of replications is $(1/2)$, 17 a result significant at the 0.00001 level.[32]

Some cautions are in order. First, the validity of this computation, as of the ordinary test of significance, rests on the elimination of correlated biases. Since one can almost always conceive of relevant variables that have not been controlled and since there is no randomization to turn these correlated biases into random events, this condition is never fully satisfied. However, by applying this test only within series of replications, some, at least, of the correlated biases are controlled. The more variables that are controlled in any one replication, the more convincing this test of significance becomes.

Because he is dealing with official statistics that seldom are classifiable according to more than three variables, Durkheim's control over the correlated biases is relatively loose. Survey analysts, on the other hand, can more easily control these variables. For example, to test the hypothesis that socioeconomic status affects voting behavior, one would compare subgroups of high and low status that are similar on as many relevant variables as can be manipulated simultaneously. Such a test might compare two groups of young, single, urban, Protestant, male high-school graduates, one group of high socioeconomic status, the other of low status. This comparison would be repeated for all possible com-

binations of these six variables; if enough of these comparisons are in the same direction as the original relationship, one can be reasonably confident that the original relationship is not the result of random errors, assuming, of course, that there are no other important correlated biases.

In controlling for correlated biases, the subgroups should be formed on relevant variables; in testing for statistical significance, the subgroups should be independent. Consequently, if both criteria are satisfied, replications will tend to accomplish both tasks simultaneously. Relevance depends on the implicit or explicit theory that is being used, and no rules can guarantee it. On the other hand, independence can in general be insured by seeing that no individual appears in more than one subgroup in a given replication. For example, it would not be efficient to replicate Durkheim's religion-suicide relationship by studying it first among married and single men and then among older and younger men in the same country, for some men will appear in both sets of comparisons.[33]

One empirical procedure used by Durkheim appears at first glance to be another form of replication. In demonstrating that the relationship previously found between time of day and the suicide rate really depends on the "intensity of social life," he musters a variety of indicators of social activity—accidents, rail travel, and express receipts.[34] Social activity and suicide turn out to be highly associated, thus supporting his interpretation of the time-of-day relationship. Although this seems to be another type of replication, serving the same ends as those discussed above, this kind of item replication lacks one essential element of the unit replications: independence of observations. In fact, one does not even seek independence in item replications. These replications help to demonstrate

---

[32]Samuel A. Stouffer, "Quantitative Methods," in Joseph B. Gittler (ed.), Review of Sociology (New York: John Wiley & Sons, 1957), pp. 45-46. Stouffer's use of replications in The American Soldier (Princeton: Princeton University Press, 1949), I, 92-95, is a notable example (he refers to replications there as the "method of matched comparisons"). See also Selvin, The Effects of Leadership Climate, pp. 43-47, 183-204.

[33]Note that two or more time replications in the same table of Suicide are always separated by a period of years, thus increasing the independence of the replications.

[34]Suicide, pp. 118-20.

that an indicator is valid—in other words, that it means what the analyst says it means. The greater the variety of indicators of social activity that Durkheim can relate to suicide, the greater his assurance that social activity—and not some accidental correlate of it—is what accounts for the variations in suicide.[35]

Replications thus serve Durkheim as a means of testing and refining his empirical hypotheses. The preceding discussion has suggested that they may serve these functions even better in survey research, where large numbers of variables can be easily manipulated. Another function of replications, of less general application but often of crucial importance in studies based on "ecological" data, will be examined in the following section.

REPLICATION AND THE "ECOLOGICAL FALLACY"

Robinson[36] first called the attention of sociologists to the fallacy of assuming that associations computed from group means or group proportions are valid estimates of the associations that would be obtained from individual data.[37] Most of Durkheim's tables are based on such fallacious reasoning. Thus he reports that the rate of suicide in departments of France varies according to the proportion of "persons of independent means."[38] This result is consistent with either of the following hypotheses: none of the people who commit suicide has independent means, or all of them have independent means. In this table the ecological association between characteristics of departments reveals nothing about the individual association between a person's wealth and whether or not he commits suicide.

Every case of ecological associations does not entail the ecological fallacy. Menzel has shown that ecological associations are not only permissible but necessary when the "unit of analysis" is a group rather than the individuals in it.[39] However, Durkheim never theorizes about wealthy and poor departments, only about wealthy and poor individuals. And if he were interested in group characteristics—at the level, say, of departments or provinces—why would he replicate for successively finer subdivisions within these groups, in two cases carrying the replications down to individual data?[40] It is clear that Durkheim was guilty of the ecological fallacy.

To say that Durkheim's procedures were fallacious does not detract from his conclusions.[41] They may be true, even if they do not necessarily follow from his data. In effect, Durkheim recognized this problem and attempted to solve it in the only way open to him—the systematic use of replications for units smaller than those in his original relationship. When he was able to carry the replications down to individual data, there was, of course, no ecological fallacy: the hypothesis stated for group data is confirmed for individual data. However, even when Durkheim did not have individual data,

---

[35] Item replication is, in a sense, the inverse of scaling. In item replication, one begins with a concept and seeks a variety of indicators to clarify its meaning. In scaling, one begins with a set of items and asks whether there is a single underlying concept that accounts for them.

[36] William S. Robinson, "Ecological Correlations and the Behavior of Individuals," *American Sociological Review*, XV (1950), 351-57. This problem seems to have been discovered and treated independently in psychology, statistics, and economics, as well as in sociology, although not so fully as in Robinson's paper (see Edward L. Thorndike, "On the Fallacy of Imputing the Correlations Found for Groups to the Individuals or Smaller Groups Composing them," *American Journal of Psychology*, LII (1929), 122-24; Yule and Kendall, op. cit., pp. 310-15; Kenneth H. Arrow, "Mathematical Models in the Social Sciences," in Daniel Lerner and Harold D. Lasswell (eds.), *The Policy Sciences* (Stanford: Stanford University Press, 1951), p. 134).

[37] Robinson's paper concentrates on linear regression and correlation, but the same problem arises, whatever the measure of association.

[38] *Suicide*, p. 245.

[39] Herbert Menzel, "Comment on Robinson's Ecological Correlations and the Behavior of Individuals,'" *American Sociological Review*, XV (1950), 674; see also the discussion of the "modifiable unit" in Yule and Kendall, op. cit.

[40] *Suicide*, pp. 154, 175.

[41] Andrew F. Henry and James F. Short, Jr., have made the most recent attempt to formulate a comprehensive theory of suicide in their *Suicide and Homicide* (Glencoe, Ill.: Free Press, 1954).

the procedure of replicating in smaller units may lead, as Duncan and Davis have shown,[42] to useful estimates of the individual association.

Durkheim's data cannot be used to illustrate this procedure, for a reason to be stated shortly. Consider, instead, the following ecological data from a hypothetical city in which there are 20 election districts of 100 voters. Each of the first 10 districts has 10 per cent Republicans and 20 per cent voting for Eisenhower. (These are group attributes; nothing is said about the number of individuals who are both Republicans and for Eisenhower.) The other 10 districts are 80 per cent Republicans and 90 per cent for Eisenhower. However one chooses to measure association—by product-moment correlation, percentage differences in a fourfold table, or any other index—this is a perfect ecological association: all the districts with many Republicans are for Eisenhower, as against none of the districts with few Republicans. This is formally the kind of relationship studied by Durkheim.

Now consider any one of the first 10 districts. The number of Republicans for Eisenhower is not known, but it is easy to see that it must be between a maximum of 10 and a minimum of zero. The corresponding values for the other 10 districts are 80 and 70. If each district had the maximum possible number of Republicans for Eisenhower, the total for the city would be $(10 \times 10) + (10 \times 80) = 900$; the minimum total for the city would be $(10 \times 0) + (10 \times 70) = 700$. Table 2 shows the maximum and minimum values for the four cells of the individual association. If the association between Republicanism and preference for Eisenhower is a maximum in each district, then, for the city as a whole, 100 per cent of the Republicans and 18.2 per cent of the Democrats prefer Eisenhower, a difference of 81.8 per cent. This is something less than the perfect ecological associa-

tion; there, every Republican district was for Eisenhower and every Democratic district for Stevenson. Similarly, if the within-district associations are as small as possible, then 77.8 per cent of the Republicans and 36.4 per cent of the Democrats are for Eisenhower, a difference of 41.4 per cent.

The ecological data for the districts thus lead to bounds for the individual association in the city as a whole. Durkheim's procedure of replications in successively smaller units would likewise seem to generate bounds for the intellectual associations on which his analysis is really based. In fact, Goodman has shown that the smallest units give the closest possible bounds; nothing would be gained in the example above by aggregating the districts into larger areas.[43] Durkheim's reason for replicating at several levels instead of going directly to the smallest units is probably that his data were uneven (i.e., that he did not have comparable figures for the provinces in all his countries).

Table 2. Party Affiliation and Vote
(Hypothetical Data)

Presidential Candidate Choice		Individual Party Affiliation		
		Republican	Democratic	Total
Eisenhower	Max.	900	200	1,100
	Min.	700	400	
Stevenson	Max.	0	900	
	Min.	200	700	900

The only difficulty in applying this procedure to Durkheim's data is that it will not work. Goodman's analysis indicates that bounds can be inferred only when the points in the ecological scatter plot are located in at least two of the four regions in Figure 1. The two sets of points for the hypothetical election data are located in regions A and D, as shown. But if the proportion for Eisenhower is replaced by the suicide rate and the pro-

[42]Otis Dudley Duncan and Beverly Davis, "An Alternative to Ecological Correlation," *American Sociological Review*, XVIII (1953), 665–66.

[43]Leo A. Goodman, "Some Alternatives to Ecological Correlation" (Chicago: Statistical Research Center, University of Chicago, 1957) (dittoed). This comprehensive paper also includes another method for estimating the "individual regression" from ecological data under certain assumptions. Unfortunately, these assumptions are not met in Durkheim's data.

portion Republican by any one of Durkheim's independent variables (say, the proportion of Protestants), than all Durkheim's data are located in region <u>B</u>. (This is the region in which the suicide rate is less than the proportion of Protestants and also less than the proportion of non-Protestants.) No amount of replication, therefore, will lead to bounds for the individual association between suicide and Protestantism or between suicide and any of Durkheim's independent variables. Suicide is too rare an event, compared with the rates of the other variables he used. Ecological reasoning in <u>Suicide</u> is not limited to geographical data. "A proof of the slight effect of marriage [on suicide] is the fact that the marriage rate has changed very little since the first of the [nineteenth] century, while suicide has tripled."[44] Here, again, the real question is whether married people are more or less likely than single people to commit suicide. With these data, however, a positive, negative, or zero individual association is possible. Data aggregated over time can lead to false interpretations, just as can data aggregated over geographical units. In both cases the difficulty is removed by studying the data within units rather than "ecologically." There is no ecological fallacy when the independent variable and suicide are examined for individuals within each geographical area or for individuals within each time period. In other words, both versions of the ecological fallacy can be considered as cases of "spurious association." This, it will be recalled, is an erroneous inference that is "explained away" by holding constant a variable that accounts for both the items being studied. The association between region and religion and between region and suicide may account for the ecological association between religion and suicide; holding region constant removes any possibility of a false inference from this association. Similarly, the association between suicide and the marriage rate may lead to false inferences unless it is examined

within relatively short time periods.[45] There is thus a close methodological connection between problems of ecological association and procedures of multivariate analysis.

Proportion of District
for Eisenhower

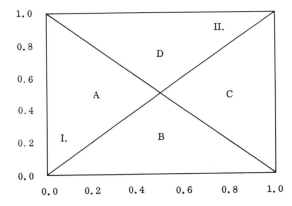

Proportion of District
Voting Republican

Figure. 1. Conditions under which ecological associations yield bounds for individual associations.

This section has considered the uses of replications in testing sociological hypotheses and in making valid inferences from characteristics of groups to characteristics of their members. In both cases attention has been focused on the relationship of groups and subgroups; the description of the group, as given by Durkheim, has been taken for granted. But here, too, there are useful lessons to be learned from a careful examination of Durkheim's procedures.

A PROBLEM IN DESCRIBING GROUPS

The first section of the chapter on anomic suicide begins: "It is a well-known fact that economic crises have an aggravating effect on the suicidal tendency."[46] Durkheim then establishes that

---

[44]<u>Suicide</u>, p. 185.

[45]This is explanation in which the "ordering principle" is not "time" but "level of aggregation" or "level of complexity" (cf. Kendall and Lazarsfeld, <u>op. cit.</u>, p. 196).

[46]<u>Suicide</u>, p. 241.

poverty is not the link between economic crises and suicide. He argues that poverty "tends rather to produce the opposite effect. There is very little suicide in Ireland, where the peasantry leads so wretched a life. Poverty-stricken Calabria has almost no suicide; Spain has a tenth as many as France."[47] Here is an association between groups (countries) and individual behavior, in which the relationship is attributed to one property of the groups—their poverty. But Calabria, Ireland, and Spain are not only poorer than France; they are also more Catholic than France and, as Durkheim was at pains to show in his analysis of egoistic suicide, less educated. There is no necessary reason why poverty should be singled out as the cause of the lower suicide rate in these countries. Religious or educational differences would have accounted equally well for the variations in suicide.

Essentially this same problem appears in different guise when one tries to infer the intensity of some form of behavior from data about its incidence. For example, Durkheim assumes that districts with high divorce rates have many families that are near divorce.[48] This statement may be true; it is not necessarily true. Two countries with the same average intensity of marital unhappiness may, because of their legal codes, have very different rates of divorce. To move legitimately from incidence to intensity in this way, one must take into account the other group characteristics that affect the dependent variable.

The source of these difficulties is clear. It is the oversimple description of a group according to a single variable. What can be done to avoid such problems? The obvious answer is to hold the other group characteristics constant by cross-tabulation, just as one does with individual characteristics. To study the influence of poverty on suicide, Durkheim would have had to find areas that were alike on other variables, such as religion, urbanization, and education, and different only in relative wealth. As a practical matter, this is impossible. Murdock's cross-cultural comparisons are based on as many as 250 different cultures, but even this number is too small to allow more than one variable to be held constant in any table.[49] The smaller the groups, the easier such statistical manipulation of group variables becomes, at least in principle. But surveys that study the joint effects of group and individual characteristics on behavior seldom have the resources to include the hundreds of groups that would be necessary if group characteristics were to be manipulated by cross-tabulation (Studies based on census data can easily handle thousands of groups, but they do not often have data on the joint effects of individual and group variables.)

If groups differing in only a single characteristic are practically impossible to find in survey research and if large numbers of groups are impossibly expensive is there any alternative? The most attractive alternative—perhaps the only one is to abandon the attempt to deal with one group characteristic at a time and to describe the groups with as many variables as necessary. Where the number of groups is too small for cross-tabulation, they should be described in terms of a multivariate typology.[50] In the first example above, for instance, Calabria, Ireland, and Spain would have been described not simply as poor but as poor, Catholic, and having a bad level of education. Theoretical simplicity is thus sacrificed for theoretical and empirical accuracy. These countries would differ from France on three or more independent variables instead of one, but they would be described in all their relevant aspects.[51]

---

[47]Ibid., p. 245; italics added.
[48]Ibid., p. 263.

[49]George Peter Murdock, Social Structure (New York: Macmillan Co., 1949).
[50]Allen H. Barton, "The Concept of Property-Space in Social Research," in Lazarsfeld and Rosenberg, op. cit., pp. 40-53.

[51]When the number of variables and the number of groups is as large as fifteen or twenty, it becomes economical to use factor-analytic procedures for determining the dimensions of the typology (see Andrew W. Halpin, The Leadership Behavior of

It is only fitting to close this argument for the typological analysis of group characteristics by noting that here, too, Durkheim pointed the way. In his chapter "How To Determine Social Causes and Social Types" (Book II, chap. i), he argues for the classification of suicides, not as the simple act of killing one's self, but according to "morphological types" determined by the psychological and other characteristics of each suicide. It is only because the necessary data were not available that he was compelled to use his "etiological types." The same

School Superintendents [Columbus: College of Education, Ohio State University, 1956], pp. 3-10; Selvin, The Effects of Leadership Climate, pp. 11-39). The descriptions of group characteristics in these two works indicate that factor analysis is ideally suited to the study of groups (while it is, at best, a crude tool for the study of individuals). Briefly, the reason is that the correlations of group means and group proportions are virtually free from the idiosyncratic and random errors that attenuate the correlations of individual data, so that relatively few factors account for most of the variation in a large number of variables.

logic and the greater ease with which group data may now be gathered suggest that groups be described as multivariate types rather than by a single variable.

Despite its occasionally archaic language ("suicidogenic current"), the empirical analysis in Suicide is as vital today as it was in 1897—perhaps more so, since the quantitative approach that Durkheim pioneered has since become widely accepted among sociologists. But overemphasis on the quantitative aspects of Suicide would be as dangerous as total neglect, if it furthered the current tendency to substitute technical virtuosity for hard thinking about empirical data, thinking that is guided by theory and is directed toward enriching theory. This, after all, is the essential message of Suicide: that methodology is valuable insofar as it springs from the needs of theory and that theory is most fruitful when it is continually tested and refined in empirical research.

Ecological Correlations and the Behavior of Individuals

W. S. Robinson

SOURCE: *American Sociological Review*, Vol. 15, (June, 1950), pp. 351–57.

INTRODUCTION

An individual correlation is a correlation in which the statistical object or thing described is indivisible. The correlation between color and illiteracy for persons in the United States, shown later in Table 1, is an individual correlation, because the kind of thing described is an indivisible unit, a person. In an individual correlation the variables are descriptive properties of individuals, such as height, income, eye color, or race, and not de-

scriptive statistical constants such as rates or means.

In an ecological correlation the statistical object is a group of persons. The correlation. between the percentage of the population which is Negro and the percentage of the population which is illiterate for the 48 states, shown later as Figure 2, is an ecological correlation. The thing described is the population of a state, and not a single individual. The variables are percentages, descriptive properties of groups, and not descriptive properties of individuals.

Ecological correlations are used in an impressive number of quantitative sociological studies, some of which by now have attained the status of classics: Cowles' "Statistical Study of Climate in Relation to Pulmonary Tuberculosis";[1] Gosnell's "Analysis of the 1932 Presidential Vote in Chicago,"[2] "Factorial and Correlational Analysis of the 1934 Vote in Chicago,"[3] and the more elaborate factor analysis in Machine Politics;[4] Ogburn's "How Women Vote,"[5] "Measurement of the Factors in the Presidential Election of 1928,"[6] "Factors in the Variation of Crime Among Cities,"[7] and Groves and Ogburn's correlation analyses in American Marriage and Family Relationships;[8] Ross' study of school attendance in Texas;[9] Shaw's Delinquency Areas study of the correlates of delinquency,[10] as well as the more recent analyses in Juvenile Delinquency in Urban Areas;[11] Thompson's "Some Factors Influencing the Ratios of Children to Women in American Cities, 1930";[12] Whelpton's study of the correlates of birth rates, in "Geographic and Economic Differentials in Fertility";[13] and White's "The Relation of Felonies to Environmental Factors in Indianapolis."[14]

Although these studies and scores like them depend upon ecological correlations, it is not because their authors are interested in correlations between the

properties of areas as such. Even out-and-out ecologists, in studying delinquency, for example, rely primarily upon data describing individuals, not areas.[15] In each study which uses ecological correlations, the obvious purpose is to discover something about the behavior of individuals. Ecological correlations are used simply because correlations between the properties of individuals are not available. In each instance, however, the substitution is made tacitly rather than explicitly.

The purpose of this paper is to clarify the ecological correlation problem by stating, mathematically, the exact relation between ecological and individual correlations, and by showing the bearing of that relation upon the practice of using ecological correlations as substitutes for individual correlations.

THE ANATOMY OF AN ECOLOGICAL CORRELATION

Before discussing the mathematical relation between ecological and individual correlations, it will be useful to exhibit the structural connection between them in a specific situation. Figure 1 shows the scatter diagram for the ecological cor-

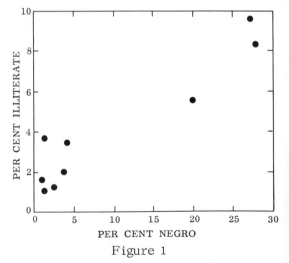

Figure 1

relation between color and illiteracy for the Census Bureau's nine geographic divisions of the United States in 1930. The

[1] Journal of the American Statistical Association, 30 (Sept., 1935), 517-536.

[2] American Political Science Review, 24 (Dec., 1935), 967-984.

[3] Journal of the American Statistical Association, 31 (Sept., 1936), 507-518.

[4] Chicago, 1938.

[5] Political Science Quarterly, 34 (Sept., 1919), 413-433.

[6] Social Forces, 8 (Dec., 1929), 175-183.

[7] Journal of the American Statistical Association, 30 (Mar., 1935), 12-34.

[8] New York, 1928.

[9] School Attendance in the United States: 1920, a supplementary report to the 1920 U.S. Census, Washington, 1924.

[10] Chicago, 1929.

[11] Chicago, 1942.

[12] American Journal of Sociology, 45 (Sept., 1939), 183-199.

[13] Annals of the American Academy of Political and Social Science, 188 (Nov., 1936), 37-55.

[14] Social Forces, 11 (May, 1932), 498-513.

[15] In Shaw's Delinquency Areas, for example.

X-coordinate of each point is the percentage of the divisional population 10 years old and over which is Negro. The Y-coordinate is the percentage of the same population which is illiterate.[16] The Pearsonian correlation for Figure 1, i.e., the ecological correlation, is .946.

Table 1 is a fourfold table showing for the same population the correlation between color and illiteracy considered as properties of individuals rather than geographic areas. The Pearsonian (fourfold-point) correlation for Table 1, i.e., the individual correlation, is .203, slightly more than one-fifth of the corresponding ecological correlation.

Table 1. The Individual Correlation Between Color and Illiteracy for the United States, 1930

(for the population 10 years old and over)[17]

	Negro	White	Total
Illiterate	1,512	2,406	3,918
Literate	7,780	85,574	93,354
Total	9,292	87,980	97,272

Ordinarily, such an ecological correlation would be computed on a county or state basis, instead of the divisional basis used here to simplify numerical presentation.

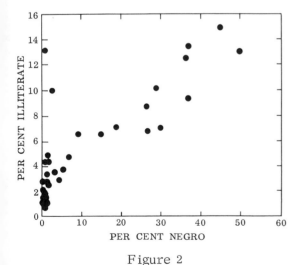

Figure 2

sentation. Whether the ecological areas are counties, states, or divisions, however, the results are similar. Figure 2, for example, shows the ecological correlation on a state rather than a divisional basis. When the ecological areas are states, as in Figure 2, the ecological correlation is .773, to be compared with .946 when the ecological areas are divisions.

The connecting link between the individual correlation of Table 1 and the ecological correlation of Figure 1 is the individual correlations between color and illiteracy within the nine geographic divisions which furnish the nine observations for the ecological correlation. These are the within-areas individual correlations, a selection from which is given in Table 2.

Table 2. The Within-Areas Individual Correlations Between Color and Illiteracy for the United States, 1930[18]

		Negro	White	Total
New England	Illiterate	4	240	244
	Literate	72	6,386	6,458
	Total	76	6,626	6,702
Middle Atlantic	Illiterate	32	719	751
	Literate	836	19,958	20,794
	Total	868	20,677	21,545
East North Central	Illiterate	36	392	428
	Literate	735	19,443	20,178
	Total	771	19,835	20,606
. . . .				
Pacific	Illiterate	2	71	73
	Literate	75	6,332	6,407
	Total	77	6,403	6,480

Both the individual correlation and the ecological correlation depend upon the within-areas individual correlations, but in different ways. The individual correlation (Table 1) depends upon the internal or cell frequencies of the nine within-areas individual correlations. Its cell frequencies are sums of the nine corresponding divisional cell frequencies.

[16] These percentages were computed from the marginal totals of the fourfold tables given in Table 2.

[17] The source for this and all following tables is the 1930 U.S. Census. All figures are in thousands.

[18] The tables for the West North Central, South Atlantic, East South Central, West South Central, and Mountain divisions are omitted to save space.

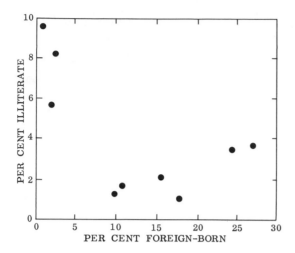

Figure 3

For example, in the upper left cell of Table 1 the frequency is 1,512 = 4 + 32 + 36 + ...+ 2.

The ecological correlation (Figure 1) also depends upon the nine within-areas individual correlations, but only upon their marginal totals. For example, in Table 2 the marginal total for the first table shows 76,000 Negroes in the New England division. Since the total population for this division is 6,702,000, the percentage of Negroes is 100(76)/6,702 = 1.1. The percentage of illiterates in New England is computed from the other marginal total in the same way.

In brief, the individual correlation depends upon the internal frequencies of the within-areas individual correlations, while the ecological correlation depends upon the marginal frequencies of the within-areas individual correlations. Moreover, it is well known that the marginal frequencies of a fourfold table do not determine the internal frequencies. There is a large number of sets of internal frequencies which will satisfy exactly the same marginal frequencies for any fourfold table. Therefore there are a large number of individual correlations which might correspond to any given ecological correlation, i.e., to any given set of marginal frequencies. In short, the within-areas marginal frequencies which determine the percentages from which the ecological correlation is computed do

not fix the internal frequencies which determine the individual correlation. Thus there need be no correspondence between the individual correlation and the ecological correlation.

An instance will document this conclusion. The data of this section show that the individual correlation between color and illiteracy is .203, while the ecological correlation is .946. In this instance, the two correlations at least have the same sign, and that sign is consistent with our knowledge that educational standards in the United States are lower for Negroes than for whites.

However, consider another correlation where we also know what the sign ought to be, viz., that between nativity and illiteracy. We know that educational standards are lower for the foreign born than for the native born, and therefore that there ought to be a positive correlation between foreign births and illiteracy. This surmise is corroborated by the individual correlation between foreign birth and illiteracy, shown in Table 3. The individual correlation for Table 3 is .118.

Table 3. The Individual Correlation Between Nativity and Illiteracy for the United States, 1930

(for the population 10 years old and over)

	Foreign Born	Native Born	Total
Illiterate	1,304	2,614	3,918
Literate.	11,913	81,441	93,354
Total	13,217	84,055	97,272

However, the ecological correlation between foreign birth and illiteracy, shown in Figure 3, is −.619! When the ecological correlation is computed on a state rather than a divisional basis, its value is −.526.

THE MATHEMATICAL RELATION BETWEEN ECOLOGICAL AND INDIVIDUAL CORRELATIONS

Individual and ecological correlations, along with other correlations which also play a part in the situation, are functionally related by one of the basic equations of the analysis of covariance.[19] This equation can be derived from the following assumptions, which merely describe in mathematical terms the situation underlying an ecological correlation:

(1) There is a total group of N persons, who are characterized by two variable properties X and Y. These properties may be genuine variables such as age or income, or they may be dichotomous attributes such as sex or literacy.

(2) The N members of the total group can be put into m distinct sub-groups according to their geographic position, whether by census tracts, townships, counties, states, or divisions. It is convenient to think of these m sub-groups as defined by m values of a third variable A (= Area) which is really an attribute, viz., geographic region.

The numerical values from which the ecological correlation is computed describe these m sub-groups. They may be means, medians, or percentages, and in fact all three are sometimes involved in a single ecological correlation analysis. Usually, however, they are percentages. While the mathematics applies to means as well, and approximately to medians also, it will simplify the present discussion to assume that X and Y are dichotomous properties, and therefore that the ecological correlation is a correlation between m pairs of percentages.

In the preceding section, three distinct correlations were shown to be involved in the ecological correlation situation. In mathematical terms, these correlations are described as follows:

The total individual correlation (r) is the simple Pearsonian correlation between X and Y for all N members of the total group, computed without reference to geographic position at all. If X and Y are dichotomous properties, the total individual correlation will be a fourfold-point correlation based on a fourfold table (Table 1).

[19]The derivation of this equation is not given here because of space limitations. Readers wishing a copy may secure one by sending a stamped, self-addressed envelope to W. S. Robinson, Department of Anthropology and Sociology, University of California, Los Angeles 24, California.

The ecological correlation (r_e) is the weighted correlation between the m pairs of X- and Y-percentages which describe the sub-groups. In the example of Section 2, r_e is the correlation between the nine percentages of Negroes and the nine corresponding percentages of illiterates. However, each cross-product of an X- and Y-percentage is weighted by the number of persons in the group which the percentage describes, to give it an importance corresponding to the number of observations involved.

Ordinarily, ecological correlations are computed without the refinement of weighting. While the weighted form is theoretically more adequate, and is required by the mathematics of this section, the numerical difference between the two is negligible. The weighted ecological correlation for Figure 1, which involves few observations and should therefore be very sensitive to weighting, is .946, while the corresponding unweighted value is .944.

The within-areas individual correlation (r_w) is a weighted average of the m within-areas individual correlations between X and Y, each within-area correlation being weighted by the size of the group which it describes.

Two correlation ratios, η_{XA} and η_{YA}, are also involved in the relation. Their purpose is to measure the degree to which the values of X and Y show clustering by area. If X is a dichotomous property, say illiteracy, then a large value of η_{XA} indicates wide variation in the percentage of illiterates from one area to another.

With these definitions, the relation between individual and ecological correlations may be written as

$$r_e = k_1 r - k_2 r_w, \qquad (1)$$

where
$$k_1 = 1/\eta_{XA}\,\eta_{YA} \qquad (1a)$$
and
$$k_2 = \sqrt{1 - \eta_{XA}^2}\,\sqrt{1 - \eta_{YA}^2}/\eta_{XA}\,\eta_{YA}. \qquad (1b)$$

That is, the ecological correlation is the weighted difference between the total individual correlation and the average of the m within-area individual correlations. In this weighted difference, the weights of the total individual correlation and the within-areas individual correlation depend upon the degree to which the values of X and Y show clustering by area.

Investigation of the relation given in (1) shows that an individual and ecological correlation will be equal, and the equivalency assumption will therefore be valid, when

$$r_w = k_3 r, \qquad (2)$$

where

$$k_3 = \frac{1 - \eta_{XA}\,\eta_{YA}}{\sqrt{1 - \eta_{XA}^2}\,\sqrt{1 - \eta_{YA}^2}} \qquad (2a)$$

However, the minimum value of k_3 in (2) is unity. Therefore (2) will hold, and the individual and ecological correlations will be equal, only if the average within-areas individual correlation is not less than the total individual correlation. But all available evidence is that (whatever properties X and Y may denote) the correlation between X and Y is certainly not larger for relatively homogeneous subgroups of persons than it is for the population at large. In short, the equivalency assumption has no basis in fact.

The consistently high numerical values of published ecological correlations in comparison with the smaller values ordinarily got in correlating the properties of individuals suggest that ecological correlations have some reason for being larger than corresponding individual correlations. The relation given in (1) shows what this reason is, for it gives as the condition for the numerically larger value of the ecological correlation

$$r_w < k_3 r, \qquad (3)$$

where k_3 is given by (2a). Since the minimum value of k_3 is unity, equation (3) implies that the ecological will be numerically greater than the individual correlation whenever the within-areas individual correlation is not greater than the total individual correlation, and this is the usual circumstance.

Habitual users of ecological correlations know that the size of the coefficient depends to a marked degree upon the number of sub-areas. Gehlke and Biehl, for example, commented in 1934[20] upon the positive relation between the size of the coefficient and the average size of the areas from which it was determined. This tendency is illustrated in Section 2, where the ecological correlation between color and illiteracy is .773 when the sub-areas are states and .946 when the sub-areas are the Census Bureau's nine geographic divisions. The same tendency is shown by the correlations between nativity and illiteracy, the value being −.526 on a state basis and −.619 on a divisional basis.

Equation (1) shows why the size of the ecological correlation depends upon the number of sub-areas, for the behavior of the ecological correlation as small sub-areas are grouped into larger ones can be predicted from the behavior of the variables on the right side of (1) as consolidation takes place. As smaller areas are consolidated, two things happen:

(1) The average within-area individual correlation increases in size because of the increasing heterogeneity of the sub-areas. The effect of this is to decrease the value of the ecological correlation.

(2) The values of η_{XA} and η_{YA} decrease because of the decrease in the homogeneity of values of X and Y within sub-areas. The effect of this is to increase the value of the ecological correlation.

However, these two tendencies are of unequal importance. Investigation of (1) with respect to the effect of changes in the values of η_{XA}, η_{YA}, and r_w indicates that the influence of changes in the η's is considerably more important than the influence of changes in the value of r_w. The net effect of changes in the values of the η's and of r_w taken together, therefore, is to increase the numerical value of the ecological correlation as consolidation takes place.

[20] "Certain Effects of Grouping upon the Size of the Correlation Coefficient in Census Tract Material," Journal of the American Statistical Association, 24 (Mar., 1934, Supplement), 169-170.

CONCLUSION

The relation between ecological and individual correlations which is discussed in this paper provides a definite answer as to whether ecological correlations can validly be used as substitutes for individual correlations. They cannot. While it is theoretically possible for the two to be equal, the conditions under which this can happen are far removed from those ordinarily encountered in data. From a practical standpoint, therefore, the only reasonable assumption is that an ecological correlation is almost certainly not equal to its corresponding individual correlation.

I am aware that this conclusion has serious consequences, and that its effect appears wholly negative because it throws serious doubt upon the validity of a number of important studies made in recent years. The purpose of this paper will have been accomplished, however, if it prevents the future computation of meaningless correlations and stimulates the study of similar problems with the use of meaningful correlations between the properties of individuals.

Comment on Robinson's *"Ecological Correlations and the Behavior of Individuals"*

Herbert Menzel

SOURCE: *American Sociological Review*, Vol. 15, (October, 1950), p. 674.

W. S. Robinson[1] demonstrates both logically and mathematically that ecological correlations cannot validly be used as substitutes for individual correlations. As an illustration he points out that the ecological (linear) correlation of color and illiteracy, state by state for the year 1930 is .773, while the individual (four-fold-point) correlation of color and illiteracy for the United States as a whole is only .203.

This is a valid and extremely important warning against a very common fallacy. It removes one more prop from the old saw that personal disorganization is merely a reflection of social disorganization.

On the other hand I believe Mr. Robinson is incorrect in his statement that "in each study which uses ecological correlations ... ecological correlations are used simply because correlations between the properties of individuals are not available" and "not because their authors are interested in correlations between the properties of areas as such." It seems to me that ecological correlations may be of great value even without reflecting individual correlations, and that they are indeed used by many researchers without any thought of serving as substitutes for the latter.

A common case in point is the establishment of area-by-area correlations of various so-called indexes of social disorganization. A high ecological correlation of, say, arrests and divorces may be (fallaciously) advanced to imply that the very individuals who are arrested are particularly prone to obtain divorces; but more commonly it is used as an argument for the claim that both arrests and divorces are functions of a common underlying cause inherent not in the indi-

[1] W. S. Robinson, "Ecological Correlations and the Behavior of Individuals," <u>American Sociological Review</u>, 15 (June 1950), 351-357.

viduals as such but in interindividual differences and relationships—"properties of areas as such"—termed culture conflict, social disorganization, or what have you. It can hardly be said that a researcher correlating women's court cases[2] does so in order to imply that the very individuals who land in women's court are especially likely to land in the boys' court also!

Mr. Robinson's own illustration—the state-by-state correlation of per cent population Negro and per cent population illiterate—retains its value even after it is recognized that the corresponding individual correlation is very much lower. It points to the fact that identical historical circumstances and aspects of economic development have caused certain states both to (a) import and retain a large Negro population and (b) neglect their school systems.

Furthermore, ecological correlation

may retain validity not only where it is argued that the variables correlated are functions of a common cause, but also where it is claimed that one of them is a cause of the other. Take the (hypothetical) case of an ecological correlation, within certain limits, of the per cent population Jewish and the per cent population registering high on a scale measuring anti-Semitism. This would hardly indicate that Jews are anti-Semitic, yet it would demonstrate a significant relationship. Or take another hypothetical case, the ecological correlation of the number of physicians per capita and the infant death rate. This correlation may be expected to be high and negative, and loses none of its significance for the fact that a corresponding individual correlation would be patently impossible.

Needless to say, none of those arguments detracts in the least from the value and importance of Mr. Robinson's contribution in those cases where ecological correlations are indeed used as substitutes for individual correlations, explicitly or implicitly.

---

[2]E.g., Ernest R. Mowrer, Disorganization, Personal and Social, 1942.

The Exportability of the "Labor Force" Concept

Wilbert E. Moore

SOURCE: *American Sociological Review*, Vol. 18 (1953), pp. 68–72.

Every attempt at comparative statistical analysis through space and often through time, is likely to be plagued by at least two problems: the availability and the comparability of data. The concept of "labor force" or other rubric designed to distinguish economically "active" and "inactive" sectors of a population is a particular example of this troublesome generality.

Official and scholarly interest in various aspects of economic development has given new emphasis to the relationship

between demographic and economic trends. Unlike the older treatments of the population problem, contemporary discussion stresses the population of producers as well as consumers, and attempts to assess labor potential as well as caloric demand.

These problems arise in acute degree precisely with reference to the "undeveloped" areas of the world. In such areas census enumerations and other statistical information tend to be old, irregular, incomplete, crude, or non-existent. Attempts to provide or improve current data are being made in many areas, with various degrees of local heroism and outside technical assistance. The results of these attempts still leave large areas of ignorance of even the most elementary social quantities.

The problem of comparability of data on population and social structure derives in part from differing statistical standards and from categories of enumeration peculiarly local or simply whimsical in origin. Most discussions of the problem of comparability across national boundaries and through time have been devoted to the essentially administrative aspects of collecting and processing information. These problems are by no means inconsequential, and the perversity of all things is such that temporal comparisons are weakened by every "improvement" in method and classification, and spatial comparisons are not immune to attack from the same honorable source.

It is possible to imagine, and in part to achieve, solutions to the problem of administrative uniformity. A greater difficulty remains. This remaining difficulty is not likely to be overcome by improvements in the techniques of enumerators, in the minds and morals of census administrators, or in the skills of social analysts. Social behavior and the organization of life are genuinely and importantly different in various areas of the world. In these circumstances standard classification and uniform coding can only obscure and delude. It is the thesis of this paper that precisely this situation applies to the concept of the labor force and many associated classificatory devices relating to economic activity. Some faintly happy notes will be sounded later, but only as limited ways of avoiding the consequences of social variability.

THE ECONOMICALLY "ACTIVE" AND "INACTIVE"

In the historical development of statistical data on the populations of western countries, a variety of concepts and classifications have been adopted. Those of present interest center about the distinction between the sector of the population that is in some sense active, or productive, in the economy, and the sector that is for various reasons inactive.

Within that portion of the population that is deemed "active," attention has been centered on industry, occupation, status (that is, employer, employee, self-employed, unpaid family worker, etc.) and on actual employment or unemployment at the time of the enumeration.

The older concepts relating to this portion of the population as a whole were generally "active" or "gainfully occupied."

The labor force concept has many of its own difficulties, even in advanced market economies.[1] The part-time worker, the unpaid family worker, and the producer of possibly marketed goods and services that do not actually go through market arrangements, all provide problems of inclusion or exclusion. For comparisons through time, however, a uniformly defined labor force and its age and occupational composition provide fairly useful indicators of labor potential, of the relation between labor supply and the state of the labor market, and of the ratio between workers and dependents. For similarly constituted economies, international comparisons of the same type are possible.

The real difficulty is the impossibility of defining "labor" in any way that will refer to the same class of human activities in all societies. Let us assume a situation that is only an extreme degree of that prevailing in agrarian societies generally. We are initially concerned with sorting out "economic" activities or functions. We may think this can be done by confining our attention to physical production: the gathering, growing, or fabricating of food, clothing, shelter, and any other valued physical objects. But

---

[1] See Wilbert E. Moore, "Persistent Problems of Labor Force Analysis," Population Index, 17 (April, 1951), pp. 78-91. The discussion in subsequent paragraphs of application of the "labor force" concept to undeveloped areas is also based in part on this earlier paper.

how are these produced? Let us further assume that there is a division of labor at least by age and sex, and that such exchange as takes place is strictly determined by kinship obligations. Everyone except infants and the completely infirm takes some part in these activities, but also engages in some portion of the total range of activities that comprises social existence. The very activity that involves "production" is likely to entail esthetic, magical, or religious elements, entails kinship elements by definition, and must entail the allocation of power and responsibility.[2]

Now even if our unit were the man-hour and not the person, it is difficult in these circumstances to distinguish work from non-work. And the distinction has no particular value for comparison with a markedly different economy. Given careful observation and coding, it might be possible to assess the "productivity" of labor for the same class of products, but it is not likely that the "economic" value of other functions performed by the same person at the same time can adequately be assessed.

The conceptual problem becomes even more acute when one turns attention to services, which constitute a major proportion of all labor in industrial economies. "Almost any form of human activity that affects other persons may be a 'service' and be remunerated as a commodity in a highly developed market economy, although even in such economies not all activities of given types actually reach the market."[3] Indeed, it is not even necessary to insist on the effects on other persons, as services performed for oneself may be assigned the market value they would have if performed by others.

Discovering what constitutes labor in an undeveloped area is part of the more general problem of defining the "economic." In any society an economic activity or structure is only "predomi-

nantly" so, as such activities or organizations cannot be concretely separated from other functions.[4]

In modern western economies there is, however, a kind of operational test of what is economically valuable activity— the market test. This test does not meet all conceptual difficulties, but does make possible a distinction between labor and other activities, or between workers and non-workers. These distinctions will serve many practical and analytical purposes.[5] The inapplicability of this test for major proportions of the world's population provides an intrinsic barrier to comparisons of labor force or any similar measure.

THE RATIONALE AND HAZARDS OF COMPARISON

Why does one want to compare the "economically active" proportions of populations anyway? The most general answer is, to use number of active and potential producers as an index of productive potential. For example, the ratio of producers to dependents is variable from one time and place to another.[6] This ratio and its shifts as a consequence of trends in birth and death rates, have repercussions for the productive potential of an economy.

The number of workers, even assuming they can be identified, is scarcely significant. The number of workers must be related to dependents, capital and resources, or some other basis of comparison. Even for military man power, it is a commonplace that each man does not automatically count as one.

Numbers or proportions of workers obviously constitute data of comparative value in direct measure with the similarity of other relevant conditions. Hours of

---

[2]See Marion J. Levy, Jr., The Structure of Society, Princeton: Princeton University Press, 1952, pp. 88-99.

[3]Moore, op. cit., p. 81.

[4]Levy, op. cit., especially pp. 88-98, 330-332, 389-467.

[5]In addition to Moore, op. cit., see A. J. Jaffe and Charles D. Stewart, Manpower Resources and Utilization, New York: John Wiley & Sons, 1951, pp. 17-33.

[6]John D. Durand, "Manpower and Dependency in Under-Developed Countries," paper presented at the annual meeting of the American Sociological Society, September 3-5, 1952.

labor, skill, the organization of production, and the supply of other factors of production (especially capital) affect the "labor supply" for any inference concerning production.

Any comparison of labor supply should also take into account the product structure of an economy. Physical goods called by the same name are difficult enough to compare with regard to style and quality. The difficulties increase as markedly different goods are produced, and become acute when services are involved. "Labor supply" and "economic output" may both increase artifactually through a transfer of activities from the home to the market.

These differences in relevant elements of an economy increase as one moves from the extreme of the urban-industrial societies to the extremes of tribal or village forms of productive organization.

For some purposes the range of variation in economies may be divided at some point into two sectors, and "labor force" and related measures may then be applied within the group of countries that is considered "industrial." This procedure still entails the hazards indicated, although in lesser degree, and does not meet the problem of getting some factual and analytical tools for the study of the potentialities of undeveloped areas. For these purposes some other bases of comparison are needed, and not totally lacking.

COMPARISONS FOR LIMITED PURPOSES

If ascertaining the number of workers, with or without multipliers of time and skill and divisors of dependents or total population, is an impossible aspiration, what approaches to comparative analysis can we adopt?

Two general bases for comparison can be adopted, the utility of their specific variants being dependent upon the limited purpose at hand. The one basis is essentially demographic and rests upon the circumstance that age and sex are universal attributes of mankind. The other aims at some form of quantitative description of the "economically relevant" features of a population or some sector of it, under various present or possible conditions of socioeconomic structure.

Age and sex always have some relevance to the pattern of social activities, if only on ultimately biological grounds. It follows that the age-sex composition of a population, and the way this structure is affected by migration and changes in birth and death rates, may be used for making inferences concerning the "productive potential" of a population.

On grounds of the variability both of statistical practice and of actual social organization, the productive role of women poses serious difficulties of analysis. Though marital, maternal, and domestic activities of women are difficult or impossible to evaluate economically in a highly developed market economy, the problem is magnified in an agrarian economy. Data on labor force participation rates of women (by age, marital status, and size of family) are not totally useless, where labor force itself has any meaning. Such data can be used at some risk for appraisal of what would be the experience in an undeveloped country if it were to move toward modern economic organization. Indeed, there is no particular scientific harm in attempts to appraise the unused labor potential of females who are "under-employed" because of the uneconomically small scale of household operations. No sociologist, however, would allow such an economic analysis to stand as anything more than an inconsequential exercise.

Age also is a limiting but not determining element in role assignment. The age composition of a population and its observed or hypothetical changes yield valid bases for a number of inferences about productive potential when coupled with observed or hypothetical characteristics of the social structure. Given a usable test of economic activity, labor force participation rates by age and variations in dependency ratios may be calculated, and inferences drawn concerning possible trends. In the absence of the "market test," arbitrarily assigned age limits may be adopted (for example, 15

and 65) as a more abstract and hypothetical index of "productive potential."

Once one leaves the reasonably reliable concepts of age and sex, the hazards of comparison multiply. Several
forms of partial quantitative description
of the socioeconomic characteristics of
a population may still be attempted. Here
a further pair of alternatives may be
posed—crude measures applying to the
entire population, or more refined measures applying to that greater or lesser
segment of the social order where the
market test of economic activity applies.

Census enumeration and other sources
may yield some usable information or
estimates for many undeveloped countries
if one is not too particular about the purity of the definition of economic activity.
One approach is to distinguish "agricultural" and "non-agricultural" sectors of
an economy by use of approximate measures of "population dependent on" or
"males engaged in" agriculture.[7] However crude this distinction may be, it
does yield an approximate ordering of
areas in the degree to which the economy is differentiated, market-based, and
industrialized, as the "agricultural" sector of the population tends to decrease
with economic development. It thus permits both static and temporal comparisons, and by the same token provides an
approximate index for analysis of the
structural features of societies in various
"stages" of industralization.

The use of "agriculturalism" as an
index is essentially a simplified variant
of "primary, secondary, and tertiary production," as used by Colin Clark.[8] This
classification also presents difficulties,
such as the union of agriculture and
mineral extraction as "primary," although mining is generally commercial-

ized. It does, however, provide a possibly
useful distinction with the "non-agricultural" sector between manufacturing and
services. Highly industrialized societies
are characterized by an increasing number of services, particularly of non-
domestic services. This trend derives in
part from the process of moving services into the market, noted earlier, in
part from new services required in a
highly specialized and integrated productive system. The point of present
concern is simply the possible utility of
the threefold classification as an index
of the changing structure of a society or
its economy.

The other alternative previously indicated is to settle for less than an entire
population for comparative purposes. No
area of the world is now wholly untouched
by the market system. Thus some persons everywhere can be caught by the
same conceptual apparatus found useful
in modern economies. Unfortunately reasonable kinds of census enumeration do
not prevail because of the attempt to
force occupational or industrial classifications on entire populations. With such
data, however, it would be interesting to
calculate the proportions of various populations within the market system.

Though census data may yield essentially fictitious occupational data, some
comparison of occupational structure with
various indexes of economic development
may be made. The reliability of any such
comparison is likely to be enhanced by
the elimination of "agriculture" and "domestic service" altogether, although
handicrafts and manufacturing also furnish adequate opportunities for confusion.
Were data available the total number of
distinguishable full-time "occupations"
might serve as an index of specialization.
The use of some system of weights for
differences in skills is difficult, but at
least avoids the assumption that each
worker counts for one in production.

An approximation of the proportion of
the population that is appropriately to be
viewed in "labor force" terms may be
made by considering wage and salary
earners as an index of the development

---

[7]This approach is used by Davis. See Kingsley
Davis, "Population and the Further Spread of Industrial Society," <u>Proceedings of the American Philosophical Society</u>, 95 (February, 1951), pp. 8-19.

[8]See Colin Clark, <u>Conditions of Economic Prog-
ress</u>, London: Macmillan and Co., 1940; Australia,
Queensland Bureau of Industry, "The Distribution
of Labour between Industries: I-IV," <u>Review of
Economic Progress</u>, 2 (April, May, June, and July,
1950), pp. 1-4, 1-4, 1-4, and 1-8.

Table 1. Male Wage and Salary Earners as a Proportion of All Males Aged 15-64 in Selected Countries*

Country and Year	Proportion (Per Cent)
England and Wales, 1931	74.6
Netherlands, 1930	73.2
Australia, 1947	72.4
Denmark, 1940	70.9
Germany, 1939	69.6
Sweden, 1940	66.3
Austria, 1939	65.8
United States, 1940	65.5
Switzerland, 1941	65.1
Czechoslovakia, 1947	63.8
New Zealand, 1945	63.7
Belgium, 1930	61.2
Norway, 1930	57.8
France, 1936	57.5
Japan, 1930	55.7
Canada, 1941	54.5
Portugal, 1940	54.3
Italy, 1936	53.9
Venezuela, 1941	52.7
Mexico, 1940	52.5
Eire, 1936	52.4
Colombia, 1938	52.2
Jamaica, 1943	52.1
Malaya, British, 1947	50.6
Peru, 1940	44.5
Latvia, 1935	41.5
Estonia, 1934	38.8
Poland, 1931	35.7
Philippines, 1939	35.3
Yugoslavia, 1931	27.4
Bulgaria, 1934	25.5
Roumania, 1930	20.6
U.S.S.R., 1926	19.3

*Based on official national and international sources.

of a labor market. This number leaves out of account business proprietors, the self-employed in general, and unpaid family workers. However, the category itself is subject to fairly rigorous definition. Such a figure may be taken as an indicator not only of the importance of a labor market but also of the specialization and organization of economic activities, which varies even among industrialized countries.

The use of wage and salary earners as a basis of comparison is illustrated by Table 1, which shows the number of male wage and salary earners in various countries as a proportion of the total male population aged 15-64. It is possible to pick up from the table not only the markedly wide range of proportions employed, but also some interesting comparisons within the range. France as the country of northwestern Europe most characterized by small-scale enterprise, whether rural or urban, properly appears well down in the list. Denmark and The Netherlands, which are commonly and erroneously supposed to be predominantly agricultural countries, are shown to have highly organized economies.[9]

The goal of economic growth in undeveloped areas may be expressed as the attempt to create a "labor force" in the technical sense. The data useful for implementing policy would appear to include such descriptions of the population essentially outside the market system as would be relevant to estimates of capacity and availability of labor for a changed mode of general economic organization. To the degree that the attempt is successful, more and more of the world's populations will come within the characteristic social system of industrial societies. Meanwhile, the administrative policy of data gathering should take into account the kinds of information that can and cannot be meaningfully obtained, and that not only to help the suffering social scientist.

[9] No precise significance can be attached to the order of the countries as they are listed, in view of the wide differences in effective date. Were contemporary data available for the Soviet Union, for example, it would probably appear about midway on the list, not at the bottom. Similarly, if Australian data for 1933 were used, its position (53.4) would approximate that of Japan and Italy for that period.

Individual and Organizational Research in Sociology

Alfred McClung Lee

SOURCE: *American Sociological Review*, Vol. 16, (1951), pp. 701–07.

Both "individual" and "organizational" research have grown with the sociological field.[1] Both have made notable contributions.

What would contemporary sociology be without the findings of such significant "individual" researchers as William Graham Sumner, Ferdinand Tönnies, Emile Durkheim, Georg Simmel, William Isaac Thomas, Max Weber, and Charles Horton Cooley? Their work still has vitality that demands quotation and re-interpretation today both in introductory textbooks and in careful scientific monographs. The growing influence of so recently deceased a colleague as Willard Waller suggests that such independents can still make strikingly useful additions to our knowledge of human relationships.

What would contemporary sociology be without the contributions of organized investigators and so-called group researchers? The social bookkeeping reports of governmental units and the special surveys of civic bodies and business firms have a long and fruitful history. Their description of artifacts, populations, and human behavior are part of the backdrop against which sociological knowledge has evolved since Auguste Comte and Herbert Spencer. Questions, suggestions, and occasionally plans and guidance from sociologists have helped such censuses and surveys to gain in accuracy and in social and scientific utility.

What is usually called group research rather than just organized investigation grew out of the work of individuals such as Frederic Le Play, Franklin Henry Giddings, Robert Ezra Park, Ernest W. Burgess, and F. Stuart Chapin as well as of the groups headed by such persons as Charles Booth, Paul U. Kellogg, A. L. Bowley, Robert S. and Helen M. Lynd, W. Lloyd Warner, Louis Wirth, Samuel A. Stouffer, and Paul F. Lazarsfeld. As part of this group research development, especially since the 1920s, came subsidies for group projects by foundations and special interests and the establishment of research institutes and bureaus in connection with academic departments of sociology and anthropology as well as with the related departments of psychology, economics, and government.[2]

---

[1] The terms, investigation and research, are used in this paper in a commonly accepted manner. Investigation refers to any systematic fact-gathering. This would include organized investigation for news reports, public opinion surveys, and censuses. Research refers to investigation for the purpose of constructing, testing, or modifying scientific theory. When it is independent research, it is research upon the responsibility of individual researchers. When it is group research, it is upon the joint responsibility of a group of professional researchers. When it is organizational research, it is research carried on as an organizational function. When an investigation or research is institutionalized, it is adjusted and assimilated into the modes of operation of institutional functionaries and their routines in a given association.

[2] See V. L. Parrington, Main Currents in American Thought, New York: Harcourt, Brace and Co., 1930, vol. 3, pp. xxvii, 401-413; U. S. Federal Trade Commission, Efforts by Associations and Agencies of Electric and Gas Utilities to Influence Public Opinion, 70th Congress, 1st Session, Senate Document 92 Part 71A, Washington: Government Printing Office, 1934, pp. 173, 393; R. S. Lynd,

Concomitant with this development, opinion and attitude studies have become a sizable element in industrial, distributive, and political planning in the United States and to an increasing extent in other Western countries.[3] Industrialists have learned that "attitudes" have something to do with personnel morale, efficiency, and productivity and with the ways in which present and potential employees are likely to react in crisis situations. Consumer acceptance tests have helped distributors of items packaged and advertised for retail sale to select more effective labels, cartons, and advertisements.[4] The relative accuracy of poll predictions of elections gave politicians and businessmen some respect for poll reports of all sorts prior to the failure of the commercial polls to predict correctly the November 2, 1948 federal election results. But this set-back only temporarily placed commercial polling in a more accurate perspective. Public relations counselors, who once proved their worth to clients with bulging scrapbooks of press clippings, find a wide range of surveys and polls now available to them to attest to their accomplishments, all of course "scientifically" certified and some bearing the imprimaturs of renowned universities.

Before going further with what must in part be a comparison of "individual" and "organizational" research, let me offer further definitions of these terms.

By "individual" research, I refer to research carried on as nearly as possible as a personal venture on free time by (1) a teacher, (2) a person otherwise employed, or (3) a person with independent funds or so subsidized that he feels relatively free to pursue his own interests as he sees them. As R. S. Lynd[5] has put it, "Upon those teachers who are on what is called, probably increasingly optimistically, 'permanent tenure,' there would appear to rest the special obligation to carry for their less-secure junior colleagues the main brunt of hard-hitting, constructive thought that spares no one, least of all themselves."

The "individual" researcher may or may not use clerical and mechanical aids. That depends upon his needs and resources. He may or may not relate his efforts to those of other researchers. If he is well trained and has the emotional and intellectual qualifications to be a scientist, he will be eager to accept, modify, or reject the findings of others and to relate his own work to theirs. He may base his conclusions and test and retest his theories primarily on his own first-hand observations, including his own experiments. For these purposes, his observations may be of few or many cases, and the cases may be a random choice or a carefully developed sample. Or the individual researcher may assess and use observations of others, such as census, ethnographic, court, legislative, administrative, sample-survey and case-study reports. In order that he may have maximal flexibility and minimal embedment in institutional obligations, tensions, and other influences during his hours of research, the individual researcher needs to feel above all and as much as possible that his only criteria of achievement in research are those he associates with (1) his own drive to satisfy his own curiosity, (2) his own desire to extend or broaden human knowledge of society, and (3) his own conception of a scientist's personal integrity.

By "organizational" research, I refer to research that is carried on in an institutional setting and as an institutional function, in other words upon institutional rather than personal responsibility. This is something more ambitious than what is labeled above as organized investigation. Group research usually involves an effort

Knowledge for What? Princeton: Princeton University Press, 1939, chap. 1; H. M. Baus, "How to Get Publicity," chap. 26, esp. pp. 593-595, and Marion Harper, Jr., "Finding the Facts," chap. 29, in Philip Lesly, ed., Public Relations Handbook, New York: Prentice-Hall, 1950.

[3] See esp. files of Public Opinion Quarterly, Princeton, 1937- and International Journal of Opinion and Attitude Research, Mexico City, 1947-.

[4] See D. B. Lucas and S. H. Britt, Advertising Psychology and Research, New York: McGraw-Hill Book Co., 1950.

[5] Knowledge for What? Princeton: Princeton University Press, 1939, p. 10.

to modify sociological theory. It is to group research rather than mere organized investigation that especial attention is to be given here. Allyn A. Young[6] has described group research as "a common attack upon a particular problem or set of problems, by an organized body of investigators who apportion their work so as to get some of the advantages of the division of labor, and who may be able to turn over routine parts of their tasks to a corps of clerical assistants." To such a description, Donald Young[7] adds this significant qualification: "It is assumed with good historical reason that basic innovations in social science may rarely be expected from large-scale projects; initiation of such projects has usually been stimulated by the findings of some previous innovator working on a modest scale. There seems to be no alternative to continued dependence on the individual worker for new ideas and pioneering studies."

Even in such a highly institutionalized type of research as that in the electron-tube industry, a researcher[8] points to much the same situation when he notes. "The conception of an original idea, the finding of a basic principle, is essentially an individual effort." He reinforces this by asserting, "When the problem has been stated—always the most difficult step—and a sound approach to its solution is indicated, a group effort will bring the most rapid solution." In other words, he would allot only routine efforts to a "research task force."

What advantages to researchers and to scientific development does subsidized and institutionalized group research provide? Group-researchers contend that a research organization should be nothing more or less than a medium through which capable researchers are freed from extraneous activities and responsi-

bilities and given the essentials of modern research—specialized associates, technical and clerical assistants, and expensive machinery. The group brings together trained persons with diverse backgrounds and skills who benefit from interstimulation. Such association is especially productive, it is claimed, when the group specialists focus their efforts upon the solution of a common theoretical or practical problem or group of problems. Once a research organization designs a research project, the human and mechanical machine as a whole can start to function. The machine can carry out controlled observations on adequate samples of large populations. It can process these observations with precision and efficiency. Its top staff specialists can join not only in planning such a project but also in assuring adequate execution and thorough analyses, criticisms, and interpretations of results.[9]

These are brief favorable descriptions of independent and institutionalized research. For the purposes of characterization, fairly extreme rather than intermediate types are selected. It might be argued, to illustrate, that certain work done by graduate students is of an independent sort, and this may be so. It depends upon the graduate student and the graduate department in which he is working. It might also be argued that a professor "has given heavy hostages to fortune: he has a family to rear, usually on a not too ample salary; his income depends upon the academic advancements he can win, and these in turn depend upon 'productive research.'...He lives in a world which, by and large, is not asking, 'Is Smith trying to get at the facts? Is he trying to be fair and constructive at the same time that he is unwilling to pull his

---

[6] In Wilson Gee, ed., Research in the Social Sciences, New York: Macmillan Co., 1929, p. 68.

[7] "Organization for Research in the Social Sciences in the United States," UNESCO International Social Science Bulletin, Paris, 1 (1949), 99-107 (p. 100 quoted).

[8] Walter H. Kohl, "The Human Element in Research and Industry," Proceedings of the I.R.E., 39 (1951), 228-229 (p. 228 quoted).

[9] On this, see especially S. A. Stouffer and others, The American Soldier, Princeton: Princeton University Press, 1949, chap. 1; Daniel Katz and others, Human Relations Program of the Survey Research Center, Ann Arbor: Institute for Social Research, University of Michigan, 1950; Wilson Gee, Social Science Research Methods, New York: Appleton-Century-Crofts, 1950, chap. 12; and John McDonald, "The War of Wits:...the Story of the Rand Corporation," Fortune, April 1951, pp. 99-102, 144, 147, 148, 150, 152, 156, 158.

punch?' but which asks, 'Are you for us, or against us?'"[10] But there are now, as there have been for many generations in many countries, academic and other social scientists who, to be picturesque with V. L. Parrington,[11] "decline to block the path to the Promised Land with retainer-fees."

Unfavorable descriptions of what are derisively called "lone wolf" research and "assembly-line" research need also be given.

A great many see the individual sociological researcher in the mid-twentieth-century world as a lone and primitively equipped David going forth to meet a vastly expanded and awesomely armored Goliath, modern society. The analogy is appealing to group-research partisans. Apologists for "assembly-line" research say that their teams outfitted with modern machinery and drilled to precision in techniques have become as essential to sociological research as are Panzer divisions to modern international relations.

A great many others would, significantly enough, reject both this statement and its analogy. They see group research as a profitable but bungling and overrated bureaucratic device which comes to end-products of greater political than scientific significance. If all the clashes of views, facts, and personalities within a group were published, the gain to science would be far greater than vague unified end-products are likely to yield. As in the U. S. Supreme Court, minority reports might stand the tests of subsequent experience and verification far more substantially than those of the majority. But minority statements and "minutes of proceedings" in which differences of view within the group are ironed out seldom appear in the publications of group research organizations.

More systematically, what are principal criticisms leveled against contemporary individual research? Here are two common ones of some weight. It is said that individual researchers are likely to be more intuitive, impressionistic, and subject to the use of the Verstehen[12] operation than group researchers. The necessarily individualistic individual researchers are also likely to be thought impudent, imprudent, repugnant, confusing, or confused by the more socialized or bureaucratic group researchers: The individualists "do not fit in." They do not know "how to sell their ideas." They do not know "how to sell themselves." They are "lone wolves." They live in "ivory towers" or now, more probably, "white farmhouses." They "lack savvy." For any of many combinations of possible life-history factors, they are what Robert Ezra Park[13] called "marginal men." At any rate, they are not, as it has been said of many group researchers in social science, "assimilated members of the American business community."

What are the principal criticisms made against contemporary group research? Here, as with individual research, a comprehensive list is not attempted. Of these criticisms, two contrast especially with those mentioned for individual research, and two are more peculiar to group operation. These criticisms have to do with (1) observation, (2) decision-making processes, (3) interests, and (4) organizational imperatives. Let us look at each of these briefly in turn.

1. Observation. Sociological group research typically underrates the importance of firsthand observation and relegates it to minor staff members. It exaggerates the importance of a priori constructions arrived at in committee: hypotheses, definitions, specifications of data to be sought, procedures, research or experiment designs. Relatively unskilled and underpaid workers carry out

---

[10] R. S. Lynd, Knowledge for What? Princeton: Princeton University Press, 1939, p. 10.

[11] Main Currents in American Thought, New York: Harcourt, Brace and Co., 1930, vol. 3, p. xxvii.

[12] Theodore Abel, "The Operation Called Verstehen," American Journal of Sociology, 54 (1948-49), 211-218. See also Willard Waller, "Introduction," to E. C. Jandy, Charles Horton Cooley, New York: Dryden Press, 1942, pp. 1-6, and E. C. Hughes, "Preface," to R. E. Park, Race and Culture, Glencoe, Illinois: Free Press, 1950, pp. xi-xvii.

[13] "Human Migration and the Marginal Man," American Journal of Sociology, 33 (1927-28), 881-893.

in a prescribed and routine manner what observations are made. It has frequently been said in opinion research that when an interviewer becomes competent he can make a great deal more doing something other than opinion interviewing. In scientific work generally, a great many would agree with W. H. Hudson[14] that "an observer is a rarer thing than a genius" and would add that he is far more productive in contributions to science.

In order to explain away and to adjudge unscientific the first-hand observings and the careful weighings of data by a Sumner or a Cooley, their ability to make what Francis Bacon[15] so long ago called "a fresh examination of particulars" must be labeled "intuitive," "impressionistic," or "Verstehen," as is suggested above. It does not seem to occur to rationalists for the exclusive superiority of "assembly-line" methods that basic to all scientific research are sense impressions of phenomena. These are basic to and underlie whatever processing might later be given to reports of sense data. If observations are inferior, partial, or badly recorded, all else in the research effort is impaired. If observation turns up one verified and verifiable fact at odds with existing theory, the whole project gains more therefrom than from any amount of statistical manipulation, except to the extent that the latter might help to reveal novelty in observation. As Irving Langmuir[16] notes, scientists "have to be prepared for the unexpected, for things that don't make sense according to our old ideas," and he adds, "the more you try to dominate scientists the less they can deal with the unforeseen."

2. Decision-making processes. In group research, the prestige, aggressiveness, and plausibility of the advocate of an idea frequently give that idea weight out of all proportion to its scientific significance. One thus has in group decision-making processes the phenomena associated with "committee thinking." These phenomena are quite useful in democratic decision-making for political or business purposes, but they have little relevance or pertinence to scientifically useful assessments, analyses, and generalizations of systematic sense impressions.

The prestige factor in decision-making gains much from a person's ability to bring funds into the group. Here as elsewhere not only he who pays the piper but also he who takes the money from the paymaster to the piper—the go-between—both exert direct and indirect influences upon the selection of both piper and tune.

It is of course a commonplace in polite discussion to ignore many consequences of the go-between's entrepreneurial role. Members of a group ordinarily maintain an oral ritual in which the go-between's preëminence in the group is attributed to his alleged fruitfulness as a source of ideas or of administrative wisdom rather than to the overshadowing fact that he is the principal channel of power and hence the dominant instrument of control. He may also, it should be admitted, be a stimulating theorist and a wise administrator.

A great many foundations create and build entrepreneurism in research by preferring to make sizable grants to institutions for group research rather than to individuals. Notable exceptions are, as examples, the Wenner-Gren Foundation and, in part, the Social Science Research Council.

3. Interests. As a result of skilled leadership in "committee thinking" and of the need to offer commercially understandable services to potential clients and foundations, groups develop a lack of flexibility rather quickly. They acquire vested interests in personnel, in one or several personalities, in methods, and in theories. This problem afflicts individual researchers more acutely than groups, but the greater power and persistence of

---

[14] As quoted by C. H. Ward in his Builders of Delusion, Indianapolis: Bobbs-Merrill, 1931, p. 223.

[15] "Magno Instauratio: Aphorisms Concerning the Interpretation of Nature and the Kingdom of Man," no. xcvii, in Essays, selected and edited by R. F. Jones, New York: Odyssey Press, 1937, p. 313.

[16] As quoted by John Pfeiffer, "Scientist of Light and Weather," New York Times Magazine, January 28, 1951, pp. 11, 33.

groups makes such inflexible vested interests the more serious in the cases of groups. Individuals rise and fall with their methods and theories. The brief span of a person's professional career delimits the period during which prestige and control can maintain useless theories. But groups can give methods and theories a sanction, a dignity, a following, an authority long after they are seen by outsiders to have little or no scientific merit.

4. Organizational imperatives. To keep group research going, constant attention must be given by one or more of the group to the cultivation of sources of income. These are the go-betweens mentioned above. In all cases that have come to my attention and about which I have been able to gain fairly adequate data, including a great many group researches in social, biological, and physical fields for a range of sponsors, this ever-present necessity pervades much of the thinking of the whole staff whether they like it or not and whether their income source is private industry, a government agency, a foundation, a university committee, or a combination of several such. This consciousness of payroll problems is not as conducive to detached and objective research as group research is usually claimed to be.

The operational imperatives of both independents and group researchers tend, as A. H. Maslow[17] indicates, to place premiums upon means-centering in investigations rather than upon scientific-problem-centering. By means-centering, he refers "to the tendency to consider that the essence of science lies in its instruments, techniques, procedures, apparatus and its methods rather than in its problems, questions, fuctions or goals." This especially "tends to push into a commanding position in [what is called] science the technicians and the 'apparatus men,' rather than the 'question-askers' and the problem-solvers." It is easier to gain institutional support for a

technology that stresses, as Maslow observes, "elegance, polish, 'technique,' and apparatus" rather than for the irritating questionings and novel observations of scientists.

If the foregoing were the only problems associated with individual and organizational research, few would be greatly concerned. In competition, individual research would continue to outpace the organizational in the ways indicated in my quotation above from Donald Young, an advocate of group research. But the primary problem is this: Group research has now so absorbed the interests, aspirations, and resources of graduate departments of sociology that the training of individual well-rounded journeymen in sociological research is being eclipsed. The situation has thus now arisen that it is becoming fairly difficult to locate young staff members for a college or university who are trained to be liberal arts college and graduate school professors and to carry on the independent research that needs to go therewith.

This situation is not unique to sociology. It arrived much earlier in the physical and biological sciences, Writing in Chemical and Engineering News, Harry A. Toulmin, Jr.,[18] states in part as follows:

Freedom of the scientist—as of any individual—means his right to hold his own social, political, and economic opinions ....

Freedom of the scientist should also mean the right to select the things in which he wishes to do his research and the privilege, subject only to considerations of national security, to publish such scientific information as he wishes.

I do not go along with the present trend in some universities toward regimenting scientific and engineering personnel by preventing them from doing research work unless it is controlled by a government, a foundation, or by rigid corporate policies. I do not go along with arbitrary control of patent rights of university personnel as the result of their own work. I do not go along with the contention of some universities that their research foundations can properly participate in studies lead-

---

[17]"Problem-Centering Vs. Means-Centering in Science," Philosophy of Science, 13 (1946), 326-331 (pp. 326-327 quoted).

[18]"The Freedom of Science—Its Opportunities and Responsibilities," Chemical and Engineering News, 27 (1949), 980-982 (p. 980 quoted).

ing to Ph.D. degrees, accept compensation from commercial sponsors who seek this cheaper form of doing their research, and agree to suppress the publication of the resulting theses until the convenience of the commercial sponsor is served. That is not freedom of science—that is not a true university.

Toulmin is speaking primarily of chemistry. He might just as well, as it is becoming increasingly apparent, have been speaking of abuses now rapidly mushrooming in sociology.

We sociologists are presumably students of scientific methodology and of the stultifying as well as the useful influences of bureaucracy and institutionalism. We are also presumably committed primarily to scientific rather than commercial or manipulative goals, or we would have found an easier and more direct route to financial rewards. Why, therefore, are we sociologists—of all specialists—now permitting our graduate training programs to be distorted by the same anti-scientific tendencies against which Toulmin inveighs in chemistry?

There is certainly a need for the training of social engineers, social technicians for employment by business management, government, trades unions, and others. These include both skilled organizational investigators and analyst-counselors. But there is an even greater need for the scientist-professor, for professors who are sociological scientists and for scientists who can conduct their independent researches as concomitants of their instructional work with students. There is also, it should be emphasized, a need for the training of group researchers[19] as well as—but not to the exclusion of—well-rounded journeymen of the individualistic and independent sort.

To cut my discussion short, I shall point merely to a few factors against which even we students of human relationships apparently cannot maintain very

effective defenses. As Gerald Wendt[20] observes in a recent book review, and many other writers on science have discerned the same thing, "American culture...is essentially unscientific, although the products of science are everywhere." He would have been more accurate, in my estimation, if he had said, "Human cultures are unscientific." After all, when the scientist struggles to overcome the handicaps Francis Bacon[21] characterized as the "idols and false notions which are now in possession of human understanding, and have taken deep root therein," he is fighting especially the preconceptions in any given culture which look upon innovations, innovators, and questioners as annoying and even subversive.

Overriding all else in mass society—East and West—is preoccupation with the control and manipulation of social power by elite groups and by their hired technical specialists. The unsettling consequences of scientific observation are far more difficult to sell to power-seekers than dependable techniques, dependable research teams, and dependable and supposedly scientific ammunition for political, legal, and industrial competition and conflict. Thus, to a very large extent, professionals in our society find it expedient to become peddlers not of knowledge and wisdom but of techniques. They develop and merchandise managerial techniques to entrepreneurs of large social power, techniques that at least appear to be useful tools and weapons.

That is the "big time" aspect of technique peddling. Related to this is what Jessie Bernard[22] refers to as "an almost insatiable demand for techniques today." This is the mass aspect of the same general development. As Bernard notes, "Scarcely a single issue of any popular

---

[19]See useful discussion of graduate training for group researchers by Talcott Parsons, "Graduate Training in Social Relations at Harvard," *Journal of General Education*, 5 (1950-51), 149-157.

[20]New York *Herald Tribune Book Review*, February 18, 1951.

[21]"Magna Instauratio: Aphorisms Concerning the Interpretation of Nature and the Kingdom of Man," nos. xxxviii-lxix, in *Essays*, selected and edited by R. F. Jones, New York: Odyssey Press, 1937, pp. 278-295 (p. 278 quoted).

[22]"The Art of Science: A Reply to Redfield," *American Journal of Sociology*, 55 (1949-50), 1-9 (p. 2 quoted).

journal appears without rules for something or other: how to stay young and beautiful; how to win friends and influence people; how to stop worrying and live; how to secure peace of mind; how to achieve salvation; how to find God."

No inference should be drawn from what is said that I am arguing in any sense against an appropriate use of the very best techniques available to scientists. As A. H. Maslow[23] puts it, "The working scientist must, of course, be concerned with his techniques, but only because they can help him achieve his proper ends. Once he forgets this, he becomes like the man spoken of by Freud who spent all his time polishing his glasses instead of putting them on and seeing with them."

Sociological research is necessarily a marginal, extra-moral, and extra-class-

mores calling. Scientific sociologists somehow succeed in resisting the overwhelming societal and class compulsions to forego curiosity and to manufacture salable weapons of power-conflict and plausible sedatives for tension-worn humanity. In my estimation, those who succeed in contributing to the science of sociology will be the ones who continue to resist those influences today as they have been such persons in the past. In this work, however, more aid is needed from graduate departments in the development of journeymen sociologists rather than merely of compatible and clever group researchers. This would facilitate the achievement of more substantial gains in sociology.

Only through more keen and precise observations of human relations, only through the devoted work of more and more keen and curious observers can sociology as a science increase its potentialities for service to humanity.

[23]"Problem-Centering Vs. Means-Centering in Science," Philosophy of Science, 13 (1946), 326-331 (p. 327 quoted).

CULTURE AND SOCIETY: THE CREATION AND MAINTENANCE OF CULTURAL PATTERNS

Priorities in Scientific Discovery: A Chapter in the Sociology of Science

Robert K. Merton

SOURCE: *American Sociological Review*, Vol. 22, (1957), pp. 635–59.

We can only guess what historians of the future will say about the condition of present-day sociology. But it seems time to anticipate one of their observations. When the Trevelyans of 2050 come to write that history—as they well might, for this clan of historians promises to go on forever—they will doubtless find it strange that so few sociologists (and historians) of the twentieth century could bring themselves, in their work, to treat science as one of the great social institutions of the time. They will observe that long after the sociology of science became an identifiable field of inquiry,[1] it remained little cultivated in a world where science loomed large enough to present mankind with the choice of destruction or survival. They may even suggest that somewhere in the process by which social scientists take note of the world as it is and as it once was, a sense of values appears to have become badly scrambled.

This spacious area of neglect may therefore have room for a paper which tries to examine science as a social institution, not in the large but in terms of a few of its principal components.

A Calendar of Disputes over Priority. We begin by noting the great frequency with which the history of science is punctuated by disputes, often by sordid disputes, over priority of discovery. During the last three centuries in which modern science developed, numerous scientists, both great and small, have engaged in such acrimonious controversy. Recall only these few: Keenly aware of the importance of his inventions and discoveries, Galileo became a seasoned campaigner as he vigorously defended his rights to priority first, in his Defense against the Calumnies and Impostures of

[1] The rudiments of a sociology of science can be found in an overview of the subject by Bernard Barber, Science and the Social Order, Glencoe: The Free Press, 1952; Bernard Barber, "Sociology of Science: A Trend Report and Bibliography," Current Sociology, Vol. 5, No. 2, Paris: UNESCO, 1957.

Baldassar Capar, where he showed how his invention of the "geometric and military compass" had been taken from him, and then, in The Assayer, where he flayed four other would be rivals; Father Horatio Grassi, who tried "to diminish whatever praise there may be in this [invention of the telescope for use in astronomy] which belongs to me"; Christopher Scheiner, who claimed to have been first to observe the sunspots (although, unknown to both Scheiner and Galileo, Johann Fabricius had published such observations before); an unspecified villain (probably the Frenchman Jean Tarde) who "attempted to rob me of that glory which was mine, pretending not to have seen my writings and trying to represent themselves as the original discovers of these marvels"; and finally, Simon Mayr, who "had the gall to claim that he had observed the Medicean planets which revolve about Jupiter before I had [and used] a sly way of attempting to establish his priority."[2]

The peerless Newton fought several battles with Robert Hooke over priority in optics and celestial mechanics and entered into a long and painful controversy with Leibniz over the invention of the calculus. Hooke,[3] who has been described as the "universal claimant" because "there was scarcely a discovery in his

time which he did not conceive himself to claim," (and, it might be added, often justly so, for he was one of the most inventive men in his century of genius), Hooke, in turn, contested priority not only with Newton but with Huygens over the important invention of the spiral-spring balance for regulating watches to eliminate the effect of gravity.

The calendar of disputes was full also in the eighteenth century. Perhaps the most tedious and sectarian of these was the great "Water Controversy" in which that shy, rich and noble genius of science, Henry Cavendish, was pushed into a three-way tug-of-war with Watt and Lavoisier over the question of which one had first demonstrated the compound nature of water and thereby removed it from its millennia-long position as one of the elements. Earthy battles raged also over claims to the first discovery of heavenly bodies, as in the case of the most dramatic astronomical discovery of the century in which the Englishman John Couch Adams and the Frenchman Urban Jean LeVerrier inferred the existence and predicted the position of the planet now known as Neptune which was found where their independent computations showed it would be. Medicine had its share of conflicts over priority; for example, Jenner believed himself first to demonstrate that vaccination afforded security against smallpox, but the advocates of Pearson and Rabaut believed otherwise.

Throughout the nineteenth century and down to the present, disputes over priority continued to be frequent and intense. Lister knew he had first introduced antisepsis, but others insisted that Lemaire had done so before. The sensitive and modest Faraday was wounded by the claims of others to several of his major discoveries in physics: one among these, the discovery of electro-magnetic rotation, was said to have been made before by Wollaston; Faraday's onetime mentor Sir Humphrey Davy (who had himself been involved in similar disputes) actually opposed Faraday's election to the Royal Society on the ground that his was

---

[2]Galileo, The Assayer, 1623, translated by Stillman Drake in Discoveries and Opinions of Galileo, New York: Doubleday, 1957, pp. 232-233, 245. Galileo thought it crafty of Mayr to date his book as published in 1609 by using the Julian calendar without indicating that, as a Protestant, he had not accepted the Gregorian calendar adopted by "us Catholics" which would have shifted the date of publication to January 1610, when Galileo had reported having made his first observations. Later in this paper, I shall have more to say about the implications of attaching importance to such short intervals separating rival claims to priority.

[3]For scholarly reappraisals of Hooke's role in developing the theory of gravitation, see Louis Diehl Patterson, "Hooke's Gravitation Theory and Its Influence on Newton," Isis, 40 (November, 1949), pp. 327-341; 41 (March, 1950), pp. 32-45; and E. N. da C. Andrade, "Robert Hooke," Wilkins Lecture, Proceedings of the Royal Society, Series B, Biological Sciences, 137 (24 July, 1950). The recent biography by Margaret 'Espinasse is too uncritical and defensive of Hooke to be satisfactory; Robert Hooke, London: Heinemann, 1956.

not the original discovery.[4] Laplace, several of the Bernoullis, Legendre, Gauss, Cauchy were only a few of the giants among mathematicians embroiled in quarrels over priority.

What is true of physics, chemistry, astronomy, medicine and mathematics is true also of all the other scientific disciplines, not excluding the social and psychological sciences. As we know, sociology was officially born only after a long period of abnormally severe labor. Nor was the postpartum any more tranquil. It was disturbed by violent controversies between the followers of St. Simon and Comte as they quarreled over the delicate question of which of the two was the father of sociology and which merely the obstetrician. And to come to the very recent past, Janet is but one among several to have claimed that they had the essentials of psycho-analysis before Freud.

To extend the list of priority fights would be industrious and, for this occasion, superfluous. For the moment, it is enough to note that these controversies, far from being a rare exception in science, have long been frequent, harsh, and ugly. They have practically become an integral part of the social relations between scientists. Indeed, the pattern is so common that the Germans have characteristically compounded a word for it, Prioritätsstreit.

On the face of it, the pattern of conflict over priority can be easily explained. It seems to be merely a consequence of the same discoveries being made simultaneously, or nearly so, a recurrent event in the history of science which has not exactly escaped the notice of sociologists, or of others, at least since the definite work of William Ogburn and Dorothy Thomas. But on second glance, the matter does not appear quite so simple.

The bunching of similar or identical discoveries in science is only an occasion[5] for disputes over priority, not their cause or their grounds. After all, scientists also know that discoveries are often made independently. (As we shall see, they not only know this but fear it, and this often activates a wish to ensure their priority). It would therefore seem a simple matter for scientists to acknowledge that their simultaneous discoveries were independent and that the question of priority is consequently beside the point. On occasion, this is just what has happened, as we shall see in that most moving of all cases of noblesse oblige in the history of science, when Darwin and Wallace tried to outdo one another in giving credit to the other for what each had separately worked out. Fifty years after the event, Wallace was still insisting upon the contrast between his own hurried work, written within a week after the great idea came to him, and Darwin's work, based on twenty years of collecting evidence. "I was then (as often since) the 'young man in a hurry,' " said the reminiscing Wallace; "he, the painstaking and patient student seeking ever the full demonstration of the truth he had discovered, rather than to achieve immediate personal fame."[6]

On other occasions, self-denial has gone even further. For example, the incomparable Euler withheld his long sought solution to the calculus of variations, until the twenty-three-year-old Lagrange, who had developed a new method needed to reach the solution, could put it into print, " 'so as not to deprive you,' Euler informed the young man, 'of any part of the glory which is your due.' "[7] Apart from these and many

---

[4] Bence Jones, The Life and Letters of Faraday, London: Longmans, Green, 1870, Vol. I, pp. 336-352.

[5] And not always even the occasion. Disputes over priority have occurred when alleged or actual anticipations of an idea have been placed decades or, at times, even centuries or millennia earlier, when they are generally described as "rediscoveries."

[6] This remark is taken from Wallace's commentary at the semi-centenary of the joint discovery, a classic of self-abnegation that deserves to be rescued from the near-oblivion into which it has fallen. For a transcript, see James Marchant, Alfred Russel Wallace: Letters and Reminiscences, New York: Harper, 1916, pp. 91-96.

[7] E. T. Bell, Men of Mathematics, New York: Simon and Schuster, 1937, pp. 155-156. And see the

other examples of generosity in the annals of science, there have doubtless been many more that never found their way into the pages of history. Nevertheless, the recurrent struggles for priority, with all their intensity of affect, far overshadow these cases of noblesse oblige, and it still remains necessary to account for them.

Alleged Sources of Conflicts over Priority. One explanation of these disputes would regard them as mere expressions of human nature. On this view, egotism is natural to the species; scientists, being human, will have their due share and will sometimes express their egotism through self-aggrandizing claims to priority. But, of course, this interpretation does not stand up. The history of social thought is strewn with the corpses of those who have tried, in their theory, to make the hazardous leap from human nature to particular forms of social conduct, as has been observed from the time of Montesquieu, through Comte and Durkheim, to the present.[8]

A second explanation derives these conflicts not from the original nature shared by all men, but from propensities toward egotism found among some men. It assumes that, like other occupations, the occupation of science attracts some ego-centered people, and assumes further that it might even attract many such people, who, hungry for fame, elect to enter a profession that promises enduring fame to the successful. Unlike the argument from nature, this one, dealing with processes of self-selection and social selection, is not defective in principle. It is possible that differing kinds of personalities tend to be recruited by various occupations and, though I happen to doubt it, it is possible that quarrelsome or contentious personalities are

especially apt to be attracted to science and recruited into it. The extent to which this is so is a still unanswered question, but developing inquiry into the type of personality characteristic of those entering the various professions may in due course discover how far it is so.[9] In any event, it should not be difficult to find some aggressive men of science.

But even should the processes of selection result in the recruitment of contentious men, there are theoretical reasons for believing that this does not adequately account for the great amount of contention over priority that flares up in science. For one thing, these controversies often involve men of ordinarily modest disposition who act in seemingly self-assertive ways only when they come to defend their rights to intellectual property. This has often been remarked, and sometimes with great puzzlement. As Sir Humphrey Davy asked at the time of the great Water Controversy between Cavendish and Watt, how does it happen that this conflict over priority should engage such a man as Cavendish, "unambitious, unassuming, with difficulty ... persuaded to bring forward his important discoveries ... and ... fearful of the voice of fame."[10] And the biographer of Cavendish, writing about the same episode, describes it as "a perplexing dilemma. Two unusually modest and unambitious men, universally respected for their integrity, famous for their discoveries and inventions, are suddenly found standing in a hostile position towards each other . . . ."[11] Evidently, ingrained egotism is not required to engage in a fight for priority.

---

comparable act of generosity on the part of the venerable Legendre toward the mathematical genius, Niels Abel, then in his twenties, *ibid.*, p. 337.

[8] Émile Durkheim had traced this basic theme in sociological theory as early as his Latin thesis of 1892, which has fortunately been translated into French for the benefit of some of us later sociologists. See his *Montesquieu et Rousseau: Précurseurs de la Sociologie*, Paris: Marcel Rivière, 1953, esp. Chapter I.

[9] Information about this is sparse and unsatisfactory. As a bare beginning, a study of the Thematic Apperception Test protocols of 64 eminent biological, physical, and social scientists found no signs of their being "particularly aggressive." Anne Roe, *The Making of a Scientist*, New York: Dodd, Mead, 1953, p. 192.

[10] Sir Humphrey Davy, *Collected Works*, VII, p. 128, quoted by George Wilson, *The Life of the Honorable Henry Cavendish*, London, 1851, p. 63.

[11] Wilson, *op. cit.*, p. 64. There can be little doubt about the unassuming character of Cavendish, the pathologically shy recluse, whose unpublished notebooks were crowded with discoveries disproving

A second strategic fact shows the inadequacy of explaining these many struggles as owing to egotistic personalities. Very often the principals themselves, the discoverers or inventors, take no part in arguing their claims to priority (or withdraw from the controversy as they find that it places them in the distasteful role of insisting upon their own merits or of deprecating the merits of their rivals). Instead, it is their friends and followers, or other more detached scientists who commonly see the assignment of priority as a moral issue that must be fought to a conclusion. For example, it was Wollaston's friends, rather than the distinguished scientist himself, who insinuated that the young Faraday had usurped credit for the experiments on electromagnetic rotation.[12] Similarly, it was Priestley, De Luc and Blagden, "all men eminent in science and of unblemished character," who embroiled the shy Cavendish and the unassertive Watt in the Water Controversy.[13] Finally, it was the quarrelsome, eminent, and justly esteemed scientist François Arago (whom we shall meet again) and a crowd of astronomers, principally in France and England but also in Germany and Russia, rather than "the shy, gentle and unaffected" co-discoverer of Neptune, Adams, who stirred the pot of conflict over priority until it boiled over and then simmered down into general acknowledgment that the planet had been independently discovered by Adams and LeVerrier.[14] And so, in one after another of the historic quarrels over priority in science.

Now these argumentative associates and bystanders stand to gain little or nothing from successfully prosecuting the claims of their candidate, except in the pickwickian sense of having identified themselves with him or with the nation of which they are all a part. Their behavior can scarcely be explained by egotism. They do not suffer from rival claims to precedence. Their personal status is not being threatened. And yet, over and again, they take up the cudgels in the status-battle[15] and, uninhibited by any semblance of indulging in self-praise, express their great moral indignation over the outrage being perpetrated upon their candidate.

This is, I believe, a particularly significant fact. For, as we know from the sociological theory of institutions, the expression of disinterested moral indignation is a signpost announcing the violation of a social norm.[16] Although the indignant bystanders are themselves not injured by what they take to be the mis-

---

then widely-held theories and anticipating discoveries not made again for a long time to come. He stands as the example *a fortiori*, for even such a man as this was drawn into a controversy over priority.

The history of science evidently has its own brand of chain-reactions. It was the reading of Wilson's <u>Life of Cavendish</u> with its report of Cavendish's long-forgotten experiment on the sparking of air over alkalis which led Ramsay (just as the same experiment led Rayleigh) to the discovery of the element argon. Both Rayleigh and Ramsay delicately set out their respective claims to the discovery, claims not easily disentangled since the two had been in such close touch. They finally agreed to joint publication as "the only solution" to the problem by assigning appropriate credit. The episode gave rise to a great controversy over priority in which neither of the discoverers would take part; the debate is continued in the biographies of the two: by the old friend and collaborator of Ramsay, Morris W. Travers, in <u>A Life of Sir William Ramsay</u>, London: Edward Arnold Ltd., 1956, pp. 100, 121-122, 292, passim; and by the son of Lord Raleigh, <u>John William Strutt: Third Baron Rayleigh</u>, London: Edward Arnold, 1924, Chapter XI.

[12] Jones, <u>op. cit.</u>, pp. 351-352; see also the informative book by T. W. Chalmers, <u>Historic Researches: Chapters in the History of Physical and Chemical Discovery</u>, New York: Scribner's 1952, p. 54.

[13] This is the contemporary judgment by Wilson, <u>op. cit.</u>, pp. 63-64.

[14] Sir Harold Spencer Jones, "John Couch Adams and the Discovery of Neptune," reprinted in James R. Newman, <u>The World of Mathematics</u>, New York: Simon and Schuster, 1956, II, pp. 822-839. A list of cases in which associates, rather than principals, took the lead in these conflicts is a very long one. I do not include it here.

[15] Sometimes, of course, they act as judges and arbitrators rather than advocates, as was true of Lyell and Hooker in the episode involving Darwin and Wallace. But, as we shall see, the same institutional norms are variously called into play in all these cases.

[16] For an acute analysis of the theoretical place of moral obligation, and its correlate, moral indignation, in the theory of institutions, particularly as this was developed in the long course of Durkheim's

behavior of the culprit, they respond with hostility and want to see "fair play," to see that behavior conforms to the rules of the game. The very fact of their entering the fray goes to show that science is a social institution with a distinctive body of norms exerting moral authority and that these norms are invoked particularly when it is felt that they are being violated. In this sense, fights over priority, with all their typical vehemence and passionate feelings, are not merely expressions of hot tempers, although these may of course raise the temperature of controversy; basically, they constitute responses to what are taken to be violations of the institutional norms of intellectual property.

INSTITUTIONAL NORMS OF SCIENCE

To say that these frequent conflicts over priority are rooted in the egotism of human nature, then, explains next to nothing; to say that they are rooted in the contentious personalities of those recruited by science may explain part, but not enough; to say, however, that these conflicts are largely a consequence of the institutional norms of science itself comes closer, I think, to the truth. For, as I shall suggest, it is these norms that exert pressure upon scientists to assert their claims, and this goes far toward explaining the seeming paradox that even those meek and unaggressive men, ordinarily slow to press their own claims in other spheres of life, will often do so in their scientific work.

The ways in which the norms of science help produce this result seem clear enough. On every side, the scientist is reminded that it is his role to advance knowledge and his happiest fulfillment of that role, to advance knowledge greatly. This is only to say, of course, that in the institution of science originality is at a premium. For it is through originality, in greater or smaller increments, that

knowledge advances. When the institution of science works efficiently, and like other social institutions, it does not always do so, recognition and esteem accrue to those who have best fulfilled their roles, to those who have made genuinely original contributions to the common stock of knowledge. Then are found those happy circumstances in which self-interest and moral obligation coincide and fuse.

Recognition of what one has accomplished is thus largely a motive derived from institutional emphases. Recognition for originality becomes socially validated testimony that one has successfully lived up to the most exacting requirements of one's role as scientist. The self-image of the individual scientist will also depend greatly on the appraisals by his scientific peers of the extent to which he has lived up to this exacting and critically important aspect of his role. As Darwin once phrased it, "My love of natural science...has been much aided by the ambition to be esteemed by my fellow naturalists."

Interest in recognition,[17] therefore, need not be, though it can readily become, simply a desire for self-aggrandizement or an expression of egotism. It is, rather, the motivational counterpart on the psychological plane to the emphasis upon originality on the institutional plane. It is not necessary that individual scientists begin with a lust for fame; it is enough that science, with its abiding and often functional emphasis on originality and its assigning of large rewards for originality, makes recognition of priority uppermost. Recognition and fame then become symbol and reward for having done one's job well.

---

work, see Talcott Parsons, The Structure of Social Action, Glencoe: The Free Press, 1949, pp. 368-470; for further formulations and citations of additional literature, see R. K. Merton, Social Theory and Social Structure, Glencoe: The Free Press, 1957 (rev. ed.), pp. 361 ff.

[17] It is not only the institution of science, of course, that instills and reinforces the concern with recognition; in some degree, all institutions do. This is evident since the time W. I. Thomas included 'recognition' as one of what he called "the four wishes" of men. The point is, rather, that with its emphasis on originality, the institution of science greatly reinforces this concern and indirectly leads scientists to vigorous self-assertion of their priority. For Thomas's fullest account of the four wishes, see The Unadjusted Girl, Boston: Little, Brown, 1925, Chapter I.

This means that long before we know anything about the distinctive personality of this or that scientist, we know that he will be under pressure to make his contributions to knowledge known to other scientists and that they, in turn, will be under pressure to acknowledge his rights to his intellectual property. To be sure, some scientists are more vulnerable to these pressures than others—some are self-effacing, others self-assertive; some generous in granting recognition, others stingy. But the great frequency of struggles over priority does not result merely from these traits of individual scientists but from the institution of science, which defines originality as a supreme value and thereby makes recognition of one's originality a major concern.[18]

When this recognition of priority is either not granted or fades from view, the scientist loses his scientific property. Although this kind of property shares with other types general recognition of the "owner's" rights, it contrasts sharply in all other respects. Once he has made his contribution, the scientist no longer has exclusive rights of access to it. It becomes part of the public domain of science. Nor has he the right of regulating its use by others by withholding it unless it is acknowledged as his. In short, property rights[19] in science become whittled down to just this one: the recognition by others of the scientist's distinctive part in having brought the result into being.

It may be that this concentration of the numerous rights ordinarily bound up in other forms of property into the one right of recognition by others helps produce the great concentration of affect that commonly characterizes disputes over priority. Often, the intensity of affect seems disproportionate to the occasion; for example, when a scientist feels he has not been given enough recognition for what is, in truth, a minor contribution to knowledge, he may respond with as much indignation as the truly inventive scientist, or even with more, if he secretly senses that this is the outermost limit of what he can reasonably hope to contribute.[20] This same concentration of property-rights into the one right of recognition may also account for the deep

---

[18] In developing this view, I do not mean to imply that scientists, any more than other men, are merely obedient puppets doing exactly what social institutions require of them. But I do mean to say that, like men in other institutional spheres, scientists tend to develop the values and to channel their motivations in directions the institution defines for them. For an extended formulation of the general theory of institutionalized motivation, see Talcott Parsons, Essays is Sociological Theory, Glencoe: The Free Press, 1954 (rev. ed.), esp. Chapters II and III.

[19] That the notion of property is part and parcel of the institution of science can be seen from the language employed by scientists in speaking of their work. Ramsay, for example, asks Rayleigh's "permission to look into atmospheric nitrogen" on which Rayleigh had been working; the young Clerk Maxwell writes William Thomson, "I do not know the

Game laws and Patent laws of science...but I certainly intend to poach among your electrical images"; Norbert Wiener describes "differential space, the space of the Brownian motion" as "wholly mine in its purely mathematical aspects, whereas I was only a junior partner in the theory of Banach spaces." Borrowing, trespassing, poaching, credit, stealing, a concept which "belongs" to us—these are only a few of the many terms in the lexicon of property adopted by scientists as a matter of course.

[20] Some of this had occurred to Galileo in his counterattack on Sarsi (pseudonym for Grassi): "Only too clearly does Sarsi show his desire to strip me completely of any praise. Not content with having disproved our reasoning set forth to explain the fact that the tails of comets sometimes appear to be bent in an arc, he adds that nothing new was achieved by me in this, as it had all been published long ago, and then refuted, by Johann Kepler. In the mind of the reader who goes no more deeply than Sarsi's account, the idea will remain that I am not only a thief of other men's ideas, but a petty, mean thief at that, who goes about pilfering even what has been refuted. And who knows; perhaps in Sarsi's eyes the pettiness of the theft does not render me more blameworthy than I would be if I had bravely applied myself to greater thefts. If, instead of filching some trifle, I had more nobly set myself to search out books by some reputable author not as well known in these parts, and had then tried to suppress his name and distribute all his labors to myself, perhaps Sarsi would consider such an enterprise as grand and heroic as the other seems to him cowardly and abject," (Galileo, The Assayer, op. cit., pp. 261-262.)

This type of reaction to what I describe as the "professional adumbrationist" (in the unpublished part of this paper) was expressed also by Benjamin Franklin after he had suffered from claims by others that they had first worked out the experiment of the lightning kite. As he said in part (the rest of his

moral indignation expressed by scientists when one of their number has had his right of priority denied or challenged Even though they have no personal stake in the particular episode, they feel strongly about the single property-norm and the expression of their hostility serves the latent function of reaffirming the moral validity of this norm.

National Claims to Priority. In a world made up of national states, each with its own share of ethnocentrism, the new discovery redounds to the credit of the discoverer not as an individual only, but also as a national. From at least the seventeenth century, Britons, Frenchmen, Germans, Dutchmen, and Italians have urged their country's claims to priority; a little later, Americans entered the lists to make it clear that they had primacy.

The seventeenth-century English scientist Wallis, for example, writes: "I would very fain that Mr. Hooke and Mr. Newton would set themselves in earnest for promoting the designs about telescopes, that others may not steal from us what our nation invents, only for the neglect to publish them ourselves." So, also, Halley says of his comet that "if it should return according to our prediction about the year 1758 [as of course it did], impartial posterity will not refuse to acknowledge that this was first discovered by an Englishman."[21]

Or to move abruptly to the present, we see the Russians, now that they have taken a powerful place on the world-scene, beginning to insist on the national character of science and on the importance of finding out who first made a discovery. Although the pattern of national claims to priority is old, the formulation of its rationale in a Russian journal deserves quotation if only because it is so vigorously outspoken:

Marxism-Leninism shatters into bits the cosmopolitan fiction concerning supra-class, non-national, "universal" science, and definitely proves that science, like all culture in modern society, is national in form and class in content. . . . The slightest inattention to questions of priority in science, the slightest neglect of them, must therefore be condemned, for it plays into the hands of our enemies, who cover their ideological aggression with cosmopolitan talk about the supposed non-existence of questions of priority in science, i.e., the questions concerning which peoples [here, be it noted, collectivities displace the individual scientist] made what contribution to the general store of world culture. . . . [And summarizing the answers to these questions in compact summary] The Russian people has the richest history. In the course of this history, it has created the richest culture, and all the other countries of the world have drawn upon it and continue to draw upon it to this day.[22]

Against this background of affirmation, one can better appreciate the recent statement by Khrushchev that "we Russians had the H-bomb before you" and the comment by the New York Times that "the question of priority in the explosion of the hydrogen bomb is . . . a matter of semantics," to be settled only when we know whether the "prototype-bomb" or the "full fledged bomb" is in question.[23]

observations are almost equally in point), "The smaller your invention is, the more mortification you receive in having the credit of it disputed with you by a rival, whom the jealousy and envy of others are ready to support against you, at least so far as to make the point doubtful. It is not in itself of importance enough for a dispute; no one would think your proofs and reasons worth their attention: and yet if you do not dispute the point, and demonstrate your right, you not only lose the credit of being in that instance ingenuous, but you suffer the disgrace of not being ingenuous; not only of being a plagiary but of being a plagiary for trifles. Had the invention been greater it would have disgraced you less; for men have not so contemptible an idea of him that robs for gold on the highway, as of him that can pick pockets for half-pence and farthings." (Quoted in the informed and far-reaching monograph by I. B. Cohen, Franklin and Newton, Philadelphia: The American Philosophical Society, 1956, pp. 75-76.)

[21] Louis T. More, Isaac Newton, New York: Scribner's, 1934, pp. 146-147, and pp. 241; 477-478.

[22] An editorial, "Against the Bourgeois Ideology of Cosmopolitanism," Voprosy filosofi, 1948, No. 2, as translated in the Current Digest of the Soviet Press, February 1, 1949, Vol. 1, No. 1, pp. 9-10, 12. For an informed account, see David Joravsky, "Soviet Views on the History of Science," Isis, 46 (March, 1955), pp. 3-13, esp. at pp. 9n. and 11, which treat of changing Russian attitudes toward priority and simultaneous invention; see also Merton, Social Theory and Social Structure, op. cit., pp. 556-560.

[23] New York Times, July 27, 1957, p. 3, col. 1.

The recent propensity of the Russians to claim priority in all manner of inventions and scientific discoveries thus energetically reduplicates the earlier, and now less forceful though far from vanished, propensity of other nations to claim like priorities. The restraint often shown by individual scientists in making such claims becomes rather inconspicuous when official or self-constituted representatives of nations put in their claims.

THE REWARD-SYSTEM IN SCIENCE

Like other institutions, the institution of science has developed an elaborate system for allocating rewards to those who variously live up to its norms. Of course, this was not always so. The evolution of this system has been the work of centuries, and it is probably far from finished. In the early days of modern science, Francis Bacon could explain and complain all in one by saying that "it is enough to check the growth of science, that efforts and labours in this field go unrewarded.... And it is nothing strange if a thing not held in honour does not prosper."[24] And a half-century later, much the same could be said by Thomas Sprat, the Bishop of Rochester, in his official history of the newly-established Royal Society:

...it is not to be wonder'd, if men have not been very zealous about those studies, which have been so farr remov'd, from present benefit, and from the applause of men. For what should incite them, to bestow their time, and Art, in revealing to mankind, those Myster-

ies for which, it may be, they would be onely despis'd at last? How few must there needs be, who will be willing, to be impoverish'd for the common good? while they shall see, all the rewards, which might give life to their Industry, passing by them, and bestow'd on the deserts of easier studies?[25]

The echo of these complaints still reverberates in the halls of universities and scientific societies, but chiefly with regard to material rather than honorific rewards. With the growth and professionalization of science, the system of honorific rewards has become diversely elaborated, and apparently at an accelerated rate.

Heading the list of the immensely varied forms of recognition long in use is eponymy,[26] the practice of affixing the name of the scientist to all or part of what he has found, as with the Copernican system, Hooke's law, Planck's constant, or Halley's comet. In this way, scientists leave their signatures indelibly in history; their names enter into all the scientific languages of the world.

At the rugged and thinly populated peak of this system of eponymy are the men who have put their stamp upon the science and thought of their age. Such men are naturally in very short supply, and these few sometimes have an entire epoch named after them, as when we speak of the Newtonian epoch, the Darwinian era, or the Freudian age.

The graduations of eponymy have the character of a Guttman scale in which those men assigned highest rank are also assigned lesser degrees of honorific recognition. Accordingly, these peerless scientists are typically included also in the next highest ranks of eponymy, in

---

[24] Francis Bacon, *Novum Organum,* trans. by Ellis and Spedding, London: Routledge, n. d. Book I, Aphorism XCI. The ellipsis in the text above was for brevity's sake; it should be filled out here below because of the pertinence of what Bacon went on to say: "For it does not rest with the same persons to cultivate sciences and to reward them. The growth of them comes from great wits, the prizes and rewards of them are in the hands of the people, or of great persons, who are but in very few cases even moderately learned. Moreover this kind of progress is not only unrewarded with prizes and substantial benefits; it has not even the advantage of popular applause. For it is a greater matter than the generality of men can take in, and is apt to be overwhelmed and extinguished by the gales of popular opinions."

[25] Thomas Sprat, *The History of the Royal Society,* London, 1667, p. 27.

[26] Galileo begins his "Message from the Stars," announcing his discovery of the satellites of Jupiter, with a pacan to the practice of eponymy which opens with these words: "Surely a distinguished public service has been rendered by those who have protected from envy the noble achievements of men who have excelled in virtue, and have thus preserved from oblivion and neglect those names which deserve immortality." (Op. cit., p. 23.) He then proceeds to call the satellites "the Medicean Stars" in honor of the Grand Duke of Tuscany, who soon becomes his patron.

which they are credited with having fathered a new science or a new branch of science (at times, according to the heroic theory, through a kind of parthenogenesis for which they apparently needed no collaborators). Of the illustrious Fathers of this or that science (or of this or that specialty), there is an end, but an end not easily reached. Consider only these few, culled from a list many times this length:

Morgagni, the Father of Pathology
Cuvier, the Father of Palaeontology
Faraday, the Father of Electrotechnics
Daniel Bernoulli, the Father of Mathematical
    Physics
Bichat, the Father of Histology
van Leeuwenhoek, the Father of Protozoology
    and Bacteriology
Jenner, the Father of Preventive Medicine
Chladni, the Father of Modern Acoustics
Herbart, the Father of Scientific Pedagogy
Wundt, the Father of Experimental Psychology
Pearson, the Father of Biometry;
    and, of course,
Comte, the Father of Sociology.

In a science as farflung and differentiated as chemistry, there is room for several paternities. If Robert Boyle is the undisputed father of Chemistry (and, as his Irish epitaph has it, also the Uncle of the Earl of Cork), then Priestley is the Father of Pneumatic Chemistry, Lavoisier the Father of Modern Chemistry, and the nonpareil Willard Gibbs, the Father of Physical Chemistry.

On occasion, the presumed father of a science is called upon, in the persons of his immediate disciples or later adherents, to prove his paternity, as with Johannes Müller and Albrecht von Haller, who are severally regarded as the Father of Experimental Physiology.

Once established, this eponymous pattern is stepped up to extremes. Each new specialty has its own parent, whose identity is often known only to those at work within the specialty. Thus, Manuel Garcia emerges as the Father of Laryngoscopy, Adolphe Brongiart as the Father of Modern Palaeobotany, Timothy Bright as the Father of Modern Shorthand, and Father Johann Dzierson (whose important work may have influenced Mendel) as the Father of Modern Rational Beekeeping.

Sometimes, a particular form of a discipline bears eponymous witness to the man who first gave it shape, as with Hippocratic medicine, Aristotelian logic, Euclidean geometry, Boolean algebra, and Keynesian economics. Most rarely, the same individual acquires a double immortality, both for what he achieved and for what he failed to achieve, as in the cases of Euclidean and non-Euclidean geometries, and Aristotelian and non-Aristotelian logics.

In rough hierarchic order, the next echelon is comprised by thousands of eponymous laws, theories, theorems, hypotheses, instruments, constants and distributions. No short list can hope to be representative of the wide range of these scientific contributions that have immortalized the men who made them. But a few examples in haphazard array might include the Brownian movement, the Zeeman effect, Rydberg's constant, Moseley's atomic number, and the Lorenz curve or to come closer home, where we refer only to assured contemporary recognition rather than to possibly permanent fame, the Spearman rank-correlation coefficient, the Rorschach inkblot, the Thurstone scale, the Bogardus social-distance scale, the Bales categories of interaction, the Guttman scalogram and the Lazarsfeld latent-structure analysis.

Each science, or art based on science, evolves its own distinctive patterns of eponymy to honor those who have made it what it is. In the medical sciences, for example, the attention of posterity is assured to the discoverer or first describer of parts of the body (as with the Eustachian tube, the circle of Willis, Graffian follicles, Wharton's duct, and the canal of Nuck) though, oddly enough, Vesalius, commonly described as the Father of Modern Anatomy has been accorded no one part of the body as distinctly his own. In medicine, also, eponymy registers the first diagnostician of a disease (as with Addison's, Bright's, Hodgkin's, Menière's and Parkinson's diseases); the inventor of diagnostic tests (as with Romberg's sign, the Wasser- mann reaction, the Calmette test, and the Babinski reflex); and the inventor of in- struments used in research or practice (as with the Kelly pad, the Kelly clamp, and the Kelly rectoscope). Yet, however numerous and diversified this array of eponyms in medicine,[27] they are still re- served, of course, to only a small frac- tion of the many who have labored in the medical vineyard. Eponymy is a prize that, though large in absolute aggregate, is limited to the relatively few.

Time does not permit, nor does the occasion require, detailed examination of eponymous practices in all the other sci- ences. Consider, then, only two other patterns: In a special branch of physics, it became the practice to honor great physicists by attaching their names to electrical and magnetic units (as with volt, ohm, ampere, coulomb, farad, joule, watt, henry, maxwell, gauss, gilbert and oersted). In biology, it is the long-stand- ing practice to append the name of the first describer to the name of a species, a custom which greatly agitated Darwin since, as he saw it, this put "a premium on hasty and careless work" as the "spe- cies-mongers" among naturalists try to achieve an easy immortality by "miser- ably describ[ing] a species in two or three lines."[28] (This, I may say, will not be the last occasion for us to see how the system of rewards in science can be stepped up to such lengths as to get out of hand and defeat its original purposes.)

Eponymy is only the most enduring and perhaps most prestigious kind of recog- nition institutionalized in science. Were

the reward-system confined to this, it would not provide for the many other dis- tinguished scientists without whose work the revolutionary discoveries could not have been made. Graded rewards in the coin of the scientific realm—honorific recognition by fellow-scientists—are distributed among the stratified layers of scientific accomplishment. Merely to list some of these other but still considerable forms of recognition will perhaps be enough to remind us of the complex structure of the reward-system in sci- ence.

In recent generations, the Nobel Prize, with nominations for it made by scien- tists of distinction throughout the world, is perhaps the pre-eminent token of rec- ognized achievement in science.[29] There is also an iconography of fame in sci- ence, with medals honoring famous sci- entists and the recipients of the award alike (as with the Rumford medal and the Arago medal). Beyond these, are mem- berships in honorary academies and sci- ences (for example, the Royal Society and the French Academy of Sciences), and fellowships in national and local soci- eties. In those nations that still preserve a titled aristocracy, scientists have been ennobled, as in England since the time when Queen Anne added laurels to her crown by knighting Newton, not, as might be supposed, because of his superb ad- ministrative work as Master of the Mint, but for his scientific discoveries. These things move slowly; it required almost two centuries before another Queen of England would, in 1892, confer a peerage of the realm upon a man of science for his work in science, and thus transform the pre-eminent Sir William Thomson into the no less eminent Lord Kelvin.[30]

---

[27] It has been suggested that, in medicine at least, eponymic titles are given to diseases only so long as they are poorly understood. "Any disease desig- nated by an eponym is a good subject for research." (O. H. Perry Pepper, Medical Etymology, Phila- delphia: W. B. Saunders Co., 1949, pp. 11-12.)

[28] Exercised by the excesses eponymy in natural history had reached, the usually mild Darwin re- peatedly denounced this "miserable and degrading passion of mere species naming." What is most in point for us is the way in which the pathological exaggeration of eponymizing highlights the normal role of eponymy in providing its share of incentives for serious and sustained work in science. Francis Darwin, ed., The Life and Letters of Charles Dar- win, New York: Appleton, 1925, Vol. I, pp. 332-344.

[29] On the machinery and results of the Nobel and other prize-awards, see Barber, Science and the Social Order, op. cit., pp. 108 ff.; Leo Moulin, "The Nobel Prizes for the Sciences, 1901-1950," British Journal of Sociology, 6 (September, 1955), pp. 246- 263.

[30] For caustic comment on the lag in according such recognition to men of science, see excerpts from newspapers of the day in Silvanus P. Thomp- son, The Life of William Thomson: Baron Kelvin of Largs, London: Macmillan, 1910, Vol. II, pp. 906-907.

Scientists themselves have distinguished the stars from the supporting cast by issuing directories of "starred men of science" and universities have been known to accord honorary degrees to scientists along with the larger company of philanthropists, industrialists, businessmen, statesmen and politicians.

Recognition is finally allocated by those guardians of posthumous fame, the historians of science. From the most disciplined scholarly works to the vulgarized and sentimentalized accounts designed for the millions, great attention is paid to priority of discovery, to the iteration and reiteration of 'firsts.' In this way, many historians of science help maintain the prevailing institutional emphasis on the importance of priority. One of the most eminent among them, the late George Sarton, at once expresses and exemplifies the commemorative function of historiography when he writes that "... the first scholar to conceive that subject [the history of science] as an independent discipline and to realize its importance was ... Auguste Comte." He then goes on to propose that great scholar, Paul Tannery, as most deserving to be called "the father of our studies," and finally states the thesis that "... as the historian is expected to determine not only the relative truth of scientific ideas at different chronological states, but also their relative novelty, he is irresistibly led to the fixation of <u>first</u> events."[31]

Although scientific knowledge is impersonal, although its claim to truth must be assessed entirely apart from its source, the historian of science is called upon to prevent scientific knowledge from sinking (or rising) into anonymity, to preserve the collective memory of its origins. Anonymous givers have no place in this scheme of things. Eponymity, not anonymity, is the standard. And, as we have seen, outstanding scientists, in turn, labor hard to have their names inscribed in the golden book of firsts.[32]

Seen in composite, from the eponyms enduringly recording the names of scientists in the international language of science to the immense array of parochial and ephemeral prizes, the reward-system of science reinforces and perpetuates the institutional emphasis upon originality. It is in this specific sense that originality can be said to be a major institutional goal of modern science, at times, the paramount one, and recognition for originality a derived, but often as heavily emphasized, goal. In the organized competition to contribute to man's scientific knowledge, the race is to the swift, to him who gets there first with his contribution in hand.

<u>Institutional Norm of Humility.</u> If the institution of science placed great value <u>only</u> on originality, scientists would per-

[31] George Sarton, <u>The Study of the History of Science</u>, Cambridge: Harvard University Press, 1936, pp. 3-4, 35-36. Sarton goes on to observe that this practice of identifying first events "never fails to involve him [the historian] in new difficulties, because creations absolutely <u>de novo</u> are very rare, if they occur at all; most novelties are only novel combinations of old elements and the degree of novelty is thus a matter of interpretation, which may vary considerably according to the historian's experience, standpoint, or prejudices....It is always risky, yet when every reasonable precaution has been taken one must be willing to run the risk and make the challenge, for this is the only means of being corrected, if correction be needed." (<u>Ibid.</u>, p. 36.) This is a telling sign of the deep-rooted sentiment that recognition for originality in science must be expressed, that it is an obligation— "the historian is expected ... "—to search out the 'first' to contribute an idea or finding, even though a comprehensive view of the cumulative and interlocking character of scientific inquiry suggests that the attribution of 'firsts' is often difficult and sometimes arbitrary. For a further statement on this matter of priority, see George Sarton, <u>The Study of the History of Mathematics</u>, Cambridge: Harvard University Press, 1936, pp. 33-36.

I cannot undertake here to examine the attitudes commonly manifested by historians of science toward this emphasis on searching out priorities. It can be said that these too are often ambivalent.

[32] This was presumably not always so. As is well known, medieval authors often tried to cloak their writings in anonymity. But this is not the place to examine the complex subject of variations in cultural emphases upon originality and recognition. For some observations on this, see George Sarton, <u>A Guide to the History of Science</u>, Waltham, Mass.; Chronica Botanica Co., 1952, p. 23, who reminds us of ancient and medieval practices in which "modest authors would try to pass off their own compositions under the name of an illustrious author of an earlier time," ghost-writing in reverse. See also R. K. Merton, <u>Science, Technology and Society in Seventeenth Century England</u>, Bruges, Belgium: Osiris, 1938, pp. 360-632, at p. 528.

haps attach even more importance to recognition of priority than they do. But, of course, this value does not stand alone. It is only one of a complex set making up the ethos of science—disinterestedness, universalism, organized scepticism, communism of intellectual property, and humility being some of the others.[33] Among these, the socially enforced value of humility is in most immediate point, serving, as it does, to reduce the misbehavior of scientists below the rate that would occur if importance were assigned only to originality and the establishing of priority.

The value of humility takes diverse expression. One form is the practice of acknowledging the heavy indebtedness to the legacy of knowledge bequeathed by predecessors. This kind of humility is perhaps best expressed in the epigram Newton made his own: "If I have seen farther, it is by standing on the shoulders of giants" (this, incidentally, in a letter to Hooke who was then challenging Newton's priority in the theory of colors.)[34] That this tradition has not always been honored in practice can be inferred from the admiration that Darwin, himself lavish in such acknowledgments, expressed to Lyell for "the elaborate honesty with which you quote the words of all living and dead geologists."[35] Exploring the literature of a field of science becomes not only an instrumental practice, designed to learn from the past, but a commemorative practice, designed to pay homage to those who have prepared the way for one's work.

Humility is expected also in the form of the scientist's insisting upon his personal limitations and the limitations of scientific knowledge altogether. Galileo taught himself and his pupils to say, "I do not know." Perhaps another often-quoted image by Newton most fully expresses this kind of humility in the face of what is yet to be known:

I do not know what I may appear to the world, but to myself I seem to have been only like a boy playing on the seashore, and diverting myself in now and then finding a smoother pebble or a prettier shell than ordinary, whilst the great ocean of truth lay all undiscovered before me.[36]

If this contrast between public image ("what I may appear to the world") and self-image ("but to myself I seem") is fitting for the greatest among scientists, it is presumably not entirely out of place for the rest. The same theme continues unabated. Laplace, the Newton of France, in spite of what has been described as "his desire to shine in the constantly changing spotlight of public esteem," reportedly utters an epigrammatic paraphrase of Newton in his last words, "What we know is not much; what we do not know is immense."[37] Lagrange summarizes his lifetime of discovery in the one phrase, "I do not know." And Lord Kelvin, at the Jubilee celebrating his fifty years as a distinguished scientist in the course of which he was honored by scores of scientific societies and academies, characterizes his lifelong effort to develop a grand and comprehensive the-

[33]For a review of other values of science, see Barber, op. cit., Chapter IV; Merton, Social Theory and Social Structure, op. cit., pp. 552-561; H. A. Shepard, "The Value System of a University Research Group," American Sociological Review, 19 (August, 1954), pp. 456-462.

[34] Alexander Koyré, "An unpublished letter of Robert Hooke to Isaac Newton," Isis, 43 (December, 1952), pp. 312-337, at p. 315.

[35]Darwin, op. cit., I, p. 263.

[36]David Brewster, Memoirs of the Life, Writings, and Discoveries of Sir Isaac Newton, Edinburgh and London, 1855, Volume II, Chapter xxvii. For our purposes, unlike those of the historian, it is a matter of indifference whether Newton actually felt acutely modest or was merely conforming to expectation. In either case, he expresses the norm of personal humility, which is widely held to be appropriate. I. B. Cohen, (op. cit., pp. 47, 58, passim) repeatedly and incisively makes the point that both admirers and critics of Newton have failed to make the indispensable distinction between what he said and what he did.

[37]Bell, op. cit., p. 172. Bell refers also to "a common and engaging trait of the truly eminent scientist in his frequent confession of how little he knows...." What he describes as a trait of the scientist can also be seen as an expectation on the part of the community of scientists. It is not that many scientists happen to be humble men; they are expected to be humble. See E. T. Bell, "Mathematics and Speculation," The Scientific Monthly, 32 (March, 1931), pp. 193-209, at p. 204.

ory of the properties of matter by the one word, "Failure."[38]

Like all human values, the value of modesty can be vulgarized and run into the ground by excessive and thoughtless repetition. It can become merely conventional, emptied of substance and genuine feeling. There really can be too much of a good thing. It is perhaps this excess which led Charles Richet, himself a Nobel laureate, to report the quiet self-appraisal by a celebrated scientist: "I possess every good quality, but the one that distinguishes me above all is modesty."[39] Other scientists, for example, the great Harvard mathematician, George Birkhoff, will have no truck with modesty, whether false, prim, or genuine. Having been told by a Mexican physicist of his hope that the United States would continue "to send us savants of your stature," Birkhoff sturdily replied. "Professor Erro, in the States I am the only one of my stature." And as Norbert Wiener is reported to have said in his obituary address for Birkhoff, "He was the first among us and he accepted the fact. He was not modest."[40] Nevertheless, such forthright acknowledgement of one's eminence is not quite the norm among scientists.

It would appear, then, that the institution of science, like other institutions, incorporates potentially incompatible values: among them, the value of originality, which leads scientists to want their priority to be recognized, and the value of humility, which leads them to insist on how little they have been able to accomplish. These values are not real contradictories, of course—" 'tis a poor thing, but my own"—but they do call for opposed kinds of behavior. To blend these potential incompatibles[41] into a single orientation, to reconcile them in practice, is no easy matter. Rather, as we shall now see, the tension between these kindred values—kindred as Cain and Abel were kin—creates an inner conflict among men of science who have internalized both of them and generates a distinct ambivalence toward the claiming of priorities.

AMBIVALENCE TOWARD PRIORITY

The components of this ambivalence are fairly clear. After all, to insist on one's originality by claiming priority is not exactly humble and to dismiss one's priority by ignoring it is not exactly to affirm the value of originality.[42] As a result of this conflict, scientists come to despise themselves for wanting that which the institutional values of science have led them to want.

With the rare candor that distinguishes him, Darwin so clearly exhibits this agitated ambivalence in its every detail that this one case can be taken as paradigmatic for many others (which are matters of less detailed and less candid rec-

[38]G. F. Fitzgerald, Lord Kelvin, 1846-99. Jubilee Commemoration Volume, with an Essay on the Works, 1899; S. P. Thompson, Life of William Thomson, Vol. II, Chapter XXIV.

[39]See the gallery of trenchant pen-portraits of scientists in Charles Richet, The Natural History of a Scientist. trans. by Sir Oliver Lodge, New York: Doran, 1927, p. 86.

[40]Carlos Graef Fernandez (as transcribed by Samuel Kaplan), "My Tilt with Albert Einstein," American Scientist, 44 (April, 1956), pp. 204-211, at p. 204.

[41]For further examination of the problem of blending incompatible norms into stable patterns of behavior, in this case among physicians, see R. K. Merton, "Some Preliminaries to a Sociology of Medical Education," in R. K. Merton, G. G. Reader and P. L. Kendall, eds., The Student-Physician, Cambridge: Harvard University Press, 1957, p. 72 ff. As is well known, R. S. Lynd has set forth the general notion that institutional norms are organized as near-incompatibles; see his Knowledge for What?, Princeton: Princeton University Press, 1939, Chapter III.

[42]Strictly speaking, originality and priority are of course not the same thing. Belated independent rediscoveries of what was long since known may represent great originality on the part of the rediscoverer, as is perhaps best shown in the remarkable case of the self-taught twentieth-century Indian mathematician, Srinivasa Ramanujan, who, all unknowing that it had been done before, recreated much of early nineteenth-century mathematics, and more besides. Cf. G. H. Hardy, Ramanujan: Twelve Lectures Suggested by His Life and Work, Cambridge: Harvard University Press, 1940. Edwin G. Boring, who has long been interested in the subject of priority in science, has, among many other perceptive observations, noted the lack of identity between originality and priority. See, for example, his early paper, "The Problem of Originality in Science," American Journal of Psychology, 39 (December, 1927), pp. 70-90, esp. at p. 78.

ord). In his Autobiography, he writes that, even before his historic voyage on the Beagle in 1831, he was "ambitious to take a fair place among scientific men— whether more ambitious or less so than most of my fellow-workers, I can form no opinion."[43] A quarter of a century after this voyage, he is still wrestling with his ambition, exclaiming in a letter that "I wish I could set less value on the bauble fame, either present or posthumous, than I do, but not, I think, to any extreme degree. . . ."[44]

Two years before the traumatizing news from Wallace, reporting his formulation of the theory of evolution, Darwin writes his now-famous letter to Lyell, explaining that he is not quite ready to publish his views, as Lyell had suggested he do in order not to be forestalled, and again expressing his uncontrollable ambivalence in these words: "I rather hate the idea of writing for priority, yet I certainly should be vexed if any one were to publish my doctrines before me."[45]

And then, in June 1858, the blow falls. What Lyell warned would happen and what Darwin could not bring himself to believe could happen, as all the world knows, did happen. Here is Darwin writing Lyell of the crushing event:

[Wallace] has today sent me the enclosed, and asked me to forward it to you. It seems to me well worth reading. Your words have come true with a vengeance—that I should be forestalled. . . . I never saw a more striking coincidence; if Wallace had my MS. sketch written out in 1842, he could not have made a better short abstract! Even his terms now stand as heads of my chapters. . . . So all my originality, whatever it may amount to, will be smashed. . . .[46]

Humility and disinterestedness urge Darwin to give up his claim to priority; the wish for originality and recognition urges him that all need not be lost. At first, with typical magnanimity, but without pretense of equanimity, he makes the desperate decision to step aside altogether. A week later, he is writing Lyell

again; perhaps he might publish a short version of his long-standing text, "a dozen pages or so." And yet, he says in his anguished letter, "I cannot persuade myself that I can do so honourably." Torn by his mixed feelings, he concludes his letter, "My good dear friend, forgive me. This is a trumpery letter, influenced by trumpery feelings." And in an effort finally to purge himself of his feelings, he appends a postscript, "I will never trouble you or Hooker on the subject again."[47]

The next day he writes Lyell once more, this time to repudiate the postscript. Again, he registers his ambivalence: "It seems hard on me that I should lose my priority of many years' standing, but I cannot feel at all sure that this alters the justice of the case. First impressions are generally right, and I at first thought it would be dishonourable in me now to publish."[48]

As fate would have it, Darwin is just then prostrated by the death of his infant daughter. He manages to respond to the request of his friend Hooker and sends him the Wallace manuscript and his own original sketch of 1844, "solely," he writes, "that you may see by your own handwriting that you did read it. . . . Do not waste much time. It is miserable in me to care at all about priority."[49]

Other members of the scientific community do what the tormented Darwin will not do for himself. Lyell and Hooker take matters in hand and arrange for that momentous session in which both papers are read at the Linnean Society. And as they put it in their letter prefacing the publication of the joint paper of "Messrs. C. Darwin and A. Wallace," "in adopting our present course . . . we have explained to him [Darwin] that we are not solely considering the relative claims to priority of himself and his friend, but the interests of science generally."[50] Despite

---

[43] Darwin, op. cit., p. 54.
[44] Ibid., p. 452.
[45] Ibid., pp. 426-427.
[46] Ibid., p. 473.

[47] Ibid., pp. 474-475.
[48] Ibid., p. 475.
[49] Ibid., p. 476.
[50] "On the Tendency of Species to Form Varieties and on the Perpetuation of Varieties and Species by Natural Means of Selection," by C. Darwin and A. R. Wallace. Communicated by Sir C. Lyell and J. D. Hooker, Journal of the Linnean Society, 3 (1859), p. 45. Read July 1, 1858.

this disclaimer of interest in priority, be it noted that scientific <u>knowledge</u> is not the richer or the poorer for having credit given where credit is due; it is the social <u>institution</u> of science and individual men of science that would suffer from repeated failures to allocate credit justly.

This historic and not merely historical episode so plainly exhibits the ambivalence occasioned by the double concern with priority and modesty that it need not be examined further. Had the institutionalized emphasis on originality been alone in point, the claim to priority would have invited neither self-blame nor self-contempt; publication of the long antecedent work would have proclaimed its own originality. But the value of originality was joined with the value of humility and modesty. To insist on priority would be to trumpet one's own excellence, but scientific peers and friends of the discoverers, acting as a third party in accord with the institutional norms, could with full propriety announce the joint claims to originality that the discoverers could not bring themselves to do. Underneath it all lies a deep and agitated ambivalence toward priority.

I have not yet counted the recorded cases of debates about priority in science and the manner of their outcome. Such a count, moreover, will not tell the full story for it will not include the doubtless numerous instances in which independent ideas and discoveries were never announced by those who found their ideas anticipated in print. Nevertheless, I have the strong impression that disputes, even bitter disputes, over priority outnumber the cases of despondent but unreserved admission that the other fellow had made the discovery first.

The institutional values of modesty and humility are apparently not always enough to counteract both the institutional emphasis upon originality and the actual workings of the system of allocating rewards. Originality, as exemplified by the new idea or the new finding, is more readily observable by others in science and is more fully rewarded than the often unobservable kind of humility that keeps an independent discoverer from reporting that he too had had the same idea or the same finding. Moreover, after publication by another, it is often difficult, if not impossible, to demonstrate that one had independently arrived at the same result. For these and other reasons, it is generally an unequal contest between the values of recognized originality and of modesty. Great modesty may elicit respect, but great originality promises everlasting fame.

In short, the social organization of science allocates honor in a way that tends to vitiate the institutional emphasis upon modesty. It is this, I believe, which goes far toward explaining why so many scientists, even those who are ordinarily men of the most scrupulous integrity, will go to great lengths to press their claims to priority of discovery. As I have often suggested, perhaps too often, any <u>extreme</u> institutional

emphasis upon achievement—whether this be scientific productivity, accumulation of wealth or, by a small stretch of the imagination, the conquests of a Don Juan—will attenuate conformity to the institutional norms governing behavior designed to achieve the particular form of "success," especially among those who are socially disadvantaged in the competitive race.[51]

[51]Merton, <u>op. cit.</u>, p. 166. Scientists do not all occupy similar positions in the social structure; there are, consequently, differentials in access to <u>opportunity</u> for scientific achievement (and, of course, differences of individual capacity for achievement). The theory of the relations of social structure to anomie requires us to explore differential pressures upon those scientists variously located in the social structure. Contrast only the disputatious Robert Hooke, a socially mobile man whose rise in status resulted wholly from his scientific achievements, and the singularly undisputatious Henry Cavendish, high-born and very rich (far richer, and, by the canons of Burke's peerage, more elevated even than that other great aristocrat of science, Robert Boyle) who, in the words of Biot, was "<u>le plus riche de tous les savans; et probablement aussi, le plus savant de tous les riches.</u>" Or consider what Norbert Wiener has said of himself, "I was competitive beyond the run of younger mathematicians, and I knew equally that this was not a very pretty attitude. However, it was not an attitude which I was free to assume or to reject. I was quite aware that I was an out among ins and I would get no shred of recognition that I did not force." (<u>I Am a Mathematician</u>, New York: Doubleday, 1956, p. 87).

Or more specifically and more completely, great concern with the goal of recognition for originality can generate a tendency toward sharp practices just inside the rules of the game or sharper practices far outside. That this has been the case with the behavior of scientists who were all-out to have their originality recognized, the rest of this paper will try to show.

TYPES OF RESPONSE TO CULTURAL EMPHASIS ON ORIGINALITY

Fraud in Science. The extreme form of deviant behavior in science would of course be the use of fraud to obtain credit for an original discovery. For reasons to be examined, the annals of science include very few instances of downright fraud although, in the nature of the case, an accurate estimate of frequency is impossible. Darwin, for example, said that he knew of only "three intentionally falsified statements" in science.[52] Yet, some time before, his contemporary, Charles Babbage, the mathematician and inventor of calculating machines (one of which prophetically made use of perforated cards), had angrily taken a classified inventory of fraud in science.[53]

At the extreme are hoaxes and forgery: the concocting of false data in science and learning—or, more accurately, in pseudo-science and anti-scholarship. Literary documents have been forged in abundance, at times, by men of previously unblemished reputation, in order to gain money or fame. Though no one can say with confidence, it appears that love of money was at the root of the forgery of fifty or so rare nineteenth-century pamphlets by that prince of bibliographers, that court of last appeal for the authentication of rare books

and manuscripts, Thomas J. Wise. Of quite another stripe was John Payne Collier, the Shaksperian scholar who, unrivalled for his genuine finds in Elizabethan drama and "encouraged by the steadily growing plaudits of his colleagues," could not rest content with this measure of fame and proceeded to forge, with great and knowledgeable skill, a yet-uncounted array of literary papers.[54] But these rogues seem idle alongside the fecund and audacious Vrain-Lucas who, in the space of eight years, created more than 27,000 pieces of manuscript, all duly sold to Michel Chasles, perhaps the outstanding French geometer of the mid-nineteenth century, whose credulity stretches our own, inasmuch as this vast collection included letters by Pontius Pilate, Mary Magdalene, the resurrected Lazarus, Ovid, Luther, Dante, Shakespeare, Galileo, Pascal and Newton, all written on paper and in modern French. Most provocative among these documents was the correspondence between Pascal and the then eleven-year-old Newton (all in French, of course, although even at the advanced age of thirty-one Newton could struggle through French only with the aid of a dictionary), for these letters made it plain that Pascal, not Newton, had, to the greater glory of France, first discovered the law of gravitation, a momentous correction of history, which for several years excited the interest of the Académie des Sciences and usurped many pages of the Comptes Rendus until, in 1869, Vrain-Lucas was finally brought to book and sentenced to two years in prison. For our purposes, it is altogether fitting that Vrain-Lucas should have had Pascal address this maxim to the boy Newton: "Tout homme qui n'aspire pas à se faire un nom n'exécutera jamais rien de grand."[55]

But these are only straws in the wind; once again, limitations of space allow me only to identify a problem, not to examine it.

[52]Darwin, op. cit., p. 84.
[53]Charles Babbage, The Decline of Science in England, London, 1830, pp. 174-183. George Lundberg has independently noted that "a scientist's greed for applause [sometimes] becomes greater that his devotion to truth." [Social Research, New York: Longmans Green, 1929, p. 34 (and in less detail, in the second edition, 1946, p. 52).]

[54]I have drawn these examples of frauds in anti-scholarship from the zestful and careful account by Richard D. Altick, The Scholar Adventurers, New York: Macmillian, 1951, Chapters 2 and 6.
[55]The definitive reports on the Vrain-Lucas affair by M. P. Faugère and by Henri Bordier and Mabille are not available to me at this telling; substantial details, including extracts from the court-proceedings, are given by the paleographer, Étienne

Such lavish forgery is unknown to science proper, but the pressure to demonstrate the truth of a theory or to produce a sensational discovery has occasionally led to the faking of scientific evidence. The biologist Paul Kammerer produced specimens of spotted salamanders designed to prove the Lamarckian thesis experimentally; was thereupon offered a chair at the University of Moscow where in 1925 the Lamarckian views of Michurin held reign; and upon proof that the specimens were fakes, attributed the fraud to a research assistant and committed suicide.[56] Most recently, the Piltdown man—that is, the skull and jaw from which his existence was inferred—has been shown, after forty years of uneasy acceptance, to be a carefully contrived hoax.[57]

Excessive concern with "success" in scientific work has on occasion led to the types of fraud Babbage picturesquely described as "trimming" and "cooking." The trimmer clips off "little bits here and there from observations which differ most in excess from the mean, and [sticks] . . . them on to those which are too small . . . [for the unallowable purpose of] 'equitable adjustment.'" The cook makes "multitudes of observations" and selects only those which agree with an hypothesis and, as Babbage says, "the cook must be very unlucky if he cannot pick out fifteen or twenty which will do

for serving up." This eagerness to demonstrate a thesis can, on occasion, lead even truth to be fed with cooked data, as it did for the neurotic scientist, described by Lawrence Kubie, "who had proved his case, but was so driven by his anxieties that he had to bolster an already proved theorem by falsifying some quite unnecessary additional statistical data."[58]

The great cultural emphasis upon recognition for original discovery can lead by gradations from these rare practices of outright fraud to more frequent practices just beyond the edge of acceptability, sometimes without the scientist's being aware that he has exceeded allowable limits. Scientists may find themselves reporting only "successful experiments or results, so-called, and neglecting to report 'failures,'" Alan Gregg, that informed observer of the world of medical research, practice, and education, reports the case of

the medical scientist of the greatest distinction who told me that during his graduate fellowship at one of the great English universities he encountered for the first time the idea that in scientific work one should be really honest in reporting the results of his experiments. Before that time he had always been told and had quite naturally assumed that the point was to get his observations and theories accepted by others, and published.[59]

Yet, these deviant practices should be seen in perspective. What evidence there is suggests that they are extremely infrequent, and this temporary focus upon them will surely not be distorted into regarding the exceptional case as the typical. Apart from the moral integrity of scientists themselves and this is, of course, the major basis for honesty in science, there is much in the social organization of science that provides a further compelling basis for honest work. Scientific research is typically, if not

---

Charavay, <u>Affair Vrain-Lucas: Étude Critique</u>, Paris, 1870; a more accessible summary that does not, however, do full justice to the prodigious inventiveness of Vrain-Lucas is provided by J. A. Farrer, <u>Literary Forgeries</u>, London: Longmans Green, 1907, Chapter XII. The biographer of Newton, Sir David Brewster, at the age of 87, did his share to safeguard the integrity of historical scholarship, but this did not prevent Chasles from prizing the three thousand letters of Galileo which he had acquired from his friend, although they happened to be in French, rather than in the Latin or Italian in which Galileo wrote.

[56]Martin Gardner, <u>In the Name of Science</u>, New York: G. P. Putnam's Sons, 1952, p. 143; W. S. Beck, <u>Modern Science and the Nature of Life</u>, New York: Harcourt, Brace, 1957, pp. 201-202; Conway Zirkle, "The Citation of Fraudulent Data," <u>Science</u>, 120 (30 July, 1954), pp. 189-190.

[57]William L. Straus, Jr., "The Great Piltdown Hoax," <u>Science</u>, ·119 (26 February, 1954), pp. 265-269.

[58]Lawrence S. Kubie, M.D., "Some Unsolved Problems of the Scientific Career," <u>American Scientist</u>, 41 (1953), pp. 596-613; 42 (1954), pp. 104-112, at p. 606.

[59]Alan Gregg, <u>Challenges to Contemporary Medicine</u>, New York: Columbia University Press, 1956, p. 115.

always, under the exacting scrutiny of fellow-experts, involving, as it usually though not always does, the verifiability of results by others. Scientific inquiry is in effect subject to rigorous policing, to a degree perhaps unparallelled in any other field of human activity. Personal honesty is supported by the public and testable character of science. As Babbage remarked, "the cook would [at best] procure a temporary reputation . . . at the expense of his permanent fame."

Competition in the realm of science, intensified by the great emphasis on original and significant discoveries, may occasionally generate incentives for eclipsing rivals by illicit or dubious means. But this seldom occurs in the form of preparing fraudulent data; instead, it appears in quite other forms of deviant behavior involving spurious claims to discovery. More concretely, it is an occasional theft rather than forgery, and more often, libel and slander rather than theft that are found on the small seamy side of science.

Plagiary: Fact and Slander. Deviant behavior most often takes the form of occasional plagiaries and many slanderous charges or insinuations of plagiary. The historical record shows relatively few cases (and of course the record may be defective) in which one scientist actually pilfered another. We are assured that in the Mécanique céleste (until then, outranked only by Newton's Principia) "theorems and formulae are appropriated wholesale without acknowledgement" by Laplace.[60] Or, to take a

marginal case, Sir Everard Home, the distinguished English surgeon who was appointed custodian of the unpublished papers of his even more distinguished brother-in-law, John Hunter, published 116 papers of uncertain origin in the Philosophical Transactions after Hunter's death, and burned Hunter's manuscripts, an action greatly criticized by knowledgeable and suspicious contemporaries.[61] It is true also that Robert Boyle, not impressed by the thought that theft of his ideas might be a high tribute to his talent, was in 1688 driven to the desperate expedient of printing an "Advertisement about the Loss of many of his Writings," later describing the theft of his work and reporting that he would from then on write only on loose sheets, in the hope that these would tempt thieves less than "bulky packets" and, going on to say that he was resolved to send his writings to press without extensive revision in order to avoid prolonged delays.[62] But even with such cases of larceny on the grand scale, the aggregate of demonstrable theft in modern science is not large.

What does loom large is the repeated

---

when he himself was beginning his career, Laplace introduced him at the Institute for the purpose of explaining his supposed discovery of equations of mixed differences, and afterwards showed him, under a strict pledge of secrecy, the papers, then yellow with age, in which he had long before obtained the same results." (Vol. XVI, pp. 201-202). As we shall see, Gauss, who was meticulous in acknowledging predecessors, treated the young Bolyai as did Laplace the young Biot.

[61] Ralph H. Major, A History of Medicine, Oxford: Blackwell Scientific Publications, 1954, Vol. II, p. 703.

[62] The account by A. M. Clerke in the article on Boyle in the Dictionary of National Biography is somewhat mistaken in attributing charges of plagiary to the published Advertisement. This speaks only of losses of manuscript through "unwelcome accidents" (e.g., the upsetting of corrosive liquors over a file of manuscripts) and at most hints at less impersonal sources of loss. But a later unpublished paper by Boyle, dug up by his biographer Birch, is levelled against the numerous plagiarists of his works. This document, running to three folio pages of print, is a compendium of the ingenious devices for thievery developed by the grand larcenists of seventeenth-century science. See The Works of the Honourable Robert Boyle, in six volumes, to which is prefixed The Life of the Author, by J. Birch, London, 1772, Volume I, pp. cxxv-cxxviii, ccxxii-ccxxiv.

---

[60] As stated by the historian of astronomy, Agnes Mae Clerke, in her article on Laplace in the eleventh edition of the Encyclopaedia Britannica. Some of Clerke's further observations are much in point: "In the delicate task of apportioning his own large share of merit, he certainly does not err on the side of modesty; but it would perhaps be as difficult to produce an instance of injustice, as of generosity in his estimate of others. Far more serious blame attaches to his all but total suppression in the body of the work—and the fault pervades the whole of his writings—of the names of his predecessors and contemporaries . . . a production which may be described as the organized result of a century of patient toil presents itself to the world as the offspring of a single brain." And yet, since these matters are seldom all of a piece, "Biot relates that,

practice of charging others with pilfering scientific ideas. Falsely accused of plagiarizing Harvey in physiology, Snell in optics, and Harriot and Fermat in geometry, Descartes in turn accuses Hobbes and the teen-age Pascal of plagiarizing him.[63] To maintain his property, Descartes implores his friend Mersenne, "I also beg you to tell him [Hobbes] as little as possible about what you know of my unpublished opinions, for if I'm not greatly mistaken, he is a man who is seeking to acquire a reputation at my expense and through shady practices."[64] All unknowing that the serene and unambitious Gauss had long since discovered the method of least squares, Legendre, himself "a man of the highest character and scrupulously fair," practically accuses Gauss of having filched the idea from him and complains that Gauss, already so well-stocked with momentous discoveries, might at least have had the decency not to adopt his brainchild.[65]

At times, the rivalrous concern with priority can go so far as to set, not the Egyptians against the Egyptians, but brother against brother, as in the case of the great eighteenth-century mathematicians, the brothers Jacob and Johannes Bernoulli, who repeatedly and bitterly attacked one another's claims to priority. (Johannes improved on this by throwing his own son out of the house for having won a prize from the French Academy on which he himself had had his eye.)[66]

Or to turn to our own province, Comte, tormented by the suggestion that his law of three stages had really been originated by St. Simon, denounces his one-time master and describes him as a "superficial and depraved charlatan."[67] Again, to take Freud's own paraphrase, Janet claims that "everything good in psychoanalysis repeats, with light modifications, the views of Janet—everything else in psychoanalysis being bad."[68] Freud refuses to lock horns with Janet in what he describes as "gladiator fights in front of the noble mob," but some years later, his disciple, Ernest Jones, reports that at a London Congress he has "put an end to" Janet's pretensions, and Freud applauds him in a letter that urges him to "strike while the iron is hot," in the interests of "fair play."[69]

So the almost changeless pattern repeats itself. Two or more scientists quietly announce a discovery. Since it is often the case that these are truly independent discoveries, with each scientist having separately exhibited originality of mind, the process is sometimes stabilized at that point, with due credit to both, as in the instance of Darwin and Wallace. But since the situation is often ambiguous with the role of each not easy to demonstrate and since each knows that he had himself arrived at the discovery, and since the institutionalized stakes of reputation are high and the joy of discovery immense, this is often not a stable solution. One or another of the discoverers—or frequently, his colleagues or fellow-nationals—suggests that he rather than his rival was really first, and that the in-

[63] For the case of Harvey, see A. R. Hall, The Scientific Revolution, 1500-1800, London: Longmans, Green, 1954, p. 148; for Hobbes, see Descartes, Oeuvres, (edited by Charles Adam and Paul Tannery), Correspondance, Paris, 1899, Vol. III, pp. 283 ff.; for Pascal, see ibid., 1903, Vol. V, p. 366.

[64] Descartes, ibid., Vol. III, p. 320.

[65] Bell, op. cit., pp. 259-260. Legendre seems to have been particularly sensitive to these matters, perhaps because he was often victimized; note Clerke's remark that between Laplace and Legendre "there was a feeling of 'more than coldness,' owing to his appropriation, with scant acknowledgment, of the other's labors." Encyclopaedia Britannica, Vol. XVI, p. 202.

[66] Bell, op. cit., p. 134.

[67] Frank E. Manuel, The New World of Henri Saint-Simon, Cambridge: Harvard University Press, 1956, pp. 340-342; also Richard L. Hawkins, Auguste Comte and the United States, Cambridge: Harvard University Press, 1936, pp. 81-82, as cited by Manuel.

[68] Sigmund Freud, History of the Psychoanalytic Movement, London: Hogarth Press; also, Freud, An Autobiographical Study, London: Hogarth Press, 1948, pp. 54-55, where he seeks "to put an end to the glib repetition of the view that whatever is of value in psycho-analysis is merely borrowed from the ideas of Janet . . . historically psycho-analysis is completely independent of Janet's discoveries, just as in its content it diverges from them and goes far beyond them." For Janet's not always delicate insinuations, see his Psychological Healing, New York: Macmillan, 1925, I, pp. 601-640.

[69] Ernest Jones, Sigmund Freud: Life and Work, London: Hogarth Press, 1955, Vol. II, p. 112.

dependence of the rival is at least un-proved. Then begins the familiar deterioration of standards governing con-flictful interaction: the other side, group-ing their forces, counter with the opinion that plagiary had indeed occurred, that let him whom the shoe fits wear it and furthermore, to make matters quite clear, the shoe is on the other foot. Reinforced by group-loyalties and often by chauvin-ism, the controversy gains force, mutual recriminations of plagiary abound, and there develops an atmosphere of thoroughgoing hostility and mutual distrust.

On some occasions, this can lead to outright deceit in order to buttress valid claims, as with Newton in his controversy with Leibniz over the invention of the cal-culus. When the Royal Society finally es-tablished a committee to adjudicate the rival claims, Newton, who was then pres-ident of the Royal Society, packed the committee, helped direct its activities, anonymously wrote the preface for the second published report—the draft is in his handwriting—and included in that preface a disarming reference to the old legal maxim that "no one is a proper witness for himself [and that] he would be an iniquitous Judge, and would crush un-derfoot the laws of all the people, who would admit anyone as a lawful witness in his own cause."[70] We can gauge the im-mense pressures for self-vindication that must have operated for such a man as

Newton to have adopted these means for defense of his valid claims. It was not be-cause Newton was so weak but because the institutionalized values were so strong that he was driven to such lengths.

This interplay of offensive and de-fensive maneuvers—no doubt, students of the theory of games can recast it more rigorously—thus gives further emphasis to priority. Scientists try to exonerate themselves in advance from possible charges of filching by going to great lengths to establish their priority of dis-covery. Often, this kind of anticipatory defense produces the very result it was designed to avoid by inviting others to show that prior announcement or publica-tion need not mean there was no plagiary.

The effort to safeguard priority and to have proof of one's integrity has led to a variety of institutional arrangements de-signed to cope with this strain on the sys-tem of rewards. In the seventeenth cen-tury, for example, and even as late as the nineteenth, discoveries were sometimes reported in the form of anagrams—as with Galileo's "triple star" of Saturn and Hooke's law of tension—for the double purpose of establishing priority of con-ception and of yet not putting rivals on to one's original ideas, until they had been further worked out.[71] Then, as now, com-plex ideas were quickly published in ab-stracts, as when Halley urged Newton to do so in order to secure "his invention to himself till such time as he would be at leisure to publish it."[72] There is also the long-standing practice of depositing sealed and dated manuscripts with scien-tific academies in order to protect both priority and idea.[73] Scientific journals

---

[70] There is a sizeable library discussing the New-ton-Leibniz controversy. I have drawn chiefly upon More, op. cit., who devotes the whole of Chapter XV to this subject; Auguste de Morgan, Essays on the Life and Works of Newton, Chicago: Open Court Pub. Co., 1914, esp. Appendix II; and Brewster, op. cit., Chapter XXII; cf. Cohen, op. cit., who is properly critical of the biography by More at var-ious points (e.g., pp. 84-85). On the basis of his examination of the Portsmouth Papers, More con-cludes that "the principals, and practically all those associated with them wantonly made statements which were false; and not one of them came through with a clean record." (P. 567.) E. N. da C. Andrade has aptly summed up Newton's ambivalence in this judgment: "Evidence can be cited for the view that Newton was modest or most overweening; the truth is that he was a very complex character . . . when not worried or irritated he was modest about his achievements." See also Andrade's Sir Isaac New-ton, London: Collins, 1954, esp. pp. 131-132.

[71] The earlier widespread use of anagrams is well-known. As late as the 19th century, the physi-cists Balfour Stewart and P. G. Tait reintroduced this practice and "to secure priority . . . [took] the unusual step of publishing [their idea] as an anagram in Nature some months before the publication of their book." Sir J. J. Thomson, Recollections and Reflections, London: G. Bell, 1936, p. 22.

[72] Thomas Birch, The History of the Royal Society of London, London, 1756-1757, Vol. IV, p. 437.

[73] For a recent instance, see the episode described by Wiener in which the race between Bouligand and Wiener to contribute new concepts "in potential

often print the date on which the manuscript of a published article was received, thus serving, even apart from such intent, to register the time it first came to notice. Numerous personal expedients have been developed: for example, letters detailing one's own ideas are sent off to a potential rival, thus disarming him; preliminary and confidential reports are circulated among a chosen few; personal records of research are meticulously dated (as by Kelvin). Finally, it has often been suggested that the functional equivalent of a patent-office be established in science to adjudicate rival claims to priority.[74]

In prolonged and yet overly quick summary, these are some of the forms of deviance invited by the institutional emphasis on priority and some of the institutional expedients devised to reduce the frequency of these deviations. But as we would expect from the theory of alternative responses to excessively emphasized goals, other forms of behavior, verging toward deviance though still well within the law and not as subject to moral disapproval as the foregoing, have also made their appearance.

Alternative Responses to Emphasis on Originality. The large majority of scientists, like the large majority of artists, writers, doctors, bankers and bookkeepers, have little prospect of great and decisive originality. For most of us artisans of research, getting things into print becomes a symbolic equivalent to making a significant discovery. Nor could science advance without the great unending flow of papers reporting careful investigations, even if these are routine rather than distinctly original. The indispensable reporting of research can, however, become

converted into an itch to publish that, in turn, becomes aggravated by the tendency, in many academic institutions, to transform the sheer number of publications into a ritualized measure of scientific or scholarly accomplishment.[75]

The urge to publish is given a further push by the moral imperative of science to make one's work known to others; it is the obverse to the culturally repudiated practice of jealously hoarding scientific knowledge for oneself. As Priestley liked to say, "whenever he discovered a new fact in science, he instantly proclaimed it to the world, in order that other minds might be employed upon it besides his own."[76] Indeed, John Aubrey, that seventeenth-century master of the thumbnail biography and member of the Royal Society, could extend the moral imperative for communication of knowledge to justify even plagiary if the original author will not put his ideas into print. In his view it was better to have scientific goods stolen and circulated than to have them lost entirely.[77]

To this point (and I provide comfort by reporting that the end of the paper is in

---

[75]There is not space here to examine the institutional conditions which lead the piling up of publications to become a virtually ritualistic activity.

[76]Priestley's remark as paraphrased by his long-time friend, T. L. Hawkes, and reported by George Wilson, op. cit., p. 111. The 17th-century Dutch genius of microscopy, Anton van Leeuwenhoek, also adopted a policy, as he described it, that "whenever I found out anything remarkable, I have thought it my duty to put down my discovery on paper, so that all ingenious people might be informed thereof." (Quoted by Major, History of Medicine, Vol. I, p. 531.) The same sentiment was expressed by St.-Simon, among many others. Cf. Manuel, op. cit., pp. 63-64.

[77]Aubrey could say, irresponsibly and probably without malice, that the mathematician John Wallis "may stand with much glory upon his owne basis, and need not be beholding to any man, for Fame, yet he is so greedy of glorie, that he steales feathers from others to adorn his own cap; e.g. he lies at watch, at Sir Christopher Wren's discours, Mr. Robert Hooke's, &c.; putts down their notions in his note booke, and then prints it, without owneing the authors. This frequently of which they complaine. But though he does an Injury to the Inventors, he does good to Learning, in publishing such curious notions, which the author (especially Sir Christopher Wren) might never have the leisure to write of himselfe," (John Aubrey, Brief Lives, ed. by Andrew Clark, Oxford, 1898, Vol. II, pp. 281-282.)

---

theory" ended in a "dead heat," since Bouligand had submitted his "results to the [French] Academy in a sealed envelope, after a custom sanctioned by centuries of academy tradition," (Wiener, op. cit., p. 92.)

[74] J. Hettinger, "Problems of Scientific Property and Its Solution," Science Progress, 26 (January, 1932), pp. 449-461; also the paper by Dr. A. L. Soresi, of the New York Academy of Medicine, cited by Bernhard J. Stern, Social Factors in Medical Progress, New York: Columbia University Press, 1927, p. 108.

sight), we have examined types of deviant responses to the institutional emphasis on priority that are active responses: the fabrication of "data," aggressive self-assertion, the denouncing of rivals, plagiary, and charges of plagiary. Other scientists have responded to the same pressures passively or at least by internalizing their aggressions and directing them against themselves.[78] Since these passive responses, unlike the active ones, are private and often not publicly observable, they seldom enter the historical record. This need not mean, of course, that passive withdrawal from the competition for originality in science is infrequent; it might simply mean that the men responding in this fashion do not come to public notice, unless they do so after their accomplishments have qualified them for the pages of history.

Chief among these passive deviant responses is what has been described, on occasion, as retreatism, the abandoning of the once-esteemed cultural goal of originality and of practices directed toward reaching that goal. In such instances, the scientist withdraws from the field of inquiry, either by giving up science altogether or by confining himself to some alternative role in it, such as teaching or administration. (This does not say, of course, that teaching and administration do not have their own attractions, or that they are less significant than inquiry; I refer here only to the scientists who reluctantly abandon their research because it does not measure up to their own standards of excellence.)

A few historical instances of such retreatism must stand in place of more: The nineteenth-century physicist Waterston, his classic paper on molecular velocity having been rejected by the Royal Society as "nothing but nonsense," becomes hopelessly discouraged and leaves science altogether.[79] Deeply disappointed by the lack of response to his historic papers on heredity, Mendel refuses to publish the now-permanently lost results of his further research and, after becoming abbot of his monastery, gives up his research on heredity.[80] Robert Mayer, tormented by refusals to grant him priority for the principle of conservation of energy, tries a suicide leap from a third-story window and succeeds only in breaking his legs and being straitjacketed, for a time, in an insane asylum.[81]

Perhaps the most telling instance of retreatism in mathematics is that of Janos Bolyai, inventor of one of the non-Euclidean geometries. The young Bolyai tries to obey his mathematician-father who, out of the bitter fruits of his own experience, warns his son to give up any effort to prove the postulate on parallels—or, as his father more picturesquely put it, to "detest it just as much as lewd intercourse; it can deprive you of all your leisure, your health, your rest, and the whole happiness of your life." He dutifully becomes an army officer instead, but his demon does not permit the twenty-one-year-old Bolyai to leave the postulate alone. After years of work, he develops his geometry, sends the manuscript to his father who in turn transmits it to Gauss, the prince of mathematicians, for a magisterial opinion. Gauss sees in the work proof of authentic genius, writes the elder

---

[78] The distinction between active and passive forms of deviant behavior is drawn from Talcott Parsons, The Social System, Glencoe: The Free Press, 1951, pp. 256-267.

[79] Murray, op. cit., pp. 346-348; and David L. Watson, Scientists are Human, London: Watts & Co.,

1938, pp. 58, 80; Baron Rayleigh, op. cit., 169-171. Evidently, Sidney Lee, the editor of the Dictionary of National Biography by the time it reached the volume in which Waterston should have had an honored place, could not penetrate the obscurity into which the great discoverer was plunged by the unfounded rejection of his work; there is no biography of Waterston in the DNB.

[80] Hugo Iltis, Life of Mendel, New York: W. W. Norton, 1932, pp. 111-112; and see Mendel's prophetic remark, "My time will come," p. 282.

[81] Mayer's having been rejected by his liberal friends who took part in the revolution of 1848, which he as a conservative opposed, may have contributed to his disturbance. For some recent evidence on how Mayer's priority was safeguarded by the lay-sociologist Josef Popper, see Otto Bluh, "The Value of Inspiration: A Study on Julius Robert Mayer and Josef Popper-Lynkeus," Isis, 43 (September, 1952), pp. 211-220. Bluh's opinion that claims of priority in science are no longer taken seriously seems exaggerated.

Bolyai so, and adds, in all truth, that he cannot express his enthusiasm as fully as he would like, for "to praise it, would be to praise myself. Indeed, the whole contents of the work, the path taken by your son, the results to which he is led, coincide almost entirely with my meditations, which have occupied my mind partly for the last thirty or thirty-five years. . . . I am very glad that it is just the son of my old friend, who takes the precedence of me in such a remarkable manner." Delighted by this accolade, the elder Bolyai sends the letter to his son, innocently saying that it is "very satisfactory and redounds to the honor of our country and our nation." Young Bolyai reads the letter, but has no eye for the statements which say that his ideas are sound, that in the judgment of the incomparable Gauss he is blessed with genius. He sees only that Gauss has anticipated him. For a time, he believes that his father must have previously confided his ideas to Gauss who had thereupon made them his own.[82] His priority lost, and, with the further blow, years later, of coming upon Lobachevsky's non-Euclidean geometry, he never again publishes any work in mathematics.[83]

Apart from historical cases of notable scientists retreating from the field after denial of the recognition owing them, there are many contemporary cases that come to the notice of psychiatrists rather than historians. Since Lawrence Kubie is almost alone among psychiatrists to have described these in print, I shall draw upon his pertinent account of the maladaptations of scientists suffering from an unquenched thirst for original discovery and ensuing praise.

When the scientist's aspirations become too lofty to be realized, the result sometimes is apathy, imbued with fantasy. In Kubie's words,

> the young scientist may dwell for years in secret contemplation of his own unspoken hope of making great scientific discoveries. As time goes on, his silence begins to frighten him; and in the effort to master his fear, he may build up a secret feeling that his very silence is august, and that once he is ready to reveal his theories, they will shake the world. Thus a secret megalomania can hide among the ambitions of the young research worker.[84]

Perhaps most stressful of all is the situation in which the recognition accorded the scientist is not proportioned to his industry or even to the merit of his work. He may find himself serving primarily to remove obstacles to fundamental discoveries by others. His " negative experiments clear the road for the steady advance of science, but at the same time they clear the road for the more glamorous successes of other scientists,

---

[82] The principal source on the Bolyais, including the germane correspondence, is Paul Stackel, <u>Wolfgang und Johann Bolyai</u>, <u>Geometrische Untersuchungen</u>, Leipzig: 1913, two vols. which was not available to me at this writing. An excellent short account is provided by Roberto Bonola, <u>Non-Euclidean Geometry</u> (trans. by H. S. Carslaw), La Salle, Illinois: Open Court Publishing Company, 1938, 2d rev. ed., pp. 96-113; see also Dirk J. Struik, <u>A Concise History of Mathematics</u>, New York: Dover Publications, 1948, Vol. II, pp. 251-254; Franz Schmidt, "Lebensegeschichte des Ungarischen Mathematikers Johann Bolyai de Bolya," <u>Abhandlungen zur Geschichte der Mathematik</u>, 8 (1898), pp. 135-146.

[83] Two letters provide context for Bolyai's great fall from the high peak of exhilaration into the slough of despond. In 1823, he writes his father: ". . . the goal is not yet reached, but I have made such wonderful discoveries that I have been almost overwhelmed by them, and it would be the cause of continual regret if they were lost. When you will see them, you too will recognize it. In the meantime I can say only this: <u>I have created a new universe from nothing</u>. All that I have sent you till now is but a house of cards compared to the tower. I am as fully persuaded that it will bring me honor, as if I had already completed the discovery." And just as,

a generation later, Lyell was prophetically to warn Darwin of being forestalled, so does the elder Bolyai warn the younger: "If you have really succeeded in the question, it is right that no time be lost in making it public, for two reasons: first, because ideas pass easily from one to another, who can anticipate its publication; and secondly, there is some truth in this, that many things have an epoch, in which they are found at the same time in several places, just as the violets appear on every side in spring. Also every scientific struggle is just a serious war, in which I cannot say when peace will arrive. Thus we ought to conquer when we are able, since the advanage is aways to the first comer." (Quoted by Bonola, <u>op. cit.</u>, pp. 98, 99.) Small wonder that though young Bolyai continued to work sporadically in mathematics, he never again published the results of his work.

[84] Kubie, "Some Unsolved Problems of the Scientific Career," <u>op. cit.</u>, p. 110.

who may have used no greater intelligence, skill or devotion; perhaps even less."[85] Like other men, scientists become disturbed by the pan-human problem of evil, in which "the fortunes of men seem to bear practically no relation to their merits and efforts."[86]

Kubie hazards some further observations that read almost as if they were describing the behavior of delinquents in response to a condition of relative anomie. "Success or failure, whether in specific investigations or in an entire career may be almost accidental, with chance a major factor in determining not what is discovered, but when and by whom. . . . Yet young students are not warned that their future success may be determined by forces which are outside their own creative capacity or their willingness to work hard."[87] As a result of all this, Kubie suspects the emergence of what he calls a "new psychosocial ailment among scientists which may not be wholly unrelated to the gangster tradition of dead-end kids. Are we witnessing the development of a generation of hardened, cynical, amoral, embittered, disillusioned young scientists?"

Lacking the evidence, this had best be left as a rhetorical question. But the import of the question needs comment. There have been diagnoses of the ways in

which a culture giving emphasis to aspirations for all, aspirations which cannot be realized by many, exerts a pressure for deviant behavior and for cynicism, for rejection of the reigning moralities and the rules of the game. We see here the possibility that the same pressures may in some degree be at work in the institution of science. But even though the pressures are severe, they need not produce deviant behavior. There are great differences between the social structure of science and other social structures in which deviance is frequent. Among other things, the institution of science continues to have an abiding emphasis on other values that curb the culturally induced tendency toward deviation, an emphasis on the value of truth by whomsoever it is found, and a commitment to the disinterested pursuit of truth. Simply because we have focused on the deviant behavior of scientists, we should not forget how relatively rare this is. Only a few try to gain reputation by means that will lose them repute. Scientists may feel the pressures whose institutional sources I have tried to describe, but we can suppose that most will continue in the future as they manifestly have done in the past to abide by the institutional norms.

FUNCTIONS AND DYSFUNCTIONS OF EMPHASIS ON PRIORITY

It has sometimes been said that the emphasis upon recognition of priority has the function of motivating scientists to make discoveries. For example, Sir Frederick Banting, the major figure in the discovery of insulin-therapy for diabetes, was long disturbed by the conviction that the chief of his department had been given too much credit for what he had contributed to the discovery. Time and again, Banting returned to the importance of allocating due credit for a discovery: ". . . it makes research men," he said. "It stimulates the individuality and develops personality. Our religion, our moral fabric, our very basis of life are centered round the idea of reward. It is not abnormal therefore that the research

---

[85] Ibid.

[86] Gilbert Murray, quoted in a similar theoretical context by Merton, op. cit., p. 147.

[87] Ibid., pp. 111-112. This reading of the case is not inconsistent with the facts of multiple independent discoveries and inventions. As the long history of multiple discoveries makes clear, and as W. F. Ogburn and D. S. Thomas among the sociologists have shown, certain discoveries become almost "inevitable" when the cultural base cumulates to a certain level. But this still leaves some indeterminacy in the matter of who will first make the discovery. Kubie mentions some "near-misses" of discoveries that suggest undoubted merit is not all when it comes to the first formulation of a discovery, and this list can be greatly extended. In the nature of the case, moreover, we often do not know of those scientists who have abandoned a line of inquiry that was moving toward a particular discovery when they found it had been made and announced by another. These "personal tragedies" of near-discovery—tragedy in terms of the prevailing cultural belief that all credit is due him who is "first,"—are the silent tragedies that leave no mark in the historiography of science.

man should desire the kudos of his own work and his own idea. If this is taken away from him, the greatest stimulant for work is withdrawn."[88]

From this, it would seem that the institutional emphasis is maintained with an eye to its functional utility. But as I have tried to show, the emphasis upon priority is often not confined within functional limits. Once it becomes established, forces of rivalrous interaction lead it to get out of hand. Recognition of priority, operating to reward those who advanced science materially by being the first to make a significant discovery, becomes a sentiment in its own right. Rationalized as a means of providing incentives for original work and as expressing esteem for those who have done much to advance science, it becomes transformed into an end-in-itself. It becomes stepped up to a dysfunctional extreme far beyond the limits of utility.[89] It can even reach the revealing extreme where, for example, the permanent secretary of the French

Academy of Sciences, François Arago, could exclaim (apropos of the controversy involving Cavendish and Watt) that to describe discoveries as having been made "'about the same time' proves nothing; questions as to priority may depend on weeks, on days, on hours, on minutes."[90]

When the criteria of priority become as finely discriminated as this—and Arago only put in words what many others have expressed in behavior—then priority has lost all functional significance. For when two scientists independently make the same discovery months or weeks apart, to say nothing of days or hours, it can scarcely be thought that one has exhibited greater originality than the other or that the short interim that separates them can be used to speed up the rate of scientific achievement.

CONCLUSION

The interpretation I have tried to develop here is not, I am happy to say, a new one. Nor do I consider it fully established and beyond debate. After all, neither under the laws of logic nor under the laws of any other realm, must one become permanently wed to an hypotheses simply because one has tentatively embraced it. But the interpretation does seem to account for some of the otherwise puzzling aspects of conflicts over priority in science and it is closely bound to a body of sociological theory.

In short review, the interpretation is this. Like other social institutions, the institution of science has its characteristic values, norms, and organization. Among these, the emphasis on the value of originality has a self-evident rationale, for it is originality that does much to advance science. Like other institutions also, science has its system of allocating rewards for performance of roles. These rewards are largely honorific, since even today, when science is largely professionalized, the pursuit of science is cul-

---

[88] Quoted in Lloyd Stevenson, Sir Frederick Banting, London: Heinemann Medical Books, 1947, p. 301. Two hundred years before, John Morgan, the celebrated founder of the first American medical school, had expressed the same conception, but in sociologically more acceptable terms. To his mind, personal motivation for fame was linked with the social benefit of the advancement of science. Men of science, he said, "have the highest motive that can animate the pursuits of a generous mind. They consider themselves as under the notice of the public, to which every ingenious person labours to approve himself. A love of fame and a laudable ambition allure him with the most powerful charms. These passions have, in all ages, fired the souls of heroes, of patriots, of lovers of science, have made them renowned in war, eminent in government and peace, justly celebrated for the improvement of polite and useful knowledge." In effect, "other-directedness" can be functional to the society, providing that the criteria of judgment by others are sound. See John Morgan, A Discourse upon the Institution of Medical Schools in America, photo-offset reprint of first edition, Philadelphia, 1765, Baltimore: The Johns Hopkins Press, 1937, pp. 59-60.

[89] For suggestive observations on the process of "stepping up patterns to unanticipated extremities," a process which he called "perseveration," see W. I. Thomas, Primitive Behavior, New York: McGraw-Hill, 1937, p. 9 and passim; see also, Merton, op. cit., pp. 199 ff. As I have tried to show in this paper, science has experienced this stepping-up of functional norms to an extreme at which they become dysfunctional to the workings of the institution.

[90] M. [F.] Arago, Historical Éloge of James Watt, trans. by J. P. Muirhead, London, 1839, p. 106. The whole of this document and Arago's role in the Adams-LeVerrier controversy clearly exemplify the forces producing conflicts over priority.

turally defined as being primarily a disinterested search for truth and only
secondarily, a means of earning a livelihood. In line with the value-emphasis,
rewards are to be meted out in accord
with the measure of accomplishment.
When the institution operates effectively,
the augmenting of knowledge and the
augmenting of personal fame go hand in
hand; the institutional goal and the personal reward are tied together. But these
institutional values have the defects of
their qualities. The institution can get
partly out of control, as the emphasis
upon originality and its recognition is
stepped up. The more thoroughly scientists ascribe an unlimited value to originality, the more they are in this sense
dedicated to the advancement of knowledge, the greater is their involvement in
the successful outcome of inquiry and
their emotional vulnerability to failure.

Against this cultural and social background, one can begin to glimpse the
sources, other than idiosyncratic ones, of
the misbehavior of individual scientists.
The culture of science is, in this measure, pathogenic. It can lead scientists to
develop an extreme concern with recognition which is in turn the validation by
peers of the worth of their work. Con-
tentiousness, self-assertive claims, se-
cretiveness lest one be forestalled, reporting only the data that support an
hypothesis, false charges of plagiarism,
even the occasional theft of ideas and in
rare cases, the fabrication of data,—all
these have appeared in the history of
science and can be thought of as deviant
behavior in response to a discrepancy be-

tween the enormous emphasis in the culture of science upon original discovery
and the actual difficulty many scientists
experience in making an original discovery. In this situation of stress, all
manner of adaptive behaviors are called
into play, some of these being far beyond
the mores of science.

All this can be put more generally. We
have heard much in recent years about
the dangers brought about by emphasis on
the relativity of values, about the precarious condition of a society in which
men do not believe in values deeply
enough and do not feel strongly enough
about what they do believe. If there is a
lesson to be learned from this review of
some consequences of a belief in the absolute importance of originality, perhaps
it is the old lesson that unrestricted belief in absolutes has its dangers too. It
can produce the kind of fanatic zeal in
which anything goes. In its way, the abso-
lutizing of values can be just as damaging
as the decay of values to the life of men
in society.[91]

_____

[91]Limitations of time and space do not allow me to
do as I originally intended: to examine patterns of
rediscovery, that is, the independent but considerably later discovery of something that had been
found before but was since lost to view. These patterns have their own sociological characteristics
which have not been considered here. A systematic
sociological investigation of priority and rediscovery in science is being planned to test the validity of the interpretations set out in this paper and
of other hypotheses mercifully omitted from it.

It is of some interest that just when this paper
was in galley proof, all the world came to experience the social, political, and scientific repercussions of a spectacular "first" in science, when Russian scientists put a man-made sphere into space.

An Analysis of Sect Development

Bryan R. Wilson

SOURCE: *American Sociological Review*, Vol. 24, (Feb., 1959), pp. 3–15.

The tendency for sects to become denominations has frequently been noted, and on the basis of this tendency the generalization has sometimes been made that a sect-type organization can exist for only one generation, that in the second generation the sect (and the cult in Becker's use of the term) becomes a church or a denomination.[1] Yet, if one surveys existing religious organizations, it is evident that, in both the sociological and the everyday use of the term, some sects persist as such over several generations. In view of the fact that some sects have undeniably gravitated towards a denominational structure, however we need to know just what factors in the organization and circumstances of sects promote or retard this development.[2]

Since sects are not all of a piece, we need to distinguish and delineate certain sub-types which should prove of greater predictive utility than does the grosser concept of the sect, and with which we may pass from crude hypothesis to more fully developed theory. Once these sub-types have been identified we may turn to the elements in sect organization which are focal points of tension. It is here hypothesized that sects experience different types of tension which vary according to their own constellation of values, as well as the circumstances of their origin. In response to such tensions, in the attempt at their management, we may expect to find the genesis of processes which cause some sects to develop into denominations, others to wither, some to be exterminated, some to fragment, and some to remain, over several generations, as sects.[3] This paper considers the following elements: the circumstances of sect emergence, the internal structure of sect organization, the degree of separateness from the external world, the coherence of sect values, and group commitments and relationships.

---

[1] H. Richard Niebuhr, The Social Sources of Denominationalism, New York: Holt, 1929, p. 19; Howard Becker, Systematic Sociology on the Basis of the Beziehungslehte and Gebildelehre of Leopold von Wiese, New York: Wiley, 1932; Liston Pope, Millhands and Preachers, New Haven: Yale University Press, 1942, pp. 118 ff.

[2] J. M. Yinger, Religion in the Struggle for Power, Durham: Duke University Press, 1946, suggested an alternative development for the sect, into an "established sect." More recently Yinger has suggested that established sects develop because they emphasize the evil nature of society, while denominationalizing sects are those which stress the reduction of individual anxiety and guilt—a conclusion generally consistent with the analysis proposed here; see Yinger's Religion, Society and the Individual, New York: Macmillan, 1957, pp. 151-152. Recognition of the limitations of the Niebuhr hypothesis is offered in the context of a discussion somewhat different from the above by Benton Johnson, "A Critical Appraisal of Church-Sect Typology,"

American Sociological Review 22 (February, 1957), pp. 88-92. For another approach to this process, see Harold W. Pfautz, "The Sociology of Secularization: Religious Groups," American Journal of Sociology 61 (September, 1955), pp. 121-128.

[3] The type of analysis to be followed owes much to the work and the suggestions of Philip Selznick; see especially his book, The Organizational Weapon, New York: McGraw-Hill, 1952.

CHARACTERIZATION OF SECT AND
DENOMINATION

Typically a <u>sect</u> may be identified by
the following characteristics: it is a
voluntary association; membership is by
proof to sect authorities of some claim to
personal merit—such as knowledge of
doctrine, affirmation of a conversion experience, or recommendation of members
in good standing; exclusiveness is emphasized, and expulsion exercised against
those who contravene doctrinal, moral,
or organizational precepts; its self-conception is of an elect, a gathered remnant, possessing special enlightenment;
personal perfection is the expected standard of aspiration, in whatever terms this
is judged; it accepts, at least as an ideal,
the priesthood of all believers; there is
a high level of lay participation; there
is opportunity for the member spontaneously to express his commitment; the
sect is hostile or indifferent to the secular society and to the state.[4]

In elaboration of this general identification of the sect, it might be added that
although sects differ among themselves
in their characteristic social relationships, the commitment of the sectarian
is always more total and more defined
than that of the member of other religious
organizations. The ideology of the sect
is much more clearly crystallized, and
the member is much more distinctly
characterized than is the adherent of the
larger denomination or church. The behavioral correlates of his ideological
commitment also serve to set him and
keep him apart from "the world." Sects
have a totalitarian rather than a segmental hold over their members: they
dictate the member's ideological orientation to secular society; or they rigor-

ously specify the necessary standards of
moral rectitude; or they compel the
member's involvement in group activity.
Ideological conformity may be achieved
by compulsory participation, but the system of control varies widely.[5] Not only
does the sect discipline or expel the
member who entertains heretical opinions, or commits a moral misdemeanor,
but it regards such defection as betrayal
of the cause, unless confession of fault
and appeal for forgiveness is forthcoming.

The <u>denomination</u>, in contrast, shows
the following features: it is formally a
voluntary association; it accepts adherents without imposition of traditional prerequisites of entry, and employs purely
formalized procedures of admission;
breadth and tolerance are emphasized;
since membership is laxly enrolled, expulsion is not a common device for dealing with the apathetic and the wayward;
its self-conception is unclear and its
doctrinal position unstressed; it is content to be one movement among others,
all of which are thought to be acceptable
in the sight of God; it accepts the standards and values of the prevailing culture
and conventional morality; there is a
trained professional ministry; lay participation occurs but is typically restricted to particular sections of the
laity and to particular areas of activity;
services are formalized and spontaneity
is absent; education of the young is of
greater concern than the evangelism of
the outsider; additional activities are
largely non-religious in character; individual commitment is not very intense;
the denomination accepts the values of the
secular society and the state; members
are drawn from any section of the community, but within one church, or any
one region, membership will tend to

---

[4] The characterization of the sect here proposed
is in many respects more general than the "type-
constructs" offered by Becker, Yinger, and Pope
in the works cited above, and by E. D. C. Brewer,
"Sect and Church in Methodism," <u>Social Forces</u> 30
(May, 1952), pp. 400-408. It omits such characteristics as subjectivism, informality, the expression
of fervor, and poverty, since these characteristics
appear to belong to certain sub-types only.

[5] Thus in Christian Science, for example, doctrinal purity is maintained without members being
compelled to participate in an intense round of
group activity. Illustrative material is largely from
the writer's own research into sects and sect literature in England; for these cases and for cases
where the facts are widely known or well established, specific citations are omitted.

limit itself to those who are socially compatible.[6]

CHARACTERIZATION OF TYPES OF SECT

Given these general types of organization, we need to distinguish the sub-types of sects.[7] The basis of the present classification is the characterization of types of mission which might be discerned among sects. Generally these types of mission rest on the ideological and doctrinal character of sects, and serve as useful indicators of the clusters of other characteristics to be found in each type. For our purposes, within the framework of Protestant Christianity, four broad types may be discerned. Such a classification is not necessarily exhaustive, nor necessarily exclusive of alternative types. It rests essentially on the response of the sect to the values and relationships prevailing in society. This response, in the nature of sectarianism as we have already described it, is necessarily one of greater or lesser rejection. The Conversionist sects seek to alter men, and thereby to alter the world; the response is free-will optimism. The Adventist sects predict drastic alteration of the

world, and seek to prepare for the new dispensation—a pessimistic determinism. The Introversionists reject the world's values and replace them with higher inner values, for the realization of which inner resources are cultivated. The Gnostic sects accept in large measure the world's goals but seek a new and and esoteric means to achieve these ends—a wishful mysticism. This classification is sociological rather than psychological; the responses are built into particular institutions. The implications of these four depictions are elaborated in the following characterizations, and although the empirical correlates of each type are not explored, the implications themselves are not simply logical extensions of the hypothesized types of response. What is here suggested is that, given particular responses within the context of Christianity, these further corollaries may be expected.[8]

1. The Conversionist sect is one whose teaching and activity centers on evangelism; in contemporary Christianity it is typically the orthodox fundamentalist or pentecostal sect. It is typified by extreme

---

[6] This characterization of the denomination stresses many points similar to those suggested by Pope, op. cit., pp. 120 ff., but avoids making a direct comparison of sect traits and denominational traits, as well as the implication that sect characteristics automatically undergo mutation and become denominational traits.

[7] An earlier categorization of sects is offered by E. T. Clark in The Small Sects in America, Nashville: Abingdon Press, 1937, which uses rather diverse criteria, including attitudinal, doctrinal, and organizational elements. In the classification offered here the distinction advanced by Howard Becker, op. cit., between sects and cults, and more recently employed by W. E. Mann, Sect, Cult and Church in Alberta, Toronto: University of Toronto Press, 1955, is abandoned; movements styled as cults by Becker and Mann are here subsumed in a more generalized typification of the sect, and as a subtype could figure principally among gnostic sects. For an extremely suggestive classification of sects, which has come to my notice since this paper was written, but which shares certain similarities with the categorization here proposed, see Peter L. Berger, "The Sociological Study of Sectarianism," Social Research 21 (Winter, 1954), pp. 467-485.

[8] The basic types of response here proposed may be compared to the typology of modes of individual adaptation in Robert K. Merton's "Social Structure and Anomie" (Social Theory and Social Structure, Glencoe, Ill.: Free Press, 1957, pp. 131 ff.). There is some correspondence between introversionist sects and the retreatist response, revolutionist sects and the rebellious response, and gnostic sects and the innovative type. Merton's conformist case is clearly not appropriate to sects, nor is the ritualist, unless one admits some schisms of the Catholic church and even then the case is doubtful. See also, Karen Horney, The Neurotic Personality of Our Time, New York: Norton, 1937.
It is clear that a given sect may well shift in its response to the external society, and whilst remaining a protest group, alter the terms of its protest. Our analysis here is primarily concerned with the process of accommodation—the conditions under which sects become denominations or fail to do so. A development unexplored here is the sect which, whilst remaining a sect, changes character by changing its response; frequently the shift will be of emphasis rather than of complete transformation. There is some evidence to show that revolutionist sects, under circumstances of external duress, have altered their response to one of introversion. The processes here involved would require further analysis in the light of the sociological variables underlying such changes, both as internal and external factors.

bibliolatry: the Bible is taken as the only guide to salvation, and is accepted as literally true. Conversion experience and the acceptance of Jesus as a personal saviour is the test of admission to the fellowship; extreme emphasis is given to individual guilt for sin and the need to obtain redemption through Christ. Despite the theoretical limit on the number who can gain salvation, the sect precludes no one and revivalist techniques are employed in evangelism. It is distrustful of, or indifferent towards, the denominations and churches which at best have diluted, and at worst betrayed, Christianity; it is hostile to clerical learning and especially to modernism; it is opposed to modern science, particularly to geology and to evolutionary theories; it disdains culture and the artistic values accepted in the wider society. Examples are to be found in the Salvation Army and the Pentecostal sects.

2. The Adventist—or revolutionist—sect focuses attention on the coming overturn of the present world order: in contemporary Christianity it is the adventist movement. It is typified by its emphasis on the Bible, and particularly of its exegesis of the allegorical and prophetic books from which the time and circumstances of the second advent of Christ is discerned. The conventional eschatological ideas of heaven and hell are regarded as false, and the resurrection of the dead for judgment is accepted as the principal eschatological event. Christ is regarded as a divine commander, not only as a saviour, and a high moral standard is based on the moral precepts of Jesus. Participation in the new kingdom will be limited and only those who have maintained doctrinal and moral rectitude will be eligible; admission to the fellowship is by thorough understanding of necessary doctrine, and not by affirmation of conversion. Evangelism is undertaken by way of preaching the word but quick conversions are not sought and revivalism is despised as emotional and misguided. The established church is regarded as fulfilling the role of the anti-Christ: clerical learning is despised (but science is depreciated only in so far as its doctrines conflict with adventist biblical exegesis) and the professional ministry is vigorously opposed. Separation from the world is a more crucial interdiction than are restrictions placed upon certain worldly activities. The sect is hostile towards the wider society and looks forward to its overthrow.[9] Examples are Jehovah's Witnesses and the Christadelphians.

3. The Introversionist—or pietist—sect directs the attention of its followers away from the world and to the community and more particularly to the members' possession of the Spirit; in recent Christianity it is exemplified in the pietist sect. Such a sect is typified by reliance on inner illumination, whether this be regarded as the voice of conscience or the action of the Holy Ghost. The Bible is a source or stimulant of inner inspiration and ethical insight; doctrine is of lesser importance in that the letter has surrendered to the spirit, the deepening of which is a central preoccupation. The sect develops a particular Weltanschauung and considers itself an enlightened elect; inner values may be regarded as incommunicable and eschatological ideas are unarticulated or of little significance. No evangelism is undertaken and a strong ingroup morality is developed; the sect withdraws from the world, or allows its members to be active in the world only for human betterment at the behest of conscience and at the periphery of social concern. It is indifferent to other religious movements. It admits of no spiritual directors or ministers. Examples include some Holiness movements, Quakers, and the Society of the Truly Inspired (Amana Community).

---

[9] The similarities of the adventist type sect and the revolutionary political movement have been brought out by Donald G. MacRae in "The Bolshevik Ideology," *The Cambridge Journal*, 3 (December, 1954), pp. 164-177, and are also dealt with in Bryan R. Wilson, *Minority Religious Movements in Modern Britain* (forthcoming). See also Werner Cohn, "Jehovah's Witnesses as a Proletarian Movement," *The American Scholar*, 24 (Summer, 1955), pp. 281-298.

4. The Gnostic sect emphasizes some special body of teaching of an esoteric kind. In contemporary Christianity it is a sect offering a new or revived interpretation of Christian teaching. It accepts the Bible as allegorical and complementary to its own gnosis; conventional Christian eschatology is replaced by a more optimistic and esoteric eschatology; Christ is a wayshower, an exemplar of truth, rather than a saviour. Christian mystical teachings, such as the Trinity, are replaced by other more exclusive mysticism, the significance of which the adherent can hope only gradually to penetrate; doctrine includes teachings which replace secular scientific explanations, and offer a cosmology, an anthropology, and a psychology of their own. The utility of the gnosis for everyday life is emphasized, particularly in the achievement of worldly success, self-realization, health, material well-being and happiness. Conversion is an alien concept to the Gnostic sect, but instruction and guidance is offered to the outsider or the neophyte; there are stages in understanding: enlightenment "unfolds." There is a charismatic leader (or a succession of such leaders) who pronounces wisdom; ministers are usually styled as teachers or guides, and ministerial functions are subdivided among laity with appropriate qualification. Other churches are regarded with indifference as ignorant or backward; secular knowledge is seen as valid and useful relatively, except where it contravenes sect teaching. The cultural standards of the society are accepted and even utilized: the Gnostic sectarian does not withdraw from the world but seeks to use his special knowledge for his own advancement, or that of the movement, in the world. These traits are found, for example, in Christian Science, New Thought sects, Koreshanity, and the Order of the Cross.[10]

---

[10] The types here hypothesized are primarily Christian, and each type finds some support within Christian scriptures. Whether such a classification could be usefully employed for other major religions is doubtful in that, although revolutionist and introversionist sects appear to be common to many

CIRCUMSTANCES OF SECT EMERGENCE

The conditions under which sects emerge may, for analytical purposes, be divided into three elements: the method by which the sect comes into being, the specific factors of stimulus, and the external social conditions prevailing.

1. The principal methods of sect emergence are by spontaneous development around a local charismatic leader, by schism, and by organized revival. In the case of a sect emerging around a leader much will depend on his teaching and his organizational ability. Some such sects disappear when the leader dies or departs. Others, particularly those in which the leader offers a new gnosis which is consonant with the age, spread and retain their identity. The gnosis may be a new combination of ideas or the retailing of older ideas to a new audience.[11] Thus the optimism, feminism, and success-orientation of the New Thought sects and of Christian Science fitted well with American ideals at the end of the nineteenth century. If the leader offers a variant of traditional Christianity, however, then such a group is likely to remain local and, if persisting, eventually to make common cause with other fundamentalist movements or with the fundamentalist wing of one of the larger denominations, usually the Baptists. Many independent missions of this type joined with the pentecostal sects in England during the first three decades of this century. But if such sects spread they appear to be particularly likely to be-

---

religions, and the gnostic sects occur in some, conversionism is perhaps less widespread. The situation is sometimes confused with regard to the relative positions of orthodoxy and sectarianism, and by the difference between the relationship of religion and the state which prevails in many non-Christian countries and the pattern which has generally obtained in the West.

[11] This syncretistic approach is typical of gnostic sects: many such movements have drawn on diverse sources for their teachings. See, for example, Bryan R. Wilson, "The Origins of Christian Science," *The Hibbert Journal*, forthcoming.

come denominationalized, as the distinctive needs of members change—assuming that there is no constant stream of new admissions to keep alive the pristine spirit of the movement.

The schismatic sect tends to be vigorous as long as its protest against the parent body remains significant, and as long as the rival group exists as a challenge; in this period it is likely to grow only by accretions from the parent body. Subsequently, as the issue of disagreement wanes in importance, such a schismatic group may adjust to continuance as a sect, may decay in the absence of opposition, or may partially and gradually rejoin the parent body. Illustrations of such processes are afforded in the history of the Plymouth Brethren in England, and of the Christadelphians in England, the United States, Canada, and Australia.

Organized revival is the method of development most usual to fundamentalist sects, and may well begin in a non-denominational spirit. Success, however, tends to impose organizational responsibilities and, if there are distinctive teachings, sects tend to emerge. The Full Gospel Testimony and the Elim Four-square Gospel Church in England are examples of this development, the teachings being pentecostal. Such groups usually experience rapid growth and high turnover of personnel; since they rely on revivalists for stability and permanence there is, in the nature of the case, an acceptance of trained functionaries, and in this respect a tendency towards denominational development.

2. The specific factors of stimulus of sect emergence are usually found in the stresses and tensions differentially experienced within the total society. Change in the economic position of a particular group (which may be a change only in relative position); disturbance of normal social relations, for instance in the circumstances of industrialization and urbanization; the failure of the social system to accommodate particular age, sex, and status groups—all of these are possible stimuli in the emergence of sects.

These are the needs to which sects, to some extent, respond. Particular groups are rendered marginal by some process of social change; there is a sudden need for a new interpretation of their social position or for a transvaluation of their experience. Insecurity, differential status anxiety, cultural neglect, prompt a need for readjustment which sects may, for some, provide. The maladjusted may be communities, or occupational groups, or dispersed individuals in similar marginal positions. The former cases are more typical for the emergence of Conversionist, Adventist, and Introversionist groups, the latter for the Gnostic sects. Sudden social dislocation, as experienced in urbanization and industrialization, appears to be a frequent circumstance in which Conversionist sects emerge, while Adventists and Introversionists have arisen in the midst of longer persisting deprivation.

3. The external social conditions are not easily distinguished from the stimulus factors considered above, but taken in their widest sense it is evident that there are different consequences for sects according to the political and moral character of the society in which they emerge. In feudal, authoritarian, or totalitarian societies, the sect is persecuted; if it persists it will do so only as a clandestine organization. It will tend to be hostile to the world (whether or not this was its original orientation) and may, in reality or in fantasy, project this hostility upon society. The very early Quakers, the Fifth Monarchy Men, and the numerous pietist and millennial movements in Europe from the thirteenth to the eighteenth centuries, illustrate this reaction.[12] An alternative development in the past has been for the sect to migrate and seek an environment where it could live according to its own standards. The achievement of such isolation has, in itself, consequences for sect organization and promotes communistic arrangements. Examples here are the Rappites,

---

[12]On European millennial movements see Norman Cohn, The Pursuit of the Millennium, London: Secker and Warburg, 1957.

Amana Society, and other movements flourishing in eighteenth and nineteenth century America after migrating from Germany.[13] In such circumstances, to which more specific reference is made below, the sect is unlikely to show marked denominational tendencies.

In democratic or pluralist societies the sect is not pushed into the search for isolation, and although revolutionary type movements (Adventist) may emerge, they are likely to maintain their separation from the world by other methods. Clearly, during rapid social change the various stimulus factors discussed above are more likely to become operative, and it is empirically well established that sects proliferate in periods of social unrest. In this connection, some very general propositions have been offered on the basis of data drawn from the United States in the period from 1800 to the present time. This was a society undergoing almost uninterrupted expansion, rapid social change, high mobility, intense urbanization, and successive waves of immigration (from which its proletariat was continually re-recruited). In the face of these developments the original social values were undergoing constant modification through differential acceptance by diverse ethnic and religious groups. In short, this was a highly atypical context from which to make generalizations concerning the development of sects. The absence of tradition and of stable class differences, the promotion of denominational competition, and the expectation of growth and development resulted in extreme accommodation which helped sects rapidly to evolve into denominations—almost as part of a "success-pattern." In this situation even the Quakers could develop a schism which accepted a ministry and became virtually a denomination. The external social circumstances, rather than the intrinsic nature of the sect as such, must here be invoked to explain why sects become denominations.[14]

THE INTERNAL STRUCTURE OF SECT ORGANIZATION

A feature of sects in contemporary society is that they tend to develop some sort of centralized organization, however minimal. This development has been prompted by the need for communication between dispersed communities, the increase in mobility, and the growing impact of legislation on sects, particularly in wartime. Central organization in itself, however, is not to be equated with a denominational tendency, since control may be effectively employed to prevent such trends, as with Jehovah's Witnesses.[15] On the other hand, such agencies may be a departure from the original sect ideal —their development may be a response to some external threat to the sect's values, but they also imply the surrender of other values. The most significant question about this development would seem to be whether or not those who acquire responsibilities in the central agencies of the sect become professional public functionaries—where functions become institutionally differentiated and specialization of roles occurs.

The initial position of the sect, where there is no local charismatic leader, is the occupation of offices by members in rotation, by lot, or by seniority, and subsequently to institute the lay leader, usually chosen by the group for his particular abilities. Once the concept of special training of such leaders is admitted then a step to denominationalism has been taken. Training implies lack of parity between leaders and members, it

---

[13]For a recent brief account of such movements, see Henri Desroche, "Micromillenarismes et Communautorismes Utopique en Amérique du Nord du XVIIe au XIXe Siècle," *Archives de Sociologie des Religions*, 4 (Juillet-Décembre, 1957), pp. 57-92.

[14]For a discussion of internal and external factors in a clinical, as distinct from a typological, examination of sect development, see Bryan R. Wilson, "Apparition et Persistence des Sectes dans un Milieu Social en évolution," *Archives de Sociologie des Religions*, 5 (Janvier-Juin, 1958), pp. 140-150.

[15]See H. H. Stroup, *Jehovah's Witnesses*, New York: Columbia University Press, 1945; also E. Royston Pike, *Jehovah's Witnesses*, London: Watts, 1954; Werner Cohn, *op. cit.*

compromises the radical democracy of the sect and the ideal of the priesthood of all believers. Spontaneity disappears, and leaders employ the status symbols of their profession, seeking equal esteem with the pastors of other movements.[16]

Such a radical departure from sect values does not normally occur abruptly, nor does denominational character rest on this one factor alone. Obviously, different types of sect show a different proclivity to this development. We can fully expect sects highly concerned with evangelism and revivalism to be most prone to evolve in this way. If missionaries and revivalists are being supported by the group, the value of special training is likely to be accepted and will probably be provided within and by the organization itself. The economies of scale may well induce the movement to train more people than can readily be absorbed in the mission field, or than can be supported there, whilst there is also a limit to the number of active revivalists who can operate on behalf of a particular movement. The replacement of local lay pastors by trained ministers is then a likely consequence. Something like this sequence can be seen in the development of pentecostal sects in Britain. Of other groups, the sect known as the Church of God in the British Isles and Overseas has full-time itinerant revivalists who preach in the meeting houses in place of local lay leaders. This development may be regarded as a stage in the same general process, retarded in this instance by the sect's strong anti-ministerial ideology.

This type of development is most probable in the Conversionist sects. The orthodox fundamentalist sect stands nearest to traditional Christianity and may have had its own origins in some larger movement with a ministry, whose or-

ganization might be accepted even if its teachings are rejected. The Adventist sect resists organizational change in its confident expectation of an early end to the present dispensation and is, in any case, hostile to any institution associated with the established order. Similarly, the pietist (Introversionist) sect is ideologically resistant to the development of a ministry and, moreover, is not concerned with evangelism. In that the adventists evangelize they do so without the use of revivalist techniques. The Gnostic sect, while usually instituting a system of special instruction, does so for the private and personal benefit of the member and not as a qualification for any particular office in the movement, even though in practice the more highly taught are likely to gain easier admission to leadership positions. Worship is not usually of major importance to the Gnostic sect and when professional functionaries do arise they are more likely to be private counsellors than public ministers.

Elites emerge in sects both at the local level and, once centralized agencies have arisen, also at the center. They may be elected by the generality, but they tend to become self-recruiting both locally and at the center. Central control of local leaders may also occur, and when it does the local elite will be the group which interprets, explains, and rationalizes the activity of the central group. In such movements there is a distinct centripetal tendency of responsibility: allegiance is to "headquarters," "the central board," "the executive." Christian Science and Jehovah's Witnesses both typify this organizational structure. The existence of such elites has no specific implication for the development of the sect into a denomination for the crucial matters are whether the elite is specially trained and whether its function becomes that of a professional ministry. What may be noted, however, is that centralized movements appear to be better able to prevent schism than movements in which the central agencies are less well articulated and in which centripetal responsibility has not developed.

---

[16] The equivocal position of the ministry emering within a sect which is undergoing transformation to a denomination, is discussed in Bryan R. Wilson, "Role Conflicts and Status Contradictions of the Pentecostal Minister," *American Journal of Sociology* (forthcoming).

Schism is a feature of sects and of churches more than of denominations (expect in the early period of denominational development). (This is partly because sects and churches tend to possess a much more clearly articulated structure of doctrine and organization than do denominations.) Otherwise, schism usually centers on the question of purity of doctrine, and successful schism usually finds its leader in the very inner elite of the movement.[17] Schism of this kind serves to preserve the distinctive sectarian character of the organization since the schismatic groups tend to become the keepers of each other's consciences in relation to the maintenance of traditional values. The two groups compete for the same public, and frequently appeal to the same sources and authorities in legitimation of their position, thus engendering a competitive struggle to prove the purity of their doctrine and social practice. The Plymouth Brethren, the Mennonites, and the Christadelphians provide illustrations of this development.

DEGREE OF SEPARATENESS FROM THE WORLD

The relationship which a sect permits itself and its members to the external world is of vital importance to the nature of its continuance. In some measure, and by some methods, the sect is committed to keeping itself "unspotted from the world": its distinctness must be evident both to its own members and to others. To this end there are two principal types of mechanism, isolation and insulation. Isolation may be consciously designed, or unconsciously accepted. It may be vicinal isolation in which social isolation is necessarily implied, but this is readily achieved only by groups which accept a communistic type of organization; such organization, in turn, acts as a further isolating device. Sects which have aspired to be self-contained in this

way, and have sought to avoid the "alien" even in those spheres where most sects are prepared to treat with him, have usually been of the Introversionist type. Clearly, such a radical mechanism for the achievement of self-maintenance would mean too profound a change in sect character for Conversionist sects, while the expectation of an early overturn of normal social relations makes such action premature for Adventists. Gnostic sects usually lack the community basis for such a venture and seek their separateness from the world in different ways. Isolation may also be linguistic, a condition illustrated by the various bodies of Mennonites, Hutterites, and Doukhobors. Finally, isolation may be simply the injunction to maintain social separateness from the alien; this is urged by most sects, even the evangelical.

Insulation consists of behavioral rules calculated to protect sect values by reducing the influence of the external world when contact necessarily occurs. Of course, insulation may be a latent function of the moral demands of sect teaching, the justification for which is biblical or revealed prescription; the sect leaders and the members themselves, however, often become aware of the real value of such precepts. Distinctive dress is such an insulating device, characteristic of some Mennonites, early Quakers, and Hutterites. Group endogamy is a more widely used method of insulation and is the rule for most Adventist and Introversionist sects, the expectation in many Conversionist sects, and the preferred form, if marriage is approved at all, in Gnostic sects.

THE COHERENCE OF SECT VALUES

Separateness from the world is clearly a part of the general constellation of values embraced by sects. The coherence of such values and the tensions which their acceptance involves are discussed below. However, it is analytically possible to distinguish between tensions arising from the conflict of this particular value and others embraced by the sect and the tensions resulting from the

[17]For an excellent illustration of this point, see A. K. Swihart, Since Mrs. Eddy, New York: Holt, 1931; for further examples in Christian Science and other movements, see Wilson, "Minority Religious Movements . . ." op. cit.

conflict between sect ideals and the ideals of the wider society, and ultimately with those of the state.

The principal tension between the demand for separateness and other sect values arises in the injunction, accepted by many sects, to go out and preach the gospel. Evangelism means exposure to the world and the risk of alienation of the evangelizing agents. It means also the willingness to accept into the sect new members. This throws a particular weight on the standards of admission if, through the impact of recruitment, the sect itself is not to feel the effect of members who are incompletely socialized from the sect's point of view. The more distinctive are sect doctrines and the more emphatic the insistence on strict standards of doctrinal understanding, the less likely it is that the sect will suffer from its evangelism. The Introversionist and Gnostic sects do not experience this type of tension since they do not evangelize the alien, or seek to do so only by formalized procedures. The Adventist sect regards it as one of its responsibilities to preach the kingdom, to forewarn the world of events portending, and to gather a remnant, but it sends its evangelizing agents into the world only after their doctrinal understanding has been thoroughly tested and their allegiance well tried. Equally it does not expect rapid returns, but subjects those who wish to join the movement to examination of their doctrinal knowledge. The Conversionist sects, which are fundamentalists, experience this tension most fully and have evolved least protection for themselves on these vulnerable points. Their agents are young, their doctrine often less sharply distinguished from that of the denominations, and their tests of good faith inadequate, subordinate to conversionist enthusiasm, and easily, if unwittingly, counterfeited by the emotionally overwrought in the revivalist situation.

The recruitment of the second generation is also an aspect of evangelism. There are similar problems of the tests of admission and the process of social-izing the in-comers. Niebuhr, and subsequently Pope, pin-pointed a key tension for sect organization in recognizing the significance of accepting the second generation.[18] It is an oversimplification to say, however, that the second generation makes the sect into a denomination. As indicated above, such development depends on the standards of admission imposed by the sect, the previous rigor with which children have been kept separate from the world, and on the point at which a balance is struck between the natural desire of parents to have their children included in salvation and their awareness of the community view that any sort of salvation depends on the maintenance of doctrinal and moral standards. Obviously, whether the sect tends to embrace whole families or simply individuals is a significant matter. In general, Gnostic sects, which tend to have an individualistic appeal and do not emphasize the normal type of separation from the world, have more difficulty in winning the allegiance of the second generation than have other sects. Pietistic and Adventist sects, enjoying both doctrinal distinctiveness and the allegiance of whole families (supported by endogamous injunctions) and also tending to have exacting standards for would-be joiners, are apt to hold their second generation without damage to sect identity. The fundamentalist Conversionist groups—who often appeal to individuals, have a less clearly articulated difference of doctrine from the denominations, and whose standards of admission are simple acceptance of a Saviour—are most likely to be affected by the degree of adherence of the second generation.[19]

The sect's desire to be separate from the world and its concerns—and the values which express that separateness—results in certain distinct tensions for the organization and for its members.

---

[18] Niebuhr, op. cit.; Pope, op. cit.

[19] Both Niebuhr and Pope base their generalizations on the examinations of what we have called Conversionist sects; the present classification has thus prevented or decreased errors in prediction.

versionist sects (which may or may not have recognized leaders, and whose leaders may or may not claim distinctive charisma) add to the commitment of the member a distinct moral commitment: certain types of behavior are expected, and there is a strong commitment to the fellowship itself. The Adventist group demands commitment to specific doctrine and specific morality, which further implies commitment to the brethren themselves. The Conversionist sects, while expecting doctrinal and moral rectitude, are less sharply exclusive in demands towards the fellowship as such and are even prepared to extend their general idea of community to embrace "all born-again believers."

Introversionist and Adventist sects are distinctly <u>Gemeinschaften</u>. Fellowship is an important value for all members: fellow-members are "brethren;" relationships as far as possible are primary; the local meeting is a face-to-face group. The individual is a sect-member before he is anything else, he is expected to find his friends within the group, group endogamy is the rule, and there is expulsion of the wayward and lax. The membership is a membership of families rather than of individuals and sect values are mediated by the kin-group. The Introversionists are sharers of an inner and unseen truth; the Adventists are participants in revolutionary intrigue. The Conversionist sect shares these general characteristics only partially: its concept of brotherhood extends beyond sect boundaries and its standards are less rigorous. It accepts individuals more lightly, socializes them less intensely, and loses them easily—all of which disturbs the strong sense of community. Its appeal is to the individual seeking salvation, and consequently it is less typically composed of families. The Gnostic sect is much more frankly a <u>Gesellschaft</u>: the individual's relationships to other devotees are secondary to his commitment to the ideology and the leadership. Brotherhood is an alien concept. Discipline is for disloyalty, not for specific moral misdemeanor. The impersonality of relationships may even

be regarded as ideal, since the gnosis, "the principle," is what matters. Since there are fewer behavioral correlates of sect affiliation, the member, socially, may hide his membership and so avoid the disapproval of the outside world.

CONCLUSIONS

Our analysis has brought out a number of items which are subject to variation as between different types of sect and which help to determine the likely development of such movements. Thus it is clear that sects with a general democratic ethic, which stress simple affirmation of intense subjective experience as a criterion of admission, which stand in the orthodox fundamentalist tradition, which emphasize evangelism and use revivalist techniques, and which seek to accommodate groups dislocated by rapid social change are particularly subject to denominationalizing tendencies. These same tendencies are likely to be intensified if the sect is unclear concerning the boundaries of the saved community and extends its rules of endogamy to include any saved person as an eligible spouse; if its moral injunctions are unclearly distinguished from conventional or traditional morality; and if it accepts simple assertion of remorse for sin as sufficient to re-admit or to retain a backslidden member. Denominationalization is all the more likely when such a sect inherits, or evolves, any type of preaching order, lay pastors, or itinerant ministers; when revivalism leads to special training for the revivalists themselves (and so leads to a class of professionals who cease to rely on "love-offerings" but are granted a fixed stipend); and when the members are ineffectively separated from the world, a condition enhanced by proselytizing activities.

It is clear that the types of sect which we described as Conversionist are most likely to fulfil the conditions which transform sects into denominations and are least likely to enjoy the circumstances preventing this process. The Adventist and the Introversionist types appear to be best protected from this development, although by different mechanisms: they fulfil few of the conditions supporting this evolution and often enjoy or create the factors which retard it. The Gnostic sect is in some ways less clearly protected, but its distinctive ideology performs in some measure the functions which social insulating mechanisms perform for other types.

In a broad way, we can see why certain earlier studies of sects fell into errors of prediction, since the conclusions rested on the experience of certain types of sects, sects which existed in very particular social circumstances, and accommodated people whose social marginality and sense of anomie were often temporary and a consequence of inadequate readjustment to rapidly changing social conditions. Of course, to predict the development of any given sect requires examination in close detail of its circumstances. Once these are known, however, the foregoing analysis should provide a guide for the interpretation of these facts.

Revitalization Movements

Anthony F. C. Wallace

SOURCE: *American Anthropologist*, Vol. 58 (1956), pp. 264–81.

INTRODUCTION

Behavioral scientists have described many instances of attempted and sometimes successful innovation of whole cultural systems, or at least substantial portions of such systems. Various rubrics are employed, the rubric depending on the discipline and the theoretical orientation of the researcher, and on salient local characteristics of the cases he has chosen for study. "Nativistic movement," "reform movement," "cargo cult," "religious revival," "messianic movement," "utopian community," "sect formation," "mass movement," "social movement," "revolution," "charismatic movement," are some of the commonly used labels. This paper suggests that all these phenomena of major cultural-system innovation are characterized by a uniform process, for which I propose the term "revitalization." The body of the paper is devoted to two ends: (1) an introductory statement of the concept of revitalization, and (2) an outline of certain uniformly-found processual dimensions of revitalization movements.

The formulations are based in major part on documentary data, mostly published. Library research on the project began in 1951 with a study of the new religion initiated by Handsome Lake, the Seneca prophet, among the nineteenth century reservation Iroquois. The Handsome Lake materials being unusually ample (a number of manuscript journals and diaries were found) provided a useful standard with which to compare the various other movements which have since been investigated. Our files now contain references to several hundred religious revitalization movements, among both western and nonwestern peoples, on five continents. These represent only a small portion, gathered in a quick preliminary survey of anthropological literature. An earnest attempt to collect all revitalization movements described in historical, anthropological, and other sorts of documents, would without question gather in thousands. Movements on which we have substantial data include: in North America, the Handsome Lake case (Seneca, 1799-1815), the Delaware Prophet (associated with Pontiac, 1762-1765), the Shawnee Prophet (associated with Tecumseh, 1805-1814), the Ghost Dance (1888-1896), and Peyote; in Europe, John Wesley and early Methodism (1738-1800); in Africa, Ikhnaton's new religion (ancient Egypt), the Sudanese Mahdi (the Sudan, 1880-1898), and the Xosa Revival (South Africa, 1856-1857); in Asia, the origin of Christianity, the origin of Mohammedanism (c610-650), the early development of Sikhism (India, c1500-c1700), and the Taiping Rebellion (China, 1843-1864); in Melanesia, the Vailala Madness (New Guinea, c1919-c1930); in South America, a series of terre sans mal movements among the forest tribes, from early contact to recent times.[1]

Accordingly, the formulations presented here are in an intermediate stage: a species has been recognized and certain characteristics (selected, of course, in the light of the author's theoretical interests) described, after the fashion of natural history. More abstract descriptions, in terms of the interaction of analytic variables, can only be suggested

here, and other papers will present details of the dynamics of the revitalization process.

THE CONCEPT OF REVITALIZATION

A revitalization movement is defined as a deliberate, organized, conscious effort by members of a society to construct a more satisfying culture. Revitalization is thus, from a cultural standpoint, a special kind of culture change phenomenon: the persons involved in the process of revitalization must perceive their culture, or some major areas of it, as a system (whether accurately or not); they must feel that this cultural system is unsatisfactory; and they must innovate not merely discrete items, but a new cultural system, specifying new relationships as well as, in some cases, new traits. The classic processes of culture change (evolution, drift, diffusion, historical change, acculturation) all produce changes in cultures as systems; however, they do not depend on deliberate intent by members of a society, but rather on a gradual chain-reaction effect: introducing A induces change in B; changing B affects C; when C shifts, A is modified; this involves D... and so on ad infinitum. This process continues for years, generations, centuries, millennia, and its pervasiveness has led many cultural theorists to regard culture change as essentially a slow, chain-like, self-contained procession of superorganic inevitabilities. In revitalization movements, however, A, B, C, D, E... N are shifted into a new Gestalt abruptly and simultaneously in intent; and frequently within a few years the new plan is put into effect by the participants in the movement. We may note in passing that Keesing's assessment of the literature on culture change (1953), while it does not deal explicitly with the theoretical issue of chain-effects versus revitalization, discusses both types. Barnett (1953) frankly confines his discussion to innovations of limited scope in the context of chains of events in acceptance and rejection. As Mead has suggested, cultures can change within one generation (Mead

[1]The Handsome Lake project, supported largely by a Faculty Research Fellowship of the Social Science Research Council, with supplemental funds from the Behavioral Research Council and Committee for the Advancement of Research of the University of Pennsylvania, has served as a pilot study, and the larger investigation is now largely financed by the National Institute of Mental Health (U. S. Public Health Service), Grant M-883, with supplemental funds from the American Philosophical Society and the Eastern Pennsylvania Psychiatric Institute. I should like to express my appreciation to Sheila C. Steen (who has been the "field director" of the project, responsible for much of the empirical research and participant in conceptual formulation), and to research and clerical assistants Josephine H. Dixon, Herbert S. Williams, and Ruth Goodenough. Persons whose comments and suggestions on the first draft of this paper have been of value in its revision include Margaret Mead, Theodore Schwartz, Walter Goldschmidt, A. I. Hallowell, David F. Aberle, Betty S. Wallace and Ward Goodenough. The Handsome Lake movement will be described in detail in a book the writer is now preparing. For other treatments now in print, see Parker, 1913; Deardorff, 1951; Voget, 1954; and Wallace, 1952a and 1952b.

1955); and the process by which such transformations occur is the revitalization process.

The term "revitalization" implies an organismic analogy.[2] This analogy is, in fact, an integral part of the concept of revitalization. A human society is here regarded as a definite kind of organism, and its culture is conceived as those patterns of learned behavior which certain "parts" of the social organism or system (individual persons and groups of persons) characteristically display. A corollary of the organismic analogy is the principle of homeostasis: that a society will work, by means of coordinated actions (including "cultural" actions) by all or some of its parts, to preserve its own integrity by maintaining a minimally fluctuating, life-supporting matrix for its individual members, and will, under stress, take emergency measures to preserve the constancy of this matrix. Stress is defined as a condition in which some part, or the whole, of the social organism is threatened with more or less serious damage. The perception of stress, particularly of increasing stress, can be viewed as the common denominator of the panel of "drives" or "instincts" in every psychological theory.

As I am using the organismic analogy, the total system which constitutes a society includes as significant parts not only persons and groups with their respective patterns of behavior, but also literally the cells and organs of which the persons are composed. Indeed, one can argue that the system includes nonhuman as well as human subsystems. Stress on one level is stress on all levels. For example, lowering of sugar level (hunger) in the fluid matrix of the body cells of one group of persons in a society is a stress in the

[2]This article is not the place to present a general discussion of the notions of order and field, function and equilibrium, the organismic analogy, the concept of homeostasis, and certain ideas from cybernetics, learning and perception, and the physiology of stress, which would be necessary to justify and fully elucidate the assumptions on which the revitalization hypothesis is based. See however, Wallace 1953, 1955, and 1956 for further development of the holistic view and more extended discussions of the mazeway concept.

society as a whole. This holistic view of society as organism integrated from cell to nation depends on the assumption that society, as an organization of living matter, is definable as a network of intercommunication. Events on one subsystem level must affect other subsystems (cellular vis-a-vis institutional, personal vis-a-vis societal) at least as information; in this view, social organization exists to the degree that events in one subsystem are information to other subsystems.

There is one crucial difference between the principles of social organization and that of the individual person: a society's parts are very widely interchangeable, a person's only slightly so. The central nervous system cells, for example, perform many functions of coordinating information and executing adaptive action which other cells cannot do. A society, on the other hand, has a multiple-replacement capacity, such that many persons can perform the analogous information-coordination and executive functions on behalf of society-as-organism. Furthermore, that regularity of patterned behavior which we call culture depends relatively more on the ability of constituent units autonomously to perceive the system of which they are a part, to receive and transmit information, and to act in accordance with the necessities of the system, than on any all-embracing central administration which stimulates specialized parts to perform their function.

It is therefore functionally necessary for every person in society to maintain a mental image of the society and its culture, as well as of his own body and its behavioral regularities, in order to act in ways which reduce stress at all levels of the system. The person does, in fact, maintain such an image. This mental image I have called "the mazeway," since as a model of the cell-body-personality-nature-culture-society system or field, organized by the individual's own experience, it includes perceptions of both the maze of physical objects of the environment (internal and external, human and nonhuman) and also of the ways in which this maze can be manipulated by the self and others in order to minimize stress. The mazeway is nature, society, culture, personality, and body image, as seen by one person. Hallowell (1955) and Wallace (1955 and 1956) offer extended discussions of the mazeway and the related concepts of self, world view, and behavioral environment.

We may now see more clearly what "revitalization movements" revitalize. Whenever an individual who is under chronic, physiologically measurable stress, receives repeated information which indicates that his mazeway does not lead to action which reduces the level of stress, he must choose between maintaining his present mazeway and tolerating the stress, or changing the mazeway in an attempt to reduce the stress. Changing the mazeway involves changing the total Gestalt of his image of self, society, and culture, of nature and body, and of ways of action. It may also be necessary to make changes in the "real" system in order to bring mazeway and "reality" into congruence. The effort to work a change in mazeway and "real" system together so as to permit more effective stress reduction is the effort at revitalization; and the collaboration of a number of persons in such an effort is called a revitalization movement.

The term revitalization movement thus denotes a very large class of phenomena. Other terms are employed in the existing literature to denote what I would call subclasses, distinguished by a miscellany of criteria. "Nativistic movements," for example, are revitalization movements characterized by strong emphasis on the elimination of alien persons, customs, values, and/or materiel from the mazeway (Linton 1943). "Revivalistic" movements emphasize the institution of customs, values, and even aspects of nature which are thought to have been in the mazeway of previous generations but are not now present (Mooney 1892-93). "Cargo cults" emphasize the importation of alien values, customs, and materiel into the mazeway, these things being

expected to arrive as a ship's cargo as for example in the Vailala Madness (Williams 1923, 1934). "Vitalistic movements" emphasize the importation of alien elements into the mazeway but do not necessarily invoke ship and cargo as the mechanism.[3] "Millenarian movements" emphasize mazeway transformation in an apocalyptic world transformation engineered by the supernatural. "Messianic movements" emphasize the participation of a divine savior in human flesh in the mazeway transformation (Wallis 1918, 1943). These and parallel terms do not denote mutually exclusive categories, for a given revitalization movement may be nativistic, millenarian, messianic, and revivalistic all at once; and it may (in fact, usually does) display ambivalence with respect to nativistic, revivalistic, and importation themes.

Revitalization movements are evidently not unusual phenomena, but are recurrent features in human history. Probably few men have lived who have not been involved in an instance of the revitalization process. They are, furthermore, of profound historical importance. Both Christianity and Mohammedanism, and possibly Buddhism as well, originated in revitalization movements. Most denominational and sectarian groups and orders budded or split off after failure to revitalize a traditional institution. One can ask whether a large proportion of religious phenomena have not originated in personality transformation dreams or visions characteristic of the revitalization process. Myths, legends, and rituals

---

[3] After we had coined the term "revitalization movement," we discovered that Marian Smith in an article on the Indian Shakers (Smith 1954) uses the closely related term "vitalistic movements" ("a vitalistic movement may be defined as ' any conscious, organized attempt on the part of a society's members to incorporate in its culture selected aspects of another culture in contact with it"). However, she uses this term for what I would call nonnativistic revitalization movements with important (rather than revivalistic) emphasis.

[4] I should like to express my appreciation to Dr. Arthur P. Noyes, Superintendent, and Drs. Warren Hampe and Kenneth Kool of the staff of Norristown (Pa.) State Hospital, for their assistance in making this survey possible.

may be relics, either of the manifest content of vision-dreams or of the doctrines and history of revival and import cults, the circumstances of whose origin have been distorted and forgotten, and whose connection with dream states is now ingnored. Myths in particular have long been noted to possess a dream-like quality, and have been more or less speculatively interpreted according to the principles of symptomatic dream interpretation. It is tempting to suggest that myths and, often, even legends, read like dreams because they <u>were</u> dreams when they were first told. It is tempting to argue further that culture heroes represent a condensation of the figures of the prophet and of the supernatural being of whom he dreamed.

In fact, it can be argued that all organized religions are relics of old revitalization movements, surviving in routinized form in stabilized cultures, and that religious phenomena per se originated (if it is permissible still in this day and age to talk about the "origins" of major elements of culture) in the revitalization process—i.e., in visions of a new way of life by individuals under extreme stress.

THE PROCESSUAL STRUCTURE

A basic methodological principle employed in this study is that of event-analysis (Wallace 1953). This approach employs a method of controlled comparison for the study of processes involving longer or shorter diachronic sequences (vide Eggan 1954 and Steward 1953). It is postulated that events or happenings of various types have genotypical structures independent of local cultural differences; for example, that the sequence of happenings following a severe physical disaster in cities in Japan, the United States, and Germany, will display a uniform pattern, colored but not obscured by local differences in culture. These types of events may be called behavioral units. Their uniformity is based on generic human attributes, both physical and psychological, but it requires extensive analytical and comparative study to elucidate the structure of any one. Revitalization movements constitute such a behavioral unit, and so also, on a lower level of abstraction, do various subtypes within the larger class, such as cargo and revival cults. We are therefore concerned with describing the generic structure of revitalization movements considered as a behavioral unit, and also of variation along the dimensions characteristic of the type.

The structure of the revitalization process, in cases where the full course is run, consists of five somewhat overlapping stages: 1. Steady State; 2. Period of Individual Stress; 3. Period of Cultural Distortion; 4. Period of Revitalization (in which occur the functions of mazeway reformulation, communication, organization, adaptation, cultural transformation, and routinization), and finally, 5. New Steady State. These stages are described briefly in the following sections.

I. <u>Steady State.</u> For the vast majority of the population, culturally recognized techniques for satisfying needs operate with such efficiency that chronic stress within the system varies within tolerable limits. Some severe but still tolerable stress may remain general in the population, and a fairly constant incidence of persons under, for them, intolerable stress may employ "deviant" techniques (e.g., psychotics). Gradual modification or even rapid substitution of techniques for satisfying some needs may occur without disturbing the steady state, as long as (1) the techniques for satisfying other needs are not seriously interfered with, and (2) abandonment of a given technique for reducing one need in favor of a more efficient technique does not leave other needs, which the first technique was also instrumental in satisfying, without any prospect of satisfaction.

II. <u>The Period of Increased Individual Stress.</u> Over a number of years, individual members of a population (which may be "primitive" or "civilized," either a whole society or a class, caste, religious, occupational, acculturational, or other definable social group) experience increasingly severe stress as a result of the decreasing efficiency of certain stress-reduction techniques. The culture may remain essentially unchanged or it may undergo considerable changes, but in either case there is continuous diminution in its efficiency in satisfying needs. The agencies responsible for interference with the efficiency of a cultural system are various: climatic, floral and faunal change; military defeat; political subordination; extreme pressure toward acculturation resulting in internal cultural conflict; economic distress; epidemics; and so on. The situation is often, but not necessarily, one of acculturation, and the acculturating agents may or may not be representatives of Western European cultures. While the individual can tolerate a moderate degree of increased stress and still maintain the habitual way of behavior, a point is reached at which some alternative way must be considered. Initial consideration of a substitute way is likely, however, to increase stress because it arouses anxiety over the possibility that the substitute way will be even less effective than the original, and that it may also actively interfere with the execution of other ways. In other words, it poses the threat of mazeway disintegration. Furthermore, admission that a major technique is worthless is extremely threatening because it implies that the whole mazeway system may be inadequate.

III. The Period of Cultural Distortion. The prolonged experience of stress, produced by failure of need satisfaction techniques and by anxiety over the prospect of changing behavior patterns, is responded to differently by different people. Rigid persons apparently prefer to tolerate high levels of chronic stress rather than make systematic adaptive changes in the mazeway. More flexible persons try out various limited mazeway changes in their personal lives, attempting to reduce stress by addition or substitution of mazeway elements with more or less concern for the Gestalt of the system. Some persons turn to psychodynamically regressive innovations; the regressive response empirically exhibits itself in increasing incidences of such

things as alcoholism, extreme passivity and indolence, the development of highly ambivalent dependency relationships, intragroup violence, disregard of kinship and sexual mores, irresponsibility in public officials, states of depression and self-reproach, and probably a variety of psychosomatic and neurotic disorders. Some of these regressive action systems become, in effect, new cultural patterns.

In this phase, the culture is internally distorted; the elements are not harmoniously related but are mutually inconsistent and interfering. For this reason alone, stress continues to rise. "Regressive" behavior, as defined by the society, will arouse considerable guilt and hence increase stress level or at least maintain it at a high point; and the general process of piecemeal cultural substitution will multiply situations of mutual conflict and misunderstanding, which in turn increase stress-level again.

Finally, as the inadequacy of existing ways of acting to reduce stress becomes more and more evident, and as the internal incongruities of the mazeway are perceived, symptoms of anxiety over the loss of a meaningful way of life also become evident: disillusionment with the mazeway, and apathy toward problems of adaptation, set in.

IV. The Period of Revitalization. This process of deterioration can, if not checked, lead to the death of the society. Population may fall even to the point of extinction as a result of increasing death rates and decreasing birth rates; the society may be defeated in war, invaded, its population dispersed and its customs suppressed; factional disputes may nibble away areas and segments of the population. But those dire events are not infrequently forestalled, or at least postponed, by a revitalization movement. Many such movements are religious in character, and such religious revitalization movements must perform at least six major tasks:

1. Mazeway reformulation. Whether the movement is religious or secular, the reformulation of the mazeway generally seems to depend on a restructuring of elements and subsystems which have

already attained currency in the society and may even be in use, and which are known to the person who is to become the prophet or leader. The occasion of their combination in a form which constitutes an internally consistent structure, and of their acceptance by the prophet as a guide to action, is abrupt and dramatic, usually occurring as a moment of insight, a brief period of realization of relationships and opportunities. These moments are often called inspiration or revelation. The reformulation also seems normally to occur in its initial form in the mind of a single person rather than to grow directly out of group deliberations.

With a few exceptions, every religious revitalization movement with which I am acquainted has been originally conceived in one or several hallucinatory visions by a single individual. A supernatural being appears to the prophet-to-be, explains his own and his society's troubles as being entirely or partly a result of the violation of certain rules, and promises individual and social revitalization if the injunctions are followed and the rituals practiced, but personal and social catastrophe if they are not. These dreams express: 1. the dreamer's wish for a satisfying parental figure (the supernatural, guardian-spirit content), 2. world-destruction fantasies (the apocalyptic, millennial content), 3. feelings of guilt and anxiety (the moral content), and 4. longings for the establishment of an ideal state of stable and satisfying human and supernatural relations (the restitution fantasy or Utopian content). In a sense, such a dream also functions almost as a funeral ritual: the "dead" way of life is recognized as dead: interest shifts to a god, the community, and a new way. A new mazeway Gestalt is presented, with more or less innovation in details of content. The prophet feels a need to tell others of his experience, and may have definite feelings of missionary or messianic obligation. Generally he shows evidence of a radical inner change in personality soon after the vision experience: a remission of old and chronic physical complaints, a more active and purposeful way of life, greater confidence in interpersonal relations, the dropping of deep-seated habits like alcoholism. Hence we may call these visions "personality transformation dreams." Where there is no vision (as with John Wesley), there occurs a similarly brief and dramatic moment of insight, revelation, or inspiration, which functions in most respects like the vision in being the occasion of a new synthesis of values and meanings.

My initial approach to the understanding of these visions was by way of psychoanalytic dream theory. This proved to be of some use in elucidating the meaning of the vision. From an analysis of its manifest content and from the circumstances of the dreamer's history and life situation, it is possible to make more or less plausible interpretations of the nature of the prophet's personal preoccupations and conflicts. But conventional dream theory was designed to explain the conflicts represented in ordinary night dreams. Prophetic visions, while essentially dream formations, differ in several respects from ordinary symptomatic dreams: they often occur during a waking state as hallucinatory experiences, or in an ecstatic trance rather than in normal sleep; they impress the dreamer immediately as being meaningful and important; the manifest content is often in large part rational and well considered intellectual argument and cogent moral exhortation; and recollection of them is in unusually rich detail. This brings to mind Fromm's position (1951), that many dreams are not so much symptomatic of unconscious neurotic conflict as insightful in a positive and creative sense. But this additional consideration did not seem adequately to account for the most remarkable feature of all: the transformation of personality, often in a positive therapeutic sense, which these dreams produced. Prophetic and ecstatic visions do express unconscious conflict: they sometimes reveal considerable insight, but they also work startling cures.

We therefore became interested in pursuing the dynamics of personality transformation dreams. As a type of event, they would seem to belong to a general clinical category of sudden and radical changes in personality, along with transformations occurring in psychotic breaks, spontaneous remissions, narcosynthesis, some occasions in psychotherapy, "brainwashing," and shock treatments. There are, incidentally, some interesting similarities between the physical state of prophets and converts in the vision-trance, and patients undergoing shock (Sargant 1949, 1951). Physical stress and exhaustion often seem to precede the vision-trance type of transformation, and it seems probable that chemical substances produced in the body under stress may be important in rendering a person capable of this type of experience (Hoffer, Osmond, and Smythies, 1954). The relationship of this sort of sudden personality change to slower maturational processes, on the one hand, and to what happens in rites of passage, on the other, should be points of interest to social scientists generally.

Nonclinical anologues of the prophet's personality transformation vision appear in several contexts: in accounts of individual ecstatic conversions and experiences of religious enthusiasm; in the guardian spirit quest among American Indians and elsewhere; and in the process of becoming a shaman, which is similar in many cultures all over the world. Conversion, shamanism, and the guardian-spirit vision seem to be phenomena very similar in pattern. All three of these processes are distributed globally; in many cultures all three are normal phenomena; all involve persons who are faced with the opportunity (if not necessity) of assuming a new cultural role and of abandoning an earlier role in order to reduce stress which they will not be able to resolve if they stand pat. A precipitating factor in many cases is some sort of severe physical stress, such as illness, starvation, sleeplessness, or fatigue. After the vision experience, the individual is often able to assume a new role

requiring increased or differently phrased emotional independence. In the vision experience, he has invented a fictitious, nurturing, parent-like supernatural figure who satisfies much of his need for authority and protection; thus he is presumably able to loosen emotional ties to certain cultural objects, roles, and persons, and to act without undue inhibition and anxiety. Inconvenient wishes are displaced onto a fictitious but culturally sanctioned supernatural pseudo-community, leaving the personality free for relatively healthy relationships to the real world. An essential function of the vision is that the demands for energy made by transference wishes are minimized by displacement onto supernatural objects which can in fantasy be perceived as uniformly supporting and protective.

Inasmuch as many prophets were suffering from recognizable and admitted mental disorders before their transformation, which they achieved by means of a type of experience (hallucination) that our culture generally regards as pathological, the relevance of psychopathology to the vision experience needs to be explored. We have under way some observations on the case histories of a series of persons in a state mental institution who have been known to attendants for their excessive religiosity.[4] This survey, which we hope to extend to include interview materials, is not complete, but I can summarize our initial impressions. Chronic schizophrenics with religious paranoia tend to believe that they are God, Jesus, the Virgin Mary, the Great Earth Mother, or some other supernatural being. Successful prophets, on the other hand, usually do not believe that they are the supernatural, only that they have communicated with him (although their followers may freely deify them). Prophets do not lose their sense of personal identity but psychotics tend to become the object of their spiritual longing.

There are in this institution several persons who were hospitalized during the course of an experience which resembles in many respects the process of becoming a prophet. A man, burdened with a sense of guilt and inadequacy, and sensible of the need to reform his life, has a religious conversion in which he sees God or hears his voice; thereafter he displays a changed and in some ways healthier (or at least less rapidly deteriorating) personality; he undertakes an evangelistic or prophetic enterprise which is socially inconvenient to spouse, relatives, employer, warden, or other closely associated persons; he is thereupon certified as insane and hospitalized. Such frustrated prophets, being unable any longer to satisfy important human needs and suffering the obvious disapproval of the community, may also lose confidence in their relationship to the supernatural pseudo-community. They cannot return to their preconversion state because the hospital situation makes anything remotely approaching normal cultural and social participation impossible. Many therefore take the emotionally logical but unfortunate next step, and become the guardian spirit.

At this time, then, we would tentatively conclude that the religious vision experience per se is not psychopathological but rather the reverse, being a synthesizing and often therapeutic process performed under extreme stress by individuals already sick.

2. Communication. The dreamer undertakes to preach his revelations to people, in an evangelistic or messianic spirit; he becomes a prophet. The doctrinal and behavioral injunctions which he preaches carry two fundamental motifs: that the convert will come under the care and protection of certain supernatural beings: and that both he and his society will benefit materially from an identification with some definable new cultural system (whether a revived culture or a cargo culture, or a syncretism of both, as is usually the case). The preaching may take many forms (e.g., mass exhortation vs. quiet individual persuasion) and may be directed at various sorts of audiences (e.g., the elite vs. the downtrodden). As he gathers disciples, these assume much of the responsibility for

communicating the "good word," and communication remains one of the primary activities of the movement during later phases of organization.

3. Organization. Converts are made by the prophet. Some undergo hysterical seizures induced by suggestion in a crowd situation; some experience an ecstatic vision in private circumstances; some are convinced by more or less rational arguments, some by considerations of expediency and opportunity. A small clique of special disciples (often including a few already influential men) clusters about the prophet and an embryonic campaign organization develops with three orders of personnel: the prophet; the disciples; and the followers. Frequently the action program from here on is effectively administered in large part by a political rather than a religious leadership. Like the prophet, many of the converts undergo a revitalizing personality transformation.

Max Weber's concept of "charismatic leadership" well describes the type of leader-follower relationship characteristic of revitalization movement organizations (1947). The fundamental element of the vision, as I have indicated above, is the entrance of the visionary into an intense relationship with a supernatural being. This relationship, furthermore, is one in which the prophet accepts the leadership, succor, and dominance of the supernatural. Many followers of a prophet, especially the disciples, also have ecstatic revelatory experiences; but they and all sincere followers who have not had a personal revelation also enter into a parallel relationship to the prophet: as God is to the prophet, so (almost) is the prophet to his followers. The relationship of the follower to the prophet is in all probability determined by the displacement of transference dependency wishes onto his image; he is regarded as an uncanny person, of unquestionable authority in one or more spheres of leadership, sanctioned by the supernatural. Max Weber denotes this quality of uncanny authority and moral ascendency in a leader as charisma. Followers defer to

the charismatic leader not because of
his status in an existing authority structure but because of a fascinating personal
"power," often ascribed to supernatural
sources and validated in successful performance, akin to the "mana" or
"orenda" of ethnological literature. The
charismatic leader thus is not merely
permitted but expected to phrase his call
for adherents as a demand to perform
a duty to a power higher than human.
Weber correctly points out that the "routinization" of charisma is a critical issue
in movement organization, since unless
this "power" is distributed to other personnel in a stable institutional structure,
the movement itself is liable to die with
the death or failure of individual prophet,
king, or war lord.

Weber, however, is essentially discussing a quality of leadership, and one which
is found in contexts other than that of
revitalization movements. In consequence, his generalizations do not deal
with the revitalization formula itself, but
rather with the nature of the relationship
of the early adherents to their prophet.
Furthermore, there is a serious ambiguity in Weber's use of the charisma
concept. Weber seems to have been uncertain whether to regard it as an unusual quality in the leader which is recognized and rationalized by his adherents,
or whether to regard it as a quality
ascribed to the leader by followers and
hence as being a quality of their relationship to him, determined both by the
observed and the observer in the perceptual transaction. We have used it to
denote the libidinal relationship which
Freud described in Group Psychology and
the Analysis of the Ego (1922).

It would appear that the emotional appeal of the new doctrine to both the
prophet and his followers is in considerable part based on its immediate
satisfaction of a need to find a supremely
powerful and potentially benevolent leader.
For both the prophet and his followers,
this wish is gratified in fantasy (subjec-
tively real, of course); but the follower's
fantasy is directed toward the person of
the prophet, to whom are attributed

charismatic properties of leadership
(Weber 1946, 1947).

4. Adaptation. The movement is a
revolutionary organization and almost inevitably will encounter some resistance.
Resistance may in some cases be slight
and fleeting but more commonly is determined and resourceful, and is held either
by a powerful faction within the society
or by agents of a dominant foreign society. The movement may therefore have
to use various strategies of adaptation:
doctrinal modification; political and
diplomatic maneuver; and force. These
strategies are not mutually exclusive nor,
once chosen, are they necessarily maintained through the life of the movement.
In most instances the original doctrine
is continuously modified by the prophet,
who responds to various criticisms and
affirmations by adding to, emphasizing,
playing down, and eliminating selected
elements of the original visions. This re-
working makes the new doctrine more
acceptable to special interest groups, may
give it a better "fit" to the population's
cultural and personality patterns, and may
take account of the changes occurring in
the general milieu. In instances where
organized hostility to the movement
develops, a crystallization of counter-
hostility against unbelievers frequently
occurs, and emphasis shifts from cultivation of the ideal to combat against the
unbeliever.

5. Cultural Transformation. As the
whole or a controlling portion of the
population comes to accept the new religion with its various injunctions, a noticeable social revitalization occurs, signalized by the reduction of the personal
deterioration symptoms of individuals, by
extensive cultural changes, and by an
enthusiastic embarkation on some organized program of group action. This
group program may, however, be more or
less realistic and more or less adaptive: some programs are literally suicidal; others represent well conceived
and successful projects of further social,
political, or economic reform; some fail,
not through any deficiency in conception

and execution, but because circumstances made defeat inevitable.

6. <u>Routinization.</u> If the group action program in nonritual spheres is effective in reducing stress-generating situations, it becomes established as normal in various economic, social, and political institutions and customs. Rarely does the movement organization assert or maintain a totalitarian control over all aspects of the transformed culture; more usually, once the desired transformation has occurred, the organization contracts and maintains responsibility only for the preservation of doctrine and the performance of ritual (i.e., it becomes a church). With the mere passage of time, this poses the problems of "routinization" which Max Weber discusses at length (Weber 1946, 1947).

V. <u>The New Steady State.</u> Once cultural transformation has been accomplished and the new cultural system has proved itself viable, and once the movement organization has solved its problems of routinization, a new steady state may be said to exist. The culture of this state will probably be different in pattern, organization or <u>Gestalt</u>, as well as in traits, from the earlier steady state; it will be different from that of the period of cultural distortion.

VARIETIES AND DIMENSIONS OF VARIATION

I will discuss four of the many possible variations: the choice of identification; the choice of secular and religious means; nativism; and the success-failure continuum.

1. <u>Choice of Identification.</u> Three varieties have been distinguished already on the basis of differences in choice of identification: movements which profess to <u>revive</u> a traditional culture now fallen into desuetude; movements which profess to <u>import</u> a foreign cultural system; and movements which profess neither revival nor importation, but conceive that the desired cultural end-state, which has never been enjoyed by ancestors or foreigners, will be realized for the first time in a future <u>Utopia</u>. The Ghost Dance,

the Xosa Revival, and the Boxer Rebellion are examples of professedly revivalistic movements; the Vailala Madness (and other cargo cults) and the Taiping Rebellion are examples of professedly importation movements. Some formulations like Ikhnaton's monotheistic cult in old Egypt and many Utopian programs, deny any substantial debt to the past or to the foreigner, but conceive their ideology to be something new under the sun, and its culture to belong to the future.

These varieties, however, are ideal types. A few movements do correspond rather closely to one type or another but many are obvious mixtures. Handsome Lake, for instance, consciously recognized both revival and importation themes in his doctrine. It is easy to demonstrate that avowedly revival movements are never entirely what they claim to be, for the image of the ancient culture to be revived is distorted by historical ignorance and by the presence of imported and innovative elements. Importation movements, with professed intentions to abandon the ancestral ways, manage to leave elements of the ancestral culture intact, if unrecognized, in large areas of experience. And movements which claim to present an absolutely new conception of culture are obviously blinding themselves to the fact that almost everything in the new system has been modeled after traditional or imported elements or both. Although almost every revitalization movement embodies in its proposed new cultural system large quantities of both traditional and imported cultural material, for some reason each movement tends to profess either no identification at all, a traditional orientation, or foreign orientation. This suggests that the choice of identification is the solution of a problem of double ambivalence: both the traditional and the foreign model are regarded both positively and negatively.

Culture areas seem to have characteristic ways of handling the identification problem. The cargo fantasy, although it can be found outside the Melanesian area, seems to be particularly at home there; South American Indian prophets frequently preached of a migration to a heaven-on-earth free of Spaniards and other evils, but the promised-land fantasy is known elsewhere; North American Indian prophets most commonly emphasized the revival of the old culture by ritual and moral purification, but pure revival ideas exist in other regions too. Structural "necessity" or situational factors associated with culture area may be responsible. The contrast between native-white relationships in North America (a "revival" area) and Melanesia (an "importation" area) may be associated with the fact that American Indians north of Mexico were never enslaved on a large scale, forced to work on plantations, or levied for labor in lieu of taxes, whereas Melanesians were often subjected to more direct coercion by foreign police power. The Melanesian response has been an identification with the aggressor (vide Bettelheim 1947). On the other hand, the American Indians have been less dominated as individuals by whites, even under defeat and injustice. Their response to this different situation has by and large been an identification with a happier past. This would suggest that an important variable in choice of identification is the degree of domination exerted by a foreign society, and that import-oriented revitalization movements will not develop until an extremely high degree of domination is reached.

2. <u>The Choice of Secular and Religious Means</u>. There are two variables involved here: the amount of secular action which takes place in a movement, and the amount of religious action. Secular action is here defined as the manipulation of human relationships; religious action as the manipulation of relationships between human and supernatural beings. No revitalization movement can, by definition, be truly nonsecular, but some can be relatively less religious than others, and movements can change in emphasis depending on changing circumstances. There is a tendency, which is implicit

in the earlier discussion of stages, for movements to become more political in emphasis and to act through secular rather than religious institutions, as problems of organization, adaptation, and routinization become more pressing. The Taiping Rebellion, for instance, began as religiously-preoccupied movements; opposition by the Manchu dynasty and by foreign powers forced it to become more and more political and military in orientation.

A few "purely" political movements like the Hebertist faction during the French Revolution, and the Russian communist movement and its derivatives, have been officially atheistic, but the quality of doctrine and of leader-follower relationships is so similar, at least on superficial inspection, to religious doctrine and human-supernatural relations, that one wonders whether it is not a distinction without a difference. Communist movements are commonly asserted to have the quality of religious movements, despite their failure to appeal to a supernatural community, and such things as the development of a Marxist gospel with elaborate exegesis, the embalming of Lenin, and the concern with conversion, confession, and moral purity (as defined by the movement) have the earmarks of religion. The Communist Revolution of 1917 in Russia was almost typical in structure of religious revitalization movements: there was a very sick society, prophets appealed to a revered authority (Marx), apocalyptic and Utopian fantasies were preached, and missionary fervor animated the leaders. Furthermore, many social and political reform movements, while not atheistic, act through secular rather than religious media and invoke religious sanction only in a perfunctory way. I do not wish to elaborate the discussion at this time, however, beyond the point of suggesting again that the obvious distinctions between religious and secular movements may conceal fundamental similarities of socio-cultural process and of psycho-dynamics, and that while all secular prophets have not had personality transformation visions, some probably have, and others have had a similar experience in ideological conversion.

Human affairs around the world seem more and more commonly to be decided without reference to supernatural powers. It is an interesting question whether mankind can profitably dispense with the essential element of the religious revitalization process before reaching a Utopia without stress or strain. While religious movements may involve crude and powerful emotions and irrational fantasies of interaction with nonexistent beings, and can occasionally lead to unfortunate practical consequences in human relations, the same fantasies and emotions could lead to even more unfortunate practical consequences for world peace and human welfare when directed toward people improperly perceived and toward organs of political action and cultural ideologies. The answer would seem to be that as fewer and fewer men make use of the religious displacement process, there will have to be a corresponding reduction of the incidence and severity of transference neuroses, or human relationships will be increasingly contaminated by character disorders, neurotic acting out, and paranoid deification of political leaders and ideologies.

3. Nativism. Because a major part of the program of many revitalization movements has been to expel the persons or customs of foreign invaders or overlords, they have been widely called "nativistic movements." However, the amount of nativistic activity in movements is variable. Some movements—the cargo cults, for instance—are antinativistic from a cultural standpoint but nativistic from a personnel standpoint. Handsome Lake was only mildly nativistic; he sought for an accommodation of cultures and personalities rather than expulsion, and favored entry of certain types of white persons and culture-content. Still, many of the classic revivalistic movements have been vigorously nativistic, in the ambivalent way discussed earlier. Thus nativism is a dimension of variation rather than

an elemental property of revitalization movements.

A further complication is introduced by the fact that the nativistic component of a revitalization movement not uncommonly is very low at the time of conception, but increases sharply after the movement enters the adaptation stage. Initial doctrinal formulations emphasize love, co-operation, understanding, and the prophet and his disciples expect the powers-that-be to be reasonable and accepting. When these powers interfere with the movement, the response is apt to take the form of an increased nativistic component in the doctrine. Here again, situational factors are important for an understanding of the course and character of the movement.

4. Success and Failure. The outline of stages as given earlier is properly applicable to a revitalization movement which is completely successful. Many movements are abortive; their progress is arrested at some intermediate point. This raises a taxonomic question: how many stages should the movement achieve in order to qualify for inclusion in the category? Logically, as long as the original conception is a doctrine of revitalization by culture change, there should be no requisite number of stages. Practically, we have selected only movements which passed the first three stages (conception, communication, and organization) and entered the fourth (adaptation). This means that the bulk of our information on success and failure will deal with circumstances of relatively late adaptation, rather than with such matters as initial blockage of communication and interference with organization.

Two major but not unrelated variables seem to be very important in determining the fate of any given movement: the relative "realism" of the doctrine; and the amount of force exerted against the organization by its opponents. "Realism" is a difficult concept to define without invoking the concept of success or failure, and unless it can be so defined, is of no use as a variable explanatory of success or failure. Nor can one use the criterion of conventionality of perception, since revitalization movements are by definition unconventional. While a great deal of doctrine in every movement (and, indeed, in every person's mazeway) is extremely unrealistic in that predictions of events made on the basis of its assumptions will prove to be more or less in error, there is only one sphere of behavior in which such error is fatal to the success of a revitalization movement: prediction of the outcome of conflict situations. If the organization cannot predict successfully the consequences of its own moves and of its opponents' moves in a power struggle, its demise is very likely. If, on the other hand, it is canny about conflict, or if the amount of resistance is low, it can be extremely "unrealistic" and extremely unconventional in other matters without running much risk of early collapse. In other words, probability of failure would seem to be negatively correlated with degree of realism in conflict situations, and directly correlated with amount of resistance. Where conflict-realism is high and resistance is low, the movement is bound to achieve the phase of routinization. Whether its culture will be viable for long beyond this point, however, will depend on whether its mazeway formulations lead to actions which maintain a low level of stress.

SUMMARY

This programmatic paper outlines the concepts, assumptions, and initial findings of a comparative study of religious revitalization movements. Revitalization movements are defined as deliberate, conscious, organized efforts by members of a society to create a more satisfying culture. The revitalization movement as a general type of event occurs under two conditions: high stress for individual members of the society, and disillusionment with a distorted cultural Gestalt. The movement follows a series of functional stages: mazeway reformulation, communication, organization, adaptation, cultural transformation, and routinization. Movements vary along several dimensions, of which choice of identification, relative degree of religious and secular emphasis, nativism, and success or failure are discussed here. The movement is usually conceived in a prophet's revelatory visions, which provide for him a satisfying relationship to the supernatural and outline a new way of life under divine sanction. Followers achieve similar satisfaction of dependency needs in the charismatic relationship. It is suggested that the historical origin of a great proportion of religious phenomena has been in revitalization movements.

BIBLIOGRAPHY

Barnett, H. G., 1953, "Innovation: The Basis of Culture Change," New York.

Bettleheim, B., 1947, "Individual and Mass Behavior in Extreme Situations." In Newcomb, Hartley, et al., eds., Readings in Social Psychology. New York.

Cantril, Hadley, 1941, The Psychology of Social Movements. New York.

Deardorff, M. H., 1951, "The Religion of Handsome Lake: Its Origin and Development." In Symposium on Local Diversity in Iroquois Culture, edited by W. N. Fenton, Bureau of American Ethnology Bulletin 149: 79-107. Washington.

Eggan, Fred, 1954, "Social Anthropology and the Method of Controlled Comparison." American Anthropologist 56:743-63.

Freud, Sigmund, 1922, Group Psychology and the Analysis of the Ego. London.

Fromm, Erich, 1951, The Forgotten Language. New York.

Hallowell, A. I., 1955, "The Self and Its Behavioral Environment." In A. I. Hallowell, Culture and Experience. Philadelphia.

Hoffer, A., H. Osmond, and J. Smythies, 1954, "Schizophrenia: A New Approach. II. Result of a Year's Research." Journal of Mental Science, 100:29-45.

James, William, 1902, Varieties of Religious Experience. New York.

Keesing, Felix M., 1953, Culture Change: An Analysis and Bibliography of Anthropological Sources to 1952. Stanford.

Knox, R. A., 1950, Enthusiasm: A Chapter in the History of Religion, with Special Reference to the XVII and XVIII Centuries. Oxford.

Linton, Ralph, 1943, "Nativistic Movements." American Anthropologist 45:230-40.

Lowe, Warner L., 1953,"Psychodynamics in Religious Delusions and Hallucinations." American Journal of Psychotherapy 7:454-62.

Mead, Margaret, 1954, "Nativistic Cults as Laboratories for Studying Closed and Open Systems." Paper read at annual meeting of the American Anthropological Association. 1955,"How Fast Can Man Change?"Address presented to Frankford Friends Forum, Philadelphia, 4 Dec. 1955.

Mooney, James, 1892-93, The Ghost Dance Religion. Bureau of American Ethnology Annual Report. Washington.

Parker, Arthur, 1913, The Code of Handsome Lake, the Seneca Prophet. New York State Museum Bulletin 163. Albany.

Sargant, William, 1949,"Some Cultural Group Abreactive Techniques and Their Relation to Modern Treatments." Proceedings of the Royal Society of Medicine 42:367-74. 1951, "The Mechanism of Conversion." British Medical Journal 2:311 et seq.

Schwarz, Theodore, 1954,"The Changing Structure of the Manus Nativistic Movement." Paper read at annual meeting of the American Anthropological Association.

Smith, Marian, 1954,"Shamanism in the Shaker Religion of Northwest America." Man, August 1954, #181.

Steward, Julian N., 1953,"Evolution and Process." In A. L. Kroeber, ed., Anthropology Today. Chicago.

Voget, Fred W., 1954,"Reformative Tendencies in American Indian Nativistic Cults". Paper read at annual meeting of the American Anthropological Association.

Wallace, Anthony F. C., 1952a, "Handsome Lake and the Great Revival in the West." American Quarterly, Summer: 149-65. 1952b, "Halliday Jackson's Journal to the Seneca Indians, 1798-1800." Pennsylvania History 19: Nos. 2 and 3. 1953, "A Science of Human Behavior." Explorations No. 3. 1955, "The Disruption of the Individual's Identification with His Culture in Disasters and Other Extreme Situations." Paper read at National Research Council, Committee on Disaster Studies, Conference on Theories of Human Behavior in Extreme Situations. Vassar College. 1956,"The Mazeway." Explorations No. 6.

Wallis, Wilson D., 1918, Messiahs—Christian and Pagan. Boston. 1943, Messiahs—Their Role in Civilization. Washington.

Weber, Max, 1930, The Protestant Ethic and the Spirit of Capitalism. Translated by Talcott Parsons, New York. 1946, From Max Weber: Essays in Sociology. Translated and edited by H. Gerth and C. W. Mills. New York. 1947, The Theory of Social and Economic Organization. Translated and edited by A. M. Henderson and Talcott Parsons. New York.

Williams, F. E., 1923, The Vailala Madness and the Destruction of Native Ceremonies in the Gulf Division. Port Moresby: Territory of Papua, Anthropology Report No. 4. 1934,"The Vailala Madness in Retrospect." In Essays Presented to C. G. Seligman. London.

The Meaning of the Coronation

Edward Shils and Michael Young

SOURCE: *Sociological Review*, Vol. 1, (1953), pp. 63–81.

I

The heart has its reasons which the mind does not suspect. In a survey of street parties in East London nothing was more remarkable than the complete inability of people to say why they thought important the occasion they were honoring with such elaborate ritual, and the newspapers naturally took for granted the behavior on which this essay is a comment. What is perhaps more strange is that on the monarchy, at a Coronation or any other time, political science and philosophy too are silent. About this most august institution there is no serious discussion at all.

Some political scientists, as if sure that the end of so many nineteenth century reformers has been achieved, tend to speak as if Britain is now an odd kind of republic,[1] which happens to have as its chief functionary a Queen instead of a President. It seems that even the most eminent scholars lose their sureness of touch when they enter the presence of Royalty. Sir Ivor Jennings has nothing to say in his volume on <u>Parliament</u>,[2] and in his <u>Cabinet Government</u>,[3] pausing only to note that the Sovereign still possesses considerable influence on legislation and that the King is also an important part of the "social structure," he gives nearly all his space on this subject to an historical treatment of the Victorian period. The late Professor Harold Laski was more discerning, even though his preferences belong to the more rationalistic phase of recent intellectual history. "Eulogy of its habits," he says, speaking of the monarchy, "has reached a level of intensity more comparable with the religious ecstasy of the seventeenth century, when men could still believe in the divine right of kings, than of the scientific temper of the twentieth, which has seen three great imperial houses broken, and the King of Spain transformed into a homeless wanderer."[4] For the rest, while lightly attributing this change in attitude to the imperial propaganda conducted since Victoria was proclaimed Empress of India, he too devotes himself to constitutional history, with

special reference to the tangled events of 1911 and 1931. Recent British political philosophy is as applicable to a republic as it is to a monarchy, whose place in a modern society is a subject most studiously avoided.[5]

Kingsley Martin is almost the only modern political writer to concern himself[6] with the theme to which Walter Bagehot gave such prominence when he set out in 1867 to trace "how the actions of a retired widow and an unemployed youth become of such importance."[7] Bagehot firmly recognized that the role of the Crown was not so much constitutional as "psychological." He supported the monarchy for the precise reason that republicans opposed it: because it enabled the educated ten thousand to go on governing as before. By commanding their unbounded loyalty, it tamed the uncouth "laborers of Somersetshire" who, in their simplicity, needed a person to symbolize the State. In this way "the English Monarchy strengthens our government with the strength of religion . . . It gives now a vast strength to the entire constitution, by enlisting on its behalf the credulous obedience of enormous masses."[8] Mr. Martin in our day, does not, of course, share Bagehot's outlook. But up to a point he puts the same stress on the psychological functions which the Sovereign performs so well because of the sacredness with which he is invested. Once this assertion is made even he falls back, for in the greater part of the book, on the amusing story of the relations of the Sovereign with Lord Melbourne, Lord Beaconsfield, Mr. Gladstone, and the glittering host whose lives are the constitutional history of the realm.

[1] The virtual disappearance of republican sentiment is obvious. John Gollan (<u>Communist Review</u>, June 1953) and Emrys Hughes, M.P., are indeed unorthodox. The current Labor attitude was expressed by Mr. Attlee in the House of Commons on 9 July, 1952. Speaking against sweeping economies in Royal expenditure, he said "It is a great mistake to make government too dull. That, I think, was the fault of the German Republic after the First World War. They were very drab and dull; the trouble was that they let the devil get all the best tunes." See also Sir Stafford Cripps (<u>Hansard</u>, 17 December 1947).

[2] "Of the King we need say nothing. His part in the process of legislation has become little more than formal." <u>Parliament</u>. Cambridge, 1939, p. 3.

[3] <u>Cabinet Government</u>. Cambridge, 1947.

[4] <u>Parliamentary Government in England</u>. Allen & Unwin, London, 1938, p. 389.

[5] Sir Ernest Barker scarcely refers to Monarchy in his <u>Reflections on Government</u> (Oxford, 1942) and passes over it entirely in his brief "Reflections on English Political Theory" (<u>Political Studies</u>, I, 1. Oxford, 1953, pp. 6-12.)

[6] <u>The Magic of Monarchy</u>. Nelson, London, 1937. The article by J. G. Weightman, "Loyal Thoughts of an Ex-Republican," and other articles in the June 1953 issue of <u>The Twentieth Century</u> must also rank as shining exceptions.

[7] <u>The English Constitution</u>. Oxford, 1936, p. 30.

[8] <u>Op. cit.</u>, pp. 35, 39.

The careful avoidance of the monarchy's role in British life appears, to the authors of this essay, to be the consequence of an "intellectualist" bias. It is avoided because the monarchy has its roots in man's beliefs and sentiments about what he regards as sacred. The decline in the intensity of religious belief, especially in the educated classes, has produced an aversion towards all the sentiments and practices associated with religion. They do not acknowledge the somewhat alarming existence of these sentiments within themselves and refuse to admit that these are at work in others. They are acknowledged only when they are derogated as "irrational"[9]—a charge which is both true and misleading, because it serves to dismiss them from further consideration.

The frequency with which the Coronation was spoken of by ordinary people as an "inspiration,"[10] and as a "rededication" of the nation, only underscores the egregiousness of the omission. This essay, using the Coronation as a point of departure, seeks to advance, in some slight measure, the analysis of a neglected subject.

II

In all societies, most of the adult members possess some moral standards and beliefs about which there is agreement. There is an ordering and assessment of actions and qualities according to a definite, though usually unspoken, conception of virtue. The general acceptance of this scale of values, even though vague and inarticulate, constitutes the general moral consensus of society.

[9]See, for instance, Percy Black, The Mystique of Modern Monarchy. Watts, London, 1953.
[10]Not only in Britain and the Commonwealth. Sebastian Haffner speaks of the way in which the Coronation has "taken hold of the public consciousness of America, France and Germany.... There is, instead, an absorbed participation which almost, momentarily, removes the barriers of statehood—as if these foreign countries were celebrating, with mourning or rejoicing, great events in their own ruling Houses, or as if the British Monarchy had become a common possession of the Western world at large." The Twentieth Century, June 1953, p. 418.

Only philosophical intellectuals and prophets demand that conduct be guided by explicit moral standards. In the normal way, the general moral standards are manifested only in concrete judgments, and are seldom abstractly formulated. Persons who conduct themselves in accordance with rigorous and abstract schemes of moral value, who derive and justify every action by referring it to a general principle, impress most others as intolerable doctrinaires. To the doctrinaires, of course, the ordinary man is even more shocking; they would shake the homme moyen sensuel from his spiritual slothfulness and elevate him to a higher plane on which he would act knowingly only in the service of the highest good. To the doctrinaire, to the ideological intellectual, the ordinary sociable man is a poor thing—narrow, unprincipled, unmoral. The ordinary man, is, of course, by no means as poor a thing as his educated detractors pretend. He too is a moral being, and even when he evades standards and dishonors obligations, he almost always concedes their validity. The revivalist reassertion of moral standards in highly individualistic frontier groups, or among detribalized primitive societies in the process of yielding before the pressure of a modern economy, are instances of the respect vice pays to virtue. The recourse to the priestly confessor and the psychoanalyst testify to the power of moral standards even in situations where they are powerless to prevent actual wrongdoing.

We do not claim that men always act in conformity with their sense of values, nor do we claim that the measure of agreement in any society, even the most consensual, is anywhere near complete. Just as no society can exist without moral consensus, without fairly far-reaching agreement on fundamental standards and beliefs, so is every society bound to be the scene of conflict. Not only is there a clash of interests, but moral and intellectual beliefs too are in collision. Yet inter-twined with all these conflicts are agreements strong enough to keep society generally peaceful and coherent.

What are these moral values which restrain men's egotism and which enable society to hold itself together? A few can be listed illustratively: generosity, charity, loyalty, justice in the distribution of opportunities and rewards, reasonable respect for authority, the dignity of the individual and his right to freedom. Most people take these values so much for granted that argument about them seems neither necessary nor possible. Their very commonplaceness may seem to place them at the very opposite pole from the sacred. Yet these values are part of the substance of the sacred, and values like them have sacred attributes in every society.

Life in a community is not only necessary to man for the genetic development of his human qualities. Society is necessary to man as an object of his higher evaluations and attachments, and without it man's human qualities could not find expression.[11] The polis or community is not just a group of concrete and particular persons; it is, more fundamentally, a group of persons acquiring their significance by their embodiment of values which transcend them and by their conformity with standards and rules from which they derive their dignity. The sacredness of society is at bottom the sacredness of its moral rules, which itself derives from the presumed relationship between these rules in their deepest significance and the forces and agents which men regard as having the power to influence their destiny for better or for worse.

Man, as a moral creature with the capacity to discriminate among degrees of rightness and wrongness, feels not only safe but also terribly unsafe in the presence of the abstract symbols of these moral rules. This is one reason why there is a recurrent need in men to reaffirm the rightness of the moral rules by which they live or feel they ought to live. The reaffirmation of the moral rules of society serves to quell their own hostility towards these rules and also reinforces states them in the appropriate relations with the greater values and powers behind the moral rules.

The need to reaffirm the moral rules comes then, not only from their sacred character, which require that they and their sources be respected in the most serious manner, but also from the struggle against morality being continuously enacted in the human mind. Dr. Ernest Jones, in a perceptive essay,[12] has pointed to the fundamental ambivalence in the attitude to authority—first towards the parents, then towards the wider authorities of State and Church, and finally towards the rules which emanate from these authorities. This ambivalence can be overcome in a number of ways of which reaction-formation and displacement are the most prominent. In order to curb an impulse to contravene a moral law, men will sometimes put all their energy into the fulfillment of the contrary impulse. Connection with the symbols of morality or proximity to them helps in this exertion and reinforces the strength which the individual can muster from his own resources to keep the moral law uppermost. It re-establishes the preponderance of positive devotion to the moral rules to enter into contact with them in their purest form. Contact with them in their most sacred form—as principles, or when symbolized in ritual activities, or when preached in moving sermons or speeches—renews their potency and makes the individual feel that he is in "good relations" with the sacred, as well as safe from his own sacrilegious tendencies.

If this argument be accepted, it is barely necessary to state the interpretation of the Coronation which follows from it: that the Coronation was the ceremonial occasion for the affirmation of the moral values by which the society lives. It was an act of national communion. In this we are merely restating the interpretation, in a particular context, of a more general view (which can apply to Christmas,

---

[11] *The Politics of Aristotle*, trans. by Sir Ernest Barker, Oxford, 1946, p. 2.

[12] Jones, Ernest. "The Psychology of Constitutional Monarchy" in *Essays in Applied Psychoanalysis*, Vol. I. Hogarth, London, 1951.

Independence Day, Thanksgiving Day, May Day, or any other great communal ritual) expressed by a great sociologist. "There can be no society," said Durkheim, "which does not feel the need of upholding and reaffirming at regular intervals the collective sentiments and the collective ideas which make its unity and its personality. Now this moral remaking cannot be achieved except by the means of reunions, assemblies and meetings where the individuals, being closely united to one another, reaffirm in common their common sentiments; hence come ceremonies which do not differ from regular religious ceremonies, either in their object, the results which they produce, or the processes employed to attain these results. What essential difference is there between an assembly of Christians celebrating the principal dates of the life of Christ, or of Jews remembering the exodus from Egypt or the promulgation of the decalogue, and a reunion of citizens commemorating the promulgation of a new moral or legal system or some great event in the national life?"[13]

The Coronation is exactly this kind of ceremonial in which the society reaffirms the moral values which constitute it as a society and renews its devotion to those values by an act of communion.

In the following pages, this interpretation of the Coronation will be illustrated by a brief analysis of the Service itself and of some aspects of public participation in it.

III

The Coronation Service itself is a series of ritual affirmations of the moral values necessary to a well-governed and good society. The key to the Coronation Service is the Queen's promise to abide by the moral standards of society. The whole service reiterates their supremacy above the personality of the Sovereign. In her assurance that she will observe

[13]*Elementary Forms of Religious Life*. Allen & Unwin. London. 1915, p. 427. Cf. also Radcliffe-Brown, A. R., *The Andaman Islanders*, Cambridge, 1922, Ch. V.

the canons of mercy, charity, justice and protective affection, she acknowledges and submits to their power. When she does this, she symbolically proclaims her community with her subjects who, in the ritual—and in the wider audience outside the Abbey—commit themselves to obedience within the society constituted by the moral rules which she has agreed to uphold.

This intricate series of affirmations is performed in the elaborate pattern which makes up the Coronation ceremony.

The Recognition. When the Archbishop presents the Queen to the four sides of the "theatre," he is asking the assembly to reaffirm their allegiance to her not so much as an individual as the incumbent of an office of authority charged with moral responsibility and for which she has the preliminary qualifications of a blood-tie. The "People" who signify their willingness to "do homage and service" were once the actual members and representatives of the Estates whose participation was necessary for the security of the realm. Now, those within the Abbey, although many of great power stand among them, are no longer its exclusive possessors. The "homage and service" of the entire society is far more important than it was in earlier Coronations and their offering is no more than a dramatic concentration of the devotion which millions now feel.

The Oath. The Queen is asked whether she will solemnly promise and swear to govern the people of the United Kingdom and the Dominions and other possessions and territories in accordance with their respective laws and customs. When she does so, she clearly acknowledges that the moral standards embodied in the laws and customs are superior to her own personal will. The Queen agrees to respect justice and mercy in her judgments, and to do her utmost to maintain the laws of God and the true profession of the Gospel. In doing this, she acknowledges once more the superiority of the transcendent moral standards and their divine source, and therewith the sacred character of the moral standards of British society.

Apart from the momentary appearance of the Moderator of the General Assembly of the Church of Scotland, the Church of England administers the entire ceremony (though the Duke of Norfolk—a Roman Catholic—organised it), and yet there is no indication that this was regarded as anomaly in a country where only a small proportion of the population actively adheres to that church. Britain is generally a Christian country, it is certainly a religious country, in the broad sense, and in the Coronation Service the Church of England served the vague religiosity of the mass of the British people without raising issues of ecclesiastical jurisdiction or formal representation. As with so much else in the Coronation Service, behind the archaic façade was a vital sense of permanent contemporaneity.

Presenting the Holy Bible. When the Moderator presents the Bible to the Queen, the Archbishop says that this act is performed in order to keep Her Majesty "ever mindful of the Law." The Bible is a sacred object which contains in writing the fundamental moral teachings of the Christian society. Since this Bible is to go with her always, her moral consciousness is to be kept alive by means of continuous contact with the Book in which God's will is revealed. As the Moderator says, "Here is Wisdom; This is the royal Law;[14] These are the lively Oracles of God." The Bible which is handed to the Queen is not simply a closed and final promulgation of moral doctrine. It is the "lively Oracles of God," in which moral inspiration and stimulus for the mastery of constantly emerging new events are to be found. The Bible is the vessel of God's intention, a source of continuous inspiration in the moral regulation of society.

The Anointing. When the Queen is di-

[14] It is the law which is to govern Royalty, and only in this way does it refer to the law made by Royalty for the government of society.

vested of her regalia, she is presented as a frail creature who has now to be brought into contact with the divine, and thus transformed into a Queen, who will be something more and greater than the human being who has received the previous instruction. When the Queen sits in the saintly King Edward's Chair she is anointed by the Archbishop with consecrated oil which sanctifies her in her regal office. When he makes the cross on both her hands, her breast and the crown of her head, he places her in the tradition of the Kings of Israel and of all the rulers of England. He anoints her saying " And as Solomon was anointed king by Zadok the priest and Nathan the prophet, so be thou anointed, blessed, and consecrated Queen over the Peoples." It is not merely an analogy; it is a symbolization of reality, in conformity with sacred precedent. She shows her submission before the Archbishop as God's agent, kneeling before him while he implores God to bless her.

Presenting the Sword and the Orb. The Queen is then told that she will be given power to enforce the moral law of justice and to protect and encourage those whose lives are in accordance with the law. She is commanded to confirm what is in good order, and to restore to order what has fallen away from it. The sword is an instrument of destruction. It is as dangerous as the sacred foundations of the moral rules themselves and its terrible power, for evil, as well as good, must never be forgotten by the Queen. To stress this dual potentiality of authority, it is, throughout the rest of the ceremony, carried naked before her by the peer who redeemed it. In this way, the terrible responsibilities and powers of royal authority are communicated to the Queen and the people. The people are thus made aware of the protection which a good authority can offer them when they themselves adhere to the moral law, and of the wrathful punishment which will follow their deviation. She is next invested with the bracelets of sincerity and wisdom and is dressed in the Robe Royal, which enfolds her in righteousness. With these dramatic actions, she is transformed from a young woman into a vessel of the virtues which must flow through her into her society. Thus transformed, she is reminded of the wide sphere of her power, and of the responsibilities for its moral and pious use, by the Orb which she takes in her hand and places on the altar which is the repository of the most sacred objects. In doing this, she resanctifies her own authority. She is told to execute justice but never to forget mercy.

The Benediction. The communal kernel of the Coronation becomes visible again in the Benediction when the duties of the subjects are given special prominence by the Archbishop. In his blessing, he says: "The Lord give you faithful Parliaments and quiet Realms; sure defence against all enemies; fruitful lands and a prosperous industry; wise counsellors and upright magistrates; leaders of integrity in learning and labour; a devout, learned, and useful clergy; honest, peaceable, and dutiful citizens." The circle of obligation is completed: the Queen to God's rule, and to her subjects in the light of God's rule, and then, her subjects to her by the same standard.

IV

The Coronation Service and the Procession which followed were shared and celebrated by nearly all the people of Britain. In these events of 2nd June the Queen and her people were, through radio, television and press and in festivities throughout the land, brought into a great nation-wide communion. Not only the principals and the spectators inside the Abbey, but the people outside also, participated in the sacred rite. There is no doubt about the depth of the popular enthusiasm. Only about its causes is there disagreement. Some claim that it is the product of commercially interested publicity, others that it is the child of the popular press, others simply dismiss it as hysteria or "irrationality." There are those who claim (with rather more

justice) that the involvement in the Coronation was no more than an expression of an ever-present British love of processions, uniforms, parades and pageants. Still others see the whole affair as a national "binge," or an opportunity for millions of people to seize the occasion for a good time. The youth and charm of the Queen and the attractiveness of her husband and children are also cited to explain the absorption of the populace.

Which of these explanations is correct? All of them, it seems to us, are at best partial answers. They all overlook the element of communion with the sacred, in which the commitment to values is reaffirmed and fortified. As we said earlier the rationalistic bias of educated persons in the present century, particularly those of radical or liberal political disposition, is liable to produce abhorrence towards manifestations of popular devotion to any institution which cannot recommend itself to secular utilitarianism.

The collision between the latter viewpoint and the devoted gravity of the popular attitude was revealed most strikingly in the uproar which followed the publication of Mr. David Low's cartoon in the Manchester Guardian on 3rd June. This cartoon showed a Blimp-like figure, "the morning after," a paper crown awry on his head, the remains of the tinsel and crepe paper of a gay party littered about him, a television receiver in the corner and over it all a grim reminder that £100,000,000 had been spent on the spree. It was in the radical "debunking" tradition. It called forth a storm of denunciation. Moral sentiments had been affronted by Mr. Low's frivolity at a time when they were at a high pitch of seriousness.[15]

[15]Durkheim, to whose understanding of the function of great communal rituals we have already referred, designated the side of life which includes action on behalf of or in accordance with the sacred moral values as "la vie serieuse." Durkheim might have been referring to the "Low crisis" when he wrote: "What social danger is there in touching a tabooed object, an impure animal or man, in letting the sacred fire die down, in eating certain meats, in failure to make the traditional sacrifice over the graves of parents, in not exactly pronouncing the ritual formula, in not celebrating

The first flood of letters expressed indignation that a cynical reference to monetary costs should intrude upon a state of exhilaration, of "inspiration," of "uplift," upon "a unique and inspiring experience" of "heartfelt national rejoicing," upon a "spirit of service and dedication and the inspiring unity of all the people who rejoiced together (and who rededicated themselves) on this wonderful occasion." The second stage of the correspondence was no less significant. Although the anti-Low letters continued, the outburst of sentiment affirming the sacred character of the national participation in the Coronation made the more sceptical uncomfortable. Some of those who sprang to Low's defence found the expression of such intensely serious moral indignation "frightening."

The solemn sense that something touching the roots of British society was involved found expression in many other ways as well. An experienced observer of the London crowd said that the atmosphere on 1st June was like that of Armistice Day 1918 and of VE and VJ Days 1945: there was an air of gravity accompanied by a profound release from anxiety. The extraordinary stillness and tranquillity of the people on the route all through the early morning of 2nd June was noted by many who moved among them. Churches received many persons who came to pray or to meditate in the quiet, and in at least one famous London church—All Hallows Barking—communion services were held every hour.

Just as the Coronation Service in the Abbey was a religious ceremony in the conventional sense, so then the popular participation in the service throughout the country had many of the properties of the enactment of a religious ritual. For one thing, it was not just an extraordinary spectacle, which people were interested in as individuals in search of enjoyment. The Coronation was throughout a collective, not an individual experience.

W. Robertson Smith in his great work, Lectures on the Religion of the Semites[16], points out that acts of communion (of which the Coronation can be regarded as an example) are never experienced by individuals alone: they are always communal occasions. They are acts of communion between the deity or other symbols of the highest values of the community, and persons who come together to be in communion with one another through their common contact with the sacred. The fact that the experience is communal means that one of the values, the virtue of social unity or solidarity, is acknowledged and strengthened in the very act of communion.

The greatly increased sensitivity of individuals to their social ties, the greater absorption of the individual into his group and therewith into the larger community through his group found expression not only on the procession route but in the absent people as well, notably through their families. The family, despite the ravages of urban life and despite those who allege that it is in dissolution, remains one of the most sinewy of institutions. The family tie is regarded as sacred, even by those who would, or do, shirk the diffuse obligations it imposes. The Coronation, like any other great occasion which in some manner touches the sense of the sacred, brings vitality into family relationships. The Coronation, much like Christmas, was a time for drawing closer the bonds of the family, for re-asserting its solidarity and for re-emphasizing the values of the family—generosity, loyalty, love— which are at the same time the fundamental values necessary for the well being of the larger society. When listening to the radio, looking at the television, walking the streets to look at the decorations, the unit was the family, and neither mother nor father were far away when their children sat down for cakes and

certain holidays, etc.? We know, however, what a large place in the repressive law of many peoples ritual regimentation, etiquette, ceremonial, and religious practices play".... "An act is criminal when it offends strong and defined states of the collective conscience." The Division of Labor in Society, Macmillan, New York, 1933, pp. 72; 80.

[16] Lectures on the Religion of the Semites, Black, London, 1927.

ice-cream at one of the thousands of street and village parties held that week. Prominent in the crowds were parents holding small children on their shoulders and carrying even smaller ones in cradles. In all towns over the country, prams were pushed great distances to bring into contact with the symbols of the great event infants who could see or appreciate little. It was as if people recognized that the most elementary unit for entry into communion with the sacred was the family, not the individual.

The solidarity of the family is often heightened at the cost of solidarity in the wider community. Not so at the Coronation. On this occasion one family was knit together with another in one great national family through identification with the monarchy. A general warmth and congeniality permeated relations even with strangers. It was the same type of atmosphere, except that it was more pronounced, that one notices at Christmas time when, in busy streets and crowded trains, people are much more warm-hearted, sympathetic and kindly than they are on more ordinary occasions. Affection generated by the great event overflowed from the family to outsiders, and back again into the family. One correspondent of the Manchester Guardian, reporting the Coronation procession, observed: "The Colonial contingents sweep by. The crowd loves them. The crowd now loves everybody." Antagonism emerged only against people who did not seem to be joining in the great event or treating with proper respect the important social values—by failing, for example, to decorate their buildings with proper splendor. A minor example of the increase in communal unity was the police report that, contrary to their expectations, the pickpockets, usually an inevitable concomitant of any large crowd, were entirely inactive during Coronation Day.

An occurrence in a new housing estate on the outskirts of London provides another instance. There the organizer of a street party had for many months been engaged in a feud with a neighbor so violent that they had at one time sum-

moned each other to the local court. The origin of the feud—a minor quarrel about trespassing by children—was forgotten, and there were continuous outbursts of aggression which reached a climax in May when the neighbor poured hot water over the fence on to some flowers which had just been planted. The neighbor's children were not enrolled for the Coronation party until near the day itself. Then the neighbor came to the organizer and asked in a very humble way whether her own children might be included. They were accepted, and the two who had not exchanged friendly words for so long began to greet each other in the streets as they passed. On the day itself, the organizer, out of her generosity for everyone, went so far as to ask the neighbor to come in and watch her television set. When the neighbor had been in the house for half an hour she asked whether her husband, who was waiting alone next door, could join them. He came in, and when the Service was over, the long standing feud was finally ended over a cup of tea.

Something like this kind of spirit had been manifested before—during the Blitz, the Fuel Crisis of 1947, the London smog of 1952, even during the Watson—Bailey stand in the Lord's Test or Lock's final overs at the Oval—and to some extent the broad reasons were probably the same. There was a vital common subject for people to talk about; whatever the individual's speciality, the same thought was uppermost in his mind as in everyone else's, and that made it easier to overcome the customary barriers. But not less important than the common subject is the common sentiment of the sacredness of communal life and institutions. In a great national communion like the Coronation, people became more aware of their dependence upon each other, and they sensed some connection between this and their relationship to the Queen. Thereby they became more sensitive to the values which bound them all together. Once there is a common vital object of attention, and a common sentiment about it, the feelings apt for the occasion spread by a kind of contagion. Kindness, met with on every side, reinforces itself, and a feeling of diffuse benevolence and sympathy spreads; under these circumstances the individual loses his egoistic boundaries and feels himself fused with his community.

The need to render gifts and sacrifices, so central in religious ceremonies, was also apparent in various forms. Many persons sent gifts directly to the Queen, and the vast scale of individual and collective gifts to persons known and unknown has been the occasion of much comment. Very many muncipalities arranged "treats for old folks," local authorities gave gifts to school children and gift-giving within and between families was very widespread. The joint viewing of the Coronation Service and Procession on the television called forth many presentations. The universal decorations attest not merely to the sense of festivity but also to the disposition to offer valuable objects on such an occasion of entry into contact with the sacred values of society. Low's cartoon in the Manchester Guardian certainly portrayed one aspect of the truth when he saw the whole thing as "one gigantic binge." But it was not just a "good time" or an "opportunity for a good time," as some persons grudgingly said in justification for giving themselves up to the Coronation. There was an orgy, in a certain sense, but it was not just one of self-indulgence. Students of comparative religion have shown that an orgy following an act of communion with the sacred is far from uncommon. It aids the release of tension and reduces the anxiety which intense and immediate contact with the sacred engenders. Moreover, what appears to be simply an orgy of self-indulgence is often one of indulgence with goods which have been consecrated or which have some sacred, communally significant properties.

Surcease from drabness and routine, from the commonplaceness and triviality of daily preoccupation, is certainly one reason for the exaltation. There is surely wisdom in the remark of a philosophical Northern villager: "What people like is the sheer excess of it. We lead niggling enough lives these days. Something a bit lavish for a change is good for the soul."[17] But he did not go far enough. The British love of processions, of uniforms, and ceremonial is not just simple-minded gullibility—it is the love of proximity to greatness and power, to the charismatic person or institution which partakes of the sacred. The crowds who turned out to see the Queen, who waited in the rain in quiet happiness to see the Queen and her soldiers, were waiting to enter into contact with the mighty powers who are symbolically and to some extent, really responsible for the care and protection of their basic values and who on this day had been confirmed in these responsibilities. The crowds who clamored for the Queen outside Buckingham Palace or who lined the streets on the days following Coronation Day when she made her tours of London were not just idle curiosity-seekers. They were, it is probably true, looking for a thrill but it was the thrill of contact with something great, with something which is connected with the sacred, in the way that authority which is charged with obligations to provide for and to protect the community in its fundamental constitution is always rooted in the sacred.

V

Let us now assume that this interpretation of the Coronation is at least plausible and perhaps correct. Why then, should it have taken place in this way in Great Britain at this time? Not all coronations, British or foreign, have drawn such deep sentiments of devoted participation. Whereas a century ago republicanism had numerous proponents in England, it is now a narrow and eccentric sect. Although the stability of the British monarchy became well established in the course of the nineteenth century, persons who have lived through or studied the four coronations of the present century seem to agree that the Coronation of

---

[17] Manchester Guardian, 3 June 1953.

Elizabeth II stirred greater depths in the people than any of its predecessors.

Over the past century, British society, despite distinctions of nationality and social status, has achieved a degree of moral unity equalled by no other large national state. The assimilation of the working class into the moral consensus of British society, though certainly far from complete, has gone further in Great Britain than anywhere else, and its transformation from one of the most unruly and violent into one of the most orderly and law-abiding is one of the great collective achievements of modern times. Whatever its origins, the past century has certainly witnessed a decline in the hostility of the British working and middle classes towards the symbols of the society as a whole and towards the authorities vested with those symbols and the rules they promulgate and administer.

It is true that the discredit into which the British "ruling class" fell as a result of the First World War, the General Strike and the Great Depression, diminished this moral unity. But consensus on fundamental values remained. The Second World War greatly contributed to the strengthening of attachment to society. The care which officers, junior and senior, took to avoid the waste of life, the provision for families at home, the steadiness of the emergence of victory, made for widespread solidarity and for absence of rancor even across gaps in that solidarity. The subsequent General Election was soberly fought. Following that, the Labor Government, by its concern for the under-privileged, by its success in avoiding the alienation of the middle and upper classes, and by the embodiment of certain prized British virtues in its leaders, brought this moral unity of British society to a remarkably high level. Moreover, many British intellectuals who in the 1920's and 1930's had been as alienated and cantankerous as any, returned to the national fold during the War.[18] Full

employment and Government patronage on a large scale, as well as a growing repugnance for the Soviet Union and a now exacerbated but hitherto dormant national pride or conceit also played their part in this development. The central fact is that Britain came into the Coronation period with a degree of moral consensus such as few large societies have ever manifested.

VI

The combination of constitutional monarchy and political democracy has itself played a part in the creation and maintenance of moral consensus, and it is this part which we shall now briefly consider. The late John Rickman and Ernest Jones have argued that the deep ambivalence towards authority and towards moral rules has promoted the widespread acceptance of the monarchy in Britain and other countries where constitutional monarchy has become firmly established. Whereas the lands where personal or absolute monarchy prevailed were beset by revolution, countries of constitutional monarchy became politically stable and orderly, with a vigorously democratic political life. Hostility against authority was, it is said, displaced from royalty onto the leaders of the opposition party and even onto the leaders of the government party. Constitutional monarchies and their societies were fortified by drawing to themselves the loyalties and devotion of their members while avoiding the hostility which is always, in varying measure, engendered by submission to morality. When protected from the full blast of destructiveness by its very <u>powerlessness</u>, royalty is able to bask in the <u>sunshine</u> of an affection unadulterated by its opposite. The institution of the constitutional monarchy is supported by one of the mechanisms by which the mind defends itself from conflict, namely, by the segregation of mutually antagonistic sentiments, previously directed towards a single object, onto discrete and separate objects.[19]

---

[18]Cf. Arthur Koestler's penetrating article on Richard Hillary in <u>The Yogi and the Commissar</u>, Cape, London, 1945, <u>pp. 46-67.</u>

[19] Anna Freud. <u>The Ego and the Mechanisms of Defence</u>. Hogarth, London, 1937.

It might therefore be said that the vigor of British political life is actually rendered possible by the existence of the constitutional monarchy. But the aggressiveness which is channelled into the political arena is in its turn ameliorated and checked by the sentiments of moral unity which the Crown helps to create. Here it is not only the symbolism of the Crown but also the painstaking probity of Kings George V and VI in dealing with the Labor Party, both when it was in opposition and when it formed the Government, which have helped to weld the Labor Party and its following firmly into the moral framework of the national life.

An effective segregation of love and hatred, when the love is directed towards a genuinely love-worthy object, reduces the intensity of the hatred as well. Just as the existence of a constitutional monarchy softens the acerbity in the relations between political parties, so it also lessens the antagonism of the governed towards the reigning government. Governments are well known to benefit whenever the virtues of Royalty are displayed.[20] It appears that the popularity of the Conservative Administration was at least temporarily increased by the Coronation, and at the time much newspaper speculation centred on the question whether Mr. Churchill would use the advantage to win a large majority for his Party at a General Election.

Thus we can see that the image of the monarch as the symbolic custodian of the awful powers and beneficent moral standards is one weighty element in moral consensus. But the monarch is not only symbol. Personal qualities are also significant. Hence it is appropriate at this point to refer to the role of the Royal Family in attaching the population to the monarchy. Walter Bagehot said: "A family on the throne is an interesting idea

also. It brings down the pride of sovereignty to the level of petty life."[21] More and more has this become true since then. Where once to mention the family of the King, like Charles II or George IV, would have provoked laughter, it is now common form to talk about the Royal Family. The monarchy is idealised not so much for the virtue of the individual sovereign as for the virtue which he expresses in his family life.

Devotion to the Royal Family thus does mean in a very direct way devotion to one's own family, because the values embodied in each are the same. When allowance is also made for the force of displacement, if it is accepted that a person venerates the Sovereign partly because he is associated, in the seat of the emotions, with the wondrous parents of phantasy, and if it is accepted that there is also a sort of re-displacement at work, whereby the real parents and wives and children are thought of more highly because they receive some of the backwash of emotion from their Royal counterparts,[22] it is easy to see that the emotional change is a reciprocal one, and all the more powerful for that. Some aspects of this relationship become clear in the Christmas broadcast in which the Sovereign year after year talks about the Royal Family, the millions of British families, and the nation as a whole, as though they are one.[23] On sacred occasions, the whole society is felt to be one large family, and even the nations of the Commonwealth, represented at the Coronation by their prime ministers, queens, and ambassadors, are conceived of as a "family of nations."

---

[20] The Secretary of the Labor Party once told one of the authors of this essay that he had always been confident that Labor would win the hotly contested Gravesend by-election in 1947 because the then Princess Elizabeth had been married a short time before.

[21] Op. cit. p. 34.

[22] One of the authors, during an interview in a London slum district, asked a mother the age of her small son. "Just the same age as Prince Charles," she replied, looking at him with a smile of pride and love.

[23] We have mentioned above the significance of the reconciliation between the intellectuals and the monarchy as part of the general re-acceptance of society by the intellectuals. With respect to the family, the change is equally impressive. Who among the figures of the high intelligentsia would now accept the critical views on the family of Shaw, Wells, Havelock Ellis, Edward Carpenter,

In other ways the monarchy plays on more ordinary occasions the same kind of role as it does at a Coronation—only in a far less spectacular way. Thus British society combines free institutional pluralism with an underlying moral consensus. The universities, the municipalities, the professional bodies, the trades unions, the business corporations—all seek to enforce and protect their internal standards and to fend off external encroachment. Yet they coexist and cooperate in a remarkable atmosphere of mutual respect and relative freedom from acrimony. There are many reasons for this (which we hope to treat more elaborately and with adequate documentation in subsequent publications). In the present context we wish only to stress the unifying function of the monarchy and the orders of society which derive their legitimacy from connection with it. Every corporate body which has some connection with the sacred properties, the charisma, of the Crown thereby has infused into it a reminder of the moral obligations which extend beyond its own corporate boundaries. It is tied, so to speak, to the central value system of the society as a whole through its relationship with Royalty. Quite apart from the Armed Forces, with their multiplicity of royal connection, by fleet, regiment and squadron, a thousand institutions of all kinds are also recognized by the presence of a member of the Royal Family as Patron, President, or Visitor. Royalty presides over such diverse organizations as the Royal Society and the Royal Institute of British Architects, the Royal Academy and the Royal College of Vet-

erinary Surgeons, the British Medical Association and the Institution of Civil Engineers, the Marylebone Cricket Club and the Lawn Tennis Association, the Red Cross and the National Playing Fields Association, St. Mary's Hospital and the Royal Yacht Squadron, the Royal Forestry Society and the University of London.[24] There are the Royal Charters, the patronage of charities, the inaugural ceremonies of hospitals and ships, gardens and factories. The monarchy is the one pervasive institution, standing above all others, which plays a part in a vital way comparable to the function of the medieval Church as seen by Professor Tawney—the function of integrating diverse elements into a whole by protecting and defining their autonomy[25].

Even where the monarchy does not assume ceremonial offices of the type just referred to, the function of holding together the plurality of institutions is performed in some measure by the peerage and the system of honors. In all institutions and professions, all forms of individual achievement and merit are recognized and blessed by this system. The outstanding actors and poets, doctors and scientists, leaders of trade unions and trade associations, scholars and sportsmen, musicians and managers, the brave, the brilliant and the industrious, all receive confirmation of their conformity with the highest standards of society by an honour awarded by the Sovereign. The Sovereign acts as agent of the value system, and the moral values of the society are reinforced in the individuals honored.

To sum up: A society is held together by its internal agreement about the sacredness of certain fundamental moral

D. H. Lawrence or the Bertrand Russell of the 1920's? Who among well known British intellectuals today would be sympathetic with H. G. Wells' pronouncement?: "The family can remain only as a biological fact. Its economic and educational autonomy are inevitably doomed. The modern state is bound to be the ultimate guardian of all children, and it must assist, replace or subordinate the parents as supporter, guardian and educator; it must release all human beings from the obligation of mutual proprietorship and it must refuse absolutely to recognize or enforce any kind of sexual ownership." Experiment in Auto-Biography, Vol. II. Gollancz and Cresset Press, London, 1934, p. 481.

[24] The Queen is Visitor to all the Universities in England, Wales and Ulster except Oxford, Cambridge and Durham; and even in Scotland one University, Edinburgh has the Duke as Chancellor. In the Dominions the Queen's representative often plays the same part—at McGill, for instance, the Governor General is Visitor and at Melbourne the Governor of Victoria.
[25] "Religion . . . . the keystone which holds together the social edifice. . . " Religion and the Rise of Capitalism. John Murray, London, 1926, p. 279.

standards. In an inchoate, dimly perceived, and seldom explicit manner, the central authority of an orderly society, whether it be secular or ecclesiastical, is acknowledged to be the avenue of communication with the realm of the sacred values. Within its society, popular constitutional monarchy enjoys almost universal recognition in this capacity, and it is therefore enabled to heighten the moral and civic sensibility of the society and to permeate it with symbols of those values to which the sensitivity responds. Intermittent rituals bring the society or varying sectors of it repeatedly into contact with this vessel of the sacred values. The Coronation provided at one time and for practically the entire society such an intensive contact with the sacred that we believe we are justified in interpreting it as we have done in this essay, as a great act of national communion.

Does Literature Reflect Common Values?

Milton C. Albrecht

SOURCE: *American Sociological Review*, Vol. 21, (1956), pp. 722–29.

The relationship of literature and society has been variously conceived. Three general assumptions are that literature reflects society and culture, that it serves as a means of social control, and that it influences attitudes and behavior of people in ways considered in some respects desirable, in others undesirable.[1] For the present article, research was oriented to the reflection theory.

Like other arts, literature has in the past been assumed to reflect cultural norms and values, the ethos and the stresses of a society, the process of dialectical materialism, and the historical development of a society or culture.[2] Recently, divorce and prejudice in fiction have been studied, and some research has attempted to determine agreement between literary content and statistical data on occupations and population distribution in the United States.[3] The results have pointed to an emphasis on widespread American attitudes and ideals, reinforcing the idea that literature reflects common cultural values. It is this conception, also, which is logically consistent with the theory of social control.[4] The present research was focused, consequently, on the problem of literature reflecting cultural norms and values. It was limited, however, to the area of the American family and to short stories in large circulation magazines.

The principal hypothesis was that short stories read by large audiences, even though representing distinct reading levels, will express essentially the same basic values and ideals of the American family. It was anticipated, nevertheless, that variations in selection and emphasis of these values would occur among the several levels, derived probably from sub-cultural differences, but the precise

---

[1] M. C. Albrecht, "The Relationship of Literature and Society," American Journal of Sociology, 59 (March, 1954), pp. 425-436.

[2] Ibid., pp. 425-431.

[3] See J. H. Barnett and R. Gruen, "Recent American Divorce Novels, 1938-1945," Social Forces, 26 (March, 1948), pp. 332-337; B. Berelson and P. Salter, "Majority and Minority Americans: An Analysis of Magazine Fiction," Public Opinion Quarterly, 10 (Summer, 1946), pp. 168-190; R. Inglis, "An Objective Approach to the Relationship Between Fiction and Society," American Sociological Review, 3 (August, 1938), pp. 526-531.

[4] Albrecht, op. cit., pp. 430-431.

nature of these variations was not predicted. This aspect of the study was regarded as exploratory.

The magazines should obviously represent as distinct cultural reading strata
or social classes as possible. Warner's
ranking of magazines according to their
popularity in each of the six social
classes was relied on chiefly.[5] His general results are strongly supported, for
middle and lower levels especially, by
Kass's technique of overlapping reading
which in turn has a high correlation with
the ranking of cultural levels of magazines by the judgment of experts.[6] On the
basis of these studies, True Story and
True Confessions were selected for the
lower level, the American and the Sat-
urday Evening Post for the middle level,
the Atlantic and the New Yorker for the
upper level. Sampling was limited to issues for the year 1950 and included only
"regular" short stories.[7]

In order to avoid the fallacy of assuming that values found concentrated in fiction must inevitably be widespread in
society, a framework derived from
sources independent of literary materials
was necessary. For this framework the
"configurations" of Sirjamaki were
chosen, although his list of eight was
modified slightly and extended to ten

moral ideas or values of the American
family,[8] stated as follows:

1. Marriage is a dominating life goal, for
   men as well as for women.
2. Marriage should be based on personal
   affection and on individual choice.
3. The family should be a small independent unit, having a home of its own.
4. The exercise of sex should be contained
   within wedlock.
5. The criterion of successful marriage is
   personal happiness of husband and wife.
6. Marriage should be monogamous and
   permanent, but if mates are very unhappy, divorce is sanctioned.
7. The family roles of husband and wife
   should be based on a sexual division of
   labor, but with male status superior.
8. Individual values are esteemed in family living, though affection should be
   strong.
9. Children should be reared in a child's
   world and shielded from too early participation in adult woes and tribulations.
10. The best years of life are those of
    youth, and its qualities are the most
    desirable.

To prevent selective bias and to test as
fully as possible for values other than
those listed, two or more alternatives for
each of the ten were formulated which
modified and opposed the original statement. Alternatives for marriage being a
dominant goal, for example, are that
marriage is less important than a successful career, that marriage should be
rejected as too limiting emotionally and
too restricting in terms of mobility, and
that love should be a dominating goal,
avoiding marriage.

---

[5] W. L. Warner and P. S. Lunt, The Social Life
of a Modern Community, New York: Harcourt Brace
and Company, 1941, pp. 386-406.

[6] B. Kass, "Overlapping Magazine Reading: A New
Method of Determining the Cultural Levels" in P.
Lazarsfeld and F. Stanton, Communications Re-
search, 1948-49, New York, Harper and Brothers
1949, pp. 130-151. See also W. L. Morgan and A. M.
Leahy, "The Cultural Content of General Interest
Magazines," Journal of Educational Psychology, 25
(October, 1934), pp. 530-536. W. A. Kerr and H. H.
Remmers, "Cultural Value of 100 Representative
Magazines," School and Society, 54 (November,
1941), pp. 476-480; J. H. Foster, "An Approach to
Fiction Through the Characteristics of Its Readers,"
Library Quarterly, 6 (April, 1936), pp. 124-174.

[7] The year 1950 was selected for its avoidance
of war influences and its closeness to recent research on cultural reading levels as well as on
families. Omitted from the sample were "book-
lengths," "short-shorts," serials, autobiographical
reminiscences and informational pieces in the guise
of fiction.

[8] J. Sirjamaki, "Culture Configurations in the
American Family," American Journal of Sociology,
53 (May, 1948), pp. 464-471. His list is based on a
variety of sources which show general agreement.
The order of items was changed and numbers three
and six added after consulting standard texts and
specific studies: A. B. Hollingshead, Elmtown's
Youth, New York: John Wiley and Sons, 1949; M. P.
Redfield, "The American Family: Consensus and
Freedom," American Journal of Sociology, 52 (Sep-
tember, 1946), pp. 175-183; M. Mead, "The Con-
temporary American Family as an Anthropologist
Sees It," American Journal of Sociology, 53 (May,
1948), pp. 453-459; M. Mead, Male and Female,
New York: William Morrow and Company, 1949;
P. J. Campisi, "Ethnic Family Pattern: The Italian
Family in the United States," American Journal of
Sociology, 53 (May, 1948), pp. 443-449.

Whenever possible, modifications were drawn from values known to occur among groups at one or another social level. An alternative to marriage being based on personal affection and individual choice is that marriage should be based primarily on parental preference and in-group solidarity—values fostered by upper-class families.[9] Or, instead of the exercise of sex being contained within wedlock, that the exercise of sex outside of wedlock should be permissible or condoned, that the exercise of sex before, if not after, marriage is expected. These alternatives were derived in part from Whyte's "A Slum Sex Code" and from other studies.[10] Alternatives for each of the ten original statements were formulated in the same way.

A schedule was devised of the original ten, together with the sets of alternatives.

The sample totaled 189 stories, from which 36 were discarded as inappropriate in content or setting, leaving a final sample of 153 stories: 62 from the lower level, 59 from the middle, and 32 from the upper.

As the stories were read, direct or positive approval of values and goals was noted in authors' statements, in descriptions of characters' thoughts and behavior and in the plot resolution. The approved values were recorded on a schedule card, whether for a listed value, for an alternative, or for any unlisted value. The principal value and theme were differentiated from subsidiary values and from certain implied or unquestioned values. The plot was also summarized, the main conflict described, and a selection made of statements representing the values strongly supported.

Table 1. Percentage Distribution of Family Values Occurring as Main Themes in Short Stories of Three Cultural Reading Levels

Value Number	Lower Level		Middle Level		Upper Level		All Levels	
	N	Percentage	N	Percentage	N	Percentage	N	Percentage
1	8	11.26	10	16.13	0	0.00	18	11.11
2	26	36.62	33	53.22	3	10.33	62	38.27
3	2	2.81	0	0.00	0	0.00	2	1.24
4	3	4.23	0	0.00	2	6.90	5	3.09
5	15	21.12	4	6.45	7	24.14	26	16.05
6	1	1.41	0	0.00	1	3.45	2	1.24
7	3	4.23	3	4.84	1	3.45	7	4.32
8	9	12.68	6	9.68	6	20.69	21	12.96
9	1	1.41	0	0.00	2	6.90	3	1.85
10	0	0.00	3	4.84	0	0.00	3	1.85
Total Approved Values	68	95.77	59	95.16	22	75.86	149	91.98
Total Alternative Values	3	4.23	3	4.84	7	24.14	13	8.02
Totals	71*	100.00	62*	100.00	29†	100.00	162	100.00

*Total exceeds sample because of double themes in some stories.
†Total less than sample because themes of three stories not on family value.

[9] Hollingshead, op. cit., p. 85; A. Davis, B. Gardner and M. Gardner, Deep South, Chicago: University of Chicago Press, 1941, pp. 87-88, 95-99. See also C. Amory, The Proper Bostonians, New York: E. P. Dutton and Company, 1947; F. Lundberg, America's 60 Families, New York: The Citadel Press, 1946.

[10] W. F. Whyte, "A Slum Sex Code," American Journal of Sociology, 49 (July, 1948), pp. 24-31; Hollingshead, op. cit., pp. 418-423.

The story, "A Place of Our Own,"[11] for instance, begins with a scene in which the embrace of husband and wife is interrupted by relatives passing through the front room to their quarters. This disturbs the wife so that she blurts out: "All right. You've got a job, and a wife and

[11] True Story, December, 1950, p. 42 ff.

baby. When are we going to have a home?" This idea of a home of their own is repeated in varying forms more than twenty times, and obligations to the husband's mother and other relatives, the main opposing value, being stated seventeen times. Out of this conflict the plot is made, and it is resolved by husband and wife moving to their own home.

Thus the principal value of the family as a small independent unit in a home of their own (No. 3) is upheld by the plot resolution as well as by the sheer quantity of direct statements,[12] and indirectly by the repudiation of the opposing value. These conclusions were recorded, together with marks or indices, showing support for two subsidiary values: the necessity of happiness in marriage, and insistence on the dominant role of the husband. Tabulated also was the fact that marriage as an important goal in life was implied throughout the story.

The values in all the stories were identified and indices recorded in the same way. When all the evidence had been gathered, the values associated with main themes and story endings were examined first to determine the extent to which the ten listed values were approved as compared with alternatives. The results are presented in Table 1. Of 162 themes, 91.98 per cent upheld the basic values as stated, 8.02 per cent supported alternatives.

The detailed evidence of approval for basic and alternative values, apart from main themes, is shown in Table 2. Of 737 indices, 88.47 per cent were for the listed values, 11.53 per cent for alternative values. The overall quantitative evidence of our sample favors the conclusion that the cultural norms and values of the American family are strongly upheld in the short stories of wide-circulation

magazines, even though they represent distinct cultural reading levels.

These summary results, however, tend to obscure somewhat the differences between levels. As shown in Table 1, the total percentage of themes supporting basic values is only 75.86 for the upper level as compared with 95.16 for the middle and 95.77 for the lower. (Both comparisons are significant at the 5 per cent level.) On the other hand, Table 2, a more complete tabulation of approval for basic and for alternative values, does not indicate these striking variations. In fact, the differences in total percentage of approval for basic values between the levels are not statistically significant. These results still support the hypothesis primarily, but to some extent they set apart the upper level in its treatment of themes.

The fluctuation in frequency of themes, however, appears to be a special phenomenon common to all levels, as Table 1 indicates. The reflection theory (in its rather simplified state) seems to imply that cultural norms and values are expressed in literature about equally. From the variation in the occurrence of themes, it is obvious that basic values are not "reflected" directly and mechanically, as if they were of equal "weight." Certain values do not appear as main themes in stories at some levels, while others occur with a high degree of frequency. Although the intra-level difference—from zero to over 53 per cent—is highest for the middle level, the difference between extremes is statistically significant for all levels at the 1 per cent level of confidence.

Although these differences within levels are rather startling, the question most pertinent to our inquiry is whether the selective concentrations of themes are similar for each level. According to our hypothesis, a positive correlation should exist between the rank orders of frequency of each level. The coefficient of rank order correlation between the lower and the middle level is .76, between the lower and the upper is .65—both significant at the 5 per cent interval. The correlation between the middle and upper

---

[12] As D. Jones observed about movies, the goals striven for by the chief characters are limited and are developed scene by scene so that they can easily be determined. This quantitative procedure was somewhat less applicable to stories from the Atlantic and the New Yorker, which in general involved fewer scenes for making their "point." See "Quantitative Analysis of Motion Picture Content," Public Opinion Quarterly, 6 (Fall, 1942), p. 419.

levels, however, is .32—not significant. If "expression" of basic values, therefore, is interpreted in terms of frequency of occurrence, there is positive correlation between levels except the middle and the upper. While largely supporting the main hypothesis, this result again sets apart the upper level, but from the middle, not the lower level.

But why the concentration of frequencies on a relatively few themes? Combining all levels, four values occur with greatest frequency: marriage as a goal (No. 1), personal choice of marriage partner (No. 2), happiness in marriage (No. 5), and esteem for individuals along with strong affection (No. 8). Value No. 2 is overwhelmingly greatest in frequency, the percentage being more than twice that of its nearest rival, No. 5. In their historical study of "mass periodical fiction," Johns-Heine and Gerth also observe a typical clustering of themes. They think that such themes, once stabilized, "express national traditions and values tacitly supported by all."[13] This conclusion is probably true, but also highly inadequate in view of our results, since certain important family values are relatively neglected or omitted as themes in stories at some levels.

Clustering of themes, therefore, is probably a function of other variables besides widespread acceptance of the values represented—variables that must also account for the absence from each level of certain subjects. The broadly "romantic" character of our society is fairly appropriate to the dominant themes. The age of audiences may play a part, since younger readers presumably would be interested in marriage and the choice of marriage partner, and an older audience might account for the lack of themes on marriage at the upper level,[14] but these factors cannot also account for

the absence of themes on the value of youth in the lower and on sex in the middle level. Taboos might explain the absence of themes on sex, but not on a family having a home of its own. The concern with happiness and with affectional problems in marriage may reflect certain stresses in modern families, but other strains—on older members, for example—are not equally developed. Leisure-time interests cannot adequately justify the concentrations, as Lowenthal thought accounted for the selection of heroes in popular biographies.[15] These varied suppositions show, in fact, little consistency and suggest that complex factors are at work for which no general explanation as yet exists.

The question of valid indices in stories to values that are widespread in society remains. If clustering of themes fails to indicate such values adequately, then one logical answer may be the general degree of approval of basic as compared with alternative values, as shown in Table 2. As mentioned earlier, there is no significant difference between the total percentages of any level, but the middle level conforms the most, followed by the lower, then the upper. In fact, only two of the basic values in the middle level receive approval less than 90 per cent, while the lower shows four and the upper, nine. If at least 80 per cent approval is selected as a standard, the middle level again shows only one or at most two values below this degree of support, while the lower has three and the upper, five. These results, for family values, may confirm in part the general observation that the dominant values in American society are derived from the middle class.

If the arbitrary standard of at least 80 per cent approval is used to indicate those values that are most widely accepted, then examination of the least accepted values may reveal the influence of sub-cultural differences, as well as the

---

[13] P. Johns-Heine and H. H. Gerth, "Values in Mass Periodical Fiction, 1921-1940," Public Opinion Quarterly, 13 (Spring, 1949), p. 105.

[14] See Johns-Heine and Gerth, op. cit., footnote, p. 107; P. F. Lazarsfeld and R. Wyant, "Magazines in 90 Cities, Who Reads What?" Public Opinion Quarterly, 1 (October, 1937), pp. 35-37.

[15] L. Lowenthal, "Biographies in Popular Magazines," in P. Lazarsfeld and F. Stanton, Radio Research, 1942-43, New York: Harper and Brothers, 1944, pp. 517-518.

Table 2. Percentage Distribution of Approval for Basic and for Alternative Values, Apart from Main Themes, in Stories of Three Reading Levels

Value Number	Lower Level		Middle Level		Upper Level		All Levels	
	Basic	Alternative	Basic	Alternative	Basic	Alternative	Basic	Alternative
1	96.30	3.70	97.83	2.17	82.61	17.39	94.31	5.69
2	100.00	0.00	100.00	0.00	86.36	13.64	96.15	3.85
3	94.82	5.18	95.74	4.26	96.00	4.00	95.38	4.62
4	94.87	5.13	100.00	0.00	69.23	30.77	90.00	10.00
5	96.88	3.12	96.43	3.57	75.00	25.00	92.12	7.88
6	73.33	26.67	80.95	19.05	83.33	16.67	78.26	21.74
7	93.10	6.90	95.45	4.55	85.71	14.29	92.31	7.69
8	57.14	42.86	76.47	23.53	69.23	30.77	65.62	34.48
9	60.00	40.00	100.00	0.00	50.00	50.00	64.28	35.72
10	86.67	13.33	90.00	10.00	60.00	40.00	86.00	14.00
Totals	88.13	11.87	93.52	6.48	81.05	18.95	88.47	11.53
Total Indices	297	40	231	16	124	29	652	85

direction of non-conformity or of change. Together, the least accepted values may reveal the influence of sub-cultural differences, as well as the direction of non-conformity or of change. Together, the least accepted values are 4, 5, 6, 8, 9, 10. Of these, only 8 is common to all levels. Number 9 is strongly non-conformist at both the lower and the upper levels, number 6 at the lower and middle levels, and 4, 5, and 10 only at the upper level.

As one might expect, a statistically significant difference exists in the proportion of support for values 4 and 5 between the upper level and both the lower and middle levels—at the 1 and 5 per cent interval respectively. For number 4 the modification given marked support (30.77 per cent) is that sex expression outside of wedlock is permissible or condoned. Although this alternative was expected primarily among lower-level stories, only one story supported this value, and then rather ambivalently. If the slum sex code operates in society at lower cultural levels, this fact is not reflected in lower-level stories. Whether the degree of non-conformity in stories of the upper level accurately reflects the attitude of upper-class families is uncertain. At any rate, the middle-level stories are the most consistent in showing no support for any modifications in this area, and in fact, for generally avoiding any direct references to the subject. As for number 5, the kind of alter-

native upheld to some degree at the upper level, and insignificantly at the lower and middle levels, is an emphasis on duty in marriage and a concern for status. These modifications are consistent with values predominant in upper-class families.[16]

For value 10 the statistical significance is the same as for 4, though the small number of stories expressing this value at the upper level (only five) makes this result questionable. At any rate, the nature of the modification supported is the same at all levels: the recognition of the value of maturity as against that of youth. Sub-cultural differences, then, are not represented, except that middle-level stories are somewhat more ambivalent in their support of maturity, continuing to give the strongest approval to youth.

Value 6 shows a considerable degree of support for alternatives, the lower and middle levels 26.67 and 19.05 per cent respectively, the upper, 16.67 per cent. As expected, there are no significant differences between levels, and the modification supported at all levels is the same: an insistence on marriage being permanent, a rejection of divorce. This high degree of agreement between levels suggests that the idea of divorce is not fully approved in society, which agrees

---

[16] Hollingshead, op. cit., pp. 85, 88; Davis, Gardner and Gardner, op. cit., pp. 90-91, 95 ff. See also original materials in R. Cavan, American Family, New York: Thomas Crowell Company, 1953, pp. 138-140.

with Goode's assertion that "there are many strong, if gradually weaker, moral prescriptions against it."[17] Perhaps the original statement should be somewhat modified. The data indicate also that the lower level is the most conservative in attitude, the middle more tolerant and the upper the most liberal of all. These differences, it should be noted, are a matter of verbal representation, and express perhaps greater "predisposition" toward acceptance of divorce among middle-and upper-level groups, but the actual incidence of divorce shows an inverse correlation with social classes.[18] Perhaps literary materials at the different levels operate as compensatory mechanisms to reality while still principally supporting basic values.

Values 8 and 9 are closely related, the one being concerned with affection in the family and esteem for individual values, the other with the shielding of children from adult problems. Statistically there is a significant difference at the 1 per cent interval between the middle and both the lower and the upper levels, for number 9. The middle level gives unquestioned support to this value, although only four evidences occur in nearly sixty stories. The subject appears as a main theme only in lower and upper-level stories. In both of these levels the type of modification supported is the same: that although children should be shielded, they should also be allowed full scope for emotional development. Stories portray the unfortunate consequences of overprotection, of parental neglect and dominance. These difficulties seem to derive primarily from patriarchial family systems, which are more characteristic of the lower and the upper than of the middle class.[19] But there is little or no overt

approval of the idea that children should assume adult responsibilities as soon as possible, as one might expect from social conditions in the lower class, or that they should be extremely shielded, as seems to be true in the upper classes. In fact, the implication of the stories is that these families should be more individualistic, and this indirectly supports value 8, suggesting that the original statement of 9 should be revised.

Value 8, although among the highest in percentage occurring as main themes, ranks lowest in support of the basic value at both the lower and middle levels, though the proportion of non-conformity varies: lower, 42.86 per cent; middle, 23.53 per cent; upper, 30.77 per cent. Only the difference between the lower and the middle levels is statistically significant, at the 5 per cent interval. Nevertheless, the modification supported at all levels is that of subordinating individual values to family unity, with the lower level showing the greatest approval. Since lower-class families are in fact the least stable,[20] the degree of emphasis in stories on sacrifices of parents and children to keep the family together may again, as for value 6, operate as a compensatory mechanism while reflecting the basic value of unity. In stories, as in life, individual values threaten family stability, not only at the lower but also at the upper level, and to a lesser extent even at the middle level. But insistence on unity, as in a patriarchal system, leads to frustration of children, as mentioned for value 9. The approval of modifications for both 8 and 9 shows inherent contradictions and conflicts, which apparently reflect general uncertainty of family roles and inadequately institutionalized family relationships.

Altogether, the support for alternative values does not seem to derive primarily from sub-cultural family values, except possibly for value 5. Although a number of statistically significant differences oc-

---

[17] W. J. Goode, *After Divorce*, Glencoe, Illinois: The Free Press, 1956, p. 10.

[18] *Ibid.*, pp. 44-48, 66-68.

[19] See references in notes 9 and 16, above. Also, A. Davis and R. J. Havighurst, *Father of the Man*, Boston: Houghton Mifflin Company, 1947; A. Davis, "Child Rearing in the Class Structure of American Society," in The Family in Democratic Society: Anniversary Papers of the Community Service Society of New York, New York: Columbia University Press, 1949, pp. 56-69.

[20] Hollingshead, *op. cit.*, p. 106, 117; A. B. Hollingshead, "Class Differences in Family Stability," The Annals of the American Academy of Political and Social Science, 272 (November, 1950), pp. 39-46.

cur between levels, the direction of non-conformity is usually similar at all levels, and this similarity is especially marked for value 6, where no significant differences between levels exist. Though the alternative for value 9 apparently reflects the more patriarchal family systems of lower and upper classes, the emphasis tends to support indirectly value 8. These values that are most "deviant" at each level seem principally to point up areas of change, though neither the extent nor the direction can be determined without further research. They contrast with the relatively small proportion of non-conformity at any level for numbers 3 and 7, which show unquestioned support for nuclear families having homes of their own, and for males having some superior status, though the degree is occasionally in question. These areas contrast specifically with values 6 and 8, which, although generally upholding basic values, seem also to represent compensatory mechanisms to reality.

There is still the question of the upper level as a whole, which was set apart from other levels in its relatively smaller support of basic values as main themes and in its inadequate correlation between rank order of frequencies of themes. Certain differences of specific values have also been mentioned. In addition, for values 1 and 2, a significant difference exists between the upper and the middle level, which is born out by stories which deal with deviant groups, such as hobos and homosexuals, who avoid marriage, and by stories that show some marriage choices being determined more by status considerations than by romantic attachment.

These distinctions deserve explanation. In respect to differences in frequency of themes, the crucial fact seems to be the range of subjects in stories, which is far greater for the upper than for the other levels. This greater range results in less concentration. For a single theme, as shown in Table 1, the highest percentage at the upper level is 24.14 per cent; while in the middle it is 53.22 per

cent, which largely accounts for the lack of significant correlation between these levels. Incidentally, the wider range accounts also for the high rejection rate (43 per cent) and consequently for the relatively smaller sample of upper-level stories.[21] The greater range of subject matter is itself not a function of subcultural differences in family values, but probably of more education and wider perspective of readers. At any rate, family relationships in stories of the upper level are often placed in the context of a larger world, whereas the outlook in stories at the other levels—the lower particularly—is confined to the "world" of the family.[22]

The smaller percentage of support in upper-level stories for certain main themes, such as values 1 and 4, is probably determined by the way in which subjects are treated artistically. Deviant characters, including hobos and homosexuals, are usually presented in terms of their own values, with no plot resolution or conventional ending to indicate clearly the author's own value commitments or those of society. In other words, subjects are treated more objectively, certainly less moralistically, than at the other two levels. As Barnett says about "divorce" novels that are best in a literary sense, they are more "autonomous" than those that are written as popular fiction.[23] The stories are intended, apparently, to foster perspective and insight rather than a direct reinforcement of generally accepted values.

Except for the emphasis on status in respect to choice of mate (number 2) and in marriage situations (number 5), and possibly the greater familistic orientation, which is shared with the lower level, the upper-level stories do not seem to

---

[21] The discard from the middle level was only 20 per cent (for adventure stories) and none from the lower level.

[22] Similar differences in intellectual horizon were pointed out by W. L. Warner and W. E. Henry, "The Radio Daytime Serial: A Symbolic Analysis," Genetic Psychological Monographs, 37 (February, 1948), pp. 3-73.

[23] J. H. Barnett, Divorce and the American Divorce Novel, 1858-1937, Philadelphia: (Privately printed) 1939, p. 139.

reflect subcultural family values. They express freedom in dealing with subjects that are socially taboo—a freedom that is often interpreted as license. Verbal or artistic non-conformity is commonly mistaken for the actual behavior of the upper class, as illustrated by the liberal attitude toward divorce, described earlier. It may be said, then, that in part at least, the larger percentage of non-conformity in stories of the upper level is determined by differences not in family values but in literary tradition.

In conclusion, our main hypothesis is largely upheld: short stories in wide-circulation magazines, though representing distinct reading levels, reflect cultural norms and values of the American family. In its simplified form, however, this concept of reflection fails to account for significant differences in the frequency with which values occur as main themes. Frequency of themes is unreliable as a basis for determining widespread values, which seem to be indicated more certainly by detailed indices. These may provide a method of distinguishing the more firmly accepted from the more fluctuating and unsettled values. The evidence seems to indicate that the original statements for values 6 and 9 should be modified.

Competing ideas, however, were identified from analysis of stories, which in some respects distinguished the several levels. Familistic trends were found more marked in stories of the upper and lower levels, and concern for status was more emphasized at the upper and family unity at the lower level. But other expected variations from subcultural family differences failed to appear; the same type of non-conformity sometimes occurred at all levels. For some values the variations were in inverse ratio to reality, suggesting the operation of compensatory mechanisms in stories.

As a whole, the upper level differed most from the other levels, partly due to a few variations in family values, but considerably due to differences in general outlook and in literary tradition. The middle level, on the other hand, conformed the most closely with the basic values as originally formulated, which may in part confirm the general idea that the values most dominant in society are middle-class values.

A Content Analysis of "Little Orphan Annie"

Donald Auster

SOURCE: *Social Problems*, Vol. 2, (1954), pp. 26–33.

The most significant characteristic associated with comic strips is their huge audience which includes four-fifths of all adult newspaper readers.[1] If, in the face of this popularity, modern comic strips show a tendency to deal with events and issues of the real world, then cognizance must be taken of the emergence of the comic strip as an important mass communication medium. In view of these conditions an analysis was made to determine the nature and extent to which a measurable, social, political and economic ideology was contained in "Little Orphan Annie," a nationally syndicated strip.

"Little Orphan Annie" was launched

[1] The 138 Study Summary, <u>The Continuing Study of Newspaper Readership</u>, New York: The Advertising Research Foundation, 1951, p. 10.

August 5, 1924 in the Chicago Tribune. Meeting with rapid success, the strip was soon syndicated and ranks sixth among the nation's most popular comic strips.[2] Though official figures will not be released by the syndicate, its Sunday circulation has been estimated at twenty million in three hundred forty-five newspapers.[3]

The major characters in this strip are Orphan Annie, an appealing eleven-year-old orphan girl; Sandy, her dog; Daddy Warbucks, heroic industrial colossus, and Annie's guardian; and Punjab, Warbuck's inscrutable Asiatic follower.

THE METHOD

Four areas were selected for study: 1. social class, 2. political ideology, 3. justice, and 4. business success. A number of hypotheses were then constructed. Since the cartoonist was purported to have strong leanings in a conservative direction[4] which might be reflected in the comic strip, the hypotheses were formulated in such a manner that their substantiation would function as a measure of conservatism. They were then tested by means of a detailed content analysis of a rotating sample of eleven time periods, each containing three months' releases of the strip. The sample was taken from the New York Daily News, one of the syndicate's key newspapers. A pre-test, indicating that only dilatory action occurred during the week, made it possible to eliminate the daily issues in favor of the more widely circulated Sunday strips.[5] It further revealed that a sample of three consecutive months was sufficient to ascertain the nature of the episode and the delineation of character. The three month sample unit of Sunday releases was taken every two and a half years from 1925 to 1950 totaling 141 releases and 1623 panels. The panel (the small connecting pictures which form the

comic strip) was chosen as the unit of analysis since it was the smallest unit containing both pictorial and verbal material.

In view of the complexity of coding verbal-pictorial combinations and in consideration of the nature of the investigation, it was decided to utilize a simple directional method of classification. The general directional categories of Favorable, Unfavorable and Neutral were employed. However, each panel was first coded under one of a number of specific themes which constituted sub-categories under the broad categories of Favorable, Unfavorable and Neutral. For example, Altruism was a sub-category under a general category of Favorable social class character traits. Since comic strip panels consist of integrated verbal-pictorial combinations, the theme was defined as the dominant net impression created by this dual communications device. In most of the areas examined the thematic analysis was based on categories which had been constructed in terms of the probable character and behavioral traits of the comic strip figures who represented various classes of people such as Middle and Working Class Americans, Nazis and Communists, and American Judges. Any figure who dominated or shared either the verbal or pictorial content was considered a thematic figure and his characterization in that panel was classified. The integration of the verbal and pictorial components of the panel prevented any conflict in characterization.[6] One episode was analyzed both quantitatively and qualitatively. All hypotheses were examined in accordance with a detailed set of coding instructions.[7]

Since content analysis as a method of investigation implies objectivity, it is necessary to test inter-rater reliability. That is, different coders should secure the same results when they apply the same set of categories to the same con-

---

[2] Ibid., p. 57.

[3] Time, XLII, No. 9, August 30, 1943, p. 48.

[4] Ibid.

[5] Sunday circulation is 4,000,000 greater than weekday (Time, XLII, No. 9, August 30, 1943, p. 48).

[6] In view of the somewhat subjective nature of any thematic analysis, the high reliability secured here was essential as well as gratifying.

[7] Coding instructions are available upon request.

tent.[8] Despite the difficulties created by the presence of both written and pictorial material, the following results were obtained by comparing the agreement between the author and two judges on randomly selected pages chosen from each of the sample years. All figures are for triple agreement.

1. Thematic agreement at the indicator (smallest sub-category) level was 91.8%. Directional agreement was 100%.

2. Thematic agreement on panels included by any one of the three coders was 75.5%. This figure is the net agreement remaining after deductions for both inclusion-exclusion and theme disagreements.

3. The symbol analysis of the social class hypothesis resulted in 86.4% agreement.

THE FINDINGS

Social Class: Hypothesis—That in this comic strip in which one of the major figures is an industrial colossus there is an inadequate and unfavorable presentation of the working class as compared with the portrayal of the middle class.

Two methods of analysis were employed to test this hypothesis. In addition to the customary thematic analysis, a symbol analysis was utilized in order to compare the frequency, whether thematic or not, with which middle class and working class figures appeared in the strip. Occupation was used as a determinant of class. The criteria by which occupations were ascribed to various classes were based on Centers' study.[9]

The thematic analysis focussed on the character traits of the two classes mentioned above. A number of ideal American character traits, such as altruism, for-

bearance, self-reliance, industriousness, bravery and practicality were used as categories.[10]

The thematic comparison of character traits shows 101 panels which can be classified under a <u>Favorable</u> heading for the middle class while only four working class panels can be so classified.

Forty-two additional panels dealing with the middle class were classified as <u>Neutral</u>; seven working class panels were placed under this heading. An insignificant number of panels dealt with each class <u>Unfavorably</u>.

The symbol analysis compared the number of panels in which middle and and working class figures appeared or were mentioned. The total number of panels tabulated here includes in addition to the thematic panels many other pertinent panels which could not fulfill the criteria of being thematic. The results showed a better than ten to one (226 to 22) ratio of middle class panels to working class panels (panels in which members of these classes appeared.)

In no panel was a worker identified by name and in most of the twenty-two panels the portrait was typically of an indistinguishable group of men. The result is a dehumanized portrait.[11] Middle class figures, on the other hand, occupy major roles, are known by name and have the opportunity to express their attitudes, values and aspirations.

An examination of the locale of the eleven sample periods indicated six to be rural and small town, two urban and three mixed. This finding is in agreement with the fact that the most common Fa-

---

[8] According to Berelson, only 15-20% of all content analyses report reliability results. Bernard Berelson, <u>Content Analysis in Communication Research</u>, Glencoe, Illinois: The Free Press, 1952, p. 172.

[9] Richard Centers, <u>The Psychology of Social Classes</u>, Princeton, New Jersey: The Princeton University Press, 1949, pp. 80-83.

[10] Ideal character traits were taken from <u>The Boy Scout Handbook</u>, New York: Boy Scouts of America, 1945, pp. 33-36 and also from Robert S. and Helen M. Lynd, <u>Middletown in Transition</u>, New York: Harcourt, Brace and Company, 1937, pp. 402-486.

[11] Arnheim in his analysis of the radio daytime serial finds, "The complete absence of the working class proper is striking... There is no case of a worker ... playing an important role..." Rudolph Arnheim, "The World of the Daytime Serial," in Wilbur Schramm, ed., <u>Mass Communications</u>, Urbana: The University of Illinois Press, 1949, p. 362. For the working class there apparently is no respite in radio or comic strips from the prevailing middle and upper class orientation.

vorable characteristic was Altruism with 29% of the Favorable middle class panels being so coded. For this trait to occur so frequently in a comic strip whose locale is often rural or small town is not surprising. Lynd speaks of the emphasis on neighborliness and being a "good fellow" which he found in Middletown.[12] The heroine of the strip contributes directly to this view by her own observation that "If folks in big cities felt the same friendship for poor folks that small folks feel, ther'd be a lot less sufferin' I betcha." (December 11, 1932)

Psychologically, altruism may serve the function of providing a theoretical sense of security. Since the value system of the society frowns on charity, the need for security, especially against financial crisis, must be met in some other manner. In such a milieu a preoccupation which both real and imaginary deeds of an altruistic nature may tend to create a belief on the part of the donor that his acts somehow assure him of reciprocal aid should he be in need.

The second most frequently encountered Favorable trait was Forbearance. In a comic strip where one of the characters states, "Most of our calamities are blessings in disguise . . ." (April 10, 1938) There is need for forbearance during the inevitable metamorphosis of misfortune into fortune. Space does not permit a discussion of the other character traits.

The 1935 sample period was one of the most interesting examined. Consequently, a detailed qualitative analysis was made in addition to the usual quantitative study. The current episode dealt with the efforts of Slugg and Claptrap to ruin Warbucks by convincing the public that his Eonite factory belonged to the people. Eonite was a new material. The production of this substance apparently was to solve the unemployment of that era for as Warbucks put it, ". . . men are going back to work by the tens of thousands. Thanks to 'Eonite' everything is getting better and everyone is happier . . ." (July 21, 1935).

In the meantime an aroused mob destroys the factory but is finally quelled by the National Guard.[13]

A unique spatial anomaly was encountered in this episode. The August 11, 1935 release contained a panel approximately twice as large as the average panel. It was the largest of the 1623 panels examined. This powerful panel depicts an aroused mob storming Warbucks' factory. The implications of this panel are not revolutionary but counterrevolutionary for in the end we see that the mob is quelled by the State and in addition has destroyed its only source of employment, the Eonite factory.

An analysis of this sample period in the light of the economic chaos prevailing at the time permits a psychological evaluation of the function of this episode. The method for solving the depression is seen to be a magical one. It is the result of a chance encounter by Warbucks with the hermit, Old Eli, the inventor of Eonite. The production of this substance is supposed to do the rest. The actual depiction of the mass violence could have had a cathartic effect on the reader of that period who might well have been one of the hard pressed legion of unemployed. Using Lasswell's definition of catharsis as the dissipation of insecurity without change in symbol or practice,[14] the cathartic nature of this episode becomes more apparent. The desire to strike out against the economic system was quite in evidence during this decade.[15] The portrayal of antisocial behavior in a favorite comic strip presented an opportunity for the dissipation of frustration and insecurity through empathy and identification while at the same time

---

[12] Lynd and Lynd, op. cit., p. 404.

[13] Twice during this episode the strip appears on page one of the comic section of the New York Daily News. These are the only instances in the 141 releases examined in which the comic strip occupies a prominent position.

[14] Harold D. Lasswell and Dorothy Blumenstock, World Revolutionary Propaganda, New York: Alfred A. Knopf, 1939, p. 342.

[15] For example, the bonus army marched on Washington in 1932 and was finally driven off by the Army; there were also numerous strike riots during this period. See the New York Times, June 24, and July 30, 1936.

no real action is undertaken. And to increase the value of the educational lesson, it is evident that the mob destroyed its own source of salvation and was dispersed by the authority of the state. The social order dominates. The process is:

Catharis ⟶ Coercion ⟶ Re-education = Social Control

Lasswell states:

Those against whom the protest movement is directed [big business of which newspapers are a member] further facilitate catharsis by providing channels for substitutive response, bread and circuses, face saving symbols of acquiescence, alternative targets ... Guided catharsis is a major means of social control.[16]

To this group we may add comic strip riots.

Political Ideology: Hypothesis—That Communism is more frequently and vigorously attacked than Nazism. Communism is subject to a more persistent and vitriolic attack than was Nazism even during the period when the United States was at war with the nation representing the latter ideology.

Although almost the same number of panels, 106 and 107 dealt with each ideology, all of the panels with Communism as a theme were in the Unfavorable category while on the other hand eleven panels portrayed Nazism Favorably. However, most of the panels with Nazi themes were also Unfavorable. But an examination of the Unfavorable categories reveals a sharp contrast in the presentation of these two enemies of the United States. Though a considerable number of panels, 82, depict comic strip figures battling the Nazis, the fighting is restricted and confined. The impression is of a chess battle rather than total war. For example, the ideological aspect of warfare is hardly in evidence. A comparison of ideological themes reveals that only 13% of the Unfavorable Nazi panels utilized ideological warfare as a technique while 50% of the Unfavorable Communist panels were coded under this category. Since the re-

maining half of the Unfavorable Communist panels indicate no reluctance to portray open warfare with the Communist nation, the difference cannot be explained on this basis. When the international situation in 1943 is recalled the contrast in ideological panels increases in significance. Deep in the midst of war one might expect that both ideological and physical warfare themes would be intensified. In contrast, our relations with the Communists (during the panels studied) had not reached the low point of relations between the United States and Nazi Germany—open warfare, and yet many panels illustrate both physical and psychological warfare against the Communist nation in the strip.[17] This lack of ideological anti-Nazi panels may be indicative of an insufficiently formulated understanding of why the war against Nazism was being waged. In contrast the variety of Unfavorable Communist themes is evident of an acute awareness of the threat to democracy posed by Communism.

The level of sophistication in the presentation of the theme is another distinction between the treatment of Nazism and Communism. The anti-Nazi themes are on a primitive level—we are good and the Nazis are bad; they try to kill Annie by throwing her to the sharks. (June 27, 1943) The anti-Communist themes on the other hand are presented with a great deal of variety and often a remarkable subtlety. They vary from such psychologically terrifying statements as, "Ivan has plans of unbelievable danger to us . . ." (June 25, 1950) which leave the reader's imagination to play on the wildest interpretation of these dangers, to the subtle use of a parable. One particular parable concerns Warbucks' response to Annie's provocative query: "Should we ever start a war?" In reply Warbucks tells the story of a quick-drawing sheriff named Smith whose wife, fearful that he would kill some bandit since he could outdraw all of them, partially sewed up his gun holster to slow down his "draw." One day Smith

[16] Harold D. Lasswell and Abraham Kaplan, Power and Society, New Haven: Yale University Press, 1950, p. 9.

[17] In the strip the communist nation is known by the pseudonym "Franaston" and its leader is known as Ivan.

found himself up against a desperate bandit and needed his gun quickly— "What happened?" Annie asks excitedly. Warbucks' answer is brief but powerful— "His wife is now known as 'Widow Smith.' " (April 30, 1950)

American justice: Hypothesis—That justice and the legal process are demonstrated to be unwieldy and corrupt and as a consequence extra-legal substitutes are frequently employed.

Panels treating both justice and judges were coded since the one was considered representative of the other.

Flexibility is the most frequent Favorable characteristic with which justice is endowed. A number of instances occur in the strip during which good people are for a time exploited by the malfunction or misuse of justice. To the extent to which the law or its servants are flexible and humane the panels are Favorably coded. However, humane treatment of evil-doers is not accepted in the strip. In fact it is severely criticized.

Many of the panels in the largest Unfavorable category, Criminal, are from an episode in which a judge knowingly commits a sane man to a mental hospital and later is an accessory to his murder. In the second largest Unfavorable category justice is represented as Circumscribed. e.g., a villainous wife deserter securing custody of their son declares to his tearful wife, "It was all legal . . . the kid is legally mine . . ." (November 24, 1940)

With justice described Unfavorably, the opportunity avails itself for the cartoonist to present a substitute for the judicial system. It consists of Punjab and Warbucks. Punjab, even more impatient than Warbucks, declares outright: "Laws so often bind the hands of justice." (August 22, 1935) It is characteristic that Punjab makes this assertion for he frequently assumes the role of judge, jury and executioner. Warbucks, although usually remaining aloof from Punjab's "hangman" activities, seems to lend them tacit approval. He rarely questions the disappearance of Punjab's victims. In one panel he gave open support to these

extra-legal proceedings. In this particular panel Warbucks cautions Punjab after the Asiatic has evaporated several Communists, "Don't let it get you Punjab . . . and don't let their bodies ever be found." Punjab replies, "Quite so Sahib—Those who strike at us never are seen or heard again—It becomes a pattern." (May 25, 1950).[18] Warbucks' warning seems to acknowledge that his behavior is illegal. It is a justice rendered in terms of the situation and follows the schema, "It is written but I say unto you." It is the antitraditional justice of the charismatic leader.[19]

Business success: Hypothesis—That comic strip success operates on the basis of the Horatio Alger legend.

While the number of panels coded under this hypothesis was small, it proved to be one of the most interesting investigated because of the contradictions disclosed by comparing some sections of the sample with others.

In various panels Warbucks states his formula for success, a prescription which emphasizes the need for intelligence and determination. And yet an analysis of success revealed that the most frequent determinant of success was luck.

Merton, analyzing the functions of luck, declares that in addition to being an expression of modesty it has ". . . the dual function of explaining the frequent discrepancy between merit and reward while keeping immune from criticism a social structure which allows this discrepancy to become frequent."[20]

For those who are not as successful as Warbucks the comic strip provides an interesting rationalization. Orphan Annie's friend Spike Spangle indicates

---

[18] The importance of these two incidents warrants their inclusion although they occurred in the weekday rather than the customary Sunday release of the comic strip.

[19] This kind of justice is what Max Weber calls "kadi-justice." See H. H. Gerth and C. Wright Mills, trans. and eds., From Max Weber, Essays in Sociology, New York: Oxford University Press, 1947, p. 218.

[20] Robert K. Merton, Social Theory and Social Structure, Glencoe, Illinois: The Free Press, 1949, p. 139.

the nature of his rationalization. Annie points out:

Daddy took to th' big time! Long chances! High stakes! Big money! and he won! Spike liked small towns—quiet peaceful living—security... Spike worked hard and when he was forty he owned a little store. O'course he owned his own home too, a home, some ground... (October 8, 1943)

She concludes with the thought,

It makes people with not too much happy to think about how much rich and successful folks have to worry about and how much better off they are with a little. (October 8, 1943)

The theme seems to be that the road to success is fraught with danger and thus a reduction of goals provides greater happiness and security.

The emphasis on financial success as a major cultural goal so evident in the real society is also reflected in this comic strip. The frustration created by the lack of sufficient legitimate avenues for attaining this objective is probably reduced by the adoption of an attitude which emphasizes the importance of luck in attaining success and which also characterizes success as a troublesome and dangerous state of existence.

The type of social structure depicted in this comic strip contains a number of conditions favoring the development of Charisma. On a societal level the dysfunction of customary procedures such as those attaining success and justice fits in with the Weberian definition of Charisma[21] as resulting from the breakdown of traditional forms of social organization. On the personal level, Warbucks' omniscience, phenomenal luck and power, so great that even the geni Punjab fears him (May 7, 1950) endow him with supernatural qualities that distinguish

him from ordinary men and which in essence are charismatic.

Warbucks' popularity with his readers despite his fabulous wealth may be due in part to the fact that he uses his wealth and power for such unquestionable purposes as creating employment and fighting his country's enemies. This is in accord with the Protestant ethic wherein wealth is evil only when used for wasteful or sinful living.

CONCLUSION

Although examined separately, these sections are closely linked to each other, for together they reflect the social structure as it may appear to the cartoonist and imply a kind of ideal society. A society in which a favored rural middle class lives in a foreboding frustrating world threatened by domestic and foreign enemies, where success is an unpredictable, hard-to-come-by goal and even the judicature cannot be fully relied upon. It is a world in which the only rational and powerful source of ideas and action stems from the industrial colossus Daddy Warbucks, a leader who once described his aims and philosophy in this manner:

We're not fighting for a new world Annie—not for a new world for Americans—we're fighting for the world we've grown up and prospered in—for the old world of free America. (August 1, 1943)

This research has demonstrated that a measurable social, political and economic ideology is present in this entertainment medium. The import of these findings lies not merely in the nature of the content nor in the fact that a comic strip contains a definite ideology within its framework. More significantly, as the commonplace sources of ideas and ideological viewpoints become recognized, the more innocuous forms of mass media may take on greater significance as communicators of particular points of view.

[21]Max Weber, The Theory of Social and Economic Organization, translated by A. M. Henderson and Talcott Parsons, New York: Oxford University Press, 1947, p. 71.

The Theme of Social Isolation in American Painting and Poetry[1]

Jiri Kolaja and Robert N. Wilson

SOURCE: *Aesthetics and Art Criticism*, Vol. 13, (1954), pp. 37–45.

This report describes a content analysis of American paintings and poems exhibited and published in the middle of the twentieth century. The most conspicuous finding for both arts is the small amount of social interaction—interplay of activities and emotions between individuals—expressed in their themes.

Underlying this research was the assumption that the two fields of aesthetics would display certain similarities of content. Such an assumption is based upon the notion of culture as a more or less coherent system of meanings. Some theorists treat culture as a thing-in-itself which is cohesive because it has a unified, coherent existence independent of the whims of particular individuals. Thus, in one approach to artistic creativity, A. L. Kroeber[2] tends to submerge the question of individual talent or genius by looking instead at broad patterns of artistic fluctuation. The great flowering of English literature in the Elizabethan age, then, to put it crudely, is seen as the result of the time's being ripe for literary experiment rather than as a consequence of the birth of a disproportionate number of gifted writers. When culture is seen as an entity in this manner, then it is obvious that its component patterns—artistic, ideological, or whatever—should bear an established relationship to one another. And so one speaks of symmetry (or asymmetry) in culture, and expects major patterns to exhibit a defined congruence. It would be highly unusual, building on such a theory, to encounter widely disparate characteristics in the arts of one country at one point in time.

If one starts from the other pole, and focuses attention on the individual creator, artistic patterns are seen less as a unitary system-in-themselves, and more as a series of sub-group products which overlap to some discoverable degree. Here the emphasis is on individual or group engaged in concrete activity, rather than on the results of such activity exclusively. Yet this conception of cultural reality points toward the influence of artists on one another, and their possible attempts to incorporate more than one artistic sub-system. Under its postulates one would look for mutual influences; there is clear evidence that in modern America such influences are many. Painters and poets know something of one another's work. More than a few individuals have attained a respectable competence in both areas. This approach to culture also directs attention to the individual artist's social position, and once again it is apparent that practitioners of the two arts share many environmental elements: a lack of popular recognition; a paucity of economic reward; a status as the follower of something less than a "full-time job."

We find, therefore, that virtually any

---

[1] The authors would like to express their appreciation for the criticism of Dr. Robin Williams and for the library help of Miss Etta Arntzen, both of Cornell University.

[2] A. L. Kroeber, Configurations of Culture Growth (Berkeley and Los Angeles: 1944).

conceptual representation of culture lends credence to the expectation that art forms will have some common characteristics in any particular society. Furthermore, studies in non-literate societies show that different arts, e.g., sandpainting and ritual dances, evince common forms and symbols.

Artists are probably endowed with a greater-than-average sensitivity to new ideas and social change. At any rate, they are able to give expression to such things more readily than their less expert fellows. Contrary to one common belief, the artist does not necessarily give voice or color to the most popular themes in his society, does not speak only "for the people." He always speaks first for himself; under special conditions he may speak for a group (e.g., odes to victory in the manner of Pindar). Eventually, if his voice has had maximum relevance, it may be seen in retrospect that he was in fact representing something like a majority mood, although the majority are rarely alert to this at the time the art product is put forth. A global condition like social anomie, the widespread recognition of individual loneliness, may be so pervasive that the artist does actually express a core theme in the contemporary human drama.[3]

Some forms of art may represent popular beliefs more strikingly than others, especially the conscious themes of a society. Certainly the "mass art" of the film expresses current fashions in a much more patent manner than poetry or painting.[4] The latter are products of restricted sub-cultures, and tend to give a specialized fragmentary picture of society, along with a picture of the artist himself. Yet this sub-culture may well be a style leader whose views are later to be more generally accepted. And the

greater skill, the long-run integrity, of the serious painter or poet who devotes his life—often literally—to his work, means that his product has a greater potential of ultimate survival. It may thus come to "stand for" his society when the more explicit and popular indices have been forgotten, and so engender a certain historical truth.[5]

The paintings studied for this research consisted of 228 pictures reproduced in Art Digest during 1950. One hundred poems were taken from Poetry, 1950-1951. Paintings were selected on the basis of a list of artists who have regular gallery representation in one or more of six large U. S. cities. Only paintings embracing American themes were included. All paintings meeting these two criteria were then drawn in the sample. Poems were taken at random, but the limitation to American themes was not followed because it was felt this would distort the dynamic nature of poetic imagery.

The categories of analysis were not precisely similar for the two samples, since the investigators worked independently; the autonomous character of the arts would be gravely "forced" if one tried to make exactly parallel comparisons. However, since the authors were both working from a sociological perspective, and since the agreed-upon major category was that of social interaction, a substantial correspondence of analysis was found.[6]

---

[3]See Werner Ziegenfuss' article i on Art in A. Vierkandt et al. eds., Handwörterbuch der Soziologie (Stuttgart: 1931), p. 326. "The novel has become an expression of the deep crisis of society."

[4]The works of Flinders Petrie, Paul Ligetti, J. Combarieu, and many others maintain that each artistic medium dominates the social scene for a limited period of time. See Vol. I of P. Sorokin's Social and Cultural Dynamics (New York: 1937).

[5]For a fuller consideration of the ways in which art may be related to society, see R. N. Wilson's "Literature, Society and Personality," Journal of Aesthetics and Art Criticism, (June, 1952).

[6]The present research has several methodological deficiencies, and it may be well to point out the more important ones:

(a) The sampling technique does not exclude the possibility that the exhibits we analyzed are less than fully representative. Although leading periodicals in the two arts were consulted, the editorial selection of the journals themselves may have imposed a bias. Few critics, presumably, could agree on what is or is not truly typical of modern art.

(b) The analysts worked alone, so that the validity and reliability of their conclusions are of course open to question in this notoriously difficult area of aesthetic judgment. Different categories, used by different investigators, would almost certainly result in some conclusions at variance with theirs.

To begin with the analysis of the paintings, it was assumed that the degree to which visual reality was distorted promised to serve as a good index of the artist's attitude toward the world surrounding him. Hence for our research purposes a continuum of reality-abstractness was constructed. Applying it to the 228 analyzed pictures, we constructed four analytical categories. There are, in the first place, abstract pictures: by definition, these are all the paintings which do not denote any object of our common social experience. In this category are included also pictures whose denotation of some common object becomes clear only after the reading of the caption. In the second category are imaginary pictures. These denote some objects of our common experience in a realistic way, but taken altogether the whole scene is unreal, impossible. The third category consists of stylized pictures which display a high degree of distortion. They differ from abstract pictures in that their denotatum, speaking in Charles Morris' terms, can be understood without the help of a caption.[7] Finally, in the last category are "realistic" pictures. This category covers all pictures which were not classified within the previous three categories. It overlaps to some degree with the stylized paintings category.

Classifying the paintings into the above four categories we get the following figures:

1. Abstract paintings   50
2. Imaginary paintings   10
3. Stylized paintings   67
4. Realistic paintings 101

These figures show that about three-fourths of the sample denote visual objects of our common social experience, while only one-fourth of the paintings go beyond the limits of such an average vision.

Abstract paintings. The category of abstract paintings was divided into three classes. In the first place there are two mutually exclusive classes, the dynamic and the static patterns. By the dynamic pattern is meant any pattern which stimulates in the onlooker an idea of motion, action, conflict, disequilibrium, etc.[8] A static pattern suggests the opposite of these concepts. Numerically we get:

1. Dynamic pattern . . . . 34 paintings
2. Static pattern . . . . 16 paintings

However, the classification was based on the apperceptive judgment of one analyst only, and is, consequently subjected to individual variations. Nevertheless the numerical difference between the two classes seems to us so great that we feel entitled to conclude that a significant majority of the abstract paintings display a dynamic pattern.

The third class of the abstract pictures contains paintings that possess a potential similarity to reality. Some abstract paintings show certain similarities with common visual reality when the caption is read. Altogether there were 15 such pictures.

Imaginary paintings. There were only 10 pictures that fell into this category. But almost all of them clearly depicted spatial depth. Two captions suggest that an increased sensitivity to time accompanies a great sensitivity to space.[9] In general these visionary pictures show great consciousness of the dimensions of the cosmos as if the authors were aware

---

(c) The discussion lacks a comparative dimension. It speaks of painting and poetry in contemporary America, but does not demonstrate how these differ from similar expressions in other societies or at other points in time. It would be a logical step to extend the analysis toward a comparison with an earlier American period, say the Golden Age of Concord, or with the two arts in contemporary France or England. An example of the added power of the comparative approach is found in McGranahan's study of German and American drama.

Cf. D. V. McGranahan and I. Wayne, "German and American Traits Reflected in Popular Drama," Human Relations, Vol. I, (1947-48), pp. 429-455.

[7] See Charles Morris, Signs, Language, Behavior (New York: 1946), p. 347.

[8] The dynamic nature of these paintings is often suggested by their captions, such as "Pulsion," "Arithmetic of Wind," "Vacillating Progression," "Rhythmic Form," etc.

[9] For example, "Mother of Time."

that they create a new space and time through their imagination. Often this perception is expressed by some visual symbol. Correspondingly, of 10 captions 8 are symbolic in the sense that they refer to something which we cannot directly see in the picture.

Stylized paintings. The stylized pictures represent an eclectic collection containing pictures with different formal tendencies. The most conspicuous fact is their abstraction from any locale. Twenty-eight pictures placed their objects with no reference, and 28 with only faint references to some locale. Hence in contrast to the imaginary paintings this category is almost completely blind to the dimension of space.

Now, classifying the paintings according to the social relationship represented and according to the subject matter, we get the following two tables:

Social Relationship (mutually exclusive)
    No people represented . . . . 38 paintings
    At least one person . . . . 12 paintings
    At least two persons. . . . . 17 paintings
Subject Matter (not mutually exclusive):
    Still life . . . . 15 paintings
    Open nature . . . . 13 paintings
    Elements of sea. . . . . 10 paintings
    Movement or some activity . . . . . 16 paintings

The most interesting additional fact concerning the depiction of social relationships is that the persons, if they are represented, do not interact with each other.[10] The great number of pictures without any people at all seems to us also significant.

Realistic paintings. The category of realistic pictures bears formal and subject matter characteristics similar to the stylized pictures. Of 101 realistic pictures 36 were significantly distorted, thus representing a transition from the previous category. The only other major difference between the abstract and the realistic categories is that the latter has a more or less clear design of locale.

Classifying the pictures according to social relationship and subject matter, we obtain the following figures:

Social Relationship (mutually exclusive):
    No people represented . . . . 41 paintings
    At least one person . . . . 29 paintings
    At least two persons. . . . . 31 paintings
Subject Matter (not mutually exclusive):
    Still life . . . . 14 paintings
    Open nature . . . . 23 paintings
    Cities . . . . 15 paintings
    Elements of sea. . . . . 17 paintings
    Movement or some activity . . . . . 16 paintings

When analyzing the pictures showing social interaction, we find again that the persons, with an exception of some two or three instances, do not interact mutually at all. And again there are pictures whose captions suggest the interest in isolated or spoiled or old objects.[11] Characteristically, night scenes receive relatively more attention than sun-bathed joyful morning scenes.

Hence neither the realistic nor stylized pictures display any of the visual vitality and optimism expressed by the nation-wide periodicals such as Life or Time. The painters of our sample show a different attitude. Their world seems to be highly private and yet not secret. The majority of the captions simply describe what we see within the frame. There are only 15 captions that could be called more or less explicative. And probably only 2 pictures could be classified as symbolic.[12]

Finally as could be anticipated, the paintings do not refer by their subject matter to any social problems of American society. Social criticism, such as painters produced after 1930[13] is absent from our sample. The painters seem to be making statements about the small

---

[10]A typical example is the picture called "The Incident." All four men look in different directions without paying attention to each other. Characteristically, the painters are also interested in old and desolate objects such as factory windows or chimneys, etc.

[11]For examples, "The Lonesome Valley," "Abandoned Mill," "Three Chairs on Sunday," "The Torn Sail," "The Wreck," etc.

[12]These are the pictures, "Shattered Image" and "Sentinelle." The first shows a broken looking glass with a reflection of a face in it, and the second some sea gulls sitting in military order on a wooden ladder. Hence the symbolism, if there is any, is an unsophisticated "concrete symbolism."

[13]See John I. Baur, Revolution and Tradition in Modern American Art (Harvard University, 1951), esp. pp. 21-22.

things of life, without any specific desire to convince the onlooker about their attitudes. To achieve this they use a wide variety of techniques; reflecting in this way the pluralistic character of American society.

Summarizing the categories, let us bring together only the stylized and realistic paintings. They are by their nature similar to a certain degree, and therefore they can be summed up, making up together three-fourths of the sample. Hence from 168 pictures there are:

No people represented	79
At least one person	41
At least two persons	48

The fact that only one-fourth of all paintings show at least two persons is by itself significant. But if we realize that from this number only some 3 or 4 pictures show something that may be called interaction, the almost complete lack of interaction becomes evident.

Summarizing the categories according to the subject matter, let us recall that the pertinent classes were not exhaustive. The stylized pictures were in most cases without any identification of the locale. Nevertheless, it seems significant that "Open nature" pictures (36) appeared twice as often as the "Cities" paintings (17). Is this an anticipation of future deurbanization?

Now turning our attention to the analysis of 100 poems, let us recall that a number of generalizations have been made by critics of modern poetry, although most such statements would be hard to document from a truly representative sample. Among the more tenable, and more frequently expressed are these:

1. Contemporary poetry is "difficult;" that is, for the casual reader, it seems to require an effort of concentration and often a degree of erudition which the reader is unable or unwilling to supply.

2. Related to the first proposition, today's poetry is often laden with associations whose import is so "private," restricted in significance to one person or small group, that most readers find it

impossible or not worthwhile to disentangle the general meaning from the idiosyncratic statement.

3. The modern poet is subjective in approach, describing his own ideas and feelings to the exclusion of topical themes or comments on the public scene. In Browning's phrase, the modern poet is one who "digs where he stands."

4. Contemporary poetry is "odd" or "complex" or "haphazard" in style. That is, its rhymes are not often obvious, its rhythm is seldom pronounced and repetitive, and its language is more suited to conceptual than to musical communication.

The poems examined showed the following gross characteristics:

I. Relationships. The categories of analysis here attempt to determine what kinds of interpersonal content are displayed in the poem. Four categories were employed; they are not mutually exclusive. From the 100 poems, these figures were obtained:

a. More than 2 persons (present in the poem)	30
b. 2 persons (present in the poem)	19
c. 1 person (objectively described)	18
d. 1 person (subjectively explored)	21
e. Interaction (description of people acting on one another)	19

Perhaps the most striking evidence is the paucity of poems in the final category, Interaction. The relationships among and between people are overtly described in fewer than one-fifth of the poems. Although the verse is well-peopled, the individuals do not act upon one another; rather, they are analyzed in a kind of sociological vacuum. It is interesting that poems dealing with a single person constitute the largest category (c + d). The next largest number, found in the first category, More than 2 persons, do not usually deal with groups in the sense of multi-related persons. Rather, they tend to describe a series of discrete personalities or a mass of faceless ciphers. When the small number of poems presenting 2 persons (b) are taken into account, it may be seen that the interplay of personality, the social-relatedness of human beings, is not a prominent feature of the poetic landscape.

II. <u>Themes and Textures</u>. This, the most loosely-defined set of categories, is concerned with the essential content of the poem. What seem to be the objects of the poet's interest, and how may the dominant mood, the prevailing motif of the verse be characterized?

Again, the divisions are not mutually exclusive.

f. <u>Social Concepts and Subjects</u> (interests which might be roughly called political, economic, or sociological; including, but not confined to, the literature of amelioration or social protest) 11

g. <u>Physical Objects and Animals</u> (when the trees, rocks, birds, etc., are the key to metaphor or imagery, not when they are casually mentioned) 31

h. <u>Pictorial</u> (concerned in the first place with sensuous reception of visual stimuli; overlapping often, but not identical with, "g" the above category) 30

i. <u>Emotional</u> (dealing with affectively-toned responses to situations, individuals, and memories of them; criterion of a rather overt level since nearly all poetry is in some sense emotional) 30

j. <u>Philosophic-Ideational</u> (concerned with ideas, concepts, moral judgments, thoughtful examination of life) 52

Here the slight emphasis is on "social consciousness." A comparative analysis of the poetry of the mid-thirties might be instructive, since that was apparently the zenith of "proletarian" artistic effort in the West. Certainly the other arts, especially the novel, also exhibit a striking lack of interest in sociological matters. This is particularly true of the <u>avant garde</u>, with whom it is nowadays somewhat gauche to be seriously concerned with the fate of groups or societies, since the individual is so demonstrably all-important. The large total under "j", <u>Philosophic-Ideational</u>, may indicate several things. When contrasted with "i", it points up the cerebral nature of much contemporary verse. Again, it may complement the current tendency to examine first principles, to search for a guiding (often an absolute) philosophy in a time of unrest and cultural flux.

III. <u>Time Sense</u>.

k. <u>Chronological Cross-Section</u> (the "frozen" slice of time, present tense, which lacks temporal flow or chronological direction) . . . 51

l. <u>Narrative</u> (events following one another in time; recognition of past and future tenses). . 49

This category has at least two facets of significance. Poets seem to be concerned like physicists with the relativity of time. Note the "stream of consciousness" novel, the "flashback" technique, the fact that <u>Ulysses</u> occurs in twenty-four hours only. Time is a coiled rope rather than an extended single strand.

IV. <u>Activity</u>.

m. <u>Motion</u> (objects and persons in movement; active transition; dynamic notion of process). 60

n. <u>Stasis</u> (passive state; motionless; description of fixed entities, static situations) 40

There is relatively a greater tendency to depict motion than immobility. This reminds one of abstract painting where the dynamic pattern was numerically more significant than the same pattern.[14]

Summarizing the analysis of the poems, let us point out the relative lack of interaction. Only one-fifth of all the poems have been classified as containing interaction. Compared with the scores achieved by the paintings in the same category, the poems show a very great interest in at least one person. Nearly all the poems dealt with some person. On the contrary, only one-half of the paintings represented one person or persons.

With regard to the subject matter the poems show the same lack of interest in social problems as the paintings. The poet's story is a private story similar to that of the painter.

A somewhat plausible comparison can be drawn between the philosophic-ideational themes of the poems (one-half of the poems) and the abstract and visionary paintings (one-fourth of the sample). The abstract paintings in most cases contain a conceptual element because the painter creates something that he does not see. In most cases this is a "constructed picture."

[14] Allen S. Weller characterizes modern American painting as displaying a greater interest in internal structure than in surface, in motion rather than isolated objects as such, and in the aerial viewpoint and tendency to look behind the horizon. See his "Truth and Vision in Contemporary Painting," <u>Contemporary American Painting</u> (1952), p. 16.

Provided that the analogy between the philosophic-ideational poetry and abstract and visionary paintings can be accepted, the difference between their proportions in the sample seems to us significant. How should one account for the greater interest of poetry in the philosophic-conceptual subjects? In our opinion the explanation can be offered in terms of the material nature of the pertinent vehicle. The verbal statement lends itself better to the expression of processes and concepts than does a single picture.[15]

As a result of our analysis we have found that paintings and poems tend to possess certain common meanings. Both painters and poets take their point of departure from the individual who is mostly isolated, being perceived without any relationship toward other persons. The poets, however, do deal most of the time with the individual, as their attention is primarily directed toward the man's "inside." The painters, on the contrary, tend to explore the world outside the individual, getting along in half of the cases without any reference to the individual at all.

Contrary to the common belief, our sample has shown that half of the poems use the traditional narrative presentation of events. The proportion of paintings that use "normal" three-dimensional presentation of the scene is even higher, falling within the range of some one-half to two-thirds of all the pictures. Hence this question occurs: Which of the halves may be more significant? The traditional order or the new freely-coordinated order of time or space dimensions? The

students of arts and literature would doubtlessly give a preference to the new phenomena. But a sociologist has to ask whether the proportion of products following the more or less established ways is not as significant as the "new order." The student of social change may attempt to tie the proportion (of the vehicles with changed meanings to those with relative unchanged meaning) to considerations of social structure. Could we, for example, say that when one-half of the cultural vehicles is meaningfully new in some respect while the other half follows the established order, that there is a sign of "healthy equilibrium?" Would it be a case of a society in which a change is achieved in a normal "healthy" way?

The differences in proportion of particular meanings of pertinent vehicles can be traced to the social conditions under which the vehicles were created. For example, the greater tendency of the painters to take account of the common "objective" experience may be partially accounted for by the fact that paintings are usually sold while poems are rarely rewarded. And if the poet is rewarded, the rewarding agency is again a highly specialized and selective group.

Both pictures and poems, whatever their differences, may be evidence of a position of specialization in which American painters and poets find themselves today. It is our opinion that this specialization also brings about the feeling of isolation that is so significantly projected into contemporary American painting and poetry.[16]

---

[15]For the differences between the verbal and pictorial signs see J. Kolaja: The Problems of the Film (Prague: 1948), in Czech.

[16]A bibliographical note: An interesting example of how different media may be compared to a mutual advantage of interpretation was recently offered by Helmut A. Hatzfeld, Literature Through Art, A New Approach to French Literature (New York, 1952).

PERSONALITY AND SOCIETY: THE FORMATION OF PERSONALITY THROUGH SOCIALIZATION AND EDUCATION

The Life Cycle of the Family

Paul C. Glick

SOURCE: *Marriage and Family Living*, Vol. 17, (1955), pp. 3–9.

Within the life of a given family, a host of demographic and economic changes take place that require continuous readjustments of the habits and values of the family members. Moreover, the secular and cyclical changes in age at marriage, size of completed family, and length of life have greatly affected the patterns of family formation, development, and dissolution. In this paper, some of the implications of these several types of change are analyzed with respect to the family in the United States.[1]

In the discussion which follows, frequent reference is made to both "married couples" and "families." The former is defined by the U. S. Bureau of the Census as a married man and his wife who are living together. A "family" is defined as two or more persons related to each other who are living together; thus, if two married couples live together and are mutually related, they are counted as one family. The source materials include numerous reports of the decennial censuses of population, the

Current Population Surveys (sample surveys covering about 25,000 households), and annual vital statistics.[2] In

[2] A selected bibliography of census and vital statistics reports used is as follows: U. S. Bureau of the Census, U. S. Census of Population: 1950, Vol. 11. Characteristics of the Population, Part 1, U. S. Summary (tables on marital status and relationship to head of household); Vol. IV, Special Reports, Part 2, Chapter D, Marital Status: and Vol. IV, Special Reports, Part 1, Chapter A, Employment and Personal Characteristics. U. S. Bureau of the Census, U. S. Census of Housing: 1950, Vol. II, Nonfarm Housing Characteristics, Chapter 1. U. S. Bureau of the Census, Current Population Reports, "Marital Status, Number of Times Married, and Duration of Present Marital Status: April 1948," Series P-20, No. 23; "Marital Status and Household Characteristics: (date)," Series P-20, Nos. 33 (March 1950), 38 (April 1951), and 44 (April 1952); "Fertility of the Population: April 1952," Series P-20, No. 46; "Marital Status, Year of Marriage, and Household Relationship: April 1953." Series P-20, No. 50; "Household and Family Characteristics: April 1953," Series P-20, No. 53; "Marital Status of Workers: April 1953," Series P-50, No. 50; and "Family Income in the United States: 1952," Series P-60, No. 15. U. S. Bureau of the Census, Differential Fertility, 1940 and 1910—Fertility for States and Large Cities. National Office of Vital Statistics, U. S. Public Health Service, Department of Health, Education and Welfare, Vital Statistics of the United States, reports for selected years from 1917 to 1950.

A closely related report was published by the National Office of Vital Statistics shortly after the

[1] A similar analysis, based largely on date for 1940 and earlier dates, was published by the author as "The Family Cycle" in the American Sociological Review, XII: 164-174, April, 1947.

some instances, the available data are fragmentary; in other instances, they provide only approximations to the information desired. The shortcomings are not sufficiently serious, however, to invalidate the central point of the discussion, namely, that married couples now have many more years of family life remaining after their children have married than did couples of earlier generations.

STAGES OF THE LIFE CYCLE OF THE FAMILY

Marriage. The average young man in the United States in 1950 entered marriage for the first time at about the age of 23 years and his wife at about the age of 20. (See table 1 and figure 1.) Both the groom and the bride in 1950 were more than a year younger, on the average, than the corresponding young persons who were entering their first marriage a decade earlier. This decline stands in contrast with the fact that during the entire 50-year period from 1890 to 1940, the average (median) age at first marriage for grooms had declined only about two years and that for brides only about one-half year, according to the best estimates available.[3]

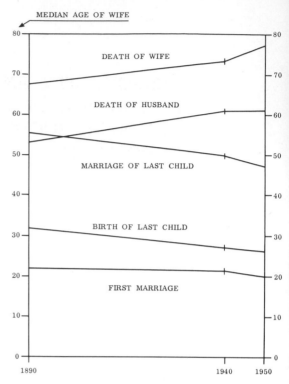

Figure 1. Stages of the life cycle of the family in the United States: 1890, 1940, and 1950.

Earlier marriages have become more common during recent years when married women have found it easier to gain

Table 1. Median Age of Husband and Wife at Selected Stages of the Life Cycle of the Family, for the United States: 1950, 1940, and 1890

Stage of the life cycle of the family	Median age of husband			Median age of wife		
	1950	1940	1890	1950	1940	1890
A. First marriage	22.8	24.3	26.1	20.1	21.5	22.0
B. Birth of last child	28.8	29.9	36.0	26.1	27.1	31.9
C. Marriage of last child	50.3	52.8	59.4	47.6	50.0	55.3
D. Death of one spouse[1]	64.1	63.6	57.4	61.4	60.9	53.3
E. Death of other spouse[2]	71.6	69.7	66.4	77.2	73.5	67.7

[1]Husband and wife survive jointly from marriage to specified age.
[2]Husband (wife) survives separately from marriage to specified age.

meeting in 1954 of the World Population Conference; this report is entitled "Demographic Characteristics of Recently Married Persons: United States, April 1953," Vital Statistics—Special Reports, Vol. 39, No. 3. It contains the results of a sample survey conducted for the National Office of Vital Statistics by the Bureau of the Census.

[3]Averages are in terms of medians and represent estimates based on marital status and age distributions from decennial census reports for

the respective dates. For an explanation of the methodology, see Current Population Reports, Series P-20, No. 38, P. 7. The report, "Demographic Characteristics of Recently Married Persons" (see footnote 2), shows median ages at first marriage for men (23.2) and women (20.4) who married in 1950. These figures are quite close to those shown in table 1 of this paper; both sets of figures are based on census data by single years of age. In Vol. I of the 1950 Vital Statistics

employment outside the home. More and more women now work for a period before marriage, continue their employment after marriage until they start the childbearing period, then in a few years return to work outside the home. Women who are in the labor force have received more education, on the average, than those not in the labor force. In the marriage boom of the last decade, greater gains in the proportion married in the United States were made by the more-educated than by the less-educated sections of the population.[4]

An interesting sidelight on the changing age at marriage is an apparent decline in the gap between the median ages of husbands and wives at first marriage. The average husband of recent years is his wife's senior by about three years, whereas his grandfather was likely to have been senior by about four years.[5]

To simplify the treatment of our subject, we have limited our discussion to first marriages. It is recognized, of course, that many of these marriages

become broken within a relatively short time[6]; in such cases, most of the marriage partners are at ages when remarriage rates are relatively high. In 1948, about 13 per cent of the married women living with their husbands had remarried after the dissolution of an earlier marriage; in 1910, the corresponding proportion was probably about seven or eight per cent.[7] Among persons who married since the end of World War II, about one fifth were entering a second or subsequent marriage.[8]

Childbearing. The average mother who was having her first child in 1950 was 22.5 years old, according to vital statistics data on order of birth by single years of age of mother. The difference between the median age at first marriage based on census data and the median age at birth of first child based on vital statistics data, however, provides an unsatisfactory measure of the average interval between marriage and the birth of the first child. Similar data are used here to approximate the average interval between marriage and the birth of the last child only because the relative error is much less in this case. More precise measurement of child-spacing intervals is now being undertaken by the Bureau of the Census in cooperation with the National Office of Vital Statistics, on the basis of data from the 1950 Census of Population and from the Current Population Survey.[9]

---

of the United States, the median ages at first marriage for grooms (23.9) and brides (21.5) in 19 reporting states were computed from distributions of marriages by 5-year age groups and are therefore somewhat higher. The differences between the various sets of medians may be attributed not only to the use of different age groupings but also in part at least to the use of different types of basic data and in part to the over-representation of highly urbanized states among the 19 reporting.

[4]John Hajnal, "Differential Changes in Marriage Patterns," *American Sociological Review*, 19: 148-154, April, 1954. Similar findings were reported by Calvin L. Beale in "Some Marriage Trends and Patterns Since 1940," an unpublished paper which was presented at a special meeting of the District of Columbia Sociological Society, May 3, 1952.

[5]The median difference between the ages of husbands and wives in their first marriages in 1948 was 2.8 years (See Paul C. Glick and Emanuel Landau, "Age as a Factor in Marriage," *American Sociological Review*, XV: 517-529, August, 1950.) This figure is of approximately the same order of magnitude as the difference (3.3 years) between the median age of husband at first marriage and the median age of wife at first marriage derived from the same census data. In the absence of a direct measure of the difference between the ages of spouses in 1890, it is assumed that the difference between the median ages of spouses provides a usable approximation for that date.

[6]Paul H. Jacobson, "Differentials in Divorce by Duration of Marriage and Size of Family," *American Sociological Review*, XV: 236-244, April, 1950.

[7]Paul C. Glick, "First Marriages and Remarriages," *American Sociological Review*, XIV: 726-734, December, 1949.

[8]Op. cit., and Current Population Reports, Series P-20, No. 53.

[9]Several studies have provided significant information about child spacing for selected areas within the United States. For example, see P. K. Whelpton and Clyde V. Kiser, "Social and Psychological Factors Affecting Fertility. VI. The Planning of Fertility," *The Milbank Memorial Fund Quarterly*, XXV: 63-111, January, 1947. See also Harold T. Christensen and Hanna H. Meisner, "Studies in Child Spacing: III—Premarital Pregnancy as a Factor in Divorce," *American Sociological Review*, 18: 641-644, December, 1953.

For women who had married and had reached the end of their reproductive period (45 to 49 years old) by 1952, the average number of children born per woman was about 2.35. By making use of this fact in conjunction with 1950 statistics on order of birth, it is estimated that approximately half of the women have borne their last child by the time they are 26 years old. Thus, the median length of time between marriage and the birth of the last child is probably close to six years.[10]

Because families have declined so sharply in size, the usual span of the childbearing years has become only about half as long as it was two generations ago. The average mother whose family reached completion in 1890 had borne 5.4 children, with an estimated interval of ten years between marriage and the birth of the last child. She had not given birth to her last child until she was about 32 years old. For 1940, the last of three (3.0) children was born when the mother was about 27 years old.

Women who had never borne a child constituted only about eight per cent of all women who had married and completed their period of fertility by 1890. This percentage approximately doubled by 1940 (15 per cent); it continued to rise by 1952 to 19 per cent for women

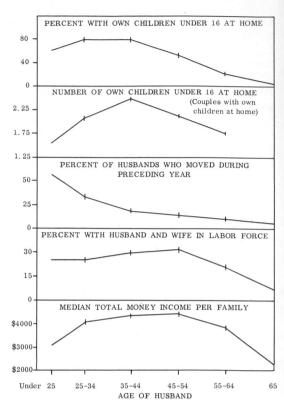

Figure 2. Characteristics of married couples by age of husband, for the United States: 1952.

45 to 49 years old but there was evidence that it would fall sharply for younger women.

During the next decade or two the average number of children per completed family is likely to rise moderately and the proportion of women who remain childless throughout their reproductive years is certain to decline. Changes in patterns of marriage and childbearing which have developed since about the beginning of World War II will apparently have the effect of reversing, at least temporarily, the 150-year decline in the average size of completed family.

<u>Children Leaving Home.</u> From the time the last child is born until the first child leaves home, the size of family usually remains stable. Changes in family living during this period are those related to the growth and maturation of the children and the changing economic status of the parents.

---

[10]For each stage of the life cycle of the family, the ages given in table 1 for a given year are based on experience relating to marriages, births, or deaths as near to that year as available nationwide data permit. The average number of children per ever-married woman 45 to 49 years old in 1952 (2.35) was used as an estimate of the average number of children that women who married in 1950 will have. Women who married in 1950, however, will not be at the end of their childbearing period until about 1975. If they were to bear, say, 2.8 children, on the average, instead of 2.35 as assumed, the estimated median age of mother at birth of the last child (and at the time the last child leaves home) would be increased about one year. As the practice of family limitation becomes more nearly universal, the number and spacing of children may vary more widely with changes in economic conditions. For a valuable analysis of past and probable future changes in size of completed families, see P. K. Whelpton, <u>Cohort Fertility: Native White Women in the United States</u> (Princeton, N. J.: Princeton University Press, 1954).

If we make some allowance for mortals, among the children, and if we assume that the children will marry and leave home at the same age that their parents married, we find that the average woman who married in 1950 will be about 48 years of age when her last child leaves home. By comparison, the average woman of her grandmother's day was about 55, if she lived that long, when her last child got married.

Dissolution of the Family. The combined effects of earlier marriages, smaller families, and longer average length of life have produced a remarkable change in the length of time that married couples live together after their children have set up homes of their own. Under condi-

spouse or the other would die at least two years before their youngest child married.

Because men are usually older than their wives at marriage and have higher mortality rates, age for age, wives generally outlive their husbands. The wife can expect to live much longer after her husband's death if she is the survivor than the husband can expect to live after his wife's death if he is the survivor.[11] In this final stage of the family life cycle, the length of time that the remaining marriage partner survives has not changed greatly in the last two generations, but the expected ages during which the lone survivor is in this phase have been advanced several years.

Table 2. Characteristics of Married Couples by Age of Husband, for the United States: 1952

Age of Husband	Per Cent of Couples With No Own Children Under 18 at Home	Own Children Under 18 at Home Per Couple With Children	Per Cent of Husbands Who Moved During the Preceding Year	Per Cent of Couples With Husband and Wife in Labor Force[1]	Median Total Money Income Per Family[2]
All ages	44.8	2.15	20.2	24.5	$3,890
Under 25 years	42.4	1.51	55.8	24.9	$3,069
25 to 34 years	20.9	2.08	32.9	24.9	$4,030
35 to 44 years	20.9	2.46	18.2	29.5	$4,339
45 to 54 years	49.4	2.08	⎰10.3	30.9	$4,355
55 to 64 years	79.6	1.71	⎱	20.5	$3,805
65 years and over	96.2	[3]	6.6	6.5	$2,276

[1]Based on 1953 data.
[2]Income in 1952, for families surveyed in 1953.
[3]Fewer than 100 cases in sample.

tions existing in 1950, a couple could expect to have about 41 years of married life before either the husband or the wife died; during their last 14 years together, the couple would ordinarily have no unmarried children remaining with them. Thus, the couple would have half as many years of married life with no young children at home as they would have with children at home.

By contrast, conditions existing in 1890 assured only about 31 years of joint survival for the husband and wife; in fact, the chances were 50-50 that one

[11]All estimates of age at death were based on chances of survival from age at marriage. Age at "death of one spouse" is the age to which half of the married couples are expected to survive jointly. Age at "death of other spouse" is the age to which half of the husbands (wives) are expected to live, without regard to the age to which their spouse lives. The difference between age at "death of one spouse" and age at "death of other spouse" is somewhat less than the expected period of widowerhood (widowhood) for the surviving marriage partner who does not remarry; but if age at "death of other spouse" had been calculated with age at "death of one spouse" as the point of departure, the overall length of the family cycle would have been somewhat elongated. United States life tables for all races in 1890 and 1940, and abridged life tables for whites in 1950, were used.

CHANGES IN COMPOSITION AND ECO-NOMIC CHARACTERISTICS

As the family proceeds through its life cycle, it expands in size with the addition of each child and eventually contracts as the children marry and depart from their parental home. Many variations in this pattern exist, of course. Some families have no children; in others, one or more ,children remain at home longer than usual, often after marriage; and in still other cases, one or more of the parents or parents-in-law spend their later years with their children. Adjustments in living accommodations are commonly made in order to meet the needs of the family and changes in the economic activity of the family members generally occur as conditions make such changes feasible and advantageous.

These dynamic aspects of family living are traced in this section by studying changes in characteristics of married couples as the age of the husband advances. (See table 2 and figure 2.)

Family Composition. On the basis of data for a recent year (1952), about 45 per cent of the married couples of all ages combined have no sons or daughters under 18 years of age in their homes. About four tenths of the husbands below the age of 25 years have no dependent children, but only 21 per cent of those between 25 and 44 have none in the home. Above the age of 45, the proportion of husbands without young children of their own at home rises sharply and continuously until, among those above the age of 65, nearly all have none living with them.

The number of children in homes with children rises until it reaches two or three, on the average, by the time the husband is 35 to 44 years old, then declines. Thus, the average family group, comprising the husband, wife, and young children, grows from two persons to four or five and then diminishes gradually to the original two parents.

There are seldom any additional relatives living with the couple while the husband is under 40 years of age. From that time until old age approaches, however, there are likely to be one or more adult relatives (usually grown children of their own) in about one half of the homes and one or more other young relatives (usually grandchildren) in about one home out of ten. When a young married couple lives with the husband's or wife's parents, the chances are nearly two out of three that the couple will stay with the wife's parents. This arrangement is most common perhaps largely because the wife is likely to spend more time in the home than her husband, and because close daily contacts between a mother and her daughter are less likely to create tensions than similar contacts between a mother-in-law and her daughter-in-law.

Residential Location. About four fifths of the persons who marry change residences at the time of marriage or within the ensuing year. Thereafter, the mobility rate decreases sharply as the number of years married increases. By the time couples have been married 10 to 15 years, only about 20 per cent move to another home in the course of a year's time. By this time, most of the changes of residence required to provide room and a measure of privacy for the various family members have been made. Moreover, the difficulty of moving all of the belongings of the family when it is at its maximum size probably serves as a deterrent to residential changes during this stage of family life. The continued decline, rather than an increase, in mobility during the later years of life perhaps suggests, among other things, that families do not ordinarily move into smaller quarters after their children have left home. Data from the 1950 Census of Housing also suggest that the shifts to smaller homes are relatively few in number during this period of life and that most of them take place after the husband reaches 65 years of age.

Labor Force Participation. Half of the young men have begun employment by the time they are about 18 years of age, that is, five years before the median age at marriage. Between the ages of 25 and 60, about 85 per cent or more of the men are in the labor force, and close to half of them remain in the labor force until they reach the age of 70.[12]

Although it is characteristic of husbands to be in the labor force from marriage until the age of retirement, at no time does the proportion of wives in the labor force exceed one half. In 1953, one fourth of all women living with their husbands were in the labor force, that is, had a job (or were seeking work) other than their own home housework. In 1940, the corresponding proportion was only 15 per cent. This striking change has taken place despite the fact that the average number of children that married women under 35 years of age have borne has increased by about 20 per cent.

During the first year after marriage about 40 per cent of the wives have jobs away from home. During the second or third year many drop out of economic activity to have children and the proportion of working wives falls to about 30 per cent. For the period when women have children of preschool age (under 6 years old), only about 15 per cent are labor force participants. After all of the children have reached school age, nearly one third of the wives are in the labor force. Aside from the first couple of years of marriage, this is the period when the wife is most likely to be supplementing the husband's earnings by working outside the home; it is probably also the period when women are most likely to contribute volunteer service to their communities.

Among older couples, whose children have married and left home, it seems probable that fewer wives feel the necessity to remain in the labor force. Furthermore, as the situation exists at present, the average wife who has reached her upper fifties probably lacks the necessary skills, experience, and other qualifications for remunerative employment. Since many more of the younger wives now than formerly have had work experience, it seems reasonable to expect that a larger proportion of those who advance to later middle age in future years will be qualified to contribute to the family income by engaging in work away from home.

In 1952, one third of the families had two earners—usually the husband and the wife. In one tenth of the families, there were three or more earners, usually including the wife and/or young adult children.

Family Income. The median income of families in 1952 was about $3,900.[13] Although family incomes had increased about 50 per cent over the 1944 level, the gain was largely absorbed in higher prices paid to meet the rising cost of living. During this period, the increases have been distributed fairly evenly among families in various stages of the life cycle; recently, however, the older families have shown the largest proportionate gain in income.

For families that are newly formed, there are many demands for household goods to equip the home and, in some cases, to start a business. Furthermore, within a short time the wife is likely to be preoccupied with child rearing and unable to help her husband make a living. During this period, while the husband's work experience is still limited, the family income is relatively low. Within about ten years, however, the family income generally has increased about one third. Between the ages of 35 and 54, when the wife may have returned to the labor force and some of the older

---

[12]See U. S. Bureau of the Census, U. S. Census of Population: 1950, Vol. IV, Special Reports, Part 1, Chapter A, Employment and Personal Characteristics. Also, see U. S. Department of Labor, Bulletin No. 1001, Tables of Working Life: Length of Working Life for Men, on pages 4 and 36 of which are data for 1940 and 1947.

[13]The income figures used here are based on data for all families, in the absence of data for all married couples and in the absence of data for husband-wife families by age of the husband. The median income of husband-wife families in 1952 ($4,061) was about $175 higher than that of all families. The median income of married couples and their unmarried children living at home is probably lower than that of husband-wife families.

children who live with their parents may be working, the family income is at its peak, about 40 per cent above the level for newly-formed families. After the family head has passed age 65, the family has only about half the income it had at its peak.

Partly as a consequence of declining income in old age and partly as a means of being better cared for at that time, the proportion of married couples who live in the homes of others increases somewhat from a low point of less than three per cent in their late 50's but amounts to only about five per cent for couples above the age of 65 years. Some older couples invite a married son or daughter to move in with them for similar reasons.

Concluding Statement. From the foregoing analysis, it is evident that the average family in the United States undergoes many significant changes in the course of its life cycle. At the same time, the pattern of these changes is different in important respects from that which prevailed a generation or two ago.

The effects of most of the changes since 1890 have been cumulative. Trends toward earlier marriage, smaller families, and longer length of life have culminated in the fact that couples now spend one third of their married life with no unmarried children of their own in the home. In 1890, the average married couple did not survive jointly to see their last child get married.

The recent upsurge in the number of births has resulted from increases in the number of women of childbearing age, in the proportion of persons in this age group who have married, and in the average number of children per married couple. The rise in the birth rate since 1940 is less significant for its effect on the current pattern of family development, however, than it is for its implications that more of the young adults are marrying and having a moderate-sized family.

Family Role Structure and Self-Blame

Andrew F. Henry

SOURCE: *Social Forces*, Vol. 35, (1956), pp. 34–38.

This paper reports findings supporting the hypothesis that male subjects who perceive their mother as playing the principal disciplinary role in the family will rank higher on attitudinal measures of self-blame than male subjects who perceive their father as playing the principal disciplinary role.

THEORY AND HYPOTHESIS

Dollard,[1]   Menninger,[2]   Rosenzweig,[3]

and others have suggested that anger aroused by frustration may flow either outwardly against other persons or inwardly against the self. Anger roused by experimental frustration is accompanied by one type of cardiovascular reaction when it is discharged outwardly against others and a different type of cardiovascular reaction when it is discharged

[1] John Dollard et al., Frustration and Aggression (New Haven: Yale University Press, 1939).

[2] Karl Menninger, Man Against Himself (Harcourt, Brace and Company, 1938).

[3] S. Rosenzweig, "The Picture Association Method and Its Application in a Study of Reactions to Frustration," Journal of Personality, 14, (1945), pp. 3-23.

inwardly in the form of anxiety or self blame.[4] Subjects experiencing the type of cardiovascular reaction associated with the inward discharge of anger report their mother as the principal disciplinarian in the family.[5] This finding suggested the hypothesis that subjects who report on attitudinal measures that they would blame themselves will be more likely to perceive mother as principal disciplinarian than subjects who report on the same measures that they would not blame themselves. This hypothesis was tested in the course of a larger study with Louis Guttman to examine certain methodological hypothesis about higher components of attitudes generated by Guttman's scaling theory.[6]

THE QUESTIONNAIRE AND THE SAMPLE

A 34-page questionnaire was administered to a sample of enlisted personnel at a United States Air Force Base. Testing conditions were poor. Eight hundred subjects at a time gathered in a theatre and were asked to fill in the questionnaire during a period of normally "free" time. The large size of the groups and the lack of motivation forced the removal of 17 percent of the schedules which were incompletely filled out. Five percent of the sample was female and these schedules were not analyzed. Another nine percent failed to answer the question, "Who was the principal disciplinarian in your family?" Data here reported were gathered from 765 males who had completed at least a 4-year high school education.

The questionaire included two 5-item Guttman scales—one designed to measure tendencies to blame the self and one designed to measure tendencies to blame the other person. Each of the scales poses a hypothetical conversation between the respondent and another person. The subject is asked to assume that the other person gets hurt by something which is said during the conversation. For example, the five items composing the "blame self" scale are as follows:

> The questions on this page assume that the other person gets hurt by something which is said during a conversation with you.
> 1. Suppose the other person felt very deeply hurt. Would you have much feeling that you were to blame?
> 2. Suppose, in the heat of the discussion, you deliberately hurt the other person. Would you have much feeling that you were to blame?
> 3. Suppose the situation did not show the other person quite at his best. Would you have much feeling that you were to blame?
> 4. Suppose the situation made the other person look like quite a fool. Would you have much feeling that you were to blame?
> 5. Suppose, in the heat of the discussion, that the other person provoked you so that you said something which hurt his pride. Would have much feeling that you were to blame?

FINDINGS

Scales. Guttman's "image" technique was used in constructing the self-blame scale.[7] Since there is no simple summary statistic for assessing the reproducibility of an "image" scale, the conventional Guttman scale also was built using all five of the original items. It has a coefficient of reproducibility of 91.4 with 62 percent of the cases falling into perfect scale types. Intensity computed by the "fold-over" technique[8] provided a rationale for dividing respondents into three groups. On the blame-self scale, 55

[4] Stanley H. King, "Emotional and Cardiovascular Responses During Stress—An Experimental Study" (unpublished Ph. D. dissertation, Department of Social Relations, Harvard University, 1953).

[5] Stanley H. King and Andrew F. Henry, "Aggression and Cardiovascular Reactions Related to Parental Control over Behavior," _Journal of Abnormal and Social Psychology_, 50 (March 1955), pp. 206-210.

[6] Louis Guttman and Andrew F. Henry, "An Empirical Study of Some Higher Components of Attitudes" (in preparation).

[7] Louis Guttman, "The Israel Alpha Technique for Scale Analysis," _Sociological Studies in Scale Analysis_, ed. by N. W. Riley, J. W. Riley, Jr. and J. Toby (New Brunswick, N. J.: Rutgers University Press, 1954), chap. XIX.

[8] S. A. Stouffer et. al., "Measurement and Prediction," _The American Soldier_ (Princeton, N. J.: Princeton University Press, 1950), IV, pp. 249-253.

percent of the respondents fall on the positive side of the zero point established by the plot of intensity of self-blame against content position on the self-blame scale. Thirteen percent fall at the zero point and 32 percent fall on the negative side of the zero point. In other words, about half of the subjects say they would blame themselves, a third say they would not blame themselves, and the rest beg the question. Forty-five percent of those saying they would blame themselves report their mother as principal disciplinarian. Thirty-eight percent of those falling at the zero point or on the negative side of the zero point report their mother as principal disciplinarian.[9] On the "blame other" scale, 25 percent fall on the positive side of the zero point saying they would blame the other person. A third say they would not blame the other person and 42 percent beg the question.

Blame of self and blame of another. There is some positive correlation between our measure of self-blame and our measure of blame of the other person. Of other person. Those reluctant to blame the self also are reulctant to blame the other person. Given this correlation, it is possible that our relation between blame of self and perception of mother as disciplinarian only reflects a relation between perception of mother as disciplinarian and the tendency to assign blame irrespective of its target. Table 1 permits us to see whether the relation between self-blame and perception of mother as disciplinarian persists when tendency to blame the other person is held constant. Since subjects coming from homes broken either by divorce, separation or death of one or both parents are more likely to report mother as principal disciplinarian than subjects from unbroken homes, Table 1 includes only those subjects coming from unbroken homes. Among those who would blame the other person, the relation between blame of self and perception of mother as disciplinarian disappears. But the relation is significant beyond the .01 level among those who say they would not blame the other

Table 1. Perception of Principal Disciplinarian by Self Blame and Other Blame: Male High School Graduates from Unbroken Homes

Would You Blame Yourself?	Would You Blame the Other Person?						Total
	Would not			Would			
	Mother	Father	Total	Mother	Father	Total	
Would.	60	52	112	42	70	112	224
Would Not	38	70	108	28	38	66	174
Total.	98	122	220	70	108	178	398

Note: Those falling at the zero point on either of the two scales are omitted. Self-blame and disciplinarian among those who would not blame the other person, X^2 - 7.5107, p < .01; self-blame and disciplinarian among those who would blame the other person, X^2 not significant at the .05 level; other blame and disciplinarian among those who would blame self, X^2 - 5.8322, p < .02; other blame and disciplinarian among those who would not blame self, X^2 not significant at the .05 level.

those saying they would blame themselves, 27 percent say they would not blame the other person. Of those saying they would not blame themselves, 44 percent say they would not blame the other person.[10] Those who are willing to blame the self are willing also to blame the person. Among those saying they would not blame the other person, 53.6 percent of those who would blame themselves perceive mother as disciplinarian compared with 35.2 percent of those who would not blame themselves. Subjects saying they would blame themselves and would not blame the other person are most likely to perceive mother in the principal disciplinary role.

---

[9] Significant beyond the .05 level.

[10] The 3 x 3 X = 30.4399, p   .001.

Relation between behavioral and normative aspects of self-blame. In addition to our content scales, a projective scale was built to measure the normative dimension of self-blame. The content scale asks the question "How much would you blame yourself?" The normative scale asks the question "How much should one blame himself?" One of the items in the normative scale is the following:

Suppose two men, Mack and Larry, were talking excitedly about something important to both of them. In the heat of the discussion, Mack deliberately said something which hurt Larry very much. Some people would think it right, and others would think it wrong, if Mack felt he (Mack) was to blame for Larry getting hurt. In your opinion, how much should Mack feel that he himself was to blame?

Response categories ranged from "a great deal" to "not at all." Intensity also was computed for the normative scale providing a methodological rationale for dividing respondents into three groups. Those who say they would blame themselves tend to say that one should blame himself. And those who say they would not blame themselves tend to think one should not blame himself. But the correlation is far from perfect. One-fourth of those saying they would blame themselves also say that one should not blame one's self. And a third of those who say they would not blame themselves also say that one should blame one's self.[11] Those viewing mother as disciplinarian were more likely to reveal a discrepancy in what they think one should do and what they say they actually would do than those viewing father as principal disciplinarian. Twenty-seven percent of subjects perceiving mother as disciplinarian report this discrepancy between what they would do and what they should do. Only 22 percent of those perceiving father as disciplinarian report this discrepancy.

Let us define as a "deviant" (1) a respondent who says one should blame one's self but who also says he would not blame himself; or (2) a respondent who says one should not blame one's self but also says he would blame himself. Deviants are respondents who say that their actual behavior fails to conform with the norms or values to which they subscribe. Conformists are those who say they would do what they think one ought to do; i.e., those whose reported behavior conforms with their verbalized norms. Those who perceive the mother as the principal disciplinarian tend to be deviants; those who see the father in the

Table 2. Perception of Principal Disciplinarian by Content and Normative Aspects of Self Blame: Male High School Graduates From Unbroken Homes

Blame Self?	Principal Disciplinarian		Total	Percent Mother
	Mother	Father		
Should Not				
Would (deviants)	35	30	65	53.8
Would not (conformists) .	25	64	89	28.1
Should				
Would (conformists). . . .	57	100	157	36.3
Would not (deviants). . . .	16	38	54	29.6

Note: Those falling at the zero point on either of the two scales are omitted. Self-blame and principal disciplinarian among those saying one should not blame himself, $X^2 = 10.5333$, $p < .01$; self-blame and principal disciplinarian among those saying one should blame himself, X^2 not significant at the .05 level; normative self-blame and principal disciplinarian among those who would blame self, $X^2 = 5.8828$, $p < .02$; normative self-blame and principal disciplinarian among those who would not blame self, X^2 not significant at the .05 level. The 2 x 4 $X^2 = 12.2650$ and is significant beyond the .01 level.

[11] The 3 x 3 X - 49.1868, p   .001.

disciplinary role tend to be conformists.

Table 2 shows the relation between self-blame and perception of disciplinarian holding constant the "should" or normative aspect of self-blame. Among those saying they would blame themselves, 53.8 percent of the "deviants" and 36.3 percent of the "conformists" perceive mother as disciplinarian. Among those saying they would not blame themselves, only 29.6 percent of the "deviants" and 28.1 percent of the "conformists" perceive mother as disciplinarian. We noted above that subjects perceiving mother as disciplinarian were more likely to give a "deviant" response than subjects perceiving father as disciplinarian. The data of Table 2 show that perception of mother as disciplinarian is concentrated in only one of

component" of blame.[12] Closure indexes whether the subject is clear in his own mind or unclear about whom he would blame. An example of one of the items in the closure on blame scale is the following:

Assume you and another person are talking excitedly about something important to both of you. Suppose, in the heat of the discussion, you deliberately hurt the other person. Now it is possible to have feelings that you were to blame, that the other person was to blame, that both of you were to blame, or that the situation was to blame. Is it clear to you against which of these you would have the strongest feelings of blame?

Response categories ranged from "yes, extremely clear" to "no, not at all clear."

In 10 out of the 12 tests, those who

Table 3. Percent Perceiving Mother as Principal Disciplinarian and Self-Blame by Closure, Normative Self-Blame, and Other Blame: Male High School Graduates From Broken and Unbroken Homes

Closure and Other Blame	(1) Should Blame Self		(2) Should Not Blame Self	
	Would blame self	Would not blame self	Would blame self	Would not blame self
Clear whom to blame				
(a) Would blame other	25.0 (48)	45.8 (24)	75.0 (16)	52.0 (25)
(b) Neutral.	45.3 (53)	38.9 (18)	51.5 (33)	27.3 (22)
(c) Would not blame other.	67.6 (34)	48.3 (29)	61.9 (21)	41.7 (24)
Not clear whom to blame				
(d) Would blame other	34.5 (29)	36.4 (11)	42.1 (19)	36.4 (22)
(e) Neutral.	48.1 (52)	41.7 (24)	38.9 (54)	32.8 (61)
(f) Would not blame other.	33.3 (24)	23.8 (21)	48.5 (33)	35.3 (68)

Note: Subjects falling at the zero point of the normative scale are included with those saying one should not blame himself and subjects falling at the zero point of the blame self content scale are included with those saying they would not blame themselves. Subjects were split into two roughly equal groups on the closure scale. The association between blame of self and perception of mother as disciplinarian is significant beyond the .20 level in four of the six comparisons among those clear about whom they would blame. Neither of the two reversals of the predicted relationship (1a and 1d) is significant at the .05 level.

the two "deviant" groups——those saying they would blame themselves but should not. Among those saying they would not blame themselves, there is no difference in perception of disciplinarian between "deviants" and "conformists."

Self-blame, blame of another, and closure on blame. Table 3 presents 12 tests of the relation between self-blame and perception of mother as disciplinarian holing constant three variables——blame of another, the normative dimension of self-blame, and "closure" or the "third

would blame themselves are more likely to perceive mother as principal disciplinarian than those who would not blame themselves. And among those clear about whom they would blame and saying they both would and should blame themselves (1a, 1b and 1c in Table 3) the percent perceiving mother as disciplinarian rises steadily from a low of 25.0 percent for those willing to blame the other person to

[12] Louis Guttman, "The Principal Components of Scale Analysis," in Vol. IV, *The American Soldier* by S. A. Stouffer et al., chap. 9.

a high of 67.6 percent for those unwilling to blame the other person.

DISCUSSION

Subjects reporting that they would blame themselves and would not blame the other person are most likely to perceive mother as the principal disciplinarian. This finding is congruent with our research hypothesis derived from the fact that subjects experiencing the type of cardiovascular reaction associated with the outward discharge of anger report their father as the principal disciplinarian while those experiencing the type of cardiovascular reaction associated with the discharge of anger inwardly in the form of anxiety or self-blame report their mother as disciplinarian. Reluctance to blame the other person as well as willingness to blame the self both increase the likelihood that the mother will be viewed as principal disciplinarian.

Further, subjects reporting that they would blame themselves yet think one should not blame himself are most likely to perceive mother in the principal disciplinary role. The degree of correspondence between questionnaire reports of how a person would act and the way the person actually would act is unknown. Wide divergence often is assumed. This assumed divergence between questionnaire behavior and overt or actual behavior has led to the criticism that questionnaire research yields conventional or expected answers rather than true answers. Answers of the conformist— the subject who says he would do what he thinks one should do—are always suspect. His report of what he would do may merely reflect what he thinks one ought to do in the particular situation and has little or no relation to what he actually does. Unlike the conformist, the deviant cannot be accused of distorting reports of what he would do in favor of what he thinks one ought to do. In fact, we characterize him as a deviant because his report of what he would do does not correspond with what he thinks one ought to do. Therefore, on purely methodological grounds, we would have greater con-

fidence in the report of the deviant than in the report of the conformist. If a subject tells us that he would blame himself even though he thinks one should not blame himself, we have more reason for believing him than if he tells us he would blame himself and thinks that one should blame himself.

There is a second possibility. Our findings indicate that the intropunitive subject is most likely to perceive mother as disciplinarian; further, that "deviant" subjects are more likely to perceive mother as disciplinarian. Is it not reasonable to suggest that a discrepancy between a statement of what one would and should do is in itself an instance of intropunitive behavior? But we are forced to reject this alternative. For if it were the true explanation, "deviant" subjects should be most likely to perceive mother as disciplinarian irrespective of their position on the content scale. This is not true. Deviance increases the likelihood of viewing mother as disciplinarian only among those who would blame themselves. It has no effect whatever among those who would not blame themselves.

Experimental data have shown a relation between perception of mother as disciplinarian and intropunitive behavior on the psycho-physiological level. Our data very tentatively suggest a relation between perception of mother as disciplinarian and intropunitive tendencies on the attitudinal level. The inference of causality from associated phenomena must always be avoided and the interpretation of this relationship—if buttressed by further supporting research— must await elaboration of the interaction between sociological or structural states on one hand and psycho-physiological states on the other. Yet one or two speculative remarks may be in order.

The emotion of anger has its roots in the physiological organism, and its discharge or inhibition is associated with the biochemistry of the autonomic nervous system. But the emotion of anger also is aroused by frustrations inherent in the interactive relationships between persons. And its control also is a function of the system of expectations operative in the subgroup and the sanctions imposed in their behalf. Perception of principal disciplinarian is related to birth order within the family.[13] The eldest child is exposed to a social environment radically different from that of the youngest child. Much further research is needed to see whether the locus of the

person in the family structure is related to the control of the emotion of anger of the person and perhaps to the biochemical processes operating within his physiological structure. If these connections between sociological structures and physiological states become established, the balance of forces within the social system may prove to be one important determinant of the balance of forces within the physiological system.

[13]A. F. Henry, "Sibling Structure and Disciplinary Roles." Paper prepared for the 1956 meetings of the American Sociological Society.

Factors in the Relationship Between Social Status and the Personality Adjustment of the Child *

William H. Sewell and A. O. Haller

SOURCE: *American Sociological Review*, Vol. 24 (1959), pp. 511–20.

In an earlier paper the writers demonstrated the existence of a significant relationship between social status and measured personality adjustment of school children when other variables

*The writers gratefully acknowledge the help of Chester W. Harris on technical aspects of the factor analysis and the computational assistance of Masako I. Yamada and the staff of the Numerical Analysis Laboratory of the University of Wisconsin. The research reported in this paper is part of a larger project under the direction of William H. Sewell which is supported by the Agricultural Experiment Station and the Research Committee of the University of Wisconsin.

Other published papers reporting research on the larger project include: William H. Sewell, "Field Techniques in Social Psychological Study in a Rural Community," American Sociological Review, 14 (December, 1949), pp. 718-726; Sewell, "Infant Training and the Personality of the Child," American Journal of Sociology, 58 (September, 1952), pp. 150-159; Sewell and P. H. Mussen, "The Effects of Feeding, Weaning and Scheduling Procedures on Childhood Adjustment and the Formation of Oral Symptoms," Child Development, 13 (September, 1952), pp. 185-191; Sewell and B. F. Ellenbogen, "Social Status and the Measured Intelligence of Small City and Rural Children," American Sociological Review, 17 (October, 1952), pp. 612-616;

known to be related either to social status or personality adjustment were controlled.[1] This confirmed the findings of a number of less rigorously designed studies which had shown that children of lower social status tend to rank somewhat below middle- and upper-status children on personality tests.[2] The present paper explores the nature of this relationship through further examination and analysis of personality test items which were found to be most highly associated with the social status of the children in the original sample.

Sewell, P. H. Mussen, and C. W. Harris, "Relationships Among Child Training Practices," American Sociological Review, 20 (April, 1955), pp. 137-148; Sewell and A. O. Haller, "Social Status and the Personality Adjustment of the Child," Sociometry, 19 (June, 1956), pp. 114-125; and Sewell, "Some Observations on Theory Testing," Rural Sociology, 21 (March 1956), pp. 1-12.

[1] Sewell and Haller, op. cit.

[2] An extensive bibliography appears in the review article by B. F. Auld, Jr., "Influence of Social Class on Personality Test Response," Psychological Bulletin, 49 (July, 1952), pp. 318-332. Aditional references are given in Sewell and Haller, op. cit., pp. 121-125.

The research reported here is exploratory in that it starts with no fixed notions to account for the relationship between status and personality. Its purpose is to re-examine the data already at hand in an attempt to learn which of the items in the personality test employed in the original study are most highly associated with social status, the extent to which such items are intercorrelated, whether or not any pattern can be found among intercorrelated items, the manifest content of any such constellations of items, the extent to which any factors discovered may be related to each other and to social status, and finally, to relate the results to current views regarding social structure and personality. It is believed that such analysis will help to indicate some possible directions for research on status and personality, and perhaps, may suggest a pattern for the examination of the bearing of other social structure variables on personality.

RESEARCH PROCEDURE

The sample upon which the research is based has been discussed elsewhere; in brief, it consists of 1462 children in grades 4-8 who live in a typical midwestern rurban community characterized by a fairly wide range of social status levels.[3] The social status of the child was determined by an index consisting of a linear combination of father's occupational level, parental educational attainment, and the prestige of the child's family in the local community. These status indicators are among those most widely accepted in the sociological literature.[4] The information on parents' education and occupation was taken from school records; the prestige ratings were obtained from local informants. The California Test of Personality—Elementary Form A (hereafter referred to as the CTP) was administered to the children as a part of the testing program of the schools, under the direct supervision of persons with considerable experience and training in testing techniques.[5] The CTP consists of 144 questions which the child reads and answers "yes" or "no." These questions deal with a broad range of behavior and appear to be quite similar in content to those found in numerous other paper-and-pencil tests of personality. Thus they provide a wide range of test response data for the analysis attempted in this study. Each child's answers to these questions, along with his status index score, were punched on IBM cards so as to facilitate statistical analysis.

The analysis included the following steps: (1) The association of each of the personality test items with social status was determined by simple chi-square analysis, in which the social status scores were separated into three equal-sized categories and responses to the test items were dichotomized into favorable and unfavorable responses. The thirty test items most highly associated with social status were selected for further analysis. For the thirty items, all of the relationships appeared to be approximately linear and in all instances lower-status children were more likely than those of higher status to give test responses indicating less favorable adjustment.[6] The retained items or questions, numbered and stated exactly as on the printed form of the test, are given in Table 1. (2) These items were then intercorrelated using phi-coefficients.[7] The resulting matrix of inter-

---

[3] A brief description of the community and information about the social status background of the children is given in Sewell and Haller, op. cit., pp. 115-117.

[4] See H. F. Kauffman, N. Gross, O. D. Duncan and William H. Sewell, "Problems of Theory and Method in the Study of Social Stratification in Rural Society," *Rural Sociology*, 18 (March, 1953), pp. 12-24.

[5] *The California Test of Personality—Elementary Form A, No. 1*, Los Angeles: The California Test Bureau, 5916 Hollywood Blvd., 1942.

[6] This particular technique for selecting the test items was used because of ease of computation, although it may not be strictly applicable to these data. If one wished to apply a level of significance criterion, all of the retained items surpass the .001 level. An additional fifty items, not included in this analysis because of practical and computational considerations, are between the .05 and .001 levels.

[7] G. U. Yule and M. G. Kendall, *An Introduction to the Theory of Statistics*, London: Griffin, 1948, pp. 252-253.

Table 1. CTP Items Most Highly Associated With Social Status

CTP Item No.	CTP Item	Unfavorable Response	CTP Item No.	CTP Item	Unfavorable Response
14.	Do most of your friends and classmates think you are bright?	No	71.	Do you often have dizzy spells?	Yes
16.	Do you wish that your father (or mother) had a better job?	Yes	72.	Do your eyes hurt you often?	Yes
21.	Do your folks seem to think that you are doing well?	No	88.	Does it make you feel angry when you lose in games at parties?	Yes
25.	May you usually choose your own friends?	No	93.	Do you usually forget the names of people you meet?	Yes
30.	Do you have a chance to see many new things?	No	104.	Is it hard to make people remember how well you can do things?	Yes
39.	Do your classmates think you cannot do well in school?	Yes	109.	Do you have a hard time because it seems that your folks hardly ever have enough money?	Yes
45.	Do you have just a few friends?	Yes	111.	Are you unhappy because your folks do not care about the things you like?	Yes
46.	Do you often wish you had some other parents?	Yes	114.	Do you like both of your parents about the same?	No
47.	Are you sorry you live in the place you do?	Yes	115.	Does someone at home pick on you much of the time?	Yes
48.	Do your friends have better times at home than you do?	Yes	117.	Do you try to keep boys and girls away from your home because it isn't as nice as theirs?	Yes
57.	Do people often try to cheat you or do mean things to you?	Yes	120.	Have you often felt that your folks thought you would not amount to anything?	Yes
61.	Do you often have sneezing spells?	Yes	124.	Is school work so hard that you are afraid you will fail?	Yes
62.	Do you often have bad dreams?	Yes	144.	Do you dislike many of the people who live near your home?	Yes
63.	Do you bite your fingernails often?	Yes			
66.	Do you often find you are not hungry at meal time?	Yes			
68.	Do you often feel tired in the forenoon?	Yes			
70.	Do you often feel sick at your stomach?	Yes			

correlations is shown in Table 2. (3) This matrix was then factor analyzed according to Rao's canonical factor method.[8] Nine orthogonal factors were required to reduce the significant residual variation to zero, as indicated by Lawley's maximum likelihood criterion.[9] Only the first four of these factors were judged to have any meaningful content; since these four accounted for approximately 90 per cent of the common variance among the items, the remaining factors were dropped from the analysis. The four retained factors were then rotated obliquely to yield Thurstone's simple structure.[10] The resulting oblique rotated factor matrix is shown in Table 3. (4) The interrelationships among the factors were determined by intercorrelating the factors. The resulting correlations are shown in Table 4. (5) Finally, each of the four factors was then correlated with the social status index to determine the direction and extent of any relationship which might obtain between the derived factors and social status. These correlation coefficients are presented at appropriate points in the following discussion.

RESULTS OF THE FACTOR ANALYSIS

The factorial matrix in Table 3 may be

[8]C. R. Rao, "Estimations and Tests of Significance in Factor Analysis," _Psychometrica_, 20 (June, 1955), pp. 99-111.

[9]D. N. Lawley, "The Maximum Likelihood Method of Estimating Factor Loadings," in G. H. Thomson, _The Factorial Analysis of Human Ability_, New York: Houghton Mifflin, 1948, pp. 324-326.

[10]L. L. Thurstone, _Multiple Factor Analysis_, Chicago: University of Chicago Press, 1946, pp. 319-343.

Table 2. Intercorrelations of the Status Related Personality Test Items*

** Item No.	14	16	21	25	30	39	45	46	47	48	57	61	62	63	66	68	70	71	72	88	93	104	109	111	114	115	117	120	124	144
14																														
16	140																													
21	233	093																												
25	113	072	117																											
30	141	192	106	052																										
39	247	167	229	068	164																									
45	166	140	140	104	177	254																								
46	037	049	127	058	077	075	051																							
47	127	193	120	057	167	170	181	152																						
48	137	214	156	100	242	212	195	190	216																					
57	225	191	096	060	166	221	229	073	154	249																				
61	082	100	032	066	118	097	047	105	063	137	202																			
62	142	063	046	031	106	097	128	068	052	165	259	342																		
63	092	072	050	036	097	054	093	028	053	097	127	127	131																	
66	140	065	051	026	072	094	077	062	078	128	179	210	258	112																
68	094	165	062	016	068	148	096	062	069	201	206	255	254	121	257															
70	139	127	070	065	120	126	112	059	116	183	267	284	325	129	257	337														
71	082	116	089	035	063	152	046	152	141	150	199	177	270	093	171	214	294													
72	084	126	093	063	050	119	092	094	115	146	125	162	156	105	171	184	252	244												
88	105	084	114	074	055	118	114	112	092	154	113	065	076	053	060	126	134	063	096											
93	176	114	123	101	107	146	079	032	082	183	211	199	231	139	166	196	190	172	107	112										
104	177	159	112	052	106	175	179	077	100	213	235	114	161	128	114	155	144	122	074	169	186									
109	163	303	125	062	254	147	107	135	181	319	226	115	113	046	055	134	136	090	101	125	136	188								
111	156	191	149	088	135	162	137	149	144	272	182	134	128	050	136	175	172	179	138	132	127	244	271							
114	033	083	145	102	033	120	064	133	136	124	096	062	037	020	009	110	052	031	104	138	061	085	115	170						
115	162	119	123	069	135	146	150	075	127	214	257	216	197	127	152	221	208	176	164	181	214	231	227	233	115					
117	085	113	122	099	108	166	119	088	318	181	100	000	072	070	059	114	089	082	086	091	075	117	241	170	217	110				
120	131	123	200	156	146	177	118	152	130	273	183	153	141	047	096	150	144	133	083	105	128	171	160	260	102	211	152			
124	253	164	227	094	097	206	172	113	131	252	196	180	215	111	140	216	189	129	146	160	161	133	172	203	083	226	113	224		
144	100	095	111	027	088	199	111	695	135	156	095	062	089	040	078	095	075	102	101	105	112	005	050	152	117	110	127	064	134	

*Decimal properly preceding each entry have been omitted.
**Items numbered as in CTP. For item descriptions see table 1.

Table 3. Oblique Rotated Factor Matrix*

Item No.	Item**	Factors			
		I	II	III	IV
14	Do most of your friends and classmates think that you are bright?	000	373	000	000
16	Do you wish that your father (or mother) had a better job?	388	-010	005	023
21	Do your folks seem to think that you are doing well?	-087	331	212	-098
25	May you usually choose your own friends?	-004	139	134	-043
30	Do you have a chance to see many new things?	365	049	-070	-030
39	Do your classmates think you cannot do well in school?	019	297	149	-010
45	Do you have just a few friends?	100	273	021	-039
46	Do you often wish you had some other parents?	050	-038	295	053
47	Are you sorry you live in the place you do?	264	-108	346	017
48	Do your friends have better times at home than you do?	255	100	135	089
57	Do people often try to cheat you or do mean things to you?	149	160	-052	232
61	Do you often have sneezing spells?	043	-049	-009	481
62	Do you often have bad dreams?	-006	038	-081	504
63	Do you bite your fingernails often?	106	010	-116	221
66	Do you often find you are not hungry at meal time?	-042	030	-013	410
68	Do you often feel tired in the forenoon?	003	-005	069	459
70	Do you often feel sick at your stomach?	002	-014	035	506
71	Do you often have dizzy spells?	-034	-069	176	422
72	Do your eyes hurt you often?	-039	-045	208	327
88	Does it make you feel angry when you lose in games at parties?	-021	148	161	064
93	Do you usually forget the names of people you meet?	053	164	-010	257
104	Is it hard to make people remember how well you can do things?	104	223	000	094
109	Do you have a hard time because it seems that your folks hardly ever have enough money?	445	-039	065	-003
111	Are you unhappy because your folks do not care about the things you like?	145	083	213	101
114	Do you like both of your parents about the same?	000	000	380	000
115	Does someone at home pick on you much of the time?	069	146	053	234
117	Do you try to keep boys and girls away from your home because it isn't as nice as theirs?	229	-139	395	-001
120	Have you often felt that your folks thought you would not amount to anything?	044	178	195	072
124	Is school work so hard that you are afraid you will fail?	-027	284	095	142
144	Do you dislike many of the people who live near your home?	-038	124	235	033

*Decimals properly preceding each entry have been omitted.
**Unfavorable.

examined by columns in order to interpret the meaningful content of the factors. For purposes of this analysis any item with a factor loading of .200 or greater was arbitrarily considered to make a sufficient contribution to the factor to be retained. To clarify the meaning of the factors, all of the items meeting this criterion were transformed from questions into positive, first-person statements indicating the supposedly unfavorable response in terms of personality adjustment. Thus, for example, item 14—"Do most of your friends and classmates think you are bright?"—to which the unfavorable response is "no," became "Most of my friends and classmates do not think I am bright."

Factor 1. The six items which comprise the first factor in order of magnitude of the loadings are:

Loading	CPT Items	Content
.445	109	I often have a hard time because it seems that my folks hardly ever have enough money.
.388	16	I wish my father (or mother) had a better job.
.365	30	I don't have a chance to see many new things.
.264	47	I am sorry I live in the place I do.
.255	48	My friends have better times at home than I do.
.229	117	I try to keep boys and girls away from my home because it isn't as nice as theirs.

These six items seem to reflect the concern of the child with his family's social status. An examination of all 144 items in the test reveals no others which directly refer to the child's perception of his family's social status. In its negative form the factor manifests itself in the child's concern over the social status of his family; its more favorable manifestation indicates his freedom from such concern. In the present context it may be called <u>concern over social status.</u> That the child's perception and concern with his social status, as measured by this factor, are associated with social status is revealed by its correlation (—.312) with the social status index used in this study. This indicates that children from lower-status families tend to show more concern about their social status than children from higher-status families. Thus one of the elements in the correlation of social status and personality adjustment test scores, namely concern over social status, has been tentatively isolated and identified.

Factor 2. The following items have the greatest loading on this factor:

Loading	CTP Items	Content
.373	14	Most of my friends and classmates do not think I'm bright.
.331	21	My folks do not seem to think I'm doing well.
.297	39	My classmates think I cannot do well in school.
.284	124	School work is so hard I am afraid I will fail.
.273	45	I have just a few friends.
.223	104	It is hard to make people remember how well I can do things.

The six items most heavily saturated with this factor seem to deal with the child's concern with how others rate his ability and achievements. Three of the items (14, 39, and 124) have specific reference to the school situation. Two (21 and 104) have no specific reference, but in the context of the child's usual tasks may well be seen by him to refer to school work. One item (45) has no direct reference to the child's perception of how others view his ability or performance. Again, examination of the CTP reveals no other items which appear to relate directly to the child's concern about his ability and achievements. Since the child who is concerned over the negative way in which others evaluate his abilities and achievements scores high on this factor, the factor may be simply labeled <u>concern over achievement.</u> In its more favorable manifestation it takes the form of freedom from concern over the way others evaluate one's ability and performance. This factor has a low negative correlation (—.178) with social status. This means that children of lower status are somewhat more likely than those of higher status to manifest concern over their ability to perform up to the levels expected of them. The isolation and identification of this factor provides another element in the association between social status and personality test performance.

Factor 3. The third factor is made up of the following eight items:

Loading	CTP Items	Content
.395	117	I try to keep boys and girls away from my home because it is not as nice as theirs.

.380	114	I like one of my parents more than the other.
.346	47	I am sorry I live in the place I do.
.295	46	I often wish I had some other parents.
.235	144	I dislike many of the people near my home.
.213	111	I am unhappy because my folks do not care about the things I like.
.212	21	My folks do not seem to think I am doing well.
.208	72	My eyes hurt me often.

The five items (117, 114, 47, 46, and 144) which have the greatest projection on this factor all seem quite clearly to deal with the child's rejection of his home and parents. Two of the remaining items (111 and 21) may well be interpreted as representing essentially a complementary reaction to the child's rejection of his family, namely his conviction that they in turn reject him. However, the remaining item (72) does not fit the general pattern of family rejection manifest in the other variables which comprise this factor. The factor may be called rejection of family, as it appears in its negative form. The children who score high on this factor tend to express attitudes of rejection of their families, while those with low scores are relatively free from these negative attitudes. The correlation between social status and this factor is —.117, indicating some tendency for lower-status children to reject their parents and their homes. This factor may also be considered tentatively as another element in the relationship between status and personality, at least with respect to the children under study.

Factor 4. Eleven of the 30 items included in the analysis have loadings of .200 or higher on the fourth factor, as follows:

Loading	CTP Items	Content
.506	70	I often feel sick at my stomach.
.504	62	I often have bad dreams.
.481	61	I often have sneezing spells.
.459	68	I often feel tired in the forenoon.
.422	71	I often have dizzy spells.

.410	66	I often find I am not hungry at meal time.
.327	72	My eyes hurt often.
.257	93	I usually forget the names of people I meet.
.234	115	Someone at home picks on me much of the time.
.232	57	People often try to cheat me or do mean things to me.
.221	63	I bite my fingernails often.

All of the items, but particularly the seven with the heaviest loadings on the factor (70, 62, 61, 68, 71, 66, and 72), clearly deal with what are commonly termed neurotic symptoms in the clinical literature. Sick stomach, bad dreams, sneezing spells, tired feeling, dizzy spells, lack of appetite, sore eyes, nail biting, and feeling "picked on" are widely interpreted as psychosomatic symptoms associated with underlying personal anxieties. Consequently, this factor may be termed nervous symptoms. Those scoring high on this factor tend to display symptoms of nervousness, while those scoring low are relatively free from such symptoms. The correlation between scores on this factor and social status is —.236, indicating that lower-status children tend to exhibit more nervous symptoms than those of higher status. The isolation of this rather clear-cut factor provides still another element in the correlation between social status and the measured personality of the children studied.

Intercorrelation of factors. The interrelationships among the factors are shown in Table 4. Each of the factors is moderately and positively correlated with each of the other factors. The correlations range from +.249 (factor 3 with factor 4) to +.587 (factor 1 with factor 2). There is thus a consistent tendency for those children in the sample who are concerned about the social status of their

Table 4. Intercorrelation of Factors

	I	II	III	IV
I. Concern over social status	1.000			
II. Concern over achievement	.587	1.000		
III. Rejection of family	.383	.391	1.000	
IV. Nervous symptoms	.401	.447	.249	1.000

family to be worried also about their own achievements, to reject their families, and to display nervous symptoms.

DISCUSSION

The isolation of four interrelated factors which seem to account for most of the relationship between social status and personality test scores in this sample of grade school children has several implications for theory and research in the general area of social structure and personality.

An examination of the content of the factors and of their correlations with social status indicates that much of the behavior represented by the items can be interpreted as expressions of anxiety on the part of lower-status children. The items included in the first factor appear to deal with the concern that the child has over the status of his family in the community. Such concern is most commonly expressed by children of lower status. The variables comprising the second factor seem to indicate the child's concern about his ability to perform up to acceptable standards, particularly in the school situation. Again, the lower-status child is most likely to manifest this concern. The variables in the third factor indicate the extent to which the child rejects his family and home environment and may be interpreted as a sign of anxiety on the part of the child. Certainly the norms of our society require that the child, especially the young child, accept and defend rather than reject his family. This rejection is likely to be fraught with considerable anxiety. Its correlation with the other factors lends further support to this interpretation. The lower-status child, once more, is most likely to reject his family. The various nervous symptoms making up the fourth factor may be at least in part products of the anxieties of the child. The intercorrelation among the factors and their correlations with social status permit the tentative inference that it is generally the lower-status child in the supposedly middle-class environment of the school who is most likely to be concerned about the social status of his family in the community, to be anxious about his ability to perform up to expectations—particularly in school, to reject his family and home environment, and to display nervous behavior.

These findings do not square with the conclusion reached by some sociologists and anthropologists, based upon their observations of and views concerning the socialization of children in our society, to the effect that middle-class children are subjected to more frustrations in learning and are more anxious as a result of these pressures than are lower-class children.[11] Yet there is considerable evidence from other studies which in general supports the results of the present research. Most of the investigations which have attempted directly to relate the child's social status to his personality adjustment, rather than to infer personality effects from observed status-related patterns of socialization, have clearly shown that lower-status children are less well adjusted than those from middle- and high-status families.[12] Moreover, a study by Gough, of particular significance because it includes cor-

[11] See e.g., A. W. Green, "The Middle-Class Male Child and Neurosis," American Sociological Review, 11 (February, 1946), pp. 31-41; M. C. Ericson, "Child Rearing and Social Status," American Journal of Sociology, 52 (November, 1946), pp. 190-193; A. Davis and R. J. Havighurst, Father of the Man, Boston: Houghton Mifflin, 1947. Chapter 5; and A. Davis and R. J. Havighurst "Color Differences in Child-Rearing," American Sociological Review, 11 (December, 1946), pp. 698-710. It should be noted that recent studies have presented evidence which contradicts the earlier conclusions; their findings indicate that middle class parents are more permissive than lower class parents in their child rearing practices. See E. E. Maccoby and P. K. Gibbs, "Methods of Child Rearing in Two Social Classes" in W. E. Martin and C. B. Stendler, editors, Readings in Child Development, New York: Harcourt, Brace, 1954; R. R. Sears, E. E. Maccoby, and H. Levin, Patterns of Child Rearing, Evanston, Ill.: Row, Peterson, 1957; R. A. Littman, R. C. A. Moore, and J. Pierce-Jones, "Social Class Differences in Child Rearing: A Third Community for Comparison with Chicago and Newton," American Sociological Review, 22 (December, 1957), pp. 694-704; and M. S. White, "Social Class, Child Rearing Practices, and Child Behavior," American Sociological Review, 22 (December, 1958), pp. 704-712.

[12] See Auld, op. cit., p. 330; and Sewell and Haller, op. cit., p. 119.

relations between social status and certain MMPI scales which are similar to the factors isolated in this study, reports results in agreement with the present findings.[13]

Finally, there seems to be good reason on theoretical as well as empirical grounds to expect the results obtained. A general explanatory formulation for the findings of this study might well take the following form: (1) The early socialization of the lower-status child results in the internalization of values and the development of behaviors characteristic of the lower-status family and neighborhood in which he is reared. (2) When the lower-status child extends his activities into the larger social environment of the school and the community, he encounters many values and behavior expectations that are quite different from those of his family and neighborhood. (3) He is made to feel that some of these values and behaviors are superior to those of his own family and neighborhood, so he tries to adopt them. (4) Since these values and behaviors are in conflict with those of his family and neighborhood and since the low status position of his family in many ways inhibits the behavior dictated by them, he experiences tension states which may be manifested in (a) concern about the social status of his family; (b) concern over his ability to perform up to expected levels, particularly in school; (c) rejection of his family, since its members are perceived by him as responsible for his inability to behave according to his higher status values; and

finally, (d) a syndrome of nervous behaviors indicative of general anxiety. Further field research is required to test this general formulation. But at least it offers a plausible explanation for the pattern of results found in this study and is consistent with current social psychological theory and research.

Another plausible and more specific explanation of the results of the present study is that the relatively low negative association between social status and the isolated factors may be due to the presence of some children among the lower-status group who are striving hard for upward social mobility, encountering a great deal of frustration, and consequently are showing significantly greater anxieties than their status peers or their peers from middle and higher status levels who are not experiencing as serious frustrations in attaining their goals. This possibility cannot be tested with the limited data at hand but should be carefully examined in future studies of status and personality.

Of course, status-related anxieties are not necessarily dysfunctional for the lower-status child.[14] From other evidence it appears that the lower-status children in this sample did not generally suffer from serious personality problems. Moreover, if he is to be spurred on to the achievements that upward social mobility demands, it is probably necessary for the lower-status child to experience a certain amount of anxiety regarding his social status and his present performance levels, and even to reject the standards of his parents. The question of the extent to which socially derived anxieties may be functionally effective in stimulating achievement-striving, without concomitantly creating pathological personality patterns, is one of the most important and intriguing problems of theory and research in the

[13]Gough constructed a status scale from items included in the MMPI which differentiated significantly between students of different status levels as measured by other status scales. H. G. Gough, "A New Dimension of Status: I. Development of a Personality Scale," American Sociological Review, 13 (August, 1948), pp. 401-409. He subsequently correlated the status measurements produced by the scale with the scales of the MMPI and found that students of higher status when compared with those of lower status show less tendency toward serious personality disturbances, less insecurity, less social introversion, fewer somatic complaints, and more satisfactory over-all adjustment. Gough, "A New Dimension of Status: II. Relationship of the St. Scale to other Variables," American Sociological Review, 13 (October, 1948), pp. 534-537.

[14]For an excellent discussion of the function of social anxiety in upward social mobility, see A. Davis, "Socialization and Adolescent Personality," Forty-third Yearbook of the National Society for the Study of Education, Chicago: National Society for the Study of Education, 1944, Part I, Chapter 11.

field of social structure and personality. The data of this study do not bear directly on this problem and additional research will be necessary to approximate an answer to this question. An equally important problem to students of social structure—and again one with which this research is not adequate to cope—is the question of how open the channels of social mobility must remain in order to provide lower-status persons with sufficient incentive to struggle for higher positions in the social structure; what will be the consequences for society if the anxieties here assumed to be necessary for upward social mobility are generated in lower-status persons without some good chance of its attainment? This is a problem of great practical as well as sociological significance.

From the methodological point of view, the writers believe that the general design used in this research could be employed fruitfully in the examination of the relationship between other structural variables and personality. Data on such variables as age, sex, religious affiliation, race, ethnic origins, and rural-urban backgrounds are usually obtained in personality studies. Application of the model developed for this research, with appropriate variations depending on the available data and the specific problem, might provide a means of further analysis of the nature of the relationship between these variables and personality. This could result in verification and extensions of existing theories and in the formulation of new theoretic leads for further development of knowledge and research on social structure and personality.

A last word of caution is in order concerning the results of the present study. First, it should be remembered that practical considerations precluded a complete factor analysis of all of the personality test items related to social status or to extract completely all of the possible factors from the more limited matrix that was analyzed. Therefore, it may be that additional status-related factors of importance would be found in a more complete factor analysis of the personality test items used in this study. Secondly, it should be clear that the results of the type of analysis undertaken here are necessarily conditioned by the content of the personality test employed. Another test with a different set of items might produce different factors from those isolated in this study. It might be suggestive to determine the factor content of the status-related items of other commonly used personality tests and, particularly, to determine whether or not factors with similar manifest content can be isolated and identified. In this case, theoretical and research effort could be directed quite profitably to further examination of the functional relationship between social status and anxiety. Finally, it should be pointed out that, because of the exploratory nature of this study and the limitations of the sample, the data, and the analysis, the usual cautions regarding the tentative nature of empirically derived conclusions should be especially observed.

Residential Segregation of Social Classes and Aspirations of High School Boys

Alan B. Wilson

SOURCE: *American Sociological Review*, Vol. 24, (1959), pp. 836–45.

Consistent and strong evidence has been accumulated showing that members of different socio-economic strata, as groups, adhere to differing values which reinforce their respective statuses.[1] Members of the working class tend to devalue education and to aspire to modest but secure occupations and income levels. Through familial socialization and divergent perceptions of their opportunities these aspirations are transmitted to the younger generation. The social inheritance of such values and attitudes tends to inhibit social mobility.

Many investigations have shown the relevance of individual personality characteristics to aspirations. These aspects of personality have been linked in turn to such variations in the familial socialization of children as direct exhortation and positive valuation of education and status, early independence training, the level of adult-child contact indicated by the size of family or the child's position in the order of siblings, and matriarchal versus patriarchal authority structure within the family.[2] Since the familial characteris-

tics which are conducive to a high level of aspirations are more typical of the middle class than of the working class, these variates can be viewed, at least in part, as intervening between the parent's social class and his children's aspirations.

While the association between youths' educational and occupational aspirations and their parents' class position is strong, regardless of what dimension of social stratification is employed, there is considerable variation in aspirations among youths within a single class. This study is concerned with a related matter: the derivation of values from the immediate social milieu—the climate of the school society.

A variety of experimental and descriptive investigations have demonstrated the influence of social context upon judgments, attitudes, and aspirations.[3] Berenda, using the technique developed by Solomon Asch, found that when a child is confronted with classmates giving unanimous, incorrect judgments, only seven per cent of the younger children (ages 7 to 10) and 20 per cent of the older children (ages 10 to 13) remained independent.[4] A series of studies have shown the homogenization of certain social and

---

[1] See, e.g., H. H. Hyman, "The Value Systems of Different Classes: a Social Psychological Contribution to the Analysis of Stratification," R. Bendix and S. M. Lipset, editors, Class, Status and Power, Glencoe, Ill.: Free Press, 1953, pp. 426–442; J. A. Kahl, "Educational and Occupational Aspirations of 'Common Man' Boys," Harvard Educational Review, 23 (Summer, 1953), pp. 186–203; W. H. Sewell, A. O. Haller, and M. A. Straus, "Social Status and Educational and Occupational Aspiration," American Sociological Review, 22 (February, 1957), pp. 67–73.

[2] See especially, S. M. Lipset and R. Bendix, Social Mobility and Industrial Society, Berkeley: University of California Press, 1959, Chapter 9.

[3] See, e.g., R. K. Merton, Social Theory and Social Structure, Glencoe, Ill.: Free Press, 1957, Chapters 8 and 9; E. Katz and P. F. Lazarsfeld, Personal Influence, Glencoe, Ill.: Free Press, 1955, passim.

[4] R. W. Berenda, The Influence of the Group on the Judgment of Peers, New York: King's Crown, 1950; the technique is presented in S. E. Asch, Social Psychology, New York: Prentice-Hall, 1952, pp. 450–501.

political attitudes at college.[5] Herbert Hyman also has suggested that a current reference group, such as one's current co-workers, may provide a systematic factor accounting for differences in values among individuals with common class-origins.[6]

Because of the sifting of like social types into specific zones within an urbanized area, school districting tends to segregate youths of different social strata. Consequently school populations have modally different attitudes toward educational achievement and aspirations for a college education. The proposition that the aspirations of the bulk of the students in a high school district provide a significant normative reference influencing the educational aspirations of boys from varying strata is investigated in this paper bv comparing the aspirations of students with similar social origins who attend schools characterized by different climates of aspiration. Concretely, are the sons of manual workers more likely to ·adhere to middle-class values and have high educational aspirations if

they attend a predominantly middle-class school, and, conversely, are the aspirations of the sons of professionals more modest if they attend a predominantly working-class school?

PROCEDURE

The data for this study are provided by a survey of students' interests as related to their success in school and their decisions about educational and occupational specialization. This survey gathered information on students in thirteen high schools in and around the San Francisco-Oakland Bay area.[7] Five of these schools, located in cities and places outside the urbanized area, are excluded from the present analysis; and the study is confined to boys, since the educational and occupational aspirations of girls are more homogeneous and are conditioned by different factors.

A high degree of concordance (W=.92) is found among the several rank orders of occupational and educational stratification obtained from the census data describing the populations from which the

Table 1. Census and Sample Distribution of Educational and Occupational Variates by Schools

| | 1950 Census | | | High School Sample | | | |
| | | | | College Graduates | | Fathers' Occupation | |
Schools	Median Years of Schooling	Pro-fessional	Laborers	Fathers	Mothers	Pro-fessional	Manual
Group A: Upper white collar							
1. Private boys' school	*	*	*	65%	53%	30%	6%
2. Residential	13.3	26%	2%	51	35	22	2
3. Sub-urban	12.3	13	8	28	23	14	22
Group B: Lower white collar							
4. Metropolitan	12.0	13	5	27	21	8	32
5. Metropolitan	11.1	11	9	21	17	13	38
Group C: Industrial							
6. Predominantly Catholic	10.7	5	10	11	5	1	53
7. Heterogeneous	9.6	4	12	2	2	4	56
8. Predominantly Negro	8.7	2	32	9	7	6	72

*The private school's population is drawn from scattered tracts.

[5] T. H. Newcomb, "Attitude Development as a Function of Reference Groups: the Bennington Study," in E. E. Maccoby, T. H. Newcomb, and E. L. Hartley, editors, Readings in Social Psychology, New York: Henry Holt, 1958, pp. 265-275. Several studies are summarized by P. E. Jacob, Changing Values in College, New Haven: Hazen Foundation, 1957.

[6] Hyman, op. cit., pp. 441-442.

[7] The schools were selected purposively from those accessible which had been stratified on the basis of census data. Confidence in the findings depends upon their internal consistency and their congruence with the body of parallel research and relevant theory. Ultimately, the generalizability of the study must depend upon replication with other populations rather than statistical inference to a population of schools which, necessarily, would also be arbitrarily limited by their accessibility.

student bodies were recruited, and the data from the observed sample of students at the seven public schools.[8] The entire population of a private boys' school, the students of which are not recruited from continuous tracts, was sampled. The sample distributions obtained clearly place this school in the first rank (group A) in Table 1. The schools are grouped, for this study, on the basis of these rank orders, as well as congruent distinctions not reflected in the statistics—impressions of the school "atmospheres" obtained while observing students in the classrooms, halls, and playgrounds. Because of the high concordance between the various dimensions of stratification, the grouping would be the same whichever combination one might choose to emphasize.[9]

Detailed contrasts between the three groups of schools (designated A, B, and C, respectively) in the distribution of several dimensions of stratification are shown in Table 2. The distributions show the gross correlation between these various dimensions of stratification, and reflect the extent of segregation between strata due to school districting along lines of social concentration. While only 10 per cent of the students in the group A schools are children of manual workers, one-half of the boys in the group C schools are manual workers' sons; and while 65 per cent of the fathers in the group A schools have at least some college education, only 14 per cent of the fathers of students at the group C schools

Table 2. Distributions of Selected Variates by School Groups

Variate	School Group		
Category	A	B	C
Fathers' occupation			
Professional	22%	8%	2%
White collar	42	29	25
Self employed	17	20	8
Manual	10	30	49
Not Available	9	12	15
Fathers' Education			
Some college or more	65	35	14
High school graduate	20	29	26
Some high school or less	14	32	54
Not available	2	3	6
Mothers' education			
Some college or more	56	31	12
High school graduate	34	41	39
Some high school or less	9	25	45
Not available	1	3	4
Residence in California			
Over 25 years	58	48	32
Race			
White	98	78	66
Religion			
Catholic	21	27	38
Number of cases	(418)	(480)	(457)

have any college training. Other comparisons show similar contrasts. (It is interesting to note that the families of the students in the group A schools have resided in California longer than those in the group C schools. This reflects the predominantly working-class origins of the recent large-scale immigration into California and the upward mobility of the established urban residents.)

FINDINGS

It was found, as anticipated, that there is a great divergence between the schools in the proportions of students aspiring to

---

[8] The census data use different classifications, based upon a wider population (not limited to the parents of high school boys), and were gathered at an earlier date than the sample data. The concordance of ranks rather than the correlation of actual percentages is all that is pertinent, in any event, to confirm the appropriateness of the ordering and grouping of schools.

[9] The grouping of schools on the basis of occupational and educational dimensions of stratification, and the subsequent pooling of a predominantly Catholic with a predominantly Negro school as working-class schools might be unjustified if religion and race were independently associated with the dependent variable, i.e., educational aspirations. Altogether, 58 per cent of the Protestants and only 47 per cent of the Catholics in the sample aspire to go to college. But within educational and occupa-

tional strata the difference between Protestants and Catholics is small and unsystematic, while within each religious group the differences between occupational and educational strata are large. For example, among the children of professionals with at least some college education, 87 per cent of both Protestants and Catholics· wish to go to college; among the children of manual workers who are high school graduates, 44 per cent of the Protestants and 46 per cent of the Catholics so wish; 34 per cent of the Protestants and 28 per cent of the Catholics whose fathers are manual workers who have not finished high school, want to go to college.

Similarly, the overall differences in educational aspirations between Negroes and Whites are "explained" by the predominantly working-class and low educational status of the Negroes.

Table 3. Percentages Aspiring to Go to College
by School Groups and Fathers' Occupations

| | School Group | | |
Fathers' Occupation	A	B	C
Professional	93%	77%	64%
	(92)	(39)	(11)
White collar	79	59	46
	(174)	(138)	(111)
Self employed	79	66	35
	(68)	(90)	(37)
Manual	59	44	33
	(39)	(140)	(221)
Weighted mean of per cents	80	57	38
Total	(373)*	(407)*	(380)*

*The total number of cases on which these percentages are based is less than the totals shown in Table 2 because cases for which data were unavailable for either the control or dependent variates are not shown. Variation in the total number of cases in the succeeding tables is for the same reason unless otherwise noted.

a college education.[10] Eighty per cent of the students in the A schools, 57 per cent in the B schools, and only 38 per cent in the C schools want to go to college. (See the bottom row of Table 3.) This difference is due to a great extent, of course, to attributes of the parents who serve as reference individuals for

---

[10]Educational aspirations were inferred from the following question:

After I graduate from high school (and, if necessary, serve in the military forces)—
1. ....I plan to get a job right away
2. ....I plan to be a housewife
3. ....I plan to go to a technical or trade school
4. ....I plan to go to a junior college
5. ....I plan to go first to a junior college, and then to a four-year college or university
6. ....I plan to go directly to a four-year college or university
7. ....I have other plans

....
(What are they?)

Responses 5 and 6 were considered as indicating an aspiration to go to college. Since there are several free junior colleges in the area which are open to all high school graduates regardless of past scholarship, poor students can and often do use them as a means of remedying their academic deficiencies. Any student who wants to go to college can plan to do so, unless, of course, he does not believe he is capable of improving and, therefore, has no intention of trying. A student might value higher education without aspiring to attain a higher education. However, differences in school achievement do not account for the differences between schools in aspirations. (See Tables 11 and 12.)

the students. This is seen by making vertical comparisons in Table 3: many more children of professionals have collegiate aspirations than children of manual workers in each school group. But within occupational strata, reading across the table, we see that attributes of the reference group—the norms of the school society—symmetrically modify attitudes: while 93 per cent of the sons of professionals in the group A schools want to go to college, less than two-thirds of the sons of professionals in the group C schools wish to do so; whereas only one-third of the sons of manual workers wish to go to college if they attend a predominantly working-class school, more than one-half of such sons so wish in the middle-class schools. This isotropic relationship provides prima facie confirmation of the cumulative effects of the primary and contextual variates—the boys' own class origins and the dominant class character of the high schools' student body.

It is possible, however, that these differences between schools reflect uncontrolled systematic variation in the attributes of the parents. Within each of these broad occupational strata there is considerable variation of occupational status, income, education, habits of consumption and the like, each of which makes a cumulative impact upon values. The more successful and better educated professionals tend to move to more exclusive residential areas, send their children to private schools, or both; among the "white collar" occupations more prosperous executives reside in the group A school districts, clerks in the group C districts, and so on. Differences of this kind between schools within roughly defined occupational strata are shown in Table 4.

If the apparent effects of the school climate were in fact due to such uncontrolled variation along several dimensions of familial status, then one would expect the differences between the aspirations of the students at the different schools to diminish as the control categories are progressively refined—that

Table 4. Percentages Within Each Occupational Category With High Status Jobs and High Education by School Groups

Occupational Stratum Sub-stratum and Education	School Group		
	A	B	C
Professional			
"Free" (self employed)	59%	55%	27%
Some college or more	96	98	73
Number of cases	(92)	(40)	(11)
White collar			
"Executive"	42	14	3
Some college or more	65	47	20
Number of cases	(177)	(141)	(113)
Self employed			
Merchants (e.g., retail)	51	41	30
Some college or more	62	36	14
Number of cases	(71)	(95)	(38)
Manual			
Skilled	60	52	43
Some college or more	21	14	9
Number of cases	(40)	(144)	(225)

is, as the students are compared within more homogeneous background categories. The refinement of any one or a few dimensions of stratification will result in groups which one may reasonably assume are also somewhat more homogeneous with respect to uncontrolled correlated dimensions.

This question is considered in Table 5, which is designed to show the impact of school norms upon students from more homogeneous occupational strata. This table is not, of course, "independent" of

Table 5. Percentages Within Occupational Sub-Strata Aspiring to Go to College by School Groups

Fathers' Occupation	School Group		
	A	B	C
"Free" professional	94%	67%	...
	(54)	(21)	(3)
Salaried professional	92	89	...
	(38)	(18)	(8)
Executive	88	79	...
	(75)	(19)	(3)
Upper white collar	79	59	55
	(68)	(64)	(40)
Lower white collar	55	53	40
	(31)	(55)	(68)
Self employed: merchants	88	77	18
	(33)	(35)	(11)
Self employed: artisans	73	60	44
	(33)	(53)	(25)
Manual: skilled	75	46	40
	(24)	(74)	(93)
Manual: semi- and unskilled	33	42	29
	(15)	(66)	(128)

Table 3, which can be reproduced by recombining the sub-strata shown in Table 5. But it indicates that the refinement—the homogenization, so to speak—of the control categories, does not systematically modify the effect of the school society upon aspirations. For example, three-fourths of the children of self-employed artisans and skilled manual workers aspire to go to college at the group A schools, while considerably fewer than one-half of them do so at the group C schools.[11]

The education of the parents is likewise known to have a strong independent effect upon students' aspirations. Fathers' and mothers' educations are controlled in Tables 6 and 7, respectively. The effect of the school society upon aspirations is still found to be operative and strong when holding constant the influence of

Table 6. Percentages Aspiring to Go to College by School Groups and Fathers' Education

Fathers' Education	School Group		
	A	B	C
College graduate	88%	73%	73%
	(207)	(109)	(30)
Some college	79	68	58
	(61)	(56)	(33)
High school graduate	74	51	35
	(81)	(138)	(115)
Some high school	63	39	30
	(32)	(74)	(109)
Grammar school or less	32	29	33
	(22)	(76)	(131)

Table 7. Percentages Aspiring to Go to College by School Groups and Mothers' Education

Mothers' Education	School Group		
	A	B	C
College graduate	87%	77%	67%
	(64)	(88)	(24)
Some college	87	54	53
	(67)	(57)	(30)
High school graduate	74	54	35
	(140)	(191)	(170)
Some high school	50	35	39
	(20)	(69)	(120)
Grammar school or less	44	34	24
	(16)	(47)	(33)

---

[11] The largest irregularities—the sons of merchants at the group C schools, and the sons of semi- and un-skilled manual workers at the group A schools—are based upon very few cases.

Table 8. Percentages Aspiring to Go to College by Fathers' and
Mothers' Education

Fathers' Education	Mothers' Education			
	Col.	H.S.	Less than H.S.	Total*
Some college or more	85%	72%	53%	79%
	(309)	(149)	(36)	(495)
High school graduate	71	50	37	51
	(65)	(191)	(75)	(334)
Some high school or less	40	38	31	35
	(50)	(154)	(239)	(445)
Total*	77	53	35	56
	(430)	(501)	(355)	(1311)

*Marginal totals include those cases for which information is unavailable on the respective control variates.

either parent's education. A comparison of these two tables does not substantiate the notion that the mother's education is more influential than the father's upon the high school boy's educational aspirations. Hyman suggests the importance of the woman's role in the transmission of educational values on the basis of the fact that youths and adult women both recommended college more frequently than adult men.[12] Perhaps women directly exhort educational values more frequently, independently of their own educational background. But these data do not suggest that the mother's role is

more significant than the father's with respect to the more subtle and indirect effects of the parents' own education.

Looking more closely at the effect on educational aspirations of the interaction between the education of the two parents, it can be seen, in Table 8, that each makes an independent and cumulative impact of about the same degree. The only asymmetrical effect lies in the extreme combinations: if the father has not completed high school it makes little difference whether the mother has gone to college or not, but it makes considerable difference whether or not the father has

Table 9. Percentages Aspiring to Go to College by School Groups Within
Educational and Occupational Strata

Fathers' Occupation	Mothers' Education						
	College Graduate		High School Graduate			Less than High School	
	School Group		School Group			School Group	
Fathers' Occupation	A	B	A	B	C	B	C
College graduate							
Professional	92%	78%	—	—	—	—	—
	(52)	(18)	—	—	—	—	—
Upper white collar	86	94	83%	62%	—	—	—
	(57)	(17)	(24)	(13)	—	—	—
High school graduate							
Upper white collar	—	—	85	65	—	—	—
	—	—	(20)	(20)	—	—	—
Lower white collar	—	—	—	50	20%	—	—
	—	—	—	(10)	(15)	—	—
Manual	—	—	60	54	32	32%	35%
	—	—	(10)	(26)	(25)	(25)	(48)
Less than high school							
Lower white collar	—	—	—	60	27	—	—
	—	—	—	(10)	(15)	—	—
Manual	—	—	—	—	—	36	26
	—	—	—	—	—	(45)	(86)

[12]Hyman, op. cit., pp. 431-432.

gone to college even though the mother has not completed high school. Since these extreme combinations are the rarest, however, their effects are the least reliable.

The possibilities of holding several variates constant simultaneously are limited in tabular analysis, due to the rapid reduction of the number of cases which can be matched. The homogenization of categories is carried as far as is feasible within the limitations of the size of our sample in Table 9. In this table the educational and occupational attributes of the parents are simultaneously held constant while comparisons are made between the educational aspirations of students in different groups of schools. While the reduced numbers of cases makes these percentages less reliable, of the nine comparisons available,[13] seven clearly substantiate the hypothesis, while the two reversals are small. The average percentile differences between adjacent schools are as great within these homogeneous groups as in the coarser groupings of Tables 3, 6, and 7, where the fathers' occupations and parents' education are controlled separately. The only comparison available for all three school groups is among the sons of manual workers both of whose parents have a high school education. Among these boys, 60 per cent in the A schools, 54 per cent in the B schools, and 32 per cent in the C schools seek to go to college.

ACHIEVEMENT AND EDUCATIONAL VALUES

Educational values and achievement interact and reinforce one another. On the one hand, those who devalue education are poorly motivated to achieve; on the other, those who have been poor achievers will defensively devalue education, and perhaps realistically, modify their educational aspirations. A much

Table 10. Percentages Attaining High ("A" or "B") Median Grades by School Groups and Fathers' Occupations

Fathers' Occupation	School Group		
	A	B	C
Professional	66%	50%	18%
	(91)	(40)	(11)
White collar	50	28	18
	(176)	(138)	(111)
Self employed	51	35	11
	(71)	(95)	(37)
Manual	35	13	11
	(40)	(141)	(221)
Weighted mean of per cents	52	27	13
	(378)	(414)	(380)

higher proportion of students in the middle-class schools obtain "A's" and "B's" than do those in the working-class schools. In addition to the influence of the family and school norms upon achievement, with which hitherto we have been concerned, there is the possibility that teachers grade more liberally at the middle-class schools—either for entirely extraneous reasons or, more plausibly, because the parents' expectations and the students' aspirations place pressure on them to raise the grading curve.

If the latter interpretation is sound, then the students who are high achievers of the group C schools will be higher achievers on an absolute basis, than those at the group A schools. But, holding grades constant and reading across the rows in Table 11, we see that even under these conditions more students receiving the same grade in the middle-class schools want to go to college.[14] Virtu-

Table 11. Percentages Aspiring to Go to College by School Groups and Grades

Median Academic Grade	School Group		
	A	B	C
"A"	98%	96%	78%
	(60)	(24)	(9)
"B"	90	89	72
	(152)	(90)	(46)
"C"	72	55	41
	(145)	(207)	(184)
"D"	43	21	25
	(47)	(120)	(169)

---

[13] Percentages are shown in Table 9 for each classification where there are ten or more cases in two school groups on which to base a comparison. The empty cells and categories not shown have fewer than ten cases.

[14] The number of cases on which these percentages are based reflects the fact, shown in Table 10, that far fewer students do receive "A's" at the group C schools.

Table 12. Percentages Aspiring to Go to College
By School Groups and IQ Scores

	School Group		
IQ Score	A	B	C
120+	96%	83%	33%
	(100)	(81)	(18)
110-119	93	72	51
	(128)	(108)	(53)
110-109	76	52	41
	(87)	(89)	(82)
90-99	47	24	35
	(30)	(63)	(68)
89-	25	29	25
	(12)	(69)	(111)

ally all of those who receive "A's" at the group A schools want to go to college, but only three-fourths of the "A" students at the group C schools want to go to college.[15]

Using IQ scores as an index of achievement which is standardized across school lines, and thus eliminating the possibility of systematic differences between school grading policies, we see in Table 12 that high achievers are less likely to wish to go to college if they attend a working-class school and, conversely, that low achievers are more apt to want to go to college if they attend a middle-class school.[16] Almost all of the students with IQ scores over 120 at the group A schools hope to go to college, whereas only one third of those with such scores at the group C schools want to do so. Those who adhere to the interpretation of intelligence test scores as more or less valid measures of innate capacity will see the "waste" of talent implicit in the horizontal contrasts in Table 12, from the stance of the prevalent concern with the conservation of talent.

Comparing the effect of the school climate upon grades and upon educational aspirations in Tables 10 and 3, we can

see that the devaluation of education in the working-class schools affects academic achievement as much as it is reflected in educational aspirations. In fact, it adversely affects the achievement of the sons of professional and white-collar workers more than it does their aspirations.

TANGENTIAL CONFIRMATION

The imputation of the variation in educational aspirations and behavior between schools to the "moral force" of the normative values within the school society is of course inferential.[17] This interpretation has been argued, up to this point, by holding constant other factors known to affect educational attitudes and attributing the residual difference to the hypothetical factor. The hypothesis, moreover, is theoretically congruent with a considerable accumulation of research on small groups, studies of peer-group influences, and of the differential effects of contrasting community structures: it has been shown that the perception of the opportunity for upward mobility by lower-strata youth is facilitated by the economic and occupational heterogeneity of the community.[18] Yet, if Occam's razor is to be scrupulously applied against the contextual hypothesis, it might be argued that, however homogeneous the students' familial backgrounds may be in terms of all available external indices, those working-class families living in predominantly middle-class districts are showing "anticipatory socialization" in their values and are inculcating them in their children.

While the latter interpretation is reasonable, it is not so persuasive to argue the corollary that middle-class families would act to depress the aspirations of their children if they lived in a predominantly working-class neighborhood. "... inherent in the very existence of a

[15]Note that the aspirations of the students who receive high grades at the group B schools resemble those of the students of the group A schools, while those who get low grades have aspirations similar to those students at the group C schools. This suggests the possibility of two dominant norms in the intermediate schools providing alternative normative references.

[16]This relationship disappears among those with IQ's below 89—that is, those for whom collegiate aspirations are unrealistic.

[17]This requires no apology—the step from data to a theoretical proposition is always inferential. One does not see a cause.

[18]Lipset and Bendix, Social Mobility . . . , op. cit., pp. 220-224.

stratification order, of higher and lower valuations of social positions, is the motivation to move up in the social structure if one's position is low, or to retain one's position if it is high."[19] It is plausible to assume that middle-class youth, even when living in a predominantly working-class neighborhood, will be stimulated by their families toward educational diligence and to aspire to high-status occupations. The fact that the aspiration of these children is depressed when they attend a working-class school is more compelling evidence for the effect of the school milieu and peer-group norms than is the fact of the upward mobility of working-class youths in middle-class schools.

It has been reported frequently that students from middle-class families are generally over-selected for peer-group leadership positions. But "in order to become a leader ... one must share prevailing opinions and attitudes."[20] This view has led to a presumption of the universality of upward aspirations. It was found in the present study, however, that one-half of those who had held peer-group offices in the group C schools were children of manual workers, while only eight per cent of those in the group A schools were the sons of manual workers (see Table 13). The distribution of peer-group offices among occupational

strata is very close to that of the student bodies at large at each school group (as can be seen by comparing Table 13 with the first distribution in Table 2). But, consequently, the leaders who reflect, express, and mold the attitudes of the school society reinforce and extend the pre-existing differences in group characteristics.

THE IMPACT OF SCHOOL NORMS UPON OTHER VALUES

Sociologists concerned with intergenerational mobility and the formation of social attitudes might well direct more attention to the investigation of contextual variables—attributes of membership groups which serve as references during the adolescent period of socialization—particularly to the society of the school. While the importance of both the family and the peer-group in the development of the economic and political values of the adolescent have been pointed out, most investigations have concentrated upon the influence of the family.[21] That the influence of the school climate is not confined to educational aspirations is shown by brief explorations, presented in Tables 14 and 15, into the differences between schools in occupational aspirations and in

Table 13. Distribution of Peer-Group Offices Among Occupational Strata by Schools

Fathers' Occupation	School Group		
	A	B	C
Professional	25%	9%	3%
White collar	49	38	40
Self employed	18	29	7
Manual	8	24	50
Number of cases*	154	160	92

*Percentages are based on the number of students who have held some peer-group office—either within the school, such as team captain, student council member or class president, or outside of school, as an officer of "De Molay," "Teen-age Club," or similar group.

Table 14. Percentages Aspiring to Professional Occupation by School Groups and Fathers' Occupation

Fathers' Occupation	School Group		
	A	B	C
Professional	78%	60%	60%
	(81)	(35)	(10)
White collar	61	37	35
	(160)	(120)	(31)
Self employed	44	47	23
	(62)	(79)	(106)
Manual	44	31	27
	(36)	(121)	(198)
Weighted mean of per cents	60	39	30
	(339)	(355)	(345)

[19]Ibid., p. 203

[20]Katz and Lazarsfield, op. cit., p. 52.

[21]Richard Centers, "Children of the New Deal: Social Stratification and Adolescent Attitudes," in Class, Status and Power, op. cit., pp. 359-370; S. M. Lipset et al., "The Psychology of Voting: An Analysis of Political Behavior," in G. Lindsey, editor, Handbook of Social Psychology, Cambridge: Addison-Wesley, 1954, Vol. II, pp. 1124-1175.

Table 15. Percentages Expressing Preference for
the Republican Party by School Groups and
Fathers' Occupations

Fathers' Occupation	School Group		
	A	B	C
Professional	81%	71%	33%
	(73)	(31)	(9)
White collar	72	64	36
	(120)	(98)	(72)
Self employed	80	62	39
	(56)	(68)	(23)
Manual	50	32	24
	(26)	(107)	(161)
Weighted mass of per cents	74	53	29
	(275)*	(304)*	(265)*

*Percentages are based on the number of students expressing preference for the Republican or Democratic party, omitting those who indicated "other," "none," or failed to respond.

CONCLUSION

Whether the modification of attitudes by the normative climate of the school society persists or a reversion toward familial norms in later life takes place cannot be determined on the basis of static comparisons. But certainly the student's high school achievement and his decision for or against college entrance have irreversible consequences in channeling him into the stream of economic and social life, and in biasing the probability of future intimate contact with countervailing reference groups.

The Supreme Court has found that, even though the "tangible" provisions of schools are the same, schools segregated along racial lines are inherently unequal. The "sense of inferiority affects the motivation of the child to learn." The de facto segregation brought about by concentrations of social classes in cities results in schools with unequal moral climates which likewise affect the motivation of the child, not necessarily by inculcating a sense of inferiority, but rather by providing a different ethos in which to perceive values.

political preferences. These tables provide prima facie evidence, comparable to that of Table 3, suggesting that the dominant climate of opinion within a school makes a significant impact upon students' occupational goals and their political party preferences.

Personalities of Public and Private School Boys

Charles McArthur

SOURCE: *Harvard Educational Review*, Vol. 24, (1954), pp. 256–61.

We are already warned by the Chicago group of sociologists[1] that we unrealis-

[1]A. Davis, Social Class Influences Upon Learning. Cambridge: Harvard Univ. Press, 1948; K. Eells, "Some Implications for School Practices of the Chicago Studies of Cultural Bias in Intelligence Tests." Harvard Educ. Rev., 1953, 23, No. 4, 284-297; A. A. Hollingshead, Elmstown's Youth. New York: John Wiley & Sons, 1949; W. S. Warner, R. J. Havighurst, and M. R. Loeb, Who Shall Be Educated? New York: Harper & Bros., 1944.

tically impose our middle-class values upon students we educate, test, and counsel who come from the lower class. May not the same middle-class bias encroach upon our teaching, testing, and counseling of upper-class students as well? Not rarely, an Ivy college counselor finds a Boston "white shoe boy" waiting in the outer office, seated next to the son of an unemployed Kansas laborer, the pair of them showing in tableau both the permeability and the reality of American social class. What does the counselor know about the differences between these two students? Will the same tests provide useful information about both? Should they be judged against separate norms? Or, perhaps, is it best in one case to use no tests at all? The purpose of this paper is to bring together scattered observations and fragmentary theories from which these questions may one day be answered.

Public school students consistently achieve higher college grades than do boys with a private school background. At Harvard, the Dean of the College[2] remarked that when the depression raised all grades appreciably, it was unable to disturb this public-private school contrast. Nor can we accept the usual polite rationalizations by which deans explain away this difference[3], Seltzer[4] matched groups on scholastic aptitude and still found the public school grades higher. At Yale[5] it is also true that, "intelligence held constant, college grades showed a consistent inverse relation to 'economic advantage.'" Similar reports[6] came from seven other colleges. What is more, when Dyer[7] set up excellent rules for predicting freshman grades at Harvard, he found that public and private school grades were not only different in value but had to be predicted from different formulae.

What other differences exist? Novelists

like the two Marquands[8] and Weller[9] dramatize the fact that private and public school boys have different values. No systematic theory from social science helps us to understand these differences, however. The most relevant ideas are provided by Dr. Florence Kluckhohn's[10] description of American subcultures. Like most social scientists[11] she feels that the dominant value system is the "official" American "success culture," radiating from a focus somewhere in the lower-middle class. Dominant values emphasize the Future as the important time, the Individual as the important person, and Doing as the important aspect of personality. However, many alternative values are permitted, even required, in our very complex society: consider those held by corner gangs, intellectuals—or women! The alternative system relevant to the present problem is one radiating from some point in the Eastern upper class. There the time most valued is the Past, the persons who matter bear a Lineal relation to oneself, and Being is the most valued aspect of the person.

Dr. Kluckhohn's contrast of Doing vs. Being orientations illuminates other observations such as Jersild's[12] public school children who checked "studies" as their "greatest problem" and private

[2]Reports of the president and treasurer of Harvard College, 1939-40. Official Register of Harvard University, 1941, 38 (20), 140.

[3]Reports of the president of Harvard College and reports of departments, 1947-8. Official Register of Harvard University, 1950, 47 (12), 152-153.

[4]C. C. Seltzer, "Academic Success in College of Public and Private School Students: Freshman Year at Harvard." J. Psychol., 1948, 25, 419-431.

[5]A. B. Crawford, Incentives to Study. New Haven: Yale Univ. Press, 1929.

[6]P. Harris, "The Relation of College Grades to Some Factors Other Than I. Q." Arch. Psychol., New York, 1931, 20, No. 131; P. Harris, "Factors Affecting College Grades: a Review of the Literature: 1930-1937." Psychol. Bull., 1940, 37, 125-151.

[7]H. S. Dyer, The Proper Use of Objective Test Scores. Cambridge: Office of Tests, Harvard College, 1951.

[8]J. P. Marquand, The Late George Apley. Boston: Little Brown & Co., 1937; J. Phillips, (Pseud.), The Second Happiest Day. New York: Harper & Bros., 1953.

[9]G. A. Weller, Not to Eat, Not for Love. New York: H. Smith & R. Haas, 1933.

[10]Florence R. Kluckhohn, "Dominant and Substitutive Profiles of Cultural Orientations: their Significance for the Analysis of Social Stratification." Social Forces, 1950, 28, 376-393; Florence R. Kluckhohn, "Dominant and Variant Value Orientations." In C. Kluckhohn, and H. A. Murray, (Ed.), Personality in Nature, Society, and Culture. (2nd Ed.) New York: Alfred A. Knopf, 1953, pp. 342-366.

[11]A. Davis, op. cit.; K. Eells, op. cit.; G. Gorer, The American People, New York: Norton, 1948; A. B. Hollingshead, op. cit.; Margaret Mead, Male and Female, New York: William Morrow, 1950.

[12]A. T. Jersild, F. V. Markey, and C. J. Jersild, "Children's Fears, Dreams, Wishes, Daydreams, Likes, Dislikes, Pleasant and Unpleasant Memories." Child Develop. Monogr., 1933, No. 12.

school children who checked various items having to do with their "personalities." To measure oneself by achievement must feel quite different from the way it feels to measure oneself by one's acceptability. Not that the latter cannot lead to as much anxious conformity as the former. "Honey," said Kitty Foyle's father in a novel[13] studded with little essays on mores, "those folks are so pedigreed they'd be ashamed to press their pants. They hire someone to drive the Rolls for a year before they use it, so it won't look too fresh." More realistically, Marquand[14] has two generations of Apleys advise their sons to "bear in mind that the friendships and associations which you are now making at Harvard will be with you for the rest of your life," and that "your first object must be to 'make' the Club . . . everything else, even including your studies, should be secondary."

Being and Doing values define quite different meanings of education. At Harvard, more Doing-oriented boys make an A in Chem 20, while more Being-oriented boys settle for "Gentlemen's C's." Often enough, Doing boys enter Harvard with a clear choice of major—usually pretechnical—and, often enough, Being boys come with a vague choice—usually in the Humanities. It was a Doing boy whose uncle insisted that be become a pre-Med because "scientists only make thirty dollars a week" and a Being boy whose grandfather settled on Classics for the boy's major "because Classics prepares one for anything." That reminds us of Marquand's[15] creation, John Grey, who felt that, "Going to a lawyer is like going to a doctor. No matter how well or how long you know them personally, they always put you at a disadvantage with their specialized knowledge." The juxtaposition of social acquaintance (Being) and specializing (Doing) is very nice there and not unlike the plaints heard from faculty members who resent the sciences and would, like John Grey, "rather have a good dry chat with a clergyman," because "God and sin are sort of in the public domain." The quintessence of this Being orientation to education is Marquand's favorite quotation, which he puts in the mouth of the fictitious George Apley[16] and later himself uses in a speech[17] at a Harvard commencement. According to Marquand, it was the late Justice Holmes who felt that facts should be secondary to "an aroma of high feeling" at Harvard. All this might lead, in one's wilder speculative moments, to toying with the theory that General Education simply institutionalizes private school values

More practically, the counseling psychologist must wonder how Doing and Being values alter a boy's post-college career. There is a parallel notion of the industrial sociologists Miller and Form[18] whose typology of work histories included two types, called Ambitious and Responsive Careers. When upward mobility is steady, both between and within generations, they speak of Ambitious Careers, but we may also see the effects of Doing orientation. When mobility is absent or irrelevant, so that one generation simply reproduces the standards of another, they speak of Responsive Careers, but we may also speculate upon the operation of a Being orientation. Responsive Careers are found at many points in our society (e.g., the lower class), but they are also common among members of the Eastern upper class. Indeed, it has been argued that propriety limits a young Brahmin to but three choices: he may become a Doctor, a Lawyer, or a Trustee.

The relevance of testing for "vocational interests" should therefore vary according to whether the subject is pursuing an Ambitious or Responsive career. Sometimes it does. The Study of

[13]C. Morley, Kitty Foyle. New York: The New American Library, 1944.

[14]J. P. Marquand, op. cit.

[15]J. P. Marquand, Point of no Return. Boston: Little Brown & Co., 1949.

[16]J. P. Marquand, The Late George Apley, op. cit.

[17]J. P. Marquand, "A Confession of an Educated Man." Harvard Alumni Bull., 1953, 55, No. 18, 755.

[18]D. C. Miller, and W. H. Form, Industrial Sociology. New York: Harper & Bros., 1951.

Adult Development[19] followed for fifteen years the careers of students who had taken the Strong Vocational Interest Blank. For public school boys the test predicted both choice of job and subsequent contentment. For private school boys it predicted nothing at all! The way[20] to predict private school boys' careers was to ask them, when they were still undergraduates, what they were going to do after they finished college. Inventoried interests were valid predictors for public school boys; expressed interests were valid for private school boys. Or, with even cleaner statistics, inventories were predictive for men with Ambitious and interviews for men with Responsive Careers.

Just how "deep" do such differences go? We can explain all the facts reported so far in terms of differing values. It is well to be wary of values as explanations. For values are superficial aspects of the total personality; already, too much thinking about the effects of culture on personality thus remains superficial, though more properly[21] "to the psychologist, personality is both broader and deeper than values and attitudes."

A few studies go deeper. The author[22] contrasted public and private school Thematic Apperception Tests in ways that were congruent with the Kluckhohn theory. No one has discovered, however, whether his findings are repeatable. Although Davidson[23] reported no differences between Rorschachs collected in a public and a private school in New York, Spinley[24] found significant differences between Rorschachs collected in a housing project and in one of the better schools in England. Her finding of more emotional constriction in the upper classes can be duplicated at Harvard both from the Study of Adult Development and from a more recent sample of a Harvard class. (These data have not yet been published.) Further, it appears from the Harvard samples that Rorschach signs of constriction or expansion have reversed implications for academic over-and under-achievement among public and private school boys. For the public school boy, the crucial question is apparently, "Has he enough control to be able to work effectively?" For the private school boy the question seems to be, "Has he enough freedom to be able to express himself?"

If these groups have different character structures, there should have been a difference in their infantile training. Study of Adult Development data show just such a difference. The pattern is best phrased in terms of social class. Lower-middle class families, whose sons come to Harvard as part of an Ambitious Career leading to social mobility, trained their infants very early in every respect. Upper-middle class families, whose sons, as a recent article[25] in this Review implied, may profit from Harvard more in terms of cultivation than of mobility, trained their infants strikingly late. In the upper class, early training re-occurs, but with the interesting exclusion of age of learning to read. It could be argued that early training that includes reading is done in terms of an inclusive demand to achieve, while the less comprehensive program involves only the early acquisition of proper behavior. On this basis, one might infer that both the lower-middle and the upper

[19] C. C. McArthur, "Long-term Validity of the Strong Test in Two Subcultures." J. Appl. Psychol., 1954, 38, 346-353.

[20] C. C. McArthur and Lucia B. Stevens, "The Validation of Expressed Interests as Compared with Inventoried Interests: a Fourteen-year Follow-up," J. Appl. Psychol., in press.

[21] Mirra Komarovsky, and S. S. Sargent, "Research into Subcultural Influences upon Personality." In S. S. Sargent, (Ed.), Culture and Personality. New York: The Viking Fund, 1950, pp. 143-162.

[22] C. C. McArthur, Cultural Values as Determinants of Imaginal Productions. Unpublished doctor's dissertation, Harvard Univ., 1951; C. C. McArthur, "Personality Differences between Middle and Upper Classes." J. Abnorm. Soc. Psychol., in press.

[23] Helen H. Davidson, Personality and Economic Background. New York: King's Crown Press, 1943.

[24] Betty M. Spinley, The Deprived and the Privileged. London: Routledge & Kegan Paul Ltd., 1953.

[25] M. R. Loeb, "Implications of Status Differentiation for Personal and Social Development." Harvard Educ. Rev., 1953, 23, No. 3, 168-174.

class family define their expectations for the boy early and in a manner consistent with later reinforcements.

All this has practical consequence. Super[26] recently warned counselors that the consequence of a lifetime of decisions must be honored if one is to give effective guidance. The counselor will decide, then, to use different techniques in guiding boys from middle and upper-class backgrounds. For a middle-class boy, the Strong and probably all the usual testing paraphernalia can be used; a Doing-oriented boy has wide latitude in choice of job title, so long as he maximizes his chances of success. For an upper-class boy, the counselor will remain skeptical of test scores, especially when they point to a vocation outside those the boy has foreseen; a Being-oriented boy is limited in choice of job title by considerations of propriety. Neither boy should be guided into a vocation not consistent with the values of his subculture, lest he pay too heavily in social isolation. However, mobility can still be managed, since pathways like medical school are institutionally provided that do not require a traumatic change of values.

Practical as the division between private and public school boys may be, the counselor should be aware that it is not necessarily the most meaningful dichotomy he can make. In the first place, no evidence suggests that the schools themselves are the main cause of the observed personality differences. In the second place, there are many choices of dividing lines.

Are there, for example, meaningful gradations in private schools? For certain personality studies[27], it has been helpful to distinguish the six most snobbish "St. Grottlesex Schools" from the rest. For predicting adjustment to military service, Monks[28] found that he had to distinguish boarding students from day students. Then, too, one has to ask whether parochial schools ought to be considered separately and what one is to do with the "public and private" boy, who shifted from one to the other during his last year or two of secondary education. Again, there may be gradations in public schools. Riesman[29] cites the unique properties of "those model schools, such as New Trier or Scarsdale, where a suburban community, prosperous and enlightened, chooses to run its own private school at its own public expense."

The true difference of which the public-private dichotomy is but a symptom may be one of social class. If so, the dividing lines that yield the best predictions of behavior seem to fall just below the upper-upper and just below the upper-middle. Or it may be that Miller and Form's distinction between career types or Kluckhohn's value profiles, will turn out to be the most explanatory concept. All these typologies overlap to a considerable degree, though no pair exactly corresponds. Which has the most explanatory power is an empirical question as yet undecided. What is clear is that there are private school types of personality, educational values, and career patterns that are very different from the personalities, values, and careers of graduates from public schools. The need for tailoring guidance techniques to social background may be stated not only for the case of the lower-class pupil but for upper-class students as well.

Of course, most counselors realize that they would be wiser to act on these rules but refrain from discussing them. The public-private comparison is one especially calculated to arouse moral indignation on both sides. Why bother, then? One can only plead that, practical import aside, these observations constitute a test case for the newer theories about the interaction of "culture and personality." Little has been learned about "subcultural personalities," despite recent pleas[30] that it would be theoret-

[26]D. E. Super, "Career Patterns as a Basis for Vocational Counseling." J. Counsel. Psychol., 1954, 1, No. 1, 12-20.

[27]C. C. McArthur, "Cultural Values as Determinants of Imaginal Productions," op. cit.

[28]J. P. Monks, College Men at War (In preparation).

[29]D. Riesman, "The Teacher Amid Changing Expectations." Harvard Educ. Rev., 1954, 24, No. 2, 106-117.

[30]Mirra Komarousky and S. S. Sargent, op. cit.

ically consequential to make such studies. The private-public dichotomy constitutes a crucial "natural experiment" in the effects of subculture upon the personality. The scattered facts reviewed here can, if further study is made, be brought to bear upon hypotheses of strategic importance in today's science of man.

The Fate of Idealism in Medical School

Howard S. Becker and Blanche Geer

SOURCE: *American Sociological Review*, Vol. 23 (1958), pp. 50–56.

It makes some difference in a man's performance of his work whether he believes wholeheartedly in what he is doing or feels that in important respects it is a fraud, whether he feels convinced that it is a good thing or believes that it is not really of much use after all. The distinction we are making is the one people have in mind when they refer, for example, to their calling as a "noble profession" on the one hand or a "racket" on the other. In the one case they idealistically proclaim that their work is all that it claims on the surface to be; in the other they cynically concede that it is first and foremost a way of making a living and that its surface pretensions are just that and nothing more. Presumably, different modes of behavior are associated with these perspectives when wholeheartedly embraced. The cynic cuts corners with a feeling of inevitability while the idealist goes down fighting. The Blackboard Jungle and Not as a Stranger are only the most recent in a long tradition of fictional portrayals of the importance of this aspect of a man's adjustment to his work.

Professional schools often receive a major share of the blame for producing this kind of cynicism—and none more than the medical school. The idealistic young freshman changes into a tough, hardened, unfeeling doctor; or so the popular view has it. Teachers of medicine sometimes rephrase the distinction between the clinical and pre-clinical years into one between the "cynical" and "precynical" years. Psychological research supports this view, presenting attitude surveys which show medical students year by year scoring lower on "idealism" and higher on "cynicism."[1] Typically, this cynicism is seen as developing in response to the shattering of ideals consequent on coming face-to-face with the realities of professional practice.

In this paper, we attempt to describe the kind of idealism that characterizes the medical freshmen and to trace both the development of cynicism and the vicissitudes of that idealism in the course of the four years of medical training. Our main themes are that though they develop cynical feelings in specific situations directly associated with their medical school experience, the medical students never lose their original idealism about the practice of medicine; that the growth of both cynicism and idealism are not simple developments, but are instead complex transformations; and that the very notions "idealism" and "cynicism" need further analysis, and must be seen

---

[1]Leonard D. Eron, "Effect of Medical Education on Medical Students," Journal of Medical Education, 10 (October, 1955), pp. 559-566.

as situational in their expressions rather than as stable traits possessed by individuals in greater or lesser degree. Finally, we see the greater portion of these feelings as being collective rather than individual phenomena.

Our discussion is based on a study we are now conducting at a state medical school,[2] in which we have carried on participant observation with students of all four years in all of the courses and clinical work to which they are exposed. We joined the students in their activities in school and after school and watched them at work in labs, on the hospital wards, and in the clinic. Often spending as much as a month with a small group of from five to fifteen students assigned to a particular activity, we came to know them well and were able to gather information in informal interviews and by overhearing the ordinary daily conversation of the group.[3] In the course of our

observation and interviewing we have gathered much information on the subject of idealism. Of necessity, we shall have to present the very briefest statement of our findings with little or no supporting evidence.[4] The problem of idealism is, of course, many-faceted and complex and we have dealt with it in a simplified way, describing only some of its grosser features.[5]

THE FRESHMEN

The medical students enter school with what we may think of as the idealistic notion, implicit in lay culture, that the practice of medicine is a wonderful thing and that they are going to devote their lives to service to mankind. They believe that medicine is made up of a great body of well-established facts that they will be taught from the first day on and that these facts will be of immediate practical use to them as physicians. They enter school expecting to work industriously and expecting that if they work hard enough they will be able to master this body of fact and thus become good doctors.

In several ways the first year of medical school does not live up to their expectations. They are disillusioned when they find they will not be near patients at all, that the first year will be just like another year of college. In fact, some feel that it is not even as good as college because their work in certain areas is not as thorough as courses in the same fields in undergraduate school. They come to think that their courses (with the exception of anatomy) are not

---

[2] This study is sponsored by Community Studies, Inc., of Kansas City, Missouri, and is being carried on at the University of Kansas Medical School, to whose dean, staff, and students we are indebted for their wholehearted cooperation. Professor Everett C. Hughes of the University of Chicago is director of the project.

[3] The technique of participant observation has not been fully systematized, but some approaches to this have been made. See, for example, Florence R. Kluckhohn, "The Participant Observer Technique in Small Communities," *American Journal of Sociology*, 45 (November, 1940), pp. 331-343; Arthur Vidich, "Participant Observation and the Collection and Interpretation of Data," *ibid.*, 60 (January, 1955), pp. 354-360; William Foote Whyte, "Observational Field-Work Methods," in Maria Jahoda, Morton Deutsch, and Stuart W. Cook (editors), Research Methods in the Social Sciences, New York: Dryden Press, 1951, II, pp. 393-514; and Street Corner Society (Enlarged Edition), Chicago: University of Chicago Press, 1955, pp. 279-358; Rosalie Hankey Wax, "Twelve Years Later: An Analysis of Field Experience," *American Journal of Sociology*, 63 (September, 1957), pp. 133-142; Morris S. Schwartz and Charlotte Green Schwartz, "Problems in Participant Observation," *ibid.*, 60 (January, 1955), pp. 343-353; and Howard S. Becker and Blanche Geer, "Participant Observation and Interviewing: A Comparison," Human Organization (forthcoming). The last item represents the first of a projected series of papers attempting to make explicit the operations involved in this method. For a short description of some techniques used in this study, see Howard S. Becker, "Interviewing Medical Students," *American Journal of Sociology*, 62 (September, 1956), pp. 199-201.

[4] A fuller analysis and presentation of evidence will be continued in a volume on this study now being prepared by the authors in collaboration with Everett C. Hughes and Anselm L. Strauss.

[5] Renée Fox has shown how complex one aspect of this whole subject is in her analysis of the way medical students at Cornell become aware of and adjust to both their own failure to master all available knowledge and the gaps in current knowledge in many fields. See her "Training for Uncertainty," in Robert K. Merton, George G. Reader, and Patrick L. Kendall, eds., The Student Physician: Introductory Studies in the Sociology of Medical Education, Cambridge: Harvard University Press, 1957, pp. 207-241.

worth much because, in the first place, the faculty (being Ph.D.'s) know nothing about the practice of medicine, and, in the second place, the subject matter itself is irrelevant, or as the students say, "ancient history."

The freshmen are further disillusioned when the faculty tells them in a variety of ways that there is more to medicine than they can possibly learn. They realize it may be impossible for them to practice medicine properly. Their disillusionment becomes more profound when they discover that this statement of the faculty is literally true.[6] Experience in trying to master the details of the anatomy of the extremities convinces them that they cannot do so in the time they have. Their expectation of hard work is not disappointed; they put in an eight-hour day of classes and laboratories, and study four or five hours a night and most of the weekend as well.

Some of the students, the brightest, continue to attempt to learn it all, but succeed only in getting more and more worried about their work. The majority decide that, since they can't learn it all, they must select from among all the facts presented to them those they will attempt to learn. There are two ways of making this selection. On the one hand, the student may decide on the basis of his own uninformed notions about the nature of medical practice that many facts are not important, since they relate to things which seldom come up in the actual practice of medicine; therefore, he reasons, it is useless to learn them. On the other hand, the student can decide that the important thing is to pass his examinations and, therefore, that the important facts are those which are likely to be asked on an examination; he uses this as a basis for selecting both facts to memorize and courses for intensive study. For example, the work in physiology is dismissed on both of these grounds, being considered neither relevant to the facts of medical life nor

important in terms of the amount of time the faculty devotes to it and the number of examinations in the subject.

A student may use either or both of these bases of selection at the beginning of the year, before many tests have been given. But after a few tests have been taken, the student makes "what the faculty wants" the chief basis of his selection of what to learn, for he now has a better idea of what this is and also has become aware that it is possible to fail examinations and that he therefore must learn the expectations of the faculty if he wishes to stay in school. The fact that one group of students, that with the highest prestige in the class, took this view early and did well on examinations was decisive in swinging the whole class around to this position. The students were equally influenced to become "test-wise" by the fact that, although they had all been in the upper range in their colleges, the class average on the first examination was frighteningly low.

In becoming test-wise, the students begin to develop systems for discovering the faculty wishes and learning them. These systems are both methods for studying their texts and short-cuts that can be taken in laboratory work. For instance, they begin to select facts for memorization by looking over the files of old examinations maintained in each of the medical fraternity houses. They share tip-offs from the lectures and offhand remarks of the faculty as to what will be on the examinations. In anatomy, they agree not to bother to dissect out subcutaneous nerves, reasoning that it is both difficult and time-consuming and the information can be secured from books with less effort. The interaction involved in the development of such systems and short-cuts helps to create a social group of a class which had previously been only an aggregation of smaller and less organized groups.

In this medical school, the students learn in this way to distinguish between the activities of the first year and their original view that everything that happens to them in medical school will be impor-

---

[6]Compare Fox' description of student reaction to this problem at Cornell (op. cit., pp. 209-221).

tant. Thus they become cynical about the the value of their activities in the first year. They feel that the real thing—learning which will help them to help mankind—has been postponed, perhaps until the second year, or perhaps even farther, at which time they will be able again to act on idealistic premises. They believe that what they do in their later years in school under supervision will be about the same thing they will do, as physicians, on their own; the first year had disappointed this expectation.

There is one matter, however, about which the students are not disappointed during the first year: the so-called trauma of dealing with the cadaver. But this experience, rather than producing cynicism, reinforces the student's attachment to his idealistic view of medicine by making him feel that he is experiencing at least some of the necessary unpleasantness of the doctor's. Such difficulties, however, do not loom as large for the student as those of solving the problem of just what the faculty wants.

On this and other points, a working consensus develops in the new consolidated group about the interpretation of their experience in medical school and its norms of conduct. This consensus, which we call student culture,[7] focuses their attention <u>almost completely</u> on their day-to-day activities in school and obscures or sidetracks their earlier idealistic preoccupations. Cynicism, griping, and minor cheating become endemic, but the cynicism is specific to the educational situation, to the first year, and to only parts of it. Thus the students keep their cynicism separate from their idealistic feelings and by postponement protect their belief that medicine is a wonderful thing, that their school is a fine one, and that they will become good doctors.

LATER YEARS

The sophomore year does not differ

greatly from the freshman year. Both the work load and anxiety over examinations probably increase. Though they begin some medical activities, as in their attendance at autopsies and particularly in their introductory course in physical diagnosis, most of what they do continues to repeat the pattern of the college science curriculum. Their attention still centers on the problem of getting through school by doing well in examinations.

During the third and fourth, or clinical years, teaching takes a new form. In place of lectures and laboratories, the students' work now consists of the study of actual patients admitted to the hospital or seen in the clinic. Each patient who enters the hospital is assigned to a student who interviews him about his illnesses, past and present, and performs a physical examination. He writes this up for the patient's chart, and appends the diagnosis and the treatment that he would use were he allowed actually to treat the patient. During conferences with faculty physicians, often held at the patient's bedside, the student is quizzed about items of his report and called upon to defend them or to explain their significance. Most of the teaching in the clinical years is of this order.

Contact with patients brings a new set of circumstances with which the student must deal. He no longer feels the great pressure created by tests, for he is told by the faculty, and this is confirmed by his daily experience, that examinations are now less important. His problems now become those of coping with a steady stream of patients in a way that will please the staff man under whom he is working, and of handling what is sometimes a tremendous load of clinical work so as to allow himself time for studying diseases and treatments that interest him and for play and family life.

The students earlier have expected that once they reach the clinical years they will be able to realize their idealistic ambitions to help people and to learn those things immediately useful in aiding people who are ill. But they find themselves working to understand cases as

---

[7]The concept of student culture is analyzed in some detail in Howard S. Becker and Blanche Geer, "Student Culture in Medical School," <u>Harvard Educational Review</u> (forthcoming).

medical problems rather than working to help the sick and memorizing the relevant available facts so that these can be produced immediately for a questioning staff man. When they make ward rounds with a faculty member they are likely to be quizzed about any of the seemingly countless facts possibly related to the condition of the patient for whom they are "caring."

Observers speak of the cynicism that overtakes the student and the lack of concern for his patients as human beings. This change does take place, but it is not produced solely by "the anxiety brought about by the presence of death and suffering."[8] The student becomes preoccupied with the technical aspects of the cases with which he deals because the faculty requires him to do so. He is questioned about so many technical details that he must spend most of his time learning them.

The frustrations created by his position in the teaching hospital further divert the student from idealistic concerns. He finds himself low man in a hierarchy based on clinical experience, so that he is allowed very little of the medical responsibility he would like to assume. Because of his lack of experience, he cannot write orders, and he receives permission to perform medical and surgical procedures (if at all) at a rate he considers far too slow. He usually must content himself with "mere" vicarious participation in the drama of danger, life, and death that he sees as the core of medical practice. The student culture accents these difficulties so that events (and especially those involving patients) are interpreted and reacted to as they push him toward or hold him back from further participation in this drama. He does not think in terms the layman might use.

As a result of the increasingly technical emphasis of his thinking the student appears cynical to the non-medical

outsider, though from his own point of view he is simply seeing what is "really important." Instead of reacting with the layman's horror and sympathy for the patient to the sight of a cancerous organ that has been surgically removed, the student is more likely to regret that he was not allowed to close the incision at the completion of the operation, and to rue the hours that he must spend searching in the fatty flesh for the lymph nodes that will reveal how far the disease has spread. As in other lines of work, he drops lay attitudes for those more relevant to the way the event affects someone in his position.

This is not to say that the students lose their original idealism. When issues of idealism are openly raised in a situation they define as appropriate, they respond as they might have when they were freshmen. But the influence of the student culture is such that questions which might bring forth this idealism are not brought up. Students are often assigned patients for examination and follow-up whose conditions might be expected to provoke idealistic crises. Students discuss such patients, however, with reference to the problems they create for the student. Patients with terminal diseases who are a long time dying, and patients with chronic diseases who show little change from week to week, are more likely to be viewed as creating extra work without extra compensation in knowledge or the opportunity to practice new skills than as examples of illness which raise questions about euthanasia. Such cases require the student to spend time every day checking on progress which he feels will probably not take place and to write long "progress" notes in the patient's chart although little progress has occurred.

This apparent cynicism is a collective matter. Group activities are built around this kind of workaday perspective, constraining the students in two ways. First, they do not openly express the lay idealistic notions they may hold, for their culture does not sanction such expression; second, they are less likely to have

<hr>

[8]Dana L. Farnsworth, "Some Observations on The Attitudes and Motivations of the Harvard Medical Student," *Harvard Medical Alumni Bulletin*, January, 1956, p. 34.

thoughts of this deviant kind when they are engaged in group activity. The collective nature of this "cynicism" is indicated by the fact that students become more openly idealistic whenever they are removed from the influence of student culture—when they are alone with a sociologist as they near the finish of school and sense the approaching end of student life, for example, or when they are isolated from their classmates and therefore are less influenced by this culture.[9]

They still feel, as advanced students, though much less so than before, that school is irrelevant to actual medical practice. Many of their tasks, like running laboratory tests on patients newly admitted to the hospital or examining surgical specimens in the pathology laboratory, seem to them to have nothing to do with their visions of their future activity as doctors. As in their freshman year, they believe that perhaps they must obtain the knowledge they will need in spite of the school. They still conceive of medicine as a huge body of proven facts, but no longer believe that they will ever be able to master it all. They now say that they are going to try to apply the solution of the practicing M.D. to their own dilemma: learn a few things that they are interested in very well and know enough about other things to pass examinations while in school and, later on in practice, to know to which specialist to send difficult patients.

Their original medical idealism reasserts itself as the end of school approaches. Seniors show more interest than students in earlier years in serious ethical dilemmas of the kind they expect to face in practice. They have become aware of ethical problems laymen often see as crucial for the physician—whether it is right to keep patients with fatal diseases alive as long as possible, or what should be done if an influential patient demands an abortion—and worry about them. As they near graduation and student culture begins to break down as

the soon-to-be doctors are about to go their separate ways, these questions are more and more openly discussed.

While in school, they have added to their earlier idealism a new and peculiarly professional idealism. Even though they know that few doctors live up to the standards they have been taught, they intend always to examine their patients thoroughly and to give treatment based on firm diagnosis rather than merely to relieve symptoms. This expansion and transformation of idealism appear most explicitly in their consideration of alternative careers, concerning both specialization and the kind of arrangements to be made for setting up practice. Many of their hypothetical choices aim at making it possible for them to be the kind of doctors their original idealism pictured. Many seniors consider specialty training so that they will be able to work in a limited field in which it will be more nearly possible to know all there is to know, thus avoiding the necessity of dealing in a more ignorant way with the wider range of problems general practice would present. In the same manner, they think of schemes to establish partnerships or other arrangements making it easier to avoid a work load which would prevent them from giving each patient the thorough examination and care they now see as ideal.

In other words, as school comes to an end, the cynicism specific to the school situation also comes to an end and their original and more general idealism about medicine comes to the fore again, though within a framework of more realistic alternatives. Their idealism is now more informed although no less selfless.

DISCUSSION

We have used the words "idealism" and "cynicism" loosely in our description of the changeable state of mind of the medical student, playing on ambiguities we can now attempt to clear up. Retaining a core of common meaning, the dictionary definition, in our reference to the person's belief in the worth of his

---

[9] See the discussion in Howard S. Becker, "Interviewing Medical Students," op. cit.

activity and the claims made for it, we have seen that this is not a generalized trait of the students we studied but rather an attitude which varies greatly, depending on the particular activity the worth of which is questioned and the situation in which the attitude is expressed.

This variability of the idealistic attitude suggests that in using such an element of personal perspective in sociological analysis one should not treat it as homogeneous but should make a determined search for subtypes which may arise under different conditions and have differing consequences. Such subtypes presumably can be constructed along many dimensions. There might, for instance, be consistent variations in the medical students' idealism through the four years of school that are related to their social class backgrounds. We have stressed in this report the subtypes that can be constructed according to variations in the object of the idealistic attitude and variations in the audience the person has in mind when he adopts the attitude. The medical students can be viewed as both idealistic and cynical, depending on whether one has in mind their view of their school activities or the future they envision for themselves as doctors. Further, they might take one or another of these positions depending on whether their implied audience is made up of other students, their instructors, or the lay public.

A final complication arises because cynicism and idealism are not merely attributes of the actor, but are as dependent on the person doing the attributing as they are on the qualities of the individual to whom they are attributed.[10] Though the student may see his own disregard of the unique personal troubles of a particular patient as proper scientific objectivity, the layman may view this objectivity as heartless cynicism.[11]

Having made these analytic distinctions, we can now summarize the transformations of these characteristics as we have seen them occuring among medical students. Some of the students' determined idealism at the outset is reaction against the lay notion, of which they are uncomfortably aware, that doctors are money-hungry cynics; they counter this with an idealism of similar lay origin stressing the doctor's devotion to service. But this idealism soon meets a setback, as students find that it will not be relevant for awhile, since medical school has, it seems, little relation to the practice of medicine, as they see it. As it has not been refuted, but only shown to be temporarily beside the point, the students "agree" to set this idealism aside in favor of a realistic approach to the problem of getting through school. This approach, which we have labeled as the cynicism specific to the school experience, serves as protection for the earlier grandiose feelings about medicine by postponing their exposure to reality to a distant future. As that future approaches near the end of the four years and its possible mistreatment of their ideals moves closer, the students again worry about maintaining their integrity, this time in actual medical practice. They use some of the knowledge they have gained to plan careers which, it is hoped, can best bring their ideals to realization.

We can put this in propositional form by saying that when a man's ideals are challenged by outsiders and then further strained by reality, he may salvage them by postponing their application to a future time when conditions are expected to be more propitious.

---

[10] See Phillip Selznick's related discussion of fanaticism in TVA and the Grass Roots, Berkeley: University of California Press, 1953, pp. 205-213.

[11] George Orwell gives the layman's side in his essay, "How the Poor Die" in Shooting an Elephant and Other Essays, London: Secker and Warburg, 1950, pp. 18-32.

Role, Personality, and Social Structure in the Organizational Setting[1]

Daniel J. Levinson

SOURCE: *The Journal of Abnormal and Social Psychology*, Vol. 58, (1959), pp. 170–80.

During the past 20 years the concept of role has achieved wide currency in social psychology, sociology, and anthropology. From a sociopsychological point of view, one of its most alluring qualities is its double reference to the individual and to the collective matrix. The concept of role concerns the thoughts and actions of individuals, and, at the same time, it points up the influence upon the individual of socially patterned demands and standardizing forces. Partly for this reason, "role" has been seen by numerous writers as a crucial concept for the linking of psychology, sociology, and anthropology.[2] However, while the promise has seemed great, the fulfillment has thus far been relatively small. The concept of role remains one of the most overworked and underdeveloped in the social sciences.

My purpose here is to examine role theory primarily as it is used in the analysis of organizations (such as the hospital, business firm, prison, school). The organization provides a singularly useful arena for the development and application of role theory. It is small enough to be amenable to empirical study. Its structure is complex enough to provide a wide variety of social positions and role-standardizing forces. It offers an almost limitless opportunity to observe the individual personality in vivo (rather than in the psychologist's usual vitro of laboratory, survey questionnaire, or clinical office), selectively utilizing and modifying the demands and opportunities given in the social environment. The study of personality can, I submit, find no setting in which the reciprocal impact of psyche and situation is more clearly or more dramatically evidenced.

Organizational theory and research has traditionally been the province of sociology and related disciplines that focus most directly upon the collective unit. Chief emphasis has accordingly been given to such aspects of the organization as formal and informal structure, administrative policy, allocation of resources, level of output, and the like. Little interest has been shown in the individual member as such or in the relevance of personality for organizational functioning. The prevailing image of the

[1]This is an expanded version of a paper presented at the meetings of the American Sociological Association in August, 1957. I am indebted to Peter D. Watson, Elizabeth Watson, and George Grosser for helpful criticism of the initial version. The ideas presented here stem in part from research supported by Grants M-687 and M-1000 from the National Institute of Mental Health, of the National Institutes of Health, Public Health Service.

[2]H. H. Gerth and C. W. Mills, Character and Social Structure. New York: Harcourt, Brace, 1953; N. Gross, W. S. Mason, and A. W. McEachern, Explorations in Role Analysis. New York: Wiley, 1958; E. L. Hartley and Ruth E. Hartley, Fundamentals of Social Psychology. New York: Knopf, 1952; R. Linton, The Cultural Background of Personality. New York: Appleton-Century, 1945; G. H. Mead, Mind, Self and Society. Chicago: University of Chicago Press, 1934; R. K. Merton, Social Theory and Social Structure (rev. ed.). Glencoe, Ill.: Free Press, 1957; T. Parsons, The Social System. Glencoe, Ill.: Free Press, 1951; T. R. Sarbin, "Role Theory," in G. Lindzey (ed.), Handbook of Social Psychology. Cambridge, Mass.: Addison-Wesley, 1954.

organization has been that of a mechanical apparatus operating impersonally once it is set in motion by administrative edict. The prevailing conception of social role is consonant with this image: the individual member is regarded as a cog in the apparatus, what he thinks and does being determined by requirements in the organizational structure.

This paper has the following aims: 1. To examine the traditional conception of organizational structure and role and to assess its limitations from a sociopsychological point of view. 2. To examine the conception of social role that derives from this approach to social structure and that tends, by definition, to exclude consideration of personality. 3. To provide a formulation of several, analytically distinct, role concepts to be used in place of the global term "role." 4. To suggest a theoretical approach to the analysis of relationships among role, personality, and social structure.

TRADITIONAL VIEWS OF BUREAU-
CRATIC STRUCTURE AND ROLE

Human personality has been virtually excluded from traditional organization theory. Its absence is perhaps most clearly reflected in Weber's theory of bureaucracy, which has become a major source of current thought regarding social organization and social role.[3] I shall examine this theory briefly here, in order to point up some of its psychological limitations but without doing justice to its many virtues. In Weber's writings, the bureaucratic organization is portrayed as a monolithic edifice. Norms are clearly defined and consistently applied, the agencies of role socialization succeed in inducing acceptance of organizational requirements, and the sanctions system provides the constraints and incentives needed to maintain behavioral conformity. Every individual is given a clearly defined role

and readily "fills" it. There is little room in this tightly bound universe for more complex choice, for individual creativity, or for social change. As Gouldner has said of the studies carried out in this tradition: "Indeed, the social scene described has sometimes been so completely stripped of people that the impression is unintentionally rendered that there are disembodied social forces afoot, able to realize their ambitions apart from human action."[4]

For Weber, bureaucracy as an ideal type is administered by "experts" in a spirit of impersonal rationality and is operated on a principle of discipline according to which each member performs his required duties as efficiently as possible. Rationality in decision-making and obedience in performance are the pivots on which the entire system operates. In this scheme of things, emotion is regarded merely as a hindrance to efficiency, as something to be excluded from the bureaucratic process.

The antipathy to emotion and motivation in Weber's thinking is reflected as well in his formulation of three types of authority: traditional, charismatic, and rational-legal. The rational-legal administrator is the pillar of bureaucracy. He receives his legitimation impersonally, from "the system," by virtue of his <u>technical</u> competence. His personal characteristics, his conception of the organization and its component groupings, his modes of relating to other persons (except that he be fair and impartial)— these and other psychological characteristics are not taken into theoretical consideration. There is no place in Weber's ideal type for the ties of affection, the competitive strivings, the subtle forms of support or of intimidation, so commonly found in even the most "rationalized" organizations. It is only the "charismatic" leader who becomes emotionally important to his followers and who must personally validate his right to lead.

---

[3]M. Weber, <u>Essays in Sociology</u>, ed. by H. H. Gerth and C. W. Mills. New York: Oxford University Press, 1946; M. Weber, <u>The Theory of Social and Economic Organization</u>, ed. by T. Parsons. New York: Oxford University Press, 1947.

[4]A. W. Gouldner, <u>Patterns of Industrial Bureaucracy</u>. Glencoe, Ill.: Free Press, 1954, p. 16.

While Weber has little to say about the problem of motivation, two motives implicitly become universal instincts in his conception of "bureaucratic man." These are conformity (the motive for automatic acceptance of structural norms), and status-seeking (the desire to advance oneself by the acquisition and exercise of technical competence). More complex motivations and feelings are ignored.

There has been widespread acknowledgment of both the merits and the limitations of Weber's protean thought. However, the relevance of personality for organizational structure and role-definition remains a largely neglected problem in contemporary theory and research.[5] Our inadequacies are exemplified in the excellent Reader in Bureaucracy, edited by Merton, Gray, Hockey, and Selvin.[6] Although this book contains some of the most distinguished contributions to the field, it has almost nothing on the relation between organizational structure and personality. The editors suggest two lines of interrelation: first, that personality may be one determinant of occupational choice; and second, that a given

type of structure may in time modify the personalities of its members. These are valuable hypotheses. However, they do not acknowledge the possibility that personality may have an impact on social structure. "The organization" is projected as an organism that either selects congenial personalities or makes over the recalcitrant ones to suit its own needs. This image is reflected in the editors' remark: "It would seem, therefore, that officials not initially suited to the demands of a bureaucratic position, progressively undergo modifications of personality."[7] In other words, when social structure and personality fail to mesh, it is assumed to be personality alone that gives. Structure is the prime, uncaused, cause.

The impact of organizational structure on personality is indeed a significant problem for study. There is, however, a converse to this. When a member is critical of the organizational structure, he may maintain his personal values and traits, and work toward structural change. The manifold impact of personality on organizational structure and role remains to be investigated. To provide a theoretical basis for this type of investigation we need, I believe, to re-examine the concept of role.

"SOCIAL ROLE" AS A UNITARY CONCEPT

The concept of role is related to, and must be distinguished from, the concept of social position. A position is an element of organizational autonomy, a location in social space, a category of organizational membership. A role is, so to say, an aspect of organizational physiology; it involves function, adaptation, process. It is meaningful to say that a person "occupies" a social position; but it is inappropriate to say, as many do, that one occupies a role.

There are at least three specific senses in which the term "role" has been used, explicitly or implicitly, by different writers or by the same writer on different occasions.

[5] Contemporary organization theory has benefited from criticisms and reformulations of Weber's theory by such writers as C. I. Bernard in The Functions of the Executive, Cambridge, Mass.: Harvard University Press, 1938; C. V. Friedrich in Constitutional Government and Democracy, Boston: Little Brown, 1950; Gerth and Mills, op. cit.; A. W. Gouldner, op. cit.; R. Y. Merton, op. cit.), T. P. Parsons (in his introduction to Weber, op. cit.), Selznick in his Leadership in Administration, Evanston, Ill.; Row-Peterson, 1957, has recently presented a conception of the administrative-managerial role that allows more room for psychological influences, but these are not explicitly conceptualized. There is growing though still inconclusive evidence from research on "culture and personality" work that social structures of various types both "require" and are influenced by modal personality, but his approach has received little application in research on organizations. (A. Inkeles and D. J. Levinson, "National Character: The Study of Modal Personality and Socio-Cultural Systems," in G. Lindzey (ed.), Handbook of Social Psychology. Cambridge, Mass.: Addison-Wesley, 1954). An attempt at a distinctively socio-psychological approach, and a comprehensive view of the relevant literature, is presented by C. Argyris in Personality and Organization. New York: Harper, 1957.

[6] R. K. Merton, A. P. Gray, Barbara Hockey, and H. C. Selvin, Reader in Bureaucracy. Glencoe, Ill.: Free Press, 1957.

[7] Ibid., p. 352.

a. Role may be defined as the <u>structurally given demands</u> (norms, expectations, taboos, responsibilities, and the like) associated with a given social position. Role is, in this sense, something outside the given individual, a set of pressures and facilitations that channel, guide, impede, support his functioning in the organization.

b. Role may be defined as the member's <u>orientation</u> or <u>conception</u> of the part he is to play in the organization. It is, so to say, his inner definition of what someone in his social position is supposed to think and do about it. Mead is probably the main source of this view of social role as an aspect of the person, and it is commonly used in analyses of occupational roles.[8]

c. Role is commonly defined as the <u>actions</u> of the individual members—actions seen in terms of their relevance for the social structure (that is, seen in relation to the prevailing norms). In this sense, role refers to the ways in which members of a position act (with or without conscious intention) <u>in accord with or in violation of a given set of organizational norms</u>. Here, as in (b), role is defined as a characteristic of the actor rather than of his normative environment.

Many writers use a definition that embraces all of the above meanings without systematic distinction, and then shift, explicitly or implicitly, from one meaning to another. The following are but a few of many possible examples.[9]

Each of the above three meanings of "role" is to be found in the writings of Parsons: (a) "From the point of view of the actor, his role is defined by the normative expectations of the members of the group as formulated in its social traditions"[10] (b) "The role is organized sector of an actor's orientation which constitutes and detines his partici-

pation in an interactive process."[11] (c) "The status-role (is) the organized subsystem."[12]

More often, the term is used in a way that includes all three meanings at once. In this <u>unitary</u>, all-embracing conception of role, there is, by assumption, a close fit between behavior and disposition (attitude, value), between societal prescription and individual adaptation. This point of view has its primary source in the writings of Linton, whose formulations of culture, status, and role have had enormous influence. According to Linton, a role "includes the attitudes, values and behavior ascribed by the society to any and all persons occupying this status."[13] In other words, society provides for each status or position a single mold that shapes the beliefs and actions of all its occupants.

Perhaps the most extensive formulation of this approach along sociopsychological lines is given by Newcomb.[14] Following Linton, Newcomb asserts, "Roles thus represent ways of carrying out the functions for which positions exist—ways which are generally agreed upon within (the) group."[15] And, "Role is strictly a sociological concept; it purposely ignores individual, psychological facts."[16] Having made this initial commitment to the "sociological" view that individual role-activity is a simple mirroring of group norms, Newcomb later attempts to find room for his "psychological" concerns with motivation, meaning, and individual differences. He does this by partially giving up the "unitary" concept of role, and introducing a distinction between "prescribed role" and "role behavior." He avers that prescribed role is a so-

<hr/>

[8] G. H. Mead, <u>op. cit.</u>

[9] An argument very similar to the one made here is presented by Gross, Mason, and McEachern in a comprehensive overview and critique of role theory (<u>Explorations in Role Analysis</u>. New York: Wiley, 1958). They point up the assumption of high consensus regarding role-demands and role-conceptions in traditional role theory, and present empirical evidence contradicting this assumption. Their analysis is, however, less concerned than the present one with the converging of role theory and personality theory.

[10] T. Parsons, <u>Essays in Sociological Theory</u> (rev. ed.). Glencoe, Ill.: Free Press, 1945 p. 230.

[11] T. Parsons and E. A. Shils (eds.), <u>Toward a General Theory of Action</u>. Cambridge, Mass.: Harvard University Press, 1951, p. 23.

[12] T. Parsons, <u>The Social System</u>, p. 26.

[13] R. Linton, <u>op. cit.</u>

[14] T. M. Newcomb, <u>Social Psychology</u>. New York: Dryden-Holt, 1950.

[15] Ibid., p. 281.

[16] Ibid., p. 329.

ciological concept, "referring to common factors in the behaviors required,"[17] whereas role behavior is a psychological concept that refers to the activities of a single individual. The implications of this distinction for his earlier general definition of role are left unstated.

Whatever the merits or faults of Newcomb's reformulation, it at least gives conceptual recognition to the possibility that social prescription and individual adaptation may not match. This possibility is virtually excluded in the definition of social role forwarded by Linton and used by so many social scientists. In this respect, though certainly not in all respects, Linton's view is like Weber's: both see individual behavior as predominantly determined by the collective matrix. The matrix is, in the former case, culture, and in the latter, bureaucracy.

In short, the "unitary" conception of role assumes that there is a 1:1 relationship, or at least a high degree of congruence, among the three role aspects noted above. In the theory of bureaucratic organization, the rationale for this assumption is somewhat as follows. The organizationally given requirements will be internalized by the members and will thus be mirrored in their role-conceptions. People will know, and will want to do, what is expected of them. The agencies of role socialization will succeed except with a deviant minority—who constitute a separate problem for study. Individual action will in turn reflect the structural norms, since the appropriate role-conceptions will have been internalized and since the sanctions system rewards normative behavior and punishes deviant behavior. Thus, it is assumed that structural norms, individual role-conceptions and individual role-performance are three isomorphic reflections of a single entity: "the" role appropriate to a given organizational position.

It is, no doubt, reasonable to expect some degree of congruence among these aspects of a social role. Certainly, every

organization contains numerous mechanisms designed to further such congruence. At the same time, it is a matter of common observation that organizations vary in the degree of their integration; structural demands are often contradictory, lines of authority may be defective, disagreements occur and reverberate at and below the surface of daily operations. To assume that what the organization requires, and what its members actually think and do, comprise a single, unified whole is severely to restrict our comprehension of organizational dynamics and change.

It is my thesis, then, that the unitary conception of social role is unrealistic and theoretically constricting. We should, I believe, eliminate the single term "role" except in the most general sense, i.e., of "role theory" as an over-all frame of analysis. Let us, rather, give independent conceptual and empirical status to the above three concepts and others. Let us investigate the relationships of each concept with the others, making no assumptions about the degree of congruence among them. Further, let us investigate their relationships with various other characteristics of the organization and of its individual members. I would suggest that the role concepts be named and defined as follows.

ORGANIZATIONALLY GIVEN ROLE-DEMANDS

The role-demands are external to the individual whose role is being examined. They are the situational pressures that confront him as the occupant of a given structural position. They have manifold sources: in the official charter and policies of the organization; in the traditions and ideology, explicit as well as implicit, that help to define the organization's purposes and modes of operation; in the views about this position which are held by members of the position (who influence any single member) and by members of the various positions impinging upon this one; and so on.

It is a common assumption that the structural requirements for any position

---

[17]*Ibid.*, p. 459.

are as a rule defined with a <u>high degree of explicitness, clarity</u>, and <u>consensus</u> among all the parties involved. To take the position of hospital nurse as an example: it is assumed that her role-requirements will be understood and agreed upon by the hospital administration, the nursing authorities, the physicians, etc. Yet one of the striking research findings in all manner of hospitals is the failure of consensus regarding the proper role of nurse.[18] Similar findings have been obtained in school systems, business firms, and the like.[19]

In attempting to characterize the role-requirements for a given position, one must therefore guard against the assumption that they are unified and logically coherent. There may be major differences and even contradictions between official norms, as defined by charter or by administrative authority, and the "informal" norms held by various groupings within the organization. Moreover, within a given-status group, such as the top administrators, there may be several conflicting viewpoints concerning long range goals, current policies, and specific role-requirements. In short, the structural demands themselves are often multiple and disunified. Few are the attempts to investigate the sources of such disunity, to acknowledge its frequency, or to take it into conceptual account in general structural theory.

It is important also to consider the specificity or <u>narrowness</u> with which the normative requirements are defined. Norms have an "ought" quality; they confer legitimacy and reward-value upon certain modes of action, thought and emotion, while condemning others. But there are degrees here. Normative evaluations cover a spectrum from "strongly required," through various degrees of qualitative kinds of "acceptable," to more or less stringently tabooed. Organizations

differ in the width of the intermediate range on this spectrum. That is, they differ in the number and kinds of adaptation that are normatively acceptable. The wider this range—the less specific the norms—the greater is the area of personal choice for the individual. While the existence of such an intermediate range is generally acknowledged, structural analyses often proceed as though practically all norms were absolute prescriptions or proscriptions allowing few alternatives for individual action.

There are various other normative complexities to be reckoned with. A single set of role-norms may be internally contradictory. In the case of the mental hospital nurse, for example, the norm of maintaining an "orderly ward" often conflicts with the norm of encouraging self-expression in patients. The individual nurse then has a range of choice, which may be narrow or wide, in balancing these conflicting requirements. There are also ambiguities in norms, and discrepancies between those held explicitly and those that are less verbalized and perhaps less conscious. These normative complexities permit, and may even induce, significant variations in individual role-performance.

The degree of <u>coherence</u> among the structurally defined role-requirements, the degree of <u>consensus</u> with which they are held, and the degree of <u>individual choice</u> they allow (the range of acceptable alternatives) are among the most significant properties of any organization. In some organizations, there is very great coherence of role-requirements and a minimum of individual choice. In most cases, however, the degree of integration within roles and among sets of roles appears to be more moderate.[20] This struc-

[18]C. Argyris, <u>Human Relations in a Hospital.</u> New Haven: Labor and Management Center, 1955; T. Burling, Edith Lentz, and R. N. Wilson, <u>The Give and Take in Hospitals.</u> New York: Putnam, 1956.

[19]N. Gross et al., <u>op. cit.</u>; A. hornhauser, R. Dubin, and A. M. Ross, <u>Industrial Conflict.</u> New York: McGraw-Hill, 1954.

[20]The reduced integration reflects in part the tremendous rate of technological change, the geographical and occupational mobility, and the diversity in personality that characterize modern society. On the other hand, diversity is opposed by the standardization of culture on a mass basis and by the growth of large-scale organization itself. Trends toward increased standardization and uniformity are highlighted in Whyte's analysis (W. F. Whyte, <u>The Organization Man.</u> New York: Simon & Shuster, 1956).

tural pattern is of especial interest from a sociopsychological point of view. To the extent that the requirements for a given position are ambiguous, contradictory, or otherwise "open," the individual members have greater opportunity for selection among existing norms and for creation of new norms. In this process, personality plays an important part. I shall return to this issue shortly.

While the normative requirements (assigned tasks, rules governing authority-subordinate relationships, demands for work output, and the like) are of great importance, there are other aspects of the organization that have an impact on the individual member. I shall mention two that are sometimes neglected.

Role-Facilities. In addition to the demands and obligations imposed upon the individual, we must also take into account the techniques, resources, and conditions of work—the means made available to him for fulfilling his organizational functions. The introduction of tranquillizing drugs in the mental hospital, or of automation in industry, has provided tremendous leverage for change in organizational structure and role-definition. The teacher-student ratio, an ecological characteristic of every school, grossly affects the probability that a given teacher will work creatively with individual students. In other words, technological and ecological facilities are not merely "tools" by which norms are met; they are often a crucial basis for the maintenance or change of an organizational form.

Role-Dilemmas or Problematic Issues. In describing the tasks and rules governing a given organizational position, and the facilities provided for their realization, we are, as it were, looking at that position from the viewpoint of a higher administrative authority whose chief concern is "getting the job done." Bureaucracy is often analyzed from this (usually implicit) viewpoint. What is equally necessary, though less often done, is to look at the situation of the position-members from their own point of view: the meaning it has for them, the feelings it evokes,

the ways in which it is stressful or supporting. From this sociopsychological perspective, new dimensions of role analysis emerge. The concept of role-dilemma is an example. The usefulness of this concept stems from the fact that every human situation has its contradictions and its problematic features. Where such dilemmas exist, there is no "optimal" mode of adaptation; each mode has its advantages and its costs. Parsons in his discussion of "the situation of the patient," explores some of the dilemmas confronting the ill person in our society.[21] Erikson and Pine and Levinson have written about the dilemmas of the mental hospital patient; for example, the conflicting pressures (from without and from within) toward cure through self-awareness and toward cure through repressive self-control.[22] Role-dilemmas of the psychiatric resident have been studied by Sharaf and Levinson.[23] Various studies have described the problems of the factory foreman caught in the conflicting cross-pressures between the workers he must supervise and the managers to whom he is responsible. The foreman's situation tends to evoke feelings of social marginality, mixed identifications, and conflicting tendencies to be a good "older brother" with subordinates and an obedient son with higher authority.

Role-dilemmas have their sources both in organizational structure and in individual personality. Similarly, both structure and personality influence the varied forms of adaptation that are achieved. The point to be emphasized here is that every social structure con-

---

[21]T. Parsons, The Social System.

[22]K. T. Erikson, "Patient Role and Social Uncertainty: A Dilemma of the Mentally Ill," Psychiatry, 1957, 20, 263-274; F. Pine and D. J. Levinson, Problematic Issues in the Role of Mental Hospital Patient. Mimeographed: Center for Sociopsychological Research, Massachusetts Mental Health Center, 1958.

[23]M. R. Sharaf and D. J. Levinson, "Patterns of Ideology and Role Definition among Psychiatric Residents," in M. Greenblatt, D. J. Levinson, and R. H. Williams (eds.), The Patient and the Mental Hospital. Glencoe, Ill.: Free Press, 1957.

fronts its members with adaptive dilemmas. If we are to comprehend this aspect of organizational life, we must conceive of social structure as having intrinsically psychological properties, as making complex psychological demands that affect, and are affected by, the personalities of its members.

PERSONAL ROLE-DEFINITION

In the foregoing we have considered the patterning of the environment for an organizational position—the kind of sociopsychological world with which members of the position must deal. Let us turn now to the individual members themselves. Confronted with a complex system of requirements, facilities, and conditions of work, the individual effects his modes of adaptation. I shall use the term "personal role-definition" to encompass the individual's adaptation within the organization. This may involve passive "adjustment," active furthering of current role-demands, apparent conformity combined with indirect "sabotage," attempts at constructive innovation (revision of own role or of broader structural arrangements), and the like. The personal role-definition may thus have varying degrees of fit with the role-requirements. It may serve in various ways to maintain or to change the social structure. It may involve a high or a low degree of self-commitment and personal involvement on the part of the individual.[24]

For certain purposes, it is helpful to make a sharp distinction between two levels of adaptation: at a more ideational level, we may speak of a role-conception; at a more behavioral level, there is a pattern of role-performance. Each of these has an affective component. Role-conception and role-performance are independent though related variables; let us consider them in turn.

Individual (and Modal) Role-Conceptions. The nature of a role-conception may perhaps be clarified by placing it in relation to an ideology. The boundary between the two is certainly not a sharp

one. However, ideology refers most directly to an orientation regarding the entire organizational (or other) structure—its purposes, its modes of operation, the prevailing forms of individual and group relationships, and so on. A role-conception offers a definition and rationale for one position within the structure. If ideology portrays and rationalizes the organizational world, then role-conception delineates the specific functions, values, and manner of functioning appropriate to one position within it.

The degree of uniformity or variability in individual role-conceptions within a given position will presumably vary from one organization to another. When one or more types of role-conception are commonly held (consensual), we may speak of modal types. The maintenance of structural stability requires that there be at least moderate consensus and that modal role-conceptions be reasonably congruent with role-requirements. At the same time, the presence of incongruent modal role-conceptions may, under certain conditions, provide an ideational basis for major organizational change.

Starting with the primary assumption that each member "takes over" a structurally defined role, many social scientists tend to assume that there is great uniformity in role-conception among the members of a given social position. They hold, in other words, that for every position there is a dominant, modal role-conception corresponding to the structural demands, and that there is relatively little individual deviation from the modal pattern. Although this state of affairs may at times obtain, we know that the members of a given social position often have quite diverse conceptions of their proper roles.[25] After all, individual role-conceptions are formed only partially

----

[24]R. Selznick, op. cit.

[25]M. Greenblatt, D. J. Levinson, and R. H. Williams (eds.), The Patient and the Mental Hospital. Glencoe, Ill.: Free Press, 1957; N. Gross et al., op. cit.; L. Reissman and J. J. Rohrer (eds.), Change and Dilemma in the Nursing Profession. New York: Putnam, 1957; R. Bendix, Work and Authority in Industry. New York: Wiley, 1956.

within the present organizational setting. The individual's ideas about his occupational role are influenced by childhood experiences, by his values and other personality characteristics, by formal education and apprenticeship, and the like. The ideas of various potential reference groups within and outside of the organization are available through reading, informal contacts, etc. There is reason to expect, then, that the role-conceptions of individuals in a given organizational position will vary and will not always conform to official role-requirements. Both the diversities and the modal patterns must be considered in organizational analysis.

Individual (and Modal) Role-Performance. This term refers to the overt behavioral aspect of role-definition—to the more or less characteristic ways in which the individual acts as the occupant of a social position. Because role-performance involves immediately observable behavior, its description would seem to present few systematic problems. However, the formulation of adequate variables for the analysis of role-performance is in fact a major theoretical problem and one of the great stumbling blocks in empirical research.

Everyone would agree, I suppose, that role-performance concerns only those aspects of the total stream of behavior that are structurally relevant. But which aspects of behavior are the important ones? And where shall the boundary be drawn between that which is structurally relevant and that which is incidental or idiosyncratic?

One's answer to these questions probably depends, above all, upon his conception of social structure. Those who conceive of social structure rather narrowly in terms of concrete work tasks and normative requirements, are inclined to take a similarly narrow view of role. In this view, role-performance is simply the fulfillment of formal role-norms, and anything else the person does is extraneous to role-performance as such. Its proponents acknowledge that there are variations in "style" of performance but

regard these as incidental. What is essential to role-performance is the degree to which norms are met.

A more complex and inclusive conception of social structure requires correspondingly multi-dimensional delineation of role-performance. An organization has, from this viewpoint, "latent" as well as "manifest" structure; it has a many-faceted emotional climate; it tends to "demand" varied forms of interpersonal allegiance, friendship, deference, intimidation, ingratiation, rivalry, and the like. If characteristics such as these are considered intrinsic properties of social structure, then they must be included in the characterization of role-performance. My own preference is for the more inclusive view. I regard social structure as having psychological as well as other properties, and I regard as intrinsic to role-performance the varied meanings and feelings which the actor communicates to those about him. Ultimately, we must learn to characterize organizational behavior in a way that takes into account, and helps to illuminate, its functions for the individual, for the others with whom he interacts, and for the organization.

It is commonly assumed that there is great uniformity in role-performance among the members of a given position. Or, in other words, that there is a dominant, modal pattern of role-performance corresponding to the structural requirements. The rationale here parallels that given above for role-conceptions. However, where individual variations in patterns of role-performance have been investigated, several modal types rather than a single dominant pattern were found.[26]

Nor is this variability surprising, except to those who have the most simplistic conception of social life. Role-performance, like any form of human behavior, is the resultant of many forces. Some of these forces derive from the organizational matrix; for example, from

---

[26]C. Argyris, *Personality and Organization*. New York: Harper, 1957; M. Greenblatt et al., op. cit.

role-demands and the pressures of authority, from informal group influences, and from impending sanctions. Other determinants lie within the person, as for example his role-conceptions and role-relevant personality characteristics. Except in unusual cases where all forces operate to channel behavior in the same direction, role-performance will reflect the individual's attempts at choice and compromise among diverse external and internal forces.

The relative contributions of various forms of influence to individual or modal role-performance can be determined only if each set of variables is defined and measured independently of the others. That is, indeed, one of the major reasons for emphasizing and sharpening the distinctions among role-performance, role-conception, and role-demands. Where these distinctions are not sharply drawn, there is a tendency to study one element and to assume that the others are in close fit. For example, one may learn from the official charter and the administrative authorities how the organization is supposed to work—the formal requirements—and then assume that it in fact operates in this way. Or, conversely, one may observe various regularities in role-performance and then assume that these are structurally determined, without independently assessing the structural requirements. To do this is to make structural explanations purely tautologous.

More careful distinction among these aspects of social structure and role will also, I believe, permit greater use of personality theory in organizational analysis. Let us turn briefly to this question.

ROLE-DEFINITION, PERSONALITY,
   AND SOCIAL STRUCTURE

Just as social structure presents massive forces which influence the individual from without toward certain forms of adaptation, so does personality present massive forces from within which lead him to select, create, and synthesize certain forms of adaptation rather than others. Role-definition may be seen from

one perspective as an aspect of personality. It represents the individual's attempt to structure his social reality, to define his place within it, and to guide his search for meaning and gratification. Role-definition is, in this sense, an ego achievement—a reflection of the person's capacity to resolve conflicting demands, to utilize existing opportunities and create new ones, to find some balance between stability and change, conformity and autonomy, the ideal and the feasible, in a complex environment.

The formation of a role-definition is, from a dynamic psychological point of view, an "external function" of the ego. Like the other external (reality-oriented) ego functions, it is influenced by the ways in which the ego carries out its "internal functions" of coping with, and attempting to synthesize, the demands of id, superego, and ego. These internal activities—the "psychodynamics" of personality—include among other things: unconscious fantasies; unconscious moral conceptions and the wishes against which they are directed; the characteristic ways in which unconscious processes are transformed or deflected in more conscious thought, feeling, and behavioral striving; conceptions of self and ways of maintaining or changing these conceptions in the face of changing pressures from within and from the external world.

In viewing role-definition as an aspect of personality, I am suggesting that it is, to varying degrees, related to and imbedded within other aspects of personality. An individual's conception of his role in a particular organization is to be seen within a series of wider psychological contexts: his conception of his occupational role generally (occupational identity), his basic values, life-goals, and conception of self (ego identity), and so on. Thus, one's way of relating to authorities in the organization depends in part upon his relation to authority in general, and upon his fantasies, conscious as well as unconscious, about the "good" and the "bad" parental authority. His ways of dealing with the stressful aspects of organizational life are influenced by the impulses, anxieties, and modes of defense that these stresses activate in him.[27]

There are variations in the degree to which personal role-definition is imbedded in, and influenced by, deeper-lying personality characteristics. The importance of individual or modal personality for role-definition is a matter for empirical study and cannot be settled by casual assumption. Traditional sociological theory can be criticized for assuming that individual role-definition is determined almost entirely by social structure. Similarly, dynamic personality theory will not take its rightful place as a crucial element of social psychology until it views the individual within his sociocultural environment. Lacking an adequate recognition and conceptualization of the individual's external reality—including the "reality" of social structure—personality researchers tend to assume that individual adaptation is primarily personality-determined and that reality is, for the most part, an amorphous blob structured by the individual to suit his inner needs.

Clearly, individual role-conception and role-performance do not emanate, fully formed, from the depths of personality. Nor are they simply mirror images of a mold established by social structure. Elsewhere, I have used the term "mirage" theory for the view, frequently held or implied in the psychoanalytic literature, that ideologies, role-conceptions, and behavior are mere epiphenomena or by-products of unconscious fantasies and defenses.[28] Similarly, the term "sponge" theory characterizes the view, commonly forwarded in the sociological literature, in which man is merely a passive, mechanical absorber of the prevailing structural demands.

Our understanding of personal role-definition will remain seriously impaired as long as we fail to place it, analytically, in both intrapersonal and structural-environmental contexts. That is to say, we must be concerned with the meaning of role-definition both for the individual personality and for the social system. A given role-definition is influenced by, and has an influence upon, the psyche as well as the socius. If we are adequately to understand the nature, the determinants, and the consequences of role-definition, we need the double perspective of personality and social structure. The use of these two reference points is, like the use of our two eyes in seeing, necessary for the achievement of depth in our social vision.

Theory and research on organizational roles must consider relationships among at least the following sets of characteristics: structurally given role-demands and -opportunities, personal role-definition (including conceptions and performance), and personality in its role-related aspects. Many forms of relationship may exist among them. I shall mention only a few hypothetical possibilities.

In one type case, the role-requirements are so narrowly defined, and the mechanisms of social control so powerful, that only one form of role-performance can be sustained for any given position. An organization of this type may be able selectively to recruit and retain only individuals who, by virtue of personality, find this system meaningful and gratifying. If a congruent modal personality is achieved, a highly integrated and stable structure may well emerge. I would hypothesize that a structurally congruent modal personality is one condition, though by no means the only one, for the stability of a rigidly integrated system. (In modern times, of course, the rapidity of technological change prevents long-term stability in any organizational structure.)

---

[27]C. Argyris, op. cit.; E. H. Erikson, Childhood and Society. New York: Norton, 1950; W. E. Henry, "The Business Executive: The Psychodynamics of a Social Role," American Journal of Sociology, 1949, 54, 286-291; F. H. Blum, Toward a Democratic Work Process. New York: Harper, 1933; and F. Pine and D. J. Levinson, "Two Patterns of Ideology," Role Conception, and Personality among Mental Hospital Aides," in M. Greenblatt et al., op. cit.

[28]D. J. Levinson, "Idea Systems in the Individual and Society," Paper presented at Boston University, Founder's Day Institute, 1954. Mimeographed: Center for Sociopsychological Research, Massachusetts Mental Health Center.

However, an organization of this kind may acquire members who are not initially receptive to the structural order, that is, who are <u>incongruent</u> in role-conception or in personality. Here, several alternative developments are possible.

1. The "incongruent" members may change so that their role-conceptions and personalities come better to fit the structural requirements.

2. The incongruent ones may leave the organization, by choice or by expulsion. The high turnover in most of our organizations is due less to technical incompetence than to rejection of the "conditions of life" in the organization.

3. The incongruent ones may remain, but in a state of apathetic conformity. In this case, the person meets at least the minimal requirements of role-performance but his role-conceptions continue relatively unchanged, he gets little satisfaction from work, and he engages in repeated "sabotage" of organizational aims. This is an uncomfortably frequent occurence in our society. In the Soviet Union as well, even after 40 years of enveloping social controls, there exist structurally incongruent forms of political ideology, occupational role-definition, and personality.[29]

4. The incongruent members may gain sufficient social power to change the organizational structure. This phenomenon is well known, though not well enough understood. For example, in certain of our mental hospitals, schools and prisons over the past 20-30 years, individuals with new ideas and personal characteristics have entered in large enough numbers, and in sufficiently strategic positions, to effect major structural changes. Similar ideological and structural transitions are evident in other types of organization, such as corporate business.

The foregoing are a few of many possible developments in a relatively monolithic structure. A somewhat looser organizational pattern is perhaps more commonly found. In this setting, structural change becomes a valued aim and innovation is seen as a legitimate function of members at various levels in the organization. To the extent that diversity and innovation are valued (rather than merely given lip-service), variations in individual role-definition are tolerated or even encouraged within relatively wide limits. The role-definitions that develop will reflect various degrees of synthesis and compromise between personal preference and structural demand.

In summary, I have suggested that a primary distinction be made between the structurally given role-demands and the forms of role-definition achieved by the individual members of an organization. Personal role-definition then becomes a linking concept between personality and social structure. It can be seen as a reflection of those aspects of individual personality that are activated and sustained in a given structural-ecological environment. This view is opposed both to the "sociologizing" of individual behavior and to the "psychologizing" of organizational structure. At the same time, it is concerned with both the psychological properties of social structure and the structural properties of individual adaptation.

Finally, we should keep in mind that both personality structure and social structure inevitably have their internal contradictions. No individual is sufficiently all of a piece that he will for long find any form of adaptation, occupational or otherwise, totally satisfying. Whatever the psychic gains stemming from a particular role-definition and social structure, there will also be losses: wishes that must be renounced or made unconscious, values that must be compromised, anxieties to be handled, personal goals that will at best be incompletely met. The organization has equivalent limitations. Its multiple purposes cannot all be optimally achieved. It faces recurrent dilemmas over conflicting requirements: control and freedom; centralization and decentralization of authority; security as against the risk of failure; specialization and diffusion of work function; stability and change; collective unity and diversity. Dilemmas such as these arise anew in different forms at each new step of organizational development, without permanent solution. And perpetual changes in

---

[29] A. Inkeles, Eugenia Hanfmann, and Helen Beier, "Modal Personality and Adjustment to the Soviet Political System," <u>Human Relations</u>, 1958, 11, 3-22.

technology, in scientific understanding, in material resources, in the demands and capacities of its members and the surrounding community, present new issues and require continuing organizational readjustment.

In short, every individual and every sociocultural form contains within itself the seeds of its own destruction—or its own reconstruction. To grasp both the sources of stability and the seeds of change in human affairs is one of the great challenges to contemporary social science.

PHYSICAL AND BIOLOGICAL BOUNDARIES: ECOLOGY AND DEMOGRAPHY

Cultural, Behavioral, and Ecological Perspectives in the Study of Social Organization

Otis Dudley Duncan and Leo F. Schnore

SOURCE: *American Journal of Sociology*, Vol. 65, (1959), pp. 132–46; also pp. 146–53.

Although there are various understandings as to the scope and problems of sociology, many would grant that the study of society as a system or pattern of organization constitutes the core problem, whatever other preoccupations it may have. As a result, a rather amorphous area, usually called "social organization," seems to provide sociology's central concern. Admittedly, the boundaries of the area are indistinct, and its conceptual apparatus is notably eclectic.

Tangential to this central area, three distinctive approaches to the study of society have developed within American sociology within the last few decades—the cultural, behavioral, and ecological. The terms may recall the tripartite scheme of Sorokin and Parsons: society, culture, and personality.[1] The purposes of these authors differ from ours. Focusing on the nature of society as the explanandum of sociological theory, we attempt to make clear that the concepts and assumptions in use in sociology today were fashioned largely from these different ways of regarding society. However, no prospect of integrating them into a "socio-cultural" theory or a "general theory of action" is here entertained; the relationships among the three are not taken as evidence that they are special cases of some master scheme.

"Cultural sociology," whose "father" might be identified as Sumner, was picked up as a label in the 1920's following the popularization of concepts of culture by Ogburn, Chapin, and others who leaned heavily on such authorities in

[1] Pitirim Sorokin, Society, Culture, and Personality (New York: Harper & Bros., 1947); Talcott Parsons, The Social System (Glencoe, Ill.: Free Press, 1951); Talcott Parsons and Edward A. Shils (eds.), Toward a General Theory of Action (Cambridge, Mass.: Harvard University Press, 1951). In some respects the perspectives identified here correspond more closely to those sketched by Harold W. Pfautz in his "Social Stratification and Sociology," Transactions of the Second World Congress of Sociology (London: International Sociological Association, 1954), II, 311-20.

anthropology as Kroeber, Lowie, and Wissler. The pervasive impact of cultural sociology as a school of thought has waned, but virtually all general texts on sociology continue to give considerable play to concepts derived from culture theory. Znaniecki's recent magnum opus, Cultural Sciences, persuasively restates his position that social systems are a subclass of cultural systems and that the methods of studying social and cultural systems are generically the same. However, Znaniecki's work draws heavily on European sources of culture concepts and stands somewhat outside the main stream of cultural sociology in this country.[2] A splendid statement that is of greater relevance to developments within American sociology is given in the collection of Kroeber's papers, The Nature of Culture.[3]

"Behavioral science," of course, is little more than a new label for what has long gone under the name of "social psychology." The current popularity and even dominance of "behavioral" studies in sociology reflect, in part, the vigor of recently developed sociometric and small-group interests, the convergence of certain social-psychological concepts, stemming, respectively, from sociological and psychological traditions, and the current preoccupation of sociologists with such problems of method as scaling, experimental design, and analysis of opinion-survey data. The contemporary version of behavioral science seems to find little place for the older tradition of "collective behavior." This is unfortunate, inasmuch as the latter was explicitly an approach to the study of society, as distinguished from the study of attitudes, personality, socialization, and the processes of interaction emphasized in recent social psychology. It is in the relatively unstructured collective behavior of aggregates that we are sometimes able to observe organization in an incipient form. Thus the study of social move-

ments may give clues to the emergence of organizational forms prior to their becoming viable, that is, before they possess unit character. This possibility assumes some practical importance when it is recognized that most societal origins are lost in the past. The recent appearance of a comprehensive treatise on collective behavior and the apparent renewal of interest in the study of social movements may indicate that this tradition has more vitality than seemed apparent for some time.[4] Should this prove to be the case, perhaps it would be well to regard collective behavior as a fourth major perspective.

"Human ecology" has had a curious history, arising as it did in the context of a series of specialized empirical studies of contemporary urban life. Its early exponents can hardly be said to have grasped its possibilities and implications. In fact, the leading spokesman of the first sociological version of ecology denied that he and the other early writers were attempting to construct a theory.[5] Consequently, when the urban studies lost their novelty, ecology was relegated to a minor theoretical role at best and virtually became identified with a rather narrow preoccupation with urban areal distributions and the elementary techniques applied to their analysis. The belated summary of this "classical" point of view appeared in 1950 in Quinn's Human Ecology.[6] By coincidence, the same year witnessed the appearance of Hawley's Human Ecology, which developed human ecology as "a theory of community structure."[7] This treatise presented not only a systematic account of human ecology as

---

[2]Florian Znaniecki, Cultural Sciences (Urbana: University of Illinois Press, 1952).

[3]A. L. Kroeber, The Nature of Culture (Chicago: University of Chicago Press, 1952).

[4]Ralph H. Turner and Lewis M. Killian, Collective Behavior (Englewood Cliffs, N. J.: Prentice-Hall, Inc., 1957); Rudolf Heberle, Social Movements (New York: Appleton-Century-Crofts, 1951); Herbert Blumer, "Collective Behavior," in J. B. Gittler (ed.), Review of Sociology: Analysis of a Decade (New York: John Wiley & Sons, 1957).

[5]Robert E. Park's review of Milla A. Aliban's Social Ecology in the Annals, CCII (March, 1939), 264-65.

[6]James A. Quinn, Human Ecology (Englewood Cliffs, N. J.: Prentice-Hall, Inc., 1950).

[7]Amos H. Hawley, Human Ecology (New York: Ronald Press Co., 1950).

the study of social organization but also a statement of its basic assumptions, elaborated in a number of important conceptual contributions and a host of researchable hypotheses. In the light of subsequent thinking the fact that Hawley's volume tended to stop short at the community level of organization must be viewed as a temporary expedient, for there is nothing in the basic framework of ecology that precludes its attention to more-inclusive forms of organization. A flurry of interest in the ecological viewpoint on the part of disciplines other than sociology seems certain to force human ecologists working in the sociological tradition into more ambitious conceptions of their task.

None of the three perspectives can be regarded as an exclusively sociological specialism. Certainly, each has ramifications carrying it into a whole range of problems lying well beyond the study of society, which is the focus of interest here. Unless sociology is willing to revert to a Comtean encyclopedism, it will hardly wish to claim the entirety of behavioral science, culture theory, and human ecology. In discussing their contributions to the study of society, therefore, one must avoid the appearance of evaluating them as fields or disciplines in their own right—on their "home territory," so to speak. At the same time the character of their extra-sociological preoccupations manifestly directs and limits their mode of attack on the core problems of sociology. This is seen readily in their key problems.

The cultural approach is derived from classical anthropological theory, which conceives of culture as a more or less integrated totality, comprising cultural patterns or sub-systems of which society is one, along with art, religion, language, technology, and others. A volume such as Kroeber's Configurations of Cultural Growth, for example, scarcely makes reference to social structure and can hardly be called a contribution to knowledge of social change, except indirectly.[8]

The original intention of the cultural sociologists was to bring over from culture theory its general concepts and major hypotheses, demonstrating their applicability and fruitfulness in the study of society and social change in particular. Thus society, like other parts of culture, was described in terms of cultural continuity ("social heritage"), invention, cultural diffusion, and the like.

The enduring contribution of this school, as it turned out, was not the strangely static "cultural determinism" of certain of its epigoni, or the theory which explains social systems in terms of "institutions" derived from "cultural value patterns," or yet the abortive effort to construct a global "socio-cultural" theory. It was rather the interpretation of social change as an adjustment to cultural, and particularly technological, accumulation. (As is suggested below, the ecological perspective is perhaps a more congenial milieu for this type of interpretation than culture theory per se.) Hence the theoretical weakness of behavioralism in regard to change is not characteristic of the best cultural sociology. The latter has a well-developed interest—at least on the conceptual level—in innovation and invention and in diffusion and borrowing, all conceived as processes. In practice, except for the global theorists, cultural sociologists seldom concerned themselves with such problems of culture theory as the structure and evolution of linguistic systems, movements in styles of art and philosophy, or diffusion of items of ceremonial culture. But culture theory, insofar as it suggests an effort to treat these matters as aspects of an integrated whole, may distract the student whose business is to deal with social organization.

The behavioral approach (we shall refer primarily to the social-psychological version rather than that of "collective behavior") is centrally concerned with how the individual participates in social life: how the person reconciles himself to the necessity of living with others, how he relates to other persons, how he is socialized, how his behavior is controlled

---

[8]A. L. Kroeber, Configurations of Culture Growth (Berkeley: University of California Press, 1944).

or influenced by that of others, and how all these problems are related to the structure of his personality and the content of his attitudes, commitments, orientations, and personal adjustment. The sociological viewpoint appropriate for this range of problems regards society as a pattern of interpersonal relationships or as an arena of social interaction. Here, however, the relevant "structure" is that which is perceived by the individual, just as the relevant "environment" is the social environment, which is again conceived in terms of individual perceptions. One searches this literature in vain for more than superficial reference to the brute facts that men live in a physical environment and that they employ material technology in adapting to it. More important, adaptation itself is conceived in individualistic terms rather than as a collective process.[9]

As a consequence of the behavioralists' focus on the individual, his motivation, and his "tensions . . . as he fits himself into the social system,"[10] they find little need for structural or organizational concepts, nor do they like.to entertain hypotheses calling for an explanation of social change other than through such in-

tervening variables as dispositional changes or modifications of character structure. Many behavioralists have a thoroughly nominalistic view of societies and groups; as a result, they are methodical reductionists and have a trained incapacity to view social organization as a reality sui generis in functional and evolutionary terms. (These remarks do not apply so forcefully to the student of collective behavior, who examines social organization in the process of its emergence from relatively unstructured interaction. But this view, of course, has a built-in bias that precludes its yielding an adequate account of society as a going concern or the underlying factors of social change.)

In fact, the most glaring weakness of the behavioral approach to problems of organization can be seen in the treatment accorded change. One is hard put to find the source of societal dynamics—the causes of the changing objective circumstances perceived by the individual, to which he attends. Thus the overwhelming stress upon the individual's "adjustment" to altered external circumstances and the almost total lack of attention to the mainsprings of change, wherever they may reside. Actually, by adopting a patently static conception of culture as "that which is socially transmitted between generations," the behavioral approach is forced to an impasse: it can "explain" stability over time, but it is unable to cope with change within its own frame of reference without invoking "deviation" from norms. A circular argument often results, for social change is defined as a new pattern of individual behavior, which is brought about by "deviation"—a new pattern of behavior.

The ecological viewpoint likewise is easily deflected, in its turn, into studies of the environment in strictly geographic terms or into exercises in formal demography. However, its view of social organization as the collective adaptation of a population to its environment avoids the reductionism of behavioral concepts and the etherealism of the "value-pattern" concepts of some culture theorists.

---

[9]The Handbook of Social Psychology, ed. Carl Murchison (Worcester, Mass.: Clark University Press, 1935), contained a long chapter on "The Physical Environment" by the ecologist V. E. Shelford. But in the two-volume Handbook of Social Psychology, ed. Gardner Lindzey (Cambridge, Mass.: Addison-Wesley Publishing Co., 1954), only 2 out of 1,175 pages are explicitly devoted to physical-environmental features (see Henry W. Riecken and George C. Homans, "Psychological Aspects of Social Structure," section on "Social Structure and the Environment," ibid., pp. 801-2). Clyde Kluckhohn dismisses the relevance of the physical environment for human activities by quoting Margaret T. Hodgen, that "the historically important thing in regard to natural resources is man's attitude toward them" ("Culture and Behavior," ibid., p. 922).

[10]Phraseology attributed to Wilbert E. Moore by Clyde V. Kiser in a summary of a round table on "Exploration of Possibilities for New Studies of Factors Affecting Size of Family," Milbank Memorial Fund Quarterly, XXXI (October, 1953), 477. (Moore is singled out for the aptness of his language, not necessarily because of his theoretical position.)

In this sense ecology deals with society in somewhat more concrete terms than either of the other approaches. The concept of a "population" as a system with emergent properties is not found in the behavioral or cultural perspectives, nor is the version of the functions of social organization to which this concept leads.

Judged by their research interests and theoretical concerns, as mirrored in current publications, most sociologists today are inclined to be behavioralists. Some have a familiarity with culture theory, and they eclectically accept elements of the cultural approach; few have an acquaintance with human ecology that goes beyond the chapters on urban ecology in their undergraduate textbooks. A brief exposition of this perspective may be appropriate at this point.

In the most general terms the framework of human ecology embraces four main referential concepts: population, environment, technology, and organization, which define what may be called the "ecological complex."[11] Organization is assumed to be a property of the population that has evolved and is sustained in the process of adaptation of the population to its environment, which may include other populations. Insofar as it is amenable to ecological study, organization tends to be investigated as a ramification of sustenance activities, broadly conceived, which utilize whatever technological apparatus is at the population's disposal or is developed by it.

While in its crudest version this framework suggests that organization is to be viewed as the "dependent variable," influenced by the other three "independent variables," upon a more sophisticated view, organization is seen as reciprocally related to each of the other elements of the ecological complex. In fact, to define any of the elements of this complex adequately, one has to take account of their relationship with organization. The notion of an "ecosystem" may be used as a heuristic designation for the ecological complex in order to bring out this aspect of interrelatedness which some writers have identified as the most fundamental premise in ecological thinking. That to others this notion is one of the central postulates of sociology itself only serves to underscore the sociological character of ecology—whether in its plant, animal, or human version. Darwin's conception of the "web of life" refers to a system of organization first and foremost.

Although ecology is not to be identified with the study of areal distributions, and its subject matter is by no means limited to the "territorial arrangements that social activities assume,"[12] the study of spatial relationships continues to play a key role in ecology for several reasons. First, territoriality is a major factor giving unit character to populations. Second, space is simultaneously a requisite for the activities of any organizational unit and an obstacle which must be overcome in establishing interunit relationships. Finally, space—like time—furnishes a convenient and invariant set of reference points for observation, and observed spatiotemporal regularities and rhythms furnish convenient indicators of structural relationships.[13]

In comparing the three alternative approaches, it is instructive to raise two closely related questions: What are the unit parts that are analytically manipulated? What emerges as a "system" when these unit parts are ordered?

In the case of the cultural approach, the units turn out to be "cultural traits," such as the elements of language, aes-

---

[11] If one needs a mnemonic device, the initial letters of these terms spell p-o-e-t (see Otis Dudley Duncan, "Human Ecology and Population Studies," in Philip M. Hauser and Otis Dudley Duncan [eds.], The Study of Population [Chicago: University of Chicago Press, 1959], pp. 678–716, and Leo F. Schnore, "Social Morphology and Human Ecology," American Journal of Sociology, LXIII [May, 1958], 620–34).

[12] Walter Firey, Land Use in Central Boston (Cambridge, Mass.: Harvard University Press, 1947), p. 3.

[13] Hawley, op. cit., and his succinct account of "The Approach of Human Ecology to Urban Areal Research," Scientific Monthly, LXXIII (July, 1951), 48–49.

thetic values, or material artifacts, and they are organized into "trait complexes" and less frequently, cultural and subcultural systems. With respect to the behavioral perspective, the ultimate focus is upon one or another variety of mental behavior (e.g., attitudes, aspirations, and expectations), and these elements are organized most often into "personality systems" or "character types." From the ecological standpoint, however, the elementary unit of analysis—the "atom" so to speak—is the "pattern of activity," or simply "activity." The system envisioned is an organization of activities, arranged in overlapping and interpenetrating series of activity constellations, or groups.

From the standpoint of the individual engaged in it, the activity or the individual's share in the activity is commonly designated as his "role." This term would be quite serviceable for ecological analysis[14] were it not for the psychological connotations that have become attached thereto in the work of writers like Linton, Parsons, and Stouffer. The ecologist is interested in the pattern of observable physical activity itself rather than the subjective expectations that individuals may entertain of their roles. Ecological analysis does not attempt to explain the individual's feelings of obligation, the stresses he suffers as a consequence of performing several roles simultaneously or sequentially, or his motivational syndromes when he is engaged in different sorts of activities. At the common-sense level the closest approximation to the ecological conception of "activity" is the notion implied by the term "occupation," although our interest includes activities that do not ordinarily receive monetary compensation (e.g., those found within the household complex). "Functionary" is a less frequently used term that carries a similar conno-

tation, and—within general ecology—the concept of "niche" designates practically the same.[15]

Although the matter of subjective obligation emphasized in role theory is irrelevant for our purposes, there is a strong emphasis upon reciprocity in the ecological conception of activity, for the activity is not conceived individualistically or in vacuo. It cannot be conceived of apart from other activities. The logic of ecological theory compels the analyst to view distinctive activities—their numbers and kinds—as properties of aggregates or populations. Thus an aggregate may be labeled as relatively "undifferentiated" if it is found to engage in few distinctive activities. Actually, however, that portion of the ecological notion of activities that points to their interdependence is perhaps the crucial element of the concept. This stress, it might be added, indicates the intrinsically sociological character of ecological thought, for, if sociology can be credited with any one major insight, it is its recognition of the inescapable interdependence of human activities.

Such a conception gives immediate rise to a range of essentially taxonomic problems. Most abstractly, what are the generic forms of activity constellations or groups? Unfortunately, this basic taxonomic work has been studiously avoided by sociologists in general and by ecologists in particular. Ecologists themselves are currently obliged, for example, to work with crude polar types of communities and societies. In many respects a perusal of the recent literature suggests that taxonomic work is being carried forward largely by anthropologists, economists, geographers, and political scientists rather than by sociologists.[16]

---

[14] Amos H. Hawley, in "Some Remarks on the Relation of Social Psychology and Human Ecology," a paper read at the 1950 meetings of the American Sociological Society, defines "role" as "a routinely performed activity which depends for its continuity on the routine performance of other activities." We are greatly indebted to this paper and to his other published and unpublished work.

[15] Odum writes that "the habitat is the organism's 'address,' and the niche is its 'profession,' biologically speaking" (Eugene P. Odum, Fundamentals of Ecology [Philadelphia: W. B. Saunders Co., 1953], p. 15).

[16] See Hawley, Human Ecology, chap. xii: "Community Structure," for a discussion of types of activity constellation; the household, the production unit, and the community itself are treated in some detail. One misses, however, a formal treatment of

Another line of inquiry is to ask to what extent the alternative approaches might serve to inform major areas of current interest for students of social organization. For illustrative purposes we may raise this question with respect to three topics of much current theoretical and empirical interest: bureaucracy, stratification, and urbanization. We shall then allude to the issue of functional analysis.

In the case of the cultural approach to these three topics there seem to be almost no immediate contributions in view, beyond certain broad generalities regarding the indigenous appearance of such "trait complexes" as written language, monetary systems, and rational techniques and devices for the measurement of time, space, and weight with the emergence of urban forms of organization. If it offers any special contribution to an understanding of bureaucracy, it escapes most writers on the subject. With respect to stratification, the only relevant contribution is the notion of distinctive "subcultures" in various strata; this term, however, merely provides another label for the phenomena under investigation.

As to the behavioral approach, to the extent that it is employed in these areas of investigation, the main focus is upon the effects upon the individual of a position in a bureaucratic setting, of a particular locus in the stratification system, or of living in an urban area. When behavioralists study bureaucracy, they study the stresses on the individual in a bureaucratic context and his accomodations thereto rather than the functions of bureaucratic systems as such or the societal and technological matrix within which bureaucracy evolves. In the analysis of stratification, behavioralists avoid the problem of the determinants of sys-

tems of rank. Rather their overwhelming concern is with such matters as the criteria employed by individuals in their evaluations of others, the processes of socialization in the various strata, or the development of stratum-specific clusters of attitudes, values, and modes of thought. Regarding urbanization, behavioralists have not proceeded very far beyond the hypotheses sketched by Wirth in his essay, "Urbanism as a Way of Life," in which he suggested certain consequences for the individual living in a community of great size, density, and heterogeneity.[17] As yet no one has seriously put forward a causal account of the rise of cities in which social-psychological factors take precedence, although there has been some recent effort to deal thus with "suburbanization."[18] In each of these problems, then, the focus is almost inevitably upon the <u>consequences</u> for the individual of the very forms that the student would like to explain.

In contrast, the <u>ecological</u> perspective apparently holds great promise for the student of organization, although, frankly, it is at present largely a matter of potential rather than of solid performance in the areas of stratification and bureaucracy. But in the study of urbanization, of course, a well-documented case can be argued that ecology provides an appropriate mode of causal analysis; for this reason, we shall not elaborate the point. However, ecologists themselves are not entirely satisfied with the present state of their own research on urbanization. Much more work is required, detailing

---

systems of local communities, regions, and societies, for which see Rutledge Vining, "A Description of Certain Spatial Aspects of an Economic System," <u>Economic Development and Cultural Change</u>, III (January, 1955), 147-95, and the comment by Edgar M. Hoover, "The Concept of a System of Cities," <u>Economic Development and Cultural Change</u>, III (January, 1955), 196-98.

[17]Louis Wirth, "Urbanism as a Way of Life," <u>American Journal of Sociology</u>, XLIV (July, 1938), 1-24.

[18]Fava and Bell, respectively, stress a propensity for "neighboring" and "familistic values" in their discussions of the development of suburbs; both, however, eventually admit that they are attempting to account for the selectivity of migration to suburbs (even in the absence of controls) and that they are not presuming to explain the rise of suburbs themselves (see Sylvia Fleis Fava, "Suburbanism as a Way of Life," <u>American Sociological Review</u>, XXI [February, 1956], 34-37, and Wendell Bell, "Familism and Suburbanization: One Test of the Social Choice Hypothesis," <u>Rural Sociology</u>, XXI [September-December, 1956], 276-83).

the precise technological, demographic, and environmental conditions under which various urban forms of organization may be expected to appear and—once established—to develop at given rates.[19] But the absence of comparative data of historical depth and on a world-wide scale poses a major problem.

In the two remaining areas—bureaucracy and stratification—the ecological conception of "activity constellations" could be fruitfully extended, to the benefit of the analysis of social organization and to ecology itself. If one does not become deflected by an interest in certain institutional mechanisms, such as provisions for promotion and job security, the salient features of a bureaucracy are its great size, its high degree of differentiation, and its internal stratification—properties of the aggregate itself which suggest that the bureaucracy, as a mode of organization, shares certain key features with the urban community and the urban society in which it typically appears. Further, these common formal characteristics suggest that the causation may be similar and that the study of a bureaucracy in terms of the ecological complex may be more than an idle exercise. On the face of it, the impact of technological developments would appear to warrant further study. It is a commonplace to speak of the historical emergence of the factory, a large, differentiated, hierarchically organized system, as an organizational response to the development of steam power and other technological innovations. Longitudinal study of growing business enterprises or governmental bureaus might also establish whether or not mounting numbers and spatial expansion of functions tend to exert a pressure in the direction of increasing "bureaucratization."[20] Boulding's recent attempt to account for the rise of the type of large-scale social

unit that lends itself to bureaucratic organization makes explicit reference to what the author regards as an "ecological" framework.[21] Had his argument availed itself more explicitly of the ecological conceptions of sociologists, it might have provided even more convincing evidence of their relevance. Reference may also be made to a study which demonstrates the mutual relevance of studies in bureaucratic organization and in metropolitan dominance.[22]

In the area of stratification, of course, the "prestige dimension" in the subjective sense in which it is generally understood is beyond ecology's immediate purview. The primary contribution would consist of aiding the student of organization in attacking the problem of power. However, precisely this aspect of stratification is widely regarded as the most neglected in American sociological thought.[23] For the moment, the ecologist's contribution to the analysis of power may be confined to the context of the local community. Hawley has suggested that "dominance" in the local community attaches to those functional units that control the flow of sustenance into it.[24] Comparative analysis would be required to test this hypothesis adequately; however, informal observation leads one to conclude that cities of different size and functional type do comprise significantly different arenas for the struggle between contending power groups. The "town-and-gown" splits in small university towns present somewhat different situations from those in the traditional "company town," and both differ significantly from the complexities

[19]Duncan, op. cit.

[20]Frederic W. Terrien and Donald L. Mills, "The Effect of Changing Size upon the Internal Structure of Organizations," American Sociological Review, XX (February, 1955), 11-13.

[21]Kenneth E. Boulding, The Organizational Revolution (New York: Harper & Bros., 1953).

[22]Donnell M. Pappenfort, "The Ecological Field and the Metropolitan Community: Manufacturing and Management," American Journal of Sociology, LXIV (January, 1959), 380-85.

[23]Seymour M. Lipset and Reinhard Bendix, "Social Status and Social Structure: A Re-examination of Data and Interpretations, I and II," British Journal of Sociology, II (June and September, 1951), 150-68 and 230-54.

[24]Hawley, Human Ecology, pp. 229-30.

of the metropolis, where dominance is diffused.

Indeed, there are striking formal similarities between the very concept of "power" and that of "dominance" which, in general ecology, is treated as a subcategory of symbiotic relation between dissimilar functions and is ordinarily given a species referent. Both concepts point to the ability of one cluster of activities or niches to set the conditions under which others must function. One promising line of inquiry is the elaboration of the related ecological concepts of "subdominant" and "influent." These are also positional concepts that refer to a system of interdependent relationships between activities. Consideration of their formal analogues in the study of stratification in the human community might eliminate the too-frequent conceptualization of power as a "one-way street." In this connection a problem that has yet to be adequately explored is the relationship between occupational differentiation and stratification: occupations hold central positions in theories of stratification that are otherwise strikingly dissimilar.

Coming at the problem in another way, strata may be viewed as assemblages of household units, although the precise conditions under which they are likely to act in concert have yet to be specified. In another guise this is the question of whether strata are "really" groups or merely statistical categories.[25] An unequivocal answer is, of course, impossible; rather it seems that under certain circumstances households do act together to such an extent that they can be literally regarded as groups. "Castes" are cases in point, although probably too much attention has been given such institutional mechanisms as caste endogamy and occupational inheritance. A somewhat related problem—although it requires analysis outside the confines of the local community—is that of the circumstances under which occupational coalitions appear. The standard answer is that they emerge in response to some external threat. Systematically overlooked, however, is the simple matter of spatiotemporal accessibility. The difficulty of unionizing workers in industries widely scattered or subject to seasonality is instructive.

One recent approach to stratification that has come into some prominence is by way of the concept of "class crystallization."[26] Although the form of the data with which most investigators of this phenomenon have worked (the products of sample surveys) has tended to turn them in the direction of analyzing the extent to which the individual's ranked roles may be in alignment, the writers seem to appreciate fully the possibility of characterizing whole aggregates—communities and even societies—as more or less crystallized. Just as an aggregate may be more or less differentiated by the number of its distinctive activities, it seems possible that degrees of stratification may be shown by the extent of its crystallization. The usual approach, of course, is to conceive societies as possessing varying degrees of permeability between strata, with "open" and "closed" societies as polar types; individual mobility is used as an index. However, this method requires "dynamic" data, for example, career mobility or father's occupation—measures that inevitably involve thorny methodological problems, including controls for age and estimates of structurally induced mobility. In contrast, crystallization can be used with data referring to only one point in time; however, this does not

---

[25]Gerhard Lenski, "American Social Classes: Statistical Strata or Social Groups?" *American Journal of Sociology*, LVIII (September, 1952), 139-44.

[26]Hawley, *Human Ecology*, p. 231; Ronald Freedman, Amos H. Hawley, Werner S. Landecker, Gerhard E. Lenski, and Horace M. Miner, *Principles of Sociology* (rev. ed; New York: Henry Holt & Co., 1956), chaps. vii and xiii; Gerhard Lenski, "Status Crystallization: A Non-vertical Dimension of Social Status," *American Sociological Review*, XIX (August, 1954), 405-13, and his "Social Participation and Status Crystallization," *American Sociological Review*, XXI (August, 1956), 458-64; Ralph Spielman, "A Study of Stratification in the United States" (unpublished doctoral dissertation, University of Michigan, 1953).

prevent its use in longitudinal analysis. Given comparable data of appropriate form, a series of "snap-shot" observations would provide a "moving picture" and might incidentally settle the current controversy over whether the United States is tending toward a "closed" society.

But the point is that the concept of crystallization permits one to define stratification operationally as a variable property of the aggregate, without further reference to the individual. For ecological analysis this may then be related to other attributes of the aggregate—for example, its size, rate of growth, degree of urbanization, and technological equipment.[27] However, it soon becomes evident that there will be inevitable difficulties in the analysis of stratification in the absence of a well-defined taxonomy of societies. Moreover, a coherent typology of communities would also be of enormous value, especially in view of the usual research strategy of making case studies of single communities. Again, the single-industry town presumably reveals a different degree of class crystallization from that of the metropolis.[29] At this point the ecologists can be of some assistance, for at least they have done some exploratory typing of communities according to major functions.

The human ecologist is, of course, in a unique position by virtue of his skills and preoccupations to contribute to

knowledge of the sheerly demographic and territorial aspects of stratification.[30] But the test of ecological theory is its ability to clarify issues and suggest hypotheses. One issue which has been much discussed in the last decade is that of the relation between patterns of stratification in the local community and those of the mass society[31] or of the reasons for variation in stratification patterns.[32] It is difficult to see how a behavioral approach can explain such variation, while the cultural viewpoint has contributed little more than the virtually tautological suggestion that differences among communities or their deviations from a national pattern may be regarded as "substitute profiles of cultural orientation."[33] But, if social stratification is conceived to be related to other aspects of organization, the ecologist is in a position to indicate reasons for both similarities and differences in a community's patterns of stratification. On the one hand, modern communities are highly interrelated by function, as is shown by the volume of intercommunity economic and migratory flows; they share a common technology for the most part; and communities of comparable size have fairly similar local service structures and perform fairly similar reportories of services for outlying areas. On the other hand, each community holds a more or less specialized position in the complex of intercommunity relationships, reflected in variations in occupational structure and levels of living. Moreover, given unequal rates of change in the several sectors of the economy, com-

---

[27]For an interesting use of census and other mass data in a "crystallization" framework see Leonard Blumberg, "The Relationship among Rank Systems in American Society," in Freedman *et al.*, *op. cit.*, pp. 540-44. In both the mobility and the crystallization approaches, of course, the sheer number of strata recognized by the observer will affect his judgment of the degree of "openness" or "crystallization" that obtains.

[28]Pfautz (*op. cit.*) makes a similar observation with respect to mobility. For a provocative discussion of stratification in the context of types of community and society see Gideon Sjoberg, "Folk and 'Feudal' Societies," *American Journal of Sociology*, LVIII (November, 1952), 231-39, and his related discussion of "The Preindustrial City," *American Journal of Sociology*, LX (March, 1955), 438-45.

[29]Lipset and Bendix, *op. cit.*

[30]Otis Dudley Duncan and Beverly Duncan, "Residential Distribution and Occupational Stratification," *American Journal of Sociology*, LX (March, 1955), 493-503.

[31]Paul K. Hatt, "Stratification in the Mass Society," *American Sociological Review*, XV (April, 1950), 216-22.

[32]Otis Dudley Duncan and Jay W. Artis, "Some Problems of Stratification Research," *Rural Sociology*, XVI (March, 1951), 17-29.

[33]Florence Kluckhohn, "Dominant and Substitute Profiles of Cultural Orientations: Their Significance for the Analysis of Social Stratification," *Social Forces*, XXVIII (May, 1950), 376-93.

munities with differing economic bases are expected to evidence differing rates of growth and hence differential opportunities for social mobility. Finally, ecologists have amassed a considerable amount of information on variation in social structure according to community size, which is highly relevant to the differences in stratification pattern. In short, it seems good scientific strategy to couch analysis of structural variation in structural terms, at any rate until such time as it is shown that the only recourse is to another level or type of abstraction.[34]

We believe that the acceptance of an ecological approach would go far toward clarifying contemporary issues in organizational theory concerning "functionalism." Although "functional analysis" arose in the cultural approach to society, it has been taken over by the behavioralists. Consequently, recent statements of the "functional requisites of society" have been confounded by the attempt of their authors to proceed simultaneously from both an individual and a social perspective. What are called "functions" are, as often as not, aspects of individual motivation, and the necessity for a clear distinction between motivation and function has yet to be clearly recognized.[35] A coherent statement of functionalist principles as applied to the study of society will follow from the recognition that functions should be attributed to units of social organization—activity constellations—and not to individuals as persons or to symbols, values, or other cultural items.

Ecological structure is conceived as an organization of functions—activities that are dependent upon other activities. Ecologists have usually bypassed the question of "contributions to the maintenance of the system," although this problem logically does not lie beyond their purview. However, they have deliberately avoided the blind alley of exploring "functions versus dysfunctions," recognizing that what is functional for one part of the total system is often dysfunctional for another. (This fact, incidentally, appears to be the source of many conflicts of power.) Moreover, the ecologist makes no use of the distinction between latent and patent functions since this rests with the individual's knowledge and judgment, and the individual's personal view of things is, as such, of no ecological interest. Parenthetically, it might be remarked that the ecologist—for all his lack of skill in social-psychological matters—has come to recognize that what is obvious, intended, and anticipated by one person may be unknown, unanticipated, and unintended by another. Perhaps his acumen has been fortified by wrestling with what now appears to be an irrelevant distinction between "natural" and "planned" processes. At any rate, it is clear to the contemporary ecologist, though it was not to the classical, that the subject matter of human ecology cannot be defined residually in terms of an unmanageable psychological distinction.

It is significant that, while theorists of culture and behavioralists have been propounding confused hypothetical versions of functionalism, ecologists have been busy making inductive studies of the functions of communities and correlating functions with aspects of organization, location, and demographic structure. This suggests that the ability to manipulate ideas about function effectively in research develops rather easily after an ecological perspective is adopted.

The ecological approach, in comparison with the two alternatives, holds out special promise of enriching the fund of systematic knowledge on social change—here conceived as the transformations of patterns of social organization occurring over time rather than as, say, shifts in value systems or modal character structure. Recent contributions exhibit a wide range of ecological hypotheses which illuminate broad patterns of social evolu-

---

[34]Duncan and Artis, op. cit., pp. 28-29.

[35]See David Aberle et al., "The Functional Prerequisites of a Society," *Ethics*, LX (January, 1950), 100-111.

tion, help to explain contemporary social trends, and provide a sociological matrix for studies of "economic development." In contrast, the efforts of present-day behavioralists contribute little to our understanding of where modern society came from or where it is going, and the limited potentialities for providing a comprehensive account of social change within the framework of "collective behavior" remain largely latent, as a recent statement admits.[36] Culture theory, too, except as it implicitly or explicitly incorporates an ecological viewpoint, fails to come to grips with many salient aspects of social change, particularly insofar as it remains preoccupied with global theories of cultural evolution or sociocultural dynamics.[37]

Ogburn's theory of social change continues to be the most influential one in American sociology.[38] Although it developed in the tradition of cultural sociology, actually it has assumed a quite different emphasis. Ogburn's theory falls into two main parts: the theory of cultural accumulation, expounded with primary reference to technology, and the hypothesis that a large part of social change amounts to an adjustment to technological change. In the first part, the theory depends upon such concepts as invention, culture base, cultural accumulation, and, quite incidentally, cultural diffusion. Invention is regarded as fundamental and is viewed, in turn, as a function of "demand," the culture base, and mental ability. The last-named is regarded as essentially a constant, while the inability of demand to stimulate invention in the absence of an adequate culture base is emphasized.

Ogburn's theory of invention could doubtless be improved by casting it in

ecological terms, that is, by examining technological innovation as a response to demographic, environmental, and organizational variations over space and time. "Demand," for example, may be viewed as rather sensitive to population change. Moreover, while the relative distribution of mental ability may be viewed as a constant, the absolute number of persons of superior ability is, of course, directly related to size of population. Moreover, ability as such makes no inventions, but organized ability does, for the more and more elaborate organization of inventive effort is a trend nearly equal in importance to technological accumulation itself. Studies of such organization would reveal the role of mobilized resources in making inventions possible; no amount of progress in pure science accomplished through the exercise of "mental ability" would have produced the atom bomb without a tremendous mobilization of resources and personnel. Finally, the character of the problem of collective adjustment facing a population rather than "demand"—in the somewhat anemic sense of the economist—may be what gives direction to invention. Thus the environment itself must be taken into account from the standpoint of the limitations and the possibilities that it presents: the arts of navigation are not perfected by landlocked peoples; and the irrigation systems developed where there are monsoons differ from those devised in arid regions.

The second part of Ogburn's theory—social adjustment to technological change—requires little restatement to bring it well within the compass of an ecological framework. In fact, the voluminous evidence that he has amassed on behalf of this general hypothesis is one of the major claims of technology to its status as a prime element in the ecological complex, along with population, environment, and organization. Here again, however, Ogburn's analysis of the implications of technology for organization seems to require supplementary exploration of the demographic situations and environmental contexts in which tech-

[36]Turner and Killian, op. cit., chap. xxii, pp. 515-29.

[37]Sorokin, op. cit. A "culturological" view that has had less influence in sociology is that of Leslie A. White (see his The Science of Culture [New York: Farrar & Straus, 1949]).

[38]William F. Ogburn, Social Change (New York: B. W. Huebsch, 1922; rev. ed., New York: Viking Press, 1950).

nology modifies organization.[39]

The most recent theory of cultural change to attract widespread attention is one that espouses a frankly ecological view: Steward's "cultural ecology" and his theory of "multilinear evolution."[40] Steward's position differs in a number of details from the ecological perspective as it has developed within sociology. The key difference, however, can be seen in his choice of "culture," in the usual broad sense, as his dependent variable. This is not to say, however, that he fails to offer a great deal to the student of social organization, for organizational arrangements comprise part of the totality of culture that he sets out to explain. Thus, in the course of his analysis of the culture of the Great Basin Shoshone, Steward includes an admirably lucid account of the forms of community and family organization and how they evolved in response to technological, demographic, and environmental forces. In short, a great deal of his empirical work makes use of the "ecological complex" described above. Moreover, he does not feel compelled to invoke subjective "values" or any other attributes of individuals in detailing his causal explanation.

Steward apparently does consider his version of ecology as significantly different from the sociological variety, as shown by his choice of the "cultural ecology" rubric. From his brief remarks on the difference between his viewpoint and that of the human ecologist, one gathers that he is especially critical of human ecologists like Hawley for giving too little recognition to the physical environment as a causal factor. His different emphasis is very probably the result of his greater interest, as an anthropologist, in smaller and technologically less advanced societies, where adaptations to the environment are more direct and immediately evident. In his discussion of other larger and more complex societies (e.g., Puerto Rico) the environment receives notably less weight. And, further, Steward accuses the human ecologists of seeking "universal" relationships and thus tending to develop hypotheses that resemble those of the unilinear evolutionists of the late nineteenth century.[41]

It must be abundantly clear by now that the ecological view—alone among these three perspectives—focuses upon organization as a property of an aggregate or population. Eschewing a formulation of his problem in terms of the individual or the culture trait, the ecologist takes the aggregate as his frame of reference and deliberately sets out to account for the forms that social organization assumes in response to varying demographic, technological, and environmental pressures. In this way, the ecologist seems to be contributing to the maintenance of a traditional sociological interest in explaining forms of organization and changes therein. Were it not for the recent ascendancy of the behavioral approach, one would be tempted to say that these two problems—structure and change—pose the key questions for sociology. However, the behavioral approach has shifted the focus of sociological attention to an individualistic frame of reference.

Our intention here is not to engage in bootless argument regarding the "ultimate reality" of either the individual or the aggregate. Suffice it to say that both are abstractions and thus unreal in equal

---

[39]At least three of Ogburn's essays deal explicitly with population as a variable, although in different ways. In his "Inventions, Population and History," in Percy Long (ed.), Studies in the History of Culture (Menasha, Wis.: George Banta Publishing Co. [for the American Council of Learned Societies], 1942), pp. 232-45, population size is explicitly treated as the dependent variable. A more general discussion is contained in his essay, "On the Social Aspects of Population Changes," British Journal of Sociology, IV (March, 1953), pp. 25-30. Finally, "Population, Private Ownership, Technology, and the Standard of Living," American Journal of Sociology, LVI (January, 1951), 314-19, contains a formulation almost identical with the "ecological complex" discussed above.

[40]Julian Steward, Theory of Culture Change (Urbana: University of Illinois Press, 1955).

[41]Ibid., p. 34.

degree. As Cooley noted, and as many of his alleged followers choose to forget, the individual and the group are but aspects of the same reality.[42] Nor is it our intention to establish false divisions where none exist. None of these perspectives is independent of the others. Empirically, they all examine the same thing—society—albeit different aspects of that "thing." As frames of reference each must borrow certain assumptions from the empirical generalizations of the others or else substitute "homemade" versions. Underlying any elaboration of ecological theory, for example, are certain minimal assumptions about the plasticity of the individual's behavior, permitting him to engage in numerous activities. From the cultural approach, ecology borrows presuppositions about cultural continuity and the diffusibility of culture patterns, as well as assumptions regarding the cumulative character of technological change. The uses made of such premises, however, are unlikely to be the same by the borrower as by the lender, inasmuch as they are combined with other assumptions and empirical generalizations to yield distinctive hypotheses.

Consequently, emphasis on the indebtedness of each perspective to the others must not obscure the genuine distinctiveness of their concepts and assumptions: the behavioral scientist studies society as a system of social interaction and interpersonal relations, the culture theorist approaches it as a culture pattern or value system, and the human ecologist examines society as the functional organization of a population in process of achieving and maintaining an adaptation to its environment. If our experience is typical, these perspectives are not only different; they are so different that it is difficult to explain and justify one of them to a sociologist committed to another. The usual reaction is that the other two perspectives are

[42]See Charles Horton Cooley, Human Nature and the Social Order (New York: Charles Scribner's Sons, 1902; rev. ed., Glencoe, Ill.: Free Press, 1956), esp. chap. i, "Society and the Individual."

wrong, or at least incomplete, whereas the favored one is sufficient for virtually all purposes of sociological research. Let it be very clear that our intention is not to assert the superiority of the ecological approach per se, for all sociological uses, except perhaps for the particular range of organizational problems emphasized here.

Our intention, rather, is to argue—with as much force as may be at our disposal—that a point of view that transcends the view of the individual as the ultimate significant unit, and that confines attention to a limited aspect of the totality of culture, is not somehow doomed from the outset, nor is it to be dismissed out of hand as intrinsically incapable of a very high degree of predictive power. On the contrary, the partial results available at this point lead us to the conclusion that an aggregate approach—not framed in terms of the individual or value systems—holds more promise for exploring problems of organization than any alternative yet put forward.

It is true that the behavioral approach, in particular, will probably continue to illuminate the human situation, offering insight into the nature of life in society, but it does not promise to yield much in the way of explanation of social organization per se. These two approaches may be expected to make further contributions, respectively, to theories of personality and of culture, but their current preoccupations are such that they offer relatively little promise of advancing the study of society itself. Needless to say, this point of view is subject to empirical test. We are unable to wait for a happy millennium, when "all the evidence is in." The internal dynamics of the cultural system called "social science" seem to demand that theory and research press forward even in the absence of complete logical closure.

One further observation may be pertinent to our argument for the fruitfulness of an ecological approach. While behavioralists have recently emphasized the advantages of interdisciplinary cooperation, ecologists for a long time have been engaged in cross-disciplinary activity. A comprehensive bibliography of work embodying the ecological approach would show titles from economics, demography, geography, and biology, along with contributions of sociologists (the latter representing a minority). Not only do the several disciplines add to the general stock of ecological research but, in regard to many specific problems, the contributions of each discipline are hard to isolate.[43] That an ecological outlook lends itself so well to fruitful exchanges among disciplines is due to its strong empirical base and its relatively concrete view of society, which brings sociological investigation down from the spaceless, timeless abstractions of culture theory but preserves it from the aimless empiricism of detailing the manifold behavioral nuances of interpersonal relations. The cross-disciplinary tendency of human ecology also accounts for the fact that one need not call himself an ecologist to do ecological research or to employ essentially ecological concepts. Thus geographers balked when urged to regard geography as human ecology, but, first and last, they have not been able to pursue geographic research without making notable contributions to ecological knowledge.[44] The

same can be said, of course, about those sociologists who (as implied in respect to Ogburn) are at least half-ecologist, in spite of their labels.

At any rate, this paper is no mere prolegomenon to ecology or a statement of a suspicion that an ecological perspective might be a valuable way to look at society. Contributions of the highest importance to an understanding of the nature of social organization and social change are being made by investigators more or less explicitly adopting an ecological outlook.[45] The performance and promise of human ecology should be judged in terms of the caliber of such contributions, and judgments should be based on an analysis of patterns of inquiry, not on slogans. It matters little if an investigator, breaking somewhat with anthropological tradition but wishing to maintain his affiliation with it, attaches importance to the rubric "cultural ecology" as distinct from "human ecology." What does matter is whether an important insight has been gained by taking an ecological perspective.

---

[43]E.g., the recent work on the functions of communities has been carried forward by land economists, location economists, human and urban geographers, political scientists, and sociologists (see the references cited in Leo F. Schnore, "The Functions of Metropolitan Suburbs," *American Journal of Sociology*, LVII [March, 1956], 453-58). An earlier contribution was made by a sociologist who was a "territorial demographer" before he became a behavioralist interested in the looking-glass self (see Charles Horton Cooley, "The Theory of Transportation," *Publications of the American Economic Association*, Vol. IX [May, 1894]; reprinted in Robert Cooley Angell [ed.], *Sociological Theory and Social Research* [New York: Henry Holt & Co., 1930], pp. 17-118).

[44]See H. H. Barrows, "Geography as Human Ecology," *Annals of the Association of American Geographers*, XIII (March, 1923), 1-14. Barrows' view has not been widely accepted by geographers.

[45]Among the more significant recent contributions are the following: Francis R. Allen et al., *Technology and Social Change* (New York: Appleton-Century-Crofts, 1957); Donald J. Bogue, *The Structure of the Metropolitan Community* (Ann Arbor: University of Michigan Press, 1949); Boulding, op. cit.; Fred Cottrell, *Energy and Society: The Relation between Energy, Social Change and Economic Development* (New York: McGraw-Hill Book Co., 1955); William F. Ogburn and Meyer Nimkoff, *Technology and the Changing Family* (Boston: Houghton Mifflin Co., 1955); Julian Steward et al., *Irrigation Civilizations: A Comparative Study* (Washington, D. C.: Pan-American Union, 1955); William L. Thomas, Jr. (ed.), *Man's Role in Changing the Face of the Earth* (Chicago: University of Chicago Press, 1956); and Erich W. Zimmerman, *World Resources and Industries* (rev. ed.; New York: Harper & Bros., 1951). Only Bogue (a demographer), Boulding (an economist), Steward (an anthropologist) and a few of the contributors to the Thomas volume employ explicitly ecological approaches, and these differ.

COMMENT
Peter H. Rossi

The proper study of sociology is social organization. On this perspective there is probably the greatest degree of agreement in our discipline. That the studies we make rarely attend to this major commitment is not only a measure of our youthful deficiencies as a discipline but also indicates how easily we have been deflected into fascinating but peripheral side issues.

The shortcomings of our discipline are cogently, if somewhat righteously, pointed out by Duncan and Schnore. There is no doubt that they have made a most valuable contribution by reaffirming so strongly the perspective to which we all ultimately subscribe. Whether they have with equal cogency pointed out the reasons why sociology has not followed through to its major goal or offered a reasonably promising means to attain it are other matters.

It is in the best Durkheimian tradition to set up your opponents in their weakest posture and then push them over with your strongest arguments. The descriptions given of the three perspectives by Duncan and Schnore hardly do complete or even adequate justice to any. And yet, as in any stereotype, there is some truth in each description. It is true that, when "culture" is used as an explanatory variable, we often get explanations of the order that things are so because they have been so. But this description hardly fits the work of Whiting and Child,[1] who show how the myths current in a society are related to the means of subsistence through the impact of the latter on personality formation in early childhood.

Similarly, the "behaviorists" are given very short shrift. For example, the major references are to the Handbook of Social Psychology[2] and to a remark by Wilbert Moore as reported by Clyde Kiser. Such presumed behaviorists as Weber, Merton, Lipset, and Blau,[3] who have very directly tackled problems of social organization in studying bureaucracies and labor unions, are not mentioned. The impression intended is that all behaviorists are concerned only with "feelings" and "mental states" which are somehow separate from and more ephemeral than "activities."

Nor are the ecologists given their fair due. The impression given by Duncan and Schnore is that the ecologists have faced squarely the study of social organization, have made considerable headway, and have eschewed work which has not led in the right direction. In fact, it is probably the case that sociologists or others who invoke the label of ecologists are not more likely than anyone else to tackle the problems of understanding social organization. (Although it is true that some, for example, Amos Hawley,[4] have given primary attention to the organized aspects of society, the focus on organization is on too broad a level to be of much use.) Ecological theory appears to be no more suited than any other variety or theory to generate propositions about organization.

Duncan and Schnore also show a rather distressing tendency toward intellectual "imperialism." The ecological perspective is so loosely defined that it can be stretched to include what is regarded as

---

[1] J. Whiting and Irving Child, Child Training and Personality (New Haven, Conn.: Yale University Press, 1953).

[2] Gardner Lindzey (ed.), Handbook of Social Psychology (Cambridge, Mass.: Addison-Wesley Publishing Co., 1955).

[3] E.g., H. H. Gerth and C. W. Mills, From Max Weber (Oxford: Oxford University Press, 1948); S. M. Lipset et al., Union Democracy (Glencoe, Ill.: Free Press, 1956); P. M. Blau, Dynamics of Bureaucracy (Chicago: University of Chicago Press, 1955).

[4] Amos Hawley, Human Ecology (New York: Ronald Press Co., 1950).

praiseworthy (e.g., Lenski's work on status crystallization) and contracted to avoid the apparently faulty (e.g., Quinn's Human Ecology). While it is convenient to have a fairly flexible perspective, if you use up all your degrees of freedom, you arrive only at tautologies.

In short, we are equally culpable (or equally praiseworthy). The fact of the matter is that some sociologists attend to this problem and that some do not. Those who do are relatively infrequently encountered not because they do not have the proper methodology but because, given our present level of theory and research methods, it is easier to attend to other problems.

Duncan and Schnore give the impression that the central problem in the study of social organization is the latter's relationship to the environment, a term which is not very well specified. "Environment" along with "activity" are the central concepts of their discussion. However, when they make suggestions about how an ecological perspective may contribute to the study of social organization, these terms are not used as frequently as their central position would indicate. Furthermore, when they get specific, it appears that there are central problems in this field other than the relationships between environment and forms of social organization.

There is no doubt that organization-environment relationships constitute a central problem for sociology. That this calls for a comparative frame of reference and is particularly crucial in the study of preindustrial societies is suggested by the authors' strong regard for the works of Julian Steward. (Kardiner's earlier work suggesting strong relationships among environment, personality, and social structure is, strangely, not mentioned.[5]) But organization-environment relationships are not the only area of concern in social organization.

One is surprised that Duncan and Schnore have not followed through further

on the model presented by general ecology. Plant and animal ecologists give the physical characteristics of species a central place in their conceptual schemes, while Duncan and Schnore apparently would leave the human animal out of theirs. Certainly, man's biological makeup is part of the scheme of things severely conditioning responses to environmental conditions. Indeed, the search for the functional requisites of societies may be viewed as an attempt to indicate the limits imposed on social organization by the givens of the human species.

The nature of the species plays a crucial role in human social organization through psychological processes. It is strange that Duncan and Schnore wish to read the behavioralists (social psychologists) out of the sociological fraternity when their activities are among the most crucial to our field, for the forms of social organization are not merely reactions to environmental exigencies but reactions with definite psychological characteristics. Behavior, whether "activity" or "mental states," is motivated, and men seek goals through social organization—goals which cannot be irrelevant to social organization. Indeed, this is the lesson we learn from Weber and Merton and their students, as the cogent analysis of March and Simon indicates.[6]

The authors' illustrations of important substantive problems in social organization are strangely inappropriate to their main point that an ecological perspective is peculiarly suited to the study of social organization. Certainly, there are more central issues in the study of bureaucracy than merely to suggest that the rise of bureaucratic organizations may have the same explanation as the rise of cities. An ecological approach to the study of social stratification may certainly add much to our understanding, but it is difficult to see the precise directions it may take from the discussions the authors supply. For example, every

[5]A. Kardiner et al., The Individual and His Society (New York: Columbia University Press, 1939).

[6]J. March and H. Simon, Organizations (New York: John Wiley & Sons, 1958).

student of community power structures has guessed that communities will vary widely according to the kinds of economic structures found within them, but no one as yet has provided a fruitful comparative study of communities on the organizational level. The issues Duncan and Schnore have pointed up are well known; the lack of progress stems not from the wrong methological perspective but from something far more prosaic, namely, the lack of a good technical apparatus for categorizing social organizations.

In their discussion of the potentialities of the ecological perspective for the study of social change, Duncan and Schnore make their strongest case. In any adequate theory of social change, the environment is bound to play a central role. Certainly, any study of social change among relatively primitive peoples will inevitably give a primary place to environment, as Steward illustrates.[7]

Duncan and Schnore's central thesis is that the reason sociologists have not paid enough attention to problems of social organization is their inappropriate methodologies, represented by the behavioral and cultural approaches. In contrast, the ecological approach, because of its central concern with the properties of aggregates, is more suitable. While there is some justification for this statement, it is too idealistic in that it gives too important a place to ideas, a criticism which the authors themselves make of other viewpoints.

General orientations of the order of broad methodologies are usually too vague to be the most important determinants of what researchers are working on in specific detail. Perhaps they are best interpreted as the post hoc rationalization of activity rather than as specific guides. Indeed, ecological theory, as represented in Hawley's work, postdated much of the work in this area.

The lack of a strong body of research on social organization, in my view, stems from three interrelated causes. To begin

with, if we view social organization as a system of relationships, we may immediately recognize that the stuff with which we must be concerned is not directly observable. Relationships are defined in terms of reciprocating sets of activities among units and are therefore observable only through the activities themselves. The discernment of a relationship therefore becomes a job of abstraction. Hence the development of adequate conceptual schemes for the study of social organization is a task of formidable magnitude for which a first approximation in the form of an adequate common-sense vocabulary is largely missing.

A second, and perhaps more important, obstacle is the lack of an adequate research technology for the study of social organization. Our best-developed and most frequently employed techniques are based ultimately on data gathered from individuals. Censuses, sample surveys, and their variations rest, in the final analysis, on the answers given by individual respondents. The simplest and, for that reason, the most attractive way of analyzing these data is in terms of individual differences. Thus we study how different individuals react to a bureaucratic organization or how the power system of a community looks from different individual points of view and the like. To get from the study of the individual to that of social organization requires a development of ways of aggregating individual data into organizational measures. It is true that some data are already aggregated, as, for example, the data on the output of firms or the rates employed by demographers. Aggregation of individual data to form measures of aspects of social organization going beyond notions of social climate, rough measures of output, and the like seem, at present, to be largely beyond our ken.

This last is perhaps the most serious problem facing the sociologist who wishes to study social organization. It is not that he does not give enough attention to the environment or to the technology; it

[7]Julian Steward, Theory of Culture Change (Urbana: University of Illinois Press, 1955).

is that he does not know how to develop empirical measures of the forms of organization.

A final source of difficulty lies in the research designs appropriate to the study of social organization. All too often the designs we employ are adequate to the study of individuals but not of organizations. Thus most studies of community power structures lead nowhere because they are usually case studies of individual communities. Community organization can be studied only comparatively, so the study of the individual community generally turns out to be a study of how different residents vary in their definition of the local power structure. Similarly, studies of a bureaucracy based on a case tend to focus primarily on subunits within the structure or on individuals.

The appropriate designs are those which allow comparisons among the kinds of social organizations to be studied. Unfortunately, this often means research on a much larger scale than we are used to.

While it must be abundantly clear at what points this critic disagrees with Duncan and Schnore, it must be equally clear how much agreement there is on one central point: the study of social organization is disgracefully neglected in sociology.

REJOINER
Otis Dudley Duncan and Leo F. Schnore

Manifestly, this kind of discussion can have no immediately definitive outcome. If our paper and Rossi's thoughtful commentary encourage some readers to reexamine their preconceptions about what aspects of social organization need investigation and to reconsider the generic relevance of human ecology for the study of society, we shall be more than satisfied.

It is not surprising that a lightly documented compression of the recent history of American sociological thought into a typology of "perspectives" fails to flatter all points of view. Yet we doubt that we have overestimated the dominance of "behavioral" premises in current research on social organization. One of the acknowledged leaders of the school to which Rossi refers has put the matter plainly enough: Social structures, according to Homans, must ultimately be composed of elementary social behavior, and such behavior is to be explained by propositions of behavioral psychology. To hold such a view consistently, one must accept the position of an "ultimate psychological reductionist."[1] While human ecol-

ogists, as Rossi avers, may not be "more likely than anyone else to tackle the problems of understanding social organization," they generally do not get sidetracked from these problems for the particular reasons that Rossi enumerates in the third section of his commentary.

It is irrelevant to raise the charge of "imperialism" against our view that an adequate conception of the task of human ecology leads to a central concern with problems of social organization. The argument is surely not about boundaries and labels, and to elaborate some implications of a point of view is not to "use up all your degrees of freedom." As we try to make clear, the version of human ecology that seems consistent with both the very idea of ecology and the best contemporary sociological research does represent a shift from the "classical" view in certain important particulars. Moreover, it does not entail the environmental determinism that Rossi seems to attribute to it in referring repeatedly to "environment" but overlooking our statements on the place of technology and population in the ecological complex.

Given the nominal agreement between our position and that of our commentator as to the central problem of sociological

[1]George C. Homans, "Social Behavior as Exchange," *American Journal of Sociology*, LXIII (May, 1958), 597-606.

theory, it is somewhat disconcerting to find him voicing such a long series of objections. But quite possibly the agreement is more apparent than real; neither document states adequately what may be the actual but implicit issues. We have two guesses about these underlying disagreements.

The first is suggested by Rossi's rather sententious pronouncement that "behavior . . . is motivated, and men seek goals through social organization—goals which cannot be irrelevant to social organization." Whatever the basis for this statement, it. does not have to be accepted as an axiom. Indeed, it raises problems of grave import which go well beyond the scope of either discussion. In very brief summary, our position is that the merits of such "teleological" or motivational assumptions, as compared with those in our own frame of reference, have not been put to conclusive empirical test. It is therefore premature to proclaim that any and all study of social organization must be couched in terms of the goals that men supposedly seek.

Though we cannot here document the point, there is strong reason to believe that many critics of ecology are guilty of uncritical application of the method of residues. Let a human ecologist set forth a tentative and exploratory analysis of some organizational pattern, employing the crudest sort of indicators and leaving obvious gaps in the empirical coverage of relevant ecological variables. The critic, noting that the ecological contribution does not provide an exhaustive explanation of the observed pattern, draws the conclusion that the unexplained residual should be attributed to values, motives, or normative limitations on the exercise of "rationality" or the influence of supra-empirical goals on social behavior. But the method of residues effectively tests the explanatory potential of an ecological scheme only on the assumption that all relevant ecological variables have been taken into account, that they are measured with sufficiently high validity and reliability, and that they are combined with the proper weights. (We

note further the related practice of citing illustrative exceptions to presumed ecological generalizations. Instead of being regarded as possibly fruitful "negative instances" leading to an improvement of ecological theory, casually adduced exceptions are accepted as prima facie evidence that such theory cannot be viable.)[2]

A second hidden issue may underlie Rossi's dissatisfaction with our statement. In all likelihood he does not mean what we mean in declaring that the job of sociology is to explain social organization. Perhaps Rossi really means by "social organization" a fabric of mutual understandings and consensual meanings shared by a set of persons. If this is the case, it is difficult indeed to reach any fundamental agreement, since the conception of social organization set forth in our paper does not involve such subjective elements. It is perhaps more likely that Rossi considers the aspects of social organization of greatest interest to the ecologist—for example, division of labor, sustenance structure of communities, and systems of intercommunity relationships—too abstract, too obvious, too general, or too poorly defined to be problems for the general sociologist. (This is suggested by his rather casual evaluation of Hawley's contribution.) If this supposition is correct, we can only emphasize the need for a great deal more discussion between ecologists and other students of social organization.

It is our conviction that most current research on social organization, soi-disant, carries the burden of a strong microscopic bias and an almost studied disinterest in the classical problem of understanding society and societies. It manifests, moreover, an intense intellectualistic preoccupation with the intricate for its own sake and a disinclination to work with the kinds of gross and obvious, but accessible, indicators and variables that are within our power to

---

[2]Cf., further, Leo F. Schnore and Otis Dudley Duncan, "A Review of the Critical Literature in Human Ecology," a paper presented at the 1958 meeting of the American Sociological Society.

manipulate here and now. Where, for example, are the sociological studies of bureaucracy capitalizing on the voluminous census data concerning form of organization, size of employment, volume of business, location, and differentiation of commercial and industrial establishments? Rossi doubts that drawing analogies between bureaucratization and urbanization will be fruitful. But has anyone really made a determined attempt to follow out these analogies in a meticulous empirical inquiry? Or are we correct in suspecting that Rossi is curious only about problems more esoteric than that of uncovering the conditions under which bureaucracies arise?

Considering that the discipline is presumed to be centrally concerned with social organization, the current literature of sociology is perplexing. Why should the comparative analysis of aggregates be so consistently ignored in sociology, the very specialty that is responsible for such inquiry? The methodological problems which Rossi enumerates undoubtedly are important. Another difficulty, however, stems from the widespread failure to appreciate the abstract character of science in general and of theory construction in particular. In any science the proximate objective is not an exhaustive description of anything, and we should strive for a deliberately incomplete (i.e., abstract) account. Instead, too many of us have adopted what amounts to a vulgarization of statistical theory, holding the goal of science to be a complete explanation of ("accounting for") the variance of a concrete set of observations. When we deplore the partial character of our descriptions and explanatory propositions about social organization—as compared with some elusive completeness—we cease to be scientists and become historians or artists.

Another possible explanation, Rossi suggests, is that we lack sufficient practice in what may be called "aggregative thinking." This is surprising in view of the statistical sophistication of many contemporary sociologists. We experience no particular difficulty in handling some properties of some aggregates (e.g., size), and we do not feel compelled endlessly to reiterate the fact that individuals (human or other) serve as the original counting units. Yet we find it hard to conceptualize operationally such abstract structural attributes of populations as the division of labor.[3] As Rossi notes, individuals ordinarily serve not only as units of enumeration but also as the original sources of data on organization. But what is often considered to be the unique advantage of social scientists—our ability to communicate with the phenomena observed—may equally well turn into an enormous disadvantage. Impressed by the obvious fact that human beings often have feelings about their behavior and that much behavior is goal-oriented, we are too ready to assume that personal feelings and orientations must inevitably have a place in every account of human activity, whatever the level of analysis. It is all too easy to let a simple matter of convenience of observation obscure our view. Hence most of us find it hard to see how the ultimate product of our inquiries and enumerations can be anything but a description of the individuals queried and counted. We forget that other disciplines are clearly able to conduct analyses of social and cultural phenomena without becoming preoccupied with individual behavior. Thus whole linguistic systems and monetary systems are studied without reference to the fact that only individual human organisms manipulate verbal symbols and engage in getting and spending. Is social structure entirely resistant to analogous modes of inquiry?

---

[3] This problem has been left to others, notably anthropologists (see, e.g., Raoul Naroll, "A Preliminary Index of Social Development," *American Anthropologist*, LVIII [August, 1956], 687-715), and references there cited. A remarkably similar but quite independent study by a sociologist—significantly enough, likewise based on data from the Human Relations Area Files—is partially reported in Stanley Udy, Jr., "'Bureaucratic' Elements in Organizations: Some Research Findings," *American Sociological Review*, XXIII (August, 1958), 415-18.

Rossi states succinctly the semantic obstacles to treating the familiar—concrete human behavior and its observable products—in an unfamiliar fashion. Propositions about organization are raised above the level of colloquial discourse only with difficulty. But we should recall that sociologists have reached some degree of consensus regarding properties of collectivities, groups, and populations: the population per se has no sensorium and thus no mind, no values, no attitudes, and no goals. To speak of the "goals of organizations" or the "attitude of the group" is to speak metaphorically and not literally. Such phrases might better be construed as denoting certain attributes of persons, not of organized populations. The careless use of language should not lead us into attributing properties to aggregates that they cannot possess by definition.

Contempory American sociologists are surely agreed that much of individual human behavior is incomprehensible without reference to data regarding position in some system of social relationships. Social organization is thus properly accepted as a powerful predictor of individual behavior, and most studies described as dealing with social organization actually come down to the formulation and testing of predictions of behavior. A separate and more difficult question is the extent to which properties of individuals may influence the aggregates of which they appear to be "parts." With little difficulty one may assemble persuasive, if impressionistic, evidence for an extreme answer to this broad question. By focusing upon cases in which certain key individuals appear to exert profound influence upon a group and by pointing to changes that ensue upon their departure, one can construct the argument for an individualistic interpretation. By pointing to other instances where aggregates persist in the face of high rates of personnel turnover, however, an equally compelling case can be made for a radically different view—one in which the individual does not serve as the unit of analysis or as the agent of efficient causation. The dilemma is perhaps closer to resolution, once we fashion a suitable concept of the "aggregate" not as a mere collection of individuals or as a simple distribution of personal traits but as an organized population which can be characterized by its patterns of activities.

In summary, human ecologists are so impressed with the persuasive evidence of the importance of social organization—evidence assembled largely by behavioralists—that they are moved to undertake a related but distinctive form of inquiry. Granted that a substantial portion of the variation in individual behavior is demonstrably conditioned by variation in social structure—we ought then to be curious about the determinants of social structure itself.

Size, Shape, and Function in Industrial Organizations

Mason Haire

SOURCE: *Human Organization*, Vol. 14, (1955), pp. 17–22.

INTRODUCTION

There has been a great deal of discussion, in recent years, of the growth of very large business and of the problems that this makes for the national economy, as well as for the political and social organization of the country. There has also been some suggestion that this bigness in itself is evil, although the nature of the evil is never made very clear, nor is it clearly stated at what point in growth the size becomes bad. From the point of view of management's problem, there seems to be no necessary liability in simple size, but there are special problems connected with it, and it is well to look at the implications of growth in an industrial organization for its shape and function.

In the development of living organisms, size, shape, and function are very closely linked together; the problems of their inter-relation have concerned a small group of biologists since D'Arcy Thompson first published his monumental Growth and Form in 1917.[1] Let us look at some of their speculations and consider what they may mean for an analysis of size in industrial organizations. It will pay us to examine the problem of growth and form in living organisms, keeping in mind the business organization as an analogous problem. Let us continue to ask: Do these principles apply, and how do they apply to the development of companies? It is quite possible that the relationship between the two sets of problems is more than merely an analogue; if it is possible to translate the structures and the forces, we may see something of the principles underlying social organizations. In any case, the analogy seems a stimulating one both for the industrial manager and for the social scientist.

SIZE, SHAPE, AND FUNCTION IN LIVING ORGANISMS

Living organisms tend to be the shape they are because they are the size they are, and both their size and shape are made possible by the way certain functions are performed within them. For instance, in considering the relation between size and shape, let us ask how big a man can be. The mythical monster whom Jack the Giant Killer met is pictured as being 60 feet tall and well proportioned. Thus, he is 10 times as tall as Jack, and also 10 times as broad and 10 times as thick through. His volume and mass are 1,000 times as great as Jack's, since he is 10 times as big in each dimension. However, since he is proportioned in much the same way that Jack is, we might expect his leg bones to be 10 times as broad across and 10 times as thick through, or the cross section of his bone to be a 100 times that of Jack's. This means that his weight, has increased 1,000-fold, must be borne by supports which have increased only 100-fold. The human bone will barely support 10 times the weight that is normal, and consequently if the giant ever got up to pursue Jack, his legs would very likely break at the first step, being unable to support the additional weight that accrued when he changed his size so radically without having the foresight to change his shape appropriately. The poor giant is trapped by what is often called the square-cube law. As size increases, the mass grows according to a cube function[2] (since it increases in three dimensions), while the surface or cross-section only grows by a square function, increasing as it does in only two dimensions. This balance between mass and cross-section places a simple engineering limitation on the size of a man, unless he changes his shape to handle the increased load. We might ask similarly what a deer would look like if it were as large as a rhinoceros. The answer is that it very likely would look like a rhinoceros. It would have to give up its graceful legs and develop short stubby legs, angled out to support the tremendous increase in mass involved.

It seems clear from these examples that a certain shape only fits a par-

---

[1] D'Arcy Thompson, Growth and Form, MacMillan & Co., New York, 1942.

[2] This is why the Lilliputians had to feed Gulliver such tremendous amounts. When they had a half-pint to drink, they gave him 108 gallons. And quite rightly! They reasoned well that since he was 12 times their height, from the similarity of their bodies he would need 12^3 or 1728 times as much as they, and 1728 of their half-pints made a drink of 108 gallons. Their arithmetic was correct, even though their engineering principles may be strained by the disparity in size.

ticular size, and that the appropriate size may be rather narrowly limited and defined by rigorous physical laws. The same kind of thing is true in the relation between size and function. Particular ways of accomplishing certain functions are suited to one size, but are not at all appropriate as the size increases, and new solutions must be found. For example, a microscopic worm has a smooth skin, through which all the oxygen it needs soaks in directly. This system works well because the permeability of the tissues is sufficient to absorb oxygen, and the distance from front to back of the organism, or from head to toe is so small that the oxygen can be diffused throughout all the tissues. Consider again, however, what happens when the organism increases 10-fold. The mass is now 10 times 10 times 10, or 1,000 times as big, but the surface is only 10 times 10, or 100 times increased. The skin can no longer absorb sufficient oxygen to supply the mass with its vital requirements. If it were to function it would have to absorb 10 times as much oxygen through every square inch to care for the new size, and the characteristics of the gas and the tissue do not permit this. The worm, like the giant, is brought up short by the inflexible square-cube law. The problem presented is how to increase the surface without running into the prohibitively expensive increase in mass which was the original stumbling block. As we look at other species we can see other solutions to the problem. Specialized folds of skin are pleated and wrinkled to provide a maximum of surface and a minimum of volume, so that the absorption can continue within the limitations of the permeability of the tissue, and still provide sufficient oxygen for the larger body. These specialized pleats are sometimes constructed in different ways and attached somewhat differently, but the function is the same. Whether they are called gills or lungs, their development is an attempt to meet the problems of increased size by modifying function appropriately.

We begin to see, by these examples,

the close inter-relation between size and shape and function. A particular shape limits the possible size; a particular function will only work well for a particular size and shape. As size increases the shape must be changed to meet the new forces implied, and the functions modified appropriately. It has been suggested that the study of morphology and comparative anatomy is a study of the problem of getting a shape that will fit the size that has grown, and of adapting functions to the shape and size. The survival of the species depends on the solution to these problems. The organisms who retain their original size survive because their shape and function remain appropriate. Those which grow much larger survive only if they develop at the same time new solutions to the problem of shape and function. Organisms which grow and attempt to retain their original shape and functions are eliminated through the blind evolutionary processes of natural selection.

SIZE, SHAPE, AND FUNCTION IN INDUSTRIAL ORGANIZATION

When we look at the natural history of industrial organizations we see much the same thing. The size of companies varies through somewhat the same limits as the size of warm-blooded mammals. In history, many of them have grown through similar evolutionary processes, and there has been some of the same kind of elimination of inefficient solutions through natural selection. Organizations have similar inter-related demands on size and shape and function, and it seems wise to try to make these relations explicit, because in this case, unlike the development of organisms, we can plan in advance some of the changes that will come with growth, and thus eliminate certain forms which have little survival value. Instead of being at the mercy of blind evolutionary processes and a ruthless natural selection, we can, by understanding the implications of size for shape and function, avoid inefficient solutions, and direct the development of organizations with conscious planning toward rational ends.

If we think of an industry on the analogy of an organism, we see it embedded in a particular vital context. It must have a regular supply of raw materials and it can only afford to spend a certain amount of energy (or money) in acquiring them. It must transform these materials in much the same way as the body transforms food into energy, and to do this it requires a group of specialized functions. Within it, it must have a particular distribution of functions such as authority, control, communication, and skill. As it grows larger it makes new demands on its environment in terms of natural resources, labor requirements, and customers. Internally it also makes new demands. As the business grows, the old face-to-face techniques are no longer adequate. Just as the microscopic worm in growing requires lungs to absorb oxygen, so the company in growing may have to develop entirely new techniques to accomplish functions that were easily encompassed when it was smaller. In many cases these new techniques are not merely more of the same, but really involve things that are different in kind as well as in degree. Such things as the kinds of skill and the location of pools of skill within the organization, the decentralization of authority, and the development of new kinds of communication networks may change radically as the company grows.

Unfortunately, there is a great tendency, in human activity, to perpetuate solutions that were successful in the past, and to try to solve tomorrow's problems with the techniques that worked yesterday. For a specific example, this tendency is nowhere clearer than in the history of small restaurants all over the country. No business has as high a proportion of failures, and much of this seems to come from the problems of the inter-relation of size and shape and function of the sort that we have just discussed. Typically, an enterprising man starts a diner. He is cook and counterman and cashier, as well as public relations

man dealing with his customers. As he prospers he moves to a bigger place. Now he needs more people—separate individuals to be cook, counterman, cashier, and greeter. His success at this point demands two skills of him that were not required in his first endeavor. First, much of his future depends on a keen analysis by him of the nature of his business and of his own strengths and weaknesses, so that he can assign himself to the proper job in this more complicated organization. Secondly, he has taken on a new function that was not required in the original business. He is the boss. This requires a new skill—that of handling people, and of running his organization in such a way that the cook as well as he himself cooked, the counterman will wait as well as he did, and the cashier be as honest and careful as he was. Here the size implies a new shape and the size and shape a new function. This is the point at which the businesses typically fail, still in the flush of their success, because it is impossible to make the transition to the new functions that are required by increased size. If it succeeds, the same kind of new problems will continue to be presented as the size increases and shape changes, requiring new functions. Now the boss must build an organization which will delegate such functions as the cashier-control job, the purchasing job, and the production responsibility; he will face technical problems in labor relations which he never knew before; he will have all the problems involved in maintaining a harmonious functioning group of suborinates. The persistence of his success through growth depends on his ability to meet very rapidly the changes in shape and function that are implied by the growth of his business. If he tends to apply to today's problems in techniques that were responsible for yesterday's success, he may be developing a form with no survival value. He must be maximally alive to changing requirements.

The example from a growing restaurant is not out of line with similar problems in other industries. In a large manufacturing industry such as the aircraft industry, fluctuations in the external environment require many and rapid changes in size. Often these changes come so fast that it is difficult to retailor the shape and function of the organization to meet them. In other areas, we all have seen businesses which hung on to a centralization of authority long after growth dictated its delegation, and that paid for this lack of adaption of shape and function in terms of an organization which was very much less efficient than was possible. Similarly, many companies, as they grow, feel the need for new formal communications systems— for house organs, foremen's meetings, managerial conferences, and the like. Many large companies are beginning to realize the increased demand for a formal public relations program to maintain their contact with the environment in which they live. All of these are responses to the pressures of size and shape which must be met quickly and well for optimal effectiveness.

In many cases we may have to find solutions that are radically different. We may have to give up the old notion of an organization chart looking like a family tree, with the branches leading up to a single central trunk. It may be better to set up relatively autonomous organizations within the company which compete with one another, as has happened in the automobile industry and elsewhere. It may be necessary to re-examine the traditional assumptions about the span of control—the number of men one man can supervise—and radically alter them. Instead of 10 or 20 men reporting to an officer, we may need 50 or 75, as has happened in some places in retailing. Instead of relying on a suggestion box to provide upward communication about the organization, we may need to consider more elaborate committees spreading across lines of authority. It is never safe to rely entirely on the solutions that worked before, depending on having more of the same to allow for greater size. To keep healthy organisms, as industry grows, we must be sensitive to the im-

plications that size has for shape and function, and we must anticipate the possibility of entirely different solutions to managerial problems.

In the beginning, we raised the question concerning the harmful effects of size, and took the position that size, of itself, is not necessarily harmful. However, the appearance of size has a seductive quality in that it seems to arouse the feeling that a thing is strong and powerful just because it is big. This feeling is dangerous. It is not only not true, but it may well be exactly the opposite of the truth. Consider, for example, the construction of a bridge. As was the case in the example of Jack and the Giant, the strength of the bridge's girders will increase in proportion to the square of the girder's cross-sectional dimensions. Its weight, however, varies as the cube of its linear dimensions. If two bridges are built of the same shape— that is, geometrically similar—but one is bigger than the other, the larger bridge will be the weaker for just this reason. The strength of its members has not increased as fast as its own weight. To match the strength of the smaller bridge, the larger will have to increase the size of its girders much faster than the size of its length, for instance, and this will soon become prohibitive and impractical. The other alternative is to change the geometrical structure of the larger bridge, and gain increased strength from the new shape. The strength comes from the appropriateness of the shape to the size, not from the size alone. Similarly, the industrial colossus will break from its own weight if it tries to retain the original form and function, and its strength will come from the proper solution of the size-shape-function balance, rather than simply from sheer size.

One other implication of size needs to concern us here. In living organisms it seems clear that the larger the animal the more difficult job it has in adapting itself to sudden changes in the environment. The small animal seems to maintain an agility and flexibility, not only in moving, running, and jumping, but indeed, a similar flexibility in adapting to changed environmental conditions. Superficially, it is easy to see the same loss in flexibility in very large industrial organizations. The implications of size may be somewhat the same, and should be taken into account. Quoting an earlier writer, Thompson says, "In proportion to the bulk of species is the difficulty of the contest which, as a living organized whole, the individual of each species has to maintain against the surrounding agencies that are ever tending to dissolve the vital bond, and subjugate the living matter to the ordinary chemical and physical forces. Any changes, therefore, in such external conditions as a species may have been originally adapted to exist in, will militate against that existence in a degree proportional, perhaps in geometrical ratio, to the bulk of the species. If a dry season be greatly prolonged, the large mammal will suffer from the drought sooner than the small one; if any alteration of climate affects the quantity of vegetable food, the bulky Herbivore will be the first to feel the effects of stinted nourishment." (pp. 29-30). A large size becomes cumbersome in almost any exigency. Perhaps we should contemplate large industrial organizations, considering their survival value, in their present form, in the face of radically changed environmental conditions.

Not all of the implications of size are liabilities. To return to the analogy of living organisms, one of the real advantages of size is that it is easier to keep a large organism warm than it is a small one. Some of the problems of function arise from the fact that volume increases faster than surface, and consequently the oxygen absorption of the skin becomes insufficient, or the bearing strength of bones is too little as size increases. The same fact, however, makes it easier to keep large bodies warm. Heat loss is proportional to skin surface, since the heat radiation is largely directly from the skin. The animal 10 times as big as his smaller

neighbor has 1,000 times the volume to warm, but only 100 times the skin through which to lose heat. This means that he has to take in proportionately less food to survive, since the food provides fuel for warming. For example, a mouse eats about a quarter of its weight daily to supply itself with fuel. A human eats something on the order of one-seventieth. He has gained considerably in efficiency by gathering under one skin all of the volume he is trying to fuel. If a number of small animals were gathered together until the total weight was as much as a man's, their fuel requirement would by 15 or 20 times as much because of the inefficiency of their operation as separate organisms. Large industrial organizations are reaping the benefits of similar savings resulting from the operation of increased mass within a single skin. These benefits, too, must be recognized and exploited as fully as possible, to maximize the advantage of size. Properly used, they can provide the return for the difficulties that arise with new problems which accompany growth. Throughout periods of increasing and decreasing size, we need to be alert to the demands on shape and function, to anticipate new methods, and also to be alert to the benefits that are possible from the new size, to draw the fullest measure of return from them. The history of the development of living organisms is one in which a series of changes are made, and the most favorable of the changes survive. If we are to avoid this kind of blind evolutionary selection in industrial growth, we must take advantage of our understanding of the process to anticipate the requirements and implications of changes in size. There are no simple rules for doing this. The main requirement seems to be an increased sensitivity to the way the organization is presently functioning and the reasons for its success, together with a thoughtful appraisal of the demands that tomorrow's changes may put upon it.

Many present problems in management point to the demand for new functions occurring with changes in size and shape.

Our national genius is for technological change. Usually this kind of change is paid for by large volume operations—by increased size. The de-skilling that accompanies technological change (to minimize the cost of turnover) and the growth of the organizations, have both pointed up a group of problems related to motivation and morale at work. The considerable current interest in "human relations in industry" is evidence of management's attempt to deal with this problem.

Both the fact of increased size and the kind of work implied by rationalized and engineered jobs have created new management problems which require a rethinking of the psychological bases of human behavior at work. There was an opportunity, 40 years ago, to anticipate these implications and to take them into account. By and large this opportunity was missed, and we are hurrying now to make up for the deficiency with a great deal of current interest in the area. To look elsewhere, the growth of large organizations has outrun the available supply of executive talent, and many companies are scrambling to institute executive development programs to correct the deficiency. Here we exhausted a resource without anticipating it, and without a careful program in advance to develop the material that is needed today.

Can we avoid this kind of thing in the future? Only to the extent that we can anticipate the implications of developments that seem certain to arise in industry. There is a growing interest in automation in industry. What will be the implications in terms of managerial techniques and personnel policy? As accounting machines take over more of the control function in banking operations, it will make it possible to change the duties of tellers so that their customer relations become more important. As automatic production techniques in manufacturing approach the production lines of the automobile industry or the dial-watching of the process industries, such as oil and paper, the size and char-

acter of the work-force will change, and with these changes will come changes in the problem of supervision and management. Finally, in the past we have typically reaped from technical change a benefit that has been largely paid off in terms of increased leisure time for the worker. In this way, changes within industry have altered the nature of the environment in which it is imbedded. If automation extends these same benefits we need to anticipate the implications they will have in terms of such diverse things as customer demand, the motivation of workers on the job, and the availability of a part-time labor force.

The rough shape of a good many other problems of this sort is discernible. Labor relations have certainly entered a new phase, in which the concerns of labor and management will be very different. Labor is still making a transition from an organization geared to fighting for representation to one geared to a continuing relationship. Management is developing new skills in dealing with the changed relation. Increased social security at the government level, and the security of contractual pension and health benefits are both changing the motivational context in which everyone works. Even within the individuals themselves, changes are taking place. Medical advances are extending the life-span of the population so that we are living longer and longer. When this is coupled with the tendency toward early retirement, it means that we not only have a larger proportion of older people, but we may have a larger segment of non-producing pure consumers in the population. These changes will have implications in the realm of economics, politics, and motivation. The rough general shape of these and many other changes can already be seen. To trim our organizations to fit them requires a good deal of thoughtful planning. It is perhaps too much to suggest that every company needs a Department of Philosophy to meditate on the future (although this is not an outlandish suggestion); but at least every manager, at whatever level he finds himself, should take as part of his job the setting aside of a certain amount of time to put his feet up and look out the window while he considers the nature of his job and his subordinates, and the changes that he may anticipate in them.

IMPLICATIONS OF SIZE, SHAPE, AND FUNCTION FOR THE SOCIAL SCIENTIST

In addition to the suggestive parallels between size, shape, and function in organisms and in organizations, there are a few somewhat more concrete threads that can be drawn which may have real promise for the social scientist's investigation of the nature of social organization. In discussing the form of animals, it becomes clear that the form is not accidental or arbitrary, but is what it is because of a number of definite and identifiable forces playing on it, and further that the form is prescribed closely within certain limits by these forces. In this sense, the form itself is an index of the kinds of forces playing on the organism, and the shape of the form is a first clue to the nature of the forces. Thompson says of this, "The form, then, of any portion of matter, whether it be living or dead, and the changes of form which are apparent in its movements and in its growth, may in all cases alike be described as due to the action of force. In short, the form of an object is a 'diagram of forces' in this sense, at least, that from it we can judge of or deduce the forces that are acting or have acted upon it: in this strict and particular sense, it is a diagram—in the case of a solid, of the forces which have been impressed upon it when its conformation was produced, together with those which enable it to retain its conformation. . . . " (p. 16). If we could expand this principle to apply to social organizations, the form of the organization and the history of its changing form would provide an excellent beginning to the identification of the forces in which it exists, and the nature of their operation.

This approach finds some interesting applications in morphology which provide suggestive illustrations of the possibilities elsewhere. It often happens, for instance, that fossilized animals are discovered that have been radically distorted in shape under the very great shear forces in the rocks in which they were imbedded. In order to reconstruct the original shape of the animal, it is necessary to correct these forces, and to push the organism back into shape, at least in theory. This process of "righting" the shape is indeed a process of returning to rectilinear coordinates a form which is presented to us on distorted coordinates. Let us assume that the horizontals on which our fossil appears are unchanged, but the verticals of the grid are oblique at an angle of 70 degrees. The transformation then, would be to straighten the vertical coordinates to 90 degrees, and to reproduce the fossil in the adjusted rectilinear system. However, suppose the problem were reversed. If we knew the proper form of the fossil and were given the distorted version, we could, by the discrepancy, infer the size and direction of the forces that must have been present to produce the distortion. If we had a time series of such fossils, distorted at different times, we could deduce quite a history of the forces which played on the rocks.

If instead of thinking of shear forces in rocks acting on fossils, we think of environmental forces acting on the change in form of various animals, we have such a time series, and one by which we can make some inferences about the forces associated with changing form. For instance, if a porcupine fish (Diodon) is pictured on a set of simple rectilinear Cartesian coordinates, some transformations can be made. If the vertical coordinates are transformed into a system of concentric circles and the horizontal coordinates into a system of hyperbolas, with the pictured fish reproduced point for point and space by space, the new picture is not a senseless jumble or an impossible form, but a good representation of a closely allied, but very differént looking sunfish (orthagoriscus mola). (See Thompson, pp. 1026-95). This transformation immediately suggests that we will have a foot in the door of understanding the evolutionary process if we can now identify the forces that acted on the fish in its development—what made circles of the verticals and hyperbolas of the horizontals in this form. Julian Huxley, in his Problems in Relative Growth,[3] has very much elaborated this analysis in an attempt to define growth gradients and growth centers in organisms. He points out (p. 104 et seq.) that this kind of transformation is not merely an exercise in higher geometry, but, biologically, the clue to the origin of very active growth-centers and to the fish's adaption to life on the surface of the sea.

To apply this process to the matter at hand: Suppose we knew how to draw a picture of an industrial organization. (We don't, but let us let that problem wait a moment.) By tracing the history of a company through time we could see a series of changes whose regular nature would give us a clue to the kinds of forces playing on it. By comparing industries similar in size but different in process, product, resource, location, or age, we could, similarly, begin to infer from the systematic variation, the kinds of forces that are associated with these different conditions. A summary pictorial history, of, say, the process industries in comparison with the retail companies, would seem to promise an additional understanding of their natures and their differences.

Part of the rub here is that we don't know how to draw a picture of an industry. Certainly we do not want the old family-tree style of organization chart. Probably we don't even want that type of representation if the formal published description is corrected to agree with the way the plant really functions. We need something that will reflect the changes in size. That is not so hard. Probably some combination of numbers

[3]Julian Huxley, Problems in Relative Growth, Dial Press, New York, 1932.

of people, investment per worker, gross volume, capitalization, and the like will do the job. Beyond this, we need something to define the shape. Where are the pools of skill and the pools of authority? What kind of internal bonds connect the parts in terms of authority? Of communication? What kind of specialized functions are there, and when did they develop, and what kind of relation do they have to other parts? How big was the company when a separate personnel function was established? Did it hire? Fire? Or merely record and plan vacation schedules? At what size did a control function emerge, and what has been the history of its duties, authority, and connection with other parts? Questions of this sort must be answered by our final picture. It must show the size, the shape, the components, and their relation to one another. It must have the functional meaning of the organization chart and the internal connectedness of the sociogram. At the moment we don't have such a picture, but there doesn't seem to be any necessary reason why we can't have one. It would seem to be simply an empirical matter of collecting variables and a creative job of putting them together tentatively time after time. It is a long task, but if it will lead to the evolutionary forces in the development of social organizations, it is well worth it. It could give us the first real understanding of the nature of the growth of groups.

There is one other asset which might be derived from such an analysis: We have spoken glibly, so far, of the forces that act on an industrial organization to change it, but we have no real understanding of what those forces are. In examining the morphological history of organisms it becomes perfectly clear that very different forces apply, and that they can be inferred from the problems of size and shape and function. For instance, in the case of animals of the general size of man, the chief external force is gravity. Gravity broke the giant's legs (in the form of gravitational mass), and ultimately limited his size. In historical perspective, the sagging in human shapes is an eloquent witness to the force of gravity in determining form. Small insects are very little influenced by gravity. Their surface is so large in comparison with their mass that, for instance, in falling the frictional resistance is sufficient to protect them from the harm of the bump we receive under the influence of gravity. Such small insects, however, have their size and shape determined primarily (in external terms) by their problems with surface tension. The ratio of surface to volume which protected the insect in falling is a tremendous liability if he gets wet. Man's wet weight is imperceptibly more than dry; a fly's wet weight is double his dry weight. A form which will not break the surface tension is indispensable, and

much of the shape and size is traceable to this. When we go still smaller, to the order of magnitude of the bacillus, the kinds of forces change again. Now the viscosity of liquids, molecular shocks of Brownian movement, and the electrical characteristics of the medium become predominant. In these cases, a study of the history of growth and the relation between size and shape has given us a lead to the primary forces in the environment in which the organism lives. One might hope, similarly, that an historical analysis of the growth of business, and a detailed understanding of the relation between size and shape and function in an industrial organization would give us similar insight into the kinds of forces in its environment which shape its existence.

The Effect of Declines in Mortality on Age Distribution

Ansley J. Coale

SOURCE: *Trends and Differentials in Mortality*, Papers presented at 1955 Annual Conference of Milbank Memorial Fund (1956).

It is common knowledge that the average age of the population has increased in the United States and in most countries of Western culture. As part of the changing age profile, the number of persons over 65 has increased much more rapidly than the total population. Most of us would assume offhand that the increase in the fraction over 65 and in average age has been caused mostly, if not wholly, by the increasing average longevity of individuals—by increases in the probability of surviving accompanying the rapid development of better medicine and higher levels of living. However, this explanation is an instance in which common sense leads us into error. In most Western countries the fraction over 65 would

be larger than it is if mortality rates had remaincd at their 1900 level. The average age of the population would be greater if mortality had not improved.

Common sense gives the wrong answer because it takes account of only part of the effect of improved mortality. It is immediately clear that lower death rates yield more older people than unchanged rates would produce. It is equally true— but not quite so immediately apparent— that lower death rates can produce more babies and more young people. If there are more old people and more young people, the population is surely larger than it would have been, but whether the number over 65 has grown faster than the total is uncertain. The kinds of mortality improvement that have actually occurred would in fact make the number of younger persons grow more rapidly than the number over 65.

Mortality improvement can produce more children even if childhood mortality rates are not themselves changed. We will show this effect by means of a simple example. Consider a hypothetical female population with the following characteristics:

1. Women 20 and over give birth to girl babies at an average rate of one birth per five women per annum.

2. No births occur to women under 20.

3. The death rate from birth to age 25 is zero, but all women die on reaching exact age 25.

4. The population size is 250,000. There are 10,000 births per annum, 10,000 women at each age through 24, and 10,000 deaths— the number of women reaching age 25 during the year.

This hypothetical population is in a stable equilibrium, with an unchanging age distribution and no growth. It is what is known technically as a stationary population. Now suppose that through a medical discovery the zero death rate is suddenly extended to exact age 30 (where 100 per cent die) with no other change. One year after this change, there will be 10,000 women over 25, but these 10,000 women will be giving birth to extra children at a rate of 2,000 per year. After five years there will be 50,000 women over 25 and 25,000 extra children under 5. The proportion under 5 will rise from 20 per cent to 23.1 per cent during these five years. This result follows because the extra women over 25 bear children. After many years of the new mortality regime, the population would grow steadily at about 2.8 per cent per annum, and the age distribution would taper continuously from 4.9 per cent under 1 year of age to about 2.1 per cent between 29 and 30. Thus an extension of life from 25 to 30 years with no other change would increase the number

of children under 5 faster than it would increase the population total. (Figure 1.)

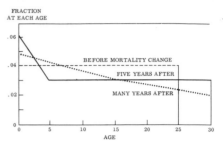

Figure 1. Three age distributions showing effect of mortality change.

This result comes about because a growing population tapers with increasing age, even with no deaths (as in our example there are no deaths under age 30). The faster the growth, the greater the tapering effect. If the population is growing at a rate of 2.8 per cent per annum, each annual birth crop tends to be 2.8 per cent larger than the next older cohort. But the more steeply a population tapers with increasing age, the younger is its average age. Thus any change in death rates which tends to produce a long-run rise in the growth rate has a tendency, at least, to make the population younger.

An increase in the probability of surviving, in other words, can produce two effects opposite in direction on the general shape of the age distribution. By increasing the fraction who survive to older ages, it tends to increase the average age of the population; while by raising the growth rate, it tends to lower the average age. Which of these tendencies dominates depends on the age pattern of the improvement in mortality. Indeed a pattern of improvement can be specified which has no effect whatever on the age distribution—where the increased probability of surviving is precisely offset by the greater growth rate. What is required is the same proportional increase at all ages in the probability of surviving. Suppose that the probability of surviving one year were suddenly raised by 1/2 per cent at all ages. A year later there would be 1/2 per cent more 1-year olds, 2-year olds, etc.—at every age 1/2 per cent more persons than there would have been. There would also be 1/2 per cent more births, since there would be precisely 1/2 per cent more parents at all ages. Since all age groups are multiplied by the same factor, the proportionate age distribution would not be affected.

Improvements in mortality rates can have a variety of effects on the age distribution, the nature of the effect depending on the ages at which the probability of surviving is most improved. I shall not try to describe here the rather involved analysis by which one can determine, under certain initial conditions, the age-distribution effects of any given mortality change.[1] I shall attempt to show instead the effects of typical observed age patterns of mortality improvement. It turns out when the available data are assembled that there is a general pattern of mortality improvement by age which holds very widely, especially for females. This pattern is roughly U-shaped when the increase in the probability of surviving is plotted as a function of age. The per cent increase in the probability of surviving is in a typical instance relatively low from age 5 to 50. It is usually high at age 0, and declines sharply until about age 5. It frequently but not universally rises above age 50 or 60. The "U" is not always very flat bottomed, and may be missing its right leg—resembling a J written backward, rather than a U. (Figure 2.)

The effect of this pattern on the age distribution can be understood at least qualitatively by decomposing the pattern into three components. The first component is the per cent improvement in the probability of surviving at the bottom

[1]Coale, A. J.: "The Effects of Changes in Fertility and Mortality on Age Composition." Milbank Memorial Fund Quarterly. January, 1956, XXXIV, No. 1, pp. 79-114. In this article, extensive work on the same subject by Alfred J. Lotka, Frank Lorimer, Alfred Sauvy, and by the Population Division of the United Nations is cited.

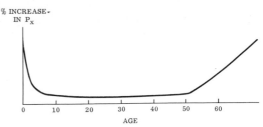

Figure 2. Typical pattern of improvement in the probability of surviving.

tom of the U. We will approximate the bottom of the U by a horizontal straight line. This line represents the minimum increase in the probability of surviving. We may extend this line until it reaches from age 0 to the oldest age, and then subtract the minimum increase from the increases above the minimum to obtain the other two components. The three components are shown by Figure 3.

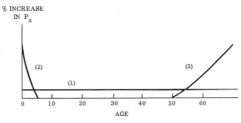

Figure 3. Components of the typical pattern of per cent increase in the probability of surviving.

The first component—the horizontal straight line—has no effect whatever on the age distribution since it is a uniform per cent increase in the probability of surviving at all ages.

The second component—the excess increase in the probability of surviving at the youngest ages—affects primarily the growth rate of the population. It is clear that the long-term growth rate of the population is increased because of component (2)—there will be coincident with the improvement more children surviving to age 5, but after a few years there will be more people surviving to the ages of parenthood, and hence an increased flow of births. On the other hand, since each cohort experiencing the lower mortality will be larger than it would have been at all ages above 5, component (2) has no tendency to increase the <u>fraction</u> at ages over 65. Thus the extra improvement in childhood survivorship—the first leg of the U—will in the long run make the population taper more rapidly with age. In fact an improvement in infant survivorship has an effect on the age distribution almost exactly the same as a rise in fertility.

The third component—the second leg of the U, or the excess improvement in survivorship above age 50—has no effect on the long term growth rate,[2] since it has no effect on births. However, component (3) increases both the number and the fraction surviving to the older ages.

The overall effect of an improvement in survivorship depends on which of the two legs of the U dominates, since one tends to make the age distribution taper more rapidly (eventually at all ages), while the other tends to make the population taper <u>less</u> rapidly above age 50. The flat part of the U tends only to make the population grow more rapidly, with no effect on the age distribution.

We have surveyed mortality records[3] among a group of relatively low-mortality European areas during the last half of the nineteenth century, a group of low-mortality areas (European and otherwise) in the interval 1900 to 1940, a smaller group of low-mortality areas before and after World War II, and a group with relatively high mortality in the interval from 1900 to the present. This survey shows that had fertility remained constant at pre-1900 levels, the median age of the population would have been lowered in 40 out of 44 of the recorded declines in mortality. The fraction over 65 would have been decreased in about half the instances surveyed. In other words, in over 90 per cent of these changes in mortality the higher growth associated with the left leg of the U would have a stronger negative effect on the median age than the positive effect of extra mortality improvements in the older

ages. In about half the mortality improvements, the tapering effect of childhood mortality improvements would be strong enough to <u>reduce</u> the proportion of the population over 65.

These remarks describe the effects of mortality changes in the low-mortality regions of the world during the past century, and during recent years in relatively high-mortality regions. What are the likely age-distribution effects of current and future mortality changes? The answer can be determined by looking at the survivorship rates already achieved in the areas with the best mortality records. There simply is not much room for much of a left-hand leg on the U-shaped pattern of any further improvements in survivorship. If the per cent improvement in survivorship to age 5 that occurred in Sweden between 1935 and 1948 were to be repeated, the probability of surviving would exceed unity—a patent impossibility. Thus future improvements in mortality must necessarily be characterized by small per cent improvements in infant survivorship. On the other hand, there is ample room left for improvements in survivorship at ages above 50. The four instances in the survey cited above where a mortality change would raise the median age of the population were all changes from before to after World War II in low-mortality countries. In short, improvements which would raise the median age and increase the fraction over 50 have been occurring recently and are likely to become increasingly prominent.

A final point is worth noting. Since the bottom of the U-shaped curve of improvement in survivorship has no effect on age distribution, and since the two legs have more or less opposing effects, mortality improvement has typically had a rather small overall effect on the per cent age distribution. The effect of future changes—which must be concentrated in the older ages if they are to be of any magnitude—will be more pronounced.

Our principal theme has been that increases in the probability of surviving do not necessarily increase the relative

---

[2] It produces a temporary rise in the rate of growth, which ends when the fraction over 50 stops increasing.

[3] See Coale. <u>op. cit.</u>, for a fuller description.

size of older age groups. To the contrary, the net effect of improvements can be, and typically has been, in the direction of a reduced median age, and a decreased or only slightly increased proportion over 65. If declines in mortality have not produced an older population, what factor does account for the marked aging of Western populations? In two words: declining fertility.

A General Typology of Migration

William Petersen

SOURCE: *American Sociological Review*, Vol. 23, (1958), pp. 256–66.

Most studies of international migration are focused on the movement from or to one particular country, and virtually all of the other, somewhat broader works are concerned with a single historical era. Moreover, the emphasis is usually on description rather than analysis, so that the theoretical framework into which these limited data are fitted is ordinarily rather primitive. In this paper, an attempt is made to bring together into one typology some of the more significant analyses of both internal and international migration, as a step toward a general theory of migration.

The best known model for the analysis of migration is the typology constructed some years ago by Fairchild.[1] He classifies migration into invasion, of which the Visigoth sack of Rome is given as the best example; conquest, in which "the people of higher culture take the aggressive;" colonization, when "a well established, progressive, and physically vigorous state" settles "newly discovered or thinly settled countries;" and immigration, or the individually motivated, peaceful movement between well established countries "on approximately the same stage of civilization." That is to say, Fairchild uses, more or less clearly, two main criteria as his axes— the difference in level of culture and whether or not the movement was predominantly peaceful. His four types, thus, can be represented schematically as follows:

Migration from	Migration to	Peaceful Movement	Warlike Movement
Low culture	High culture		Invasion
High culture	Low culture	Colonization	Conquest
Cultures on a level		Immigration	

[1] Henry Pratt Fairchild, Immigration: A World Movement and Its American Significance, Rev. edition, New York: Macmillan, 1925, pp. 13 ff. In spite of the fact that it has all the faults of a pioneer effort, this classification has been adopted uncritically in several other works on the subject. See, for example, Maurice R. Davie, World Immigration with Special Reference to the United States, New York: Macmillan, 1949, pp. 2-3; Julius Isaac, Economics of Migration, London: Kegan Paul, Trench, Trubner, 1947, p. 1. The most recent and in many respects the best text in the field takes over Fairchild's four types and adds a fifth, compulsory migration; see Donald R. Taft and Richard Robbins, International Migrations: The Immigrant in the Modern World, New York: Ronald Press, 1955, pp. 19-20.

Several other discussions are decidedly better

Reducing the implicit underlying structure to this schematic form has the immediate advantage of indicating its incompleteness. Two types are lacking from the classification,[2] although they are well represented in history.

Such a paradigm, moreover, suggests even more strongly than the dozen pages of text it summarizes that the two axes are not the best that could have been chosen. An attempt to distinguish between "high" and "low" cultures is an invitation to ethnocentrism, which Fairchild does not always avoid. The contrast between "progressive" England and "newly discovered" India, for example, can hardly be termed a scientific analysis of colonization. Similarly, Rome's conquest of her empire was not merely the migration of a people of higher culture: much of Rome's culture was adapted from that of conquered Greece. Nor is the distinction between "peaceful" and "warlike" always an unambiguous one. Colonization is ordinarily neither one nor the other;[3] and the Visigoths' invasion of

Rome, Fairchild's main example of this type, was predominantly a peaceful interpenetration of the two cultures, accomplished (as Fairchild points out) over more than two centuries.[4]

This criticism of Fairchild's classification illustrates two general points: that it is useful to make explicit the logical structure of a typology, and that the criteria by which types are to be distinguished must be selected with care.

PSYCHOLOGICAL UNIVERSALS

Together with most other analysts of migration, Fairchild implies that man is everywhere sedentary, remaining fixed until he is impelled to move by some force. Like most psychological universals, this one can be matched by its opposite: man migrates because of wanderlust. And like all such universals, these cannot explain differential behavior: if all men are sedentary (or migratory) "by nature," why do some migrate and some not? If a simplistic metaphor is

---

than Fairchild's, though not nearly so well known. I found two particularly stimulating—Rudolf Heberle, "Theorie der Wanderungen: Sociologische Betrachtungen," Schmollers Jahrbuch, LXXV:1 (1955); and Ragnar Numelin, The Wandering Spirit: A Study of Human Migration, London: Macmillan, 1937. See also Howard Becker, "Forms of Population Movement: Prolegomena to a Study of Mental Mobility," Social Forces, 9 (December, 1930), pp. 147-160 and 9 (March, 1931), pp. 351-361.

[2] It is patent that this omission was not intentional; this is not an example of what Lazarsfeld terms "reduction"—that is, the collapsing of a formally complete typology in order to adjust it to reality. See Paul F. Lazarsfeld, "Some Remarks on the Typological Procedures in Social Science," mimeographed translation of an article that appeared originally in Zeitschrift für Sozialforschung, vol. VI, 1937.

[3] According to Fairchild, "while the resistance of the natives may be so weak as to make the enterprise hardly a military one, yet colonization is carried on without the consent, and against the will, of the original possessors of the land, and is, consequently, to be regarded rightly as a hostile movement. . . . [Moreover,] not infrequently the rivalry of two colonizing powers for some desirable locality may involve them in war with each other" (op. cit., p. 19). In spite of this hedge, classifying colonization as "peaceful" is in accord with his main argument, for this is how he distinguishes it from conquest.

[4] On the one side, Germans were taken into the Roman army, granted land in the border regions and civil rights in the city; on the other side, after Wulfilas's translation of the Bible into Gothic, Roman culture made deep inroads among the Germans through their conversion to Christianity. The relation between the two cultures, therefore, was expressed not merely in a sharp confrontation on the field of battle, but also in the divided loyalties of marginal types. Alaric, leader of the Visigoths, was a romanized German, a former officer in the Roman army, a Christian; and Stilicho, the de facto emperor after Theodosius's death, was a German-Roman, a German by descent who had reached his high post through a successful army career. Alaric's purpose was not to overthrow Rome but, within the framework of the Empire, to get land and increased pensions (!) for his followers; Stilicho's purpose, similarly, was not to oust the Visigoths, whom he sought as allies against Constantinople, but to keep them under control. The interpenetration of the two cultures, that is to say, was a complex and subtle process, not too different from the present-day acculturation of immigrant groups. That Alaric put pressure on the Senate by marching his army into Italy was not the characteristic of "a rude people on a low stage of culture," but the time-honored mode of lobbying used by Roman generals. Historical studies substantiate this account of the facts; I have used principally J. B. Bury, The Invasion of Europe by the Barbarians, London: Macmillan, 1928.

used, it should be at least as complex as its mechanical analogue, which includes not only the concept of forces but also that of inertia.

Thus one might better say that a social group at rest, or a social group in motion (e.g., nomads), tends to remain so unless impelled to change; for with any viable pattern of life a value system is developed to support that pattern. To analyze the migration of Gypsies, for example, in terms of push and pull is entirely inadequate—no better, in fact, than to explain modern Western migration, as Herbert Spencer did, in terms of "the restlessness inherited from ancestral nomads."[5] If this principle of inertia is accepted as valid, then the difference between gathering and nomadic peoples, on the one hand, and agricultural and industrial peoples, on the other hand, is fundamental with respect to migration. For once a people has a permanent place of residence, the relevance of push and pull factors is presumably much greater.

Sometimes the basic problem is not why people migrate but rather why they do not. The vast majority of American Negroes, for example, remained in the South until the First World War, in spite of the Jim Crow pattern and lynch law that developed there from the 1870's on and, as a powerful pull, the many opportunities available in the West and the burgeoning northern cities.[6]

If wanderlust and what might be termed sitzlust are not useful as psychological universals, they do suggest a criterion for a significant distinction. Some persons migrate as a means of achieving the new. Let us term such migration innovating. Others migrate in response to a change in conditions, in order to retain what they have had; they move geographically in order to remain where they are in all other respects. Let us term such migration conservative. When the migrants themselves play a passive role, as in the case of African slaves being transported to the New World, the migration is termed innovating or conservative depending on how it is defined by the activating agent, in this case the slave-traders.

The fact that the familar push-pull polarity implies a universal sedentary quality, however, is only one of its faults. The push factors alleged to "cause" emigration ordinarily comprise a heterogeneous array, ranging from an agricultural crisis to the spirit of adventure, from the development of shipping to over-population. Few attempts are made to distinguish among underlying causes, facilitative environment, precipitants, and motives.[7] In particular, if we fail to distinguish between emigrants' motives and the social causes of emigration— that is, if we do not take the emigrants' level of aspiration into account—our analysis lacks logical clarity. Economic hardship, for example, can appropriately be termed a "cause" of emigration only if there is a positive correlation between hardship, however defined, and the propensity to migrate.[8] Often the relation has been an inverse one; for example, the mass emigration from Europe in modern times developed together with a marked rise in the European standard of living. As has been shown by several studies, the correlation was rather with the business cycle in the receiving coun-

[5] Herbert Spencer, The Principles of Sociology, 3rd edition, New York: Appleton, 1892, I, p. 566.

[6] See Gunnar Myrdal, An American Dilemma: The Negro Problem and Modern Democracy, New York: Harper, 1944, Chapter 8, for an extended discussion of this point. For an international example, see William Petersen, Planned Migration, Berkeley: University of California Press, 1955, Chapter 3, which discusses the several factors in prewar Holland that seemingly should have induced a large emigration, but did not.

[7] Cf. R. M. MacIver, Social Causation, Boston: Ginn, 1942.

[8] Similarly, no principled difference is usually made between what is sometimes termed "absolute overpopulation," which results in hunger and starvation, and milder degrees of "overpopulation," which reflect not physiological but cultural standards. In the first case the aspiration of emigrants can be ignored, for it is a bare physiological minimum that can be taken as universal; but in the second case it is the level of aspiration itself that defines the "overpopulation" and sets an impetus to emigrate.

try,[9] and even this relation explains fluctuations in the emigration rate more than
its absolute level. Nor can the class
differential in the rate of emigration be
ascribed simply to economic differences.
The middle class lived in more comfortable circumstances, but for many a
move to America would have meant also
a definite material improvement. During
the period of mass emigration, however,
this was stereotyped as lower-class behavior, as more than a bit unpatriotic
for the well-to-do. For a middle-class
person to emigrate meant a break with
the established social pattern; therefore
in the middle class, especially marginal
types like idealists or black sheep left
the country, and these for relevant personal reasons. Once a migration has
reached the stage of a social movement,
however, such personal motivations are
generally of little interest.

This kind of confusion is not limited
to economic factors. Religious oppression
or the infringement of political liberty
was often a motive for emigration from
Europe, but before the rise of modern
totalitarianism emigrants were predominantly from the European countries least
marked by such stigmata. An increasing
propensity to emigrate spread east and
south from Northwest Europe, together
with democratic institutions and religious tolerance. Again, we are faced with
the anomaly that those who emigrated
"because" of persecution tended to come
from countries where there was less
than elsewhere.

When the push-pull polarity has been
refined in these two senses, by distinguishing innovating from conservative
migration and by including in the analysis
the migrants' level of aspiration, it can
form the basis of an improved typology
of migration. Five broad classes of migration, designated as primitive, forced,
impelled, free, and mass, are discussed
below.

PRIMITIVE MIGRATION

The first class of migration to be
defined is that resulting from an ecological push, and we shall term this primitive migration. Here, then, primitive migration does not denote the wandering of
primitive peoples as such, but rather a
movement related to man's inability to
cope with natural forces. Since the reaction to a deterioration in the physical
environment can be either remedial action or emigration, depending on the
technology available to the people concerned, there is, however, a tendency for
primitive migration in this narrower
sense to be associated with primitive
peoples.

Many of the treks of preindustrial
folk seem, moreover, to have been conservative in the sense defined above.
"There is often a tendency for [such] a
migrating group to hold conservatively
to the same type of environment; pastoral people, for example, attempt to
remain on grasslands, where their accustomed life may be continued."[10] Such
conservative migrations are set not by
push and pull, but by the interplay of
push and control. The route is shaped by
both natural and man-made barriers:
mountains, rivers, or rainfall or the
lack of it; and the Great Wall of China
or other, less monumental, evidences of
hostility toward aliens. If they are indifferent about where they are going, men
migrate as liquids flow, along the lines
of least resistance. Conservative migrants seek only a place where they can
resume their old way of life, and when
this is possible they are content. Sometimes it is not possible, and any migration, therefore, may be associated with
a fundamental change in culture.

The frequent designation for migrations of prehistoric primitives used to be
"wandering of peoples," a translation
from the German that, however inelegant,
is nevertheless appropriate, for it de-

---

[9]Harry Jerome, Migration and Business Cycles,
New York: National Bureau of Economic Research,
1926; Dorothy Swaine Thomas, Social and Economic
Aspects of Swedish Population Movements, 1750-
1933, New York: Macmillan, 1941, Chapter 9.

[10]Roland B. Dixon, "Migrations, Primitive," Encyclopedia of the Social Sciences, New York: Macmillan, 1934, Vol. X, pp. 420-425.

notes two of the characteristics that define it. For usually peoples as a whole migrate, not merely certain families or groups, and they leave without a definite destination, as "wander" implies in English. Let us, then, term migrations induced by ecological pressure as the <u>wandering of peoples</u>. Unintended movements over the ocean—an analogous type of primitive migration, which can be termed <u>marine wanderings</u>—have occurred more frequently than was once supposed.

> There are countless examples . . . [of] more or less accidental wanderings from island to island over oceanic expanses of water, brought about by winds and currents. The space of time and extent of these voyages seem to play a subordinate part. Journeys covering 3,000 miles are not unusual. They may last six weeks or several months. Even without provisions the natives can get along, as they fish for their food and collect rainwater to drink.[11]

Contemporary primitives also often move about in a way directly related to the low level of their material culture. A food-gathering or hunting people cannot ordinarily subsist from what is available in one vicinity; it must range over a wider area, moving either haphazardly or back and forth over its traditional territory. Such movements can be called <u>gathering.</u> The analogous type of migratory movements of cattle-owning peoples is called <u>nomadism</u>, from the Greek word meaning to graze. Gatherers and nomads together are termed <u>rangers.</u>

The way of life of rangers is to be on the move, and their culture is adapted to this state. Their home is temporary or portable; some Australian peoples have no word for "home" in their language. Their value system adjudges the specific hardships of their life to be good; the contempt that the desert Arab feels for the more comfortable city Arab is traditional. Although their ordinary movement is usually over a restricted area, bounded by either physical barriers or peoples able to defend their territories, rangers are presumably more

likely to migrate over longer distances (apart from differences in the means of transportation) simply because they are already in motion. Whether any particular nomad people settles down and becomes agricultural does not depend merely on geography. Geography determines only whether such a shift in their way of life is possible—it is barely feasible on the steppe, for example; but even when physical circumstances permit a change, the social pattern of ranging may be too strong to be broken down. The Soviet program of settling the Kirghiz and other nomad peoples on collective farms, for example, succeeded because it was implemented by sufficient terror to overcome their opposition.[12] That is to say, ranging, like wandering, is typically conservative.

A primitive migration of an agrarian population takes place when there is a sharp disparity between the produce of the land and the number of people subsisting from it. This can come about either suddenly, as by drought or an attack of locusts, or by the steady Malthusian pressure of a growing population on land of limited area and fertility. Persons induced to migrate by such population pressure can seek another agricultural site, but in the modern era the more usual destination has been a town: the migration has ordinarily been innovating rather than conservative. The Irish immigrants to the United States in the decades following the Great Famine, for example, resolutely ignored the Homestead Act and other inducements to settle on the land; in overwhelming proportion, they moved to the cities and stayed there. Let us term such an innovating movement <u>flight from the land</u> (again, an inelegant but useful translation from the German).

To recapitulate, primitive migration may be divided as follows:

---

[11]Numelin, <u>op. cit.</u>, pp. 180-181.

[12]For a documentation from two sources of divergent political views, see Rudolf Schlesinger, <u>The Nationalities Problem and Soviet Administration</u>, London: Routledge & Kegan Paul, 1956; Walter Kolarz, <u>The Peoples of the Soviet Far East</u>, New York: Praeger, 1954.

Primitive	Wandering	Wandering of peoples
		Marine wandering
	Ranging	Gathering
		Nomadism
	Flight from the land	

These are the types of migration set by ecological push and controls, usually geographical but sometimes social.

FORCED AND IMPELLED MIGRATIONS

If in primitive migrations the activating agent is ecological pressure, in forced migrations it is the state or some functionally equivalent social institution. It is useful to divide this class into impelled migration, when the migrants retain some power to decide whether or not to leave, and forced migration, when they do not have this power. Often the boundary between the two, the point at which the choice becomes nominal, may be difficult to set. Analytically, however, the distinction is clearcut, and historically it is often so. The difference is real, for example, between the Nazis' policy (roughly 1933-38) of encouraging Jewish emigration by various anti-Semitic acts and laws, and the later policy (roughly 1938-45) of herding Jews into cattle-trains and transporting them to camps.

A second criterion by which we can delineate types of forced or impelled migration is its function, defined not by the migrant but by the activating agent. Persons may be induced to move simply to rid their homeland of them; such a migration, since it does not ordinarily bring about a change in the migrants' way of life, is analogous to conservative migration and can be subsumed under it. Others are induced to move in order that their labor power can be used elsewhere; and such a migration, which constitutes a shift in behavior patterns as well as in locale, is designated as innovating.

Four types are thus defined, as follows:

In all of human history, flight has been an important form of migration. Whenever a stronger people moves into a new territory, it may drive before it the weaker former occupants. The invasion of Europe during the early centuries of the Christian era thus was induced not only by the power vacuum resulting from the disintegration of the Roman Empire, but also by a series of successive pushes, originating from either the desiccation of the Central Asian steppes (Huntington) or the expansion of the Chinese empire still farther east (Teggart).[13]

Many more recent migrations have also been primarily a flight before invading armies.[14] In modern times, however, those induced to flee have often been specific groups among the population, rather than everyone occupying a particular territory. Political dissidents, of course, always were ousted when they became a danger to state security; but with the growth of nationalism ethnic as well as political homogeneity has been sought. The right of national self-determination proclaimed by the Treaty of Versailles included no provision for the minorities scattered through Central Europe; and in the interwar period the League of Nations negotiated a series of population transfers designed to eliminate national minorities from adjacent countries or, more usually, to legitimate expulsions already effected.[15] The sep-

[13]Ellsworth Huntington, Civilization and Climate, New Haven: Yale University Press, 1951; Frederick Teggart, Rome and China: A Study of Correlations in Historical Events, Berkeley: University of California Press, 1939.

[14]See, for example, Eugene M. Kulischer, Europe on the Move, New York: Columbia University Press, 1948.

[15]Cf. Stephen P. Ladas, The Exchange of Minorities: Bulgaria, Greece and Turkey, New York: Macmillan, 1932, p. 721: "Both conventions [of Neuilly and Lausanne], and especially that of Lausanne, proved to be agreements confirming accomplished facts," and the Greek-Turkish exchange, while "voluntary in theory, became in fact to a great extent compulsory."

	Impelled	Forced
To be rid of migrants (conservative)	Flight	Displacement
To use migrants' labor (innovating)	Coolie trade	Slave trade

aration of Pakistan from India, another example, was accompanied by one of the largest migrations in human history, in part induced by terrorist groups on both sides and in part arranged under official auspices.

It is useful to distinguish between two classes of those who have fled their homeland—emigrés, who regard their exile as temporary and live abroad for the day when they may return, and refugees, who intend to settle permanently in the new country. Under otherwise similar circumstances, the acculturation of the latter would presumably be much more rapid than that of persons still living spiritually in another country.

Frequently, even the pretense that the movement is voluntary has been lacking. As part of its European population policy, Nazi Germany exported Jews to camps and imported forced laborers from all occupied countries. The latter movement was a modern variant of the earlier slave-trade, but the largely successful attempt to kill off some millions of persons because of their supposed racial inferiority was something new in history. In the jargon of official bureaus, those that survived such forced migration have been termed "displaced persons," a designation that clearly implies their passive role. The forced movement itself is here called displacement.

The forced migrations under Soviet auspices have typically served two purposes, to remove a dissident or potentially dissident group from its home[16] and

to furnish an unskilled labor force in an inhospitable area. During the first two five-year plans, several million "kulaks" were removed en masse to the sites of cities-to-be, and the inhabitants of the five national units of the USSR abolished during the war were deported wholesale to forced-labor camps.[17] Such movements combine displacement with slave trade, or the forcible migration of laborers. While the overseas shipment of Africans during the mercantile age differed in some respects from the use of forced labor in an industrial economy, the two criteria that define the type are the same—the use of force and the supply of labor power.

The analogous form of impelled migration is termed coolie trade. This includes not only the movement of Asians to plantations, the most typical form, but also, for example the migration of white indentured servants to the British colonies in the 18th century. Such migrants, while formally bound only for the period of a definite contract, very often are forced into indebtedness and thus to extend their period of service indefinitely.[18] But as in

[16]For example, after Poland was divided between Nazi Germany and Communist Russia in 1939, the more than a million Poles deported to Asiatic Russia were chosen not merely on the basis of actual or alleged opposition to their country's invasion but more often as members of a large variety of occupational groups, which were defined as potentially oppositionist. "Regarded as 'anti-Soviet elements,' and so treated, were administrative officials, police, judges, lawyers, members of Parliament, prominent members of political parties, non-communist non-political societies, clubs, and the Red Cross; civil servants not included above, retired military officers, officers in the reserve, priests, tradesmen, landowners, hotel and restaurant owners, clerks of the local Chambers of Commerce, and any class of persons engaged in trade

or correspondence with foreign countries—the latter definition extending even to stamp collectors and Esperantists—were also deported. Many artisans, peasants, and laborers (both agricultural and industrial), were banished too, so that, in effect, no Polish element was spared." Edward J. Rozek, Allied Wartime Diplomacy: A Pattern in Poland, New York: Wiley, 1958, p. 39.

[17]The Volga-German ASSR, the Kalmyk ASSR, the Chechen-Ingush ASSR, the Crimean ASSR, and the Karachayev Region were designated as "disloyal nationalities," and the major portion of the 2.8 million inhabitants were removed from their immemorial homeland. The million or so Tatars brought into Crimea to replace the deportees also proved to be unreliable, and in 1945 most of these were also deported to forced labor. See David J. Dallin and Boris I. Nicolaevsky, Forced Labor in Soviet Russia, New Haven: Yale University Press, 1947, pp. 274-277. According to a decree dated January 9, 1957, the survivors among five of the uprooted peoples are to be shipped back to their homes over the next several years. Even under this new policy, however, the Volga Germans and the Tatars are presumably to be left in their Siberian exile (New York Times, February 12, 1957).

[18]See, for example, Victor Purcell, The Chinese in Southeast Asia, London: Oxford University Press, 1951, p. 345.

other cases of impelled and forced migration, even when the difference between historical instances becomes blurred, the analytical distinction is clear. Another important difference between slave and coolie migration is that many coolies eventually return to their homeland. The total emigration from India from 1834 to 1937, for example, has been estimated at slightly more than 30 million, but of these almost 24 million returned, leaving a net emigration over the century of only six million.[19]

FREE MIGRATION

In the types of migration discussed so far, the will of the migrants has been a relatively unimportant factor. A primitive migration results from the lack of means to satisfy basic physiological needs, and in forced (or impelled) migration the migrants are largely passive. We now consider the types in which the will of the migrants is the decisive element, that is, free migrations.

Overseas movements from Europe during the 19th century afford important illustrations of this class of migration. Because of the excellence of its formal analysis, Lindberg's monograph on emigration from Sweden[20] has been chosen as an example. Lindberg distinguishes three periods, each with a characteristic type of emigrant. During the first stage, beginning around 1840, emigrants came principally from the two university towns of Upsala and Lund; they were "men with a good cultural and social background, mostly young and of a romantic disposition" (p. 3). Since the risks in emigration were great and difficult to calculate, those who left tended to be adventurers or intellectuals motivated by their ideals, especially by their alienation from European society during a period of political reaction. The significance of this pioneer movement was not in its size, which was never large, but in the example it set: "It was this emigration that helped to break the ice and clear the way for the later emigration, which included quite different classes" (p. 7). These pioneers wrote letters home; their adventures in the new world were recounted in Swedish newspapers. Once settled in the new country, they helped finance the passage of their families or friends.

Imperceptibly, this first stage developed into the second, the period of group migration—the emigration, for example, of Pietist communities under the leadership of their pastor or another person of recognized authority. Even when not associated through their adherence to a dissident sect, emigrants banded together for mutual protection during the hazardous journey and against the wilderness and the often hostile Indians at its end. Again, the significance of this group migration lay not in its size but in the further impulse it gave. During the decade beginning in 1841, an average of only 400 persons left Sweden annually, and during the following decade, this average was still only 1,500.

MASS MIGRATION

Free migration is always rather small,[21] for individuals strongly motivated to seek novelty or improvement are not commonplace. The most significant attribute of pioneers, as in other areas of life, is that they blaze trails that others follow, and sometimes the number who do so grows into a broad stream. Migration becomes a style, an established pattern, an example of collective behavior. Once it is well begun, the growth of such a movement is semiautomatic: so long as there are people

---

[19] Kingsley Davis, The Population of India and Pakistan, Princeton: Princeton University Press, 1951, p. 99.

[20] John S. Lindberg, The Background of Swedish Emigration to the United States: An Economic and Sociological Study in the Dynamics of Migration, Minneapolis: University of Minnesota Press, 1930.

[21] As in general throughout this essay, the words used to designate the classes or types of migration are terms in common usage rather than Neologisms. Since they are here more precisely defined than in most contexts, however, they denote a narrower range of meaning; thus free migration is not all unforced migration, for it is one of five rather than two classes.

to emigrate, the principal cause of emigration is prior emigration. Other circumstances operate as deterrents or incentives, but within this kind of attitudinal framework; all factors except population growth are important principally in terms of the established behavior. As we have already noted, when emigration has been set as a social pattern, it is no longer relevant to inquire concerning the individual motivations. For the individual is, in Lindberg's phrase, in an "unstable state of equilibrium," in which only a small impulse in either direction decides his course; hence the motives he ascribes to his emigration are either trivial or, more likely, the generalities that he thinks are expected.[22]

The development of migration as collective behavior is aptly illustrated by the Swedish case. During the decade 1861-70, when the average number of emigrants jumped to 9,300 per year, the transition to the third stage of mass emigration began. Transportation facilities

improved: railroads connected the interior with the port cities, and the sailing ship began to be replaced by the much faster and safer steamer. While its relation to mass migration was important, this improvement in transportation facilities was not a cause; rather, it is "possible and even probable that emigration and the development of transportation were largely caused by the same forces" (p. 15, n. 17). Not only was the geographical distance cut down but also what Lindberg terms the social distance: as communities in the new country grew in size and importance, the shift from Sweden to America required less and less of a personal adjustment. Before the migrant left his homeland, he began his acculturation in an American-Swedish milieu, made up of New World letters, photographs, mementoes, knickknacks. There developed what the peasants called "America fever": in some districts, there was not a farm without some relatives in America, and from many all the children had emigrated. According to a government report that Lindberg quotes, children were "educated to emigrate," and he continues—

> When they finally arrived at a decision, they merely followed a tradition which made emigration the natural thing in a certain situation. In fact, after the imagination and fantasy had, so to speak, become "charged with America," a positive decision not to emigrate may have been necessary if difficulties arose. (pp. 56-57.)

The Swedes who migrated to Minnesota became farmers or small-town craftsmen or merchants. In a more general analysis, it is useful to distinguish two types of mass movement according to the nature of the destination—settlement, such as Lindberg described, and urbanization, or mass migration to a larger town or city. No distinction in principle is made here between internal and international migration, for the fundamentals of the rural-urban shift so characteristic of the modern era are generally the same whether or not the new city-dwellers cross a national border.

[22] Hansen has pointed out that the migrant's motivation was likely to be pruned to suit the person asking for it. The official in the home country was told of material difficulties, but to cite these in America would confirm the natives' belief that the foreigner was a dangerous economic competitor. The village clergyman, should he attempt to dissuade a prospective migrant, was told that his sons were growing up without a future and becoming lazy and shiftless; but in America these moral motives would give point to the argument that immigrants were depraved. Hence, "the newcomer said, 'I came to the United States to enjoy the blessings of your marvelous government and laws,' [and] the native warmed to him and was likely to inquire whether there was not something he could do to assist him. Immigrants soon learned the magic charm of this confession of faith. They seized every opportunity to contrast the liberty of the New World with the despotism of the Old." Marcus Lee Hansen, The Immigrant in American History, Cambridge: Harvard University Press, 1940, pp. 77-78.

This is a good example of why public opinion polling can be deficient as a method of social—rather than social psychological—analysis. Each respondent queried replies in terms of his own norms, and for the whole sample these may differ considerably, depending on how heterogeneous the respondents are with respect to the subject of the poll. To sum up the Yes's and No's without taking into account the criteria that determined these replies is appropriate only when we are interested solely in the sum, as in an election.

CONCLUSIONS

The typology developed in this paper is summarized in the attached table. Such a typology is a tool, and it is worth constructing only if it is useful. What is its utility?

This question may be answered against a perspective of the present undeveloped status of migration theory. Classifications of modern migrations tend to derive from the statistics that are collected, whether or not these have any relevance to theoretical questions. It is as if those interested in the causes of divorce studied this matter exclusively with data classified according to the grounds on which divorces are granted. Even the principal statistical differentiation, that between internal and international migration, is not necessarily of theoretical significance.[23] Similarly, when the species migrant is set off from the genus traveler by arbitrarily defining removal for a year or more as "permanent" migration, such a distinction clearly has little or no theoretical basis, and it is not even certain that it is the most convenient one that could be made.[24] The preferable procedure in any discipline is to establish our concepts and the logical relation among them, and to collect our statistics in terms of this conceptual framework. The principal purpose of the typology, then, is to offer, by such an ordering of conceptual types, a basis for the possible development of theory. "Since sound sociological interpretation inevitably implies some theoretic paradigm, it seems the better part of wisdom to bring it out into the open," first of all because such a paradigm "provides a compact parsimonious arrangement of the central concepts and their interrelations as these are utilized for description and analysis."[25]

Migration differs from fertility and mortality in that it cannot be analyzed, even at the outset, in terms of non-cultural, physiological factors, but must be differentiated with respect to relevant social conditions. This means that the general statement that one makes concerning migration should be in the form of a typology, rather than a law.[26] While few today would follow Ravenstein's example by denoting their statements "laws,"[27] most treatments of migratory selection still imply a comparable degree of generality. Even the best discussions[28] typically neglect to point out that selection ranges along a continuum, from total migration to total non-migration, or that the predominance of females in rural-urban migration that Ravenstein noted must be contrasted with male predominance in, for example, India's urbanization. As we have seen, the familiar push-pull polarity implies a universal sedentary tendency, which has little empirical

[23] The movement westward across the United States, for example, included a swing northward to the western provinces of Canada at the turn of the century, and today American cities attract both Americans and Canadians. In both cases, one may interpret English-speaking North America as a single labor market, with the international border acting primarily as an added friction to free mobility. See Brinley Thomas, Migration and Economic Growth: A Study of Great Britain and the Atlantic Economy (National Institute of Economic and Social Research), London: Cambridge University Press, 1954, pp. 134-138.

[24] Thus in his recent study of British migration, Isaac found it useful to distinguish between those who intend to settle elsewhere permanently and what he termed "quasi-permanent" migrants or those who leave for a year or more but intend to return. See Julius Isaac, British Post-War Migration (National Institute of Economic and Social Research), Occasional Paper XVII, Cambridge University Press, 1954, p. 2.

[25] Robert K. Merton, Social Theory and Social Structure, Glencoe, Ill.: Free Press, 1949, p. 14. For an interesting article exemplifying the usefulness of such a typology, see Merton, "Intermarriage and the Social Structure: Fact and Theory," Psychiatry, 4 (August, 1941), pp. 361-374.

[26] This point is very effectively argued by Heberle, op. cit.

[27] E. G. Ravenstein, "The Laws of Migration," Journal of the Royal Statistical Society, XLVIII (June, 1885), pp. 167-235; LII (June, 1889), pp. 241-305.

[28] See, for example, Dorothy Swaine Thomas (ed.), Research Memorandum of Migration Differentials, New York: Social Science Research Council, Bulletin 43, 1938; E. W. Hofstee, Some Remarks on Selective Migration, The Hague: Nijhoff, 1952.

Relation	Migratory Force	Class of Migration	Type of Migration	
			Conservative	Innovating
Nature and man	Ecological push	Primitive	Wandering	Flight from the land
			Ranging	
State (or equivalent) and man	Migration policy	Forced	Displacement	Slave trade
		Impelled	Flight	Coolie trade
Man and his norms	Higher aspirations	Free	Group	Pioneer
Collective behavior	Social momentum	Mass	Settlement	Urbanization

basis in either history or psychology. Analogously, the distinction between conservative and innovating migration challenges the usual notion that persons universally migrate in order to change their way of life.

Sometimes an analytical problem can be clarified by defining more precisely the two more or less synonymous terms that denote a confusion in concepts. For example, the question of whether the secular decline in the Western birth rate was due to a physiological deterioration or to new cultural standards was often not put clearly until fecundity was precisely distinguished from fertility. Several such pairs of terms are differentiated here. Whether a movement from the countryside to towns is urbanization or flight from the land can be a very important distinction; the discussion of Canada's immigration policy, for example, has largely centered on this point.[29] While the distinction between urbanization and settlement would seem to be so obvious that it can hardly be missed, one can say that the national-quota system of American immigration law is based in part at least on neglect of the implications of this differentiation.[30] The most useful distinction in the typology, perhaps, is that between mass migration and all other types, for it emphasizes the fact that the movement of Europeans to the New World during the 19th century, the migration with which we are most familiar, does not constitute the whole of the phenomenon. When this type of migration declined after the First World War, largely because of new political limitations imposed by both emigration and immigration countries, this was very often interpreted, not as a change to a different type, but as the end of significant human migration altogether.[31] A world in which hardly anyone dies in the place where he was born however, can hardly be termed sedentary.

[29] See Petersen, op. cit., pp. 202 ff.

[30] The main source of immigration to the United States shifted from Northwest Europe to Southern and Eastern Europe at about the same time that the American economy underwent a fundamental transformation from an agrarian to an industrial base; consequently some of the observed differences between the "old" and the "new" immigration were due not to variations among European cultures, as is assumed in the law, but to the different rate of acculturation of peasants undergoing settlement or urbanization.

[31] The two best known statements of this point of view are W. D. Forsyth, The Myth of Open Spaces, Melbourne: Melbourne University Press, 1942, and Isaiah Bowman (ed.), Limits of Land Settlement, New York: Council on Foreign Relations, 1937.

Social Structure and Fertility: An Analytic Framework

Kingsley Davis and Judith Blake

SOURCE: *Economic Development and Cultural Change*, Vol. 4 (1956), pp. 211–235.

A striking feature of underdeveloped areas is that virtually all of them exhibit a much higher fertility than do urban-industrial societies. This well-documented but insufficiently analyzed fact is known to be connected with profound differences in social organization as between the two types of society, and is therefore significant for the comparative sociology of reproduction. The clarity and importance of the contrast, however, should not be allowed to obscure the equally important fact that underdeveloped areas themselves differ markedly in social organization, and that these differences appear to bring about variations in fertility. Though the demographic statistics of backward regions have generally been so poor as to place in doubt the validity of reported differences, there are cases in which the evidence is reliable (e. g., as between Puerto Rico and Jamaica, or Arab Palestine and Ceylon). Of equal interest are the cases in which societies with differing social organization have the same level of fertility, for they may reach this common result by quite different institutional mechanisms. All told, ample opportunity exists for the comparative analysis of social structure as it affects fertility. In view of the bearing of future population trends on economic development, the pursuit of such analysis has a practical as well as a theoretical significance.

The present paper represents an attempt to set forth and utilize an analytical framework for the comparative sociology of fertility. It first presents a classification of the intermediate variables through which any social factors influencing the level of fertility must operate. It next tries to show, in broad outline, how some types and elements of social organization, acting through these variables, appear to enhance or depress societal fertility. Our hope is that as more sociological and demographic information becomes available, the theories advanced can be refined further and tested empirically.

THE INTERMEDIATE VARIABLES

The process of reproduction involves three necessary steps sufficiently obvious to be generally recognized in human culture: (1) intercourse, (2) conception, and (3) gestation and parturition.[1] In analyzing cultural influences on fertility, one may well start with the factors directly connected with these three steps. Such factors would be those through which, and only through which, cultural conditions can affect fertility. For this reason, by way of convenience, they can be called the "intermediate variables" and can be presented schematically as follows:

I. Factors Affecting Exposure to Intercourse ("Intercourse Variables").

    A. Those governing the formation and dissolution of unions in the reproductive period.[2]

        1. Age of entry into sexual unions.

        2. Permanent celibacy: proportion of

---

[1] Although the physiologist sees more steps in the process, these can all be subsumed under the three headings given here. We are concerned only with the steps in reproduction as they may be socially recognized and utilized.

[2] Since sexual intercourse is not confined to wedlock, the term "sexual union" seems preferable to "marriage." A union is here defined as any

women never entering sexual unions.
3. Amount of reproductive period
   spent after or between unions.
   a. When unions are broken by div-
      orce, separation, or desertion.
   b. When unions are broken by death
      of husband.
B. Those governing the exposure to intercourse within unions.
   4. Voluntary abstinence.
   5. Involuntary abstinence (from impo-
      tence, illness, unavoidable but tem-
      porary separations).
   6. Coital frequency (excluding periods
      of abstinence).
II. Factors Affecting Exposure to Conception
    ("Conception Variables").
    7. Fecundity or infecundity, as af-
       fected by involuntary causes.
    8. Use or non-use of contraception.
       a. By mechanical and chemical
          means.
       b. By other means.[3]
    9. Fecundity or infecundity, as af-
       fected by voluntary causes (steri-
       lization, subincision, medical treat-
       ment, etc.).
III. Factors Affecting Gestation and Suc-
     cessful Parturition ("Gestation Vari-
     ables").
     10. Foetal mortality from involuntary
         causes.
     11. Foetal mortality from voluntary
         causes.

---

heterosexual relationship in which either actual
intercourse occurs or orgasm is produced for at
least the male partner. Every society has a type
of union (marriage) in which reproduction is expected, approved, and even enjoined. At the same
time every society runs the risk of unions in which
reproduction is condemned, either because they
lack the legal form of marriage or because they
violate one or more institutional taboos (adultery,
incest, caste, or class endogamy, etc.—see K.
Davis, "The Forms of Illegitimacy", Social Forces,
Vol. 18, October 1939, pp. 77-89). Between the
fully approved and the strongly proscribed unions,
there may be other types which have a lesser
grade than marriage but in which reproduction
normally occurs. Such unions may be frequent,
in some cases representing the majority of reproductive unions. Any satisfactory sociological
analysis of reproduction must keep straight the
different types of unions.

[3]Means of contraception other than mechanical
and chemical include the "rhythm" method (which
can also be classed as voluntary abstinence), withdrawal, simulated intercourse without penetration,
various "perversions," etc.

It is clear that any cultural factor that
affects fertility must do so in some way
classifiable under one or another of our
eleven intermediate variables.[4] Hence
the latter provide a framework in terms
of which the relevance of cultural factors
to fertility can be judged. In fact, attempts to explain causal relationships
between institutions and fertility without
such a framework have led to inconclusive and confused writing on the subject.[5] The cultural factors, or "conditioning variables", are presumably many,
and no effort is made here to classify
them; but the "intermediate variables"
offer a means of approach to selecting
and analyzing these factors.

It is also clear that each of the eleven
variables may have a negative (minus)
or a positive (plus) effect on fertility.
If by examining all societies we could
find the range of influence of a given
variable, any effect more negative than
the midpoint of this range would be on
the minus side, and any influence more
positive would be on the plus side. If,
for example, a society uses contraception successfully, it has a minus value
with respect to variable number 8; if it
uses no contraception, it has a plus
value on this variable. The value of each
variable refers to how it affects fertility
in each case; so a positive use of something (e. g., contraception, abortion, abstinence) may mean that it has a "minus" fertility-value.

[4]The reader will note that our list of variables
does not include infanticide or child care. The
reason for this omission is that our analysis is
focused on factors affecting fertility strictly defined. Infanticide does, of course, affect family
size and natural increase and may serve as an
alternative to factors affecting fertility. It is therefore discussed briefly at a later point.

[5]For instance, Frank Lorimer, Culture and
Human Fertility, Paris, 1954, by failing to make
clear the ways in which fertility can be affected,
gives in some ways a confused picture of how it
is affected. The reader may wish to compare
our framework with a half-page outline of direct
and indirect factors affecting fertility given by
Raymond Pearl at the end of an article on "Biological Factors in Fertility," Annals of the American Academy of Political and Social Science, Vol.
188, November 1936, p. 24.

One cannot say, as is frequently implied in the literature, that some of these variables are affecting fertility in one society but not in another. All of the variables are present in every society. This is because, as mentioned before, each one is a variable—it can operate either to reduce or to enhance fertility. If abortion is not practiced, the fertility-value of variable number 11 is "plus". In other words, the absence of a specific practice does not imply "no influence" on fertility, because this very absence is a form of influence. It follows that the position of any society, if stated at all, must be stated on all eleven variables.

Societies differing in their social organization do not necessarily have different fertility-values with respect to all the variables. On some of the variables they may exhibit quite similar values. A nomadic tribe may have the same age at marriage as a settled agrarian village; a primitive group may practice the same rate of abortion as an industrial society. Two contrasting societies are not likely, however, to manifest similar values for all the variables; they are not likely to do this even when their general fertility level is practically the same. The actual birth rate depends on the net balance of the values of all the variables. Though societies which generate a high fertility tend to be predominantly on the plus side, no society has the highest plus value on all eleven variables; and societies with low fertility turn out to be amazingly positive on a number of them.

It should, of course, be mentioned that cultural influences affecting our eleven variables do not necessarily represent rational attempts to govern fertility. Many fertility consequences stemming from socio-cultural conditions (especially in underdeveloped regions) are by-products, being unanticipated and unrealized by members of the society. Surely by now social scientists know that they cannot confine their attention only to rational actions or treat non-rational actions as somehow defying systematic analysis. The requirements of a given society can be met just as well, and just as ill, by an unintentional level of fertility as by an intentional one.

INSTITUTIONAL PATTERNS AND THE INTERMEDIATE VARIABLES: A PRELIMINARY ANALYSIS

From the standpoint of comparative sociology, an important question is how the fertility-values of our intermediate variables distribute themselves in different kinds of societies. A preliminary generalization is that underdeveloped societies tend to have high fertility-values for numbers 1, 2, 8, and 9 on the list; they may have high values for 3a, 3b, and 10; and they often have low values for 4 and 11. As for the remaining variables—5, 6, and 7—it is hard to prove that there are any consistent differences between pre-industrial and industrial societies. If this generalization is roughly accurate, then it becomes meaningful to re-group the eleven variables as follows:

The Intermediate Variables According to Their Values in Pre-Industrial Societies

Usually High Values
1. Age of entry into unions.
2. Permanent celibacy.
8. Contraception.
9. Sterilization, etc.

Usually Low Values
4. Voluntary abstinence.
10. Foetal mortality—involuntary

High or Low Values
3a. Time between unstable unions.
3b. Post-widowhood celibacy.
11. Foetal mortality—voluntary.

Indeterminate
5. Involuntary abstinence.
6. Frequency of coitus.
7. Involuntary sterility.

In attempting to analyze in a preliminary way how different institutional patterns affect the variables, we shall find it convenient to follow the order just given.

Number 1. Age of Entry into Unions. In beginning with age of entry into unions, we are dealing with one of the variables governing exposure to intercourse. It should be noted that these particular variables, however favorable they may be to fertility in themselves, may be counteracted in practice by other factors governing conception and gestation. For example, even though sexual unions begin early, pregnancy or childbirth may be prevented. This is often the case when the sexual union is not a marriage. Many societies, even though they permit premarital intercourse, strongly forbid illegitimate pregnancy.[6] With respect to marital unions, however, reproduction is specifically sanctioned, indeed expected. As already mentioned, there may be, in addition, non-marital unions in which reproduction also normally occurs. Consequently, in dealing with age of entry into unions, we shall separate those unions in which offspring normally appear (including both marital and non-marital types) from those in which reproduction is so strongly condemned that it is infrequent. We shall now deal with the first general class (paying attention mostly to marriage itself), leaving until later the discussion of non-reproductive sexual unions.

Since in pre-industrial societies the age of entry into reproductive unions is generally young, the question must be raised as to why the fertility-value of

this variable is usually positive when on certain other variables it is often negative. From a broad functional standpoint, the explanation stems from high mortality. Not only does a high death rate normally prevail in underdeveloped societies from year to year, but there is always the danger of a sudden catastrophic rise in mortality. Early marriage therefore represents the maximum possible hedge against the threat of failure in population replacement. Entering a union at a young age does not commit one irretrievably to a large family, because all other means of reducing fertility come <u>after</u> this point. If a particular union is resulting in progeny that are too numerous under current circumstances, this eventuality can be obviated by abstinence, contraception, abortion, or infanticide. These means, precisely because they come later, can be utilized at a time closer to the actual impingement of new individuals on the resources of those responsible. If, on the other hand, the age of entry into unions is late, the potential fertility that is lost can never be recovered. The threat of mortality, from a societal standpoint, has reference not only to the potential offspring but also to the parents themselves. Early formation of unions helps to guarantee that the young adults will achieve at least some reproduction before they die.

This broad functional explanation does not, however, enlighten us concerning the specific institutional mechanisms by which early marriage is insured. These can best be understood in terms of family and kinship organization (involving rules of residence and rules of descent) and the control of property. Such mechanisms apply most clearly to formal marriage, although they may apply as well, though in lesser degree, to informal reproductive unions.

From the standpoint of kinship organization, an essential distinction is that between a joint household and/or clan system, on the one hand, and an independent nuclear family organization on the other. When the clan is the unit controlling the property (whether the lat-

---

[6]Among the 250 societies for which he had information, Murdock found that, apart from incest taboos, "premarital relations are fully permitted in 65 instances, and are conditionally approved in 43 and only mildly disapproved in 6, whereas they are forbidden in only 44. In other words, premarital license prevails in 70 per cent of our cases. In the rest, the taboo falls primarily upon females and appears to be largely a precaution against childbearing out of wedlock rather than a moral requirement." George P. Murdock, *Social Structure*, New York, 1949, p. 265. On p. 5 the author gives slightly different figures, but the majority of his societies still permit premarital sexual relations.

ter consists in herds or land), the question of inheritance does not normally arise, because the clan is immortal. When the joint family is the controlling unit, the question arises only when the joint family divides; the joint family, however, does not divide when the offspring marry, but rather, at the earliest, when the father dies. Thus, in societies having a joint household (and a fortiori in those having a strong clan organization), marriage is in no way made contingent on the possession of separate property by the newly married pair.

Furthermore, with strong clan or joint-household control (or both), marriages are usually arranged by the elders, who are often motivated to make the arrangements early in the lifetime of the prospective mates, i. e., before puberty. Religious prescription may require this result, and the economic exchanges involved in betrothal may be structured in such a way as to yield an advantage to the parents who marry their daughter early. If the system is one of patrilocal residence, for example, a grown daughter remaining in her parental home is an anomaly. Not only does her presence run counter to the normal division of labor by sex, which assumes the complementarity of husband and wife, but she must adjust to the wives of her brothers coming into the household. Add to this fact that the daughter, as a prospective spouse, is most in demand by other families when she is young, first because she then has a greater potential fertility ahead of her, and, second, because she is more attractive sexually and fits more easily into a subordinate status in her husband's parental home. If, then, there is a substantial brideprice or groomprice at marriage, the girl's kin stand a better chance of a favorable bargain if they marry her off early. This may help them in procuring wives for their sons.

In societies having neither a strong clan nor a joint family, the forces leading to early marriage may be overbalanced by others. The Irish family, for instance, has long been organized in terms of neolocal residence and hence marital rather than filial solidarity. This being true, land had to be obtainable or marriage postponed. During the greater part of the eighteenth century land was scarce and could not be subdivided because the economy was predominantly pastoral. Consequently, an obstacle to early marriage "was the difficulty of acquiring a settlement upon which a new family might depend."[7] Later, during the sixty years before the Famine, when the potato became the staple food and the economy shifted from pastoralism to cultivation, couples could get property at marriage by subdivision of the land, thus removing temporarily the main obstacle to early marriage. But with the crisis of the Famine, the futility of progressive subdivision led to the Land Purchase Acts stipulating that the loans which transformed tenants into owners were granted only on condition that no subdivision would take place. Since the annuities ran for 35 years, this represented some restraint on subdivision.[8] A more powerful restraint was the fact that, once the tenants became owners, they grew unwilling to subdivide in behalf of their sons. The tendency was to retain only one on the paternal land, the remainder of the children being dispersed, partly through migration abroad. The independent nuclear family was maintained, but the son who remained at home could not establish such a family until the father was willing to resign both authority and property. As a result the average age at marriage in Ireland became extremely advanced, reaching 29.1 for women by 1926.[9]

Lest our characterization of Irish family organization as neolocal appear sur-

---

[7] K. H. Connell, The Population of Ireland, 1750-1845, Oxford 1950, p. 89 [underscoring ours].

[8] See Elizabeth R. Hooker, Readjustments of Agricultural Tenure in Ireland, Chapel Hill, 1938, esp. pp. 55-57, 106, 151, 208.

[9] A. M. Carr-Saunders, World Population, Oxford, 1936, p. 91. Cf. James Meenan, "Some Causes and Consequences of the Low Irish Marriage Rate", Journal of the Statistical and Social Inquiry Society of Ireland, 86th session, 1932-33, pp. 19-27.

prising, it should be noted that although the Irish have been interpreted as having a joint household and patrilocal residence,[10] the opposite seems to be true. Even if one or two sons remain at home, the resulting menage is not what is ordinarily called a joint household; because in Ireland marriage implies the independence of the son. When the son brings a bride into what was the paternal homestead, he brings her into a home that has been redefined as his, no longer his father's. The father has relinquished both ownership of the farm and authority over the son. As long as the father continues to own the land, the son who remains at home cannot marry because the land is necessary for the "match".[11] If marriage occurs, therefore, the fact that the parents are still in the home is merely adventitious—they have entered "the age grade of the dying".[12] Significantly, if irreconcilable conflict develops in the shared household, it is the parents, not the son and his wife, who must leave. "The bond between them [husband and wife] is stronger than that between son and parent."[13] Thus in Ireland the fact of sharing a house with the parents is not a reflection of the joint family ideal but of the force of circumstances. The fact of a common menage is socially defined in such a way as to comply with the ideal of a neolocal and independent nuclear family.

This independent nuclear family organization is neither unique to Ireland nor modern in development. In Northwestern Europe the custom of impartible inheritance (e. g., by promigeniture or ultimogeniture) was found in many areas during the Middle Ages. In some sections it was apparently customary for the old people to give their land to the heir before they died. Surrendering their authority, they expected only their keep off the land. The heir's marriage was contingent on the land being turned over to him; if his sisters and brothers stayed on, they could claim their keep but not the privilege of marriage.[14] The principle of no holding, no marriage,[15] operated to advance the average age beyond what it otherwise would have been. Furthermore, the notion of the independence of the nuclear family also manifested itself in the master-apprentice relationship within the medieval guilds; for marriage often did not occur until an adequate guild status had been acquired by inheritance, purchase, or dower.[16] There is thus evidence that European society has long emphasized the marital rather than the filial bond as the basis of family organization, with a consequent tendency to delay marriage.[17]

The emphasis on marital rather than filial solidarity, on neolocal rather than patrilocal residence, which appears to have delayed marriage in Ireland and Northwestern Europe contrasts sharply with the forces operating to precipitate marriage in an extended family system. In a truly joint household the authority of the elders continues <u>after</u> marriage; the marital bond is therefore subordinate to the filial bond and does not require economic independence on the part of those getting married. Such a family pattern is well known as the ideal one in traditional China, India, Bantu Africa, and many other peasant or primitive cultures. In the Chinese case, the father maintains his tutelage over the married

---

[10]E. g., Conrad M. Arensberg and Solon T. Kimball, Family and Community in Ireland, Cambridge, 1938, p. 80.

[11]Arensberg and Kimball, op. cit., pp. 107-122.

[12]Ibid., p. 123.

[13]Ibid., p. 128.

[14]George C. Homans, English Villagers of the Thirteenth Century, Cambridge, 1942, Chs. 9-10.

[15]Josiah C. Russell, "Demographic Values in the Middle Ages", Studies in Population, George F. Mair, ed., Princeton, 1949, p. 104.

[16]Josiah C. Russell, British Medieval Population, Albuquerque, 1948, pp. 163-164.

[17]Of course, not every society with neolocal residence shows a retarded age at marriage. In a primitive economy with high mortality, where no formal training or other obstacles to adult status must be hurdled, and where scarcity of persons rather than scarcity of land is the felt need, independent nuclear families may be formed by early marriage, e. g., the Netsilik Eskimos, Fox Indians, Andaman Islanders, Ruthenians.

son and his control over the familial property until death. He consequently need not fear the marriage of his son as a threat to his authority, and therefore, unlike the Irish father, has no motive (at least in this regard) for postponing such marriage. On the contrary, to the extent that his son brings a wife into the house and has children, the old man's authority is extended. Indeed, it is only by the marriage of his son that the patriarch can fulfill <u>his</u> filial obligation to <u>his</u> father.[18]

<u>Number 2. Extent of Permanent Celibacy.</u> If late marriage can have a minus effect on fertility, so can permanent non-marriage. In both cases, if this effect is to be produced, there must be either continence outside of marriage, or the use of means to prevent intercourse from resulting in childbirth. In practice, non-marriage usually does produce a low rate of reproduction among the unmarried, because, as mentioned already, marriage in all societies is the preferred institutional arrangement for having chilren. It seems wise, therefore, to discuss "celibacy" primarily in terms of nonmarriage, and to consider sexual continence only in so far as it illuminates that factor.

Although permanent non-marriage is obviously a more potent factor than mere postponement of marriage, it actually occurs less frequently and hence has less negative influence on fertility. Only rarely can a population be found where more than 20 per cent of the women complete the reproductive period without ever having married. Ireland is an extreme case, with 26.3% of its women aged 45-49 in 1946 still single.[19] If we assume that these women, had they married, would have had the same completed fertility as those who did, then their proportion represents an estimate of the loss of fertility due to non-marriage (excluding illegitimate births).[20] Thus the loss due to permanent non-marriage seems, even in the extreme case, scarcely to exceed one-fourth. Such a loss in fertility is greatly exceeded by that due to late age at marriage. For example, in Switzerland (where the data are readily available), if all women in 1941 who had ever married by ages 40-44, had married at ages 15-19 and had subsequently manifested the same age-specific fertility as those who had actually married then or did marry at some point prior to age 40, the reproduction would have been 75% greater than it actually was![21] In other words, the gain in fertility if late marriage had been eliminated would have been approximately three times the gain (25%) if permanent non-marriage had been eliminated.

It is mainly in urban-industrial societies that the proportion of women never marrying by the end of the reproductive span exceeds 10%. In India in 1931 it was only 0.6%, in Ceylon in 1946, 3.4%; and in Malaya in 1947, 3.3%. Thus the underdeveloped areas generally show a very high plus value for fertility with respect both to variable number 1 (age at marriage) and variable number 2 (proportion ever married), whereas industrial

---

[18]Marion J. Levy, Jr., <u>The Family Revolution in Modern China</u>, Cambridge, 1949, pp. 168-170. When the family head dies there is the problem of one of the sons assuming authority over the others. It is precisely at this point that the joint household often dissolves; but if it survives this crisis, as it may, it does so because of the past institutionalization of relative age as a factor in authority.

[19]Other cases of high proportions never married are Sweden (1945) 20.9%, Switzerland (1941) 20.1%, England and Wales (1931) 16.8%, Belgium (1930) 13.3%.

[20]Differences in mortality and possible fecundity as between married and unmarried women may introduce a small but probably not serious error into this estimate.

[21]This calculation excludes non-marriage as a factor, because the women who had never married by age 40-44 were subtracted from the women under consideration in each age group. In other words, 21.4% of Swiss women at ages 40-44 had never married. But the remaining 78.6% had married at various ages. If this 78.6% had all married at ages 15-19 and had from that age experienced the same age-specific fertility as those ever married at each age, their total fertility would have been 76% greater. Stated in terms of the potential fertility lost by late marriage, the figure is approximately 64%. The calculation is rough, because the data refer to 1941 and thus do not represent a true cohort analysis; but a refined calculation on a cohort basis should yield rather similar results.

societies often show rather low fertility-values on these.

We thus have to answer two questions: Why do all societies generally make less use of non-marriage than of late marriage in depressing fertility? Why do underdeveloped peoples make less use of both of these mechanisms than do industrial societies? Let us attempt to answer these two questions in order.

Given the low fecundity of the human species, no society can hope to replace itself unless either a majority of its women participate in reproduction or its mortality is rigorously controlled. Since most of man's history has occurred under conditions of heavy mortality—conditions which still prevail for many of the world's peoples—all viable societies have evolved social mechanisms that lead the majority of women to participate in reproduction. Their participation is organized through the institution of marriage, which links sex and reproduction to the care and socialization of children. This institution is in turn supported by its articulation with the rest of the social order. The marital relation thus becomes a general norm in terms of which the hopes and expectations of virtually all individuals are channelized. If for some reason the pressure of mortality is relaxed, the norm still continues in effect. Not only do normative systems change slowly, but there still remains the necessity for a family organization in terms of which reproduction and child-rearing are provided for. Thus individuals continue to anticipate marriage as a normal and important part of life, an event more easily postponed than foregone altogether.

In any case, an increase in non-marriage would not reduce fertility unless either coitus outside of wedlock were successfully banned or contraception and abortion were freely used. If the latter were readily available, they could be used within marriage, and the consequent reduction in marital fertility would obviate the necessity of denying marriage to a substantial portion of the population. If contraception and abortion were not readily available, non-marriage would be an effective brake on fertility only at the price of permanent sexual celibacy. Everything we know about human society indicates that this price is so high that no population is willing to pay it.

Since no society has ever attempted to incorporate permanent celibacy as a widespread custom, we have no conclusive evidence as to what it would do to a social system. We can, however, obtain some clues by examining countries in which permanent celibacy has appeared to an unusual extent and by examining organizations which have enjoined it as a rule. We can also say something on purely theoretical grounds concerning what it might do if utilized as the chief means of reducing fertility to a modern level. Limitations of space prevent our giving a complete treatment along these lines, but something can be said about each of them.

Because Ireland has an unusually late age at marriage and a high proportion who never marry, together with a strong prejudice against coitus outside of marriage, it provides the main example of a rather extensive practive of celibacy.[22] Has this adjustment exacted a price? To answer such a question is difficult. A puritanical attitude toward sex cannot be listed as a consequence, because this is part of the celibacy itself. That the Irish avoid reproduction outside of marriage is shown by their low illegitimacy rate—2.8% of all live births in 1921-1930 and 3.3% in 1931-1940.[23] However, such descriptions as we have suggest that a great amount of attention, community effort, and personality conflict go into controlling sexual expression. Having a social system that emphasized the mar-

[22]David Glass, Introduction to Malthus, New York, 1953, pp. 27-54, shrewdly notes that Ireland is the only country which has come close to following Malthus' rules of conduct--"moral restraint" and no birth control. In other countries of Northwestern Europe, such as Sweden and Norway, a late age at marriage does not imply sexual abstinence, not only because illegitimacy is more tolerated but also because contraception is more freely practiced.

[23]Ibid., p. 37.

ital bond and the nuclear family, the Irish
cannot completely segregate unmarried
females, as is done in Moslem countries.
The young people must have some chance
to participate in courtship and mate selection. But, given this system, the Irish
seem to make an unusually strong effort
to control sexual behavior. For a country
not living under a dictatorship, the official censorship of literature and ideas
is exceptionally rigid, and has as its
main purpose the suppression of material
pertaining to sex and reproduction.[24] Furthermore, the data on mental illness,
which show a high rate for Ireland, indicate a possible consequence of such repression.[25] There appear to be few fea-

tures in Irish life that compensate for
whatever is lost through celibacy. Ireland
has, for example, the lowest level of
living of any nation in Northwestern Europe. All told, there is some ground for
the hypothesis that Ireland is paying a
price for its unusual degree of celibacy.

Celibacy as an <u>organizational</u> rule has
almost solely applied to religious personnel. Among those few religions which
have adopted such a rule for their clergy,
our evidence is most readily available
for the Roman Catholic priesthood. As
is well known, the application of the rule
in this case encountered great difficulties. It required nearly nine centuries
before the edict of non-marriage itself
could be enforced with relative success.
Priests were first commanded to separate from their wives and remain continent in 385 A. D. After that date there
were periods when the ban against marriage could be safely ignored by priests,
followed by periods when the Church was
militantly purging its married clergy.
Pope Gregory (Hildebrand) encountered
such obstacles in enforcing the rule of
non-marriage that he ordered the laity
to withdraw their obedience from all
members of the clergy who disregarded
the papal canons on simony and incontinence. By so doing, he undermined a
basic principle of the Church—clerical
immunity—and thus as early as 1074
directly laid one of the foundations of the
Reformation. Only by placing the sacra-
ment of marriage in a lower position
than that of the religious vow (Lateran
Council of 1123) did the Church finally
settle the issue of clerical marriage,
although in practice such marriages occurred with some frequency after that—
as late as the nineteenth century in some
parts of Latin America, for example. In
periods when the ban against marriage
was being enforced, the Church still had
to deal with sexual incontinence among
its priests and nuns. "Solicitation" (the

[24]For attitudes toward sexual behavior see
Arensberg and Kimball, op. cit., Ch. 11; and also
such literary and popular sources as Frank O'Connor, "Ireland", Holiday, Vol. 6, December 1949,
p. 40; Sean O'Faolain, "Love Among the Irish",
Life Magazine, Vol. 34, March 16, 1953, pp. 140-
157. Regarding censorship, the following passage
from O'Faolain is pertinent: "...Our censorship of
books and publications, instigated by the clergy
and submitted to, willy-nilly, by everybody, is a
symbol of this fear of sex...In the 150 close-
packed pages of the official register of books and
periodicals banned by the Irish Censorship Board
we find the names of almost every single Irish
writer of note, some for one book, some for several. The banning is done in secret. There is no
appeal to the courts of law..." See also an article,
"Irish Challenge Censors' Methods", The New York
Times, August 14, 1955, where it is pointed out
that the Irish Censorship Board "has banned books
by the most reputable Irish authors, including
Sean O'Casey, Liam O'Flaherty, Sean O'Faolain,
and Ireland's most brilliant short story writer,
Frank O'Connor. Nobel prize winners have even
come under the interdict...many works of worth
are condemned on a few isolated marked passages, while the general tenor of the book is
ignored...Even the works of Roman Catholic authors approved by the church authorities in Britain
have not escaped the five Irish Roman Catholic
Censors."

[25]In 1949 the proportion of hospital beds devoted
to mental cases was 57% in Ireland, whereas it
was only 49% in the United States. The rate of
mental patients per 100,000 population in 1948 was
603 in Ireland as contrasted to 382 in the United
States. Adventitious circumstances seem not to
account for this result. Though Ireland has a
larger percentage of persons in the advanced ages
than does the United States (24.7% at ages 50 and
over as against 22.4% at these ages in the United
States), she has a higher proportion under age 30.
The fact that Irish medical services are less
developed than in this country suggests that the

comparison understates the difference in mental
illness. In 1949 Ireland had only one hospital bed
per 1,000 inhabitants, whereas the United States
has 9.6, so that a higher proportion of mental
cases in Ireland may never appear in the statistics.

seduction of female penitents), concubinage, and other violations were so common as to cause chronic public scandal. In some areas priestly concubinage became, for long periods, a customary practice, and the sons of priests received preferment.[26] We can thus see that the enforcement of celibacy even for that small fraction of the population represented by the clergy was anything but easy.

If we imagine a society in which celibacy is institutionalized and becomes a norm rivaling marriage, we can see that the result would be paradoxical and impossible. Should the celibate class be large enough to reduce the birth rate to a modern level without other means, it would have to contain at least half the population. For individuals on such a scale to be induced to make the sacrifice of celibacy, they would not only have to be firmly controlled (perhaps segregated from the rest of the community and thus divorced from the temptations of everyday life), but would also have to be ideologically indoctrinated, and, above all, socially rewarded. If the rewards were great enough to recruit people for the numerous celibate portion of the population, this class would inevitably occupy the top of the social ladder. But the celibate class would be too big to be an elite. Furthermore, the sheer fact of

celibacy would not represent in itself a contribution to the productive capacity of the society. If the celibate population were given useful tasks to perform, the variety of functions would necessarily be great; and if all these received an indiscriminately high reward, some celibates would be receiving this return not because of their productive contribution but because of their celibacy. In this way, seeking to give half or more of its population advantages that at best only a few can be given (and doing so regardless of productive merit), the society would suffer an intolerable economic and social burden.[27]

After this analysis of the relatively minor role of permanent celibacy in fertility limitation, we are now ready for our second question: Why are late marriage and non-marriage more frequent in industrial than in pre-industrial societies?

Perhaps non-marriage occurs more often in industrial societies because these societies depend less upon kinship and the family as bases of social organization. The fact of being or not being married affects less the individual's economic chances. In pre-industrial societies, where the family is a productive unit, marriage has a high value for the individual. Also, where the partners to marriage are self-selected by a competitive process of courtship, as in modern countries, there tends to be a substantial proportion who are not successful in attracting a suitable mate.

The greater postponement of marriage in urban-industrial nations can be similarly explained. The necessity of lengthy training for skilled positions in an industrial economy, the often lengthy trial-and-error process of courtship, the nec-

---

[26]For the history of clerical celibacy in Europe, see Henry C. Lea, <u>History of Sacerdotal Celibacy in the Christian Church</u>, London, 1932, and <u>A History of the Inquisition of the Middle Ages</u>, Vol. 1, New York, 1888, pp. 31-32; Alexander C. Flick, <u>The Decline of the Medieval Church</u>, New York, 1930, Vols. 1-2, <u>passim</u>.; J. R. Tanner et al. (eds.), <u>Contest of Empire and Papacy</u>, Vol. 5 of <u>Cambridge Medieval History</u>, New York, 1926, esp. pp. 11-14, 40, 61-62, 73, 695; Eileen Power, <u>Medieval English Nunneries</u>, Cambridge, 1922, Ch. 11; Geoffrey Baskerville, <u>English Monks and the Suppression of the Monasteries</u>, New Haven, 1937, pp. 261-266; Joseph McSorley, <u>An Outline History of the Church by Centuries</u>, St. Louis, 1944, pp. 83, 154, 206-207, 237; H. J. Schroeder, <u>Disciplinary Decrees of the General Councils</u>, St. Louis, 1937, p. 193. For Latin America, see J. Lloyd Mecham, <u>Church and State in Latin America</u>, Chapel Hill, 1934, p. 48; Mary Watters, <u>A History of the Church in Venezuela, 1810-1930</u>, Chapel Hill, 1933, p. 211; Gilberto Freyre, <u>The Masters and the Slaves</u>, New York, 1946, pp. 446-452.

[27]Of course, a society could be imagined in which half or more of the women were forced to be celibate, the rest of the people living in polyandrous marriage. But such a speculation would evoke more paradoxes than that already sketched. A society capable of such deliberate organization could scarcely be expected to use celibacy alone as its means of controlling fertility. With other less drastic means available, the end would hardly justify the means.

essity of economic self-sufficiency on the part of the newly married couple—all are conducive to marital postponement.

But in neither type of society is non-marriage likely to be as important a depressant of fertility as late marriage, because marriage remains the institutional norm in both cases. Wedlock may be postponed with some equanimity, but individuals who actually never marry have, in most cases, hoped that this would not be their fate. In Ireland, for example, clerical celibacy is certainly valued, but not permanent celibacy among laymen.[28]

Once again let us note that neither the postponement nor the total abjuration of marriage necessarily implies sexual celibacy. Hence no industrial society today is required to use either method as a dominant means of controlling fertility, because other less drastic, less sacrificial, methods are available. It is clear that marital postponement, non-marriage, and abstinence within marriage, if they are effective in limiting fertility, all have a common feature—sexual denial; and all share the difficulties that this entails.

Number 8. Use or Non-Use of Contraception. Whereas the "intercourse variables" have a negative effect on fertility only through abstinence, neither the conception nor the gestation variables require this drastic behavior by the individual or the institutionalization necessary to insure such behavior. With the "conception variables" (of which the use or non-use of contraception is one), the pleasure of intercourse is not foregone. The individual, thus released from paying a heavy appetitive penalty for the decision not to have children, is much freer to decide this issue in terms of his economic and social interests alone.

With reference to contraception in particular, its apparent efficiency might lead one to expect a widespread use of it as a depressant of fertility. Yet we have already stated that this is one of the three variables which almost universally have

a strong plus fertility-value in pre-industrial societies. Why, then, do these societies so widely exhibit the non-use of contraception? To answer this question, we must consider separately the two types of contraception.

8a. Contraception by chemical or mechanical means. In many primitive and peasant cultures the idea of chemical and mechanical contraception is known and attempts are made to apply it. Yet, even in situations motivating the individual to limit his fertility, this is not usually the means adopted, simply because the technology of underdeveloped societies cannot supply effective methods. In the absence of a knowledge of reproductive physiology, people in these societies have little sense of even the kind of instrumentalities to look for. Similarly, there is not enough knowledge of chemistry to give command over materials. The methods, therefore, tend to be hit or miss, with magic rather than science playing a prominant role. Lack of experimental technique leads one method to be valued as highly as another.[29] Even the methods that would actually accomplish the purpose of contraception are apt to be clumsy, sexually unsatisfactory, and unhealthful, e. g., insertion of an okra-like seed pod in the vagina (Bush Negroes of British Guiana); insertion of rags or finely chopped grass (Bapindas and Bambundas in Central Africa); insertion of dung (Egypt and other societies).[30] Furthermore, granted that a really satisfactory method is hit upon, such as possibly the use of a douche containing lemon juice or a decoction of the husks of mahogany nut (Martinique or Guiana),[31] the materials are likely to be available only in one locale or in certain seasons of the year. Thus the technology

---

[28]Arensberg and Kimball, op. cit., p. 69.

[29]Norman E. Himes, Medical History of Contraception, Baltimore, 1936, pp. 53-54, 99. See also Clellan S. Ford, A Comparative Study of Human Reproduction, New Haven, 1945, pp. 40-42.

[30]Himes, op. cit., pp. 10, 18-19, 63.

[31]Ibid., p. 17. Also see M. Soors, "La dénatalité chez les Mongo", Zaire, Vol. 4, May 1950, pp. 525-532.

and economy of pre-industrial societies have not been equal to the task of providing a chemico-mechanical contraceptive that would be at once cheap, satisfactory, effective, and readily available.

8b. Contraception without chemical or mechanical means. Clearly such methods as withdrawal, intercourse without penetration, and various heterosexual "perversions" do not depend on scientific and technological progress. They are known and practiced in one form or another in nearly all societies.[32] Yet they seem to be insufficiently employed to represent a major control over fertility. They may be so employed in a few primitive societies, but apparently not in the civilizations such as that of China, India, and the Near East where huge population aggregates are found. For the most part, it seems, they are employed in extra-marital relations or in those cases where premarital intercourse is permitted but

premarital pregnancy forbidden. But it is doubtful that such practices represent an important contribution to fertility control in whole societies. Numerous societies—some with a good share of the world's people—either do not permit the ordinary female to engage in premarital intercourse, or have such a young age at marriage that such intercourse would play a small role in any case. As for extra-marital relations, those societies which permit them under certain circumstances are not particularly concerned about the woman's becoming pregnant, because biological paternity is not stressed. Only those societies branding adulterous children as illegitimate would condemn the married woman's pregnancy by another man than the husband, and these would be societies which restrict extra-marital intercourse. For these reasons, to have an independent and significant effect on fertility, non-mechanical contraceptive methods would have to be used within marriage. We are therefore forced to ask why such methods are not more widely used within wedlock in pre-industrial societies.

The reader should recall that any society with a high mortality must in general motivate its members to view legitimate reproduction favorably. Under this pressure the cultures in question, as already pointed out, are so organized as to maximize fertility values in the early stages of the reproductive process—e. g., by early marriage. Although intercourse is one step later, it is still so early as to involve a risk of inadequate fertility. If conditions subsequently make children undesirable, measures can still be taken after conception.

An additional consideration is that the physical burden and danger of childbearing, and the responsibility for nourishing and rearing the child, fall mainly on the mother. If therefore there is a wish to avoid childbirth, this wish is apt to be hers rather than her husband's. It happens, however, that the non-chemico-mechanical methods of contraception are the ones requiring the co-operation and partial frustration of the male. Since he

---

[32]Himes, speaking of Europe, says that "coitus interruptus is doubtless the most popular, widely diffused method of contraception...and has been for centuries...[It] is probably nearly as old as the group life of man." Op. cit., pp. 183-184. He also cites numerous primitive tribes in which coitus interruptus is practiced. I. Schapera, writing of the Kgatla of Bechuanaland, says: "The commonest method of contraception locally practiced is coitus interruptus...It is widely employed not only by married people, but also by unmarried lovers." Sometimes the woman, by moving her hips so as to extrude the penis just before ejaculation, accomplishes coitus interruptus without the male's cooperation. Married Life in an African Tribe, New York, 1941, pp. 222-223. Coitus inter femora is practiced in many societies, particularly by the Bantus in Africa. Girls may wear special girdles designed to avoid penetration. C. Daryll Forde, Marriage and the Family among the Yakö of South-Eastern Nigeria, London, 1941, p. 14. Bantu tribes, permitting sexual relations but not pregnancy before marriage, teach (or did teach) their young people how to have intercourse without penetration, the unbroken hymen in some tribes being regarded as an important index of virginity, insisted on at marriage.

Alfred C. Kinsey et al. found "petting to climax" to have been practiced by 24% of the male sample (blown up to represent the U. S. male population) by age 21, and by 50% of college-educated males. The cumulative incidence among females was less but still substantial, being 24% for the college-educated at age 20. Sexual Behavior in the Human Male, Philadelphia, 1948, pp. 531-542, and ...in the Human Female, 1953, p. 270.

is not under the pressures that affect his wife in this matter, he may be reluctant to aid her in avoiding pregnancy.

The social insulation of the two sexes is often carried so far that communication between them is difficult. This insulation is particularly observable in regard to sexual behavior, which tends to be surrounded by taboos and rituals. As between husband and wife, sexual intercourse, by virtue of being the special bond and therefore the focus of anxiety and conflict between them, may be the topic they discuss with least freedom. Thus the cooperation necessary for contraception is made difficult.

In such terms we can understand why the available methods of contraception receive scant use in underdeveloped societies. Which of the considerations mentioned plays the greatest role is hard to say, but the fact should be emphasized that not all the reasons for limiting births are predictable at the time of intercourse—particularly in simple societies that live close to the environment and are threatened by quick catastrophe. The individual couple may, therefore, as we shall see later, limit fertility <u>after</u> rather than <u>at</u> the time of intercourse.

Number 9. Voluntary Control over Fecundity. Like chemical and mechanical contraception, satisfactory control of fecundity is beyond the technical capacity of pre-industrial societies. Neither the reduction nor the enhancement of fecundity by harmless medical measures appears possible in such cultures. Operations on the male external genitalia can be performed, such as subincision and castration, but these are either too drastic to be harmless or have little effect on fedundity.[33]

We may conclude, then, that pre-industrial societies are plus on variable number 9. But so are industrial societies. The latter may have even more of a plus fertility-value on this variable than simple societies because they can, and usually do, forbid sterilization and, at the same time, foster medical treatment for sterility, thus enhancing the fecundity of partially sterile couples.

Although modern science makes harmless sterilization possible, it has not yet been used, except in Puerto Rico, as a popular method of avoiding children.[34] The Puerto Rican case suggests, however, that sterilization may in the future become more widely diffused in underdeveloped areas. If the operational technique were improved to the point where it could be easily reversed—so that it could be used for the spacing, as well as for limiting the total number, of children—it might become the principal means of reducing fertility in backward areas.

Number 3a. Time Between Unstable Unions. Any negative effect on fertility from variable 3a is a function of both the rate of dissolution of unions and the time lost between them. If unions are stable, or if they are unstable but no time is lost between them, fertility will not be affected adversely.

With reference to <u>marital</u> unions, pre-industrial societies seem generally to have a low rate of dissolution. True, there are certain exceptions to this rule. Some of the Islamic peoples show a tendency toward marital instability, and in some primitive societies the clan or joint household takes such precedence over the nuclear family that the latter tends to be somewhat unstable.[35] On the

---

[33]Castration is so drastic that it is apparently never used with enough frequency to affect group fertility. Subincision, the splitting of the penis in such a way that the semen is expelled from the lower part rather than through the glans, seemingly has little effect on fecundity, depending in part on the position assumed during intercourse. Also the practice has a very limited distribution even in primitive society and seems unknown in more advanced pre-industrial societies. Among the Australian aborigines, where it is found, opinion differs as to its effects. German theorists, ac-

cording to Himes, have generally held that the operation lowers fertility and is so intended. Modern anthropologists, on the other hand, have denied both these contentions. Himes himself believes it may have some negative effect of this kind. <u>Op. cit.</u>, pp. 41-51.

[34]See J. M. Stycos, "Female Sterilization in Puerto Rico," <u>Eugenics Quarterly,</u> Vol. 1, June 1954, pp. 3-9.

[35]See Ralph Linton, <u>Study of Man</u>, New York, 1936, Ch. 10. Murdock, <u>op. cit.</u>, p. 3, criticizes

whole, however, the institutional structure of pre-industrial groups buttresses marriage in such ways as to give it considerable stability.

When a society has a significant proportion of informal unions which it regards as inferior to legal marriage but in which reproduction is nevertheless expected (e. g., "consensual unions" in Latin America and "common law" unions in the British West Indies), one of the features of such unions is that they tend to be unstable. In such cases the woman may wait some time before entering a new union, and the fertility lost may be substantial. For a small sample of women in Jamaica (where around 70% of the births are illegitimate) the reduction in fertility due to the instability of unions was approximately 37%.[36] The informal type of union arises as an institutional form from various historical causes. In societies that have been disorganized by Western contact, they may appear abundantly, and legal marriage itself may become unstable.[37] In other instances where the social order has grown largely out of a former slave class, informal unions may be both more numerous and more unstable than legal marriages.[38]

Linton for holding that in some societies organized on a "consanguine" basis the nuclear family plays an insignificant role, but the fact is that in such cultures marital instability may have little disorganizing effect. See K. Davis, "Children of Divorced Parents", Law and Contemporary Problems, Vol. 10, Summer 1944, pp. 700-710.

[36] Judith Blake, "Family Instability and Reproductive Behavior in Jamaica", Current Research in Human Fertility, Milbank Memorial Fund, New York, 1955, pp. 26-30.

[37] Margaret Mead, Changing Culture of an Indian Tribe, New York, 1932, pp. 14-15, Ch. 10. Schapera, op. cit., Ch. 10; Migrant Labour and Tribal Life, London, 1947, pp. 183-189; and "Cultural Changes in Family Life", The Bantu-Speaking Tribes of South Africa, London, 1937, pp. 380-385. The literature covering the impact of Western culture on native peoples is so enormous that one could document indefinitely the tendency of such contact to produce illicit sexual unions and instability in such unions and in marriage.

[38] T. S. Simey, Welfare and Planning in the West Indies, Oxford, 1946, passim. F. M. Henriques, Family and Colour in Jamaica, London, 1953,

With reference to premarital unions, there is every evidence that in the many societies where these are permitted they are, as a rule, highly unstable, amounting in many cases to adolescent promiscuity. However, there is ordinarily little time lost between such liaisons; few societies permit reproduction in them; and, given a young age at marriage, most such unions occur at an age when adolescent sterility seemingly reduces the number of conceptions.

It follows that pre-industrial societies generally have a plus fertility-value with respect to variable number 3a, but the exceptions are more numerous than was the case with the other variables so far considered.

Number 3b. Post-Widowhood Celibacy. What effect the high rate of widowhood found in pre-industrial societies has on fertility depends on the institutional position of the widow. In many such societies she loses little time from exposure to intercourse, because she soon marries again. In other pre-industrial cultures, however, the widow either must wait for a protracted period or is subject to a distinct prejudice against remarrying at all. An important problem in analyzing the institutional impingements on fertility is the discovery of why some societies take one course in this regard and others take the opposite course.

If we study those societies in which remarriage occurs universally and soon, we find that they are the ones requiring the widow to marry a kinsman of the deceased husband (levirate). Such societies are usually primitive, practicing a shifting cultivation, hunting, or pastoral pursuits, and are characterized by strong clan or lineage organization. Marriage involves substantial economic exchanges and, if the system is patrilineal and patrilocal, these are weighted in favor of the bride's lineage (brideprice). The wo-

---

passim. G. W. Roberts, "Some Aspects of Mating and Fertility in the West Indies", Population Studies, Vol. 8, March 1955, pp. 199-227. R. T. Smith, "Family Organization in British Guiana", Social and Economic Studies, Vol. I, February 1953, pp. 87-111.

man brought into the clan or lineage as a wife is conceived as belonging to this clan, which has paid the brideprice; her children, who are automatically members of the husband's lineage, represent her contribution in return for the cost of procuring her. When the woman is widowed, the lineage retains control over her, not only because a price has been paid for her but also because her children must remain with the lineage. If she still is fecund, the lineage feels it would be losing potential children if she did not remarry. But remarriage to an outsider would be unsatisfactory, because the children of that union would belong to another lineage. Hence the remarriage must be within the clan. Since in the exchanges cementing the first marriage, the husband's nearest relatives bore the main cost, it is natural that his close kin (notably his brothers) should have first claim on the widow. If the deceased husband has no actual brothers, one of his "classificatory brothers" can be substituted. In anticipation of her possibly entering a leviratic union, a woman's relation with her husband's actual and classificatory brothers is often one of privileged familarity. The term for "husband's brother" may be the same as that for "husband." The social structure clearly demonstrates that the clan is thinking of the widow in terms of her potential production of children. Among the Nuer, for instance, even if the widow should take as a lover a person outside the clan (she cannot legally marry outside), the children are viewed as the descendents of the dead husband and therefore as members of his, not the lover's, clan.[39]

In many societies, on the other hand, the widow is forbidden to marry a close relative of the deceased husband. These seem to be cases in which the clan, however important it may once have been, has receded in economic and political significance, seemingly as a result of technological advance and greater class stratification. The economy is that of a more stable agriculture in which the same land is intensively cultivated year in and year out. Under such circumstances the joint household acquires more independence and more significance as an economic unit than it seems to have in most primitive societies. The distinction between relatives in different households thus takes precedence over their solidarity as members of the same lineage or clan. To be sure, the woman marrying into the joint household may do so in terms of some form of economic exchange, but this exchange is between individual households rather than clans. The widow and her children accordingly belong to the deceased husband's household. Remarriage to one of her dead mate's brothers or other close male relatives, however, would be structurally inappropriate, because the joint household is always subject to dissolution and must be so organized as to minimize the complications of such dissolution. Unlike the clan or lineage, which is immortal and indefinitely expandable, the household is a residential economic unit which can easily grow too large for its immediate resources. With stable agriculture, the household must be near the land it works. If its memberships increases, it must ultimately break up because the land required for sustenance will be too distant. When the household does break up, usually at the death of the male head, it does so by the separation of its nuclear families.[40] Accordingly, even when the nuclear family forms part of a joint household, it is visualized not only as a separate unit but also as one that may in the future have its own independent residence. A widow's remarriage to one of her husband's relatives within the household would conflict with this idea of potential independence. It would inextricably merge two nuclear families. It would require polygyny and would emphasize the solidarity of the

---

[39] E. E. Evans-Pritchard, Kinship and Marriage among the Nuer, Oxford, 1951, pp. 112-123.

[40] For mention of the joint household's vulnerability to change and its consequent fissive tendency, see Murdock, op. cit., p. 36.

sibling relationship rather than the father-son relation so central to the independent joint household.

Stable agrarian societies not only forbid the widow to marry within the circle of her husband's kin but also often frown on her marrying anyone at all. This additional prejudice seems likewise to be explicable in structural terms. For the widow to marry outside would require that some agency make a match for her, because marriages in traditional agrarian societies are arranged by persons other than the parties to the union. However, her family of orientation is no longer responsible for her. The family of her deceased husband is restrained from taking the responsibility for several reasons. It would, in seeking a mate for the widow, have to treat her as a daughter, which might interfere with the rights of the actual daughters. Furthermore, since she is a widow and is older, she has become less valuable than upon her first marriage, so that it is difficult to get her married at a social level reflecting favorably on the family's prestige. If the widow has children, her marriage outside the immediate kin would require her separation from them. It is thus understandable why traditional agrarian societies, especially where the joint household is normally preferred, should exhibit a prejudice against widow remarriage. Such unions certainly do occur, particularly in the lower classes which cannot carry out the joint family ideal, but the prejudice may be strong enough to prevent a high proportion of widows in the upper classes from remarrying.[41] In India the caste controls reinforce those of the joint household in preventing widow remarriage. Since such unions are thought to lower the caste's prestige, and since marriage is endogamous within the caste, both parties to a remarriage are condemned. For this reason the reduction of fertility due to widow agamy is probably greater in India than in any other country, especially because of the early age at marriage and the high mortality there.

Number 11. Voluntary Control over Foetal Mortality. Underdeveloped societies have few means for lessening foetal mortality, but they do have readily available means, through abortion, for increasing such mortality. In fact, abortion is widely practiced in pre-industrial societies, being the individual's principal means of limiting fertility.[42] Since medical measures to avoid foetal mortality do not, at least as yet, have as much influence on fertility as voluntary abortion can and does, we can say that whether a society has a plus or minus fertility-value with respect to variable 11 depends primarily on the extent to which it practices abortion. Accordingly, some pre-industrial societies are on the "plus" side (forbidding abortion and practicing it little) but many others are on

---

[41]Levy, *op. cit.*, p. 46, points out that although the Chinese gentry have always frowned on widow remarriage, the peasants have usually practiced it. In fact, if a peasant widow was young and lacked grown sons, remarriage was inevitable. As the peasantry is said to comprise as much as 80% of the population (p. 44), widow celibacy is hardly characteristic of China as a whole, although gentry patterns set the ideals for the entire society. Olga Lang, without distinguishing between gentry and peasantry, says that remarriage is frowned on. *Chinese Family and Society,* New Haven, 1946, p. 53. She says (p. 126) that poor men often marry widows because they are easier to get than virgins.

Any divorcee or widow can find a husband if she is willing to marry beneath her status. With regard to the absence of anything like the levirate in China, it is interesting to note that Miss Lang says (p. 21) that "early in the feudal period, under the Chou dynasty (ca. 1027-256 B. C.), the clan began to divide into economic families." Today, even in the South where clans are of some importance, they have no real authority in family matters. The strongest clans in Central and North China lack the essential of clan life, a fair amount of common property (pp. 177-178).

[42]Ford, *op. cit.*, pp. 50-51, found that most of his tribes took cognizance of abortion. In eleven it was specifically stated to be forbidden, and in eight it could be inferred to be forbidden; in 21 it was permitted to the young girl who finds herself pregnant, and in 4 this could be inferred to be the case; and in 12 a married woman was allowed to practice abortion if she believed that she had become pregnant through an adulterous intrigue. Himes regards abortion as widespread in primitive societies (*op. cit.*, p. 52). A recent study by George Devereaux, *Abortion in Primitive Society,* New York, 1955, pp. 25-26, cites cases of tribes where abortion is quite frequent.

the "minus" side (practicing abortion to a considerable extent). If we grant that interference with conception is less hazardous to health than interference with pregnancy, an important question for us is why abortion is so much more frequently used in underdeveloped societies than contraception.

In answering this question, one can point to the following considerations: (a) as compared to mechanical and chemical means of contraception, abortion is technically simple;[43] (b) In contrast to such non-chemico-mechanical methods as coitus interruptus or coitus inter femora, abortion is not applied at the time of intercourse and does not require co-operation between man and woman. It is a woman's method and can be practiced without the man's knowledge. (c) Unlike contraception, it is completely effective. (d) Once an undesired pregnancy has occurred, the need for abortion is certain, whereas at the time of intercourse there is always the chance that pregnancy will not eventuate anyway. (c) Although a child may be desired at the time of intercourse, subsequent events may alter this attitude, at which time abortion rather than contraception is a remedy.

A Note on Infanticide. Although infanticide is not dealt with as an integral part of our analysis because it does not affect fertility, one should note that it is virtually a functional equivalent of abortion in controlling family size, and that it too is practiced widely in pre-industrial societies, much more so than contraception. The rationale for its use is much the same as that for abortion, but it does differ from the latter in at least three respects. First, infanticide allows the progeny to be selected by sex, as shown by the custom of female infanticide. The logic of this practive is exemplified by the Netsilik Eskimos:

The most glaring consequences of the struggle for existence is manifested in the way in which they try to breed the greatest possible number of boys and the fewest possible girls ... girls are killed at birth, if they have not already been promised to a family where there is a son who some day is to have a wife ... They hold the view that if a woman is to suckle a girl child it will be two or three years before she may expect her next confinement ... A hunter must take into consideration that he can only subject himself and his constitution for comparatively few years to all the strain that hunting demands ... Now if he has sons, they will as a rule be able to step in and help just when his own physique is beginning to fail. Thus it is life's own inexorability that has taught them the necessity of having as many sons as possible. Only by that means may they be certain that they will not need to put the rope around their own neck too early; for it is the common custom that old people, who can no longer keep themselves, prefer to put an end to their life by hanging ...[44]

Olga Lang discusses the persistence of the immemorial custom of female infanticide in China. The hospital records used for her study "contained matter-of-fact references to infanticide made by Chinese social and medical workers indicating that it was taken for granted. Much more often, however, infant daughters have not been killed outright. What happens is that the small amount of food available for the family is unequally distributed: the son gets the larger share and the daughters are practically starved. Hence the frequent epidemics have taken a heavier toll of girls than of boys."[45] Much the same could be said of India.

Second, infanticide also allows the offspring to be selected according to physical status, weeding out those with deformities, bad health, or unacceptable physical or racial characteristics.[46] Third, it can be practiced when the circumstances of birth are considered to be

---

[43]Premature labor can be induced by killing the foetus. This can be done by beating, pressing, or massaging the abdomen; by drinking poisons or strong emetics or laxatives; by piercing the foetus or amniotic sac with sharp reeds or instruments; or by wearing a tight belt. See Ford, op. cit., p. 52; Devereaux, op. cit., pp. 27-42.

[44]Knud Rasmussen, The Netsilik Eskimos, Copenhagen, 1931, pp. 139-140.

[45]Lang, op. cit., p. 150.

[46]Hutton Webster, Taboo: A Sociological Study, Stanford, 1942, pp. 59-61.

abnormal and ritualistically taboo. Twins, children born with feet first or with teeth, infants whose mothers died at their birth,[47] and offspring born on unlucky days are typical victims.[48] Fourth, whereas abortion may injure the health of the mother, infanticide obviously does not.

A disadvantage of infanticide may seem to be that since a child has already been born, a living person is being killed. However, the newborn child is often not viewed as a member of society until he has passed through some sort of ceremony (amphidromia in ancient Greece, presentation of the child to the father in China) which defines him as such. The destruction of the child is therefore viewed psychologically in much the same light as abortion.

Number 4. Voluntary Abstinence within Unions. Abstinence within unions is practiced much more, on the average, in preindustrial than in industrial societies. The effect of such abstinence on fertility, however, depends on the circumstances; for there are at least four types of restriction—post partum, occasional, gestational, and menstrual. The first two types tend to limit fertility, while the last two, if they have any effect at all, tend to increase it.

Post-partum abstinence occurs in nearly all societies, including our own. The amount of time involved, however, varies greatly—all the way from one to two weeks in some societies to two to three years in others. Many pre-industrial societies insist upon abstinence for an arbitrary period of time after birth, usually for several weeks or months. In a few instances the duration of abstinence is fixed by some developmental stage of the child—e. g., when the baby first crawls, sits up, walks, or cuts its teeth. In many cases the taboo on coitus extends through the lactation period, which may last two to three years.[49] Not all of the time involved, of course, represents a loss of fertility, because ovulation is often delayed or occurs sporadically for a time after parturition. It is only when the period of abstinence extends to two months or more that a loss of fertility can be assumed, although even then it may not be quite commensurate with the amount of time covered. These longer periods, though found frequently in primitive and peasant societies,[50] are not customary in industrial countries.

Long post-partum taboos on intercourse obviously help to space out children, but this is not the reason usually given in communities that practice such taboos. Instead, a violation of the taboo is viewed as being magically dangerous to the child or the parents.[51] Such notions probably lead to the observance of the abstinence rules. In addition, it should be noted that in many instances the male has access to another wife (if he is polygynous) or to a concubine or other available woman. The social structure may encourage observance of the taboo in another way. When, as in India, the wife customarily goes to her parents' home to bear each of her first two or three children and stays there for a few months after the confinement, the taboo is enforced with ease. Thus the fact that 80% of Indian villagers in one study reported post-partum abstinence of six months or more indicates a significant loss of fertility from this cause.[52] Doubtless similar or greater losses occur in many other agrarian societies.

The "occasional" restrictions on sexual intercourse are those occurring in con-

---

[47]Ibid., pp. 59-65.

[48]Linton , Study of Man, op. cit., pp. 194-195, with reference to the Tanala of Madagascar. In a letter to W. Lloyd Warner quoted by Himes, op. cit., p. 8, Linton says: "I do not think that there was any idea of limiting population in it [infanticide], but the losses were severe. In at least one tribe all children born on three days in each week were killed."

[49]Clellan S. Ford and Frank A. Beach, Patterns of Sexual Behavior, New York, 1951, p. 219.

[50]Webster, op. cit., pp. 67-71.

[51]Ford and Beach, op. cit., p. 219.

[52]C. Chandrasekaran, "Cultural Patterns in Relation to Family Planning in India", Proceedings of the Third International Conference on Planned Parenthood, 1952, Bombay, p. 78.

nection with regular holidays and special ceremonies, tabooed days of the week, and important communal tasks (war, economic undertakings,[53] etc.) The exact amount of time lost to reproduction in this way has seldom been calculated, but the Indian field study just cited found that the average number of days of avoidance for religious reasons was 24 per year in a rural village, while in a middle class housing project it was 19.[54] If these days occur sporadically, they hardly represent much loss of fertility, because they are practically comprised within the normal frequency of intercourse; but in many societies the abstentions extend over substantial periods. "The natives of the Mortlock Islands, a part of the Caroline group, proscribe any sexual intercourse in time of war; a man who violated the rule would die a sudden death. During the fishing season, which lasts for six to eight weeks, every Yap fishermen is subject to many restrictions....Women are very strictly tabooed to him..."[55]

In contrast to post-partum and "occasional" taboos on coitus, gestational abstinence obviously cannot diminish fertility. The only question is whether it may slightly increase fertility. Most societies proscribe intercourse during some part, but seldom during all or even the major portion, of the gestation period. Only seven of the primitive groups in Ford's sample extended the taboo to the greater part of the period.[56] Usually it is toward the end of the pregnancy that the prohibition applies. If intercourse during the later stages occasionally induces miscarriage or causes puerperal infection, as is sometimes claimed,[57] then the taboo may enhance fertility, but only slightly.

---

[53]Ford, Comparative Study of Human Reproduction, op. cit., pp. 28-29. Webster, op. cit., pp. 132-139.

[54]Chandrasekaran, op. cit., p. 78.

[55]Webster, op. cit., p. 134.

[56]Ford, op. cit., p. 48.

[57]Ibid., p. 49.

Similarly, the almost universal prohibition of coitus during menstruation can have little or no negative effect on fertility. Such abstention, when fertilization is least likely, tends to concentrate sexual activity in the more fertile part of the menstrual cycle. In some pre-industrial cultures the taboo is extended for a few days after the menstrual flow has ceased (as among the ancient Hebrews), which has the effect of concentrating coital activity still more directly on the days when conception is most likely.

On the whole, primitive and peasant societies appear to have a greater fertility loss through intra-marital abstinence (variable number 4) than do industrial societies. They have considerably more post-partum and "occasional" abstinence, and the effect of these in inhibiting reproduction is not fully counterbalanced by the fact that underdeveloped societies also occasionally have longer menstrual and gestational taboos (which may slightly enhance fertility).

The Other Intermediate Variables. There remain four variables—number 10 (which usually has a low fertility-value in non-industrial societies) and numbers 5, 6, and 7 (which seem indeterminate in their values). All four of these variables appear not to be clearly determined by institutional patterns in different cultures. If there is any difference in their fertility-values as between one type of society and another, the difference seems to be more a function of the general level of living than of the specific institutional structures. Perhaps one clue to this circumstance lies in the fact that three of the four variables (10, 5, and 7) are defined as involuntary in the sense of not being under control and hence not amenable to motivational determination. The other variable (number 6, frequency of coitus), though subject to individual control, is possibly too private and too linked up with organic capacity to be culturally controlled.

With respect to number 10—foetal mortality from involuntary causes—we have said that the fertility-value is generally low in pre-industrial societies;

because the data available indicate that stillbirth rates are greater in such societies. However, the conclusion is tentative, because adequate comparative information does not exist for miscarriage rates.

Number 5—involuntary abstinence—presumably varies according to several disparate factors. In so far as health or sickness may be involved, the non-industrial peoples would probably exhibit a higher degree of such abstinence. The same inference might be drawn with regard to impotency, except that this condition if often caused by psychological determinants which may be more prevalent in industrial cultures. Another cause of involuntary abstinence, the separation of couples due to migration, would seem to vary according to the particular historical circumstances of the society. Except under conditions of European contact, indigenous groups apparently have little individual mobility. Clearly, these divergent influences affecting involuntary abstinence can run counter to each other. It is therefore difficult to claim, for this variable, any consistent overall differences between societies. We are also handicapped by an almost total lack of data, for no comparative information has been collected with this issue in mind.

Variable number 6—frequency of intercourse—possibly favors fertility more in underdeveloped than in industrial societies. But at best the evidence for this view is indirect, drawn solely from a few advanced societies where coital frequency appears greater among the manual than among the sedentary classes. Such direct evidence as we have supports no view at all. Average figures on "coital frequency" given in the literature, usually stated as so many times per week, are ambiguous, because it is unclear whether they mean _every_ week or only those weeks when coitus is not impossible because of sickness, absence, menstrual, or other taboos, etc. Also, the comparative frequency figures cited in the literature are fantastic, showing variations from one society to another that are

wholly inexplicable.[58] We have found no reliable evidence that the average frequency of intercourse for comparable age groups varies significantly as between one society and another, and certainly none which indicates that this is a significant factor in inter-societal variations in fertility.

With respect to variable number 7 (involuntary sterility) we again have little evidence. The hard conditions of life in pre-industrial societies may give rise to a considerable amount of low fecundity or absolute sterility—particularly in the latter part of the woman's reproductive span; and in given instances, after contact with highly civilized peoples, venereal disease may have a pronounced effect of this sort. On the other hand, the nervous tension and artificial modes of life in urban-industrial populations may possibly tend to lower fecundity to some extent.

Patently, the comparative fertility-values of the four intermediate variables just discussed are unknown. Not only is evidence lacking, but there is no sound line of reasoning by which the behavior of these variables can be linked up with specific institutional patterns. At most, there may be some connection in each case with the general level of living. The evidence for this is best with respect to number 10, but the other three must be left for the time being as indeterminate.

CONCLUSION: THE GENERAL PATTERN

Any analysis of institutional factors in

---

[58]Thus Ford and Beach report as an apparent fact that "the Aranda of Australia have intercourse as often as three or five times nightly, sleeping between each sex act", and that for Chagga men "intercourse ten times in a single night is not unusual". Nothing is said about how these bizarre statistics are gathered, or about what age groups in the population are being considered. The authors say simply, "it is reported that", or "it is not unusual that", etc. Such reports are all the more questionable since societies apparently with a similar level of living are said to have extremely different figures—some at "once a week" or "once or twice a week"—without any explanation of why they should be so low and others fifteen or twenty times as high. Op. cit., pp. 78-79.

fertility must first explain the well known fact that underdeveloped societies in general have a higher rate of reproduction than industrial societies. The explanation, in brief, is that the pre-industrial peoples, in the face of high mortality, have had to develop an institutional organization which would give them sufficient reproduction to survive. However, analysis at this level does not carry us very far. In order to study the effects of institutional factors, one needs to break down the reproductive process itself so as to distinguish clearly the various mechanisms through which, and only through which, any social factor can influence fertility. In trying to do this, we have found eleven "intermediate variables". When analysis is made along those lines, it can be seen that the generally high fertility of underdeveloped areas does not mean that these areas encourage high fertility in every respect. As we have seen, they do not have high plus values on all the intermediate variables. Why, then, do they have low values in some respects and not in others?

It is possible to discern a systematic difference between underdeveloped and developed societies with reference to the eleven variables. In general, the pre-industrial societies have high fertility-values for those variables farthest removed from the actual moment of parturition and which, therefore, imply an overall outlook favorable to fertility. To a much greater degree than industrial societies, they tend to encourage early exposure to intercourse—exhibiting a far younger age at marriage and a higher proportion married. They thus lose little potential fertility by delaying or avoiding the formation of unions. After unions have been formed, these societies tend to enjoin more abstinence than industrial societies do (and therefore have lower values on variable number 4), but such "sexual fasting" arises from religious and magical motives rather than as a deliberate fertility control measure, and it does not appear to be great enough to have a substantial negative effect on fertility.

Underdeveloped societies also have high fertility-values for the conception variables. They practice little contraception and virtually no sterilization. Consequently, the tendency is to postpone the issue of controlling pregnancy until a later point in the reproductive process, which means that when a couple wishes to avoid children, those methods nearest the point of parturition—abortion and infanticide—are employed. These have the advantage, in societies living close to privation, of being nearer to the actual moment when the child must be supported.

Industrial societies, on the other hand, exhibit low fertility-values for those variables involving the early stages of the reproductive process, especially age at marriage, proportion married, and contraception; and they manifest high fertility-values for the variables in the later stages, especially infanticide. It follows that for many of the variables the two types of society exhibit opposite values. This is true for age of entry into unions, permanent celibacy, voluntary abstinence, contraception, and (if included as a variable) infanticide. It is not necessarily true of the time spent between or after unions, of sterilization, or of abortion; and it, of course, is not true of those variables characterized as "indeterminate"—involuntary abstinence, frequency of coitus, or involuntary infecundity. But the general contrast is sufficiently clear to require explanation.

A key to the position of the industrial societies lies in the fact that, as compared to pre-industrial cultures, they have achieved their lower reproduction, not by acquiring low fertility-values for all the intermediate variables, but by singling out particular ones as the means to that result. They took those means of reducing fertility which involved the least institutional organization and re-organization and which involved the least human cost. In the secular decline of the birth rate they relied more heavily on the mere postponement of marriage than on non-marriage. They relied less on abstinence, which makes heavy demands on the individual, and more on contraception and abortion, which do not. They dropped infanticide altogether and, in the later stages, tended to reduce abortion. In other words, they have undertaken to lower fertility, not primarily by extending further the negative effect of the variables by which fertility was lowered in the pre-industrial stage, but by using readily available institutional mechanisms with respect to marriage and by employing the possibilities of their advanced technology for conception con-

trol. Marital postponement was easily extended in the early and middle stages of industrialization because the basis for it already existed in Western society and because contraception and relatively safe abortion freed those who married late from the necessity of premarital celibacy. Gradually, in the late stages of industrial development, contraception has gained such predominance that it has made low fertility-values on the other variables (including abortion and late marriage) unnecessary.

ECONOMIC STRUCTURES AND PROCESSES

*Efficiency and "The Fix": Informal Intergroup
Relations in a Piecework Machine Shop* [1]

Donald Roy

SOURCE: *American Journal of Sociology*, Vol. 60, 1955), pp. 255-66.

As part of a broader examination and appraisal of the application of piecework
incentive to the production line of an
American factory this paper essays the
simple but largely neglected task of exploring the network of intergroup relations in which the work activity of machine operatives is imbedded. Exploration will be restricted to a limited sector
of the total web of interaction in one
shop; description will center upon those
relationships that provide support to the
operator group in its resistance to and
subversion of formally instituted managerial controls on production. It is hoped
that observations reported here not only
will bear upon the practical problem of
industrial efficiency but will also contribute to the more general study of institutional dynamics.

This could be considered the third in a

series of attempts to make more careful
discriminations in an area of research
that has been characteristically productive of sweeping generalizations, blanket
conceptualizations, or algebraic gymnas-
tics that tend to halt inquiry at the same
time that they lay a fog over otherwise
easily discerned reality. Data for all
three papers were acquired in an investigation of a single work situation by a
single technique of social inquiry, participant observation. The writer was employed for nearly a year as radial-drill
operator in one of the machine shops of
a steel-processing plant, and he kept a
daily record of his observations and experiences relating to work activity and
social interaction in the shop. His major
interest lay in the phenomenon of restriction of output, or "systematic sol-
diering," the practice of which various
sociological soundings have revealed in
the lower depths of our industrial organization. To complete the analogy: the
writer donned a diving suit and went
down to see what it looked like on the
bottom.

---

[1] This report is drawn from materials presented
in the writer's doctoral dissertation, "Restriction
of Output in a Piecework Machine Shop" (University of Chicago, 1952), under the direction of
Everett C. Hughes.

One conclusion has already been set forth,[2] namely, that the usual view of output restriction is grossly undifferentiating. Different kinds of "institutionalized underworking" were practiced, each with its characteristic pattern of antecedents and consequences. The blanket term "restriction" was found to cloak all-important contrarieties of work behavior. Machine operatives not only held back effort; sometimes they worked hard. The very common failure to note such contrarieties has tended, of course, to impede the progress of research by checking consideration of the specific conditions under which differences in behavior occur.

A second finding was the discovery of complexity where simple lines of relationship had generally been assumed to exist.[3] When inconsistencies in the operator's behavior seemed to contradict the hypothesis that variations in application of economic incentive could account for the variations in work effort, a more intensive examination of response to piecework was undertaken. This disclosed that piecework incentive was not equivalent to economic incentive and that attainment of piecework "quotas" afforded machine operators a complex of rewards in which the strictly economic might or might not play a part.

The third set of observations, to be here discussed, again exhibits complication in a picture that has come to be accepted as simple in design. Here the focus of interest is the structure of "informal" intergroup connections that bear directly upon work behavior at the machine level. The material will not deny the hypothesis that the willingness of operatives to put forth effort is a function of their relationship with management or the widely held affirmation that this relationship is mediated by the organization of operatives into "informal groups." It will indicate, however, that further advances in the understanding of work behavior in the factory may involve attention to minor as well as major axes of intergroup relations. It will show that the relevant constituents of problematic production situations may include "lateral" lines of interaction between subgroups of the work force as well as "vertical" connections between managerial and worker groups.

It will be seen, in other words, that the interaction of two groups in an industrial organization takes place within and is conditioned by a larger intergroup network of reciprocal influences. Whyte has called attention to the limitations of studying groups in "isolation," without regard for the "perspectives of large institutional structures."[4] A second warning might be: The larger institutional structures form networks of interacting groups.

As a bona fide member of an informal group of machine operatives the writer had an opportunity to observe and experience management-work group conflict in its day-to-day and blow-by-blow particulars. Also, he participated in another kind of social process, intergroup co-operation. Not only did workers on the "drill line" co-operate with each other as fellow-members of a combat team at war with management; they also received considerable aid and abetment from other groups of the shop. This inter-group co-operation was particularly evident when operators were trying to "make out," or attain "quota" production, on piecework jobs.

It has been noted in another connection that machine operators characteristically evinced no reluctance to put forth effort when they felt that their group-defined piecework quotas were attainable.[5] It might seem, at first glance, that the

---

[2]Donald Roy, "Quota Restriction and Goldbricking in a Machine Shop," *American Journal of Sociology*, LVII (March, 1952), 427-42.

[3]Donald Roy, "Work Satisfaction and Social Reward in Quota Achievement: An Analysis of Piecework Incentive," *American Sociological Review*, XVIII (October, 1953), 507-14.

[4]William F. Whyte, "Small Groups and Large Organizations," in *Social Psychology at the Crossroads*, ed. John R. Rohrer and Muzafer Sherif (New York: Harper & Bros., 1951) pp. 297-312.

[5]Roy, "Work Satisfaction and Social Reward in Quota Achievement," *op. cit.*

supporting of operators during intensive application to "getting the work out" would represent co-operation <u>with</u> and not <u>against</u> management. However, the truth is that operators and their "allies" joined forces in certain situations in a manner not only unmistakably at variance with the carefully prepared designs of staff experts but even in flagrant violation of strongly held managerial "moral principles" of shop behavior. In short, machine operators resorted to "cheating" to attain their quotas; and since this often involved the collusion of other shop groups, not as mere "accessories after the fact" but as deeply entangled accomplices, any managerial suspicion that swindling and conniving, as well as loafing, were going on all the time was well founded. If the workers' conviction that the echelons of management were packed with men addicted to the "dirty deal" be additionally considered, it might appear that the shop was fairly overrun with crooks. Since a discussion of "contrast conceptions"[6] cannot find a place within the limited scope of this paper, it must suffice at this point merely to declare that the kind of effort made by operators and their aids to expedite production, when they did try to expedite it, was actually in many respects conflict with management.

One belief, universally accepted in the work group, may be phrased thus: "You can't 'make out' if you do things the way management wants them done." This gem of shop wisdom thus negatively put is hardly a prescription for action, but its obverse, "You've got to figure the angles," gave all hands plenty to do.

According to Al McCann (all names used are fictitious), the "Fagan" of the drill line, "They time jobs to give you just base rates. It's up to you to figure out how to fool them so you can make out. You can't make any money if you run the job the way it's timed."

---

[6]See L. Copeland, "The Negro as a Contrast Conception," in Race Relations and the Race Problem, ed. E. T. Thompson (Durham: Duke University Press, 1939), and S. Kirson Weinberg, "Aspects of the Prison's Social Structure," American Journal of Sociology, XLVII (March, 1942), 717-26.

We machine operators did "figure the angles"; we developed an impressive repertoire of angles to play and devoted ourselves to crossing the expectations of formal organization with perseverance, artistry, and organizing ability of our own. For instance, job timing was a "battle all the way" between operators and and time-study men. The objective of the operators was good piecework prices, and that end justified any old means that would work. One cardinal principle of operator job-timing was that cutting tools be run at lower speeds and "feeds" than the maximums possible on subsequent production, and there were various ways of encouraging the institution of adequate differentials. Also, operators deemed it essential to embellish the timing performance with movements only apparently functional in relation to the production of goods: little reachings, liftings, adjustings, dustings, and other special attentions to conscientious machine operation and good housekeeping that could be dropped instanter with the departure of the time-study man.

However, the sophistication of the time-study men usually matched the strategy employed against them. The canniest operators often gave of their best in timing duels only to get "hopeless prices" for their pains:

Gus Schmidt was timed early in the evening on a job, and given a price of $1.00 per 100 for reaming one hole, chamfering both sides of three holes, and filing burrs on one end of one hole. All that for one cent!

"To hell with them," said Gus.

This not to say that the "hopeless price" was always truly hopeless. Since the maintenance of an effective control over job-timing and hence price-setting was an uncertain, often disheartening matter, operators were forced to develop skills for turning bad into good. Under the shaping hands of the "angle-applicators" surprising metamorphoses sometimes took place. Like the proverbial ugly duckling that finally feathered out into a beautiful swan, piecework jobs originally classified in operator vernacular as "stinkers" came to give off the delightful aroma of "gravy." Without going into the particulars of the various types of operation, one might say that jobs were "streamlined." This streamlining was, of course, at times "rough on the tools" and adverse in its effects on the quality of output. The jettisoning of quality called, necessarily, for a corresponding attention to ways and means of shielding supervisors and inspectors from discovering the sacrifices and consequently brought into further play the social graces of equivocation, subterfuge, and prestidigitation.

Still, the adroitness of the machine operators, inventing, scheming, and conniving unto themselves to make quotas attainable, was not enough. Many "stinkers" would not yield before the whitest heat of intelligence or the most cavalier disregard for company property. An appreciable incidence of failure should not be surprising when it is kept in mind that the black arts of "making out" were not only responses to challenge from management but also stimulations, in circular interaction, to the development of more effective countermagic in the timing process. It would be hard to overestimate the wizardry of the time-study men with pencil and paper in computing "angle-tight" piecework prices. During the latter months of his employment, months that marked the peak of his machine performance, the writer was able to achieve quota earnings approximately half the time that piecework jobs were offered. If this experience is roughly representative of the fortunes of the drill-line group, the battle with the stopwatch men was nip and tuck.

It is to be expected that a group of resourceful operatives, working with persistent intent to "make out" at quota levels, and relying heavily upon illegal practices, would be alert to possibilities of assistance from groups that were able and willing to give it and would not hesitate at further flouting the rules and regulations in cultivating it. It is also to be expected that the upholders of a managerial rational and moral order would attempt to prevent corruptive connections

and would take action to stamp out whatever subversive organization did develop. During the eleven-month study, machine operators, including the drill-line men, were enjoying the co-operation of several other shop groups in an illegal facilitation of the "make-out" process. This intergroup network effectively modified certain formally established shop routines, a too close attachment to which would handicap the operators. The "syndicate" also proved adequate in circumventing each of a series of "new rules" and "new systems" introduced by management to expurgate all modifications and improvisations and force a strict adherence to the rules.

The shop groups that conspired with the operators were, namely, the inspectors, the tool-crib men, the time-checkers, the stock-men, and the setup men. With a single exception, these "service" groups stemmed from lines of authority distinct from the one for which the operators formed the base. The one exception was the setup group; it was subordinate to the same set of officials in the "production" line of authority that controlled the operators. A brief description of the duties of each of these service groups and a rough tracing of the sequences of interaction involved in the prescribed work routine of the drill men will indicate the formal pattern of intergroup relations within which informally instituted variations were woven.

THE SETUP MEN

A chief function of the setup men was to assist machine operators in the "setting-up" of jigs and fixtures preparatory to operation of machines in the processing of materials. It included the giving of preliminary aid and advice at the beginning of the production process, at which time the setup men would customarily "run the first piece" to show operators how to do it and to indicate that the setup was adequate to meet work specifications. The duties of the setup men also included "trouble-shooting" on occasions when operators encountered difficulties that effected a lowering of the quality of output below inspection standards or a reduction of the rate of output unsatisfactory to operators or supervisors.

THE INSPECTORS

The chief function of the inspectors was to pass judgment on the quality of the output of the machine operators, either accepting or rejecting work turned out, according to blueprint specifications. Their appraisals came at the beginning of operations, when especially thorough examinations of the first pieces processed were made, and subsequently at varying intervals during the course of a job.

THE TOOL-CRIB MEN

The tool-crib attendants served the operators as dispensers of jigs, fixtures, cutting tools, blueprints, gauges, and miscellaneous items of equipment needed to supplement basic machinery and operator-owned hand tools in the processing of materials. They worked inside a special inclosure conveniently located along one of the main arterials of shop traffic and did most of their dispensing across the wide sill of a "window," an aperture which served, incidentally, as locus of various and sundry transactions and communications not immediately relevant to tool-dispensing. There were two other openings into the crib, a door, two steps from the window, and a wide gate, farther down the corridor.

THE STOCKMEN

The stockmen were responsible for conducting a steady flow of materials to the machines for processing. Their work called for the removal of finished work as well as the moving-up of fresh stock and involved a division of labor into two specializations: "stock-chasing" and "trucking." The chief duties of the stock-chasers were to "locate" unprocessed materials in the various storage areas, when operators called for stock, and to direct the activities of the truckers, who attended to the physical transportation.

THE TIME-CHECKERS

The time-checkers worked in another special inclosure, a small "time cage," from which they distributed to the operators the work orders "lined up" by the schedulemen of the Planning Department and within which they registered the starting and completion times of each job. There were four time-registering operations for every work order. First, upon presenting an operator with a work-order slip, the checker would "punch" him "on setup" by stamping a separate order card with a clocking mechanism that registered the hours in tenths. Later, when the operator would call at the cage window to announce completion of all preparatory arrangements for the actual processing of materials, the checker would punch him "off setup" and "on production." Finally, following another operator announcement, the checker would clock the termination of the machining process with a fourth punch. At the time of his terminal punch the operator would report the number of "pieces" completed on the job just concluded and would receive a new work order to start the cycle over again. And, since the terminal punch on the completed job would be registered at the same time as the initial punch on the new one, hours on shift would be completely accounted for.

OPERATOR INTERACTION WITH SERVICE GROUPS

The machine operator's performance of each individual job or order assigned to him involved formal relationships with service groups in well-defined sequences or routines.

First, the operator would receive his work order from the time-checker. Next, he would present the work order to a tool-crib attendant at the crib window as a requisite to receiving blueprints, jigs, cutting tools, and gauges. At the same time, that is, immediately before or after approaching the crib attendant, sometimes while waiting for crib service, the operator would show his work order to a stock-chaser as a requisite to receiving materials to work on. The stock-chaser, after perusing the order slip, occasionally with additional reference to the blueprint, would hail a trucker to bring the necessary stock to the operator's machine. If there were no delay in contacting a stock-chaser or in locating and moving up the stock, a load of materials would await the operator upon his arrival at his machine with equipment from the tool crib.

Upon returning to his machine, the operator would proceed with the work of "setting up" the job, usually with the assistance of a setup man, who would stay with him until a piece was turned out whose quality of workmanship would satisfy an inspector. In appraising a finished piece, the inspector would consult the blueprint brought from the crib for work specifications and then perform operations of measurement with rules, gauges, micrometers, or more elaborate equipment. The inspector might or might not "accept" the first piece presented for his judgment. At any rate, his approval was requisite to the next step in the operator's formal interactional routine, namely, contacting the time-checker to punch "off setup" and "on production."

The operator would ordinarily have further "business" contact with a setup man during the course of production. Even if the job did not "go sour" and require the services of a "trouble-shooter," the setup man would drop around of his own accord to see how the work was progressing. Likewise, the operator would have further formal contact during the course of his job with inspectors and tool-crib attendants. Each inspector would make periodic "quality checks" at the machines on his "line"; and the operator might have to make trips to the tool crib to get tools ground or to pick up additional tools or gauges. He might also have to contact a stock-chaser or truckers for additional materials.

Upon completion of the last piece of his order the operator would tear down his setup, return his tools to the tool crib, and make a final report to the time-checker. Should the job be uncompleted at the close of a shift, the operator would merely report the number of pieces finished to a checker, and the latter would register a final punchout. The setup would be left intact for the use of the operator coming in to work the next shift.

MAJOR JOB CATEGORIES

Certain variations in types of jobs assigned to operators are pertinent to a discussion of intergroup collusion to modify formal work routines. These variations could be classified into four categories: (1) piecework; (2) time study; (3) rework; and (4) setup.

Each piecework job carried a price per 100 pieces, determined by the timing operations mentioned earlier. Time-study and rework jobs carried no prices. The time-study category included (a) new jobs that had not yet been timed and (b) jobs that had once carried a piecework price. As the label indicates, rework jobs involved the refinishing of pieces rejected either by inspectors or in the assembly process but considered salvageable by reprocessing.

Since time-study and rework jobs carried on piecework prices, operators engaged in these two types of work were paid "day rates," that is according to an hourly base rate determined in collective bargaining. The base rates represented minimal wage guaranties that not only applied to "day work" but also covered piecework as well. If an operator on piecework failed to exceed his base rate in average hourly earnings on a particular day, he would be paid his base rate. Failure to produce at base rate or above on the first day of a piecework job did not penalize an operator in his efforts to earn premium pay on the second day; nor did failure to attain base rate on one piecework job on a given day reduce premiums earned on a second job performed that day.

Not a fourth type of job, but measured separately in time and payment units, were the setup operations. Piecework jobs always carried piecework setups; failure to equal or exceed base rate on setup did not jeopardize chances to earn premium on "production," and vice versa. Time-study jobs frequently carried piecework setups; rework never.

Obviously, these formal work routines may easily be modified to fit the perceived needs of machine operators. Possibilities for the development of "make-out angles" should be immediately apparent in a work situation characterized by job repertoires that included piecework and day-work operations; minimum-wage guaranties uniform for all work done; and separate payment computations by jobs and days worked. If, for instance, time formally clocked as day work could be used to gain a "head start" on subsequent piecework operations, such a transferral might mean the difference between earning and not earning premiums on doubtful piecework jobs. Similarly, time on "hopeless" piecework jobs might be applied to more promising operations; and the otherwise "free time" gained on "gravy" jobs might be consumed in productive anticipation of the formal receipt of ordinarily unrewarding piecework. Especially lush "gravy" jobs might even contribute extra time enough to convert "stinkers" into temporary "money-makers." Realization of such possibilities in any given case would necessarily involve obtaining, without a work order, the following: (1) identification of future operations as listed in sequence on the schedule board inside the time cage; (2) jigs, blueprints, and cutting tools appropriate to the work contemplated; (3) stock to work on; (4) setup help and advice; (5) inspection service; and (6) "trouble-shooting" assistance as needed. Obviously, this sequence of accomplishments would call for the support of one or more service groups at each step. That the required assistance was actually provided with such regularity that it came to be taken for granted, the writer discovered by obser-

vation and personal experience.

The following diary recording of interaction between the writer and a time-checker may be indicative of the extent to which service-group collaboration with the operators in perverting the formal system of work routine had become systematized:

When I came to punch off the rework, the time-cage girl said, "You don't want to punch off rework yet, do you?"—suggesting that I should get a start on the next job before punching off rework.

Even line foremen, who, in regard to intergroup collusion preferred the role of silent "accessory after the fact," became upset to the point of actual attempted interference with formal rules and regulations when the naïve neophyte failed to meet the expectations of his own informal system.

Art [foreman] was at the time cage when I punched off the day work of rereaming and on to the piecework of drilling. He came around to my machine shortly after.
"Say," he said, "when you punch off day work onto piecework, you ought to have your piecework already started. Run a few; then punch off the day work, and you'll have a good start. You've got to chisel a little around here to make money."

Acceptance of such subversive practices did not extend, however, to groups in management other than local shop supervision. The writer was solemnly and repeatedly warned that time-study men, the true hatchet men of upper management, were disposed to bring chiselers to speedy justice.

Gus went on to say that a girl hand mill operator had been fired a year ago when a time-study man caught her running one job while being punched in on another. The time-study man came over to the girl's machine to time a job, to find the job completed and the girl running another.

NEW RULES AND NEW SYSTEMS

During the near-year that he spent in the shop the writer felt the impact of several attempts to stamp out intergroup irregularities and enforce conformity to managerial designs of procedure. He co-incidentally participated in an upholding of the maxim: "Plus Ca change, plus c'est la même chose."

Attempts to tighten controls came in a series of "new rules" or "new systems" promulgated by bulletin-board edicts. How far the beginning of the series antedated the writer's arrival is not known. Old-timers spoke of a "Golden Age" enjoyed before the installation of the "Booth System" of production control; then operators "kept their own time," turning in their work orders as they saw fit and building "kitties" on good jobs to tide them over rainy days on poor jobs.

The first new rule during this study went into "effect" less than two months after the writer was hired. It was designed to tighten controls in the tool-crib sector, where attendants had not only been passing out setups ahead of time but allowing operators or their setup men to enter the toolroom to make the advance pickups themselves. An aim of the new rule was also to curb the operators' practice of keeping "main setups" at the machines instead of turning them in at the completion of operations.

A new crib ruling went into effect today. A memorandum by Bricker [superintendent] was posted on the side of the crib window. Those who check out tools and jigs must sign a slip in triplicate, keeping the pink one and turning it in with the tools in exchange for the white original, which would constitute proof that the tools had been returned. No new setups would be issued until the old ones had been turned in.

An optimistic perception of the new procedures was expressed by young Jonesy, a tool-crib attendant and otherwise willing conniver with the operators: "Tools are scattered all over the shop. This way we'll have them all in order in the crib, and the fellows can get them anytime they need them."

But multiple-drill operator Hanks, old-timer on the line, drew upon his lengthy experience with managerial efficiency measures and saw the situation differently:

Hanks commented unfavorably on the new ruling. He and the day man [his machine partner on the other shift] had been keeping the tools for their main setups at their bench, or, rather, under it. This practice, according to Hanks, was to insure their setting up promptly without inordinate waste of time and to insure their having all the tools needed. Hanks said that on a previous occasion he was told to turn in one of his main setups, which included over a dozen drills, reamers, taps, etc., of varying sizes. He did so, but, when he needed this setup again, the crib man couldn't locate all the tools. He asked Hanks to come back in the crib and help him find them. Hanks refused. After several hours of futile search, Hanks was finally induced to "come back and find his tools." He did so on condition that it would not be on his own time. The foreman agreed to this.

"The same thing is going to happen again," predicted Hanks. "And I'm not going back there to find my tools they scatter all over, on my own time."

Though the operators went through the formality of an exchange of slips when they exchanged setups, the new procedures did not modify the practice of getting setups from the crib ahead of time. Appreciable effects of the new ruling included making more paper work for crib attendants at the same time that more work at assembling setups was thrust upon them. Jonesy's happy prediction did not materialize: the tools were not "always in order." Subsequent events confirmed Hanks's gloomy forebodings:

It took Paul [setup man] and me several hours to get set up for the sockets, as the setup given was incomplete.

Some time was spent in looking for an angle plate that was specially made for the job. Both Paul and Steve [superintendent] were irritated because the crib men could not find the plate.

We spent an hour setting up because we could not find the jig.

Included in the new ruling was a stipulation that blueprints and gauges be turned in by the operators at the end of each shift, though setup paraphernalia other than prints and gauges were to be left at the machines as long as jobs were in operation. Calling for prints and gauges at the beginning of the shift, waiting at the crib window in the line that naturally formed, even when these items were "located" immediately, consumed operator time.

Owing to the new crib ruling, he [Joe Mucha, the writer's machine partner on another shift] turned in the tap gauge. I spent 20 minutes trying to get it back again. The crib man could not find it and claimed that Joe had not turned it in. Joe stayed after three o'clock to help me get it, countering the arguments of the crib with the slip that he retained as evidence. Finally the gauge was located in the crib.

I started out a half-hour late on operation 55 on the pedestals, due to delay at the crib waiting to check out the print and gauge that Joe had just turned in.

Four months later the new crib ruling was modified by another that canceled the stipulation regarding the turning-in of blueprints and gauges and called for changes in the paper work of operator-crib-attendant relations. These changes were featured by a new kind of work order, duplicates of which became involved in tool-crib bookkeeping. The change reduced the waste of operator time at the start of shifts, but to the burden of the crib attendants paper-work irritations were now added.

When I punched in on the rework and asked Walt [crib attendant] for a print, he fumed a bit as he sought a duplicate of my new-type yellow work order in a new file of his.

"I haven't been able to find more than one in five duplicates so far," he said. "And there's supposed to be a duplicate for every one."

Walt said tonight, when I presented him with a work-order card for tools, "That makes the twelfth card I've had and no duplicate!"

The tool crib under the new system is supposed to have duplicate work orders in their file of all jobs given operators. These duplicates are to be put in the toolroom files as soon as they are put on the board; and the operators are to sign these duplicates when checking out setups.

The "new system" did operate to handicap operators in that they were not to receive new setups from the crib until they received the new yellow work orders from the time cage to check with the duplicates in the crib. However, setup men roamed at will in the toolroom, grinding tools and fixing jigs, and were able to help the operators by picking up setups ahead of time for them. Their detailed knowledge of the various setups made it possible for them to assemble the necessary tools without the use of setup cards.

"This is a good job," I said to McCann [now setup man]. "I wish I could get it set up ahead of time, but I guess it's no use trying. I can't get the setup now from the toolroom until I get the new work order from the time girls."

McCann thought a moment. "Maybe I can get the jig and tools out of the crib for you."

McCann did get the jig and tools, and I got a half-hour's head start on the job.

The writer had found Ted, a stock-chaser, and his truckers, George and Louie, willing conivers in the time-chiseling process. They moved up stock ahead of time, even after the new system made presentation of the new work order to the stock-chaser a prerequisite to getting stock. Contrary to first impressions, for all practical purposes the situation was unchanged under the new system.

I could not go ahead with the next order, also a load of connecting rods, because the new ruling makes presentation of a work order to the stock-chaser necessary before materials can be moved up. So I was stymied and could do nothing the rest of the day.

About an hour before I was to punch off the connecting rods, I advised Ted that I would soon be needing another job. He immediately brought over a head of reservoir casings.

The new system also included complication of operator-inspector relations. Inspectors were now to "sign off" operation from completed jobs before new work orders could be issued at the time booth. The "signing-off" process included notation by the inspector of the time of operation completion, a double check on the time-checker's "punch out." This added, of course, to the paper work of inspectors.

Drill-man Hanks's first response to this feature of the new system was "individualistic":

Hanks commented on the new system tonight. He thinks that its chief purpose is to keep the operators from getting ahead on an operation and starting the next job on saved time. He said that the inspector checked him off a job tonight at 4:40, and he was not due to punch in on the next one until 6:10. He changed the time recorded by the inspector on his work slip to 6:10 and went ahead as usual. If he had not done so, there would have been a "gap" of an hour and a half unaccounted for in the records.

The writer found himself "stymied" at first but soon discovered that the new obstacle could be overcome without engaging in such a hazardous practice as "forging."

It was ten o'clock when we were ready to punch off setup, and Johnny [setup man] asked Sam [inspector] to sign me off setup earlier, so that I could make out on setup. "Punch me off at nine o'clock," I said, not expecting Sam to check me off earlier, and purposely exaggerating Johnny's request.

Sam refused. "I can't do that! If I do that for you, I'll have to do it for everybody!"

Sam seemed somewhat agitated in making the refusal.

A few minutes later he said to Johnny, "Why did you ask me to do that when Hanks was standing there?"

Hanks had been standing by my machine, watching us set up.

"I can't take you off an hour back. Go find out when you punched in on this job in the first place."

Johnny consulted the time-cage girl as to the time I punched in on the job, later talked to Sam at Sam's bench while I was working, and came to me with the announcement that it was "fixed up" so that I made out on setup and was credited with starting production at 9:30. This gave me an hour and a half of "gravy."

By the time the "new system" was a month old, Sam was not only doing this for everybody but actually taking the initiative:

When I punched off setup for the eight pieces, Sam asked me if I wanted him to take me off setup at an earlier time in order that I might make out on the setup. I refused this offer, as it wasn't worth the trouble for me to stop to figure out the time.

Instead of looking at the clock when an operator asks to be taken off setup, Sam usually asks the operator, "When do you want to be taken off?"

No sooner had the shop employees adjusted to this "new system" and settled down to normal informal routine than they were shocked by a new pronunciamento that barred admittance to the toolroom to all save superintendents and toolroom employees:

A new crib ruling struck without warning today. Typewritten bulletins signed by Faulkner [shop manager] were posted on the toolroom door, barring admittance to all save the toolroom employees and the two departmental foremen [superintendents], Bricker and Steve. Other foremen and setup men are not to be admitted without permission from Milton, toolroom supervisor.

Hanks predicts that the new ruling won't last out the week.

Stimulated by Hanks's prediction, the writer kept an eye on the toolroom door. The rule seemed to be enforced.

On one occasion tonight Paul [setup man] asked Jonesy to let him into the crib; he was in a hurry about something. But Jonesy shook his head, and Paul had to wait at the crib window with the rest of us.

Johnny, the setup man, predicted that the new ruling would be "tough on" the tool-crib employees, not on setup men.

Johnny says that the new rule is going to be tough on grinders and crib attendants, because setup men and foremen have been doing rework of the grinding and have made it easier for them by coming in to help themselves to tools, jigs, etc.

Johnny says that the new rule suits him fine. Now he can just stand at the window and talk, and let the toolroom employees do the work.

The line foremen seemed to take offense at the new "exclusion act" and threatened reprisals to the crib attendants.

At quitting time I noticed Gil [line foreman] talking to Walt at the crib window. Gil
seemed very serious; Walt was waving his
arms and otherwise gesturing in a manner
indicating rejection of responsibility. I didn't
catch any words but gathered that Gil was
voicing disapproval or warning, and after Gil
left I said to Walt, "Looks like you're behind
the eight-ball now!"
I noticed that Walt's hair was mussed, and
he looked a little wild. He denied that he
was in any trouble whatsoever; nor was he
worried about anything whatsoever.
"I'm just working here!" he exclaimed. "I
just go by the cards, and beyond that. I've
got no responsibility!"
I was curious as to what Gil had told him
and asked Johnny later, on the way home. I
had noticed that Johnny was standing near by
when Gill was talking to Walt. Johnny said
that Gil was telling Walt that from now on the
crib was going to be charged with every
minute of tool delay to the operators—that,
if there was any waiting for tools, Gil was
going to make out allowance cards charging
these delays to the crib.

Contrary to Hanks's prediction, the
new rule did "last out the week," and
crowds milled around the crib window.

The boys seemed very much disgusted with
the slow service at the tool crib. They crowd
around the window (always a crowd there)
and either growl or wisecrack about the service.

It was at this time that Jonesy, erstwhile optimist and regarded by shop employees as the most efficient of the crib
attendants, decided that he had "had
enough." He transferred to the quiet
backroom retreat of tool-grinding. But
several days later, just ten days since
the new rule was promulgated, the sun
began to break through the dark clouds of
managerial efficiency. Hanks's prediction
was off by four days.

While I was waiting for tools at the crib
window tonight, I noticed the jockey [turret-
lathe man] dash into the tool crib through a
door that was left ajar; he was followed soon
after by Gil. Later, when the door was closed,
Paul shook it and shouted to the attendant,
"Let me in!" He was admitted.

Steve [superintendent] called out, "Hey!"
when he saw the jockey go into the crib. When
the jockey came out, he spoke to him, and the
jockey joshed him back. Steve did not seem to
be particularly put out about it.

Soon the boys were going in and out of
the crib again, almost at will, and setup
men were getting setups ahead of time
for operators, ignored by the crib attendants.

I noticed that Johnny and others seemed to
be going in and out of the crib again, almost
at will.
I noticed tonight that Johnny got into the
tool crib by appearing at the door and saying
to the attendant, "Let me in!"
So much for Faulkner's order—until he
makes a new one!
When I asked Walt for some jaws to fit the
chuck I had found, he said, "We've got lots
of jaws back here, but I wouldn't know what to
look for. You'd better get the setup man to
come back here and find you some."
Walt said to me, "I break the rules here,
but not too much, just within reason to keep
the boys on production."
Faulkner's order still hangs at eye level
on the crib door.

"So much for Faulkner's order!" The
"fix" was "on" again, and operators and
their service-group allies conducted
business as usual for the remaining
weeks of the writer's employment.

CONCLUSIONS

This rough sketch of the operation of
one shop "syndicate" has been no more
than indicative of the existence of intergroup co-operation in the lower reaches
of factory social structure. No attempt
has been made here to account for the
aid extended by service groups, though
suggestion that this assistance might be
part of a larger system of reciprocal obligations has been implicit. It is apparent, for instance, that tool-crib attendants benefited from their practice of
admitting operators and setup men to the
toolroom to seek and pick up equipment.
A more complete picture of intergroup
relations would include conflict, as well
as co-operation, between operators and
the various service groups. It could be

shown, if space permitted, that changes in relationship accompanied, in cyclical fashion, changes in basic conditions of work.

Furthermore, attention has not been drawn to intragroup role and personality variations in intergroup relations. Such additional discriminations and the questions that they might raise in regard to the study of institutional dynamics must be left for future discussion.

As for their possible bearing on practical industrial administration, materials presented here seem to challenge the view held in some research circles that the "human" problem of industrial efficiency lies in faulty communication between an economically "rational" or "logical" management and "nonrational" or "nonlogical" work groups. While nothing has been offered to deny linkage between communication and efficiency, observations reported here suggest examination of the stereotypes of the two parties.[7] And questioning the fitness of the stereotypes may lead to a more fruitful conceptualization of the process that is reputedly in need of attention: communication.

Do we see, in the situation studied, an economically "rational" management and an economically "nonrational" work group? Would not a reversal of the labels, if such labels be used, find justification? Does it not appear that operatives and their allies resisted managerial "logics of efficiency" because application of those "logics" tended to produce something considerably less than "efficiency"? Did not worker groups connive to circumvent managerial ukase in order to "get the work out"? Did not Walt, for instance, break the rules "to keep the boys on production"? May not the common query of industrial workers, "What in the hell are they trying to do up there?" be not merely reflective of faulty communication but also based on real managerial inadequacy, quite apart from a failure in

"explanation"? May it not be assumed that managerial inefficiency is and has been for some time a serious problem to those who labor?

If managerial directives are not the guides to efficient action that they are claimed to be, then, perhaps, "logics of efficiency" would be better designated as "sentiments of efficiency." When failure to "explain" is additionally considered, perhaps bulletin-board pronunciamentos might properly be classified with the various exorcisms, conjurations, and miscellaneous esoteric monkey-business of our primitive contemporaries.

If we conceive of "logical" behavior not as self-contained ratiocinative exercises but as intellectual operations in continuous reciprocal interplay with concrete experience, machine operators and their service-group allies would appear the real holders of "logics of efficiency." Like big-city machine politicians, they develop plans for action that, under given conditions of situational pressures, "work."

But this rejection of commonly held stereotypes cannot lead to mere reversal of invidious distinctions; the situation is far too complex for that. The group life that the writer shared was by no means devoid of "sentiments." To the contrary, operator interaction was rich in shared feelings, attitudes, and practices not only of doubtful bearing on getting the work out but often undeniably preventing production maximization. Nor can it be maintained that management, in applying its "sentiments of efficiency," was always ineffective. Perhaps solution to the human problem of industrial efficiency would best be expedited by abandoning altogether the use of contrasted caricatures handed down to us from a preindustrial social class structure. Instead of concerning ourselves with such blind-alley issues as who is "rational" and who is not, we might recognize with John Dewey that both intellectual and emotional activity are essentials of goal-directed behavior[8] and that the develop-

---

[7] William F. Whyte, "Semantics and Industrial Relations," *Human Organization*, VIII (Spring, 1949), 1-7

[8] *Art as Experience* (New York: Minton, Balch & Co., 1934), p. 55.

ment of effective communication focusing on production goals is a matter of instituting interactional processes that engender ideas, sentiments, and plans for action held in common.

Framework for the Analysis of Industrial Relations: Two Views[1]

John T. Dunlop and William F. Whyte

SOURCE: *Industrial and Labor Relations Review*, Vol. 3 (1950) pp. 383–402

I

The purpose of this exchange of views is to sharpen and clarify explanations of industrial relations behavior. There is no interest here in polemics, tactical points, or in debate for its own sake. In view of the growing and extensive amount of research in industrial relations, however, it may be constructive at this stage for those working in this field—in a variety of disciplines—to consider the implications of these contending frameworks of analysis.

THE ALTERNATIVE FRAMEWORKS

Mr. Whyte holds that the system of communications within a management organization or within a union is the more fruitful analytical framework in which to explain the behavior of these organizations. Similarly, the interaction of the systems of communication in labor and management organizations is the preferred framework in which to explain collective bargaining. The communications pattern or human relations between worker and foreman, foreman and steward, steward and worker, and similar

relations throughout the organizations constitute an explanation of the operations of unions and managements.[2] Significant principles of behavior can be developed from a study of these human relations which are valid as among various organizations and among different collective bargaining relationships.

I shall contend that the analytical framework more fruitful for the explanation of collective bargaining behavior involves the interaction and accommodation of union and management organizations in an economic, technological, and social context. Attention to the internal communications system of an organization, or the interaction of such systems between unions and managements in collective bargaining, without frequent re-

---

[1] This discussion developed from a conference sponsored by the Social Science Research Council. See Charles A. Myers and John G. Turnbull, <u>Research on Labor Management Relations: Report of a Conference Held on February 24-25, 1949, at the Industrial Relations Section, Princeton University, Princeton, New Jersey</u> (New York: Social Science Research Council, 1949), pp. 10-17.

[2] The "human relations" approach is more or less identified here with the study of communications. While the study of human relations might be identified with all social science, the term has more specialized meanings. Those who write of "human relations" have an obligation, as yet unfulfilled, to define the field and the term more explicitly. (a) At times human relations is used generally to contrast human beings with inanimate things. In this sense it is said that managements "need to pay greater attention to human relations in industry." (b) At other times the term implies an emphasis upon all forms of interactions among individuals in a group in contrast to concern with individuals in isolation from their social context. (c) On other occasions the term human relations is limited to those forms of interaction in a continuing group which relate to "official" business of the group.

sort to the environmental setting, can have only limited use as explanation for industrial relations behavior. From this vantage point the "human relations approach" must be cut to size—to a minor role—in any full explanation of industrial relations behavior.

At this point it is essential to examine more carefully what is meant by "industrial relations behavior." The analytical framework will necessarily vary with the precise form of behavior to be explained. There are at least three types of industrial relations behavior that have frequently been examined:

(1) The collective bargaining process creates agreements periodically and administers them on a day-to-day basis. The whole complex of interactions between the two organizations centering around the agreement and its administration is the behavior to be explained. This perspective raises such questions as: Why has the bituminous coal industry had many strikes? Why do some contracts provide for piecework and others for an hourly method of wage payment? Why is arbitration over the terms of new agreements used so extensively in the transit industry in comparison to others? Why have relations been relatively peaceful in the clothing industry in recent years?

(2) The management organization involves a whole series of relationships between employees and supervisors. The union organization involves relations between members and a hierarchy of elected and appointed officials. The characteristics of these relations, including their effects upon output of the enterprise and policies of the unions, is the behavior to be explained. Industrial relations behavior here is the separate activity of either organization.

(3) The conduct of individual workers in the work situation is the behavior to be explained. Interest is centered upon the tensions and satisfactions of individuals. The following questions illustrate this concept of industrial relations behavior: Why do some waitresses cry and break down under pressure of work?[3] How do problems of the family affect performance in the work community? How account for absenteeism? Why are some workers more susceptible to accidents than others?

The choice among these forms of industrial behavior as fields of research has frequently proceeded from more general interests. The attention to collective bargaining processes springs from concern with industrial peace or warfare between the two organizations and from interest in the consequences for the community of the terms of agreements reached between the parties. The examination of the internal administration of a management or a union is related to interest in morale, productivity, and personnel policy on the one hand or to democracy and decision-making in the union on the other. Consideration of the problems of workers as individuals derives from concern with personal adjustments in the face of tensions and insecurities.

It is not to be denied that each one of these types of industrial relations behavior, and the broader perspectives from which an inquiry into each proceeds, are in some sense legitimate. They are all appropriate areas of fruitful research. The critical question is rather which of the analytical frameworks briefly sketched at the outset of this section is more adequate to explain the first two types of industrial behavior— collective bargaining and the operation of union and management organizations.

The choice between two theoretical frameworks is a recurring problem in all scientific inquiry. Which model provides the better fit? Which model provides the more fruitful framework for case studies, such as those undertaken by the National Planning Association on the "causes of industrial peace"? The present contention is not that the study of communications and human relations

---

[3]See the interesting study by William F. Whyte, Industry and Society (New York: McGraw-Hill Book Company, Inc.), 1946, pp. 123-47.

is without interest. Nor is it that such investigations have no contribution to make to understanding collective bargaining and management or union organizations. The issue is not even economics versus sociology. The point of view advocated here is rather that the communications and human relations approach is not the most fruitful framework in which to explain industrial relations behavior (first two types defined above). Communications and human relations are to be embraced within the larger framework which follows.

THE CASE FOR THE INTERACTION OF ORGANIZATIONS IN AN ENVIRONMENT

Collective bargaining is the process of accommodation of management and union organizations in a particular environment. In the simplest case there is one organization on each side; in complex situations there may be a group of unions interacting with a group of managements. The term "accommodation" is not intended to imply any judgment as to the results of the bargaining.[4] There are no overtones implying that the adjustment process is "successful," "desirable," or "constructive." Thus, continuous conflict, an armed truce, containment, domination of one side by the other, or co-operation, are all forms of accommodation.[5] The point can be underlined by recalling that many forms of insanity represent a form of adjustment of a personality to tensions.

It is to be emphasized that the accommodation is between organizations. They can be depicted as social systems

with a continuing existence apart from the particular individuals who compose the group. The relations between individuals within each organization are structured. There are lines of responsibility and authority; there are different statuses and roles. In management there is the line of command from foreman to president with staff organization. In unions there is the hierarchy of elected officers from steward to international president, and the appointed line and staff officers. Formal and informal lines of communication surely exist within both organizations. These organizations develop a folklore. A body of ideas and beliefs emerges indicating the purpose of the management or the union for the wider community. These social systems have their founding fathers and their crises. In a word, each organization is a community in miniature.

The relations between union representatives are also structured. They do not deal with each other as isolated individuals. They each have a role to fulfill in their respective organizations. The management representative is ordinarily an administrator. The union representative is in part administrator, politician, and leader. The points of contact between the union and management organizations are only certain facets of the two social systems. The interactions at the points of contact will reflect total developments within the organizations and cannot be isolated from all aspects of the life of the organization.

It is also to be emphasized that the accommodation between the two organizations takes place in a particular environment. They do not interact in a vacuum. The environment may be stable or may be changing rapidly. The term "environment" refers to the total context in which the two organizations accommodate to each other. Although there are a great many aspects of this environment, for general purposes it is useful to distinguish four facets: (1) the technological and physical conditions of the work community; (2) the conditions in the labor market in which the labor services

---

[4] See John T. Dunlop, Collective Bargaining: Principles and Cases (Chicago: Richard D. Irwin, Inc., 1949), pp. 38-66. The term "accommodation" is used in a definition of collective bargaining at p. 66.

[5] Professor Benjamin M. Selekman, "Varieties of Labor Relations," Harvard Business Review, XXVII (March 1949), 175-99, uses the term "accommodation" to refer to one of eight "prototypes of joint dealings"; see also "'Some Implications and Problems of Collective Bargaining," in The New Industrial Relations (Ithaca, N. Y.: Cornell University Press, 1945). pp. 33-65.

are purchased by the management, and the conditions in the product market in which the output or service is sold; (3) the industrial relations setting of the parties which includes the relations of the union to other unions and the management to other managements in its labor relations policies; and (4) the ideas, beliefs, and value judgments in the community and in the industry in which the parties bargain. The environment of the parties denotes the total external context of the union and the management as they accommodate to each other. In any particular case some aspects of the environment will be more decisive than others.

The main features of the analytical framework here proposed to explain industrial relations behavior (collective bargaining or the operation of unions and managements) can now be outlined. In a cross section or static view the framework consists of: (1) The union and management organizations and their respective internal procedures for decision making; (2) the total context in which the parties accommodate to each other, conceived in terms of the four elements of the environment outlined above. Collective bargaining is envisaged as an adjustment of the two organizations to the problems, difficulties, and opportunities posed by the environment.

The cross-section view needs to be supplemented by two additional elements of an analytical framework in order to consider industrial relations behavior over time:

(3) The origins and the beginnings of a collective bargaining relationship are institutionalized and come to have a continuing effect upon the parties. The early years are frequently reflected in the mature collective bargaining relation. Thus, the opposition to the speed-up and piecework in the automobile assembly plants was a factor associated with the birth of the union in the early 1930's. The speed-up was an effective organizing slogan. It became institutionalized in the union constitution. It persists in the thinking of the founding fathers. It is still an effective force in the collective bargaining

relations. The origins and beginnings of a collective bargaining relationship must be understood.

(4) Collective bargaining between a union and a management cannot grow in all directions at once. In each situation the relationship follows particular axes of development. It may be a safety program, a wage incentive scheme, a quality problem, or a job evaluation procedure. Among the problems and opportunities posed by the environment, the parties will come to select particular axes or directions along which their relationship will grow.

In summary, then, the analytical framework proposed to explain a collective bargaining relationship involves: (1) two or more organizations (social systems); (2) the total environment as conceived above; (3) the beginnings of the relationships; and (4) the continuing axes of development.

This discussion may appear excessively formal. But the problem centers in alternative analytical frameworks. In the final analysis the choice among such frameworks must depend on how well they explain industrial relations behavior. An illustration or two may be in order.

Consider the problem of factionalism in the United Automobile Workers, CIO, and its effects on collective bargaining behavior in that industry.[6] How is this industrial relations behavior to be explained? A very brief statement of the application of the framework just outlined yields the following factors: (a) The labor force of the industry in Detroit has its antecedents in the border states and the Midwest with strong traditions of rural values and individualism. (b) The city of Detroit was a center of "radical" sects in the depression period. (c) The negotiations in the industry must deal separately with at least three major producers. There is no single "bargain" as in basic steel. (d) There was no tradition of unionism prior to the mid-thirties.

[6] I am indebted to an unpublished paper by Philip Taft on a comparison of the steelworkers' and automobile workers' unions.

(e) The organization from "outside" was attempted by organizers (Dillon) without prestige in the labor movement. It is to be noted that in this list the first three factors reflect the environment and the last two the origins of organization. A more complete statement would show the way factionalism, once begun, was reflected in the internal organization of the union and even in managements in the industry.

Consider the problem of explaining jurisdictional disputes in the construction industry. The human relations approach, it seems to me, has virtually nothing to offer toward explaining these disputes.[7]

While the analytical framework here proposed has perhaps never been quite so explicitly stated, at least in this form, it represents an approach that has been widely applied and has yielded fruitful results. Professor Slichter's treatment of the problems of union and management policies is in this tradition.[8] Why have some unions opposed technological change and others encouraged it? Why do some collective bargaining agreements provide for seniority and others equal division of work in layoffs? Why do some union-management co-operation plans succeed and others fail? The same framework is congenial to a number of recent studies of particular union-management relations, such as those undertaken by Clark Kerr,[9] Frederick Harbison, and Robert Dubin.[10]

While the framework needs to be refined and made explicit, in my view the approach has yielded the most significant explanations of industrial relations behavior that we have. I submit that this framework is also congenial to the habits of thought and techniques that are widely used by arbitrators and mediators. Their understanding of industrial relations must be adequate to provide the basis for important decisions. They do not make decisions in terms of the communications framework. As practitioners they come to have a "feel" for such personal aspects of industrial relations. Yet they must operate with the larger framework.

The framework sketched in this section has the further advantage of concentrating attention upon the longer-run consequences of collective bargaining. The parties are not only affected by their environment, but as collective bargaining becomes more extensive, its processes also shape and mold the environment. The interactions are both ways. The framework suggests the need of investigating the impact of trade unions upon the internal organization of managements and the countereffects of changes in management organization upon union administrative practices and structure. It is indeed strange that the "human relations" approach should have failed to emphasize the extent of the "revolution" within managements which have been required to deal with a union. Thus, the union requires management to standardize practices between departments or be "whipsawed." The role of the foreman is altered; the industrial relations department arises. The management needs to develop an improved intelligence system.

The framework has the further merit that it also points to the impact of collective bargaining upon the environment of the parties, all four aspects distinguished above. I have developed elsewhere, for instance, the ways in which collective bargaining has reshaped labor markets and product markets.[11] Collective bargaining is also in the process of significantly reshaping the ideas and beliefs of the community.

---

[7]For an explanation in terms of the framework here advocated, see John T. Dunlop, "Jurisdictional Disputes," in New York University Second Annual Conference on Labor, Emanuel Stein, ed. (Albany, N. Y.: Matthew Bender & Company, 1949).

[8]Sumner H. Slichter, Union Policies and Industrial Management (Washington: Brookings Institution, 1941).

[9]Clark Kerr and Roger Randall, Crown Zellerbach and the Pacific Coast Pulp and Paper Industry (Washington: National Planning Association, 1948).

[10]Frederick H. Harbison and Robert Dubin, Patterns of Union-Management Relations (Chicago: Science Research Associates, 1947).

[11]John T. Dunlop, Wage Determination under Trade Unions (New York: Macmillan Co., 1944, pp. 45-73; 95-121.

THE CASE AGAINST THE COMMUNICATIONS OR HUMAN RELATIONS FRAMEWORK

The caption may appear almost irreverent in the day of the great popularity of "human relations." Yet I am convinced that the "human relations and communications" viewpoint has very little to offer as an <u>analytical framework to explain industrial relations and collective bargaining behavior.</u> The approach yields useful insights to supplement the larger framework outlined in the previous sections. It offers promising methods of measuring some behavior. Yet the approach needs to be seen in perspective: it must be cut to size. The major points against the communications and human relations framework as a comprehensive explanation of industrial relations behavior may be summarized as follows:

(1) The system of communications within a management or a union is in itself very largely a product of other characteristics of the organization and its environment. Both the structure of communications and the pattern of exchange between superiors and subordinates are themselves to be explained. There may be some problems for which it will be appropriate to take the communications system as given. But for a generalized framework of industrial relations, this system must be treated as a variable; the features of the particular communications pattern need to be explained.

Consider the diverse communication problems within either the union or management organization in the construction industry, the fishing industry,[12] the shipping and longshore industries, the railroad industry, the airlines, a national news service, or the harvesting of commercial agriculture. The system of communication would in each case have to be

quite different. It is difficult to see how comparative studies of the flow of communications in these situations could reveal very much about the quality of industrial relations. The communication systems themselves reflect the environments. There has been a tendency for students of "human relations" to concentrate upon industrial plant situations.[13]

If attention be concentrated upon the flow of communication between the union and a management at various levels, rather than within each, this communications pattern is also to be seen as derived largely from other features of the two organizations and from their environment. Would the study of the communication system between the coal operators and the United Mine Workers, for instance, provide a fruitful framework for explaining industrial relations in the coal mines? The question seems rhetorical to me. It would no doubt provide interesting information and useful leads. But as an <u>analytical framework</u> it would certainly not explain the industrial relations behavior of the industry.

It may be suggested that since environmental factors are reflected within organizations, they are adequately observed in the internal communications of unions and managements. That internal systems of communication are structured by the environment is the basic point here insisted upon. An analytical framework for the study of industrial relations, however, should make the influence of the context explicit rather than conceal it in the "human relations" within organizations. The "human relations" approach might make a real contribution in indicating the mechanisms by which the pressures and opportunities of the environment affect organizational decisions.

(2) In order to explain behavior an analytical framework must set forth the behavior to be explained, the independent

---

[12]See Donald J. White, <u>Union Policies in the New England Fish Industry,</u> dissertation for Ph.D. degree, Harvard University, May 1949.

[13]Mr. Whyte's study of the restaurant industry is a notable exception. <u>See Human Relations in the Restaurant Industry</u> (New York: McGraw-Hill Book Company, Inc., 1948).

variable, and then specify the dependent variables that produce the observed behavior. By this test, it seems to me, the communications or human relations approach has provided no analytical framework of collective bargaining. What behavior of union or management organizations is explained by what variables? Some fruitful suggestions have emerged for the industrial relations behavior of individual workers[14] (type 3), but few have been developed for the behavior of unions and management organizations (types 1 and 2).

It is precisely in the area of the relation of individuals to organizations that it is to be hoped that disciplines like sociology and psychology have a contribution to make to industrial relations. There are very large gaps which need to be filled between the ideas, beliefs, and conduct of individual workers and the policies of unions, or between the ideas and conduct of foremen and the policies of companies. Decisions are made by organizations; the relation of those decisions to individuals who compose the organizations is not simple or direct. Neither are the decisions of either group to be understood simply by summarizing the preferences of individuals who compose the group. Any enlightenment the human relations approach can throw on these problems will be a real contribution. Work in this area is to be encouraged.

(3) The interest and ideas regarding communications have been derived, with few exceptions, largely from studies in which no union was present.[15] The analysis of communications is more simple and probably more useful in the absence

of the union. It is difficult under these circumstances to see how communications can provide an adequate framework for the analysis of collective bargaining. It is no accident that the great interest in communication arises in management circles.[16] It is no doubt a useful tool of administration. But as a framework for industrial relations analysis it can be only very limited.

Even greater significance must be attached to the affinity of the communications and human relations approach to the primary work community. As union organization becomes more extensive, the behavior of workers even in the primary work community of the factory becomes more closely tied to organizational decisions. The same development emerges on the side of management. Behavior in even the primary work community under union conditions is structured within narrow limits by the union and management organizations.

(4) The communication and human relations approach seems to proceed from the premise that conflict can be reduced in industrial relations if individuals have more accurate information. I shall not deny that more adquate knowledge of the views of others in the work community can result in a somewhat more "efficiently" administered enterprise. There may be less waste motion. But this approach is highly inadequate as a framework for industrial relations generally. Consider, for example, the problem of the knowledge of workers about the financial conditions of a business. Much has been made of the grossly exaggerated views which most workers and the public generally have of profits per dollar of sales. The communications approach is mobilized for passing out more "accurate" figures. But is not this somewhat naïve? The union member takes the views of his organization about company profits over the views of any company officer. It matters not that the

---

[14]See, for instance, Douglas McGregor, "The Staff Function in Human Relations," Journal of Social Issues, IV (Summer 1948), and Irving Knickerbocker, "Leadership: A Conception and Some Implications," ibid.

[15]See Productivity, Supervision and Employee Morale, A Report from the Survey Research Center of the University of Michigan (Survey Research Center Study no. 6, 1948). Also refer to C. W. M. Hart, "Industrial Relations Research and Social Theory," Canadian Journal of Economics and Political Science, XV (February 1949), 4-8.

[16]V. W. Bladen, "Economics and Human Relations," Canadian Journal of Economics and Political Science, XIV (August 1948), 301-11.

financial report of the company is attested to by a C.P.A., and the union view may be only the assertion of one who is unembarrassed by a formal education. Views about profits, and behavior oriented toward profits by workers, are structured. They are organizationally determined. The problems of conflict derive not from lack of knowledge or information, but rather from the difficulties of accommodating the two organizations in a particular context.

Fundamentally, the conduct of individual workers, union officers or representatives, or management is not autonomous even in the primary work community. The higher one proceeds in either organization the more certain does this fact become. The accommodation of two organizations in collective bargaining cannot fundamentally be a matter of communications, or simply adjusting human relations, or "treating people right." The accommodation must reflect adjustment to stubborn problems posed by the total environment.

(5) The philosophic basis of the communications and human relations framework needs to be examined. The point is relevant to the writings of Mayo and others, rather than to those of Mr. Whyte. As has been developed elsewhere,[17] the Mayo approach abhors conflict and seeks a unity in the community akin to that in a primitive society. Yet conflict and competition between individuals and groups is one of the cornerstones of democratic Western society. The communications framework advocates a single unity and corporateness in the work community which is basically incompatible with collective bargaining and democratic traditions. An analytical framework oriented toward the individual worker in his relationships to a single community of interests cannot provide a basis for a full explanation of the facts of collective bargaining.

John T. Dunlop

---

[17] Reinhard Bendix and Lloyd H. Fisher, "The Perspectives of Elton Mayo," Review of Economics and Statistics, November 1949.

II

The "human relations approach" to union-management problems is now the center of heated controversy. Some see in it a means of laying a scientific foundation for the field of industrial relations. Others condemn it as an escape from the "real issues" of the field.

Interest in industrial relations research is now so keen that it may be worthwhile to try to clear away some of the confusion and to state the issues as clearly and as unemotionally as possible. That is the task Mr. Dunlop and I have undertaken.

As a relatively new field, human relations is today very much in a state of flux. That point should be emphasized, for some critics seem to be trying to discredit the field through attacking Elton Mayo, who may well be considered its founder. So much has been done since Mayo's pioneering research that arguments over what he did and thought are out of touch with present-day realities.

With such a wide variety of activity now going on in this general field, no one can presume to speak for all human relations research men. While I speak only for myself,[18] some of my comments may serve to state the issues that divide research men in industrial relations.

SOCIAL SYSTEMS: A THEORETICAL STATEMENT

I look upon a company and the union with which it deals in a given plant as two interrelated and interdependent social systems. The parts of the social system are the relations among the members of the organization. These parts are also interdependent.

Two propositions flow from that statement:

1. A change in one part of a social system affects all other parts. (Since

---

[18] I had one seminar with Elton Mayo, who seems to me one of the great pioneers in social science. However, my thinking has been much more strongly influenced by Conrad M. Arensberg, Eliot D. Chapple, Burleigh B. Gardner, Everett C. Hughes, Alexander H. Leighton, and W. Lloyd Warner.

the union and management systems interlock at several points, a change in one part of one system tends to affect not only other parts of that system but also the interlocking system.) Some changes will have such slight effects on other parts that they can be disregarded for most purposes, but there are cases in which an apparently small change in one part of a social system disrupts the equilibrium of that system and precipitates a crisis.

2. To determine how parts of a social system relate to each other, we need to study people with emphasis upon the time dimension.

What are the parts of these social systems that particularly require attention in studies of union-management relations? I would point to the following areas of human relations:

(a) Up and down the line of authority from top management to worker.

(b) Up and down the union hierarchy, from worker to top union officer. This area should also include what is generally known as informal organization among workers.

(c) Cross relations between union and management at every point of contact.

(d) Staff and control organizations in relation to the line of authority. Especially we need to observe the role of personnel or industrial relations, engineering, accounting and cost control, and industrial engineering.

(e) Work flow relations. The relations that arise among workers and among members of management in the flow of work from receiving the raw materials to shipping the finished products.

Research on such relationships involves the study of interaction, sentiments, and actions.

By actions I mean simply the things people do while participating in the social system. There are, of course, an endless variety of possible actions. For research purposes, it is well to concentrate upon those which can be most objectively observed and even measured; for example, productivity, absenteeism, labor turnover, presence or absence of work stoppages, and so on.

By sentiments I mean the way the people who are interacting express their feelings about each other, about their organizations, and about the jobs they are doing. Such data can be derived from personal interviews or, on a statistical basis, from questionnaires.

By interaction I am referring to all personal contacts between two individuals or among three or more individuals. There are these aspects of interaction that can be objectively observed: Origination: does A originate action for B, or does B originate for A? Duration: for how long a period do A and B interact with each other? Frequency: how often (in a given time period) do A and B interact? And how often does A originate for B compared with B's originations for A?

Further research may indicate a need to classify interaction into various types, but so far that definition has proved highly serviceable.

According to this approach, actions and sentiments are the items to be explained: Why do workers increase (or decrease) their productivity? Why do they stay on the job—or go out on strike? Why do they express hostile (or favorable) sentiments toward management? And the analysis of patterns of interaction seems to me the most effective means of explaining actions and sentiments. A number of studies have shown how quantitative changes in the pattern of interaction go together with changes in action and sentiments.[19]

---

[19]Many examples could be cited. See, for example, the author's "Who Goes Union and Why," Personnel Journal, Dec. 1944; or "From Conflict to Cooperation" by B. B. Gardner, A. H. Whiteford, and W. F. Whyte, special issue of Applied Anthropology, Fall 1946.

For an application of this theoretical scheme to a particular body of data, see my forthcoming article in Human Organization (formerly Applied Anthropology): "Structures of Union-Management Relations."

For a more thorough discussion of the interaction concept, see Eliot D. Chapple and Conrad M. Arensberg, "Measuring Human Relations," Genetic Psychology Monographs, Vol. 22, 1940, and Arensberg and A. B. Horsfall, "Teamwork and Productivity in a Shoe Factory," Human Organization, Winter 1949, pp. 13-25.

APPLICATION OF THIS FRAMEWORK

Before going into further detail, I should make clear the claims that are being made for this framework. I feel that it has been useful for studies of the relationship between management and industrial unions. It has been used particularly to investigate such relations at the plant level. That does not mean that its utility is limited to small organizations; later I shall show how a study focused primarily at the plant level can add to our knowledge of large organizations.

I have made no attempt to apply the scheme to craft unions, such as the building trades, nor have I tested it out in industry-wide bargaining situations, such as we find in coal. I am not saying that the scheme has no value in such areas. I am simply saying that I make no claims beyond the area where I have done research.

This limitation is certainly in accord with the traditions of science. I feel that it is fruitless to seek a framework which will explain all industrial relations situations. If we begin that way, we will have such a vague, general theory that it will do us no good in specific instances. On the other hand, if we develop a theory which works reasonably well in a restricted area, we can then proceed step-by-step to modify and reshape that theory, so that it will be serviceable in broader areas.

WHY A HUMAN RELATIONS APPROACH TO INDUSTRIAL RELATIONS?

Since research in human relations arose partly in response to a presumed inadequacy of the work of economists in union-management relations, it may be well to spell out some of those criticisms before illustrating further the application of this particular human relations approach.

Most students have concentrated upon top level union-management relationships, arguing that this is where the key decisions are made. This sometimes leads to mistaking the formal policy statements of the parties for the actual motivations of people. It also leads to a gross over-simplification of organizational problems. We find a "tendency to personify such complex entities as the union and the business firm and to reason about group behavior on individualistic lines."[20]

Actually all of these "key people" have their specific places in this network of interdependent relations that we call a social system. Their behavior can only be understood as we develop and apply methods for analyzing such social systems. Neither classical nor institutional nor Keynesian economics supplies any of the tools necessary to cope with such a system of relationships. Consequently the economist cannot operate effectively in this area, unless he also acquires some of the tools of anthropology, sociology, or psychology. Since an increasing number of young economists are moving in this direction, we may hope that this particular criticism will lose its force as time goes on.

This top-level approach seems to assume that the formal agreements reached at this level set the pattern for the entire company in its relations with the union. The extent to which this is true varies greatly from organization to organization. Even in some very large companies top management allows a high degree of autonomy to the local plant managements. And even where top management centralizes its industrial relations policies, the actual working out of those policies will vary widely from plant to plant.

This is not to say that it is useless to study top level relationships. It is simply an argument against conclusions drawn about reactions of "management" or "the union" based largely, if not exclusively, upon study of the top officers. Social systems are just too complicated to submit to that approach.

Some union-management studies concentrate attention upon the so-called sub-

[20]Lloyd G. Reynolds, "Economics of Labor," in Howard S. Ellis, ed., A Survey of Contemporary Economics, p. 285.

stantive issues (seniority, wages, management prerogatives, etc.). This approach yields significant conclusions on the relationship between certain contract clauses and the economic and other environmental conditions of the industry.[21] However, if our problem is to explain the degree of harmony or conflict between union and management—and this is the popular problem today—then the substantive issue approach offers us very little.

We may have a number of different union-management relations, all equally harmonious, in which a particular substantive issue is handled quite differently. Therefore it does us little good to be told just what the agreement was on this point, and the logical arguments given by people on both sides for this agreement. On the other hand, it can be exceedingly valuable to us to get a play-by-play account of the relations developed among the various individuals in the solving of this problem. It is on the level of relationships that we will find uniformities from case to case. I am not suggesting that we throw the substantive issues out altogether. I am saying that we must develop means of showing the people in action in the process of solving their problems.

Some studies are particularly faulty in dealing with the relationship between economic conditions and human relations. We are told that "favorable economic conditions . . . contribute to satisfactory labor relations"[22] and that economic crises tend to stimulate co-operation.[23] Why such a disagreement?

The most obvious answer is that the authors were simply studying cases at different periods of the business cycle. But that criticism in itself indicates that "economic conditions" were viewed as a broad, general factor, and no attempt was made to show how such conditions specifically affected the people involved in the cases.

If some of these studies fall down in relating economic factors to the union-management picture, they are even more grossly inadequate in dealing with the so-called "psychological" factors leading to or preventing union-management co-operation. We may be told that "personalities" play an important role in the process without being given any explanation of what the author means by "personalities" and how the role they play may be submitted to objective analysis. Or we may be told that "mutual trust" is important in achieving union-management co-operation. What we need to know is: How does this mutual trust come into being? Statements on the importance of mutual trust merely state the problem—in a vague way—and contribute nothing to its solution.

Many studies are inadequate because they present the picture in static terms. All of us recognize that the present has a past, but too often this is covered by a brief discussion of "past history" and a description of the present situation; with no convincing demonstration of how the present has evolved out of the past. People live through time. Our analysis must cope with this fundamental fact.

Finally, this concentration on "the big picture" prevents the researcher from testing his conclusions experimentally.

In industrial relations we should be able to predict the outcomes of certain actions, given a known set of conditions. The man who is able to get his own design of action acted upon, and then can follow through to determine the extent to which the results match the predictions, and study the factors which cause such conformity to or deviation from predictions, has a learning opportunity whose importance is hard to over-estimate. For the academic man accustomed to operate several levels of abstraction above the data of observation, the discipline of having to lay the theories on the line for the test of field experience can lead to very fruitful results.

If we seek to gain these advantages in

[21]See particularly Sumner H. Slichter, Union Policies and Industrial Management (Washington: Brookings Institution, 1941).

[22]R. A. Lester and E. A. Robie, Constructive Labor Relations (Industrial Relations Section, Princeton University), p. 113.

[23]Slichter, op. cit.

a top level union-management study of a large corporation and an international union, we run into serious practical difficulties.

Even assuming that we were able to persuade such key management or union people to try out a new line of action—quite a large assumption indeed—the results of such action would extend in so many directions that it would be next to impossible to determine what results flowed from the planned action and what arose from quite different stimuli. To connect actions and outcomes firmly is a difficult enough problem in a single plant. The task of doing that job on a big business or big union basis staggers the imagination.

THE CASE FOR INTENSIVE HUMAN RELATIONS STUDIES

By contrast, human relations studies have tended to concentrate upon plant level relationships. While more attention may profitably be given to higher level relationships, there are good practical and scientific reasons for concentrating in this area at the present time.

To do an effective social science job, we must know where to draw the line. We cannot study everything significant at once. We can study all of the sets of relations making up the interdependent parts of the social systems of the plant and local union. We can examine them at first hand and at close range—as we never could if we sought to encompass a large-scale organization.

I say "we can," but I should add that it has not yet been fully done. Human relations studies in the past have concentrated upon some of the five areas listed above and have presented only fragmentary information about others; for example, the area of work flow relations was almost completely neglected until the recent Richardson and Walker study[24] showed how such data could be developed. But now the parts have been identified, the methods for their study have been

developing, and we should be able to do an increasingly adequate job at analyzing such social systems.

Such studies can be and are being carried on through <u>time,</u> so that we can see how a change in one part of the social system is accompanied by changes in other parts. We have had field workers who have been able to observe and interview freely at all levels from workers to top plant management and from rank-and-file union members up to international representatives. In such studies, we have been able to sit in on union meetings, on management meetings, and on union-management meetings. While we have supplemented this by occasional interviews with higher management and higher union officials, we feel that this area of intensive work at the plant level provides opportunities for interviewing and observation that are difficult to match at higher levels.

Working at the plant level, we are able to test some of our conclusions experimentally. Perhaps "experimentally" is too big a word. We cannot carry on the closely controlled laboratory experiments characteristic of the natural sciences. Nevertheless, we can outline a course of action that should lead to certain results, persuade key people to embark on the course of action, and make careful observations of the results. If the results are as predicted the first time, we are encouraged but not convinced. If we observe similar results in similar situations several times, we are inclined to think that the theories on which we based our predictions are more or less sound. If the results do not meet our expectations, then we are forced to re-examine the data, question our assumptions, and reshape our theories. This sort of discipline is essential for establishing industrial relations on a scientific foundation.

These values of the in-plant study may perhaps be granted, and yet there will still be serious questions raised against it.

Recognizing that much behavior within the plant arises in response to actions of

---

[24]*Human Relations in an Expanding Company* (Labor-Management Center, Yale University).

higher levels in union and management, will we not distort the picture if we study the plant as an isolated unit? Furthermore, since the plant is subject to the influences of the community social environment in which it is located and also to the pressures of the economic environment, will we not distort the picture if we treat the plant in isolation?

The answer, of course, is "yes" in both cases. We must have a means of dealing with influences from outside the plant. But at the same time, we are not dealing with influences in general. We must study them at the point of contact: where they actually enter the plant.

Suppose we are studying one plant of a large corporation. We concentrate on the relations we can observe in the plant and within the local union. We recognize that the plant manager is also part of a larger organization. Some managers have a high degree of autonomy; others are subjected to very tight controls. In either case, we must give close attention to these controls, so that we can understand the manager's behavior. We interview him concerning the policies that are passed down to him from top management and the personal influences upon him from above. We supplement this by interviewing one or more of the top management people having jurisdiction over activities in this plant, in order to get their perspective upon top management pressures on the plant.

In that way, we take into account the higher management influences that play upon the social system we have under observation. But—and this is the key point—we accept those influences as given. We do not seek to explain the motives of higher management people in exercising those influences. Suppose the plant manager has the primary responsibility for negotiating a contract with his local union. He will always act within certain limitations set from above; for example, it may be corporation policy that management will not arbitrate incentive rates. To understand how rate problems are handled, we must, of course, know of this policy, but we must go on to observe how all the parties involved react to this limitation in thrashing out their rate problems. For an analysis of the in-plant processes, it is not necessary to know why top management reached this particular decision.

The same point applies to the union. We cannot assume that the local president or international representative is completely free to make whatever agreement seems best to him. He is subject to certain policies and personal influences at higher levels in the union. To understand his behavior, we need to be fully aware of these policies and influences. But we do not need to explain them. We can accept them as given and go on to see how they are reflected in the behavior of the people in the local situation.

Of course, it would be interesting to know how top management reached its decision on incentive rates, but that is another study. The industrial relations field is so large and complex that we must rigorously cut our study areas down to manageable size. Only as we develop more systematic knowledge of these smaller units will it be profitable for us to tackle large organizations as a whole.

The relation of the plant to its social and economic environment can be dealt with in the same way. We need to examine how this environment comes to bear upon the behavior of people in the social system.

There have been case studies in which the researchers have checked off a number of points about the economic or community environment and have rested their case at that point without showing how that environment comes into the plant through the actual behavior of people in the observed situation. This is not to deny that these so-called environmental influences do come into the plant; of course, they do. The plant manager who finds the market for his product suddenly dropping away responds either to the reports of salesmen assigned to that plant or to directives from higher management, and makes decisions which may drastically alter the relations among people in the plant. But, if that is the case, then the effect of the environment must be noted in those terms rather than in the highly general discussion of the nature of the product market and of the effect of cyclical fluctuations upon management and union. In other words, we need to translate these so-called environmental influences into specific items of observed behavior.

The same can be said of the influence of the social environment. For example, if we were to study a plant having Negro and white workers in, e.g., Detroit, it is obvious that the race-relations situation in the community would have a bearing upon in-plant behavior. However, it is not obvious just what form such influences would take. We cannot assume that because the community race-relations pattern is so-and-so, it has contributed to such-and-such a situation within the plant. It is our task to fight shy of such assumptions and instead investigate carefully just how these community influences crop up in the in-plant behavior.

Whether we shall consider the environment, is not, I believe, the central issue. A man trained in sociology and anthropology would be the last one to deny the importance of the community environment. The problem is to discover the most effective ways of taking the environmental factors into account. I am simply proposing that we take the social systems of union and management as the central items for study. I am suggesting that we will make progress faster if we study small, manageable units, even when they are parts of large organizations. The influences flowing down from top management and top union can be noted as they are manifested in the behavior of the people under observation. Similarly, the community influences must be noted in exactly the same way: as they come out in specific items of behavior within the social system.

William F. Whyte

Shop Society and the Union

Joseph Kovner and Herbert J. Lahne

SOURCE: *Industrial and Labor Relations Review*, Vol. 7, (1953), pp. 3–14.

A current and continuing interest in problems of democracy within unions, and in questions concerning participation in and control of union affairs, is evident to anyone who has followed the literature in the past few years. The objective of this interest has been to determine the attitudes of union members toward the union, toward its activities, and toward participation in union affairs. Most of these studies, so far as we have been able to discern, have been concerned with "the union" in a general sense and with "the local" where there has been a particularization. There is a very important aspect of union life which warrants more than passing mention—but which has had no more than this heretofore. We refer to the "shop" level of union life.

The actual relationship between active and passive members, the full meaning of participation in union affairs, is a pyramid based on union activity in the shop. Study of this "grass roots" level of activity has been too long neglected. We propose to look into the shop, to examine its society, its affairs, and its interests, and to relate the shop to the union local in terms of formal and informal participation. We shall also, of necessity, have something to say about the local itself in these same terms, and about the theory of participation in general and its relationship to participation in union affairs.

The term "shop" is used here to refer to the place where workers are gathered in the course of their employment to perform their work. "Shop society" refers to the group of workers who are brought together in a common place of employment and, more particularly, to that part of a larger force of employees who are in close enough touch with each other for conversation or shoptalk.

Close examination of shop society throws a fresh light on a basic problem of union affairs: the extent of and nature of participation in, and awareness of, union activities on the part of union members. Our observations suggest that participation in formal union activity— such as attendance at meetings, voting in elections, and serving in office—is not the full measure of awareness and interest on the part of the membership; that on the contrary, these formal activities, although carried on by only a few of the members, are outward manifestations of an interest and awareness of union affairs of most of the shop society. The so-called "active members" who participate in union affairs are also in close touch with the rest of their fellows in the shop. There is no organized selection of the active participants, but they are in fact representatives of the whole group, and so we call them "informal representatives." The shop society and the union organization are related to each other through the informal representation of the members in the shop by the active participants in formal union affairs.

SHOP SOCIETY AND SHOPTALK

The job relationships of the members are the elemental stuff of union life. The society of union members begins with the facts of their ways of earning a living, and the government of the union grows out of the need for a rule-making authority to regulate job relations among the members and with the employer. But it is the society which comes first—the government follows. Each day the society forms itself about the gathering together

in common pursuits, and the laws and procedures are resumed. The formal methods of action are preceded by informal talk and informal action. The union lives not because it has formal laws and procedures, but because it is present in the minds and feelings of its members. The first proof of its existence is the place it holds in the talk of the shop.

The shop is not only a place of employment; it is also a social meeting place—a place of talk. Union affairs are one of the more frequent topics of conversation, ranking high with sex, sports, political affairs, and personal gossip. Members who do not attend meetings hear in the shop about what happened at the meeting from those who were there. In one instance, when a shop chairman reported to a unit meeting on the new contract demands, his report was received without comment from the attendants. He scolded them, saying that he knew that there would be no lack of discussion in the factory washrooms. A staff representative of the Steelworkers said, "If we could do away with the bathhouse meetings, we would get more members out to the regular union meeting." (One does not have to know parliamentary law to discuss a subject in a bathhouse!) A Telephone Workers local found that only 30 percent of its twenty-five hundred members voted in an important referendum on its relation with a strengthened national federation. But the subject was thoroughly discussed by nearly every employee. The operators and office help talked about it in the rest rooms and at lunch, and in snatches between working moments. The repair and installation crews work in twos and threes, and they discussed it as they worked and traveled from one working spot to another. The decision on the proposal was formulated in these talks among the employees at work, and the referendum merely registered a developed sentiment. Many members did not take the trouble to vote because they knew what the result was going to be. In discussing whether or not the Rubber

Workers would vote to strike in 1947, a shop chairman of one local said,

There were some people in the National Office who thought that the vote would be against a strike, or that it would be close; but I said it would be 10 to 1 for the strike. I knew because I was in the plant; I knew what the workers were talking [about] in the plant. And it came out 12 to 1 for the strike.

The extent of shoptalk varies with the nature of the work. There are many jobs on which the worker is alone, for example bus drivers and deliverymen. The same is true of craftsmen such as those represented by the Asbestos Workers. Shoptalk for these workers is carried on at assembly points such as terminals, loading platforms, or places where they receive their assignments. Where shoptalk is difficult or restricted, there is often some compensation in the form of better attendance at union meetings. Most jobs, however, are in groups, and even on the most mechanized assembly line the workers can chat as machines are being set or repaired or the flow of material slows. Opportunities for talk are, of course, provided by lunch and relief periods, which are now accepted features of industrial practice. The area of shoptalk also includes the coming-to-work and going-home periods, and other places outside the shop itself, as when fellow employees meet over the back fence, at the corner tavern, or at any sort of social meeting.

The degree to which a job permits talk may be an important factor not only in the initial organization of a union, but also in its continued strength as well. Skilled workers who have a chance to converse on the job have often been the most active union members among a group. The higher degree of participation among the members of the International Typographical Union as against those of the Pressmen is not unrelated to the fact that the former can talk while they work, whereas presswork discourages conversation.

Shoptalk covers a wide variety of subjects. It includes topics of union interest such as grievances, contracts, and union politics, but it also covers many other subjects in which workers are interested simply as human beings and citizens. And the strength of the specifically union topics lies in being set in a background of varied talk. Carried on in small groups of contiguous workers, it is full of personals—but there is always someone willing to discourse on the union issues of the day. Efforts to promote participation in union affairs, educational classes, social and recreational programs all seek to capture the intimate qualities of shoptalk and its companionship. Many unions also recognize this factor in the "personal" items of their journals and newspapers. Such stories as "Pop Nelson is back from his Missouri trip," thanks from a sick brother, the golden wedding anniversary of an old-timer, all appear curious to the outside reader and unrelated to the "real business" of the union. They should be viewed, however, for what they are: an attempt to bring into a formal organization the informal personal exchanges of the shop which are elusive and really resist such treatment.

Shoptalk and companionship exert an intense influence in a small circle, but by their nature they cannot be easily extended without losing considerable force. Yet to prosper and survive, a union must, despite obstacles of size and spatial considerations, organize the specific union interests that are present and immediate to the workers on the job in the shop—those who in the talk and contact of the small shop societies hold the key to the life of the union. These interests are usually referred to as shop rules and grievances.

SHOP ORGANIZATION AND FUNCTION

Union power is the power of government, namely rule-making and administration, and the specific subject matter of union rule-making is relations of members to their jobs and to each other. Some rules, especially among craft unions, are exclusively union-made, but in modern collective bargaining most job rules are the result of contracts between unions and employers. Most of the business of a union is to promote the interests of its members by the creation and administration of rules favorable to them. For both craft and industrial unions—new and old, big and small—the heart of the union is its handling of job rules and grievances in the shop. Grievances are the most important membership interest, except perhaps at contract negotiation time; even then much of the negotiating is often concerned with rule-making based on past or existent grievances.

The best way to measure the influence of grivances in union life is simply to observe how much they displace other points of interest. Grievances absorb the major energies of union members in the shops and emerge as the determinant of union life in any conflict with other interests. Employee representation plans by the score were defeated and absorbed by the CIO in the early days because the plan representatives could not get favorable settlements of grievances. The telephone workers' unions were built on grievances, without the aid of professional organizers. The grievance builds the union; over a period of time, practically every employee will be drawn into a grievance transaction affecting his job.

The Shop Unit. The talk and companionship of the shop provide the society out of which union governments are formed, the shop rules and their administration provide the specific subject matter of union business, and the shop unit provides the primary cell of union government. In its elementary form, the shop organizaton is represented by a single official. He is commonly called a steward—the simple ancient title of the official of a household, the primal unit of social organization. This title is still used by many unions, though there are other titles such as the "chapel chairman" in the printing trades, the "patrolman" of the maritime unions, and the "committeeman" of various industrial unions. A few unions are notable for the absence of any such functionary. The Asbestos Workers, for example, fre-

quently does not have them because the craftsmen often work singly. In some of the older unions, the function of the job steward has lost much of its former importance as full-time business agents have taken over the responsibility of policing union contracts and rules.

In most cases, the shop steward is elected, but whether elected or appointed he must, in the final analysis, be acceptable to the shop society within which he operates. For the steward really serves two masters—the society of employees from which he is selected and the union authority. Though others also often serve dually the workers and "the union," this characteristic is strikingly apparent in the steward's job. Moreover, this dual relationship of the stewards—to the members they serve and to the union authority—is a key one in the life of the union. Many successful organization drives and NLRB election victories have not yielded permanent results because of the difficulty of finding capable workers willing to serve as shop stewards. This was a major factor in the failure of the Southern organizing campaign, but it is true everywhere that the union dies or lives in the shop—not in the local office or national office, which are built upon the place which the union holds in the shop society. A new union tries to reduce the turnover of shop stewards, for the increasing stability of the body of shop officials is proof of the stability of the local and the union.

The shop steward has to solve the elemental problem of government—the relation of the member to authority. Self-rule and authority both play their part, for a steward is close to his constituency and is tested by the intimate personal knowledge of the members he represents. The office of shop steward is the first opportunity for the exercise of skills and talents which the union affords to men who need more than their job for self-expression. It is the first step for ambitious men who want to rise to union power, and it carries honors and privileges—the simple honor to be the leader of one's shopmates. Literally, it also carries a badge of office—the steward's button. The steward is the first line of division between officials and citizens, but the gap is not very wide, for the steward must live with his constituency.

As the first-line officer of the union, the steward in a small shop constitutes the entire shop executive. In the printing trades, the "chapel chairman" is leader of the minimum body of three printers. But in shops of any size there are usually several stewards who are organized into an official body which meets regularly and has an executive head. A shop unit of any size becomes a well-developed governing unit with bylaws, funds, and a complement of officers. This development reaches its highest form in the large amalgamated locals, where each plant constitutes a distinct unit within the local. In large "single-plant" locals, union structure usually corresponds to management's operating departments and divisions, with department committeemen under divisional chairmen as the shop's first line of union officialdom.

Whatever its form, the important fact is that this organization of the shop society is devoted to the business of handling grievances as a separate and distinct branch of local union government. Despite differences in name, size, or hierarchic grades, the grievance committee is the focal point of shop government, and shop government is the direct product of the social and personal interests out of which union organizations are fashioned. Like many other societies, a union becomes an end in itself, and the interests which the organization is intended to serve have to yield some place to the interests of the organized body itself. Though this organizational interest is present in the shop machinery for handling grievances, it must in this instance (with very few exceptions) be subordinate to the interest of the membership if the union is to live.

The Shop Meeting. The will of the shop society is expressed through the shop meeting. These shop meetings are well known so far as the Typographical Union is concerned, where under the name of chapel meetings they have been credited with a large role in the democratic tradition of this union. The roles of similar shop meetings and shop government structure are less well known in other fields, despite the fact that practically every local which encompasses more than one shop provides for such meetings, either formally or informally. Shop meetings are invariably better attended than local meetings because they are closer to the membership, but by the same token it is unnecessary for all to attend. Those who attend will know and express the shop sentiments, and the formal actions of the meeting are quickly communicated to the others in the shop by the attendants.

Perhaps one reason for the neglect of shop meetings in the literature of union government and structure is that they are, at first glance, trivial affairs. A shop meeting of a unit of the UAW-CIO's giant Local 12 in Toledo provides an apt illustration of this first impression. This local had thirty-five thousand members at the time, and the unit in question comprised some three hundred employees in a small machine plant. The unit had a three-man executive, a shop chairman, vice-chairman, and secretary. The shop committee consisted of these three officers and seven stewards. Yet there were only about forty members at this meeting in one of the rooms of the local's building. First came communications: a letter from the president of Local 12 thanking the unit for their support in re-electing him; a letter to the Labor Board asking if it was all right for the employer to buy tickets to the union baseball game. Then came an authorization to buy new stationery. The new shop committee was sworn in, the local secretary coming in from his office, in his shirt sleeves, to administer the obligation. Then the officers of the unit recommended setting up four new committees. A motion was passed leaving the negotiations on a new contract in the hands of the shop committee, with the amount of wage increase left open because no pattern had yet been set by autos and steel. Then there was discussion about asking for a bonus based on profits, more chairs for the plant recreation room—and then adjournment.

Certainly this meeting can hardly be called impressive or its actions "important." But set the meeting in its background and a different picture emerges. This unit was organized by the men in the shop, with help from a Local 12 organizer. Union affairs are a common topic of shop conversation. The employer tries to avoid hiring men who are hostile to the union. One such did happen to be hired and this is what happened, according to our informant:

His father had filled him up with stuff against unions. Well, he started to work, and the first thing he needed was tools, since each man in the shop supplies his own. The supervisor was going to lend him some, but the fellows called the supervisor and said that each man had to buy his own. Well, the boy had to fumble along. Then little things would happen. He would ask a fellow worker to help him lift a bucket—the other would say "I'm not helping a scab!" I felt sorry for him, watching him. But he wouldn't give in and he quit.

Few workers can stay long in a shop when excluded from its fraternity—its helping hands and its conversations. Here the union lived in the shop, was an integral part of the mores of the shop, and the worker who refused to conform had been rejected by the shop society— which was essentially a union-oriented society.

So if we look at this shop meeting again, we can see it as one of the most important institutions of self-government. Behind the "trivia" of the meeting, the seeming fumbling, the writing of a letter about trifles to the government in Washington, and the busying with little things, lies a unit which in the years since it was organized has called on the big local for help only once. Its members are very competent about their own affairs, about matters within the realm of their own experience. They like the formalities of government and their slight hierarchy; and those with authority among them are trusted to do the right thing. At this first line between members

and officials, which is also the gap between the active and the passive members, the constant testing of the officials by the personal knowledge of the members does not permit much arbitrary action. But all the human elements and outward circumstances of high policy and great power are rooted here in this unit—it is the soil which nourishes the upper branches.

THE SHOP AND THE LOCAL

We may now turn to a consideration of the relationship of the shop society to the local, where formal union activities are carried on outside the shop. All local union bodies are combinations of the shop-cell unit of union life. Some locals consist of only one small shop; the shop and the local are the same unit. On the other hand, there are huge amalgamated locals which, however, are only magnified pictures of the common structure of all locals. The differences are almost entirely those of size. The small local has much of the cohesiveness and unity of the shop society, with its common talk and companionship. The large local tries to achieve the same solidarity by drawing it from its units.

The local, however, rarely can achieve the same degree and character of unity as the shop. Yet it is under a compelling need to make up for this lack just because it does not have the benefit of informal directness and immediacy. The art of formal government is one of the contrivances to get over the void of impersonality. The "impressiveness" of government begins with the local. This impressiveness takes many forms and uses many pressures. Its first cry is that it is the important affair, that the local deals with the big things that shape the life of the individuals down below. Coupled with this avowal of importance is the assertion that the local alone has the power to deal with the important factors, that the individual and the shop unit are helpless. Union constitutions vest local governing powers in the local body and whatever powers the unit has are subject to control by the local body. The power of the shop unit rests upon the fact that it is the place where rules are applied, but it is the local which has the power to make rules, to review the original application of rules by the unit, and to link the unit to the authority of the parent organization.

Sources of Local Power. Generally speaking, the full authority of the local is exercised by the membership meeting, and we can study the local union meeting as a clue to the relationship between the local and the shop society. Local membership meetings are meetings of the body politic, duly constituted to act in the name of the local. The power of this body is supreme in local affairs, its decisions binding unless reversed or modified by higher union authorities. In theory, all the authority of the local officers flows from the meeting, since all official action must either be authorized or ratified by a membership meeting. In most locals, this theory is actually carried out in practice: formal authorization or approval is secured at a meeting for nearly every item of union business, from the payment of bills and answering of letters to the settlement of grievances and the negotiation of new contracts. There are, of course, cases where the local does not itself have many powers, where the negotiation of agreements or the handling of grievances has been taken over by district or national officials and bodies. But whatever powers the local has are vested in the membership body, and except for individual referenda actions like elections, the membership exercises its power in a meeting, through the parliamentary procedure of a motion and a vote or order. Substantially, therefore, local union government rests upon a basic plan of direct democracy.

Local Meetings. That actual participation by attendance at local meetings is limited to a small part of the membership has been established beyond peradventure of doubt. Our own field investigations, the investigations by others, and the recurrent discussions in union journals all support the conclusion that with rare exceptions, only a small part of the

local membership formally exercises its democratic right of self-government by attending the local meeting. Moreover, the fraction of the membership which does attend is a regular or steady group, with only a few occasional attendants. These "regulars" are the same individuals who are active in other affairs of the local. They are the officers-at-large of the local, the officers of shop units, the stewards, committee members, and the activists who hold no official union office. The latter are frequently those who are at the center of shop discussions of the union and union affairs; they have an informal leadership or quasi-leadership status in the shop or some segment thereof.

"Why should it be so difficult to get a good turnout at monthly union meetings?" asks a correspondent to the journal of the AFL Electrical Workers. This question is repeated again and again in union literature. All the reasons are marshalled to prove that the union would be so much stronger and better if there were a larger attendance, the officers would have the benefit of full advice; the employer would realize that the union membership is solidly behind its official actions, and so forth. Poor attendance is often regarded as a sign of a poor union by the union itself. A retiring secretary of a Papermakers local tried to figure out why his local of three hundred members could only draw twenty-five to the meetings:

Is it not possible that the fault lies within the officials ourselves? The method by which debates and motions are carried out. The fact that the "gashouse politicians" attend meetings regularly, yet are unable to voice their opinions at the proper time and place. Is it that the meetings are not interesting enough or attractive? Or is it a natural desire to pass the buck? It would require an expert to diagnose the ailment, for sure.

But the secretary himself was something of an expert. Undoubtedly, union officials, like other "professionals," make a mystery of participation. They often become fond of the technicalities of parliamentary law and enjoy practicing them. Parliamentary tangles are sure to bedevil meetings even if the officers wish to avoid them. They arise out of the sheer difficulty of stating the issue for debate and reaching a meeting of minds on points at issue. They often arise out of errors of understanding. And if there is any factional dispute, long drawn-out parliamentary maneuvers are inevitable. Whatever the cause, the result is that meetings are lengthy and debate tends to be not on the merits of an issue, but on procedures. Such affairs can be endured if one is both patient and aggressive. The only other alternative would be to conduct meetings without taking formal action, but resting upon the sense of the meeting. Informal conferences, and caucuses of the groups who plan the decision of formal meetings, are usually conducted on the basis of discussion, from which the sense of the meeting will be taken and a motion is only used at the end to register the sense of the meeting. Small committees also often proceed in this fashion.

In contrast to the informal talk of the shop and to the talk of the shop unit meeting, where formality (if it exists at all) is relieved by the day-to-day closeness of the participants, the local meeting is a place of formal talk, and the special quality required of attendants is the ability to talk. Even at conventions of the international, which are really meetings of active individuals, the talk is often monopolized by a small handful of delegates and officials. The same fact is noticeable at local meetings, where the officials or two or three members do most of the talking. On the other hand, if an issue excites many members, then time prevents everyone from being heard. Or if those who participate have violent feelings, the meeting becomes disorderly, ends in confusion, and scares away timid members. Since local meetings for the most part involve a great deal of routine business, their very function of passing on all actions involves the review of trifling details as well as of general policies. Some people like both routine and talk, and the active individ-

uals who become known to each other in this way enjoy the play of personalities which goes on all the time. To them, the routine has the same interest as household details to friendly neighbors. The occasional attendant is either bored by the details or can make neither head nor tail of the proceedings because of the frequent references by the "regulars" to what happened at the last meeting, the one before that, or even to one held months previously.

Participation or Representation? If the unions themselves tend to attach too much importance to the local membership meeting, it is not surprising that many outside the labor movement interpret poor attendance to mean either that unions do not have a strong hold upon their membership or that they are controlled by a small clique.

Both of these views, and the ideas of union officials on the subject of meetings, overemphasize the importance of the formal meeting and ignore its informal background. Far from being a sign of weakness, small meeting attendance is often a sign that members are in close touch with each other about union affairs and that the union is strongly established in their minds. A native Southern organizer said that union meetings were at first well attended in one town by an enthusiastic membership, freed from outrageous suppression. But now that the union runs the town— the mayor and councilmen are good union members— only the "regulars" show up. More important is the fact that the individuals who attend local and unit meetings are informal representatives of a larger number of members. It is impossible to specify the size of the represented group; in a small one-shop local, it includes practically all of the employees. This status of representative is a quasi-official one for stewards and shop officers, who attend meetings as part of their duties and as a further sign of their interest in union affairs. Whether stewards and shop-unit officers are required to attend or not is immaterial—it remains that the shop membership expects them to attend <u>and to report back</u> to the shop on the happenings at the meeting. And the factions, whether personal or ideological, are sure to be represented by a few of each party. On a test vote, all the adherents are summoned to attend, but they keep informed of the ordinary meetings through an informal representation system, just as the rank-and-file membership does through its stewards and shop unit officers.

The informal representative nature of a membership meeting is an adjustment to size and limits on actual participation. In a few large unions, this fact is recognized, and the membership meeting has been displaced by a delegate body, elected under a formal scheme of representation. This body is found in the amalgamated locals of the UAW-CIO; and the large River Rouge local of this union, though it is not an amalgamated local, has the permission of the international to act in this form. It is also used by the New York Newspaper Guild local, which has over seven thousand members working on many newspapers scattered over the five boroughs. In numerous other unions, similar subdivisions of the local have been observed— whether formally recognized or not. The Hotel Workers, the Pressmen, the Brewery Workers, and the Locomotive Engineers are examples. The use of a delegate body in an amalgamated local of the UAW-CIO is not mandatory, but the international may order the use of this form upon the petition of two units in an amalgamated local. UAW-CIO Local 12 in Toledo, for example, does not have a council, but its general membership meeting is usually attended by only one-tenth of 1 per cent of its over thirty-five thousand members. The local president said that members had considered a delegate body but felt that a general membership meeting open to all was more democratic. "No one is prevented from attending," he declared, and added, "of course if the bulk of the membership decided to attend meetings why they would become too big, and I suppose we

would then have to adopt a representative scheme." There is no opposition group in Local 12. There is a functioning opposition in big Local 174 and in Local 600 of the UAW-CIO, where units select representatives to a general council.

It is, of course, true that a small clique can (at least for a time) run a union by attending meetings regularly and with advance preparations. The machinery of democracy is vulnerable to careful manipulation. But the real problem lies not so much in the size of the group which attends meetings as in the character of those who attend and in the freedom of those who attend to speak. The open formal meeting of the local is not in itself a guarantee of democracy— no one feature is—but it is certainly indispensable.

Perhaps formal representative bodies should be used more commonly in locals. The shop steward structure, however, converts many union meetings into a quasi-representative body, and those who attend often informally represent the rest by communication in the shop. In a sense, it is as if the citizens in a neighborhood were to discuss civic affairs daily with the policeman, who not only enforced the law, but was also the representative of the neighborhood in the municipal government. Moreover, any member can become an active participant in union affairs; all he has to do is to attend union meetings regularly, but it takes interest and will to sit and listen, and then to act. The Washington Newspaper Guild of one thousand members considered setting up a representative body, but though actual attendance was less than 5 percent, the members did not want to confine the membership meeting to official and exclusive attendants. Just as the individual does not wish to lose his right to attend meetings even if he does not exercise it, so the removal of local union meetings from the institutional life of unions would transform them into executive and managerial organizations much like the business corporation.

THE DYNAMICS OF UNION PARTICIPATION

What we have just said of the local union meeting holds true for other formal union affairs. The relation of a member to his union has many fine connections which can be easily missed if one regards only participation in meetings and formal occasions, for much of the relation lies in sympathetic action and common signals, not in the area of direct and explicit communication. Union members are not in a mass relation to their union nor do they stand in any simple linear or one-to-one relation.

Actually, the picture of passive and active members is a moving, complex series of relations. In any given group of union members gathered in any unit of union affairs, there are at any given moment a number of individuals whose personal worlds lie at the center of union activities. They are the small percentage of the total number in the union who are continuously active in its affairs. Directly outside the center, a number of individuals occasionally take an active interest. Their personal world gives an important place to the union, they know what it means, they consider it valuable, they will defend it in any danger, and they will answer calls to action coming from the center group. The rest of the members stretch out toward the edge of the union world, some of them hardly doing more than belonging with a very low degree of interest, while those at the very edge are completely ignorant of the union's meaning and actions. The degree of interest and positions of the members in several groups are relative and constantly changing. A member once active gives up his interest, and one long passive is suddenly stirred by some incident in his personal world, so that he moves to the very center of union activity. Each unit of union life always contains active and passive members, but their numbers and proportions are expressed through formal and <u>informal</u> methods of participation, at different points of interest, on frequent and periodic occasions.

The ideal of full participation seems attractive, but it is unnecessary. Social action for all its importance has a repetitive, cumulative effect so that the participation of a few is enough to determine a matter. Each individual by himself is unique, but in the pursuit of a common social interest one member represents another and one can stand for many. The notion of political equality as the basis of democracy, which makes each person an equal one with all other persons, also makes it unnecessary for each one individually to participate. A sample is enough for most purposes. We do not mean, of course, a sample in terms of a deliberate selection (as by a statistician) of members chosen as representative on the basis of their age, sex, or skill. What is indicated is that the whole of the membership, in a sense, picks its own sample for meeting attendance and activity. On the job, whether in mine, mill, or factory, the "shoptalk" about the union and union issues gives everyone a notion as to the consensus on the issues. And so the "full" local meeting becomes, informally in most cases, a delegate meeting of the activists. Of course, when the issue is important and the division of opinion is close, the meeting is enlarged by the attendance of the occasionally active members.

Full participation, moreover, is not only unnecessary but also a practical impossibility; there simply is not enough space or time to afford an opportunity for every member to take a part. Except for a few very small locals, union offices and meeting halls are not built to accommodate all members. Even if they were enlarged, there is no time to hear everyone. Social or group talk is noteworthy for the high percentage of irrelevancies and repetitions of individual speakers. Each individual expresses himself through a maze of personal quirks and habits of speech. If every member of a union of any size were with equal fervor to pour his energies into the common life of the group, a mass of energy beyond the capacity of the organization to contain would be formed. The organization would break down under the collision of so many opposing wills and temperaments collected in one place. Organizational life, except for occasional celebrations or events like elections, disperses itself into a series of small units. Some of these units are formal arrangements, like committees and membership divisions or departments; others are informal, like caucuses and conferences. In the case of unions, the most common primary unit of the membership where common interests are discussed and acted upon, is on the job, in the mine, mill, or factory; thus we come full circle back to this primary unit of union activity, the shop society and its shoptalk.

CONCLUSIONS

Our conclusions may perhaps be better understood by reference to the course that studies of unionism have taken over the years. A good while ago those interested in unionism studied locals as the clue to understanding the labor movement. Later, as the internationals grew in size and authority, interest shifted to these bodies and to questions of centralization of functions and power. More recently the pendulum of interest has swung back to the local, with analyses of members' attitudes toward the locals and statistical tables of attendance at local meetings. We believe, however, that the back swing has not gone far enough. There is much room for work at the shop level—at the "grass roots" of unionism. What was done for nonunion shop society and, from a different point of view, in the famous Hawthorne studies has yet to be really undertaken with respect to the role of the union in the shop.

The problems of democracy and participation in unions have received much misdirected attention because of a failure to perceive and assess properly the relationship between the shop unit and the local and between the active and passive members. What is needed is a better and more realistic theory of participation based on these relationships. We have already observed that the shop unit and shop society, when carefully studied, provide the ground for findings that "participation" is something that exists aside from the physical motions of the members. It exists in the daily talk of the society and in the emotions and mores of the workers. We have also observed that the physical manifestations of participation are strongest at the shop level; such as better attendance at shop unit meetings than at local meetings (except possibly when the local and shop are conterminous). Even such manifestations, however, are not crucial because of the quick communication between the shop society and the shop meeting and the closeness of those who attend in person and those who do not. These observations are the basis for a theory of the shop society, and of informal representation which links the shop society to the formal union organization. This discussion is only a beginning, both observationally and theoretically, but we hope that it will stimulate further work along these lines.

The Housemaid—An Occupational Role in Crisis

Vilheim Aubert

SOURCE: *Acta Sociologica*, Vol. 1, (1955–56), pp. 149–58.

> *Burge-Lubin.* What's a parlormaid?
> *Mrs. Lutestring:* An extinct species.
>   A woman in a black dress and white apron who opened the house door when people knocked or rang, and was either your tyrant or your slave. *
>
>   G. B. Shaw, *Back to Methuselah*

This article is an incidental product of a survey of the impact of labor-legislation upon the working conditions of house-maids in Oslo.[1] It is intended as a contribution to the sociology of occupations. Its main thesis is this: The occupational relationship and the role expectations between a family and its domestic servants were patterned throughout a long tradition in a society with a preponderance of Gemeinschaft-characteristics. In Sir Henry Maine's terms, it was for a very long time a status-relationship and not one based upon contract. The Gesellschaft-characteristics that today dominate in most other occupations of industrial society have not left the same marks on this time-honored relationship. But neither do present conditions permit a continuation of a relationship on a genuine Gemeinschaft-basis. While the role of the housemaid is wavering between these two occupational models, its incumbents are escaping from the field as statistics show beyond any doubt. Attempts to restore the balance in the relationship through legislation has not been very successful in reversing this trend.

The significance of our problem is twofold. It is based upon the assumption that the employer and employee are not "free" to arrange their relationship in any way they want. There is certainly room for great variation, and the personalities of the parties have a determining influence on the success and satisfaction in the relationship, probably more so than in most occupational relationships. But the arrangements made have repercussions and premises that go way beyond the factors controlled by the housemaid and her employer. They are both caught in the web of role-expectations that are traditionally given or imposed by present economic and material conditions, legislation, etc. These expectations may be more or less psychologically compatible seen from the individual's point of view. Our main thesis implies that the psychological compatibility is doubtful in the case of the modern housemaid. Certain elements in her role encourage her to wish for avenues of satisfaction which other elements in her role deny her. Although a psychological problem, it can probably not be satisfactorily solved without modifications on the social level. That is one reason why a "structural" sociological analysis seems called for.

---

* Reprinted by permission of The Public Trustee and The Society of Authors, London.

[1] V. Aubert, T. Eckhoff, and K. Sveri, En lov i sokelyset (A Law in the Searchlight), Akademisk Forlag, Oslo 1952.

On the other hand, an analysis of a microcosmic social system like that of employer-housemaid has general sociological implications. It follows from the above that the concrete arrangements and conflicts to be observed in this microcosmos mirror far-reaching structural features of society at large. Without any claims to representativeness, we nevertheless felt during the analysis of the housemaid's role, that we were studying something more general. To put this problem in its most abstract form we have felt that we were in touch with the general way in which our existing social institutions deal with the task of keeping some kind of a motivational balance between "work" and "private life."

First of all this task consists in securing some motivation both for "work" and "living." That is not so hard. But how does "society" solve the problem of encouraging people to invest in work that kind of motivation which can be satisfied in work and to invest in private life that kind of motivation which can best be satisfied in private life? The concrete solution of this problem in each individual is very much a question of personality. But not altogether. The individual is guided by the clues given, e.g. by the occupational culture. These clues, both as they appear from the outside to the new recruit and as they appear from the inside of the role to the veteran, may, by their consistency or inconsistency, encourage realistic or unrealistic attachments of needs to environmental situations.

A few examples of culturally determined displacement of motivation might clarify the nature of the problem. Around the occupational role of the seaman have risen a number of myths that must be assumed to play their part in the recruitment to the occupation. Among these myths are several that are heavily loaded with "private" motives. A sailor has a girl in every harbor, it is often said. No doubt this aspect of the role as seen from the outside gets attached to the need for sexual and intimate contact in the motivation of quite a few novices who

go to sea. There is good reason to believe that this motivation in most cases is tragically misplaced. The occupational culture induces a disturbance in the motivational balance between work and private life. A parallel disturbance, which has to do with certain expectations to a family role, a role in private life, can be found among housewives. Many housewives, deprived of any opportunity to seek work outside their homes, develop a certain professional attitude towards their housework. That is to say, they attribute autonomous value to objective standards of performance in cleaning, cooking, and mending, irrespective of the emotional implications in their relationships to husband and children. No doubt, many elements in the role of the housewife and current expectations encourage her to pursue a kind of professional ambition within this role. At the same time the role makes demands upon her which conflict with a professional attitude. This conflict indicates a disturbance in the motivational balance between work and private life.

Against the general background outlined above, it will probably be seen that a study of the role of the housemaid, with its marginal character, may offer new insights into problems of general significance. As tools of analysis I shall use in a liberal way some of the concepts developed by Talcott Parsons in his scheme of "pattern variables."[2] In this scheme the value-orientations characterized as affectivity, diffuseness, particularism, and ascription seem to have an affinity to private life. Work seems in our society to be more connected with affective neutrality, functional specificity, universalism, and achievement.

The modern housemaid is a species of the genus "servant." In order to trace the historical development of the specific occupational role of the housemaid it will be useful to throw a glance at the position of servants in general in Norwegian society from the Middle Ages until this century. Few occupations have

[2] *The Social System*, Glencoe, Illinois, (1951) p. 58 ff.

a longer tradition, and in few do more traditional patterns survive. An ahistorical approach to this occupational role would therefore of necessity be misleading.

The role of the free servant displaced the role of the serf when serfdom was abolished towards the end of the 12th century. Since then, the legislative authorities have been constantly occupied by the problem of how to secure an adequate supply of servants and agricultural workers. A general prescription was issued in 1291 making it a legal duty for all able-bodied men and women, under threat of penalties, to seek employment in the service of others. This duty is clearly reaffirmed in the Law of Christian V of 1687. It states that servants who leave their service, together with vagrants, are to be caught and sentenced to forced labor for as long a period as they have shirked the job. A prescription from 1754 made it a duty for all unmarried sons and daughters of farmers, who didn't themselves run a farm (as owner or tenant), to seek employment for the duration of at least one year. This prescription remained in force until 1854. Parallel to these prescriptions ran statutory determination of the days of notice, twice a year, the so-called hiring days.

These various legal enactments show very clearly that the occupational role of the servant was largely based upon an ascribed status. It was not, even in principle, a matter of achievement and free choice to become a servant. "Servant" was more or less a born characteristic of the person. In this respect the role of servant was more closely related to some of the family roles than to modern occupational roles. This kinship with family roles is clearly acknowledged in Blackstone's Commentaries, where he makes this illuminating statement: "The three great relations in private life are 1) That of master and servant . . . . . . 2) That of husband and wife . . . . . 3) That of parent and child."[3] In Norwegian ju-

risprudence from the middle of the 19th century, the legal status of servants is treated as part of the Law of Persons.[4] To be a servant was a lasting quality ascribed to a person irrespective of his free choice. His relationship to the Master was, as already mentioned, one based predominantly upon status and not upon contract.[5]

The kinship between the occupational role of the servant and the family roles is not, however, limited to the pattern variable achievement-ascription. It is also evident in relation to the patterns of universalism and particularism. Modern occupational roles of the service-kind, e.g. doctor, lawyer, dance-musician,[6,7] are based upon criteria of performance that are relatively independent of the recipient of the service. The incumbent's duties are not to any great extent dependent upon the particular relationship to this or that client. Not so with the role of the servant in 19th century Norway or earlier. The strong particularistic element is brought out in the treatment of a leading legal authority of the servant's duty to obey the master.[8] Only under two conditions may the servant decline to obey an order. To define the duties negatively in this way is in itself the clearest indication that we deal with a particularistic relationship. There are no set objective standards of performance in which the servant can legitimately refuse to obey unreasonable orders. The two exceptions to the rule of unconditional obedience bring this out even more clearly. A master cannot prevent his servant from performing legal duties to the state, such as doing military service, and a servant may refuse to obey an

---

[3]William Blackstone, Commentaries of the Laws of England, Vol. 1, Ch. 14, p. 422 (1st edition 1765. Here quoted from 15th edition, London, 1809).

[4]P. J. Collett, Forelæsninger over Personretten I, Christiania, 1865, pp. 331 ff.

[5]Sir Henry Sumner Maine, Ancient Law, London, 1861.

[6]T. Parsons, The Social System, pp. 428 ff.

[7]Howard S. Becker, "The Professional Dance Musician and his Audience," American Journal of Sociology, Vol. LVII, 1951-52, pp. 136 ff.

[8]Collett, 1. c., p. 337-38.

order to do something which is obviously unlawful. That the legality is doubtful, is not sufficient ground for refusal. A servant cannot demand permission to exercise his rights as a citizen, e. g. by casting his vote, if it collides with his duties as a servant. The master had, until 1891, a legal right to punish his servants just as he could punish his children. The particularistic element in the master-servant relationship is very onesidedly expressed in the legislation. There is reason to believe, however, that the good servant had a moral, if not legal, right to expect a particularistic attachment on the part of his master too.

The nature of the domestic servant's work was functionally diffuse. This was partly contingent upon the nature of the task itself. Neither in terms of time limitations nor with regard to qualitative differentiation is it easy to limit the duties along lines of functional specificity. This was particularly true in relatively small households without specialized cooks, chambermaids, or the like. Practically unlimited duty to obey the Master was in itself also an indication that the relationship would be functionally diffuse.

One implication of the preceding analysis is that the servant was exposed to a constant threat of invasion of his or her "private life." The role arrangements made no solid safeguards against complete domination of the servant's private life by his or her occupational role. First of all, the ascription pattern made it impossible, not only economically difficult, to keep out of the occupation even if it clashed with the most important "private needs." Once in the role, the particularistic pattern made it impossible to legitimate a defense of the private sphere by the claim that the job is done according to generally accepted objective standards of occupational performance. The diffuseness of the role had similar repercussions. Under such conditions the basic question is not to secure a motivational balance between work and private life. The two are not sufficiently differentiated for that. Rather, the problem is

how the occupational situation in itself may, if necessary, give satisfaction to needs that belong to the private sphere, since "private life" is something which does not exist for everyone.

The saving grace in such an occupational situation must be sought in a certain emotional security and opportunity for affective expression. From literary and biographical evidence we know that servants were often "members of the family" in this sense. Particularly the relationship to the children offered avenues of immediate emotional gratification; avenues that in certain periods in certain strata were less open to the parents themselves. Whether the patterns of affectivity also comprised security valves for release of aggressive emotions is more doubtful. The nature of the affective element in the role is poignantly expressed in the following quotation from a book, For Housemaids, from the middle of the 19th century. It was widely read and we can interpret this "Bible of the housemaids" as an authoritative expression of the ethos of this occupational role in the 19th century. The quotation weaves together the patterns of ascription, particularism, diffuseness and affectivity in a convincing total picture.

The master and mistress must, if they want to obey the word of the Lord, look out for their servant's welfare, care for them in case of sickness and other accidents, warn them when they see them on off-paths, and on the whole show an affectionate disposition towards them and set a good example, and not load them with more work than their strength permits them to carry.

The housemaids must obey their master and mistress both for their own and for the sake of the Lord, who commands servants to love and to obey their masters and mistresses. They (the housemaids) should in all things look for what is best for their masters, and must have a loving and pliable disposition towards them like a good and obedient child has towards strict, but honorable parents.

You ought never to sulk if unexpected or unpleasant business turns up, and this may infringe a little on your spare time. A good mistress knows how to make up for this on another occasion and she does it so much the more when you serve her without hesitancy in busy moments.

Your position in life implies much exertion and self-denial. But you ought not to be dissatisfied therewith because you can rest assured that the Lord has put every one of us in the position best suited for trying us and leading us to His Kingdom.[9]

What prevented the role of the servant, e. g. the housemaid, from becoming part of the social system of an individual family in spite of its close affinity to family roles, was the status differential. The role of the servant is essentially a feudal role, developed during a period of rigid social stratification, a Ständersociety. Characteristic of such a society is the possibility of close physical, even emotional proximity, without minimization of status differentials. Not only the status of the servant was ascribed, but also that of the master and his family. They belonged normally by birth to the "conditioned" class of the privileged landowners, the class that set the pattern for the housemaid role. Nothing that the housemaid could observe through her intimate contact with the family was highly relevant to its social status. Human frailties, ignorance, laziness, even poverty were irrelevant from the point of view of status, although they might be important in other respects. This ascriptive status pattern is brought out in the Norwegian novelist, Trygve Andersen's book I kansellirådens dager. It describes the relationship between the state officials and other members of the "conditioned" class on the one hand, and the farmers on the other about the year 1800 in Hedemarken. Among other sociological characteristics of this interesting period in our history, it communicates some very perceptive insights into the relationship between servants and their masters. In some ways it was a close relationship and it certainly gave the servants ample opportunity to observe the human frailties, alcoholism, dishonesty, laziness, etc. among some of their

unhappy and culturally isolated masters. This did not, however, change the status of the master. However close the relationship, the status difference and the concomitant element of distance remained unaltered. This particular status system, still heavily dominated by ascription patterns, made it possible to keep the housemaid in a role dominated by the ethos of the family role, and yet not running any risk of assimilating her into the social system of any one family. Concrete evidence of this might sometimes be difficult to trace when the household was functioning as a group. But as soon as the household ceased functioning and went into a latency phase, the evidence would be striking. The family members would move into social groupings that tended to reaffirm the values, interests, and "culture" they had in common with the other members of their family. The servants, however, would move into social interaction within their social stratum, being constantly reminded of the gap between their "culture" and that of their master.

From the preceding analysis it can be surmised that the role of the housemaid entered into a state of very precarious balance when status criteria were increasingly perceived in achievement terms, of the individual's toil, ability, and performance. We can read the uneasiness of the situation out of the various abortive attempts around the turn of the century to restore balance through legislation. The housewives' organization suggested legislation that was, at least on important points, an attempt to solidify the old patterns. The housemaids' organization made recommendations that, on a very minor scale, would introduce a contractual pattern resembling other occupational roles.

In the official publications from around 1900 we can perceive an interest in introducing achievement, universalism, and functional specificity as patterns governing the housemaid's role. Achievement patterns were expressed in the emphasis upon the freedom of contract, functional specificity in the limitation of work hours

---

[9]Hanna Winsnes, For Tjenestepiger, 2nd edition, Christiania 1868.

and time off, universalism in the emphasis upon education and objective standards of performance. Paradoxically the strong emphasis upon that particular pattern of achievement which is called "freedom of contract" prevented the legislators from furthering the goals of universalism and functional specificity. Under the impact of other occupational models and the scarcity of supply of housemaids, these patterns became nevertheless more prevalent from 1900 onwards, and were given legal sanction in 1948 and even more explicit recognition in the preamble of the law.

Today the role of the housemaid is in acute crisis. Between 1930 and 1952 the statistics show a decline in the number of housemaids from 115,000 to 49,000 for all of Norway. In Oslo the decline seems to have been even sharper. The same trend is apparent in the increasing average age of the housemaids. Between 1938 and 1950 it seems to have increased by close to 10 years. According to certain statistics from 1938, 76% of the housemaids were under 30 years old. In our investigation, which is not strictly comparable, only 45% were under 30. Another symptom of the precarious position of this occupational role became apparent in this survey which was conducted with a representative sample of housewives and housemaids in Oslo. Questioned whether there was any other kind of job they would rather have, 61% answered yes, and 50% even mentioned a specific job which they would prefer to their present one. We might also mention as a similar symptom that only 1% of our sample were organized in the housemaids' union, which is generally known to have very weak support.

As mentioned already, the new law on working conditions for housemaids attempts to narrow the gap between this occupational role and the more "advanced" ones (e. g. in industry). The survey did, however, reveal that realities are lagging behind the legislative attempts. In spite of the law and the general economic and social development, the working conditions of many house-maids have preserved many important traits from the old Gemeinschaft-pattern. Others have gone quite far in approaching the work-models from industry, with important modifications. We shall attempt to analyze some aspects of this empirical material in terms of the pattern variables already applied to the historical material from the study.

Recruitment to the housemaid role is no longer a matter of ascription as it was according to the old prescriptions. It is a matter of "free choice" to become a domestic servant. The legislators also debated how to secure a new kind of recruitment and selection through formal education in domestic work. There was a general agreement that it would be highly desirable to have more education for housemaids, but also that this problem could not be solved by this law. In our sample of housemaids only 17% had attended school in domestic work. If we go beyond the question of how these occupational roles are filled we must say that the enactment of a law regulating domestic work has introduced a new element of ascription. Given that a certain work-relationship is established, certain rights and duties for the parties involved flow from the law irrespective of the choice, agreements, or achievements of these. This contrasts with the period immediately preceding the law. As Karl Renner put it in his general analysis of employer-employee relations: ". . . . the labor relationship has now developed into a ' position,' just as property has developed into public utility. If a person occupies a 'position,' this means that his rights and duties are closely circumscribed, and the position' has become a legal institution in character much like the fee of feudal times."[10] In this respect, however, the housemaid's role is no different from other labor roles, except in the frequency of deviations from this pattern of legal ascription. There is in our material ample evidence on the widespread ignorance of the law and the rights and duties established by the law.

[10]Karl Renner, The Institutions of Private Law and Their Social Functions, London, 1949, p. 121.

Hardly more than 10—15% of all the surveyed work-relationships are in full conformity with the law.

We have also evidence of an ascriptive element in the housemaid role from a different and negative point of view. The law has attempted to institute more formalized contracts in the area of domestic work. According to Section 2 in the law, both parties have a right to demand a written contract. Forty-one per cent of the housemaids claim, however, that they do not have any contract at all. Barely 3% of the work-relationships surveyed are based upon a written contract. Nevertheless, 82% of the housemaids and 70% of the housewives believe that the parties are free to arrange their relationship the way they want.

The minimum rights of the housemaids are defined in the new law in universalistic terms. That is, irrespective of their particular relationships there are certain demands they can make according to objective, universally applicable criteria. As already mentioned, we find frequent, and sometimes gross, deviations from these universalistic norms. In cases where the deviations are striking, we are also least likely to find a contractual agreement which might set up an alternative norm. What then determines the rights of the housemaids in such cases? It is difficult to escape the conclusion that the parties are strongly orientated towards the peculiarities of their particular relationship. Whether this particularism should be viewed as institutionalized or just as deviations from a universalistic norm is debatable.

The question of functional specificity is vital in any analysis of occupational roles. As we have pointed out before, the role of the servant has traditionally been defined as diffuse in its orientation. This involved both the dimensions of time and space and dimension of work-content. Even today we find that 92% of the housemaids in Oslo live with the family in which they are employed.[11] Their place

of work is not separated on the basis of function from their own homes. This is, no doubt, a sociological fact with considerable psychological importance, tying the occupation to old work models.

How pressing this problem of diffuseness along the space-dimension has been, is borne out by Section 5 of the law. It states that the housemaid should have her own bed, that it should be possible for her to lock her room, and that she cannot be ordered to sleep in the same room as the children. This is obviously intended as a defense against symbiosis between work and private life as far as space is concerned.

The major aim of the present legislation has been to introduce functional specificity along the dimension of time. The housemaid has a right to demand a limitation of her working hours which will give her an opportunity to spend some of her own time awake. In this area, however, we find frequent, and sometimes very marked deviations from the rules of the law. Ten per cent of the housemaids claim they work 12 hours a day or more, which is pretty much the same as saying that the working day has no specific limits. Nearly half of the relationships examined exhibited a break of the law which puts a 10 hour limit on housework. A sizeable group of employers violated the rules about free days or about limitation of overtime. It is, in other words, still difficult for many housemaids to protect their private life by referring to universalistic standards concerning the nature of the work. Although such universalistic standards are to be found in the law, they are still insufficiently institutionalized or internalized in the actual interaction between housewives and housemaids.

The results of our study indicate that there is a move in the direction of more universalism and more specificity also on the level of internalized norms for

---

[11]Our sample excluded, in accordance with the law, the increasingly numerous groups of housemaids who work less than three days a week with one family and who do not live at their place of work. Actually, the development of this type of housemaid may afford the best solution to many of the emotional problems inherent in the more traditional housemaid role.

interpersonal behavior. The younger housemaids and the younger housewives show more conformity with legal norms than do the older ones. In one respect, however, this trend towards "occupationalization" will probably not emerge for a long time to come. The housemaid who wants to avoid emotional conflicts has to do the job the way her particular mistress wants her to do it, irrespective of which one of the two is better from an occupational point of view. Under present conditions, this problem is hard to settle. Its ultimate settlement may depend upon the future solution of another problem; how far should one go towards making the housewife's role an occupational role? This involves very intricate emotional problems as I mentioned in the introduction.

In a nutshell, the situation of the housemaid seems to be this: She will in many cases find it difficult or impossible to evaluate her own work in terms of recognizable objective standards of performance. Although the work may have other satisfying features, she often lacks this essential source of self esteem. Concomitant with this comes her lack of informal emotional contact with colleagues at the place of work. She cannot satisfy her craving for companionship in this way and she does not have a role in a work-group as a possible substitute for direct work-satisfaction.

At the same time as the housemaid is bound to be frustrated by these aspects of her work situation, she is constantly encouraged by the peculiarities of this situation to invest some of her "private" emotions in the family with which she works. Both the content of her work, the proximity of her employer, and the uncertain boundaries (in many cases) between work hours and time off operate in this direction. Since there are obvious dangers for the housemaid in getting too emotionally involved with the family, she may solve her problem by creating internal barriers against such involvement.

POLITICAL STRUCTURES AND PROCESSES

An Approach to the Analysis of Political Systems

David Easton

SOURCE: *World Politics*, Vol. 9, (1957), pp. 383–400.

I. SOME ATTRIBUTES OF POLITICAL SYSTEMS

In an earlier work I have argued for the need to develop general, empirically oriented theory as the most economical way in the long run to understand political life. Here I propose to indicate a point of view that, at the least, might serve as a springboard for discussion of alternative approaches and, at most, as a small step in the direction of a general political theory. I wish to stress that what I have to say is a mere orientation to the problem of theory; outside of economics and perhaps psychology, it would be presumptuous to call very much in social science "theory," in the strict sense of the term.

Furthermore, I shall offer only a Gestalt of my point of view, so that it will be possible to evaluate, in the light of the whole, those parts that I do stress. In doing this, I know I run the definite risk that the meaning and implications of this point of view may be only superficially communicated; but it is a risk I shall have to undertake since I do not know how to avoid it sensibly.

The study of politics is concerned with understanding how authoritative decisions are made and executed for a society. We can try to understand political life by viewing each of its aspects piecemeal. We can examine the operation of such institutions as political parties, interest groups, government, and voting; we can study the nature and consequences of such political practices as manipulation, propaganda, and violence; we can seek to reveal the structure within which these practices occur. By combining the results we can obtain a rough picture of what happens in any self-contained political unit.

In combining these results, however, there is already implicit the notion that each part of the larger political canvas does not stand alone but is related to each other part; or, to put it positively, that the operation of no one part can be fully understood without reference to the way in which the whole itself operates. I have suggested in my book, The Political System,[1] that it is valuable to adopt this implicit assumption as an articulate premise for research and to view political life as a system of inter-related activities. These activities derive their relatedness or systemic ties from the fact that they all more or less influence the way in which authoritative decisions are formulated and executed for a society.

Once we begin to speak of political life as a system of activity, certain consequences follow for the way in which we can undertake to analyze the working of a system. The very idea of a system suggests that we can separate political life from the rest of social activity, at least for analytical purposes, and examine it as though for the moment it were a self-contained entity surrounded by, but clearly distinguishable from, the environment or setting in which it operates. In much the same way, astronomers consider the solar system a complex of events isolated for certain purposes from the rest of the universe.

[1]New York, 1953.

Furthermore, if we hold the system of political actions as a unit before our mind's eye, as it were, we can see that what keeps the system going are inputs of various kinds. These inputs are converted by the processes of the system into outputs and these, in turn, have consequences both for the system and for the environment in which the system exists. The formula here is very simple but, as I hope to show, also very illuminating: inputs—political system or processes—outputs. These relationships are shown diagrammatically in Figure I. This diagram represents a very primitive "model"—to dignify it with a fashionable name—for approaching the study of political life.

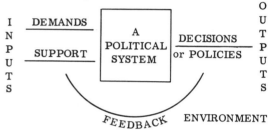

Figure 1

Political systems have certain properties because they are systems.[2] To present an over-all view of the whole approach, let me identify the major attributes, say a little about each, and then treat one of these properties at somewhat greater length, even though still inadequately.

(1) Properties of identification. To distinguish a political system from other social systems, we must be able to identify it by describing its fundamental units and establishing the boundaries that demarcate it from units outside the system.

[2]My conceptions relating to system theory have been enriched through my participation in the Staff Theory Seminar of the Mental Health Research Institute at the University of Michigan. There has been such thorough mingling of ideas in this Seminar that rather than try to trace paternity, I shall indicate my obligation to the collective efforts of the Seminar.

(a) Units of a political system. The units are the elements of which we say a system is composed. In the case of a political system, they are political actions. Normally it is useful to look at these as they structure themselves in political roles and political groups.

(b) Boundaries. Some of the most significant questions with regard to the operation of political systems can be answered only if we bear in mind the obvious fact that a system does not exist in a vacuum. It is always immersed in a specific setting or environment. The way in which a system works will be in part a function of its response to the total social, biological, and physical environment.

The special problem with which we are confronted is how to distinguish systematically between a political system and its setting. Does it even make sense to say that a political system has a boundary dividing it from its setting? If so, how are we to identify the line of demarcation?

Without pausing to argue the matter, I would suggest that it is useful to conceive of a political system as having a boundary in the same sense as a physical system. The boundary of a political system is defined by all those actions more or less directly related to the making of binding decisions for a society; every social action that does not partake of this characteristic will be excluded from the system and thereby will automatically be viewed as an external variable in the environment.

(2) Inputs and outputs. Presumably, if we select political systems for special study, we do so because we believe that they have characteristically important consequences for society, namely, authoritative decisions. These consequences I shall call the outputs. If we judged that political systems did not have important outputs for society, we would probably not be interested in them.

Unless a system is approaching a state of entropy—and we can assume that this is not true of most political systems—it must have continuing inputs to keep it going. Without inputs the system can do no work; without outputs we cannot identify the work done by the system. The specific research tasks in this connection would be to identify the inputs and the forces that shape and change them, to trace the processes through which they are transformed into outputs, to describe the general conditions under which such processes can be maintained, and to establish the relationship between outputs and succeeding inputs of the system.

From this point of view, much light can be shed on the working of a political system if we take into account the fact that much of what happens within a system has its birth in the efforts of the members of the system to cope with the changing environment. We can appreciate this point if we consider a familiar biological system such as the human organism. It is subject to constant stress from its surroundings to which it must adapt in one way or another if it is not to be completely destroyed. In part, of course, the way in which the body works represents responses to needs that are generated by the very organization of its anatomy and functions; but in large part, in order to understand both the structure and the working of the body, we must also be very sensitive to the inputs from the environment.

In the same way, the behavior of every political system is to some degree imposed upon it by the kind of system it is, that is, by its own structure and internal needs. But its behavior also reflects the strains occasioned by the specific setting within which the system operates. It may be argued that most of the significant changes within a political system have their origin in shifts among the external variables. Since I shall be devoting the bulk of this article to examining some of the problems related to the exchange between political systems and their environments, I shall move on to a rapid description of other properties of political systems.

(3) Differentiation within a system. As we shall see in a moment, from the environment come both energy to activate a

system and information with regard to which the system uses this energy. In this way a system is able to do work. It has some sort of output that is different from the input that enters from the environment. We can take it as a useful hypothesis that if a political system is to perform some work for anything but a limited interval of time, a minimal amount of differentiation in its structure must occur. In fact, empirically it is impossible to find a significant political system in which the same units all perform the same activities at the same time. The members of a system engage in at least some minimal division of labor that provides a structure within which action takes place.

(4) Integration of a system. This fact of differentiation opens up a major area of inquiry with regard to political systems. Structural differentiation sets in motion forces that are potentially disintegrative in their results for the system. If two or more units are performing different kinds of activity at the same time, how are these activities to be brought into the minimal degree of articulation necessary if the members of the system are not to end up in utter disorganization with regard to the production of the outputs of interest to us? We can hypothesize that if a structured system is to maintain itself, it must provide mechanisms whereby its members are integrated or induced to cooperate in some minimal degree so that they can make authoritative decisions.

II. INPUTS: DEMANDS

Now that I have mentioned some major attributes of political systems that I suggest require special attention if we are to develop a generalized approach, I want to consider in greater detail the way in which an examination of inputs and outputs will shed some light on the working of these systems.

Among inputs of a political system there are two basic kinds: demands and support. These inputs give a political system its dynamic character. They furnish it both with the raw material or

information that the system is called upon to process and with the energy to keep it going.

The reason why a political system emerges in a society at all—that is, why men engage in political activity—is that demands are being made by persons or groups in the society that cannot all be fully satisfied. In all societies one fact dominates political life: scarcity prevails with regard to most of the valued things. Some of the claims for these relatively scarce things never find their way into the political system but are satisfied through the private negotiations of or settlements by the persons involved. Demands for prestige may find satisfaction through the status relations of society; claims for wealth are met in part through the economic system; aspirations for power find expression in educational, fraternal, labor, and similar private organizations. Only where wants require some special organized effort on the part of society to settle them authoritatively may we say that they have become inputs of the political system.

Systematic research would require us to address ourselves to several key questions with regard to these demands.

(1) How do demands arise and assume their particular character in a society? In answer to this question, we can point out that demands have their birth in two sectors of experience: either in the environment of a system or within the system itself. We shall call these the external and internal demands, respectively.

Let us look at the external demands first. I find it useful to see the environment not as an undifferentiated mass of events but rather as systems clearly distinguishable from one another and from the political system. In the environment we have such systems as the ecology, economy, culture, personality, social structure, and demography. Each of these constitutes a major set of variables in the setting that helps to shape the kind of demands entering a political system. For purposes of illustrating what I mean, I shall say a few words about culture.

The members of every society act within the framework of an ongoing culture that shapes their general goals, specific objectives, and the procedures that the members feel ought to be used. Every culture derives part of its unique quality from the fact that it emphasizes one or more special aspects of behavior and this strategic emphasis serves to differentiate it from other cultures with respect to the demands that it generates. As far as the mass of the people is concerned, some cultures, such as our own, are weighted heavily on the side of economic wants, success, privacy, leisure activity, and rational efficiency. Others, such as that of the Fox Indians, strive toward the maintenance of harmony, even if in the process the goals of efficiency and rationality may be sacrificed. Still others, such as the Kachins of highland Burma, stress the pursuit of power and prestige. The culture embodies the standards of value in a society and thereby marks out areas of potential conflict, if the valued things are in short supply relative to demand. The typical demands that will find their way into the political process will concern the matters in conflict that are labeled important by the culture. For this reason we cannot hope to understand the nature of the demands presenting themselves for political settlement unless we are ready to explore systematically and intensively their connection with the culture. And what I have said about culture applies, with suitable modifications, to other parts of the setting of a political system.

But not all demands originate or have their major locus in the environment. Important types stem from situations occurring within a political system itself. Typically, in every on-going system, demands may emerge for alterations in the political relationships of the members themselves, as the result of dissatisfaction stemming from these relationships. For example, in a political system based upon representation, in which equal representation is an important political norm, demands may arise for equalizing representation between ur-ban and rural voting districts. Similarly, demands for changes in the process of recruitment of formal political leaders, for modifications of the way in which constitutions are amended, and the like may all be internally inspired demands.

I find it useful and necessary to distinguish these from external demands because they are, strictly speaking, not inputs of the system but something that we can call "withinputs," if we can tolerate a cumbersome neologism, and because their consequences for the character of a political system are more direct than in the case of external demands. Furthermore, if we were not aware of this difference in classes of demands, we might search in vain for an explanation of the emergence of a given set of internal demands if we turned only to the environment.

(2) How are demands transformed into issues? What determines whether a demand becomes a matter for serious political discussion or remains something to be resolved privately among the members of society? The occurrence of a demand, whether internal or external, does not thereby automatically convert it into a political issue. Many demands die at birth or linger on with the support of an insignificant fraction of the society and are never raised to the level of possible political decision. Others become issues, an issue being a demand that the members of a political system are prepared to deal with as a significant item for discussion through the recognized channels in the system.

The distinction between demands and issues raises a number of questions about which we need data if we are to understand the processes through which claims typically become transformed into issues. For example, we would need to know something about the relationship between a demand and the location of its initiators or supporters in the power structures of the society, the importance of secrecy as compared with publicity in presenting demands, the matter of timing of demands, the possession of political skills or know-how, access to channels of communication, the attitudes and states of mind of possible publics, and the images held by the initiators of demands with regard to the way in which things get done in the particular political system. Answers to matters such as these would possibly yield a conversion index reflecting the probability of a set of demands being converted into live political issues.

If we assume that political science is primarily concerned with the way in which authoritative decisions are made for a society, demands require special attention as a major type of input of political systems. I have suggested that demands influence the behavior of a system in a number of ways. They constitute a significant part of the material upon which the system operates. They are also one of the sources of change in political systems, since as the environment fluctuates it generates new types of demand-inputs for the system. Accordingly, without this attention to the origin and determinants of demands we would be at a loss to be able to treat rigorously not only the operation of a system at a moment of time but also its change over a specified interval. Both the statics and historical dynamics of a political system depend upon a detailed understanding of demands, particularly of the impact of the setting on them.

III. INPUTS: SUPPORT

Inputs of demands alone are not enough to keep a political system operating. They are only the raw material out of which finished products called decisions are manufactured. Energy in the form of actions or orientations promoting and resisting a political system, the demands arising in it, and the decisions issuing from it must also be put into the system to keep it running. This input I shall call support.[3] Without support, demands could not be satisfied or conflicts in goals composed. If demands are to be acted upon, the members of a system undertaking to pilot the demands through to their transformation into binding decisions and those who seek to influence the relevant processes in any way must be able to count on support from others in the system. Just how much support, from how many and which members of a political system, are separate and important questions that I shall touch on shortly.

What do we mean by support? We can say that A supports B either when A acts on behalf of or when he orients himself favorably toward B's goals, interests, and actions. Supportive behavior may thus be of two kinds. It may consist of actions promoting the goals, interests, and actions of another person. We may vote for a political candidate, or defend a decision by the highest court of the land. In these cases, support manifests itself through overt action.

On the other hand, supportive behavior may involve not external observable acts, but those internal forms of behavior we call orientations or states of mind. As I use the phrase, a supportive state of mind is a deep-seated set of attitudes or predispositions, or a readiness to act on behalf of some other person. It exists when we say that a man is loyal to his part, attached to democracy, or infused with patriotism. What such phrases as these have in common is the fact that they refer to a state of feelings on the part of a person. No overt action is involved at this level of description, although the implication is that the individual will pursue a course of action consistent with his attitudes. Where the anticipated action does not flow from our perception of the state of mind, we assume that we have not penetrated deeply enough into the true feelings of the person but have merely skimmed off his surface attitudes.

Supportive states of mind are vital inputs for the operation and maintenance of

[3] The concept support has been used by Talcott Parsons in an unpublished paper entitled "Reflections on the Two-Party System." I am pleased to note that in this article Professor Parsons also seems to be moving in the direction of input-output analysis of political problems, although the extent to which he uses other aspects of system theory is not clear to me.

a political system. For example, it is often said that the struggle in the international sphere concerns mastery over men's minds. To a certain extent this is true. If the members of a political system are deeply attached to a system or its ideals, the likelihood of their participating in either domestic or foreign politics in such a way as to undermine the system is reduced by a large factor. Presumably, even in the face of considerable provocation, ingrained supportive feelings of loyalty may be expected to prevail.

We shall need to identify the typical mechanisms through which supportive attitudes are inculcated and continuously reinforced within a political system. But our prior task is to specify and examine the political objects in relation to which support is extended.

(1) <u>The Domain of Support</u>. Support is fed into the political system in relation to three objects: the community, the regime, and the government. There must be convergence of attitude and opinion as well as some willingness to act with regard to each of these objects. Let us examine each in turn.

(a) The political community. No political system can continue to operate unless its members are willing to support the existence of a group that seeks to settle differences or promote decisions through peaceful action in common. The point is so obvious—being dealt with usually ·under the heading of the growth of national unity—that it may well be overlooked; and yet it is a premise upon which the continuation of any political system depends. To refer to this phenomenon we can speak of the political community. At this level of support we are not concerned with whether a government exists or whether there is loyalty to a constitutional order. For the moment we only ask whether the members of the group that we are examining are sufficiently oriented toward each other to want to contribute their collective energies toward pacific settlement of their varying demands.

The American Civil War is a concrete illustration of the cessation of input of support for the political community. The war itself was definitive evidence that the members of the American political system could no longer contribute to the existence of a state of affairs in which peaceful solution of conflicting demands was the rule. Matters had come to the point where it was no longer a question of whether the South would support one or another alternative government, or whether it could envision its demands being satisfied through the normal constitutional procedures. The issue turned on whether there was sufficient mutual identification among the members of the system for them to be able to work together as a political community. Thus in any political system, to the extent that there is an in-group or we-group feeling and to the extent that the members of the system identify one another as part of this unit and exclude others according to some commonly accepted criteria, such as territoriality, kinship, or citizenship, we shall say that they are putting in support for the political community.

(b) The regime. Support for a second major part of a political system helps to supply the energy to keep the system running. This aspect of the system I shall call the regime. It consists of all those arrangements that regulate the way in which the demands put into the system are settled and the way in which decisions are put into effect. They are the so-called rules of the game, in the light of which actions by members of the system are legitimated and accepted by the bulk of the members as authoritative. Unless there is a minimum convergence of attitudes in support of these fundamental rules—the constitutional principles, as we call them in Western society—there would be insufficient harmony in the actions of the members of a system to meet the problems generated by their support of a political community. The fact of trying to settle demands in common means that there must be known principles governing the way in which resolutions of differences of claims are to take place.

(c) The government. If a political system is going to be able to handle the conflicting demands put into it, not only must the members of the system be prepared to support the settlement of these conflicts in common and possess some consensus with regard to the rules governing the mode of settlement; they must also be ready to support a government as it undertakes the concrete tasks involved in negotiating such settlements. When we come to the outputs of a system, we shall see the rewards that are available to a government for mobilizing support. At this point, I just wish to draw attention to this need on the part of a government for support if it is going to be able to make decisions with regard to demands. Of course, a government may elicit support in many ways: through persuasion, consent, or manipulation. It may also impose unsupported settlements of demands through threats of force. But it is a familiar axiom of political science that a government based upon force alone is not long for this world; it must buttress its position by inducing a favorable state of mind in its subjects through fair or foul means.

The fact that support directed to a political system can be broken down conceptually into three elements—support for the community, regime, and government—does not mean, of course, that in the concrete case support for each of these three objects is independent. In fact we might and normally do find all three kinds of support very closely intertwined, so that the presence of one is a function of the presence of one or both of the other types.

For example, withdrawal of support from the government of Louis XVI in effect also meant that members of the French monarchical system were challenging at least the regime; as it turned out in the ensuing revolution and civil war, there was even doubt whether the members of the system would continue to support a unified political community. In this case, what was initially opposition to the ruling sovereign—that is, to the government—quickly turned out to signify a lack of sufficient support for the regime and ultimately, to some extent, for the political community. But this is not always so and fortunately, from the point of view of social order, it is not typically the case. We are accustomed to calling for a change of government without thereby suggesting dissatisfaction with the regime or community. And at times, although this is less frequently true, the community shows sufficient intention to continue as a cooperating group to be able to accept a challenge to the regime. From 1832 to the 1880's England underwent a serious modification in its regime, introducing the basic elements of a system of popular democracy, without serious diminution of input of support at the community level. It is always a matter for empirical enquiry to discover the degree to which support at any one level is dependent upon support at the others.

This very brief discussion of support points up one major fact. If a system is to absorb a variety of demands and negotiate some sort of settlement among them, it is not enough for the members of the system to support only their own demands and the particular government that will undertake to promote these demands. For the demands to be processed into outputs it is equally essential that the members of the system stand ready to support the existence of a political community and some stable rules of common action that we call the regime.

(2) Quantity and Scope of Support. How much support needs to be put into a system and how many of its members need to contribute such support if the system is to be able to do the job of converting demands to decisions? No ready answer can be offered. The actual situation in each case would determine the amount and scope required. We can, however, visualize a number of situations that will be helpful in directing our attention to possible generalizations.

Under certain circumstances very few members need to support a system at any level. The members might be dull and apathetic, indifferent to the general operations of the system, its progress or decisions. In a loosely connected system such as India has had, this might well be the state of mind of by far the largest segment of the membership. Either in fact they have not been affected by national decisions or they have not perceived that they were so affected. They may have little sense of identification with the present regime and government and yet, with regard to the input of demands, the system may be able to act on the basis of the support offered by the known 3 per cent of the Western-oriented politicians and intellectuals who are politically active. In other words, we can have a small minority putting in quantitatively sufficient supportive energy to keep the system going. However, we can venture the hypothesis that where members of a system are putting in numerous demands, there is a strong probability that they will actively offer support or hostility at one of the three levels of the system, depending upon the degree to which these demands are being met through appropriate decisions.

Alternatively, we may find that all the members of a system are putting in support, but the amount may be so low as to place one or all aspects of the system in jeopardy. Modern France is perhaps a classic illustration. The input of support at the level of the political community is probably adequate for the maintenance of France as a national political unit. But for a variety of historical and contemporary reasons, there is considerable doubt as to whether the members of the French political system are putting in anything but a low order of support to the regime or any particular government. This low amount of support, even though spread over a relatively large segment of the population, leaves the French political system on somewhat less secure foundations than is the case with India. There support is less widespread but more active—that is, quantitatively greater—on the part of a minority. As this illustration indicates, the amount of support is not necessarily proportional to its scope.

It may seem from the above discussion as though the members of a political system either put in support or withhold it—that is, demonstrate hostility or apathy. In fact, members may and normally do simultaneously engage in supportive and hostile behavior. What we must be interested in is the net balance of support.

IV. MECHANISMS OF SUPPORT

To this point I have suggested that no political system can yield the important outputs we call authoritative decisions unless, in addition to demands, support finds its way into the system. I have discussed the possible object to which support may be directed, and some problems with regard to the domain, quantity, and scope of support. We are now ready to turn to the main question raised by our attention to support as a crucial input: how do systems typically manage to maintain a steady flow of support? Without it a system will not absorb sufficient energy from its members to be able to convert demands to decisions.

In theory, there might be an infinite variety of means through which members could be induced to support a system; in practice, certain well-established classes of mechanisms are used. Research in this area needs to be directed to exploring the precise way in which a particular system utilizes these mechanisms and to refining our understanding of the way in which they contribute to the making of authoritative policy.

A society generates support for a political system in two ways: through outputs that meet the demands of the members of society; and through the processes of politicization. Let us look at outputs first.

(1) Outputs as a Mechanism of Support. An output of a political system, it will be recalled, is a political decision or policy. One of the major ways of strengthening the ties of the members to their system is through providing decisions that tend to satisfy the day-to-day demands of these members. Fundamentally this is the truth that lies in the aphorism that

one can fool some of the people some of the time but not all of them all of the time. Without some minimal satisfaction of demands, the ardor of all but the most fanatical patriot is sure to cool. The outputs, consisting of political decisions, constitute a body of specific inducements for the members of a system to support that system.

Inducements of this kind may be positive or negative. Where negative, they threaten the members of the system with various kinds of sanctions ranging from a small monetary fine to physical detention, ostracism, or loss of life, as in our own system with regard to the case of legally defined treason. In every system support stems in part from fear of sanctions or compulsion; in autocratic systems the proportion of coerced support is at a maximum. For want of space I shall confine myself to those cases where positive incentives loom largest.

Since the specific outputs of a system are policy decisions, it is upon the government that the final responsibility falls for matching or balancing outputs of decisions against input of demand. But it is clear that to obtain the support of the members of a system through positive incentives, a government need not meet all the demands of even its most influential and ardent supporters. Most governments, or groups such as political parties that seek to control governments, succeed in building up a reserve of support. This reserve will carry the government along even though it offends its followers, so long as over the extended short run these followers perceive the particular government as one that is in general favorable to their interests. One form that this reserve support takes in Western society is that of party loyalty, since the party is the typical instrument in a mass industrialized society for mobilizing and maintaining support for a government. However, continuous lack of specific rewards through policy decisions ultimately leads to the danger that even the deepest party loyalty may be shaken.

For example, labor has continued to support the Democratic Party even though much of the legislation promoted by members of that party has not served to meet labor's demands. In some measure, large sections of labor may continue to vote and campaign vigorously on behalf of the Democratic Party because they have no realistic alternative other than to support this party; but in addition the Democrats have built up in recent years, especially during the Roosevelt era, a considerable body of good will. It would take repeated neglect of labor's demands on the part of the Democratic Party to undermine the strong urban working-class support directed toward it and the government that the party dominates from time to time.

Thus a system need not meet all the demands of its members so long as it has stored up a reserve of support over the years. Nor need it satisfy even some of the demands of all its members. Just whose demands a system must seek to meet, how much of their demands, at what time, and under what conditions are questions for special research. We can say in advance that at least the demands of the most influential members require satisfaction. But this tells us little unless we know how to discover the influentials in a political system and how new sets of members rise to positions of influence.[4]

The critical significance of the decisions of governments for the support of the other two aspects of a system—namely, the political community and the regime—is clear from what I have said above. Not all withdrawal of support from a government has consequences for the success or failure of a regime or community. But persistent inability of a government to produce satisfactory outputs for the members of a system may well lead to demands for changing of the regime or for dissolution of the political community. It is for this reason that the input-output balance is a vital mechanism in the life of a political system.

(2) Politicization as a Mechanism of Support. It would be wrong to consider

[4] See C. W. Mills, The Power Elite, New York, 1956.

that the level of support available to a system is a function exclusively of the outputs in the form of either sanctions or rewards. If we did so conclude, we could scarcely account for the maintenance of numerous political systems in which satisfaction of demands has been manifestly low, in which public coercion is limited, and yet which have endured for epochs. Alternately, it might be difficult to explain how political systems could endure and yet manage to flout or thwart urgent demands, failing thereby to render sufficient quid pro quo for the input of support. The fact is that whatever reserve of support has been accumulated through past decisions is increased and reinforced by a complicated method for steadily manufacturing support through what I shall call the process of politicization. It is an awkward term, but nevertheless an appropriately descriptive one.

As each person grows up in a society, through a network of rewards and punishments the other members of society communicate to and instill in him the various institutionalized goals and norms of that society. This is well known in social research as the process of socialization. Through its operation a person learns to play his various social roles. Part of these goals and norms relate to what the society considers desirable in political life. The ways in which these political patterns are learned by the members of society constitute what I call the process of politicization. Through it a person learns to play his political roles, which include the absorption of the proper political attitudes.

Let us examine a little more closely something of what happens during the process of politicization. As members of a society mature, they must absorb the various orientations toward political matters that one is expected to have in that society. If the expectations of the members of society with regard to the way each should behave in specific political situations diverged beyond a certain range, it would be impossible to get common action with regard to the making

of binding decisions. It is essential for the viability of an orderly political system that the members of the system have some common basic expectations with regard to the standards that are to be used in making political evaluations, to the way people will feel about various political matters, and to the way members of the system will perceive and interpret political phenomena.

The mechanism through which this learning takes place is of considerable significance in understanding how a political system generates and accumulates a strong reserve of support. Although we cannot pursue the details, we can mention a few of the relevant dimensions. In the first place, of course, the learning or politicization process does not stop at any particular period for the individual; it starts with the child and, in the light of our knowledge of learning, may have its deepest impact through the teen age. The study of the political experiences of and the influences operating on the child and the adolescent emerges as an important and neglected area of research.[5]

In the second place, the actual process of politicization at its most general level brings into operation a complex network of rewards and punishments. For adopting the correct political attitudes and performing the right political acts, for conforming to the generally accepted interpretations of political goals, and for undertaking the institutionalized obligations of a member of the given system, we are variously rewarded or punished. For conforming we are made to feel worthy, wanted, and respected and often obtain material advantages such as

---

[5] I am happy to say that, since I wrote this statement, the neglect has begun to be remedied. My colleagues at the University of Chicago, Robert Hess of the Committee of Human Development and Peter Rossi of the Department of Sociology, and I have undertaken a questionnaire-interview study of the development of the political attitudes, opinions, and images held by children and adolescents. This research is an attempt to develop some useful generalizations about major aspects of the processes of politicization in the American political system and to formulate a design that, for comparative purposes, could be applied in other political systems as well.

wealth, influence, improved opportunities. For deviating beyond the permissible range, we are made to feel unworthy, rejected, dishonored, and often suffer material losses.

This does not mean that the pattern of rewards and punishments is by any means always effective; if it were, we would never have changed from the Stone Age. A measure of non-conformity may at certain stages in the life history of a political system itself become a respected norm. Even where this is not the case, the most seductive rewards and the severest punishments will never succeed in preventing some of the members of a system from pursuing what they consider to be their inextinguishable interests and from seeking, with varying degrees of success, to change the goals and norms of the system. This is one of the important sources of political change closely associated with changes in the inputs of demands that are due to a changing environment. But we cannot pursue this crucial matter of the nature of political change, as it would lead us off in a new direction.

In the third place, the means used for communicating the goals and norms to others tend to be repetitive in all societies. The various political myths, doctrines, and philosophies transmit to each generation a particular interpretation of the goals and norms. The decisive links in this chain of transmission are parents, siblings, peers, teachers, organizations, and social leaders, as well as physical symbols such as flags or totems, ceremonies, and rituals freighted with political meaning.

These processes through which attachments to a political system become built into the maturing member of a society I have lumped together under the rubric of politicization. They illustrate the way in which members of a system learn what is expected of them in political life and how they ought to do what is expected of them. In this way they acquire knowledge about their political roles and a desire to perform them. In stable systems the support that accrues through these means adds to the reservoir of support being accumulated on a day-to-day basis through the outputs of decisions.[6] The support obtained through politicization tends to be relatively—although, as we have seen, not wholly—independent of the vagaries of day-to-day outputs.

When the basic political attachments become deeply rooted or institutionalized, we say that the system has become accepted as legitimate. Politicization therefore effectively sums up the way in which legitimacy is created and transmitted in a political system. And it is an empirical observation that in those instances where political systems have survived the longest, support has been nourished by an ingrained belief in the legitimacy of the relevant governments and regimes.

What I am suggesting here is that support resting on a sense of the legitimacy of a government and regime provides a necessary reserve if the system is to weather those frequent storms when the more obvious outputs of the system seem to impose greater hardships than rewards. Answers to questions concerning the formation, maintenance, transmission, and change of standards of legitimacy will contribute generously to an understanding of the way in which support is sufficiently institutionalized so that a system may regularly and without excessive expenditure of effort transform inputs of demand into outputs of decisions.

That there is a need for general theory in the study of political life is apparent. The only question is how best to proceed. There is no one royal road that can be said to be either the correct one or the best. It is only a matter of what appears at the given level of available knowledge to be the most useful. At this stage it appears that system theory, with its sensitivity to the input-output exchange between a system and its setting offers a fruitful approach. It is an economical way of organizing presently disconnected political data and promises interesting dividends.

---

[6] In primitive systems, politicization, not outputs of decisions, is normally the chief mechanism.

A Critique of the Ruling Elite Model

Robert A. Dahl

SOURCE: *American Political Science Review*, Vol. 52, (1958), pp. 463–69.

A great many people seem to believe that "they" run things: the old families, the bankers, the City Hall machine, or the party boss behind the scene. This kind of view evidently has a powerful and many-sided appeal. It is simple, compelling, dramatic, "realistic." It gives one standing as an inside-dopester. For individuals with a strong strain of frustrated idealism, it has just the right touch of hard-boiled cynicism. Finally, the hypothesis has one very great advantage over many alternative explanations: It can be cast in a form that makes it virtually impossible to disprove.

Consider the last point for a moment. There is a type of quasi-metaphysical theory made up of what might be called an infinite regress of explanations. The ruling elite model <u>can</u> be interpreted in this way. If the overt leaders of a community do not appear to constitute a ruling elite, then the theory can be saved by arguing that behind the overt leaders there is a set of covert leaders who do. If subsequent evidence shows that this covert group does not make a ruling elite, then the theory can be saved by arguing that behind the first covert group there is another, and so on.

Now whatever else it may be, a theory that cannot even in principle be controverted by empirical evidence is not a scientific theory. The least that we can demand of any ruling elite theory that purports to be more than a metaphysical or polemical doctrine is, first, that the burden of proof be on the proponents of the theory and not on its critics; and, second, that there be clear criteria according to which the theory could be disproved.

With these points in mind, I shall proceed in two stages. First, I shall try to clarify the meaning of the concept "ruling elite" by describing a very simple form of what I conceive to be a ruling elite system. Second, I shall indicate what would be required in principle as a simple but satisfactory test of any hypothesis asserting that a particular political system is, in fact, a ruling elite system. Finally, I shall deal with some objections.

I. A SIMPLE RULING ELITE SYSTEM

If a ruling elite hypothesis says anything, surely it asserts that within some specific political system there exists a group of people who to some degree exercise power or influence over other actors in the system. I shall make the following assumptions about power:[1]

1. In order to compare the relative influence of two actors (these may be individuals, groups, classes, parties, or what not), it is necessary to state the scope of the responses upon which the actors have an effect. The statement, "A has more power than B," is so ambiguous as to verge on the meaningless, since it does not specify the scope.

2. One cannot compare the relative influence of two actors who always perform identical actions with respect to the group influenced. What this means as a practical matter is that ordinarily one can test for differences in influence only where there are cases of differences in initial preferences. At one extreme, the

[1]See Robert A. Dahl, "The Concept of Power," <u>Behavioral Science</u>, Vol. 3 (July 1957), pp. 201-215.

difference may mean that one group prefers alternative A and another group prefers B, A and B being mutually exclusive. At the other extreme, it may mean that one group prefers alternative A to other alternatives, and another group is indifferent. If a political system displayed complete consensus at all times, we should find it impossible to construct a satisfactory direct test of the hypothesis that it was a ruling elite system, although indirect and rather unsatisfactory tests might be devised.

Consequently, to know whether or not we have a ruling elite, we must have a political system in which there is a difference in preferences, from time to time, among the individual human beings in the system. Suppose, now, that among these individuals there is a set whose preferences regularly prevail in all cases of disagreement, or at least in all cases of disagreement over key political issues (a term I propose to leave undefined here). Let me call such a set of individuals a "controlling group." In a full-fledged democracy operating strictly according to majority rule, the majority would constitute a controlling group, even though the individual members of the majority might change from one issue to the next. But since our model is to represent a ruling elite system, we require that the set be <u>less than a majority in size.</u>

However, in any representative system with single member voting districts where more than two candidates receive votes, a candidate <u>could</u> win with less than a majority of votes; and it is possible, therefore, to imagine a truly sovereign legislature elected under the strictest "democratic" rules that was nonetheless governed by a legislative majority representing the first preferences of a minority of voters. Yet I do not think we would want to call such a political system a ruling elite system. Because of this kind of difficulty, I propose that we exclude from our definition of a ruling elite any controlling group that is a product of rules that are actually followed (that is, "real" rules) under

which a majority of individuals could dominate if they took certain actions permissible under the "real" rules. In short, to constitute a ruling elite a controlling group must not be a pure artifact of democratic rules.

A ruling elite, then, is a controlling group less than a majority in size that is not a pure artifact of democratic rules. It is a minority of individuals whose preferences regularly prevail in cases of differences in preference on key political issues. If we are to avoid an infinite regress of explanations, the composition of the ruling elite must be more or less definitely specified.

II. SOME BAD TESTS

The hypothesis we are dealing with would run along these lines: "Such and such a political system (the U. S., the U.S.S.R., New Haven, or the like) is a ruling elite system in which the ruling elite has the following membership." Membership would then be specified by name,' position, socio-economic class, socio-economic roles, or what not.

Let me now turn to the problem of testing a hypothesis of this sort, and begin by indicating a few tests that are sometimes mistakenly taken as adequate.

The first improper test confuses a ruling elite with a group that has a high <u>potential for control</u>. Let me explain. Suppose a set of individuals in a political system has the following property: there is a very high probability that if they agree on a key political alternative, and if they all act in some specified way, then that alternative will be chosen. We may say of such a group that it has a <u>high potential for control</u>. In a large and complex society like ours, there may be many such groups. For example, the bureaucratic triumvirate of Professor Mills would appear to have a high potential for control.[2] In the City of New Haven, with which I have some acquaintance, I do not doubt that the leading business figures together with the

---

[2] C. Wright Mills, The Power Elite (New York, 1956), <u>passim.</u>

leaders of both political parties have a high potential for control. But a potential for control is not, except in a peculiarly Hobbesian world, equivalent to actual control. If the military leaders of this country and their subordinates agreed that it was desirable, they could most assuredly establish a military dictatorship of the most overt sort; nor would they need the aid of leaders of business corporations or the executive branch of our government. But they have not set up such a dictatorship. For what is lacking are the premises I mentioned earlier, namely agreement on a key political alternative and some set of specific implementing actions. That is to say, a group may have a high potential for control and a low potential for unity. The actual political effectiveness of a group is a function of its potential for control and its potential for unity. Thus a group with a relatively low potential for control but a high potential for unity may be more politically effective than a group with a high potential for control but a low potential for unity.

The second improper test confuses a ruling elite with a group of individuals who have more influence than any others in the system. I take it for granted that in every human organization some individuals have more influence over key decisions than do others. Political equality may well be among the most Utopian of all human goals. But it is fallacious to assume that the absence of political equality proves the existence of a ruling elite.

The third improper test, which is closely related to the preceding one, is to generalize from a single scope of influence. Neither logically nor empirically does it follow that a group with a high degree of influence over one scope will necessarily have a high degree of influence over another scope within the same system. This is a matter to be determined empirically. Any investigation that does not take into account the possibility that different elite groups have different scopes is suspect. By means of sloppy questions one could easily seem to dis-

cover that there exists a unified ruling elite in New Haven; for there is no doubt that small groups of people make many key decisions. It appears to be the case, however, that the small group that runs urban redevelopment is not the same as the small group that runs public education, and neither is quite the same as the two small groups that run the two parties. Moreover the small group that runs urban redevelopment with a high degree of unity would almost certainly disintegrate if its activities were extended to either education or the two political parties.

III. A PROPOSED TEST

If tests like these are not valid, what can we properly require?

Let us take the simplest possible situation. Assume that there have been some number—I will not say how many—of cases where there has been disagreement within the political system of key political choices. Assume further that the hypothetical ruling elite prefers one alternative and other actors in the system prefer other alternatives. Then unless it is true that in all or very nearly all of these cases the alternative preferred by the ruling elite is actually adopted, the hypothesis (that the system is dominated by the specified ruling elite) is clearly false.

I do not want to pretend either that the research necessary to such a test is at all easy to carry out or that community life lends itself conveniently to strict interpretation according to the requirements of the test. But I do not see how anyone can suppose that he has established the dominance of a specific group in a community or a nation without basing his analysis on the careful examination of a series of concrete decisions. And these decisions must either constitute the universe or a fair sample from the universe of key political decisions taken in the political system.

Now it is a remarkable and indeed astounding fact that neither Professor Mills nor Professor Hunter has seriously attempted to examine an array of specific cases to test his major hypothesis.[3] Yet I suppose these two works more than any others in the social sciences of the last few years have sought to interpret complex political systems essentially as instances of a ruling elite.

To sum up: The hypothesis of the existence of a ruling elite can be strictly tested only if:

1. The hypothetical ruling elite is a well-defined group.
2. There is a fair sample of cases involving key political decisions in which the preferences of the hypothetical ruling elite run counter to those of any other likely group that might be suggested.
3. In such cases, the preferences of the elite regularly prevail.

IV. DIFFICULTIES AND OBJECTIONS

Several objections might be raised against the test I propose.

First, one might argue that the test is too weak. The argument would run as follows: If a ruling elite doesn't exist in a community, then the test is satisfactory; that is, if every hypothetical ruling elite is compared with alternative control groups, and in fact no ruling elite exists, then the test will indeed show that there is no minority whose preferences regularly prevail on key political alternatives. But—it might be said—suppose a ruling elite does exist. The test will not necessarily demonstrate its existence, since we may not have selected the right group as our hypothetical ruling elite. Now this objection is valid; but it suggests the point I made at the outset about the possibility of an infinite regress of explanations. Unless we use the test on every possible combination of individuals in the community, we cannot be certain that there is not some combination that constitutes a ruling elite. But since there is no more a priori reason to assume that a ruling elite does exist than to assume that one does not exist, the burden of proof does

not rest upon the critic of the hypothesis, but upon its proponent. And a proponent must specify what group he has in mind as his ruling elite. Once the group is specified, then the test I have suggested is, at least in principle, valid.

Second, one could object that the test is too strong. For suppose that the members of the "ruled" group are indifferent as to the outcome of various political alternatives. Surely (one could argue) if there is another group that regularly gets its way in the face of this indifference, it is in fact the ruling group in the society. Now my reasons for wishing to discriminate this case from the other involve more than a mere question of the propriety of using the term "ruling elite," which is only a term of convenience. There is, I think, a difference of some theoretical significance between a system in which a small group dominates over another that is opposed to it, and one in which a group dominates over an indifferent mass. In the second case, the alternatives at stake can hardly be regarded as "key political issues" if we assume the point of view of the indifferent mass; whereas in the first case it is reasonable to say that the alternatives involve a key political issue from the standpoint of both groups. Earlier I refrained from defining the concept "key political issues." If we were to do so at this point, it would seem reasonable to require as a necessary although possibly not a sufficient condition that the issue should involve actual disagreement in preferences among two or more groups. In short, the case of "indifference vs. preference" would be ruled out.

However, I do not mean to dispose of the problem simply by definition. The point is to make sure that the two systems are distinguished. The test for the second, weaker system of elite rule would then be merely a modification of the test proposed for the first and more stringent case. It would again require an examination of a series of cases showing uniformly that when "the word" was authoritatively passed down from the designated elite, the hitherto indifferent

---

[3]Mills, op. cit.; Floyd Hunter, Community Power Structure (Chapel Hill, 1953).

majority fell into ready compliance with an alternative that had nothing else to recommend it intrinsically.

Third, one might argue that the test will not discriminate between a true ruling elite and a ruling elite together with its satellites. This objection is in one sense true and in one sense false. It is true that on a series of key political questions, an apparently unified group might prevail who would, according to our test, thereby constitute a ruling elite. Yet an inner core might actually make the decisions for the whole group.

However, one of two possibilities must be true. Either the inner core and the front men always agree at all times in the decision process, or they do not. But if they always agree, then it follows from one of our two assumptions about influence that the distinction between an "inner core" and "front men" has no operational meaning; that is, there is no conceivable way to distinguish between them. And if they do not always agree, then the test simply requires a comparison at those points in time when they disagree. Here again, the advantages of concrete cases are palpable, for these enable one to discover who initiates or vetoes and who merely complies.

Fourth, it might be said that the test is either too demanding or else it is too arbitrary. If it requires that the hypothetical elite prevails in <u>every single case</u>, then it demands too much. But if it does not require this much, then at what point can a ruling elite be said to exist? When it prevails in 7 cases out of 10? 8 out of 10? 9 out of 10? Or what? There are two answers to this objection. On the one hand, it would be quite reasonable to argue, I think, that since we are considering only key political choices and not trivial decisions, if the elite does not prevail in <u>every</u> case in which it disagrees with a contrary group, it cannot properly be called a ruling elite. But since I have not supplied an independent definition of the term "key political choices," I must admit that this answer is not wholly satisfactory. On the other hand, I would be inclined to suggest that

in this instance as in many others we ought not to assume that political reality will be as discrete and discontinuous as the concepts we find convenient to employ. We can say that a system approximates a true ruling elite system, to a greater or lesser degree, without insisting that it exemplify the extreme and limiting case.

Fifth, it might be objected that the test I have proposed would not work in the most obvious of all cases of ruling elites, namely in the totalitarian dictatorships. For the control of the elite over the expression of opinion is so great that overtly there is no disagreement; hence no cases on which to base a judgment arise. This objection is a fair one. But we are not concerned here with totalitarian systems. We are concerned with the application of the techniques of modern investigation to American communities, where, except in very rare cases, terror is not so pervasive that the investigator is barred from discovering the preferences of citizens. Even in Little Rock, for example, newspaper men seemed to have had little difficulty in finding diverse opinions; and a northern political scientist of my acquaintance has managed to complete a large number of productive interviews with White and Negro Southerners on the touchy subject of integration.

Finally one could argue that even in a society like ours a ruling elite might be so influential over ideas, attitudes, and opinions that a kind of false consensus will exist—not the phony consensus of a terroristic totalitarian dictatorship but the manipulated and superficially self-imposed adherence to the norms and goals of the elite by broad sections of a community. A good deal of Professor Mills' argument can be interpreted in this way, although it is not clear to me whether this is what he means to rest his case on.

Even more than the others this objection points to the need to be circumspect in interpreting the evidence. Yet here, too, it seems to me that the hypothesis cannot be satisfactorily confirmed without something equivalent to the test I have proposed. For once again either the consensus is perpetual and unbreakable, in which case there is no conceivable way of determining who is ruler and who is ruled. Or it is not. But if it is not, then there is some point in the process of forming opinions at which the one group will be seen to initiate and veto, while the rest merely respond. And we can only discover these points by an examination of a series of concrete cases where key decisions are made: decisions on taxation and expenditures, subsidies, welfare programs, military policy, and so on.

It would be interesting to know, for example, whether the initiation and veto of alternatives having to do with our missile program would confirm Professor Mills' hypothesis, or indeed any reasonable hypothesis about the existence of a ruling elite. To the superficial observer it would scarcely appear that the military itself is a homogeneous group, to say nothing of their supposed coalition with corporate and political executives. If the military alone or the coalition together is a ruling elite, it is either incredibly incompetent in administering its own fundamental affairs or else it is unconcerned with the success of its policies to a degree that I find astounding.

However I do not mean to examine the evidence here. For the whole point of this paper is that the evidence for a ruling elite, either in the United States or in any specific community, has not yet been properly examined so far as I know. And the evidence has not been properly examined, I have tried to argue, because the examination has not employed satisfactory criteria to determine what constitutes a fair test of the basic hypothesis.

Power Relations in Three-Person Groups

Theodore M. Mills*

SOURCE: *American Sociological Review*, Vol. 18, (1953), pp. 351–57.

In drawing his fundamental distinction between two-person groups and all groups of larger size, Simmel[1] called attention to certain characteristics of the three-person situation. It was important to him the way the position of the third person impinged upon the other two, whether this position be as mediator, as holder of the balance of power, or as constant disturber of the solidarity enjoyed by the other two. He described how a conflict between two could bring satisfaction and strength to a third, and how the sense of unity within a pair could be threatened by the mere presence of another person.

More recently, and on quite another plane, Von Neumann and Morgenstern[2] have made an important contribution by making room, in their theory, for the

*The author gratefully acknowledges the contributions, in the form of critical review of a preliminary draft, of Professors Talcott Parsons and Samuel A. Stouffer, Dr. Robert F. Bales, Dr. Andrew F. Henry, Dr. Duncan MacCrae and other members of the Harvard Laboratory, and of Mary E. Roseborough and Christoph Heineke in scoring the interaction.

[1] Kurt H. Wolff (translator and editor), The Sociology of Georg Simmel, Glencoe, Illinois: The Free Press, 1950, Chapters 2, 3, and 4.

[2] John Von Neumann and Oskar Morgenstern, Theory of Games and Economic Behavior, Princeton, New Jersey: Princeton University Press, 1944, Chapter 5.

three-person game and, in their solution, by allowing for a coalition between two parties to the game. Their model has a place within it for this alliance, whether it be collusion in the market place, a strong emotional tie, or simply a gentleman's agreement.

In this respect, Simmel and Von Neumann and Morgenstern share common ground. One assumes and the others plan for an elementary differentiating tendency in the threesome; namely, segregation into a <u>pair</u> and an <u>other</u>.

Whether or not this segregation generally occurs, and just what position the third party <u>does</u> take (or is given) in the face of conflict or alliance between the others, are empirical questions. They are precisely the sort of questions that are easier to investigate now than they were before recent developments in the observation of behavior in small groups.

Simmel's principle of segregation is the first of three questions examined in the paper. The second is the extent to which relationships are interdependent. The problem is whether the nature of one relationship determines to any appreciable degree the nature of the other relationships. The third follows naturally from these: when is it found that interdependence develops into a sharply differentiated and rigidly set power structure, and when is it found that relationships are in a state of fluctuation?

PROCEDURES

<u>Observation Setting.</u> The data consist of observations made of interaction in forty-eight three-person discussion sessions. Subjects were student volunteers, recruited through the Harvard Student Employment Service. Groups were assembled in a room equipped with an adjacent observation room. Subjects had not previously interacted with one another, and there were no marked status differences between them. A group performed in two sessions, each lasting around thirty minutes.

Each group was asked to create, from three pictures selected from the T.A.T. series, a single dramatic story upon which they all agreed. In the experimental setting there was a minimum of restraints; no limit was placed upon the kind of story, or its content, or upon what member should play what role in its telling.

<u>Collection of Data.</u> Each act was scored in sequence according to Bales' method of interaction process analysis.[3] This score shows, first, who initiates the act and to whom it is directed. In addition, it indicates the relevance of the act either to the solution of the problem confronting the group or to the state of integration of the group. Acts classified as relevant primarily to the group problem (categories four through nine) are for present purposes combined and called "contributions." Positive acts (categories one through three) directed specifically to others in the group are called acts of "support"; negative acts (categories ten through twelve) directed specifically to others are called acts of "non-support." In this manner interaction is divided into items offered to the group's solution and into positive or negative responses to what is offered.

A summary tabulation of scores for the entire discussion provides two important sets of data; first, the relative number of contributions made by each member, and, second, the exchange of supportive and non-supportive responses between members.

<u>Ordering the Data.</u> These data are ordered in a matrix illustrated in Table 1. The member in the group who is highest in contributions is assigned, as initiator, to the first row of the matrix, and, as recipient, to the first column. Others are assigned to succeeding rows and columns according to the rank order of their contributions. Within matrix cells are placed the rates of support between members. In the illustration, the rate from the most active member to the medium active member is 22.1, and this may be taken to read roughly that the former overtly supports 22 per cent of

---

[3]Robert F. Bales, <u>Interaction Process Analysis</u>, Cambridge, Massachusetts: Addison-Wesley Press, 1950.

Table 1. Illustration of Matrix, Showing Rates of Support According to Rank Order of Contributions

(Experimental Group No. 40; Total Acts: 493)

| As Initiator | As Recipient | | | Rate of Total Support Output |
	Most Active	Medium Active	Least Active	
Most Active	.....	22.1	3.2	15.0
Medium Active	24.2	.....	11.1	20.9
Least Active	.5	1.0	.....	.8
Rate of Total Support Received	24.8	23.0	14.3	.....

the latter's contributions. The rate in the adjacent cell indicates that the most active member supports around three per cent of the least active member's contributions.[4] Rates of total support output

---

[4]More precisely, the rates indicate the preponderance of supportive versus non-supportive acts, for the calculation of the rate of support takes into account both classes of acts. Support is assumed to range from positive (where supportive acts outnumber non-supportive) through zero (where supportive and non-supportive acts are equal) to negative (where non-supportive outnumber supportive acts). Details in the calculation of rates to specific persons in the group and of total output and intake rates are given in the following formulae:
(A) The rate at which member 1 supports member 2 (RS_{12}) is given, for example, by the equation:

$$RS_{12} = 100 \cdot \frac{A_{12} - D_{12}}{B_2 + C_2}$$

Where: A_{12} refers to the frequency of supportive acts initiated by member 1 and directed to member 2.
D_{12} refers to the frequency of non-supportive acts initiated by member 1 and directed to member 2.
B_2 and C_2 combined refer to the frequency of "contributions" (as defined above in the text) initiated by member 2 regardless of the recipients of the acts.
(B) The rate of total support of member 1 ($RTSO_1$) is given by the following equation:

$$RTSO_1 = 100 \cdot \frac{(A_{12} + A_{13} + \ldots A_{1n}) - (D_{12} + D_{13} + \ldots D_{1n})}{(B_2 + B_3 + \ldots B_n) + (C_2 + C_3 + \ldots C_n)}$$

Where the letter symbols have the same meaning in respect to classes of acts as in the equation above, and where the subscripts, as above, indicate the initiator and the recipient in that order. A single subscript indicates that all initiations, regardless of recipient, are included.

are recorded to the right of the matrix; rates of total support intake, below the matrix.

These procedures result in a standardized matrix presenting two components that are taken together as a first approximation to the definition of the power position of a member; first, the relative number of contributions, and second, the relative frequency of support others give to the author of these contributions. It is inferred, in other words, that a high rate of participation coupled with high support intake means that a member is in a relatively strong position, while low participation coupled with a low rate of support means a relatively weak position.

Moreover, for any pair of members, the magnitude of the rates of support are taken as manifestations of the nature of the relationship existing within that pair. Thus in the group illustrated in Table 1, it may be said, tentatively at least, that the two more active members are in a solidary alliance, the most and the least in conflict, and the medium and least active in an unbalanced, non-reciprocal relationship. The most active member is in the strongest power position, the least active, in the weakest.

A matrix, like the one illustrated, is calculated for each session, and these matrices form the base for further steps in ordering the data. In the discussion of central tendencies in the following section, they are combined into a "median matrix," and later on they are split into time segments to show trends from the beginning to the end of the sessions.

FINDINGS

Central Tendencies in Exchange of Support. Taking the sample of forty-eight

---

(C) The rate of total support intake of member 1 ($RSTI_1$) is given by the following equation:

$$RTSI_1 = 100 \cdot \frac{(A_{21} + A_{31} + \ldots A_{n1}) - (D_{21} + D_{31} + \ldots D_{n1})}{B_1 + C_1}$$

Where letter symbols and subscripts have the same reference as in the above equations. Note that the use of the letters corresponds to Bales' designation, op. cit., p. 9.

sessions as a whole, what evidence is there to confirm or to refute Simmel's observation that the elementary differentiating tendency is for the threesome to segregate into a pair and a third party? In order to represent the central tendencies in a simple manner, a median matrix is constructed as follows: rates for all cases in any one cell of the matrix (for example, the cell from the most active to the medium active) are taken to form a single distribution, rates in another cell another distribution, so that for exchange and total rates there are a total of twelve distributions, each with forty-eight cases. The medians of these distributions are recorded in a single matrix, shown in Table 2.

Table 2. Median Rates of Support According to Rank Order of Contributions of Members

(N = 48 cases)

As Initiator	As Recipient			Rate of Total Support Output
	Most Active	Medium Active	Least Active	
Most Active	.....	12.0	7.0	9.7
Medium Active	11.1	.....	3.8	8.9
Least Active	4.0	2.5	.....	3.5
Rate of Total Support Intake	15.2	15.0	12.4	.....

The highest rates of support are those exchanged between the two more active members and the rates are very near the same. Moreover, the frequency distributions, represented here only by the medians, are almost identical in every respect. All other distributions of rates are significantly different from these two. This is to say that as far as exchange of support is concerned, the relationship between these two members is sharply differentiated from the other relationships. The results for this sample confirm Simmel's observation. The two more active members form the pair and the least active member is the relatively isolated third party.

Interdependence of Relationships. The question of interdependence of relationships is examined by holding constant deviations from respective medians in the most active pair and testing the association with deviations in the other two relationships. The classification of support rates above or below respective medians renders four types of relationships in the most active pair which are called: (1) solidary, when both rates are above; (2) conflicting, when both rates are below; (3) dominant, when the more active is below and the lesser active above; and (4) contending, when the former is above and the latter below.

Results of a standard chi-square test for association show that: (1) In the 15 sessions where the most active pair is solidary, there is association: the least active member opposes both members of the pair, and the medium active member reciprocates the opposition (chi-square values are 4.44, which is significant beyond the .05 level). Reciprocation from the most active member is not so regular (chi-square value is 2.28, significant at about the .16 level). (2) In the 13 sessions where the strongest pair is conflicting, there is no association whatsoever. The same is true for the 11 sessions where the relationship is dominant. (3) In the 9 sessions where the relationship is contending, the least active tends to support both other members (chi-squares are 3.56, significant at about the .07 level), but there is no association in rates of support given to him by others.

A comparison of average rates of support in respect to the least active member shows that they are lowest in the solidary pattern (intake: 6.57; output: 0.97) and highest in the contending pattern (16.10 and 6.84), with these latter rates not significantly different from those in the conflict pattern (15.17 and 5.37).

In summary, relationships are both differentiated and interdependent when the general tendency for segregation into a pair and an other becomes accentuated, the solidary pattern being the case in point. Here the least active tends to oppose the pair and the pair tends to reciprocate the opposition. Support to and from the least active is lower in this pattern than in others. However, when the tendency for segregation is reversed, as in the conflict pattern, there is neither differentiation nor interdependence. The least active member may not regularly depend upon support from either of the others and apparently no regular pressures figure in his support of them. His position is indeterminant. With certain exceptions this is the case in the remaining patterns as well.

These results probably mean that Simmel's proposition of intitial segregation is more relevant to the analysis of small group structures than his famous exemplification of _tertius gaudens_, for while the third member fares better when facing a conflict than when facing a solidary bond, he fares no better facing the conflict than he does in other patterns. The important interdependent pattern consists of the solidary pair in reciprocal opposition to the third member.

Tests for the Existence of a Power Structure. Before a pattern of relationships between members may legitimately be called a power structure it is suggested that it possess at least the following characteristics: (1) _internal differentiation in acceptance_; some members must receive more support than others, (2) _interdependence_; the differentiated elements must be related so that a change in one relationship will result in changes in others, (3) _stability of position_ of members within the pattern through time, and (4) _stability of the pattern_ itself through time.

Internal Differentiation and Interdeterminancy. Tests reported in the previous paragraphs show that differentiation is sharpest in the solidary pattern and weakest in the conflicting; that interdetermination is strongest in the solidary, next strongest in the contending, and non-existent in the conflicting and dominant patterns.

Stability of Activity Position. To test the constancy of activity position, the rank order of output of contributions during the first third of the session is compared with the rank order for the final third. Comparisons are made separately for each type of pattern. The probability of remaining in the same rank is tested by the following model:[5] given $\underline{NS}$ as the number of non-shifts in rank order, $\underline{R}$ as the number of ranks (in this case, three), and $\underline{n}$ as the total number of members in all groups of a given type of pattern, then $\underline{p}$ is $1/R$; $\underline{q}$ is $R-1/R$; $\underline{np}$ is the mean number of non-shifts in rank order; and, the variance of non-shifts is npq $(n/n-1)$.

Results show that: (1) Activity positions are most stable in the solidary pattern; the probability of the observed number of non-shifts (34) is less than .01. (2) Activity position is least stable in the conflict pattern; the probability of the observed number of non-shifts (18) is greater than .05. (3) A large number of non-shifts for the most active members in the dominant and contending patterns render the probabilities of the observed number of non-shifts (20 in the dominant and 16 in the contending) less than .05.

In summary, all positions are stable beyond chance expectations in the solidary pattern, all positions unstable in the conflicting pattern, and, in the other types, while the position of the most active is relatively stable, positions of other members fluctuate.

Trends in Support Received. To test stability in this respect, gain or loss of support through time is calculated for positions in each of the four types of patterns.

It is found in the solidary pattern that though there is a considerable change in support rates from the first to the final third of the session, the changes amount to an accentuation of the pattern of support at the beginning of the session. The two or more active members gain in support (9.3 and 14.0 respectively), while the third member loses (−9.3). These

---

[5]The model is derived from the one used for the matching problem by Robert. R. Bush and C. Frederick Mosteller, reported in the chapter, "Selected Quantitative Techniques," in _Handbook of Social Psychology_, Gardner Lindzey, editor (to be published by the Addison-Wesley Press, Inc., Cambridge, Mass.).

trends, combined with the stability of activity position reported above, show that the "coalition" grows stronger through time as the position of the third member becomes weaker.

Again, trends in the conflict pattern are in contrast with the solidary. There is little gain or loss for any position (most active, -1.5; medium, -3.8 and least, 1.8). However, this stability is not only at a low rate but is largely a function of the rapid turnover in activity position, reported above. There is fluctuation in who takes part in the conflict, but the state of conflict remains fairly constant.

In the other two patterns, the most active member gains while the less active members lose; these gains and losses are more pronounced in the contending pattern.

Thus, in most general terms, it is found that fluctuation of activity position is related to either a low rate or a loss of support, and that stability is associated with gain. The striking and important exception to this is the position of the third man in the solidary pattern; he both remains fixed in his position and loses support through time.

Stability of Patterns. Those patterns that maintain themselves throughout the session and toward which others shift are assumed to be stable, as distinguished from those that dissolve quickly and toward which no others shift.

Comparisons of patterns during the first phase with patterns in the third phase show that: (1) Of the 13 sessions with the solidary relationship, 10 remain solidary and three shift each to one of the other types of patterns. (Chi-square, in a test assuming equal likelihood of final pattern, is 15.9 which is significant beyond the .01 level). (2) Of the 19 sessions with the conflict pattern only 8 remain in conflict, while 5 shift to the solidary and 3 each to the other types. (3) Of the 7 with the dominant pattern, 5 shift to the conflicting pattern, and of the 9 sessions with the contending pattern, 4 shift to the conflicting, the others being distributed over the remaining types.

The single stable pattern is the soli-

dary one; next in stability is the conflict pattern. The more transient patterns, the dominant and the contending, tend to shift to the conflicting. Temporally, the solidary and the conflicting patterns seem to be terminal tendencies.

Summary of Findings. Medians of support rates exchanged between three members in a series of 48 problem-solving sessions confirm Simmel's proposition that the primary tendency in the threesome is segregation into a pair and an other: the more active members form the solidary bond and the least active member is isolated. Tests for more detailed structural characteristics show that when this initial tendency is accentuated, there forms a genuine power structure, with internal differentiation, interdependence of relationships between members, stability of activity position, steady trends in receipt of support that are congruent with the initial differentiation, and, finally, stability of the pattern itself. This structure, in its ideal form of one positive relationship and two hostile relationships is called the "true coalition structure." Other patterns have some but not all characteristics of a power structure—when the relationship between the stronger members is non-reciprocal, the pattern lacks temporal stability and when the relationship is conflicting there is rapid turnover in activity position and lack of interdetermination.

In so far as they represent divergent poles toward which groups may develop, the solidary and conflicting patterns seem the more interesting ones. In one direction power relations are structured with a steady maximization of the predictability of how members will act toward one another. In the other direction, there is maximization of uncertainty—uncertainty as to how one person's acts will affect another's, uncertainty as to who will lead and who will follow. In one direction there is differentiation, stability, predictability; in the other, lack of clear form, rapid fluctuation, unpredictability. The central relationship in one is positive, in the other, negative.

DISCUSSION

It has already been said that the findings confirm Simmel's basic point that the threesome tends to break up into a pair and another party. However, they do more than this; they enable us to add several points to his discussion. First, in his analysis of the dyad, Simmel was struck by the possibility of a sense of complete solidarity between the members, and, in progressing to the next larger size group, he assumed, in effect, the existence of this bond. Quite understandably, the added member became important primarily as an intruder or the disturber of this solidarity. It is possible but hardly necessary that fear of the third party accounts for the coalition formation, but, in any case, it seems plausible that once formed the coalition's intensity increases simply because there is a common object of opposition for each member of it. The third party, as scapegoat, as common enemy, or whatever he might be called, may serve to cement the coalition as much as he threatens it.

The second point is in reference to the case of tertius gaudens which Simmel presents as a particular set of circumstances where conflict between two members results in benefit to the third.[6] From the above observations, it is found that though this may have occurred in one or two groups it is not a general tendency. However, the principle does seem involved in the case of the genuine power structure, the true coalition structure. As just stated, there is apparently a secondary gain for the coalition when one member of it opposes the third party. But note that this gain is directly dependent upon the existence of the coalition, for without it, the pattern develops into conflict and fluctuation of positions associated with conflict. This suggests that the principle of tertius gaudens can better be seen as an important dynamic aspect of the true coalition structure than

as a principle underlying a type of structure all its own.

In view of these points, two simple propositions are suggested as additions to Simmel's principle of initial segregation: (1) The development most threatening to the position of any member in the threesome is the solidarity between the other two. (2) The condition most conducive to the intensification of a solidary bond, once formed, is the presence of a common object of opposition.

Another major point of Simmel's may be paraphrased to the effect that the three-person group is inherently unstable.[7] If by unstable, he meant absence of a power structure, the findings are a clear contradiction of his position. If, on the other hand, he meant that in spite of a structure there are always residual strains, the question remains quite open. There is probably a basic incompatibility of interests and gratifications in the threesome, but to contend from this that residual tensions within members will result in a change in group structure is to assume a less rigid structure than shown by the data. Specification of the conditions under which residual tensions within members do result in a change in group structure is an important problem for further research.

Before they are of general use these propositions need further test. In fact, a rather long road of research seems required in order to determine to just what extent the above findings may be generalized either to other laboratory groups or, more important, to groups in less artificial settings, such as the family, the mediation situation, the tri-partite board, the play group, the therapy group, and the like. Not all groups of three are like the ones in this sample, and not all groups of similar composition operate under the same sets of conditions. Meaningful generalizations can be made only after the significant conditions are taken into account. No attempt is made here to carry out this task, even if it could be done with the present knowledge of

[6]Kurt H. Wolff, op. cit., pp. 154-162.

[7]Ibid., pp. 135-136.

groups. Instead, the writer should like to list some of the conditions surrounding the groups in this sample and conclude by posing several questions that should be answered in extrapolating to other three-person situations.

To mention some of the more important and obvious conditions: (1) the groups were <u>short-lived</u>—none lasted longer than two hours; (2) they were of <u>unusual composition</u>—all subjects were adult males, within a narrow age range, from a single and immediate academic community and all in need of part-time work; (3) the groups were of <u>unknown composition</u>—particularly in respect to personalities and admixtures of these in given groups; (4) the groups' <u>internal, functional organization was amorphous</u>; (5) they worked on <u>one task</u> and it was an unusual one; (6) while being observed they were kept <u>immune from most external influences and pressures</u>, other than those they brought with them; and, finally, (7) their performance was <u>divorced from reward and disapproval</u> from outside the group.

The list might be extended, but it is enough to say that unless other groups duplicate these conditions any extension of the findings requires an investigation of the differences in accentuating or counteracting the tendencies observed for this sample. We must ask: (1) in spite of the differences in conditions, do the findings hold? (2) if not, what factors in the new setting account for the negative result? An example in respect to the present findings might be the family where coalitions are commonplace but intensive and continued rejection is rare. What factors not present in the laboratory groups account for this fact? For another example, it is clear that mediation collapses if coalitions <u>do</u> form. Is the hypothesis irrelevant in this case, or are there special, formal provisions that insure a check against "normal" tendencies in the three-party situation? Once these variables are specified, one may in turn ask a further question: (3) how may these variables that either intensify or negate originally observed tendencies be introduced into the group setting in the laboratory so that their effects may be measured?

It is in the light of these subsequent steps that the above findings are presented. They were not predicted, nor are they tests of a body of general theory. They are, however, relevant to Simmel's insights and it is hoped they will lend economy to the small groups researcher.

"Bureaucratic" Elements in Organizations: Some Research Findings

Stanley Udy, Jr.

SOURCE: *American Sociological Review*, Vol. 23, (1958), pp. 418–20.

During the course of a general comparative study of work organization in nonindustrial society, the data under analysis quite unexpectedly yielded a highly consistent pattern of relationships between certain "bureaucratic" organizational characteristics.[1] If these relationships prove to have general validity, they imply a possibly highly fruitful reformulation

---

[1] See the writer's unpublished doctoral dissertation, <u>The Organization of Production in Nonindustrial Culture</u>, Princeton University, 1958.

of the Weberian model of "rational bureaucracy." Therefore they are presented
here, despite the small number of cases
on which they are based and the peripheral, "accidental" nature of the findings.

The analysis is based on 25 examples
of bureaucratic production organizations
in 19 different societies, using data collected from the Human Relations Area
Files, supplemented by additional ethnographic materials. The 25 cases utilized
here represent a portion of a larger
sample of 321 nonindustrial production
organizations, used in the broader study
referred to above. Owing to gaps in the
data, as well as to the fact that bureaucracy is in any case fairly rare in nonindustrial production systems, only 38 of
the original 321 cases could be definitely
classified as bureaucratic according to
criteria which we shall presently discuss. And only 25 of these 38 examples
offered sufficiently complete data on all
relevant points to enable their use in the
present analysis. For these reasons, as
well as those noted above, our conclusions may be regarded as no more than
suggestive.

A production organization is defined
here as any social group oriented to the
combination or transformation of raw
materials into material goods. Such an
organization is designated as bureaucratic if it possesses three or more levels of authority such that all members on
one level are subordinate to one or more
members on the next higher level, and so
on until the topmost level is reached.
This definition departs from conventional
usage in specifying only one, rather than
several, distinguishing characteristics.
Such a procedure involves no assumption
of simultaneous covariation of several
diverse elements, and hence, we believe,
avoids "ideal-type" rigidity. Operationally, production organizations are classified as bureaucratic or otherwise by re-
constructing organization charts from
ethnographic materials and counting the
number of authority levels.

This minimal definition further permits us to treat the presence or absence
of other purported "bureaucratic" at-

tributes as a purely empirical question.
In the present report, we are concerned
with four such frequently cited attributes:
specialized division of labor, segmental
participation of members, "compensatory" rewards, and an emphasis on performance. Division of labor is considered
specialized if three or more qualitatively
different operations are carried on concurrently by different members. Participation of members is deemed segmental
if its terms are defined by some explicit
contractual agreement. Rewards are said
to be compensatory if money or goods in
kind are allocated by higher authority to
members of lower authority in return for
participation. A performance emphasis is
considered to be present if the quantity of
the reward, whether allocated by a compensatory system or otherwise, is expected in any respect whatever to be proportional to the amount of work done, the
amount of effort expended, or both.[2]

The presence or absence of each of
these attributes in each of our 25 cases
had previously been determined from
ethnographic descriptions as part of the
larger project. Initial examination of this
information revealed that not every bureaucratic organization possesses all
four, or even any, of these characteristics. This fact is hardly surprising, especially in view of the type of organizations studied. However, if we arrange
these 25 cases, starting with those possessing all four attributes and proceeding
to those possessing none of them, the resulting array forms a scale, with only
one exceptional case, as indicated by Table 1.

In Table 1, X denotes the presence of
an attribute, and O, its absence. An as-

----

[2] These attributes were adapted from specifications alleged by Max Weber in various parts of his
work to apply to "rational bureaucracy." They are
not, however, necessarily those specifications conventionally cited in this connection, nor are they
intended to exhaust all those given by him. See his
Theory of Social and Economic Organization, New
York: Oxford University Press, 1947, pp. 225-226;
From Max Weber: Essays in Sociology, New York:
Oxford University Press, 1946, pp. 196ff.; General
Economic History, Glencoe, Ill.: Free Press, 1950,
p. 95.

Table 1. Bureaucratic Elements in Twenty-Five Nonindustrial Production Organizations

Society	Activity	Segmental participation	Performance emphasis	Specialization	Compensatory rewards
Navaho[1]	hunting I	X	X	X	X
Navaho[1]	hunting II	X	X	X	X
Paiute[2]	hunting	X	X	X	X
Sanpoil[3]	hunting	X	X	X	X
Lobi[4]	construction I	X	X	X	X
Kabyles[5]	construction I*	O	X	X	X
Betsileo[6]	agriculture	O	O	X	X
Haitians[7]	agriculture	O	O	X	X
Lobi[8]	hunting	O	O	X	X
Kaybles[5]	construction II	O	O	X	X
Solomon Islanders[9]	construction*	O	O	X	X
Bantu (southeast)[10]	agriculture I	O	O	O	X
Bemba[11]	agriculture I	O	O	O	X
Bemba[11]	agriculture II	O	O	O	X
Dahomey[12]	agriculture*	O	O	O	X
Hopi[13]	agriculture	O	O	O	X
Iroquois[14]	agriculture*	O	O	O	X
Muong[15]	fishing	O	O	O	X
Crow[16]	construction	O	O	O	X
Kikuyu[17]	construction	O	O	O	X
Lobi[4]	construction II	O	O	O	X
Bantu (southeast)[18]	agriculture II*	O	O	O	O
Tibetans[19]	agriculture*	O	O	O	O
Basuto[20]	hunting*	O	O	O	O
Samoans[21]	fishing	O	O	X	O

[1]W. W. Hill, The Agricultural and Hunting Methods of the Navaho Indians, New Haven: Yale University Publications in Anthropology, No. 18, 1938, pp. 96-182.

[2]Isabel T. Kelly, Ethnography of the Surprise Valley Paiute, Berkeley: University of California Publications in American Archaeology and Ethnology, 31, 3, 1934, p. 88; Robert H. Lowie, Notes on Shoshonean Ethnography, New York: Anthropological Papers of the American Museum of Natural History, Vol. XX Pt. III, p. 197.

[3]Verne F. Ray, The Sanpoil and Nespelem, Seattle: University of Washington Press, 1933, pp. 77-82.

[4]Henri Labouret, Les Tribus du Rameau Lobi, Paris: Institut d'Ethnologie, 1931, pp. 153-157.

[5]Rene Maunier, La Construction collective de la maison en Kabylie, Paris: Institut d'Ethnologie, 1926, passim.

[6]H. M. DuBois, S. J., Monographie des Betsileo, Paris: Institut d'Ethnologie, 1938, pp. 434-440.

[7]Melville J. Herskovits, Life in a Haitian Valley, New York: Alfred A. Knopf, 1937, pp. 70-75.

[8]Labouret, op. cit., pp. 122-124.

[9]W. G. Ivens, Melanesians of the South-east Solomon Islands, London: Kegan Paul, Trench, Trubner & Co., 1927, pp. 149-154.

[10]I. Schapera and A. J. H. Goodwin, "Work and Wealth," in I. Schapera (editor), The Bantu-speaking Tribes of South Africa, London: Routledge and Kegan Paul, 1950, pp. 151-153, 222ff; D. M. Goodfellow, Principles of Economic Sociology, London: George Routledge and Sons, 1939, p. 242.

[11]Audrey I. Richards, Land, Labour and Diet in Northern Rhodesia, New York: Oxford University Press, 1939, pp. 145-151, 383ff.

[12]Melville J. Herskovits, Dahomey, New York: J. J. Augustin, 1938, pp. 63-77.

[13]Ernest Beaglehole, Notes on Hopi Economic Life, New Haven: Yale University Publications in Anthropology No. 15, 1937, pp. 29-43; C. Daryll Forde, "Hopi Agriculture and Land Ownership," Journal of the Royal Anthropological Institute, 41 (1931), pp. 357-405.

[14]B. H. Quain, "The Iroquois" in Margaret Mead (editor), Cooperation and Competition among Primitive Peoples, New York: McGraw-Hill, 1937, pp. 257-258; Carrie A. Lyford, Iroquois Crafts, Lawrence, Kansas: Haskell Institute, 1945, p. 15.

[15]Jeanne Cuisinier, Les Muong, Paris: Institut d'Ethnologie, 1948, pp. 176-179.

[16]Robert H. Lowie, The Crow Indians, New York: Farrar and Rinehart, 1935, p. 88.

[17]Jomo Kenyatta, Facing Mount Kenya, London: Secker and Warburg, 1937, esp. pp. 76-84.

[18]Audrey I. Richards, Hunger and Work in a Savage Tribe, London: George Routledge and Sons, 1932, p. 146; Goodfellow, op. cit., p. 244.

[19]Sir Charles Bell, The People of Tibet, Oxford: Clarendon Press, 1928.

[20]E. Casalis, Les Bassoutos, Paris: Librairie de Ch. Meyrueis et Cie., 1859, pp. 179-183.

[21]Margaret Mead, "The Samoans" in Mead, op. cit., pp. 242-243.

terisk (*) indicates some ambiguity leading to certain difficulties of classification, the nature of which will be explained presently. Roman numerals indicate either alternative ways of organizing the same activity, or the presence of different organizational forms at different stages of the process. Each entry corresponds to a single instance of work organization reported in the literature; the forms indicated in no sense purport to be exhaustive of all ways in which the activity in question may be carried on in the society concerned.

One of the major difficulties of any comparative institutional analysis of this sort is the problem of classifying concrete examples according to precise abstract criteria where institutionalization is, in reality, quite flexible and diffuse. As explained above, only cases involving what appear to be precise descriptions of the status of the four attributes under analysis were used in the study. But where the data clearly indicate diffuse or uncertain institutionalization of any of the four attributes under study, we have reported the case as "ambiguous." The data themselves are not ambiguous; but institutionalization is reported as being so. The interesting fact in this connection is that none of these ambiguities appear to be inconsistent with the scale suggested by our array. Rather, the question in each instance seems to be the precise point at which the example should appear on the scale. In the case of Kabyle construction I, for example, there is no doubt about the presence of compensatory rewards and specialization. For the majority of positions, there is likewise some emphasis on performance. It appears, however, that in most cases an individual building a house hires a mason under a rather explicit contractual agreement. To this extent, segmental participation is institutionalized, but can hardly be said to be general to the entire organization. Thus in a sense our classification of this case is somewhat arbitrary: compensatory rewards and specialization are present, a performance emphasis is widespread but not univer-

sal, while segmental participation seems to be restricted to one position only. The point is that despite this ambiguity, and regardless of which "cutoff point" one prefers, the case remains consistent with the alleged general model.[3]

Our other ambiguous cases are similar. In construction among the Solomon Islanders, compensatory rewards and specialization are present generally, but a "master builder" is likely to be engaged, with some performance emphasis and segmental participation on his part. Dahomean agriculture may at times involve specialization, in addition to compensatory rewards. Iroquois agriculture does not appear to involve specialization strictly according to our definition, but each person on the authority level next to the top is held responsible for a certain part of the field. In Southeastern Bantu agriculture II (a corvee for the chief), there is some indication that the chief frequently provides a feast for the workers, i.e., a compensatory reward. On the other hand, there appear to be instances where the chief does not do so, but commands the work simply by virtue of his authority. An analogous situation seems to obtain in Tibetan agriculture: a feast is sometimes provided, although in general contributions to the lord of the manor are required by virtue of the latter's authority position.[4] In the Basuto hunting example, distribution of rewards seems not to be compensatory; hunters are required to make contributions to higher authority. Some redistribution may take place, however, and generally does indirectly, in that each hunter is allowed to keep much of his own game.

None of the ambiguities reported, then, is inconsistent with the scale suggested by our array. Although the problem of

---

[3]René Maunier, La Construction collective de la maison en Kabylie, Paris: Institut d'Ethnologie, 1926. Similarly, for the other cases described below, see the references cited in Table 1.

[4]Provision of a feast, however, may extend only to instances of intra-village reciprocity, and thus may belong to a different organizational form from the one reported here. See David MacDonald, The Land of the Lama, London: Seeley Service and Co., 1929, p. 240.

spurious accuracy may remain present in other respects, it is significant that the suggested model does not appear to stand or fall on the question of diffuse institutionalization.

If the pattern suggested by our data is generally valid, it has some far-reaching implications. It suggests, for example, that in order for segmental participation to be institutionalized in any bureaucratic production organization, performance emphasis, specialized division of labor, and compensatory rewards must also be institutionalized. It similarly suggests an order in which different characteristics must be introduced in the course of organizational development under conditions where they cannot be introduced simultaneously, as is often the case in underdeveloped areas.

This pattern is of course in effect a scale, with the response patterns in accord with the criteria for Guttman scaling. At the present stage of research, we merely note this fact. However, there is some indication from our data that the application of scaling techniques in comparative social analysis might provide a means for dealing with diffuse institutionalization without sacrificing theoretical precision—long a major problem in this area of research. Our results further suggest the usefulness of a new ap-

proach to Weber's construct of "rational bureaucracy." Reformulation of this construct along lines similar to those indicated, using more items and proceeding from more cases, might aid in isolating those structural variables most strategic to organizational development, and enable the eventual construction of a tenable scale of organizational characteristics on this basis.[5]

We have already noted certain biases in the selection of our cases. Furthermore, some societies are represented more than once. In addition, it is apparent that our "sample" is not very representative on a cross-cultural basis. Moreover, the fact that the pattern was discovered accidentally, ex post facto, indicates that it might well have occurred by chance. Thus there is no claim of definitive general validity for our results. Despite these methodological shortcomings, we believe that the consistency of the pattern and its possible implications are suggestive and warrant consideration.

[5] Freeman and Winch have already demonstrated the feasibility of this general procedure in broader comparative institutional analysis, using the Guttman technique. See Linton C. Freeman and Robert F. Winch, "Societal Complexity: an Empirical Test of a Typology of Societies," American Journal of Sociology, 62 (March, 1957), pp. 461-466.

The Study of Corruption

Eric L. McKitrick

SOURCE: *Political Science Quarterly*, Vol. 72 (1957), pp. 502–14.

The investigation of corruption (in the analytical sense) does not seem to present a subject of very intense interest to social scientists these days. Past research in this area has for the most part taken its stimulus from a basic commitment to reform, rather than from the in-

trinsic charm of the subject, and most of it has tended to be done during times when a general concern with reform was fairly high. We are not living in such a period today. Actually such periods have been very productive, yielding rich materials in the form of journalism, histories, memoirs of reformers, and treatises on "good government" which, in their very devotion to the overthrow of the "machine" system, could hardly help producing, in the course of things, a number of insights into the nature of that system. Such bursts of energy have, in their turn, even begotten certain idiosyncratic by-products, such as an occasional "apology" for the system, or occasional sympathetic sketches of the more legendary "bosses," showing the genial side of their activities—all of which has not only multiplied the raw data, but has also given them depth.[1]

----

[1]The work which combines all the best in the tradition is, of course, that of Lincoln Steffens: The Shame of the Cities (New York, 1904), and especially the Autobiography (New York, 1951). Early inquiries (more or less theoretical) from a reform viewpoint are Robert C. Brooks, Corruption in American Politics and Life (New York, 1910); John J. Hamilton, Government by Commission: The Dethronement of the City Boss (New York and London, 1911); Frank J. Goodnow, City Government in the United States (New York, 1904); and Frederic C. Howe, The City: The Hope of Democracy (New York, 1906). A more recent summation of early reform efforts is Clifford W. Patton, The Battle for Municipal Reform (Washington, 1940). That "muck-raking" itself is not quite dead, even today, is evident in Estes Kefauver's Crime in America (Garden City, 1951). The machine, on the other hand, had its literary apologists as early as the 1890s; Daniel Greenleaf Thompson, Politics in a Democracy (New York, 1898); Alfred Henry Lewis, Richard Croker (New York, 1901) and The Boss (New York, 1903). Material on Tammany Hall is very rich. It includes Denis Tilden Lynch, "Boss" Tweed (New York and London, 1927) and The Wild Seventies (New York and London, 1941); M. R. Werner, Tammany Hall (New York, 1928); Roy V. Peel, The Political Clubs of New York City (New York and London, 1935); William L. Riordon, Plunkitt of Tammany Hall (New York, 1948); and especially Lothrop Stoddard's fascinating Master of Manhattan: The Life of Richard Croker (New York and Toronto, 1931). A number of active reformers have left us their memoirs. Outstanding among them are Brand Whitlock, Forty Years of It (New York, 1914); Fremont Older, My Own Story (San Francisco, 1919); Tom L. Johnson, My Story (New York, 1911); and Carter Harrison, Stormy Years (Indianapolis and New York, 1935). An attempt to deal "scientifically" with city politics is Harold F. Gosnell, Machine Politics: Chicago Model (Chicago, 1937); also in this vein is Sonya Forthal, Cogwheels of Democracy: A Study of the Precinct Captain (New York, 1946). More humane, and consequently more illuminating, is John T. Salter, Boss Rule: Portraits in City Politics (New York and London, 1935).

It may be regrettable—in the interest of sustained energy—that the moral tensions which formerly served to foster such investigation are at present so noticeably relaxed. But, on the other hand, there may also be reason to think that this very relaxed emotional climate itself offers a peculiarly promising setting in which future work might take a new and fruitful turn. In this setting, we are now able to recognize that further "reform" activity, for its own sake, will probably yield us very little that we do not already have in the way of insights; it is difficult, for instance, to mistake the indiscriminate Kefauver diggings for much that resembles "knowledge." Moreover, in this setting, we have perceived that, amid the conflicting claims of a disorderly democratic political society, the corrupt machine system has historically performed certain stabilizing functions: it was David Riesman who referred to the local politician as "soaked in gravy which we can well afford." And finally, it is in this same setting of detachment that we are free to appreciate the attributes of that remarkable technician—and gentleman—DeSapio of Tammany Hall. These, at any rate, are a few of the straws in the wind.[2]

What we ought to see in the future—assuming a picking-up of interest—will be various studies in which political machines and their auxiliary activities are examined in a structural and functional way: that is, in terms of such questions as, what have they done for society—how do they work—what gaps have they filled in our political life—what has been needed to maintain them—what are the limits within which they have had to operate—what sort of future may be expected for them?

The closest approach to a theoretical model for dealing with such questions has been that offered by Robert K. Merton in his Social Theory and Social Structure,[3] and no new investigation could very well afford not to take this model as its start-

----

[2] Another such "straw," surely, is the immense popularity of Edwin O'Connor's novel, The Last Hurrah (Boston, 1956).

[3] Glencoe, Ill., 1949. See pp. 71-81.

ing point. So far as I know, very little, if anything, has been done with it. I am not even sure that it has been subjected to critical examination.

An important thing to note with regard to the Merton scheme is that it seems to have been postulated for what might be called a "classical" period in the history of American machine politics. The most perceptive field work ever done in this area is still probably that of Lincoln Steffens—and since it is from Steffens that Mr. Merton has taken his major cues, it is inevitable that the balance and arrangement of his categories should be most appropriate to a state of things which existed about fifty years ago: a period roughly centering on the year 1905.

This is not meant to intimate that the model does not apply today. It is valid and accurate in all its major details. It is so set up that any alterations in it would have to be more in the nature of refinements than of basic changes. But the subject matter itself has changed in a great many ways since Steffens' time, and I emphasize this in order to make my key point. In the absence of outside stimuli—such as a general public interest in "reform" (or, for that matter, a primary <u>need</u> for reform)—pressure for new work and new insights will have to come from somewhere within the social sciences, and, specifically, I would say that it will have to come from the field of American history. Its raw data will be found in the form of substantial materials which must now be called "historical": material covering the period in which our cities underwent their most phenomenal phases of growth—material which dates back at least to the end of the Civil War. Any theoretical model for the explanation of social phenomena has a tendency, in spite of all precautions, to be static. But if there is anything about our social scene that is insistently dynamic, it is the tempo of our political life—and to get the sense of dynamism in political structures (that is, <u>change</u>, and the things that produce it), one needs the sense of time. We know a great deal about the functions of such structures at given points in time. But of equal, if not greater, importance to political sociology today is the course of transformation which these structures—these "machines"—have undergone over the past two generations. This is now what makes "history" such a vital dimension. An understanding of such change, and of the reasons for it, is bound to "feed back" into one's understanding and judgment of the very functions themselves.

What are—or have been—these "functions"? To repeat, they have been no better itemized than by Mr. Merton, and probably the best way to set up points of reference for the present discussion would be to recapitulate very briefly the principal elements of his model.

A "structural context" is first established: a general setting or environment in which, for one reason or another, the "need" for such an establishment as the political machine has arisen. The principal element in this environment is the diffusion and fragmentation of power— and therefore of responsibility—which tends to be inherent in a transitory, non-authoritarian, elected, democratic officialdom. It is easy to see how this could emerge as a critical limitation in the mushrooming cities of the United States during the seventies, eighties and nineties, amid an urban life proliferating in complexity and tangled with a bewildering maze of conflicting needs and claims. Here an alternative, informal focus of responsibility was located in the "boss," a leader of unofficial executive status who had a freedom and flexibility made possible by his ability to work, as it were, in the back room. Another element in this context—if I myself may add one —would be the fact that any organization of a political nature which did have the power and numbers to furnish these needs and umpire these claims was bound to have no more than a semiprofessional status. Such an organization, constantly requiring money to keep itself going, would have to derive a certain amount of it from sources no more than quasi-official in nature. All this would follow in the absence of centralized, professionalized, bureaucratic tradition of administration.[4]

In this setting, Mr. Merton enumerates four of the major "latent functions" which have been performed by the machine system, in relation to the various subgroups making up its constituency. The first of these functions involves various kinds of welfare services for the poor and powerless; such services would include the widest range of things—farm jobs, intercession with the law in times of difficulty, and so forth. Their price, quite logically, would be votes. Another set of functions appears in response to some of the manifold and perennial problems of business men—such problems as the need of smaller business men for protection against each other, the occasional need for larger business men to have cumbersome and expensive projects expedited, and the constant need of all classes of business men for unofficial protection against a snarl of contradictory and overlapping terms, codes and regulations. The prices here, graded as they would be according to the services, add up to "routine graft"—the "oil" that keeps the machine in running order. A third type of function is one which requires a certain conceptual subtlety to recognize. For certain critical ethnic groups, and for groups situated in lower social brackets generally, the large urban political machine has traditionally afforded very important channels of social mobility—avenues to personal advancement—which would doubtless otherwise be closed.[5]

For example, the availability of careers in politics served as a significant

safety valve for the surplus social energies of the New York Irish from the 1870's on. The price which these groups were asked to pay was, from their viewpoint, hardly excessive: unstinting party loyalty—unquestioning devotion to the organization. A final category of functions is one in which services analogous to those performed for "legitimate" business were also made available to the underworld—to "illegitimate" business. Here the machine could actually operate as a kind of stabilizing mechanism: by maintaining communication—and actual connections—with the underworld, it could act as an umpire for activities carried on outside the law; it maintained, in effect, a measure of control; it could set standards and define limits. The price, of course, was the familiar "protection money"—the kickback.

Such, then, is the pattern. To what extent does it hold today? It is a pattern whose formal outlines are still in some way to be recognized in all our major cities. However, the specific activities and operations represented by these formal categories have been so immeasurably altered and transformed as to change the very symmetry of the pattern, and to raise certain very crucial questions. Has the old system for practical purposes (as some writers have begun to assert) really "broken down"? Or does it continue to operate within a more limited area? What has been the effect of the reform tradition? Has the boss "gone straight"? What kind of loyalties can the machine command today? What kinds of things can it still do—and are there things that it can no longer do?

Certain kinds of historical problems immediately suggest themselves—problems having to do with the persistence of the "corrupt machine." For instance: under what conditions has it been possible for a reform movement to be successful? We find that it has never quite been a matter of civic affairs reaching a given point of "rottenness," with the honest citizens at that point making common cause to strike down the machine. What seems to have been required, as a matter

---

[4]Max Weber, acutely sensitized to bureaucracy and its implications, was very impressed by the responsibility of the American "boss," recognizing that in him and in his organization lay the natural functional substitute for bureaucracy in a growing democratic political culture. See "Politics as a Vocation," in From Max Weber: Essays in Sociology, translated and edited by H. H. Gerth and C. Wright Mills (New York, 1945), pp. 108-111.

[5]The significance of this function may be confused unless an important analytical distinction is made. It should be thought of in terms, not of the "number" of careers it provides for these groups at large, but rather of a critical ratio of outlets for the potential leadership among such groups.

of historical experience, is the combining of other factors, fairly complex and not always easy to identify. Such factors include points at which the machine has ceased to serve its clients responsibly—points at which services could no longer be considered worth the prices asked. The arrival of hard times could quickly precipitate such a situation. An even more sensitive point could be the one at which (for whatever reason) the machine's internal solidarity had become weakened—because of power struggles, some temporary loss of internal responsibility, perhaps a weakening of loyalties resulting from inequitable distribution of spoils. Variations on these themes will be found, if one is looking for them, recurring again and again in the literature. They are admirably spelled out in the downfall of the Tweed machine. Here we see the Boss having lost all bearings, all sense of proportion, launching a series of insane depredations, and alienating his followers by refusing to distribute the loot honorably. The Ring had become virtually a personal operation, with Tweed's raids upon the city treasury far exceeding what could reasonably be afforded. Here, moreover, we see the critical increment of reform energy coming from within: Samuel Tilden's success was in large measure due to strategic assistance from the Tammany organization, and to the invaluable inside knowledge which was the product of having himself worked, for years, with Tammany Hall.

A situation of this sort may undoubtedly be matched by numerous others—and, in fact, by still others turned, as it were, inside out. For, conversely, it may be assumed that a reform government which offers nothing as a substitute for the functions performed by the machine will find itself very shortly in a state of paralysis. The mayorality of Seth Low in New York in the early 1900s furnishes such a case; another is found in the efforts of Joseph Folk to "reform" St. Louis in 1902; and numerous others may be located all through the reform annals of the Progressive Era.

Such might be called the "functional" approach on the simplest and most

straightforward plane. But it leads into parallel problems of even greater interest and greater subtlety. Take this question: what is the function of the reform movement—not for destroying the machine but for reinvigorating it, for renewing its vitality, for helping it to persist? At this point the "machine" metaphor itself becomes misleading. It has in no case, apparently, been a thing that could be smashed in the way that an engine can be rendered useless by the destruction of a few key parts. Rather, its very complexity, the very functional autonomy of so many of its parts, makes it more like an organism. For instance, solidarity at the ward level seems to persist almost by habit: Plunkitt of Tammany Hall—then a ward leader—survived the destruction of Tweed and flourished, and his experience must have been reënacted by many another in comparable circumstances. How might this be explained?

Taking this situation as the focal point for a whole range of problems, one might attempt to picture the scene at local headquarters the day after an election in which smashing victories had been won by the reform ticket. One may picture the post-mortem (a proceeding built into American politics); it would most surely include a highly critical reappraisal of the power situation in the ward—and those present would be the first to understand why the organization had lost. A further result would compare very closely with Durkheim's analysis of what happens at funerals: a ritual reaffirmation of group solidarity. Still another consequence would be that the demands normally made on the machine would (in view of lean times to come) tend to drop off. Therefore—assuming that the lean period did not last too long—it might be predicted that the aftermath of defeat would coincide with precisely that phase of the machine's greatest moral solidarity.[6] Some highly interesting conclusions

---

[6] I have been told that some of the Wallace groups reached the high point of their solidarity about a month after the 1948 election. After this high point—with nothing to look forward to—the groups tended to disintegrate.

might be expected to flow from this. Granting any other functions remaining for the machine to perform—and by definition they always exist—might not these be precisely the conditions in which they would be discovered? A crude example is afforded by the breakup of the Whisky Ring in Grant's time; the "army of termites" (as Matthew Josephson put it) promptly marched into the Post Office Department. Or, let the setting be a little less extreme and more refined: such conditions as those just described might simply serve as a test for activities whose style must be altered from time to time in order to remain acceptable. Boss Kelly of Chicago, according to legend, was always pleased to have Paul Douglas somewhere on the scene; his use of Douglas was as a standing threat to "any of the boys who got too hungry." A final point to be made along these lines is that the very informal nature of the machine will set limits at any time upon its stability—which would mean that its internal leadership must remain aggressive and dynamic to keep from being unhorsed by disaffected henchmen. The most natural alliance that an insurgent group could reach for would be an alliance with reformers. Other factions standing by could then, like Lord Stanley on Bosworth field, take their choice. The machine, in other words, has been anything but a torpid institution: a perennial state of internal "yeastiness" has made it a dynamic one.

Another set of problems, in which historical analysis and the use of historical materials are indispensable, would have to do with long-term changes in the entire system of machine rule. Here the reform tradition must be given its due in another way, for the very process of evolution in civic politics has been accompanied by reform groups taking up the slack and calling the turn as change occurs. The city manager and city commission plans never quite produced—in themselves—the effects hoped for by their early exponents, but they may still be considered as symptoms of a long-term process whose tendency has been toward ever-continued extension, ration-

alization and stabilization of official administrative agencies. Probably the most specific and most important single expression of this has been the extension of civil service into municipal government. Today, for example, a considerable sector of Tammany's former patronage preserves in New York City is blanketed by a very efficient system of civil service.

The notion of evolutionary change could be carried directly into the specific functions enumerated in Mr. Merton's conceptual scheme. Upon the welfare functions, for instance, time has unquestionably left its mark. Here, a considerable number of the services once performed for unassimilated immigrant groups and for the economically underprivileged are today no longer needed. The need has been eroded away by the assimilation process itself, by the development of scientific welfare on municipal and state-federal levels, and, most especially, by a relatively long period of full-employment capitalism. The result has been mobility, a constant turnover of population in urban areas—all of which has been deeply subversive of neighborhood solidarity.[7] Or, take those functions performed for legitimate business. If it is kept in mind that the protection, the controls, and the umpiring have been "unofficial," as opposed to "official," there can be little doubt as to which direction the curve has gone over time, since one of the most dramatic features of our political history since 1933 has been the extension of official public controls into every aspect of business and over all kinds of businesses. Such change is, of course, anything but absolute; the old pattern, in some form, is still there. I am only indicating what the time dimension has been doing to it.

The most fascinating changes ·of all, and by far the most complex and difficult to trace down, are those connected with Mr. Merton's other two functions—the

---

[7]Some present-day consequences of this mobility are discussed in G. Edward Janosik, "Suburban Balance of Power," American Quarterly, VII, 123-141 (Summer 1955); and Harvey Wheeler, "Yesterday's Robin Hood," American Quarterly, VII, 332-344 (Winter 1955).

functions involving social mobility and relationships with the underworld. One of the most remarkable of recent discoveries in the social sciences has been the manner in which these two areas are related—the manner in which (whether the political machine is directly involved or not) they grade into one another. Somewhere along the way a conceptual block has been removed, and we are now able to see that not only do the values of mobility, status and respectability operate in the underworld in a way precisely analogous to their workings in the "upperworld," but also, that the extent to which the two worlds overlap in shared values is considerable. All of this furnishes us a final set of problems directly related to those already touched upon.

In drawing a pattern of corruption (loosely used here as a generic term covering a wide variety of things) might it not be possible to trace not only the obvious shifts and transformations but also a pattern of energy? What happens when obstacles are placed in a particular area of corruption? Is the result an alternative pattern? Perhaps—but what about the stabilization of existing patterns? The same question could be put in another way—in terms of the social-mobility function (either in politics or the underworld) for socially deprived ethnic groups. Is there a possible correlation between the rise to social acceptability and the stabilization of particular forms of corruption in which members of these groups have specialized? Might not the very high value which American society at large sets upon mobility serve over time as a built-in check—as a stimulus for (say) "cleaning up" the rackets?[8] This surely goes back at least to the days of Plunkitt—he was the man who made the virtuous distinction between "honest" and "dishonest" graft.[9]

The Italian community of a generation ago may provide the clue to the way the mechanism works. Assume at the outset a series of status gradations all the way up through narcotics, prostitution, and ultimately gambling—and in which the gamblers would be, as it were, the "gentlemen." Costello would handle the gambling, Luciano the girls and dope. Now what has, in fact, happened between then and today? As the entire Italian community was moved up, the higher-status brackets of the underworld have apparently come under tremendous crowding and pressure (gambling at large having become almost respectable), whereas the lower grades have been vacated to unorganized riffraff. No one of comparable prestige has arisen to fill the shoes of Lucky Luciano, and probably no one will. Moving up, then, into politics, we see the New York civic scene today liberally dotted with substantial citizens of Italian origin.[10] Indeed, it appears that the same mechanism just described (simple mobility—with or without an

---

[8] A real landmark of analysis in this area, one whose importance cannot be too much emphasized, is Daniel Bell's brilliant essay, "Crime as an American Way of Life", Antioch Review, XIII, 131-154 (Summer 1953).

[9] There have, of course, been exceptions, but it appears that city bosses (who have by definition "risen to the top") have in general tended to be men

who were fairly honest personally, and who remained aloof from police corruption (the "shaking down) of disorderly houses and other illegal enterprises"), even while tolerating it among their vassals. Such activity was considered dirty and disreputable, and beneath their personal dignity. "Honest graft", on the other hand (business dealings to which the city was a party, and in which the politician, as business man, had advantages of prior knowledge), was on a considerably higher moral plane. See Riordon, Plunkitt, pp. 3-8. For a comparative survey in standards of honesty—standards surprisingly high—see Harold Zink, City Bosses in the United States (Durham, 1930).

[10] Throughout William Foote Whyte's Street Corner Society (enlarged ed., Chicago, 1955) are examples of how the universally coercive values of respectability and the drive for status and success operated among the Italian community both in the rackets and in politics, as well as elsewhere. Especially illuminating is Mr. Whyte's story of how a leading racketeer of "Cornerville" forbade his son to play with the riffraff of the neighborhood, and how gratified he himself was to associate with a Harvard professor—until he discovered the "professor" hanging out with the street-corner and poolroom crowd. Very perceptive observations on the social, political and geographical mobility of the Italian community are also to be found in chapter 4 ("The Frontier Reappears") of Samuel Lubell's The Future of American Politics (New York, 1952), pp. 62-80.

"ethnic" dimension) has been at work within Tammany Hall itself. One of Mr. DeSapio's current problems seems to be the presence of significant numbers of liberal, civic-conscious young people working in the local clubs simply for the fun of it. The "Boss" is not finding it easy to give away what patronage he has, since the very people to be rewarded are turning out to be better placed elsewhere, in business and in the professions.[11]

Let me now return to my original point. I would like to repeat my belief that those studies which can most appropriately embrace the kinds of questions I have raised will come more and more to have a historical framework. An excellent type of investigation, simple in format but with the flexibility needed for moving into any number of related areas, would be the life-study of a machine. Here, with the historical dimension, one could get the very crucial sense of a cy-cle. For cycles are long, and they embrace much change. One might further predict that the historian to whom this kind of project will be of interest will tend more and more to come into it equipped with analytical tools which he has appropriated from elsewhere but domesticated for his own special requirements. They may not ease his task, but they will make him sensitive to a whole range of vital connections which, admittedly, past historical studies (and many "scientific" ones as well) have left untouched.[12]

I cannot resist a final question. Is the machine headed for extinction? Is it getting "cleaner and cleaner"? Conceivably not—not necessarily. New predictions could very well center on a new mobility-cycle for ethnic groups still not yet "arrived"; and this might involve a period of renewed machine activity in which the tone of politics could once more drop quite noticeably. For instance, what might happen when municipal patronage and civil service jobs are no longer attractive to (say) bright young Jewish and Italian lawyers—no longer within their dignity? One clear sign of rising mobility among Negro and Puerto Rican groups would be the appearance of substantial numbers of them in minor political leadership roles. Along with it would come, of course, a great deal of tension as such groups increased in power and numbers, and the first phase would probably not be attractive in its quality and style. We might expect, moreover, that the very same liberal, socially conscious groups now urging a "fair shake" for our minorities may themselves soon be embarking on new reform crusades without quite realizing what was happening. It has all happened in the past.

But what would be happening? It would be the same process of assimilation and socialization, the same "mobility-cycle" (though they did not call it that) which was undergone by the Irish after the Civil War, and after them the Jews and Italians. It is a process full of corruption and full of vitality. What we know about those groups may well give us the clues we need for plotting what is still to come.

---

[11]See Robert L. Heilbroner, "Carmine G. De-Sapio: The Smile on the Face of the Tiger," *Harper's Magazine*, July 1954, pp. 23-33.

[12]Since the above was written, an excellent and illuminating monograph, conceived along these very lines, has come to my attention. It is A. Theodore

Brown's "The Politics of Reform: Kansas City's Municipal Government 1925-1950" (Ph.D. Thesis, University of Chicago, 1956).

Social Status in Jury Deliberations*

Fred L. Strodtbeck, Rita M. James, and Charles Hawkins

SOURCE: *American Sociological Review*, Vol. 22 (1957), pp. 713–19.

Occupational specialization has two distinguishable effects. First, it increases productivity and, second, it provides the basis for a status hierarchy. It is less commonplace to think of role differentiation in face to face groups as arising from a similar economic process and resulting in similar status differences. For groups to define and achieve their goals, they must control the use of their primary group resource, their common time together. Only one, or, at most, a few persons can talk at any given instant and be understood. Who talks and how much he talks is, within limits, determined by the reactions of the remainder of the group to the speaker. Acts that are perceived as relevant to the solution of the group's problems are generally favorably received and the responsible speaker is encouraged to continue. Over the long run participation tends to become differentiated with a small fraction of the group's members accounting for most of the participation.

For the purposes of the present study into the relationships between occupation and selected aspects of role differentiation, it is desirable that the focus of the small group discussion not be that narrowly circumscribed by status prerogatives. For example, a group of officers and enlisted men discussing military problems or a group of doctors and nurses discussing a medical problem would not provide the circumstance we require. A greater presumption of equality is desired.

In the jury situation there is not only the wide-spread norm that group members should act toward one another as equals but also the reinforcement of the presumption of equality by the requirement that the verdict be unanimous. Equal and responsible participation in the deliberation is an institutionalized expectation. Therefore, if there is evidence that the status differences of the larger community become manifest in the deliberation, then it may be expected that a similar generalization of status will be found in other interactional contexts where hierarchical considerations are more prominent.

It is essential for our study that wide background differences be present within the juror population. This is assured by the fact that in metropolitan areas such as Chicago, St. Louis, and Minneapolis where our experimental jury research has been conducted, jurors are selected by a random process from voting registration lists. The resultant jury pool population compares closely with the expected population computed from census reports, although there are several known sources of bias. Lawyers, doctors, teachers, policemen and other local and federal employees, including elected officials, are excused from jury service. Aliens, foreign visitors, recent migrants and persons under 21, who are not eligible to vote, do not appear on the jury lists. Finally, men who operate "one

*A report of the experimental jury investigation conducted as part of the Law and Behavioral Science Project with funds granted by the Ford Foundation at the Law School, The University of Chicago.

Lee H. Hook and Dathleen Beaufait, current staff members, and Margaret R. McDonald, Leo Lynch, and Noreen Haygood, former staff members, are appreciatively acknowledged for their contribution toward the accumulation of the data on which this report is based.

man" businesses and prospective jurors with pressing personal problems can ordinarily have their jury service deferred or cancelled. The net effect is that the professions and the very low education and occupation groups are slightly underrepresented.

Occupations are classified in four groups: proprietors, clerical, skilled and labor. "Proprietor" includes the census category[1] of Proprietors, Managers and Officials as well as professionals such as architects, accountants, and engineers who are not excluded from service. "Clerical" and "skilled" categories correspond to the census categories and "labor" subsumes the census categories semi-skilled workers, non-farm laborers and servant classes. Farm owners and laborers are absent from our populations, and retired persons have been classified by their occupations prior to retirement. Women are classified by their stated occupations, except that housewives are classified by their husbands' occupations.

Previous studies indicate that power and participation in face to face situations are related to status. Caudill[2] observed the daily exchange of information at administrative conferences among the staff of a small psychiatric hospital and found that the relative participation by the director of the service, the residents, the head nurse, the nurses and the occupational therapist were ordered by their statuses in the hospital even though the lower status persons ordinarily spent more time with the patients. Torrance[3] used nonmilitary problems but found that pilots, navigators, and gunners recognized a power hierarchy in the contrived situation which paralleled that ordinarily

in effect in airship operation. Strodtbeck[4] demonstrated that the greater economic and religious power of Navaho in contrast with Mormon women was reflected in their greater power in husband-wife decision-making. More pertinent, perhaps, is a study[5] relating to the continuation in jury deliberations of a strong emphasis by women on expressive and integrative acts. The components that had been found descriptive of women's roles in family interaction situations were found to characterize women's roles in jury deliberations.

It is important to stress that while the related studies are consistent insofar as they suggest a parallel between generalized status and status in face to face systems, they do not provide a firm basis for generalizing to the situation at hand, at least in terms of the measure of correspondence. In Torrance's experiment the pilots probably dominated to a lesser degree in the experimental situation than they would have when the airship was in operation. Thus, while the ordering was preserved, it was undoubtedly attenuated. In the present case, what differences are to be expected? Relations between roles like pilot-gunner and clerical worker-laborer are not equally clear in the interaction differences they imply. There is no compelling reason to believe that clerical workers and laborers will have had sufficient experience together to evolve a stable pecking order. Further, once jurors have completed their deliberations, there is no expectation of continued relations that would provide opportunity for external status differences to become manifest. If status differences are present in the jury room, it is almost certain that they arise in part because the varied requirements of the deliberation re-create within the jury the need for the differential experiences associated with status. Whether or not

---

[1] Alba M. Edwards, *Bureau of the Census Alphabetical Index of Occupations by Industries and Social-Economic Groups*, Washington, D. C.: U. S. Department of Commerce, 1937.

[2] William Caudill, *The Psychiatric Hospital as a Small Society*, Cambridge: Harvard University Press, 1957.

[3] E. P. Torrance, "Some Consequences of Power Differences on Decision Making in Permanent and Temporary Three-Man Groups," *Research Studies*, Pullman: State College of Washington, 1954, 22, pp. 130-140.

[4] F. L. Strodtbeck, "Husband-Wife Interaction Over Revealed Differences," *American Sociological Review*, 16 (August, 1951), pp. 141-145.

[5] F. L. Strodtbeck and R. D. Mann, "Sex Role Differentiation in Jury Deliberations," *Sociometry*, 19 (March, 1956), pp. 3-11.

the determinants from the external system are great enough to become apparent in a one to two hour deliberation is the empirical question we seek to answer.

SOURCE OF DATA

Mock jury deliberations were conducted in which the participants were jurors drawn by lot from the regular jury pools of the Chicago and St. Louis courts. The jurors listened to a recorded trial, deliberated, and returned their verdict—all under the customary discipline of bailiffs of the court. The jury deliberations were recorded, fully transcribed, and scored in terms of interaction process categories.

This paper is based primarily upon 49 deliberations for which interaction process analysis has been carried out. Although further work is in process on more than 100 additional deliberations which have been collected by the project during the past three years, the present report is final in that further interaction process analysis of the type here reported is not contemplated. Two civil trials were used as the basis for the deliberations. In the first (29 deliberations), the plaintiff, a secretary, seeks compensation for injuries incurred in a two-car collision, and in the second (20 deliberations), a young child seeks compensation for facial disfigurement incurred in a fire alleged to have been caused by a defective vaporizer. A total of 49 x 12, or 588 different jurors were involved. Data on 14 vaporizer cases and 28 recent experimental trials are utilized in other portions of the paper. In total, data from 91 juries are used in the examination of different status effects.

SELECTING A FOREMAN

After the jury listened to the case, they were told to select their foreman and begin their deliberation. In more than half of the deliberations, the foreman was nominated by one member and then quickly accepted by the remainder of the group. In about a third of the deliberations the man who opened the discussion

Table 1
Occupational Status of 49 Jury
Foremen

Occupation	Expected*	Observed	Index
Proprietor	9.73	18	185
Clerical	15.03	15	100
Skilled	9.56	8	84
Labor	14.68	8	54

*Computed under assumption that foremen will be proportional to portion of sample in the given occupation.

and sought either to nominate another, or to focus the group's attention on their responsiblity to select a foreman, was himself selected foreman. However, in all instances the selection of a foreman was quickly and apparently casually accomplished. There was no instance in which mention of any socio-economic criteria was made, but this is not to say that socio-economic criteria were not involved. For example, Table 1 shows that some foremen were selected from all strata, but the incidence was three and a half times as great among proprietors as among laborers. In addition, although the details are not given in the table, tabulation shows that only one-fifth as many women were made foreman as would be expected by chance.

RELATIVE PARTICIPATION

The deliberations were recorded with two microphones to facilitate binaural identification of individual participants. The protocols were fully transcribed, and from the protocol each speaker's contributions were unitized into discrete acts. These acts are roughly the equivalent of a simple declarative sentence. Identification of the speaker was checked with the original observer's notes and scoring was done by an assistant with the aid of the recording plus indications of nonverbal gestures made by the original observer.

Since there are 12 persons in the jury, one-twelfth or 8 1/3 per cent, of the total acts is the pro rata percentage for each juror's acts. This provides the base-line against which the effects of external status may be appraised. The

Table 2
Percentage Rates of Participation in
Jury Deliberation by Occupation and
Sex of Juror

| Sex | Occupation | | | | |
	Proprietor	Clerical	Skilled	Laborer	Combined
Male	12.9	10.8	7.9	7.5	9.6
	(81)	(81)	(80)	(107)	(349)
Female	9.1	7.8	4.8	4.6	6.6
	(31)	(92)	(28)	(62)	(213)
Combined	11.8	9.2	7.1	6.4	8.5
	(112)	(173)	(108)	(169)	(562)*

*Numbers of jurors are shown in parentheses. Twenty-six of 588 jurors from the 49 juries used were not satisfactorily classified by occupation and are omitted.

higher the average participation of an occupational group, the greater their relative share of the common resource of time. It may be seen in Table 2 that in all occupations males talked more than females and the amount of participation was sharply differentiated between higher than expected values for proprietors and clerical workers and lower than expected values for skilled and unskilled laborers.

While the moderately differing values in Table 2 are averages based upon the scores of more than 500 persons, within any particular deliberation there was a very steep differentiation between the most- and least-speaking jurors. For example, in 82 per cent of the juries the top three participators account for one-half or more of the total acts with the remainder distributed among the other nine members. It is to be emphasized that the averages of Table 2 are descriptive of the relative participation of the occupation and sex groups, but do not reflect the wide variation within a jury.

One of the sources of differences in participation within the jury may be attributed to the election of one member to play the role of foreman. The foreman was responsible for approximately one-fourth of the total acts, and as previously shown, was more frequently selected from the higher status groups, but when foreman scores were eliminated the average participation values were as follows: proprietor, 8.9; clerical, 7.0 skilled, 6,3; labor, 5.9. The gap between clerical and skilled workers is narrower but the rank order is unchanged.[6]

The latent premise in the study of participation is that high participation indicates greater ability to influence others in keeping with the actor's goals. Earlier research supports such an interpretation for ad hoc problem-solving groups and for families. Further evidence is available from the present research. Jurors were asked before the deliberation what, if anything, they would award the plaintiff. A detailed examination of pre-deliberation awards of the individual juror with the subsequent group awards in 29 deliberations reveals that the more active jurors shifted their pre-deliberation positions less than less active jurors in the process of agreeing with the group verdict.[7] This interpretation of the relation between participation and influence or status level may be documented by comparing the average pre-deliberation award by occupational group with the jury verdict. The correlations are as follows: proprietor .50, (P < .05); clerical .11; skilled .29; labor

[6]A further check was made on the effects of being on a jury with differing numbers of one's own occupation group. For juries in which at least two of each occupational group are present, the values are quite similar to Table 2, and while there is some tendency for higher status persons to talk more when they are alone, or in a marked minority, further corrections have minor effects.

[7]Allen Barton, "Persuasion and Compromise in Damage Awards," December, 1956. Unpublished ms.

.02. Members from the same occupational group sometimes initially favored different verdicts, and in this case not all the members of this group achieved their desired outcome. Nonetheless, the proprietors showed a significant correlation between their average and the jury verdicts. This result, which separates proprietors from other occupations, corresponds to the participation values after they have been corrected by eliminating the foreman. Since our content analyses clearly show that foremen were more neutral in the discussion of how much money to award the plaintiff than other high participating jurors, the corrected participation values are probably a more satisfactory measure of influence in the damage award discussion.

The meaning of levels of participation may be viewed from still another perspective. After the deliberation, the jurors were asked to answer a battery of questions reporting their personal satisfaction with the quality of the deliberation and the tone of interpersonal relations. The level of an individual's satisfaction was positively correlated with the level of his own participation (r=.52, P < .05). The involvement that high participation represents in the jury is not unlike the investment in the affairs of the larger community by higher status persons; both are instruments for group-derived satisfactions.

As a further commentary upon the interpretation of participation levels, responses to the post-deliberation question, "Who do you believe contributed most to helping your group reach its decision?" were tabulated by occupation of the target person. The average number of helpfulness votes received by occupation groups (see Table 3) closely parallels the participation by occupation groups (see Table 2). The correlation between votes received and participation is about .69 when sets of individual values are correlated. Male clerical workers get slightly fewer votes than their participation would appear to warrant and male skilled workers net slightly more, but the overwhelming impression is that votes received as a helpful juror, like participation, influence, and satisfaction parallels status differentiation in the larger society.

PERCEIVED FITNESS AS JURORS

Where is the quality of justice to be found? The Courts Martial reform, which permitted enlisted men to request other enlisted men for their trial panels, was largely nullified by their preference to leave their cases in the hands of officers. How do jurors react? A departure from random selection might tend toward over-selection of the higher occupations as it had in the helpfulness nominations, or, as one might predict in terms of class theory, departure from randomness might be in the direction of enlightened choice for the chooser's own occupation. How these counter tendencies might be balanced is a question for which we have no theoretical answer and therefore must investigate empirically.

Table 3
Average Votes Received as Helpful
Juror by Occupation and Sex

Sex	Occupation				
	Proprietor	Clerical	Skilled	Laborer	Combined
Male	6.8 (113)	4.2 (108)	3.9 (115)	2.7 (143)	4.3 (479)
Female	3.2 (34)	2.7 (116)	2.0 (36)	1.5 (76)	2.3 (262)
Combined	6.0 (147)	3.4 (224)	3.5 (151)	2.3 (219)	3.6 (741)*

*This number includes 14 additional cases for which interaction process scores are not available.

In an effort to probe deeper for evidence of class identifications, the following question was asked of 28 juries.

The jury pool is made up of people from all walks of life. However, if a member of your family were on trial and you had your choice, which of the following kinds of people would you prefer to make up the majority of the jurors who would hear your case?
(Business and professional people; clerical and white collar workers; skilled workers; unskilled workers.)

The expected values, determined by assuming that each status group is equally likely to be chosen, have been divided into the observed values and the resultant ratio multiplied by 100 to give the index numbers shown in Table 4. All groups, except laborers, would prefer to have a member of their family tried before a jury, the majority of whose mem-

Table 4 .
Choice of Juror If Member of Respondent's Family Were on Trial, Based Upon Occupation Stereotypes (Pro Rata Expected is 100)*

Respondent's Occupation	Preferred Occupation			
	Proprietor	Clerical	Skilled	Laborer
Proprietor (63)	241	95	51	13
Clerical (107)	206	112	71	11
Skilled (72)	172	55	139	33
Laborer (76)	126	42	147	84

*These data were collected from jurors in our 28 most recent experimental juries. See fn. 8.

bers were proprietors. Like other groups, laborers were also upwardly oriented as to their preference rank, but their first choice was skilled workers, then proprietors. Clerical and skilled workers chose persons from their own occupation group as their second choice. All groups except laborers ranked laborers last. Laborers placed themselves third and clerical persons last. It is to be stressed that Table 4 represents the choice of jurors in terms of occupational stereotypes. It is what a member of one occupational group perceives in terms of his generalized conception of his own and other occupational groups.

We also asked jurors to choose "four of your fellow jurors whom you would

best like to have serve on a jury if you were on trial." This latter question asks jurors not for generalized conceptions of other occupational groups but for evaluations of particular persons. We wished to know if the selections when jurors chose on the basis of face to face contact were similar or different from stereotype choices.[8] If a prototype of a social system had grown during deliberation, jurors might come to regard one another more in terms of performance in the task at hand than in terms of general social status. It was also possible for the deliberation to reveal status-based ideologies that would open latent schisms. The data suggest that differences were ordinarily not magnified by the deliberation and the jurors came to be convinced that a just job had been done. The special thrust of the question "If a member of your family were on trial" could have sensitized jurors to think in terms of personal interests rather than abstract principles such as competence or justice. Heightened sensitivity of personal interests could have caused respondents to turn away from those who had been the arbiters of consensus in their deliberation.

Table 5 shows a preference for proprietors but at a somewhat lower level. More detailed effects of the face to face experience in contrast with the response to occupational categories may best be illustrated by subtracting Table 4 from Table 5. It is to be noted that while Tables 4 and 5 are based on different populations, the respondents in both cases are random samples from the population available in successive weeks in the jury pool.

When Table 4 is subtracted from Table 5 (see Table 6) a positive value in the matrix represents an increase in index value associated with the face to face experience. The boldface diagonal shows that "own group" choices were lower at

---

[8] The stereotype juror preference question was not asked the juries in Table 5. The 28 juries of Table 4 are a wholly different set, so that the possible bias of face to face choices by the prior administration of the stereotype choices is avoided.

Table 5
Choice of Juror if Respondent Were on Trial Based Upon Deliberation Experience (Pro Rata Expected is 100)*

Respondent's Occupation	Preferred Occupation			
	Proprietor	Clerical	Skilled	Laborer
Proprietor (78)	169	110	119	39
Clerical (129)	145	100	101	75
Skilled (74)	147	104	84	73
Laborer (130)	162	100	112	74

*The expected values used to form the index numbers have been determined by assuming that each person distributes his four choices under conditions that give an equal chance of each of the 11 fellow juror's being chosen. For example, for 2 proprietors, 4 clerical, 2 skilled, and 4 labor, the expected distribution of the 8 proprietor votes would be 2/11(B), 8/11(B), 4/11(B) and 4/11(B). It is assumed that no fellow juror can be chosen twice by the same subject. The expected and observed choices for individuals on one jury are combined by status groups and accumulated for the different juries. Only 6 randomly selected jurors in the 20 vaporizer cases were asked this form of the question, so the 411 responses come from a potential population of (29 × 12) (20 × 6), or 468.

each occupation level, particularly among proprietors and skilled laborers. That is, choices after the deliberation experience are not determined by a narrow "interest group." In addition, all values above the main diagonal are positive. That is, face to face experience caused lower status persons to be evaluated more highly. As shown below the main diagonal, proprietors were reduced in the evaluation of clerical and skilled workers and increased in the evaluation of laborers; clerical persons were rated more highly by both skilled workers and laborers; and laborers decreased their former preference for skilled workers. The lower range of index values in the face to face situation arises in part from the effects of forcing the distribution of 4 votes among the 11 jurors who were members of the respondent's particular

Table 6
Change in Index Value Associated with Deliberation Experience (Value of Table 4 Subtracted from Table 5)

Respondent's Occupation	Preferred Occupation			
	Proprietor	Clerical	Skilled	Laborer
Proprietor	−72	15	68	26
Clerical	−61	−12	30	64
Skilled	−35	49	−55	40
Laborer	36	58	−35	−10

jury. Notwithstanding this flattening effect, it still appears that the face to face experience (1) results in fewer proprietor and skilled worker "own group" choices; and (2) brings the choice gradients into smoother conformity with the observed contribution of each status group to the deliberation.

DISCUSSION

Jury deliberations have been used to examine the intersection of occupational status and sex with the typically small group measures of participation, influence, satisfaction, and perceived competence. The null assumption that there is no relation between these modes of classification can be safely rejected. Men, in contrast with women, and persons of higher, in contrast with lower, status occupations have higher participation, influence, satisfaction and perceived competence for the jury task.

The present study does little to explain the cause of this differentiation. Insofar as selection of the foreman may be taken as a guide to more general expectations concerning desirable attributes for the jury task, it appears that the foreman is expected to be a male, preferably, a male of higher occupational status. Although we know of no empirical studies, we assume that the business discipline and related experiences of higher status occupations involve both substantive knowledge and interactional skills that may be used during the deliberation. Hence, in the competition for the available deliberation time, higher status males may rise to prominence because their comments are perceived to have greater value. On the other hand, since the cues of status—dress, speech, and casual references to experiences—are easily read, the differentiation may in part be explained by these expectations instead of actual performance.

Jurors who used more of the group's scarce resource, their common time together, were perceived by respondents to be the jurors desired if they were on trial. This finding suggests that whatever the criteria used by the groups to regulate the contributions of their members, these criteria were broadly held. The differential distribution of speaking time was achieved without serious violation of developing group norms. Further, face to face experience, in contrast with occupational stereotypes, tended to smooth post-meeting choices into a gradient parallel to both activity rates and status. These findings and others reported constitute a preliminary clarification of the small group process within the deliberation.

While our data do little to illuminate how differentiation arises, the status gradients emerge clearly in as brief a time as the one or two hour discussions under study. Though careful study will be required to determine the degree to which one may generalize from status in the larger social system to a particular interaction context, the demonstration of the continuity of status in the present case should be noted in any theory directed to the description of the process of status affirmation and maintenance.

The Voter and the Non-Voter

Philip K. Hastings

SOURCE: *American Journal of Sociology*, Vol. 62 (1956), pp. 302–7.

The off-year, non-presidential elections bring into sharp focus the widespread political apathy of the American electorate, whose chronic non-voting is so common that it may fairly be considered one of the defining attributes of American democracy. During the past quarter-century the proportion of eligible voters failing to go to the polls has ranged as high as 45 per cent in presidential elections and even higher in other contests. Why?

Among the earliest contributions to an understanding of non-voting were the demographic analyses of non-voters undertaken in both community or regional and national studies. The Survey Research Center's 1948 analysis,[1] based on a national sample, indicated a relatively high proportion of nonvoters between the ages of twenty-one and thirty-four, among individuals with only a grade-school educa-

tion, who earned under $2,000 per year and who were Negroes, unskilled laborers, or farmers. Similar data have been obtained in other studies, including those of Erie County, Ohio (1940),[2] Elmira, New York (1948),[3] and Pittsfield, Massachusetts (1952).[4] The high level of agreement both between geographical regions and in time is particularly noteworthy.

More recent studies of non-voters have shifted from a simple enumeration of various descriptive characteristics to the identification and measurement of both psychological and overt correlates of non-voting. One might infer that investigations of this nature arise from at least two assumptions: that underlying the various demographic characteristics known to be roughly definitive of non-voters is a

---

[1] A. Campbell and R. L. Kahn, The People Elect a President (Ann Arbor: Survey Research Center, Institute for Social Research, University of Michigan, 1952).

[2] P. Lazarsfeld, B. Berelson, and H. Gaudet, The People's Choice (New York: Columbia University Press, 1948).

[3] B. Berelson, P. Lazarsfeld, and W. McPhee, Voting (Chicago: University of Chicago Press, 1954).

[4] P. Hastings, "Politics Laboratory—1952," Journal of Higher Education, XXIV (January, 1953), 12-17.

distinctive psychological makeup and that failure to vote (or political apathy generally) is but one indication of a highly consistent pattern of behavior. Witness the Survey Research Center's 1952 national study of voting[5] and the continuing community study of Pittsfield, Massachusetts. In the latter investigation, for example, the following correlates of non-voting were established: (1) comparatively rare membership in voluntary associations; (2) minimum exposure to political communication; (3) meager information; (4) little identification with political organizations; (5) low frequency of substantive assumptions regarding the voting behavior of various political organizations; and (6) indefinite attitudes toward current politicio-economic issues.[6] It is also known that political apathy is found predominantly among certain strata of the population.

One of the primary questions raised in light of existing research, however, is the nature of the relationship between the demographic and the psychological characteristics. Do they vary concomitantly? For example, are the non-voter's low level of political awareness and vagueness of attitude governed by his small amount of education? Does his tendency to identify himself with those of low income reflect his own economic status? The failure to examine such variables independently has been a notable deficiency in many non-voter studies. Clearly, there still remain the tasks of attempting not only to identify further psychological correlates but also to study their significance apart from the demographic variables. This paper, based on data obtained in the 1954[7] continuation of

the Pittsfield Project, undertakes to do so.

With certain demographic factors held constant, three groups of Pittsfield respondents differing from one another in frequency of voting were compared as to replies to the following:

1. Do voters and non-voters differ in the nature and extent of their political identification with a number of local leader (or authority) symbols?

2. With what income class do they identify themselves?

3. Is there a difference between them in degree of crystallization of their political attitudes?

4. Do voters and non-voters differ in their evaluation of political issues?

5. To what extent is general social isolation and immobility characteristic of the non-voter?

6. Is the non-voter significantly less informed than the voter on political matters?

As a preliminary, each of the Pittsfield respondents who had been an eligible voter since 1948 was assigned to one of three groups divided on the basis of replies to two questions requiring them to recall how they voted and one on their voting intention. Group I, the voters, was composed of those who claimed that they had voted for President in 1948 and 1952 and who, as of September, 1954, expressed intention to vote in the 1954 Massachusetts senatorial, congressional, and gubernatorial elections. Group II, the non-voters, was made up of persons who said that they had not voted in either 1948 or 1952 for President and who in September, 1954, had made no decision regarding any of the 1954 elections about which they were questioned.[8] Group III, the occasional voter, consisted of individuals who indicated actual or intended voting participation in at least two of the three elections. On a proportional basis, the three groups were equated as to age, sex,

[5]A. Campbell, G. Gurin and W. E. Miller, The Voter Decides (Evanston, Ill.: Row, Peterson & Co., 1954).

[6]P. Hastings, "The Non-Voter in 1952: A Study of Pittsfield, Massachusetts," Journal of Psychology, XXXVIII (Fall. 1954), 301-12.

[7]Begun in 1952, this is a continuing detailed study of the political attitudes and behavior of the residents of Pittsfield, Massachusetts (pop. 55,000). The 1956 phase of the project is under way, financed by the Ford Foundation.

[8]The November post-election survey showed that a large majority of them did not vote in 1954.

religion, education, and income.[9]

That non-voting is but one indication of political apathy and a general withdrawal from community life was an assumption in the study. We expected that the non-voter's social isolation would be evident both in his overt behavior and in certain psychological attributes. We aimed to demonstrate empirically, with certain demographic factors held constant, that on both counts the non-voter differs significantly from the voter.

A composite measure dealing with different types of behavior was designed to test the non-voter's hypothesized isolation. As shown in Table 1, the sample was asked a series of questions designed to throw light on its involvement in community life. The questions touched on (1) physical or geographical mobility; (2) political behavior, aside from voting; (3) formal group activity; (4) exposure to politics in a medium of mass communication; and (5) vocational behavior. It was felt not only that the various questions should be simple and direct but that special care should be taken to avoid obliging the respondent to place himself in an unfavorable light. Further, since we sought a single index of general level of social involvement, by definition, it was necessary to devise a set of items with a wide range. Finally, it was clear that the value

---

[9]The proportions established after the interviews were in each case:

1. Male : female . . . . —5:5
2. Under forty years : over forty years . . . . —2:3
3. Catholic : Protestant : other. . . —5:4:1
4. Grades I-VIII : Grades IX-XII : college : other . . . . —2:5:2:1
5. Under $4,000 per year : $4,000-$7,000 : over $7,000 . . . . —5:4:1

While in the total cross-section the subsamples of occasional voters and non-voters differed insignificantly in each of the five dimensions, the voter group contained significantly larger proportions of Protestants over forty years old. Consequently, to make the three groups match, a total of 23 Protestant respondents over forty years old were removed from the original voter group. The 23 were the only persons who could be so removed without altering the already-matching proportions on sex, education, and income and at the same time effect a matching on the religion and age variables.

TABLE 1

DEGREE OF SOCIAL WITHDRAWAL AND IMMOBILITY*

QUESTION: Have you ever—

a) Lived anywhere else but Pittsfield?
b) Had a job other than your present one?
c) Read a travel book?
d) Felt at election time that your vote didn't really count?
e) Openly disagreed with your boss on something?
f) Visited Canada?
g) Written to your congressman?
h) Thought of changing your present line of work?
i) Wished you were in politics?
j) Visited New York City?
k) Been a member of some Pittsfield group like the Red Cross, the P.T.A., the Elks', etc.?
l) Visited Chicago?
m) Listened to (or on TV) a news commentator like Elmer Davis, for example?
n) Read a newspaper editorial all the way through?

	Group I Voters ($\underline{N}$=112)	Group II Non-Voters ($\underline{N}$=44)	Group III Occasional Voters ($\underline{N}$=57)
Mean score . . .	9.0	6.1†	7.9

*With the exception of item (d), each affirmative answer was assigned a score of 1. The score range was from 0 to 14, with the higher score indicating greater social involvement.

†The difference between the mean scores of Groups I and II is significant at the 5 per cent level of confidence.

---

of the measure depended in part upon its power of discrimination within the total sample, specifically, between the voters and the non-voters.

The replies (Table 1) indicate, at least within the limits of our measure, a significant difference in the social involvement of the non-voter in comparison with the voter. This relationship is strengthened by data on Group III (the occasional voters), showing an average social involvement score which falls between those of the first two groups. With age, income, education, sex, and religion held constant, as voting decreased, so did social involvement in general.

The frequently demonstrated relationship between infrequent voting, uncertain attitudes, and meager information has often been accounted for by limited education. But we argued that failure to vote involves considerably more: that the non-voter literally does not perceive political

stimuli whether factual data or controversial issues.

As Table 2 shows, the apathetic individual's ability to give correct answers
to questions of fact on well-publicized
political events was limited. Of eleven
questions, Pittsfield's non-voters, on the
average, could answer only three correctly, compared with seven correct replies by the voters. One might have expected that, with education held constant
in the three groups, there would be insignificant differences in level of information. Yet this was not the case.

TABLE 2

LEVEL OF INFORMATION*

QUESTION: I wonder if you happen to remember —
a) About how many people live in Pittsfield?
b) Whether Eisenhower or Stevenson won in Pittsfield in the 1952 elections?
c) Who Roy Cohn is?
d) Who ran against Governor Herter in 1952?
e) Who L. K. Miller is?†
f) Whether a pay raise for post-office workers
was approved by Congress recently?
g) Who Ralph Zwicker is?
h) Whether Congress recently changed the Taft-
Hartley Law?
i) Who is running against Heselton this year?
j) Whether Congress voted, during the past year,
to lower our taxes?
k) Who Leonard Hall is?

	Group I Voters (N=112)	Group II Non-Voters (N=44)	Group III Occasional Voters (N=57)
Mean score ..	13.0	5.7‡	10.0

*Each item was scored as follows: 0 = incorrect;
1 = partly correct; and 2 = totally correct. The score
range was from 0 to 22.

†Editor of Pittsfield's only newspaper, The Berk-
shire Eagle (by and large, Republican-oriented).

‡The difference between the mean scores of
Groups I and II is significant at the 5 per cent level
of confidence.

A third variable hypothesized as correlated with non-voting was the crystallization of attitudes. As frequency of voting
decreased, one would expect replies of
"No opinion" to increase. And this is the
case, as Table 3 shows.

What empirical data would give a more
positive picture of the non-voter? To gain
a better idea of the non-voter's personality, we went into each of the following

TABLE 3

CRYSTALLIZATION OF ATTITUDES

(Per Cent)

	Group I Voters (N= 112)	Group II Non- Voters (N= 44)	Group III Occasional Voters (N= 57)
A. In your opinion does organized labor have a great deal of influence in the politics of this country, or doesn't it have very much influence?			
Great deal......	65	43	58
Not much	22	25	25
No opinion......	13	32*	17
B. Would you like to have McCarthy on your party ticket as the candidate for senator from Massachusetts?			
Yes	13	20	14
No............	79	36	60
Depends	5	7	9
No opinion......	3	37*	17
C. Would you favor making our Army and Navy smaller if this meant that you wouldn't have to pay so many taxes?			
Yes	6	14	11
No............	89	55	81
Depends	2	9	7
No opinion......	3	22*	1

*Items in which a percentage difference signifi-
cant at the 5 per cent level of confidence or better
exists between Groups I and II.

questions: Are there differences between
the voter and the non-voter in their selection and assessment of political issues
of maximum concern? With which local
economic stratum does the non-voter
most frequently identify himself psychologically? What subjective relation exists
between the non-voter and recognized
community leaders?

We anticipated that the non-voter would
tend to be a self- rather than environ-
ment-centered individual whose interest
would focus primarily upon the political
issues of most immediate and practical
concern to him. Further, we expected
that the non-voter experiences a sense of

insecurity and inadequacy manifested in a comparatively great subjective dependence upon the local leaders. Definitive verification would require more than the techniques employed in the Pittsfield Project, and the following data are offered as the initial and tentative results.

It seemed likely that one indication of the non-voters' greater immediate and material self-interest would be the frequency with which they stress political issues of 1954 directly bearing on their economic well-being. The respondents were therefore presented a list of eight issues (Table 4), to be ranked in order of importance. The politically active respondents proved to be more concerned with foreign affairs; the non-voters, with taxation and the cost of living.

TABLE 4

EVALUATION OF POLITICAL ISSUES

	Percentage Difference Between Groups I and II*	
Political Issue	Group I Voters (N=112)	Group II Non-Voters (N=44)
More aggression by Communist China (e.g., an invasion of Formosa)	+ 25	. . . .
Threat of another world war	+ 19	. . . .
Corruption in government . .	+ 7	. . . .
Government spending	+ 4	. . . .
Amount of money I can earn (wages)	. . . .	+ 1
McCarthy	. . . .	+ 1
Level of taxation	. . . .	+ 7
Cost of living	. . . .	+ 29

*The question on which Table 4 is based was: "[HAND CARD] Here is a list of problems that both the Democrats and the Republicans will be talking about during the election campaign this fall. As of now, which of these problems worries you most? Which worries you second most? Third, etc.?" The card contained the issues as enumerated above. All the voters and non-voters replied, and the percentage differences here shown are differences in the frequency with which the issue was ranked No. 1 and No. 2 by the individuals in each group.

A corroborating finding was that six out of ten of the non-voters, when asked whether they considered themselves as wealthy, earning a little more than average, earning a little less than average, or poor, claimed to belong to one or the

TABLE 5

ECONOMIC STRATA IDENTIFICATION

(Per Cent)

	Group I Voters (N= 112)	Group II Non-Voters (N= 44)	Group III Occasional Voters (N= 57)
Wealthy, or income a little above average . .	65	40	52
Income a little below average, or poor	35	60*	48

*The percentage difference between Groups I and II is significant at the 5 per cent level of confidence.

other of the latter two (Table 5). Essentially the opposite was found among the voters.

Those who are highly active politically tend to concern themselves with broad political issues that only indirectly and in the long run affected their daily lives and, although no different from non-voters in economic composition, identify themselves more frequently with the classes with higher incomes. For the comparatively inactive group, the findings on these two counts indicated an opposite tendency.

To test our expectation that voters and non-voters would differ in the extent to which they demonstrated a measure of political dependence upon individuals with comparatively high status (authority symbols), the following question was asked:

[Hand Card] Here is a list of people whose opinions on politics you may or may not agree with. Could you tell us which people you tend to agree with most and, also, which you tend to disagree with most?

  a) Other members of your family
  b) Your priest or minister
  c) Your boss (or your husband's)
  d) The editor of the Eagle
  e) Your close friends
  f) Local labor union leaders
  g) People who live in your neighborhood
  h) Your (or your husband's fellow workers

Of the eight individuals or groups included in the question, four were selected as having essentially equal status with the respondent and four as occupying relatively high status both in the community at large and in relation to most of the respondents. We anticipated that there would be insignificant differences in the

TABLE 6

POLITICAL IDENTIFICATION PATTERN

(Per Cent)

	Group I Voters (N= 112)	Group II Non-Voters (N= 44)	Group III Occa-sional Voters (N= 57)
Agree with Most			
High status:			
The editor of the Eagle	41	79*	56
Your boss (or your husband's)	65	83*	85
Local labor union leaders	31	47*	39
Your priest or minister	86	78	92
Equal status:			
People who live in your neighbor-hood	74	69	83
Members of your family.	85	81	76
Your (or your hus-band's) fellow workers.	74	74	88
Your close friends	80	77	81

*The percentage differences between Groups I and II are significant at the 5 per cent level of confidence.

comparative proportions of voters and non-voters indicating political agreement with those who were their equals in status but that among the non-voters significantly higher percentages would agree with their "superiors." With one exception ("your priest or minister"), the results (Table 6) bear out these expectations.

What can be inferred from these results? One might argue that they further reinforce the observation that the non-voter is generally a non-participant: these data suggest that he is perhaps not even willing to think for himself as far as political matters are concerned. An alternative interpretation, however, is that the non-voter actually views those with high status in his community, whether they be the editor of the local paper, a labor leader, or his job superior, as politically knowledgeable people with whom to identify himself and to follow. One might speculate, although the Pittsfield data provide no empirical basis for this, that, to the extent that the non-voter depends politically upon the local authority or leader symbols, he betrays a personal sense of inadequacy and insecurity. Conceivably, this is a pervasive personality trait that in part defines the politically apathetic individual.

THE DISTRIBUTION OF PRESTIGE

Some Principles of Stratification

Kingsley Davis and Wilbert E. Moore

SOURCE: *American Sociological Review*, Vol. 10 (1945), pp. 242–49.

In a previous paper some concepts for handling the phenomena of social inequality were presented.[1] In the present paper a further step in stratification theory is undertaken—an attempt to show the rela-

tionship between stratification and the rest of the social order.[2] Starting from

[1]Kingsley Davis, "A Conceptual Analysis of Stratification." American Sociological Review. 7: 309-321, June 1942.

[2]The writers regret (and beg indulgence) that the present essay, a condensation of a longer study, covers so much in such short space that adequate evidence and qualification cannot be given and that as a result what is actually very tentative is presented in an unfortunately dogmatic manner.

the proposition that no society is "class-less," or unstratified, an effort is made to explain, in functional terms, the universal necessity which calls forth stratification in any social system. Next, an attempt is made to explain the roughly uniform distribution of prestige as between the major types of positions in every society. Since, however, there occur between one society and another great differences in the degree and kind of stratification, some attention is also given to the varieties of social inequality and the variable factors that give rise to them.

Clearly, the present task requires two different lines of analysis—one to understand the universal, the other to understand the variable features of stratification. Naturally each line of inquiry aids the other and is indispensable, and in the treatment that follows the two will be interwoven, although, because of space limitations, the emphasis will be on the universals.

Throughout, it will be necessary to keep in mind one thing—namely, that the discussion relates to the system of positions, not to the individuals occupying those positions. It is one thing to ask why different positions carry different degrees of prestige, and quite another to ask how certain individuals get into those positions. Although, as the argument will try to show, both questions are related, it is essential to keep them separate in our thinking. Most of the literature on stratification has tried to answer the second question (particularly with regard to the ease or difficulty of mobility between strata) without tackling the first. The first question, however, is logically prior and, in the case of any particular individual or group, factually prior.

THE FUNCTIONAL NECESSITY OF STRATIFICATION

Curiously, however, the main functional necessity explaining the universal presence of stratification is precisely the requirement faced by any society of placing and motivating individuals in the social structure. As a functioning mechanism a society must somehow distribute its members in social positions and induce them to perform the duties of these positions. It must thus concern itself with motivation at two different levels: to instill in the proper individuals the desire to fill certain positions, and, once in these positions, the desire to perform the duties attached to them. Even though the social order may be relatively static in form, there is a continuous process of metabolism as new individuals are born into it, shift with age, and die off. Their absorption into the positional system must somehow be arranged and motivated. This is true whether the system is competitive or non-competitive. A competitive system gives greater importance to the motivation to achieve positions, whereas a non-competitive system gives perhaps greater importance to the motivation to perform the duties of the positions; but in any system both types of motivation are required.

If the duties associated with the various positions were all equally pleasant to the human organism, all equally important to societal survival, and all equally in need of the same ability or talent, it would make no difference who got into which positions, and the problem of social placement would be greatly reduced. But actually it does make a great deal of difference who gets into which positions, not only because some positions are inherently more agreeable than others, but also because some require special talents or training and some are functionally more important than others. Also, it is essential that the duties of the positions be performed with the diligence that their importance requires. Inevitably, then, a society must have, first, some kind of rewards that it can use as inducements, and, second, some way of distributing these rewards differentially according to positions. The rewards and their distribution become a part of the social order, and thus give rise to stratification.

One may ask what kind of rewards a society has at its disposal in distributing its personnel and securing essential services. It has, first of all, the things that contribute to sustenance and comfort. It has, second, the things that contribute to humor and diversion. And it has, finally, the things that contribute to self-respect and ego expansion. The last, because of the peculiarly social character of the self, is largely a function of the opinion of others, but it nonetheless ranks in importance with the first two. In any social system all three kinds of rewards must be dispensed differentially according to positions.

In a sense the rewards are "built into" the position. They consist in the "rights" associated with the position, plus what may be called its accompaniments or perquisites. Often the rights, and sometimes the accompaniments, are functionally related to the duties of the position. (Rights as viewed by the incumbent are usually duties as viewed by other members of the community.) However, there may be a host of subsidiary rights and perquisites that are not essential to the function of the position and have only an indirect and symbolic connection with its duties, but which still may be of considerable importance in inducing people to seek the positions and fulfill the essential duties.

If the rights and perquisites of different positions in a society must be unequal, then the society must be stratified, because that is precisely what stratification means. Social inequality is thus an unconsciously evolved device by which societies insure that the most important positions are conscientiously filled by the most qualified persons. Hence every society, no matter how simple or complex, must differentiate persons in terms of both prestige and esteem, and must therefore possess a certain amount of institutionalized inequality.

It does not follow that the amount or type of inequality need be the same in all societies. This is largely a function of factors that will be discussed presently.

THE TWO DETERMINANTS OF
POSITIONAL RANK

Granting the general function that in-

equality subserves, one can specify the two factors that determine the relative rank of different positions. In general those positions convey the best reward, and hence have the highest rank, which (a) have the greatest importance for the society and (b) require the greatest training or talent. The first factor concerns function and is a matter of relative significance; the second concerns means and is a matter of scarcity.

Differential Functional Importance. Actually a society does not need to reward positions in proportion to their functional importance. It merely needs to give sufficient reward to them to insure that they will be filled competently. In other words, it must see that less essential positions do not compete successfully with more essential ones. If a position is easily filled, it need not be heavily rewarded, even though important. On the other hand, if it is important but hard to fill, the reward must be high enough to get it filled anyway. Functional importance is therefore a necessary but not a sufficient cause of high rank being assigned to a position.[3]

Differential Scarcity of Personnel. Practically all positions, no matter how acquired, require some form of skill or

[3]Unfortunately, functional importance is difficult to establish. To use the position's prestige to establish it, as is often unconsciously done, constitutes circular reasoning from our point of view. There are, however, two independent clues: (a) the degree to which a position is functionally unique, there being no other positions that can perform the same function satisfactorily; (b) the degree to which other positions are dependent on the one in question. Both clues are best examplified in organized systems of positions built around one major function. Thus, in most complex societies the religious, political, economic, and educational functions are handled by distinct structures not easily interchangeable. In addition, each structure possesses many different positions, some closely dependent on, if not subordinate to, others. In sum, when an institutional nucleus becomes differentiated around one main function, and at the same time organizes a large portion of the population into its relationships, the key positions in it are of the highest functional importance. The absence of such specialization does not prove functional unimportance, for the whole society may be relatively unspecialized; but it is safe to assume that the more important functions receive the first and clearest structural differentiation.

capacity for performance. This is implicit in the very action of position, which implies that the incumbent must, by virtue of his incumbency, accomplish certain things.

There are, ultimately, only two ways in which a person's qualifications come about: through inherent capacity or through training. Obviously, in concrete activities both are always necessary, but from a practical standpoint the scarcity may lie primarily in one or the other, as well as in both. Some positions require innate talents of such high degree that the persons who fill them are bound to be rare. In many cases, however, talent is fairly abundant in the population but the training process is so long, costly, and elaborate that relatively few can qualify. Modern medicine, for example, is within the mental capacity of most individuals, but a medical education is so burdensome and expensive that virtually none would undertake it if the position of the M.D. did not carry a reward commensurate with the sacrifice.

If the talents required for a position are abundant and the training easy, the method of acquiring the position may have little to do with its duties. There may be, in fact, a virtually accidental relationship. But if the skills required are scarce by reason of the rarity of talent or the condition of training, the position, if functionally important, must have an attractive power that will draw the necessary skills in competition with other positions. This means, in effect, that the position must be high in the social scale—must command great prestige, high salary, ample leisure, and the like.

How Variations Are to Be Understood. In so far as there is a difference between one system of stratification and another, it is attributable to whatever factors affect the two determinants of differential reward—namely, functional importance and scarcity of personnel. Positions important in one society may not be important in another, because the conditions faced by the societies, or their degree of internal development, may be different.

The same conditions, in turn, may affect the question of scarcity; for in some societies the stage of development, or the external situation, may wholly obviate the necessity of certain kinds of skill or talent. Any particular system of stratification, then, can be understood as a product of the special conditions affecting the two aforementioned grounds of differential reward.

MAJOR SOCIETAL FUNCTIONS AND STRATIFICATION

Religion. The reason why religion is necessary is apparently to be found in the fact that human society achieves its unity primarily through the possession by its members of certain ultimate values and ends in common. Although these values and ends are subjective, they influence behavior, and their integration enables the society to operate as a system. Derived neither from inherited nor from external nature, they have evolved as a part of culture by communication and moral pressure. They must, however, appear to the members of the society to have some reality, and it is the role of religious belief and ritual to supply and reinforce this appearance of reality. Through belief and ritual the common ends and values are connected with an imaginary world symbolized by concrete sacred objects, which world in turn is related in a meaningful way to the facts and trials of the individual's life. Through the worship of the sacred objects and the beings they symbolize, and the acceptance of supernatural prescriptions that are at the same time codes of behavior, a powerful control over human conduct is exercised, guiding it along lines sustaining the institutional structure and conforming to the ultimate ends and values.

If this conception of the role of religion is true, one can understand why in every known society the religious activities tend to be under the charge of particular persons, who tend thereby to enjoy greater rewards than the ordinary societal member. Certain of the rewards and special privileges may attach to only the highest religious functionaries, but others usually apply, if such exists, to the entire sacerdotal class.

Moreover, there is a peculiar relation between the duties of the religious official and the special privileges he enjoys. If the supernatural world governs the destinies of men more ultimately than does the real world, its earthly representative, the person through whom one may communicate with the supernatural, must be a powerful individual. He is a keeper of sacred tradition, a skilled performer of the ritual, and an interpreter of lore and myth. He is in such close contact with the gods that he is viewed as possessing some of their characteristics. He is, in short, a bit sacred, and hence free from some of the more vulgar necessities and controls.

It is no accident, therefore, that religious functionaries have been associated with the very highest positions of power, as in theocratic regimes. Indeed, looking at it from this point of view, one may wonder why it is that they do not get <u>entire</u> control over their societies. The factors that prevent this are worthy of note.

In the first place, the amount of technical competence necessary for the performance of religious duties is small. Scientific or artistic capacity is not required. Anyone can set himself up as enjoying an intimate relation with deities, and nobody can successfully dispute him. Therefore, the factor of scarcity of personnel does not operate in the technical sense.

One may assert, on the other hand, that religious ritual is often elaborate and religious lore abstruse, and that priestly ministrations require tact, if not intelligence. This is true, but the technical requirements of the profession are for the most part adventitious, not related to the end in the same way that science is related to air travel. The priest can never be free from competition, since the criteria of whether or not one has genuine contact with the supernatural are never strictly clear. It is this competition that debases the priestly posi-

tion below what might be expected at first glance. That is why priestly prestige is highest in those societies where membership in the profession is rigidly controlled by the priestly guild itself. That is why, in part at least, elaborate devices are utilized to stress the identification of the person with his office— spectacular costume, abnormal conduct, special diet, segregated residence, celibacy, conspicuous leisure, and the like. In fact, the priest is always in danger of becoming somewhat discredited—as happens in a secularized society—because in a world of stubborn fact, ritual and sacred knowledge alone will not grow crops or build houses. Furthermore, unless he is protected by a professional guild, the priest's identification with the supernatural tends to preclude his acquisition of abundant wordly goods.

As between one society and another it seems that the highest general position awarded the priest occurs in the medieval type of social order. Here there is enough economic production to afford a surplus, which can be used to support a numerous and highly organized priesthood; and yet the populace is unlettered and therefore credulous to a high degree. Perhaps the most extreme example is to be found in the Buddhism of Tibet, but others are encountered in the Catholicism of feudal Europe, the Inca regime of Peru, the Brahmanism of India, and the Mayan priesthood of Yucatan. On the other hand, if the society is so crude as to have no surplus and little differentiation, so that every priest must be also a cultivator or hunter, the separation of the priestly status from the others has hardly gone far enough for priestly prestige to mean much. When the priest actually has high prestige under these circumstances, it is because he also performs other important functions (usually political and medical).

In an extremely advanced society built on scientific technology, the priesthood tends to lose status, because sacred tradition and supernaturalism drop into the background. The ultimate values and common ends of the society tend to be expressed in less anthropomorphic ways, by officials who occupy fundamentally political, economic, or educational rather than religious positions. Nevertheless, it is easily possible for intellectuals to exaggerate the degree to which the priesthood in a presumably secular milieu has lost prestige. When the matter is closely examined the urban proletariat, as well as the rural citizenry, proves to be surprisingly god-fearing and priest-ridden. No society has become so completely secularized as to liquidate entirely the belief in transcendental ends and supernatural entities. Even in a secularized society some system must exist for the integration of ultimate values, for their ritualistic expression, and for the emotional adjustments required by disappointment, death, and disaster.

Government. Like religion, government plays a unique and indispensable part in society. But in contrast to religion, which provides integration in terms of sentiments, beliefs, and rituals, it organizes the society in terms of law and authority. Furthermore, it orients the society to the actual rather that the unseen world.

The main functions of government are, internally, the ultimate enforcement of norms, the final arbitration of conflicting interests, and the overall planning and direction of society; and externally, the handling of war and diplomacy. To carry out these functions it acts as the agent of the entire people, enjoys a monopoly of force, and controls all individuals within its territory.

Political action, by definition, implies authority. An official can command because he has authority, and the citizen must obey because he is subject to that authority. For this reason stratification is inherent in the nature of political relationships.

So clear is the power embodied in political position that political inequality is sometimes thought to comprise all inequality. But it can be shown that there are other bases of stratification, that the following controls operate in practice to keep political power from becoming complete: (a) The fact that the actual holders of political office, and especially those determining top policy must necessarily be few in number compared to the total population. (b) The fact that the rulers represent the interest of the group rather than of themselves, and are therefore restricted in their behavior by rules and mores designed to enforce this limitation of interest. (c) The fact that the holder of political office has his authority by virtue of his office and nothing else, and therefore any special knowledge, talent, or capacity he may claim is purely incidental, so that he often has to depend upon others for technical assistance.

In view of these limiting factors, it is not strange that the rulers often have less power and prestige than a literal enumeration of their formal rights would lead one to expect.

Wealth, Property, and Labor. Every position that secures for its incumbent a livelihood is, by definition, economically rewarded. For this reason there is an economic aspect to those positions (e.g. political and religious) the main function of which is not economic. It therefore becomes convenient for the society to use unequal economic returns as a principal means of controlling the entrance of persons into positions and stimulating the performance of their duties. The amount of the economic return therefore becomes one of the main indices of social status.

It should be stressed, however, that a position does not bring power and prestige *because* it draws a high income. Rather, it draws a high income because it is functionally important and the available personnel is for one reason or another scarce. It is therefore superficial and erroneous to regard high income as the cause of a man's power and prestige, just as it is erroneous to think that a man's fever is the cause of his disease.[4]

The economic source of power and

---

[4] The symbolic rather than intrinsic role of income in social stratification has been succinctly summarized by Talcott Parsons, "An Analytical Approach to the Theory of Social Stratification," American Journal of Sociology. 45: 841–862, May, 1940.

prestige is not income primarily, but the ownership of capital goods (including patents, good will, and professional reputation). Such ownership should be distinguished from the possession of consumers' goods, which is an index rather than a cause of social standing. In other words, the ownership of producers' goods is properly speaking, a source of income like other positions, the income itself remaining an index. Even in situations where social values are widely commercialized and earnings are the readiest method of judging social position, income does not confer prestige on a position so much as it induces people to compete for the position. It is true that a man who has a high income as a result of one position may find this money helpful in climbing into another position as well, but this again reflects the effect of his initial, economically advantageous status, which exercises its influence through the medium of money.

In a system of private property in productive enterprise, an income above what an individual spends can give rise to possession of capital wealth. Presumably such possession is a reward for the proper management of one's finances originally and of the productive enterprise later. But as social differentiation becomes highly advanced and yet the institution of inheritance persists, the phenomenon of pure ownership, and reward for pure ownership, emerges. In such a case it is difficult to prove that the position is functionally important or that the scarcity involved is anything other than extrinsic and accidental. It is for this reason, doubtless, that the institution of private property in productive goods becomes more subject to criticism as social development proceeds toward industrialization. It is only this pure, that is, strictly legal and functionless, ownership, however, that is open to attack; for some form of active ownership, whether private or public, is indispensable.

One kind of ownership of production goods consists in rights over the labor of others. The most extremely concentrated and exclusive of such rights are found in slavery, but the essential principle remains in serfdom, peonage, encomienda, and indenture. Naturally this kind of ownership has the greatest significance for stratification, because it necessarily entails an unequal relationship.

But property in capital goods inevitably introduces a compulsive element even into the nominally free contractual relationship. Indeed, in some respects the authority of the contractual employer is greater than that of the feudal landlord, inasmuch as the latter is more limited by traditional reciprocities. Even the classical economics recognized that competitors would fare unequally, but it did not pursue this fact to its necessary conclusion that, however it might be acquired, unequal control of goods and services must give unequal advantage to the parties to a contract.

Technical Knowledge. The function of finding means to single goals, without any concern with the choice between goals, is the exclusively technical sphere. The explanation of why positions requiring great technical skill receive fairly high rewards is easy to see, for it is the simplest case of the rewards being so distributed as to draw talent and motivate training. Why they seldom if ever receive the highest rewards is also clear: the importance of technical knowledge from a societal point of view is never so great as the integration of goals, which takes place on the religious, political, and economic levels. Since the technological level is concerned solely with means, a purely technical position must ultimately be subordinate to other positions that are religious, political, or economic in character.

Nevertheless, the distinction between expert and layman in any social order is fundamental, and cannot be entirely reduced to other terms. Methods of recruitment, as well as of reward, sometimes lead to the erroneous interpretation that technical positions are economically determined. Actually, however, the acquisition of knowledge and skill cannot be accomplished by purchase, although the opportunity to learn may be. The control of the avenues of training may inhere as a sort of property right in certain families or classes, giving them power and prestige in consequence. Such a situation adds an artificial scarcity to the natural scarcity of skills and talents. On the other hand, it is possible for an opposite situation to arise. The rewards of technical position may be so great that a condition of excess supply is created, leading to at least temporary devaluation of the rewards. Thus "unemployment in the learned professions" may result in a debasement of the prestige of those positions. Such adjustments and readjustments are constantly occurring in changing societies; and it is always well to bear in mind that the efficiency of a stratified structure may be affected by the modes of recruitment for positions. The social order itself, however, sets limits to the inflation or deflation of the prestige of experts: an over-supply tends to debase the rewards and discourage recruitment or produce revolution, whereas an under-supply tends to increase the rewards or weaken the society in competition with other societies.

Particular systems of stratification show a wide range with respect to the exact position of technically competent persons. This range is perhaps most evident in the degree of specialization. Extreme division of labor tends to create many specialists without high prestige since the training is short and the required native capacity relatively small. On the other hand it also tends to accentuate the high position of the true experts —scientists, engineers, and administrators—by increasing their authority relative to other functionally important positions. But the idea of a technocratic social order or a government or priesthood of engineers or social scientists neglects the limitations of knowledge and skills as a basis for performing social functions. To the extent that the social structure is truly specialized the prestige of the technical person must also be circumscribed.

VARIATION IN STRATIFIED SYSTEMS

The generalized principles of stratification here suggested form a necessary preliminary to a consideration of types of stratified systems, because it is in terms of these principles that the types must be described. This can be seen by trying to delineate types according to certain modes of variation. For instance, some of the most important modes (together with the polar types in terms of them) seem to be as follows:

(a) The Degree of Specialization. The degree of specialization affects the fineness and multiplicity of the gradations in power and prestige. It also influences the extent to which particular functions may be emphasized in the invidious system, since a given function cannot receive much emphasis in the hierarchy until it has achieved structural separation from the other functions. Finally, the amount of specialization influences the bases of selection. Polar types: Specialized, Unspecialized.

(b) The Nature of the Functional Emphasis. In general when emphasis is put on sacred matters, a rigidity is introduced that tends to limit specialization and hence the development of technology. In addition, a brake is placed on social mobility, and on the development of bureaucracy. When the preoccupation with the sacred is withdrawn, leaving greater scope for purely secular preoccupations, a great development, and rise in status, of economic and technological positions seemingly takes place. Curiously, a concomitant rise in political position is not likely, because it has usually been allied with the religious and stands to gain little by the decline of the latter. It is also possible for a society to emphasize family functions—as in relatively undifferentiated societies where high mortality requires high fertility and kinship forms the main basis of social organization. Main types: Familistic, Authoritarian (Theocratic or sacred, and Totalitarian or secular), Capitalistic.

(c) The Magnitude of Invidious Differences. What may be called the amount of social distance between positions, taking into account the entire scale, is something that should lend itself to quantitative measurement. Considerable differences apparently exist between different societies in this regard, and also between parts of the same society. Polar types: Equalitarian, Inequalitarian.

(d) The Degree of Opportunity. The familar question of the amount of mobility is different from the question of the comparative equality or inequality of rewards posed above, because the two criteria may vary independently up to a point. For instance, the tremendous divergences in monetary income in the United States are far greater than those found in primitive societies, yet the equality of opportunity to move from one rung to the other in the social scale may also be greater in the United States than in a hereditary tribal kingdom. Polar types: Mobile (open), Immobile (closed).

(e) The Degree of Stratum Solidarity. Again, the degree of "class solidarity" (or the presence of specific organizations to promote class interests) may vary to some extent independently of the other criteria, and hence is an important principle in classifying systems of stratification. Polar types: Class organized, Class unorganized.

EXTERNAL CONDITIONS

What state any particular system of stratification is in with reference to each of these modes of variation depends on two things: (1) its state with reference to the other ranges of variation, and (2) the conditions outside the system of stratification which nevertheless influence that system. Among the latter are the following:

(a) The Stage of Cultural Development. As the cultural heritage grows, increased specialization becomes necessary, which in turn contributes to the enhancement of mobility, a decline of stratum solidarity, and a change of functional emphasis.

(b) Situation with Respect to Other Societies. The presence or absence of open conflict with other societies, of free trade relations or cultural diffusion, all influence the class structure to some extent. A chronic state of warfare tends to place emphasis upon the military functions, especially when the opponents are more or less equal. Free trade, on the other hand, strengthens the hand of the trader at the expense of the warrior and priest. Free movement of ideas generally has an equalitarian effect. Migration and conquest create special circumstances.

(c) Size of the Society. A small society limits the degree to which functional specialization can go, the degree of segregation of different strata, and the magnitude of inequality.

COMPOSITE TYPES

Much of the literature on stratification has attempted to classify concrete systems into a certain number of types. This task is deceptively simple, however, and should come at the end of an analysis of elements and principles, rather than at the beginning. If the preceding discussion has any validity, it indicates that there are a number of modes of variation between different systems, and that any one system is a composite of the society's status with reference to all these modes of variation. The danger of trying to classify whole societies under such rubrics as caste, feudal, or open class is that one or two criteria are selected and others ignored, the result being an unsatisfactory solution to the problem posed. The present discussion has been offered as a possible approach to the more systematic classification of composite types.

Social Stratification and the Functional Theory of Social Differentiation

Walter Buckley

SOURCE: *American Sociological Review*, Vol. 23 (1958), pp. 369-75.

There has been no dearth of criticism of the Davis-Moore theory of social stratification since its publication over a decade ago.[1] Particularly disturbing is the fact that what this theory views as virtues (eufunctions) are the very factors that others overwhelmingly see as vices (disfunctions). The former characterize it in terms of competitive achievement of position; a close correlation between superior capacities, importance of position, and high rewards; and its functional necessity to maintenance of the social system. The critics associate the theory with role-ascription and restriction of opportunity; absence of correlation between superior capacities, rewards, and positional importance; and disruption or discontinuity of the society. This gross difference of views has led several sociologists to seek out and find deficiencies in the functional theory. Among other shortcomings, its critics[2] have pointed out that the Davis-Moore theory is inadequate in its treatment of the concept of "functional importance"; it ignores possible disfunctions and functional alternatives of stratification; it reifies "society" as "inducing" its members to assume positions and play roles; and in general it accepts outmoded concepts and assumptions of classical economics, such as "inherent scarcity" of social ends and the inviolability of competition, all of which results in a picture of theoretical necessity that reproduces with remarkable faithfulness a culturally circumscribed ideology. The view expressed by Lester F. Ward over half a century ago would seem to be still relevant:

... here we encounter the great sullen, stubborn error, so universal and ingrained as to constitute a world view, that the difference between the upper and lower classes of society is due to a difference in their intellectual capacity, something existing in the nature of things, something pre-ordained and inherently inevitable. Every form of sophistry is employed to uphold this view. We are told that there must be social classes, that they are a necessary part of the social order.[3]

The widespread acceptance of this theory in introductory sociology texts,[4] along with the recent appearance of Berard Barber's detailed presentation of essentially the Davis-Moore functional view, demands further thought on the question of why the many cogent critic-

---

[1] Kingsley Davis. and Wilbert E. Moore, "Some Principles of Stratification," American Sociological Review, 10 (April, 1945), pp. 242-249.

[2] Cf. especially the critique of Melvin Tumin, "Some Principles of Stratification: A Critical Analysis," American Sociological Review, 18 (August, 1953), pp. 387-394. See also Melvin Tumin, "Rewards and Task-Orientations," American Sociological Review, 20 (August, 1955), pp. 419-423; Richard D. Schwartz, "Functional Alternatives to Inequality," American Sociological Review, 20 (August, 1955), pp. 424-430; Richard L. Simpson, "A Modification of the Functional Theory of Social Stratification," Social Forces, 35 (December, 1956), esp. p. 137.

[3] Lester F. Ward, Applied Sociology, Boston: Ginn and Company, 1906, p. 96.

[4] For example, see Arnold W. Green, Sociology, New York: McGraw-Hill, 1952. He states, on page 217: "Stratification is universal because it is necessary." It is of interest to note, however, that in the second edition, 1956, of this text the above statement is changed to read merely: "Stratification is universal."

isms remain unanswered, and especially why so much of current American sociological theory in this area remains isolated from and incompatible with the voluminous European and earlier American literature.

The present paper is concerned, not to review or revive earlier criticisms, but to point out what we believe to be a heretofore neglected basic conceptual flaw in the current functional theory of stratification and a problem focus that has still to be faced by an adequate theory. Whereas the excellent critique of Tumin and others was aimed mainly at the substantive content of this theory, the present analysis is aimed primarily at its methodological deficiencies.

To put the issue simply, and as the title of this paper suggests, the current functional theory of stratification is not a theory of stratification at all but something that more closely resembles a theory of certain aspects of social differentiation and hierarchical organization —a distinction, our argument insists, that is not merely one of arbitrary terminology.[5]

To begin with, it will be recalled that the Davis-Moore theory specifies the central defining criterion of the concept of stratification as follows: "If the rights and perquisites of different positions in a society must be unequal, then the society must be stratified; because that is precisely what stratification means."[6] We shall argue, however, that this is not precisely what stratification has meant to most students. It is (or was) rather firmly embedded in usage that stratification involves the existence of <u>strata</u>, generally agreed to refer to specifiable collectivities or subgroups that <u>continue through several generations</u> to occupy the same relative positions and to receive the same relative amounts of material ends, prestige, and power. The statement quoted above, on the other hand, refers only to the fact of the differentiation of social positions as seen at any one point of time, and implies nothing about the existence of strata, which, to extend our above definition, implies groupings of individuals with biological and social continuity whose movements into the differentiated positions can be predicted to some degree (if only statistically).

Past stratification studies of importance have usually viewed strata, whether implicitly or explicitly, as historical developments. Without going back further, we recall the Marxian framework:

From the serfs of the Middle Ages sprang the chartered burghers of the earliest towns. From these burgesses the first elements of the bourgeoisie were developed. . . .

We see, therefore, how the modern bourgeoisie is itself the product of a long course of development, of a series of revolutions in the modes of production and exchange . . .

In proportion as the bourgeoisie, i.e., capital, is developed, in the same proportion is the proletariat, the modern working class, developed. . . .[7]

And certainly Pareto's "circulation of the elites," Veblen's "leisure class," and Weber's "life-chances" and "life-style" lose much of their meaning outside of a developmental framework.

Turning to the early American sociological pioneers, we note that Ward and Cooley stressed continuity and inheritance of position as basic to class. Thus, for example, Cooley—who preferred the term "caste" or "caste principle" to refer to what we mean by strata or stratification—wrote:

---

[5] The distinction between stratification and differentiation has been made in some detail by, among others, Wiese-Becker, <u>Systematic Sociology</u>, New York: John Wiley and Sons, 1932, and Cecil C. North, <u>Social Differentiation</u>, Chapel Hill: The University of North Carolina Press, 1926. The latter uses "social differentiation" as the generic term, subsuming under it the four main types: differences of function, of rank, of culture, and of interests.

And at least one other student of stratification has noted this basic flaw in Davis' theory: "Davis attempts a functional explanation of social stratification but, in fact, explains only social differentiation." Harold Pfautz "Social Stratification and Sociology," <u>Transactions of the Second World Congress of Sociology</u>, Vol. II, London: International Sociological Association, 1954, p. 320, footnote 18.

[6] Davis and Moore, <u>op. cit.</u>, p. 243.

[7] Karl Marx and Friedrich Engels, "The Communist Manifesto," in V. F. Calverton (editor), <u>The Making of Society</u>, New York: Random House, Inc., 1937, pp. 340, 341, 346.

When a class is somewhat strictly heredi- tary, we may call it a caste—a name origi- nally applied to the hereditary classes of India, but to which it is common, and cer- tainly convenient, to give a wider meaning. . . .

On every side we may see that differences arise, and that these tend to be perpetuated through inherited associations, opportunities, and culture. . . . . Unlikeness in the constitu- ents, a settled system and a low state of communication and enlightenment favor the growth of caste, and vice versa. The first provides natural lines of cleavage and so makes it easier to split into hereditary groups; the second gives inheritance time to consoli- date its power, while the third means the absence of those conscious and rational forces which are its chief rivals.[8]

Charles Page's study of the treatment of class by the American "Fathers" shows a similar general conception underlying the views of Small, Ross, and even Sum- ner.[9]

Of the contemporary students of strati- fication, we may mention R. H. Tawney, C. C. North, Wiese-Becker, Sorokin, Gerth and Mills, R. M. Williams, Jr., MacIver and Page, Harold Pfautz, and Kurt Mayer as a few of those (some, like Williams, with a functional orientation) who describe stratification as implying stratum permanence and hereditary in- equality and not merely "achieved ine- quality."[10] Thus, North has argued:

It is frequently urged that this emergence of the class of those who control modern eco- nomic processes through the ownership of capital is not a case of privilege but of a nat- ural evolution, whereby those whose abilities are adapted to the creation of capital and to the occupation of management and control naturally find their places in this position of power. In order to substantiate such a view

it would have to be shown that the creation of capital was the work of such individuals and that they entered their vocations through a process of competitive adaptation. As a mat- ter of fact all historical evidence points in exactly the opposite direction. . . .

Private property and the family, conserva- tive government, legalization of class, occu- pational and religious differences, primogeni- ture, peonage, an aristocratic educational system, these are some of the socially created factors that tend to fasten upon the coming generations distinctions that have once be- come prevalent. In so far, as these factors operate there are given to the members of the newer generations their respective places in the social system without reference to their own inherent qualities. But there is always the pretense that the inherent worth of the in- dividual is the determining factor.[11]

For MacIver and Page,

A system or structure of social classes in- volves, first, a hierarchy of status groups, second, the recognition of the superior-infe- rior stratification, and finally, some degree of permanency of the structure.[12]

And Mayer has recently stated:

Permanence is an important characteristic of social stratification. Rank hierarchies, like everything human, are changeable, but they tend to be relatively stable and enduring. Only those positions, therefore, which permit the exercise of power based on durable criteria, such as the possession of valuable material goods or the control of non-material values like magic formulas or religious symbols, can become the bases of permanent social strata.[13]

In our judgment Davis and Moore have in effect disclaimed any interest in the problem of stratification per se by claim- ing to concern themselves only with the system of positions of a society. As if attempting to justify their avoidance of what has been the central conception of stratification, they state emphatically:

---

[8]Charles H. Cooley, Social Organization, Glen- coe, Illinois: The Free Press, 1956, pp. 211, 217. ·

[9]Charles Hunt Page, Class and American Soci- ology, New York: The Dial Press, 1940.

[10]R. H. Tawney, Equality, London: George Allen and Unwin, Ltd., 4th ed., 1952; Wiese-Becker, op.; cit.; Pitirim A. Sorokin, Social Mobility, New York: Harper and Bros., 1927; Hans Gerth and C. Wright Mills, Character and Social Structure, New York: Harcourt, Brace and Company, 1953; Robin M. Williams, Jr., American Society, New York: Alfred A. Knopf, 1955, p. 89; Harold Pfautz, op. cit., p. 314.

[11]Cecil C. North, op. cit., pp. 222, 265.

[12]R. M. MacIver and Charles H. Page, Society: An Introductory Analysis, New York: Rinehart and Company, Inc., 1949, pp. 348-349.

[13]Kurt B. Mayer, Class and Society, Garden City, N. Y.: Doubleday and Company, Inc., 1955, p. 5.

Throughout, it will be necessary to keep in mind one thing—namely, that the discussion relates to the system of positions, not to the individuals occupying those positions. It is one thing to ask why different positions carry different degrees of prestige, and quite another to ask how certain individuals get into those positions. Although . . . . both questions are related, it is essential to keep them separate in our thinking. . . . The first question . . . is logically prior and, in the case of any particular individual or group, factually prior.[14]

Leaving aside the debatable assertion of priority, it should be noted that concern for the system of positions alone would have to stop with an analysis of their possible relations to and consequences for the system as a whole. When Davis and Moore go on, however, to speculate about processes motivating actors to fill these positions, and the relation between the[10] superior capacities or the training of actors and the highly rewarded positions they must fill, then Davis and Moore must relinquish their claim since they are clearly concerning themselves with characteristics of individuals and how these aid such persons in attaining certain positions. Whereas we concur in the view that differentiation of position on the one hand and the problem of individual attainment of those positions on the other are analytically distinct concerns, we are arguing that, not only must the distinction be consistently maintained, but, even more important, we cannot entertain a theory of stratification unless it focuses directly on the latter concern.

If we can agree that the term "social strata" refers to social groups or collectivities, and not positions, and that stratification refers to the existence of strata in a society, then perhaps we should, logically, insist that stratification be defined in terms of groups or collectivities, not positions. It might help to avoid confusion if we resist the current tendency to say, "Social stratification refers to the existence of a graded hierarchy of social positions" and to declare, instead, "Social stratification refers to

the existence of a graded hierarchy of continuous social groups or collectivities." The difference of emphasis here can be crucial, since the distinction between hierarchy of positions and hierarchy of groups opens up important questions. For example: To what extent, and how, does the former determine the latter, and vice versa? Would the range and particular structure of differential rewards and perquisites attaching to positions be what they are if it were not for the differential distribution of wealth, prestige, and power attaching to groups?

Failure to make and maintain the distinction between differentiation and stratification is brought out even more clearly in the recent volume by Bernard Barber, who builds the former concept into his definition of the latter. For Barber, stratification is "the product of the interaction of social differentiation and social evaluation."[15] It is "the result of the evaluations made of functionally important and differentiated social roles."[16] Thus, "a system of stratification can be seen as a system of facilities, rewards, and punishments allocated to the members of a society for the ways in which they perform its functionally essential and valued roles."[17] It follows then that "Position in the system of stratification is determined on the whole by performance in functionally essential roles. . . ."[18] And further, Barber concludes that stratification is inevitable because, first, some differentiation is essential in any society—it would be too wasteful to train all men for every specialized role, even if all were capable; and, second, differential evaluation of roles cannot be eliminated—not all roles are equally important. In sum, since Barber has defined stratification in terms of differentiation, and since we can all generally agree that some social differentiation is essential, if not inevitable, then it logically follows that "Some system of stratification is a

---

[14] Davis and Moore, op. cit., p. 242.

[15] Bernard Barber, Social Stratification, New York: Harcourt, Brace and Company, 1957, p. 2.
[16] Ibid., p. 54.
[17] Ibid., p. 20.
[18] Ibid., p. 60.

functional requirement of societies."[19]

But Barber fails to include the central notion of strata in his definition of stratification and thus, like Davis and Moore, ignores the distinction between stratification and differentiation. This distinction may perhaps be brought out more clearly by the consideration that a non-stratified society (if the functionalist can, for the moment, grant such a possibility) containing no intergenerationally continuous strata: (1) would nevertheless be differentiated in terms of duties, rights, and perquisites, (2) might, without being inconsistent, recognize differential evaluation of roles (though not necessarily of persons), and (3) would still have the problem of training and selecting the new members for the various roles. The classlessness of the society would have nothing directly to do with its differentiation but would be manifested in the fact that a person's initial social position or milieu at birth would not be correlated with his adult social position, except perhaps to the very small extent that current fact and theory allow us to correlate validly the individual's biologically based capacities or talents with his biological background. Stratified societies, on the other hand, have been viewed historically (as we have noted above) in terms of just such a correlation between individuals' initial social positions at birth and their adult social positions, giving rise to· castes, estates, or classes. This is why the several recent empirical studies of intergenerational mobility, as distinct from career patterns per se, are crucial in establishing the fact and the extent of stratification.

The manner in which the functionalists present the stratification system as actually operating is rather the way in which many persons desire and believe that it would work in contemporary society if only the class structure did not exist to hinder it! As Mayer states,

According to democratic ideology a person's social position should depend solely upon his

own qualities and achievements and he should be free to rise above or fall below his parents' class and status groups in accordance with his personal capacities. Correspondingly, social classes should consist merely of temporary aggregates of individuals who happen to have achieved similar social positions at any particular time.[20]

Thus, it is precisely the issue of equality or inequality of initial opportunity to acquire the qualifications socially defined as necessary for achievement of functionally important positions that is conspicuously absent from the functionalists' theory.

The fact that differentiation and stratification are analytically distinct does not imply that they are not closely interrelated. Social differentiation accompanied by great inequalities in the distribution of wealth, power, and prestige, can be seen to promote the development of more or less permanent strata; these, in turn, seem to promote the maintenance of large inequalities. Put otherwise, a classless society that nevertheless maintained great inequalities would seem to be as sociologically improbable as a stratified society maintaining no significant inequalities. Anthropological studies suggest, however, at the preliterate level at least, that such types of societies have existed. An important case in point is the Kwakiutl society of rank without class. Here is a society, according to a recent analysis,[21] with a proliferation of differentiated ranks and titles, but with each passed on from individual to individual, such that during his lifetime a person may be anything from a chief to a commoner. The result is that no classes can develop since no subgroup maintains a stable status over a long enough period for material, psychological, or subcultural distinctions to develop and persist.

Support for our basic argument is provided by the difficulties faced by the functionalist in attempting to square his theoretical formulation with research evi-

[19]Ibid., p. 19.

[20]Mayer, op. cit., p. 27.
[21]Cf. Helen Codere, "Kwakiutl Society: Rank without Class," American Anthropologist, 59 (June, 1957), pp. 473-486.

dence. Thus, Barber, in discussing ethnic, racial, and religious criteria of stratification, drops his theoretical guard by suggesting that "There is no necessary reason why a member of a society born into any given ethnic, racial, or religious group in that society cannot learn to perform adequately in any social role that society includes, whether high-ranking or low-ranking."[22] If we extend this formulation to include any economic or social group in general, and no reason is given why we may not, we arrive at the proposition that stratification is not necessary, or inevitable, after all. For an explanation of its ubiquity, then, we must turn, not to any functional necessity, but to the sociocultural dynamics of particular times and places.

A second difficulty is involved in Barber's claim that "Position in the system of stratification is determined on the whole by performance in functionally essential roles. . . ." Although Barber dedicates his book to Robert Merton he apparently overlooks a telling point made by his mentor. After pointing out the great difficulties involved in trying to establish a "clear minimum inventory of 'functional needs' of social systems," Merton writes:

> Much the same can be said of the formally described need for motivating people to perform "the essential social roles" in a society. The criteria of the "essential" are of course heavily dependent on the social system as it exists at a given time. In actual practice, functional sociologists devote little attention to alternative roles "essential" to the modification of a social system in determinate directions.[23]

Furthermore, the empirical data Barber gathers together in later chapters show over-whelmingly that, even in modern democratic societies, the social positions of the majority of adults are at the same or very similar levels in the hierarchy as those of their parents. In other words, positions are determined on the whole by

social inheritance, and only secondarily, within this pattern, by "performance." Although "performance" by itself may be important, it is the chance to perform that is at stake here.

Barber himself reaches this conclusion, although he fails to make explicit its implications for his functional theory: ". . . it happens that every child is born into the social class of his parents, is socialized accordingly, and derives greater or fewer advantages or disadvantages from his initial class position. . . . The family restricts equality of opportunity."[24] Barber seems to be trying to have and eat his cake. On the one hand, he states that position in a system of stratification is determined primarily by performance in functionally important roles. On the other hand, he declares that in no society can this be the case because it is inevitable that the family plays a central (according to his own interpretation, the central) role in determining position in the system; any other arrangement, he claims, would destroy the family (another confused but widely held hypothesis that we cannot discuss here).[25]

We note further that Barber's theory holds that social stratification is integrative for society "to the extent that it expresses a common and shared set of values."[26] But the empirical materials he uses show, in his own words, how

> Family solidarity will cause the members of different classes to have different interests in social mobility . . . different political interests . . . different attitudes toward income and inheritance-tax laws . . . obviously, have different economic interests . . . different educational interests. . . . And so it will be with every other kind of social interest—recreational, 'cultural,' and even religious.[27]

Barber's conclusion from all this, however, is: "Thus the upper and the lower classes will have opposed interests be-

---

[22]Barber, op. cit., p. 60 (emphasis in original).
[23]Robert K. Merton, "Discussion," *American Sociological Review*, 13 (April, 1948), p. 168.

[24]Barber, op. cit., p. 74.
[25]Cf. Codere, op. cit., for evidence that wide differences of rank could and did typically exist within the Kwakiutl family with no particular stress noted.
[26]Barber, op. cit., p. 9.
[27]Ibid., pp. 256-257.

<u>cause</u> they share a fundamental value consensus." [28] Unless we have missed a subtle point here, we believe that a more warranted conclusion is that stratification, in principle as well as in practice, is incompatible with value consensus on any level. [29]

Finally, Barber's theoretical orientation and conceptual commitment lead him to see a direct correlation between functional differentiation and inequality:

When we examine the evidence from many different societies, we discover a positive correlation between the amount of role differentiation and the development of a system of stratification. . . . Modern industrial societies, of course, are so highly differentiated that they all have elaborate systems of stratification. . . . [30]

But, we must ask, in what sense do modern societies have more highly developed and elaborated systems of stratification than, for example, India, Classical China, or feudal Europe? Do we not hold up such

societies to students as models of highly elaborate stratified systems? Thus R. H. Tawney writes:

A community which is marked by a low degree of economic differentiation may yet possess a class system of which the lines are sharply drawn and rigidly defined, as was the case, for example, in many parts of the agricultural Europe of the eighteenth century. It may be marked by a high degree of economic differentiation, and yet appear, when judged by English standards, to be comparatively classless, as is the case, for example, with some British Dominions. [31]

In sum, it would not seem unjust to say that the functionalists' [32] unique definition of stratification jetisons much of the previous work done in this area and promotes an insuperable discontinuity in sociological research. [33]

---

[28] <u>Ibid.</u>, p. 257 (emphasis in original).

[29] Most students of society with a strong historical sense should find little difficulty in supporting the view that stratification has been, on balance, an actual or potential disruptive force. The fact that highly stratified societies like India have survived for many centuries proves, not that stratification is integrative as some claim, but only that a high degree of stratification can persist and the society "survive" at a certain level under such conditions as autocracy, little functional differentiation, and a low state of communication and enlightenment.

The question of whether functional differentiation <u>per se</u> is also, on balance, disintegrative is complicated by the difficulty of separating out the effects of stratification that, in practice, are closely intermingled with differentiation. Thus, it would seem that functional specialization, while leading to differences in <u>some</u> spheres of activity and outlook, need to lead to gross cleavages of a subcultural character such as stratification promotes. We might well subscribe to the perspective of C. C. North who, accepting Durkheim's argument that increasing division of labor leads to organic solidarity of cohesive interdependence, notes also the disruptive potential of overspecialization and of individualistically oriented interest groups. North, <u>op. cit.</u>, Part IV.

[30] Barber, <u>op. cit.</u>, pp. 14-15.

---

[31] Tawney, <u>op. cit.</u>, pp. 52-53.

[32] Merton's view that the functional approach does not <u>logically</u> entail the difficulties discussed above is without doubt sound. (See R. K. Merton, <u>Social Theory and Social Structure</u>, Glencoe, Ill.: The Free Press, 1949, Chapter 1.) Yet the frequent stress of functionalism on the "survival of society" easily leads one to look very hard for, or find very easily, some existing structural arrangement which, under the guise of explaining the survival of "society" (a very difficult concept to specify apart from the <u>status quo</u>), succeeds only in justifying the persistence of some existing <u>structure</u>, e.g., a class system. When we work in the other direction, however, starting with existing structures and seek their <u>consequences for or determinate relationships</u> to the total system in the present or future (a non-functionalist orientation), we are more easily humbled before the enormity of the task.

In any case, the student of sociology of knowledge might well argue that when we add to the logical structure of functionalism the factors of "human nature" and ethnocentrism, the probability is very great that some misuse will occur. Past experience would lend this some support. Cf. the writer's "Structural-Functional Analysis in Modern Sociology," in Howard Becker and Alvin Boskoff (editors), <u>Modern Sociological Theory in Continuity and Change</u>, New York: The Dryden Press, 1957, Chapter 8.

[33] A similar conclusion is reached by Jean Floud in her trenchant criticism of Theodore Geiger's functional orientation and concomitant confusion of social differentiation with social stratification. See "Social Stratification in Denmark" (Review Article), <u>British Journal of Sociology</u>, 3 (June, 1952), especially pp. 176-177.

Status Crystallization: A Non-Vertical Dimension of Social Status*

Gerhard E. Lenski

SOURCE: *American Sociological Review*, Vol. 19 (1954), pp. 405-13.

In recent years there have been numerous indications that, in the analysis of social stratification, sociology is rapidly outgrowing the classical conceptual schemes inherited from the past. Critically inclined students have come increasingly to recognize the inability of the older schemes to incorporate many of the findings of present day research, or to adapt themselves to newer theoretical concerns.

This trend is evident even with respect to such a basic matter as the manner in which the vertical structure of groups is conceived. From Aristotle to Marx to Warner, most social philosophers and social scientists have described the vertical structure of human groups in terms of a single hierarchy in which each member occupies a single position. Different exponents of this traditional scheme have not always agreed regarding the nature or characteristics of this hierarchical structure. Nevertheless, all have shared the common conception of a unidimensional structure.

Since Max Weber's day, however, this traditional approach has come to be criticized by a growing number of sociologists, who have argued that the uni-dimensional view is inadequate to describe the complexities of group structure. These critics have mentioned that the structure of human groups normally involves the coexistence of a number of parallel vertical hierarchies which usually are imperfectly correlated with one another.

If this newer approach is sound, the traditional conception of individual or family status will require radical revision. Instead of being a single position in a uni-dimensional hierarchy, it becomes a series of positions in a series of related vertical hierarchies.

An important question which is raised immediately by such a view is the question of how these several positions are interrelated. Theoretically it becomes possible to conceive of a non-vertical dimension to individual or family status —that is, a consistency dimension. In this dimension units may be compared with respect to the degree of consistency of their positions in the several vertical hierarchies. In other words, certain units may be consistently high or consistently low, while others may combine high standing with respect to certain status variables with low standing with respect to others.[1]

*This article is the first of a projected series on status and class crystallization growing out of a research project conducted jointly by Professor Warner S. Landecker and the present writer. Grateful appreciation is expressed to Professor Ronald Freedman and his Detroit Area Study Staff for their assistance in collecting the data, and to the Horace H. Rackham School of Graduate Studies of the University of Michigan for financial assistance.

[1] This possibility has also been noted in recent years by Emile Benoit-Smullyan, "Status, Status Types and Status Interrelationships," American Sociological Review, 9 (1944), pp. 151-61; Pitirim A. Sorokin, Society, Culture, and Personality, New York: Harper & Brothers, 1947, pp. 289-94; Harold F. Kaufman, et al., "Problems of Theory and Method in the Study of Social Stratification in Rural Society," Rural Sociology, 18 (1953), p. 15; and Stuart Adams, "Status Congruency as a Variable in Small Group Performance," Social Forces, 32 (1953), pp. 16-22.

While it is one thing to conceive of new theoretical models, it is another matter to demonstrate their utility. This article reports the results of an empirical study designed to test the significance and utility of this non-vertical dimension of status. More specifically, this study was designed to discover whether an analysis employing this new dimension would be capable of accounting for some of the variance in political behavior which is left unexplained by traditional methods of stratification analysis.

THE RESEARCH DESIGN

The basic hypothesis tested in this study is as follows: <u>individuals characterized by a low degree of status crystallization[2] differ significantly in their political attitudes and behavior from individuals characterized by a high degree of status crystallization, when status differences in the vertical dimensions are controlled.</u>

The data were gathered in the first Detroit Area Study.[3] In the spring of 1952, a random sample of the residents of the metropolitan Detroit area was interviewed.[4] A total of 749 interviews was obtained. Comparisons with 1950 census data indicated that the sample obtained was highly representative of the total population of the metropolitan area.[5]

Two basic variables employed in the present study require operational definition. These are (1) social status, and (2) status crystallization.

<u>Social status.</u> For operational purposes, the statuses of respondents were defined in terms of their relative positions in four vertical hierarchies: the income hierarchy; the occupation hierarchy; the education hierarchy; and the ethnic hierarchy. These four were chosen both because of their great importance and also because of the relative ease with which necessary information relating to them could be obtained.

With respect to income and education, there was no problem in defining the structure of the hierarchy. Both hierarchies are quantitative in nature. With respect to occupation and ethnic background there was, unfortunately, no such built-in scale. Thus, the construction of scales of relative rank had to be undertaken.

In ranking occupations, the Edwards classificatory scheme was considered and rejected on the grounds that it does not constitute a sufficiently precise scale of status. Top business executives, for example, enjoy greater prestige than many professional men. At the same time, very small proprietors (who are classified with top executives in the Edwards scheme) may enjoy no more prestige than skilled workers. Furthermore, recent empirical studies indicate that skilled workers today enjoy greater prestige than many clerical and sales workers.[6] In short, the overlap between occupational categories when judged by the criterion of relative prestige seemed too great in the Edwards scheme.

The best empirical basis for constructing a scale of occupational rank seemed to have been provided by the National Opinion Research Center's study of occupational prestige.[7] Using the occupations evaluated in that study as a basis, five occupational prestige levels were defined, and an attempt was made to

[2]The term "status crystallization" will be used throughout the remainder of the article as a synonym for "status consistency."

[3]For details regarding the Detroit Area Study, see Ronald Freedman, "The Detroit Area Study: A Training and Research Laboratory in the Community," American Journal of Sociology, 59 (1953), pp. 30-33.

[4]Respondents were selected by the area sampling method. In general, the sampling procedure involved: (1) random selection of a sample of blocks in the community; (2) within these blocks a random selection of households; and (3) within each household a random selection of persons to be interviewed. For a more detailed description of the methods employed, see Leslie Kish, "A Two-Stage Sample of a City," American Sociological Review, 17 (1952), pp. 761-69, and Kish, "A Procedure for Objective Respondent Selection Within the Household," Journal of the American Statistical Association, 44 (1949), pp. 380-87.

[5]For detailed comparisons with census data, see A Social Profile of Detroit: 1952, Ann Arbor: University of Michigan Press, 1952, pp. 34-47.

[6]See "Jobs and Occupations A Popular Evaluation," Opinion News, 9 (1947), p. 3 ff.

[7]Op. cit.

extrapolate from the rated occupations to others not rated in that study. Slightly over 50 per cent of the occupations of the family heads in the Detroit sample required such extrapolation. Coding reliability in these cases was better than 90 per cent.[8]

No national sample of public opinion was available for the construction of the ethnic scale. In the circumstances, the best solution seemed to be an evaluation of the various ethnic groups by Detroit-area residents. For this purpose a sample of 195 Detroit area students enrolled in introductory sociology courses at the University of Michigan was obtained during the academic year 1951-52. These students were asked to rate all of the major ethnic groups found in the Detroit area on the basis of what they thought to be the general community evaluation, as distinguished from their own personal evaluation.[9] As was expected, the northwest European groups were ranked ahead of the south and east European groups, and these in turn were generally ranked ahead of the colored groups.[10]

For respondents who were not themselves the family head, the status characteristics of the head were used to define their position in the four hierarchies. This procedure was followed for two reasons. First, current literature, both theory and research, indicates that the family is normally a status unit and that the social attributes of the family head are the chief determinants of status for all dependent relatives in the domicile.[11] Second, this procedure ren-

dered the data collected from wives and other dependent relatives comparable with that for individuals who were themselves family heads.[12] This latter consideration was quite important due to the relatively small size of the sample.

Status Crystallization. Having established the structure of these vertical hierarchies, the next problem was to establish common scales for all of them, so that the relative position of respondents in the several hierarchies might be compared. Without common scales, a measure of status crystallization would be impossible.

To this end, frequency distributions were established for each hierarchy. Using these distributions as a basis, scores were assigned for each of the various positions (or intervals) in each hierarchy on the basis of the midpoint of the percentile range for that position (or interval). Table 1 below illustrates the pro-

Table 1
Frequency Distribution of Respondents by Income of Family Head, and Assigned Percentile Scores for Each Income Range

Annual Income of Family Head	Number of Respondents	Cumulative Percentile Range	Assigned Score
$10,000 or more	29	95.4—100.0	98
8,000—9,999	15	93.0— 95.3	94
7,00 —7,999	19	90.0— 92.9	91
6,000—6,999	58	80.7— 89.9	85
5,000—5,999	82	67.6— 80.6	74
4,000—4,999	137	45.6— 67.5	57
3,000—3,999	191	15.0— 45.5	30
2,000—2,999	57	5.9— 14.9	10
1,000—1,999	21	2.5— 5.8	4
1— 999	10	0.9— 2.4	2
No income	5	0.0— 0.8	0
Total	624*		

*This figure includes only those who were themselves currently in the labor force or respondents who were members of families in which the head was in the labor force, and for whom income data were available.

---

[8]Admittedly this technique was not wholly satisfactory. It seemed, however, the most satisfactory approximation which could be achieved within the financial and temporal limitations of the project.

[9]Student evaluations of their own ethnic group were not included, in order to minimize personal biases which might not be consistent with community biases.

[10]Separate ranks were determined for each of the specific groups within these general categories. In the case of respondents of mixed ethnic backgrounds, the scores of the several ethnic groups (see below) were averaged.

[11]See, for example, Talcott Parsons, "A Revised Analytical Approach to the Theory of Social Stratification," in Class, Status and Power, edited by

Reinhard Bendix and Seymour Lipset, Glencoe: The Free Press, 1953, pp. 166-67; Kingsley Davis, Human Society, New York: The Macmillan Company, 1949, p. 364; W. Lloyd Warner and Paul S. Lunt, The Social Life of a Modern Community, New Haven: Yale University Press, 1941, p. 90.

[12]If this were not done, comparisons of nonemployed dependent relatives would be most difficult, since such respondents could not be ranked in terms of income and occupation.

cedure as it was employed in assigning scores to the various income intervals.[13]

Having obtained comparable scores for the four hierarchies, the last remaining step was to establish the quantitative measure of status crystallization. This was accomplished by taking the square root of the sum of the squared deviations from the mean of the four hierarchy scores of the individual and subtracting the resulting figure from one hundred.[14] The more highly consistent or crystallized an individual's status, the more nearly his crystallization score approached one hundred; the less consistent or crystallized his status, the more nearly his crystallization score approached zero.

The study group. Of the original 749 respondents, it was necessary to eliminate 136 from the study group, either because of incomplete or inadequate data on one of the four key status variables, or because the family head was not in

the labor force.[15] Due to the small number of cases, it seemed advisable to divide the study group into only two crystallization categories—a high crystallization category and a low crystallization category. Those with crystallization scores of 53 or more were placed in the former category (N=439) while those with scores of 52 or less were placed in the latter category (N=174). This line of division was selected because in the course of the analysis it was discovered that something roughly approximating a natural breaking point was discernible here.

FINDINGS

As a first test of the basic hypothesis, the voting behavior and preferences of the two categories of respondents were compared. Data relating to three elections were used: (1) the 1948 presidential election; (2) the 1950 Michigan gubernatorial election; and (3) the 1952 presidential election. For the first two elections comparisons were made on the basis of the respondents' reports of their behavior. For the 1952 election, it was necessary to make the comparison on the basis of the respondents' indications of their party preferences, since the interviews were conducted eight to ten months before the election.

In each election, the proportion of respondents supporting the Democratic party was substantially greater in the low crystallization category than in the high crystallization category. As may be seen from Table 2, below, these differences were significant at the five per cent level in all but the 1952 election.[16]

---

[13] In computing the educational scores of the respondents, one variation was introduced. Respondents forty years of age and over were separated from those younger. This was considered necessary in view of the rapid changes in educational expectations and attainments in American society in recent times. Direct comparisons of older persons with younger persons in terms of educational attainments would be unrealistic, since failure to complete high school, for example, is a far more serious handicap for members of the younger generation than for members of the older. Some allowance for this difference is usually made in the evaluative process in contemporary society. The division of the sample at age forty seemed the most effective simple method for taking recognition of this fact, since by this means the sample was divided into approximately equal halves.

[14] The use of squared deviations from the mean rather than simple deviations was employed to emphasize the effect of larger deviations and to minimize the effect of smaller deviations. This was considered desirable since the techniques employed in quantifying positions (or intervals) in the several hierarchies were sufficiently crude so that no great importance could be attached to small deviations.

The technique of subtracting the resulting figure from one hundred was employed so that respondents whose status was highly crystallized would have -numerically higher crystallization scores than those whose status was poorly crystallized. This was done solely to avoid semantic difficulties.

[15] It seemed desirable to remove those respondents in families in which the family head was not currently in the labor force due to retirement, prolonged illness, or extended unemployment, since serious difficulties arose in any attempt to compare them with the remainder of the sample with respect to their position in the occupational hierarchy.

[16] It will be noted in Table 2 that the proportion of persons supporting the Democratic party is far above the national average in all three elections. Some difference in this direction was to be expected, since the sample was drawn from the

Table 2
Voting Behavior and Preferences in the 1948,
1950, and 1952 Elections, by Degree of
Status Crystallization
Per Cent of Voters
Supporting Democrats

Election Year	Low Crystallization	High Crystallization	Prob. Less Than
1948	81.3*	69.0*	.03
1950	84.0	68.4	.01
1952	73.2**	64.7**	.11

*Includes supporters of the Progressive party, since 70 per cent of these individuals (N=10) were normally Democratic voters; none gave any indication of ever having supported a Republican candidate.

**Refers to the percentage expressing a _preference_ for the Democratic party.

Although the data in Table 2 suggest that the basic hypothesis is sound, no conclusions can be drawn until controls

are established for status differences in the four vertical dimensions. This is necessary in the present problem because of the well established fact that variations in these four dimensions are closely associated with variations in political behavior and attitudes. Thus, the variations between the two crystallization categories observed in Table 2 might be due simply to failure to control vertical status differences between the two categories.

A check of the mean scores of the two categories of respondents in the four vertical dimensions revealed, as shown in the upper half of Table 3, that low crystallization respondents had higher _mean_ education and ethnic scores than high crystallization respondents. At the same time, however, high crystallization respondents had higher _mean_ income and occupation scores.

Table 3
Mean Income, Occupation, Ethnic, and Education Scores by
Crystallization Categories, Before and After Correction
to Control Status Differences in the
Vertical Dimensions

Crystallization Category	N	Mean Income Score	Mean Occupation Score	Mean Ethnic Score	Mean Education Score
Uncorrected					
Low crystallization	174	46.6	49.5	50.1	54.1
High crystallization	439	51.3	50.2	50.0	46.1
Corrected					
Low crystallization	166	48.6	50.0	49.7	53.7
High crystallization	413	48.4	48.2	48.4	44.1

metropolitan Detroit area, which is the stronghold of the Democratic party in Michigan. This, however, does not entirely account for the preponderance of Democratic voters. In the 1948 election, for example, slightly less than 60 percent of the major party vote in the metropolitan Detroit area went to the Democratic party. However, slightly more than 70 percent of the respondents in the study group reported that they voted for the Democratic party that year. This discrepancy seems to be due to the fact observed by polling organizations that many persons report on interviews that they voted in a previous election, when careful checking of the voting lists reveal they did not. This seems to be more frequently a characteristic of Democrats than of Republicans of the larger cities.

Some evidence of this tendency was discovered in the present study. In cases where the respondent resided at the same address in 1948 or 1950, the accuracy of his response was checked. Such checks revealed that at least 13 per cent of those who claimed to have voted in 1948, had not, in fact,

voted. Eighty-five per cent of those who erroneously claimed to have voted reported voting for either the Democratic or Progressive parties, while only 15 per cent reported voting for the Republican party. While these respondents were not counted as voters in Table 2, others undoubtedly remained who gave erroneous reports, but for whom no check was possible due to a change in residence during the intervening period.

Among the erroneous reports discovered, the proportion of erroneous Democratic reports was somewhat greater in the high crystallization category while the proportion of erroneous Republican reports was somewhat greater in the low crystallization category. If it is assumed that comparable proportions of Republican and Democratic voters would be found in the undiscovered erroneous reports, this would mean that the present uncorrected error in the data works _against_ the basic hypothesis, since it tends to make the difference in voting behavior between the two categories of respondents appear less than it actually was.

This latter fact is important, since it might be argued that income and occupation are the chief determinants of political behavior, while education and ethnic background are of negligible importance. If this were so, the tendency of high crystallization respondents to favor the Republican party might then be simply a function of their higher average income and superior occupational status.

To test this alternative hypothesis, 26 respondents with the highest incomes in the high crystallization category and eight respondents with the lowest incomes in the low crystallization category were dropped from the study group. The elimination of these respondents had the effect of controlling status differences simultaneously in all of the four vertical dimensions as shown in the lower half of Table 3. In other words, after the elimination of these 34 cases, respondents in the low crystallization category had a higher mean score than respondents in the high crystallization category with respect to each of the four status variables. Thus, any Democratic bias remaining after the elimination of these respondents could not be attributed to a failure to control status differences in these vertical dimensions. On the contrary, whatever differences might remain after this control was applied would remain in spite of the fact that respondents in the low crystallization category had slightly higher mean scores than respondents in the high crystallization category.

As may be seen by an inspection of Table 4, the application of this rigorous control tended to reduce the margin of difference in political behavior between the two crystallization categories. With the exception of the 1952 election, however, a statistically significant margin of difference remained. Even in the 1952 election, the direction of the difference was consistent with the pattern observed in the other two elections.

The significance of the differences between the two crystallization categories became more apparent when a further test of the basic hypothesis was made,

Table 4
Voting Behavior and Preferences in the 1948, 1950, and 1952 Elections, by Degree of Status Crystallization, After Correction
Per Cent of Voters
Supporting Democrats

Election Year	Low Crystallization	High Crystallization	Prob. Less Than
1948	82.2*	71.4*	.05
1950	83.5	71.3	.04
1952	72.2**	68.0**	.46

*Includes supporters of the Progressive Party.
**Refers to the percentage expressing a preference for the Democratic Party.

using other data. A 50 per cent subsample of the respondents (N=311) were asked their views on (a) a government-sponsored health insurance program, (b) price controls, and (c) a general extension of governmental powers. As shown in Table 5 below, respondents in the low crystallization category took a more liberal (i.e. leftist) stand on each of these questions than did respondents in the high crystallization category. In two of the three cases, the difference was significant at the two per cent level.

As in the analysis of the data on voting behavior and preferences, the application of controls for differences in the four status hierarchies reduced slightly the margin of differences between the two crystallization categories. It should be noted, however, that even with the application of these controls, the difference between the two categories was still significant at the five per cent level for both the health insurance question and

Table 5
Frequency of Strongly Liberal Responses on Controversial Issues, by Degree of Status Crystallization

Issue	Per Cent Strongly Liberal		Prob. Less Than
	Low Crystallization	High Crystallization	
Government health insurance	26.7	14.9	.02
Price controls	31.1	25.8	.35
Extension of government powers	40.0	25.8	.02

the question regarding the extension of governmental powers.

On the basis of the data described above, it would therefore appear that a definite association existed between low crystallization and political liberalism among respondents in this cross-section sample of metropolitan Detroit. Before such a relationship could be asserted with confidence, one further problem required examination. Briefly stated, the problem was whether the differences observed between the two crystallization categories were due to the lack of status

To test this alternative hypothesis, a detailed analysis of the low crystallization category was made. All of the respondents in this category were classified on the basis of the various relationships between the income, occupation, education, and ethnic hierarchies. Thus, for example, respondents whose income score was markedly higher than their education score (i.e., 30 or more points higher) were placed in one category, while those whose education score was markedly higher than their income score were placed in a second category. Each

Table 6
Summary Comparison of Voting Records and Attitudes on Controversial
Issues of Twelve Categories of Low Crystallization Respondents
with Crystallization Respondents

Paired Variables[1]			Complete Sample Per Cent Strongly		Subsample Per Cent Strongly
High	Low	N	Democratic[2]	N	Liberal[3]
Income	—Ethnic	53	56.6	23	34.8
Occupation	—Ethnic	53	50.9	28	39.3
Education	—Ethnic	68	50.0	34	32.4
Occupation	—Education	36	47.2	16	25.0
Education	—Occupation	56	42.8	28	17.8
Income	—Occupation	28	39.6	21	4.8
Education	—Income	67	38.8	31	25.8
Income	—Education	41	36.6	21	28.6
Ethnic	—Occupation	53	35.8	29	17.2
Ethnic	—Education	48	35.4	26	19.2
Ethnic	—Income	63	34.9	32	21.9
Occupation	—Income	32	34.4	17	29.4
All high crystallization		413	34.2	207	15.5

[1]In the case of each comparison respondents had an assigned percentile score 30 or more points higher for the high variable than for the low variable.
[2]Includes all those who supported Democratic (or Progressive) Candidates at least twice between 1948 and 1952.
[3]Includes all those who took strongly liberal stand on at least two of the three controversial issues.

crystallization per se, or rather were a function of particular patterns of status inconsistency which were present in large numbers in the low crystallization category. Thus, for example, it might be argued that the combination of extensive education and limited income is associated with strong liberal biases, while the reverse combination is not, and that the differences observed in Tables 4 and 5 were due to the fact that persons possessing the former combination were extremely numerous in the low crystallization category, giving the category as a whole a liberal bias which was not due to lack of status crystallization per se.

of the twelve resulting categories of low crystallization respondents were then compared with high crystallization respondents in terms of their voting record and their views on the three controversial issues.[17] The results of this analysis are shown in Table 6.

Two tentative conclusions may be drawn from a careful analysis of Table 6. First, liberal political tendencies are associated with a low degree of status

[17]This comparison was made after the correction to control for status differences in the four hierarchies.

crystallization regardless of the specific relationship of the status variables. This conclusion seems justified in view of the fact that despite the relatively small number of cases involved, 23 out of 24 of the comparisons made yielded differences in the predicted direction. In short, regardless of whether income rank was high and educational rank low, or the reverse, or what the particular nature of the status inconsistency was, the fact of imperfect status crystallization per se seems to have been related to political liberalism.

The data in Table 6 also suggest the tentative conclusion that certain types of status inconsistencies are more closely related to political liberalism than others. For example, relatively low ethnic status in combination with relatively high income, occupational, or educational status was more closely associated with liberal tendencies than the reverse. Also, the data suggest that status inconsistencies involving high occupational rank and low educational rank are more closely associated with liberal tendencies than the reverse. However, in view of the small number of cases in each cell it is necessary to use considerable caution in drawing conclusions from the present data regarding which patterns of relationships are most closely associated with political liberalism.

DISCUSSION

Not only do the findings in the preceding section suggest that a recognition of this non-vertical dimension of social status may help account for some of the previously unexplained variance in political behavior, but also they hint at a more basic relationship between social structure and social change. Extrapolating from these findings, one might predict that the more frequently acute status inconsistencies occur within a population the greater would be the proportion of that population willing to support programs of social change.[18]

Apparently the individual with a poorly crystallized status is a particular type of marginal man, and is subjected to certain pressures by the social order which are not felt (at least to the same degree) by individuals with a more highly crystallized status. Conceivably a society with a relatively large proportion of persons whose status is poorly crystallized is a society which is in an unstable condition. In brief, under such conditions the social system itself generates its own pressures for change.

Some insight into the manner in which such pressures for change may be generated by status inconsistencies has been supplied by Hughes in his excellent discussion of "Dilemmas and Contradictions of Status."[19] The Negro doctor, by virtue of the fact that in his person he combines two roles of grossly discrepant status, is apt to be subjected with some frequency to social experiences of an unpleasant or frustrating nature. The same will tend to be true of the highly educated man with limited income, or the business executive with a grammar school education.

Not all such individuals would be expected to react against the social order which produces such unpleasant experiences in their lives. For various reasons the individual may develop other reactions. For example, the individual may react by blaming other individuals as individuals rather than as agents of the social order. Such a reaction might be common among persons raised in an individualistic tradition or who, because

---

[18] It might be argued that conservatives advocate programs of social change just as do liberals, especially in periods of liberal control. Strictly

speaking, this is true, but it must be noted that such changes are usually put forward as a program of return to former conditions. Although experts might challenge this claim in many respects, it is a claim which is accepted by the general public. Thus, in the public mind the liberal or left-wing parties are usually thought of as the parties advocating change, while the conservative parties are thought of as the supporters of the present order (or the old order).

[19] *American Journal of Sociology*, 50 (1944), pp. 353-57. It should be noted that Hughes uses the term "status" differently from the use made in this article. It is not difficult, however, to relate his discussion to the present problem if this fact is kept in mind.

of limited educational opportunities, have not learned to relate individual experiences to the social order. Another possibility open to the individual with a poorly crystallized status is that he will react to resulting unpleasant experiences by blaming himself. Finally, there is the possibility that the individual may withdraw in such a manner as to diminish the frequency and the seriousness of the socially disturbing experiences which arise as a result of his status inconsistencies. Such alternative types of reactions may very well explain a part of the variance in responses among individuals in the poorly crystallized category in the present study. It should be noted, however, that the tendency to react by advocating change in the social order seems to have been a frequent type of reaction in the present sample.

Building on this foundation, the political liberalism of several diverse groups in American society begins to appear as a common expression of a common social experience. In recent years political observers have reported relatively strong support for liberal political programs from such diverse groups as college professors, Jewish businessmen, Hollywood actors, and the Protestant clergy. All four of these categories of persons, it must be noted, are characterized by a relatively low degree of status crystallization. Professors and clergymen enjoy high occupational and educational rank, yet their income is sometimes less than that of skilled manual workers. Screen stars frequently combine high income rank with low educational rank, and sometimes with low ethnic rank as well. Jewish businessmen combine high income and occupational rank (and often high educational rank) with low ethnic rank. If the foregoing analysis is sound, one would be led to expect a relatively high frequency of liberal biases among the members of such groups, and for the same fundamental reason.

Building on the present foundation, it also becomes possible to predict one of the sources of leadership of successful revolutionary movements. Years ago Marx and Engels noted that successful revolutionary movements are usually characterized by the combination of broad support from the masses or lower strata, and leadership recruited from the higher strata in the old order.[20] The present study suggests that persons of poorly crystallized status may be an important source from which such leadership is recruited. Quite often such persons combine the personal skills necessary for effective leadership with the equally necessary motivation.

Finally, it may be noted that if the conception of social status presented in this paper is as fruitful as the findings of this pilot study would seem to indicate, some considerable modification of the traditional conception of social class will also be required. This point will be developed more fully in subsequent papers based on the present project.

One methodological implication of the present study remains to be discussed. During the past two decades it has become fashionable in social science circles to construct indices of socio-economic status by averaging up in some manner several status variables.[21] The findings of this present study indicate that such constructions are seriously deficient in characterizing the social status of a significant minority of the population. Such techniques for classifying individuals fail to take into account what appears to be an important dimension of status, and thus may frequently fail to account for an important part of the variance in the phenomena under investigation.

CONCLUSIONS

The conclusions which are drawn from a pilot study such as the present one

[20] *Manifesto of the Communist Party*, New York: International Publishers, 1932, p. 19.

[21] See, for example, W. Lloyd Warner, et al., *Social Class in America*, Chicago: Science Research Associates, 1949, Part 3; or Clyde V. Kiser and P. K. Whelpton, "Social and Psychological Factors Affecting Fertility, IX. Fertility Planning and Fertility Rates by Socio-Economic Status," *Milbank Memorial Fund Quarterly*, 27 (1949), pp. 214-16.

should be concerned primarily with questions of the advisability of pursuing further the projected line of research, and the methods appropriate to further research, if such is warranted. Conclusions concerning the validity of given hypotheses about social relationships are hardly warranted, except insofar as they relate to the question of the advisability of further research.

In the present case the writer feels that the findings fully warrant further exploration of the crystallization dimension of status. This view seems justified not only on the ground that status crys-

tallization seems a useful tool for reducing the range of unexplained variation in American political behavior, but also because of the broader theoretical and methodological implications which were outlined in the preceding section.

Future research in this area should be directed not only to the checking and rechecking of the relationship of status crystallization and political liberalism, but also to the exploration of the relationship of status crystallization to variations in other areas of behavior, and in personality development as well. Possibly fruitful new discoveries will result.

Migration and Occupational Mobility in Norristown, Pennsylvania

Sidney Goldstein

SOURCE: *American Sociological Review*, Vol. 20 (1955), pp. 402–8.

INTRODUCTION

Norristown, Pennsylvania, a medium-sized city twenty miles northwest of Philadelphia, is currently the focus of an intensive study of the changing size, composition, and demographic behavior of its population. This is a report on one phase of this overall study—an attempt to utilize local data to determine the changing patterns of occupational mobility among the male members of the Norristown labor force over the last forty years and to determine what relationship, if any, exists between these patterns of occupational mobility and the patterns of migration into and out of Norristown. For purposes of analysis, four time periods were used: 1910-1920, 1920-1930, 1930-1940, and 1940-1950.

DATA AND METHOD

The labor force of an industrialized locality such as Norristown undergoes con-

tinuous changes in size and in composition. Among the factors contributing to these changes are: (1) selective migration into and out of the area; (2) the entrance of new persons into the labor force as the children of residents reach adulthood, and the exit from the labor force of residents who become disabled, who retire, or who die; (3) internal changes within the occupational structure itself, resulting from the movement of residents from one occupational group to another.

Decennial censuses show the net changes that have taken place in the size and composition of both the population and the labor force during intercensal periods. They are not sufficient, however, to indicate the gross changes that characterized the intervening years, and they cannot separate the effects of migration from the changes resulting from occupational mobility on the part of the non-migrant population of the community.

What is needed for this type of intensive analysis is a source that provides the basis for identifying the separate streams of in- and out-migration and the occupational attachment of the members of these streams, as well as the occupations of the non-migrant population at the beginning and at the end of the decade.

The only comprehensive sources available for this project in Norristown were vital statistics records, school records, and city directories. An unbroken series of city directories covers the last one hundred years; school records date to the turn of the century; and complete files of birth and death certificates exist for the last sixty years. These sources were used, in part because they have the requisite historical depth, but largely because tests showed that these three quite distinct types of data, when combined in the process of analysis, give an accurate record of the Norristown population now and forty years ago, and make it possible to study the effect of migration and occupational mobility on the labor force composition of the community. With such sources available, the method for obtaining the data necessary for this analysis was a comparatively simple one.

The city directories of Norristown contain the names, addresses, and occupations of all adult male residents of the community. These directories have been compiled and issued every second year since 1860. For this analysis, two samples were drawn from the directories of each decade from 1910 to 1950, one from the first directory of the decade, and the other from the last directory of the decade. Each sample consisted of a ten per cent random selection of all male residents listed. Tests[1] indicated that they were representative both of the total size of the adult male population of Norristown and of its occupational composition.

The sample drawn from the first directory of the decade served as the basis

for measuring migration out of the community during the ensuing decade. By tracing the individuals in this sample through the five succeeding directories of that decade, it became possible to note changes of residence within Norristown and changes in occupation. A large number of individuals were found in all directories, but others disappeared in the course of being traced. These disappearances were attributable either to death or to out-migration. All of the disappearances were, therefore, checked, name by name, in the death certificates. After those who were no longer listed because of death had been identified, the remaining disappearances were classified as out-migrants.

Correspondingly, the sample drawn from the last directory of the decade provided the basis for determining in-migration during the previous decade. By tracing the individuals in this sample through all the five preceding directories of the decade, it became possible to note all changes in residence and occupation. As in the case of the forward traced samples, a large number of these individuals were listed in all directories. Others did not appear as they were traced back in time. These were the potential in-migrants—potential because it was also possible that some were not found in the earlier directories because they were not old enough to be covered by directory entries. All of these "disappearances" were, therefore, checked, name by name, in the school records and birth certificates. After those who entered the directory because of aging were identified, the remaining "disappearances" were classified as in-migrants.

Combination of the results obtained from both the forward and backward tracings through each decade provided data for analyzing the patterns of both migration and occupational mobility during the decade. The data indicated how many and what segments of the population resident in the community at the beginning of the decade moved out by the end of the decade, and how many and what segments of the population resident in

---

[1] See Sidney Goldstein, "City Directories as Sources of Migration Data," The American Journal of Sociology, 60 (September, 1954), pp. 169-176.

the community at the end of the decade had moved in during the previous ten years. In addition, for all these persons in both samples who were continuous residents of Norristown throughout the decade, these data made possible the analysis of patterns of occupational mobility by comparison of the occupational attachment of each individual at the beginning of the decade with his occupational attachment at the end of the decade. By joint analysis of the migrants and the residents, it was possible to evaluate changes in the labor force structure from one census to another in terms of both the occupational mobility of the resident population of Norristown as an adjustment to the changing economic needs of the community, and the in- and out-movement of persons of particular occupations, largely in response to the push and pull of employment opportunities in Norristown and elsewhere. In making possible these analyses, this method provided a basis for obtaining data on the changing roles and interrelations of migration and occupational mobility in affecting the size and composition of the labor force structure of the Norristown male population from 1910 to 1950.

SOME SUBSTANTIVE FINDINGS

Migration. The major emphasis of this paper is on the patterns of occupational mobility and its relation to migration in each of the last four decades. The results of the migration analysis will therefore be summarized briefly.[2]

For the forty year period from 1910 to 1950, migration accounted for 79 per cent of the population growth of the adult male population of Norristown, the remaining growth being attributable to a surplus of young males entering the adult cohort over those lost to it by death. This heavy contribution of migration to population growth was not, however, uniform throughout the forty year period. Its importance declined steadily from the 1910-1920 decade when the opposing streams of in- and out-migration[3] resulted in a net gain to the community of 213 persons per 1,000 population, to the decade of 1940-1950 when the net gain was only 35 per 1,000 population. In the 1920-1930 decade the net migration gain was 119 per 1,000 and in 1930-1940 it was only 4.

Despite the fact that migration has come to play a decreasing role in the population and labor force growth of Norristown, the actual volume of the separate streams of movement into and out of the community remained at very high levels throughout the forty year period. Whereas the in-migration rate of the two earlier decades was significantly higher than the out-migration rate, in the two later decades the gap between the rates was greatly reduced. In the 1910-1920 decade, for example, out of every 1,000 adult males living in Norristown, 270 had moved out by 1920, and in that interval 483 out of every 1,000 had moved into the community. In contrast, 369 out of every 1,000 adult males living in Norristown in the 1940-1950 decade had moved out by 1950, and 404 per 1,000 had moved in during the same ten year period. Thus, despite the fact that the overall pattern of migration had changed, the total rates of movement were high for all four periods.

While these high rates of in- and out-migration have not greatly affected the total size of the Norristown population in more recent decades, the fact that the opposing streams of movement were selective of persons in the different occupational groups meant that migration served to alter the occupational composition of the male labor force. The begin-

---

[2]For a fuller discussion of migration patterns in Norristown see, Sidney Goldstein, "Patterns of Internal Migration, Norristown, Pennsylvania, 1910-1950," Philadelphia: Behavioral Research Council, 1953, dittographed.

[3]The decennial migration rates were based on the adult male population resident in Norristown at the midpoint of the decade. The midpoint population was attained through averaging the two decennial populations. By using this base, the in-, out-, and net-migration rates of each decade were all based on the same population group.

Table 1

Decennial Rates of In-, Out-, and Net-Migration, Norristown, Pennsylvania, 1910-1950, by Occupational Group*

	1910-1920	1920-1930	1930-1940	1940-1950
In-Migration Rates				
Professionals	455	489	518	338
Managers	471	542	273	333
Clerical and sales	308	410	309	286
Skilled laborers	410	456	285	362
Semi-skilled	508	475	481	480
Unskilled	678	623	418	461
All groups	483	501	381	404
Out-Migration Rates				
Professionals	152	267	250	415
Managers	143	365	455	280
Clerical and sales	269	343	335	464
Skilled laborers	282	335	352	286
Semi-skilled	317	436	333	372
Unskilled	288	385	490	373
All groups	270	382	377	369
Net-Migration Rates				
Professionals	303	222	268	− 77
Managers	328	177	−182	53
Clerical and sales	39	67	− 26	−178
Skilled laborers	128	121	− 67	76
Semi-skilled	191	39	148	108
Unskilled	390	238	− 72	88
All groups	213	119	4	35

*Rates represent the number of adult male migrants per 1,000 males in each occupational group at the midpoint of each decade.

ning of the forty year period was characterized by gains through migration by all occupational groups, as examination of the data of Table 1 will indicate. For three groups—professionals, proprietors, and unskilled laborers—these net gains amounted to over 300 per 1,000 persons in each group. Only for the clerical and sales workers was the net rate of gain below 100 per 1,000 workers in this category. These net rates of gains and losses of individual occupational groups showed no consistent patterns of change decade by decade. By 1930-1940, however, the significant reduction in the total net effect of migration was reflected in the different occupational groups. In this decade all groups except professionals and semi-skilled workers experienced net losses through migration, and the rates of these two groups, while still positive, were lower than in the first decade of this forty year period. This same pattern of either net losses or low net rates of gain as compared to the 1910-1920 decade continued into 1940-1950. Thus, in both 1930-1940 and 1940-1950, migration played a less significant role in altering the size of each occupational group than it did in 1910-1920.

Migration, as indicated earlier, is only one among several factors responsible for changes in the occupational composition of the Norristown population, the others being the entrance of young persons into the labor force, the exodus of old ones through retirement and death, and occupational mobility. Within the limits of this paper, it is not possible to discuss the role of maturation, death, and retirement in changing the labor force structure. The discussion which follows is limited to an analysis of the decennial occupational mobility patterns of those Norristown males who resided in the community throughout the decade and who were members of its labor force at both the beginning and the end of each ten year period of residence.

Occupational Mobility. The analysis of occupational mobility, like that of migration, was based on directory data. In both the forward and backward tracings of each decade, relatively large numbers of individuals were identified as having been continuous residents of Norristown throughout each decade. Data for these persons included information on the job held at the time of each biennial directory enumeration of the population. Each job attachment was classified into the appropriate occupational category as defined by the Bureau of the Census' "Alphabetical Index of Occupations and Industries."[4] Occupational mobility was then defined as movement from one major occupational group to another, whether for the same or for a different employer. It does not include change in jobs involving movement within the same oc-

---

[4] The categories used were professionals, managers, clerical and sales workers, skilled laborers, semi-skilled laborers, and unskilled laborers.

cupational category. By a comparison of the occupational identification of each resident at the beginning of the decade with that at the end of the decade, it was possible to determine for each ten year period whether he had been occupationally mobile, and if so, the type of move involved. Among the main findings were the following:

1. The stability rate of the Norristown male labor force, as measured by the proportion of the resident population remaining in the same occupational category during each decennial period, has decreased steadily from 1910-1920 to 1940-1950.[5] Of the sample population of the 1910-1920 decade, 75.9 per cent were in the same occupational group at the beginning and at the end of the decade. The stability rates in the three following decades were 71.4, 65.9, and 65.1, respectively. Thus over the forty year period under consideration, there was an increase of approximately 10 per cent in the proportion of males in the labor force who had changed occupational affiliation by the end of each ten year period. It is significant for our later discussion to note here that there was very little change in stability rates from the 1930-1940 to the 1940-1950 decades.

2. The decrease in stability from 1910-1920 to 1940-1950 characterized all occupational groups except the semi-skilled, whose stability rate in 1940-1950 was approximately the same as in 1910-1920. Among professionals, managers, and skilled workers, the stability rates of 1940-1950 were approximately 10 per cent lower than in 1910-1920. Among clerical and sales workers and unskilled laborers, the 1940-1950 rates were approximately 20 per cent lower than those of 1910-1920.

3. In each decade, professionals, managers, and skilled laborers, in that order, consistently represented the most stable occupations. This is explainable, no

doubt, by the positions these three categories occupy on the occupational hierarchy, the professionals and the managers being at the top of the white collar hierarchy and the skilled laborers at the top of the manual labor groups. As the data in Tables 3-6 show, the stability rate of these three groups never went below 74.8. The stability rates of the three remaining groups were never above 75. In relation to each other, however, they showed no consistent pattern.

4. For the total labor force, despite the increased amount of occupational mobility, the direction of movement[6] among those who were mobile remained approximately the same. Thus in 1940-1950, as in 1910-1920, approximately twice as many of the mobile persons moved up the occupational ladder as moved down. (See Table 2.)

Table 2
Occupational Mobility, Resident Male Labor
Force of Norristown, 1910-1950, by Decades

Decade	Up- ward Mo- bility*	Same Occu- pation	Down- ward Mo- bility*	Total Per Cent	Total Number
1910-1920	15.8	75.9	8.3	100.0	781
1920-1930	17.5	71.4	11.1	100.0	760
1930-1940	21.1	65.9	13.0	100.0	907
1940-1950	22.8	65.1	12.1	100.0	972

*See Footnote 6 for a definition of upward and downward mobility.

5. The patterns of upward and downward movement differed significantly among the different occupational groups, partly because of their relative positions on the occupational hierarchy. Professionals who were mobile could move only down to positions lower on the scale. Among managers, in all four decades, the proportion who moved down was significantly greater than the proportion

---

[5]The directory listings did not include any data on the age of the persons analyzed in this study. It was not possible, therefore, to control the age factor in the analyses of either migration or occupational mobility.

[6]For purposes of analyzing direction of movement, occupations were arranged in the order used by the United States Bureau of the Census, i.e., professionals, managers, clerical and sales, skilled, semi-skilled, and unskilled laborers. Movement from a job in one category to a job in another category higher in the list is defined here as upward mobility. Contrariwise, movement to a job belonging to a category lower on the list is defined as downward mobility.

Table 3
Occupational Mobility, Male Residents of Norristown, 1910-1920

Occupation in 1910	Occupation in 1920							
	Professional	Manager	Clerical and Sales	Skilled	Semi-skilled	Unskilled	Total Per Cent	Total Number
Professional	94.7	—	5.3	—	—	—	100.0	38
Manager	2.7	89.2	4.1	2.7	1.3	—	100.0	74
Clerical and sales	2.5	15.0	67.5	3.3	5.9	5.8	100.0	120
Skilled worker	0.5	1.7	1.7	86.2	4.4	5.5	100.0	182
Semi-skilled worker	0.5	4.5	4.9	11.9	67.8	10.4	100.0	202
Unskilled worker	—	5.5	4.2	6.1	13.9	70.3	100.0	165

who moved up. Reflecting their middle position in the hierarchy, the mobile clerical and sales workers moved in large numbers both up and down the occupational scale; except for the 1930-1940 decade, more of these mobile persons moved up into higher white collar occupational categories than down into manual labor groups. Mobile members of the three laboring groups were consistent in their mobility patterns in all four decades. Reflecting their top position among manual laborers, a majority of the skilled laborers who were mobile moved down into less skilled manual labor occupations rather than up into white collar positions; more semi-skilled workers moved up into skilled labor and white collar positions than down into unskilled jobs; unskilled laborers who were mobile necessarily moved up because of their position at the bottom of the hierarchy.

6. Examination of the specific occupational group into which mobile persons of each occupational category moved indicates that if the general increase in mobility in the later periods is taken into account, the patterns of 1940-1950 closely resembled those of 1910-1920. In general the greatest amount of movement was into those occupational groups

most closely related to those to which the individuals originally belonged. Reflecting this, most movement took place between occupations within the two major classes of occupations, i.e., white collar and manual labor categories, rather than between jobs belonging to different major categories. It is important to recognize, nonetheless, that in all four decades there was a minority of persons who made major changes in occupational affiliation and thereby significantly altered their position in the socio-economic scale.

In review, almost all segments of the Norristown labor force have been characterized by an increased amount of mobility in 1940-1950 as compared to 1910-1920. However, the direction and range of movement in these two extreme decades has not changed significantly. For most groups, the mobility in the 1930 and 1940 decades was similar and, therefore, represented a leveling off of of the earlier trends toward increased instability in occupational affiliation. These being the major patterns of occupational mobility from 1910 to 1950, let us now see, what relationship, if any, they bear to the patterns of migration.

Interrelationships Between Migration and Occupational Mobility. Although it is assumed that economic conditions are

Table 4
Occupational Mobility, Male Residents of Norristown, 1920-1930

Occupation in 1920	Occupation in 1930							
	Professional	Manager	Clerical and Sales	Skilled	Semi-skilled	Unskilled	Total Per Cent	Total Number
Professional	91.4	—	5.7	—	2.9	—	100.0	35
Manager	2.9	77.1	11.5	4.3	2.8	1.4	100.0	70
Clerical and sales	3.6	12.5	75.0	0.9	3.6	4.4	100.0	112
Skilled worker	—	6.3	4.0	76.9	6.9	5.9	100.0	173
Semi-skilled worker	1.1	2.2	8.1	10.3	59.4	18.9	100.0	185
Unskilled worker	—	4.9	2.7	4.7	17.4	70.3	100.0	185

Table 5
Occupational Mobility, Male Residents of Norristown, 1930-1940

Occupation in 1930			Occupation in 1940				Total Per Cent	Total Number
	Professional	Manager	Clerical and Sales	Skilled	Semi-skilled	Unskilled		
Professional	88.0	—	6.0	4.0	2.0	—	100.0	50
Manager	—	75.0	10.4	2.1	10.4	2.1	100.0	96
Clerical and sales	3.0	12.1	60.6	5.3	11.4	7.6	100.0	132
Skilled worker	2.4	2.9	5.3	74.8	9.2	5.4	100.0	206
Semi-skilled worker	—	2.7	9.1	7.5	66.8	13.9	100.0	187
Unskilled worker	0.4	3.0	4.7	9.7	30.1	52.1	100.0	236

largely responsible for both migration and occupational mobility, it is not possible within the limits of this paper to evaluate the changing economic conditions and their relation to these two processes. Discussion will necessarily be limited to what relationship these two processes bear to each other.

It will be recalled that net rates of migration were much higher in the earlier decades of the twentieth century than they were in the last two decades. In the 1910-1920 decade the net rate of migratory gain was 213 persons per 1,000 population, and in 1920-1930 it was 119. In the 1930-1940 decade, however, it touched a low of 4 and in 1940-1950 it remained at this low level. This forms a pattern of a decreasing net rate of migration with a tendency to level off during the last twenty years. Whereas in 1910-1920 all but the clerical and sales group experienced large net rates of gain through migration, by 1940-1950 two groups were experiencing net losses and the rates of gain of the remaining groups were significantly lower than they were in 1910-1920. Between these same two periods, the rates of occupational mobility of all occupational groups except the semi-skilled laborers increased among the continuous residents of Norristown.

These data on migration and occupational mobility suggest the possibility that to the extent Norristown is able to meet either its increased or its changing labor force needs by attracting persons from outside the borough, to that extent will there be less need and/or opportunity for occupational mobility by those who are gainfully employed in the local economic structure. On the other hand, once this outside supply ceases to be attracted, then the labor force needs of the local area are met by a constant readjustment within the resident population.

When the volume of mobility was high in the first decade, it can be assumed that most of the needs of the expanding Norristown economy were met by drawing migrants into the borough. As this period of rapid expansion slowed and the economy became more stable, the attractiveness of Norristown as a place of economic opportunity diminished. As a result, the net rate of migration decreased to a point where by the 1930-1940 and the 1940-1950 decades the number of in-migrants just about balanced the number of out-migrants. During this period, however, while the economy may not have been expanding, its internal structure was changing as new types of

Table 6
Occupational Mobility, Male Residents of Norristown, 1940-1950

Occupation in 1940			Occupation in 1950				Total Per Cent	Total Number
	Professional	Manager	Clerical and Sales	Skilled	Semi-skilled	Unskilled		
Professional	83.8	6.5	6.5	1.6	1.6	—	100.0	62
Manager	2.6	79.2	13.0	—	3.9	1.3	100.0	77
Clerical and sales	8.0	18.5	49.4	6.2	15.4	2.5	100.0	162
Skilled worker	1.6	5.3	3.1	76.8	12.1	1.1	100.0	190
Semi-skilled worker	0.7	4.5	4.5	9.7	69.4	11.2	100.0	268
Unskilled worker	1.4	5.2	5.2	11.8	25.7	50.7	100.0	213

jobs were created and old ones were eliminated. The response to these changing needs is reflected in the selective character of the in- and out-movement and in the increased amount of occupational mobility on the part of those who remained in the community throughout the decade.

Of course, such an explanation does not rule out the possibility that over the last forty years there has been a decreasing amount of job attachment on the part of the labor force members to their original occupational positions. The data, indeed,

suggest that this is so. Whether this is related in a causal manner to the reduced volume of net migration cannot be conclusively determined. It is clear, however, that as a concomitant of decreased net migration, there has been an increased amount of occupational mobility. This suggests, therefore, that migration and occupational mobility have served to complement each other and in so doing have jointly served to meet the changing needs of the local economy and thereby to effect changes in the labor force structure.

A Note on the "Trickle Effect"

Lloyd A. Fallers

SOURCE: *Public Opinion Quarterly*, Vol. 18 (1954), pp. 314–21.

Much has been written—and much more spoken in informal social scientific shop talk—about the so-called "trickle effect" —the tendency in U. S. society (and perhaps to a lesser extent in Western societies generally) for new styles or fashions in consumption goods to be introduced via the socio-economic elite and then to pass down through the status hierarchy, often in the form of inexpensive, mass-produced copies.

In a recent paper, Barber and Lobel have analyzed this phenomenon in the field of women's clothes.[1] They point out that women's dress fashions are not simply irrational shifts in taste, but that they have definite functions in the U. S. status system. Most Americans, they say, are oriented toward status mobility.

Goods and services consumed are symbolic of social status. In the family division of labor, the husband and father "achieves" in the occupational system and thus provides the family with monetary income. Women, as wives and daughters, have the task of allocating this income so as to maximize its status-symbolic value. Since women's clothing permits much subtlety of expression in selection and display, it becomes of great significance as a status-mobility symbol.[2] The ideology of the "open class" system, however, stresses broad "equality" as well as differential status. The tendency of women's dress fashions to "trickle down" fairly rapidly via inexpensive reproductions of originals created at fashion centers helps to resolve this seeming inconsistency by preventing the

[1] Barber, Bernard and Lyle S. Lobel, " 'Fashion' in Women's Clothes and the American Social System," Social Forces, Vol. 31, pp. 124-131. Reprinted in Bendix, Reinhard and S. M. Lipset, Class, Status and Power: A Reader in Social Stratification, Free Press, 1953. pp. 323-332.

[2] It is not suggested that women are solely in charge of status-symbolic expenditure, merely that they play perhaps the major role in this respect. See also: Parsons, Talcott, Essays in Sociological Theory, Free Press, 1949, p. 225.

development of rigid status distinctions.[3]

In the widest sense, of course, the "trickle effect" applies not only to women's dress but also to consumption goods of many other kinds. Most similar to women's dress fashions are styles in household furnishings. A colleague has pointed out to me that venetian blinds have had a similar status career—being introduced at relatively high levels in the status hierarchy and within a few years passing down to relatively low levels. Like women's dress styles, styles in household furnishings are to a substantial degree matters of taste and their adoption a matter of "learning" by lower status persons that they are status relevant. The trickling down of other types of consumption goods is to a greater degree influenced by long-term increases in purchasing power at lower socio-economic levels. Such consumers' durables as refrigerators and automobiles, being products of heavy industry and hence highly standardized over relatively long periods and throughout the industries which produce them, are much less subject to considerations of taste. They do, however, trickle down over the long term and their possession is clearly status-relevant.

The dominant tendency among social scientists has been to regard the trickle effect mainly as a "battle of wits" between upper-status persons who attempt to guard their symbolic treasure and lower-status persons (in league with mass-production industries) who attempt to devalue the status-symbolic currency. There is much truth in this view. Latterly we have observed a drama of this sort being played out in the automotive field. Sheer ownership of an automobile is no longer symbolic of high status and neither is frequent trading-in. Not even the "big car" manufacturers can keep their products out of the hands of middle- and lower-status persons "on the make." High-status persons have therefore turned to ancient or foreign sports-cars.

It seems possible, however, that the trickle effect has other and perhaps more far-reaching functions for the society as a whole. Western (and particularly U. S.) society, with its stress upon the value of success through individual achievement, poses a major motivational problem: The occupational system is primarily organized about the norm of technical efficiency. Technical efficiency is promoted by recruiting and rewarding persons on the basis of their objective competence and performance in occupational roles. The field of opportunity for advancement, however, is pyramidal in shape; the number of available positions decreases as differential rewards increase. But for the few most competent to be chosen, the many must be "called," that is, motivated to strive for competence and hence success. This, of course, involves relative failure by the many, hence the problem: How is the widespread motivation to strive maintained in the face of the patent likelihood of failure for all but the few? In a widely-quoted paper, Merton has recognized that this situation is a serious focus of strain in the social system and has pointed to some structured types of deviant reaction to it.[4] I should like to suggest the hypothesis that the trickle effect is a mechanism for maintaining the motivation to strive for success, and hence for maintaining efficiency of performance in occupational roles, in a system in which differential success is possible for only a few. Status-symbolic consumption goods trickle down, thus giving the "illusion" of success to those who fail to achieve differential success in the opportunity and status pyramid. From this point of view, the trickle effect becomes a "treadmill."

There are, of course, other hypotheses to account for the maintenance of motivation to strive against very unfavorable odds. Perhaps the most common is the notion that the "myth of success," perhaps maintained by the mass-communications media under the control of the

[3]Our thinking concerning the status-symbolic role of consumption patterns owes a great debt, of course, to Veblen's notion of "conspicuous consumption" and more recently to the work of W. L. Warner and his colleagues.

[4]Merton, R. K. "Social Structure and Anomie," reprinted as Chapter IV, Social Theory and Social Structure, Free Press, 1949.

"vested interests," deceives peoples into believing that their chances for success are greater than is in fact the case. Merton seems to accept this explanation in part while denying that the ruse is entirely effective.[5] Somewhat similar is another common explanation, put forward, for example, by Schumpeter, that though the chances for success are not great, the rewards are so glittering as to make the struggle attractive.[6] Undoubtedly both the "success myth" theory and the "gambling" theory contain elements of truth. Individual achievement certainly is a major value in the society and dominates much of its ideology, while risk-taking is clearly institutionalized, at any rate in the business segment of the occupational system. Taken by themselves, however, these explanations do not seem sufficient to account for the situation. At any rate, if it is possible to show that the system does "pay off" for the many in the form of "trickle-down" status-symbolic consumption goods, one need not lean so heavily upon such arguments.

It seems a sound principle of sociological analysis to assume "irrationality" as a motivation for human action only where exhaustive analysis fails to reveal a "realistic" pay-off for the observed behavior. To be sure, the explanation put forward here also assumes "irrationality," but in a different sense. The individual who is rewarded for his striving by the trickling-down of status-symbolic consumption goods has the illusion, and not the fact, of status mobility among his fellows. But in terms of his life history, he nevertheless has been rewarded with things which are valued and to this degree his striving is quite "realistic."[7] Though

---

[5]Ibid.

[6]Schumpeter, J. A., Capitalism, Socialism and Democracy, Harpers, 1947, pp. 73-74.

[7]By "irrationality" is meant here irrationality within the framework of a given value system. Values themselves, of course, are neither "rational" nor "irrational" but "non-rational." The value of individual achievement is non-rational. Action directed toward achievement may be termed rational to the degree that, in terms of the information available to the actor, it is likely to result in achievement; it is irrational to the degree that this is not so.

his status position vis-a-vis his fellows has not changed, he can look back upon his own life history and say to himself (perhaps not explicitly since the whole status-mobility motivational complex is probably quite often wholly or in part unconscious): "I (or my family) have succeeded. I now have things which five (or ten or twenty) years ago I could not have had, things which were then possessed only by persons of higher status." To the degree that status is defined in terms of consumption of goods and services one should perhaps say, not that such an individual has only the illusion of mobility, but rather that the entire population has been upwardly mobile. From this point of view, status-symbolic goods and services do not "trickle-down" but rather remain in fixed positions; the population moves up through the hierarchy of status-symbolic consumption patterns.

The accompanying diagram illustrates the various possibilities in terms of the life-histories of individuals. The two half-pyramids represent the status hierarchy at two points in time (X and Y). A, B, C and D are individuals occupying different levels in the status hierarchy. Roman numerals 1 through V represent the hierarchy of status-symbolic consumption patterns. Between time periods X and Y, a new high-status consumption pattern has developed and has been taken over by the elite. All status levels have "moved up" to "higher" consumption patterns. During the elapsed time, individual C has "succeeded', in the sense of having become able to consume goods and services which were unavailable to him before, though he has remained in the same relative status level. Individual B has been downwardly mobile in the status hierarchy, but this blow has been softened for him because the level into which he has dropped has in the meantime taken over consumption patterns previously available only to persons in the higher level in which B began. Individual D has been sufficiently downwardly mobile so that he has also lost ground in the hierarchy of consumption patterns. Finally, individual A, who has been a spectacular success, has risen to the very top of the status hierarchy where he is able to consume goods and services which were unavailable even to the elite at an earlier time period. Needless to say, this diagram is not meant to represent the actual status levels, the proportions of persons in each level or the frequencies of upward and downward mobility in the U. S. social system. It is simply meant to illustrate diagrammatically the tendency of the system, in terms of status-symbolic consumption goods, to reward even those who are not status mobile and to provide a "cushion" for those who are slightly downward mobile.

Undoubtedly this view of the system misrepresents "the facts" in one way as much as the notion of status-symbolic goods and services "trickling down" through a stable status hierarchy does in another. Consumption patterns do not retain the same status-symbolic value as they become available to more people. Certainly to some degree the "currency becomes inflated". A more adequate diagram would show both consumption patterns trickling down and the status hierarchy moving up. Nonetheless, I would

suggest that to some degree particular consumption goods have "absolute" value in terms of the individual's life history and his motivation to succeed. To the degree that this is so, the system pays off even for the person who is not status-mobile.

This pay-off, of course, is entirely dependent upon constant innovation and expansion in the industrial system. New goods and services must be developed and existing ones must become more widely available through mass-production. Average "real income" must constantly rise. If status-symbolic consumption patterns remained stationary both in kind and in degree of availability, the system would pay off only for the status-mobile and the achievement motive would indeed be unrealistic for most individuals. Were the productive system to shrink, the pay-off would become negative for most and the unrealism of the motivation to achieve would be compounded. Under such circumstances, the motivational complex of striving-achievement-occupational efficiency would be placed under great strain. Indeed, Merton seems to have had such circumstances in mind when he described "innovation," "ritualism," "rebellion," and "passive withdrawal" as common patterned deviations from the norm.[8]

This suggests a "vicious circle" relationship between achievement motivation and industrial productivity. It seems reasonable to suppose that a high level of achievement motivation is both a cause and a result of efficiency in occupational role performance. Such an assumption underlies much of our thinking about the modern Western occupational system and indeed is perhaps little more than common sense. One British sociologist, commenting upon the reports of the British "Productive Teams" which have recently been visiting American factories, is impressed by American workers' desire for status-symbolic consumption, partly the result of pressure upon husbands by their wives, as a factor in the greater

HIERARCHY OF CONSUMPTION PATTERNS	STATUS HIERARCHY: TIME X	STATUS HIERARCHY: TIME Y
V		A
IV	D	C
III	C	D
II	B	B
I	A	

---
[8] Merton, R. K. op. cit.

"per man hour" productivity of American industry.[9] Greater productivity, of course, means more and cheaper consumption goods and hence a greater pay-off for the worker. Conversely, low achievement motivation and inefficiency in occupational role performance would seem to stimulate one another. The worker has less to work for, works less efficiently, and in turn receives still less reward. Presumably these relationships would tend to hold, though in some cases less directly, throughout the occupational system and not only in the sphere of the industrial worker.

To the degree that the relationships suggested here between motivation to status-symbolic consumption, occupational role performance, and expanding productivity actually exist, they should be matters of some importance to the theory of business cycles. Although they say nothing about the genesis of up-turns and down-turns in business activity, they do suggest some social structural reasons why upward or downward movements, once started might tend to continue. It is not suggested, of course, that these are the only, or even the most important, reasons. More generally, they exemplify the striking degree to which the stability of modern industrial society often depends upon the maintenance of delicate equilibria.

The hypotheses suggested here are, it seems to me, amenable to research by a number of techniques. It would be most useful to discover more precisely just which types of status-symbolic consumption goods follow the classical trickle-down pattern and which do not. Television sets, introduced in a period of relative prosperity, seem to have followed a different pattern, spreading laterally across the middle-income groups rather than trickling down from above. This example suggests another. Some upper-income groups appear to have shunned television on the grounds of its "vulgarity"

—a valuation shared by many academics. To what degree are preferences for other goods and services introduced, not at the upper income levels, but by the "intelligensia," who appear at times to have greater pattern-setting potential than their relatively low economic position might lead one to believe? Finally, which consumption items spread rapidly and which more slowly? Such questions might be answered by the standard techniques of polling and market analysis.

More difficult to research are hypotheses concerning the motivational significance of consumption goods. I have suggested that the significance for the individual of the trickling down of consumption patterns must be seen in terms of his life-history and not merely in terms of short-term situations. It seems likely that two general patterns may be distinguished. On the one hand, individuals for whom success means primarily rising above their fellows may be more sensitive to those types of goods and services which must be chosen and consumed according to relatively subtle and rapidly changing standards of taste current at any one time at higher levels. Such persons must deal successfully with the more rapid devaluations of status-symbolic currency which go on among those actively battling for dominance. Such persons it may be who are responsible for the more short-term fluctuations in consumption patterns. On the other hand, if my hypothesis is correct, the great mass of the labor force may be oriented more to long-term success in terms of their own life-histories—success in the sense of achieving a "better standard of living" without particular regard to differential status. Interviews centered upon the role of consumption patterns in individuals' life aspirations should reveal such differences if they exist, while differences in perception of symbols of taste might be tested by psychological techniques.

Most difficult of all would be the testing of the circular relationship between motivation and productivity. Major fluctuations in the economy are relatively long

[9] Balfour, W. "Productivity and the Worker," British Journal of Sociology, Vol. IV, No. 3, 1953, pp. 257-265.

term and could be studied only through research planned on an equally long-term basis. Relatively short-term and localized fluctuations, however, do occur at more frequent intervals and would provide possibilities for research. One would require an index of occupational performance which could be related to real income and the relationship between these elements should ideally be traced through periods of both rising and falling real income.

National Comparisons of Occupational Prestige

Alex Inkeles and Peter H. Rossi[1]

SOURCE: *American Journal of Sociology*, Vol. 61, (1956), pp. 329–39.

During the latter part of the nineteenth and the first half of the twentieth centuries the factory system of production was introduced, at least on a small scale, to most areas of the world. The factory has generally been accompanied by a relatively standard set of occupations, including the factory manager (sometimes also owner) and his administrative and clerical staff, engineering and lesser technical personnel, foremen, skilled, semiskilled, and unskilled workers. In the factory, authority and responsibility are allocated largely according to the degree of technical or administrative competence required for the job. In addition, the allocation of material and social rewards, the latter generally in the form of deference, is closely adjusted to levels of competence and degrees of authority and responsibility. The pattern of differentiation of authority is undoubtedly functionally necessary to the productive activity of the factory, and it may be that the associated pattern of reward differentiation is also functionally necessary.

There is, however, no clear-cut imperative arising from the structure of the factory as such which dictates how the incumbents of its typical statuses should be <u>evaluated</u> by the population at large. One possibility is that in popular esteem the typical occupations will stand relative to one another in a rank order strictly comparable to their standing in the formal hierarchy of competence, authority, and reward in the factory. It is also possible, however, that the popular evaluation of these occupations will be quite different. Indeed, where the factory system has been introduced into societies like those of Spain or Japan, with well-established values based on tradition and expressive of the culture, one might expect significant differences between an occupation's standing in the formal hierarchy of the industrial system and its position in the popular ranking scheme.

Thus the interaction of the two systems —the standardized modern occupational system and the individual national value pattern for rating occupations—presents an interesting and important problem in comparative sociology.

We may posit two extreme positions in this interaction, while granting that it might be difficult to find live exponents of either. The extreme "structuralist" would presumably insist that the modern industrial occupational system is a highly coherent system, relatively impervious

[1] We wish to express our appreciation to Edward A. Tiryakian for his voluntary services as research assistant and to Alice S. Rossi for a critical reading.

to influence by traditional culture patterns. Indeed, he might go so far as to insist that the traditional ranking system would in time have to be subsumed under, or integrated into, the industrial system. Consequently, his argument would run, even such occupations as priest, judge, provincial governor, not part of the modern occupational system and often given unusual deference, would come in time to have roughly the same standing relative to one another and to other occupations, no matter what their national cultural setting.

By contrast, an extreme "culturalist" might insist that within each country or culture the distinctive local value system would result in substantial—and, indeed, sometimes extreme—differences in the evaluation of particular jobs in the standardized modern occupational system. For example, he might assume that in the United States the company director would be rated unusually high because of our awe of the independent businessman and large corporations or that in the Soviet Union the standing of industrial workers would be much higher relative to managerial personnel than in Germany, with its emphasis on sharply differentiated status hierarchies. Furthermore, he might argue that the more traditional occupational roles assigned special importance in particular cultures would continue to maintain their distinctive positions in the different national hierarchies. Indeed, he might hold that the characteristic roles of the modern industrial system would come to be subsumed within the traditional rating system, each factory occupation being equated with some traditional occupation and then assigned a comparable rank.

A systematic test of these contrasting positions is not beyond the capacity of contemporary social research. A standard list of occupations—say thirty or forty in number—might be presented for evaluation to comparable samples from countries presenting a range of culture types and degrees of industrialization. The list should contain both standard industrial occupations and the common,

but differentially valued, traditional roles (e.g., priest, legislator, etc.).

Data are available which, though far from completely adequate, will carry us a long way beyond mere speculation on these matters. In the postwar years studies of occupational ratings have been conducted in and reported on five relatively industrialized countries: the United States, Great Britain, New Zealand, Japan, and Germany.[2] In addition, the authors have available previously unpublished data for a sixth country, the Soviet Union.

Since these six studies[3] were, on the whole, undertaken quite independently, our ideal research design is clearly far from being fulfilled. Nevertheless, the data do permit tentative and exploratory cross-national comparisons.

I. THE COMPARABILITY OF RESEARCH DESIGNS

The elements of similarity and difference in the six studies may be quickly assessed from the following summary of their essential features:

A. Population studied United States: National sample of adults fourteen years and over; 2,920 respondents

Japan: Sample of males twenty to sixty-eight years of age in the six large cities of Japan; 899 respondents

Great Britain: Written questionnaires distributed through adult-education centers and other organizations; 1,056 returns (percentage returned unspecified)

---

[2]Additional studies of occupational prestige are available for the United States and for Australia. The authors decided to restrict the United States data to the most comprehensive study available. The Australian case (Ronald Taft, "The Social Grading of Occupations in Australia," British Journal of Sociology, Vol. IV, No. 2 [June, 1953]) was not included in this report because it was felt that little was to be gained by the inclusion of another Anglo-Saxon country.

[3](1) A. A. Congalton, "The Social Grading of Occupations in New Zealand," British Journal of Sociology, Vol. IV, No. 1 (March, 1953) (New Zealand data); (2) John Hall and D. Caradog Jones, "The Social Grading of Occupations," British Journal of Sociology, Vol. I, No. 1 (January, 1950) (Great Britain); (3) National Opinion Research Center, "Jobs and Occupations: A Popular Evaluation," in

U.S.S.R.: Sample of displaced persons, mostly in DP camps near Munich, Germany, and some former DP's now residing on eastern seabord of U.S.; 2,100 written questionnaires

New Zealand: Sample collected mainly by interviews with inhabitants of town of 2,000, partly by mailed questionnaires (12 per cent returns) sent out to town of 4,000; 1,033 questionnaires and interviews used

in each research was matched, when possible, with an occupation in the data gathered in the other country. In many cases it was necessary to disregard the information about an occupation in one of the paired countries no comparable occupation was studied in the other. In other instances, in order to increase the number of occupations which could be compared for any given pair of countries, occupations were matched which were only very

TABLE 1

NUMBER OF IDENTICAL OR SIMILAR OCCUPATIONS
RATED BETWEEN SIX COUNTRIES

	U.S.	Great Britain	U.S.S.R.	Japan	New Zealand	Germany
United States	...	24	10	25	24	20
Great Britain...................	...	...	7	14	30	12
U.S.S.R.	...	...	...	7	7	8
Japan	...	...	...	...	14	19
New Zealand...................	...	...	...	...	...	12
Total occupations studied	88	30	13	30	30	38

Germany: 1,500 Schleswig-Holsteiners: vocational-school students, university students, and male adults (not otherwise specified); adult sample only used here

B. Overlap among occupations studied

Each study involved a different number of occupations, ranging from 88 in the case of the National Opinion Research Center American study to 13 in the Soviet research. Only the New Zealand and the British groups studied exactly the same occupations. Each of the remaining four studies used a different, but partially overlapping, set of occupations.

In order to make comparisons between pairs of countries, each occupation studied

roughly comparable, e.g., Buddhist priest and minister, or collective farm chairman and farm owner and operator. In most cases, however, a direct correspondence characterizes the pairs of occupations which are being equated. The reader is invited to turn to Table 5 (below), where the lists of occupations used from each of the researches are printed. The occupations listed on any row or line were matched. The number of pairs of similar or identical occupations for each cross-national comparison is shown in Table 1.

C. Nature of rating task

United States: Respondents were asked: "... Please pick out the statement that best gives your own personal opinion of the general standing that such a job has. Excellent standing, good standing, average standing, somewhat below average, poor standing."

Japan: Respondents were given a set of thirty cards and asked: "... Think of the general reputations they have with people, and sort them into five or more groups, from those which people think highly of to those which are not thought so well of."

Great Britain: Respondents were told: "We should like to know in what order, as to their social standing, you would grade the occupations in the list given to you. [Rate them]... in terms of five main social classes... ABCDE."

U.S.S.R.: Respondents were asked: "Tak-

Reinhard Bendix and S. Martin Lipset, Class, Status and Power (Glencoe, Ill.: Free Press, 1953) (United States data); (4) the Schleswig-Holstein data are taken from an article published in Der Spiegel, June 30, 1954, reporting a study by Professor Karl-Martin Bolte, of Christian-Albrecht University, in Kiel, Germany, to be published early in 1955; (5) Research Committee, Japan Sociological Society, "Report of a Sample Survey of Social Stratification and Mobility in the Six Large Cities of Japan" (mimeographed; December 1952) (the authors are grateful to Professor Kunio Odaka, of the University of Tokyo, for bringing this valuable study to their attention); and (6) the Soviet materials were collected by the Project on the Soviet Social System of the Russian Research Center at Harvard University. The authors plan to publish several articles dealing with the special features of the occupational ratings secured from former Soviet citizens.

ing everything into consideration, how <u>desirable</u> was it to have the job of ( ) in the Soviet Union? Very desirable? Desirable? So-so? Undesirable? Very undesirable?"

New Zealand: Same as in Great Britain.

Germany: The source is unfortunately not very specific about the rating task assigned. The respondents were apparently asked to rank-order a list of 38 occupations presented as one slate.

D. Computing prestige position

With the exception of the German study, each research presents a "prestige score" for each of the occupations studied. These scores, computed variously, represent in each case the "average" rating given to each of the occupations by the entire sample of raters used. The German study presented only the rank-order positions of the occupations.

tions used in another study, it is possible to compare the prestige hierarchies of occupations in pairs of countries by computing correlation coefficeints for the scores (or ranks) of occupations. The fifteen correlation coefficients which result are presented in Table 2.[4] It will be seen immediately that the levels of correlation are considerably higher than the magnitude to be expected if there were only rough agreement on placement in the top and bottom halves of the prestige hierarchy. Indeed, twelve of the fifteen coefficients are above .9, and only one is below .8. The three coefficients below .9 all concern the Soviet ratings, which, it will be recalled, involve only a very small number of occupations, maximizing the chances for lower correlations

TABLE 2*

CORRELATIONS BETWEEN PRESTIGE SCORES (OR RANKS) GIVEN TO COMPARABLE OCCUPATIONS IN SIX NATIONAL STUDIES

	U.S.S.R.	Japan	Great Britain	New Zealand	U.S.	Germany†
U.S.S.R.	....	.74	.83	.83	.90	.90
Japan	....	....	.92	.91	.93	.93
Great Britain.............	....	....	....	.97	.94	.97
New Zealand.............	....	....	....	....	.97	.96
United States	....	....	....	....	....	.96
Av. correlation	.84	.89	.93	.93	.94	.94

*See Table 1 for numbers of occupations involved in each comparison.

†All coefficients are product-moment correlations, with the exception of those involving Germany, which are rank-order coefficients.

One is not sure whether differences between nations are generated by the differences in the questionnaires or the differences in the nations themselves. However, similarities in the prestige hierarchies, particularly when they are striking, are somewhat strengthened by the same lack of comparability in research designs and in the occupations matched to one another. Similarities may be interpreted as showing the extent to which design and other differences are overcome by the comparability among the prestige hierarchies themselves.

II. COMPARABILITY OF OCCUPATIONAL PRESTIGE HIERARCHIES

Since each study included some occupa-

arising from merely one or two "mismatches."

For most of the comparisons, furthermore, the findings go beyond establishing mere comparability of rank orders. With the exception of the correlations involving Germany, each coefficient represents the relationships between prestige <u>scores</u> given to the same occupations in two different nations. Hence there is a high relationship between the relative "distance" between occupations, as expressed

---

[4] Note that the correlation coefficients are all product-moment correlations, with the exception of the five coefficients involving the German study, which are rank-order correlations. With the exception noted, these coefficients represent the degree of similarity between the prestige scores given to the occupations.

in score differences, as well. In other words, if, of two occupations, one is given a much lower score than the other by the raters in one country, this difference in prestige scores and not merely crude rank order also obtains in another country.

It should also be noted that these high correlations were obtained by using samples of occupations which were not strictly identical from country to country, including such very crude comparisons already mentioned as that of collective farm chairman and farm owner and operator. One may anticipate that if the occupations studied were more uniform, the similarities of prestige hierarchies from country to country would be even higher.

In other words, despite the heterogeneity in research design, there exists among the six nations a marked degree of agreement on the relative prestige of matched occupations. To this extent, therefore, it appears that the "structuralist" expectation is more nearly met than is the expectation based on the culturalist position.

Each of the six nations differs in the extent to which its prestige hierarchy resembles those of other nations. The average of the correlations for each nation, contained in the botton row of Table 2, expresses these differences among nations quantitatively. Thus we may see that the American and German occupational prestige hierarchies are most similar to those of other nations, while the Soviet and Japanese hierarchies are most dissimilar. When we consider that the Soviet Union and Japan are, of the six, the more recently industrialized cultures, we may see there some small degree of evidence for the culturalist position.

Furthermore, if we examine the correlations among the three nations which have the closest cultural ties and which share a common historical background and language—Great Britain, the United States, and New Zealand—we find these coefficients to be among the highest in Table 2. Again, the evidence to some extent supports the interpretation of a small "cultural" effect. However, the coefficients in question are not sufficiently distinguished in size from those involving Germany[5] and the three Anglo-Saxon nations to allow much weight to be given to the influence of the common Anglo-Saxon culture. In other words, whatever the national differences between the six, they do not greatly affect the general pattern of the prestige hierarchy.

III. NATIONAL PATTERNS OF OCCUPATIONAL PRESTIGE

Although the relationships among the six occupational hierarchies are very high, they do not indicate one-to-one correspondences among the national ranks of occupations. Each nation shows some variation from every other, and the international discrepancies may perhaps throw further light on the relationships between social structure, culture, and occupational prestige.

One possibility is that unique aspects of the culture or social structure of a particular country determine distinctive appraisals of a certain type or types of occupation. National differences are thus to be interpreted in a unique fashion for each country.

A second possible explanation is that it is the type of occupation which engenders disagreement, some occupations being similarly rated everywhere and others yielding no consistent rating. To some extent these contrasting explanations are similar, respectively, to the culturalist and structuralist positions discussed earlier.

Here again the available data place marked limits on the possibility of a definitive answer, but it is nevertheless feasible for us to go some distance in exploring the problem. In order to ob-

---

[5] Since the correlations involving Germany are rank-order correlations, it is difficult to make comparisons of such coefficients with others in Table 1. However, the relationship between rank-order correlations and product-moment correlations is rather high in the upper ranges, and it can be taken for granted that if prestige scores were available for the German ratings, the analysis shown in Table 2 would not be materially altered.

tain some means by which to assess the presence or absence of disagreement among nations, regression equations were computed to predict the prestige positions of the occupations in one country as against the prestige positions of the comparable occupations in each other country. Ten such equations were computed, interrelating the prestige hierarchies in the United States, Japan, Great Britain, New Zealand, and the Soviet Union but excluding Germany, since the published data on that country indicated only the rank order of occupations. Those occupations which lay more than one standard of the estimate off the regression lines were arbitrarily characterized as occupations over which there was a disagreement between the two nations involved.

nations, not forgetting that each comparison of a pair of countries involves a somewhat different set of occupations from the comparison of ratings for any other two countries. Only a few occupations, such as farmer, teacher, doctor, factory manager, and some form of industrial worker, were rated in all five countries and therefore appear in all the pairs of comparisons. Some occupations, such as judge, were rated in only two countries and therefore appear in only one paired comparison.[6]

Table 3 serves to highlight the special positions held by certain occupations in particular countries. For example, the Japanese Buddhist priest rates lower than a minister in each of the three available comparisons, and this undoubt-

Table 3
Discrepancies* in the Rating of Matched Occupations by Pairs of Nations

	Rated Higher in Japan	Rated Higher in U.S.	Rated Higher in Great Britain	Rated Higher in New Zealand	Rated Higher in U.S.S.R.
Rated lower in Japan		Minister, farmer, insurance agent, carpenter	Minister, farmer, insurance agent	Minister, farmer, insurance agent	Accountant
Rated lower in U.S.	Company director, labor leader, reporter (news), street sweeper, shoe shiner		Accountant, chef, street sweeper	Accountant, farmer, truck driver, street sweeper	Engineer, worker
Rated lower in Great Britain	Reporter (news), street sweeper	Civil servant, truck driver, minister, building contractor, electrician		Truck driver	Worker
Rated lower in New Zealand	Reporter (news), street sweeper	Civil servant, building contractor, bookkeeper, electrician, dock worker	Chef, bartender		Worker
Rated lower in U.S.S.R.	Factory manager, farmer	Scientist, farmer	Farmer	Farmer	

*We consistently designate any cited occupation by the title closest and most familiar to Americans. For example, we used minister in preference to Buddhist priest, electrician rather than fitter (electrical). For the exact titles see Table 5.

Applying this criterion, we have, in Table 3, presented the discrepancies in ratings between all the relevant pairs of nations. The columns show the occupations rated higher by a given country in relation to each of the other countries represented in the rows. Reading the table by rows, we find the occupations rated lower by one country than by other

edly reflects the cultural differences in structure and role between the Buddhist religion in Japan and the Judeo-Christian religion in the three Anglo-Saxon coun-

[6] Table 5 (below) will be found a useful aid in this connection, since by reading across the rows of that table one can tell quickly how many times a particular occupation was evaluated and by which national samples.

tries. Equally notable is the consistently lower position of farm manager as rated by displaced persons from the Soviet Union. While the occupation collective farm chairman is not strictly comparable to those with which it is matched, there can be no doubt that the displaced persons regard that occupation with a special ambivalence arising out of the position of agriculture in the Soviet economy during the last three decades.

Despite the clarity with which a particular occupation may stand out, it is difficult to find any definite pattern characterizing the disagreements expressed by any one country. Of course, such a pattern, if it does exist, may be obscured in our data by the modest number of occupations rated by each country. There are seldom more than one or two occupations of a given type in each of the comparisons, and it is hazardous to assume from the fact, for example, that since the Japanese rate the occupation newspaper reporter higher than Americans, Britishers, or New Zealanders, they would rate occupations of this type higher than the other three countries. Nevertheless, it will be noticed that in the country with the largest number of comparisons, the instances of disagreement involve a wide variety of quite disparate occupations. Those rated higher in the United States, for example, range from building contractor to farmer and from scientist to dock worker and appear to have little in common. The same range and absence of a common denominator are shown by the occupations rated lower in the United States. Furthermore, the discrepancies do not consistently appear in all the relevant comparisons: farm owner is out of line in only two out of four comparisons; as to truck driver, the two recorded disagreements go in opposite directions, that occupation being rated higher in comparison with Britain and lower in comparison with New Zealand.

IV. INTERNATIONAL COMPARABILITY OF TYPES OF OCCUPATION

If there is no clear-cut pattern of deviance by country, is there perhaps a tendency for certain types of occupation to be foci of disagreement? Perhaps if we classify occupations according to the features of social structure or culture to which they are most closely related, we may gain further insight into the interaction between culture, social structure, and occupational prestige hierarchies. To

Table 4
Discrepancies in Prestige Position According to Type of Occupation

Occupation Types*	Proportion of Discrepancies (Per Cent)	No. of Comparisons
Professional.	16	31
Industrial.	24	29
Political	25	16
Traditional crafts	27	11
Clerical and commercial .	32	37
Agricultural.	50	16
Service	63	20

*Examples of occupations included in each type are as follows: Professional: doctor, minister, teacher, etc.; industrial: industrial worker, company director, factory manager, engineer; political: judge, civil servant, etc.; traditional crafts: bricklayer, carpenter, fisherman; clerical and commercial: accountant, bookkeeper, salesman, small entrepreneur, etc.; agricultural: farm owner and operator, farm hand; service: shoe shiner, barber, porter, streetcar conductor, etc.

explore this question, we grouped all the occupations into seven basic types: industrial, clerical and commercial, professional, political, traditional crafts, agricultural and service occupations.[7] In Table 4 we have indicated the number of international comparisons between pairs among the five countries, again excluding Germany, which could be made involving the occupations in each class of occupations. We have also indicated the proportions of those comparisons which yielded disagreements. Disagreements were recorded on the same basis as in the preceding table, that is, on the basis of predictions from regression equations.

Because our findings so far have so strongly supported the structuralist expectation concerning the influence of industrialization in producing uniformity,

[7]See note to Table 4 for examples of occupations included in each type.

our initial expectation may well be that occupations closely allied to the industrial system will enjoy highly comparable standings from country to country, while occupations more remotely connected would be the focus of international discrepancies. Table 4 indicates that industrial occupations do enjoy comparable standing in all five countries. Nevertheless, the <u>lowest</u> proportion of disagreements is shown by the professions. In addition, other occupational types, such

as the political occupations and the traditional crafts, which are not necessarily closely allied to the industrial system, manifested levels of disagreement as low as that enjoyed by the industrial occupations. Only the agricultural and service occupations yield a degree of disagreement which sets them apart from the other occupational groups.

Accounting for these discrepancies appears to require a combination of arguments. In the first place, some types of

Table 5

Occupation	Score	Occupation	Rank	Occupation	Score	Occupation	Score	Occupation	Score	Occupation	Score
United States:		Germany:		Great Britain:		New Zealand:		Japan:		U.S.S.R.:	
Physician	93	Doctor	2	Medical officer	1.3	Medical officer	1.4	Doctor	7.0	Doctor	75
State governor	93							Prefectural gov.	3.8		
College professor	89	Univ. professor	1					Univ. professor	4.6		
Scientist	89									Scientific worker	73
County judge	87							Local court judge	4.7		
Head of dept. in state government	87	High civil servant (Regierungarat—höherer Beamter)	4	Civil servant	6.0	Civil servant	7.0	Section head of a government office	7.2		
Minister	87	Minister (Pfarrer)	6	Non-conformist minister	6.4	Non-conformist minister	5.9	Priest of a Buddhist temple	12.5		
Architect	86	(Elec. engineer)*	10					(Architect)	9.5		
Lawyer	86			Country solicitor	2.6	Country solicitor	3.8				
Member of board of directors of large corporation	86	Factory director (Fabrikdirektor)	5	Company director	1.6	Company director	3.6	Officer of large company	5.5	Factory manager	65
Civil engineer	84	Elec. engineer	10					(Architect)†	9.5	Engineer	73
Owner of factory that employs about 100 people	82							Owner of a small or medium-sized factory	10.2		
Accountant for a large business	81			Chartered accountant	3.2	Chartered accountant	5.7	(Company office clerk)‡	16.1	Bookkeeper	62
Captain in regular army	80	Major (in armed forces)	8							Officer in the armed services	58
Building contractor	79			Jobbing master builder	11.4	Jobbing master builder	10.7				
Instructor in public schools (teacher)	78	Elem.-school teacher (Volksschullehrer)	11	Elem.-school teacher	10.8	Elem.-school teacher	10.3	Elem.-school teacher	11.7	Teacher	55
Farm owner and operator	76	Farmer (Bauermittelgrosser Betrieb)	13	Farmer	7.3	Farmer	8.1	Small independent farmer	16.4	Chairman of collective farm	38
Official of international labor union	75							Chairman of national labor federation	10.8		
Electrician	73			Fitter (elec.)	17.6	Fitter (elec.)	15.8				
Trained machinist	73	Skilled industrial worker (Industriefacharbeiter)	24								
Reporter on daily newspaper	71			News reporter	11.8	News reporter	13.8	Newspaper reporter	11.2		
Bookkeeper	68	Bank teller (bookkeeper in bank)	19	Routine clerk	16.1	Routine clerk	16.4	Company office clerk	16.1	(Bookkeeper)§	62

*Used here only for comparison with Japan. For comparison with other countries, see line beginning "United States civil engineer."

†Architect is the only occupation of a technical nature in Japan and was used here as a comparison only with the Soviet Union.

‡Used here only for comparison with the Soviet Union. For comparison with other countries, see line beginning "United States bookkeeper."

§Used here only for comparison with Japan. For comparison with other countries, see line beginning "United States accountant for a large business."

TABLE 5—Continued

Occupation	Score	Occupation	Rank	Occupation	Score	Occupation	Score	Occupation	Score	Occupation	Score
United States:		Germany:		Great Britain:		New Zealand:		Japan:		U.S.S.R.:	
Insurance agent	68	Insurance agent	20	Insurance agent	14.6	Insurance agent	16.1	Insurance agent	20.2		
Traveling salesman for wholesale concern	68			Commercial traveler	12.0	Commercial traveler	14.1				
Policeman	67			Policeman	16.1	Policeman	15.5	Policeman	16.4		
Mail carrier	66	Postman	23								
Carpenter	65	Carpenter	18	Carpenter	18.6	Carpenter	17.0	Carpenter	20.2		
Corporal in regular army	60	Non-commissioned officer	31								
Machine operator in factory	60	Machine operator (Maschinenschlosser-Geselle)	26	(Composite of fitter, carpenter, bricklayer, tractor driver, coal hewer)‖	20.5	(Composite of fitter, carpenter, bricklayer, tractor driver, coal hewer)‖	20.9	Latheman	21.1	Rank-and-file worker	48
Barber	59	Barber	16					Barber	20.5		
Clerk in a store	58	Store clerk (Verkäufer im Lebensmittelgeschäft)	28	Shop assistant	20.2	Shop assistant	20.2	Department-store clerk	19.8		
Fisherman who owns own boat	58							Fisherman	22.0		
Streetcar motorman	58	Conductor	33					Bus driver	20.9		
Restaurant cook	54			Chef	13.8	Chef	21.8				
Truck driver	54			Carter	25.8	Carrier	20.2				
Farm hand	50	Farm laborer (worker)	36	Agricultural laborer	25.5	Agricultural laborer	24.4			Rank-and-file collective farmer	18
Coal miner	49			Coal hewer	23.2	Coal hewer	24.7	Coal miner	23.7		
Restaurant waiter	48	Waiter (Kellner)	30								
Dock worker	47			Dock laborer	27.0	Dock laborer	28.3				
Bartender	44			Barman	26.4	Barman	28.3				
Street sweeper	34	(Unskilled laborer)**	38	Road sweeper	28.9	Road sweeper	28.9	Road worker	24.8		
								Shoe shiner	26.9		
Shoe shiner	33	Bricklayer	27	Bricklayer	20.2	Bricklayer	19.3				
		Clothing-store owner	12					Owner of a retail store	15.3		
		Tailor	14					Tailor	17.7		
		Street peddler	35					Street-stall keeper	24.9		
				Business manager	6.0	Business manager	5.3				
				Works manager	6.4	Works manager	7.9				
				News agent and tobacconist	15.0	News agent and tobacconist	15.4				
				Tractor driver	23.0	Tractor driver	22.8				
				Railway porter	25.3	Railway porter	25.3				

‖Used here only for comparison with the Soviet Union. For comparison with other countries, see individual occupations as they appear later in the table.

†As there was no comparable occupation in New Zealand, the occupation substituted was carrier.

**Used here only for comparison with Japan.

non-industrial occupations are easily assimilated to the industrial system. The traditional crafts serve as the prime example here, since the skills involved in such occupations as bricklayer, carpenter, and plumber have a close resemblance to the skills of industrial workers. Indeed, some crafts have been partly incorporated into the industrial system, and, it may be argued, such occupations are easily placed within the hierarchy of industrial occupations and may tend to assume roughly the same position vis-à-vis industrial occupations. Likewise, some professions, such as engineering and applied scientific research, have a most immediate connection with the industrial system, and others, such as architecture, are easily equated with it.

However, closeness or assimilability to the industrial system will not suffice to explain the relatively stable position of other professions, such as doctor. Nor will it serve to explain the low proportion of disagreement concerning the political occupations. We must recognize that the nations being compared have certain structural and cultural features in common, in addition to the presence of industry. For example, they share certain needs, as for socialization, and values, such as health and systematic knowledge, which insure relatively comparable standing to doctors, teachers, and scientists. Furthermore, all the countries compared have in common the national state, with which is associated a relatively standardized occupational structure ranging from ministers of state to local bureaucrats. In addition, both the professions and the political occupations are highly "visible," and agreement as to their standing is probably facilitated by the relatively objective and easily perceived indexes of power, knowledge, and skill manifested by their incumbents.

The types of occupation which generate the greatest amount of disagreement are highly variant and unstandardized or difficult to assimilate to the industrial structure. Agriculture may be conducted, as in Japan, on relatively small holdings, on collective farms as in the U. S. S. R., or, as in the western plains of the United States, in "agricultural factories." Being a farmer means very different things in each of the five countries, quite unlike the standardized image of the machinist or the factory manager. It can be anticipated, however, that as agriculture tends to be similarly organized in different countries, agricultural occupations will achieve more uniform standing.

The "service" occupations—barber, shoe shiner, chef, street sweeper—show the greatest amount of variation. Many of them antedate the industrial system and are in agrarian as well as industrial societies. They have no fixed position relative to the industrial order, nor are they similar to typical industrial occupations, as are many of the traditional crafts. They therefore appear to be most easily evaluated according to the traditional culture. Personal service in countries like Japan and Great Britain, in which a servant class was historically well developed and benefited from intimate association with an aristocratic upper class, may still be regarded as not so degrading as in the more democratic societies, such as the United States and New Zealand. In fact, the greatest discrepancy to be found among all the comparisons involves the differences in prestige position accorded to chef in Great Britain as compared with either

the United States or New Zealand, although in the case of the former the match was poor, since the comparable occupation was "restaurant cook." As these services come to be organized and mechanized—as in modern laundries or restaurants—they will become more thoroughly integrated into the larger economic order and may in time achieve more strictly comparable status from country to country.

All told, it would appear from this examination of international discrepancies that a great deal of weight must be given to the cross-national similarities in social structure which arise from the industrial system and from other common structural features, such as the national state. The greatest incidence of discrepancies occurs for occupations which are hardest to fit into either the one or the other structure. To this extent the structuralist position which we outlined earlier seems to be more heavily borne out in these data.

V. SUMMARY AND CONCLUSIONS

To sum up, our examination of occupational ratings in six modern industrialized countries reveals an extremely high level of agreement, going far beyond chance expectancy, as to the relative prestige of a wide range of specific occupations, despite the variety of sociocultural settings in which they are found. This strongly suggests that there is a relatively invariable hierarchy of prestige associated with the industrial system, even when it is placed in the context of larger social systems which are otherwise differentiated in important respects. In addition, the fact that the countries compared also have in common the national state and certain needs or values, such as interest in health, apparently also contributes to the observed regularity of the ratings, since both professional and political occupations are foci of agreement. Perhaps the most striking finding is the extent to which the different classes of occupation have been woven together into a single relatively unified occupational structure, more or less common to the six countries. At the same time, there is strong evidence that this relatively standardized occupational hierarchy does not apply without major exception to all occupations in all large-scale industrialized societies. In some instances, important disagreement may arise from the distinctive role of a single occupation in a particular country. In the majority of cases, however, the disagreement appears to involve certain classes of occupation, notably agricultural and service, about which there is only modest agreement. Disagreement probably reflects differences in the length and "maturity" of industrialization in various countries but also clearly results from differentiations in sociocultural systems which may well be relatively enduring.

The Role of Organizational Structures: Union versus Neighborhood in a Tension Situation

Dietrich C. Reitzes

SOURCE: *Journal of Social Issues*, Vol. 9, (1953), pp. 37–44.

Much of the current work in the field of "race relations" is limited by the assumption that behavior in racial contact situations is structured by the attitudes of individuals as such. As a result racial relations are often interpreted from the perspective of the individuals who constitute the group. Two corollaries follow: One is that changes in race relations are to be brought about through changes in the individuals' attitudes: the other is that once changes have occurred in the person's attitudes in one situation, similar changes in other situations will also occur. Thus it is often felt that individuals who work with Negroes in the plant or cooperate with Negroes in the union will also accept Negroes in other situations. When observation reveals that many individuals accept Negroes in one situation reject them in others, this is interpreted as an "inconsistency" in the individual's behavior.

It is the theme of this paper that this basic assumption has to be re-examined.

This paper rests on the premise that human society is not a mere aggregation of individuals, and that the present and anticipated behavior of people in society will depend primarily on the kind of organization that exists in the given area of conduct. It follows too that an understanding of individual behavior in most situations is predicated on understanding how deliberately organized groups define those situations.

Certainly a focus on the group is necessary both in the work and community setting. At work the individual is incorporated in large organizations which mediate between him and management. Within the organization a hierarchy of officers and committees formulate policies, establish objectives, decide on strategy and tactics.[2]

A parallel development is taking place in the community. The residential neighborhood is the special locale in which individuals attempt to realize such interests as the protection of property values

---

[1]The writer is greatly indebted to Mr. Joseph D. Lobman for the conceptual framework of this study.

[2]Herbert Blumer, "Sociological Theory in Industrial Relations," American Sociological Review, 1947, v. 12.

and personal and social deference. In terms of these interests their activities are mobilized and collectively shaped. These interests bring individuals together in organizations and cause the members to reflect in themselves, as individuals, the   raison d' être of the group.

The key question is to what extent are attitudes a "product" of group membership. Our contention is that these deliberately organized groups structure and define the situation for the individual and offer him ready and available definitions of behavior.[3] Individual behavior under such conditions, therefore, cannot be explained in terms of personal attitudes toward minority groups. In the community or neighborhood it is the property owner's association which provides us with the key to the actions of individuals in situations of racial contacts. In the plant it is the union.

We tested this thesis in the midwest by analyzing the rejection or acceptance of Negroes in a residential neighborhood and on the job. The two situations mentioned involved the same white individuals. The white individuals all lived in a residential neighborhood which had a pattern of strong rejection of Negroes, and yet the same individuals participated in a union which strongly accepted Negroes on an equal basis.

The analysis was made in terms of the collective definitions of these situations by the neighborhood organization, the union and management respectively. The study of individual behavior was preceded by an intensive study of the two situations involved, with particular emphasis on their organizational structure.

THE NEIGHBORHOOD

We found that in the center of the organizational pattern of the neighborhood —let us call it Steelside—was the property owner's association, called the Civic Club. The main objective of the Civic Club was to keep Negroes out of the

community. The president of the Club stated: "Now we generally don't talk about that freely, but actually the main purpose of the Club is to keep up the bar against the colored element moving in here. That was the purpose when it was first founded and that is still the purpose today."

The Civic Club claims to reflect and carry out the wishes of the people in the neighborhood. Actually, however, it is more accurate to state that the Club formulates the sentiments and directs the actions of a large portion of the population on certain issues, namely those dealing with the residential neighborhood. This became obvious when we studied the operation of the Club in detail. Attendance at meetings was very small and the actual control of the organization lay in the hands of a few individuals who made all important decisions.

The influence of the Club, however, could not be judged by its membership or attendance at meetings. A study of the entire neighborhood revealed that all other neighborhood organizations followed the Civic Club's leadership in its rejection of Negroes in Steelside. There were definite and clear lines of communication between the other organizations and the Club. This enabled the Club to mobilize the entire neighborhood against Negroes whenever necessary.

The Civic Club was able to mobilize individuals because of the interests of the individuals in the neighborhood. These interests centered around property values and social acceptance, and the Club was effective because it provided the individual with well formulated statements, reasons and justifications for his specific acts in specific situations.

The neighborhood itself reflected the success of the Civic Club's activities. At the time the study began, in 1948, no Negroes lived in Steelside. Several Negroes had attempted to move in, but were repelled by force, including such instances as burning down back porches, etc. Impending sales of homes to Negroes were prevented through pressure on the owners or their agents.

---

[3]Joseph D. Lohman and Dietrich C. Reitzes, "Note on Race Relations in Mass Society," *American Journal of Sociology*, 1952, 58, 241-242.

A short time before the study was
made a major racial disturbance occurred in a near-by community when
Negroes sought to move into that area.
Individuals living in Steelside participated in that disturbance, and a number
were arrested by the police. There was
some evidence that the Civic Club was
active in arousing the individuals in its
own area and sending them to the scene
of the disturbance.

THE WORK SITUATION

Many of the people who lived in Steelside worked in industrial plants which
are located just outside of the neighborhood. To study the work situation we
selected two factories which had the
largest number of employees from Steelside.

The individual and collective interests
in the work situation differ, of course,
from the interests in the neighborhood.
The key organizations are the company
and the union. The local union was part
of an international affiliated with the
CIO. On all three levels, the local, the
parent union and the national CIO, there
was a clear-cut policy of non-discrimination.

This policy of equality for Negroes,
however, was not considered as an end
in itself but was definitely and consciously related to the larger union objectives. This is illustrated by a statement of the local union organizer:

We are an industrial union and we learned
years ago through bitter experience that we
cannot afford to have any disruption or break
in our Negro-white relationships among the
workers. They are all workers faced with
common problems for which the union fights
and on which they have to stay together.

Management, too, had a policy of non-
discrimination. One plant was part of a
large progressive-minded heavy manufacturing company which had pioneered a
policy of integrating Negroes into its
labor force. The second plant, belonging
to a different company, had a policy,
too, of employing Negroes, and reported

that such equality created no special
problem.

Thus in the work situation the effective
organizations defined Negro-white contact on the basis of equality. The interviews clearly revealed that as far as
race relations were concerned the white
workers were primarily influenced by
the union policy and definition of the situation. Therefore, in the analysis of individual behavior, we have emphasized the
union rather than management.

The situation in the plants and union
hall reflected this formal policy. Neither
plant had segregated facilities. Locker
rooms, lunch rooms, shower rooms, and
toilets were shared by Negroes and
whites; Negroes participated fully in
union activities, and several held important elective offices.

THE INTERVIEWS

It was against this background of the
community and work situation that the
data were analyzed. We interviewed 151
white persons all of whom lived in Steelside, worked in the two plants mentioned,
and belonged to the union.[4]

The interviews were conducted in the interviewees' homes, and the individuals were told
that it was a general community study. No
special emphasis was placed on "race relations." Our questions were directed to ascertaining the involvement of the individual
in the group life of the neighborhood, on his
rejection of Negroes in the neighborhood, on
the involvement of the individual with union
activities and his acceptance of Negroes on
the job. We used open-ended interview questions. Our main effort was to get the individual to describe situations to us, and particularly to describe his own activity in these

---

[4]Over 90 percent of the workers in the plants
were members of the union. Their names and
addresses were obtained by selecting from the
union membership lists those members who lived
in Steelside. In one local we were able to make this
check ourselves and selected all union members in
the neighborhood. In the other local we did not
have access to the list but had a union member do
the selecting for us. We attempted to interview all
individuals so selected. However, in 51 cases we
were unable to contact the person. We have no
reason, however, to believe that the loss of those
cases biased our results.

situations. We felt that by emphasizing descriptions of situations, we would get not only information about the situation but also the individual's own definition of the situation which would provide the key to his actions. This proved to be the case. Thus by asking the respondent: "Do any Negroes live here?" we would get not only factual information but also almost invariably the respondent's concept of Negroes as neighbors.[5]

Tables I to III are based on ratings made from the completed interviews.

Table II indicates the relationship between "involvement in union activities" and "acceptance of Negroes at work." The value of chi-square for this table is 86.45—while a chi-square of only 13.27 would have indicated significance at the one per cent level. Thus this table also indicates high association between these two factors.

The most significant finding is the one regarding the relationship between "re-

Table I

Relation Between Involvement in Collective Existence
of the Neighborhood and Rejection of Negroes in
Neighborhood

	Involvement in the Collective Existence of the Neighborhood			
Rejection of Negroes in Neighborhood	High	Medium	Low	Total
High	56	9	3	68
Medium	8	36	18	62
Low	1	8	12	21
Total	65	53	33	151

Table I indicates the relationship between "involvement in the collective existence in the neighborhood" and "rejection of Negroes in the neighborhood." (The value of chi-square for this table is 79.90 . In order to be significant at the one per cent level a chi-square of only 13.27 is required.) This indicates that there is a definite positive association between these two factors.

jection of Negroes in the neighborhood" and "acceptance of Negroes on the job." This relationship is shown in Table III. (The chi-square test cannot be applied to this table since the expected value in some of the squares is less than 5. Inspection of the table indicated, however, that the distribution of cases is almost random.) Tables I and II show clearly the strong association between

Table II

Relationship Between Involvement In Union Activities
and Acceptance of Negroes at Work

	Involvement in Union Activities			
Acceptance of Negroes at Work	High	Medium	Low	Total
High	45	19	?	66
Medium	7	47	13	67
Low	0	6	12	18
Total	52	72	27	151

[5]In order to test our hypothesis the completed interviews were then rated. To do this objectively we extracted from every interview all the information available pertaining to (1) the respondent's involvement in the collective existence of the neighborhood, (2) his rejection of Negroes in the neighborhood, (3) his involvement in union activities, (4) his acceptance of Negroes on the job. These data were recorded separately for each category. Then we graded one group at a time marking each case "high," "medium," or "low" in accordance with established criteria. In order to check the objec-

tivity of our own judgments we submitted the first 44 cases to three other judges. These judges were given the extractions and the criteria for judgments. The judges agreed with the writer in better than 90 per cent of the cases so that it was felt that this procedure was not necessary for the balance of the cases. However, we did compare the balance of the cases with the first group and found that the associations between the four areas did not change significantly in the cases which were not checked by other judges.

Table III
Relationship Between Rejection of Negroes in Neighborhood
and Acceptance of Negroes at Work

Acceptance of Negroes at Work	Rejection of Negroes in Neighborhood			
	High	Medium	Low	Total
High	31	25	10	66
Medium	26	32	9	67
Low	11	5	2	18
Total	68	62	21	151

individual behavior and the organizational structure of the situation. Table III shows the inadequacy of explaining this behavior in terms of individual attitudes. Thus only 11 of the 68 cases which were rated as showing "high" rejection of Negroes in the neighborhood showed "low" acceptance of Negroes on the job, while 31 persons who strongly rejected Negroes in the neighborhood showed "high" acceptance of Negroes on the job. Also only 10 of the 66 cases showing "high" acceptance of Negroes at work indicated "low" rejection of Negroes in the neighborhood, while 31 of these cases showed "high" rejection in the neighborhood.

The three tables show that knowing a person's behavior toward Negroes in one situation does not enable one to predict that person's behavior toward Negroes in another situation. But knowing the organizational definition of a situation and the involvement with this organization, prediction of behavior becomes possible.

It should be emphasized that the interviews clearly indicated that the Negro issue as such was not the determining factor in either the involvement of the individual in the community or in the involvement of the individual in the union. The controlling interests in the neighborhood were social acceptance and property values, and on the job they were wages, security and working conditions. It is in terms of these specific interests that organizations mobilized the individuals and directed their actions.

IMPLICATIONS OF THE STUDY

The findings of this study are in agreement with the hypothesis that in modern mass society the basis for individual behavior in situations of racial contacts becomes increasingly the definition of the situation provided to the individual by deliberately organized collectivities. This organizational structuring is effective to the extent that it defines the situation for the individual in terms of his specific interests in the situation.

These findings have important implications for tactics in the field of race relations. A labor union with non-discriminatory practices might be concerned with the race relations pattern in the community and attempt to influence it. In that case, the non-discriminatory behavior of union members on the job notwithstanding, it cannot be assumed that they will also follow the union's policies when it takes a stand on community issues. What is required is that the union leaders be fully aware of the organizational structuring of the community and in the development of their tactics take this into account.

Our own study provides some illustrations of this point. A few years before the study was conducted, the issue of public housing came up in the neighborhood. We interviewed the man who was at that time the president of one of the locals. He stated:

The union, that is, the national office, decided to come out in favor of it [a public housing project]. They told me that as president of one of the locals in this area I had to make an official statement in favor of it. Well, I refused. So they called me down to the national office and put me on the carpet. But I told them that we are property owners and that our property values would go down if the project would be built. I know that on that issue I had more support among the membership than the national office, so I never came out favoring [the project].

Another illustrative incident: Shortly

before our study was made, a nearby neighborhood was the scene of a near race riot. During this period the Publicity and Education Director of one of the locals wrote a letter to the local newspaper attacking the paper for its anti-Negro position. This letter was written on union letterhead and the signature included his position in the union. The members of the local reacted immediately and strongly against this "interference" by the union in local affairs. The author of the letter was severely criticized. The executive council and the president of the local had to write letters to the paper stating that the Publicity Director had acted as an individual and that his position did not represent the sentiments of the local.

The union can be effective if it can so define the community situation that non-discriminatory behavior would serve the interests of the people involved. This is, of course, less difficult when the community organizations are weak and more difficult when they are strong. The specific tactics would depend on the specific situation. The union can indicate to the individuals involved that non-discriminatory behavior in the neighborhood can serve the individuals' interests better than discriminatory behavior. It can explode the myths used by the neighborhood organizations promoting discrimination. Thus the union can point out that property values do not necessarily decline when Negroes move into a neighborhood, that crime does not necessarily increase, etc. This means that in order to be effective in the neighborhood, the union would not only have to use the same tactics that are effective in the work situation, but be prepared to enter into the neighborhood itself.

PART 4

The Balance Between Stability and Change in Society

SOCIAL DISORGANIZATION, DEVIANCE, AND SOCIAL PROBLEMS

Value-Conflict in Social Disorganization

Ralph H. Turner

SOURCE: *Sociology and Social Research*, Vol. 38, (1954), pp. 301–308.

The idea of value-conflict has played an important part in thinking about social disorganization for several years.[1] At the same time, it has remained an imprecise notion, and the implications of its use as an organizing concept in the study of social disorganization have been little developed. This paper will propose some clarification of the nature of value-conflict, with a view toward rendering it a more effective tool of theory and research.

Before exploring value-conflict, we need to note some distinctive aspects of the social disorganization approach of which it is a part. Social disorganization focuses attention on the harmonious and inharmonious aspects of the structure of society, as such. It is concerned with the ways and degrees to which the activities implicit in the organization of the society are mutually reinforcing or mutually contradictory. Consequently, its concern with the individual is incidental, and individual satisfactions, while they may turn out to be important symptomatically, do not constitute the major criteria of social organization. In the same way, social disorganization is differentiated from the study of conformity and deviancy in individuals, or the degree to which the social norms are effectively followed in individual behavior (social control).

The activities which represent the social structure are most frequently described in terms of "norms" and "values." Social disorganization may then be conceptualized in terms of some conflicts among norms and values in a society. Social disorganization deals with ways in which activities which are in some sense the product of, and legitimatized by, the social structure conflict with one another. Much the same results are obtained by

---

[1]Since Lawrence K. Frank's classic statement in "Social Problems," American Journal of Sociology, 30: 462-73, 1925, nearly all sociological writings on the subject have made use of the idea of value-conflict.

stressing either conflicts among norms or conflicts among values, but it is useful to make a distinction between these two concepts.

Social norms are prescriptions regarding behavior and belief and prohibitions against certain patterns of behavior and belief. They are statements that certain types of behavior and belief should be followed or avoided when such statements are generally accepted in a society and when each individual has the sense that they are generally accepted by others.

Social norms do not generally exist in an unequivocal sense for most activities in the society. What we conceive ideally as social norms tend in practice to be "short-circuited" into social values. Social values are objects which are regarded favorably or unfavorably, in the same manner as described for norms. As objects, values refer to something which can be secured or attained. They constitute attributes or end products of activity. Thus, the usual way of saying that one should tell the truth (norm) is to say that honesty (value) is a good thing.

Values and norms are obverse aspects of the same thing, and in some sense alternative ways of conveying the same meanings. But there are at least two important differences. First, there is generally greater agreement on values in a society than on norms, but the specific behavior meaning of values is less well defined. Thus, there will be general agreement that health, beauty, "character," and money are good things (positive values), but considerable confusion exists over what constitutes beauty and character and what particular responsibilities are imposed on the individual for the attainment of those positive values of health and money.

Second, the concept of social value is somewhat more inclusive than that of social norm. An object may be regarded as worthy of attainment, bringing its possessor social approbation, without there being any sense that others ought to pursue it. One may achieve recognition for special achievements and special

attributes of personality because these are regarded as good things by the society. But it would be hard to find a norm declaring that one should develop skill at playing baseball or collecting rare manuscripts, to correspond with the value which these activities constitute.

We shall choose to consider social disorganization primarily as conflict of values, rather than of norms. We gain thereby a more inclusive framework and one closer to the reality of the loose ordering of even the society with the least number of cultural "alternatives."

Conflict of values: difficulties of application. Social disorganization may be conceived as a state of conflict among social values.[2] This means that certain socially sanctioned values are unattainable in practice without violation or interference with the attainment of other social values, also socially sanctioned. Such conflicts exist either among values adhered to by all members and groups in the society or among values belonging to different subgroups in the society. In the latter instance, different groups within the society may seek values which are mutually contradictory, so that the activities of each group are interfered with by the activities of other groups. The clearest example of this type of conflict may be found in the existence of ethnic groups with diverse values and of economic classes with values which contradict those of other classes. But values which are generally accepted by most members and groups within the society may also come in conflict, as in the general acceptance of individualistic competition as a positive good at the same time that humanitarian cooperation is also regarded as a positive value in

[2] The present discussion should be compared with Robert C. Angell's treatment of "moral integration" in terms of compatibility and adequacy of social norms. Angell does not escape the difficulties discussed below, however. See Robert C. Angell, The Moral Integration of American Cities (Chicago: University of Chicago Press, 1951), especially pp. 115-22.

American society.[3] The problem in this instance is not that one group is exclusively identified with one of these values and another group with the other, but rather that all groups accept both values in general.

Confusion immediately arises in applying the value-conflict framework, however, if the sense in which values come into conflict is not clarified. We must distinguish between logical incompatibility of values and incompatibility in application. A subject for adolescent debate is the supposed conflict between the values of honesty and humanitarianism when the doctor gives a patient a rosier picture of his health than the facts justify. It is argued that complete honesty might kill the patient and that humanitarian values require dishonesty. One must violate one value in adhering to the other. But such discussions are purely recreational. The normally socialized person in our society encounters such a situation with no sense of having to make a crucial choice, nor does he feel guilt over having violated his values of honesty. The approved course of action is clear, the individual experiences no conflicting imperatives or indecision, and there is no major group sanction for the course of pure honesty in this situation. Thus, there is certainly a logical contradiction between these values in such a situation, but there is no contradiction in application. The orderly functioning of the society is not perceptibly disturbed by such a logical contradiction, and so the latter cannot be equated with social disorganization.

Only when social values may be called upon to support contradictory patterns of behavior in actual situations can we speak of social disorganization. Thus, Myrdal's famous study of the American Negro problem is not framed as a study of social disorganization.[4] He poses, as the "American dilemma," a logical contradiction between the "American Creed" and "the Negro's place." But it does not necessarily follow from the logical contradiction that most people in American society perceive any dilemma here. In fact, the overenthusiastic student of race relations may be distressed to find how many people and groups sincerely feel no disloyalty to democratic ideals in their support of segregation and discrimination.

How is it possible, then, for values to be in logical contradiction without coming into contradiction in application? One answer may be attempted by borrowing an idea from the study of personal disorganization. Values are not all equal in importance. Rather, they fall in hierarchies. So long as such hierarchies are clearly understood, logical conflicts of values may be easily resolved in practice in favor of the more important value. Thus, the humanitarian value may be regarded as more important than honesty, so that the individual resolves the foregoing dilemma on this basis.

While such a formulation is of some help in understanding value-conflicts, it has clear limitations. The weighing of alternative values and selection of the more important does not actually seem to take place in most situations. Furthermore, choices are not always consistent with the notion that the more important value predominates. The police officer may provoke, with public approval, a high-speed chase on crowded highways, which endangers many lives, in order to capture someone violating a relatively minor traffic rule. Yet the policeman and the public would certainly rank protection of human life a higher value than punishment for the particular minor traffic offense.

Another formulation which is a special variant of the value-conflict position is the statement of anomie by Robert Mer-

[3]Kingsley Davis, Harry C. Bredemeier, and Marion J. Levy, Jr., Modern American Society (New York: Rinehart and Company, Inc., 1948), pp. 705-06.

[4]Gunnar Myrdal, An American Dilemma (New York: Harper & Brothers, 1944), especially pp.

xlv-lii. Myrdal's entire introductory statement rests implicitly on the assumption that a logical contradiction of norms must be disturbing to the general population in America.

ton.[5] By dichotomizing values into means and ends, he observes that either means or ends may become unduly stressed in a society so that the one is not adequately qualified by the other. Money is pursued in American society as an end frequently without attention to the socially approved means for its attainment. Or it is possible for a society to become excessively formalized, emphasizing means so rigidly that they cease to be tested against ends achieved. Anomie is thus conceived as a special form of value-conflict. Socially-approved means constitute limitations on socially-approved ends, and vice versa, but value-conflict in a meaningful sense exists only when the balance between the two is lost.

This scheme is difficult to apply, however, since the distinctions between means and ends are not easily made in practice. Values become means or ends only in the context of a particular act in progress, and there are no values which constitute ends all of the time or means all of the time. To apply the scheme requires that the investigator determine what are really ends—a highly dubious process. Thus, in American society the pursuit of money (an end) without respect to the approved means can be called an excessive emphasis on goals. But it is equally logical to insist that money is regarded as a means toward more ultimate goals such as happiness, and that the excessive pursuit of money is a concentration on means at the expense of ends.

The empirical nature of values. Part of our problem may be that the nature of a social value has not been sufficiently clarified. Values are a product of ongoing behavior. While values, once conceptualized, acquire an existence prior to and partly independent of the activities to which they are applied, their general vagueness leaves much room for specific application to be adapted to the nature of

the ongoing activity and to change as the activity proceeds.

Values are generalizations, through which different acts can be related and through which a particular activity may be seen as part of a larger setting. Since every activity is unique in many respects, values are necessarily quite incomplete designators for any particular activity.

Values are conceptualizations. But the conceptualization is often misleading. Values are generally conceptualized in absolute terms, but applied with distinct situational limitations. Freedom of speech, whether presented as a value to be upheld or a norm (as in the American Constitution) is formulated in absolute terms. And yet there are laws against profanity, disturbance of the peace, libel, plagiarism, advocating overthrow of the government by violence, and laws which designate the times and places at which certain utterances are permissible. These laws do not generally trouble people as inconsistencies. Occasional discussions of this point are largely recreational; that is, they are not taken as serious discussions which should lead to rectifying action. Challenges are normally met by the statement that these are not the things which are meant by freedom of speech, or that these are not inconsistent with the spirit of free speech. Such answers are disturbing to the logical purist, but they accurately reflect the societal consensus.

Before we conclude summarily that people are inconsistent, we need to recognize that social values have two aspects which we may call the explicit and the implicit. The absolute conceptualization of the value is a symbol, an incomplete representation standing for a body of understandings regarding the value. This body of understandings defines the application of the value in different kinds of situations. We may speak of these understandings as the implicit limitations on the applications of values. On the basis of normal exposure to the culture in question, the individual acquires these understandings. They constitute the em-

[5]Robert K. Merton, "Social Structure and Anomie," *American Sociological Review*, October 1938, pp. 672-82.

pirical content of a value. But they are not logically coherent and hence are not subject to neat summarization.

Both in the social development of values and in the individual learning of values, the experience of a multitude of specific situations precedes the generalized value statement. As conditions change, large bodies of people sense that a particular course of action in a certain type of situation is rewarding or unsatisfactory. Into such a situation comes the ideologist, who offers a formulation of an established value in such a way that it sanctions the preferred course of action.

Similarly, no learning of the symbolic value formulations can be a guide to behavior in a society. The "stranger" may indeed find it more difficult to learn the effective values of a culture to the degree to which he has prepared himself with a systematic learning of the explicit value formulations. The explicit formulations are effective guides only to those who have already so fully internalized the multitude of situational directives that they have become dulled to the perception of the logical implications of the explicit value statements of the society.

The confusion arising over apparent contradictions of values which do not seem to constitute contradictions in application comes out of mistaking the absolute formulation typical of values for the actual behaviorally relevant content of the values. In fact, it is likely that the absolute logical extension of any accepted value to correspond with its conceptual formulation would necessarily bring it into conflict with many or most other values.

For the most part, the arraying of values in hierarchies of importance is an effort to conceive in rational terms the situational specificity of values. In some few ill-defined situations in which ongoing activity does not dictate the choice, the tendency to think of values in hierarchies may determine choice. Or in the case of some individuals who value an intellectual approach to situations more than do most, choice may be on this basis. Conceptualization of values into hierarchies is most frequently a technique for supporting an action under way whose legitimacy is challenged by some groups who contend that a different value is applicable to the situation in question. Thus, condemnation proceedings are justified by calling community welfare a higher value than private property. But the interest groups supporting such a definition do not support the same value-primacy in other situations and would not define the situation in this manner were not a sufficiently powerful opposition able to insist on the applicability of the value of private property in this situation.

Disorganization and the implicit content of values. While there are some values held by subgroups in a society which are not recognized as legitimate by others, most disorganization consists of conflicting interpretations of the application of certain values. There is agreement on the symbolic level of the value, but there is disagreement regarding its applicability to situations. In a smooth-functioning society, there is consensus concerning value applications, and logically contradictory values (which will always be present) are well "insulated" from one another in practice through their situational applications.

This formulation is consistent with the way in which people and organizations, in practice, deal with the logically possible application of two different values to a single situation. Rather than make judgments by weighing the importance of one value against the other, individuals and organizations make choices as to which one applies. Thus, the minister in a businessman's church who makes suggestions about employer-employee relations is not told that profits are more important than religious values. He is told, rather, that the subject matter is business, and hence is not the sphere to which religious values apply. Such partitionings of the areas which belong to different sets of values seem to be the stuff of which a smooth-functioning social order is made. The breakdown of these partitions, and the erection of different partitions by different subgroups within the society, seem to constitute most of social disorganization.

The processes of establishing and maintaining the partitioning of situations to which different values apply should accordingly be one of the major areas of investigation in the study of social disorganization. For example, in the maintenance of the separation between values which might conflict logically, certain types of imagery may be important. Thus the stereotype, as a type of imagery, may function to preserve the separation between values of racial inequality and values of general equality. The stereotype of the happy, carefree Negro plantation worker renders the value of general equality inapplicable and the value of subordination innocuous in its application.

The circumstances under which a subgroup within a society comes to sponsor a different understanding concerning the application of certain values from that held by other groups in the society should be another central concern of the study of social disorganization. The place of segmentalization of activities in the society, the limitation of communication between groups, and the tendency for organizations to be conceived as the sponsors of particular values apply here. Within the academic world, for example, the scientific method tends to be exalted and extended in its application beyond that approved elsewhere. Scientific method is a positive value throughout the society, but divergence develops regarding the situations to which it applies.

Some of the conflict between educational institutions and the rest of society seems to revolve about this sort of divergence.

Such conditions as the foregoing, which signalize disorganization in some degree, need to be differentiated from the kind of organization through which a specialized group is shielded from interaction with the rest of society at a value level. In scientific research organizations, for example, the extensive application of scientific method may prevail. Interaction with the general public, however, is not on the basis of scientific method as a value, but solely on the basis of the product of the method, which is favorably evaluated in the society. This type of value divergence does not become value-conflict and social disorganization.

Finally, social change can be meaningfully related to social disorganization by a study of its impact on the implicit or situational aspect of values. Shifts in intergroup relations, such as those accompanying war and economic dislocation, alter the significance of traditional courses of action. Instead of relinquishing the old explicit value formulations which legitimized these outmoded courses of action, people become receptive to reinterpretation of the values. A situation is thus created in which social values do not constitute effective directives to consistent action within the society. At the same time, differential interest positions and differential willingness to make reinterpretations foster group alignments about alternative definitions of the situational applications of values. The resulting state is one of value-conflict, and a degree of social disorganization characterizes the society.

Panic Theory

Paul B. Foreman

SOURCE: *Sociology and Social Research*, Vol. 37, (1953), pp. 295–304.

At least three ideas of panic are current in American social science literature. The quite standard economic interpretation holds panic to be a mass response to a market collapse, real or imagined, the purpose of which is to escape capital loss after a period of inflation or over-trading. In sociological and social-psychological literature two somewhat less clearly established conceptions appear. In the first of these, as in the writing of Cantril, Janis, Meerloo, and Sullivan,[1] panic refers either to the feelings or the overt behavior of a terrorized individual —a person utterly demoralized or distraught and then gripped by an intense state of fear and anxiety. Presumably, fear and anxiety are cued by the perception of a great, unanticipated and seemingly unmanageable crisis, and, among other possible reactions, may lead to pell-mell flight. According to the second usage, one also common in historical writing, panic is construed as a type of rout, a very ephemeral form of collective behavior occurring in face-to-face contact groups or through mediated communication in masses. Among better-known sources, this construction has appeared in the work of Lanham, La-Piere, and Reuter and Hart.[2]

The contrast between these two latter conceptions of panic has been sharpened by Janis' recent review of World War II air raid reactions.[3] Accepting the idea of panic as a terror state and as "non-adaptive" personal behavior in response to a crisis, Janis did not pause to contrast his views with panic conceived as rout. Rather, he dismissed the latter as an "a priori, stereotyped conception of mass panic."[4] He was strongly inclined to discount panic references in earlier studies of reactions at Hiroshima and Nagasaki—studies which, as he held treated panic casually but almost invariably, it would seem, in the sense of rout. Janis' views can be epitomized by the following excerpts:

The above assertions (from earlier reviews) sound like authoritative, well-established propositions, as though the panic were in the same category as the fact that there was a mass exodus from the burning cities. In the absence of precise, detailed observations of escape behavior, one cannot make an adequate evaluation of the degree of emotional control exhibited by the survivors. To stop and to attempt to extricate others in the face of a rapidly spreading conflagration would sometimes be tantamount to futile sacrifice of one's own life. We cannot be sure, therefore, that those who fled without stopping to help others were behaving impulsively since we cannot exclude the pos-

---

[1] Hadley Cantril and others, The Invasion from Mars (Princeton: Princeton University Press, 1940); Hadley Cantril, "Causes and Control of Riot and Panic," Public Opinion Quarterly, 7: 669–79, 1943; Irving L. Janis, Air War and Emotional Stress (New York: McGraw-Hill Book Company, Inc., 1951); Harry Stack Sullivan, "Psychiatric Aspects of Morale," American Journal of Sociology, 47: 277–301, 1941.

[2] C. T. Lanham, "Panic" in Joseph I. Green, The Infantry Journal Reader (Garden City: Doubleday &

Company, Inc., 1943); R. T. LaPiere, Collective Behavior (New York: McGraw-Hill Book Company, Inc., 1938); E. B. Reuter and C. W. Hart, Introduction to Sociology (New York: McGraw-Hill Book Company, Inc., 1933).

[3] Janis, op.cit., esp. pp. 1–66 on reactions to atomic blasts at Hiroshima and Nagasaki.

[4] Ibid, p. 27.

sibility that they may have been acting on the basis of a realistic appraisal of a danger situation. Our information is too incomplete to permit any fine judgments to be made; from what little is available, it would be unwarranted to conclude that there was a sizeable frequency of inappropriate, negligent, or asocial behavior merely because some instances of abandonment have been reported.[5]

Janis sought to distill inferences from World War II bombing situations which might be pertinent for the planning of postdisaster controls. Knowledge about human stampedes might be as meaningful for this interest as knowledge about the "inappropriate, negligent, or asocial" behavior which Janis identified as panic. It can be quickly demonstrated that ideas of panic as a terror state or as the overt behavior of a distraught individual and the idea of panic as rout can induce confusion. It would be consistent with Janis' premises to pay particular attention in the aftermath at Hiroshima to excited individuals huddling in the ruined city; it would be consistent with the view that panic is rout to examine the behavior of survivors fleeing toward the Hiroshima hinterlands. It is logical for Janis to hold, as he has done, that panic rarely occurs unless immediate physical danger is overwhelming and no apparent avenues of escape exist.[6] It would be equally logical for those holding panic to be a form of rout to conclude from the accounts of the General Slocum fire, for example, that panic occurs in the presence of events interpreted as acutely and uncontrollably dangerous only when avenues of possible escape are evident.[7]

Assuming the conception of panic as rout and holding the idea that knowledge about this behavior might be valuable in military operations as well as for postdisaster control of civilian populations, this paper reports the findings of an attempt to apply case study techniques for comparative analysis to a series of historical incidents in order to codify theory and to develop an initial series of propositions on panic control. Twenty-nine incidents were reviewed in detail; twenty-five other cases for which less complete information could be found were also considered. Unfortunately, no data from World War II or Korean incidents are included. If this approach is suggestive, a review of classified documents concerning such cases should permit extensive revision of or supplement to the theory developed by the present effort.

One of the most persistent problems faced in this review of panic incidents has been the need for distinguishing succinctly between antecedent and predisposing conditions on one hand and cause on the other. References to either in the literature are frequently little more than rationalizations elaborated by hind-sight imputation. By superimposing the data of case on case, however, it is possible to clarify theory at this point and to suggest that background conditions become factors in panic only as reactions to a crisis stimulus are shaped by them. In the few available accounts of mass panics, that is, stampedes induced in dispersed populations by some form of mediated communication,[8] the stimulus leading to rout clearly linked antecedent tensions with immediate shock. This was a major force in the hoax news broadcast in Paris on the day of the Bikini test. However, some stampedes in direct contact military groups—for example, in the routs at Chickamauga, Missionary Ridge, Gumbinnen, and Tannenburg—appear to be almost totally explicable in terms of the quick sequence of events following shock in the course of battle.

As cases were reviewed for this summary, a check was made on all conditions, prior to the shock stimulus, which were presumed to influence rout. They ran a long and dissonant gamut. However, all these conditions can be quickly, if

[5] Ibid, pp. 30, 37. See also his "Typical Disaster Experience," pp. 6-7 a case study which discloses flight to the Hiroshima hinterland but highlights only personal terror.
[6] Ibid., pp. 40, 193.
[7] New York Times, June 16, 1904, p.1 ff.

[8] Louis Wirth, "Consensus and Mass Communication", American Sociological Review 13: 1-15, 1948.

roughly, grouped into types: conditions such as acute fatigue which weaken individuals organically, those like worry about lack of information concerning expected attacks in war which create acute emotional tensions and anxiety, those like novice or stranger status which prevent or impoverish self-satisfying group identifications, and those like awareness of such weapons as guided missiles and napalm which incite chronic social unrest.[9]

Cause in most panics develops through the linkage of a shock stimulus and four phases of human reaction to this stimulus. The stimulus interrupts antecedent behavior and, frequently it appears, suspends action. To lead toward panic this stimulus must have sufficient duration, sequence, or repetition to command continued focused attention and to compound terror responses. Shock or the perception of the crisis as startling and crisis provoking is the initial reaction to this stimulus. In situations culminating in panic, shock is quickly followed by confusion, that is, by individual and random efforts to interpret events in terms of reasonable experiences or relatable antecedent situations. To borrow a phrase from J. T. MacCurdy, shock and confusion are phases of "indecisive inactivity occasioned by an emergency."[10] Where interpretations of the stimulus are so acutely pressing that instantaneous action is demanded, the sensing of this acuteness frequently blocks logical definition of the crisis and induces terror. Initial terror responses include shouts, screams, and excited physical movements. This is not a lull phase; it is a period of din. These indecisive acts of initial terror, if not immediately controlled by an overwhelming order-producing stimulus, compound into bedlam. Such reactions may be significant at first

as releases for overwhelming tension; quickly, however, they serve as reinforcing stimuli for the terror of others and may be reflected back, circularwise, to reinforce the frenzy of the original actor. Linked in these ways, the terror of interacting individuals is heightened. Occasionally, participant observers record the fact that these augmented terror responses serve to reduce confidence in whatever, if any, organizing interpretations of the crisis had been effected and to establish convictions of doom. Terror movements, among whatever else they may suggest, may channel attention and direct activity to flight. Actors who offer such suggestions are in this context flight models.[11] Panic is activated when interacting terrorized individuals surge away in flight.

Panic is extremely impulsive action. Frequently it is characterized as individualistic or egocentric action. This is true in the sense that panic as a design for personal survival obeys no custom. The action of people in rout is, however, given common character by at least two things: first, by circular and chain suggestions presented during flight; second, by the identity or similarity in escape opportunities afforded by the setting in which rout proceeds.

Milling and canalization of milling responses into flight by effective models continue to appear when rout is in process. Milling is accentuated wherever flight is blocked; flight proceeds when a

---

[9] A very similar typing, one which does not however distinguish background conditions and cause, appears in Anselm L. Strauss, "The Literature on Panic," Journal of Abnormal and Social Psychology, 39: 317-28, 1944.

[10] J. T. MacCurdy, The Structure of Morale (New York: The Macmillan Company, 1944).

[11] No clearer example of model suggestion for flight could be provided than this: "An American battalion holds a reserve position in a shell-torn wood. Enemy artillery has been intermittently strafing the position since dusk. The Americans in their foxholes are getting what sleep they can. At 11:00 p.m. the battalion commander, accompanied by his adjutant, starts an inspection of his lines. A runner dashes up and hands him a message. The Major reads it. He calls to his adjutant, who is a short distance away, "Come on! Let's beat it!" The two start to the rear at a dead run. Before they have covered two hundred yards the entire battalion is in wild flight behind them. It races more than ten kilometers before it can be stopped. The message to the Major had directed him to report to the regimental command post as fast as he could get there. He was complying with the order." Lanham, op.cit., p. 275.

participant hits upon some newly evident means of escape. If many avenues of escape are apparent, the terrorizing pressure of the perceived crisis is lessened; if few or no avenues of escape are evident or if available avenues are blocked, terror-accentuating pressure is augmented.

The tensions of rout are acute and tend to be short-lived. People in panic may attain safety; they may strive until death, strain, fatigue, or despair ends their participation; or, given sufficient suggestions, they may shift to some other form of collective behavior—perhaps that of a mob or an orgiastic crowd.[12] Panic in the first battle at Bull Run subsided to the dismal trek of a defeated, unorganized horde when the acute pressure of Confederate pursuit was withdrawn. Chance separations of escaping individuals from the churning aggregate of a stampede may also lessen tensions and terminate flight. The usual ending of panic clearly is not a group process; panic ends as selective influences eliminate individuals from rout. But panic behavior is not necessarily complete when flight terminates. There are common sequelae to panic—fatigue and stupor, extreme anxiety, excitability and aggression, perhaps persistent terror and, not infrequently, secondary panics.

This simple theory of panic requires at least two supplements and several specific provisos. The first supplement rests on the experience of survivors at Halifax, Hiroshima, and Nagasaki. It is that as the immediate impact of a devastating stimulus approaches the proportions of absolute incomprehensibility, this impact alone may be sufficient to trigger flight reactions. The second supplement is that if a stimulus, prior to

its occurrence, is linguistically defined as unmanageable, its name alone can induce immediate terror and panic. There are accounts indicating that the cry of "Gas!" so operated during World War I. There are accounts indicating that the cry of "Napalm!" may have operated in this way in Korea. It is also reasonable to suppose that the tactics of the Communist Chinese in Korea which call for "human wave" assaults accompanied by the sounding of bugles and other noise are somewhat similarly construed.[13]

The summary theory presented above, as a crude form of natural history derived from but a few cases, needs several specific provisos beyond the patent one that these ideas might be shaken greatly by the introduction of new evidence. First, it does not assume that all individuals interacting in a social situation culminating in panic react in the same way. Perceptions of a crisis and attempts to orient it certainly do not lead to uniform responses on the part of individuals exposed to a crisis stimulus. Differing antecedent experiences, differing immediate definitions of the crisis stimulus, and such things as differing physical abilities will encourage variable responses. Second, it does not assume that rout develops more or less automatically when certain background factors creating a condition of "panic ripeness" appear. Indeed, it assumes panic usually to be a product of a chain of reactions following a crisis stimulus, and it infers that stampedes do not develop until suggestions for flight are acted upon in a certain way. This is to say that terror does not inevitably breed

---

[12] Joseph H. Douglass ("The Funeral of Sister President," *Journal of Abnormal and Social Psychology*, 44: 217-23, 1939) called attention to one crowd which did not seem to conform to commonly indicated crowd types. What Douglass did not consider is that situational redefinitions in the period of activity of his considered group may have done precisely what is suggested above for panic groups, that is, completely changed its type as a collective behavior form.

[13] This point is briefly mentioned in Alfred L. Lindesmith and Anselm L. Strauss, *Social Psychology* (New York: The Dryden Press, 1949), p. 332. These authors go so far as to state, "Human beings usually become panicked in situations which have previously been linguistically defined as fearful or terrifying." While "usually" might be hard to prove, this hypothesis might profitably be examined when more complete testimony is available. Such theory would seem, further, to illuminate many cases of bolting by individuals: the boy who, walking by a graveyard, bolts and runs for his life because he "saw a ghost," is reacting in terms of earlier linguistic interpretations.

panic and that, perhaps with very little difference in suggestion, a terror situation might produce a mob or an orgiastic crowd rather than rout.[14] Third, this theory does not assume that panic is "nonadaptive": irrational, inappropriate, negligent, or asocial behavior. Mintz, who has recently published an objection, similar to the position taken here, to the type of panic theory that merely stresses background conditions, mutual facilitation (contagion, suggestion) leading to intense emotional excitement and regressive behavior, has made this point, although he himself describes panic as "nonadaptive group behavior." Mintz specifies:

At a theater fire if everyone leaves in an orderly manner everybody is safe and an individual waiting for his turn is not sacrificing his interests. But if the cooperative pattern of behavior is disturbed, the usual advice, "Keep your head, don't push, wait your turn, and you will be safe," ceases to be valid. If the exits are blocked the person following this advice is likely to be burned to death. In other words, if everybody cooperates there is no conflict between the needs of the individual and those of the group. However, the situation changes completely as soon as a minority of people cease to cooperate.... People are likely to recognize the threats to themselves and behave accordingly.... If a few individuals begin to push, others are apt to recognize that their interests are threatened; they can expect to win their rewards only by pressing their personal advantage at the group's expense.[15]

[14] E. Glover ("Notes on the Psychological Effects of War Conditions on Civilian Populations", *International Journal of Psychoanalysis*, 23: 17-37, 1942) and P. E. Vernon ("Psychological Effects of Air-Raids," *Journal of Abnormal and Social Psychology* 36: 457-76, 1941) confirm the point that terror does not inevitably produce panic. Lindesmith and Strauss (op.cit, p. 497) would include in panic behavior "other than that of physically running away." But this would tend to confuse panic with such distinctive behavior forms as the orgiastic crowd where physical movement and shouting are principally devices of tension release, not acute fear; the mob where action is directed at "getting" some person, group, place, or thing; or the riot where mobs meet or revelers or mobs encounter almost any sharp opposition.

[15] Alexander Mintz, "Non-Adaptive Group Behavior," *Journal of Abnormal and Social Psychology*, 46: 150-59, 1951.

The idea that panic is inappropriate, nondiscriminating behavior is age-old. It frequently appears in reviews of military incidents; clearly it has been fostered by the widespread attention given Cantril's Invasion from Mars. Cantril wrote of panic as terror produced by suggestibility and assumed that a cardinal purpose of his review was to show people how some individuals reacted unintelligently to the Welles broadcast so that they might avoid or build up resistance to similar hoodwinking.[16] This evaluative premise about panic, no matter if panic is construed as terror or as rout, ignores or underemphasizes the situational redefinitions which recast the significance of action when time is out of joint. Such moralizing appears gross when one recalls the theory behind W. I. Thomas' dictum: "If men define situations as real, they are real in their consequences."[17]

Perhaps the fact that panic is abhorred is sufficient to explain the almost universal attention given to prevention when its control is considered. Almost nothing has been written about diminution of panic or efforts to quell it once it has been activated, and even less attention has been given to panic incitement or reinforcement. It seems quite possible that obsession with prevention may have retarded panic theory. Quite possibly, panic may be a legitimate device of modern warfare, harsh as this idea may seem at first sight. Quite possibly, also, attention to control efforts, other than prevention, may result in the improvement of defensive as well as offensive tactics, whether these tactics apply to military or civilian situations. Working from such assumptions, a careful effort was made, when the cases contributing to this review were read, to conceptualize any inference about control, whatever its in-

[16] Cantril and others, op.cit., p. 8. For a review of Cantril's work, see Janis, op.cit., p. 193.
[17] Herbert Blumer, Critiques of Research in the Social Sciences: I (New York: Social Science Research Council, 1942), p. 85. See also E. H. Volkart, ed., Social Behavior and Personality (New York: Social Science Research Council, 1951), pp. 12-14 et passim.

tent might be. These inferences, not supplemented by free theorizing and cast generally in the form of inducement and reinforcement, can be presented in proposition form, as follows:

1. Although background conditions are not causal factors of panic, deliberate attempts to induce or reinforce terror or panic should succeed more readily where disturbing conditions known to be present in prior instances are clearly present and compounded.

2. Where a crisis stimulus provokes a totally incomprehensible disaster, control or selection of background conditions probably has little effect on behavior subsequent to this stimulus.

3. For an effective understanding of background conditions weakening individuals organically, producing acute tensions and anxiety, and preventing or impoverishing rewarding group identifications, considerable insight regarding human relations among target peoples in the immediate past is necessary.

4. For effective understanding of background conditions contributing to chronic social unrest in a target population, knowledge of recent developments may require considerable supplement from intimate knowledge of cultural organization and long-time social trends.

5. Any stimulus which confronts individuals in a target population with an acute sense of danger or its threat is a likely prelude to terror and panic, provided that responses to it have not been conventionalized, that it shatters immediately antecedent forms of behavior, and that it has sufficient duration, sequence, or repetition for the compounding of terror responses.

6. Any stimulus which, prior to its appearance, has been linguistically defined as acutely terrifying and unmanageable may induce immediate terror and guide action directly to flight.

7. The disruptive influences of shock appear to be greatest where surprise is most complete, where normal sensory functioning is inhibited, where the ratio of individuals suffering immediate personal or private property damage to the total population is greatest, where affected individuals respond most slowly or reluctantly to institutionalized commands, where physical protection is least adequate, and where affected individuals are in motion, particularly in retreat, at the moment of the crisis-provoking stimulus.

8. Following the initial shock produced by a crisis stimulus, a rapid sequence of inconsistent or contradictory suggestions as to the meaning of the stimulus, or what to do about it, will compound confusion.

9. Terror is compounded by effective countermeasures to panic prevention or restriction devices.

10. Terror varies inversely with the number and adequacy of available escape outlets.

11. The incidence of shock, confusion, and terror in a population acutely aware of a crisis stimulus usually decreases as distance from the stimulus increases.

12. Effective models for terror and panic behavior stress immediately personal or egocentric rather than group or team goals, and, by suggesting flight, they tend to defeat efforts to maintain or re-establish order and to counteract appeals for cooperation.

13. Panic develops only when possible avenues for escape become evident.

14. Model suggestions for the extension and direction of panic movement are effective when rout is in process as well as when it begins.

15. Terror-augmenting stimuli that appear after general rout has begun reinforce flight suggestions and thus extend panic in time and space; for example, the probability of prolonged and extended terror and panic following an air raid would presumably be increased by secondary attacks on throngs of people rushing out along traffic arteries in quest of security.

16. The actions of people in panic are given common character by the identity or similarity in escape opportunities afforded by the setting in which rout proceeds and by exposure to common chains of social interaction.

17. Panic may be extended in time and space by the absence of diminution devices or by effective countermeasures to such devices.

18. Panic may be terminated by the relaxation of threat, the attainment of safety, incapacitating injury, supervening fatigue, death, separation of individuals or small groups from an aggregate in rout, elimination of escape outlets, or effective substitution of some other action pattern.

19. Since acute fatigue, depression, anxiety, aggressive behavior, apprehensive rumors, social disruption, sickness, and injury are common, if transient, sequelae of terror and panic, these behavior forms might be most successfully provoked by directing acute danger threats to target population recently terrorized or panicked.

The inference value of a series of propositions like the above, assuming that they are as concisely drawn as data permit, should increase almost geometrically as their number increases, and with this increase propositions might well fall into prime, corollary, and subordinate series. Scrutiny of the list of propositions here included should invite challenge, refinement, and extension by others who know other literature or by those who discern logical gaps and are thus led to further formulation. The present review has suggested several free theorizing leads of this latter sort, but these are not included here for the reason that the present obligation is to present, as concisely as possible, the inferences of concrete protocols. However, with this accomplished, the conclusion Robin Williams derived from his review of intergroup relations literature can very well be brought to bear on panic theory. Williams observed:

The sole aim of the compilation is to bring together in compact and convenient form a sampling of what is known and surmised in this field... Many, if not most, of the propositions outlined are at present little more then educated guesses.... Nothing is to be gained in the current state of scientific knowledge in this field from the refusal to formulate hypotheses.[18]

The assumption, stated above, that the inference value of propositions about panic should increase almost geometrically as their number increases should hold even if the isolation of presumably relevant conditions and factors is but a first analytical step toward the end of purposive social control. Indeed, this isolation cannot specify how the concentration or combination of such elements affects the probability of the occurrence of terror or panic. This must await a much richer and tested body of principles. However, if knowledge about terror and panic must in a world of atomic bombs and guided missiles succeed sermonizing, the raw accretion of ideas and synthesis of such lore may emphasize what is not known as well as what is now known and assumed. Both may suggest next steps for development and testing of ideas.

---

[18] Robin M. Williams, Jr., The Reduction of Intergroup Tensions (New York: Social Science Research Council, 1947), pp. 49-50.

Race and Minority Riots—A Study in the Typology of Violence

H. Otto Dahlke

SOURCE: *Social Forces*, Vol. 30, (1951–52), pp. 419-25.

A constructed type is an exaggeration of actuality. Certain aspects of an historical event are abstracted in accordance with certain hypotheses. In this study we will attempt to delineate a pattern of social action in which violence is one of the essential attributes by asking: What are the essential elements of a race or minority riot? Under what conditions do these elements combine to produce the series of actions in the total event which is labeled a riot?

The underlying assumption in this study is the principle that valuations of the person and of the group organize social relations. Such valuations have been characterized as personal or categoric, intrinsic or extrinsic.[1] In those instances where intrinsic valuations in terms of respect, accountability, and inviolability are withheld, social relations are utilitarian or dissociative. Such social relations are reinforced if the content of the extrinsic categorizations is negative. These assessments, moreover, may be of long historical standing, a fact frequently overlooked, and they may become strengthened in a period of transition. When a series of negative evaluations impinges upon a group, then its situation, in the absence of mitigating norms of justice and humanitarianism, becomes extremely precarious. Violent expression of disesteem on the part of the superordinate group may readily result. Violence is more likely to occur when the minority group is not content to accept the assignment of low rank from this so-called majority group[2] and when it attempts a redefinition of the situation which will bring about assimilation or at least equal status without assimilation. This means that a redistribution of power and of opportunities is to be effected. This struggle will bring forth the opposition of the superordinate group.

Instead of defining the term riot and then finding examples to illustrate the definition we shall examine two historical events which have been defined by participants and bystanders as riots. The construction of a riot type obviously could involve many more instances. Improvement and modification of the construct arrived at in this preliminary study could be made by reference to the Nazi persecution of Jews and other groups, Polish pogroms, the Armenian pogrom in Turkey, the Huguenot massacre in France, Luddite riots in England, the recent riots in the Union of South Africa, communal riots in India, riots against Protestants in Mexico, the zoot suit riots in California, and others.

II

HISTORICAL CONDITIONS

Kiskinev Riot of 1903. A Russian official stated the case against the Jews

---

[1] E. T. Hiller, Social Relations and Structures (New York: Harper and Brothers, 1947), pp. 191-218, 631-650.

[2] The utility of the terms "minority-group" and "majority-group" is greatly limited if the terms are thought of quantitatively. Whites have frequently been dominant minorities. The crux of the matter lies in the relationship of domination and submission with the supporting valuations and power techniques.

as follows: "What can we do with them? They are the racial antithesis of our nation. A fusion with us is impossible, owing to religious and other disturbing causes. They will always be a potential source of sectarian and economic disorder in our country. We cannot admit them to equal rights of citizenship for these reasons, and, let me add, because their intellectual superiority would enable them to gain possession of most of the posts of the civil administration. . . . They are the active propagandists of the Socialism of Western Europe in our borders. Their discontent is a menace to us along the Austrian and German frontiers. The only solution to the problem of the Russian Jew is his departure from Russia."[3] In this statement there is a fairly complete negative assessment of the Jew. Various groups shared and supported this extreme disesteem, i.e., the government and especially the lower ranking officials of the political bureaucracy; the Russian Orthodox Church which was the established church; students and seminarists in the royal schools and gymnasia; the small merchant, petty trader, and working man.

This assessment, moreover, became institutionalized in a great variety of discriminatory statutes and administrative decrees. In the royal schools and gymnasia, Jews were restricted to five percent or ten percent of the total school population. From 1882 to 1903 a series of laws and administrative decrees limited property holding among Jews, restricted access to occupations, restricted education, forced unequal military service, and segregated them to the so-called Pale of Settlement.[4] These laws plus numerous local administrative decrees inhibited the economic and social

development of the Jews. They furthermore made Jews prey to the exactions of local petty officials and police. The sous prefect of police in Bessarabia in which Kishinev is located apparently was an expert at this.[5] The May law of 1882 which segregated all Jews to the Pale, i.e., from the land and villages to the towns, was not put into full effect until 1891 when the procurator of the Holy Synod, M. Podedonostev, forced the issuance of the imperial decree compelling the enforcement of the 1882 laws. Many of the fliers distributed around Kishinev advocating violence against Jews were printed by the press of the Holy Synod of St. Petersburg and passed by the church censor.[6]

Putting into effect the May law of 1882 had certain population and social consequences. These laws required that all Jews settle within the Pale, a series of provinces along the western frontier extending from Riga to the Black Sea. Those laws also excluded from agriculture all Jews except those already so engaged. Confined to the towns, the Jews had recourse only to industrial, service, and trade opportunities. Since Russia at this time was in process of becoming industrialized, occupational opportunities in industry were relatively meager. It has been estimated that 1,300,000 Jews or about one-third of the total Jewish population, were forced from the land and villages into the towns.[7] Three out of five inhabitants in urban centers of the Pale provinces were Jews.[8] In Bessarabia Jews composed 38 percent of the population. This population influx tended to increase the struggle for self-maintenance for both Jews and non-Jews, particularly among the small shopkeepers, petty middlemen, and artisans. Jews resorted to almost any means to keep

---

[3]Michael Davitt, Within the Pale (The Jewish Publication Society of America, New York: A. S. Barnes & Co., 1903), pp. 65-66.

[4]These laws and decrees are summarized in Die Judenpogrome in Russland, Zionistischen Hilisfond in London von der zur Erforschung der Pogrome Eingesetzten Kommission, judischer Verlag (Koln and Leipzig 1910), I, 97-133 (Referred to hereafter as Die Judenpogrome).

[5]Davitt, op. cit., pp. 95, 69.

[6]Die Judenpogrome, II, 10.

[7]Eugene Kolischer, Jewish Migration, American Jewish Committee, p. 23.

[8]Davitt, op. cit., p. 38.

themselves on a bare subsistence level.[9] To do so they had to resort to extra-legal and illegal means which augmented the parasitic demands of police and other officials of the bureaucracy. Extensive smuggling, for example, was one means and became so prevalent, including the entailed bribery and corruption, that Jews were forbidden to live within a stretch 35 to 40 miles from the western frontier.

Not only were Jews segregated by being forced to live in the Pale but they also tended to live in special districts within the urban centers. This local segregation apparently was on economic lines, with poor Jewish traders, shopkeepers, and laborers living close together. The more wealthy Jewish merchants and bankers had residences in the better sections of the towns. Such concentration of despised populations limits to a few focal points the outbreak of violent attacks.

A traditional anti-Jewish story, which was a very important element in the Kishinev riot, was the murder-ritual legend. This originated in the middle of the thirteenth century and spread all over Europe. This legend held that there was an annual killing of Christian children by Jews as part of the Blood Atonement in Hebrew Paschal rites.[10] The story emphasized the out-group nature of the Jew and evidently was firmly established in the cultures of Europe despite Jewish efforts to disavow it.

Social unrest, existing in many groups in Russia at this time, was attacked by the government with increasingly repressive measures. Although Jews played a role in certain movements and demonstrations, their role was exaggerated by constituted authorities as the dominant role. This repressive role of the government was expressed in the tremendous increase in death sentences for political activities, deportation to Siberia, and other tactics.[11] The fiasco of the Russo-Japanese war brought out the inefficiency and corruption of the government. In this situation Jews furnished a convenient scapegoat.[12]

Pogroms were not new in Russia. There were two large pogrom periods, the first from 1881 to 1883, and the second from 1903 to 1906. The first period involved 8 provinces and 690 pogroms.[13] Kishinev ushered in the pogroms of the second period. Local pogroms had taken place as early as 1821 in Odessa. Several isolated pogroms took place between 1884 and the second major period.[14] A pattern of violence against Jews was evidently an integral part of the culture.

Detroit Riot of 1943. The Negro came in large numbers to Detroit during tense periods, World War I and World War II. The town itself had grown meteorically, particularly after the establishment of the automobile industry. It had a large foreign-born population, including a strongly anti-Negro Polish district of around 50,000. It was estimated that 50,000 Negroes migrated to Detroit between June 1940 and June 1943, resulting in a total Negro population of about 210,000. An estimated 500,000 southern whites were living in Detroit and adjacent areas.[15] The non-white population

---

[9]This aspect is understated in *Die Judonpogrome*, particularly the relations of workers and petty traders. Davitt emphasises this aspect as important. The amount of competition varied, it would seem, in the various pogrom centers. I do not intend to overemphasize this economic factor, as the matter of religious difference was of equal, if not of greater, importance. The propaganda attack was especially based on religious differences.

[10]Josef Bloch, *Israel und Die Volker nach judischer Lehre* (Berlin: Benjamin Flairs, 1922), pp. 611-634.

[11]*Die Judenpogrome*, I, 231, and footnote, p. 232.

[12]Karl Stahlin, *Geschichte Russlands* (Konigsberg: Ost-Europa Verlag, 1939), IV, pt. 2, p. 655. The unsettled conditions in Russia, indicating a lack of consensus, struggle at new definitions of the situation, ibid., pp. 599-686. *Die Judenpogrome*, I, 267-292, discusses the organization of pogroms as a part of the function of the Russian bureaucracy as a means of intimidating revolutionary activities.

[13]*Die Judenpogrome*, I, 189, 190-191.

[14]*Ibid.*, pp. 14-15.

[15]Lee Brown, *Why Race Riot*, Public Affairs Pamphlet, No. 37 (1944), pp. 506; Cf. Bureau of Census, Series CA-3 (June 1944), pp. 7-8.

was 11 percent of the city's population in 1940 and 13 percent in 1944. The influx of Negroes and southern whites into Detroit is similar to the migration of the Jews into the Pale, except that the American migration was largely unplanned, except for the labor recruiting programs of corporations.

Just as Jews were concentrated in their ghetto in Kishinev, the Negroes were jammed into their thirty-block ghetto of Paradise Valley. This area, congested for years, had to bear the brunt of the wartime influx, an increase in population of around 33 percent. That the Negro was not content with this type of living was expressed in his effort to secure federal housing, and this attempt culminated in the Sojourner Truth Project. Bad housing, however, was not merely a Negro problem. Competition for services in housing, transportation, recreation, education, the problem of the cost of living, were common to all. All these factors, compounded with the tensions and anxieties of the war, may have interacted to lower the threshold of control and excitability. The struggle for the allocation of goods and services may have intensified the unstable relation of domination and unwilling submission between whites and Negroes.

The Negro coming to the North discovered shackles slightly less onerous than those he was trying to escape.[16] He found himself living among groups emphasizing emotionality and hate. The apocalyptic religion of the South found expression in numerous small groups. Brown estimated about 2,500 active southern-born evangelists.[17] In addition to the small fry evangelists there were the blood, sweat, and fear virtuosos such as the Rev. Gerald L. K. Smith, the Rev. J. Frank Norris, the pistol-packing parson, and others. Of the many non-religious groups indulging in violence, threats, and expressions of hate, the

most notorious was the Black Legion. When this group was broken up under FBI investigation, it diversified into many other groups, such as the Black Guards, Bullet Club, and Modern Patriots.[18]

Relations between Negroes and city officials, especially police officers, were unfavorable. There was a negative relation with those Negro leaders who endeavored to improve the lot of their group, and an essentially corrupt and parasitic relation with those Negroes involved in the policy and numbers racket. Negro arrests and treatment by police also developed mutual attitudes of suspicion and fear. Discussing the 1943 riot, Commissioner of Police Witherspoon frequently referred to this hostile relation between his department and the Negro, the perpetuation of which he blamed on the Negro.[19]

Lynchings are almost past history in this country, but riots are not, and they may in the future substitute for lynchings. The struggle with regard to superordination and subordination is thus carried from the country into the urban centers where it continues on a group rather than on an individual basis. The first series of major riots involving the Negro occurred during the period of World War I, with riots in Chicago (1919), East St. Louis (1917), and Washington, D. C. (1919). Detroit had a minor riot over Negroes in the Sweet case of 1926. Harlem broke loose in 1935 and in 1943. It was during the second World War that relations between whites and non-whites became much worse. The Negro Handbook[20] lists seven military riots, several civilian riots, and three industrial hate strikes or sit-downs in 1942; in 1943, five military riots, nine civilian riots,

---

[16]Arna Bontemps and Jack Convoy, They Sack a City (Garden City, N. Y.: Doubleday, Doran and Co., 1945), especially pp. 147-162 and 213-239.

[17]Op. cit., p. 8.

[18]Arna Bontemps and Jack Convoy, op. cit., p. 234, cf. John Carlson, Under Cover (New York: E. P. Dutton & Co., 1943); The Plotters (New York: E. P. Dutton & Co., 1946).

[19]Alfred Lee and Norman Humphrey, Race Riot (New York: Dryden Press, Inc., 1943), p. 53.

[20]Negro Handbook (1944), edited by Florence Musray (New Rochelle: Progressive Press), for articles on military and civilian riots.

five industrial hate strikes and/or riots. Mass violence against the Negro and others was nothing new to this country.

III

EVENTS LEADING TO THE RIOT

In Kishinev. The vice-governor of Bessarabia conducted an informal and active persecution of Jews on his own account for several years prior to the 1903 pogrom. He and his sub-officials traveled through Bessarabia and under any pretext or excuse or interpretation of laws and administrative decrees, they would extort money from the Jews, close their business or synagogue, or drive them away. Vice-governor Ostrogoff thus gave an apparent official sanction to Jewish persecution, and his attitude and actions encouraged the lower ranks of the bureaucracy to indulge in petty persecutions of their own.

The accusation of ritual-murder was made once in 1902 and twice in 1903. The local paper had to print a retraction of its charges but the retraction implied that Jews were securing special privilege and protection in their attacks on Christians. Fearing outbreaks, the rabbi of Kishinev asked the leading Greek bishop to issue an episcopal assurance that Jews did not practice ritual-murder and that Jews were not responsible for the local deaths. The bishop refused, implying that there were some Semitic sects that did practice such a ritual.

Six years before the riot the local paper was revived as a most violent anti-Semitic paper. As censor, the vice-governor Ostrogoff, a regular contributor under a pseudonym, could have curtailed the paper's violence on grounds of public safety and welfare. For five years the Bessarabetz fulminated against the Jews as swindlers, liars, parasites, and exploiters of the Christian population, ritual-murderers, etc. and continuously called upon the Christian population to rise and strike down the Jews. Since it was the only paper in Kishinev, counterpropaganda by the Jews was almost im-

possible. Articles in the paper were directed to the police, soldiers, workingmen, seminarists, and to the minor employees of the post office, telegraph, and other public departments. Articles were headed: "Death to the Jews," "Crusade against the Hated Race," "Down with the Disseminators of Socialism." The editors of the paper also organized a pure Christian Welfare society. Its members bought weapons and printed handbills and posters which were distributed in great quantities. One of these stated that on the basis of an ukase of the Tsar, Christians were permitted to hold a judgment of blood over Jews during the three Easter holidays.

In Detroit. Contributing to the development of the riot of 1943 was a series of minor riots. During 1941 there was an anti-Negro strike at the Ford River Rouge Plant, a student strike and fracas against Negroes at the Northwestern High School, and a series of fights between Polish youths and Negroes. The Sojourner Truth Project riot occurred in 1942. Federal troops guarded the entrance of Negroes into this housing project. This riot was not wholly spontaneous and unplanned. Local authorities, moreover, did not push an investigation, and no convictions resulted from detained "key" persons. Between March and the end of May 1943, there were hate strikes against Negroes in five different industrial plants. In the next month the major riot broke out.

DURATION OF THE RIOT

In Kishinev. From noon, Sunday, April 5 to Monday 5:00 p.m., April 6.

In Detroit. From Sunday, 10:30 p.m., June 20, to Monday, 11:00 p.m., June 21.

PERSONNEL

In Kishinev. Rioters included soldiers, policemen, civil servants, priests, peasants, laborers, students and seminarists, petit bourgeois, and a group of imported pug-uglies. Members of polite society, professional groups, and upper bourgeois participated primarily as spectators, but at times taking some of the loot, at times encouraging the rioters. With few exceptions, soldiers and policemen sided with the rioters. Peasants were especially imported from the countryside to participate. Rioters were predominantly from lower strata and their attacks were directed primarily against lower strata and moderately wealthy Jews. Rich Jews purchased immunity with bribes paid to both military and police officials. Actual leaders of the rioters were youths in the late teen ages and early twenties.

In Detroit. Both Negro and white were rioters. Both sexes were included, though the greatest proportion was male. According to the prosecutor's report, 35 percent detained in the riot were under 21 years and 63 percent under 31 years of age. Of detained Negroes, 23 percent were under 21 years and of whites 48 percent were under 21 years.[21] Youthful whites were also the leaders of mob groups, egged on in many cases by vociferous white females. Police were either helpless or negligent and on the whole took the side of the whites as demonstrated in the ratio of arrests, 12 Negro to 1 white.[22]

ORGANIZATION OF THE RIOT

In Kishinev. The pogrom was organized by a group of citizens of Kishinev with the tacit approval and support of governmental officials. Actual leaders of the riots were students and seminarists disguised as laborers and strangers. The riot began when a gang of 10 to 15 year old boys began to attack and molest Jews to test the reaction of the police. Since the police merely dispersed the gang without making any arrests, this action was interpreted favorably. Three hours later about two hundred men wearing red shirts (a working class symbol) split up into 24 sections composed of 10 to 15 men. Jewish quarters then were attacked

simultaneously in 24 parts of the city. The first effort was directed to the looting and destruction of Jewish homes and shops. In the evening a group of peasants was imported. Then all Jewish homes and stores were marked with white chalk, a process in which some policemen assisted. A system of communication between the various gangs was established with students and seminarists on bicycles. A new attack began at 3:00 a.m. on Monday. The gangs were composed of 10 to 20 persons, these numbers occasionally swelling to 80 to 100. This time not only looting, destruction, and plundering took place, but attacks on persons of all ages and sexes, murder, beating, and rape became common until the riot gradually played out, and martial law was declared.

In Detroit. The most accepted version is that the riot was precipitated by a fist fight between a Negro and a white man at Belle Isle. The major part of the rioting was concentrated in a two-mile area. In this riot, crowds of whites and crowds of Negroes fought each other, or an individual of either color would be set upon by a group of opposite color. Looting, plundering, and pillaging involved both white and Negro stores. These stores, however, were in the Negro area. Since Negroes were so concentrated, whites marched and rode in from other areas of the city to participate in the rioting. Groups gathered at street car lines, theatres, schools, and other strategic points. Actual leadership was taken over by teenage boys, who were egged on by older men. Pitched battles were fought between police and Negroes, one at the Frazer Hotel and the other at a three-story apartment building.

METHODS OF CONTROL

In Kishinev. Jews tried unsuccessfully to secure the intervention of officials and of the Greek bishop in curtailing rumors and the attacks of the Bessarabetz. Provincial officials grudgingly agreed to furnish some protection. City officials ignored the requests of Jewish delegations. Even though the criminal code

---

[21]Alfred Lee and Norman Humphrey, op. cit., p.23
[22]Negro Handbook, p. 44.

granted the governor discretion to use soldiers as a supplementary force to the police, an appeal to him on the morning of the riot was fruitless. His excuse was that he had received no order from Petersburg to use troops. The governor then forbade the sending of private telegrams and turned over the administration of the province to his assistant Ostrogoff. A telegram finally declaring martial law arrived too late.

In Detroit. As in Kishinev the police were either helpless, negligent, or actual participants in furthering the riot. Efforts of the police were predominantly directed against the Negro. Press and radio reports added to the general excitement rather than endeavoring to induce calm. Appeals by Mayor Jeffries, small neighborhood groups, Negro pastors, and leading labor officials came to nothing. Rioting stopped only when federal troops went into action. The securing of federal troops was unduly delayed because the governor did not want to declare martial law and state and city officials were hazy as to the procedure in securing troops. Police leadership appeared equally inept. The police commissioner refused to swear in Negro deputies and declared the riot under control when it was actually becoming worse.

RESULTS

In Kishinev. Killed—44; seriously wounded and injured—583; houses wrecked—700; shops and small stores looted and damaged—600; people requiring relief—10,000; families ruined in business and employment—2,000. The economic activities of the town were almost paralyzed for several days.

Ensuing trials did not result in any marked convictions. Judges and the state's attorney put all blame on the Jews. Official statements by the Russian government also placed all blame on the Jews.

In Detroit. Killed—34 (25 Negro, of which 17 were killed by the police); several hundred persons more or less

seriously wounded; two million dollars property damage.

All official government reports, whether issued by the city or state government, blamed the Negroes for causing the riot. They also exonerated the police and state militia and the city and state officials for the way in which they handled the riot.

IV

We conclude that if the conditions specified below are present, then the likelihood of rioting and violence is very high. If there is an alteration in any of these conditions, the likelihood is less; and it is even less if several of these phases are absent.

1. Historical context. A transitional period, such as industrialization, or a period involving unusual stresses and strains, such as a major war; within this period considerable horizontal and vertical mobility; a history of violence against the subordinate group.

2. The role of the subordinate group. An outstanding trait or characteristic, such as religion or color, which serves as a focal point for negative assessments, and minor constellations of value judgments and traditional negative beliefs; the subordinate group is regarded as an undesirable competitor for services, goods, control market, and the allocation of occupations; the group is officially or unofficially segregated; the group is engaged in a struggle for subsistence or is struggling to improve its status against historical traditions and controls which hold it in an inferior status.

3. The role of established authorities and law. Law assigns the minority group a second or third rate role as citizen, and the group attempts to change this legal status; violence or incipient violence (on the part of constituted authorities) is either officially approved or tacitly supported either on top levels or in some lower ranks where such sponsorship may be open and unabashed; there is a relation of hatred and suspicion between minority group and authorities, and a

pattern of petty exaction, bribery and corruption; authorities do not want to assume responsibility for control of a riot or there is administrative confusion as as to the control of a riot.

4. The role of associations. There are one or more associations whose major function is devoted to propaganda, defamation, and advocation of violence against the minority group.

5. Role of press and other means of communication. The press as official or covert policy indulges in race-minority baiting, or in general reports the group in an unfavorable way, i.e., reinforces prevailing negative assessments; the minority does not have or has limited access to the agencies of mass contact, particularly those reaching the members of the dominant group.

6. Personnel. Upper class, professionals, and more wealthy merchants contribute indirectly through the circulation of rumors, and some may participate more actively in the organization of a riot if they have an opportunity to gain by the elimination of competition; as a rule they will be morbid bystanders or by voice and gesture encourage rioters; students and marginal employed workers in the late teens and early twenties are the leaders and active participants, i.e., an older youth phenomenon; older rioters are primarily of the same social stratum as those against whom they are rioting, laborers against laborers, shopkeepers against shopkeepers, etc.

In a general way we know already the major phases given above from some studies made of riots in our country, but many of these studies deal with one incident. The significance of the cross-cultural comparison lies in a check on these findings, and this comparison corroborates them.

The race-minority riot as a type consists of the six enumerated points. The construct refers to a confluence of actions that end in violence. It is the working together of these various actions that logically culminates in a riot. These actions expressed in the many propositions about a riot pattern can be subsumed under three principles of social interaction. We understand and explain riots in the interrelation of these principles: (1) deliberately maintained opposite inclinations; (2) the augmentation of negative relations; (3) dissociative complementary inclinations.[23] These relations are buttressed by negative extrinsic valuations and the withholding of intrinsic valuations. When these apply to the racial or minority groups within a particular society, one possible and very likely consequence is a riot.[24]

---

[23]E. T. Hiller, op. cit., pp. 179-130.

[24]The use of the phrase "One possible consequence" refers to the principle of limited determinism. Cf. Alexander Goldenweiser, "The Concept of Causality in the Natural and Social Sciences," American Sociological Review (September 1938), pp. 624-636.

Deviation, Rejection, and Communication

Stanley Schachter

SOURCE: *Journal of Abnormal and Social Psychology*, Vol. 46, (1951), pp. 190-207.

The phenomenon of "group standards," uniformities of behavior and attitudes resulting from interaction among members of a group, is a widely documented finding in the social sciences. The gang studies of Shaw, Thrasher, Whyte, and Zorbaugh point up the existence of group codes and group standards.[1] Community studies such as the Yankee City Series or the Middletown books are in large part concerned with social membership and interaction.[2]

In psychological circles interest in group standards was probably first stimulated by the experiments of Sherif, which demonstrated the convergence of judgments as a function of group interaction.[3] Sherif's approach has been chiefly that of restricting experimental work to small, carefully designed laboratory studies of perceptual phenomena. The principles derived have then been extended to more complex social phenomena. Others have studied these more complex social phenomena directly; several factory studies have demonstrated the existence of group standards about production level among industrial workers;[4] Newcomb has found in a college community similarities of political attitudes which can plausibly be interpreted as group standards;[5] Merei has demonstrated that group standards arise in children's play groups and serve to increase the "strength" of the group.[6]

The means by which the group imposes and maintains conformity have been an area of speculation. It has been suggested that non-conformity results in rejection from the group. Thrasher says: "Opinion in the gang manifests its pressure in the variety of methods through which group control is exerted, such as applause, preference, and hero-worshipping as well as ridicule, scorn, and ostracism ... the member who has broken the code may be subjected to a beating or in extreme cases may be marked for death."[7] Sherif and Cantril state: "Just as good members of any organized group uphold the values or norms of the group, . . . so the good members of gangs become conscious of their own norms and react violently against deviants and nonconformists."[8]

The present study is concerned with the consequences of deviation from a group standard. Its immediate background is a study by Festinger,

[1]C. R. Shaw (ed.), Brothers in Crime. Chicago: Univ. of Chicago Press, 1938; C. R. Shaw, The Jack Roller. Chicago: Univ. of Chicago Press, 1939; F. M. Thrasher, The Gang. Chicago: Univ. of Chicago Press, 1927; W. F. Whyte, Street Corner Society. Chicago: Univ. of Chicago Press, 1943; H. W. Zorbaugh, The Gold Coast and the Slum. Chicago: Univ. of Chicago Press, 1929.

[2]W. L. Warner, and P. S. Lunt, The Social Life of a Modern Community. New Haven: Yale Univ. Press, 1941; R. S. Lynd, and H. M. Lynd, Middletown, A Study in Contemporary American Culture. New York: Harcourt, Brace, 1929; R. S. Lynd, and H. M. Lynd, Middletown in Transition. New York: Harcourt, Brace, 1937.

[3]M. Sherif, "A study of some social factors in Perception." Arch. Psychol., N. Y., 1935, No. 187; M. Sherif, The Psychology of Social Norms. New York: Harper, 1936.

[4]L. Coch, and J. R. P. French, Jr., "Overcoming resistance to change." Hum. Relat., 1948, 1,512-532; A. Zander, and J. Chabot, Unpublished Study.

[5]T. M. Newcomb, Personality and Social Change. New York: Dryden Press, 1943.

[6]F. Merei, "Group leadership in institutionalization." Hum. Relat., 1941, 2, 23-39.

[7]F. M. Thrasher, op. cit., p. 291.

[8]M. Sherif and H. Cantril, The Psychology of Ego-Involvements, p. 321. New York: Wiley, 1947.

Schachter, and Back of the relationships between group structure and group standards.[9] Findings pertinent to the present study will be briefly reviewed.

1. Within each social group in a housing community there was homogeneity of attitude toward a community-wide problem. Among these groups, however, there was marked heterogeneity of attitude.

2. There was a high positive correlation between cohesiveness of the social group (measured by per cent of in-group sociometric choices) and strength of the group standard (measured by per cent of conformers to the stand).

3. Within a social group, deviates from the group standard received far fewer sociometric choices than did conformers.

The theory developed to explain these findings is as follows: Within any social group, pressures operate toward uniformity of attitude. The origins of such pressures are at least twofold: social reality and group locomotion.

Social reality. On any issue for which there is no empirical referent, the reality of one's own opinion is established by the fact that other people hold similar opinions. Forces exist to establish uniformity and thus to create "reality" for the opinion.

Group locomotion. Uniformity may be necessary or desirable for the group to locomote toward its goal. Locomotion will be facilitated if all members agree on a particular path to the goal.

The strength of the pressures toward uniformity that a group can exercise on its members will vary with the cohesiveness of the group and the relevance of the issue to the group. "Cohesiveness" is defined as the total field of forces acting on members to remain in the group. Stemming from cohesiveness is the property called the "internal power of the group," which is defined as the magnitude of change the group can induce on its members. The degree of internal power will be equal to the magnitude of the force on the member to

remain in the group. If we assume that all groups are attempting to induce the same amount, we can derive that there will be fewer deviates from a group standard in highly cohesive groups than in less cohesive groups.

"Relevance" refers to the ordering, in terms of importance to the group, of the activities over which the internal power of the group extends. The conceptual dimension along which we can order particular activities as relevant or irrelevant to a particular group still remains unclear. There appear to be three possible bases for such ordering: the importance of the activity for group locomotion, the value which the group places upon the activity, and some hierarchy of needs common to group members in their roles as group members. Whatever the basis for ordering, we may anticipate that a group will exercise greater influence over relevant than over irrelevant activities.

It is assumed that there is a parallel between the process of induction and actual communication; that is, communication is the mechanism by which power is exerted. Therefore, one method by which deviation from a group standard may be maintained is cutting off the deviate from communication with the group. Lack of communication may result from little initial contact between the individual and the group or rejection from the group. In the latter case, if the magnitude of the change that the group attempts to induce is greater than the force on the individual to stay in the group, the deviate will want to leave the group, and/or the group will tend to push the deviate out of the group.

The present study is specifically concerned with rejection of a deviate by the group. It is probable that not all groups reject to the same degree and that rejection is a consequence of deviation on only certain kinds of issues. To delineate more carefully some of the conditions affecting rejection, this experiment examines the effect of degrees of cohesiveness of the group and relevance of the issue on the degree of rejection of a

---

[9]L. Festinger, S. Schachter, and K. Back, Social Pressures in Informal Groups: A Study of a Housing Community. New York: Harper, 1950.

deviate. The effects of these variables on communication and induction within the groups are also studied.

THE EXPERIMENT

The experiment was conducted as the first meeting of a club. Four types of clubs were set up, each representing a different degree and combination of cohesiveness and relevance. In each club paid participants' deviated from and conformed to an experimentally created group standard. Discussion in each club was systematically observed. At the end of each meeting members were nominated for committees, and sociometric questionnaires were filled out. These served as measures of rejection.

The four types of clubs set up were case-study, editorial, movie, and radio clubs. There was a total of 32 clubs, eight of each type. Each club had from five to seven members and three paid participants who were perceived as fellow club members. All of the subjects (Ss) in the clubs were male college students.

In a typical meeting, after preliminary introductions, each club member read a short version of the "Johnny Rocco" case, the life history of a juvenile delinquent, which ended as Johnny was awaiting sentence for a minor crime.[10] The case was presented as that of a real person. The leader of the club, in all instances the experimenter (E), asked the members to discuss and decide the question, "What should be done with this kid?" The discussion was guided by a seven-point scale made up of alternative suggestions ordered along a love-punishment dimension. Point 1 presented the "all-love" viewpoint, point 7 the "all-punishment" viewpoint. Between these extremes were graded variations of the two points up view.[11] This scale was used to point up the

differences of opinion within the group. It was introduced to the club members as a convenient device for learning everyone's position and for channelizing discussion.

After reading the case, each club member announced the position on the scale that he had chosen. Then the three paid participants in each club announced their positions. One paid participant, the "deviate," chose a position of extreme deviation and maintained it throughout the discussion; the second, the "mode," chose and maintained the modal position of group opinion; and the third, the "slider," chose the position of extreme deviation but allowed himself to be gradually influenced, so that at the end of the discussion he was at the modal position.

The case was written sympathetically to ensure that the deviate paid participant would be a deviate. In all clubs almost all members chose positions on the scale emphasizing love and kindness (positions 2-4), and the deviate chose the position of extreme discipline (position 7).

The discussion, limited to 45 minutes, was largely a matter of thrashing out differences of opinion among club members. After 20 minutes the leader took a census to ensure that everyone was fully aware of everyone else's position. He took no part in the discussion except to answer the few questions directed to him. At the end of the discussion a final census was taken. Then the leader turned the discussion to the future of the club. At this time the committee nomination blanks and sociometric questionnaires were filled out.

After each meeting the Ss were told that this had been an experiment and not a club, and the purposes of the experiment and the various devices used were fully explained. The Ss were asked not to disclose the true nature of these "clubs." There was no indication that anyone gave away the experiment.

---

[10] J. Evans, "Johnny Rocco." J. Abnorm. Soc. Psychol., 1948, 43, 357-383.

[11] For example, 3 point reads: "He should be sent into an environment where providing Johnny with warmth and affection will be emphasized slightly more than punishing him, but discipline and punish-

ment will be frequent if his behavior warrants it." For purposes of brevity the revised case study and the complete love-punishment scale are omitted from this paper. Interested readers may obtain copies by writing to the author.

How the Variables, Cohesiveness and Relevance Were Produced. "Cohesiveness" has been defined as the total field of forces acting on members to remain in the group. The greater the valence of the group for its members, the greater the cohesiveness. Valence of the group derives from at least two sources, the attractiveness of the activities and group mediates and the attractiveness of the members of the group. In this experiment two degrees of cohesiveness were produced by manipulating the attractiveness of the activities mediated by the groups.

Subjects were recruited for club membership from economics classes at the University of Michigan. The case-study and editorial clubs were described to half of these classes. The case-study clubs were purportedly being set up at the request of a group of lawyers, judges, and social workers to advise on the treatment and disposition of delinquents, sex offenders, etc. The editorial clubs were supposedly being organized at the request of a new national magazine to advise on feature articles, format, policy, etc. Interested students filled out a blank indicating which club they were interested in joining, and checked two rating scales indicating the extent of their interest in each club. These were four-point sclaes —"not interested at all," "only mildly interested," "moderately interested," and "extremely interested."

The movie and radio clubs were described to the other half of these classes. The movie clubs were purportedly being set up for a local theatre. The club members were to see films and decide which ones the theatre could successfully program. Radio clubs were supposedly being formed to serve a similar market research function for a local radio station. Students indicated their interest in these two clubs in the manner described above.

The case-study and movie clubs were high cohesive groups, made up of students who had checked between "moderately" and "extremely interested" on the scales for these clubs. The editorial and radio clubs were low cohesive groups, made up of students who indicated high

interest in joining the case-study or movie clubs and little or no interest in joining the editorial or radio clubs.[12] Students becoming members of clubs they were interested in joining made up the high cohesive groups. Those becoming members of clubs they were not interested in joining made up the low cohesive groups. In short, cohesiveness if defined here in terms of the valence of the activity.[13]

"Relevance" has been defined as an ordering of group activities along a dimension of "importance" to the group. Two degrees of relevance were produced experimentally. In one case, Ss were concerned with an activity corresponding to the purpose of the club. In the other case, Ss were concerned with an activity which had nothing to do with the purpose of the club.

Case-study and editorial clubs discussed a case study and a feature article, respectively. Movie and radio clubs discussed issues foreign to the purpose of the clubs; each began with an appropriate subject but was diverted to a side issue. The movie clubs saw a 15-minute film, and the radio clubs listened to a 15-minute recording. Then the leader introduced the observer as someone who had written up the Johnny Rocco case and wanted the help of the group to discuss what should be done with him. The group was assured that this had nothing to do with the club and would never happen again. With some enthusiasm from the paid participants, the group always agreed to discuss the case.

To make constant the time of interaction among Ss, radio and movie clubs

---

[12] A subject did not know which of the two clubs he had come to until the meeting was under way.

[13] This may seem a rather restricted definition of cohesiveness. Back, however, has demonstrated that cohesiveness, no matter what its source, can be considered a unitary concept. Whether cohesiveness is based on friendship, the valence of the activity mediated by the group, or group prestige, the consequences of increasing cohesiveness are identical. K. W. Back, "The exertion of influence through social communication." Unpublished Doctor's dissertation, Massachusetts Institute of Technology, 1949.

Table 1
Mean Ratings on Sign-Up Sheets

Group	Case-Study	Editorial
Hi Co Rel	3.27	2.20
Lo Co Rel	3.33	1.71
	Movie	Radio
Hi Lo Irrel	3.53	2.24
Lo Co Irrel	3.34	1.59

were chosen as a setting for the irrelevant issue. The Ss were unable to interact while looking at a movie or listening to a recording. Therefore, their discussion time was the same as that of Ss discussing relevant issues.

To compare data obtained in the four types of clubs, it was necessary that the content be constant. This was done by using the "Johnny Rocco" case and the love-punishment scale in all the clubs. In case-study clubs, "Johnny Rocco" was the case for the day. In editorial clubs, "Johnny Rocco" was part of a feature article on juvenile delinquency. In movie and radio clubs, "Johnny Rocco" was the irrelevant issue. In all clubs the scale was the basis for discussing, "What should be done with the kid?"

In summary, there were four kinds of clubs, each reproducing a different combination of the experimental variables, as follows:

1. High cohesiveness-relevant issue (Hi Co Rel): Case-Study Club
2. Low cohesiveness-relevant issue (Lo Co Rel): Editorial Club
3. High cohesiveness-irrelevant issue (Hi Co Irrel): Movie Club
4. Low cohesiveness-irrelevant issue (Lo Co Irrel): Radio Club

In the procedure used there are two possible sources of selective error. (1) Possibly students interested in the case-study and editorial clubs were selectively different from those attracted to the movie and radio clubs. However, more than 80 per cent of the students addressed asked to join one of the clubs. More than 90 per cent of these expressed preferences for case-study or movie clubs. (2) Students assigned to case-study and movie clubs rated editorial and radio

clubs slightly more favorably than students assigned to editorial and radio clubs. Possibly students in case-study and movie clubs were more attracted to the idea of a club, any kind of club. This factor, however, probably had little effect on experimental results. In the degree of rejection of the deviate, no difference was found in high cohesive groups between students who rated the nonpreferred activity high and those who rated it low.

The Validity of the Manipulation of Cohesiveness. The manipulation of cohesiveness began with the canvassing for Ss and their assignment to clubs on the basis of preliminary interest ratings. This method of assignment is summarized in Table 1, where figures were obtained by assigning numerical values to the four points of the rating scale. "Not interested at all" has the value 1; "extremely interested" has the value 4; and the two intermediate points, the values 2 and 3. The figures are the mean ratings of each club made by all Ss assigned to a particular experimental condition. There is a marked difference between Ss in high and low cohesive groups in their ratings of the clubs to which they were assigned. In the low cohesive conditions, all but two Ss rated the clubs in which they were placed between "not interested at all" and "only mildly interested." In the high cohesive conditions, all but two Ss rated the clubs in which they were placed between "extremely interested" and "moderately interested."

How successful was this method in manipulating cohesiveness? At the end of each meeting, each S filled out a cohesiveness questionnaire designed to determine his intentions toward the club. There were three questions: (1) Do you want to remain a member of this group? (2) How often do you think this group should meet? (3) If enough members decide not to stay so that it seems this group might discontinue, would you like the chance to persuade others to stay?

Table 2 summarizes the data from this questionnaire and shows marked differences between high and low cohesive groups. In high cohesive groups 101 of the 102 S̲s̲ wanted to continue their memberships; in low cohesive groups only 62 of 96 S̲s̲ wanted to do so. There are differences, too, between S̲s̲ in the two conditions who wanted to remain in their clubs. Such S̲s̲ in low cohesive groups wanted to meet less often and were less willing to persuade others to stay in the club than were S̲s̲ in high cohesive groups. The manipulation was clearly successful in producing groups with different degrees of cohesiveness.

The Paid Participants. The three paid participants in each group were perceived as fellow club members. Like the S̲s̲, they were male undergraduates. In each meeting, in each condition, they played three roles, deviate, mode, and slider. The deviate adopted the position of extreme discipline and maintained it throughout the discussion. The mode championed that position which the modal number of members supported. If during the meeting the modal position shifted, he shifted. The slider began as an extreme deviate (position 7) and during the meeting moved step by step to the modal position.

The mode and slider roles were controls. The deviate and the mode provided evidence of the effect of deviation as contrasted to conformity. Comparison of the slider and the deviate tested whether rejection was a result of having at one time, but no longer, championed a deviate position, or of simply maintaining deviancy against all attempted influence.

The three roles were systematically rotated among four paid participants so that each played each role twice in each experimental condition. To assure constancy from meeting to meeting, rules of behavior guiding the paid participants in any role were carefully defined. (1) Each paid participant had to speak once every five minutes. If during any five-minute interval no one addressed a remark to him, he initiated a communication. (2) Where possible, all communications made by the paid participants, whether initiated or in response to someone, were rephrasings of the position he was maintaining at the time. (3) When it was impossible simply to rephrase the position, the paid participants at the deviate position were permitted two standard arguments: (a) Despite the fact that Johnny was shown love and affection, he went back to stealing. (b) It could not be said that discipline would not work, since it had not consistently been applied to Johnny.

Measures of Rejection. After the discussion the leader introduced the subject of the club's future and proposed a plan by which a functioning group could be organized. To expedite such organization, each member filled out three mimeographed sheets: a committee nomination blank, a sociometric test, and the cohesiveness questionnaire described earlier.

Committee nominations. Three committees were set up, differing with respect to interest of the work, importance of the assigned functions, and delegated responsibility for club activities. They were called the Executive, Steering, and Correspondence Committees. In each club, the job of each committee was defined in much the same way, but with slightly different content. The Executive Committee was to decide what the group should discuss, to act as liaison agent between the club and its sponsoring agency, and to determine club policy. The Steering Committee was to prepare and present discussion materials and determine discussion procedure. The Correspondence Committee was to perform secretarial functions.[14]

The S̲s̲ were instructed to nominate persons whom they considered most capable of handling the work of each committee. They were not to nominate themselves or the same person for more than one committee. The number of members on each committee was manipulated so that no matter what number were present

---

[14] To check on whether or not jobs on these committees actually did vary in attractiveness, in several of the groups the members were asked to write their own names next to these committees in which they were most interested. Most requested the Executive Committee, a few the Steering, and none the Correspondence Committee.

Table 2
Breakdown of Answers to the Cohesiveness Questionnaire

Group	N	QUESTION 1 Want to remain member?		QUESTION 2 Frequency of meetings?		QUESTION 3 Want to induce others to stay in club?	
		Yes	No	Once or twice a week	Once every 2, 3, or 4 weeks	Yes	No
Hi Co Rel	53	98%	2%	61%	39%	73%	19%
Lo Co Rel	50	68	32	54	46	51	34
Hi Co Irrel	49	100	0	73	27	61	35
Lo Co Irrel	46	61	39	36	64	21	71

in any particular group, everyone had to nominate everyone else present for some committee. When ten people were present, each member nominated three people for each committee; when nine people were present, only two people were nominated for the Correspondence Committee; and, when eight people were present, two people were nominated for the Steering Committee and two for the Correspondence Committee. The importance or unimportance of the committees to which the paid participants were nominated serves as an index of acceptance or rejection.

The sociometric test. Subjects were informed that it might become necessary to reduce the number of club members or to break up the group and portion out its members to one of the other clubs, and that therefore it would be helpful to know which people would like to remain together. They were asked to rank everyone present in order of preference for remaining in the same group with themselves. In contrast to committee nomination instructions, the emphasis here was on congeniality. These data provide a sociometric index of rejection.

The Observation Schedule. An observer, introduced as a friend interested in what the club was doing and who could be imposed upon to take notes, recorded the following aspects of the group process: (1) who spoke to whom; (2) the length, in time, of the communication; (3) whether the speaker attacked or supported the position of the person to whom he spoke; (4) whether a communication, even if not addressed to a person at a specific position, implied approval or

disapproval of this position; and (5) whether the speaker talked about experiences from his own or his friends' personal histories.

Rationale. The setup described, while constituting a reasonably well controlled experimental situation, represented for the Ss a real-life situation. What was for E a method of manipulating a variable was for S a club he was interested in joining. The measuring instruments were conventional methods of electing officers; and so on. In short, the experiment was fitted within a social framework completely consistent with the idea and operation of a club with no sacrifice of experimental control. The rationale for this procedure was the assumption that it would be possible to reproduce the variables and phenomena under study with greater intensity in a purportedly "real-life situation" than in a laboratory setup that was identified as such. It is possible to produce complex social phenomena in laboratory experiments. Which procedure is more "effective" in the study of particular social phenomena can only be determined by additional investigation.

The Theoretical Relationships Among Cohesiveness, Relevance, and Rejection. The theory presented in the introduction can now be expanded to make specific derivations as to the degree of rejection anticipated in each experimental condition. The theory states that there are pressures toward uniformity of behavior and attitude among members of most social groups. If differences of opinion exist within a group, forces will arise on the members to restore uniformity. A number of corrective tendencies will develop; for example, pressures develop to change the opinions of members of the group holding opinions different from one's own; pressures arise to change one's own opinion to coincide more closely with those of other group members; a tendency develops to decrease one's dependence on deviant members as appropriate reference points in establishing the reality of one's own opinion. In any group where differences of opinion exist probably all of these tendencies exist and are, we shall say, simultaneously a function of the total pressures toward uniformity. In the present experimental situation where almost all Ss were of similar opinions and there was only one deviate, it seems reasonable to suggest that the pre-dominant tendencies acting on group members were the pressures to change the opinion of the deviate, and the tendency to decrease dependence on the deviate as a point of reference for establishing social reality.

A. Pressures to change (Pch) refer to the magnitude of pressures acting on group members to change a deviant opinion to conform more closely with their own. We make these assumptions about the relationship of Pch with the variables cohesiveness, relevance, and state of opinion:

1. With increasing difference of opinion the magnitude of Pch should increase.

If uniformity exists, Pch should have zero magnitude. As group opinion departs more and more from uniformity, Pch should correspondingly increase.

2. With increasing cohesiveness, the magnitude of Pch should increase. At any point along a scale of difference of opinion, Pch should be greater for high than for low cohesive groups.

Pressures to uniformity arise in part from a need for social reality within an appropriate reference group. A cohesive group, in which membership is valued, can be considered a more important reference group than a low cohesive group in which membership is not particularly cherished. Therefore, we can anticipate that pressures to uniformity will be greater in high than in low cohesive groups.

3. With increasing relevance of issue, the magnitude of Pch should increase.

Any set of activities can be ordered along some dimension of "importance" (relevance) for a particular reference group. It is plausible to assume that for activities which are of importance to the group, greater pressures to change will exist than for activities which are unimportant.

B. Dependence (Dep) refers to the extent to which members of a group rely on one another as reference points in establishing social reality. We make these assumptions about the relationships of dependence with the variables cohesiveness, relevance, and state of opinion:

1. With increasing difference of opinion the magnitude of Dep will decrease.

If opinions are identical, dependence will be high. When persons have different opinions, it is unlikely that they will depend on one another to establish the reality of their opinions.

2. With increasing cohesiveness, the magnitude of Dep will increase.

Members of a high cohesive group (a valued and important reference group) will be more dependent on one another than will members of a low cohesive group.

3. With relatively small differences of opinion the magnitude of Dep will increase with increasing relevance of issue. As difference of opinion increases, Dep for relevant issues decreases more rapidly than Dep for irrelevant issues, and a point of zero Dep will be reached with less difference of opinion for relevant than for irrelevant issues.

The more "important" an issue to a particular group, the greater the extent to which group members depend on one another for social reality. On relevant issues, it will be more important that the reference group which establishes social reality have similar opinions than on less relevant issues. Therefore, dependence should decrease more rapidly with increasing perceived difference and reach the point of zero dependence earlier for highly relevant issues than for irrelevant issues.

These relationships are presented graphically in Figure 1. The rising Pch curves and falling Dep curves with increasing difference of opinion express assumptions A1 and B1 above. The greater magnitude of high cohesive than of low cohesive curves (relevance held constant), and of relevant than of irrelevant Pch curves (cohesiveness held constant), expresses assumptions A2, A3,

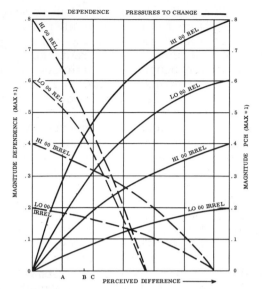

Figure 1. Theoretical curves of the relationships between dependence, pressures to change, and cohesiveness, relevance, and perceived differences of opinion.

and B2. At low levels of perceived difference with cohesiveness held constant, the magnitude of relevant Dep curves is greater than that of irrelevant Dep curves. Curves for relevant conditions drop at a faster rate and reach the point of zero dependence with far less perceived difference than do curves for irrelevant conditions. This is an expression of assumption B3.

For each condition, the maxima of the Pch and Dep curves are of the same magnitude. We assume that the maxima of both factors are similarly a function of total pressures to uniformity. The scale of magnitude along the ordinate of this graph has maximum = 1. The values assigned are, of course, arbitrary and purely illustrative.

From these curves we can make predictions concerning the interrelationships among cohesiveness, relevance, and degree of rejection.

We shall coordinate rejection to the amount of pressures to change that do not find public expression. The amount of pressures that do find public expression we call communication. Dependence defines the proportion of pressures to change that can be expressed. Multiplying

these two factors, therefore, gives the amount of pressures that will actually be exerted.[15]

$$\text{Comm} = \text{Pch} \times \text{Dep}$$

Rejection, then, which is defined as the amount of pressures not exerted, is computed by multiplying Pch by the quantity (1 — Dep).

$$\text{Rej} = \text{Pch} \times (1 - \text{Dep})$$

The number 1 represents maximum dependence, the point at which all Pch will be communicated. The greater the pressures and the smaller the dependence, the greater the rejection. In effect, this formula suggests that rejection requires relatively little dependence on a person and, at the same time, relatively high pressures to change him. If pressures to change are high but dependence is high, rejection will be relatively slight. If dependence is low but there are no pressures to change, rejection will not occur.

Applying this formula to the postulated curves in Figure 1, we find these relationships. At point A in this figure:

			$\text{Pch} \times (1 - \text{Dep}) = \text{Rej}$
Hi	Co	Rel	$.300 \times (1 - .650) = .105$
Lo	Co	Rel	$.185 \times (1 - .513) = .090$
Hi	Co	Irrel	$.110 \times (1 - .375) = .069$
Lo	Co	Irrel	$.050 \times (1 - .185) = .041$

At point B where the perceived difference is somewhat greater:

			$\text{Pch} \times (1 - \text{Dep}) = \text{Rej}$
Hi	Co	Rel	$.437 \times (1 - .487) = .224$
Lo	Co	Rel	$.295 \times (1 - .409) = .174$
Hi	Co	Irrel	$.175 \times (1 - .341) = .115$
Lo	Co	Irrel	$.075 \times (1 - .175) = .062$

These trends become clear: (1) As perceived difference increases, the degree of rejection in each of these conditions will increase. (2) At any point beyond zero, along the axis of perceived difference:

Rej in Hi Co Rel > Rej in Lo Co Rel
Rej in Hi Co Irrel > Rej in Lo Co Irrel
Rej in Hi Co Rel > Rej in Hi Co Irrel
Rej in Lo Co Rel > Rej in Lo Co Irrel[16]

---

[15] This theory of communication will be developed and expanded in the following section.

[16] It is impossible to make an exact prediction about relative rejection between the Lo Co Rel and Hi Co Irrel conditions. Though the curves imply

Thus, the set of assumptions determining the shapes of these curves leads to these experimental predictions: (a) Persons in the mode and slider roles (who at the end of a meeting are close to zero perceived difference) will be rejected less (if at all) than will persons in the deviate role. (b) From experimental condition to condition the degree of rejection of persons in the deviate role will vary in the order noted in trend 2 above. With cohesiveness constant, rejection will be greater in relevant than in irrelevant groups. With relevance constant, rejection will be greater in high than in low cohesive groups.

RESULTS

The post-meeting nominations for committees and the sociometric rankings of all club members provide two indices of rejection, i.e., nominations to the less important committees and relatively low sociometric rankings.

Sociometric Rankings. At the end of each meeting the members of each club ranked everyone in the order of his desirability as a fellow club member. The instructions emphasized congeniality and compatibility as the basis for ranking. The lower the ranking, the greater the rejection.

Table 3 presents mean sociometric rankings of each paid participant in each condition. Each figure in the table is the mean of the mean sociometric rankings in each group. The N for each figure is 8, the number of groups in each condition. Since the groups varied in size from eight to ten members, all rankings were corrected to equivalent scores by adopting the nine possible rankings in a group of ten people as a basic scale and correcting rankings in smaller groups to equivalent scores. The mean rank in every group is 5.

These relationships emerge from Table 3: (1) In any condition, mean rankings of either mode or slider are considerably below mean rankings of the deviate. All mode-deviate differences are significant by a t-test at the 7 per cent level of confidence or better. Clearly, a penalty of relative rejection is imposed on a deviate. (2) There are no significant differences in rankings of either the mode or slider when comparisons are made between conditions.[17] The variables of cohesiveness and relevance have no effects on group evaluation of individuals who are at, or who adopt, the group norms. (3) The deviate is rejected more strongly in high than in low cohesive groups. Between rankings in high and low cohesive groups, the t is significant at the 12 per cent level for the difference between Hi Co Rel and Lo Co Rel, and at the 1 per cent level for the difference between Hi Co Irrel and Lo Co Irrel.[18] As predicted, greater cohesiveness produces greater rejection.

There is, however, no immediate evidence that the variable, relevance, affects the degree of rejection. The mean sociometric rankings of the deviate in the relevant and irrelevant condition, with cohesiveness constant, are about the same. This may be attributed in part to the fact that the measurement is a relative one, indicating only an individual's relative preference for one person over another, with no indication of the absolute intensity of like or dislike. There is, however, some indication of the relative intensities of the ratings in each condition. Occasionally a subject refused to

Table 3
Mean Sociometric Rankings of the Paid
Participants

Group	Deviate	Mode	Slider
Hi Co Rel	6.44	4.65	5.02
Lo Co Rel	5.83	4.70	4.56
Hi Co Irrel	6.51	4.68	4.44
Lo Co Irrel	5.67	3.83	5.03

Rej in Lo Co Rel > Rej in Hi Co Irrel, this was done purely for illustrative simplicity. We have, of course, no way of determining the relative contributions of cohesiveness and relevance in a comparison of Lo Co Rel and Hi Co Irrel conditions.

[17]The largest difference, that between the Hi Co Irrel and Lo Co Irrel conditions for the mode, is significant by t-test at only the 28 per cent level.
[18]In all tests of significance mentioned in this section, the group rather than the individual was considered the unit.

fill in the sociometric sheet, or simply put in numbers in sequence, explaining that he was unable to discriminate among the people present. Random ranking implies that there was no genuine basis on which to express preference. If, therefore, any one experimental condition has a significantly greater number of random rankings than do the others, it may be inferred that, in general, all rankings in this condition were made with less basis for expressing preference and imply less intensity of like or dislike than in a condition where random responses are rare. More than twice as many random rankings were made in irrelevant conditions as in relevant. Of all subjects, 16 per cent ranked randomly in the irrelevant conditions and 6.8 per cent in the relevant conditions. This difference is significant by chi-square with 1 <u>d.f.</u> at the 2 per cent level. There were no significant differences between <u>Hi Co Rel</u> and <u>Lo Co Rel</u> or between <u>Hi Co Irrel</u> and <u>Lo Co Irrel</u>. Though mean rankings are about the same for relevant and irrelevant conditions, random rankings of the deviate seem to imply less strong feelings of rejection in the irrelevant groups.

These sociometric data are in the directions predicted. (1) Paid participants in the mode and slider roles were not rejected; as deviates they were definitely rejected. (2) There is greater rejection of the deviate in high than in low cohesive groups. (3) Though sociometric rankings of the deviate are about the same for relevant and irrelevant conditions, random sociometric rankings indicate that the intensity of rejection in irrelevant conditions was less than in relevant conditions.

<u>Assignment to Committees</u>. With instructions emphasizing competence for the job, the members of each club nominated people for membership on the Executive, Steering, and Correspondence Committees. Rejection is coordinated to assignment to the least desirable committee. The Executive was the most attractive committee and the Correspondence the least attractive.

Tables 4, 5, and 6 present the data on

Table 4
Percentage of Subjects Above Chance Assigning
"Mode" to Committees

Group	Executive	Steering	Correspondence
Hi Co Rel	−4.56	+6.76	−2.22
Lo Co Rel	−9.83	+20.15	−10.44
Hi Co Irrel	−0.08	+6.85	−6.93
Lo Co Irrel	+3.70	+3.70	−8.07

Table 5
Percentage of Subjects Above Chance Assigning
"Slider" to Committees

Group	Executive	Steering	Correspondence
Hi Co Rel	+1.76	−5.93	+4.16
Lo Co Rel	+7.32	−7.86	+0.50
Hi Co Irrel	−4.97	+4.38	+0.39
Lo Co Irrel	+2.69	−3.52	+0.16

Table 6
Percentage of Subjects Above Chance Assigning
"Deviate" to Committees

Group	Executive	Steering	Correspondence
Hi Co Rel	−14.00	−8.34	+22.31
Lo Co Rel	−17.58	−7.81	+25.26
Hi Co Irrel	−16.41	+4.83	+11.44
Lo Co Irrel	+10.16	−9.40	−1.30

the assignment of paid participants in the mode, slider, and deviate roles to the three committees. All figures in each table represent the percentage, above or below chance expectancy, of all <u>Ss</u> in each condition who assigned the various roles to the different committees. In Table 4, the mode was nominated for the Executive Committee by 4.56 per cent less than we would expect if nominations in the <u>Hi Co Rel</u> condition had been made on some randomly determined basis. Varying group sizes, affecting the probability of any one person being assigned to a particular committee, necessitated computation of chance expectancies.

The standard errors of all chance percentages. are close to 6.20.[19] Any

---

[19] This score was computed using $\sqrt{\frac{p\,q}{n}}$, the customary formula for computing the standard error of a percentage. Since the number of cases varied slightly from condition to condition, and <u>P</u> varied slightly with the number of people in each group, the standard error 6.20 is a convenient approximation. The obtained standard errors for each committee in each condition are all quite close to this figure.

score greater than 10.23 is significant at the 10 per cent level; greater than 12.09 is significant at the 5 per cent level; and greater than 15.93 is significant at the 1 per cent level. If the 5 per cent level is accepted, Table 5 reveals no significant fluctuations from chance in assigning the slider to any one particular committee. Similarly, for the mode, in Table 4, we find only one score that departs significantly from chance, assignment of the mode to the Steering Committee in the Lo Co Rel condition. With the large number of scores obtained, this may be interpreted as a chance fluctuation. There is no indication of systematic rejection for the mode or slider roles.

Table 6 for the deviate presents a completely different picture. In all conditions, except Lo Co Irrel, the deviate is over-nominated for the Correspondence Committee and under-nominated for the Executive Committee. Deviation results in assignment to a relatively peripheral position in the role structure of the group. Not only is the deviate considered relatively undesirable as a fellow club member, but also least capable of handling the important jobs in the club.

The degree of rejection, however, is affected by the experimental variables. Rejection is greater in both relevant conditions than in the irrelevant conditions. A t-test with 30 d.f. yields significance at the 2 per cent level of confidence for this difference. Differences between the degree of rejection in high cohesive groups and low cohesive groups, however, are less clear-cut. Although there is a difference between high and low cohesive irrelevant conditions significant by t-test at the 10 per cent level, there is no difference between the two relevant conditions. This is clearly inconsistent with theoretical expectations. Possibly the committee assignment measure should also be considered a relative measure that gives no indication of intensity of feeling. It is plausible that, though there is no difference between high and low cohesive relevant groups in the percentage of people assigning the deviate to the Correspondence

Committee, the intensity of rejection is greater in high than in low cohesive groups. In contrast to the sociometric ranking, however, no S had difficulty in making these judgments, and there is no evidence of random assignment to committees. This may possibly be attributed to the different natures of the measures. A judgment of fitness for a particular job is a fairly everyday matter. Decisions about which people should be in or out of a group appear to be a more unusual sort of judgment to make.

Except for this single inconsistency, the data support the predictions. Neither the mode nor the slider was rejected. In all conditions except Lo Co Irrel, where we anticipated very little rejection, the deviate was over-nominated for the Correspondence Committee. Rejection of the deviate was greater in the relevant than in the irrelevant conditions, and greater in the Hi Co Irrel than in the Lo Co Irrel condition.

THE PROCESS OF COMMUNICATION

The previous section has treated the relationships between experimental manipulations and post-meeting measurements. This section relates the processes of induction and communication, as they occurred during the meetings, to the experimental variables, cohesiveness and relevance, and to the post-meeting measurements.

We shall consider communication, the process of one person talking to another, as the mechanism of induction, i.e., the means by which influence is exerted. There are, of course, other reasons why people communicate, but within the confines of this experiment and theory, we shall largely limit ourselves to communication as influence.

From the theoretical elaboration of "pressures to uniformity," specific derivations may be made about certain aspects of the patterns of communication that occurred in these meetings. Let us first relate the constructs, Pch and Dep, to the occurrence of communication.

1. Pressures to change others mean

pressures to influence others, which we will consider identical with pressures to communicate. Our earlier assumptions may, therefore, be extended to communication pressures. The pressures to communicate to a deviate will rise with increasing perceived difference, increasing cohesiveness, and increasing relevance.

2. Dependence refers to the extent to which a person relies on another person or group of persons to establish social reality. It defines the proportion of pressure to change that can actually find public expression. Actual communication, then, is a function of both Dep and Pch, with dependence modifying the proportion of pressures to change that will be expressed publicly. Actual communication is formulated as Comm = Pch × Dep.

In Figure 2, the heavily dotted lines, constructed by making the proper multiplications at each point, represent the magnitude or frequency of actual communication that should be directed at positions with different degrees of perceived difference in the four experi-

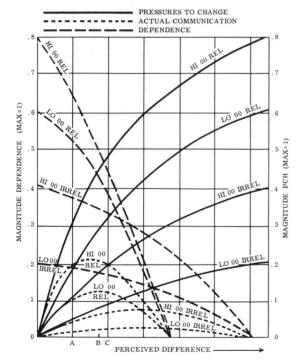

Figure 2. Derived curves of actual communication in the four experimental conditions.

mental conditions.[20] This figure is the same as Figure 1, with the curves for predicted communication added.

Let us examine more closely the meaning of "perceived difference." It refers to the phenomenological difference between two people rather than to the absolute difference between two points on the love-punishment scale. Two people may be at position 4 on the scale and perceive the difference between themselves and someone at position 7 as of very different orders of magnitude. We shall postulate that in this experiment perceived differences increased with discussion. In all club meetings the question, "How much do we really differ?" was frequently discussed, and attempts were made to reduce the distance between points on the scale. The deviates, however, were specifically instructed to resist attempts to minimize differences between themselves and people at other positions. The assumption that perceived difference increases with discussion seems reasonable, therefore, in this situation.

Accepting this assumption, we may say that the dotted curve of communication in Figure 2 represents the actual pattern of communication during the course of the meeting. From these considerations a number of testable derivations may be made about the frequency and pattern of communication to each paid participant in each condition.

Communication Patterns to the Deviate. A prediction previously developed was that rejection will increase with increasing perceived difference. Therefore, people who strongly reject the deviate perceive a greater difference be-

---

[20] The coordination of rejection to the amount of pressures that are not publicly expressed can be demonstrated graphically in Figure 2. At any point along the axis of perceived difference, rejection is equal to the difference between the height of the appropriate derived curve of actual communication and the height of the corresponding curve for Pch. This relationship is simply stated algebraically:

$$\text{Rej} = \text{Pch} \times (1 - \text{Dep})$$
$$= \text{Pch} - \text{Pch} \times \text{Dep}$$
$$\text{Comm} = \text{Pch} \times \text{Dep}$$
$$\therefore \text{Rej} = \text{Pch} - \text{Comm}$$

tween themselves and the deviate than do people who do not reject. In Figure 2, point C represents the position of a rejector at the end of a meeting, point B the position of a mild rejector, and point A the position of a non-rejector. If perpendiculars are projected from these points, they intercept the communication curves at different relative positions.

If we accept the assumption that perceived difference increases with discussion time, and postulate that points C, B, and A in Figure 2 represent, respectively, the end-of-the-meeting perceptions of people who reject the deviate strongly, reject mildly, and do not reject, then we must say that the curves of actual communication up to points C, B, and A represent the patterns of communication from these three kinds of people to the deviate during the course of the meeting. In Figure 3 these predicted curves of communication, projected from Figure 2, are drawn for these three kinds of people for each experimental condition. These curves are specific predictions about the pattern and magnitude of communication to the deviate.

In Figure 3 the ordinate represents the amount of communication during the meeting, and the abscissa, the flow of time from zero to 45 minutes. A point on these curves represents the amount of communication that will be addressed to the deviate at a particular time in the course of the meeting by either the people who reject him strongly, reject mildly, or do not reject. All curves start slightly above the zero point, for it seems likely that even at the beginning of a meeting there is some perception of difference.

In the Hi Co Rel condition, the communication curve of non-rejectors increases continuously throughout the meeting. The curve of strong rejectors reaches a peak during the meeting and then declines continuously; and the mild rejectors' curve reaches a peak somewhat later and then declines. In all other conditions, all communication curves to the deviate rise continuously throughout the meeting.

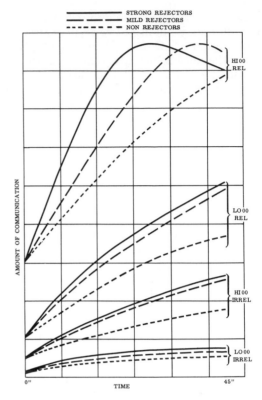

Figure 3. Theoretical curves of communications from strong rejectors, mild rejectors, and non-rejectors to the deviate in the four experimental conditions.

The data testing these derivations are presented in Table 7. The meeting is here divided into ten-minute intervals and communications to the deviate during each interval tallied. The three categories of rejectors are determined by sociometric rankings of the deviate. Non-rejectors ranked the deviate from 1.0-3.72; mild rejectors from 4.0-7.92; and strong rejectors between 8 and 9. The figures in the table represent the total number of communications in each time interval made by all people in each rejector category, divided by the number of people in this category.

Let us examine first the data for the Hi Co Rel groups in Table 7. The strong rejectors reach their peak of communication to the deviate in the 15-25 minute interval and then decline steadily. The difference between the peak interval and the final time interval is significant at

Table 7
Mean Number of Communications Addressed to
"Deviate" During the Course of the Meeting
By Subjects with Different Post-Meeting
Reactions to Him

Group	N	Time Interval in Minutes			
		5-15*	15-25	25-35	35-45
Hi Co Rel					
Non-rejectors	13	1.15	0.92	2.15	1.54
Mild rejectors	15	0.40	1.27	1.87	0.86
Strong rejectors	25	0.68	1.60	1.52	0.76
Lo Co Rel					
Non-rejectors	13	0.38	0.54	0.84	0.46
Mild rejectors	22	0.58	0.50	1.23	1.73
Strong rejectors	15	0.26	0.47	1.27	2.99
Hi Co Irrel					
Non-rejectors	9	1.32	1.44	0.99	2.44
Mild rejectors	20	1.15	1.35	1.55	1.20
Strong rejectors	20	0.75	1.15	1.60	3.42
Lo Co Irrel					
Non-rejectors	16	1.69	1.69	2.34	2.12
Mild rejectors	15	1.47	0.94	2.20	3.74
Strong rejectors	15	1.20	0.74	2.47	2.87

*Because the first few minutes of many meetings were concerned with technical problems and deciding just what was to be done, data from the 0-5 time interval are not reported.

better than the 1 per cent level.[21] Mild rejectors reach their peak somewhat later, in the 25-35 minute interval, and then decline. The difference between this peak and the final time interval is significant at the 3 per cent level. Non-rejectors seem to reach a peak and then decline, but this difference is due entirely to one case and is significant at exactly the 50 per cent level of confidence. The data, then, essentially parallel theoretical expectations.

In the other experimental conditions the theory anticipates a steady rise in the number of communications addressed to the deviate by either mild, strong, or non-rejectors. The remaining data in Table 7 indicate that this is essentially

[21]All of the levels of significance reported with this set of data were obtained by tabulating for each S in each category whether or not the number of communications he had addressed to the deviate was higher in one time interval than in the interval with which it was being compared. Probabilities were then computed by means of binomial expansion.

correct. In six of these nine breakdowns, the number of communications to the deviate rises continuously, and differences between the last two time intervals are significant at the 12 per cent level or better for all but the rising Lo Co Irrel curves. In three cases (non-rejectors in Lo Co Rel and Lo Co Irrel, mild rejectors in the Hi Co Irrel) there is a slight drop in the final interval. None of these drops is significant.

The theoretical derivations seem as well corroborated as can be anticipated with the relatively small number of cases involved. Most of the curves rise, and the only significant declines are the predicted ones.

Communication Patterns to the Mode and Slider. The position of the mode on the scale of perceived difference in Figure 2 should be at zero, the point of no perceived difference between himself and most of the others in the group. At this point $Pch = 0$, and dependence is at a maximum. There should therefore be no communications to the mode during any meeting in any experimental condition. This conclusion, however, must be qualified by two considerations. (1) As a rule, most, but not all, of the members of any one club were at the modal position. There were slight differences, therefore, between the mode and a few members of the group. (2) A paid participant in the modal role was required to speak once every five minutes. Courtesy would probably demand an occasional response.

We may anticipate, then, that the curve of communication to the mode in all experimental conditions should be a low straight line, parallel to the horizontal time axis. In Table 8, we see that this is the case. The figures in this table are computed on the same basis as those in the previous table. In all conditions only a very small number of communications was addressed to the mode at any time. Fluctuations from a straight line are all within the range of chance expectancy.

Theoretically, communications to the slider present a more complicated picture, for it is possible to predict exactly the interaction between perceived

Table 8
Mean Number of Communications Addressed to
the "Mode" and "Slider" During the Course
of the Meeting

Group	N	Time Interval in Minutes			
		5-15	15-25	25-35	35-45
Hi Co Rel					
Mode	53	0.13	0.06	0.06	0.10
Slider	53	0.53	0.55	0.21	0.17
Lo Co Rel					
Mode	50	0.06	0.10	0.14	0.22
Slider	50	0.30	0.20	0.20	0.20
Hi Co Irrel					
Mode	49	0.18	0.16	0.37	0.12
Slider	49	0.79	0.47	0.20	0.04
Lo Co Irrel					
Mode	46	0.14	0.15	0.13	0.45
Slider	46	0.72	0.63	0.41	0.30

difference and decreasing absolute difference. But it is reasonable to suggest that communications to the slider should be at about the same level as to the deviate until the slider makes his first shift, and then communications should gradually decrease until by the end of the meeting they are at about the same level for both the slider and the mode. The data presented in Table 8 essentially substantiate these expectations. About 15 minutes after the meeting started the slider shifted from 7 to 5, and finally adopted the modal position between the 35- and 40-minute marks. In all experimental conditions, communications to the slider are at first considerably above the level of communication to the mode and then decline steadily to the level of the mode in the final time interval.[22]

The Frequency of Communication. From the theoretical considerations previously formulated, additional derivations can be made about the magnitude or ab-

solute amounts of communication in each experimental condition. It may be predicted, from the curves of communication in Figure 3, that the amount of communication to the deviate will decrease from Hi Co Rel condition to Lo Co Rel to Hi Co Irrel to Lo Co Irrel. And, since the distribution of positions on the love-punishment scale is the same from condition to condition, it may also be anticipated that the mean amounts of communication for meetings, within each condition, will vary in the same order. The data collected with the present observation schedule are, however, inadequate to substantiate or disprove these derivations. It has been postulated that the magnitude or pressures to uniformity are greater on relevant than on irrelevant issues, in high than in low cohesive groups. These derivations will hold only for communications that arise from pressures to uniformity, and we can say nothing about communications that arise from other sources. However, people communicate for numberless reasons beyond that of restoring uniformity of opinion. It seems a reasonable assumption that the more irrelevant an issue, the greater will be the number of communications that have sources other than pressures to uniformity. If this analysis of the differences between the discussions of relevant and irrelevant issues is correct, supporting evidence must be found in areas other than the directions and amounts of communication.

Differences between the communication process in relevant and irrelevant conditions are shown in Table 9. Communications in the relevant groups tended to be longer. Slightly more than 30 per cent of all communications (more than 30 seconds), and only 21 per cent were long in the irrelevant conditions.[23] In addition, discussion in these two conditions went at a different clip. There were far more interruptions in irrelevant than in relevant groups.[24] An interruption is de-

---

[22] In the first time interval, though the number of communications to the slider is considerably higher than that to the mode, comparison with Table 7 reveals that the number of slider-directed communications is consistently lower than that to the deviate. Probably this is an artifact of the slider role. In preparing to shift position, the slider probably tended to be somewhat less extreme and emphatic in his defense of position 7.

[23] This difference has a $t = 2.06$, which with 30 d.f. is significant at the 5 per cent level.

[24] The difference between mean number of interruptions in relevant and irrelevant groups is sig-

Table 9
Interruptions, Pauses, Personal References, and Long Communications in All Conditions

	Hi Co Rel	Lo Co Rel	Hi Co Irrel	Lo Co Irrel
Per cent long communications	28	33	25	17
Mean interruptions per meeting	67.71	29.86	78.71	82.00
Total pauses	1	1	3	7
Personal history references	18	14	5	8

fined as any attempt to break into a speech before it is completed. Oddly enough, in the face of the greater number of communications and the more rapid clip in irrelevant groups, there was a greater number of pauses in the discussions of the irrelevant groups. Though there was no systematic notation of pause, the observer noted all particularly long, uncomfortable intervals when no one had anything to say. In short, there were marked differences in the character of discussion in the two conditions. Discussion in irrelevant groups might be characterized as cocktail party conversation, fast, brief, clipped, and in bursts; discussion in the relevant groups resembled the board meeting, slow, even-paced, long, and well considered.

Consistent with these characterizations of the process of the meeting are the additional data presented in Table 9 on the relative frequency of personal history references. Reference to personal history may be considered evidence of real involvement in the discussion. In relevant groups, there were more than two and a half times as many personal references as there were in irrelevant groups.[25] Not only were the discussions of the irrelevant groups more glib, but also apparently more superficial.

The marked differences in the manner of relevant and irrelevant groups indicate that communications in irrelevant

groups resulted in good part from sources other than pressures to uniformity. The data, therefore, do not serve as an adequate test of the derivations concerning the relative amounts of communication in the various conditions.

SUMMARY

A set of assumptions has been developed which defines the relationships of the constructs dependence and pressures to change, to cohesiveness, relevance, and state of opinion. Both communication and rejection have been coordinated to these constructs. Dependence defines the proportion of the pressures to change that can find public expression, and communication is defined as:

$$\underline{Comm} = \underline{Pch} \times \underline{Dep}$$

Rejection is coordinated to the amount of pressures to change which are not exerted and is defined as:

$$\underline{Rej} = \underline{Pch} \times (1 - \underline{Dep})$$

These coordinations and the assumptions defining $\underline{Pch}$ and $\underline{Dep}$ allow us to make a number of predictions as to the results of the experiment. Predictions about rejection and the evidence supporting them will be reviewed briefly.

1. Persons in the mode and slider roles will be rejected less (if at all) than will persons in the deviate role.

On both the sociometric and committee assignment measures there was no evidence that either the mode or slider was rejected. The deviate, on the other hand, was rejected in all experimental conditions except Lo Co Irrel. Where the magnitudes of both $\underline{Dep}$ and $\underline{Pch}$ are low, we anticipate relatively little rejection.

---

nificant at better than the .001 level of signifiance, with $\underline{t} = 5.74$ for 30 $\underline{d.f.}$ These measures of interruption and length of communication are relatively independent. Rank order correlations between the two are only +.39 in the irrelevant condition and +.45 in the relevant condition.

[25] The difference yields a $\underline{t}$ of 1.89, which with 30 $\underline{d.f.}$ is significant at the 8 per cent level.

Thus, in the Lo Co Irrel condition, the sociometric ranking of the deviate was only slightly above the mean, and he was not over-nominated for the Correspondence Committee.

2. With cohesiveness held constant, rejection will be greater in relevant groups than in irrelevant groups.

(a) On the committee assignment measure the deviate was assigned to the Correspondence Committee to a far greater extent in the relevant groups than in the irrelevant groups.

(b) Though sociometric rankings of the deviate are about the same for the relevant and irrelevant conditions, there is evidence from random sociometric rankings that the intensity of rejection is greater in the relevant than in the irrelevant conditions.

3. With relevance held constant, rejection will be greater in high cohesive than in low cohesive groups.

(a) The mean sociometric ranking of the deviate was considerably higher in both high cohesive conditions than in the corresponding low cohesive conditions.

(b) On the committee assignment measure the deviate was nominated to the Correspondence Committee to a greater extent in the Hi Co Irrel than in the Lo Co Irrel conditions. There is no difference, however, between the Hi Co Rel and the Lo Co Rel conditions. This inconsistency may be explained in terms of the relative nature of the measure. Here, too, the intensity of rejection may be stronger in Hi Co Rel than in Lo Co Rel groups. There is no immediate evidence, however, to support this argument.

Predictions about patterns of communication follow:

1. In the Hi Co Rel condition, the amount of communication addressed to the deviate by non-rejectors should increase continuously throughout the meeting. Strong rejectors should reach a peak of communication during the meeting and then decline continuously, and mild rejectors should reach a peak somewhat later and then decline.

2. In all other experimental conditions, communications to the deviate from strong, mild, or non-rejectors should increase continuously throughout the meeting.

3. In all experimental conditions, there should be relatively few communications addressed to persons in the modal role and no increase in communications during the meeting.

4. In all conditions, communications to the slider should decrease during the meeting as the slider shifts from a deviate to a modal position.

The data essentially substantiated all of these predictions. The theory leads to other predictions about the relative magnitudes of communication in each experimental condition. These derivations, however, hold only for communications arising from pressures to uniformity. Since in irrelevant conditions many communications arose from other sources, it is impossible to test these derivations.

Illness, Therapy and the Modern Urban American Family

Talcott Parsons and Renée Fox

SOURCE: *Journal of Social Issues*, Vol. 8 (1952), pp. 31-44.

The primary purpose of this paper is to show that the relations between illness and the family are to be understood only through combining sociological analysis of the structure of role-systems with psychodynamic analysis of certain processes in personalities. For we regard illness as <u>both</u> a psychological disturbance and a deviant social role.[1]

DOCTOR-PATIENT AND PARENT-CHILD: SOME ANALOGIES

We begin our analysis by suggesting that there are intimate psychodynamic relationships between the processes which occur in the normal system of family interaction, and those which obtain both in the doctor-patient relationship and in such more elaborately differentiated health-care institutions as the hospital. At the same time, we propose that the emergence of the medical profession and of the hospitals into their strategic position in contemporary society is not solely attributable to the accumulation of technical medical knowledge and its application in technological processes. Rather, it is our paramount thesis that the doctor and the hospital provide a set of institutionalized mechanisms for handling certain of the motivational problems of personality adjustment: mechanisms which, in certain respects, are functionally alternative to those of the family. Thus, the family and therapeutic institutions resemble each other; if this were not true, the kind of functional relationship between them which we wish to analyze could not exist. At the same time, they also differ in fundamental respects; if this were not the case, there would be far less reason either for the existence or for the effectiveness of these institutions.

The elements of correspondence are perhaps best approached in terms of two analogies: on the one hand, the similarity between illness and the status of the child in the family; on the other hand, the overlap between the physician's role and that of the parent. The common point of reference for the first analogy is the status of the non-sick adult member of society. Both child and sick person differ from this norm in two primary respects. The first is capacity to perform the usual functions of an adult in everyday life. The child is not yet able to do this; partly because biological maturation has not gone far enough, partly because his socialization is still incomplete. Similarly, one of our main criteria of illness is that the sick person is "incapacitated." In the usual case, he has been capable of normal functioning, but his illness, in some degree, makes him unable to carry on. The second respect in which the child and the sick actor are similar is that they are both dependent: needing and expecting

---

[1] In our submitted draft of this paper, we placed considerably more emphasis upon psychological mechanisms than this final version incorporates. All our major social structural arguments were complemented by their psychologically phrased equivalents. Space was limited, however, and so it became necessary to omit some of our more "psycholigistic" points. We hope that such deletions in no way impair our foremost intent, which is to show how the simultaneous use of psychological and sociological theory can serve to illuminate a given problem area.

to be taken care of by stronger, more "adequate" persons. Thus, in these two senses, illness is not unlike more or less complete reversion to childhood.

The analogy of physician (and other hospital personnel) and parents in part is simple and obvious. These are the stronger and more adequate persons on whom the child and the sick person, respectively, are made to rely; they are the ones to whom he must turn to have those of his needs fulfilled which he is incapable of meeting through his own resources. As we shall maintain, these analogies must not be pressed too far. But they do constitute a convenient jumping off place for our analysis.

Illness, so far as it is motivated, is a form of deviant behavior, and, as such, may be subjected to a standard sociological analysis of deviance. Compared with other types of non-conformist behavior, sickness characteristically entails passive withdrawal from normal activities and responsibilities. As such, it should be distinguished from active rebellion against the normal social expectations, and from the types of deviance characterized by compulsive conformity.[2] For it is an escape from the pressures of ordinary life. In a society such as our own, illness is a very strategic expression of deviance: first, because our culture enforces an unusually high level of activity, independence and responsibility on the average individual; and second, because it connects so closely with the residua of childhood dependency (which, we may suggest, are more intense in our society than in many others, because of the particular structure of our urban family[3]). From the point of view of the stability of the social system, therefore, too frequent resort to this avenue of es-

cape presents a serious danger. This is the primary context in which we think of illness as an institutionalized role and its relation to thereapy as an important mechanism of social control.

It should be pointed out that as a role the state of illness is partially and conditionally legitimized. That is, if a person is defined as sick, his failure to perform his normal functions is "not his fault," and he is accorded the right to exemption and to care. At one and the same time, however, the sick person is enjoined to accept the definition of his state as undesirable and the obligation to get well as expeditiously as possible.

Similarly, childhood is more than a condition. Like illness, it also is a conditionally legitimized social role. The child is permitted to be childish only temporarily. He accepts the obligation to grow up, even though at times it is very painful, and to cooperate with his parents in helping him to achieve maturity.

We feel it is largely because of this close correspondence between the status of the child and of the sick person that it is important to have the major part of illness in our society tended outside the family. However, since the family has been the principal refuge for the sick in most societies, the question arises as to why in our society we are so ready to send our sick outside the family to special medical institutions. The importance of the technological factors we grant; but, as already indicated, we feel that there is more to it than that. For family members this is primarily a "maintenance" or regulatory function: a matter of ab-

---

[2] For a grounding of this classification of types of deviant orientation, see T. Parsons, The Social System, Chap. VII, and R. K. Merton, "Social Structure and Anomie," Chap. III of Social Theory and Social Structure, Glencoe, Ill., The Free Press, 1949.

[3] Cf. "Sources and Patterns of Aggression in the Social Structure of the Western World," in Parsons, Essays in Sociological Theory (Glencoe, Ill., The Free Press 1949), Chap. XII.

[4] As we will point out in a later section of this article, despite the paring down process which our family system has undergone, its residual functions as primary socializer, social control agent, and emotional bulwark, are so crucial that this over-all importance of kinship in our society has not diminished. Indeed, as Robin Williams phrases it in his study of American Society, though "the scope of family activities has narrowed, the emotional significance of the surviving relationships has, in one sense, increased." (p. 77).

A brief analysis of these features of the American family will be found in Parsons, Bales and Shils, Working Papers in the Theory of Action, Chap. V, Sec. viii.

sorbing, easing and dealing with the consequences of various kinds of strain arising out of their life situations. For children, on the other hand, it involves the powerful process of socialization.[4]

The American family is well adapted to the exigencies of a modern industrial society. But it is also highly susceptible to many grave strains. For, though the wife-mother bears the major socio-emotional responsibilities within the family, she is largely excluded from those occupational roles which are the source of family status and socio-economic sustenance. Further, whatever her activities outside the home may be, they tend on the whole to be "representative" ones undertaken in the name of the family.

On the other hand, the husband-father as the provider and primary status bearer of the family is exposed during all the working hours of his existence to the distinctive rigors of the marketplace, wherein he carries the heavy load of responsibility for the family. In addition, he is classically a "scapegoat": the symbolic target at which the child primarily aims the hostile-aggressive impulses aroused in him as he undergoes the stressful process of socialization. It is the specialized function of the wife-mother to act as skillful mediator of the child-father relationship and thereby to assure both the perpetuation of family solidarity and the emotional security of the child.

The roles of the wife-mother and the husband-father, then, are characteristically subject to a complex of structural strains, as is the child in his role of socializee, particularly when sibling rivalry intervenes. Finally, in our society, the advent of old age brings still another set of problems in its wake: forced retirement from the occupational sphere so crucial to the male actor's sense of worth, and to the woman's status and security systems; and overwhelming socio-psychological isolation.

As a response to any one of these family-based or focussed social pressures, illness could provide a tantalizingly attractive "solution." For the sick role is a semi-legitimate channel of withdrawal—exempting the social actor from adult responsibilities and enjoining him to allow himself to be taken care of by others. As we have already emphasized, illness is very often motivational in origin. Even in those instances where the etiology of the disorder is primarily physico-chemical, the nature and severity of symptoms and the rate of recuperation are almost invariably influenced by the attitudes of the patient.

It is easy to see, therefore, how the wife-mother, for example, might "choose" the sick role as an institutionalized way out of her heavy "human relations management" responsibilities in the family; or how she might seize upon illness as a compulsively feministic way of reacting to her exclusion from the life open to a man. Similarly, the passive-dependent role of illness offers the husband-father semi-institutionalized respite from the discipline and autonomy which his occupation demands of him.

As for the child, we have already indicated that he is being pushed and pulled along a tension-ridden path which points toward adulthood. It is almost a foregone conclusion, then, that at any point along this socialization continuum, illness can provide him with a method of escape from progressively more exacting obligations to behave in a mature fashion. For sickness not only allows the child to be nurtured and cared for as the infant that he still yearns, in part, to be; but, in becoming the central focus of family solicitude and concern, the sick child also achieves temporary victory in the competition with his siblings for a lion's share of parental attention. Coming around full circle in the family's life span, we can easily see how illness might serve not only the child, and the young and middle-aged adult, but the elderly person as well. The aged individual, occupationless, and with no traditionally assured place in the families established by his daughters and sons, through illness may once again become an integral member of a meaningful social group, cared for either by his grown children or by a medical community of some sort.

FAMILY CARE OF THE SICK: A FUNCTIONAL ANALYSIS OF LIABILITIES

We turn now to consider the problem of the resources available to the family for dealing with these tendencies to make psychological use of illness. What are the probable consequences of attempting to cope with the psychological impact of serious illness within the American family—both upon the sick person himself, and upon other members of the family?

First, we note the probability that handling sickness outside the family serves to discourage falling ill in the first place. It is a method of preventing a person from "eating his cake and having it, too." Care of the sick places upon those who assume the responsibility, the obligation to accept the sick person in his state of illness. If this component of acceptance, therefore, were combined with the supportive features of the normal familial role, there would be a double reinforcement of the motivation to illness. The sick person could then enjoy good standing in the family—in the psychological sense, "all the comforts of home"—without paying the normal price for such familial acceptance: the fulfillment of role-obligations. In this respect, then, the family has an inherent tendency to set a "vicious circle" kind of interaction into motion: driving the sick actor deeper and deeper into his illness, rather than reducing his psychological investment in his disorder.

Next, what of the position of the members of the family who are not sick: what resources do they have to meet the impact of illness? We suggest that these resources are relatively weak; that consequently, the inherent social control patterns of our family would be seriously jeopardized by the strain of caring for illness. In the first place, the American family apparently operates at high levels of emotional intensity—with relatively little margin for "shock-absorp-

tion." In the second place, the specific direction of pressures from the demands of the sick strike it at what appears to be a vulnerable point. We wish to discuss each of these aspects of the problem in turn.

What we have called the isolation of the conjugal family, combined with the impersonal character of so many of our social relationships outside the family, means that we place a very large proportion of our emotional eggs in the one basket of the family. Each relationship within this small group, then, becomes critically important, both to the stability of the family itself and to each of the participants as a personality. The focal problems, in turn, center at two points: the marriage relationship and the parent-child relationship, particularly that of the mother to her children.

The constitution of our family means that there are ordinarily only two adults to take the roles of major responsibility. Further, there are no clear-cut stipulations as to which of the two is really "boss." Rather, the husband-wife relationship in the American family is defined to a very high degree in terms of equality and spontaneous emotional mutual attraction.

There are many indications that the load placed upon the marriage relationship in our family system comes closer to the maximum it can stand than is true for most other systems. We have long felt, for example, that the high American divorce rate is not an index of the "withering away" or disorganization of the family, as it is sometimes supposed. Quite to the contrary, it is our conviction that the oft-cited increase of divorce derives from the unique intensity and emotional import of the husband-wife relationship in our society, and from the heavy burden that such heightened affectivity imposes upon marriage. Similar things can be said about the parent-child relationship. How, then, does illness play into this precariously balanced, emotionally highly-charged system? This question can best be answered by following out the consequences of the serious illness of family members, one by one.

Take first the case of the husband-father. Although the exemption from adult, masculine responsibilities granted him by the sick role worsens the position of the family and makes its adaptive problems more difficult, it is the husband-father's claim to be taken care of which has the more immediately disruptive impact on the family's internal situation. The wife, of course, is the primary sick-room attendant. The most obvious consequences of her ministrations is the withdrawal of her full quota of attention from the children. The presence of the husband-father in the home at unaccustomed times is relevant here; but far more important are his greatly enhanced physical and emotional needs. The intricately balanced way in which the wife-mother normally distributes her attention between husband and children is upset, for the children are called upon to sacrifice part of their maternal support to the father.[5]

The illness of a child, on the other hand, tends to disturb family equilibrium by making it more difficult for the mother to meet the needs of the father. What is more, the mother also runs the risk of making sibling rivalries more acute.

Finally, illness of the mother herself is clearly the most disturbing of all—and this may well be the nub of the whole matter. For, in the normal course of events, the mother is the primary agent of supportive strength for the entire family unit. Her illness, therefore, subjects husband and children alike to a condition of under-support, at a time when they are suddenly being asked to meet unexpected demands of major proportions. In the light of this, a mother-wife who is motivationally inclined to cast herself in the sick role may very well constitute the greatest single source of danger that illness can inflict on the family.

To all these foregoing considerations, a more general point should be appended: the insidious effects the claims of the sick person are liable to have on the healthy members of his family—regardless of whether the stricken actor is mother, father, or child. For, if we are justified in our supposition that latent dependency needs are present in almost all normal people in our society, it follows that most individuals will also have a tendency to develop defense mechanisms against those needs. As a result, there is a high probability that our families will be inclined to over-react to the passive-dependent nature of illness, in either of two ways. On the one hand, family members may tend to be more sympathetic and supportive of the sick person than they ought: bolstering their own defense against a desire to be taken care of by projecting this need onto the sick person. Through their indulgent attitude toward the ill actor (over-emphasis on the positive aspect of the treatment; under-emphasis on the disciplinary aspect) the family may invite him to perpetuate his illness. On the other hand, the family may display an excessive intolerance with respect to the debilitating features of illness—regarding them as a sign of weakness—and impose overly harsh disciplinary sanctions on the sick member. Such hyperseverity, of course, is as unfavorable to full and rapid recovery as over-permissiveness.[6]

---

[5] We know how important (particularly at the Oedipal period) the significance of the parental marriage solidarity is to children, and how sensitive they are to a feeling of being excluded.

[6] It must not be forgotten that the sick role has a positive function in American society. There is much reason to believe that illness is less harmful to the society than other forms of deviant behavior —for example, crime and some types of political involvement. For, sickness not only exposes the actor to the counteractive therapy of the doctor and his adjuncts, .but (with the important exception of "magic-mountain-like" communities of the chronically ill) illness usually prevents the individual from attaching himself to a solidary sub-culture of similarly-oriented deviants. Thus, the inability of the family to tolerate the illness of its members runs counter to a social need to increase, rather than decrease, the relative amount of illness. This is not to say that illness is positively valued in our culture. It is merely to point out that there is pressure to divert unavoidable deviant motivation from other channels into this one—with a net

In other words, what we are suggesting here is that the optimal balance between permissive-supportive and disciplinary facets of treating illness is peculiarly difficult to maintain in the kind of situation presented by the American family. Medico-technical advances notwithstanding, therefore, therapy is more easily effected in a professional milieu, where there is not the same order of intensive emotional involvement so characteristic of family relationships.

This, of course, is a functional argument, and as such does not explain how the segregation arose in the first place. Very broadly, however, we may suggest that technological developments provided the opportunity to treat illness outside the family, while the kinds of strains we have outlined have predisposed people to take advantage of the services of medical personnel. The further we have gone in our discussion of the American family, the more apparent have become the dynamic interdependence of illness, the family, the physician; deviance, socialization, and social control.

THE DOCTOR-PATIENT RELATIONSHIP AND THE ROLES OF THE ILL

When the sick actor and his family join forces with the doctor, a therapeutic sub-system is established which, ideally speaking, should facilitate the actor's recovery from illness. At this meeting place, where the disabled individual contracts technically competent help with whom he agrees to cooperate in a concerted effort to get well, the sick role evolves into the patient role.

In spite of the fact that illness is often highly motivated, it should not be supposed that passage from health, to sickness, to the status of patient, is easily effected. From whatever socio-psychological baseline the actor enters the sick

role, adherence to the institutionalized dictates of this role is attained only by virtue of a learning process: a socialization experience not without its special problems. In the words of one patient: "It sometimes takes a long time to learn the things we have to learn..."

Even for a passive-dependent personality, the so-called exemptions of sickness usually present certain real difficulties. Since the sick individual is called upon to acknowledge the authority of medical personages over himself, the obligations of the role of the patient imply temporary relinquishment of the rights, as well as the duties, of normal adulthood. For any socialized actor, then, acceptance of this child-like status, with its attributes of inferior status and its socio-emotional skewing, entails considerable adjustment; a sort of "de-socialization" process is necessary. In the light of the motivational challenge which this unlearning entails, it would seem that the structuring of the doctor's role serves a cushioning and delimiting kind of function. For, were the doctor to treat his patient exactly as the mother and father are enjoined to treat their child, in most instances, he would be over-taxing the adult actor's capacity to tolerate dependency.[7]

It is not merely on dependency grounds alone, however, that the sick patient role involves an affect-laden learning sequence. There is also the fact that an individual in our society, when befallen with a relatively acute or severe malady, is likely to be wrenched from the reassuring familiarity of his home, his job, and his friends, and placed in a totally strange hospital bed. Illness sets him down in a new, medical-scientific

---

functional gain for the society. (The situation is analagous to the positive function of the national debt. From the point of view of private finance, debt is undesirable; but from the point of view of economy as a whole, it has certain positive functions.) On this aspect of illness, cf. Parsons, The Social System, Chaps. VII and X.

---

[7] The discomforts of the double-dependency characteristic of the patient role, would undoubtedly be experienced more acutely by an activistically-oriented personality type, for example, than by a more compliantly-organized individual. We are assuming, however, that even in the case of motivated illness, wherein the acquiescence is "chosen" by the actor, this choice is always an ambivalent one; and thus, the difficulties experienced by the patient-initiate though perhaps milder in degree, will be qualitatively the same.

world to which he must become acclimatized. And this transplantation is by no means an easy one to undergo. Though the hospital community in which he finds himself is supposedly geared to returning the patient to his full participation in life outside, it is nevertheless true that the distance between this newly-inherited sick world and the well world which he has temporarily left behind is vast indeed. As one patient phrases the dichotomy between these two universes: "when you're outside on the sidewalk there, you know there's sick people in there in the hospital. But that's breezed right through your mind. You don't know what's going on in there. Furthermore, you don't really care. Because you're out. You're walking on the street..."

The sharpness of this cleavage between sickness and wellness in our society, so problematic to the new patient, is a function of the physical and psychical separation of the hospital from the sites and activities of normal adult existence. We have already discussed some of the multiple reasons for which our society has seen fit to isolate the seriously ill patient from his family and the ranks of the non-sick in general. Most obvious among these is the phenomenal growth of scientific medicine in modern Western society—rendering the traditional home-remedy type of medical care obsolete by bringing in its wake teams of white-coated specialists, manifold test-tube procedures, an elaboration of machinery, and formal professionalized psychotherapy. Less apparent than these technological determinants, but fully as significant, are the socio-psychological reasons for which we have erected brick walls between the sick and the healthy: the special appropriateness of illness as a deviant expression in our society (hence, the dangers of exposing the non-sick to bio-psychical "infection"), and the unique defenselessness of the American urban family when faced with the illness of one of its members.

The insulation of the sick, however, not only serves passively to protect our family system and our society at large

from "contamination." Rather, it is one of the potent mechanisms which launches the patient on his recovery-directed efforts, by involving him in a complementary role-relationship with therapeutic agents. If the therapy to which he becomes subject is truly successful, the getting well process which the patient undergoes will entail meaningful attitudinal changes as well as biochemical ones.

THE DOCTOR'S ROLE IN THE THERAPEUTIC PROCESS

Sociological analysis of the therapeutic process has brought out sharply certain broad conditions of effective therapy, yielding a list of its major components and the temporal order of their utilization. Looked at from the point of view of the attitudes and manipulations of the physician[8], therapy involves four primary aspects.

In the first place, there must be permissiveness: allowing, even encouraging the patient to express deviant ideas, wishes, and fantasies. The mere privilege of being treated as sick belongs in this category, but presumably is not enough. In other words, the fact of deviant motivation must be accepted by the therapist, assuring the patient thereby that he is, in this sense, taken seriously.

The second therapeutic component is what psychiatrists often call support: a more holistic kind of acceptance. This is not so much a matter of respecting the details of the patient's troubles. Rather, it consists in valuing the sick actor as a person in his role: accepting him as a bona fide member of the therapeutic system because he is deemed worth helping. From one point of view, this is

---

[8] In outlining the components of therapy, we are assuming that not only the psychiatrist's role, but the role of the physician in the more general sense, is psychotherapeutic. Indeed, it is clear that "the basic structuring of the physician's role in our society did not come about through the application of theories of the ideal situation for psychotherapy. It was a spontaneous, unplanned development of social structure which psychiatry was able to utilize and develop . . ." (Parsons, Social System, p. 462.)

the sick person's immediate reward for trying to be a good patient.

In the light of the above analysis, it is clear that these features of the therapeutic role help to minimize inhibitions about giving way to dependency needs. In fact, through transference, the patient develops a powerful attachment to the therapist, the ingredients of which draw heavily on residua of unresolved childhood motivational structures. Thus, it becomes doubly necessary that the permissive-supportive aspects of the therapeutic process should not stand alone, if the leverage gained over the patient's motivational system is to transform, rather than confirm, his deviant motivational orientations.

The therapist applies this leverage in two primary ways. In the first place, the permissive-supportive aspect of the situation arouses the patient's expectations of positive deviant wish-fulfillment, and emboldens him to express them. The therapist must frustrate these desires by refusing the looked-for reciprocation. That is, though the patient will treat him as a parent-figure, a close friend, a lover (or, often, as a personal enemy), the therapist will adhere scrupulously to a professional attitude. Stated differently, he avoids reciprocating the patient's transference with countertransference of his own. This creates a conflict between the expectations of the patient which are encouraged in the permissive-supportive phases of therapy, and the disciplining of overt wishes that the therapist later demands of him. A secondary tension is thereby set up—which is easier for the patient to analyze than primary ones.

Concomitantly or increasingly the therapist introduces conditional rewards (of which his approval is probably the most important) for the patient's good work in the therapeutic situation. Above all, he approves the patient for gaining insight into the character and motives of his own behavior. Thus, through the therapist's denial of reciprocity and his wielding of conditional rewards, the patient is pushed out of his pathological dependency. At the same time, his dependency is positively utilized to sensitize him to the meaning of the refusal of the therapist to reciprocate, and to heighten the significance of rewards coming from that source. We may say, then, that a situation is created where conforming with the wishes of the therapist—gaining his approval for adult behavior—comes to outbalance the secondary gain of the pathological state itself. Ideally speaking, the patient gradually gives up his deviant orientation and comes to embrace maturity in its stead.

Though the basic components we have just reviewed for the case of psychotherapy are also the focus of child socialization, the differences between these two processes must be underscored. First, "classical" psychotherapy occurs in a two-person system, with one patient and one therapist. Socialization, on the other hand, entails two parents and a child, at the very least. Secondly, whereas the family milieu is a deeply affective one, the therapeutic setting is more neutrally-toned. Both these distinctions point up the fact that for all their striking similarity, the doctor-patient and parent-child relationships are not identical. Whereas the patient is a partially socialized adult who must be taught to re-assume his role-obligations, the child is learning his obligations for the first time. Because child socialization has much farther to go than the therapeutic process, rearing the child has been delegated to two adults: the primarily supportive mother, and the more disciplinary father. This division of labor lightens the parental load, and assures that both aspects of socialization will have balanced attention given them. The general protectiveness of the family, on the other hand, serves a bolstering function: endowing the child with the psychical fortitude he needs to cope autonomously with the outside world.

FAMILY CARE VS. PROFESSIONAL CARE

These facts give us a baseline from which to point out some of the main reasons why too great a predominance of family-managed treatment might not only threaten the ongoing of the family itself but also impede the recovery of the sick person as well. First, in some cases, the power of a familial therapist (e.g. the wife-mother, when either the husband-father or the child falls ill) could easily overactivate the sick person's dependency, bringing about a regression to childhood level. Extra-familial therapeutic agents have better-developed safeguards against such an eventuality. For example, contact with the therapist is restricted to stated appointments under carefully regulated conditions; and the impersonal professional character of the hospital seems to have a similar function. Even so, evidence shows that particularly in cases of severe illness it is relatively easy for the patient to acquire a very deep-seated investment in his sick role, either in the form of dependency on an individual therapist or in that of attachment to a hospital situation.[9] Though the process of desocialization in learning to become a good patient is an essential prerequisite of successful recovery in most cases, it is therefore equally important that it should not go too far;[10] and the condition under which it takes place should be carefully controlled. The American urban family, we suggest, has a strong tendency to permit desocialization excesses.[11]

Secondly, since our family is essentially non-authoritarian in nature, and the motivation to illness is so deep-rooted

in our society, the American family is a relatively weak counteractant of sickness. The professional therapist, in contrast, derives his potency from two sources. For one thing, his role is integrated with the adult world in a way that the family member in his kinship status is not.[12]

If the sick person is to be healed, then, and the well-being of our kinship system is to be assured, the modern American family cannot undertake major responsibility for care of the sick. That the doctor may easily err in the direction of under-support, however, if he too drastically extrudes the family from his sphere of operation, is cogently suggested by certain recent developments in the modern hospital. Of late, hospitals throughout the country have been experimenting with such plans as allowing the mother and her newborn infant to room together, permitting the mother to stay overnight with her hospitalized child, and extending visiting hours for all categories of patients. Since all these trial developments invite the more full-blown participation of family members in the hospital community, it appears to us that they may express a felt need for the greater inclusion of the family's permissive-supportive concern in current medical therapy.[13]

Our analysis of these particular empirical occurences may be speculative. But the larger theoretical point it is intended to illustrate is much less challangeable: Making the sick individual better calls for the well-timed, well-chosen, well-balanced exercise of the supportive and the disciplinary components of the

---

[9] In the latter type of case, a field study by the junior author of this paper of a hospital ward comprised of patients ill with chronic, progressively debilitating diseases demonstrates this phenomenon clearly.

[10] To reiterate an earlier point: the fact that the patient is a partially socialized adult, whose tolerance of dependence has upper limits is relevant here, too. What is more, the sick actor's difficulties in accepting the passive-dependent obligations of the patient role is one of the best pieces of evidence we know for correcting the common tendency to regard the child and the sick person as psychologically identical.

[11] cf. D. M. Levy, Maternal Over-Protection, New York: Columbia University Press, 1943.

---

[12] The role of the physician, however, is more closely analagous to the father role than to that of the mother. In this special sense, mother, father and therapist may be said to vary over a continuous range: with the mother giving the highest level of permissiveness and support; the physician, the greatest incentive to acceptance of discipline.

[13] It is not easy, of course, for the hospital staff —with its bureaucratic structuring and its multiple technical responsibilities to large groups of patients—to provide such personalized care. In this respect it resembles the school more than the family.

therapeutic process; and the ministrations of <u>both</u> the doctor and the family.

ILLNESS AND RECOVERY AS A LEARNING PROCESS

Our sick actor now stands poised on the threshold of recovery; and there is a deep motivational sense in which he may not be the "same" person who originally fell ill. Evidence for this hypothesis is the sizeable body of literature penned by former patients: subjective assertions of the fact that the sick role and successful emergence from it may effect a far-reaching socialization process in the recovering actor. For all the socio-psychological reasons we have been attempting to outline in this paper, it is highly probable that illness might bring an intensive learning experience in its wake. Incapacitated and emotionally disturbed; relieved of the weighty responsibilities of the well world; removed in large part from the custodianship of his family and other significant actors who would be likely to reinforce or exacerbate his psychosomatic withdrawal— the ill individual comes to live for a while in a medical-dominated sphere. Here, he is granted nurture and sustenance; but never so much as to balance out the heavy impress of deprivation, subordination and loneliness to which he is also subject. These are the penalties which give impetus to the patient's desire to re-achieve wellness: the challenges to which he responds (ideally-speaking) by re-embracing the world of health.[14]

CONCLUSION

We have given evidence which, we feel, indicates that the development of specialized professional health-care agencies, and the consequent removal of much of the treatment of illness from the family, is attributable to something more than the technological developments of modern medicine. We have tried to show that it is highly probable that certain features of the American urban family, in their impact on the personalities of its members, have tended to push the sick person out of the home. And we have argued that, on the whole, extra-familial care of the sick is positively functional for American society in at least three respects. The first is protection of the family against the disruptive effects of the illness of its members. The second is the preservation of some of the positive functions of the sick role as a mechanism of social control—primarily, by directing the passive deviance of illness into closely supervised medical channels where it finds expression, but cannot easily spread. The third is facilitation of the therapeutic process—not only technologically, but in a <u>motivational</u> sense as well.

We wish to point out that such new insights as we have been able to gain into these matters are only possible because of certain rather recent developments in the sciences of human action: above all, the possibility of bringing sociological and psychological analysis to bear upon the same set of problems in a complementary way. A simple sociological analysis of family structure and of the therapeutic system would not have helped us very much; nor, we feel, would a purist personality theory approach have proven especially enlightening. And yet when the two are put together a quite new order of understanding emerges.

We have deliberately kept our discussion on a theoretical level, without attempting to work out its possible practical import; for, within the scope of a single article, it would not have been possible to do justice to both. In conclusion, however, we would like to suggest that the potential implications of our analysis for practice ramify in several directions. For example, we think

---

[14]Even so, the restoration of the actor to his kinship unit, to his job, and to his other non-sick orbits, is usually problem-laden. For one thing, we have already shown that at this juncture we encounter the well-known phenomenon of secondary gain; a possible consequence if the transference relationship of patient and physician, and the supportive-exemptive features of illness are not adequately controlled.

that perhaps we can aid physicians and hospital administrators in their search for effective ways of dealing with the family members of their patients. Further, our material also seems relevant to the question of how visiting privileges and other forms of association with hospital patients accorded to families could be more optimally managed. It is our belief, however, that most important and far-reaching of all is the fact that both theoretically and empirically, the social and psychological sciences are now highly enough evolved to make "illness, therapy, and the family" a fruitful field of action research. We hope we can stimulate some of our readers to take advantage of this newly emergent opportunity.

Alcoholism, Crime, and Delinquency in Soviet Society

Mark G. Field

SOURCE: *Social Problems*, Vol. 3 (1955), pp. 100–109.

Under present conditions, a quantitative insight into social problems in Soviet society is unattainable because of censorship, the inability of Western social scientists to do field work in the USSR, and the lack of statistical data. Yet a qualitative study of the Soviet means of mass communication, the domestic press in particular, is not by any means impossible. Such investigation reveals that Soviet society has its full share of disturbing phenomena such as juvenile delinquency, crime and alcoholism, and that these pose definite problems to the regime both in having to cope with these aspects of social disorganization and in providing an ideologically consistent explanation. Soviet theorists maintain that their society is a new and advanced type, with full employment and no economic crises, in which "the people", having seized the means of production from capitalistic exploiters and guided by the wise hand of the Party (it used to be Stalin's), are happily advancing, arm in arm, toward the "good" society, i. e. toward communism. Soviet sources, however, hardly confirm this idealized and idyllic picture of the "workers' state."

On the contrary, Soviet society seems to be affected by many social problems that are allegedly the symptoms of a decayed capitalist system plus a few of its very own. The rather considerable amount of space devoted to these questions in Soviet Russia may be indicative of their seriousness, particularly when seen in the light of a regime-controlled press and limited newsprint. There is, furthermore, evidence that the cases reported and commented upon in the Soviet sources are not unique but typical of a general pattern affecting Soviet society as a whole.

JUVENILE AND ADOLESCENT DELINQUENCY

Juvenile delinquency which appears to be a problem of major proportions, is characterized primarily by considerable drinking among adolescents and sometimes by the formation of gangs for criminal purposes. Although Soviet law prohibits the sale of alcoholic beverages to minors, the latter do not as a rule appear to experience any difficulties in purchasing drinks either from package stores or from drink-shops.[1]

This delinquency, in turn, is abetted by the indifference of officials and private citizens who have adopted an attitude of non-interference in the criminal or semi-criminal activities of youths. For example, waitresses in taverns have no scruples in selling drinks and cigarettes to teen-agers as long as they have money; policemen will buy coal they know has been stolen by juvenile gangs; and armed railroad guards (a common feature in the Soviet Union) often do not intervene when school-children loot railroad cars.[2] In the schools, teachers are unable to stem the tide of juvenile delinquency or even to maintain discipline. There are countless examples of brutality inside and outside the schools (sometimes with fatal results), including the molesting of school personnel.[3] Soviet sources place a great deal of the responsibility for this delinquency directly at the doorstep of the Young Communist League (Komsomols) and its affiliated childrens' organizations (Pioneers, Oktobrists) for their failure to curb drinking among their members and among youths in general, for their tolerance of rowdyism[4] and for their inability to provide and devise programs that will hold children's interests and channel their energies into useful and more constructive activities.[5] At the 12th Komsomol Congress held in 1954, the Secretary of the Komsomol Central Committee declared, among other things, that

.... there are cases of unworthy behavior in public places, on the streets or in the schools, of rudeness to teachers, parents and adults . . . of hooliganism . . . . The activities [of Komsomol organizations] suffer from monotony and lack of variety.... they are too regimented and too "organized"... The work of many clubs.... does not satisfy young people . . . who lead parasitic lives. Loudly dressed young people with Tarzan haircuts, so-called "zootsuiters," roam and main streets of Moscow, Leningrad . . . and other cities. They do not work or study but spend their evenings in bars or heckling girls ... the Komsomols must proclaim relentless ... war against all kinds of zoot-suiters, "aristocrats" and other parasites and hoodlums....[6]

Parallel to the problem caused by the Komsomols' inability to cope with juvenile delinquency, is the concern caused by the emergence of a jeunesse dorée consisting primarily of the sons of powerful officials and successful intellectuals, whose life, according to the press, is an almost continuous round of pleasure, dissipation, debauchery, and sometimes crime. These adolescents are, in fact, the spoiled children of the new Soviet "aristocracy," whose parents have never denied them anything nor imbued them with a sense of responsibility.[7] Particularly revealing as an illustration is an article in Komsomolskaya Pravda, the Komsomol central organ, which describes the life of some of these young men.[8] Their night life revolved around the "Cocktail Hall" on fashionable Gorki Street in Moscow where they spent most of their evenings drinking, and carousing[9]. Leaving the Hall almost at dawn they would get into a car, "round up some girls," and then go to one of the

[1]A. Kairov, "Tasks of the Soviet school," Komsomolskaya Pravda, (August 8, 1954), 2.

[2]"An independent man," Komsomolskaya Pravda, (November 1, 1953), 2.

[3]"Incident at school," Izvestiya, (February 19, 1954), 2.

[4]"Uninhibited hoodlums and timid activists," Komsomolskaya Pravda, April 3, 1954), 3; "Why we did not like the excursion," Komsomolskaya Pravda, (July 7, 1954), 2; "Why were the Komsomols silent" Komsomolskaya Pravda, (May 8, 1954), 3.

[5]"For cultured rest and healthy life," Komsomolskaya Pravda, (July 9, 1954), 1; "For healthy life," Izvestiya, (September 17, 1954), 2.

[6]A. N. Shelepin, "Report of the Komsomol Central Committee to the 12th Congress," Komsomolskaya Pravda, (March 20, 1954), 2-4.

[7]"Mama, papa and son," Izvestiya, (December 27, 1953), 2; "Under papa's wing," Komsomolskaya Pravda, (December 21, 1953), 3.

[8]"Blight," Komsomolskaya Pravda (November 19, 1953), 3.

[9]The Hall was subsequently turned into an ice-cream parlor. Harrison I. Salisbury, "Russia Reviewed; Crime Wave Goes Unchecked," The New York Times (October 1, 1954).

gang's family summer cottages where the party would resume. Hard pressed for funds to finance their escapades, the boys stole equipment from laboratories, rings from their girl-friends or books and other valuable objects from their parents' apartment. Once, afraid an acquaintance would report them to the authorities, they murdered him; apprehended later, they were put on trial. One of the gang members' biography affords a rare view into the new Soviet gilded youth.

. . . . From childhood, Andrei never was refused anything . . . No matter what he wanted, it appeared as if at the wave of a magic wand. One day he mentioned an automobile, and soon a new "Moskvich" car stood at the door. His father's "Victory" car was also at his disposal . . . [he] was an utter parasite, but his parents, blinded with love, saw in him only a tender son . . . when he entered college, papa began to give him a thousand roubles a month for "pocket money" . . . he had to do no more than cough and they would immediately put him on a plane and send him to a southern resort even if examinations were coming up . . . the thought never entered Andrei's head that some day he would have to earn his own daily bread. His entire life he intended to remain Academician Peredery's son and enjoy all the blessings stemming from this status . . . . the fulfillment of [these youths'] every wish had accustomed them to the thought that everything is permitted to them. As is known, the so-called "gilded youth" of pre-revolutionary times were imbued with the same ideas . . . In our country everyone lives by his labor. Each one's position and his place in life depends on his labor. . . .

The reference to ascribed, as against achieved status, and implications for Soviet society and Soviet ideology are unmistakable. They are clearly a reflection of increased social stratification in Soviet society.[10] It should be noted that Andrei, in addition to the thousand roubles his father gave him as pin money, also drew a state stipend

at the university, this at the time the average worker earned in the vicinity of six to eight hundred roubles a month. Thus neither poverty nor comic books nor television programs drove Andrei and his friends to crime. What then did? According to the Soviet author, it was love for money. Yet, this same author is at a loss to explain where this love came from:

. . . . how could such blight arise in the healthy midst of our Soviet youth—these people without honor or conscience, without a goal in life. . . . for whom money was the highest ideal of happiness. . . . Whence came these corrupt types—types which seem to have stepped from American ganster films? What set these nineteen year old Moscow University students on the road to crime?[11]

One of the suggested answers is that the parents are to blame. For example, a cartoon in Krokodil, the Soviet satirical magazine, entitled "Mama's One and Only" shows a wife berating her husband for giving their son "only a measly one hundred roubles," to go out. She adds that children of "good" (solidnyi, solid) parents go to restaurants, whereas her son "like an orphan" will have to go "drink beer," obviously a sign of lower class activity.[12] Most, if not all, of these young "aristocrats" are, of course, university students, an indication of high status by itself because it exempts them from a labor draft to which children of the working classes are more readily liable, and since tuition fees must be paid in the last three years of secondary schools and all through the university.[13] It is also clear that many such students do not and cannot take their studies seriously, since they feel that "papa" and "mama" will always be there to provide for them. These students, at the same time, often manage to circumvent

[10] Alex Inkeles, "Social Stratification and Mobility in the Soviet Union: 1940-1950," American Sociological Review, 15 (August 1950), 465-479; W. W. Kulski, "Classes in the Classless State," Problems of Communism, 4 (January-February, 1955) 20-28.

[11] "Blight," Komsomolskaya Pravda (November 19, 1953), 3.

[12] "Mama's One and Only," Krokodil, (March 20, 1954), 6.

[13] James H. Meisel and Edward S. Kozera, Materials for the Study of the Soviet System, Ann Arbor: George Wahr, 1950, pp. 358-367.

assignments to the countryside and out-lying districts [14] which are the rule for those who graduate from the universities and which last from two to five years.[15] Thanks to their parents' powerful con-nections, they remain in the cities where they obtain easy jobs or may not work at all.[16] This is indeed an endemic problem which plagues the Soviet Union (it is referred to as "ruralophobia") and it seems to apply with greatest force to the children of middle and upper class parentage, and particularly to the girls whose mothers keep them home in the hope of "marrying them well." The situa-tion was neatly epitomized in another drawing in Krokodil showing a young girl yawning on a sofa, being served tea by a maid and saying: "Well, at last I have finished the institute, now I can take it easy for the rest of my life."[17] Education then, has become for some members of Soviet society a pre-rogative, a mark of prestige and "class," rather than the means to earn one's liv-ing and to be useful to society. These are disturbing trends indeed, from the viewpoint of Soviet society and Soviet ideology. On the one hand, failure to reach into all classes to discover tal-ented individuals may deprive the system of the needed services of the able but poor individual and might lead in the long-run, to a self-perpetuating ruling class steeped in mediocrity. On the other hand, this is a trend so contrary to basic ideological tenets that it may, if allowed to run its course, become threatening for a society so consciously based on an explicit doctrine.

At the same time, the increasing rig-idity of class lines may not be irrele-

vant to an understanding of the rise in crime and drinking among the less priv-ileged members of the population, as will be pointed out in the final section of this paper. But alcoholism and crime are not confined, of course, to the younger pop-ulation. They appear to have affected vir-tually all layers of Soviet society, includ-ing the upper, tone-setting "cultured" elements, particularly the writers and the artists.

DRINKING AND "WHITE COLLAR CRIM-INALITY" AMONG THE CULTURED CLASSES

One of the giants of Soviet literature, Fyodor Gladkov, the author of Cement, in an article published in the Litera-turnaya Gazeta, the organ of the Union of Soviet Writers, maintains that writers should set an example, in their personal behavior, of the "new Soviet man's moral-ity." Yet there are certain Soviet writers, who drink to excess and who generally deport themselves so as to bring dis-credit and disrepute upon the writing profession. Furthermore, writers who occupy administrative positions in the Union (of Writers) have been known to embezzle large sums of money and to have remained unpunished. What is even worse, Gladkov maintains, is that other writers view this either with in-difference or with tolerance or even some kind of benign amusement. He calls for a campaign against "violators of so-cialist ethics," against drunkenness and debauchery because "everything tolerated today becomes tomorrow's encourage-ment to further drunken hoodlumism." There are, according to him, in the healthy circle of Soviet writers some who, having closeted themselves in their cozy apartments, have lost touch with the "masses":

... Soviet writers should not be judged by these bohemian rakes and nouveau-riches with their bourgeois ways. They are alien ... unworthy of bearing the title of Soviet writer ... The Union of Writers and [its] Party Organization should genuinely rouse public opinion against petty bourgeois egotism, dis-

---

[14] Where the need for specialists with a higher education is always pressing. This applies par-ticularly to doctors, engineers, and teachers.

[15] Vladimir Gsovski, Soviet Civil Law, Ann Arbor: University of Michigan Law School, 1948. Vol. I. p. 800. (Resolution of June 23, 1936 on Higher Education).

[16] "To Moscow, to Moscow," Komsomolskaya Pravda (September 21, 1950), 2.

[17] "They raised a daughter," Krokodil, (June 20, 1954), 5.

soluteness, drunkenness and brawling. A complacent ... attitude is politically ·shortsighted .... Strict measures must be taken promptly to make unthinkable any outrage and amoral acts which are alien to our community life.[18]

In a follow-up Gladkov points out that not only writers drink to excess, but also artists and composers "whose names have become synonymous with tavern boozers and hoodlums." He reports having received letters, indicating that people in all <u>walks</u> of Soviet cultural life drink to excess. For example, at a teachers' district conference, a "respected man of letters" from Moscow was to deliver a lecture:

.... there appeared on the platform a man drunk as a lord, who talked rubbish and mixed up Euclid with Eucalyptus...[19]

One further complaint is that not only too many artists and writers drink but that too many artistic productions embody, in one form or another a glorification or at least a very passive attitude toward the problem of drinking. There is hardly a play, a movie, a radio program or a popular music record that does not encourage the listener or the reader to raise his glass and drink up.[20] And the effect of such encouragement upon younger manual workers can readily be imagined. This cannot leave the regime unconcerned because this affects industrial production, an area of vital importance in the Soviet scheme.

DRINKING AND CRIME AMONG SOVIET WORKERS

Hard drinking seems to be widespread among Soviet manual workers.[21] Apparently it is considered, in some workers' circles, a sign of manliness and serves as a badge of acceptance. The worker who can blow one hundred rou-

bles on drinks in one evening becomes something of a hero.[22] On the other hand, those who refuse to join in are accused of being "weak sisters."[23] There have been reported cases when foremen discriminated against workers or refused to hire them if they did not pay them a tribute in vodka.[24] Furthermore, it is far easier for a worker to obtain vodka and drinks than reading material. Workers who drink turn out shoddy goods, their production falls, they are often absent, and are downgraded to menial jobs or worse. While drinking appears to be more prevalent among those engaged in hazardous occupations, such as coal-mining,[25] it generally affects most manual workers, including fishermen[26] and even railroad workers. In the first five months of 1954, there were not less than nineteen cases of workers appearing drunk for work at the Moscow-Kursk railroad depot.[27] In addition, workers who drink often join criminal elements.[28] For example, <u>Trud,</u> the central organ of the trade unions, published an article early in 1954, describing the sentencing of three young unmarried workers to long terms of imprisonment for burglary and robbery. They had gone to work in a large enterprise, and lived in a dormitory. While things at work went well, life outside working hours and particularly in the dormitory, was boring. Newspapers and books were unavailable; they did not know what to do with themselves.

.... One evening an unfamiliar young man walked into the room... he smelled of vodka

[18]____, "On the subject of the writer's ethics," <u>Literaturnaya Gazeta</u>, (April 6, 1954), 2.
[19]Fyodor Gladkov, "A most evil vice," <u>Literaturnaya Gazeta</u> (July 29, 1954), 2.
[20]"Going in for the arts," <u>Komsomolskaya Pravda</u>, (July 6, 1954), 2.
[21]"A certain unpleasant phenomenon," <u>Komsomolskaya Pravda</u> (May 13, 1954), 2.

[22]"Drunkenness dishonors the miner," <u>Literaturnaya Gazeta</u>, (July 27, 1954), 2; "On false manliness..." <u>Komsomolskaya Pravda</u>, (July 27, 1954), 2.
[23]"Green sentry-boxes," <u>Komsomolskaya Pravda</u> (May 7, 1954), 3.
[24]"Shakedown," <u>Komsomolskaya Pravda</u>, (July 16, 1954), 4.
[25]"Drunkenness dishonors the miner," <u>Literaturnaya Gazeta</u> (July 27, 1954), 2.
[26]"A false tradition," <u>Literaturnaya Gazeta</u>, (August 5, 1954), 2.
[27]"The engineer was drunk," <u>Trud</u> (July 11, 1954), 4.
[28]"Always guard public order," <u>Izvestiya</u> (September 23, 1954), 2.

... The boys told the stranger about themselves and complained of boredom. The stranger said: "Bored, eh? You babies. All you need is two hundred grams of vodka apiece and things will be lively enough. Give me ten roubles." [Later] vodka... appeared on the table. The young man accompanied each glass with a comment: "You have to know how to live! Get it? Working is for fools. We'll get along without work. Get it?"

After that, evening life seemed more interesting, but in the morning heads ached and hands shook. The boys had no desire to go to work, they came late, or did not come to work at all. They would disappear in the evening, no one knew where. Soon they appeared at work every other day. The foreman decided to turn in their names to the manager for court action, as is the procedure in Soviet labor law, but before the court got to the case they were arrested for burglaries, one of which ended in a murder attempt.[29] With crime and particularly alcoholism on the increase, industrial production is bound to suffer.[30] "Even a single case of absenteeism," says an article in Trud, "thwarts the efforts of conscientious workers in conditions of complex machinery and mass production."[31]

And by the same token, the regime is also concerned with the same phenomena as they apply to the collective farmers and to agricultural production, a sensitive area in the Soviet Union.

THE SITUATION ON THE FARMS

Drinking among collective farmers appears to be prevalent, and is often sparked by festivals of all conceivable types, some celebrating local saints, others regional or national figures. Writing in Literaturnaya Gazeta V. Sapozhnikova describes, for example, the cele-

brating of St. Tikhon Day, typical of many such a holiday:

Visitors flooded the village of Polubabino from morning. They came from every direction to drink.... By all accounts a notable drinking spree was in the offing. A month previous, people had begun to make home brew and to prepare refreshments. Three days before the "holiday" fifty collective farmers, more than one-fourth of the entire working force, had gone to the nearest workers' settlement to make purchases.... glasses clinked in every house. A strong intoxicating odor of home brew pervaded the air, and discordant songs issued from the windows... "Who is this Tikhon, grandmother?" I asked an old woman "What did he do to the people to be so honored?" "Tikhon?" she replied, "Who cares? It's not for us to bother. He is home brew, that's all."... those who collapsed were dragged over a fence, doused with water, and left to lie until they came to and resumed drinking ... Zaitsev, Chairman of the Rural Consumers Cooperative (he is also secretary of the Party organization at a neighborhood collective farm) did a brisk trade in vodka ...[32]

Apparently, the regime here is caught on the horns of its own dilemma. In line with its post-Stalin policy of conciliating the population, it has toned down its anti-religious policy.[33] In the country-side, the strong-hold of religious beliefs, Party officials attempt not to antagonize the population and give permission for holidays to be celebrated. These holidays, the meaning of which, apparently, has been lost to most, often turn into drunken brawls during which, of course, none or very little of the field work gets done, and for which Party officials will later carry the responsibility. In the Moslem parts of the Soviet Union, where drinking is less of a problem, Moslem pilgrimages and holidays are also said to interfere with collective farm work.[34] In the Vologda Province,

[29]"From the courtroom: When sentence is pronounced," Trud (February 21, 1954), 2.
[30]"Gangster punished," Izvestiya (January 10, 1954), 2; "Always guard public order," Izvestiya (September 23, 1954), 2.
[31]"Old things do not disappear by themselves," Trud (June 29, 1954), 2.

[32]"St. Tikhon's Day," Literaturnaya Gazeta, (July 24, 1954), 2 (emphasis supplied).
[33]Andre Pierre, "Religion in Soviet Land," Problems of Communism, 4 (May-June, 1955), 19-28.
[34]"What a pilgrimage costs," Komsomolskaya Pravda (August 21, 1954), 2.

for example, 10,000 work-days were reportedly lost to religious festivals at the height of the 1954 harvest.[35] The persistence of religious beliefs is blamed on poor "ideological" work among collective farmers on the part of Party organizations. Party and Komsomol members are accused of compromising with "alien influences" and sometimes of participating in the religious celebrations themselves. If it is remembered that agricultural production is still very much of a critical problem in the Soviet Union, one can understand the regime's concern with the countless religious festivals celebrated in the countryside, the drinking and the attendant loss of time. There appears to be less criminality among collective farmers than among industrial workers, although there are numerous reports of collective farm chairmen abusing their authority and terrorizing the farmers. "The root of evil," writes a reader in a letter to the editor of Izvestiya "is the constant drinking of collective farm officials... Ivanov, the collective farm chairman, drinks ceaselessly. He has surrounded himself with drunkards, flatterers, and thieves, just like himself...."[36] There are also reports of the production of home brew (often abetted by collective farm chairmen themselves and sometimes with fatal results)[37] and of petty thefts of collective farm property and produce.[38]

THE OFFICIAL EXPLANATION

Social problems, and alcoholism in particular, according to official Soviet ideology are the products of a diseased and disorganized economy and society, i.e., of capitalism. This view originally derives from Engels' work in the Condition of the Working Classes in England, in which he maintains that under capitalistic conditions, the overworked, exploited, underfed, ill-housed, and ill-clothed worker seeks temporary solace and oblivion in alcohol. The exploiting classes, in addition, encourage the use and sale of alcoholic beverages not only because these bring in huge profits, but also because alcohol, just like religion, dulls the worker's social consciousness and revolutionary ardor; alcohol, is thus another tool in the capitalist arsenal. Therefore, a successful fight against alcoholism is possible only where the capitalist system has been eliminated. This means that "In the USSR where class exploitation has been ended forever, where the welfare of the population increases all the time, the social roots of alcoholism have been extirpated."[39] Yet, the incontrovertible fact remains, and the Soviet press confirms it, alcoholism and its attendant evils, rather than disappearing from the Soviet scene may, on the contrary, be on the increase. What then accounts for its existence? The theoretical explanation is one that has been used time and again to explain away certain embarrassing features of Soviet society: it is that of the famous "remnants of capitalist consciousness"[40] still existing in the minds of some Soviet citizens. It is part of the accursed heritage of the past, a legacy from a blighted period, a "lag" between changes in the "social structure" and the "consciousness of the people." Thus the Communists place the responsibility for social disorganization not on conditions existing under the Soviet system, but squarely on a political and social structure that was eliminated more than thirty-five years ago. The explanation as to how these remnants manage to exist, persist, and grow in the conditions of a socialist society is as follows:

[35] "On Saint's days," Komsomolskaya Pravda, (July 29, 1954), 2.
[36] "Out with the thistle from the kolkhoze harvest," Pravda Ukrainy (October 15, 1953), 2; "We do not need this kind of chairman," Izvestiya (July 8, 1954), 2; "With enthusiasm...," Pravda Ukrainy, (October 9, 1953), 2.
[37] "Bootleggers from Starye Algashy," Literaturnaya Gazeta (July 13, 1954), 2.
[38] S. P. Mitrichev, "Improve quality of investigations of theft of state and communal property," Sovetskoye Gosudarstvo i Pravo, 5 (1953), 91.

[39] "Alcoholism," The Great Soviet Encyclopedia, (in Russian), 2nd edition, Vol. 2, pp. 117-119 (emphasis supplied).
[40] S. Kurashov, "For a healthy life," Pravda (August 6, 1954), 2.

The Party proceeds from the viewpoint that life, worthy of socialism, does not come about by itself... automatically, but demands a struggle, a constant uprooting of the heritage of the capitalist society. The Party always considers that survivals of capitalism are still alive, that they will not disappear in the course of one generation, but may even be strengthened if a fight is not carried against them constantly.... there is evidence that quite often there is indifference.... to some of the most harmful survivals of capitalism.... Quite often... at Party meetings devoted to drunkenness at work, this problem is greeted with smiles. With such an attitude somehow we legalize drunkenness.... there is a lot of drunkenness on the collective farms... Where there is no campaign conducted against drunkenness, there are cases of drinking among adolescents, school children... but we must be careful that [in this struggle] some lecturers and authors do not exaggerate... one predicted the most terrible diseases if lumbermen drank as much as eighty to one hundred grams of vodka... this can only cause an ironic attitude.... it only weakens the struggle against alcoholism .... [41]

This then is the manner in which, officially speaking, there is a rationalization of the fact that the elimination of capitalism did not lead to the automatic elimination of alcoholism and related forms of social disorganization. What then, are some of the factors which, according to the Soviets and at a practical everyday level, facilitate, indeed even encourage, drinking and crime in contemporary Soviet society?

FACTORS FACILITATING ALCOHOLISM AND CRIME

The first factor is, of course, that of availability. Soviet citizens of all ages find it easy to purchase alcoholic drinks, and particularly vodka (its price has recently gone down.) [42] These are sold everywhere, particularly in the streets,

in booths, bars and drink stands called "green sentry boxes," and which are dotting, in increasing and alarming numbers, Soviet cities and workers' settlements. The sale of alcoholic beverages is a state monopoly and its financial contribution to the state budget is far from negligible. In addition, this serves to drain excessive purchasing power and has a salutary effect on inflationary trends. Yet Soviet authorities are obviously and genuinely disturbed about the abuse of alcohol and the increasing ease with which it has become available to the population: There are for instance many street stands which originally were designed to sell ice cream, mineral water, and tea. Many of them now dispense vodka. [43] Booths and drink shops are not, of course operated by private individuals or entrepreneurs. They belong to state food-handling trusts. These organizations, in turn, are run commercially and must show a profit at the end of their financial year. Managers have found out that it was much easier to fulfill or overfulfill their financial plans by dispensing alcoholic beverages than any other item. [44] But perhaps more important, as a contributory cause, is the boredom and drabness that seem to characterize the leisure hours of the Soviet citizenry, particularly the industrial workers and the youths. [45] One article, recently published in Izvestiya describes the almost unbelievable dreariness of a Sunday in a workers' settlement: the same movie is shown time and again, there is no entertainment.

.... Sunday is boring in Khokhol, everyone passes the time as best as he can, and the only place where there is any life is in the tearooms and the snack bars.... the district Soviet passed a resolution banning the sale of

---

[41]"Struggle for a healthy life—important task of the Soviet collectivity," Partiinaya Zhizn (August 9, 1954), 38-41 (emphasis supplied).

[42]Harrison I. Salisbury, "Russia Reviewed: Crime Wave Goes Unchecked," The New York Times (October 1, 1954),

[43]"A certain unpleasant phenomenon," Komsomolskaya Pravda (May 13, 1954), 2.

[44]"Pressing problems in the development of communal feeding," Pravda (March 2, 1954), 2; Shvernik, "Speech at the 11th Congress of the Trade Unions," Ivzestiya (June 8, 1954), 3.

[45]"On abysmal ignorance and abysmal boredom," Komsomolskaya Pravda (July 31, 1954), 3.

vodka on the premises but the strong drink addicts have managed to circumvent the resolution... people drink at home too, and not just vodka but bootleg alcohol as well .... There are always a lot of drunks on the streets on Sunday. Drunken orgies and brawls have become common at the Culture Center ....[46]

What is true of industrial workers, is also true of the youths and adolescents, who often turn to drinking, to the forming of gangs, and to criminal activities, sometimes only for the thrill and excitement. These children's predilection for the "Western" type of amusement, their imitation of "American bourgeois-gangster mannerisms" is, as noted before, a source of amazement and concern for Soviet authorities.[47]

Finally, as a contributory factor to the rise in crime, the Amnesty Decree of 1953 should be mentioned. Many of those who had been amnestied were not, for many reasons, able or willing to live as law-abiding citizens, and returned to a life of criminality. Some of these have been caught and sent back to prison or camps.[48]

PROPOSED REMEDIES

If drinking is such a problem, and given the totalitarian nature of the Soviet system, why then does the government not pass a dry law, or at least severely restrict the production of alcohol? The Soviets are not unmindful of the failure of Prohibition in the United States, and seem to have resigned themselves to the idea that people will drink, prohibition or no prohibition. Indeed, they realize that such a move would raise more problems than it would solve. They describe a dry law as something hypocritical, "a puritanical measure alien to the Soviet people."[49] They thus prefer to control drinking as much as possible and to prevent abuses. The measures advocated are: intensifying propaganda against the consumption of alcoholic beverages, particularly hard liquor (vodka), encouraging the population to drink beer and wines, a stiffening of public opinion toward habitual drunkards, increase in recreational activities, bolstering the authority of the police (militsia), and a demonstration of the harmful consequences of alcohol for the human organism. While the Ministry of Health is expected to carry this last part of the program,[50] the full weight of the regime's means of mass communication has been enlisted in that direction. Indeed, the picture of alcoholism and crime as it emerges from the Soviet press and on which this paper is based, would not be available if such a campaign had not been launched. In its campaign against crime, the death penalty has recently been reintroduced in cased of premeditated murder, and steps are being taken to reinforce the law forbidding the sale of liquor to minors. It still remains to be seen whether the regime will be successful in this, particularly in view of other factors not mentioned in the press.

SOME FURTHER HYPOTHESES

Drinking and other related social problems, particularly among the younger members of the population, may well be linked to the erosion of family functions that accompanies industrialization and the removal from the home, during working hours, of the father and, in Soviet society, quite often of the mother. Since 1936 the regime has taken drastic measures to increase family stability and to reverse the "light-minded attitude" toward family obligations which had resulted from earlier policies of easy di-

---

[46]"Day off in Khokhol," Izvestiya (August 5, 1954), 3.

[47]"Blight," Komsomolskaya Pravda (November 19, 1953), 3.

[48]"Amnestied condemned again," Pravda Vostoka (December 12, 1953), 4; "Trial: Robbers," Trud (June 24, 1954), 4.

[49]"Behind a blue fence," Komsomolskaya Pravda (March 17, 1954), 3.

[50]A. Aleksandrovsky, "A physician's note: how it [drunkenness] begins," Komsomolskaya Pravda (August 4, 1954), 2.

vorces and legalized abortions.[51] There
is as yet little evidence that such measures have been successful. Furthermore, the youths of today are part of
the "war generation," brought up without
close parental supervision, under conditions of severe deprivations, often forced
to fend for themselves without knowledge
of a peaceful, normal life. These youths
may find it difficult to adapt themselves
to a more orderly way of life, and may
prefer to keep on dodging work and
living on the fringes of Soviet society.

At the same time, alcoholism and
crime may well be linked to a general
weariness on the part of the population
with both the tempo and the drabness of
Soviet life, with unfulfilled promises,
with excessive demands put on human
beings and lack of commensurate rewards. This certainly is the burden of
much of the criticism made by refugees
who left the Soviet Union immediately
before and during the war; and from all

evidence available, this applies equally to
the postwar period. Furthermore, it may
be presumed that the hardening of the
stratification lines that has been in progress since the middle thirties has made
social mobility difficult to achieve for the
lower classes so that there is less incentive on the part of the members of these
classes to "be sober" and apply themselves in order to rise in the social
structure.[52] The presence of a "gilded
youth" of adolescents who can ride on
their parents' coat-tails and enjoy the life
of leisure of "young aristocrats" is another index of the decrease in mobility
and of careers open to those who work
hard.

And finally, as anyone acquainted with
the pre-revolutionary literature well
knows, alcoholism and its attendant evils
are not a new phenomenon in Russian
life. To say the least, the inability of
the Soviet regime to break away from
this pattern makes its claim of having
changed "society and the nature of man"
subject to certain qualifications.

---

[51]Mark G. Field, "Social Services for the Family
in the Soviet Union," Marriage and Family Living,
17 (August, 1955), 244-249; Kent Geiger and Alex
Inkeles, "The Family in the U.S.S.R.," Marriage
and Family Living, 26 (November 1954), 397-404.

[52]Alex Inkeles, "Social Stratification and Mobility in the Soviet Union: 1940-1950," American
Sociological Review, 15 (August 1950) 465-479.

SOCIAL CONTROL AND SOCIAL CHANGE

Social Control in the Newsroom: A Functional Analysis

Warren Breed

SOURCE: *Social Forces*, Vol. 33 (1955), pp. 326–35.

Top leaders in formal organizations
are makers of policy, but they must also
secure and maintain conformity to that
policy at lower levels. The situation of
the newspaper publisher is a case in
point. As owner or representative of

ownership, he has the nominal right to
set the paper's policy and see that staff
activities are coordinated so that the
policy is enforced. In actuality the problem of control is less simple, as the
literature of "human relations" and in-

formal group studies and of the professions[1] suggests.

Ideally, there would be no problem of either "control" or "policy" on the newspaper in a full democracy. The only controls would be the nature of the event and the reporter's effective ability to describe it. In practice, we find the publisher does set news policy, and this policy is usually followed by members of his staff. Conformity is <u>not</u> automatic, however, for three reasons: (1) the existence of ethical journalistic norms; (2) the fact that staff subordinates (reporters, etc.) tend to have more "liberal" attitudes (and therefore perceptions) than the publisher and could invoke the norms to justify anti-policy writing; and (3) the ethical taboo preventing the publisher from commanding subordinates to follow policy. How policy comes to be maintained, and where it is bypassed, is the subject of this paper.

Several definitions are required at this point. As to personnel, "newsmen" can be divided into "staffers" and executives. Executives include the publisher and his editors. "Staffers" are reporters, rewrite men, copy readers, etc. In between there may be occasional city editors or wire editors who occupy an interstitial status. "Policy" may be defined as the more or less consistent orientation shown by a paper, not only in its editorial but in its news columns and headlines as well, concerning selected issues and events. "Slanting" almost never means prevarication. Rather, it involves omission, differential selection and preferential placement, such as "featuring" a pro-policy item, "burying" an anti-policy story in an inside page, etc. "Professional norms" are of two types: technical norms deal with the operations of efficient news gathering, writing, and editing; ethical norms embrace the newsman's obligation to his readers and to his craft and include such ideals as

responsibility, impartiality, accuracy, fair play, and objectivity.[2]

Every newspaper has a policy, admitted or not.[3] One paper's policy may be pro-Republican, cool to labor, antagonistic to the school board, etc. The principal areas of policy are politics, business, and labor; much of it stems from considerations of class. Policy is manifested in "slanting." Just what determines any publisher's policy is a large question and will not be discussed here. Certainly, however, the publisher has much say (often in veto form) in both long-term and immediate policy decisions (which party to support, whether to feature or bury a story of imminent labor trouble, how much freespace to give "news" of advertisers' doings, etc.). Finally, policy is covert, due to the existence of ethical norms of journalism; policy often contravenes these norms. No executive is willing to risk embarrassment by being accused of open commands to slant a news story.

While policy is set by the executives, it is clear that they cannot personally gather and write the news by themselves. They must delegate these tasks to staffers, and at this point the attitudes or interests of staffers may—and often do—conflict with those of the executives.[4]

---

[2]The best-known formal code is The Canons of Journalism, of the American Society of Newspaper Editors. See Wilbur Schramm (ed.), <u>Mass Communications</u> (Urbana: University of Illinois Press, 1949), pp. 236-38.

[3]It is extremely difficult to measure the extent of objectivity or bias. One recent attempt is reported in Nathan B. Blumberg, <u>A One-Party Press?</u> (Lincoln: University of Nebraska Press, 1954), which gives a news count for 35 papers' performance in the 1952 election campaign. He concluded that 18 of the papers showed "no evidence of partiality," 11 showed "no conclusive evidence of partiality," and 6 showed partiality. His interpretations, however, are open to argument. A different interpretation could conclude that while about 16 showed little or no partiality, the rest did. It should be noted, too, that there are different areas of policy depending on local conditions. The chief difference occurs in the deep South, where frequently there is no "Republican" problem and no "union" problem over which the staff can be divided. Color becomes the focus of policy.

[4]This condition, pointed out in a lecture by Paul F. Lazarsfeld, formed the starting point for the present study.

---

[1]See, for instance, F. J. Roethlisberger and William J. Dickson, <u>Management and the Worker</u> (Cambridge· Harvard University Press, 1947); and Logan Wilson, <u>The Academic Man</u> (New York: Oxford University Press, 1942).

Of 72 staffers interviewed, 42 showed that they held more liberal views than those contained in their publisher's policy; 27 held similar views, and only 3 were more conservative. Similarly, only 17 of 61 staffers said they were Republicans.[5] The discrepancy is more acute when age (and therefore years of newspaper experience) is held constant. Of the 46 staffers under 35 years of age, 34 showed more liberal orientations; older men had apparently "mellowed." It should be noted that data as to intensity of attitudes are lacking. Some staffers may disagree with policy so mildly that they conform and feel no strain. The present essay is pertinent only insofar as dissident newsmen are forced to make decisions from time to time about their relationship to policy.[6]

We will now examine more closely the workings of the newspaper staff. The central question will be: How is policy maintained, despite the fact that it often contravenes journalistic norms, that staffers often personally disagree with it, and that executives cannot legitimately command that it be followed? The frame of reference will be that of functional analysis, as embodied in Merton's paradigm.[7]

---

[5]Similar findings were made about Washington correspondents in Leo C. Rosten, The Washington Correspondents (New York: Harcourt, Brace, 1937). Less ideological conflict was found in two other studies: Francis V. Prugger, "Social Composition and Training of the Milwaukee Journal News Staff," Journalism Quarterly, 18 (Sept. 1941), pp. 231-44, and Charles E. Swanson, The Mid-City Daily (Ph.D. dissertation, State University of Iowa, 1948). Possible reasons for the gap is that both papers studied were perhaps above average in objectivity; executives were included with staffers in computations; and some staffers were doubtless included who did not handle policy news.

[6]It is not being argued that "liberalism" and objectivity are synonymous. A liberal paper (e.g., PM) can be biased too, but it is clear that few liberal papers exist among the many conservative ones. It should also be stressed that much news is not concerned with policy and is therefore probably unbiased.

[7]Robert K. Merton, Social Theory and Social Structure (Glencoe: Free Press, 1949), esp. pp. 49-61. Merton's elements will not be explicitly referred to but his principal requirements are discussed at various points.

The present data come from the writer's newspaper experience and from intensive interviews with some 120 newsmen, mostly in the northeastern quarter of the country. The sample was not random and no claim is made for representativeness, but on the other hand no paper was selected or omitted purposely and in no case did a newsman refuse the request that he be interviewed. The newspapers were chosen to fit a "middle-sized" group, defined as those with 10,000 to 100,000 daily circulation. Interviews averaged well over an hour in duration.[8]

There is an "action" element inherent in the present subject—the practical democratic need for "a free and responsible press" to inform citizens about current issues. Much of the criticism of the press stems from the slanting induced by the bias of the publisher's policy.[9] This criticism is often directed at flagrant cases such as the Hearst Press, the Chicago Tribune and New York tabloids, but also applies, in lesser degree, to the more conventional press. The description of mechanisms of policy maintenance may suggest why this criticism is often fruitless, at least in the short-run sense.

HOW THE STAFFER LEARNS POLICY

The first mechanism promoting conformity is the "socialization" of the staffer with regard to the norms of his job. When the new reporter starts work he is not told what policy is. Nor is he ever told. This may appear strange, but interview after interview confirmed the condition. The standard remark was "Never, in my —— years on this paper, have I ever been told how to slant a story." No paper in the survey had a

---

[8]The data are taken from Warren Breed, The Newspaperman, News and Society (Ph.D. dissertation, Columbia University, 1952). Indebtedness is expressed to William L. Kolb and Robert C. Stone, who read the present manuscript and provided valuable criticisms and suggestions.

[9]For a summary description of this criticism, see Commission on the Freedom of the Press, A Free and Responsible Press (Chicago: University of Chicago Press, 1947), chap. 4.

"training" program for its new men; some issue a "style" book, but this deals with literary style, not policy. Further, newsmen are busy and have little time for recruit training. Yet all but the newest staffers know what policy is.[10] On being asked, they say they learn it "by osmosis." Sociologically, this means they become socialized and "learn the ropes" like a neophyte in any subculture. Basically, the learning of policy is a process by which the recruit discovers and internalizes the rights and obligations of his status and its norms and values. He learns to anticipate what is expected of him so as to win rewards and avoid punishments. Policy is an important element of the newsroom norms, and he learns it in much the following way.

The staffer reads his own paper every day; some papers <u>require</u> this. It is simple to diagnose the paper's characteristics. Unless the staffer is naive or unusually independent, he tends to fashion his own stories after others he sees in the paper. This is particularly true of the newcomer. The news columns and editorials are a guide to the local norms. Thus a southern reporter notes that Republicans are treated in a "different" way in his paper's news columns than Democrats. The news about whites and Negroes is also of a distinct sort. Should he then write about one of these groups, his story will tend to reflect what he has come to define as standard procedure.

Certain editorial actions taken by editors and older staffers also serve as controlling guides. "If things are blue-pencilled consistently," one reporter said, "you learn he [the editor] has a prejudice in that regard."[11] Similarly an executive may occasionally reprimand a staffer for policy violation. From our evidence, the reprimand is frequently oblique, due to the covert nature of policy, but learning occurs nevertheless. One staffer learned much through a series of incidents:

> I heard [a union] was going out on strike, so I kept on it; then the boss said something about it, and well—I took the hint and we had less coverage of the strike forming. It was easier that way. We lost the story, but what can you do?

> We used a yarn on a firm that was coming to town, and I got dragged out of bed for that. The boss is interested in this industrial stuff —we have to clear it all through him. He's an official in the Chamber. So...after a few times, it's irritating, so I get fed up. I try to figure out what will work best. I learn to try and guess what the boss will want.

In fairness it should be noted that this particular publisher was one of the most dictatorial encountered in the study. The pattern of control through reprimand, however, was found consistently. Another staffer wrote, on his own initiative, a series about discrimination against Jews at hotel resorts.

> It was the old "Gentlemen's Agreement" stuff, documented locally. The boss called me in...didn't like the stuff...the series never appeared. You start to get the idea....

Note that the boss does not "command"; the direction is more subtle. Also, it seems that most policy indications from executives are negative. They veto by a nod of the head, as if to say, "Please don't rock the boat." Exceptions occur in the "campaign" story, which will be discussed later. It is also to be noted that punishment is implied if policy is not followed.

Staffers also obtain guidance from their knowledge of the characteristics, interests, and affiliations of their executives. This knowledge can be gained in

---

[10]While the concept of policy is crucial to this analysis, it is not to be assumed that newsmen discuss it fully. Some do not even use the word in discussing how their paper is run. To this extent, policy is a latent phenomenon; either the staffer has no reason to contemplate policy or he chooses to avoid so doing. It may be that one strength of policy is that it has become no more manifest to the staffers who follow it.

[11]Note that such executives' actions as blue-pencilling play not only the manifest function of preparing the story for publication but also the latent one of steering the future action of the staffer.

several ways. One is gossip. A reporter said:

> Do we gossip about the editors? Several of us used to meet—somewhere off the beaten path—over a beer—and talk for an hour. We'd rake 'em over the coals.

Another point of contact with executives is the news conference (which on middle-sized papers is seldom called a news conference), wherein the staffer outlines his findings and executives discuss how to shape the story. The typical conference consists of two persons, the reporter and the city editor, and can amount to no more than a few words. (Reporter: "One hurt in auto accident uptown." City editor: "Okay, keep it short.") If policy is at stake, the conference may involve several executives and require hours of consideration. From such meetings, the staffer can gain insight through what is said and what is not said by executives. It is important to say here that policy is not stated explicitly in the news conference nor elsewhere, with few exceptions. The news conference actually deals mostly with journalistic matters, such as reliability of information, newsworthiness, possible "angles," and other news tactics.

Three other channels for learning about executives are house organs (printed for the staff by syndicates and larger papers), observing the executive as he meets various leaders and hearing him voice an opinion. One staffer could not help but gain an enduring impression of his publisher's attitudes in this incident:

> I can remember [him] saying on election night [1948], when it looked like we had a Democratic majority in both houses, "My God, this means we'll have a labor government." (Q: How did he say it?) He had a real note of alarm in his voice; you couldn't miss the point that he'd prefer the Republicans.

It will be noted that in speaking "how" the staffer learns policy, there are indications also as to "why" he follows it.

REASONS FOR CONFORMING TO POLICY

There is no one factor which creates conformity-mindedness, unless we resort to a summary term such as "institutionalized statuses" or "structural roles." Particular factors must be sought in particular cases. The staffer must be seen in terms of his status and aspirations, the structure of the newsroom organization and of the larger society. He also must be viewed with reference to the operations he performs through his workday, and their consequences for him. The following six reasons appear to stay the potentially intransigent staffer from acts of deviance—often, if not always.[12]

1. Institutional Authority and Sanctions. The publisher ordinarily owns the paper and from a purely business standpoint has the right to expect obedience of his employees. He has the power to fire or demote for transgressions. This power, however, is diminished markedly in actuality by three facts. First, the newspaper is not conceived as a purely business enterprise, due to the protection of the First Amendment and a tradition of professional public service. Secondly, firing is a rare phenomenon on newspapers. For example, one editor said he had fired two men in 12 years; another could recall four firings in his 15 years on that paper. Thirdly, there are severance pay clauses in contracts with the American Newspaper Guild (CIO). The only effective causes for firing are excessive drunkenness, sexual dalliance, etc. Most newspaper unemployment apparently comes from occasional economy

---

[12] Two cautions are in order here. First, it will be recalled that we are discussing not all news, but only policy news. Secondly, we are discussing only staffers who are potential non-conformers. Some agree with policy; some have no views on policy matters; others do not write policy stories. Furthermore, there are strong forces in American society which cause many individuals to choose harmonious adjustment (conformity) in any situation, regardless of the imperatives. See Erich Fromm, Escape From Freedom (New York: Farrar and Rinehart, 1941), and David Riesman, The Lonely Crowd (New Haven: Yale, 1950).

drives on large papers and from total suspensions of publication. Likewise, only one case of demotion was found in the survey. It is true, however, that staffers still fear punishment; the myth has the errant star reporter taken off murders and put on obituaries—"the Chinese torture chamber" of the newsroom. Fear of sanctions, rather than their invocation, is a reason for conformity, but not as potent a one as would seem at first glance.

Editors, for their part, can simply ignore stories which might create deviant actions, and when this is impossible, can assign the story to a "safe" staffer. In the infrequent case that an anti-policy story reaches the city desk, the story is changed; extraneous reasons, such as the pressure of time and space, are given for the change.[13] Finally the editor may contribute to the durability of policy by insulating the publisher from policy discussions. He may reason that the publisher would be embarrassed to hear of conflict over policy and the resulting bias, and spare him the resulting uneasiness; thus the policy remains not only covert but undiscussed and therefore unchanged.[14]

2. <u>Feelings of Obligation and Esteem for Superiors.</u> The staffer may feel obliged to his paper for having hired him. Respect, admiration and gratitude may be felt for certain editors who have perhaps schooled him, "stood up for him," or supplied favors of a more paternalistic sort. Older staffers who have served as models for newcomers or who have otherwise given aid and comfort are due return courtesies. Such obligations and warm personal sentiments toward superiors play a strategic role in the pull to conformity.

3. <u>Mobility Aspirations.</u> In response to a question about ambition, all the younger staffers showed wishes for status achievement. There was agreement that bucking policy constituted a serious bar to this goal. In practice, several respondents noted that a good tactic toward advancement was to get "big" stories on Page One; this automatically means no tampering with policy. Further, some staffers see newspapering as a "stepping stone" job to more lucrative work: public relations, advertising, free-lancing, etc. The reputation for troublemaking would inhibit such climbing.

A word is in order here about chances for upward mobility. Of 51 newsmen aged 35 or more, 32 were executives. Of 50 younger men 6 had reached executive posts and others were on their way up with such jobs as wire editors, political reporters, etc. All but five of these young men were college graduates, as against just half of their elders. Thus there is no evidence of a "break in the skill hierarchy" among newsmen.

4. <u>Absence of Conflicting Group Allegiance.</u> The largest formal organization of staffers is the American Newspaper Guild. The Guild, much as it might wish to, has not interfered with internal matters such as policy. It has stressed business unionism and political interests external to the newsroom. As for informal groups, there is no evidence available that a group of staffers has ever "ganged up" on policy.

5. <u>The Pleasant Nature of the Activity.</u> a. <u>In-groupness in the newsroom.</u> The staffer has a low formal status vis-a-vis executives, but he is not treated as a "worker." Rather, he is a co-worker with executives; the entire staff cooperates congenially on a job they all like and respect: getting the news. The newsroom is a friendly, first-namish place. Staffers discuss stories with editors on a

---

[13]Excellent illustration of this tactic is given in the novel by an experienced newspaperwoman: Margaret Long, <u>Affair of the Heart</u> (New York: Random House, 1953), chap. 10. This chapter describes the framing of a Negro for murder in a middle-sized southern city, and the attempt of a reporter to tell the story objectively.

[14]The insulation of one individual or group from another is a good example of social (as distinguished from psychological) mechanisms to reduce the likelihood of conflict. Most of the factors inducing conformity could likewise be viewed as social mechanisms. See Talcott Parsons and Edward A. Shils, "Values, Motives and Systems of Action," in Parsons and Shils (eds.), <u>Toward A General Theory of Action</u> (Cambridge: Harvard University Press, 1951), pp. 223-30.

give-and-take basis. Top executives with their own offices sometimes come out and sit in on newsroom discussions.[15]

b. <u>Required operations are interesting.</u> Newsmen like their work. Few voiced complaints when given the opportunity to gripe during interviews. The operations required—witnessing, interviewing, briefly mulling the meanings of events, checking facts, writing—are not onerous.

c. <u>Non-financial perquisites.</u> These are numerous: the variety of experience, eye-witnessing significant and interesting events, being the first to know, getting "the inside dope" denied laymen, meeting and sometimes befriending notables and celebrities (who are well-advised to treat newsmen with deference). Newsmen are close to big decisions without having to make them; they touch power without being responsible for its use. From talking with newsmen and reading their books, one gets the impression that they are proud of being newsmen.[16] There are tendencies to exclusiveness within news ranks, and intimations that such near out-groups as radio newsmen are entertainers, not real newsmen. Finally, there is the satisfaction of being a member of a live-wire organization dealing with important matters. The newspaper is an "institution" in the community. People talk about it and quote it; its big trucks whiz through town; its columns carry the tidings from big and faraway places, with pictures.

Thus, despite his relatively low pay, the staffer feels, for all these reasons, an integral part of a going concern. His job morale is high. Many newsmen could qualify for jobs paying more money in advertising and public relations, but they remain with the newspaper.

6. <u>News becomes a value.</u> Newsmen define their job as producing a certain quantity of what is called "news" every 24 hours. This is to be produced <u>even though nothing much has happened</u>. News is a continous challenge, and meeting this challenge is the newsman's job. He is rewarded for fulfilling this, his manifest function. A consequence of this focus on news as a central value is the shelving of a strong interest in objectivity at the point of policy conflict. Instead of mobilizing their efforts to establish objectivity over policy as the criterion for performance, their energies are channeled into getting more news. The demands of competition (in cities where there are two or more papers) and speed enhance this focus. Newsmen do talk about ethics, objectivity, and the relative worth of various papers, but not when there is news to get. News comes first, and there is always news to get.[17] They are not rewarded for analyzing the social structure, but for getting news. It would seem that this instrumental orientation diminishes their moral potential. A further consequence of this pattern is that the harmony between staffers and executives is cemented by their common interest in news. Any potential conflict between the two groups, such as slowdowns, occurring among informal work groups in industry, would be dissipated to the extent that news is a positive value. The newsroom solidarity is thus reinforced.

---

[15]Further indication that the staffer-executive relationship is harmonious came from answers to the question, "Why do you think newspapermen are thought to be cynical?" Staffers regularly said that newsmen are cynical because they get close enough to stark reality to see the ills of their society, and the imperfections of its leaders and officials. Only two, of 40 staffers, took the occasion to criticise their executives and the enforcement of policy. This displacement, or lack of strong feelings against executives, can be interpreted to bolster the hypothesis of staff solidarity. (It further suggests that newsmen tend to analyze their society in terms of personalities, rather than institutions comprising a social and cultural system.)

[16]There is a sizeable myth among newsmen about the attractiveness of their calling. For example, the story: "Girl: 'My, you newspapermen must have a fascinating life. You meet such interesting people.' Reporter: 'Yes, and most of them are newspapermen.' " For a further discussion, see Breed, <u>op. cit.</u>, chap. 17.

[17]This is a variant of the process of "displacement of goals," newsmen turning to "getting news," rather than to seeking data which will enlighten and inform their readers. The dysfunction is implied in the nation's need not for more news but for better news—quality rather than quantity. See Merton, <u>op. cit.</u>, "Bureaucratic Structure and Personality," <u>pp.</u> 154-5.

The six factors promote policy conformity. To state more exactly how policy is maintained would be difficult in view of the many variables contained in the system. The process may be somewhat better understood, however, with the introduction of one further concept—the reference group.[18] The staffer, especially the new staffer, identifies himself through the existence of these six factors with the executives and veteran staffers. Although not yet one of them, he shares their norms, and thus his performance comes to resemble theirs. He conforms to the norms of policy rather than to whatever personal beliefs he brought to the job, or to ethical ideals. All six of these factors function to encourage reference group formation. Where the allegiance is directed toward legitimate authority, that authority has only to maintain the equilibrium within limits by the prudent distribution of rewards and punishments. The reference group itself, which has as its "magnet" element the elite of executives and old staffers, is unable to change policy to a marked degree because first, it is the group charged with carrying out policy, and second, because the policy maker, the publisher, is often insulated on the delicate issue of policy.

In its own way, each of the six factors contributes to the formation of reference group behavior. There is almost no firing, hence a steady expectation of continued employment. Subordinates tend to esteem their bosses, so a convenient model group is present. Mobility aspirations (when held within limits) are an obvious promoter of inter-status bonds as is the absence of conflicting group loyalties

with their potential harvest of cross pressures. The newsroom atmosphere is charged with the related factors of ingroupness and pleasing nature of the work. Finally, the agreement among newsmen that their job is to fasten upon the news, seeing it as a value in itself, forges a bond across the status lines.

As to the six factors, five appear to be relatively constant, occurring on all papers studied. The varying factor is the second: obligation and esteem held by staffers for executive and older staffers. On some papers, this obligation-esteem entity was found to be larger than on others. Where it was large, the paper appeared to have two characteristics pertinent to this discussion. First, it did a good conventional job of news-getting and newspublishing, and second, it had little difficulty over policy. With staffers drawn toward both the membership and the reference groups, organization was efficient. Most papers are like this. On the few smaller papers where executives and older staffers are not respected, morale is spotty; staffers withhold enthusiasm from their stories, they cover their beats perfunctorily, they wish for a job on a better paper, and they are apathetic and sometimes hostile to policy. Thus the obligation-esteem factor seems to be the active variable in determining not only policy conformity, but morale and good news performance as well.

SITUATIONS PERMITTING DEVIATION

Thus far it would seem that the staffer enjoys little "freedom of the press." To show that this is an oversimplification, and more important, to suggest a kind of test for our hypothesis about the strength of policy, let us ask: "What happens when a staffer <u>does</u> submit an antipolicy story?" We <u>know</u> that this happens infrequently, but what follows in these cases?

The process of learning policy crystallizes into a process of social control, in which deviations are punished (usually gently) by reprimand, cutting one's story, the withholding of friendly comment by an executive, etc. For example, it is

---

[18]Whether group members acknowledge it or not, "if a person's attitudes are influenced by a set of norms which he assumes that he shares with other individuals, those individuals constitute for him a reference group." Theodore M. Newcomb, <u>Social Psychology</u> (New York: Dryden, 1950), p. 225. Williams states that reference group formation may segment large organizations; in the present case, the reverse is true, the loyalty of subordinates going to their "friendly" superiors and to the discharge of technical norms such as getting news. See Robin M. Williams, <u>American Society</u> (New York: Knopf, 1951), p. 476.

punishment for a staffer when the city editor waves a piece of his copy at him and says, "Joe, don't <u>do</u> that when you're writing about the mayor." In an actual case, a staffer acting as wire editor was demoted when he neglected to feature a story about a "sacred cow" politician on his paper. What can be concluded is that when an executive sees a clearly anti-policy item, he blue-pencils it, and this constitutes a lesson for the staffer. Rarely does the staffer persist in violating policy; no such case appeared in all the interviews. Indeed, the best-known cases of firing for policy reasons——Ted O. Thackrey and Leo Huberman——occurred on liberal New York City dailies, and Thackrey was an editor, not a staffer.

Now and then cases arise in which a staffer finds his anti-policy stories printed. There seems to be no consistent explanation for this, except to introduce two more specific subjects dealing first, with the staffer's career line, and second, with particular empirical conditions associated with the career line. We can distinguish three stages through which the staffer progresses. First, there is the cub stage, the first few months or years in which the new man learns techniques and policy. He writes short, non-policy stories, such as minor accidents, meeting activity, the weather, etc. The second, or "wiring-in" stage, sees the staffer continuing to assimilate the newsroom values and to cement informal relationships. Finally there is the "star" or "veteran" stage, in which the staffer typically defines himself as a full, responsible member of the group, sees its goals as his, and can be counted on to handle policy sympathetically.[19]

To further specify the conformity-de-

viation problem, it must be understood that newspapering is a relatively complex activity. The newsman is responsible for a range of skills and judgments which are matched only in the professional and entrepreneurial fields. Oversimplifications about policy rigidity can be avoided if we ask, "<u>Under what conditions</u> can the staffer defy or by-pass policy?" We have already seen that staffers are free to argue news decisions with executives in brief "news conferences," but the arguments generally revolve around points of "newsiness," rather than policy as such.[20] Five factors appear significant in the area of the reporter's power to by-pass policy.

1. The norms of policy are not always entirely clear, just as many norms are vague and unstructured. Policy is covert by nature and has large scope. The paper may be Republican, but standing only lukewarm for Republican Candidate A who may be too "liberal" or no friend of the publisher. Policy, if worked out explicitly, would have to include motivations, reasons, alternatives, historical developments, and other complicating material. Thus a twilight zone permitting a range of deviation appears.[21]

2. Executives may be ignorant of particular facts, and staffers who do the leg (and telephone) work to gather news can use their superior knowledge to subvert policy. On grounds of both personal belief and professional codes, the staffer has the option of selection at many points. He can decide whom to interview and whom to ignore, what questions to ask, which quotations to note, and on writing the story which items to feature (with an eye toward the headline), which to bury, and in general what tone to give the several possible elements of the story.

3. In addition to the "squeeze" tactic

---

[19]Does the new staffer, fresh from the ideals of college, really "change his attitudes"? It would seem that attitudes about socio-economic affairs need not be fixed, but are capable of shifting with the situation. There are arguments for and against any opinion; in the atmosphere of the newsroom the arguments "for" policy decisions are made to sound adequate, especially as these are evoked by the significant others in the system.

[20]The fullest treatment of editor-reporter conferences appears in Swanson, <u>op. cit.</u>

[21]Related to the fact that policy is vague is the more general postulate that executives seek to avoid formal issues and the possibly damaging disputes arising therefrom. See Chester I. Barnard, <u>Functions of the Executives</u> (Cambridge: Harvard University Press, 1947).

exploiting executives' ignorance of minute facts, the "plant" may be employed. Although a paper's policy may prescribe a certain issue from becoming featured, a staffer, on getting a good story about that issue may "plant" it in another paper or wire service through a friendly staffer and submit it to his own editor, pleading the story is now too big to ignore.

4. It is possible to classify news into four types on the basis of source of origination. These are: the policy or campaign story, the assigned story, the beat story, and the story initiated by the staffer. The staffer's autonomy is larger with the latter than the former types. With the campaign story (build new hospital, throw rascals out, etc.), the staffer is working directly under executives and has little leeway. An assigned story is handed out by the city editor and thus will rarely hit policy head on, although the staffer has some leverage of selection. When we come to the beat story, however, it is clear that the function of the reporter changes. No editor comes between him and his beat (police department, city hall, etc.), thus the reporter gains the "editor" function. It is he who, to a marked degree, can select which stories to pursue, which to ignore. Several cases developed in interviews of beat men who smothered stories they knew would provide fuel for policy—policy they personally disliked or thought injurious to the professional code. The cooperation of would-be competing reporters is essential, of course. The fourth type of story is simply one which the staffer originates, independent of assignment or beat. All respondents, executives and staffers, averred that any employee was free to initiate stories. But equally regularly, they acknowledged that the opportunity was not often assumed. Staffers were already overloaded with beats, assignments, and routine coverage, and besides, rewards for initiated stories were meager or non-existent unless the initiated story confirmed policy. Yet this area promises much, should staffers pursue their advantage. The outstanding case in the present study concerned a well-educated, enthusiastic reporter on a conventional daily just north of the Mason-Dixon line. Entirely on his own, he consistently initiated stories about Negroes and Negro-white relations, "making" policy where only void had existed. He worked overtime to document and polish the stories; his boss said he didn't agree with the idea but insisted on the reporter's right to publish them.

5. Staffers with "star" status can transgress policy more easily than cubs. This differential privilege of status was encountered on several papers. An example would be Walter Winchell during the Roosevelt administration, who regularly praised the president while the policy of his boss, Mr. Hearst, was strongly critical of the regime. A New York Times staffer said he doubted that any copy reader on the paper would dare change a work of the copy of Meyer Berger, the star feature writer.

These five factors indicate that given certain conditions, the controls making for policy conformity can be bypassed. These conditions exist not only within the newsroom and the news situation but within the staffer as well; they will be exploited only if the staffer's attitudes permit. There are some limitations, then, on the strength of the publisher's policy.

Before summarizing, three additional requirements of Merton's functional paradigm must be met. These are statements of the consequences of the pattern, of available alternative modes of behavior, and a validation of the analysis.

CONSEQUENCES OF THE PATTERN

To the extent that policy is maintained, the paper keeps publishing smoothly as seen both from the newsroom and from the outside, which is no mean feat if we visualize the country with no press at all. This is the most general consequence. There are several special consequences. For the society as a whole, the existing system of power relationships is maintained. Policy usually protects property and class interests, and thus the strata and groups holding these interests are better able to retain them.

For the larger community, much news is printed objectively, allowing for opinions to form openly, but policy news may be slanted or buried so that some important information is denied the citizenry. (This is the dysfunction widely scored by critics.) For the individual readers, the same is true. For the executives, their favorable statuses are maintained, with perhaps occasional touches of guilt over policy. For newsmen, the consequences are the same as for executives. For more independent, critical staffers, there can be several modes of adaptation. At the extremes, the pure conformist can deny the conflict, the confirmed deviate can quit the newspaper business. Otherwise, the adaptations seem to run in this way: (1) Keep on the job but blunt the sharp corners of policy where possible ("If I wasn't here the next guy would let all that crap go through..."); (2) Attempt to repress the conflict amorally and anti-intellectually ("What the hell, it's only a job; take your pay and forget it . . ."); (3) Attempt to compensate, by "taking it out" in other contexts: drinking, writing "the truth" for liberal publications, working with action programs, the Guild and otherwise. All of these adjustments were found in the study. As has been suggested, one of the main compensations for all staffers is simply to find justification in adhering to "good news practice."

POSSIBLE ALTERNATIVES AND CHANGE

A functional analysis, designed to locate sources of persistence of a pattern, can also indicate points of strain at which a structural change may occur. For example, the popular recipe for eliminating bias at one time was to diminish advertisers' power over the news. This theory having proved unfruitful, critics more recently have fastened upon the publisher as the point at which change must be initiated. Our analysis suggests that this is a valid approach, but one requiring that leverage in turn be applied on the publisher from various sources. Perhaps the most significant of these are professional codes. Yet we have seen the weakness of these codes when policy decisions are made. Further leverage is contained in such sources as the professional direction being taken by some journalism schools, in the Guild, and in sincere criticism.

Finally, newspaper readers possess potential power over press performance. Seen as a client of the press, the reader should be entitled to not only an interesting newspaper, but one which furnishes significant news objectively presented. This is the basic problem of democracy; to what extent should the individual be treated as a member of a mass, and to what extent fashioned (through educative measures) as an active participant in public decisions? Readership studies show that readers prefer "interesting" news and "features" over penetrating analyses. It can be concluded that the citizen has not been sufficiently motivated by society (and its press) to demand and apply the information he needs, and to discriminate between worthwhile and spurious information, for the fulfillment of the citizen's role. These other forces—professional codes, journalism schools, the Guild, critics and readers—could result in changing newspaper performance. It still remains, however, for the publisher to be changed first. He can be located at the apex of a T, the crucial point of decision making. Newsroom and professional forces form the base of the T, outside forces from community and society are the arms. It is for the publisher to decide which forces to propitiate.

SUGGESTIONS FOR VALIDATION

The Merton paradigm requires a statement concerning validation of the analysis. Checks could be forthcoming both from social science researchers and from newsmen. If the latter, the newsman should explicitly state the basis for his discussion, especially as regards the types of papers, executives, and staffers he knows. A crucial case for detailed description would be the situation in which staffers actively defied authority on policy matters. Another important test would be a comparative description of two papers contrasted by their situation as regards the six factors promoting conformity, with particular reference to the variable of obligation and esteem held toward superiors, and the factors permitting deviation. In any event, the present exploratory study may serve as a point of departure.

A second type of validation may be suggested. This would focus on the utility of the paradigm itself. Previous studies have been based on functional theory but before the development of the paradigm.[22] Studies of diverse social systems also lend themselves to functional analysis, and such comparative research could function not only to build systematic theory but to test and suggest modifications of the paradigm. Situations characterized by conflict and competition for scarce goals seem particularly well suited to functional analysis. Several points made in the present essay might have been overlooked without the paradigm.[23]

SUMMARY

The problem, which was suggested by the age-old charges of bias against the press, focussed around the manner in which the publisher's policy came to be followed, despite three empirical conditions: (1) policy sometimes contravenes journalistic norms; (2) staffers often personally disagree with it; and (3) executives cannot legitimately command that policy be followed. Interview and other data were used to explain policy maintenance. It is important to recall that the discussion is based primarily on study

of papers of "middle" circulation range, and does not consider either non-policy stories or the original policy decision made by the publishers.

The mechanisms for learning policy on the part of the new staffer were given, together with suggestions as to the nature of social controls. Six factors, apparently the major variables producing policy maintenance, were described. The most significant of these variables, obligation and esteem for superiors, was deemed not only the most important, but the most fluctuating variable from paper to paper. Its existence and its importance for conformity led to the sub-hypothesis that reference group behavior was playing a part in the pattern. To show, however, that policy is not ironclad, five conditions were suggested in which staffers may by-pass policy.

Thus we conclude that the publisher's policy, when established in a given subject area, is usually followed, and that a description of the dynamic socio-cultural situation of the newsroom will suggest explanations for this conformity. The newsman's source of rewards is located not among the readers, who are manifestly his clients, but among his colleagues and superiors. Instead of adhering to societal and professional ideals, he re-defines his values to the more pragmatic level of the newsroom group. He thereby gains not only status rewards, but also acceptance in a solidary group engaged in interesting, varied, and sometimes important work. Thus the cultural patterns of the newsroom produce results insufficient for wider democratic needs. Any important change toward a more "free and responsible press" must stem from various possible pressures on the publisher, who epitomises the policy making and coordinating role.

---

[22] References are cited in Merton, Social Theory and Social Structure, op. cit., and also in the works of Talcott Parsons.

[23] That the paradigm might serve best as a checklist or "insurance," or as a theoretical guide to fledgling scholars, is shown by the excellence of an article published before the paradigm—and quite similar to the present article in dealing with problems of policy maintenance in a formal organiza-

tion: Edward A. Shils and Morris Janowitz, "Cohesion and Disintegration in the Wehrmacht in World War II," Public Opinion Quarterly, 12 (Summer 1948), pp. 280-315.

Social Structure and Moral Reform: A Study of the Woman's Christian Temperance Union

Joseph R. Gusfield

SOURCE: *American Journal of Sociology*, Vol. 61 (1955), pp. 221–32.

Social changes affect the fortunes of organizations and movements no less than they do the fate of individuals. Movements which try to alter the manners, tastes, and daily habits of large numbers of people are peculiarly vulnerable to shifts in the culture of the population. Few social movements in American history have achieved as many successes and witnessed as many disappointments as the temperance movement. In the one hundred and fifty years during which the organized movement has been a significant part of American life, it has gone through a process of "boom and bust," from activity and success to quiescence and failure. The last seventy-five years have been particularly beset with steep rise and equally steep fall. The high point of the movement was reached in the passage of the Eighteenth Amendment and the nadir in Repeal and the period following.

This paper examines the Woman's Christian Temperance Union, one important segment· of the temperance movement, during the last eighty years. We have tried to discover the way in which the movement has changed and some of the reasons which help explain that change.

THE PROBLEM

Previous studies of social movements have dealt largely with organizations that have increased in numbers and influence. Such studies have indicated a gradual modification in the structure and ideology of the movement. As the movement grows, it tends to adapt itself to its society and to substitute the values of organizational power and prestige for its original goals. This process has been described in the now familiar theory of the "institutionalization of social movements."[1]

Recently, Messinger has shown how the adaptive process has affected a declining social movement, the Townsend Move-

---

[1] The basic statements of this approach can be found in Ernst Troeltsch, The Social Teachings of the Christian Churches, trans. Olive Wyon (London: George Allen & Unwin, Ltd., 1911), I, 331-43; Max Weber, The Theory of Social and Economic Organization, trans. A. M. Henderson and Talcott Parsons (New York: Oxford University Press, 1947), pp. 363-86; Robert Park and Ernest W. Burgess, Introduction to the Science of Sociology (Chicago: University of Chicago Press, 1921), pp. 865-74; Herbert Blumer, "Collective Behavior," in Principles of Sociology, ed. Robert Park (New York: Barnes & Noble, 1939), pp. 167-222. The general approach has been utilized in many studies. Examples of these are H. Richard Niebuhr, Social Sources of Denominationalism (New York: Henry Holt & Co., 1929); Liston Pope, Millhands and Preachers (New Haven: Yale University Press, 1943); S. D. Clark, Church and Sect in Canada (Toronto: University of Toronto Press, 1949); Roberto Michels, Political Parties, trans. Eden and Cedar Pal (new ed.; Glencoe, Ill.: Free Press, 1949); Seymour Lipset, Agrarian Socialism (Berkeley and Los Angeles: University of California Press, 1950); A. J. Muste, "Factional Fights in Trade Unions," in American Labor Dynamics, ed. J. B. S. Hardman (New York: Harcourt, Brace & Co., 1928).

ment.[2] Here the adaptation to loss of influence and adherents was in terms of the
loss of the movement's actual mission
and the emphasis on the preservation of
the organization as such. New activities
of the Townsend clubs are understandable
only as devices to perpetuate the organization's membership, income, and
power.

The WCTU cannot be called a "successful" movement. Its fundamental goal,
the changing of American drinking habits,
is less realizable today than in earlier
periods. Neither is it analogous to the
movement in decline. Membership
figures indicate that the size of the organization, while less than before Repeal,
is still above two hundred thousand and
actually growing now in membership
(Table 1).

Table 1*
WCTU Membership by Decades

Year	Member-ship
1881	22,800
1891	138,377
1901	158,477
1911	245,299
1921	344,892
1931	372,355
1941	216,843
1951	257,548

*Source: Treasurer's reports in Annual Re-
port of the National Woman's Christian Temperance Union, 1881-1951.

While the WCTU is far from decline or
death, temperance norms have lost a
great deal of their power in American
culture. Their political power, as pressure groups, is far less than before and
during Prohibition.[3] The percentage of
"dry" communities in the United States is

far less than in the period before the passage of Prohibition, and fewer Americans
are abstainers today.[4]

The change in American drinking habits and the increased permissiveness of
drinking norms have presented the WCTU
with an environment more hostile to the
doctrine of total abstinence than was true
in the years of the organization's formation and development. The reaction of the
WCTU to this changed situation forms the
subject of this paper. We want to know
whether the change in environment has
led to changes in the goals and doctrine
of the movement. We further seek to explain changes, or lack of change, in the
organization.

Several possible modes of reaction
suggest themselves to us. Faced with a
now more hostile environment, the WCTU
might change to achieve greater acceptance within the new norms. This
would entail giving up much of the earlier
mission for the sake of organizational
values, which is the adaptation suggested
by the Townsend Movement cited above.
Second, it is conceivable that we may find
little change in the face of changed conditions. Third, it is also conceivable
that we may find changes which increase
the gap between the public and the organization.

THE PRE-PROHIBITION PERIOD: TEM-
PERANCE AS SOCIAL WELFARE

Moral reform and social welfare.—The
American temperance movement during
the nineteenth century was a part of a

---

[2] Sheldon Messinger, "Organizational
Transformation: A Case Study of a Declining
Social Movement," American Sociological Re-
view, XX (February, 1955), 3-10.

[3] Odegard has analyzed the extension power
of the Anti-Saloon League during the Prohibition and pre-Prohibition periods (Peter
Odegard, Pressure Politics [New York: Columbia University Press, 1928]).

[4] E. M. Jellinek, "Recent Trends in Alcoholism and in Alcohol Consumption," Quarterly Journal of Studies on Alcohol, VIII
(1947), 1-43; "How Hard Do Americans
Drink?" Fortune, XLVII (1953), 121-25, 146-
48, 153-54. The trend toward greater permissiveness in American drinking norms is,
as we shall show, clearly recognized by the
WCTU as well as by other temperance leaders. In this regard see Harry S. Warner.
The Liquor Cult and Its Culture (Columbus,
Ohio: Intercollegiate Association, 1946), and
Albion Roy King, "Drinking in Colleges."
Christian Century, July 18, 1951, pp. 842-43,
and July 25, 1951, pp. 864-68.

general effort toward the improvement of
the worth of the human being through improved morality as well as economic
conditions. The mixture of the religious,
the equalitarian, and the humanitarian
was an outstanding facet of the moral reformism of many movements.[5] Temperance supporters formed a large segment
of movements such as sabbatarianism,
abolition, woman's rights, agrarianism,
and humanitarian attempts to improve the
lot of the poor.

In these efforts there is evident a
satisfaction with the basic outlines of the
economic and social system. What is
attempted is the extension of the system
to include the underprivileged. The reforms proposed attempt to alleviate suffering through humanitarian actions by
those in advantageous positions or to reform the habits of the suffering as a way
to the improvement of both their character <u>and</u> their material situation. There
was clearly a relationship between the
two.[6] Moral reformism of this type suggests the approach of a dominant class
toward those less favorably situated in
the economic and social structure.
Barnes has pointed out that many of the
social movements of the nineteenth
century were composed of people bent on
reforming others rather than themselves.[7] Abolitionists were rarely former

slaveowners. Except for one short
episode in the 1840's,[8] the temperance
movement has drawn to it people of little
or no experience with drinking.

The goals and doctrine of the WCTU
were part of this humanitarian moral
reform movement in the period before
Prohibition. This is most evident in the
late nineteenth century but remained a
strong aspect of WCTU activities well
into the Prohibition period.

In its auxiliary interests the WCTU revealed a great concern for the improvement of the welfare of the lower classes.
It was active in campaigns to secure
penal reform, to shorten working hours
and raise wages for workers, and to
abolish child labor and in a number of
other humanitarian and equalitarian
activities. In the 1880's the WCTU worked
to bring about legislation for the protection of working girls against the exploitation by men. During the late nineteenth century several committees were
active among lower-class groups, among
them the Department of Work with
Miners, the Department of Work with
Lumberers, and the Department of Work
among Railroadmen,[9] which directed
their efforts toward converting the
worker to Christianity, bringing him material comforts, and spreading the gospel
of temperance.

The activities of the WCTU in the pre-
Prohibition era appear to be the actions

---

[5] Cf. Arthur Schlesinger, <u>The American as
Reformer</u> (Cambridge: Harvard University
Press, 1950), pp. 3-15; Gilbert Hobbs Barnes,
<u>The Anti-Slavery Impulse</u> (New York: D.
Appleton-Century Co., 1933); Arthur Bestor,
Jr., "The Ferment of Reform," in <u>Problems
in American History</u>, ed. Richard Leopold and
Arthur Link (New York: Prentice-Hall, Inc.,
1952).

[6] Everett C. Hughes has pointed out the
moralistic elements in the attitude of George
Pullman in the construction of Pullman, Illinois, in the late nineteenth century. The material conditions of the town would, Pullman
felt, develop the moral qualities which made
better human beings as well as better workers. Such workers would have the traits of
sobriety, industry, thrift, and loyalty (cf.
Everett C. Hughes, "A Calvinistic Utopia"
[unpublished manuscript]).

[7] Op. cit.

[8] The Washingtonian movement was the response of former drunkards, who made an
organized attempt to reform drunkards. The
rest of the temperance movement would not
unite with them (cf. John Krout, <u>The Origins
of Prohibition</u> [New York: Columbia University Press, 1928], pp. 182-222).

[9] Historical material of this paper is largely
based on reading of the annual reports of the
National Woman's Christian Temperance Union and samples of the WCTU journal, the
<u>Union Signal</u>. The data cover the years 1874-
1953. For a complete statement of the material presented here cf. Joseph Gusfield,
"Organizational Change: A Study of the Woman's Christian Temperance Union" (unpublished Ph.D. dissertation, University of
Chicago).

of a socially dominant group, essentially satisfied with the major outlines of the social structure. The social welfare efforts can be viewed as attempts to raise the lower classes to a level of behavior held out to them by the dominant middle-class citizen. This view is supported by the paternalistic character of much of WCTU social welfare activity during this period. For example, in 1882 the WCTU established a Kitchen Gardens Department to train "uneducated and untrained girls" in the arts of cooking and household management. The aim of this activity was explicitly stated as the preparation of housemaids, and it was hoped that occupational training would protect the girl from the temptations of city life.[10] The same training and the same rationale are found in the WCTU industrial schools established to aid "fallen women."[11]

The WCTU played an important role in the leadership of the woman's movement in the late nineteenth century, but this was not the only concern of the organization with questions of social justice. The labor movement had strong support from the WCTU. The Knights of Labor aided the temperance activities of the WCTU. The WCTU supported the struggle for the eight-hour day and the six-day week[12] and many of the strikes of the 1890's, though it balked at the use of violence. Its support of the labor cause is illustrated in the report of the Committee on

the Relations between Temperance and Labor for 1894. Employers were urged to refrain from "kindling the spirit of animosity among those already struggling under the iron heel of oppression" and thus provoking violence.[13]

These are illustrations of the interest of the WCTU during the nineteenth century in economic and social reform. It is difficult to find activities in which moral reform is clearly distinct from economic or social reform. Prison reform, for example, was stressed as a way to rehabilitate character, to convert men to Christianity, and to prevent the suffering of prisoners.

After 1900 this humanitarian interest appears less frequently, although it is still an important aspect of WCTU activities. Two things become evident. First, the humanitarianism and the equalitarian concern for the poor have greatly decreased. The Committee on the Relation of Temperance and Labor, for example, has shifted its major concern from labor issues to the propagation of the temperance cause among workers. The reports of this committee after 1900 show an interest in the morals and character of the worker. Thus in 1909 the report of this committee stated: "Urge working men and women who work for wages to cultivate a sense of responsibility in the thoroughness of their work and to consider their employer's welfare as well as their own."

The second point is that humanitarian concerns are not ignored, although decreased in emphasis, prison reform and child welfare receiving considerable attention. Between 1900 and 1920 the WCTU allotted one of the largest segments of its budget for its center at Ellis Island devoted to aiding incoming immigrants. In 1919 a huge Americanization project was begun, reminiscent of the paternalistic pattern described above. It set aside $40,000 for the purpose, the second largest single appropriation in its history.

After 1900, however, the moral reform-

[10] Annual Report of the WCTU (1884), pp. 47-51.

[11] Annual Report of the WCTU (1889), p. 62.

[12] Not only were the speeches of Francis Willard, president of the WCTU from 1879 to 1898, very favorable to labor but the committee reports reveal similar prolabor sentiments (cf. Annual Report of the WCTU [1889], p. 144; Annual Report of the WCTU [1894], p. 147). The general attitude of the WCTU toward the six-day week was a mixture of religious sabbatarianism and social justice (cf. Union Signal, January 1, 1885). For a fuller treatment of the relations between the WCTU and the labor movement see Mary Earhart, Frances Willard: From Prayers to Politics (Chicago: University of Chicago Press, 1944), pp. 245-59.

[13] Annual Report of the WCTU (1894), p. 447.

ism of the WCTU is more frequently separated from a concern with the underprivileged. With the development of the Anti-Saloon League after 1900, temperance aims become important in the campaign for legal sanctions against the sale of alcoholic beverages. Yet the emphasis on the lower classes as the object of WCTU reform is still present.

Temperance as reform of the underprivileged.—An effort to improve the lot of the poor and the underprivileged was not only displayed in the WCTU's auxiliary concerns. The very doctrine of temperance can be seen as directed toward changing the habits of the lower classes. The materials usually depict the drunkard as a worker. Temperance is frequently presented as the solution to economic problems, the route to success, whereas drinking is seen as the path to economic and social ruin. The WCTU did make some efforts to promote temperance sentiment among socially elite groups through a Department of Drawing Room Conversion. These proved unsuccessful and were abandoned.

A popular slogan of the temperance movement, in the nineteenth century, was that "drink is the curse of the working classes." Total abstinence was viewed as the solution to the problem of poverty. A story entitled "The Strike at Dennis Moriarity's" illustrates how the WCTU saw temperance as the answer to the worker's problems.[14] Dennis, son of a workman on strike, refuses to fetch beer for the strikers, insisting that they could pay their bills, even while on strike, if they didn't drink. The strikers are impressed by his reasoning. One says, "It's the saloon that hurts and keeps us poor. I've been wondering all this while why Debs and the rest of the leaders didn't see it."

In the above story the immigrant as well as the laborer is the central character. Irish and German immigrants were often depicted in the fiction of the WCTU as drunkards or shown in the process of reformation. Often it was the son or

daughter of the immigrant who effected the reformation through his or her experiences with the WCTU.[15] This type of story again presents the idea that acceptance of temperance is a mode of assimilation into middle-class life.

That temperance is a key to class position is seen in the fates of the middle-class man who violates the temperance norms and the lower-class immigrant who accepts such norms. Lapses are punished by the loss of economic and social position. The WCTU was active, both before and after the turn of the century, in spreading the idea that "lips that have touched liquor shall never touch mine." Through its young girls' groups it tried to make sobriety in the male a prerequisite for marriage. The following story from a WCTU journal illustrates the awful consequences of drink for the middle-class male:

> Ned has applied for a job, but he is not chosen. He finds that the potential employer has judged him to be like his Uncle Jack. Jack is a kindly man but he spends his money on drink and cigarettes. Ned has also been seen drinking and smoking. The employer thinks that Ned lacks the necessary traits of industriousness which he associates with abstinence and self-control.[16]

The implications of the above story seem clear. The man who wants to succeed must have the requisite character. He must appear to possess the characteristics of sobriety which indicate the other virtues of thrift, industry, and self-control. Temperance is thus a way not only to conform to morality but to achieve social and economic welfare. The WCTU was acting as a vehicle of progress and

---

[14] Union Signal, October 11, 1984, pp. 2-3.

[15] During the agitation of the Woman's Crusades of 1873, out of which the WCTU emerged, the struggle against "demon rum" was often carried out as one between the churchwomen and German and Irish saloonkeepers. The accounts of the crusades contain many examples of the immigrant as the opponent of sobriety (cf. Annie Wittenmyer, History of the Woman's Temperance Crusade [Phildaelphia: Mrs. Annie Wittenmyer, 1878]; Eliza Stewart, Members of the Crusade [Columbus, Ohio: William G. Hubbard Co., 1888]).

[16] Union Signal, January 1, 1883, p. 6.

improvement of the poor and under-privileged.

Analysis of committee reports. — We have classified the various committee reports found in the Annual Reports of the WCTU. The treatment of issues in these reports demonstrates the existence of the humanitarian reformist orientation in earlier periods. As Prohibition struggles became fiercer, the WCTU decreased its humanitarian interest. Moral conformity appeared apart from a concern with the welfare of the downtrodden. For example, the Department of Rescue Work had been interested in the improvement of the working girls' morality, wages, and living conditions as one consistent goal. By 1916 this department was chiefly concerned with efforts to limit fashion changes in the name of morality. The social welfare interest had disappeared. The interest in temperance more frequently appears unrelated to other welfare considerations. It is not until after Repeal, however, that the reports indicate unalloyed moral reform and temperance interests more frequently than humanitarian reform unalloyed or mixed with other interests (Table 2).

Table 2*
Classification of WCTU Committee Reports
by Period and by Interests

	Humanitarian Reform (%)	Moral Reform (Unalloyed) (%)	Temperance (Unalloyed) (%)	Other (%)	N†
Period	Interests (Per Cent of Total Reports)				
1879–1903	78.6	23.5	26.5	15.3	98
1904–28	45.7	30.7	33.1	18.0	127
1929–49	25.8	37.0	48.2	1.2	81

*Source: Sample of every fifth Annual Report of the WCTU.

†Percentages total more than 100 per cent due to several interests in some committee reports.

Humanitarian reform and social dominance. — The great concern of the WCTU with the lower classes was a dominant feature of its aims during the period from its formation in 1874 to the passage of Prohibition. It is not drinking per se that is emphasized but the drinking problems of the poor and the working classes.

Even where drinking in upper classes is berated, a prime concern is the impact of upper-class drinking patterns on the lower classes.

In its temperance doctrine as well as in its alliances with social movements of a reformist nature, the WCTU attempted to cope with the problems posed for urban America by the advent or urbanism, immigration, and industry in the late nineteenth century. The large industrial working class with its alien culture clashed with the rural image of virtue. A social group whose own position was relatively secure could best react to this threat by ameliorative reforms.

The doctrine of temperance appears to function in this fashion in the pre-Prohibition period. Implicit in the logic of the activities and the doctrine of the WCTU was a basic satisfaction with the social order.[17] The problems of the underprivileged can be solved in two ways. In one, greater kindness and humanitarianism can be extended to those who have not been fortunate. This is the motif in activities such as prison reform, work with "fallen women," better labor conditions, and other reform measures described. The demand for greater equality for women is an attack on the system of male superiority, but this is not generalized into an attack on other parts of the social and economic system.

Second, the doctrine of temperance itself suggests a solution consonant with the dominance of the group and the concern with injustice and suffering. If the lower classes and the immigrants will acquire the habits and social codes of the native middle classes, their problems will be solved. In short, assimilation into middle-class, Protestant culture is the reformist solution the WCTU offered in the pre-Prohibitionist period.

---

[17] There were some efforts toward a more revolutionary position in the late nineteenth century. Frances Willard, the leader of the WCTU from 1879 to 1898, was an outspoken Socialist and tried to make the WCTU follow her position. Despite her great power and influence in the movement, she did not succeed.

It is noteworthy that, prior to the 1920's, we find no condemnation of the American middle classes in WCTU literature. The good, churchgoing people of American Protestantism are seldom depicted as drinking. It is to this class that the WCTU looks for support of its aims. In defending the canons of sobriety, the WCTU could act as a representative of this class. An article in the Union Signal in 1889 put this as follows: "The class least touched by the evil thus far is that which here, as elsewhere in the land, forms its bone and sinew—the self-respecting and self-supporting class whose chief pleasures in life center in and about the home."[18]

THE "MORALIZER-IN-RETREAT"

The political strength of the temperance movement in America has been greatest in those states with large proportions of Protestant and rural populations.[19] With the decline in supremacy of the rural culture, both in city and in country, the norms of temperance have become less respectable. The advocates of temperance now face a more hostile environment in which they cannot enunciate a moral code and assume large segments of population in agreement with them. In the phrase of David Riesman, they are "moralizers-in-retreat."[20]

With the repeal of the Eighteenth Amendment, the WCTU found itself in a radically new situation. It could no longer assume that the norms of abstinence were really supported by the dominant middle-class elements in American life. The total abstainer became a figure of disap-

proval and ridicule rather than a figure of power and respect.

WCTU leaders interviewed generally felt that the total abstainer no longer had a position of respect in the community.[21] They saw this as a change which has affected the churchgoing middle classes as well as the secularized groups. The same theme is evident in the journals and in the speeches and reports from convention proceedings. The following interview excerpts are fairly typical:

> There has been a breakdown in the middle classes. The upper classes have always used liquor. The lower classes have always used liquor. Now the middle class has taken it over. The thing is slopping over from both sides.
>
> You know that today church people drink. That's the reason for the poor showing of the WCTU. It's been that way since Prohibition. There are many that believe but won't sign the pledge. They are afraid that they might want to take a drink.

The WCTU was seen, by the leaders interviewed, as lower in prestige today than in an earlier period when temperance norms held a stronger position in the American society. Leaders contrasted the prestigeful social composition of earlier periods with the present composition. Examples such as the following appear frequently in the interviews:

> When this union was first organized, we had many of the most influential ladies of the city. But now they have got the idea that we ladies who are against taking a cocktail are a little queer. We have an undertaker's wife and a minister's wife, but the lawyer's and the doctor's wives shun us. They don't want to be thought queer.
>
> I remember when the X's lived in the house that in now the Hotel W. They were the finest people in the town, and they were temperance people.
>
> When I joined, women of prominence and social prestige were in it. They were the backbone of the churches and the schools.

The WCTU is recognized by its membership as having retreated from a past position of greater influence, power, and

---

[18] May 16, 1889, p. 3.

[19] Odegard, op. cit., pp. 24-35; cf. Harold Gosnell, Grass Roots Politics (Washington, D. C.: American Council on Public Affairs, 1942), pp. 101-2; André Siegfried, America Comes of Age (New York: Harcourt, Brace & Co., 1927), pp. 70-90.

[20] David Riesman, The Lonely Crowd (New Haven: Yale University Press, 1950), p. 195; cf. Alfred M. Lee, "Techniques of Social Reform: An Analysis of the New Prohibition Drive," American Sociological Review, IX (1944), 65-77.

[21] Interviews were conducted with forty-six local and national WCTU leaders. The local leaders were active in upstate New York and in Chicago; the national leaders, members of the staff of the WCTU National Headquarters in Evanston, Illinois.

prestige. To be a member of the WCTU is therefore harmful to social acceptability in many groups. It opens her to ridicule from people whose opinion is important to her.

This is frankly realized by the WCTU. The literature of the organization does not hide the fact. For example, a membership drive pamphlet contained the following description of one type of WCTU member, Mrs. I-Would-if-I-Could: "She wouldn't think of asking for money or inviting anyone to join. She knows the organization is not especially popular in some groups.... There are times when she prefers not to mention her membership."

Local leaders also described the low esteem of the WCTU in their communities:

People don't like us. Some of the churches don't respect us.

Well, as you have probably learned, this isn't the organization it used to be. It isn't popular, you know. The public thinks of us—let's face it—as a bunch of old women, as frowzy fanatics. I've been viewed as queer, as an old fogy, for belonging to the WCTU.... This attitude was not true thirty years ago.

The WCTU is acutely aware of what it has been and of what it has become. The present position of unpopularity might lead to several different types of reaction. One possible position would be a reversal of past doctrine and the embracing of a doctrine of moderate drinking. This would be the acceptance of the new standard of the middle classes. Another possibility might be a de-emphasis of temperance aims and a substitution of other aims, such as those of a social welfare nature or an attack on "popular" enemies, such as drug addiction or juvenile delinquency.

The alternatives considered above all imply the importance of maintaining the popularity and acceptance of the organization in middle-class circles. If the organization should attempt to maintain its old doctrines, it could no longer be representative of prestigeful segments of American life. With the social base of dominance undetermined, can the WCTU continue a reformist attitude toward lower classes, or must it become a sectarian critic of the class it once represented?

MORAL INDIGNATION: CENSURE OF THE NEW MIDDLE CLASS

The characteristic doctrine of the WCTU is no longer humanitarian reform of the underprivileged. Instead it is an indignation directed against the middle-class moderate drinker. Total abstinence is presented as behavior morally demanded, apart from social welfare considerations. The new standards of the middle class are seen as defections from the traditional morality of abstinence.

"Moral indignation" as used here is not equivalent to the use of the term by Ranulf.[22] We are not concerned with the "disinterested tendency to inflict punishment" but rather with the quality of anger generated by the failure of others to recognize standards of morality which the actor recognizes. The definition of "indignation" given by Webster's New Collegiate Dictionary accurately conveys our meaning. It is "righteous wrath" and "anger excited by that which is unworthy, base, or disgraceful." In understanding this emotion in the WCTU, we must keep in mind the fact that abstinence was once a respectable middle-class doctrine. The middle-class drinking habits are not only in conflict with WCTU norms; they are defections from past standards.

A fiction story in the Union Signal illustrates this sense of moral indignation toward the new doctrine of temperance.[23] The story is entitled "Today's Daughter." Ruth, sixteen, is taken to a party at the home of a new boy who has just moved into the neighborhood. The boy has told Ruth's family that he is glad the new house has a game room in the basement. Aunt Liz is suspicious. She knows that many of the houses in the neighborhood now have bars in the basement game

[22] Svend Ranulf, Moral Indignation and Middle Class Psychology (Copenhagen: Levin & Munksgaard, 1938), p. 13.

[23] Union Signal, December 25, 1937, pp. 5-6.

rooms. Ruth's mother tries to still these suspicions: "We're not living in the Victorian period. ... I'm sure the Barrets are alright [sic]. They joined the church last Sunday." Aunt Liz's reply greatly unnerves Ruth's mother: "As if that meant respectability these days! Many's the church member who drinks and smokes and thinks nothing of it."

This episode contains the significant parts of the current position of the WCTU. Here are people of moderate incomes, in the same neighborhood and members of the same church as the WCTU adherent, yet the indexes of social class, religion, and ethnicity are no longer good assurances of abstinence.

Conflict between the doctrine of the total abstainer and a new "middle-class psychology" is evident. The following story is an apt illustration in which the new middle class is criticized for defection from the Protestant norms which supported and sustained the temperance doctrine. The story is entitled "When Yesterday Returned."[24] Jane, the heroine, reveres her "old-fashioned, Christian grandmother" who taught her the temperance pledge. Jane's mother ridicules temperance as prudishness and says that it hinders her social position. The struggle between the two groups, the newer and more prestigeful moderate drinkers and the old-fashioned abstainers, is epitomized after Jane scolds a visitor who asked for whiskey before dinner.

> When the guest had gone her mother informed her in no uncertain tones that "such plebian mannerisms" were rude. And furthermore if there were to be any more such old-fashioned, prudish notions exploited before such persons as Mr. Forsythe, the family's opportunities for social prestige would be lost forever and Jane's visits to her grandmother curtailed.

The figures of the underprivileged poor and the laborer no longer appear as the center of WCTU interest. In their place is the middle-class, churchgoing moderate drinker. Toward him the WCTU displays resentment rather than reformist

concern. Typical remarks of interviewees stress the moderate drinker:

> We fear moderation more than anything. Drinking has become so much a part of everything—even in our church life and our colleges.
>
> Since Repeal, people are drinking who wouldn't have before. They are held in great regard. The social drinker has a greater effect on children than the drunkards.

In past decades moderate drinking might have subjected the drinker to fear of loss of reputation or damaged career.[25] Some writers have lately maintained that career routes more and more demand the skills of fellowship, personal attachments, and the ability to be the "good fellow."[26] This means that the culture may place great value on tolerance of others, in drinking as well as in other behavior. This makes the moral reformer even more reprehensible in the life of the new middle-class culture.

In reaction to this, the WCTU has poured out wrath against the defector from standards of abstinence who talks of taking an "objective" stand toward the problem. One interviewee complained of the Yale School of Alcohol Studies:

> You as a teacher must take a stand against smoking and drinking. Do you know of the Yale center? Well, I went down there one night. When they were through, you didn't know whether they were for it or against it. They didn't want to commit themselves. What can they expect students to do?

This attitude has made it difficult for the WCTU to co-operate with organizations which viewed drinking from a social

---

[24] Ibid., June 3, 1939-July 29, 1939.

[25] In some American industries this still remains true, as in the International Business Machines Corporation, under the leadership of Thomas Watson (cf. Time, March 28, 1955, p. 83). Watson may be taken as one of the last of the temperance reformers in positions of dominance. His attitude of strong disapproval toward employee drinking on or off the job is viewed as unusual enough to warrant comment both in Time and in the IBM communities.

[26] Cf. Riesman, op. cit., pp. 130-44; C. Wright Mills, White Collar (New York: Oxford University Press, 1951), pp. 91-100, 182-88.

welfare interest in curing or preventing alcoholism. Insistence on the vital importance of legal restriction of the sale of drink has continued. The president of the WCTU took an "unbending" position when she said: "Between right and wrong only one ground is possible and that is a battle ground." [27]

The fact that "good people" are drinking is a chronic complaint among interviewees and in the pages of WCTU literature. One membership pamphlet voices this lament as follows:

> The greatest difficulty to be found today among youth, in anti-alcohol education, is the fact that "good people" are using liquor. Beautifully gowned women sipping their cocktails in lavish cocktail lounges give the impression that it is an extremely cultured thing to do.... Even within some of the best homes, the bar is set up. [28]

The social position of the moderate drinker in the concern of the WCTU is not that of the poverty-striken, the socially elite, or the non-churchgoer. It is rather the class from which the WCTU formerly drew its power and which formed the base for a doctrine of social reformism. Interviewees stressed the change in the churchgoer as the cause for the new respectability of drinking:

> The churches aren't helping, some of them. We went to the home of a professor for a church meeting, and she [his wife] served sherry. The football coach's wife makes no bones about it. She serves liquor.
>
> It creeps into the official church boards. They keep it in their iceboxes... The minister here thinks that the church has gone too far, that they are doing too much to help the temperance cause. He's afraid that he'll stub some influential toes.
>
> The churches aren't doing enough.... Many nominally take a stand, but many don't follow it locally. There was one churchman in L. who had beer at his

daughter's wedding. Another churchman in H. had wine at a wedding that really flowed. And this was the Church of the Brethren!

The WCTU has not attempted to reformulate its previous temperance doctrine in the direction of popular acceptance, despite the changed milieu in which it must operate. Rather it has swung in the direction of a greater sectarianism which carries it strongly into conflict with previous sources of adherence. How can we explain this? Why has it not accommodated to the new situation? Some light may be shed on this question by the analysis of the social composition of the movement between the years 1885 and 1949.

Increasing class distance. — We have studied the social composition of local leaders in the WCTU through the use of directories of officers published in annual state WCTU reports. These list the local officers and their addresses for each city, town, and village in which there is a unit. With these lists, we then utilized city business directories, which gave us the occupation of the husband of the officer. [29] We were limited in choice of cities by availability of state reports for each of the four years chosen— 1885, 1910, 1925, 1950—and by the availability of city directories for each of the cities and years. However, we were able to compile comparative data for thirty-eight cities in five states (Table 3).

The results of this study indicate that the socioeconomic status of the local leadership has diminished during the period 1885-1950. There has been a relatively steady decrease in the percentage of professional people, proprietors, managers, and officials and a relatively steady increase in the skilled and unskilled groups. More and more, the social base of the WCTU appears to be lower middle class and lower class

---

[27] *Annual Report of the WCTU* (1952), p. 87. Recently, with the retirement of the past president, there has been a "softer" attitude toward the Prohibition question and toward co-operation with non-Prohibitionist antialcohol groups. The general condemnation of the middle-class drinker still remains the focus of WCTU doctrine, however.

[28] Roy L. Smith, *Young Mothers Must Enlist* (Evanston, Ill.: National WCTU Publishing House, 1953).

[29] In the case of widows we used the last occupation of the husband. In classifying occupations, we utilized United States Employment Service, *Dictionary of Occupational Titles* (Washington, D. C.: Government Printing Office, 1944).

Table 3
WCTU Local Leaders Classified by Husband's
Occupation for State and Year

Husband's Occupation

State and Year	Professional and Semi-professional	Proprietors, Managers, and Officials	Clerical and Sales	Skilled Labor	Unskilled and Semi-skilled	Farm	Total (%)	N
Connecticut:								
1885	25.7	20.0	22.9	22.9	5.8	2.9	100	68
1910	21.0	31.6	13.2	21.0	10.6	2.6	100	34
1925	3.8	15.4	21.2	36.6	21.1	1.9	100	51
1950	12.4	18.6	25.0	29.2	14.8	0.0	100	52
Michigan:								
1885	17.8	33.3	6.7	28.9	8.9	4.4	100	42
1910	15.3	19.4	19.4	26.4	15.3	4.1	100	72
1925	13.0	14.6	18.8	24.6	27.6	1.4	100	66
1950	13.2	7.1	16.6	26.2	36.9	0.0	100	77
Illinois:								
1885	20.0	35.6	11.2	24.4	8.8	0.0	100	50
1910	14.5	22.0	20.4	25.4	15.2	2.5	100	136
1925	11.8	19.3	23.5	19.3	24.4	1.7	100	124
1950	12.4	14.2	16.8	25.6	31.0	0.0	100	127
Minnesota:								
1885	25.6	33.3	15.4	17.9	5.2	2.6	100	38
1910	14.0	19.3	27.3	28.9	9.6	0.9	100	116
1925	12.7	22.8	20.1	28.9	15.5	0.0	100	151
1950	10.3	17.6	23.6	31.5	17.0	0.0	100	164
Maryland:								
1885	22.2	44.4	27.8	5.6	0.0	0.0	100	15
1910	13.6	36.4	40.9	9.1	0.0	0.0	100	22
1925	16.7	35.2	20.4	18.4	9.3	0.0	100	57
1950	21.4	33.3	21.4	16.8	7.1	0.0	100	41
Total:								
1885	22.6	30.4	26.1	22.1	6.5	2.3	100	193
1910	15.1	22.0	21.8	26.6	12.3	2.2	100	348
1925	12.0	21.2	21.0	25.3	19.6	0.9	100	392
1950	12.4	16.3	20.3	28.2	22.8	0.9	100	408

rather than the earlier picture of upper middle and lower middle classes.

This suggests an answer to the question posed above. The present social composition of the movement cannot duplicate the pretense to social dominance from which a reformist position is possible. Further, the very class structure of the movement accentuates the split between the upper and the lower middle classes which appears in the interviews and documentary materials. A uniform middle-class culture is less of a reality than it was in earlier periods.

One would anticipate that the groups most susceptible to norms encouraging drinking are precisely those upper-middle-class groups making up the world of the professional, business executive, and salesman—the new middle classes whose religion is less evangelical and whose norms emphasize fellowship, toleration, and leisure. These seem to be the groups who have left the WCTU. Their higher socioeconomic status would have afforded them leadership had they remained.

The data suggest that temperance norms have filtered down to lower socioeconomic groups. The moral indignation of the movement is explainable by the resentment engendered by the defection of the upper middle class. These are no longer available as models with which the religiously oriented in America can identify. The quality of "moralizing" has ceased to be respectable. The adherents of rural nineteenth-century values epitomized in the doctrine of total abstinence do not have available tangible models of success and prestige in social levels above them. Nevertheless, they nourish expectation that the values on which they have been raised will be the values of groups above them in status. Their resentment is understandable as a response to the realization that their expectations are no longer true.

CONCLUSION

This study has demonstrated a shift in the doctrine and social composition of a moral reform movement. The earlier stages of the WCTU were shown to have been characterized by an attitude of moral reform directed toward the lower classes. In this stage, social composition data indicate that the WCTU represented a socially dominant class.

Today the WCTU is an organization in retreat. Contrary to the expectations of theories of institutionalization, the movement has not acted to preserve organizational values at the expense of past doctrine. In adhering to less popular positions, it has played the role of the sect and widened the gap between WCTU membership and middle-class respectability.

Analysis of social composition in this stage indicates that the movement is today less upper middle class in composition than in earlier periods and more lower middle and lower class in composition. In this respect, as well as in the changed drinking norms of the upper middle classes, the split within American Protestant middle classes has been widened.

The moral indignation of the WCTU today is a very different approach to temperance and to the American scene from the reformism and progressivism of the late nineteenth and early twentieth centuries. The plight of the "moralizer-in-retreat" is the plight of the once powerful but now rejected suitor. The symbols at his command no longer ring true in the halls where once they were heard with great respect. He cannot identify easily with those above him in status, because they now repudiate his morality. It is the sense of the historical shift, fully as much as the absolute clash in values, that has soured his reformism and generated his resentment.

Religious Aspects of Modernization in Turkey and Japan*

Robert N. Bellah

SOURCE: *American Journal of Sociology*, Vol. 64, (1958), pp. 1–5.

The process of modernization of the "backward" nations such as Turkey and Japan, which will be considered here, involves changes in the value system as well as economic, political, and social changes. In traditional societies the value system tends to be what Howard Becker calls "prescriptive."[1] A prescriptive system is characterized by the comprehensiveness and specificity of its value commitments and by its consequent lack of flexibility. Motivation is frozen, so to

---

* I am indebted to Niyazi Berkes and Talcott Parsons for reading earlier versions of this paper.

[1]For a recent definition of "prescriptive" and "principal" see Howard Becker, "Current Sacred-secular Theory and Its Development," in Howard Becker and Alvin Boskoff (eds.), Modern Sociological Theory in Continuity and Change (New York: Dryden Press, 1957).

speak, through commitment to a vast range of relatively specific norms governing almost every situation in life. Most of these specific norms, usually including those governing social institutions, are thoroughly integrated with a religious system which invokes ultimate sanctions for every infraction. Thus changes in economic or political institutions, not to speak of family and education, in traditional societies tend to have ultimate religious implications. Small changes will involve supernatural sanctions.

Yet such a society, when faced with grave dislocations consequent to Western contact, must make major changes in its institutional structure if it is to survive. What changes must be made in the organization of the value system so that these structural changes may go forward?

We may say that the value system of such a society must change from a prescriptive type to a "principal" type, to borrow again from Becker. Traditional societies, as we have said, tend to have a normative system, in which a comprehensive, but uncodified, set of relatively specific norms governs concrete behavior. But in a modern society an area of flexibility must be gained in economic, political, and social life in which specific norms may be determined in considerable part by short-term exigencies in the situation of action, or by functional requisites of the relevant social subsystems. Ultimate or religious values lay down the basic principles of social action; thus such a normative system is called "principal," but the religious system does not attempt to regulate economic, political, and social life in great detail, as in prescriptive societies. Looking at this process another way, we may say that there must be a differentiation between religion and ideology, between ultimate values and proposed ways in which these values may be put into effect. In traditional prescriptive societies there is no such discrimination. Difference of opinion on social policy is taken to imply difference as to religious commitment.

The social innovator necessarily becomes a religious heretic. But in modern society there is a differentiation between the levels of religion and social ideology which makes possible greater flexibility at both levels.

How is the normative system in a traditional society to be changed from prescriptive to principal, and how is the differentiation of the religious and ideological levels to be effected, especially in the face of the concerted effort of the old system to avoid any changes at all? I would assert that only a new religious initiative, only a new movement which claims religious ultimacy for itself, can successfully challenge the old value system and its religious base. The new movement, which arises from the necessity to make drastic social changes in the light of new conditions, is essentially ideological and political in nature. But, arising as it does in a society in which the ideological level is not yet recognized as having independent legitimacy, the new movement must take on a religious coloration in order to meet the old system on its own terms. Even when such a movement is successful in effecting major structural changes in the society and in freeing motivation formerly frozen in traditional patterns so that considerable flexibility in economic and political life is attained, the problems posed by its own partly religious origin and its relation to the traditional religious system may still be serious indeed.

Let us turn to the example of Turkey.[2]

Ottoman Turkey in the eighteenth century was a traditionalistic society with a prescriptive value system. Virtually all spheres of life were theoretically under the authority of the religious law, the Shari'ah. Indeed, the government was supposed to have an area of freedom within the law. But this freedom had become narrowly restricted. Precedents of

---

[2] Throughout the discussion of Turkey I shall rely heavily on lectures and unpublished material of Niyazi Berkes, of the Islamic Institute at McGill University, who is undertaking a pioneering study of Turkish modernization.

governmental procedure were tacitly assimilated to the religious law.

Beginning with Selim III in the late eighteenth century, a series of reforming sultans and statesmen attempted to make major changes in Turkish society in an effort to cope with increasingly desperate internal and external conditions. While some changes were made, especially in areas remote from the central strongholds of the religious law, the reforming party was unable to attain any ultimate legitimation in the eyes of the people, and, although Turkish society was shaken to its foundation, periods of reform alternated with periods of blind reaction in which reformers were executed or banished.

The last of these reactionary periods was that of the rule of the despotic Sultan Abdul Hamid II, who was overthrown in 1908 by a coup of young army officers whom we know as the "Young Turks." By this time it had become clear to leading intellectuals that more was needed than another interim of liberal reform. They saw that a basic change in the cultural foundation of Turkish society was demanded if the long-delayed changes in economic, political, and social structure were to be effected. Some felt that a modern purified Islam could provide the new cultural basis, but orthodox Islam was so deeply imbedded in the fabric of traditional society that the Islamic modernists found little response in the religious party. Others looked to Western liberal democracy as a satisfactory foundation. Those sensitive to the mind of the Turkish masses, however, pointed out that the Turkish people would never accept a value system so obviously "made abroad" and which could so easily be condemned by the conservatives with the stigma of unbelief.

It was Ziya Gökalp, a sociologist much influenced by Durkheim, who ardently championed Turkish nationalism as the only satisfactory cultural foundation for the new Turkey.[3] Gökalp found the re-

ferent for all symbols of ultimate value in society itself. His answer to the religious conservatives was that the true Islam was that of the Turkish folk, not of the effete religious hierarchy which was largely educated in the Arabic and Persian languages rather than the Turkish language. Here at last was an ideology to which the people could respond with emotion and which could challenge religious conservatism on its own grounds.

But the course of world history did as much as Gökalp's eloquence to decide in favor of the nationalist alternative for Turkey. Not only did World War I shear Turkey of her empire, but the subsequent invasions of Anatolia threatened the very life of the nation itself. Mustafa Kemal, who led the ultimately successful effort of national resistance, partly chose and partly was impelled to make the nation the central symbol in his subsequent drive for modernization. As a result, the highest value and central symbol for the most articulate sections of the Turkish people became not Islam but Turkism, or nationalism, or Kemalism, or, simply, "the Revolution." Having a strong national and personal charismatic legitimacy, Mustafa Kemal, later known as "Ataturk," was able to create a far-reaching cultural revolution in which the place of religion in the society was fundamentally altered. We may note some of the landmarks in this revolution. In 1924 the office of caliph was abolished. In the same year all religious schools were closed or converted into secular schools. The most important change of all took place in 1926: the Muslim Civil Law was abandoned and the Swiss Civil Code adopted almost without change. Finally, in 1928, the phrase in the constitution stating that the religion of Turkey is Islam was deleted, and Turkey was declared a secular state.

That the Turks were deeply conscious of what they were doing is illustrated by the following quotation from Mahmud Essad, the minister of justice under whom the religious law was abandoned:

The purpose of laws is not to maintain the old customs or beliefs which have their

---

[3]A translation by Niyazi Berkes of selected writings of Ziya Gökalp is forthcoming.

source in religion, but rather to assure the economic and social unity of the nation.

When religion has sought to rule human societies, it has been the arbitrary instrument of sovereigns, despots, and strong men. In separating the temporal and the spiritual, modern civilization has saved the world from numerous calamities and has given to religion an imperishable throne in the consciences of believers.[4]

This quotation illustrates well enough the transition from prescriptive to principal society and the differentiation of religion and ideology as two distinct levels. It is clear that the great advances of Turkish society in economic, political, and social life are based on this new cultural foundation. But implicit in Essad's words are some of the yet unsolved problems about that new cultural pattern.

For Essad and other Turkish reformers "the Revolution" was a criterion for everything, even for the place of religion in society, and thus, whether consciously or not, they gave the revolution an ultimate, a religious, significance. The six principles upon which the constitution is based—republicanism, nationalism, populism, étatism, secularism, and revolution—are taken as self-subsisting ultimates. Thus the religious implications of the political ideology remain relatively unchecked. These express themselves in party claims to ultimate legitimacy and in an inability on the part of the party in power to accept the validity of an opposition, which are not in accord with the flexibility appropriate in a modern principal society.

On the other hand, Islam in Turkey has not on the whole been able to redefine its own self-image and face the theological issues involved in becoming a religion primarily, in Essad's words, "enthroned in men's consciences." Nor has it been able to provide a deeper religious dimension of both legitimation and judgment of the six principles which are the basis of the new social life. It remains,

on the whole, in a conservative frame of mind in which the ideological claims are considerable, thus still posing a threat, possibly a great one, to return the society to a less differentiated level of social organization. Considering the trend of the last forty years, however, we seem to be observing a differentiation in the process of becoming, but it is too soon to say that it has been entirely accomplished.

Japan, while illustrating the same general processes as Turkey, does so with marked differences in important details.[5] Premodern Japan was a traditionalistic society with a prescriptive normative system closely integrated with a religious system composed of a peculiar Japanese amalgam of Shinto, Confucianism, and Buddhism. In the immediate premodern period, however, a conjuncture of the Confucian stress on loyalty and a revived interest in Shinto began to have explosive consequences. The actual rule at this time was in the hands of a military dictator, or Shogun, hereditary in the Tokugawa family. The emperor was relegated to purely ceremonial functions in the palace at Kyoto. But, as economic and social conditions deteriorated under Tokugawa rule, important elements in the population became alienated from the political status quo. They proved extremely receptive to the religious message of the revival Shintoists and legitimist Confucians, who insisted that the true sovereign was the emperor and that the Shogun was a usurper. According to their conception, the emperor is divine, descended from the sun-goddess and his direct rule of the Japanese people could be expected to bring in a virtually messianic age.

This movement was already vigorous when Perry's ships moved into Tokyo Bay in 1853. The inability of the Tokugawa government to keep foreigners from desecrating the sacred soil of Japan added the last fuel to the flames of re-

---

[4] Quoted in Henry E. Allen, The Turkish Transformation (Chicago: University of Chicago Press, 1935); p. 34.

[5] For a more extensive treatment of the Japanese case, especially the premodern background see my Tokugawa Religion (Glencoe, Ill.: Free Press, 1957).

sentment, and with the slogan "Revere the Emperor; expel the barbarians," a successful military coup overthrew the Tokugawa and restored the emperor to direct rule.

I would suggest that Japan was at this point, in 1868, virtually at the beginning of serious Western influence, in a position that Turkey reached only in the early 1920's under Mustafa Kemal. But she reached it in quite a different way. Unlike Turkey, one of the very foundations of the old traditional order in Japan, the divine emperor, provided the main leverage for the radical reorganization of that order. The young samurai who put through the Meiji Restoration used the central value of loyalty to the emperor to legitimize the immense changes they were making in all spheres of social life and to justify the abandoning of many apparently sacred prescriptions of the traditional order. No other sacredness could challenge the sacredness inherent in the emperor's person.

Here we see an ideological movement, essentially political in nature, whose aim was the strengthening and thus the modernizing of Japan, taking a much more openly religious coloration than was the case in Turkey. There was in the early Meiji period an attempt to make Shinto into the national religion and a determined effort to root out all rival religions. Christianity was sharply discouraged, but it was on Buddhism, the chief native religious tradition with little relation to the imperial claims to divinity, that the ax fell. The Buddhist church was disestablished, and all syncretism with Shinto prohibited. In the words of D. C. Holtom:

Members of the royal family were debarred from continuing in Buddhist orders; Buddhist ceremonials in the imperial palace were prohibited; Buddhist temples all over the land were attacked and destroyed. A blind fury of misplaced patriotic zeal committed precious Buddhist writings, fine sculptures, bronzes, woodcarvings, and paintings to the flames, broke them in pieces, cast them away, or sold them for a pittance to whosoever would buy. Buddhist priests were prohibited from participating in Shinto ceremonies. They were subjected to beatings and threatened with military force. Monks and nuns in large numbers were obliged to take up secular callings.[6]

Grave foreign protests on the subject of Christianity plus serious unrest among the masses devoted to Buddhism forced the abandoning of the policy of religious persecution. Liberal elements within the country agitated for the complete separation of church and state, and the Meiji leaders were brought to understand that religious freedom was a principle of the modern society they were trying to establish. Consequently, the government included in the constitution of 1889 a clause guaranteeing freedom of religion. At the same time it continued its support of the state Shinto cult, whose main aim was the veneration of the emperor. It solved this seeming contradiction by declaring that state Shinto was not a religion but merely an expression of patriotism. Nevertheless, the existence of the national cult imposed a real limitation on the independence and effectiveness of the private religious bodies. Though in the 1920's there was a strong tendency to differentiate religion and ideology, in times of stress such as the late 1930's and early 1940's religion was completely subordinated to and fused with a monolithic ideology, an ideology which had demonic consequences both for Japan and and for the rest of the world. The new, 1946, constitution, by disestablishing Shinto and deriving sovereignty from the people rather than from the sacred and inviolable emperor, theoretically completed the process of secularization.

But, in fact, serious religious problems remain. All religious groups with the exception of the Christians were compromised by their connection with the nationalistic orgy. In the absence of any really vigorous religious life, except for the popular faith-healing cults and the small Christian community, the religious impulses of the Japanese peo-

---

[6] D. C. Holtom, Modern Japan and Shinto Nationalism (Chicago: University of Chicago Press, 1947), p. 127.

ple find expression for the more radical in the symbol of socialism, for the conservatives in a longing for a new and more innocent version of state Shinto. Here, as in Turkey, the differentiation between religion and ideology remains to be completed.

Other examples of the processes we have been discussing come readily to mind. Communism is an example of a secular political ideology which successfully came to power in the prescriptive, religiously based societies of Russia and China. But communism itself makes an ultimate religious claim, and here, as in the case of Japan, a secular ideology claiming religious ultimacy has embarked on courses of action which hinder, rather than further, the transition to modern principial society. It is perhaps safe to say that alongside the serious political and economic problems which commu-

nism faces today is the perhaps even more serious cultural problem, the problem of the differentiation of the religious and ideological levels.

In conclusion, it seems worthwhile to stress that the process of secularization, which is in part what the transition from prescriptive to principial society is, does not mean that religion disappears. The function of religion in a principial society is different from that in a prescriptive society, but it is not necessarily less important. Moreover, in the very process of transition religion may reappear in many new guises. Perhaps what makes the situation so unclear is its very fluidity. Even in highly differentiated societies, such as our own, traditional religion, so deeply associated with the prescriptive past, is still in the process of finding its place in modern principial society.

Sociological Aspects of Political Development in Underdeveloped Countries

S. N. Eisenstadt

SOURCE: *Economic Development and Cultural Change*, Vol. 5 (1957), pp. 289–307.

1. THE PROBLEM

This paper will present some hypotheses on the main sociological factors which influence political processes and institutions in underdeveloped countries. The future of democratic, representative institutions in these countries has often been debated, but most studies of these institutions have not been as systematic as others dealing with problems of economic development. Yet in many underdeveloped countries—whether of colonial, post-colonial, or independent status—the state plays a fundamental role in economic development and constitutes one of the basic factors influencing this

development. Works on the political problems in Asia and Africa center mostly around the analysis and description of formal political institutions and basic political groups, and are often based on implicit assumptions as to the relative importance of some social conditions which may influence the stability and development of the new institutions.[1]

Certain basic themes seem to recur in most studies. One is the emphasis upon traditionalism manifesting itself in the

---

[1] Among the exceptions see especially R. Emerson, Representative Government in South East Asia, Cambridge, Mass., 1955; and D. Apter, The Gold Coast in Transition, Princeton, 1956.

organization of the society on a basis of authority. This traditionalism, accompanied by a low standard of living, seems to impede the development of democratic institutions and to favor authoritarianism.[2] Another theme emphasizes aspects of the problem of transition from a traditional to a modern society. Thus Scalapino stresses the international economic and political tensions under which this transition has been made.[3] Emerson stresses such factors as lack of experience in governmental and administrative functions, the relative thinness of a modern Westernized elite and its dissociation from the traditional masses, the consequent lack of development of institutions of local government, and the continuation of traditional patterns.[4] The extent to which underdeveloped countries are internally divided is another frequently stressed theme. The division between traditional and Westernized groups, on the one hand, and the division within the Westernized groups, on the other, producing many small parties, have been discussed repeatedly.

Thus while in most works on the political problems of underdeveloped countries assumptions are made as to the social conditions which may either impede or facilitate the development of modern political institutions, the assumptions are rarely systematized. Moreover, many analyses are consciously or unconsciously focused on the extent to which political institutions, especially on the formal level, deviate from the Western political pattern. Consequently, the internal dynamics of social and political systems are sometimes lost sight of, and the ways in which the societies—successfully or unsuccessfully—accommodate themselves to various aspects of modern political institutions, and evolve relatively new forms of political organi-

zation, are misunderstood. I shall try to outline, in a systematic way, some of the main sociological factors influencing the political developments in underdeveloped countries, and the social characteristics and internal dynamics of their political systems. I shall first list some characteristics which in varying degrees are common to most colonial societies, especially to countries which have attained independence. In the last part of the paper I shall list briefly some main characteristics by which these countries differ and shall present a few basic variables which should be taken into account in trying to explain these differences. (In this way this analysis may serve as a starting point for a series of researches in which these variables and some of the hypotheses implied in them will be tested out. This will have to be done in further publications.)

2. UNEVEN CHANGE IN COLONIAL SOCIETIES

A characteristic of this whole process of transition and change in underdeveloped societies is that it has been, and continues to be, unbalanced. Certain main elements of this lack of balance have long been recognized and more or less correctly attributed to the basic nature of colonialism.[5] Although many of the underdeveloped societies did not have officially colonial status, most of the changes have occurred under the impact of the clash with the West. As a result of this, these societies have been put in an inferior, dependent, and unbalanced position in relation to European powers. This situation, moreover, has been evaluated within a framework of European institutions and values. But in order to understand some of the dynamic problems to which this process has given rise, certain additional aspects of this

[2] See Emerson, op. cit. See also E. Staley, The Future of Underdeveloped Countries, New York, 1954.

[3] R. A. Scalapino, "Democracy in Asia, Past and Future," Far Eastern Survey, Vol. XX (1951), pp. 53-57.

[4] Emerson, op. cit.

[5] Raymond Kennedy, "The Colonial Crisis and the Future," in R. Linton, ed., The Science of Man in a World Crisis, New York, 1945. See also Rita Hinden, ed., Fabian Colonial Essays, London, 1945, especially the essays by Fortes and Furnivall; and J. H. Boeke, Economics and Economic Policy of Dual Societies, New York, 1953.

uneven and unbalanced change should be analyzed.

The first major aspect is the lack of balance in processes of change and transition that can be found between the "central" level and the local level. Most changes introduced either directly or indirectly by the colonial powers (or by the "traditional" authorities of the independent societies which cooperated with the European powers) have been focused on the central institutions of the society. The most obvious changes were in the broad frameworks of political and economic institutions. In the political field, the introduction of unitary systems of administration, the unification or regularization of taxation, the establishment of modern court procedures, and at later stages, the introduction of limited types of representation, have greatly changed overall political structures and orientations. In the relatively independent states, innovation in military techniques was prevalent. The changes have introduced certain universalistic criteria, that is, orientations toward general rules and modern procedures. Even where various forms of indirect rule were practiced (as in many British South-East Asian, and particularly African territories), some change necessarily took place in political organization, though this change was much slower than in cases of direct rule.

Similarly, many changes have been effected in the economy, notably the change to a market economy.[6]

Similar attempts to change the central foci of the institutional framework were made on a more limited scale in the educational field by endeavoring to provide new types of modern education for selected local elites.[7]

The common factor in these changes was their direction toward promotion of systematic change in the society as a whole. There was a more or less conscious awareness that such change was necessary and presumably good), and

that new general institutional structures and principles should be established. At the same time, however, the colonial powers (or indigenous traditional rulers) saw it as part of their task to effect these changes only within the limits set by the existing institutions and their own interests.[8]

This is manifest in their orientation toward change at the local level, i.e., the level of the village, community, or tribal unit. Here colonial or indigenous rulers attempted to contain most changes within the limits of traditional groups and/or to limit, as much as possible, the extent of any change. But many changes did develop within the local communities, as the literature on detribalization, social and economic disorganization in villages, and disorganization of the family indicates.[9] The important thing for our analysis is that the rulers tried, insofar as was possible, to contain these changes within traditional systems, and most of their administrative efforts on the local level were aimed at the strengthening of the existing organizations and relations, at maintaining peace and order, and at reorganizing the systems of taxation. Thus, while the administration attempted to introduce innovations—particularly new taxes and improved methods of revenue administration—it tried to accomplish this within a relatively unchanging social setting, with the implicit goal of limiting changes to technical matters.[10]

---

[8] It is not of interest for our analysis here to show the exact attitudes of different groups, leaders, etc. It is only the general trend of development that is significant.

[9] See G. Wilson, An Essay on the Economics of Detribalization in Northern Rhodesia, Rhodes-Livingstone Paper 5, Livingstone, 1941. E. Hellman, Rooiyard, Rhodes-Livingstone Paper 13, Livingstone, 1948. G. Balandier, Sociologie des Brazavilles noires, Paris, 1955. See also K. Davis, The Population of India and Pakistan, Princeton, 1951. See also the papers in Sections II and IV of "Contemporary Africa," Annals of the American Academy of Political and Social Science, Vol. 298 (March 1955), and J. M. van der Kroef, Indonesia in the Modern World, Bandung, 1954, esp. Chs. 4 and 5.

[10] See, for a good description, P. Griffiths, The British Impact on India, London, 1952, Section I;

---

[6] See, for instance, Boeke, op. cit.

[7] J. S. Furnivall, Educational Progress in South East Asia, New York, 1943.

Here existed a basic contradiction: on the one hand, attempts were made to establish broad, modern, administrative, political, and economic settings, while on the other hand, these changes were to be limited and based on relatively unchanged sub-groups and on traditional attitudes and loyalties. This contradictory attitude could be found in most spheres of social action.

In the economic field, the major efforts were made to facilitate the functioning of a market-oriented economy—albeit of a very specific kind. This economy had to operate, as it were, without full development of new economic motivations, which would have disturbed the existing social order. In the field of education, where innovations were much less broad, there existed the tendency to impart rudiments of technical education without changing the system of values and aspirations.[11]

In economic and educational fields of action at least partial solutions could be found. Some indigenous groups found a place in newly established economic, educational, and professional organizations. Literacy grew to some extent, and the expectation of monetary rewards became customary and permissible for most groups.

Internal contradictions were most pronounced in the political field. Since the colonial powers or the indigenous rulers were interested in political loyalty, they aimed at maintaining a relatively passive type of obedience and identification, and were always ready, whenever possible, to utilize existing traditional loyalties or to transfer them to the new setting without much change in their basic social and cultural orientations.[12]

While the colonial powers and most indigenous rulers were interested in loyalty and were concerned with the transformation of certain institutional aspects —especially technical aspects—of the social structure, at the same time they did not want to base these innovations on new types of solidarity and general political orientations and participation of the main strata of the population. Rather they tried to base the new political-administrative structure on orientations limited to technical, administrative changes for the bulk of the population, and on more general and active identification for a very limited and select group at the center.

The full dynamic implications of this unbalanced development can only be understood if some additional aspects of the unevenness of change are analyzed. These are aspects derived from the colonial or semi-colonial political situation. Most of them were present also in the non-colonial "independent" societies (China, Ottoman Empire, Arab states) but appeared in a different light, to be analyzed in more detail later.

The two chief results derived from the colonial nexus were (1) segregation between Europeans and natives, and (2) discrimination against the natives in most of the newly developed institutions. The extent of segregation and the intensity of discrimination varied in different institutional spheres and were often coupled with attempts to maintain the traditional native culture and even to idealize and romanticize it. The attempts at "segregation" and at minimal developments of a common framework were most prominent in the fields of politics and social solidarity; they were somewhat less so in the fields of administration and the economy. But the paradox of the situation was that as the more overt attempts at segregation in the traditional as well as more

also J. Furnivall, Colonial Policy and Practice, Cambridge, 1948.

[11] See Furnivall, Educational Progress in South East Asia, op. cit., and also L. Finkelstein, "Education in Indonesia," Far Eastern Survey, Vol. 20 (1951), pp. 149-153; M. Read, "Education in Africa," ANNALS (March 1955), op. cit., pp. 170-179; S. M. Naidis, Economic Development and Education in India, New York, 1952; B. T. McCully, English Education and the Origins of Indian Nationalism, New York, 1940.

[12] See Griffiths, op. cit.; J. Furnivall, Colonial Policy, op. cit., and W. F. Wertheim, Indonesian Society in Transition, The Hague, 1956, Chs. III, IV.

modern spheres gradually were being given up, due to situational exigencies, and as more and more natives were drawn into the modern spheres, the more acute became the discrimination against them in terms of the basic premises of these institutions.

Thus the basic problem in these societies was the expectation that the native population would accept certain broad, modern institutional settings organized according to principles of universalism, specificity, and common secular solidarity, and would perform within them various roles—especially economic and administrative roles—while at the same time, they were denied some of the basic rewards inherent in these settings. They were denied above all full participation in a common political system and full integration in a common system of solidarity. In other words, they were expected to act on the basis of a motivational system derived from a different social structure which the colonial powers and indigenous rulers tried to maintain. Quite obviously these societies faced acute problems of integration which could not be solved, except momentarily, within the framework of colonial or semi-colonial societies.

These processes of uneven change did not and could not stop at a given time and freeze, as it were, a society's development at a certain stage. Many such attempts were made—as is evidenced by the attempts at indirect rule, on the one hand, and by widespread efforts of indigenous rulers to limit changes to purely technical matters, on the other. But such devices could not succeed for long. The economic needs of the colonial powers and/or of the indigenous ruling groups, their growing dependency on international markets, and on the international political system and the changes within it, precluded any freezing of development at a given stage. Thus, all these processes tended to affect "native" social systems to an increasing degree and to draw ever wider strata of these societies into the orbit of modern institutional settings. Different countries are even today at different stages of development in this process. But the greater the tempo of these changes, the greater the unevenness and lack of balance, and the greater the problems of acute mal-integration the society has to face.

As has been shown earlier, these problems of mal-integration arose at various levels and in different social spheres—in the economic and ecological spheres, in education, in family life, and others. But they were necessarily most acute in the political and solidarity spheres; there the colonial or Western impact had undermined most of the old integrative principles and organizations both at the local and at the national level. While partial solutions could sometimes be found for economic and technical problems, their very partiality only tended to emphasize the alien political framework and the mal-integration in the solidarity sphere.

3. THE INFLUENCE OF UNEVEN CHANGE ON POLITICAL MOVEMENTS IN COLONIAL SOCIETIES

It is not within the province of this paper to analyze the various attempts by colonial powers to find solutions to these problems within the framework of colonial society. Our main concern will be to analyze the repercussion of these developments on the nationalistic political and social movements which have been of prime importance for the future of these countries.[13]

These movements have their origin in the dynamic situation of change, whose imprint can be discerned in their structure and development. Naturally, most of the nationalistic and social-nationalistic

---

[13]See, for a general description of these movements, R. Emerson, L. Mills, and V. Thompson, Government and Nationalism in South East Asia, New York, 1942; J. F. Halkema-Kohl, "Colonial Nationalism," Indonesie, Vol. VII (1953), pp. 35-61; J. S. Coleman, "Current Political Movements in Africa," Annals (March 1955), op. cit., pp. 95-105; W. C. Holland, ed., Asian Nationalism and the West, New York, 1953.

movements were especially sensitive to the manifestations of lack of balance and evenness of change. Yet, at the same time, they usually could not overcome easily the problems that this imbalance had created.

This sensitivity can be discerned in two basic characteristics of these movements: first, in their strong emphasis on new secular, modern symbols of solidarity and in their strong orientation towards solidarity-political activity (aiming ultimately at political independence); and second, in their attempts, especially in the later stages of development, to break through the "freezing" at the local level and to reach the broad masses of the population. But, at the same time— and this is most important for our analysis—the common bond which they tried to create with the masses was almost entirely couched in modern solidarity-political terms and did not emphasize the solution of immediate economic and administrative problems. The political symbols used were intended to develop new, ultimate, common values and basic loyalties, rather than to relate to current policy issues within the colonial society. This emphasis was caused by their exclusion from effective power and by their fear of compromising the basic issue through participation in current affairs when opportunity arose.

A somewhat similar attitude can be observed in respect to economic, administrative and instrumental problems. Most nationalist movements did develop an economic ideology either stressing romantically the maintenance of the old village community or the necessity of state planning. All decried the injustices of the economic policies and discrimination of the colonial powers. But the nationalist leaders did not deal concretely with current economic problems or problems of daily administration. It is significant that members of the social groups among colonial peoples who participated relatively successfully in economic or administrative areas and who developed new types of social organization (as, for example, native business communities or

membership in the colonial services) usually did not participate actively in the nationalistic movements and often were looked upon as traitors, or, at least, as "compromisers," by the members and leaders of these movements. The nationalistic leaders appealed to those groups of the population which were in an acute state of transition from the traditional to the modern setting, and which therefore suffered most from social disorganization, rather than to the groups which could adapt tolerably to the new institutional spheres.[14]

Thus, most nationalistic movements, though obviously opposed to the colonial regime, inherited from it some important social characteristics. On the one hand, the leaders attempted to formulate new symbols of solidarity which would transcend the limitations of the colonial situation and which were couched in modern nationalistic and universalistic terms. But at the same time, they did not make any special efforts to transform other spheres of institutional life and to solve the problems created there by the processes of uneven change. Although the nationalist leaders did not try to prevent the development of new types of social organization, they did not explicitly deal with problems provoked by these changes. They seemed to be content to base the new movement, within the instrumental fields, either on traditional types of attitudes and organization, or on transitory types of attitudes and motivations which were not fully stabilized. Their major assumption, common to many revolutionary movements, was that all of these problems would be more or less automatically solved once political independence would be achieved.[15]

The attitudes and social characteristics of these nationalistic movements are, of course, rooted in the colonial situation. They are closely related to the

---

[14] See K. R. Bombwall, Indian Politics and Government, 1951, esp. Chs. IV, V, X, and XI; V. N. Naik, Indian Liberalism—A Study, Bombay, 1949, Chs. IV and XXI; Apter, op. cit.

[15] See abundant material in Apter, op. cit.; and van der Kroef, op. cit., Chs. 2 and 3.

social origins and processes of selection of the leaders of the nationalistic movements and the relation of the leaders to the masses of the population. The leaders usually came from sectors of the more Westernized professional and intellectual groups, from among students, lawyers, journalists, most of whom had been directly exposed to Western values, had been active in some modern institutions, but either had not been fully absorbed by them, or, though indoctrinated with Western ideologies and values, could not accept their non-realization within the colonial setting.[16]

Most of the early leaders of nationalistic movements came from relatively well-to-do families. They had adapted themselves to some aspects of Western life, without entirely losing a foothold in their own traditions, and they rarely suffered from personal oppression.[17] However, at later stages, the ranks were swelled with unemployed semi-intellectuals, semi-professionals and semi-untrained groups.[18] These new men were mostly of urban origin; at least they grew up in the new urban settings which had come into being under the colonial regime. They usually did not have many direct relations with either the rural or the urban proletarian masses. Hence, they displayed a lack of understanding of many concrete economic problems of the masses, a limited grasp of political problems on the conceptual level, because of their narrow literary and professional background, and a strong idealization of the masses and of the village. Moreover, with the development of colonial economies and nationalistic movements, urban centers tended more and more to attract the more active elements from other parts of the colonies, with the result that the countryside was depleted of potential leaders. On coming to the towns, these

potential leaders took up the symbols and orientations of the movement very quickly and often turned their backs on the acute problems of their groups or localities of origin. Whenever they returned to their points of origin, they tended to appeal in terms of overall solidarity symbols rather than in terms of specific concrete problems.[19]

The social peculiarities of nationalist movements produced various characteristics which have often been described in the literature. The emphasis on solidarity symbols, without attention to other aspects of social organization, has necessarily given rise to a relative lack of stability in the sphere of political organization itself. This is evidenced by the divisions between different political movements and between the leaders of political movements and the more traditional powers in the society, such as tribal chiefs, princes, and colonial elites. Whenever competing nationalist movements developed within any one society, they became usually totally opposed to one another in terms of ultimate values and symbols of identification, and not merely in terms of differences over policies. This was not only true in the relations between modern and traditional forces, but also—and perhaps even more so—between the different modern groups, such as nationalistic, socialistic, communistic groups. Although on certain occasions all groups entered into uneasy alliances and coalitions—this did not change greatly their basic attitudes and their mutual ideological antagonisms.[20]

A further characteristic of political structures in colonial countries is the relative weakness of various economic and professional organizations, e.g.,

[16] See A. R. Desai, Social Background of Indian Nationalism, London, 1948, Chs. XI, XIII, XVIII. See also Emerson et al, op. cit.; and Emerson, op. cit.

[17] See the autobiographies and biographies of Gandhi, Nehru, Patel, and Nkruma. For a more general analysis see McCully, op. cit.

[18] See Apter, op. cit., Chs. 7 and 8.

[19] Ibid., esp. Ch. 8 on very pertinent illustrations.

[20] See Emerson, op. cit.; Emerson et al., op. cit.; G. T. McKahin, Nationalism and Revolution in Indonesia, Ithaca, 1953; C. A. O. van Nieuwenhuijze, "The Dar ul-Islam Movement in Western Java," Pacific Affairs, Vol. XXIII (1950), pp. 169-183. See also Coleman, op. cit., and "The Emergence of African Political Parties," in C. G. Haines, ed., Africa Today, Baltimore, 1955, pp. 225ff.; J. A. Curran, Militant Hinduism in Indian Politics, New York, 1951.

trade unions, cooperatives, chambers of commerce, and the talk of their mutual integration as well as their uneasy relationship with the political movements. These weaknesses usually are of two kinds. Either the economic organizations, whatever their strength, held themselves apart from one another and from the political movements, did not participate in them, and thus did not exert their influence on them; or they became entirely subordinate to the political leaders (especially in the case of the Belfast movements) who did not take account of the specific problems and needs of economic organizations.[21]

Another characteristic of colonial politics was the way in which various interest groups, e.g., local merchants, exerted influence on the administration or on political organizations in lower levels of government. The most common techniques of exerting influence included various types of lobbying, i.e., personal pressure, and sometimes attempts at bribery. Whatever the exact nature and diversity of these activities, they were not closely related to the major political movements and did not envisage to any great extent the mobilization of public opinion. Whenever one of these issues became important for political groups and public opinion, it became transformed into an overall problem of political independence and subsumed under the general solidarity symbols.

The combination of all these factors perhaps explains the importance of the urban "mob" in the politics of many colonial countries—and the parallel weakness of organized public opinion.

The different characteristics of the political process which we enumerated varied greatly from one country to another in their concrete details and in their relative importance and intensity, and we shall later distinguish some major types. But at this stage, a general analysis with illustrations will have to

suffice. The illustrations point out some inherent weaknesses, or perhaps more accurately, the lack of balance in political developments and organizations in colonial countries. All these problems did not seem acute as long as the main issue was the attainment of political independence and as long as the movements were acting within the framework of colonial rule which was responsible for the daily running of the country. It was only when independence was attained, or when a definite transfer of power was planned and realized, that all these problems became of crucial importance for the stability of the new political system. In those countries which still retain their colonial status, the former characteristics are still predominant in different degrees. Only in those countries which have attained independence, or are in the process of attaining it, or in those areas in which a traditional ruling group has been supplanted by some more modern nationalistic elite (as in China, or some of the Middle Eastern countries), are all these problems coming to the surface.

4. THE TRANSFORMATION OF POLITICAL MOVEMENTS AFTER ATTAINMENT OF INDEPENDENCE

The full sociological significance of the attainment of independence becomes apparent and can be more exhaustively analyzed within the framework described above. Let us analyze some basic structural changes which were brought about by the attainment of independence.

A. The attainment of political independence and the establishment of a new state always entails the establishment of new spheres of power, of new power positions which exercise a strong influence on the economic structure of the society, and greatly widen the various instrumental rewards and gratifications which can be allocated through political and administrative channels.

B. The attainment of political independence necessarily also gives rise to the promotion of new collective sym-

---

[21] See V. Thompson, The Left Wing in South East Asia, New York, 1950; F. W. Galley, "The Prospect for Asian Trade Unionism," Pacific Affairs, Vol. XXIV (1951), pp. 296-306.

bols of identification, mostly borne by the new political elites which also claim special acceptance by the population because of their participation in the struggle for independence and because of the successful attainment of this aim. It may be said that because of the extension of the field of instrumental rewards and of new spheres of power, we find here also an intensification of claims by these elites to solidarity acceptance and prestige.

Let us briefly enlarge on these two points.

The enlargement of the spheres of power, and the concomitant increase in rewards through new political and administrative agencies, is self-evident. It is significant that most "new" states have attained their independence in an historical period which has witnessed a growing concentration of economic power and direction by the government. Moreover, most of the new states were relative latecomers to the international economy, and found that many of the best positions had already been monopolized by the older, long-established states. They were also relatively poor in original capital and entrepreneurial skill. For all these reasons the importance of the state and consequently its growing power in the economic sphere are evident in all former colonial societies.[22]

The growing power of the government manifests itself in the expansion of its administrative services and in the continuous growth of the bureaucratic apparatus. This expansion is not purely quantitative. It gives rise to a relatively new social group, the political elite and bureaucracy, which, whatever the extent of its internal cohesion and homogeneity, tends to claim special positions of power and prestige, and attempts to supervise many activities of other professional, economic, and cultural groups in the society.

---

[22] See M. Zinkin, Asia and the West, London, 1952, Ch. XIX; and O. Reischauer, Wanted—A Policy for Asia, New York, 1955, Ch. VII.

These claims to social importance are usually raised both by the active political top-circles and the top and middle strata of the bureaucracy. They derive their strength not only from their holding of important power positions, but also—especially among the political elite—from their close attachment to the collective solidarity values of the community, from the would-be personification of the attainment of political independence, and from the glory of the "revolutionary" days when they formed the nucleus of revolutionary political and social movements. Moreover, the elite quite often justifies its claim to power and instrumental rewards in terms of their solidarity activities and values. After the attainment of independence—unlike the pre-independence days, when their claim to prestige and influence was solely based on collective-solidarity grounds—the claims of the elite became strongly interwoven with claims based on acquisition of power and oriented to rewards in the instrumental field. The most outstanding feature of this process is the potential claim of the political and bureaucratic elite to the monopolization of the highest positions of prestige and power in the instrumental, the solidarity, and the cultural fields alike.

Generally speaking, then, the attainment of political independence has meant the extension of modern political and social institutions from the purely solidarity to the technical, adaptive, and instrumental fields, as well as the first stages in the routinization of the charisma of the older political movements. The new political system had either to incorporate within its framework the existing administrative organs and/or create new ones and had to orient itself toward various economic and instrumental problems. In other words, the sphere in which modern, universalistic principles of administration and politics prevailed became greatly extended and coordinated in one common framework with that of solidarity symbols and institutions. In a way, this constituted a total reversal of the colonial situation. But this reversal did not necessarily mean that all the problems of uneven development and change have been successfully solved. Rather, these problems became transformed, in keeping with the new framework, and constitute the main new problems of formerly dependent countries.

5. NEW PATTERNS OF POLITICAL PARTICIPATION AND MOTIVATION

With the attainment of independence the new elites faced several tasks in the area of political organization. They could not confine political participation to its former level, but had to extend its scope to the politically more passive or inarticulate groups from which new types of allegiance, political involvement, and loyalties were being demanded. The new regimes could not maintain themselves entirely on passive allegiance that had been predominant in the colonial times, since they themselves had undermined this kind of allegiance. Through their emphasis on governmental activities in many spheres of the society, they penetrated more and more into various social layers. Because of this, the new governments could not rely on traditional motivations and attitudes in the instrumental and administrative fields to the same extent the old colonial regimes had. They had, in one way or another, to foster the development of new motivations and social and political participation. Schemes for community development, for new industrial and agrarian organizations, as well as agrarian reforms, whenever they were undertaken—all implied the necessity for new orientations and incentives and the development of many new motivational patterns.[23]

The new elites had to develop the allegiance of the masses to the new symbols of solidarity and the all-embracing political system as a whole. At the same time they had also to develop in the masses some identification with and loyalty to the new administrative and bureaucratic institutions, and—even more important—to the new rules of the political game. They had to develop simultaneously a basic loyalty to the new system and to foster new types of political participation and competition within that system. They had to assume that these new patterns of competition would not disrupt the system as a whole. In other words, they had to work for the simultaneous establishment of two new kinds of ligitimization: a new solidarity one, and a new legal-rational one. Between the two there could easily develop many tensions and incompatibilities.

These tensions were due to a growing contradiction between the aspirations of various social, professional and economic groups and the policies and aspirations of the ruling elites. The attainment of independence extended the sphere and increased the value of economic, administrative, and professional activities. Moreover, most of these activities were no longer performed within the framework of an alien political system and a place had to be found for them within the new national framework.

The increase of the scope of these activities has naturally increased the potential power and the social and political aspirations of the various groups performing them. These groups constituted also the potential participants in the political game within the new states. But the aspirations of these groups have come up against the inherent tendency of the political elite and bureaucracy with respect to the monopolization of power and prestige. This tendency, which is closely related to the social transformation attendant on the attainment of independence, has manifested itself in:

(a) attempts to create a strong unified hierarchy of status in terms of political power;

(b) efforts to subject most processes of social mobility to control by the different political elites; and

(c) efforts to subject a large number of economic, professional, and cultural activities to political control.

---

[23] See, for instance, Department of Mass Education of the Ministry of Education, Mass Education in Indonesia, Djakarta, 1954; McKahin, op. cit.; van der Kroef, op. cit.

As a result, there tends to develop a continuous tension and ambivalence in the relations between the political elite, other elite groups, and potential new centers of power. The bureaucracy is inclined to belittle the importance and efficiency of purely economic activities and the claims of economic groups toward social autonomy. It tends to superimpose extra-economic criteria on economic activities and on their bearers, not only by stipulating broad, general "social goals," but also by the daily regulation and direction of activity. In other words, the bureaucracy claims great, if not absolute, power over these activities and claims greater prestige than their bearers. In this way many aspects of economic activity and entrepreneurship are stifled and discouraged. Moreover, the political elite attempts, in some cases, to undermine the autonomous development of the middle and working classes and link their positions entirely to political directives. A similar and sometimes even more intensive pattern can be found in the relations of the political elite and bureaucracy towards professional and cultural elites. If direct regimentation is not often attempted (this feature is usually limited to post-revolutionary totalitarian societies), a general tendency towards the direct linking of these activities with collective goals as represented by the elite and bureaucracy can still be found. Thus the emphasis put on cultural professions (teaching, creation of new traditional symbols) is greater than that placed on medicine, engineering, and other technical professions which seem to be more "neutral" in relation to collective goals.[24]

Closely related are the attempts of the political elite and bureaucracy to direct and control all social developments of the country, especially those relating to the standard of living and the availability of new occupations and mobility within them. In this way they tend to maintain their hold on potential centers of power and to control their evolution. But these attempts are often self-contradictory because the close control exercised by the bureaucracy undermines efforts for economic development. More aspirants are created for new posts than there are posts available, and thus the bureaucracy itself is put in an insecure position.[25]

The ambivalent position of the political elite, and especially of the bureaucracy, is clearly shown by the following facts (which are found in varying degrees in most of the countries studied): (1) the bureaucracy itself experiences difficulties in recruiting adequately trained personnel; and (2) because of financial stringency officials are underpaid with the result that corruption develops. Hence the efficient functioning of the bureaucracy becomes problematic. On the one hand, the bureaucracy increases its attempts to attain social prestige and political power; on the other hand, it alienates large parts of the population and undermines some of the social and economic aims of its activities.[26]

All these tendencies impede the development of social and institutional differentiations which would facilitate the emergence of diversified centers of power and prestige in the society. Attempts to establish a monolithic hierarchy of power and prestige have often impeded the development of relatively autonomous groups and organizations in society and weakened the development of independent public opinion. The well-known weakness of different non-specific voluntary associations in many poor countries is a case in point.

All this may be summed up by saying that the main problem in the development of the political institutions in the new

----

[24] See Apter, op. cit., Chs. 8, 10. See also L. U. Palmer, "Aspects of Indonesia's Social Structure," Pacific Affairs, Vol. 28 (1955), pp. 117-131.

[25] M. Zinkin, "Problems of Economic Development in Asia." Paper submitted to the 12th Conference of the Institute of Pacific Relations, 1954. Chs. VII and VIII (mimeographed).

[26] On some aspects of the problem of recruitment into the bureaucracy see B. Hoselitz, "The Recruitment of White-Collar Workers in Underdeveloped Countries," International Social Science Bulletin, Vol. VI, No. 3 (1954), pp. 433-442.

countries is the necessity of developing simultaneously social support for the maintenance of different and even contradictory aspects of modern, institutional frameworks.

The difficulty of a simultaneous development of different types of political institutions and of the social attitudes necessary for their maintenance and functioning is obviously rooted in the specific heritage of uneven change analyzed earlier in this paper. The unevenness of change resulted in an uneven development of different types of motivation and orientation to different aspects of a modern institutional setting. In some institutional spheres the development has, as we have seen, over-emphasized new types of motivations—especially in the solidarity field. This over-emphasis was reinforced by a relatively unorganized and unstable development of motivations and by a high extent of social disorganization in other spheres. Stabilization of these fields of action may have weakened the intensive solidarity orientation. With the attainment of independence and growing emphasis on wider administrative activities and power relations, all new developments tended to be subordinated to the activities of the political elite, which attempted also to assure its control over these new developments. Autonomous developments of outlying centers of power and the stabilization of new political groups or interests were viewed by the elite as interfering with the stabilization of the new basic institutional framework and with universal allegiance to the new common symbols. Faced with this problem, the residing elites of the new countries tended to undertake one of two possible courses of action. In some cases the elites attempted to "solve" this problem by slowing down the tempo of modern development and by maintaining, wherever possible, traditional authorities and loyalties. Perhaps the most outstanding examples of this may be found in some Middle Eastern countries, in Pakistan, and formerly in the Philippines. In other cases the new ruling elites attempted to speed up the destruction of traditional

forces and loyalties and to replace them as rapidly as possible with a new nationalism. At the same time they attempted to control this new ideology and to place it in the service of their own aims and power-positions. In these countries the ruling elites also tended to impede the development of autonomous and independent centers of social and political power. Examples of this are Indonesia, Ghana, and India. But in neither of the two cases can the ruling elites avoid the dilemma, and neither solution seems to contribute significantly to the maintenance of governmental stability.[27]

6. THE STRUCTURE OF POLITICAL INSTITUTIONS

In the formal structure of government some parallel tendencies can also be discerned, in varying degrees, in different new countries. The first is the obvious preponderance of the executive over all other branches of government. This development clearly flows from the need of the new governments to take over and to operate the governmental machinery smoothly. It is connected with the strong emphasis on governmental economic activity and the necessity to promote overall identification with and loyalty to the new state. The legislature is usually passive and subservient to the executive or so unruly as to minimize the effects of its own influence and power.[28] This does

---

[27] The analysis presented here on the different levels of motivation has some affinities with Boeke's analysis of dual societies. But it seems to me that Boeke does not realize sufficiently that the "duality" of motivation and of economic attitudes is not that between traditional and modern setting, but is a part of the whole process of change.

See J. H. Boeke, op. cit.; and "Three Forms of Disintegration in Dual Societies," *Indonesie*, Vol. 8 (1953-1954), pp. 278-295. See also B. Higgins, "The 'Dualistic Theory' of Underdeveloped Areas," *Economic Development and Cultural Change*, Vol. IV, No. 2, pp. 94-116.

[28] See McKahin, op. cit.; M. A. da Silva, "Parliamentary Government in Underdeveloped Democracies," *Parliamentary Affairs*, Vol. VII (1954), pp. 120-126; S. D. Bailey, *Naissance de nouvelles democraties*, Paris, 1953; J. H. A. Lageman, "The Indonesian Parliament," *Parliamentary Affairs*, Vol. VI (1953), pp. 346-354. See also Tuansheng Chien, *The Government and Politics of China*, Cambridge, Mass., 1950, esp. Chs. XI-XIII.

not mean that the different legislative bodies in all new countries are totally ineffective, although in some (especially the Middle East) they may be non-existent. It does indicate rather that their effective power of control over the executive and their function as mediators between the executive and the population at large are rather weak. This is closely connected with the often observed fact that in most new countries there has not existed, until recently, an effective opposition. The opposition party is too weak to constitute a real alternative (as in India), or there exists a multiplicity of parties among whom shifting coalitions are tried out (as in Indonesia), or any opposition that may arise is suppressed because it is seen as totally disloyal (as formerly in Pakistan). Closely connected with this also is the tendency for dictatorial regimes or movements with dictatorial tendencies to develop.

The judicial branch is characterized by a similar weakness. In some cases, there is no tradition of judicial independence. In others, the inability to promulgate a constitution and to organize the basic juridical norms of the state have been important factors in the absence of full legitimization of the judicial branch of government. India and Burma seem to be outstanding here, and the comparison with Pakistan and Indonesia is very instructive.[29]

But the most important manifestation of the predominance of the executive can perhaps be seen, paradoxically enough, in the uneasy relations between the executive and the administrative bureaucracies. Whatever the initial separation between the branches of government, they seem to come closer to one another and to share more values. Yet there exist many difficulties in establishing a proper division of labor between them. The two extremes of an administration engaging in political contests (or being used by the

parties in power to this end) or the executive and legislative interfering in the working of the administration are situations to be found frequently, and quite often together.[30]

Perhaps the most extreme example of this may be found in those countries where parts of the administration, expecially the military, engage in independent political action. While this is a pattern common in the Middle East, some of its embryonic manifestations may also be seen in Indonesia and Pakistan.[31] These problems indicate the relative weakness of the concept of legal-rational legitimization and of the adherence to the universalistic norms in these societies. Here, two points are of special importance. The first is the uneasy relationship between the bureaucracy and the executive, which may easily impede the smooth functioning of administrative procedures and the maintenance of a wide sphere of universal rules beyond the province of current political disputes and differing interests. In other words, the capacity of the bureaucracy to mediate according to universalistic criteria between different interests and groups may be sometimes strongly curtailed.[32]

Secondly, the weakness of the universalistic rules and of the legal-rational legitimization affects most acutely adherence to parliamentary procedures and the "rules of the game," as well as the possibility of maintaining discussion and organizing an independent public opinion. Here the two traits of "total" opposition and divisiveness, as well as of various types of direct pressures for different allocations, have been transplanted into the new political framework and have been continued in the new setting—sometimes with more intensity. They can be discerned most clearly in political par-

---

[29] Bailey, op. cit.; G. W. Choudhury, "Constitution Making Dilemmas in Pakistan," *The Western Political Quarterly*, Vol. VIII (1955), pp. 589-601.

[30] See A. D. Gorwalla, Report on Public Administration, Government of India, New Delhi, 1951; The Role of the Administrator, Poona, 1952; and P. Appleby, Public Administration in India, Delhi, 1953.
[31] M. Kadouri, "The Army.Officer: His Role in Middle Eastern Politics", in S. Fischer, ed., Social Forces in the Middle East, Ithaca, 1955.
[32] See Gorwalla, op. cit.; Apter, op. cit.

ties and movements in the new countries.[33]

7. THE DEVELOPMENT OF MEDIATING MECHANISMS, AND OF PATTERNS OF POLITICAL ENTREPRENEURSHIP

These and other aspects of the formal organization of governmental institutions clearly indicate the relative weakness of representative institutions and of the democratic process. In some countries, as in many Middle Eastern ones, such institutions are almost entirely absent or ineffective. In others, they are stronger, but the problem of their successful development is still unsolved. But it is not so much the lack of procedural experience and other formal qualifications that is so important, but rather that it is difficult for these institutions to perform one of their basic functions in a democracy: that of mediating and integrating different interests in terms of common issues and in accordance with general rules of the political game. It is relatively easy to focus the attention of public opinion and of the legislators on ultimate values and basic divisive issues, such as differences between religious creeds, problems of secularism, different social philosophies, and especially problems of foreign policies. But it is much more difficult to evolve an agreement to disagree on various secondary problems and policies. It is more difficult to focus the attention of legislators —and that of the masses—on "secondary" problems and to develop a common interest in such issues so as to organize ordered discussion around them. Both the masses and the political elite tend to shift much more between ideological discussion on basic issues and exertions of direct pressure for the allocation of different facilities by the administration and analogous objectives.[34]

With respect to parliamentarianism, there does not exist a basic difference between traditional groups and authorities, such as tribal chiefs, princes, traditional cultural elites, on the one hand, and modern parties on the other. Traditional groups may sometimes be more amenable to participating in a fairly ordered way in parliamentary institutions. While developments in Ghana indicate that traditional chiefs may develop a "total" opposition to the new regime, there are, at the same time, some indications that they may merge into a parliamentary opposition. Similarly, in Indonesia several of the older potentates did participate in nationalistic movements and the same is true of many Brahmin groups in India.

From this analysis it follows that the most important variable, from the point of view of the stability of governmental institutions in general, and of some types of representative institutions in particular, is not the scope of traditional sectors in the community. Nor is the level of economic development the most important variable; but it is found in the nature of the transition process from the traditional to the modern, from the colonial to the independent setting. What is important to identify are the elements in this process which can help in the development of autonomous social groupings and independent centers of prestige and power within the society, centers which are organized either according to modern criteria of universalism, specificity, and achievement, or which have, even if they themselves are not organized according to these principles, some basic orientations to the new institutional framework, so that their interests and points of view

---

[33] Emerson, op. cit.; J. S. Coleman, "The Problem of Political Integration in Emergent Africa," Western Political Quarterly, Vol. VIII (1955), pp. 44-58; J. Furnivall, "Twilight in Burma," Pacific Affairs, Vol. 22 (1949), pp. 22ff.

[34] See McKahin, op. cit.; da Silva, op. cit.; and L. Pye, "Communication Patterns and the Problem of Representative Government in Non-Western Society," Public Opinion Quarterly, Vol. XX (1956), pp. 249-256.

can be mediated by proper elites and representatives.[35]

I wish to stress some implications of the last point. If it is correct, a successful maintenance of modern political institutions does not require the complete abolition of traditional organization based on ascription, particularism, and diffuseness. It has already been shown that even in the sphere of economic development, where the importance of universalism, achievement, and specificity is much greater and where consideration of solidarity is not of such great importance as in the political sphere, development can take place through the utilization and organization of traditional settings if appropriate conditions prevail.[36] The same may be applied, with even greater force, to the political sphere. The rapid disorganization of traditional settings may give rise to general disorganization and instability and may enhance the development of mob-mentality and the consequent political instability. What is of greater importance is the extent to which the different traditional settings can be gradually transformed, but not abolished outright, through incorporation within a modern institutional framework, and can exist alongside more modern organizations.[37]

The strategic problem, then, is the possibility of development of various intervening mechanisms, activities, and mediating institutions which facilitate the establishment of several levels of interlinking spheres within the society. Of great importance are developments through which both the basic solidarity and identification and the contingent support for different changing policies and competing elites can be transmitted to the political institutions and through which various basic issues of political controversy and discussion can be formulated.

This is, of course, very closely related to the presence or absence of people and political leaders at various levels who are able and willing to act according to the premises of the modern political institutions and to perform, at different levels, the tasks of mediation and integration. The absence of such people is not due to ill-will or lack of "objective" ability, but rather due to the social conditions which impede the appearance of such individuals. The problem here is somewhat parallel to that of entrepreneurship in the economic field.[38] One may perhaps talk about "political entrepreneurs," persons who are able to mobilize political activities and social attitudes, and integrate them into political organizations and processes according to the premises of parliamentary institutions. Obviously, the types of activity demanded of the modern political "entrepreneur" differ from those of the economic one, although there may be some common characteristics. The political entrepreneur, as the economic entrepreneur, must orient himself according to universalistic and achievement criteria and must be able to mobilize resources and activities in terms of these criteria. He must be able to bear certain elements of uncertainty and risk as concerns the attainment of his objectives, security of his status, etc. But the nature of his "resources" as well as of the framework within which he operates is greatly different from those of the economic entrepreneur. The framework in

[35] See Apter's (op. cit.) interesting discussion in his concluding chapter; also C. Belshaw, "The Cultural Milieu of the Entrepreneur," Explorations in Entrepreneurial History, Vol. VII (1955), pp. 146-164; and S. N. Eisenstadt, "Sociological Aspects of the Economic Adaptation of Oriental Immigrants in Israel," Economic Development and Cultural Change, Vol. IV, No. 3.

[36] See Robert S. Merrill, "Some Social and Cultural Influences on Economic Growth: The Case of the Maori," Journal of Economic History, Vol. XIV, (1954), pp. 401-409.

[37] Apter, op. cit.; Merrill, op. cit.; J. Pelzel, "The Small Industrialist in Japan," Explorations in Entrepreneurial History, Vol. VII (1954), pp. 79-95; M. Levy, "Contrasting Factors in the Modernization of China and Japan," in S. Kuznets, W. Moore, and J. J. Spengler, eds., Economic Growth: Brazil, India, Japan, Durham, N. C., 1955, pp. 496-536.

[38] See A. Cole, ed., Change and the Entrepreneur, Cambridge, Mass., 1948, and the volumes of Explorations in Entrepreneurial History.

which the political entrepreneur operates is not that of the impersonal market (although he may have to take into account some of the impersonal aspects of administration and law), but that of the more personal element of political life and struggle and of social and community organization. He must be able to manipulate elements and symbols of solidarity and power relations. The main difficulty confronting the activities of such a leader stems from the lack of balance and organization of political symbols and relations. But since no modern or quasi-modern society can exist without some organization of political elements, it is very probable that some type of political entrepreneurship will emerge. The main question is whether the political entrepreneur will be able to perform the mediating and integrating functions necessary for the development of a modern representative (although not necessarily Western) type of institutional framework. Obviously such entrepreneurs do not always develop in the new countries, and instead we find more authoritarian types connected either with the executive or with outright revolutionary movements. The authoritarian types may combine, in various ways, traditional and modern elements and attitudes, using one or the other according to their audience or the group which they try to manipulate.

Another important factor in this field is the scarcity of "intermediate" entrepreneurs who can successfully mediate between the lower, and usually more traditionally oriented local groups, and the more modern ones tied to the formal institutional setting. It may perhaps be assumed, at least as a working hypothesis, that the more these authoritarian types of entrepreneurs tend to develop, the greater is the institutional instability of formal governmental institutions. In such a case, the preponderance of the executive becomes stronger simultaneously with the executive's dependence on the support of the mob and consequently the possibility of development of various extremist movements.

The problems described in this paper seem to be, to some extent, common to most underdeveloped countries. This is largely due to the basic impact of Western colonialism. But obviously there exist also many differences between these countries—conditioned by different rates and types of the impact, by different social and cultural traditions of different underdeveloped countries, and by many other factors. These differences are beyond the scope of this paper, and it is hoped that they will be dealt with in a subsequent publication.

Tepoztlán Restudied: A Critique of the Folk-Urban Conceptualization of Social Change

Oscar Lewis

SOURCE: *Rural Sociology*, Vol. 18, (1953), pp. 121–34.

THE NEED FOR RESTUDIES

Anthropologists who like to think that there is an element of science in the social sciences, including anthropology, have often called primitive societies the

"laboratory" of the social scientists, where hypotheses about the nature of man and society can be tested. While the experiments and observations of the natural scientist are generally repeated and checked independently by different observers, the reports of the anthropologists have to be accepted on their face value, and their reliability has to be judged in terms of the respect for and confidence in the author's integrity, the inner consistency of his work, and the extent to which it agrees with one's own preconceptions. If the analogy with the natural sciences is to be taken seriously, we must develop methods for checking the reliability of our observations and the validity of interpretation. Restudy is one such method. This point has been recognized by a number of anthropologists, but to date there have been very few restudies. The reasons for this are many. Perhaps most important have been the limited funds for field research, the time pressure to study tribes that were rapidly becoming extinct, the shortage of field workers, the greater appeal in studying a community never before studied, and finally, the lack of emphasis upon methodology.

Of course, there is some difference of opinion in regard to the value of restudies. Those who would emphasize the subjective element, the element of art in field work, tend to be skeptical about the methodological value of restudies. On the other hand, those who have greater faith in objective methods, in operational procedures for observation, are inclined to be more favorable toward restudies. The former would argue that all human beings make errors, that this can be taken for granted, and that we can learn more by going ahead with new studies than by concerning ourselves with past mistakes. The latter would argue that it is important to learn what kinds of errors have been made, particularly if the scientific aspect of anthropology is to grow stronger. The former would argue that we do not need to have a restudy to know that there is something wrong with a report. This can be determined in terms of our wider comparative knowledge, in terms of internal consistency, or in terms of whether it agrees with a particular school of thought. The latter would perhaps agree but add that this is not enough, that we need empirical evidence

as to just what the facts are. Finally, some would suggest that there may be a further dichotomy involved—namely, the difference between those who hold that truth is relative and subjective and that each field worker is probably correct within the limits of the problem set and the materials selected for study, and those who hold that truth is absolute and objective and can be approximated more nearly by some methods than by others.

It must be emphasized that the objective and value of restudies is not to prove one man right and another wrong. It is not a matter of listing another's errors, in itself a distasteful and painful task, but rather of finding out what kind of errors tend to be made by what kind of people under what kind of conditions. Given a sufficiently large number of restudies, it might be possible to develop a theory of error of observation which would help to evaluate the role of the personal equation, personality, and ideological or cultural variables. If we could eventually arrive at generalizations in which we could say, given an anthropologist from such and such a cultural background, we can expect that his account of tribe X will be slanted in such and such a way, then we would have made some progress.

It may be useful to distinguish four types of restudies: (1) those restudies in which a second or third investigator goes to a community with the express design of re-evaluating the work of his predecessor; (2) those in which the same or an independent investigator goes to a community studied earlier, this time to study cultural change, and utilizing the first report as a baseline against which to measure and evaluate change; (3) those in which one returns to study some aspect of the culture not studied earlier; and (4) those in which one studies more intensively, and perhaps from a new point of view, some aspect of the culture studied earlier. There is, of course, some overlapping between these types. All restudies are additive in a sense. However, it is a matter of emphasis in research design.

From the point of view of testing reliability, the first type would seem to be the most suitable, though not without its methodological difficulties. Communities change, and it is sometimes difficult to know to what extent differences in findings reflect changes in the culture. Much depends upon the area and community being restudied. In cases where many years have elapsed between the first and second study and where change has been rapid and profound, it may well be impossible to reconstruct the earlier condition with sufficient accuracy to make it useful for reliability purposes. On the other hand, there are many areas where change is relatively slow and superficial. Moreover, when too many years have not elapsed, it may be possible to interview the same informants as in the earlier study. Also, the use of village records and archive records can act as a control. Finally, much depends upon the amount of quantitative data in the first report. Where the amount is large, restudies have a more solid base for comparisons. Indeed, this is perhaps the major positive function of quantification.

To the present writer's knowledge, there is not a single published case of a restudy of the first type—i.e., where the express purpose was the interest in methodology, the interest in testing an earlier report. The recent restudy of Tepoztlán perhaps comes closest to this type, and in the following pages some aspects of this restudy will be discussed.

DIFFERENCES BETWEEN REDFIELD'S STUDY AND THE RESTUDY

In 1926, Robert Redfield first studied the village of Tepoztlán and gave us his pioneer work, Tepoztlán—A Mexican Village.[1] This book has since become a standard reference and a classic in the field of community studies. It is of particular importance in the history of community studies in that it contains Redfield's first statement on the nature of the folk society, and, at least implicitly, the concept of the folk-urban continuum,

a hypothesis of societal change later made explicit in The Folk Culture of Yucatan.[2] The folk-urban conceptualization of culture change now enjoys great prestige among sociologists and anthropologists and has served as the theoretical frame of reference for many of the community studies done by Redfield's students.

Seventeen years after Redfield's study, the writer went to Tepoztlán to take another look, with the specific objective of studying the social, economic, political, and religious life of the community, with special emphasis upon an analysis of the changes which had occurred in the village since 1926. This involved a restudy of the village and a comparison of findings. Special attention, however, was given to those aspects of village life that Redfield had merely touched upon, such as demography, the land problem, systems of agriculture, the distribution of wealth, standards of living, politics and local government, the life cycle of the individual, and interpersonal relations.

Readers who are familiar with the earlier study of Tepoztlán by Redfield will want to know how the findings compare. Such a comparison is made here, not only for a better understanding of Tepoztlán, but also because of its broader implications for anthropological method and theory. The questions are: To what extent and in what ways do the results obtained from the independent study of the same society by two anthropologists differ? What are the implications of such differences concerning the reliability and validity of anthropological reporting?

The differences in findings range from discrepancies in factual details to differences in the overall view of Tepoztecan society and its people. The impression given by Redfield's study of Tepoztlán is that of a relatively homogeneous, isolated, smoothly functioning, and well-integrated society made up of a contented and well-adjusted people. His picture of the village has a Rousseauan quality

---

[1]Robert Redfield, Tepoztlán—A Mexican Village (Chicago: University of Chicago Press, 1930).

[2]Robert Redfield, The Folk Culture of Yucatan (Chicago: University of Chicago Press, 1941).

which glosses lightly over evidence of violence, disruption, cruelty, disease, suffering, and maladjustment. We are told little of poverty, economic problems, or political schisms. Throughout his study we find an emphasis upon the co-operative and unifying factors in Tepoztecan society. The writer's findings, on the other hand, would emphasize the underlying individualism of Tepoztecan institutions and character, the lack of cooperation, the tensions between villages within the municipio, the schisms within the village, the pervading quality of fear, envy, and distrust in interpersonal relations.

Now let us consider some of these differences in more detail. Redfield's account of Tepoztlán stresses the role of communal lands as a unifying factor within the village and the municipio. While this is certainly true, it is only part of the story. With the single exception of church lands, communal lands were and are individually operated, and the ideal of every Tepoztecan is to own his private plot of land. Furthermore, the communal lands have been a source of inter-village quarrels, and during the year that Redfield was in Tepoztlán these quarrels resulted in violence. Similarly, Redfield gives the impression that the cuatequitl (a traditional form of collective labor) was part and parcel of village life. He described a cuatequitl, which occurred during his stay, as if it were a common and regular occurrence. As a matter of fact, it was the first village cuatequitl of importance since the Revolution, and there have been very few subsequent ones. The particular cuatequitl which Redfield observed was due to the curious circumstance whereby a local, socialistically oriented political faction, directed from Mexico City by a group of Tepoztecans who were members of the Confederación Regional de Obreros Mexicanos, locally known as "the Bolsheviki," revived the traditional cuatequitl. Before the Revolution, the village cuatequitl was not viewed simply as a voluntary, cooperative endeavor but was also associated

with forced labor and imposition by the local cacique groups which ruled the village during the Díaz regime. In the Colonial period, the Spaniards similarly utilized the traditional cuatequitl as a source of labor. In short, Redfield's account of the cooperative aspects of village life needs to be modified somewhat in the light of other data.

Redfield portrayed Tepoztlán as a community of landowners and did not mention a land problem. But in the re-study it was found that over half of the villagers did not own private land, and that there was an acute shortage of good land and considerable population pressure in the face of dwindling agricultural resources. Redfield gave a rather glowing picture of Tepoztlán during the Díaz regime as having reached a period of great cultural florescence, but he failed to point out that this was limited to only a few Tepoztecans, and that the vast majority of Tepoztecans were illiterate, desperately poor, landless, and living under an oppressive political regime which forbade them to utilize their own communal resources. In this connection it is interesting to note that Tepoztlán was one of the first villages in the state of Morelos to join the Zapatista revolt against the Díaz regime. Redfield apparently viewed the Mexican Revolution as having had the effect of halting the tendency for the merging of social class differences; but the writer found that the Revolution has a marked leveling influence, economically, socially, and culturally.

Redfield presented only the positive and formal aspects of interpersonal relations, such as forms of greeting and the respect-relations of compadres; he failed to deal with some of the negative and disruptive aspects of village life, such as the fairly high incidence of stealing, quarrels, and physical violence. An examination of the local records revealed that, in the year that Redfield lived in the village, there were 175 reported cases of crimes and misdemeanors in the local court. Most of these cases were offenses against person and property. Since not all cases reach the local authorities, this number is indicative of considerable conflict.

Redfield described local politics as a game, but it appears that politics was a very serious affair which frequently led to violence. The year Redfield was there, the political schisms culminated in open violence bordering on civil war, and it was this situation which finally resulted in Redfield's leaving the village.

Another important difference between the findings concerns Redfield's delineation of the social structure of the village in terms of what he called the tontos, or representative of folk culture, and the correctos, or representative of city ways. It should be pointed out that Tepoztecans do not conceive of these terms as designations of social classes, in the sense used by Redfield, nor did they twenty years ago. Tepoztecans use the words as descriptive adjectives, with tonto meaning stupid, backward, foolish, or ignorant, and with correcto meaning well-mannered, well-bred, proper, or correct. The poorest, least educated, and most conservative man may be correcto to a Tepoztecan if he is polite and behaves in the accepted manner. Similarly a well-educated, acculturated man may be called tonto if he permits himself to be fooled by others or dominated by his wife. Within any one family, some of the members may be considered tonto and others correcto, depending almost entirely upon personality traits and manners.

But, granting that the degree of exposure to and influence of city ways is an important criterion in making for status differences in Tepoztlán, it is by no means the only one, and certainly not the most significant one in terms of the actual operation of the many status distinctions in the village. Among status distinctions which were then, and are today, more meaningful to Tepoztecans are those of rich and poor, landowners and landless, owners of private lands and holders of ejidos, ejidatarios and comuneros, farmers in hoe culture and farmers in plow culture, sons of caciques and

sons of ex-Zapatistas, to mention but a few.

Furthermore, the concept of tontos and correctos, as social classes representing different cultural levels, led to misunderstanding of the local political situation. The opposing political factions in the village during Redfield's stay were not composed of tontos on the one side and correctos on the other. The leaders on both sides included highly acculturated and little acculturated individuals, as did the members at large. A study of the personnel of each of the local government administrations (ayuntamientos) from 1926 to 1947 gives no support to Redfield's statement that politics, like the religious fiestas, are in the hands of the tontos.

The use of the terms tonto and correcto to designate social groups, which did not and do not exist and operate as such, makes much of Redfield's analysis of Tepoztecan society oversimplified, schematic, and unreal. There is a much wider range of custom and belief among the so-called tontos than was reported by Redfield; and by the same token there was less of a gap between the tontos and correctos. While Redfield's concept would tend to make for two cultures, the writer sees Tepoztlán as a single culture, with more and less acculturated individuals in close and frequent contact, each influencing the other, as they have for the past four hundred years.

REASONS FOR DIFFERENCES

More important than the differences in findings is the question of how to explain these differences. In a sense, it is inevitable that different students studying the same society will arrive at different conclusions. Certainly the personal factor, and what Redfield has recently referred to as the element of art in social science, cannot be overlooked. Nevertheless the differences in findings on Tepoztlán are of such magnitude as to demand some further and more detailed explanation.

Some of the differences in the two sets of data can be explained by changes which have occurred in the village in the interim of nearly twenty years between the studies. Other differences result from the difference in the general scope of the two studies. The present study had the advantage of having Redfield's pioneer work to start with, the assistance of Mexican personnel, more than twice the amount of time for field work, and the new approaches and methods, especially in the field of culture and personality, developed during the past twenty years. The much greater emphasis upon economic analysis in this study also reflects a fairly recent trend in anthropology. In addition, this study was based on the testimony of well over one hundred informants, as compared with about a half-dozen used by Redfield. This revealed a wide range of individual differences and enabled more thorough checking of data.

Still other differences, such as those summarized, must be attributed for the most part to differences in theoretical orientation and methodology, which in turn influenced the selection and coverage of facts and the way in which these facts were organized. A reëxamination of Redfield's book, in the light of the more recent field observations in the village, suggests that the concept of the folk culture and folk-urban continuum was Redfield's organizing principle in the research. Perhaps this helps to explain his emphasis on the formal and ritualistic aspects of life rather than the everyday life of the people and their problems, on evidence of homogeneity rather than heterogeneity and the range of custom, on the weight of tradition rather than deviation and innovation, on unity and integration rather than tensions and conflict.

Redfield's interest was primarily in the study of a single cultural process: the evolution from folk to urban, rather than a well-rounded ethnographic account. He only incidentally considered Tepoztlán in its historical, geographical, and cultural context in Morelos and Mexico, and attempted rather to place Tepoztlán within the broader, more abstract context of the folk-urban continuum.

The questions he asked of his data were quite different from those asked in this study. For example, he was not concerned with determining just what Tepoztlán is typical of, in relation to rural Mexico; nor was he concerned with determining how a study of Tepoztlán might reveal some of the underlying characteristics and problems of Mexico as a whole. Thus, the Revolution in Tepoztlán is not analyzed in terms of its social, economic, and political effects upon the village, nor in terms of what light it might throw upon the nature of the Revolution as a whole, but rather in regard to the more limited question of the emergence of Zapata as a "folk hero."

COMPARISON WITH REDFIELD'S YUCATAN FINDINGS: DISORGANIZATION

To what extend does the trend of change found in the present study of Tepoztlán fall within the categories suggested by Redfield in his study, The Folk Culture of Yucatan? He postulates that with increased urban influences there is greater disorganization, secularization, and individualization. Taking each separately, we shall consider the family first, as an example of disorganization. Redfield summarized the broad trends of change in family organization as follows:

As one goes from Tusik toward Merida there is to be noted a reduction in the stability of the elementary family; a decline in the manifestation of patriarchal or matriarchal authority; a disappearance of institutions expressing cohesion in the great family; a reduction in the strength and importance of respect relationships, especially for elder brothers and for elder people generally; an increasing vagueness of the conventional outlines of appropriate behavior toward relatives; and a shrinkage in the applicability of kinship terms primarily denoting members of the elementary family toward more distant relatives or toward persons not relatives.[3]

---

[3] Ibid, p. 211.

The first generalization that can be made in the case of Tepoztlán is that, despite the increased city influences in the last seventeen years, the stability of the nuclear family has not been seriously modified. The family remains strong and cohesive, separations have not noticeably increased, and divorce is all but nonexistent. The extended family is relatively weak but continues to serve in cases of emergency. This weakness, however, is not a recent phenomenon. Quarrels between husband and wife and wife-beating occur with some frequency; but this, too, seems to be an old pattern. The tensions and quarrels within families reflect a type of family organization, as well as Tepoztecan personality, but are not necessarily symptoms of disorganization.

Parental authority remains strong in Tepoztlán despite the elimination of arranged marriages and the increase in elopements. Parents continue to have control over their children, in many cases even after marriage. On about a sixth of the house sites there are joint families, and about half of these are extended families in which married sons are treated as children subject to the authority of the parents (hijos de familia).

Although about half of the marriages now begin as elopements, which flout the authority of the parents, the old form of asking for the girl's hand by the boy's parents continues. In any case, elopements do not lead to disorganization, for most elopements end in marriage, and the couple make peace with their parents. Assuming that elopements are an old trait, as seems to be indicated, here we have a case in which urban influence has intensified an old trait rather than caused its breakdown. Moreover, because Redfield found practically no elopements in Tusik and many elopements in Merida, he associated elopements with urbanism and disorganization. But this assumes what has still to be proved. In Tepoztlán, which is much less urban than Merida, by Redfield's own standards, we find a much higher proportion of elopements than in Merida. Furthermore, in Tzintzuntzan,

an even more isolated village, Foster found that 90 per cent of the marriages began as elopements. And he cites documentary evidence for the antiquity of this pattern.[4] Beals, in another connection, has also called attention to a pattern of change different from that reported by Redfield. Beal writes:

> Cherán, like many Indian communities of Mexico, is increasingly influenced by the town and the city. Nevertheless, the process again seems significantly different from those hitherto described by Redfield. In Cherán there is no distinction of los tontos and los correctos, mestizo and indio, or ladino and indio, although such may exist in some Tarascan towns with an appreciable mestizo population. Nor does the neat diminishing order of city, town and village hold in this area. Cherán is probably more influenced by Gary (Indiana), Mexico City, and Morelia (possibly in diminishing order) than it is by Uruapan and Patzcuaro. Indeed, it is quite probable that fundamentally Cherán is more progressive, more in touch with the modern world, than is mestizo Patzcuaro with its conscious idealization of a Colonial past.[5]

The desire of young couples to become independent of their parents and to set up their own homes reflects a greater individualism but does not necessarily imply a breakdown in family life. On the contrary, the lesser role of the in-laws and the greater dependence of the husband and wife upon each other, plus the fact that they are each of their own choice, may make for better marriage relations and greater family stability.

Although it is true that some outer forms of respect have been discarded, the fundamental respect status of elders remains. Perhaps the single exception has been the decline in the respect accorded to elder brothers. But it is questionable whether the elder brother in Tepoztlán

---

[4]George M. Foster, Empire's Children: The People of Tzintzuntzan (Mexico: Imprenta Nueva Mundo, 1948), p. 429.

[5]Ralph L. Beals, Cherán: A Sierra Tarascan Village, Institute of Social Anthropology, Pub. No. 2 (Washington, D. C.: Smithsonian Institution, 1946), pp. 211 f.

ever enjoyed the special position that he had in Maya society.

There seems to be no evidence of any marked change in the reciprocal behavior of relatives, perhaps because such changes have occurred so far back in history that informants have no memory of them today. As stated previously, the extended family is weak, and seems to have been so for many generations. The same may be said for the use of kinship terms, which have not changed in recent history. In surrounding villages, which generally conserve older culture elements, kinship terms are used in substantially the same way as in Tepoztlán.

In the examples cited, it is clear that changes have occurred in the village, but these changes do not necessarily imply disorganization. Rather, they involve a new kind of organization or reorganization.

SECULARIZATION

The second conclusion of the study in Yucatan showed a clear trend toward secularization:

The conclusion has been reached that the city and town exhibit greater secularization than do the villages. The principal facts offered in support of this conclusion are...the separation of maize from the context of religion and its treatment simply as a means of getting food or money; the increase in the number of specialists who carry on their activities for a practical livelihood relative to those that carry on traditional activities which are regarded as prerogatives and even moral duties to the community; the change in the character of the institution of guardia whereby from being an obligation, religiously supported, to protect a shrine and a god it becomes a mere job in the town hall; the (almost complete) disappearance of family worship; the decline in the sacramental character of baptism and marriage; the conversion of the pagan cult from what is truly religious worship to mere magic or even superstition; the decline in the veneration accorded the santos; the change in the novena in which from being a traditional form expressive of appeal to deity, it becomes a party for the fun of the participants; the alteration in the festival of the patron saint in which it loses its predominant character as worship

and becomes play and an opportunity for profit; the separation of ideas as to the cause and cure of sickness from conceptions as to moral or religious obligation.[6]

The data from Tepoztlán do not enable a careful comparison on each of the cited points. However, many of the data are comparable and show the trend toward secularization noted. The attitude toward corn in Tepoztlán combines both the secular and religious. Certainly corn is viewed as the basic crop, both for subsistence and for trade. But the religious aspects have not been entirely lopped off. The corn is still blessed in the church on San Isidro's Day, and some families still burn incense in the home and address a prayer to the corn before planting. Some also make the sign of the cross when planting the first seed. Moreover, on the Day of San Miguel, crosses are still placed at the four corners of the milpa to ward off the winds. From informants' accounts, it appears that these customs were more widespread before the Revolution. It is difficult to say how much change has occurred since 1926, for Redfield did not report on this subject.

The study of occupational changes and division of labor in Tepoztlán showed that most of the old "folk specialists" have continued and even increased in number, side by side with the increase in the new specialists. There were more curaderos, chirimiteros, fireworks-makers, and mask-makers in 1944 than in 1926, and there seemed to be every indication that these occupations would continue. The only exceptions are the huehuechiques, who must be able to speak Nahuatl, and those chirimiteros, who are being displaced by the more modern variety. However, the rate of increase in what Redfield would call the secular specialists has been much greater than that of the "folk specialists." To this extent, the independent findings for Yucatan and Tepoztlán agree. But it should be noted that before the Revolution there were more shoemakers, carpenters, saddle-makers, and other artisans than in 1926 or 1944.

---

[6]Redfield, The Folk Culture of Yucatan, p. 352.

Were it not for the specific historical information to explain this phenomenon, one might conclude that with increasing urban contacts there is a decrease in the number of specialists. The reason for this decrease has been, rather, the destruction of many neighboring haciendas which were formerly supplied by labor from Tepoztlán, and the abolition of the cacique class which had offered a market for the products of the artisans.

In Tepoztlán there does not appear to have been any appreciable decline in the sacramental character of baptism and marriage. At any rate, both are considered important and are standard practices. Despite the legalization of secular marriage, church marriage is still considered the best marriage by most Tepoztecans.

Similarly, there is no evidence of any decline in the veneration of the santos; the novena continues to be an appeal to the diety rather than a party for fun; the patron saints of the barrios are still regarded as protectors and are worshipped as such. Nor have barrio fiestas become primarily an occasion for profit. In fact, Tepoztecans do not show the marked commercial spirit reported in Mitla by Parsons, and in communities of the Guatemalan highlands by Sol Tax. Unlike Parsons' experiences in Mitla, the researchers were never besieged by questions about the cost of things, nor did they ever witness Tepoztecans haggling among themselves or with strangers.

INDIVIDUALIZATION

The third conclusion of the Yucatan study pertains to the trend toward individualization, or individualism, as one goes from folk to urban. The specific facts found in the study of the four communities are given as follows:

...the relative decrease in importance of specialized functions which are performed on behalf of the community and the relative increase of specialties discharged for the individual's own benefit; the development of individual rights in land and in family estates; the diminution or disappearance of collective labor and of the exchange of services in connection with civic enterprises and religious worship; the decreasing concern of the family or of the local community in the making and the maintaining of marriages; the becoming less common of the extended domestic family; the lessening of emphasis and of conventional definition of the respect relationships among kin; the decline in family worship and the disappearance of religious symbols expressive of the great family; the decrease in the tendency to extend kinship terms with primary significance for members of the elementary family to more remote relatives or to persons unrelated genealogically; the increasing vagueness of the conventional outlines of appropriate behavior towards relatives; the change in the nature of marriage and baptism rites so as less to express the linkage of the families and more to concern the immediately involved individuals only; the decline in relative importance of the santo patron of the local community; the suggested relation of the increase in sorcery to the separation of individuals, especially of women, from the security of familial groups.[7]

Some of the items listed above were also listed under the categories of disorganization and secularization and have been treated earlier. The development of individual rights in land may date back to the Spanish Conquest. Cortés and his heirs owned land in Tepoztlán and rented it out to Tepoztecans as early as 1580. In the past twenty or thirty years there have been no changes in the direction of the private ownership of the communal resources. The persistence of the communal land, which still accounts for over four-fifths of all the area of the municipio, is impressive.

The trend toward the breakdown of collective labor is seen clearly in Tepoztlán, particularly in connection with the difficulty in getting barrio members to turn out for the plowing and planting of the barrio fields. In 1947, three of the barrios had rented out the land and used the rental for the barrio. On the whole, many of our findings for Tepoztlán might be interpreted as confirming Redfield's more general finding for Yucatan, particularly with regard to the trend toward secularization and individualization, perhaps less so with regard to disorganization.

[7] Ibid., p. 355.

LIMITATIONS OF THE FOLK-URBAN CONCEPT

Since the concept of the folk society as an ideal type is, after all, a matter of definition, there can be no quarrel with it as such, provided that it can be shown to have heuristic value. On the basis of the restudy of Tepoztlán, however, it seems necessary to point out a number of limitations found in the conceptual framework of the folk-urban continuum, both as a scheme for the study of culture change, and for cultural analysis. These criticisms can be discussed under seven related points.

(1) The folk-urban conceptualization of social change focuses attention primarily on the city as the source of change, to the exclusion or neglect of other factors of an internal or external nature. So-called folk societies have been influencing each other for hundreds of years and out of such interaction has come cultural change. The archaeological record in Tepoztlán, as well as in other parts of Mexico, indicates quite clearly a great mingling of people and cultures, which dates back at least a thousand years before the Spanish Conquest. Tepoztlán itself was first conquered by the Toltecs and later by the Aztecs, and with each conquest came new influences, new religious ideas, and new customs.

Another example of nonurban factors in culture change can be seen in the case of Tepoztlán and other parts of Latin America, where the introduction of rural culture elements was at least as far-reaching in effect as any changes brought about by later urban influences. Similarly, we find that the Mexican Agrarian Revolution (particularly in its Zapatista phase) was a profound influence for change, but can hardly be classified as an urban influence. It is evident that the folk-urban continuum concept covers only one of a wide variety of situations which may lead to culture change. In the case of Tepoztlán, to study the urban factors alone would give us only a partial picture of culture change.

(2) It follows that in many instances culture change may not be a matter of folk-urban progression, but rather, an increasing or decreasing heterogeneity of culture elements. For example, we have seen that the incorporation of Spanish rural elements—such as the plow, oxen, plants, and many folk beliefs—did not make Tepoztlán more urban but instead gave it a more varied rural culture. The introduction of plow culture in Tepoztlán did not eliminate the older system of hoe culture but gave the Tepoztecans an alternative and, in some ways, a more efficient method of farming, making for greater heterogeneity in the economic life and in the forms of social relationships.

(3) Some of the criteria used in the definition of the folk society are treated by Redfield as linked or interdependent variables, but might better be treated as independent variables. Sol Tax, in his study of Guatemalan societies, has shown that societies can be both culturally well organized and homogeneous and, at the same time, highly secular, individualistic, and commercialistic. He has also shown that interpersonal relations in a small and homogeneous society can be characterized by formalism and impersonality. His findings are supported by the present study. Moreover, this study shows other possible combinations of variables. Thus, whereas Tax found family disorganization as a concomitant of commercialism, in Tepoztlán the family remains strong, and there is little evidence of family disorganization. Moreover, collective forms of land tenure exist side by side with private landownership and individual working of the land.

(4) The typology involved in the folk-urban classification of societies tends to obscure one of the most significant findings of modern cultural anthropology, namely, the wide range in the ways of life and in the value systems among so-called primitive peoples. The "folk society," as used by Redfield, would group together food-gathering, hunting, pastoral, and agricultural peoples, without distinction. To apply the term "folk society" to high cultures like that of the

Aztecs (Tepoztlán was part of this high-culture area) and at the same time to apply it to simple food-gathering peoples like the Shoshone robs the term of its discriminatory value. Also, to write of a "folk element" in Tepoztlán in 1926 (the so-called <u>tontos</u>) as if it were identical with the folk element of the pre-Hispanic days neglects all the cultural influences to which this element has been subjected in the intervening four hundred years and blurs many distinctions which have to be made. Similarly, it would put into one category societies which are as different culturally and psychologically as the Arunta and the Eskimo, the Dobu and the Ba Thonga, the Zuni and the Alorese, the Dahomey and the Navaho. Indeed, one might argue that the folk-urban classification is not a cultural classification at all, since it rides roughshod over fundamental cultural differences—i.e., differences in the ethos of a people. The point is that in attitudes and value systems, folk societies may resemble some urban societies much more than they resemble other folk societies. For example, the individualism and competitiveness of the Blackfoot Indians remind one much more of American urban value systems than of Zuni values. This suggests that the criteria used in the folk-urban classification are concerned with the purely formal aspects of society and are not necessarily the most crucial for cultural analysis.

What has been said of the folk end of the folk-urban formula applies also to the urban end. Focusing only on the formal aspects of urban society reduces all urban societies to a common denominator and treats them as if they all had the same culture. Thus, Greek, Egyptian, Roman, Medieval, and twentieth-century American and Russian cities would all be put into the same class. To take but one example, there are obvious and significant differences between American and Russian urban culture, and in all probability these two "urban influences" would have a very different effect upon a preliterate society exposed to them.

It should be clear that the concept "urban" is too much of a catchall to be use-ful for cultural analysis. Moreover, it is suggested here that the question posed by Redfield—What happens to an isolated homogeneous society when it comes into contact with an urbanized society?—cannot possibly be answered in a scientific way because the question is too general and the terms used do not give us the necessary data. What we need to know is what kind of an urban society, under what conditions of contact, and a host of other specific historical data.

(5) The folk-urban classification has serious limitations in guiding field research because of the highly selective implications of the categories themselves and the rather narrow focus of problem. The emphasis upon essentially formed aspects of culture leads to neglect of psychological data and, as a rule, does not give insight into the character of the people. We have already seen how this approach has influenced the selection, interpretation, and organization of the data in Redfield's study of Tepoztlán.

(6) The folk-urban conceptualization of social change as developed by Redfield assumes a uniform, simultaneous, and unilateral change in all institutions, which is reminiscent of early evolutionary theory. Moreover, it tells us nothing about the rate of change.

(7) Finally, underlying the folk-urban dichotomy as used by Redfield is a system of value judgments which contains the old Rousseauan notion of primitive peoples as noble savages, and the corollary that with civilization has come the fall of man. This type of value system is particularly prone to influence the interpretation of a given cultural change as to whether it shall be called disorganization or simply reorganization. Since the concept of disorganization is one of the three key concepts in Redfield's folk-urban hypothesis, it can be seen how directly this value system may affect the interpretation. This is not, of course, an objection to the fact of values per se, but rather to the failure to make them explicit, as well as to this particular value system. Redfield's values suggest what Lovejoy and Boas have called "cul-

tural primitivism," which they define as "the discontent of the civilized with civilization, or with some conspicuous and characteristic feature of it."[8]

These authors show that primitivism has existed in various forms throughout the recorded history of mankind. "Of direct, or even indirect, influence of the classical primitivistic tradition there is probably little. But since the beginning of the present century, Western man has become increasingly skeptical concerning the nineteenth-century 'myth of progress,' increasingly troubled with the misgivings about the value of the outcome of civilization thus far, about the future to which it tends, and about himself as the author of it all; and similar doubts and apprehensions found expression two millenia or more ago. In spite of the more complex and sophisticated general ideology of the contemporary exponents of these moods, there are striking parallels to be observed between certain of the texts that follow (i.e., Greek, Roman, and Indian) and some passages in such writings as Freud's Civilization and Its Discontents and Spengler's Man and Technics."[9]

Again and again in Redfield's writings there emerges the value judgment that folk societies are good and urban societies bad. It is assumed that all folk societies are integrated while urban societies are the great disorganizing force. In his introduction to Miner's St. Denis study, Redfield suggests that the usual view of peasant life "as something to be escaped, an ignominy to be shunned" may be wrong. He finds that the habitant of St. Denis has order, security, faith, and confidence, "because he has culture." In another essay, "The Folk Society and Culture" in Eleven Twenty-Six, he contrasts the "organization and consistency which gives a group moral solidarity" with "the impaired moral organization of the urban society." Even in his most recent study,

which to this writer represents a great departure from his earlier thinking, in that he is less concerned with formalism and categories and more concerned with people, we find the old values reappearing. "Progress" and urbanization now are seen as inevitable, but they are still evil.[10]

CONCLUSIONS

The limitations in the folk-urban conceptualization of social change stand out even more clearly when we compare the results of this type of analysis with the results obtained by another method—namely, a combined historical-functional approach, in which the categories for analysis of change grow out of the historical data from a given situation. From this point of view, the history of culture change in Tepoztlán may be divided into three major periods: (1) from the Spanish Conquest to about 1910; (2) from 1910 to about 1930; (3) from 1930 to the present. No single formula will explain the whole range of phenomena embraced by these periods. Indeed, it appears that each period is characterized by a different rate of change and by varying degrees of change within different institutions. In some periods we find both destructive and constructive aspects, disorganization and reorganization. In one period, the technological changes affect primarily the lives of women; in another, primarily the lives of men.

During the first period, change was on the whole gradual but far-reaching, touching all aspects of life from material culture and technology to social organization, economics, and religion. The changes during this period were the result of outside influence and consisted of the transformation of the culture by the superimposition of Spanish culture—consisting of both urban and rural elements —on the native culture, with a resultant fusion of the two. During the second period, the changes were caused by a com-

---

[8]Arthur A. Lovejoy and George Boas, Primitivism and Related Ideas in Antiquity (Baltimore: Johns Hopkins Press, 1935), p. 7.

[9]Ibid., p. 10.

[10]Robert Redfield, A Village That Chose Progress, Chan Kom Revisited (Chicago: University of Chicago Press, 1950), p. 178.

bination of external and internal factors, and changes were more rapid and violent, affecting primarily the social and political organization. The third period was in a sense a continuation of the second, with the changes primarily in the fields of communication, literacy, education, consumption patterns, and values, and with economics, social organization, and religion remaining quite stable. In all periods, particularly in the field of material culture, the new culture elements tended not to supplant the old but to be added to them, thus making for a richer and more heterogeneous culture.

This discussion can be summarized in three general conclusions: (1) There is a need for more independent restudies in anthropology and, if possible, simultane-
ous studies of the same community or region by different investigators. (The writer would welcome an independent restudy of Tepoztlán twenty years hence.) (2) The approach to community and regional studies must be of the broadest possible type in which the community is seen in its geographical and historical contacts rather than as an independent isolate. (3) The checking of a specific hypothesis in the course of a community study is certainly worth while, but one must be aware of the highly selective role of the hypothesis itself in directing the gathering of data. It may be that what is left out, because of the limiting needs of the hypothesis, is all important for an understanding of the total cultural situation.